Russia

Kaliningrad
Region
p273

St Petersburg
p156

Northern European
Russia p291

Moscow
p54

Golden Ring
p125

Western European
Russia p232

The Urals
p411

Volga
Region
p332

Western
Siberia
p435

Eastern
Siberia
p475

Russian
Far East
p540

Russian
Caucasus
p369

Simon Richmond,
Mark Baker, Marc Bennetts, Stuart Butler, Trent Holden, Ali Lemer, Tatyana Leonov,
Tom Masters, Kate Morgan, Leonid Ragozin, Regis St Louis, Mara Vorhees

Contents

GUM SHOPPING MALL, MOSCOW P115

LOMONOSOV IMPERIAL PORCELAIN FACTORY P162

Contents

SAMI MAN WITH REINDEER
P318

ON THE ROAD

ROKA/SHUTTERSTOCK ©

GRAND CHORAL
SYNAGOGUE P187

Contents

UNDERSTAND

SURVIVAL GUIDE

SPECIAL FEATURES

Welcome to Russia

The world's largest country offers it all, from historic cities and idyllic countryside to artistic riches, epic train rides and vodka-fuelled nightlife.

Arty & Adventurous

Whether you're a culture vulture in search of inspiration from great artists and writers or an adventure addict looking for new horizons to conquer, Russia amply delivers. Tread in the footsteps of literary greats, including Tolstoy and Pushkin, on their country estates. Ski or climb lofty mountains in the Caucasus, go trekking or white-water rafting in the Altai Republic, hike around Lake Baikal, or scale an active volcano in Kamchatka – the variety of possibilities will make your head spin.

Historic & Contemporary

If ancient walled fortresses, glittering palaces and swirly-spired churches are what you're after, focus on European Russia. Here, Moscow and St Petersburg are the must-see destinations, twin repositories of eye-boggling national treasures, political energies and contemporary creativity. Within easy reach of these cities are charming historical towns and villages, such as Veliky Novgorod, Pskov and Suzdal, where the vistas dotted with onion domes and lined with gingerbread cottages measure up to the rural Russia of popular imagination.

Off the Beaten Track

Russia's vast geographical distances and cultural differences mean you don't tick off its highlights in the way you might those of a smaller nation. Instead, view Russia as a collection of distinct territories, each one deserving separate attention. Rather than transiting via Moscow, consider flying direct to a regional centre such as Rostov-on-Don, Irkutsk or Yekaterinburg and striking out from there. With a welcome spread of Western-style hostels and hotels around the country and the ease of booking trains and flights online, it's simple to organise this kind of trip yourself.

A Riddle Worth Solving

We won't lie: bureaucracy and occasional discomfort and inconvenience, particularly away from the booming urban centres, remain an integral part of the Russian travel experience. However, a small degree of perseverance will be amply rewarded: one of the great joys of travel in Russia is being swept away by the boundless hospitality of the people. Aleksandr Solzhenitsyn and Winston Churchill both wrote famous lines about Russia being an enigmatic riddle. Embrace this conundrum and you, too, are sure to find yourself swept away by a passion for Mother Russia.

Why I love Russia

By Simon Richmond, Writer

A traveller's relationship with Russia is never an easy one, but over two decades of exploring this multifaceted country, I've yet to tire of it or be disappointed. It's a thrill to discover the latest on the dynamic and liberal art scene in the major cities, and I particularly relish the serene countryside, with Lake Baikal and the Greater Caucasus mountains favourite locations. Above all, it has been encounters with warmly welcoming and highly educated Russians that have made the most lasting impression on me.

For more about our writers, see p718

Above: Lake Baikal (p504), Eastern Siberia

Russia

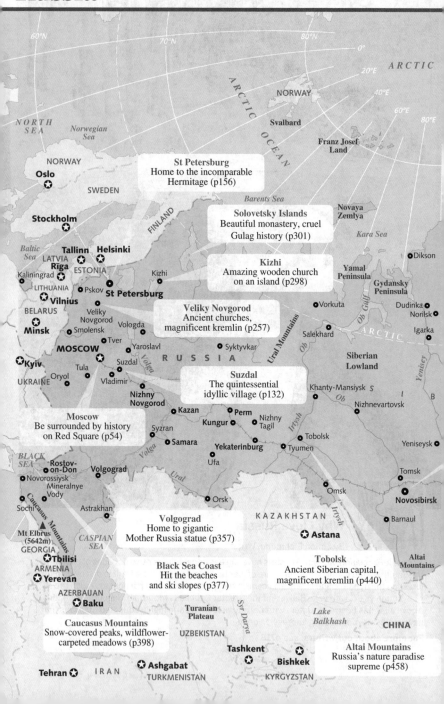

St Petersburg
Home to the incomparable
Hermitage (p156)

Solovetsky Islands
Beautiful monastery, cruel
Gulag history (p301)

Kizhi
Amazing wooden church
on an island (p298)

Veliky Novgorod
Ancient churches,
magnificent kremlin (p257)

Suzdal
The quintessential
idyllic village (p132)

Moscow
Be surrounded by history
on Red Square (p54)

Volgograd
Home to gigantic
Mother Russia statue (p357)

Black Sea Coast
Hit the beaches
and ski slopes (p377)

Tobolsk
Ancient Siberian capital,
magnificent kremlin (p440)

Caucasus Mountains
Snow-covered peaks, wildflower-
carpeted meadows (p398)

Altai Mountains
Russia's nature paradise
supreme (p458)

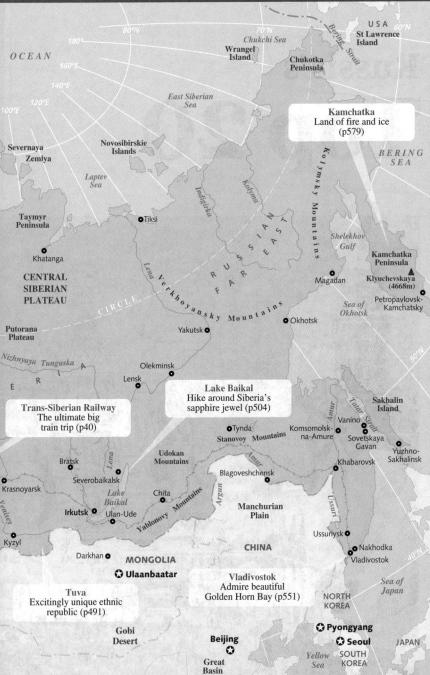

Russia's
Top 20

Walking Across Red Square

1 Stepping onto Red Square (p69) never ceases to inspire: the tall towers and imposing walls of the Kremlin, the playful jumble of patterns and colours adorning St Basil's Cathedral, the majestic red bricks of the State History Museum and the elaborate edifice of the GUM department store, all encircling a vast stretch of cobblestones. Individually they are impressive, but the ensemble is electrifying. Come at night to see the square empty of crowds and the buildings awash with lights.

The Hermitage

2 Little can prepare most visitors for the scale and quality of the exhibits at the State Hermitage Museum (p172) in St Petersburg. Comprising an almost unrivalled history of Western art, the collection includes a staggering number of Rembrandts, Rubens and Matisses – the latter being displayed in new galleries in the General Staff Building. In addition, there are superb antiquities, sculpture and jewellery on display, not to mention the stupendously decorated public halls and private apartments of the Romanovs, for whom the Winter Palace was home until 1917.

Kamchatka

3 It seems almost trite to describe Kamchatka (p579) as majestic. To many it is the most beautiful place in the world. It's Yellowstone and Patagonia rolled into one, and it teems with wildlife free to frolic in one of the world's great remaining wildernesses. Traditionally the domain of well-heeled tourists who could afford helicopter rides to view its trademark volcanoes, geysers and salmon-devouring bears, parts of Kamchatka can now be explored by independent travellers on more limited budgets. Now if only they could fix that weather... Top: Brown bears

Suzdal's Idyll

4 Ding-dong ring the bells of a few dozen churches as you ride your bike through the streets of Suzdal (p130), which are lined with wooden cottages and lush gardens. This is Russia as it would have been, if not for the devastating 20th century – unpretentious, pious and very laid-back. Some of the best religious architecture is scattered around, but you can just as well spend all day lying in the grass and watching the river before repairing to a *banya* (hot bath) for the sweet torture of heat, cold and birch twigs.

The Caucasus Mountains

5 Photos simply don't do them justice: the astonishing beauty of the Caucasus mountains (p398) is best appreciated on a trek among the jagged peaks. You can take short hikes through meadows, past waterfalls and up into alpine heights from the villages of Dombay and Arkhyz. Those seeking to conquer Europe's highest mountain set their sights on Elbrus, the twin-peaked overlord that tops out at 5642m – one of Russia's most challenging adventures. Wherever you plan to go, be sure to arrange any necessary permits well in advance.

Banya at Sanduny Baths

6 The quintessential Russian experience is visiting a traditional *banya* (hot bath). Forget your modesty, strip down and brave the steam room at the likes of Moscow's Sanduny Baths (p93). As the heat hits, you'll understand why locals wear felt hats to protect their hair. A light thrashing with a bundle of birch branches is part of the fun, as is the invigorating blast that follows the post-steam dive into an icy pool or the douse in a frigid shower – as the locals say, *S lyogkim parom!* (Hope your steam was easy!).

Exploring the Altai

7 Misty mountain passes, standing stone idols, tranquil lakes and empty roads that stretch on forever...welcome to the Altai Republic (p458), Russia's supreme natural paradise, almost twice the size of Wales. You can travel for hours without seeing another soul – unless you count wild horses and goats. From snow-capped peaks to the lunar landscapes of Kosh-Agach, desolation has never been quite so appealing. But be warned – the Altai and its mysteries possess a magnetic pull, drawing travellers back year after year.

Exploring the Black Sea

8 The serene Black Sea coast has long been a favourite of Russian holiday-makers for its seaside towns, easy-going ambience and the magnificent scenery in the nearby Caucasus mountains. The gateway to it all is Sochi (pictured below; p378), a vibrant city that reinvented itself as a first-rate international resort and host of the 2014 Winter Olympics. The looming peaks of nearby Krasnaya Polyana make a superb destination for ski lovers, while there's great hiking – past waterfalls and up to eagle-nest heights – in the Agura Valley.

Golden Horn Bay

9 Vladivostok (p551), capital of Russia's east, has a swagger in its step after being remade for an economic summit in 2012. No longer a remote satellite of Moscow, Vladivostok is Asia's rising star, and Golden Horn Bay is its heart and soul. Take it in from one of the city's myriad viewpoints, or join the frenzy of activity on the bay with a ferry cruise. Check out the impressive new suspension bridge spanning the bay. Suddenly those San Francisco comparisons don't seem quite so preposterous.

A Night at the Mariinsky

10 What could be more Russian than a night at the ballet, dressed to the nines, watching *Swan Lake* or *Romeo and Juliet*? St Petersburg's famed Mariinsky Theatre (p210) offers the ultimate in classical ballet or operatic experiences, and now has a contemporary twist as its long-awaited second stage has finally opened. Also worth a visit is Moscow's Bolshoi Theatre, looking better than ever after a long renovation. Tickets are no longer cheap, but the experience will stay with you forever.

Hiking the Great Baikal Trail

11 Already one of Russia's most successful environmental projects, the Great Baikal Trail has the ambitious aim of encircling Lake Baikal (p504) with marked hiking trails. That's still a long way from being achieved, but where trails have been etched into the landscape, donning boots for a trek along Baikal's shores is all the rage. Whichever section you choose, Baikal's gobsmacking vistas and the tough going will leave you breathless as you pass through virgin taiga (swampy coniferous forest), along isolated beaches and through cold, flowing rivers.

RASIKA108/SHUTTERSTOCK ©

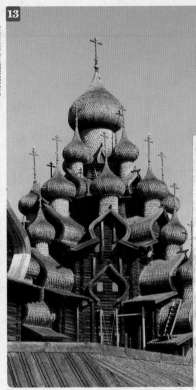

BILLAGEN I UR LOUVAIN GREMY SPLIT LEDYSTOCK

Izmaylovsky Market

12 It's a fine line between shopping and fun at the kremlin in Izmaylovo (p116). Cross the footbridge and walk through the gate to enter a Disney-like medieval village, complete with wooden church, whitewashed walls and plenty of souvenir shops. Just as in times of yore, the best shopping is in the trade rows outside the kremlin walls. Wander among the sprawling market's stalls to find an endless array of traditional handicrafts, as well as art and antiques, Central Asian carpets, Soviet paraphernalia and more.

Kizhi Island

13 Old buildings made of logs may not usually be synonymous with 'heart-stopping excitement', but the collection of wooden masterpieces on Kizhi (p298) is enough to spike the blood pressure of those blasé about even the most glorious architecture. The excitement builds as the heavenly Transfiguration Church (pictured above) is first glimpsed from the approaching hydrofoil. Up close, the church is a miracle of design and construct: legend has it that the unnamed builder destroyed his axe upon its completion, correctly assuming that its glory could not be matched.

Mamaev Kurgan

14 For history buffs, a trip to Volgograd to take in the immense Mamaev Kurgan (p358) memorial to the Battle of Stalingrad is one of those must-visit, bucket-list types of places. The sheer mass of the 72m-high statue of Mother Russia wielding a sword that extends for another 11m must be seen in person to be fully grasped. Historians regard the epic WWII battle between Nazi Germany and the Soviet Red Army as the bloodiest in human history and a turning point in Russia's ultimate victory in the war.

Olkhon Island

15 Sacred of the sacred to the shamanist western Buryats, who attach a legend or fable to every rock, cape and hillock, enchanted Olkhon (p519) sits halfway up Lake Baikal's western shore. It's obvious why the gods and other beings from the Mongol *Geser* stories chose to dwell on this eerily moving island, though today it's more likely to be a bunch of backpackers you meet emerging from a cave. The island's landscapes are spellbinding; Baikal's waters lap balmiest on its western shore and if you're after some Siberia-inspired meditation, there's no better spot.

Solovetsky Islands

16 Delve into the mysteries of the Gulag past of the Solovetsky Islands (p301) and visit one of Russia's most impressive fortress-monasteries. Some of Stalin's most brutal repressions took place on these remote, forested islands, reachable only by boat and small plane and made infamous by Solzhenitsyn's *The Gulag Archipelago*. The monastery, with its sturdy stone walls and powerful cannons, is famous for fighting off the British and withstanding an eight-year siege. Today it's a place of worship once more, the golden iconostases of its churches returned to former glories.

Tobolsk

17 The former capital of Siberia, Tobolsk (p440) is today renowned across Russia for its magnificent kremlin. Crowds are rare, though, and if you come on a weekday you're likely to have its grounds almost to yourself. The kremlin is perched high above the old town, a part of Tobolsk where you'll lose track of time as you explore the endless wooden buildings and dramatic churches. Tobolsk is off the main Trans-Siberian route, but its charms are well worth the detour. Top: St Sophia Cathedral

Trans-Siberian Railway

18 Daylight gradually fades, light illuminates the carriage, and windows turn opaque and reflect life inside the train. One of the pleasures of travelling in Russia is to board an overnight train and alight in a different city the following morning. This may be inside a deluxe carriage from St Petersburg, but for many the dream is of a cross-continent odyssey on the trans-Siberian route. One logical place to connect with this route is Novosibirsk (p444), Russia's third-largest city and home to a mammoth train station and an impressive opera house.

MALYE KARELY WOODEN ARCHITECTURE MUSEUM

Set in pretty rolling dales 25km southeast of Arkhangelsk's centre, the well-presented Malye Karely Wooden Architecture Museum (Музей деревянного зодчества и Народного Искусства Малые Корелы; www.korely.ru; Mon-Fri R500, Sat & Sun R750; ⊙10am-5pm Jul-May, to 9pm Jun; ⊟104, 108) is Arkhangelsk's foremost attraction. Featuring dozens of 16th-to-19th-century wooden buildings relocated here from rural villages during the 1970s – churches, windmills, peasant houses and barns – it's a lovely place for a stroll, especially if you possess even a passing interest in architecture. The museum is divided into four sectors, with buildings grouped according to their geographical origin.

You enter the Kargolopsko-Onezhsky sector past a series of boxy windmills, in the largest of which you can admire the complete interior workings. Cut across to the impressive 1669 Ascension Church (Вознесенская церковь) with its top-knot of wooden domes and forest-scented, icon-plastered interior. The 19th-century Tretyakov House displays curious furnishings of the era, while the quaint little Miracle Worker's Chapel (Часовня Макария Унженского, Chasovnya Makariya Unzhenskogo) has retained intact its eight-panelled octagonal ceiling icons ('skies').

To reach the other sectors, take the path heading north from the bell tower by the Ascension Church, descend the steep steps, cross the river and walk up another flight of stairs; you'll have to return the same way.

The village-like Dvinskoy sector consists of a smattering of wealthy peasant houses. Notice the curious Rusinova house, former Old Believers' home, with a tiny chapel hidden in a back room. Unlike other Russian peasants, each family member had his or her own eating utensils and a guest's utensils were thrown out. The sector's centrepiece is the enormous 1672 St George's Church (Георгиевская церковь), displaying a small but valuable selection of remarkable wayside crosses including one gigantic example that virtually fills the nave.

In both Pinezhsky sector and Mezensky sector, check out the *chyornye izby* (black cottages), so-called because their lack of a chimney resulted in smoke-stained walls. Mezensky sector's 19th-century Elkino House has an exhibition on Pomor fishing and boat-building and there's a great view over the river below.

Just 200m from the museum entrance is the holiday-hotel complex Turisticheskaya Derevnya Malye Karely (p310), which consists of modern timber cottages and apartments. The excellent restaurant has an olde-Russia theme, serving anything from grilled meats and poached fish to *vareniki*.

Every 20 to 30 minutes, little bus 104 from Troitsky pr in central Arkhangelsk runs all the way to Malye Karely (R70, 45 minutes), while bus 108 runs directly from Arkhangelsk's bus station, both terminating opposite the hotel complex. A taxi from Arkhangelsk costs around R600.

★Fine Arts Museum   MUSEUM
(Музей изобразительных искусств; pl Lenina 2; adult/student R100/60; ⊙10am-5pm Wed-Mon; ⊟1, 54) Arkhangelsk's most compelling art gallery has regularly changing exhibitions that range from modern reflections on Soviet propaganda to pop art. Upstairs are impressive icons, bone carvings and decorative art displays.

EK Plotnikova House-Museum   MUSEUM
(Усадебный Дом Е. К. Плотниковой; Pomorskaya ul 1; adult/student R150/60; ⊙10am-5pm Wed-Mon; ⊟1,11) This historical building houses an impressive collection of Russian art from the 18th to the 20th centuries, includ-

ing works by Karl Bryullov of *The Last Day of Pompeii* fame (although that one's in St Petersburg). Its main focus, however, is charting the switch to 'critical realism' in the late 19th century, when peasants and other 'common people' became the subjects of paintings.

Sovoletsky Stone
in Honour of Gulag Victims   MONUMENT
(ul Gagarina; ⊟7) This 1.5m-by-1m granite stone was brought to Arkhangelsk from the Sovoletsky Islands in 1990 as a monument to the victims of Soviet-era Gulag camps. Located in an attractive park, its inscription reads 'To the Victims of Political Repression.' There are similar stones in Moscow and St Petersburg.

Take bus 7 from the River Terminal (p312) to Prospekt Sovetskikh Kosmonavtov and it's a 300m walk down Prospekt Gagarina and through Lomonovsky Park.

Captured British Mark V Tank MEMORIAL (Troitsky pr 102; 📮1, 54) A British tank on the streets of a Russian city is an unusual sight indeed. This one, which saw service in WWI, was captured by the Red Army in 1919 after foreign forces landed in Russia in an attempt to quash the fledgling Bolshevik state before it had a chance to get going. It was first displayed as a memorial

to the Russian Civil War in 1940, and has stood in a number of locations in Arkhangelsk since.

Archangel Mikhail Cathedral CATHEDRAL (Собор Архистратига Божия Михаила; Pl Profsoyuzov; 📮1,41) The construction of this 72m-high cathedral, which stands on the site of a prerevolutionary cathedral that was destroyed by the Soviets in 1938, is due to be completed in 2018-19. Even unfinished, the cathedral, with its four golden onion domes, is already a local landmark. Construction began in 2008 as part of a drive by the Russian

Arkhangelsk

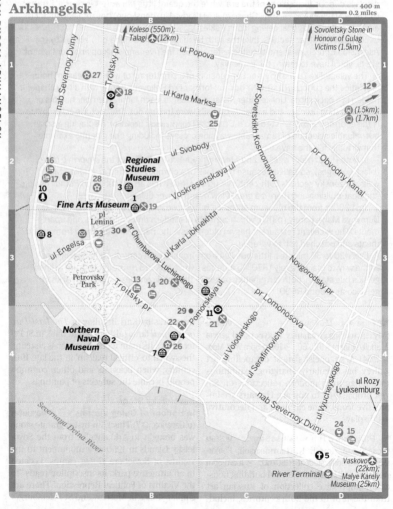

Orthodox Church to build scores of new churches across Russia.

AA Borisov Museum
MUSEUM

(Музей А. А. Борисова; Pomorskaya ul 3; R150; ⊙10am-5pm Wed-Mon; 🚌1, 11) Artwork by AA Borisov, dedicated to the Arctic scenery of Novaya Zemlya and settlement of the north.

Gostiny Dvor
HISTORIC BUILDING

(Гостиный Двор; nab Severnoy Dviny 85/86; per exhibition R90; ⊙10am-9pm Tue-Sun; 🚌1, 4) In the 17th and 18th centuries, Arkhangelsk's heart and soul was this merchants' yard, a grand, turreted brick trading centre built between 1668 and 1684. The huge, fortress-like complex has been largely restored and its exhibition rooms host anything from contemporary photography and landscape paintings by regional talent to literary displays honouring Tove Jansson, the creator of the Moomins.

Prospekt Chumbarova-Luchinskogo
STREET

(Проспект Чумбарова-Лучинского; pr Chumbarova-Luchinskogo) Arkhangelsk's appealing pedestrian street is lined with a a few surviving traditional timber houses that are in the process of being restored, cosy cafes, and a score of whimsical statues that passers-by rub for good luck.

Naberezhnaya Severnoy Dviny
PARK

(Набережная Северной Двины) Given the first hint of warm summer weather, Arkhangelskians emerge to stroll this broad promenade and loiter in any of its many seasonal beer-and-*shashlyk* (meat kebab) tents.

Lair of Art Gallery
GALLERY

(Марфин Дом; ☑8182-208 802; www.marfin. wmsite.ru; pr Chumbarova-Luchinskogo 38; R100; ⊙11am-8pm) In the fine Marfin Mansion, the Lair of Art Gallery hosts occasional mini-concerts, but is most interesting for its furnished interior and large model of how Arkhangelsk looked a century ago.

👉 Tours

★ Pomor Tur
TOURS

(Помор Тур; ☑8182-203 320; www.pomor-tur.ru; ul Voskresenskaya 99; ⊙10am-7pm Mon-Fri; 🚌1, 10) City and regional excursions, including themed tours to the Solovetsky Islands and one-week paddle-steamer cruises along the Dvina to Kotlas/Veliky Ustyug. As from 2016, Pomor Tur also offers trips on icebreakers. These last from two to five days and take place from January to April. Costs start at R23,000, and foreigners need to apply at least six weeks in advance to receive the necessary FSB clearance for travel into the Russian Arctic. Accommodation is in two-berth cabins.

Kompaniya Solovki TOURS

(Компания Соловки; ☎8182-655 008; www. solovkibp.ru; 5th fl, Troitsky pr 37; ⏰10am-6pm Mon-Fri; 🖥1, 11) Good range of tour options to the Solovetsky Islands, Kargopol and around, White Sea regional tours and more.

🛏 Sleeping

★Hostel Troika HOSTEL $

(Хостел Тройка; ☎8-818-265 0535, 8182-650 535; www.hostel-troika.ru; ul Karla Libknekhta 8; dm R550-600, dm R1600; ⊜🛜; 🖥1, 11) This friendly, centrally located hostel is perhaps the region's best budget option. Clean and bright rooms are equipped with bunk beds and shared toilet and bathroom facilities. Two double rooms also have their own toilets and bathrooms. A well-stocked kitchen has everything you need to fix yourself breakfast, as well as a good selection of books. On the 3rd floor of an office building.

Hotel Severnitsa HOTEL $$

(Отель Северница; ☎8182-430 013; nab Severnoy Dviny 32; s/d R2300/2500; ⊜🛜; 🖥1, 54) This new hotel still has that just-opened sheen and the compact, flowery rooms are good value. It is tucked away in a courtyard, just a short walk from the centre. Gets extra points for chatty, friendly staff.

Stolitsa Pomorya HOTEL $$

(Отель Столица Поморья; ☎8182-423 575; www.hotelarh.ru; nab Severnoy Dviny 88; s/d/ste from R3400/4000/5700; ⊜🛜; 🖥1, 54) Appealing business hotel with a cracking location overlooking the Dvina. The compact, modern rooms are particularly well geared towards solo travellers and perks include an on-site *banya* and massage centre. Add R400 for a river-view room.

Hotel Dvina HOTEL $$

(Гостиница Двина; ☎8182-288 888; www. hoteldvina.ru; Troitsky pr 52; s/d/ste from R3000/3400/8200; ⊜🛜; 🖥1, 11) This 13-storey pink Soviet beauty is a super-central, international-standard hotel that's been tastefully refurbished with quality linens, tiled bathrooms and a gym. Give the poor-value restaurant a miss though. Ask for mosquito netting for your window if it's missing; very helpful desk staff speak English.

Turisticheskaya Derevnya Malye Karely HOTEL $$

(Туристическая деревня Малые Карелы; ☎8182-462 472; www.karely.ru; d/apt/ste from R3200/6000/8300; ⊜🛜; 🖥104, 108) Just 200m from the Malye Karely museum entrance is this self-contained holiday-hotel complex. Bowling, billiards and fishing excursions are available, making the modern timber cottages and apartments a fun getaway alternative to central Arkhangelsk. The excellent restaurant has an olde-Russia theme, serving everything from grilled meats and poached fish to wild mushroom soup.

Pur Navolok Hotel HOTEL $$$

(Отель Пур-Наволок; ☎8182-217 200; http:// redstar-hotels.ru/hotels/arkhangelsk; nab Severnoy Dviny 88; s/d/ste incl breakfast from R5000/6500/10,500; ⊜🛜; 🖥1, 54) Though the exterior resembles an air-traffic control tower, the professionally run Pur Navolok offers bright, international-style rooms accessed by glass elevator and there's a sauna, plunge pool and hammam complex to ward off the northern chill. Rates include an extensive buffet breakfast and the panorama bar is a fun place to hang out in. Reception staff are sticklers for registration slips.

🍴 Eating

Pekarnaya na Chumbarovke CAFE $

(Пекарня на Чумбаровке; pr Chumbarova-Luchinskogo 29; business lunches R180; ⏰9am-9pm; 🛜; 🖥1, 54) This bright and cheery cafe is located halfway up pedestrianised Prospekt Chumbarova-Luchinskogo (p309). Offers great-value business lunches as well as tasty pastries to go with your tea and coffee. Can get very busy at lunchtime: a good sign!

Bratya Grill RUSSIAN $

(Братья Гриль; Troitsky pr 104; mains R295-420; ⏰9am-midnight Mon-Fri, 24hr, closed 8am-9am Sat & Sun; 🛜; 🖥1, 54) As befitting the name, buzzy 'Brothers Grill' specialises in grilled meats, though there are salads and cakes for non-carnivorous customers. The young staff are attentive, the drinks are unusual (cucumber lemonade, anyone?) and the wallpaper looks like something out of a bizarre fairy tale.

★Polina Cafe CAFE $$

(Кафе Полина; ul Troitsky 50; mains R270-450; ⏰9am-midnight Sun-Wed, 9am-7am Thu & Sat; 🛜📶; 🖥1, 11) This spacious cafe is popular with a young crowd and serves good pasta, as well as fish- and meat-based dishes. A sprouting of vegetarian dishes (such as mushroom and eggplant bake, R290) offer some welcome culinary relief for non-carnivores in provincial Russia. Also has a good selection of pastries and a decent wine list.

Chaykhona
CENTRAL ASIAN $$

(Чайхона; mains R315-945; ⊘11am-midnight Sun-Thu, 11am-1am Fri & Sat; 🔊) Spice alert in provincial Russia! This laid-back Central Asian–themed restaurant, part of a chain, serves *plov* (meat and rice, pilaf style), *kutab* (stuffed flatbread), grilled meat and good noodles.

Restoran Pomorsky
RUSSIAN $$

(Ресторан Поморский; Pomorskakay ul 7; mains R270-1200; ⊘noon-midnight; 🔊) Set in log-cabin-effect alcoves, this local favourite serves imaginatively named dishes such as 'bride of three bridegrooms' (salmon caviar *bliny*) and the 'herder bag' (pork stuffed with cheese). The affordable business lunch (R270) is filling, but not a thrill for the senses. It's hidden on the rear of the 3rd floor of an office building.

El Fuego
STEAK $$$

(pr Chumbarova-Luchinskogo 39; steak R660-4400; ⊘noon-2am; 🔊; 🚌1, 11) This Argentinian-style restaurant provides top-notch dining for the discerning carnivore. An exemplary steak menu that ranges from tender veal to Kobe rib-eye, and chefs of international calibre, make for a special night out. Its grill-scented, dark surrounds feel especially cosy in winter.

🍷 Drinking & Nightlife

Lock Stock
PUB

(www.lockstockpub.ru; nab Severnoy Dviny 30; ⊘11am-1am; 🚌1, 4, 11) Hugely popular English-style pub with authentic local-boozer decor and a hugely comprehensive list of ales, stouts and beers from the UK and elsewhere.

Biblio-Café
CAFE

(pl Lenina 3; ⊘8am-11pm; 🔊; 🚌1, 11, 54) Smart and sunny hideaway brewing strong coffees (from R140) behind the Arkhangelsk library.

Route 66
BAR

(Роут 66; pr Lomonosova 177; ⊘noon-2am; 🚌1, 6, 10) American-style diner-bar with orange leather seats and a surprisingly good selection of English beers on top of its palatable own brew. Live bands on weekends.

⭐ Entertainment

Arkhangelsk Jazz
LIVE MUSIC

(Архангельск Джаз; www.arkhangelsk-jazz.com; Pomorskaya ul 3; cover from R400; ⊘8pm-1am Sun-Thu, until 2am Fri & Sat; 🚌1, 54) This rickety-looking historic building plays host to the city's most exciting jazz and blues events. An international jazz festival takes place here in May and live gigs take place on weekends.

Philharmonia
CLASSICAL MUSIC

(Поморская филармония; 🔊8182-215 669; www.pomorfil.ru; pl Lenina 1; ⊘ticket office noon-7pm Mon-Sat; 🚌1, 54) The Philharmonia hosts orchestral concerts and operas. Its Kamerny Zal (Chamber Hall; Камерный Зал; 🔊8182-208 066; www.pomorfil.ru; ul Karla Marksa 3; ⊘ticket office 1-7pm Tue-Sun; 🚌1, 6, 10) stages organ and chamber music in the 1768 Lutheran church of St Catherine; there's a busy 'white nights' program in June.

Koleso
LIVE MUSIC

(Колесо; 🔊8182-209 799; www.arkoleso.ru; ul Gaydara 4/1; ⊘5pm-late; 🚌1, 6) The 'Wheel', an Arkhangelsk institution, hosts rock, thrash metal, folk, rockabilly and country gigs from local and visiting acts on weekends and some weeknights. Check the regularly updated website to see what's on while you're in town.

ℹ Information

Post Office (Почта; Voskresenskaya ul 5; ⊘8am-9pm Mon-Fri, 9am-6pm Sat & Sun) Main post office.

Tourist Office (Туристический информационный центр; 🔊8182-214 082; www.pomorland.info; ul Svobody 8; ⊘9am-1pm & 2-5pm Mon-Thu, to 4pm Fri; 🚌1, 54) Enthusiastic, well-informed, English-speaking staff are an inspiring source of information for the city and the whole of Arkhangelsk region. Extensive website.

The 2GIS website (www.2gis.ru) has an interactive map of the city with all transport routes marked. It's also available as a free app.

ℹ Getting There & Away

A handy ticket desk in Hotel Dvina (p310) sells rail and air tickets for a small commission.

AIR

Arkhangelsk's main airport, **Talagi** (Талаги; www.arhaero.ru), is 12km northeast of the centre. Most flights are operated by Aeroflot (www.aeroflot.com), **Nordavia** (Нордавиа; 🔊800-200 0055; www.nordavia.ru/eng) and **Rossiya** (Россия; 🔊800-444 5555; www.rossiya-air-lines.ru/en). Destinations include Moscow (1¾ hours, up to seven daily), Murmansk (two hours, six weekly), Solovetsky Islands (50 minutes, Tuesday, Wednesday, Saturday and Sunday in summer), St Petersburg (1½ hours, up to six daily).

Weather permitting, further Solovetsky Islands flights leave in small planes from **Vaskovo**

Airport (Аэропорт Васьково; ☑ 8182-462 166), 20km southwest of the city centre.

BUS

From the **bus station** (Автовокзал; ul 23-y Gvardeyskoy Divizii 13), services run to Veliky Ustyug (R1495, 11½ hours, 8am daily) and Kargopol (R1050, 13 hours, 8.15am Monday, Wednesday and Saturday).

TRAIN

Two or three daily trains run to Moscow's Yaroslavsky station (R2422, 20 to 23 hours) via Vologda (R1537, 11 to 14 hours) and Yaroslavl (R1965, 15½ to 18 hours). Daily train 009 for St Petersburg (R2574, 24½ hours) departs at 8.43pm. Train 371 heads to Kem on Tuesday, Thursday and Sunday (R2380, 13 hours), arriving at 4.03am, which will give you ample time to make the morning boats for the Solovetsky Islands. One carriage detaches en route and heads for Murmansk (R2228, 26 hours).

🛈 Getting Around

The 2GIS website (www.2gis.ru) and app offers coverage of all the city's transport routes.

Appearing as MR Vokzal (МР Вокзал) on destination boards, the **River Terminal** (Морской-речной вокзал; nab Severnoy Dviny 26) is a major hub for city buses and *marshrutky*. From here the rare bus 110 runs to Vaskovo Airport (p311) and frequent route 12 runs every few minutes to Talagi (p311) airport via pl Lenina and northern Troitsky pr.

Handy buses 4, 41 and 54 run down ul Voskresenkaya from the railway station and then turn east along Troitsky pr at pl Lenina. Bus 11 makes a loop around the city centre from MR Vokzal, and buses that run up and down Troitsky pr include 1, 4, 12 and 44.

KOLA PENINSULA
КОЛЬСКИЙ ПОЛУОСТРОВ

The Kola Peninsula is a 100,000-sq-km knob of tundra, bogs and low mountains between the White and Barents Seas. Lying almost entirely north of the Arctic Circle, its mesmerising expanses of wilderness are fabulous places to be dazzled by the aurora borealis or midnight sun.

Mineral strata beneath the Khibiny and Lovozero mountains contain a treasure trove of exotic minerals that get the world's geologists and rock collectors salivating. Apatity has secret museums, Lovozero is the heart of Russia's Sami community and Kirovsk is the gateway to pristine wilderness and has the region's best skiing. Wilderness lovers will find Central Kola particularly rewarding, with husky and reindeer sledding on offer. It's also rich hunting ground for Soviet ruin enthusiasts, with abandoned villages scattered through the region, and even a gigantic disused train station in Kirovsk.

Apatity   Апатиты

☑ 81555 / POP 56,730 / ⊘ MOSCOW

Central Kola's second-biggest town, Apatity is an *akademgorodok*, a town of chemists responsible for processing the raw product from Kirovsk's apatite mines (hence the name) and home to nine research institutes. Several of those have museums that can be visited by guided tour, such as the **Mineralogy Museum** (Минералогический музей; ☑ 8-921-665 4662; ul Fersmana 14; ⊘ by appointment 9am-5pm Mon-Fri) FREE, which has over 900 types of minerals and ores, many of them rare and unique.

The **North-Russian Exploration Museum** (Музей истории изучения и освоения Европейского севера России; Akademgorodok 40a; R70; ⊘ 2-5pm Mon-Fri) showcases the settlement of the Kola peninsula, the history of science in the region and the culture of Kola's indigenous population – the Sami.

There is no real reason to spend the night here, and you'd be much better seeking accommodation in nearby Kirovsk. There are a handful of cafes around pl Lenina, by far the best of which is **Dzhaga** (Джага; ul Fersmana 18; pizza from R330; ⊘ 11am-9pm; 🛜), which boasts arguably the region's best pizza.

The friendly **tourist information centre** (Туристский информационный центр; ☑ 8155-574 095; www.vk.com/apatity_tic; ul Lenina 3; ⊘ 10am-6pm Tue-Fri, 10am-5pm Sat) can book accommodation throughout the region, as well as organise mineral-collecting, snowmobiling and fishing trips to the White Sea and Solovetsky Islands.

From Apatity's pl Lenina, buses run to Murmansk (R555, 4½ hours, five daily), Kirovsk (R50, 25 minutes, around 12 a day) and Monchegorsk (R245, 1½ hours, four to six daily). Buy tickets in the **MTA** (Мурманское Транспортное Агентство, Murmanskoe Transportnoe Agenstvo; ul Lenina 19; ⊘ bus tickets 5.45am-1pm & 2-6pm, train tickets 10am-5pm Mon-Fri, 10am-2pm Sat) office, located in the nine-floor building behind the cinema. There are also two daily flights from Moscow (R8100, two hours) and two from St Petersburg (R6500, 90 minutes) to Apatity's small **Khibini Airport** (Аэропорт Хибины; ☎8-921 514 0015; www.hibiny.aero), which is located 15km south of the town and is used mainly by tourists heading to nearby Kirovsk. Take bus 130 (R60, every hour) from pl Lenina to get there.

Kirovsk   Кировск

☎81531 / POP 26,971 / ⊘ MOSCOW

Kirovsk is a miners' town that owes its existence to the world's purest deposits of apatite, as testified by the giant lump of the stuff on a pedestal along main ul Lenina and a cute *gornyachok* (little miner) sculpture nearby. There's a grim beauty to the industrial detritus of Kirvosk, founded in 1929, with gaping shells of abandoned Soviet buildings and open-pit mines set against the backdrop of Lake Veliky Vudyavr and the surrounding snow-covered mountains.

With its own microclimate, Kirovsk really comes into its own in the long winter, with a surprisingly good skiing scene that lasts until mid-May and local daredevils freeriding off-piste even after the ski lifts shut down for the season. In winter, ice skaters and *morzhi* (hardy Russians who swim year-round, cutting swimming holes in lakes in winter) take to the frozen lakes and sculptors take up chisels at the Snow Village.

◎ Sights

★ Abandonded Soviet Train Station   RUINS

(Kirovsk) This colossal Soviet-era train station stands abandoned and half-forgotten amid the harsh Arctic landscape. The two-platform station, which once took passengers as far as Murmansk and Leningrad (St Petersburg), was constructed in 1934 and operated until 1996. It was closed down as the local population declined following the Soviet collapse. The roof caved in long ago under the weight of winter snows. The inscription above the gradually crumbling columns reads 'Kirovsk'. It's located behind the central clock-tower.

★ Snow Village   AMUSEMENT PARK

(Снежная Деревня; www.snowderevnya.ru; Kirovsk; adult/child from R600/300; ⊙4-9pm Mon-Fri, 11am-9pm Sat & Sun Dec-Mar) Every November, ice sculptors from all over the region make their way to Kirovsk to chisel the snowy halls and tunnels of the Snow Village into existence, wowing visitors

with ice sculptures and annually changing themed displays carved into walls – from snowy pharaohs in chariots to fairy-tale creatures. For extra thrills, ride a giant banana attached to a snowmobile or marry your sweetie in the Ice Chapel. The Snow Village is located just beyond the Botanical Gardens. There are no direct buses.

Polar-Alpine Botanical Gardens   GARDENS

(Полярно-альпийский ботанический сад; ☎8-921-167 9732; www.pabgi.ru; ⊙tours by appointment at 10am, noon & 2pm; 🚌1, 12, 16, 105) **FREE** Russia's vast, northernmost botanical gardens and its special hothouses nurturing tropical plants can only be accessed on one of three tours offered daily. A 2km summer-only 'ecotrail', which climbs to the impressive alpine tundra, also awaits visitors. Take bus 1, 12, 16 or 105 (R30) towards Kukisvumchorr ('25km'), north of Lake Bolshoi Vudyavr, alight by the turnoff on the left before reaching '25km', and walk for 1.5km.

Culture Palace   THEATRE

(Дворец Культуры; ul Mira; ⊙ticket office noon-6pm Mon-Fri, 11am-4pm Sat) Everything from classical concerts to Miss Kirovsk pageants are held in this impressive, becolumned, lemon-yellow building.

⚡ Activities

There are three main skiing sites around Kirovsk; Bolshoy Vudyavr Ski Station is the best. Think hard before joining local freeriders off-piste, as every year the mountains claim lives through avalanches.

★ Bolshoy Vudyavr Ski Station   SKIING

(Горнолыжный комплекс 'Большой Вудъявр'; ☎800-200 2000; www.bigwood.ru; ski pass per 2hr/day R600/1400; ⊙Nov-early May) The best of Kirovsk's three ski stations, Bolshoy Vudyavr boasts modern lifts, downhill runs suitable for all abilities and lit-up slopes during the winter. Ski rental is R250/690 per hour/day, while snowboards are R300/830. You'll need to leave a R10000 deposit. It's

KOLA'S WHITE SEA COAST

With rafting, amethyst hunting, salmon fishing and petroglyph gawking among its offerings, the Kola Peninsula's unspoilt southern shore is one of the region's offbeat delights. The Varzuga River is famous in angling circles for its first-class fly fishing, with the prized Atlantic salmon found in remarkable abundance. Keen (and cashed-up) anglers can contact the UK-based **Roxtons** (www.roxtons.com) for information on all-inclusive six-day Varzuga packages, or head to the **Atlantic Salmon Reserve** (812-611 0417; www.kharlovka.com) where there are several fixed and tented camps with en suite facilities. Just over 140km to the northeast, river camps near the coast's biggest town, **Umba**, also offer good, and far cheaper, spots to cast a line.

Northwest of Umba, the cryptic petroglyphs (2nd to 3rd millennium BC) of **Lake Kanozero** have intrigued and bewildered experts since their discovery in 1997. Rafting tours stop at the island site. Between Umba and Varzuga, a gravel road takes rock spotters to the **Tersky Coast**, where amethyst stones litter the coastline. Contact **Kola Travel** (81536-71 313; www.kolatravel.com; pr Metallurgov 17/52, Monchegorsk) for details on mineralogical and rafting expeditions. East of Tersky coast is a patch of genuine desert where humans rarely set foot; wild horses can be spotted near there. For wildlife spotting beneath the waves, team up with the **Arctic Circle PADI Dive Center** (Туристический центр Полярный Круг; 8-925-381 2243; www.pkrug.ru; two dives from R4000, one-day ice diving R6800) to go ice diving, snorkelling with beluga whales and more.

just across the mountain east of Kirovsk, but 12km away by road (around R500 by taxi).

Can also organise snowmobile tours of the surrounding Arctic countryside (R8050 per day, per person). See the website for further details.

Kukisvumchor Ski Station   SKIING
(Кукисвумчорр Горнолыжный курорт; 8-921-154 6464; www.25chorr.ru; Kukisvumchor; ski pass per 2hr/day R500/1200; ⊙Nov-early May; 1, 104, 128) The slopes around this ski station are extremely popular with Russian freeriders. The ski station itself has three ski lifts, downhill runs suitable for every level, and lit-up slopes during winter, with skis and snowboards available for rent (R500/1200 per hour/day). The ski station is located 25km from Kirovsk. Buses 1, 104 and 128 (R50) will take you all the way there. Get out at the Pytyorochka (Пятёрочка) stop

H4U   SNOW SPORTS
(81531-54 677; www.hibiny4you.ru; ul Yubileinaya 8; ⊙10am-7pm Mon-Fri, 11am-6pm Sat & Sun) This activity operator offers snowmobile trips in the surrounding Arctic countryside, including daily travel to the top of the nearby Mt Takhtarvumchorr (R3500) and snowmobile rides on picturesque Maly Vudyavr Lake. The price includes all necessary equipment.

Kolasportland   SKIING
(Коласпортланд; 8-921-154 6464; ski-kolasport.narod.ru; ul Olimpiyskaya 81; day ski pass R950; ⊙Nov-early May; 102, 128, 135) Immediately above town, Kirovsk's highest slopes have runs for all levels, with two of the slopes lit up during winter. Skis (R80/400 per hour/day) and snowboards (R150/600) are available for rental. The resort is a short walk from the centre. Bus 102, 135 or 128 (R50) will also take you there.

Khibiny Mountains   HIKING
(Хибины) Divided by deep valleys, the bald, barren Khibiny range throws down the gauntlet to experienced hikers. Challenges include everything from strenuous day hikes to multiday wilderness expeditions. Note that though the mountains only rise to 1200m above sea level, weather can be extreme and fast changing, so go with knowledgeable locals or a tour operator such as H4U.

🛏 Sleeping

Hotel prices rise around 30% in ski season (December to May). In the brief warmer months, Kirovsk's cluster of hotels, located within walking distance of the central clocktower ('Big Ben'), makes a good springboard for rambles in the surrounding wilderness.

Hotel Gornaya Dolina
HOTEL $$

(Отель Горная Долина; ☑ 8-991-112 5011; www.gornaya-dolina.info; ul Kirova 48; s/d/tr R1970/2150/2250; ✿🖥) This orange hotel has bright and compact rooms and is ideal if you intend to spend a lot of time on the slopes at the nearby Kukisvumchor ski station. As well as ski storage space, there is also a kitchen, a washing machine and a clothes dryer for guest use. Buses 1, 104 and 128 (R50, 30 minutes) will get you here from the centre of Kirovsk.

Hotel Gornitsa
HOTEL $$

(Гостиница Горница; ☑ 81531-59 111; www.gornitsahotel.com; ul Dzerzhinskogo 19; s/d/tr/q incl breakfast R2100/3600/4650/6200; ✿🖥) This unpretentious, family-style 17-room hotel is in fantastic shape. Winter visitors will appreciate the underfloor heating in bathrooms, and the presence of the sauna (from R600 per hour).

Hotel Severnaya
HOTEL $$$

(Гостиница Северная; ☑ 81531-33 100; www.bigwood.ru; pr Lenina 11; s/d/ste from R3200/4200/6000; 🅿🖥) This forest-green, outwardly classy, neoclassical-styled hotel has 61 good-sized rooms, some of which have massive bathtubs. It's central, modern and the staff are obliging. Ski storage and transport to Bolshoi Vudyavr ski station available on request.

Hotel Ekkos
HOTEL $$$

(Гостиница Эккос; ☑ 81531-32 716; pr Lenina 12b; s/d/apt R3500/4600/7600; ✿🖥) This memorable 'castle' behind the Kirov statue may look a bit ramshackle from the outside, but the renovated rooms and four-person apartments tell a different story. Breakfast is available on request and there's a communal kitchen for self-caterers.

✕ Eating & Drinking

Cafe Schokolad
CAFE $

(Кафе Шоколад; ul Olimpiyskaya 17; mains from R200; ⊙ 11am-9pm) Cosy branch of the popular cafe chain inside the Olimp shopping centre. Come here for hot chocolate, sweet and savoury *bliny*, fried-egg-and-bacon brunches and strong coffee.

Fusion
RUSSIAN, JAPANESE $$

(mains R230-650; ⊙ 11am-1am; 🖥) Kirovsk's smartest restaurant is on the 2nd floor of an entertainment complex. The menu runs the gamut from schnitzel and *pelmeni* (Russian-style ravioli) to pizza, kimchi soup and decent sushi rolls.

Severny
RUSSIAN, EUROPEAN $$

(Северный; pr Lenina 11; mains R280-900; ⊙ 8am-11pm Sun-Thu, 8am-1am Fri & Sat; 🖥) Located on the first floor of Hotel Severnaya and serves Russian and European dishes, including *pelmeni*, deer meat, and pizza. It also has a good buffet breakfast that is open to nonguests from 8am to 11am (R350). Doubles as a bar in the evening and can get fairly noisy.

Bar Barevich
CRAFT BEER

(Бар Баревич; www.vk.com/barevichcraft; ul Leningradskaya 5; ⊙ 5pm-2am Mon-Fri, 3pm-2am Sat & Sun; 🖥) Craft beer in the Arctic Circle! This US-style bar serves a range of limited craft beers (from R250), oysters from the White Sea, and grilled meat. Also has darts and multiple TV screens that show sporting events. It's near Lake Verkhnee, a short walk from the centre of town.

ℹ Information

Tourist Office (Туристический информационный центр; ☑ 81531-55 711; www.kirovsk.ru/tourism; pr Lenina 7; ⊙ 9am-1pm & 2-5pm Mon-Fri) Useful free maps and info on the area.

You can find a super-detailed online map of Kirovsk at www.kartami.ru/kirovskmurmanskoy.

ℹ Getting There & Away

Frequent *marshrutky* and local buses to Apatity (R50, 30 minutes) pick up along ul Lenina.

A **ticket office** (Билетная касса; ☑ 81531-94 160; ul Yubileynaya 13; ⊙ 8.30am-7pm Mon-Fri, to 4pm Sat) sells tickets for buses to Murmansk (R554, 5½ hours, four daily) via Monchegorsk (R209, 1½ hours), leaving from next to the Kaskad shopping centre, across the street. It also sells train tickets to Apatity.

ℹ Getting Around

Patchy bus service means you are better off walking around the town. You'll only need buses or taxis to reach out-of-town sights or ski stations. Pick up a free map from the friendly tourist office (p315).

Lovozero   Ловозеро

☑ 81538 / POP 2871 / ⊙ MOSCOW

Under Stalin, the once-nomadic Sami people were brutally suppressed and forced into *kolkhozy* (collective farms). Today, of Russia's roughly 1600 Sami, close to 900 now live in the administrative village of Lovozero (Luyavvr). The village, which celebrated the 500th anniversary of its founding in 2017, is windswept and desolate, with numerous empty buildings. At the end of the village, the Virma River flows into the surrounding Arctic landscape.

Twenty-or-so kilometres east of Lovozero, and then 8km south, is unpretty Revda, gateway to a spectacular, rugged eight-hour hike over the Lovozyorskiye Tundry Mountains to pristine **Lake Seydozero** – holy to the Sami – where you can camp in blissful wilderness. On the way from Olenegorsk to Lovozero, look out for an abandoned Soviet military residential zone. It's just one of a number of now-forgotten villages throughout the Kola Peninsula that witnessed massive population decline after the collapse of the communist system.

◎ Sights & Activities

★ **Sami History & Culture Museum** MUSEUM
(Музей истории, культуры и быта кольских саамов; ☑ 81538-31 477; ul Sovetskaya 28; R35, guided tours R150; ☉ 9am-1pm & 2-5pm Tue-Sat) This excellent museum delves into the Sami people's troubled history and their way of life, which continues to be threatened. It also celebrates the heroic efforts to keep Sami culture alive, and the revival of the Sami language and traditional Sami crafts. Traditional costume, hunting tools and photos of ancient stone labyrinths, rock carvings and Sami fighters during WWII also feature prominently in the museum.

Sami Village 'Sam-Siyt' SNOW SPORTS
(Саамская Деревня; ☑ 8-921-169 6299, 8-911-306 0675; http://lovozero1.ru) This self-styled 'Sami cultural village' offers reindeer sledding and snowmobiling in winter, ATV rides and reindeer encounters in summer, an introduction to Sami customs, traditional Sami cuisine served in a *chumy* (tepee-shaped tent), and all manner of Sami games. There is also a small guesthouse (doubles/triples R2000/3000) with a *banya* (R3000 per three hours). Book through Kola Travel (p314).

Where the main road west of Lovozero branches in two, take the Murmansk branch; the village is 5km up the road.

Husky Park Lesnaya Elan DOG SLEDDING
(Хаски-Парк Лесная Елань; ☑ 8152-688 836, 8-921-734 0533; www.vk.com/huskypark; KM14; dog-sled ride adult/child R1000/500) At this husky farm you can go dog- and reindeer-sledding in winter, have lunch in a Sami *chum* and meet the huskies in the summer. It's located 14km east of Lovozero down an unmarked gravel road; call ahead. Visits can also be organised via Arctic Land (p319) or Kola Travel (p314).

🛏 Sleeping & Eating

Few tourists spend the night in Lovozero; accommodation here consists of just one small converted flat, **Hotel Nadezhda** (Гостиница Надежда; ☑ 8-921-150 3124, 81538-40 309; ul Danilova 21/22; r from R1300). For groceries there's **Lovozero Produkty** (Продукты; ul Sovetskaya 9; ☉ 7am-midnight).

❶ Getting There & Away

Lovozero is reached via a road that branches off the Murmansk-bound M-18 dual carriageway at the transport hub of Olenegorsk.

At the start of 2017, local authorities scrapped the subsidised Olenegorsk-Lovozero bus service, leaving Lovozero totally cut off. When we visited, the only way to get there was to take a taxi from Olenegorsk (R2000, one way). The 80km journey takes around two hours. There are shared taxis (R500, one way) but these are infrequent.

Olenegorsk is connected to Murmansk by frequent trains (R788, 2½ hours) and buses (R384, three hours). The surly staff in the nearby 24-hour canteen (it's intended for railway workers, but anyone is 'welcome') will sell you sweet black tea for just R10 while you wait.

Teriberka   Териберка

☑ 81553 / POP 1500 / ☉ MOSCOW

Hemmed in between the Barents Sea and the snow-covered hills around it, the fishing village of Teriberka is one of the most picturesque spots in Arctic Russia. With its skeletons of old boats on the shore, wooden cabins, empty shells of Soviet-era housing and a colourful seafront graveyard, this spot is easily accessed from Murmansk by car or by daily bus through spectacular Arctic scenery.

Teriberka was used as the backdrop for *Leviathan*, Russia's 2015 Golden Globe–winning and Oscar-nominated film about one man's doomed fight against corrupt officials. The film has sparked an upsurge of interest in Teriberka, and Russian and Norwegian investors are hoping to develop the village's potential.

Explore the hills and the coastline, dip your toes in the frigid waters, marvel at the midnight sun during the brief summer or simply enjoy the solitude and your proximity to the world's northernmost ocean. There are two main beaches – a sandy one right next to the village and one covered in rocks and boulders that is a 5km trek or drive away. Every summer Teriberka plays host to the **New Life festival** (Териберка. Новая жизнь; www.vk.com/newteriberka), which brings together musicians and artists from across Russia. The exact dates change every year, however. Check the website for details.

Note that some of the wilderness near Teriberka falls under Zakrytiye Administrativo-Territorialnye Obrazovania; Closed Administrative-Territorial Formations (ZATOs; p324).

🛏 Sleeping & Eating

Teribersky Bereg HUT $$
(Териберский Берег; ☎8-911-339 7869; www.teriberskybereg.ru; huts per person incl breakfast R1800; 🌂🔊) Right next to the sandy beach, Teribersky Bereg offers eye-catching accommodation in red wooden huts. The cosy huts, which are open all year round, sleep four, and are great for early morning or late night beach strolls or swims. Teribersky Bereg also runs the nearby restaurant of the same name, with great views of the sea.

Hosts can organise fishing trips, as well as travel into the surrounding Arctic wilderness.

Ter HOTEL $$
(Тер; ☎8-921-041 0581; www.vk.com/club 121694672; d incl breakfast from R3000; 🌂) A good-standard hotel with comfortable double rooms near the sandy beach. Has table-tennis and billiards for guest use, and the breakfast is tasty and filling.

Normann HOTEL $$
(Норманн; ☎8-921-513 5726; www.vk.com/club143783659; d R2000; 🌂) A friendly family-run hotel with basic, but comfortable rooms and a kitchen for guest use. Shared bathroom and toilets. The owners might show you some of their *Leviathan* props if you ask them nicely. Can also organise Barents Sea fishing trips.

ℹ Getting There & Away

From the paved main road heading east of Murmansk, a signposted gravel road branches off north after about 100km and runs through the vast tundra. It's a beautiful 60km drive that passes pristine, ice-covered lakes and a sinister Grim Reaper/skier figure wearing a gas mask.

If you don't have your own wheels, you can catch the daily bus (R496, 3½ hours) from Murmansk at 5.40pm, returning the following morning at 7am. Alternatively, taxis do the trip from Murmansk for R4000.

Travelling here in the winter months can be problematic, when the village is often cut off for days by heavy snowfalls.

MURMANSK МУРМАНСК

☑ 8152 / POP 305, 200 / TIME MOSCOW
The world's biggest Arctic city is a mere baby by Russian standards: Murmansk celebrated its 100th birthday in 2016. Murmansk's raison d'être is its port, kept ice-free by comparatively warm Gulf Stream waters. This bustling, rapidly modernising place gets much of its wealth from the cornucopia of minerals found beneath the ground of the Kola Peninsula, the controversial exploitation of natural resources

BREAKING THE ICE

It should come as no surprise that the Russians were the inventors – and perfectors – of the ice-faring vessel. The northern Pomors constructed the first ice-clearing ships (called *kochy*) in the 11th century, built with ice-resistant hardwood and used for the exploration of Arctic waters. The boats' round shape propelled them onto the ice when squeezed by floes.

Fast forward 900 years, and the development of nuclear icebreakers has literally cleared the way for northern-bound cargo ships, scientific voyages and tourist expeditions with a force hitherto thought impossible with diesel-powered predecessors. Today's vessels – mammoth double-hulled constructs comprising steel bows and two onboard reactors – power their way through ice up to 3m thick at speeds reaching 10 knots. Nuclear icebreakers are stationed at Murmansk's Atomflot base at Kola Bay.

in the Arctic and close ties with its Scandinavian neighbours.

The first glimpse of stolid Soviet-era architecture and the gritty port may not be the stuff of dreams, but beyond that, impressions get better and better. This lively city is surrounded by incomparable, often harsh Arctic scenery and is a playground for outdoor adventurers during the months of the midnight sun (late May to late July). During the winter darkness (late November to mid-January) the northern lights over the snow-covered landscape are an eerie, magical sight.

History

Founded in 1916 as Romanov-na-Murmanye, the city developed almost overnight during WWI, and was occupied until 1920 by pro-White allies fighting the Bolsheviks. Renamed Murmansk, the 'hero city' was bombed to bits in WWII.

Murmansk came to global attention in September 2013 when Russian forces seized the Greenpeace ship *Arctic Sunrise*, which was protesting against oil drilling in the Arctic, and charged its crew with piracy. In the two months that the 'Arctic 30' were kept in a Murmansk jail, the resulting media circus greatly boosted the city's businesses.

Sights

★ Ice Bathers' Hut   NATURAL POOL

(Домик моржей; ☑ 8152-242 800; Prospekt Geroev Severomortsev 2a; ⊙ 24hr Oct-May; Ⓟ; ☑ 5, 6, 10) Home to Murmansk's 'walruses' – hardy souls who swear by the health benefits of regularly bathing in icy waters – this wooden hut on the edge of Lake Semyonovskoe dates from the Soviet era. Wooden steps lead down into a hole cut into the ice for a genuinely chilled experience. Get off at the Semyonovskoe Ozero bus stop, cross the road, and track back some 250m to a path that leads to the lake. Bring a towel!

While the hut is technically only open to club members, the 'walruses' are usually happy to explain their icy passion to curious visitors, especially if you call in advance. Ice bathing is oddly exhilarating, but newcomers are advised not to put their heads under the water. Be sure to check out the photos of happy Soviet–era bathers in the changing room. A taxi here from the centre costs around R150.

★ Nuclear Icebreaker Lenin   BOAT

(Атомный ледокол Ленин; ☑ 8152-553 512; Portovy pr 25; adult/child R150/50; ⊙ Wed-Sun, tours at noon, 2pm & 4pm; ☑ 1, 4) Murmansk is a centre for nuclear icebreakers that carve their way to the North Pole, but even in port you

---

RUSSIA'S SAMI

The Kola Peninsula's indigenous people, the Sami, have been residents in this harsh land for millennia. The Sami haven't had it easy, with their semi-nomadic hunter-turned-reindeer-herdsman lifestyle under threat from everyone else who came to the Kola Peninsula after them. Exploitation by traders and settlers and forced Christianisation in the 19th century, the forced collectivisation of their reindeer in the 1920s, repression of their culture under the Soviets, and the continuous infringement of Sami land rights by mining, timber, mineral development, commercial fishing and tourism companies have all taken their toll.

While Russia's 1600-or-so Sami have set up the Association of the Kola Sami to protect and promote Sami interests, the association has no legal power under Russian law. Another problem is the lack of enforcement of existing laws, under which 'in historically established areas of habitation, Sami enjoy the rights for traditional use of nature and [traditional] activities'. In practise, they have been repeatedly forced off land to be used for mineral exploitation and had their fishing rights curtailed to make room for commercial-fishing tourism catering to foreigners. On top of that, high unemployment and alcoholism affect many members of the small community of Lovozero.

It's not all doom and gloom, though. The Sami language (Southern Sami), repressed in Soviet times, now flourishes in both written and spoken form. Credit goes to dedicated members of the community, such as writer and linguist Aleksandra Antonova, who put together the first Russian-Sami dictionary in 1982, collected oral Sami folk tales and had them compiled into storybooks. Sami *duodji* (traditional crafts such as knife-making, leatherwork, bone-carving and beadwork) has taken off, with Russian Sami masters exchanging ideas with their visiting Scandinavian brethren, the interaction between all Sami groups once again reestablished.

can give in to your wildest seafaring–Arctic explorer–Cold War spy fantasies aboard the 1957 NS *Lenin*, the world's first nuclear-powered icebreaker. You aren't allowed to wander freely, but there are three tours a day that take in the nuclear reactor (powered by uranium 235), the map room, the captain's bridge and the reception hall. Only open for tours.

★ Alyosha   MONUMENT
(Алёша; 🖼 4, 10) One of Murmansk's most memorable sights is a gigantic concrete soldier nicknamed Alyosha, erected to commemorate the Arctic fighters who perished in the Great Patriotic War (WWII). From his hilltop perch, Alyosha's stony visage stares across the Kola Inlet at the snow-speckled Arctic moors beyond. To the south, the port spreads out in all its magnificent industrial dreariness. The statue is a 20-minute ramble past Semyononvskoye Lake through the hilly park from one of the Ozero bus stops.

Regional Studies Museum   MUSEUM
(Мурманский   областной   краеведческий музей; www.mokm51.ru; pr Lenina 90; adult/student R150/25; ⏰ 11am-6pm Sat-Wed; 🖼 3, 6, 18) Comprehensive exhibits at Murmansk's oldest museum include one on Sami culture and handicrafts, a vast natural-history section with all manner of taxidermied beasts and *Wait For Me* – an exhibition on the fierce defence of the north during WWII. Delve also into the history of Arctic exploration, contemplate the region's mysterious ancient stone labyrinths, and get nostalgic over prehistoric radios and Zenit cameras in the 'Made in the USSR' section.

Fine Arts Museum   MUSEUM
(Мурманский   областной   художественный музей; www.artmmuseum.ru; ul Kominterna 13; R100; ⏰ 11am-7pm Wed-Sun; 🖼 1, 2, 4, 5) The 1927 Fine Arts Museum hosts temporary exhibitions that range from female nude photography and Kanozero petroglyphs to severe Arctic landscape painting.

Museum of the Northern Fleet   MUSEUM
(Военно-морской музей Северного флота; www.museum.ru/M2047; ul Tortseva 15; R150; ⏰ 9am-1pm & 2-5pm Thu-Mon; 🖼 10) The mass of exhibits inside this crumbling turquoise anchor-flanked building covers everything from the founding of Russia's first navy in Arkhangelsk, to 17th- and 18th-century Arctic exploration, to Murmansk convoys of WWII – a joint effort with British servicemen. A vast collection of Soviet naval equipment makes this a must for military history enthusiasts. Alight from bus 10 at the penultimate stop, Nakhimova (Нахимова), walk on for 300m then turn left and it's 80m up ul Tortseva.

Church of the
Saviour on the Waters   CHURCH
(Храм Спас на Водах; ul Chelyuskintsev; ⏰ 11am-7pm; 🖼 4, 10) FREE This gold-domed church, built in 2002 from public donations, is part of a memorial complex dedicated to the memory of Murmansk's seamen who perished in peacetime. Just below is the lighthouse monument, and next to it is part of the ill-fated submarine *Kursk*, whose entire 118-man crew perished in 2000 during naval exercises in the Barents Sea. When it sank, following an on-board explosion, the Russian government refused foreign assistance in the rescue operation until it was too late.

British Naval Cemetery   HISTORIC SITE
(ul Rogozerskaya; 🖼 10) In 1919 the British navy assisted the White Russians against the Reds – Winston Churchill, war secretary at the time, wanted to see if the Bolsheviks could be crushed before they could really get going. A few dozen British sailors found eternal rest in Russian soil, in a small 'English-style' graveyard that's remarkably well tended, even in winter. To find it, walk past the Statoil gas station on your left, and take a sharp right after 100m towards some rusty-looking sheds.

Monument To Semyon The Cat   MONUMENT
(Памятник Коту Семёну; Lake Semyonovskoe) This bronze monument to a fat little cat carrying all his worldly possessions in a knapsack was unveiled in 2013 in honour of an act of incredible feline loyalty and endurance. In 1987, after getting lost during a trip to Moscow, Semyon the cat reportedly spent the next six years travelling back to his owners' apartment in Murmansk – a journey of almost 2000km. It's on the northern bank of Lake Semyonovskoe.

☞ **Tours**

All Murmansk tour companies can arrange aurora borealis trips.

Arctic Land   TOURS
(Арктическая Земля; ☎ 8152-688 836; www.arcticland.ru; office 206, ul Knipovicha 23, in Hotel Moryak; 🖼 6, 18) Tours to Husky Park Lesnaya Elan in both summer and winter as well as fishing trips in summer.

Murmansk

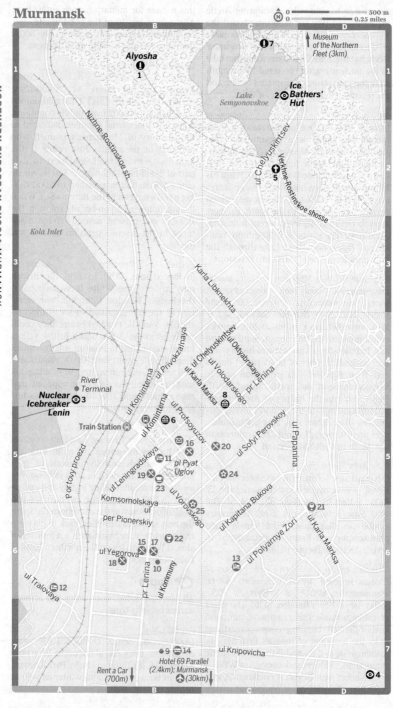

Murmansk

Nord Extreme Tour TOURS
(Норд Экстрим Тур; ☑8152-701 498; www.nor-dextreme.ru; ul Yegorova 14; ⊠3, 18) Kola Peninsula tours for active travellers, with fishing, diving, overland 4WD and snowmobiling adventures, and more.

✯ Festivals & Events

Festival of the North SPORTS
(Праздник Севера; ☉late Mar-early Apr) The annual 10-day festival includes a 'Polar Olympics', with participation from resident Scandinavians, reindeer-sled races, ski marathons, ice hockey and snowmobile contests. Many events are held at Dolina Uyuta (Cosy Valley), 25 minutes south of the train station on bus 1.

Murmansk Mile SPORTS
(Мурманская Миля; ☉Jun) Taking place on the third weekend in June, this fun festival centres around the main bridge across the Kola Bay, with a mini-marathon, swimming race across the bay, wheelchair event, volleyball, sailing and much more.

⊜ Sleeping

Most prices rise 30% during the trade exhibitions of May, June and mid-November. The Murmansk CouchSurfing community (www.couchsurfing.org) is a very active one. Besides providing free hospitality, English-speaking

Murmansk members are fantastic sources of information about the city and the region.

Hostel Prichal HOSTEL $
(Хостел Причал; ☑8152-287 560, 8-950-898-64-62; www.vk.com/club88195891; ul Tralovaya 6a; dm/s from R500/880; ⊛☏; ⊠2, 4) Basic, clean cheapie with beds rather than bunks and friendly staff. Has a decent shared kitchen.

Hotel 69 Parallel HOTEL $$
(Гостиница 69 Параллель; ☑8152-253 700; www.69parallel.ru; pr Lyzhny 14; s/d 1800-3900/2400-4900; ℙ⊛☏; ⊠18, 29) A good midrange hotel of the type that northern Russia could do with far more of. With completely refurbished rooms and an unexpectedly classy boutique(ish) vibe, it's in a good spot if you're coming for Festival of the North. Drawback: it's not exactly central; the nearest convenient bus and trolleybus stop is a 10-minute walk (trolleybus 6 and 10 also service the hotel).

Mini Hotel Rooms & Breakfast BOUTIQUE HOTEL $$
(Мини-отель Rooms & Breakfast; ☑8152-426 666; www.vk.com/hotel_murmansk; ul Polyarinye Zory 38; s/d incl breakfast from R2800/3600; ⊛☏; ⊠10) Compact rooms at this centrally located small hotel are spotless, en suite, high-tech and done up in soft pastel colours. Beds are comfortable, and there's underfloor

NORTHERN LIGHTS

Between October and March, the Kola Peninsula is one of the best places on earth to witness the aurora borealis, the natural phenomenon that has been wowing both locals and travellers alike since time immemorial. Spirals, waves and ripples of green (and sometimes yellow, white, red, blue or purple), caused by the collisions between electrically charged particles from the sun entering the earth's atmosphere, move across the dark sky.

The northern lights are the subject of many Sami legends, and the Kola Sami gather to watch the spectacle unfold above Lake Lovozero, one of the better places for viewing due to the relative lack of light pollution. Murmansk-based tour companies organise ventures into the tundra in search of the northern lights, but bear in mind that your quarry is unpredictable and not visible on a daily basis. Success depends on the weather, so you'll need plenty of time and a bit of luck.

heating. Tea and coffee are available around the clock, with freshly-prepared porridge for breakfast.

★ Azimut Hotel Murmansk HOTEL $$$

(Азимут Отель Мурманск; ☎ 8152-550 350; https://en.azimuthotels.com/Russia/azimut-hotel-murmansk; Pr Lenina 82; s/d/apt 5400/5900/8075; ☐ 3, 6, 18) Slap bang in the very centre of the city, the Murmansk branch of this international hotel chain boasts spotless rooms with underfloor heating and flat-screen, cable TV. The on-site, spacious two-room apartments are so comfy you might not want to leave. Stunning views of the city from the top floors – the highest in the entire polar region.

There is also a good on-site restaurant, a lobby bar and a cafe where guests can get a daily free cup of coffee and a pastry. Also arranges free transfers to neighbouring Norwegian cities if you are heading that way.

Park Inn Hotel Polyarnye Zori HOTEL $$$

(Парк Инн Полярные Зори; ☎ 8152-289 505; www.parkinn.ru/hotel-murmansk; ul Knipovicha 17; s/d/ste incl breakfast from R4800/7500/9950; P ❂ ✴ ☎; ☐ 3, 10, 18) This spotless business hotel has efficient, English-speaking staff, two bars, a restaurant, a nightclub with free blues gigs on Thursdays (winter only), a sauna for business room and suite dwellers and big buffet breakfasts.

Rooms come with cable TV and underfloor heating in the bathrooms. The well-stocked souvenir shop on the 1st floor has some real curios. (Life-size Lenin model anyone?)

Eating

Moroshka CAFE $

(Морошка; ul Yegorova 13; pastries R79; ⏰ 10am-10pm; ☎; ☐ 6, 18) This popular cafe hums to a soundtrack of electronic music and does great breakfasts of coffee and porridge or pastries. It also sells backpacks, if yours is feeling the strain of the road.

Northern Bakeries BAKERY $

(ul Samoylovoy 6; pastries from R75; ⏰ 9am-8pm; ☐ 18) For self-catering or a cupcake fetish, there's this tempting European-style bakery.

Evroros SUPERMARKET $

(Евророс; pr Lenina 71; ⏰ 7am-midnight; ☐ 18) Murmansk's best supermarket chain with huge variety and pre-prepared meals.

White Rabbit CAFE $

(Белый Кролик; ul Profsoyuzov 20; mains from R260; ⏰ 8am-6pm) Stylish White Rabbit has separate cafe and restaurant sections. Choose from coffee, pastries and cakes at the former, or good value pasta, fish and meat dishes at the latter. Popular with parents and their kids during the day. A warning: the throbbing disco music in the evenings might put you off your food.

★ Leto CAFE $$

(Лето; pr Lenina 61; mains R420-900; ⏰ noon-11pm; ☎; ☐ 6, 18) Don't let yourself be blinded by the in-your-face lime-green and neon-orange decor – this cafe serves some of the most imaginative food in town. Feast on the likes of crab cutlets with ginger rice, beautifully prepared *plov* with mushrooms and a selection of filling fish soups. Has a nice selection of cocktails, wines and hot drinks (including sea buckthorn tea), too.

★**Terrasa**　　　　　　　　　　FUSION $$
(Терраса; www.krugka.ru/terrasa; pr Lenina 69; mains R320-840; ⊘noon-midnight; ☑3, 18) Festooned with hams and with greenery growing out of every available crevice, this hip lounge bar with open kitchen complements its imaginative dishes (such as tagliatelle with crab sauce and venison with chocolate) with an extensive list of cocktails. Located on the 3rd floor of the shopping centre; party on at the Terrasa DJ Bar upstairs.

Dandy　　　　　　　　　　BURGERS $$
(www.krugka.ru/dandy; pr Lenina 72; burgers from R365; ⊘10am-midnight; ✳🛜) Dandy serves a wide range of burgers, including duck, deer and vegan variations, amid chilled decor and laid-back music. Staff give you black gloves to wear while eating so your hands don't get greasy. There's also a good selection of pasta, fish and meat dishes. Tables by the window are great for people-watching.

Fresh　　　　　　　　　　SUSHI $$$
(Фреш; ul Samoylovoy 6; sushi sets from R465; ⊘noon-midnight; ☑6, 18) Fresh, thankfully, lives up to its name, and delivers top-quality rolls, sushi sets and noodle dishes in hip surrounds.

Steak House Torro　　　　　STEAK $$$
(Стейк Хаус Торро; pr Lenina 80; mains from R730; ⊘noon-midnight; ☑3, 18) This elegant restaurant is a favourite with visiting businessmen and anyone with a carnivorous inclination. A special occasion treat if you've got roubles to spend, with the meat expertly prepared.

🍷 **Drinking & Nightlife**

★**7 Nebo**　　　　　　　　　　BAR
(7 Небо; www.vk.com/7sky_murmansk; pr Lenina 82; ⊘noon-2am Sun-Thu, noon-6am Fri & Sat; 🛜; ☑3, 6, 18) There are stupendous panoramic views of Murmansk on offer at 7 Nebo (Seventh Heaven), located on the 17th floor of the Azimut Hotel in the centre of the city. With imported beers and decent wine list, plus tasty pasta and pastries, this is the place to watch the sun descend languidly towards the horizon during the long summer nights.

Start-Up Cafe　　　　　　　CAFE
(Стартап Кафе; pr Lenina 67; ⊘11am-midnight Fri-Sun, 11am-11pm Mon-Thu; 🛜; ☑3, 6, 18) This centrally located cafe serves great toasted cheese sandwiches (R150) as well as the usual range of caffeine hits. There are also piles of Russian-language Marvel and DC comics

on the shelves if you feel like brushing up on your superhero vocab.

Bulldog　　　　　　　　　　PUB
(Бульдог; ul Karla Marksa 38; ⊘noon-2am; ☑10, 18) Atmospheric British-style pub, with dark-wood furniture and a good selection of imported beers.

Pinta Pub　　　　　　　　　PUB
(Паб Пинта; ul Yegorova 13a; ⊘noon-midnight Sun-Thu, to 5am Fri & Sat; ☑18) With its Germanic facade, Scottish decor and merry-old-England bathroom tiles, the Pinta seems to be in the midst of an identity crisis, but who cares when it has its own on-site microbrewery? There are regular live gigs on weekends, from rock to jazz.

☆ **Entertainment**

Philharmonia　　　　　　CLASSICAL MUSIC
(Филармония; www.murmansound.ru; ul Sofyi Perovskoy 3; ⊘most shows 7pm Sep-Jun; ☑18) For opera, folk music or classical concerts, buy tickets in advance from the on-site ticket office.

Murmansk Puppet Theatre　PUPPET THEATRE
(Мурманский областной театр кукол; www.murmanpuppet.ru; ul Sofyi Perovskoy 21a; tickets from R200; ⊘shows usually 11.30am & 2pm Fri-Sun) Keeping kids entertained since 1933.

ℹ️ **Information**

Main Post Office (Почта; pr Lenina 82a; ⊘9am-2pm & 3-7pm)

Murmansk Tourism Portal Portal (www.murmantourism.ru) For information on active tourism in the area.

Murmanout (www.murmanout.ru/events) For what's-on information.

Flait (Флайт, Flight; ☏8152-289 551; www.norge.russland.ru; in Hotel Meridian; ⊘10am-6pm Mon-Fri, to 2pm Sat) Can assist with travel bookings and visas.

ℹ️ **Getting There & Away**

AIR

Some of the airlines using **Murmansk Airport** (Аэропорт Мурманск; www.airport-murmansk.ru) include **Aeroflot** (www.aeroflot.com), **Nordavia** (www.nordavia.ru/eng) and **Rossiya** (Россия; www.rossiya-airlines.com/en). Destinations include Moscow (2½ hours, six daily), St Petersburg (two hours, four to five daily), Arkhangelsk (1¾ hours, daily except Tuesday and Saturday) and Tromsø, Norway (two hours, Monday and Friday).

BOAT

Murmansk's **River Terminal** (Portovy pr) is designed for foreign cruise vessels (around 12 a year call here), irregular boats serving remote villages in the Arctic Circle, and military vessels.

BUS

From Murmansk's **bus station** (Автовокзал; ✆ 8152-454 884; www.murmanbus.ru; ul Kominterna 16), buses run to Kirovsk (R695, 5½ hours, four daily) via Olenegorsk (R410, three hours), Monchegorsk (R510, 3½ hours) and Apatity (R585, five hours). A daily bus runs to Teriberka (R496, 4¼ hours) at 5.40pm.

Finland

A bus leaves for Ivalo (R1400, 6½ hours) at 6.45am every Saturday from outside the Park Inn Hotel (p322). Another bus to Rovaniemi (also via Ivalo) leaves on Monday, Wednesday and Friday at 7am (R2600, 11½ hours) from the bus station, where tickets can also be purchased for this and the Ivalo trip.

Norway

A daily minibus runs to Kirkenes, Norway (R2400, 4½ to six hours), managed by **Pasvikturist** (✆ in Norway 47-7899 5080; www. pasvikturist.no; Dr Wesselsgate 9, Kirkenes; ◷ 8.30am-4pm Mon-Fri). It leaves from outside the Hotel Azimut (p322) daily at 7am. Book in advance. Returning from Kirkenes, it departs daily at 3pm from Scandic Hotel.

TRAIN

From the **train station** (Железнодорожный вокзал; ul Kominterna 14) at least two daily trains run to both St Petersburg (R2879, 26¼ to 27 hours) and Moscow (R3641, 35¼ to 39 hours). All go via Apatity (R951, 3½ to 4½ hours) and Petrozavodsk (R2270, 19 to 24 hours). Daily train 15 bound for Moscow departs at 7.20pm and is ideally timed for Kem (R1979), arriving at 6.35am, just in time for you to make the 8am boat to the Solovetsky Islands.

ⓘ Getting Around

Murmansk airport is 27km southwest of the city at Murmashi, and can be reached by bus/ *marshrutka* 106, which departs from directly opposite the bus station every 30 minutes or so between 5.20am and 11.30pm. Frequent trolley-bus 6 covers the vast length of Kolsky pr, crosses the city centre on pr Lenina then swings left on ul Karla Libknekhta. Bus 18 follows almost the same route. Pr Kirova is covered by trolleybus 2 and 4, while useful bus 10 follows Kolsky pr, bypasses the centre on ul Polyarnye Zori and ul Papanina and rejoins the main drag near Lake Semyonovskoe.

Murmansk is a good place to rent a car if you want to explore the Kola Peninsula solo. Professional agency **Rent a Car** (✆ 921-285 7478, 8152-253 804; www.rentacar51.ru; office 24, pr Lenina 24) has a good selection of vehicles for hire (from R1400 per day) and can deliver to your hotel at extra cost.

VOLOGDA   ВОЛОГДА

✆ 8172 / POP 312,686 / ◷ MOSCOW

Having taken Moscow's side against all comers seemingly from its inception, Vologda was rewarded by Ivan the Terrible, who considered the quaint city perhaps worthy

---

TOP-SECRET TOWNS

During the Cold War, the Murmansk area housed the world's greatest concentration of military and naval forces. Despite drastic scale backs, the Kola Peninsula is still home to plenty of closed military zones known as ZATOs (Zakrytiye Administrativno-Territorialnye Obrazovania; Closed Administrative-Territorial Formations):

Severomorsk is headquarters of the Northern Fleet.

Shchyukozero, 8km beyond, was the scene of a potentially catastrophic near miss in 1984 when a fire swept through silos bristling with nuclear-tipped missiles.

Polyarny and Gadzhievo are nuclear-submarine bases, with more than 50 decommissioned reactor compartments stored at nearby Sayda-Guba.

Vidyaevo and Zaozersk nuclear-submarine bases are west of the Kola Inlet. Vidyaevo was the home port of the ill-fated *Kursk*.

Ostrovnoy, on the Kola Peninsula's remote eastern coast, is a former submarine base that's now a dumping and recycling centre for dismantled submarines and radioactive waste.

Access to these 'closed areas' is strictly limited to Russians who either work there or are registered, so your curiosity about Russia's secrets must remain unsated.

of his presence there – Vologdians remain steadfast in their belief that the city was a contender for Russian capital.

Until the 17th century, Vologda was an important centre of industry, commerce and arts, with Vologda lace becoming renowned as a luxury item. However, with the development of St Petersburg, Vologda was pushed into the background. At the start of the 20th century, political undesirables such as Josef Stalin and religious philosopher Nikolai Berdyaev were exiled here. Nonetheless, for just a few months in 1918, Vologda became the diplomatic capital of Russia, and today this laid-back, church-studded city is a great base for exploring the region.

⊙ Sights

★ St Sofia's Cathedral   CHURCH
(Софийский собор; Kremlyovskaya pl; adult/child R200/100; ⊙10am-6pm Wed-Sun; services 9am Wed-Sun; 🚌7) Powerful five-domed St Sofia's Cathedral has a soaring interior smothered with beautiful 1680s frescoes. The astonishingly tall iconostasis is filled with darkly brooding saintly portraiture. The massive stone cathedral was erected in just two years (1568–70) on the direct orders of Ivan the Terrible.

★ Kremlin   HISTORIC SITE
(Вологодский Кремль; Kremlyovskaya pl; ⊙10am-5pm Wed-Sun; 🚌7) FREE Vologda's multidomed, attractive kremlin is the city's historical centrepiece, a 17th-century fortified enclosure built as a church administrative centre to accompany St Sofia's Cathedral next door. Peeking into the various museums that surround the crumbling courtyard makes for a good introduction to Vologda's city history, natural history of the region and folk art.

Bell Tower   HISTORIC BUILDING
(Колокольня; Kremlyovskaya pl; adult/child R150/50; ⊙10am-4.30pm Wed-Sun; 🚌7) Climbing the 288 steps of St Sofia's Cathedral's separate 78.5m-high, gold-topped bell tower offers breathtaking views down upon the cathedral's grand onion domes. Mind your own dome on the way up: the ceilings were clearly built with gnomes in mind.

Resurrection Cathedral   CHURCH
(Воскресенский собор; Kremlevskaya pl 3; adult/child R100/50; ⊙9am-5pm Tue-Sun; 🚌7) Just outside the kremlin enclosure, the amply domed 1776 Resurrection Cathedral adds photogenic foreground to kremlin views. It also houses an art gallery of regularly changing exhibits.

Spaso-Prilutsky Monastery   MONASTERY
(Спасо-Прилуцкий монастырь; ul Monastyrskaya 12; ⊙8am-6pm; 🚌2, 28) FREE Painted in circus-tent stripes, the powerful fortress towers of this active 14th-century monastery are photogenically reflected in the river, best viewed from the nearby railway bridge. Visitors may explore the western half of the compound, including a partial rampart walk and the five-domed 16th-century Transfiguration Cathedral (Спасо-Преображенский собор).

The site is 4km north of town. Alight at Priluki (Прилуки) stop or join one of the pleasure cruises from the kremlin pier (R900 return, noon, 3pm and 6pm).

Regional Studies Museum   MUSEUM
(Вологодский областной краеведческий музей; www.vologdamuseum.ru; Kremlyovskaya pl; adult/child R100/50; ⊙10am-5pm Wed-Sun) The natural history section has clearly benefited from the untimely demise of numerous regional species of wildlife, such as the dramatically posed stuffed lynx, wolves, foxes and a tiny cub-under-glass mournfully watching his bear family from across the room. The history exhibition tells the story of the city from its very conception, while star of the rich prehistory exhibition is a 3500-year-old skeleton of a woman clasping at her modesty.

Peter the Great House   MUSEUM
(Петровский Домик; Sovetsky pr 47; adult/child R100/50; ⊙10am-1pm & 2-5pm Tue-Sat; 🚌1) Vologda's oldest museum (1885) is a compact late-17th-century stone house that belonged to the Gutman traders who hosted Tsar Peter I during his March 1724 visit to Vologda. Exhibits include a copy of Rastrelli's death mask of Peter the Great and the tsar's red tunic, underlining his remarkable height (204cm).

Art Department   MUSEUM
(Художественный отдел Кремля; Kremlyovskaya pl; adult/child R125/70; ⊙10am-5pm Wed-Sun; 🚌7) On the eastern side of the main kremlin courtyard, Muppet-style wooden dolls, lacquered wood items and embroidery briefly grab your attention before the Art Department gets down to business with some truly first-class icons and the remarkable abstract wood carvings of local artist Victor Shumilov.

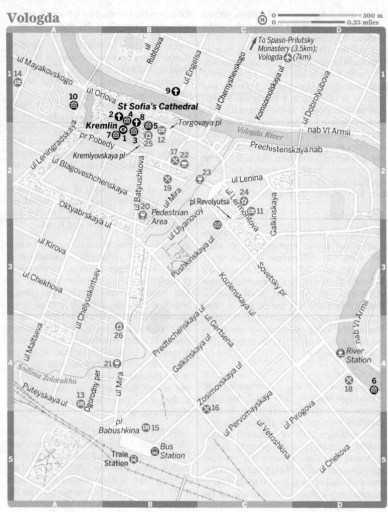

Lace Museum

MUSEUM

(Музей Кружева; www.vologdamuseum.ru; Kremlyovskaya pl 12; adult/child R150/50; ⊙10am-5pm Wed-Sun; 🚌7) The sparklingly modern Lace Museum, across the square from the kremlin, patches together some great examples of this archetypal Vologda craft, with bizarre communist-era examples incorporating tractors, hammer-and-sickle symbols and an intricate piece celebrating Russia's exploration of the cosmos.

World of Forgotten Things

MUSEUM

(Мир Забытых Вещей; www.vologdamuseum.ru; ul Leningradskaya 6; adult/child R60/30; ⊙10am-5pm Wed-Sun; 🚌7) One of several enchanting old wooden buildings at the eastern end of ul Leningradskaya, this little museum evokes the life of a 19th-century, 17-child middle-class family. Amid portraits of bewigged children and army officers is a whimsical gramophone that still plays; the beautiful landscape photography on the 1st floor is a highlight.

St John Chrysostom Church

CHURCH

(Храм Иоанна Златоуста; nab VI Armii 105; ⊙9am-4pm; 🚌2) **FREE** This attractive 17th-century church is one of Vologda's oldest constructions and contains some 200-year-old frescoes. Located on the river bank

Vologda

opposite St Sofia's Cathedral, its picturesque onion domes reflect nicely in the river. It was handed over to the army in the 1930s for use as a warehouse, but returned to the Russian Orthodox Church at the start of the 2000s.

🛏 Sleeping

Resting Rooms
HOSTEL $
(Комнаты отдыха, komnaty otdykha; ☑ 8-921-233 8323; pl Babushkina 6a; 6/12/24hr from R450/550/700; 🅿) Neat, clean shared rooms in the courtyard building across the street from the railway station. There are two twins and a triple, all of which can be rented as solo digs if you value your privacy.

Hotel Palisad
HOTEL $$
(Гостиница Палисадъ; ☑ 8172-722 761; www.palisad-vologda.ru; Torgovaya pl 17; s/d/ste incl breakfast R2800/3300/4500; 😑🏠; 🖳13) Right near the river, Hotel Palisad has compact, modern rooms, decked out in neutral tones, attentive personnel and a generous buffet breakfast featuring local produce. Proximity to the kremlin is either a boon or a bane, depending on how much you enjoy the sound of church bells.

Istoriya
HOTEL $$
(История; ☑ 8172-723 200; www.history-hotel.ru; ul Vorovskogo 28; s/d/ste from R2600/3100/3900; 🏠; 🖳7) Cute little hotel a couple of blocks from the kremlin, with classic decor in its several buildings and on-site restaurant (full board available). Rates include secure parking, reliable wi-fi, spotless rooms, and use of a sauna and a little plunge pool.

Hotel Sputnik
HOTEL $$
(Гостиница Спутник; ☑ 8172-777 975; www.sputnic-hotel.ru; Puteyskaya ul 14; s/d R2200/3100, without bathroom from R80/1000; 😑🏠) Nowhere near as grim as its institutional Soviet exterior suggests, the Hotel Sputnik's rooms are spacious and bright and even the cheapest come equipped with sinks and armchairs. The shared facilities are spotless and the reception staff are friendly and helpful. Breakfasts cost an extra R200.

★ Hotel Angliter
BOUTIQUE HOTEL $$$
(Отель Англитеръ; ☑ 8172-762 436; www.angliter.ru; ul Lermontova 23; s/tw/apt incl breakfast from R4000/3500/8000; 😑🏠; 🖳1, 6) With tirelessly helpful, multilingual staff and a super-central location, this very comfortable boutique hotel is still Vologda's top choice. Some rooms have their own saunas, and there's a good in-house restaurant (mains from R290).

🍴 Eating

Ogorod
RUSSIAN $
(Огород; pr Pobedy 10; mains R100-210; ⊘ 8.30am-11pm; 🖉; 🖳7) Grab a tray and make your way around this plant-strewn cafeteria, picking up your salads, soups and hearty mains as you go along. Wash it all down with a glass or two of *kvas*. There's an appealing summer terrace in the warmer months.

Gud'OK
RUSSIAN, ITALIAN $
(Гуд'ОК; ul Chekhova 51; mains R250-350; ⊘ noon-2am; 🏠) Gud'OK tries to ooze urban sophistication, with prints of Manhattan and red leather

seats, but doesn't quite make it. The food, on the other hand, is lovingly prepared. The prompt service is a boon for nearby railway-station departures.

★ **Sem Vecherov** RUSSIAN $$
(Семь Вечеров; pr Pobedy 13; mains R290-550; ⊘noon-midnight; 🛜🍴; 🚎7, 28) Good things come in sevens here: seven chef's specials, seven (mostly) vegetarian (постные) dishes, seven types of filled *bliny* (pancakes)... You get the picture. Downstairs is the cheery cafe section, and upstairs middle-aged couples boogie on down to live pop in the evenings.

Puzatiy Patsyuk UKRAINIAN $$
(Пузатый Пацюк; Sovetsky pr 80; mains R375-890; ⊘9am-4am; 🅿🛜🍴; 🚎1, 2) This rustic-effect nostalgia restaurant serves top-notch food such as duck in apple sauce, *draniki* (potato fritters) and goose with a honey crust. The menu (in Ukrainian with Russian translations) is a well-crafted take on a tsarist-era police report, but the ambience is lacking unless you're here on a weekend when there's live entertainment.

🍷 Drinking & Nightlife

Parizhanka CAFE
(Парижанка; pr Pobedy 8; ⊘24hr; 🛜; 🚎7) This 'Parisian' cafe is a favourite with locals for its decent coffee and delectable cakes (skip the wafer-thin pizza and the soggy pasta, though).

DJ Cafe MC2 CLUB
(ul Mira 82; ⊘8pm-6am Fri & Sat; 🛜; 🚎1, 13) Local hipsters make their way to the 5th floor of Oasis shopping centre on weekend nights to hear the resident DJs and guest talent from across Russia who specialise in deep house. If you don't feel like hitting the dance floor, the sofas are comfy, the sushi is good enough and the original cocktails pack a punch.

Arbat BAR
(Арбатъ; cnr ul Mira & ul Batyushkova; ⊘11am-1am Mon-Thu & Sun, to 4am Fri & Sat; 🛜; 🚎7, 28) A chatty verandah hang-out by day that serves a mix of European dishes and sushi, this cafe transforms into a pop-walloping bar once the sun goes down, with the local trendies taking to the dance floor.

Tonga BAR, CAFE
(Тонга; ul Mira 7; ⊘24hr; 🛜; 🚎7) This popular 24-hour bar has a decent wine list, and a wide range of cocktails. It also serves spicy Thai soups, Indian food, and European and Russian dishes. Friendly service. Can get very noisy in the evenings.

☆ Entertainment

Philharmonia CLASSICAL MUSIC
(Филармония; 🎫8172-757 513; www.volfilarmo-nia.ru; ul Lermontova 21) As well as its vibrant program of mostly classical music (October to May), the Philharmonia also organises a two-week Summer at the Kremlin festival of open-air concerts (June to July).

🛍 Shopping

Vologdskie Suveniry GIFTS & SOUVENIRS
(Вологодские Сувениры; cnr ul Mira & ul Chek-hova; ⊘10am-7pm Mon-Fri, to 5pm Sat & Sun) Sells classic *kruzhevo* (Vologda lace), colourful lacquerware, painted wooden trays and delicately carved birch wood items.

Dom Suvenirov GIFTS & SOUVENIRS
(Дом Сувениров; Kremlyovskaya pl 8; ⊘10am-7pm Mon-Sat) Well-stocked gift shop selling locally produced, high-quality linen clothing, nesting dolls, clay whistles, lace parasols and much more.

ℹ Information

Main Post Office (Почта; Sovetsky pr 4; ⊘8am-8pm Mon-Fri, 9am-6pm Sat & Sun)
Vologda Oblast (www.vologda-oblast.ru/en) The government-run website has lots of information on the region.

ℹ Getting There & Away

BUS

From the **bus station** (Автовокзал; pl Babush-kina 10) at pl Babushkina 10, next to the train station, a bus leaves at 8.10am six times a week to Petrozavodsk (R1130, 12½ hours, no buses on Tuesdays). There are up to four daily buses to Totma (R472, four hours), as well as six daily departures to Veliky Ustyug, with the most convenient (R1055) leaving at 9.20am and arriving at 6.40pm.

TRAIN

Around seven daily services run from Vologda's **train station** (pl Babushkina 8) to Moscow (eight to nine hours), of which trains 115 and 117 (R1291), leaving on alternate days at 9.54pm, are the best-timed overnighters.

Three to four trains run overnight to St Petersburg (R1431, 11½ to 12½ hours).There are four daily trains to Arkhangelsk, the most convenient over-nighter being train 16 (R1028) leaving at 6.45pm. Train 374 to Murmansk (R1767, 37 hours) leaves at 2.40pm on odd-numbered dates of the month. Arkhangelsk- and Murmansk-bound trains stop at Nyandoma (for Kargopol).

KIRILLOV-BELOZERSKY MONASTERY

In the 16th and 17th centuries, the **Kirillov-Belozersky Monastery** (Кирилло-Белозерский монастырь; www.kirmuseum.ru/en; combined ticket R450) in the lakeside town of Kirillov, 130km northwest of Vologda, was northern Russia's largest, and one of the country's most powerful. Founded in 1397 by a monk from Moscow, the monastery grew from a cave into magnificent grounds comprising 12 churches, three-storey fortress walls and the glorious Assumption Cathedral.

The prosperity of the monastery was made possible by wealthy patrons, including the Romanovs and Ivan the Terrible. Ivan had a personal room within the monastery and planned to take his own vows here. Things did not go quite as planned, however, with the tsar becoming disenchanted with what he saw as the 'lecherous' goings-on within the cloister. A prolific and polemic letter writer, Ivan penned a no-holds-barred epistle to the abbot of the time, blasting the lack of asceticism within its walls: 'Today in your cloister Sheremetyev sits in his cell like a tsar; Khabarov and other monks come to him and drink and eat as though they were laymen, and Sheremetyev – whether from weddings or births, I don't know – sends sweets and cakes, and other spiced delicacies around to all the cells, and behind the monastery is a courtyard, and in it are supplies for a year.' An anti-religion exhibition was housed in part of the monastery during the early Soviet era, and icons, engravings and other valuables were confiscated.

Entry to the grounds is free, with individual and combined ticketing for the site's exhibition rooms. Buses connect Kirillov and Vologda (R330, 2¾ hours, up to seven daily).

ⓘ Getting Around

The handy 2GIS website (www.2gis.ru) and app has up-to-date transport info. From the train station, trolleybuses 1 and 4 run up ul Mira; bus 35 takes ul Mira and then heads west along ul Gertsena.

KARGOPOL КАРГОПОЛЬ

☑ 81841 / POP 10,052 / ⊘ MOSCOW

Gently attractive Kargopol was one of Russia's richest cities in the 16th and 17th centuries, when it commanded the Onega River route to the White Sea, then Muscovy's only coastline. Once Russia had gained access to the Baltic, Kargopol lost its raison d'être and faded into obscurity, hardly helped by a devastating 1765 fire. Today, languor envelops this out-of-the-way historical town, known for its naive-style painted clay figurines (*Kargopolskiye igrushki*), and there seem to be more churches than people.

Pr Oktyabrsky and parallel ul Lenina run southwest past the hotels, pl Lenina and grassy Sobornaya Ploschad, the town's main square. Local tour agencies can organise transport to the Kenozero National Park.

⦿ Sights

★ **Nativity Cathedral** CHURCH

(Христорождественский собор; Sobornaya Ploschad; R80; ⊘ 10am-1pm & 2-5pm Tue-Sun) The

five-domed, 1562 star of Sobornaya Ploschad sports intriguing timber-encased corner buttresses and houses a splendid iconostasis on the 2nd floor (only open in summer). On a pillar, the superb 18th-century Starshni Sud (Judgment Day) icon is a who's who of saints on what looks a heavenly snakes-and-ladders board. On the 1st floor, 19th-century wooden 'skies' from the region's churches depict Adam and Eve hiding their shame, Isaac about to be killed and other biblical scenes.

John the Baptist Church CHURCH

(Церковь Иоанна Предтечи; Sobornaya Ploschad) **FREE** This 1751 church on the city's main grassy square has an impressively Gothic bulk with unusual octagonal windows and distinctive double domes on long cylindrical towers.

Bell Tower HISTORIC BUILDING

(Колокольня; Sobornaya Ploschad; R70; ⊘ 10am-1pm & 2-5pm Tue-Sun) Sweeping views from this sturdy 1778 bell tower justify the slightly claustrophobic climb from the main grassy square. Enter through a hobbit-sized door. Sometimes the caretaker only turns up at around noon to set off the merry ringing of bells.

Vvedenskaya Church CHURCH

(Введенская Церковь; Sobornaya Ploschad; R80; ⊘ 10am-1pm & 2-5pm Tue-Sun) Historically important, the 1809 Vvedenskaya Church stored the hidden chattels of the Russian

WOODEN CHURCHES

The so-called 'sky' (небо) is a unique feature of 16th- and 17th-century wooden churches in the Russian north. The church ceiling is not painted. Instead it's panelled, made up of individual wooden trapeze-shaped icons, each depicting a saint or an angel, with a circular image of Christ in the centre. The design draws its inspiration from the painted cupolas of Byzantine churches and the dominant blue colour creates an illusion of height.

Kargopol district is known for its wealth of historic wooden churches, with specialised tours running from Kargopol. The most impressive ensemble of 17th- and 18th-century wooden churches used to be beside the Pudozh road in the archetypal log-cottage village of **Lyadiny** (aka Gavrilovskaya), 35km west of Kargopol, but it perished in a fire of divine origin in 2012 when the bell tower was struck by lightning.

royals during Napoleon's 1812 attack on Moscow. Now the upstairs interior hosts changing exhibitions of local artwork.

Zosimy & Savvatiya Church CHURCH
(Церковь Зосимы и Савватия; pr Oktyabrsky 18; admission R80; ☺10am-1pm & 2-5pm Tue-Sun) A long walk down a dusty road towards the southwestern end of town, this 1819 church has a small collection of local crafts, costumes and icons, plus Saturday recitals.

Rozhdenstva Bogoroditsy Church CHURCH
(Церковь Рожденства Богородицы; ul Lenina) FREE The active 1680 Rozhdenstva Bogoroditsy Church is elegant despite the discordant red-green metallic gleam of its multiple domes. A stylistic effect? No, it's just rust.

Bereginya MUSEUM
(Берегиня; Oktyabrsky pr 72; R75; ☺9am-noon & 1-5.15pm Mon-Fri, 10am-noon & 2-4pm Sat & Sun) Bereginya displays and sells a range of folk crafts and organises all manner of masterclasses – from making clay toys to traditional weaving.

Annunciation Church CHURCH
(Благовещенская церковь; Krasnoarmeyskaya pl) FREE The disused 1692 Annunciation Church catches your eye with its unusually intricate window mouldings.

⛟ Tours

Lache Turbureau TOURS
(Турбюро Лаче; ☎81841-22 056; www.lachetur.ru; ul Akulova 23; ☺9am-6pm Mon-Sat) This accommodating tour agency organises rural accommodation and tours of the surrounding countryside – from day trips to historic wooden churches to multiday tours of Kenozero National Park in summer and winter. Also rents bicycles, canoes and rafts. Some English and French spoken. It's also possible to book train tickets here.

✯✯ Festivals & Events

Folklore Events CULTURAL
(www.kargopolmuseum.narod.ru; pr Oktyabrskaya 50; tickets R70-150; ☺events 9pm Fri-Sun Jun-Aug) Low-key musical, dance and folklore events are held outside the Museum Administration Building on most summer weekend evenings.

⊨ Sleeping

Hotel Kargopolochka HOTEL $
(Гостиница Каргополочка; ☎81841-21 264; ul Lenina 83; s/d/tr/q without bathroom R1050/1050/1350/1600, s/d with bathroom R850/1700) The landing may look like something out of *The Green Mile* and the decor may be firmly Soviet, but the basic rooms are clean enough (the priciest have their own toilets). Check-out time is 24 hours after your arrival time and the on-site cafe serves decent breakfasts, salads and mains.

Hotel Kargopol HOTEL $$
(Гостиница Каргополь; ☎81841-21 165; ul Lenina 60; s/d/ste R2600/3300/5200; ❂⑨) Kargopol's best hotel, with modern rooms, all with fridge and good bathrooms (with underfloor heating in the suites). The basement restaurant is Kargopol's best, with bargain 'business lunches' (soup R50, mains R110) and wild game dishes (R250 to R1050).

ⓘ Information

Sberbank (Сбербанк; ul Pobedy 12) has an ATM, as does the **supermarket** (Центральный магазин; ul Lenina 57; ☺24hr), and both the hotels reviewed here. This is your last chance to withdraw money if you are heading to Kenozero National Park, which has no ATMs.

For maps, try Lache Turbureau. Map-guide pamphlets sold at the hotels (R80) are in Russian but have photos.

Post Office (ul Leningradskaya 10; ☺8am-8pm Mon-Fri, to 7pm Sat, 9am-6pm Sun)

ℹ Getting There & Away

BUS

Virtually all visitors arrive by train at Nyandoma, 80km east of Kargopol on the Vologda–Arkhangelsk line. Buses to Kargopol (R245, 1½ hours) run from the car park in front of the railway station at 2.30pm and 1.30am daily, and at 7.30pm on Friday and Sunday, returning from Kargopol at noon and 9.30pm daily, and at 4pm on Friday and Sunday. Shared taxis (R600 per person, one hour) await each train.

TRAIN

Arriving at Nyandoma at 9.58am on train 118 from Moscow, you could see all of Kargopol's sights in a day, then continue to Arkhangelsk on train 116 at 12.08am (R2700, 13½ hours, every other day). Southbound from Arkhangelsk, slow train 671 runs conveniently overnight, departing at 9.49pm and arriving in Nyandoma at 7.06am. There are two or three departures for Vologda daily after midnight and at least three daily afternoon/evening arrivals from Vologda.

ℹ Getting Around

There are no bus services within Kargopol itself, although private mini buses (R30) make occasional loops of the town.

KENOZERO NATIONAL PARK
КЕНОЗЕРСКИЙ НАЦИОНАЛЬНЫЙ ПАРК

This delightful national park – parts of which have long been considered sacred by locals – is a great place to unwind amid some pristine Russian countryside. You could easily spend a few days here exploring its patchwork of forests, lakes and historic wooden churches. Be aware, though, that its remoteness means that mobile phone coverage is extremely limited, with only the Megafon operator offering service.

◉ Sights & Activities

Lekshmozero village's quirky, 3.5km Anthill Trail (Тропа Муравейников; Lekshmozero village) FREE offers a great opportunity to stretch the legs.

Lekshmozero is also the launching point for the popular Ecological Route, a one-day open-boat trip to a reconstructed traditional mill via a series of lakes and tiny linking canals – be prepared to get wet feet! Book

through an agency: Lache Turbureau (p330) in Kargopol can help.

★ St Alexander Svirsky Church on Khizhgora   CHURCH
(Храм Александра Свирского на Хижгоре; Kenozero National Park) FREE Some 2km into the national park, in an elevated clearing in the forest, stands the atmospheric St Alexander Svirsky Church on Khizhgora. This onion-domed wooden church was completed in 1866 and is located on what has been considered sacred land by locals for centuries. It is only used on special occasions. The turnoff to the church is marked by an easily-missed sign that reads Хижгора.

Church of Peter and Paul   CHURCH
(Церковь Петра и Павла; Lekshmozero village) FREE This ramshackle 19th century church stands on the edge of Lake Lekshmo, and was used as a warehouse in the Soviet era. Today it is only used for services on special occasions. From where the bus terminates, walk back 30m to a *zhurval* (shadoof-style lever-well) and turn left along ul Zapadnaya.

🛏 Sleeping

The Visitor Centre (Визит-центр Кенозерского национального парка; ☑8-921-477 9075; www.kenozero.ru; ⊙9am-9pm Jun-Aug) can arrange good accommodation in the village of Lekshmozero (aka Morschihinskaya), which sits idyllically on the shores of large Lake Lekshmo. Locals also let out rooms.

Fisherman's Hut Hotel   HOTEL $
(Рыбацкая изба; ☑8182-286 523; Lake Lekshmo; s/d R750/1500; ◉) This two-floor log cabin hotel is right on the bank of Lake Lekshmo and has great views. The cosy, compact rooms have shared bathrooms and toilets. There are also two on-site *banyas* (R800 per hour), as well as a kitchen for guest use.

ℹ Getting There & Away

Buses from Kargopol to Lekshmozero (R150, 1¾ hours) depart at 6.15am and 5.15pm on Tuesday and Friday, returning roughly two hours later. In springtime the unpaved road is impassable by bus. Taxis between Kargopol and Lekshmozero cost R2000 one-way.

ℹ Getting Around

It's around 10km from Lekshmozero village to the entrance of the national park itself, where no cars are allowed. You can hike, cycle, or take a taxi there for around R350.

Volga Region

Why Go?

The Volga (Волга), one of Europe's great rivers, winds for some 3530km through Russia's heartland and has been a part of the continent's longest 'highway' since time immemorial. The stretch of the Volga between Nizhny Novgorod and the Caspian Sea forms a rich and fascinating cultural region with over a dozen different ethnic groups, most notably the Volga Tatars. Travelling along or alongside the river you encounter spectacular hilltop kremlins in Nizhny Novgorod, Kazan and Astrakhan, bombastic architecture in Volgograd, numerous lively provincial capitals and picturesque stretches such as the Samara Bend. This natural beauty culminates in the magnificent Volga Delta south of Astrakhan, a vast region of reeds and waterways. West of the Volga River, Kalmykia takes in a windswept area of steppe that is home to the Buddhist Kalmyks, who originate from western Mongolia.

Best Places to Eat

➜ Hungry (p360)

➜ Staraya Kvartira (p351)

➜ Restoratsia Pyatkin (p338)

➜ Mindal (p364)

➜ Odessa (p356)

Best Places to Stay

➜ Astrakhanskaya Hotel (p364)

➜ Hilton Garden Inn (p349)

➜ Jouk-Jacques (p338)

➜ Hotel Giuseppe (p343)

➜ Hotel Polina (p355)

When to Go
Astrakhan

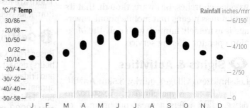

Feb Much of the Volga River is frozen over and draped in a winter landscape.

Mid–May Spring sun warms the air and the Volga finally opens for navigation.

Late Jul–Sep The river is filled with boats, and lotus flowers bloom in the delta.

History

More than 1000 years ago, the Vikings plied its waters, establishing a trade route between Baghdad and the Baltic. In the latter centuries of the first millennium, the Lower Volga was dominated by the Khazars, a Turkic tribe whose leaders converted to Judaism. The Khazar capital stood at Itil (present-day Astrakhan). The Middle Volga was the domain of another Turkic tribe, the Bulgars. Descendants of the Huns and distant relatives of the Balkan Bulgarians, they migrated eastwards, mixed with local Finno-Ugric tribes and adopted Islam in the 10th century. The river was also a vital conduit in the lucrative fur trade for Novgorod's merchants.

Volga Region Highlights

❶ **Volga Delta** (p367) Exploring the marshy waterways as the Volga approaches the Caspian Sea.

❷ **Mamaev Kurgan** (p358) Climbing the stairs and paths of Volgograd's magnificent memorial to the Battle of Stalingrad.

❸ **Volga River** (p357) Sailing the Volga on a short excursion or cruise, from any major city on the river such as Saratov.

❹ **Kazan** (p340) Strolling through one of Russia's most dynamic cities and home to a picturesque kremlin.

❺ **Elista** (p365) Rattling in a *marshrutka* (fixed-route minibus) across the grassy steppe to the capital of Europe's only Buddhist republic.

❻ **Nizhny Novgorod** (p334) Taking in some spectacular river views on a high-altitude cable car.

The Golden Horde

In the 13th century, the entire Volga region was conquered by the heirs of Chinggis (Genghis) Khaan, the Mongol-led Golden Horde, who made Saray (near present-day Volgograd and Astrakhan) their capital. For the next 200 years, the Volga's Slavic and Turkic communities swore allegiance and paid tribute to the great khan, or suffered his wrath. Challenged by the marauder armies of Timur (Tamerlane) in the south and upstart Muscovite princes in the north, the Golden Horde eventually fragmented into separate khanates: Kazan, Astrakhan, Crimea and Sibir. In the 1550s Ivan the Terrible razed Kazan and Astrakhan, and claimed the Middle and Lower Volga for Muscovy (modern-day Moscow), the capital of the new Russian state.

Cossacks

While the river trade was a rich source of income for Muscovy, it also supported gainful bandit and smuggling ventures. Hostile steppe tribes continued to harass Russian traders and settlers, and the region remained an untamed frontier for many years.

In response, the tsar ordered the construction of fortified outposts at strategic points on the river. Serfs, paupers and dropouts fled to the region, organising semi-autonomous Cossack communities that not only defended the frontier for the tsar but also operated protection rackets, plundered locals and raided Russia's southern neighbours.

Cossacks conducted large-scale peasant uprisings. In 1670 Stepan Razin led a 7000-strong army of the disaffected, which moved up the Lower Volga before meeting defeat at Simbirsk (Ulyanovsk). In 1773 Yemelyan Pugachev declared himself tsar and led an even larger contingent of Cossacks and runaway serfs on a riotous march through the Middle Volga region. The bloody revolt was forever romanticised by Alexander Pushkin in his novel *The Captain's Daughter*.

Germans in the Volga Region

Astounded by the scale of rebellion, Catherine the Great sought to bolster the economic development of the region by inviting Germany's peasants to settle here from 1763, mainly around Saratov. By the end of the 19th century, the population of ethnic Germans had reached more than 1.5 million.

In the 1920s a German autonomous republic was established along the Lower Volga, but it was dissolved amid persecutions during WWII, and German inhabitants were forced into exile. After Stalin's death, nearly a million survivors were liberated from Siberian labour camps, but were not allowed to return to their old villages.

Soviet Times & Beyond

The USSR harnessed the mighty Volga for its ambitious development plans. Eight complexes of dams, reservoirs and hydroelectric stations were constructed between the 1930s and 1960s. A network of canals connected Russia's heartland to Moscow and the Baltic and Black Seas and provincial trading towns grew into urban industrial centres closed to outsiders.

After the collapse of the USSR, each of the Volga regions went its own way. Some, like Ulyanovsk, resisted change, while others such as Samara, Saratov and Tatarstan moved quickly to liberalise markets and politics. When in 2004 the system of electing regional governors was changed to give Moscow direct control over the appointment, pluralism and dissent all but vanished from the region.

Nizhny Novgorod
Нижний Новгород

📞 831 / POP 1.25 MILLION / ⏱ MOSCOW

Russia's fifth-largest city – sometimes referred to as the country's 'third capital' – would likely go unnoticed by most travellers if not for its arresting hilltop kremlin, overlooking the confluence of two wide rivers: the Volga and Oka. This is the locale where merchant Kuzma Minin and Count Dmitry Pozharsky (men commemorated in a monument in front of Moscow's St Basil's Cathedral) rallied a popular army to repel the Polish intervention in 1612. It's also the city (then known as 'Gorky') where late Soviet scientist-dissident Andrei Sakharov was banished in the 1980s as punishment for opposing the Soviet Union's 1979 invasion of Afghanistan.

Aside from stirring views out over the river (including the possibility of a high-altitude cable-car ride), 'Nizhny' offers several very good museums, and Sakharov's former apartment is home to a quirky exhibition on the great man's life. The port offers the possibility of river excursions to nearby towns.

⊙ Sights

Nizhny Novgorod is separated into eastern and western sides by the Oka River. Most of the significant sights, including the kremlin and the best museums, are located on the eastern side of the river, while the bus and train stations are located on the western side.

⊙ Sights

★ Kremlin   HISTORIC SITE
(Нижегородский Кремль; ☑ 831-422 1080; www.ngiamz.ru; ⊙ 10am-8pm) **FREE** Built on remnants of an earlier settlement, Nizhny Novgorod's magnificent kremlin dates to 1500–15 when Italian architect Pyotr Fryazin began work on its 13 towers and 12m-high walls. Most of the buildings are government offices, though the city's two most important museums are here as well as the 17th-century **Cathedral of the Archangel Michael** and a striking **Monument to Heroes of WWII.** You can walk the walls from May to November and take in riverside views.

➤ Arsenal/National
Centre of Contemporary Art   GALLERY
(Государственный центр современного искусства; ☑ 831-422 4554; www.ncca.ru/nnovgorod; kremlin, building 6; R150; ⊙ noon-8pm Tue-Sun) Situated in the former kremlin arsenal, on the right after you enter the main gate, this top-ranking national gallery has changing exhibitions of international and Russian contemporary artists. The refurbished space also houses a cafe-restaurant and a concert venue.

➤ Nizhegorodsky
State Art Museum   MUSEUM
(Нижегородский государственный художественный музей; ☑ 831-439 1373; www.artmuseumnn.ru; kremlin, building 3; R150; ⊙ 11am-6pm Wed-Mon) The former governor's house inside the kremlin houses the Russian collection of the vast Nizhegorodsky State Art Museum. Exhibits range from 14th-century icons to 20th-century paintings by artists such as Nikolai Rerikh and Vasily Surikov.

➤ Dmitry Tower   MUSEUM
(Дмитриевская башня; ☑ 831-422 1080; www.ngiamz.ru; kremlin; museum R130, kremlin wall walk incl other towers Russian/foreigner R130/200; ⊙ 10am-5pm Tue-Sun, kremlin wall walk May-Nov) Squat Dmitry Tower, topped in green, is the main entrance to the kremlin and is visible for the length of pedestrianised Bolshaya Pokrovskaya ul. The tower has changing exhibitions on local history and is the starting point for a 1.2km walk along the kremlin walls.

★ Cable Car   CABLE CAR
(Kazanskaya naberezhe; one-way R90; ⊙ 6.45am-10pm Mon-Sat, from 9am Sun, closed 11am-1pm Mon & Thu) Connecting Nizhny Novgorod with the unattractive settlement of Bor across the Volga, this cable car offers a spectacular 13-minute ride. In winter there are views of dot-sized figures fishing on Volga ice below, and in summer there's swamp, lush greens and gentle blues. The ride peaks at over 80m and is 3.6km long. The base station is located along the embankment, 2km east of the Kremlin. Take any bus to Sennaya bus station and walk back towards the mosque.

★ Rukavishnikov Mansion   MUSEUM
(Усадьба Рукавишникова; ☑ 831-422 1050; www.ngiamz.ru; Verkhne-Volzhskaya nab 7; Russian/foreigner R80/200, tours R200/300; ⊙ 10am-5pm Tue-Thu, noon-7pm Fri-Sun) This exhibition space is located inside a 19th-century mansion once belonging to the Rukavishnikov merchant family. You can wander through the rooms on your own or join one of the hourly 40-minute tours in Russian and (less frequently) in English. Furniture and the illustrious interior of the unusual mansion are the threads running through the tours or a visit, and these are complemented by changing exhibitions – often with a focus on household furnishing and objects.

★ Memorial Apartment
of Andrei Sakharov   MUSEUM
(Музей Сахарова; ☑ 831-462 6125; pr Gagarina 214; R100; ⊙ 10am-5pm Sat-Thu) The nondescript flat where dissident scientist Andrei Sakharov, father of Russia's hydrogen bomb, spent seven years in exile after protesting the 1979 Russian invasion of Afghanistan. The Nobel laureate was held incommunicado until 1986, when Mikhail Gorbachev finally released him. Exhibits include background on Sakharov's life as well as the apartment itself. It's located 10km south of the centre. To get there, take a taxi or bus 1 from pl Minina i Pozharskogo or pl Gorkogo (stop: Muzey Akademika Sakharova).

Western European Art Collection   GALLERY
(Экспозиция западноевропейского искусства ☑ 831-439 1373; www.artmuseumnn.ru; Verkhne-

336

VOLGA REGION NIZHNY NOVGOROD

Nizhny Novgorod

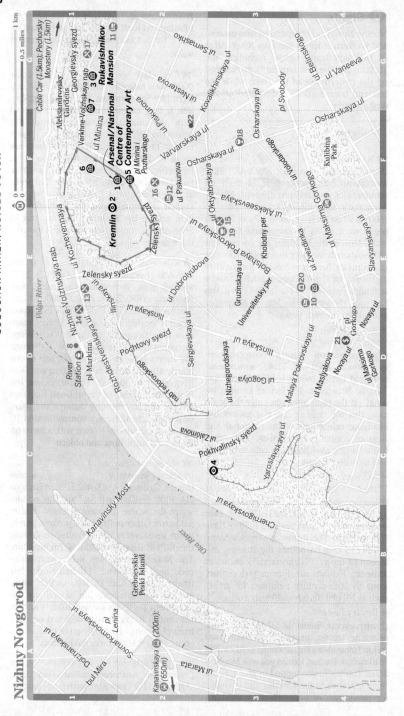

Nizhny Novgorod

Volzhskaya nab 3; R150; ⊙11am-6pm Wed & Fri-Mon, noon-8pm Thu) The Nizhegorodsky State Art Museum's collection of Western European art is exhibited a short walk from the kremlin along Verkhne-Volzhskaya nab, an attractive street lined with restored 19th-century buildings. Inside the art gallery you'll find a collection of mostly anonymous or lesser-known European painters who, despite their modest credentials, produced some remarkable works.

Pechorsky Monastery　　　MONASTERY
(☑831-436 1715; www.pecherskiy.nne.ru; Privolzhskaya sloboda 108; ⊙7am-8pm) This 17th-century monastery, overlooking the Volga, is perfect for a tranquil stroll in small but picturesque grounds. It's located about 500m east of the cable car base station and around 2.5km east of the kremlin. Take any *marshrutka* or bus from pl Minina i Pozharskogo to pl Sennaya.

**Museum of Volga
People's Architecture & Culture**　　MUSEUM
(Музей архитектуры и быта народов Нижегородского Поволжья; ☑831-422 1052; www.ngiamz.ru; Gorbatovskaya ul 41; R100; ⊙10am-5pm Tue-Sun) The open-air Museum of Volga People's Architecture & Culture has a pleasant woodland setting and a collection of traditional wooden buildings from Russian and Mordva (a Finno-Ugric people) villages. The museum is located in the remote Shchelokovsky Khutor Park, which is the final stop of bus 28 (30 minutes, every

hour), passing ul Belinskogo in the centre. *Marshrutka* 62 also stops close.

Annunciation Monastery　　MONASTERY
(Благовещенский монастырь; ☑831-430 0912; ul Garshina; ⊙7am-8pm) **FREE** Set at the foot of attractive parkland, the 13th-century Annunciation Monastery, above Chernigovskaya ul, is one of Nizhny Novgorod's oldest buildings. Most of the churches themselves are from the 17th century and are well worth visiting for their interiors.

☞ Tours

Team Gorky　　　　　　　　TOURS
(☑831-278 9404; www.teamgorky.ru) Gorky takes visitors on summer canoe and rafting tours, and winter ski treks in the Nizhny Novgorod region and beyond. See the website for a good overview of tours and options. Be flexible about dates as individuals join groups.

🛏 Sleeping

★Smile　　　　　　　　　HOSTEL **$**
(☑831-216 0222; www.smilehostel.net; Bolshaya Pokrovskaya ul 4; dm/d R450/1590; ❄@⊛) Bright, friendly and efficient, this centrally located hostel has two doubles with twin beds that can be booked as a single, and five-, six- and eight-bed dorms. There's free tea and coffee, separate male and female bathroom facilities and a nice communal area.

Ibis Hotel
HOTEL $$

(Ибис Отель; ☎831-233 1100; www.ibishotel.com; ul Maksima Gorkogo 115; r from R3100; ☻@🛜) Nizhny's Ibis offers a high standard of rooms and comforts, with the advantage that it's large enough to cope with busy periods.

★ Jouk-Jacques
BOUTIQUE HOTEL $$$

(Жук-Жак; ☎831-433 0462; www.jak-hotel.ru; Bolshaya Pokrovskaya ul 57; incl breakfast s R3000-4000, d/ste R4500/6000; ❄🛜) This cosy boutique hotel is one of the best in town. Rooms are modern and decorated in soft tones, some facing the yard. The cheapest are a bit cramped but they're neat, and breakfasts are superb.

October Hotel
HOTEL $$$

(Гостиница Октябрьская; ☎831-432 8080; www.oktyabrskaya.ru; Verkhne-Volzhskaya nab 9a; incl breakfast s R3600-4400, d R4400-7200, ste R7200-10,000; ☻@🛜) This old-timer from the Soviet era has been renovated and is a comfortable option, with bright rooms, some with great views over the Volga.

✕ Eating & Drinking

Salyut
BURGERS $

(САЛЮТ; ☎8-952-788 8558; www.salutburgers.ru; ul Oktyabrskaya 9a; burgers R250; ⊙11.50am-10pm; 🛜🖊) Just what Nizhny Novgorod needed to pull in the 21st century: a trendy, artisanal burger bar that's a nice break from Russian sit-down meals. Get in line with everyone else, order at the counter, grab a seat on the terrace and wait for your number to be called. Classic hamburgers, along with vegetarian and vegan options. Excellent chips.

Stolle
RUSSIAN $

(☎831-439 1460; www.stolle.ru; pl Minina i Pozharskogo 2/2; pastries R250; ⊙9am-9pm; 🖊) This one-trick pony does its one thing exceedingly well: making fresh-baked pastries that are stuffed with meat, mushrooms or fruit. Make your selection at the counter and carry your pie and cup of tea to your table. Perfect for lunch or a snack.

Biblioteka
ITALIAN $

(Библиотека; ☎831-433 6934; www.biblioteca-nn.ru; Bolshaya Pokrovskaya ul 46; mains R250; ⊙11am-10pm; 🖊) Upstairs from the Dirizhabl bookshop with generic but tasty Italian dishes in an informal, quirky atmosphere. There's a nice selection of salads and pastas, with a special selection of summertime cocktails. The cosy interior is meant to recall – not surprisingly, given the location – a bookshop.

★ Restoratsia Pyatkin
RUSSIAN $$

(Ресторация Пяткин; ☎831-430 9183; www.pir.nnov.ru/pyatkin; Rozhdestvenskaya ul 25; mains R500; ⊙noon-midnight; 🖫) Pyatkin makes you feel like a merchant back in his mansion after a great trading day at the fair. The menu is full of Volga fish specialities; it brews the unusual apple *kvas* (fermented rye bread water) for R75 and has a children's menu.

Bezukhov
RUSSIAN, INTERNATIONAL $$

(Безухов; ☎831-433 8763; www.bezuhov.ru; Rozhdestvenskaya ul 6; mains R600; ⊙24hr; 🛜🖊) This literary cafe with antique furnishings, stucco ceiling and the feel of a living room is part of a Nizhny Novgorod project called 'Eda i Kultura' (Food and Culture), which brings food and culture together into a delicious whole. The menu is overflowing with salads, pastas and fish, poultry and red-meat dishes, and augmented by good breakfasts.

Tiffani
INTERNATIONAL $$

(Тиффани; ☎831-419 4101; www.tiffanibar.ru; Verkhne-Volzhskaya nab 8; mains R600; ⊙noon-2am; 🛜🖊) This upmarket all-rounder is a restaurant during the day and evening, a cafe at any time and has well-known DJs some nights. The views across the Volga to the forest are spectacular.

★ Bufet
BAR

(Буфет; ☎831-218 0338; www.ekproject.ru; Osharskaya ul 14; ⊙noon-2am; 🛜) Descending the steps of this hidden art bar is to step into a bohemian world of monkey-motif wallpaper. The ambience is relaxed and alternative. There's a good range of teas and alcoholic beverages as well as a rotating menu of light bites, such as pasta and hummus. Find the entrance at the far southern end of a long building.

Traveler's Coffee
CAFE

(☎831-216 0078; www.travelerscoffee.ru; Bolshaya Pokrovskaya ul 20b; ⊙8am-midnight; 🛜) One of several American chain–style chain coffee bars along pedestrianised Bolshaya Pokrovskaya ul, but with the main difference being that the coffee is particularly good. Order a well-crafted double espresso, and sit in or take away. There's a small selection of cakes and pastries as well.

🔒 Shopping

Dirizhabl
BOOKS

(www.dirigable-book.ru; Bolshaya Pokrovskaya ul 46; ⊙10am-9pm Mon-Sat, 11am-8pm Sun) A good

GORODETS

A trip to the nearby Volga river town of Gorodets, 60km north of Nizhny Novgorod, makes for a fun day trip and, in summer, a chance to get out on the water. The town is the oldest in the region and is famous for its distinct style of folk art. The local museum quarter has been attractively preserved and can be toured in under half a day.

Gorodets earned its reputation for folk art starting around the time of the schism in the Russian Orthodox Church (1660). The town became home to a population of Old Believers seeking religious sanctuary. They became skilful craftsmen, artists and wealthy tradesmen.

In a largely illiterate society, Gorodets oil-on-wood paintings played the role of glossy magazines about lifestyle and current events. Today you can buy pictures (from R200) or a whole piece of furniture, painted in Gorodets style. The town's other speciality is *pryaniki* – hard, honey-rich cakes sold in most shops.

There are several museums in town, but some of the highlights include the **Children's Museum at the Merchants** (Детский музей на Купеческой; ☑ 831-619 4256; https://nn-welcome.ru; ul Lenina 12, Gorodets; R50; ⊗ 10am-5pm Tue-Fri, to 4pm Sat & Sun; ⛲), housed in a 19th-century schoolroom; the **House of the Countess Panina** (Дом графини Паниной; ☑ 831-619 2319; www.nnwelcome.ru/guide/museums/museum-the-countess-paninas-house; ul Rublyova 16, Gorodets; R50; ⊗ 10am-5pm Tue-Fri, to 4pm Sat & Sun), which faithfully re-creates the atmosphere of the 19th century; the **Gorodets Regional Museum** (Городецкий краеведческий музей; ☑ 831-619 2749; www.nnwelcome.ru/guide/museums/gorodets-museum-of-regional-studies; ul Lenina 11, Gorodets; R50; ⊗ 9am-5pm Tue-Fri, 10am-4pm Sat & Sun), focusing on the town's natural and social history; and the **Museum of Samovars** (Музей самоваров в Городце; ☑ 831-619 2287; nab Revolyutsii 11, Gorodets; R50; ⊗ 9am-5pm Tue-Fri, 10am-4pm Sat & Sun), which boasts the largest collection of tea-making equipment in Russia.

Several hydrofoils leave daily for Gorodets from Nizhny Novgorod's river station (R200, one hour) from late May to September. **Vodokhod Tour Office** (Водоходъ; ☑ 831-461 8030; https://volga-vodohod.ru; Nizhne-Volzhskaya nab; ⊗ 10am-9pm Mon-Fri, to 7pm Sat & Sun) in Nizhny Novgorod runs excursions for around R1000. Out of sailing season, Gorodets is accessible by bus from Nizhny Novgorod's bus station (R180, two hours, about half-hourly).

selection of maps and local guidebooks, and some books in foreign languages.

❶ Information

ВТВ24 (ВТБ24; pl Maksima Gorkogo 4/2; ⊗ 24hr; ATM; accepts major cards.

Central Post Office (Центральный почтамт; Bolshaya Pokrovskaya ul 57; ⊗ 8am-8pm Mon-Fri, 10am-5pm Sat & Sun) Just off central pl Gorkogo.

❶ Getting There & Away

VIP Travel (ВИП ТРЭВЕЛ; ☑ 831-202 1271; www.viptravelnn.ru; Kovalikhinskaya ul 8; ⊗ 9am-6pm Mon-Fri, to 4pm Sat) can help book air or rail tickets as well as plan excursions to nearby sights or around Russia.

AIR

Nizhny Novgorod International Airport (Международный аэропорт Нижний Новгород; GOJ; ☑ 831-261 8080; www.nnov-airport.ru/eng) is 15km southwest of the city centre. The airport has several flights daily to Moscow and a handful of flights to

other large cities around Russia, including to Kazan. To get to the airport, take the metro to the southern terminus at Park Kultury (Парк культу́ры) and then bus 11 or 20.

BOAT

The **river station** (Речной вокзал; Nizhne-Volzhskaya nab) is below the kremlin. All services on the Volga are cruise, day-excursion or tourist boats. Unfortunately, there are no short-hop ferries between major towns. Hydrofoils to Gorodets leave from their own pier at the river station.

BUS

Buses to Vladimir (R600, four hours, eight daily), Kostroma (R1000, nine hours, daily) and Gorodets (R200, two hours, about every half-hour) depart from the small **Kanavinskaya bus station** (Автостанция Канавинская; ☑ 831-246 2021; www.nnov.org/transport/busm/kanavinskaya; Sovetskaya ul 20a). Private operators run minibuses to Moscow (R800, six hours, at least six daily), which depart across the road from the train station; others leave from the bus station.

TRAIN

Nizhny Novgorod train station is still sometimes known as Gorky-Moskovsky vokzal, so 'Gorky' appears on some timetables. It's on the western bank of the Oka River, at pl Revolyutsii 2a. The service centre at the train station is helpful for buying rail tickets.

The train station is conveniently located above metro station Moskovskaya (Московская). From the station, take the metro one stop to Gorkovskaya (Горьковская), the main square on the eastern bank of the Oka River, and close to major sights.

Westbound

The high-speed Sapsan/Lastochka runs to Moscow's Kursky vokzal (seat R2400, four to five hours, two daily). More than a dozen other trains also serve Moscow (R1300, seven hours) via Vladimir (R800, three hours). The Volga (059) runs to/from St Petersburg (R2800, 14½ hours, daily).

Eastbound

Trans-Siberian flagships run to Perm (R3600, 14½ hours, daily) and beyond, but lesser trains do the trip for R2450 – for Kazan (R2600, nine hours, daily) the 41 is a top-flight (and only) choice. Other trains go to Yekaterinburg (R4300, 20 hours, several daily) and beyond.

❶ Getting Around

Central Nizhny Novgorod is compact enough to walk around, and a car-free pedestrian zone, ul Bolshaya Pokrovskaya, links the main square, pl Gorkogo (пл Горького), to busy pl Minina i Pozharskogo (пл Минина и Пожарского), near the kremlin.

Both the bus and train stations are located on the western side of the Oka River, about 3km from main sights (which are all situated on the eastern side). Buses and *marshrutky* run from the train station to both hubs on the eastern side: pl Gorkogo and pl Minina i Pozharskogo. The metro has a useful link between pl Gorkogo and the train station.

Uber ride-share service (www.uber.com) operates in Nizhny and rates are significantly cheaper than standard taxis.

Kazan   Казань

🚩 843 / POP 1.45 MILLION / ⏱ MOSCOW

Kazan (meaning 'cooking pot' in Tatar) is the Istanbul of the Volga, a place where Europe and Asia curiously inspect each other from the tops of church belfries and minarets. It is about 150 years older than Moscow and the capital of the Tatarstan Republic (Республика Татарстан) – the land of the Volga Tatars, a Turkic people commonly associated with Chinggis (Genghis) Khaan's hordes.

Tatar autonomy is strong here and is not just about bilingual street signs. Moscow has pumped vast sums into the republic to persuade it to remain a loyal part of Russia. It also ensures that Tatarstan benefits greatly from the vast oil reserves in this booming republic.

Although Tatar nationalism is strong, it is not radical, and the local version of Sunni Islam is very moderate. Slavic Russians make up about half of the population, and this cultural conflux of Slavic and Tatar cultures makes Kazan an all-the-more-interesting city.

History

Kazan was founded as a northeastern outpost of Volga Bulgaria around AD 1000. After the Tatar Mongols flattened Great Bulgar, it became the capital of the region and was incorporated into the Golden Horde. The independent Kazan khanate was created in 1438. It was ravaged in 1552 by Ivan the Terrible's troops and Tatar allies, and the collapse also cleared the way for Slavic Russians to move into the Urals region around Perm.

Tsar Ivan was quick to build a new – Russian – city on the ruins. Architects responsible for St Basil's Cathedral in Moscow (which honours the seizure of Kazan) were employed to plan the kremlin. Tatars were banished from the northern side of the Bulak Canal (about 500m east of the Volga shoreline) until the enlightened age of Catherine the Great, which is why the main Tatar quarter is southeast of the canal.

Kazan grew into one of Russia's economic and cultural capitals, with the country's third university opening here in 1804. Its alumni include Leo Tolstoy and Vladimir Ulyanov (Lenin), who stirred up political trouble and was expelled.

◉ Sights

⭐ **Kremlin**   HISTORIC SITE

(Казанский Кремль; ☏ 843-567 8001; www.kazan-kremlin.ru; ⏱ 8am-10pm, to 8pm in winter) **FREE** Kazan's striking kremlin is home to government offices, pleasant parks, museums, an enormous mosque and other religious buildings.

➤ **Kul Sharif Mosque**   MOSQUE

(Мечеть Кул Шариф; ☏ 843-567 8125; www.kazan-kremlin.ru; kremlin; museum R200; ⏱ 9am-

7.30pm) The Kul Sharif Mosque was completed in 2005 and is named after the imam who died defending the city against the troops of Ivan the Terrible in 1552. The museum inside tells the story of Islam, especially on the Volga, and includes manuscripts, some pieces of furniture and women's costumes.

➡ **Hermitage Kazan** MUSEUM

(Эрмитаж-Казань; ☑ 843-567 8032; www.kazan-kremlin.ru; kremlin; adult/concession R200/100; ⊙ 10am-6pm Tue-Thu, Sat & Sun, 11am-8pm Fri) Located inside the former cadet school building, the Hermitage Kazan has top-flight rotating exhibitions, many of them from the collection of St Petersburg's Hermitage.

➡ **Tatarstan Museum of Natural History** MUSEUM

(Музей естественной истории Татарстана; ☑ 843-567 8037; www.kazan-kremlin.ru; kremlin; adult/concession R200/100; ⊙ 10am-6pm Tue-Thu, Sat & Sun, 11am-8pm Fri) About a dozen rooms here tell the story of the planets, geology and minerals, and the development of life forms on earth. The most interesting sections are on dinosaurs and the rise of mammals.

➡ **Annunciation Cathedral** CHURCH

(Благовещенский собор; ☑ 843-567 8073; www.kazan-kremlin.ru; kremlin; adult/student R100/80; ⊙ 10am-6pm Tue-Thu, Sat & Sun, 11am-8pm Fri) The attractive Annunciation Cathedral, built on on the foundations of a razed eight-minaret mosque, was designed by Postnik Yakovlev, who was also responsible for St Basil's Cathedral in Moscow. It was destroyed several times over the centuries but was restored in the 1990s and finally re-opened in 2005. The museum on site tells the cathedral's story.

➡ **Syuyumbike Tower** HISTORIC BUILDING

(Башня Сююмбике; www.kazan-kremlin.ru; kremlin) The 59m-high leaning Syuyumbike Tower dates from the early 18th century and is the subject of one of the most romantic of Kazan's legends (p344).

★ **Soviet Lifestyle Museum** MUSEUM

(Музей социалистического быта; ☑ 843-292 5947; www.muzeisb.ru; Universitetskaya ul 6; adult/concession R250/150; ⊙ 10am-8pm) Kazan's most unusual museum, packed with Soviet knick-knacks, is proof that Russia's socialist epoch fostered a lively contemporary cultural scene – especially music – in the 1970s and 1980s.

★ **Chak-chak Museum** MUSEUM

(Музей чак-чака; ☑ 843-239 2231; www.chak-chak.muzeino.ru; ul Parizhskoy Kommuny 18; tours from R300; ⊙ 10am-8pm) Interactive museum dedicated to traditional Tatar food and drink, particularly sweet 'chak-chak', balls of dough that are baked in honey and served on holidays and at family festivities. Call or email in advance to book a place on a tour and leave about two hours to learn how the various foods are made and then to sample teas and sweets.

Old Tatar Settlement HISTORIC SITE

(ul Kayuma Nasyri) This assemblage of historic timbered buildings, dating mainly from the 17th and 18th centuries, marks the quarter where ethnic Tatars were forced to live following the siege of Kazan in 1552. Little of the old settlement remains, though many houses still exhibit colourful, traditional decorations. The most significant building here is the Mardzhani Mosque (ul Kayuma Nasyri 17), dating from 1767. It was the first stone mosque permitted to be built within the city limits.

National Museum of the Republic of Tatarstan MUSEUM

(Национальный музей Республики Татарстан; ☑ 843-292 8984; www.tatmuseum.ru; Kremlyovskaya ul 2; R150; ⊙ 10am-6pm Sat-Wed, 1pm-9pm Thu, 10am-5pm Fri; Ⓜ Kremlevskaya) Opposite the kremlin's main entrance, the National Museum occupies an ornate 1770 building and has a worthwhile archaeology collection as well as jewellery, weapons and exhibits on the history of the Tatar people and its literary figures. There's limited signage in English.

SS Peter & Paul Cathedral CHURCH

(Петропавловский собор; ☑ 843-292 1358; http://eng.kazan.eparhia.ru/monastyri/churches/peterpaul; ul Musy Dzhalilya 21; ⊙ services daily at 8am & 5pm) **FREE** This is Kazan's most attractive Orthodox church, built between 1723 and 1726 to commemorate Peter the Great's visit in 1722.

Epiphany Cathedral Bell Tower HISTORIC BUILDING

(ul Baumana 78; tower adult/concession R100/50; ⊙ 10am-6.30pm) This impressive bell tower, standing some 74m high, is visible all along the pedestrian promenade of ul Baumana. The tower dates from the late 19th century and can be climbed for impressive views out around the central city.

Kazan

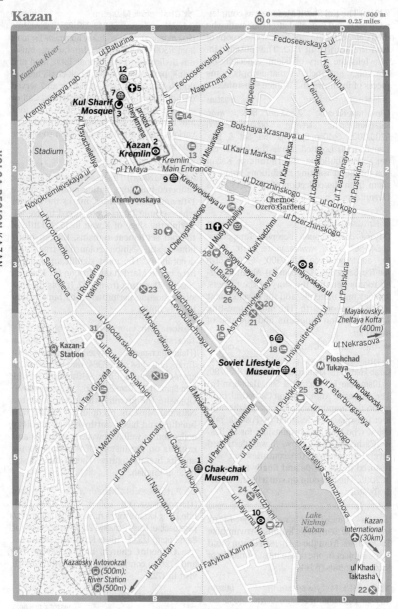

House of Zinaida Ushkova/
Tatarstan National Library LIBRARY
(Национальная библиотека Республики Татарстан; ☏ 843-292 6826; www.kitaphane.tatar-stan.ru; Kremlyovskaya ul 33; tours in English/Russian R200/100; ⊙ 9am-8pm Mon-Thu, to 6pm Sat & Sun, closed Fri) This small but extraordinary library dates from the early years of the 20th century, when several mid-19th-century houses were united and restyled to give each room its own art nouveau theme. Call ahead for English tours, or just drop by for one in Russian.

Kazan

⚒ Festivals & Events

Sabantuy　　　　　　　　　　　CULTURAL
(koresh; ⊙midsummer) Joking competitions and serious sport events – horse races and wrestling matches – feature prominently during Sabantuy, the main Tatar holiday celebrated all over Tatarstan and beyond over a long weekend in the summer. The winner of the wrestling competition is named Batyr and has to lift an overweight ram onto his shoulders for the cheering crowd.

🛏 Sleeping

Hostel Kremlin　　　　　　　　　HOSTEL $
(Хостел Кремлин; ☑843-233 0788; Bolshaya Krasnaya ul 8; dm R600-700, tw R1500; ☺@⌂) Clean, centrally located and well-run hostel with four- to eight-bed dorms and twins. Find the entrance on the far side of the building, away from the kremlin.

Hotel Ibis Kazan Centre　　　　　HOTEL $$
(Ибис Отель; ☑843-567 5800; www.ibis.com; Pravobulachnaya ul 43/1; s/d R2400/2800; ☺✱⌂) This centrally located chain hotel offers excellent value, close to ul Baumana. The reception gets high marks for English skills. Breakfast costs R420.

Hotel Shushma　　　　　　　　　HOTEL $$
(Гостиница Шушма; ☑843-292 3309; ul Narimanova 15; incl breakfast s R2100, d R2600-2700; ☺⌂) This modern hotel is a solid choice if being close to the main train station (Kazan-1) is a priority. Rooms are on the small side, but the furnishings and carpeting are clean and the welcome at the reception desk is warm.

★Hotel Giuseppe　　　　　　　　HOTEL $$$
(Гостиница Джузеппе; ☑843-292 6934; www.giuseppe.ru; Kremlyovskaya ul 15/25; incl breakfast s R2900-5300, d R3900-7000, ste R6600-14,000; ✱⌂) Run by a family with Italian ancestry, Hotel Guiseppe has spacious, comfortable rooms, with corridors decorated tastefully to give the atmosphere of a Venetian villa.

Center Hotel Kazan Kremlin　　　HOTEL $$$
(Отель 'Center Kazan Kremlin'; ☑843-210 0140; ul Karla Marksa 6; s/d R4000/5000; @⌂) This former Marriott has retained a luxury feel at reasonable rates for what's on offer. Chief advantages include well-proportioned, spotless rooms and a convenient location, about 200m from the Kazan Kremlin. The rooms at the back of the hotel have kremlin views. There's a decent restaurant, with both local favourites and international classics, such as cheeseburgers.

Shalyapin Palace Hotel — HOTEL $$$

(☑ 843-231 1000; www.shalyapin-hotel.ru; Universitetskaya ul 7/80; incl breakfast s R3100-5200, d R5900-7500, ste from R8000; ❂ ✳ ☎ ☜) Named after Russia's greatest opera singer, whose statue greets you at the door, this large hotel has rooms decorated in a classical style, a fitness centre, a sauna and a 25m pool. The location is ideal, close to the centre and just off of pedestrianised ul Baumana.

✗ Eating

Kazan is the place to try traditional Tatar food, including mains built around relatively exotic meats such as horse, duck and mutton. As in the rest of Russia, there's a mania for pastries, and Tatar cooking takes this to high art. In cafes and bakeries look for stacks of sweet and savoury pastries that can be eaten as a main course, side dish or snack. As a sampler, try the following: *echpochmak* (triangle-shaped pies stuffed with meat), *elesh* (pot pie stuffed with meat), *bekken* (crescent-shaped pie stuffed with cabbage or squash), *kystyby* (baked flatbread stuffed with potatoes), and *gubadiya* (savory pie of meat, rice, eggs, raisins and cheese). For dessert, look no further than *chak-chak*, a fried pastry coated in a honeyed sugar syrup and stuffed with almonds. Americans will find the texture not unlike that of Rice Krispie treats.

Kazan Askhane-Chai Yorty — TATAR $

(Дом чая, кафе 'Казанская ашхане'; ☑ 843-292 5654; ul Baumana 64; mains R90, pastry R50; ☉ 9am-8pm) This central, self-serve canteen offers both delicious Russian and Tatar foods at reasonable prices, and is a perfect lunch or quick-bite option. Go for stewed chicken, paired with buckwheat groats for the main, a Tatar savoury pastry as a side and a cake with tea for dessert.

Central Market — MARKET $

(Центральний рынок; ul Martyna Mezhlauka; ☉ 7am-5pm Mon, 7am-7pm Tue-Sun) The colourful, sprawling central market is good for stocking up on snacks or just for browsing.

★ Tatarskaya Usadba — TATAR $$

(☑ 8-987-225 0433; http://tatusadba.ru; ul Mardzhani 8; mains R500; ☉ 11am-1am; ☜) The 'Tatar Farmstead' is located adjacent to the Old Tatar Settlement and plays on traditional themes, both in the restaurant's decor and menu. There's a full range of Tatar classics, including several dishes with horsemeat and lamb, as well as hearty soups and stews, other mains and desserts. Good selection of Tatar pastries as well, including crunchy *chak chak*.

Dom Tatarskoy Kulinarii — TATAR $$

(Дом татарской кулинарии; ☑ 843-292 7070; ul Baumana 31; mains R600-800; ☉ 11am-11pm; ☜) The hushed, overly formal setting and mandatory coat check lend a faint whiff of tourist trap, but don't let that dissuade you. The menu is filled with Tatar specialities, such as (better than it sounds) stewed horsemeat and vegetables, you might not find elsewhere. Prices are hefty, but the quality is high too and the service faultless.

Pashmir — RUSSIAN $$

(Пашмир; ☑ 843-277 9944; www.pashmir.ru; ul Khadi Taktasha 30; mains R500-600; ☉ noon-midnight; ☜) Fusion food done very well as standard European meals are reinvented with aromatic fruits and local spices – think Italian mozzarella salad with persimmon.

THE TRUE STORY OF THE DEFIANT PRINCESS

When Ivan the Terrible seized Kazan, a local tale goes, he planned to marry Syuyumbike, the beautiful niece of the deposed khan. Nobody wants an ugly, paranoid dictator as a husband, so out of sheer desperation she agreed to marry him only if he built a tower higher than anything either of them had ever seen. Once the construction was complete, she ascended the tower and threw herself off in front of the bewildered Ivan.

A neat little tale, but residents of the small town of Kasimov, hidden in the forests of the Ryazan region on the banks of the Oka, have a different story. In medieval times, Kasimov was a Tatar stronghold and a major rival of Kazan. Therefore its khan, Shakh-Ali, was all too keen to accept Tsar Ivan's invitation to join the expedition against Kazan, especially since he was promised Syuyumbike as a trophy. When he met the captured princess, Shakh-Ali disliked her from first sight, but he eventually succumbed to Ivan's dynastic manipulations and married her. The newlyweds went to Kasimov and avoided each other for the rest of their long lives, with Syuyumbike transforming from a tiny Eastern beauty into a bulky matriarch keen on political intrigue.

The setting is upscale, though not overly formal. Book ahead.

Giuseppe
ITALIAN $$

(Джузеппе; ☑ 843-292 6934; www.giuseppe.ru; Kremlyovskaya ul 15; mains R550; ⊙10am-1am; ☎) One of Kazan's longest-running Italian restaurants is also one of the best, and close to the kremlin if you feel like a formal meal between sights or in the evening. Dress quite well for this.

Priyut Kholostyaka
INTERNATIONAL $$

(Приют холостяка; ☑843-292 0771; www. prihol.ru; ul Chernyshevskogo 27a; mains R500; ⊙11am-midnight Mon-Fri, to 2am Sat & Sun; ☎) 'Bachelor's Shelter' is a spotlessly white oasis of style with surrealist glass painting and coat hangers shaped like wild garlic flowers. International food, including the inevitable sushi, is on the menu, and it serves the best latte this side of the Volga. The restaurant is below ground, and there's a shisha bar on the ground floor.

🍷 Drinking & Nightlife

Salt Bar
BAR

(Бар Соль; ☑ 843-258 6282; www.facebook.com/solkzn; ul Profsoyuznaya 22; ⊙11am-3am Mon-Fri, from 1pm Sat & Sun) Laid-back, ultra-trendy bar and occasional club occupies a hived-out former industrial building, given a makeover of hardwood floors and exposed beam ceilings. Excellent beers on tap and a modest food menu of salads and burgers. Check the website for live events featuring popular DJs. Plan to come early, since these events tend to pack the house.

Fomin Bar & Shop
CRAFT BEER

(☑8-927-428 8114; www.facebook.com/aleandcraftkazan; ul Profsoyuznaya 10; ⊙4pm-1am; ☎) Convivial drinking spot features a daily rotating menu of craft beers on tap as well as a small selection of snacks, such as sliced horsemeat sausage. The beer shop stocks hard-to-find bottles from around the world for takeaway.

Top Hop
CRAFT BEER

(Бар 'Top Hop'; ☑8-987-226 3663; www.facebook.com/tophopbar; ul Baumana 36; ⊙noon-1am Sun-Thu, to 3am Fri & Sat) Popular spot on Kazan's pedestrianised party street serves 39 different types of beer on tap as well as a small menu of beer-friendly foods such as burgers (R350) in a welcoming, student-friendly atmosphere.

Divan
CAFE

(ДиваН; ☑8-950-313 7991; ul Mardzhani 18; ⊙9am-9pm; ☎) This tiny coffeehouse, in a ramshackle historic house on the edge of the Old Tatar Settlement, features fresh-roasted coffees as well as vegan and vegetarian snacks and a youthful vibe.

Cuba Libre
BAR

(Куба Либре; ☑843-253 5532; ul Baumana 58; ⊙noon-2am; ☎) A convivial drinking den where you can chat to friendly bartenders and other visitors while sipping Kazan's best mojitos. Wild Latin dancing may erupt at any moment. Note that the entrance is off the main street and around the corner of the building.

Beanheart's Coffee
CAFE

(Бинхартс Кофе; ☑843-296 4717; www.beanhearts.ru; ul Ostrovskogo 38; ⊙8am-midnight Mon-Fri, from 9am Sat & Sun; ☎) Cheerful, eclectic coffeeshop-restaurant, with a full coffee and tea menu as well as light bites, soups and sandwiches throughout the day (mains R400). There's a full breakfast menu (R250 to R350) served daily until noon.

Mayakovsky.Zheltaya Kofta
CLUB

(Ресторан-клуб Маяковский.Желтая кофта; ☑843-264 3980; www.zheltaya-kofta.ru; ul Mayakovskogo 24a; cover R100-1000, without band free; ⊙11am-midnight Mon-Fri, 4pm-midnight Sat & Sun) It can be Tatar rap or punk bands singing covers of Soviet soundtrack faves, or something even more experimental in this club with a youthful crowd and decor inspired by artist Kasimir Malevich.

☆ Entertainment

Smena Cultural Centre
ARTS CENTRE

(Смена; ☑843-249 5023; www.smenagallery.ru; ul Burkhana Shakhidi 7; ⊙10am-9pm) Contemporary art gallery and performance space, dedicated to the visual arts, including film, photography and painting. Check in during your visit to find out about parties or film festivals that might be going on. There's also a trendy bookstore and a branch of the Divan coffee shop.

ℹ Information

Main Post & Telephone Office (Почта и телеграф; Kremlyovskaya ul 8; internet per hour R35; ⊙8am-10pm Mon-Fri, 9am-6pm Sat & Sun)

Kazan Tourist Information Centre (Казанский туристско-информационный центр; ☑843-292 9777; http://kazantravel.ru/en; Kremlyovskaya ul 15/25; ⊙9.30am-6.30pm Mon-Fri, to 3.30pm Sat) Staff in this city-affiliated tourist office are knowledgeable and keep an excellent sheet map of town (also available in many hotels). It's also useful for booking excursions in advance.

Kazan Tourist Office branch (☑ 843-231 6798; www.kazantravel.ru/en; Hotel Tatarstan, ul Pushkina 4; ⊙ 10am-6pm Mon-Fri, from 9am Sat, 9am-1pm Sun) Branch office of the Kazan tourist information office, located in the Hotel Tatarstan. Provides maps and information, and books sightseeing tours of the city and surrounding area.

❶ Getting There & Away

AIR

Kazan International Airport (KZN; ☑ 843-267 8807; www.kazan.aero), located 30km south of the city, has good connections with the rest of Russia, including Moscow and St Petersburg. There are also useful connections to select cities in Europe, including Riga and Prague, as well as Istanbul in Turkey.

Aviakassa (☑ 8-495-970 1717; http://kazan. aviakassa.ru) is convenient for buying air tickets over the web.

To get into town from the airport, trains run from the airport to the main train stations, departing every 90 minutes or so throughout the day. The trip takes just under 30 minutes and costs R40.

Less conveniently, public bus 197 operates from 6am to 10pm and runs from the airport to a suburban stop called 'Agricultural Park Kazan', about 5km east of the centre. The fare is R20.

To travel by taxi, order a cab at a special counter at the arrivals area of Terminal 1A. The fare into town will cost about R1000 and take 25 minutes. Hotels frequently offer airport pick-up and drop-off, but expect to pay around R1500 for this.

BOAT

The Volga becomes navigable by the end of May and the boating season runs until September. Boats for both Sviyazhsk and Bolgar leave from the river station at the end of ul Tatarstan. It's best to buy tickets from the river station well in advance. Boats depart at 8.20am for Sviyazhsk and leave Sviyazhsk at 4.30pm (R200, two hours, daily); excursion boats to Sviyazhsk, with a Russian-speaking guide, leave Kazan at 9am (R400, Saturday and Sunday). For Bolgar, hydrofoils leave Kazan early morning (usually 8am) and return from Bolgar late afternoon, usually at 3pm or 4pm. Check exact times, as they tend to change from one navigation season to the next

BUS

Kazan has two bus stations, each serving different destinations.

Kazansky Avtovokzal (Казанский автовокзал; ☑ 843-293 0400; www. avtovokzal-kzn.ru; Devyataeva 15; ⊙ 5am-10.30pm), also known locally as the 'Stolichny Avtovokzal', is located near the river station and has online timetables. Most long-distance destinations depart from here, including those for Ulyanovsk (R600, five hours, 12 daily) and Samara (R900, nine hours, three daily).

Yuzhny Avtovokzal (Южный автовокзал; ☑ 843-261 5636; Orenburgsky trakt 207; ☎) is located up to an hour away (allowing for traffic

---

WORTH A TRIP

SVIYAZHSK

The Volga island of Sviyazhsk (Свияжск), about 30km west of Kazan, was a favourite escape for Kazan's artists and has some of the oldest architecture in the region. When Ivan the Terrible decided to end the Kazan khanate, he first ordered a base be built for the coming onslaught on top of Mt Kruglaya at the mouth of the Sviyaga River. A wooden kremlin was also built 700km upstream in the town of Myshkin near Yaroslavl. When finished, the builders marked each log, disassembled the fortress and sent it floating down the river to Sviyazhsk, where it was reassembled. Immediately after the Tatar defeat, Ivan's favourite architect, Postnik Yakovlev (co-creator of Moscow's St Basil's Cathedral and Kazan's Annunciation Cathedral), embarked on the construction of churches and monasteries here.

The Bolsheviks destroyed about half of Sviyazhsk's churches – wooden crosses now mark their locations – but several highlights were spared. These include the **Assumption Monastery**, where the St Nicolas Church is used for exhibitions of local artists, and **John the Baptist Monastery**, where the wooden Trinity Church looks like a modern dacha (summer country house) and is the only edifice inside the monastery from the original Myshkin-built fortress (though, rebuilt in 2002, it doesn't look anything like the original).

In the navigation season (late May to September) boats depart Kazan at 8.20am for Sviyazhsk, and leave Sviyazhsk at 4.30pm (R200, two hours, daily); excursion boats leave Kazan at 9am (R400, Saturday and Sunday). Travel here outside of summer is more problematic. The train station in Sviyazhsk is too far away from the island to be practical and buses are infrequent.

jams) from pl Tukaya by bus 37. This station serves Bolgar.

TRAIN

Kazan has two train stations. The main station for catching trains to Moscow, as well as southern destinations along the Volga, is on ul Said-Galieva in the centre. It's variously known as Kazan-1 or Kazan-Pass (passenger) on timetables. The station is composed of two buildings. The older historic building is used primarily as a waiting room, while train tickets are sold in the smaller, more modern commuter station. The entrance for accessing the trains is situated between the two buildings.

Kazan-2 (also known as Vosstanie-Pass on timetables) is located north of the centre and easily reached by metro. Many of the Siberian trains go through this station but there's little infrastructure for travellers, so check your ticket carefully.

Heading west, frequent trains connect Kazan with Moscow (from R2800, 12 hours) and Nizhny Novgorod (from R2600, nine hours). Heading south, popular destinations include Samara (R2200, 16 hours) and Volgograd (R4400, 24 hours).

ⓘ Getting Around

For the airport, bus 197 operates from 6am to 10pm and runs from the airport to a suburban stop called 'Agricultural Park Kazan', about 5km east of the centre. The fare is R20.

Kazan has a metro system, though only the central stations Kremlyovskaya (situated near the Kremlin) and Ploshchad Tukaya (centre of town) are really useful. This line also runs north to Severniy Vokzal (Kazan-2). Buy tickets at station windows.

Tram 2 and bus 53 link Kazan-1 train station with the bus and river stations. Tram 2 and bus 54 go from the river station via the bus station to pl Tukaya.

For reliable taxis, call **Taksi Tatarstan** (☑ 843-567 1567). Uber (www.uber.com) operates in Kazan, though rates are about the same as standard taxis.

Ulyanovsk УЛЬЯНОВСК

☑ 8422 / POPULATION 614,000 / ⊘ MOSCOW

The riverside city of Ulyanovsk has played an outsized role in Russian history. It's famously the birthplace of Lenin – indeed the city bears his name: Lenin was born Vladimir Ilyich Ulyanov in 1870. It's also the birthplace of one of Lenin's most formidable rivals from those early days: Alexander Kerensky. The former prime minister of the Russian provisional government of 1917 was born here in 1881.

There are several museums and memorials scattered around town dedicated to Lenin's legacy. Dig a little deeper, though, and Ulyanovsk's apolitical charms begin to emerge. The city was founded as Simbirsk in the 17th century and for a while it was a favourite retreat for young nobles. Many young aristocrats spent summers here dreaming of great endeavours while lounging between noontime breakfasts and late-afternoon naps. Their lifestyle was epitomised by Simbirsk native Ivan Goncharov in his novel *Oblomov*.

⊙ Sights

Many of the most important museums and sights are located in the old quarter of the city, west of ul Goncharova, known by the rather formal name 'State Historical and Memorial Museum-Reserve Homeland of VI Lenin'. It's a dusty but evocative part of old Simbirsk, with some pretty timber housing and a special old-world feel.

★**Goncharov Museum**   MUSEUM
(Музей Гончарова; ☑ 8422-417 966; ul Lenina 138 cnr Goncharova; R125; ⊘ 10am-6pm Tue-Sun) Writer Ivan Goncharov grew up in this three-storey house, which today is one of Ulyanovsk's most important museums. It tells the story of the house itself (dating from the late 18th century, with lots of 19th-century period-piece rooms), the writer and his era.

★**Museum Estate of Simbirsk Urban Life in the Late 19th and Early 20th Centuries**   MUSEUM
(Музей-усадьба городского быта Симбирск конца XIX - начала XX вв; www.ulzapovednik.ru; ul Lenina 90; Russian/foreigner R60/200; ⊘ 9am-5pm Tue-Sun) Among the museums dedicated to the historic quarter of town known as old Simbirsk, this is easily the most interesting. It consists of a main museum building with period furnishings and pictures of old Simbirsk, and a large yard with a series of small wooden buildings such as a kitchen and bathhouse. Lenin lived in the main building for one year in 1876–77.

Lenin Family House   MUSEUM
(☑ 8422-418 229; ul Lenina 68-70; R100; ⊘ 9.30am-5.30pm Tue-Sun) According to the plaque on the house, Lenin spent nine years here as a boy and teenager (1878–87). There's little to see inside except some simple furnishings, kids' beds and family photos, but the house itself is a window into the relatively modest lifestyle of the 19th-century middle class.

Ulyanovsk

Ulyanovsk

◎ Top Sights

◎ Sights

🛏 Sleeping

⊗ Eating

⊜ Drinking & Nightlife

**Museum of
Ulyanovsk Architecture** MUSEUM
(Музей Градостроительство и архитектура Симбирска-Ульяновска; ul Tolstogo 24a & 43; each building R60; ⊘ 9am-5pm Tue-Sun) Spread over two houses, this museum contains a wooden model of the 17th-century kremlin at ul Tolstogo 24a, the house that focuses on the 17th to 20th centuries. The branch at ul Tolstogo 43 is a brick building opposite the local FSB (former KGB) headquarters and has a full-size replica of a Simbirsk wooden fortress watchtower and specifically covers the late 19th and early 20th centuries.

Lenin Memorial Centre MUSEUM
(Ленинский Мемориальный Центр; ☑ 8422-442 080; http://leninmemorial.ru; pl 100-Letiya Lenina 1; R100; ⊘ 10am-6pm Tue-Sun, to 5pm Fri) This massive memorial centre dedicated to Ulyanovsk's most famous son is crammed with busts, photos and portraits of Lenin, from his time as a young revolutionary to his evolution as the figurehead of a Soviet cult. There's little text in English, but it's worth a visit to take in the spectacle. The centre also hosts interesting rotating exhibitions.

🛏 Sleeping & Eating

Hotel Venets HOTEL $$
(Гостиница Венец; ☑ 8422-441 870; www.venets-hotel.ru; ul Sovetskaya 15; incl breakfast s R2200-3200, d R2800-4000, ste R4000-6900; ☜) This formidable piece of Soviet hotel architecture in a towering block has clearly seen better

days, though it is clean, central to sights, and has stunning views. There are lots of cheaper rooms, but mediocre breakfasts.

Hilton Garden Inn HOTEL **$$$**
(☎8422-250 055; http://hiltongardeninn3.hilton.com; ul Goncharova 25; s/d from R3200/4000; ✳@🛜) Despite the 'Hilton' name, this beautiful four-star hotel in the centre is a surprisingly affordable option and the best lodging option in the city. Opened in 2015, the hotel occupies a newly renovated palace. The rooms are tastefully decorated with all the mod-cons and upscale toiletries you'd expect. The breakfast costs R700, though there are good coffee places nearby.

Veprevo Koleno CZECH **$$**
(☎8-951-094 5115; https://vk.com/veprevokoleno; ul Federatsii 11; mains R350-500; ◷noon-1am) The beer revolution has come slowly to Ulyanovsk, and this popular Czech restaurant features relatively rare but very good Czech brands such as Kláster and Krušovice. The food – mainly hearty meat dishes, sausages and schnitzels – is very good as well.

Cafeletto CAFE
(☎8422-441 344; www.cafeletto.ru; ul Karla Marxa 6a; ◷8.30am-midnight Mon-Fri, from 10am Sat & Sun) The ideal, refined spot to nip in for the city's best coffee and cake experience. It also does lunch foods, such as salads and quiches.

ⓘ Getting There & Away

Ulyanovsk's decrepit **central bus station** (Центральный Автовокзал; ☎842-248 5883; http://avtovokzal73.ru; ul Polbina 48; ◷5.30am-10pm) is 5km west of the centre. There are ticket offices and a large wall-mounted timetable. The bus station is reachable via trams 1, 10 and 15 as well as *marshrutka* 43. A taxi to the centre will cost R300.

Several buses run to Kazan (R600, five hours), Samara (R550, five hours) and Syzran (R300, three hours, hourly).

Ulyanovsk-Tsentralnaya train station is 6km south of the centre and is served by *marshrutka* 94 and trams 4 and 9.

WORTH A TRIP

BOLGAR

It might be the smallest town in Tatarstan, but Bolgar (Болгар) shares its name on equal terms with the country of Bulgaria. The word 'Volga' is most likely a Slavic corruption of the same name. Bolgar is the descendant of Great Bulgar, the capital of one of the most powerful states of early medieval Eastern Europe. Ruins of that city, on the outskirts of the modern town, have been turned into an open-air museum, which has become a major place of pilgrimage for Tatars in search of their roots.

The Bulgars were a Turkic tribe based south of the Don when they came under pressure from the Khazars and had to migrate. One branch headed west and occupied the eastern Balkans, but it was soon assimilated by local Slavs, leaving no trace but the name. The eastern branch settled on the Volga and mixed with local Finno-Ugric tribes. Sunni Islam became the official religion in 921.

The **Bolgar State Historical-Architectural Museum Reserve** (Болгарский Государственный историко-архитектурный музей-заповедник; ☎843-473 1632; ul Nazarovykh 67; all museums R450; ◷8am-5pm Mon-Fri, to 6pm Sat & Sun) is east of town, with a boat landing directly in front of the large Museum of Bolgar Civilisation (Музей Болгарской цивилизации), which houses the site's main exhibits on Bolgar's history.

Hydrofoils leave Kazan early morning (usually 8am) and return from Bolgar late afternoon, usually at 3pm or 4pm, giving you about three hours to look around. Check exact times, as they tend to change from one navigation season to the next (roughly from late May to September). They dock at the quay directly in front of the Museum of Bolgar Civilisation. Expect to pay around R360 each way.

Kazan Tourist Information Centre (p345) runs 11-hour boat excursions to Bolgar (twice weekly in the season, R2000 including lunch). You can stay at the **Hotel Regina** (Отель Регина; ☎843-473 1044; www.reginahotels.ru; ul Gorkogo 30; s/d R1800/2600); ask for a quiet room, as kids and loud groups can be a problem.

Buses make the 200km drive from Kazan's Yuzhny Avtovokzal bus station year-round (R350, three hours), departing at 10am and 5.45pm. Some Saturdays, Kazan Tourist Information Centre runs day excursions by bus (R2000, 11 hours) with lunch.

Trains run to Kazan (R850, six hours, two daily), Moscow (R3312, 14 hours, three daily) and Volgograd (R2000, 17 hours, two daily) via Saratov (R1038, 10 hours). Buses are a better option for Samara.

The centre is compact and walkable. **Taxis** (☎ 8422-555 000, 8422-494 949) are plentiful and reasonably priced.

Samara   Самара

☎ 846 / POP 1.16 MILLION / ⊙ MOSCOW +1HR

The Volga port city of Samara is a major hub for air, rail and river traffic, meaning that any visit to the region is likely to entail a stopover here. While there are few traditional sites beyond an impressive art museum and a quirky WWII-era bunker, the vibe is lively and the restaurants are the best around. On a summer day the riverbanks are packed with bathing beauties, in-line skaters and beer drinkers. Don't miss the chance to stroll the long and lovely riverside park. Samara also serves as the base for excursions into the nearby Zhiguli Hills.

Samara grew up where the Volga meets the Samara River, at a sharp bend across from the Zhiguli Hills. Founded as a border fortress in 1568, it saw the local governor drowned by Stepan Razin's Cossacks in 1670 and another governor flee Yemelyan Pugachev's peasant army in 1774. The Russian Civil War began in Samara, when a unit of Czechoslovakian prisoners of war commandeered their train and seized control of the city, turning it into a stronghold for the emerging White Army. During WWII a bunker was built here for Stalin but he never had to use it. In the post-WWII period Samara remained a closed city due to its strategic industries.

⊙ Sights

As well as visiting the key sights, take time to stroll along the banks of the Volga River, which is flanked by lush parks and sandy beaches.

★ **Stalin's Bunker**   HISTORIC BUILDING
(Бункер Сталина; ☎ 846-333 3571; ul Frunze 167; Russian/foreigner R80/200; ⊙11am-3pm) Samara hides a creepy piece of WWII history. This was the place Stalin was to be relocated to in the event that the Germans took Moscow. The never-used bunker was built nine storeys below the Academy of Culture and Art. Entry is by guided tour (in Russian), best booked a day in advance, though on some days you

can simply turn up. The entrance is located behind the building, in the courtyard.

Samara Art Museum   MUSEUM
(Художественный музей; ☎ 846-332 3309; www.artmus.ru; ul Kuybysheva 92; Russian/foreigner R80/120; ⊙10am-6pm Thu-Mon, to 8pm Wed) Easily the most important cultural attraction in the city, the Samara Art Museum exhibits mainly Russian art, including works by those who came to the region to paint. Look for *Boyarishina*, given by Surikov to a local doctor who treated him when he fell ill. The museum also holds an impressive collection of early Kazimir Malevich works.

Modern Museum   MUSEUM
(☎ 846-333 2498; www.samaramodern.ru; ul Frunze 15; R100; ⊙10am-6pm Tue, Wed & Fri-Sun, 1pm-9pm Thu) Modest but interesting museum dedicated to art nouveau architecture and design, which set the style tone for the city's wealthy residents in the early years of the 20th century. The setting is the central villa of the Kurlina family. Visitors take a peek into the family's living and dining rooms as well Lady Kurlina's boudoir and a couple of other rooms.

Gallereya Viktoria   GALLERY
(Галерея Виктория; ☎ 846-277 8912; www.gallery-victoria.ru; ul Nekrasovskaya 2; ⊙11am-7pm) **FREE** This private gallery is excellent for viewing (and purchasing) works by the best of the Volga region artists in regular exhibitions. Check the website for openings and down times.

Children's Art Gallery   GALLERY
(Детская художественная галерея; ☎ 846-332 4398; http://chgal.ssu.samara.ru; ul Kuybysheva 139; adult/child R100/70; ⊙9am-5.30pm; ⊛) Housed in the landmark Engineer Klodt's House (Дом инженера Клодта), which resembles a fairy-tale castle and contains a collection of children's art and art for children, who can pick up a brush here. Part of the experience is simply to see the interior of this grand house, which dates from the end of the 19th century.

Tours

Samara Intour   TOURS
(Самара Интур; ☎ 846-279 2040; www.samaraintour.ru; Samarskaya ul 51; ⊙9am-7pm Mon-Fri, 10am-5pm Sat) This highly professional travel agency has some staff who speak English and German. It can organise an individual tour into the bunker built for Stalin, and often runs excursions into the attractive Samara Bend region around Shiryaevo.

🛏 Sleeping

Volga Hotel   HOTEL $$
(Гостиница Волга; ☑ 846-242 1196; Volzhsky pr 29; incl breakfast s R2600-3000, d R3000-3800, ste R4200-4500; 🛜) This hotel gets knocked down in reviews for its location, at the northern end of the embankment and a 30-minute walk from the centre, but in a city that lacks affordable accommodation, it's an acceptable choice for a short stay. The renovated rooms have parquet flooring and dated but comfortable furniture. One virtue: the Zhiguli Brewery is nearby.

Holiday Inn Samara   HOTEL $$$
(☑ 846-372 7000; www.ihg.com; ul Alexeya Tolstogo 99; s/d R4000/5500; @🛜🏊) This reliable chain offering doesn't disappoint: large, clean rooms, good breakfasts and helpful multilingual staff. The central location is convenient to the Volga River and ferries. Some rooms have views out over the river.

Bristol-Zhiguli Hotel   HOTEL $$$
(Гостиница Бристоль-Жигули; ☑ 846-331 6555; www.bristol-zhiguly.ru; ul Kuybysheva 111; incl breakfast s R3000-4700, d R4400-7000, apt from R8000; 🍴@🛜) This art nouveau diamond in the rough recalls Samara's heyday in the late 19th and early 20th centuries, though from the outside at least the hotel has seen better days. The ornate lobby is eye-catching. The modern rooms can't match the decor, though they are clean and comfortable, and the central location is within easy walking distance of the Volga and sights.

Hotel Europe   HOTEL $$$
(Гостиница Европа; ☑ 846-270 8740; www.hoteleurope.ru; Galaktionovskaya ul 171; incl breakfast s R3300-3900, d R4000-5000, apt R7670-12,900; 🍴❄@🛜🏊) This hotel is housed in a lovely, mustard-yellow mansion from 1902 and is quirky in both good and bad ways. The stairways, corridors and rooms have unmistakable period character, though many rooms are located on the upper floors and there's no lift. The reception desk is friendly, and the in-house Irish pub on the ground floor serves very good food.

🍴 Eating

Troitsky Market   MARKET $
(Троицкий рынок; ul Galaktionovskaya 27; ⊙7am-9pm Tue-Sat, to 4pm Mon, to 6pm Sun) Stalls full of fresh fruit and veggies, and lots of fresh and smoked fish, as well as breads, meats and cheeses. Even if you're not buy-

ing, come here just to take in the piles of smoked fish on display.

⭐ Cafe Puri   GEORGIAN $$
(☑846-989 3332; https://vk.com/puri63; ul Kuybysheva 79; mains R400-500; ⊙11am-11pm; 🛜) This warm, welcoming restaurant offers authentic Georgian food and wine to an adoring public. Evening reservations are a must. Here's the place to sample *kuchmachi* (chicken innards, and walnuts and pomegranate seeds), *khachapuri* (fresh-baked bread filled with an egg), *khinkali* (meat dumplings) and many other favourites, all washed down with litres of red wine. The staff can help you choose.

⭐ Staraya Kvartira   RUSSIAN $$
(Старая квартира; ☑846-332 2260; www.oldflat.ru; Samarskaya ul 51/53; mains R500; ⊙noon-midnight) The 'Old Flat' is a total delight: a rabbit warren of tiny rooms all done up in peak Soviet-era kitsch. In keeping with the theme, the eclectic menu draws on old communist classics, such as the hamburger served with an egg on top, as well as more demanding fare. A meal to remember.

Cafe Benjamin   AMERICAN $$
(☑846-990 1576; www.benjamincafe.com; ul Kuybysheva 103; burgers & salads R400; ⊙9am-midnight Mon-Fri, from 11am Sat & Sun; 🍴) A pleasing Russian take on an American diner, chock full of cheery 1950s references and a menu that's strong on soups, salads, burgers and sandwiches. The 'Cobb' salad – with chicken breast, avocado and bacon – makes for a filling lunch in its own right. This place fills up at mealtimes, so reservations are a must.

U Palycha   RUSSIAN $$
(У Палыча; ☑846-332 3605; http://samara.palich.ru; ul Kuybysheva 100; mains R600-800) This cellar restaurant is highly recommended for its Russian cuisine, including its *pelmeni* (Russian-style ravioli). There's live Russian folk music on Thursday and Friday.

🍷 Drinking & Nightlife

⭐ Zhiguli Brewery   BREWERY
(Жигулёвское пиво; ☑846-332 6073; www.samarabeer.ru; Volzhsky pr 4) Samara's own Zhiguli Brewery, 2km north of the centre along the embankment, offers a couple of diverse drinking options. Most popular on a warm day is

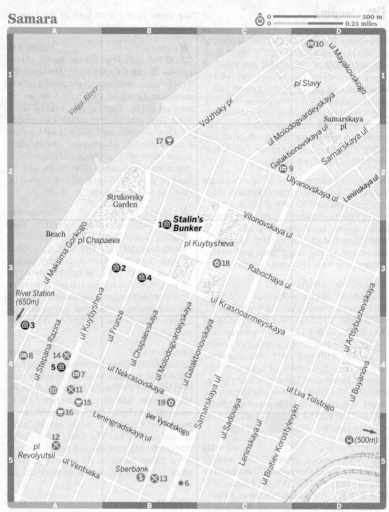

to bring an empty plastic water bottle and fill it from a small shop inside the brewery and then walk along the river. You can also purchase smoked and salted fish to eat as a snack.

There's also a pub in same complex, where you can order by the glass as well as enjoy simple pub food.

Traveler's Coffee   CAFE
(☎846-202 6008; www.travelerscoffee.ru/places/samara; ul Kuybysheva 95; ⊙8am-midnight; ☏) The perfect central spot, just off pedestrianised Leningradskaya ul, to grab a coffee or cake and connect to the web via the free

(and reliable) wi-fi. It's also possible to order food, mainly salads and sandwiches, though the strong suit here is coffee.

Kipyatok   TEAHOUSE
(Кипяток; ☎846-333 2720; Leningradskaya ul 40; ⊙11am-midnight; ☏) This funky upstairs space feels like a classic 19th-century Russian tearoom. Order from a long list of classic teas and coffees. It also does breakfasts until 2pm and offers a light menu of soups, salads, *pelmeni*, cakes and ice cream. The creative dishes are complemented by homemade *kvas* and freshly produced cranberry *mors* (fruit drink).

Samara

☆ Entertainment

Opera & Ballet Theatre THEATRE
(Театр оперы и балета; ☎ 846-332 2509; www.
opera-samara.net; pl Kuybysheva 1; tickets R150-
1000; ⊙ ticket office 10am-7pm) The main venue for ballet, classical concerts and opera.

Podval LIVE MUSIC
(Подвал; ☎ 846-332 9283; https://rock63.ru/
podval; ul Galaktionovskaya 46; cover around R200;
⊙ 7pm-3am Wed-Sun) The 'Basement' has
live rock, metal, gothic and other acts for a
youngish crowd.

◉ Information

Sberbank (ul Galaktionovskaya, opposite ul
Galaktionovskaya 29; ⊙ 9am-7pm Mon, Tue,
Thu & Fri, 10am-7pm Wed, 9am-5pm Sat)
Post Office (Почтамт; ul Kuybysheva 82;
⊙ 9am-7pm Mon-Fri, to 5pm Sat & Sun)

◉ Getting There & Away

Air and rail tickets are available at Samara Intour
(p350).

AIR

Samara's **Kurumoch International Airport**
(KUF; ☎ 846-966 5516; www.airport.samara.
ru) is located 35km north of the city and is the
region's busiest. It offers regular flights throughout Russia, Central Asia and Europe (Prague,
Barcelona and Helsinki). A special bus runs
from the airport to the centre every 20 minutes
throughout the day. Buy tickets at cashiers
inside the terminal. A taxi to the centre will cost
from R1000 to R1200.

BOAT

The **river station** (Речной вокзал; ☎ 846-222
9337; http://srpp63.ru; ul Maksima Gorkogo 82)
is at the west end of the embankment, in front
of Hotel Rossiya. Long-distance cruises operate
to various destinations along the Volga. Several
cruise agencies have kiosks here. **Infoflot**
(☎ 846-276 7491; www.infoflot.com; river station; ⊙ 9am-6pm) sells return cruises to Kazan
(from R8100, three days), Ulyanovsk via Shi-
rayevo (from R8000, three days), and Volgograd
(from R16,000, five days). Book several months
in advance for the cheapest berths. There are
also boats to closer destinations, including
Shiryaevo (about R120, 2½ hours, two daily).

BUS

The **central bus station** (Центральный
автовокзал; ☎ 846-224 1515; http://new.
avokzal63.ru; ul Avrory 207) is 7km northeast of
the centre. It's reachable via *marshrutky* 1, 4, 30
and 37. A taxi to the centre costs R300 to R400.
Watch for rush-hour traffic. A trip to/from the
centre can take up to an hour.

Samara has good connections to Kazan
(R900, nine hours, three daily), Syzran (R340,
three hours, six daily), Tolyatti (R250, two hours,
hourly) and Ulyanovsk (R550, five hours, hourly).

TRAIN

Samara's modern **railway station**
(Железнодорожный вокзал; ☎ information
800 775 0000; http://samara.dzvr.ru; pl Komsomolskaya 1) is conveniently situated in the
centre of the city, about 2km east of the riverfront. It's accessible via public transportation on
trams 1, 4, and 16. A taxi from the station to the
centre should cost no more than R200.

The flagship Zhiguli train is fastest to Moscow
(*kupe* R4000, 14 hours) but the most expensive.
Other connections are to Saratov (*kupe* R1400,
nine hours) and Volgograd (R2500, 16 hours).
For Kazan, bus is better, and for Astrakhan book
via Volgograd as direct trains pass through
Kazakhstan.

⊙ Getting Around

Most bus and *marshrutky* routes run straight as a nail in the central part of town, so it's easiest just to walk to the major street to grab one (eg ul Kuybysheva to go east to pl Slavy, or ul Samarskaya for pl Samarskaya).

Uber ride-share service (www.uber.com) operates in Samara and rates are significantly cheaper than standard **taxis** (☑ 846-302 0202).

Samara Bend

Samara sits on the left (eastern) bank of the Volga, while the right bank is dominated by the rocky Zhiguli Hills. The river loops around the hills, creating a peninsula encompassing 32,000 hectares of national forest reserve.

The **Samara Bend National Park** (Самарская Лука) is a prime area for hikes along rocky ledges and grand Volga vistas. The peaks – the highest being Strelnaya Mountain at 370m – are in the northwest corner of the reserve. These hills were the hideout of peasant rebel Stepan Razin in the 17th century.

The easiest way to reach the reserve in summer is to take a boat to any of the villages on the right bank, such as Shiryaevo. If you want to explore the area by public transport or bicycle, local hubs Tolyatti and Syzran come into the equation. Together, with Samara, they form an almost equilateral triangle and often have better connections with adjacent regions than the provincial capital.

Every year, thousands of locals raft the *zhigulyovskaya krugosvetka*, which translates as 'Zhiguli round-the-world trip'. The 10-day rafting route follows the loop in the river, then cuts back up north through a channel on the west side of the park. Samara Intour (p350) sometimes organises these trips; ask ahead.

Tolyatti   Тольятти

☑ 8482 / POP 720,000 / ⊘ MOSCOW

Much of the industrial city of Tolyatti, two hours by bus from Samara, was built in the 1960s and '70s to support the Soviet Union's burgeoning auto industry – particularly cars made by the ubiquitous Lada company. In those times, it was one of the most prosperous cities in the country. Recent days haven't been as kind, as increased competition from foreign producers has put pressure on domestic car-makers. Tolyatti has a local reputation for being a rough town, but the reality is a relatively peaceful city, with a couple of sights and a strategic position beside the giant Kuybyshev reservoir dam, with the Zhiguli Hills starting right across the water.

Tolyatti is a sprawling place, divided essentially into two large districts that are several kilometres away from each other. The central district – *Tsentralnyy rayon* – is the older of the two and sometimes called Old Town (Stary Gorod). The New Town (Novy Gorod) lies to the west. It's often referred to on maps as the *Avtozavodskiy rayon* (Auto District).

⊙ Sights & Activities

Technical Museum   MUSEUM
(☑ 8482-726 620; Yuzhnoye sh 137; R120; ⊘ 9am-5pm) Situated in the New Town, and opposite the VAZ plant that makes Ladas, this museum has a vast collection of mostly military hardware, including a nuclear submarine.

Spin Sport   CYCLING
(Спин-Спорт; ☑ 8482-489 120; www.spin-sport.ru; Komsomolskoye sh 28; tennis court hire 1hr/racquet R600/100; ⊘ 8am-11pm) This is an all-year recreational resort, offering skiing and snowboarding in the winter, and a swimming pool and tennis courts in summer. The location is a pretty, forested area near the Volga, just south of the central district.

⊨ Sleeping & Eating

Zhiguli Star   HOTEL **$$**
(Звезда Жигулей; ☑ 8482-223 311; www.lada-gam.ru; ul Mira 77; incl breakfast s R3000-4000, d R3000-5000; ⊜ ⊛) This comfortable hotel in the central district is your best option if you're staying overnight. The restaurant (mains R400) is open for breakfast, lunch and dinner.

Plan-B   BURGERS **$**
(План-Б; ☑ 8482-570 101; www.planbtlt.ru; ul Yubileynaya 8; burgers R200-280; ⊘ 10am-midnight; ⊛ ⊘) This artisanal burger bar sticks out like a sore thumb amid the communist-era, industrialised landscape of Tolyatti, yet the burgers (and fries) are seriously good. Several sizes and combinations to choose from, and even a vegan burger. Eat inside the tiny restaurant or take away. The location is in the New Town.

Izyum   CAFE
(☑ 8482-280 493; ul Gagarina 2; ⊘ 9am-11pm Mon-Fri, from 10am Sat & Sun; ⊛) Excellent coffees and cakes €/R130), as well as soups, salads and pasta dishes (mains around R300) served in a clean, contemporary setting. The location is just off the main square in the *Tsentralnyy rayon*.

❶ Getting There & Away

Buses go to/from Samara (R220, two hours, hourly), Ulyanovsk (R350, four hours, at least hourly) and Kazan (R700, 6½ hours, three daily). The main bus station is located in the Old Town (Stary Gorod).

❶ Getting Around

Taxis are the most convenient way of moving between Tolyatti's districts. Expect to pay about R250 for trips between these and less for travel within one district.

Expect to pay R150 to R200 for a **taxi** (✆ 8482-70 000) from the Old Town (Stary Gorod) bus station to the Zhiguli Star hotel.

Saratov   Саратов

✆ 8452 / POP 838,000 / ⊕ MOSCOW

Saratov is a laid-back place and has a bit of a seaside resort atmosphere, although it lacks major tourist attractions. The former name of ul Kirova is Nemetskaya (German), a sure sign that Saratov was once at the heart of the Volga German region. Wartime deportations spared few Volga Germans and only a handful returned here from exile, but their presence can be felt in the city's distinctly Central European ambience.

Across the Volga river in Engels, known as Pokrovsk when it was the capital of the Autonomous Socialist Soviet Republic of the Volga Germans, is an outstanding collection of paintings by the Volga German Yakov Veber.

The first man in space, cosmonaut Yury Gagarin, lived in Saratov and studied at the local university, which now bears his name.

◉ Sights

Gagarin Museum   MUSEUM
(Музей Гагарина; ✆ 8542-237 666; ul Sakko i Vanzetti 15; ⊕ 9am-4pm Mon-Fri, 8am-3pm Sat) **FREE** This interesting museum tells the life of the world's first man in space through photos and personal objects. Yuri Gagarin not only lived and studied in Saratov, but also landed (crashed?) his Vostok 1 capsule nearby after his much-lauded flight. The landing site, 40km out of town near the village of Kvasnikovka, is marked by a commemorative monument.

**Saratov State Museum
of Military Glory**   MUSEUM
(Саратовский Государственный Музей Боевой и Трудовой Славы; ✆ 8452-750 089; www.sargmbs.ru; Park Pobedy; R60; ⊕ 9am-5.30pm Tue-

SHIRYAEVO

In the 1870s Ilya Repin spent two years in the village of Shiryaevo (Ширяево) just north of Samara on the west bank of the Volga. Here he completed sketches for his famous painting *Barge Haulers on the Volga*, which is now in St Petersburg's Russian Museum. Today, this pleasant village welcomes art lovers and day trippers. The main formal sight of the village is the **Repin Museum** (✆ 8-960-841 3409; www.museum.ru/m1597; ul Sovetskaya 14, Shiryaevo; Russian/foreigner R120/200; ⊕ 11am-4pm Tue-Sun) and its impressive selection of Volga River paintings, though, truth be told, most visitors come here for the chance to escape busy Samara and sample a bit of village life.

Regular boats from Samara (about R120, 2½ hours, two daily) are the best way to reach Shiryaevo. You can also reach it by bus from Tolyatti (R200, 2¾ hours, daily).

Fri, 10am-6.30pm Sat & Sun May-Sep) This open-air museum filled with tanks, planes and artillery guns from the glory days of WWII is referred to locally as 'Victory Park'. Entrance to the grounds is free. There's a small exhibition filled with photos, maps and awards. In addition to the impressive firepower, the main reward for a visit here is the view out over the Volga River. The main park lane eventually leads you into an 'Ethnic Village', with houses representing numerous ethnic groups.

Radishchev Art Museum   MUSEUM
(Саратовский художественный музей имени А. Н. Радищева; ✆ 8452-261 606; http://radmuseumart.ru; ul Radishcheva 39; R150; ⊕ 10am-6pm Tue, Wed, Sat & Sun, noon-8pm Thu & Fri) This is the main branch of the city's Fine Arts Museum. It contains a good selection from the 18th to the 20th centuries, including some breathtaking examples from the Russian avant-garde period of the early 20th century.

🛏 Sleeping

★**Hotel Polina**   HOTEL **$$**
(Отель Полина; ✆ 8452-390 272; 7-y Shelkovichnyy pr 1a; s/d R2500/3000; 🅿 ❄ @ 🛜) Smallish, family-run hotel located on a quiet alley, about 2km southwest of the centre. Spotlessly clean rooms, panelled in light woods, with crisp sheets on the beds and gleaming baths.

Staff are friendly and the owners go out of their way to ensure a pleasant stay.

Hotel Volna
HOTEL $$

(Гостиница Волна; ☎8452-280 885; nab Kosmonavtov 7a; incl breakfast s R2200, d R2400-3800; ☒@🛜) With its superb location inside the river-station building and reasonable prices, this place is popular with Russian travellers. It has some very cheap rooms without bathrooms (R1500). Take bus 11 from the Saratov-1 train station, which runs east along ul Moskovskaya.

Pioner Lyux Bohemia
HOTEL $$$

(Отель Пионер-Люкс Богемия; ☎8452-454 501; www.bohemiahotel.ru; pr Kirova 15/1; incl breakfast s R2500-3400, d R4400-5400, apt R6100; ☒@🛜) This hotel offers excellent value, given the central location and quality of the rooms and service. Rooms are decorated in postmodern tones and spread over several floors. From pr Kirova, enter a small alley to the right of the old Pioner Cinema complex. Buzz to enter; the reception is on the 6th floor.

🍴 Eating

Pivnoy Zavod
RUSSIAN $

(Пивной завод; ☎8452-264 480; http://sar-brewery.com; pr Kirova 5; mains R300; ☒10am-11pm; 🛜) Beer brewed on the premises, sausages and other hearty fare are on the food and drinks menu here. Servings are not large, though – the Caucasian lamb sausage is quite decent. It also has fresh *mors*.

House of Culinary Zhulien
RUSSIAN $

(Дом кулинарии Жюльен; ☎8452-265 871; http://gulien.ru; pr Kirova 42; meals R300; ☒9am-9pm) This cafeteria, decorated in loud colours, sells inexpensive and decent ready-made dishes mostly by weight. Pick up a tray and point to the various soups, salads and main dishes on offer.

⭐ Odessa
RUSSIAN $$

(Ресторан Одесса; ☎8452-233 226; http://odessa64.ru; nab Kosmonavtov 3; mains R600; ☒noon-11pm; 🛜) This traditional restaurant serves a mix of mains and grills, drawing on Russian and Ukrainian influences. Excellent salads and soups (including a filling borsch) as well as well-done grilled pork, chicken and fish dishes. The atmosphere is folksy, with old photos on the walls and floral print tablecloths. Reserve for evenings.

Chaikhana Uzbechka
UZBEK $$

(Чайхана Узбечка; ☎8452-539 039; http://uzbechka64.ru; ul Chapayeva 93; mains R500-600; ☒11am-midnight) A charming spot to sample the Central Asian cuisines of the former Soviet Union, including Uzbek, Tajik and Kazakh national dishes. There are big plates of grilled meats, plenty of fresh-baked bread, and salad plates topped with treats such as grilled eggplant and pomegranate. Homemade lemonade and friendly servers round out the charms. Reserve in advance for evening.

Buratino
RUSSIAN $$

(Буратино; ☎8542-277 479; pr Kirova 10; mains R350; ☒11am-midnight; 🍴) This is a rustic, Saratovian cafe-restaurant themed on 'Red Count' Alexey Tolstoy's version of *Pinocchio*. The menu is filled with Russian standards, such as meat-stuffed dumplings, pancakes and grilled meats, but served in a playful setting.

WORTH A TRIP

ENGELS

Engels (Энгельс; formerly Pokrovsk) is situated across the Volga River from Saratov and became the capital of the Autonomous Socialist Soviet Republic of the Volga Germans from 1924, which survived until the republic was dissolved in 1941 and the Volga Germans were deported. It's a mostly unattractive, Soviet-style place, but worth visiting for its **regional museum** (Энгельсский краеведческий музей; ☎8453-567 073; http://ekmuzeum.ru; ul Maksima Gorkogo 4; R60; ☒10am-5pm Tue & Thu-Sun, to 9pm Wed), feeling of 'otherness' and views of the Volga as you cross the almost-3km-long bridge.

The Engels Regional Museum is part archaeology and part social-history, with exhibits showing the presence of man in the region going back to the Palaeolithic era (Old Stone Age), through the Middle Ages and eventually to the more-modern era and the Volga Germans. The museum is also strong on the art of the Volga German painter Yakov Veber (1870–1958).

Take any bus from ul Moskovskaya to the Torgoby Tsentr Lazurny in Engels. The museum is almost directly across the road.

🍷 Drinking & Nightlife

Pinup Pub   CRAFT BEER
(☑ 8452-255 898; ul Sovetskaya 73; ⊙ 2pm-3am)
Rocker bar with 15 craft beers on tap and a
short list of decent snacks and light meals,
such as salads and burgers (R350).

Klausberg   BREWERY
(Пивной Дом 'Klausberg'; ☑ 8452-930 093; http://
klausberghaus.ru; ul Rakhova 26/40; ⊙ 10am-mid-
night Sun-Thu, to 2am Fri & Sat) They also serve
food here at this German-themed tavern located inside a brewery, but Saratov residents
know to avoid the mediocre mains and stick
to the drinks: a decent range of light, dark
and wheat beers. The system is a bit confusing (you pay a drinking deposit up front), but
the beer is some of the best around.

Café Coupe   CAFE
(☑ 8452-236 759; Volzhskaya ul 34; coffee R125;
⊙ 10am-11pm) This elegant cafe in a former
burgher house evokes fin-de-siècle Paris and
serves a few inexpensive light dishes (R200)
such as soup.

⭐ Entertainment

Sobinov Conservatory   CLASSICAL MUSIC
(Саратовская государственная консерватория
имени Л. В. Собинова; ☑ 8452-230 503; www.
sarcons.ru; pr Kirova 1) One of the best conserv-
atories in Russia, holding frequent performances by resident and visiting musicians
in an architectural highlight of Saratov.

Schnittke Philharmonic Theatre   THEATRE
(Саратовская Областная Филармония им. А.
Шнитке; ☑ tickets 8452-224 872; www.sarphil.
com; Sobornaya pl 9; ⊙ box office 10am-7pm Mon-
Fri, noon-6pm Sat & Sun) This hall remains true
to the ideology of *polystylism*, fostered by
home-grown composer Alfred Schnittke, so
jazz and folk music are as much at home
here as classical music.

ⓘ Getting There & Away

BOAT
Inside the river station at the eastern end of ul
Moskovskaya, **Volga-Heritage** (☑ 8452-280
874; www.rech-vokzal.ru; nab Kosmonavtov 7a)
sells cruises in the navigation season to destinations along the Volga, such as Astrakhan (return
from R15,000, five days) and Samara (return
from R8000, three days). Staff can tell you
which boats have the best facilities and food.
Saratov–Moscow one way costs from R27,000
(eight days) and St Petersburg from R40,000
(10 days).

To find the Volga Heritage office, walk through
the small lobby of the Hotel Volna and down a
narrow corridor.

BUS
The main bus station is located just behind the
train station (ul Emlyutina 44g). Buses tend to
be slower but cheaper than trains to destinations including Samara (R900, 11 hours) and
Volgograd (R800, eight hours). The bus to Ulyanovsk costs about R1000 and takes 10 hours.

TRAIN
The train station (Privokzalnaya pl) is at the
western end of ul Moskovskaya. Train 9 (*kupe*
R5812, 14 hours, daily) is the best (but most
expensive) of the frequent trains to Moscow.
Others go to Samara (*kupe* R1400, nine hours)
and Volgograd (*platskart* R1061, seven hours).

ⓘ Getting Around
Bus 11 runs along ul Moskovskaya from the train
station to the river station. *Marshrutka* 79 connects the train station with the market in the town
centre (Krytiy Rynok). A **taxi** (☑ 8452-777 777)
from the train station to the centre will cost R200
to R300.

Volgograd   Волгоград

☑ 8442 / POP 1.02 MILLION / ⊙ MOSCOW
WWII history buffs will certainly want to
visit Volgograd, site of one of the best-known
and important battles of the war. It was here
in February 1943, when the city was known
as Stalingrad, that the relentless German advance was first halted and eventually turned
back for good. The Soviets transformed the
city, literally and figuratively, into a symbol
of their successful effort, and in the process
graced Volgograd with broad boulevards
and public buildings that show off an unmistakable Stalinesque grandeur, and an
enormous victory monument you won't
soon forget.

Volgograd was founded in 1589 as Tsarit-
syn and for centuries stood as an important
trading and military post near the southern
border. Aside from the WWII sights, including an impressive war cemetery at Rossoshka, 30km northwest of the centre, there's a
pretty waterfront and the first locks of the
impressive Volga-Don Canal.

In 2013 Volgograd was the target of several suicide bombings, including one that
caused massive damage to the main train
station and killed 17 people. Despite the
bombings, Volgograd remains a safe city for
travellers.

⊙ Sights

★ **Mamaev Kurgan**   MONUMENT
(Мамаев курган; ⊙ dawn-dusk) **FREE** Known
as Hill 102 during the Battle of Stalingrad, Mamaev Kurgan was the site of four
months of fierce fighting and is now a memorial to Soviet fighters who died in this
bloody-but-victorious fight. The complex's
centrepiece is an extraordinarily evocative
72m-high statue of Mother Russia wielding
a sword that extends another 11m above her
head. To get here take the high-speed tram
to the Mamaev Kurgan stop, 3.5km north of
the centre, and walk up the hill.

In addition to the towering victory monument, the *kurgan* (mound) is an entire
complex of statues, reflecting pools, a war
cemetery, a church and a pantheon with an
eternal flame and a stirring 'changing of the
guard' ceremony on the hour. The pantheon
is inscribed with the names of 7200 soldiers –
over one million Russian soldiers died here
in battle in WWII.

**Panorama Museum of
the Battle of Stalingrad**   MUSEUM
(Музей-панорама Сталинградская битва;
☑ 8442-236 723; http://stalingrad-battle.ru; ul Ime-
na Marshala Chuykova 47, cnr ul 13-ya Gvardeyskoy
Divizii; R250; ⊙ 10am-6pm Tue-Sun) This enormous museum has eight large display rooms
filled with exhibits on WWII and the Battle of
Stalingrad. There's little English signage but
each room has a short synopsis in English
on the room's particular theme. Audio headphones are available for a fee. A highlight
is the vivid 360-degree Battle of Stalingrad
Panorama. The museum is close to the Volga
River, several blocks north of alleya Geroyev.
The entrance is located at street level on the
side of the building facing the Volga.

The area around the museum has some
pretty views out over the river and plenty of
old tanks and planes for kids to climb around
on. Next to the museum stands the remains
of an old mill, dating from 1903, that was
destroyed in the battle. It's left standing as a
reminder of the horrific fighting.

Rossoshka Memorial Cemetery   CEMETERY
(Rossoshka; cemetery free, museum R30; ⊙ sun-
rise-sunset) This reconciliation cemetery, near
the village of Rossoshka, 35km northwest of
Volgograd, marks the final resting place of
some 20,000 fallen Soviet fighters, 60,000
Germans and 2000 Romanians who died in
the Battle of Stalingrad in 1942 and '43. The
Soviet and Russian soldiers are buried on
one side of the road, while the Germans and
Romanians are on the other. There's a small
museum that holds remnants of the battles
that have been excavated.

Museum Reserve Old Sarepta   MUSEUM
(Музей-заповедник Старая Сарепта; ☑ 8442-
673 302; http://altsarepta.ru; ul Vinogradnaya 6;
R200, tours per person from R400, minimum 3 people;
⊙ 9am-5.30pm Tue-Sun) An hour by *marshrutka* from the centre, what is now known as the
Krasnoarmeysk district was once the German
colony of Sarepta. Today the entire quarter
is a museum reserve set around a beautiful
square and Lutheran church, dating from the
late 18th century. To get here, take *marshrutka* 15a, 91a, 93a, 93c, 93 or 55a from pr Lenina
and ask the driver to stop at Vinogradnaya.

The original settlers of old Sarepta were
German Catholic missionaries from Moravia
(in the Czech Republic) who arrived here
in 1765 with the aim of proselytising the
Kalmyks. Failing that, they became the mus-
tard tycoons of Russia. The museums – one
a historic pharmacy, the other telling the history and lifestyle of the colony – are interesting but a tour in Russian, English or German
is useful, also taking you into the otherwise
closed church. Buy tickets for the two museums from the white building alongside the
church.

Volga-Don Canal   CANAL
(Волго-Донской судоходный канал имени В.
И. Ленина (Волго-Донской канал); ul Fadeeva
35a) Built in 1952, the Volga-Don Canal is
the grandiose gateway of an aquatic avenue
that now connects the White and the Black
Seas via the Volga and Don Rivers. The huge
Stalinesque neoclassical arch marks the first
lock in the Volga-Don Canal. Take *marshrutka* 15a, 91a, 93a, 93c, 93 or 55a from ul Lenina south from the centre for about 10km to
the first stop after crossing the canal.

One million people, including 236,000
Axis prisoners of war and Russian Gulag inmates, took part in the construction of the
canal, and even a planet is named after it.

Also here is a small **museum** (Музей
Волго-Донского канала; ul Fadeyeva 35a; R60;
⊙ 10am-noon & 1-4.30pm Tue, Wed & Fri), which
tells the story of the canal and gives insight
into water transport in Europe.

🏃 Activities

A popular evening stroll begins at the bottom of ul Komsomolskaya and runs north
through a park along a ridge above the Volga

THE BATTLE OF STALINGRAD

The epic WWII Battle of Stalingrad is one that nearly everyone will know something about, even if they didn't happen to major in history. It was here in late 1942 and early 1943 that the Soviet Red Army defeated Nazi Germany, along with its allies Italy, Hungary, Croatia and Romania, after a tenacious six-month battle. The victory was a key turning point in the war.

Since launching their surprise attack on the Soviet Union in 'Operation Barbarossa' in June 1941, the German army had swept over much of European Russia with relative ease, swallowing up huge amounts of territory along the way. Toward the end of 1942, Nazi Germany was closing in on the Volga River and the Red Army had switched into survival mode, with a last-ditch defence planned for Stalingrad.

The battle raged on for months, as the fortunes of both the Germans and Soviets ebbed and flowed throughout that cold winter. Much of the fighting was carried on at close quarters within the city limits. At one point, finally, the German position was successfully isolated, and the Nazi commanders had no choice but to surrender. The result was in the order of 1.5 million people killed or wounded and a city in tatters, but Soviet Russia had prevailed.

The Stalingrad victory greatly shored up Russian morale and pierced the myth of German invincibility. By the end of 1943, the Red Army had driven the Germans out of most of the Soviet Union.

River to the Panorama Museum of the Battle of Stalingrad.

A couple of local companies offer guided tours of the significant WWII sights and may be worth considering for a deeper exploration of history. Several companies offer one-hour pleasure cruises along the river for around R300 per person. Buy tickets and find the boats at the Volga river station.

Kruiz   BOATING
(Круиз; ☑ 8442-630 202; www.kruiztur.ru; 1st fl, Rechnoy vokzal; ⚓) This tour agency offers many different segments of the Volga, including to/from Astrakhan (return R11,000 to R18,000, four days) and Kazan (R25,000 to R40,000, seven days). It also offers 90-minute pleasure cruises on the Volga (R300 per person) that depart regularly from the river station from May to September.

🛏 Sleeping

⭐ **Stary Stalingrad**   BOUTIQUE HOTEL **$$**
(Отель Старый Сталинград; ☑ 8442-385 501; http://hotelstalingrad.pro34.ru; ul Ostrovskogo 4; incl breakfast s/d/ste R2800/3600/4700; 🌐) Behind the Univermag shops and part of the same building, this modern minihotel has nicely furnished rooms with individual touches. It's especially worth trying if the larger hotels are full.

Park Inn   HOTEL **$$**
(☑ 8442-268 125; www.parkinn.com/hotel-volgograd; ul Balonina 7; s/d R3000/4000; ✳ @ 🌐)

This mid-market chain is highly recommended both for its excellent location, just behind the train station and five minutes' walk from the bus station, as well as the clean, well-appointed rooms and excellent buffet breakfast. The friendly staff know some English, and the German-themed restaurant offers a welcome diversion from Russian dumplings and borsch.

Hotel Volgograd   HOTEL **$$**
(Гостиница Волгоград; ☑ 8442-551 955; www.hotelvolgograd.ru; ul Mira 12; incl breakfast s R2800, d R3600-6500, ste R5000-16,000; ✳✳🌐) South across pl Pavshikh Bortsov, this hotel has professional staff and clean and comfortable rooms in one of the few buildings remaining from Tsaritsyn times – although it was considerably altered after the war.

Hotel Intourist   HOTEL **$$$**
(☑ 8442-302 303; http://en.volgaintour.ru; ul Mira 14; incl breakfast s R3400-4200, d R5000, ste R7400-11,000; ✳✳🌐) This is a vintage Soviet-era gem with the high level of service matching the bright, welcoming lobby. Rooms are well lit and tasteful.

🍴 Eating

Central Market   MARKET **$**
(Центральный рынок; Sovetskaya ul 17; ⊘ 7am-7pm Tue-Sat, to 5pm Sun & Mon) This sprawling market, located near the corner of Sovetskaya ul and Komsomolskaya ul, stocks everything from Astrakhan watermelons to Volga fish.

★ **Hungry** RUSSIAN $$
(☑ 8442-503 973; https://vk.com/hungrycafe; alleya Geroyev 5; mains R400; ☺ 10am-midnight; 🛜) This centrally located upscale cafe is an ideal choice for lunch or dinner. Wood-fired pizzas, gourmet salads and a long list of soups as well as meat and fish dishes. Enjoy homemade cakes and ice cream for dessert, and the coffee is good as well.

Na Allee GEORGIAN $$
(На Аллее; ☑ 8442-501 375; www.naallee.gidm.ru; alleya Geroyev 3; mains R350; ☺ 9am-11pm) This very good Georgian restaurant has a family atmosphere and serves homemade wine from Georgia. It does a tasty lamb *ketsi* with vegetables (baked in an earthenware dish).

Grand Café RUSSIAN $$
(Гранд Кафе; ☑ 8442-528 140; www.grandcafe34.ru; ul Mira 12; mains R450, pizza & pasta R260; ☺ 8am-6am) Situated on the ground floor of Hotel Volgograd, this is the city's most popular spot to sip a cappuccino and scope out the scene. Part of the premises is a pizzeria open from noon to 1am daily.

Rimini ITALIAN $$
(Римини; ☑ 8442-240 908; www.trattoria-rimini.ru; ul Gagarina 9; pizza R250-350, meat mains R400; ☺ 11am-midnight; 🛜) This large, bustling Italian place has neorustic decor and a large menu offering straight-up-and-down Italian pizza, pasta and meat dishes complemented by salads. Ul Gagarina is about five blocks north of Komsomolskaya ul along pr Lenina.

Bochka GERMAN $$
(Бочка; ☑ 8-937-099 5830; http://bochka.gidm.ru; Sovetskaya ul 16; mains R400, day menu R250; ☺ 11am-midnight) Basement beer cellar and restaurant that draws a business-lunch crowd, but it's more fun in the evening, when live music is staged.

Kayfe CAFE $$
(Кайфе; ☑ 8442-244 242; pr Lenina 23a; mains R400; ☺ 9am-6am; 🛜) A cosy cafe that offers everything you might want, be it a large meal or a light snack, tea, coffee or one of the many alcoholic beverages on the menu. It's good for breakfast, lunch and especially a predawn chill-out.

Bar & Grill STEAK $$$
(☑ 8442-551 050; www.bargrill34.ru; ul Mira 5; steaks from R800; ☺ noon-midnight; 🛜) Cosy, welcoming steakhouse, situated at the front of a theater building on central pl Pavshikh Bortsov. Choose from a mouthwatering list of grilled steaks and seafood. In addition to expensive cuts of beef, there are cheaper offerings of grilled chicken and pork. The setting is romantic dark woods, though in summer there's a small outdoor terrace.

Cappuccino CAFE
(☑ 8442-235 823; www.capucino.ru; pr Lenina 22; ☺ 8.30am-10pm) Popular cafe, where the tea is actually better than the namesake cappuccino and the cakes are very good and taste homemade. The homemade ice cream is very good as well.

🔒 Shopping

Memorable Souvenir GIFTS & SOUVENIRS
(ul Ostrovskogo 4; ☺ 9am-7pm) A terrific souvenir shop with shelves of over-the-top Soviet and WWII-themed shirts, hats, medals, models, flasks and loads of other perfect take-home mementos.

ℹ Information

Sberbank (☑ 8442-742 117; ul Gogolya 5; ☺ 9.30am-7.30pm Mon-Fri, 9am-5pm Sat) Alongside the post office.

Post Office (Главпочтамт; pl Pavshikh Bortsov; internet per MB R6; ☺ 9am-5pm Mon-Fri) Post office with internet access.

Tourist Information Centre (☑ 8442-529 893; www.welcomevolgograd.com; ul Gagarina 12; ☺ 8.30am-5pm Mon-Fri) Small but helpful tourist information office can offer city maps and advise on things to do and see. Not much English spoken.

Volgograd Sputnik Travel Company (☑ 8442-502 105; www.stalingradtours.com; pr Lenina 15) All-purpose travel agency offers guided tours of the city as well as historic tours of battlefield sights and guided visits to further-afield attractions such as the Rossoshka Reconciliation Cemetery. Guided tours of the city start at about R10,000 per tour (best divided among several people). Check out the website and arrange tours in advance by email.

ℹ Getting There & Away

Tickets can be bought at **TAVS Volga** (ТАВС Волга; ☑ 8442-380 010; alleya Geroyev 5; ☺ 8am-7pm) – especially useful for picking up bus tickets to Elista.

AIR

Volgograd International Airport (Международный Аэропорт Волгоград/VOG; ☑ 8442-261 000; ul Aviatorov 161) has daily air connections with Moscow as well as to popular holiday destinations in Turkey, such as Istanbul and Antalya.

BUS

For frequent buses to Elista (R625, six hours), Astrakhan (R950, 10 hours) and Rostov-on-Don (R900, nine hours), head to the **Central Bus Station** (Центральный автовокзал; ☑ 8442-377 228; ul Mikhaila Balonina 11), a 750m walk across the tracks or through the underpass from the train station. Frequent buses leave from the train-station square to Moscow (R1500, 14 hours). Booths and offices there sell tickets.

TRAIN

Volgograd's impressive Stalinist-styled train station is located in the centre of the city, within easy walking distance of hotels, restaurants and sights. Buy tickets at counters inside the station.

Train connections from Volgograd include Astrakhan (around R1000, eight to 11 hours, two daily), Moscow (train 1, R1900, 19 hours, almost daily), Rostov-on-Don (R1200, 12½ hours, at least daily), Saratov (R1100, 7½ hours, frequent) and St Petersburg (R3000, 36 hours, at least daily) – train 79 is the best for St Petersburg.

There are cheaper but slower train connections to Moscow and St Petersburg.

ⓘ Getting Around

The city centre is accessible on foot. Kiosks sell city maps of the centre for R100. To get to Mamaev Kurgan or the Panorama Museum of the Battle of Stalingrad, take the *skorostnoy tramvay* (high-speed tram), which is a single metro line that runs along or under pr Lenina. To get to Krasnoarmeysk take *marshrutka* 15a, 91a, 93a, 93c, 93 or 55a from pr Lenina on the city side of the road (ie not the Volga side).

To get to the airport, catch express minibus 6E (R25, every 15 minutes) from the stop on pr Lenina on the Volga side of the road, or at the train station.

Astrakhan   Астрахань

☑ 8512 / POPULATION 520,500 / ⓒ MOSCOW

Astrakhan sits astride the Volga north of the Caspian Sea and is Russia's face on that multinational body of water. The city reflects much of the region's cultural and religious diversity. There are large communities of Kazakhs and Azeris, as well as Islamic Tatars. While many visitors use Astrakhan mainly as a jumping-off point for the Volga Delta, the city merits a day or two of exploration in its own right.

There's a long, handsome riverfront that's ideal for evening strolls as the sun sets across the river. The striking white kremlin, a symbol of Russian dominance since the 16th century, holds two beautiful church-es and several museums. Across the canal, north of the kremlin, the stone mansions and churches of the European and Christian centre give way to Tatar and Persian *sloboda* (suburbs) with their wooden cottages, mosques and quaint courtyards, where garlands of drying *vobla* fish flutter in the breeze.

With its position along the Volga River and just north of the Caspian Sea, Astrakhan has always been valued for its strategic military and economic position. The modern Russian city dates from 1558, after Ivan the Terrible defeated the local Tatar khanate. Historically, though, Astrakhan is the successor of two imperial capitals in the area that date back much further. These include Saray of the Golden Horde, from the 13th and 14th centuries, and Itil (sometimes called Atil), of the earlier Khazar kaganate, which adopted Judaism as its official religion and goes back to the 8th to 10th centuries. Both cities prospered thanks to their location on the Silk Route, by the sea.

◉ Sights

★ **Kremlin**   HISTORIC SITE
(Астраханский кремль; http://astrakhan-musei.ru; ⓒ 7am-7pm) **FREE** The kremlin on top of Zayachy Hill is a peaceful green haven. Its walls and gate towers were built in the 16th century using bricks from the ruins of the Golden Horde's capital Saray, which stood north of Astrakhan. Today, the kremlin encompasses several museums and two churches. The main entrance is through the impressive Prechistinsky Gate, which passes under the bell tower of the Assumption Cathedral at the western end of ul Sovetskaya.

➡ ★ **Assumption Cathedral**   CHURCH
(Успенский собор; http://astrakhan-musei.ru; kremlin; ⓒ 7am-7pm) Dating from 1698–1720, the Assumption Cathedral dominates the kremlin grounds and is decorated inside with attractive frescoes.

➡ **Guardhouse**   MUSEUM
(Гауптвахта; http://astrakhan-musei.ru; kremlin; R50; ⓒ 10am-6pm Tue-Sun May-Oct) Located inside the guardhouse from 1807, this museum gives quite a good insight into the everyday life of soldiers in 19th-century Astrakhan.

➡ **Torture Tower**   MUSEUM
(Пыточная башня; http://astrakhan-musei.ru; kremlin; R60; ⓒ 10am-6pm Tue-Sun May-Oct) Tells the story of physical torture from the 16th to the 18th centuries.

Astrakhan

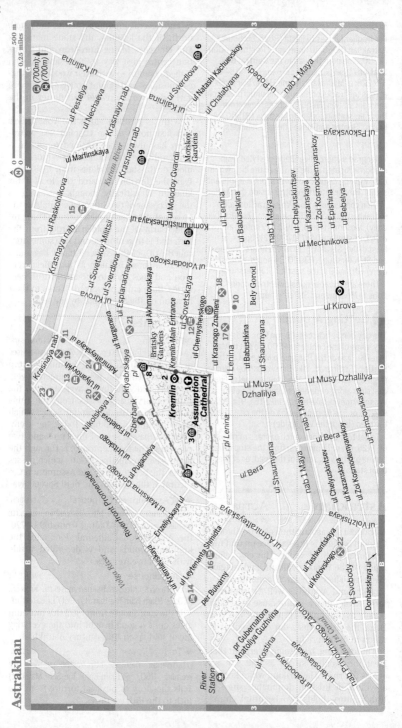

Astrakhan

➧ **Red Gates**   HISTORIC BUILDING
(Красные ворота; http://astrakhan-musei.ru; kremlin; R50; ⊙ 10am-6pm Tue-Sun May-Oct) Covers the history of Astrakhan as a southern outpost of the Russian Empire from the 16th to the 19th centuries.

PM Dogadin State Art Gallery   GALLERY
(Художественная галерея Догадина; ☑ 8512-511 121; http://agkg.ru; ul Sverdlova 81; R80, guided tours R500; ⊙ 10am-6pm Tue, Wed & Fri-Sun, 1-9pm Thu) The Dogadin State Art Gallery is especially strong on works of Astrakhan-born Boris Kustodiev, who painted lushly coloured semifolkloric scenes of merchant life, but all of the important periods of Russian art, including several masters of the Russian avant-garde, are represented. Guided tours are in English. Call ahead.

Kryusha Quarter   AREA
(Крюша) The Kryusha area of former Tatar and Persian suburbs south of the May 1st Canal is still predominantly Muslim, which is reflected in the proliferation of mosques. It's quaint in a rundown sort of way, best avoided in the evening, and a quarter where stray dogs roam along dirt roads. A nice walk to get a feel for the quarter follows Kazanskaya ul for about 2km, starting at ul Kirova and walking west to near the Tatar-Bazar.

Velimir Khlebnikov Museum   MUSEUM
(Дом-музей Велимира Хлебникова; ☑ 8512-516 496; http://agkg.ru; ul Sverdlova 53; Russian/foreigner R50/R140, bilingual tours R500; ⊙ 10am-6pm Tue-Sun) Come here for a small collection of portraits, drawings and personal objects

from this futurist poet, who lived from 1885 to 1922.

Local Studies Museum   MUSEUM
(Краеведческий музей; ☑ 8512-511 822; http://astrakhan-musei.ru; ul Sovetskaya 15; R120; ⊙ 10am-5pm Fri-Wed, to 9pm Thu) The Local Studies Museum functions as both a natural history and ethnographic museum, with permanent exhibitions dedicated to local wildlife and fish as well as the history and culture of the people in the Astrakhan region. There are occasionally interesting temporary exhibitions, though English signage is limited.

⌖ Tours

Cezar   TOURS
(Цезарь; ☑ 8512-392 992; www.zesar.ru; office 306, ul Lenina 20; ⊙ 9am-6.30pm Mon-Fri, 10am-4pm Sat) Cezar has highly professional staff with long experience in dealing with foreigners. It can organise day trips and lodge stays anywhere in the Volga Delta, as well as an excursion to Baskunchak Salt Lake and Bogdo Mountain (R1900, border permit required), sacred to Buddhists. The office is on the 3rd floor of a bank building. Ask inside for directions.

Cezar also offers a two-hour walking tour of the city (R1000 per person, with guide). In general, try to book tours well in advance, as some trips require extensive paperwork. Note that prices for trips that include an English-speaking guide tend to be much higher than similar tours for Russians. To save money, simply request the tour without a guide.

Procosta TOURS

(🖉 8512-999 812; www.procosta.ru; ul Admiral-teyskaya 43; ⊙9am-6pm) Organises tours into the Volga Delta to its own tourist base (twin cottage R2500 to R4000). A day excursion with boat and ranger from Astrakhan costs from R3500 per person, while a transfer each way costs R4000, which can be shared.

Astrintur TOURS

(Астринтур; 🖉 8512-392 406/984; www.astrintour.ru; ul Lenina 20; ⊙9am-6pm Mon-Fri, 10am-3pm Sat) This reliable agency handles hotel bookings, individual tours and boat trips to the delta, though it tends to be weaker than competitors in furnishing English-speaking guides.

🛏 Sleeping

★Astrakhanskaya Hotel HOTEL $$

(🖉 8512-488 080; www.astrakhanskaya-hotel.ru; ul Ulyanovykh 6; s/d R3000/4000; @🛜) This old luxury pile, dating from the 19th century and situated two blocks from the waterfront, has been given a thoroughly decadent makeover, with expensive carpets, crystal chandeliers and high-thread-count sheets on the beds. Yet the prices are not much higher than thoroughly inferior options. If you're looking for a modest splurge, this is the place.

Zolotoy Lotos HOTEL $$

(Золотой Лотос; 🖉 8-927-282 3007; www.astradelta.ru; near Karalat; per person per day from R3000, day excursion to Caspian Sea R5600) A good floating hotel that offers excursions. It has one building on land and another on the water.

AZIMUT Hotel Astrakhan HOTEL $$

(Гостиница Азимут; 🖉 8512-326 839; www.azimuthotels.ru; ul Kremlevskaya 4; incl breakfast s R2500-3500, d R3600-4000, ste R4400-7100; ⊖@🛜) This acceptable business and tourist hotel not only has the best river views in town, it offers some of the best value, with comfortable, refurbished rooms, good breakfasts and efficient staff. Be sure to request a room on one of the renovated upper floors (6th, 7th or 8th). Take *marshrutka* 1 from the train station to pl Lenina and walk towards the river for a few minutes.

Lotus Hotel BOUTIQUE HOTEL $$

(Лотус Отель; 🖉 8512-262 200; www.astlotushotel.ru; ul Maksima Gorkogo 44; incl breakfast s R2300-3300, d R2700-4000; 🛜▧) This is a top-quality minihotel with a small pool for sauna-goers. Rooms are modern and spacious. The location is terrific, about 5 minutes' walk from both the Volga riverfront and the kremlin.

Hotel 7 Nebo HOTEL $$

(Отель 7 Небо; 🖉 8512-160 864; www.7nebo-hotel.ru; Krasnaya nab 27; incl breakfast s R2800-3600, d R3200-4000, ste R6000; 🛜) This hotel, upstairs in a modern office building, offers good value with clean, parquet-floored rooms in tasteful colours. From the train station, take *marshrutka* 13 and ask for Krasnaya naberezhnye.

Al Pash Novomoskovskaya Hotel HOTEL $$$

(🖉 8512-271 527; www.nvmsk.com; ul Sovetskaya 4 cnr ul Kirova 18; incl breakfast s R3500-6000, d R4000-8000; ⊖🛜) This is arguably the city's most impressive hotel, occupying a late-19th-century palace situated on one of the stateliest pieces of real estate, 100m east of the kremlin. The spacious rooms cosily decorated in soft browns have marble-tiled bathrooms with bathtubs. Some rooms have views across the tranquil Bratsky Gardens.

🍴 Eating

Tatar-Bazar MARKET

(Татар-базар; pl Svobody 12 & 15; ⊙7am-5pm) For famous Astrakhan watermelons, other fresh fruit and vegetables, and meats, bread and cheese, try this market in the Kryusha neighbourhood. *Marshrutky* 1, 52 and many others run out here from Oktyabraskaya pl.

Rozmarin CAFE $

(Розмарин; 🖉 8512-299 212; ul Esplanadnaya 4a; sandwiches R200; ⊙10am-midnight; 🛜) This hipster-inspired coffee and sandwich spot is an ideal quick lunch option, and just a short walk from the main entrance to the kremlin. Choose from a long list of creative salad and sandwich combinations and enjoy an Aero-Press coffee and cherry cobbler afterward.

★Mindal CENTRAL ASIAN $$

(🖉 8512-201 212; ul Ulyanovykh 10; mains R500-600; ⊙11am-midnight) This is the ideal spot to sample the diverse cuisines of the Caspian Sea region. Choose from traditional Azeri, Persian, Kazakh and Russian dishes, starting off with a 'Tsar's fish soup', then dabbling with baked lamb or sturgeon steak, served on a bed of pomegranate seeds, and finishing with baklava. The cosy setting has a Central Asian vibe.

Cafe Izba RUSSIAN $$

(Кафе Изба; 🖉 8512-518 191; Krasnaya nab 8; mains R400; ⊙noon-midnight; 🛜) Decorated in the style of a Russian cottage, Izba is one of Astrakhan's best traditional restaurants, serving well-prepared classic cuisine popular with local office workers.

Beer Academy
PUB FOOD $$

(Академия Пива; 8512-444 940; www.academy-piva.ru; ul Lenina 7; mains R400; ⊙11am-midnight; 🛜) Among Astrakhan's pubs, this one generally serves the best food, with an extensive menu that spans Volga classics such as fish, pub fare like sausages, and steak. It also has a great selection of draught beers.

Beer House
PUB FOOD $$

(Бир Хаус; ☑8512-444 800; www.am-house.ru/beerhouse; ul Krasnogo Znameni 12; mains R400; ⊙11am-11pm Mon-Fri, from noon Sat & Sun; 🛜) The inauspicious entrance gives way to this convivial, neorustic pub upstairs, serving a competent range of salads and hot snacks (including light seafood dishes), as well as more substantial steaks and sausage dishes.

🍷 Drinking & Nightlife

La Vanile
CAFE

(Ла Ваниле; ☑8512-520 428; http://la-vanile.ru; ul Admiralteyskaya 35/37; ⊙9am-11pm Mon-Sat, 11am-11pm Sun; 🛜) Flower pots abound, water streams down a glass wall and delicious French pastries beckon from the counter to accompany your coffee or tea. It also offers a small but creative food menu (mains R350), with decent salads and soups.

Krem Café
CAFE

(Крем Кафе; ☑8512-440 400; ul Uritskogo 5; ⊙11am-11pm Sun-Thu, to midnight Fri & Sat; 🛜) Wonderful spot on the riverfront to stop for a coffee, a beer or a bite to eat. Krem does passable salads (R250) as well as sushi and meat dishes (mains R200 to R400), but the real draw is the terrace, which is best at sunset.

ℹ Information

Sberbank (ul Admiralteyskaya 21; ⊙10am-7pm Mon-Wed & Fri, to 6pm Thu, to 5pm Sat)
Post Office (Почта; cnr ul Kirova & ul Chernyshevskogo; internet per MB R3.15; ⊙8am-10pm Mon-Fri, 9am-6pm Sat & Sun) Post office with internet access.

ℹ Getting There & Away

AIR

Astrakhan's small **Narimanovo Airport** (ASF; ☑8512-393 317; pr Aeroportovskiy 1) is located 10km south of the centre in the Sovetsky Rayon. *Marshrutka* 5 runs from the airport to central pl Lenina, passing the train and bus stations and pl Oktyabrskaya. Allow at least 30 minutes for the journey from the centre by public transport. A taxi is much quicker and will cost about R400.

Two to three flights go daily to Moscow. Flights within the region require a change in Moscow.

BOAT

Astrakhan is the end point – more rarely the starting point – for cruises on the Volga. There are no regular passenger boats to the other Caspian Sea ports. Cruise ships dock at the eternally uncompleted **river station** (Речной вокзал; ul Kremlevskaya 1).

BUS

The bus station has regular services to Elista (R625, six hours) and Volgograd (R950, 10 hours).

TRAIN

Book via Volgograd (R1000, eight to 11 hours, two daily) to Moscow (R3000, at least 30 hours) to avoid passing through Kazakhstan. There are also services to Baku in Azerbaijan (R2500, 24 hours) and east to Atyrau in Kazakhstan (*kupe* R1100, 13 hours).

ℹ Getting Around

Most of the important sights, as well as hotels and restaurants, are concentrated in a relatively small area in the centre of the city and are within walking distance of each other. *Marshrutka* 1 goes from the train station to pl Oktyabrskaya and to central pl Lenina, which stands at the southern end of the kremlin.

Elista
Элиста

☑84722 / POP 103,700 / ⊙ MOSCOW

Prayer drums, red-robed monks, boiled guts and butter tea for lunch... Wait, it's still Europe! Elista is the capital of Kalmykia (Республика Калмыкия), the continent's only Buddhist region and a fragment of Mongolia thrown onto the shores of the Caspian Sea. Much of the republic consists of sparsely populated steppe occasionally punctuated by straight or squiggly lines of wooden electricity poles running to the horizon. With its colourful, Tibetan-style *khuruls* (temples), the otherwise-drab Elista is a good starting point for further exploration of this region.

History

Kalmyks are nomads (nowadays more at heart than in practice) and their history is that of migration – forced and voluntary. They descend from the Oirats, the western branch of Mongolians who embraced Buddhism in the early 17th century and soon after resolved to look for pastures green in the west.

In the last massive nomadic migration in the history of Eurasia, the Oirats traversed thousands of kilometres and ended up on the banks of the Volga, which at that time marked the border of the emerging Russian empire. Moscow initially welcomed the newcomers, allowing them to retain their way of life in return for guarding the border. But in the 18th century, the Oirats came under pressure from Russian and German settlers encroaching on their lands. One winter's night in 1771 they made a second escape – back to Mongolia. But the ice on the Volga was not strong enough for those on the western bank to cross the river, so 20,000 out of 160,000 families stayed. The flight turned into a disaster, with two-thirds of the people killed by enemies on the way.

Those who remained on the Volga lived quietly and not entirely unhappily until the 1920s, when the Bolsheviks destroyed all *khuruls,* arrested most monks and expropriated the cattle. No surprise that during the short-lived German occupation in 1942 some Kalmyks joined Hitler's army. Thousands of others fought on the Soviet side.

Stalin's reprisal was terrible. On 28 December 1943 all Kalmyks, including party members and policemen, were put in unheated cattle cars and sent to Siberia. When in 1957 Nikita Khrushchev allowed them to return, less than half the prewar population of 93,000 could make it home. The others perished in Gulag camps.

In 1993 the Kalmyks elected their first president – 31-year-old multimillionaire Kirsan Ilyumzhinov – who presided over the republic until 2010 and left his mark through his two chief fascinations: chess and a predilection for the fictional trickster Ostap Bender. This conflux of chess, fiction and the reality of Kalmyk history lends the steppe republic a rather bizarre edge. The 14th Dalai Lama has visited several times despite Moscow's reluctance to spoil relations with China. Boring it is not.

◉ Sights

The most enjoyable part of a trip to Elista is simply seeing the colourful Buddhist temples bursting with life amid the typical drabness of Soviet-era high-rises, starting with the bright red **Pagoda of Seven Days** (Пагода Семи дней; cnr ul Lenina & ul Pushkina) in the centre. A walk through the adjacent park, the **Alley of Heroes** (Аллея Героев), proceeds through a colourful Buddhist-inspired archway.

Golden Abode of
Buddha Shakyamuni   BUDDHIST TEMPLE
(Gol-Syume Burkh Bagshin Altn Syume; ☑84722-40 109; www.khurul.ru; ul Klykova; ◉ grounds & temple 8am-8pm daily, library & museum 10am-6pm Tue-Sun, daily prayer 9-10.30am, prayer for the deceased 2-4pm Fri) The Golden Abode of Buddha Shakyamuni, also called the New Khurul, was built in 2005 in the Tibetan style. The prayer hall sports an 11m-high statue of Buddha and the monk's robe of the 14th Dalai Lama. Downstairs a small museum depicts the history of Kalmyk Buddhism. The location is 1km east of the centre. Take *marshrutka* 9 or any other going east along ul Lenina.

National Museum of the
Republic of Kalmykia   MUSEUM
(Национальный музей Республики Калмыкия им. Н. Н. Пальмова; ul Dzhangara 9; Russian/foreigner R80/100, deportation exhibition extra R120, museum tour Russian/foreigner extra R120/150; ◉9am-6pm Tue-Fri, 10am-4pm Sat & Sun) The modern building of the National Museum, about 2km west of the centre, has eight large rooms covering the history, environment and culture of the Kalmyk people and republic. One room deals with the deportations during WWII. The exhibition is in Russian, so it's worth paying extra for an English (or Russian) tour for greater insight. Take *marshrutka* 5 and ask the driver to stop at the museum.

Geden Sheddup
Goichorling   BUDDHIST TEMPLE
(Syakyusn-syume; ☑84722-40 109; ◉closed to the public) Geden Sheddup Goichorling, 6km north of the centre, is the oldest *khurul* in Kalmykia and consists of a lavishly decorated large temple from 1996 and a small temple behind it containing the throne of the Dalai Lama, surrounded by the steppe. It's normally closed to the public.

The figure of Buddha Shakyamuni is at the centre of the altar, and the frescoes on the walls depict his 12 deeds and tell about his life.

Exodus & Return Memorial   MONUMENT
(www.enstudio.com; ul Khrushcheva) The striking Exodus & Return Memorial is located about 3km east of the centre on the far end of ul Khrushcheva. The work, by sculptor Ernst Neizvestny, marks the tragic, WWII-era deportation of the Kalmyk people.

Chess City   AREA
(Сити-чесс) Fans of chess will want to visit a small suburb that Kalmyk leader Kirsan Ilyumzhinov had hoped to make the world's chess capital. There's a nearly abandoned steel-and-glass 'Chess City Hall' here that played host to the 1998 Chess Olympics and several Olympic-style bungalows. The idea

THE VOLGA DELTA

The Volga Delta is the natural highlight of any trip to the region, and if you are travelling from north to south, you are likely to feel a sense of enormous achievement in reaching the point where this magnificent river flows into the Caspian Sea in Central Asia.

About 70km south of Astrakhan, the river bursts like a firecracker into thousands of streams, creating a unique ecosystem teeming with wildlife. The three symbols of the delta are the Caspian lotus flower (abundant), the sturgeon (critically threatened) and the Caspian flamingo – a semilegendary bird that the average ranger will have seen once, if at all.

The best time to visit is between late July and late September when lotus flowers blossom. April and October are major fishing seasons.

The most biologically diverse area is covered by the **Astrakhan Biosphere Reserve**. The rest of the delta is dotted with floating and land-based lodges that mostly specialise in fishing and hunting. These days operators are used to the occasional foreigner drifting down here for the simple pleasure of experiencing this beautiful wetland area and travelling by boat into the *raskaty* (the channels) to watch the birdlife.

Although the entryway into the delta region can be reached by car, the experience will be richer and easier to organise if you work with an Astrakhan-based travel agency. Not only do they offer guided tours of the most popular spots in the delta, they can help with transport, accommodation and the extensive paperwork (visas and permissions) needed to visit the region. Regardless of whether you go down to the delta on a day trip or overnight, copies of your passport main page, visa and migration card need to be presented to the tour agency or place of stay at least a week – preferably longer – in advance.

Cezar (p363) and Procosta (p364) are both highly experienced and recommended. Cezar can organise virtually any turbaza (holiday camp) or hotel on the delta. Zolotoy Lotos (p364) is a good lodging choice and is situated on the water.

Procosta takes you to its own base, which is a couple of kilometres by boat from the Caspian Sea and the nearest road, with cottages set entirely on stilts. The cottages, linked by a boardwalk, sleep two to four people. **Rybnoye Mesto** (☑8-927-070 7007; http://vipvolga.ru; ul Rybatskaya 25, Stanya; per person with full board from R3000) in Stanya (Станья), situated about 80km south of Astrakhan and a couple of kilometres from the last settlement of any size, Kamyzyak (Камызяк), is the springboard to the Procosta *turbaza* and other tourist bases in this part of the delta.

---

never caught on, and today the area is somewhat depressing. It's located about 4km southeast of the main central intersection of ul Lenina and ul Pushkina. *Marshrutka* 7 takes you there from Hotel Elista.

🖙 Tours

Kalmykia Tour   TOURS
(☑8-927-593 4530; www.kalmykiatour.com) Few tour companies are used to handling foreigners, but Kalmykia Tour can organise accommodation (from around R2000) and arrival transfer (R500) if needed. Contact by email.

Pegas Touristik   TOURS
(☑8-960-899 1705; www.pegast.ru; ul Neyman 1; ◷10am-7pm Mon-Fri, 11am-4pm Sat) Pegas can stitch together a sightseeing package with an English- or German-speaking guide and arrange accommodation. Expect to pay around R4000 for two people, excluding hotel costs and transport to/from Elista.

🎎 Festivals & Events

Dzhangariada Festival   FOLK ARTS
(◷late-Aug or Sep) The Kalmyk equivalent of the Mongolian Naadam, Dzhangariada is an annual celebration of the Kalmyk epic Dzhangar – a 12-song story about life in the blessed land called Bumba. Held on open steppe outside Elista (the location changes every year), it includes wrestling and archery contests and performances by *dzhangarchi* (traditional singers). Book accommodation early for the festival.

🛏 Sleeping

Bely Lotos   HOTEL $$
(Белый Лотос; ☑84722-34 416; ul Khoninova 7; incl breakfast s/d R2000/3000, ste R5200-7500; ❄🛜) The serene 'White Lotos' is professionally run, friendly and arguably the best of the few hotels in the city. It's tucked away on a quiet street, one block south of the Alley of Heroes

park. From the outside, the metal-and-glass building resembles an office or institute, but the rooms are clean and warmly furnished.

Hotel Ostrovok
HOTEL $$

(Отель Островок; ☑8-917-688 4248; ul Respublikanskaya 14; s/d R2000/3000; ☏) This small, family-run hotel doesn't look very promising at first glance, but it improves inside: upstairs you'll find four stylish, ultra-clean rooms. One has a small balcony and all have gleaming bathrooms and comfy beds. The location is central, about 10 minutes' walk from the main intersection of ul Lenina and ul Pushkina.

Hotel Elista
HOTEL $$$

(Отель Элиста; ☑ Korpus 1 84722-25 540; www.hotelelista.ru; Korpus 1: ul Lenina 241, Korpus 2: ul Lenina 237; incl breakfast s R2000-3300, d R4500-5200; ❂✳☏) This Soviet relic occupies two large buildings (Korpus 1 and Korpus 2), on the city's main street ul Lenina, which almost act as separate hotels. Korpus 1 has the better facilities, with a 24-hour supermarket and a coffee bar. Avoid dumpy Korpus 2. Take any *marshrutka* going to Gostinitsa (Гостиница).

✗ Eating & Drinking

Elista is the place to try Kalmyk specialities, though keep in mind that Kalmyk food tends to be far richer than what many visitors are used to. Staples include meat-filled *berg* (or *berigi*) dumplings and *hasn makhn* (sliced mutton with flat pasta). The traditional tea, *dzhomba*, is flavoured with ample amounts of butter and often taken with portions of *bortsg* (balls of dough fried in oil).

Cafeteria 'Ice'
RUSSIAN $

(Столовая 'Айс'; ul Pushkina 22; mains R200; ☺9am-7pm) Traditional no-frills, self-serve cafeteria offering very good and reasonably priced Russian and Kalmyk dishes. The location is in the centre, just off the main intersection of ul Lenina and ul Pushkina. Get in line, pick up a tray and point to the soups, salads and mains that you would like.

Cafe Chipollino
RUSSIAN $

(Кафе Чиполлино; ☑84722-44 886; ul Lenina 255a; mains R150; ☺11am-11pm) Great spot for coffee or lunch, right on the main intersection of ul Lenina and ul Pushkina. Order at the counter and choose from two daily soups and several dishes. Drink your coffee in or take away.

Gurman
KALMYK, INTERNATIONAL $$

(Гурман; ☑8-905-400 4460; http://gurman.uralan. org; ul Nomto Ochirova 9; Kalmyk dishes R200-250, mains/steaks R400/600; ☺11am-2am) Inside the

'Ural' cinema and bowling complex, a couple of blocks south of central ul Lenina, Gurman is arguably the best midrange place in town. Offers Kalmyk and Russian dishes, and international cuisine ranging from steaks to sushi.

Praga
PUB

(Прага; ☑84722-28 404; www.alyans-praga.blizko. ru; ul Nomto Ochirova 5; ☺noon-2am; ☏) This handy cellar pub, just a short stroll from the main intersection of ul Lenina and ul Pushkina, serves a nice range of Czech and other European beers and has a decent food menu that includes some traditional Kalmyk dishes.

Cafe-Bar Alyans
BAR

(Кафе-Бар Альянс; ☑84722 3-36-08; www.alyans-praga.blizko.ru; ul Nomto Ochirova 5a; ☺noon-2am) Set among a constellation of eating and drinking places along ul Nomto Ochirova – many of them popular with a very young crowd – Alyans caters to a more mixed crowd. The food (mains R250 to R450) is decent, but its chilled-out mood, small dance floor and frequent DJ nights are its main attractions.

ⓘ Information

Sberbank (Сбербанк; ul Suseyeva 13; ☺9am-7pm Mon-Sat) A central branch with ATMs and currency exchange. Other ATMs are scattered around town and inside Hotel Elista.

Main Post Office (Главпочтамт; ul Suseyeva 31; ☺8am-10pm Mon-Fri, 9am-6pm Sat & Sun)

ⓘ Getting There & Away

AIR

A handful of flights to Moscow are all that keep tiny **Elista International Airport** (Аэропорт Элиста/ESL; ☑84722-29 947; www.aero-port-elista.ru) busy. Airline tickets are available at **Elya** (☑84722-41 297; ul Lenina 247/2; one-way to Moscow R5000-8000).

BUS

The bus station is about 4km north of the centre on the outskirts of town. A taxi to the centre will cost R200. *Marshrutky* 2, 6, 9 and 17 travel to or near the station and can take you to the front of Hotel Elista in the centre.

Elista is roughly the same distance from Volgograd, Astrakhan, Mineralnye Vody (Caucasus) and Stavropol (Caucasus). A trip to any of these takes about six hours and costs around R600. Currently there are no train services to Kalmykia.

ⓘ Getting Around

Marshrutky are the only mode of public transport. Their main hub is in front of Hotel Elista (appearing as Гостиница on signs), from where you can get to any part of town. Buy tickets from the driver.

Russian Caucasus

Best Places to Eat

➡ 5642 Vsota (p397)

➡ Daki (p393)

➡ Kupol (p408)

➡ Frapp (p382)

➡ Dok (p383)

➡ Chyo? Kharcho! (p382)

Best Places to Stay

➡ LEAPrus 3912 (p410)

➡ Black Point Hostel (p408)

➡ Hostel Zhit' prosto Pyatigorsk (p392)

➡ Sanremo (p381)

➡ Park City Rose (p373)

➡ Hostel Bla Bla (p373)

Why Go?

For most Russians, the word Caucasus (Кавказ) summons up images of fiery mountain folk, the high-tempo *lezginka* dance and volatile regions such as Chechnya. But there's more to this ethnically diverse part of Russia than the stereotypes and the horror stories. Visitors to this area come to experience relaxing spa towns, breathtaking scenery and world-class ski resorts.

On top of that, there's superb trekking and horse riding amid soaring peaks, white-water rafting and paragliding, as well as the chance to climb Mt Elbrus, Europe's highest mountain. Black Sea resort towns offer sun and sea, and festive nightlife, while the Caucasus also boasts its own regional cuisines.

For anyone looking to get off the tourist trail, the Caucasus offers wide-open spaces, bustling markets and rugged mountain roads with stunning views around every corner.

When to Go
Sochi

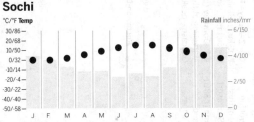

Jan Ski season reaches its peak in resorts such as Krasnaya Polyana, Arkhyz, Dombay and Elbrus.

May Enjoy sunny days and lower prices at Black Sea resorts and spa towns.

Jun-Sep Best time for climbing and hiking in the mountains. Peak season on the Black Sea.

Russian Caucasus Highlights

1 Sochi (p378) Strolling along the promenade of this post-Olympic Black Sea resort.

2 Krasnaya Polyana (p386) Soaking up scenery and checking out the ski slopes

3 Zelenaya Roscha (p383) Walking in Stalin's footsteps at the dictator's former dacha.

4 Dombay (p398) Marvelling at the Greater Caucasus' peaks and glaciers

5 Mt Elbrus (p407) Riding the gondola up Europe's highest peak for breathtaking views.

6 Kislovodsk (p394) Exploring Kurortny Park and drinking the Narzan spring waters.

7 Cherek Valley & Upper Balkaria (p405) Hiking among ruined Balkar villages in the spectacular Cherek Valley.

8 Pyatigorsk (p390) Following the footsteps of the writer Lermontov in this attractive mineral resorts spa.

9 Starocherkassk (p375) Attending the monthly fair in this old Cossack town.

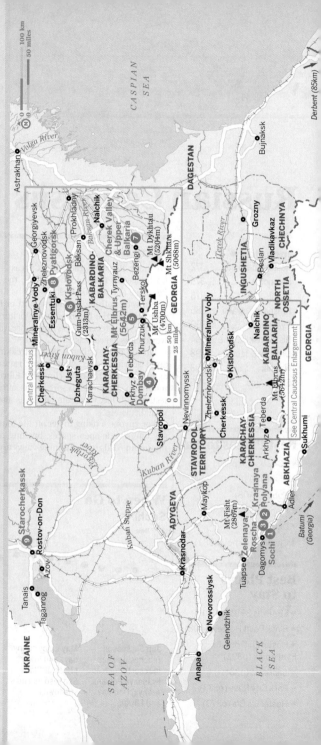

History

The Caucasus has stood at the crossroads of Asian and European cultures since the Bronze Age. The result is an extraordinary mix of races with three main linguistic groups: Caucasian, Indo-European and Turkic. The region has suffered many invasions and occupations, having been squeezed between rival Roman, Byzantine, Persian, Arab, Ottoman and Russian empires.

The earliest human traces in the Russian Caucasus date from Neolithic times, when farming was replacing hunting and gathering. The first communities evolved in Dagestan's valleys around the same time as agriculture developed in West Asia and China, establishing this region as an early cradle of civilisation.

The first dominant state was created by the Alans, ancestors of modern Ossetians. It blossomed during the 10th century AD and, at its peak, ruled most of the northern Caucasus. The Alans were Christians, probably having been introduced to the religion by the Georgians. The Alan state was conquered by the Mongol Tatar invasions of the early 13th century with nearly all remnants destroyed by the army of Timur (Tamerlane) in 1395.

The Russians Arrive

Russian adventurers and serfs escaping their masters had already settled in the lower Terek River region when Russian military power arrived here in the late 1500s. In 1696 Peter the Great captured the Turkish stronghold of Azov and expanded imperial influence southward.

Later, Catherine the Great began the subjugation of the Caucasus in earnest, assisted by the area's Cossacks. The campaign picked up steam in the early 1800s as the Caucasus became a strategically important region in the so-called 'Great Game' being played out between Russia and England.

In 1816 General Yermelov, a veteran of the Napoleonic Wars, began a ruthless campaign to pacify the mountain peoples. The predominantly Muslim populace resented this intrusion by European and Christian Russians, and bitter guerrilla-type warfare ensued, led by the Cherkess (Circassians) in the north and the legendary Dagestani leader Imam Shamil further south. Shamil united Dagestani and Chechen tribes for a 30-year fight against the Russians that ended with Shamil's surrender in 1859.

The Soviet Era

During the October Revolution, many tribes united to form the Mountain Republic. Independence lasted until 1921, when Soviet forces overran the Caucasus. Soviet policy was to divide and rule by creating small autonomous regions, often combining two totally different nationalities. The Muslim-dominated portion of the Caucasus was split into five autonomous regions: Dagestan, Adygeya, Chechnya, Kabardino-Balkaria and Karachay-Cherkessia.

In 1944 Stalin ordered the mass deportation of Balkar, Chechen, Ingush and Karachay peoples to Central Asia and Siberia, on the pretext of potential collaboration with German forces. Khrushchev allowed the exiled groups to return in 1957 but without compensation or repossession of their property. The Soviet regime smothered any potential conflict caused by this injustice, but the situation changed quickly after the collapse of the USSR in 1991.

THE CIRCASSIAN MASSACRE

One of the great tragedies of the 19th century – the complete ethnic cleansing of all Muslim peoples from the Black Sea coast and surrounding areas – is all but forgotten today and remains unacknowledged by the Russian government.

Following their surrender to the Russians in 1864, the Circassians were given a choice: leave the mountains and move to the far-off plains, or leave the country. According to 19th-century Russian historian Adolf Berzhe, some 400,000 Circassians were killed, nearly 500,000 forced to flee to Turkey, and only 80,000 permitted to settle elsewhere in Russia. Along with those who fled earlier, however, the total estimated number of expelled or slaughtered is believed to be far higher.

Today, descendants of the Circassians can be found in Turkey, Kosovo, Syria, Jordan and Israel – though you will find no trace of them in the resort towns along the Black Sea, their former ancestral homeland. Oliver Bullough's excellent book, *Let Our Fame Be Great*, explores the history of the region.

Post-Soviet Era

The sudden split of the Soviet Union triggered a spark in ethnic hostilities, as long-suppressed grudges and rivalries bubbled to the surface of the newly independent Russia. Chechnya witnessed two devastating wars (1994-96 and 1999-2000), as federal troops battled a mixture of secular separatists and Islamist fighters, with multiple atrocities committed by both sides. The violence frequently spilled over into other North Caucasus republics, including the tragic Beslan school siege in North Ossetia in 2004, Russia's worst-ever terrorist atrocity. In 2005 separatist Chechen guerrillas, led by the late warlord Shamil Basayev, launched multiple attacks on police and military posts in Kabardino-Balkaria's capital, Nalchik.

The violence in the North Caucasus was becoming increasingly jihadist in nature. In October 2007 veteran Chechen militant Doku Umarov was named emir of the 'Caucasus Emirate', a purported Islamic state that would span much of the region. Using the North Caucasus as their base, Umarov's followers launched a series of bloody attacks on Moscow and other cities in the Russian heartland. In 2011, three tourists from Moscow were killed en route from Mineralnye Vody airport to a ski resort in the Mt Elbrus area.

Today, although the northern Caucasus remains a volatile, occasionally violent region, there are indications that the security situation is improving. Terrorist attacks are on the decline, and Umarov is widely believed to have been killed during a clash with Russian security forces in late 2013 or early 2014, although details remain hazy. One obvious indication of growing stability in the region was Russia's ability to hold the 2014 Winter Olympics in Sochi, just a few hours from Chechnya. Despite fears the Games would be targeted by militant fighters, the Olympics passed peacefully.

KUBAN STEPPE

From Rostov-on-Don, the overland routes to the northern Caucasus and the Black Sea coast cross the Kuban Steppe (Кубанская Степь), named after its river flowing from Mt Elbrus into the Sea of Azov. The region is an important agricultural centre and is often referred to as the bread basket of Russia. It's also the traditional home of the Cossacks, the proud horsemen who helped protect Russia's tsarist-era borders.

Rostov-on-Don
Ростов-на -Дону

⏱ 863 / POP 1.1 MILLION / ⊘ MOSCOW

This pleasant city of green parks and monumental squares, (known simply 'Rostov' to locals) is the gateway to the northern Caucasus region, the historical hotbed of Cossack culture and peasant uprisings. It makes a pleasant stopover on the Black Sea coast and a good base for several interesting day-trips in the area.

Nowadays, Rostov is southern Russia's largest and most cosmopolitan city. Flowing through the city is the Don River, a geographic and cultural landmark. Most famously, the river is celebrated in Mikhail Sholokhov's novels of the Russian Civil War, *And Quiet Flows the Don* and *The Don Flows Home to the Sea.*

Rostov is mostly on the northern bank of the Don. The main east–west axis is Bolshaya Sadovaya ul; the bus and train stations are at its western end. Parallel to it runs the tree-lined Pushkinskaya ul.

⊙ Sights & Activities

Pushkinskaya Ulitsa   STREET
(Пушкинская улица) East of Voroshilovskiy pr, this idyllic promenade is blissfully free of traffic and sprinkled with fountains, sculptures, cafes and restaurants, with outdoor seating and music-playing buskers during the summer. It's particularly enticing at its eastern end, between the university and the October Revolution Park.

Ploshchad Sovetov   MONUMENT
(Площадь Советов; cnr Bolshaya Sadovaya ul & Voroshilovskiy pr) The 'Square of Soviets' is dominated by a colossal monument commemorating the Red Army soldiers who took part in the 1917–23 Russian Civil War. Prior to 1930, the square was home to the Alexandro-Nevsky Cathedral, which you can now see in miniature next to the monument.

Also noteworthy: excellent socialist realist tile work in the *perekhod* (underground passage) below Voroshilovskiy pr.

Don Riverside   RIVER
(Донской берег; Beregovaya ul) A statue of *And Quiet Flows the Don* author Mikhail Sholokhov depicts the writer gazing thoughtfully at the river that helped make his name. Nowa-

days, the river embankment is not so quiet, especially on summer nights, when a carnival atmosphere takes over.

Gorky Park PARK

(Парк Горького; Bolshaya Sadovaya ul 55; 🖌) Leafy Gorky Park is home to blooming gardens, open-air cafes and plenty of cheerful kiddie rides. An impressive monument to the 1917 Bolshevik Revolution is also nestled into the greenery. When the weather is fine, the park is popular with chess-playing locals, families with children and plenty of lazy cats. Accessible from Bolshaya Sadovaya or Pushkinskaya ul.

Regional Museum MUSEUM

(Ростовский областной музей краеведения; www.rostovmuseum.ru; Bolshaya Sadovaya ul 79; adult/child R120/50, special exhibits R100; ⊙10am-5.30pm Tue-Sun) The centrepiece of the regional museum are the exhibits covering the 3rd century BC until the 4th century AD, when Greek trading colonies flourished at the mouth of the Don. A large display on the 2nd floor is devoted to the Don Cossacks.

Nativity of the Virgin Cathedral CHURCH

(Ростовский Кафедральный Собор Рождества Пресвятой Богородицы; ul Stanislavskogo 58; ⊙8am-7pm) The lavish, gold-domed neo-Byzantine cathedral, built in 1856, overlooks the central market. If you approach from S;orniy per, it is framed beautifully by the elaborate buildings lining the pedestrian lane.

Don Tour CRUISE

(ДонТур; ☑863-279 7366; www.dontour.ru; Beregovaya ul 23; 1hr cruise R270-310, Starocherkassk cruise R740-790) Board a boat for a one-hour cruise along the Don, for a relaxing river tour or a party on the water (depending on what day and time you choose). There's not a lot to see, but it's a chance to get out on the river. Don Tour also offers all-day trips to Starocherkassk on summer weekends.

🛏 Sleeping

Hostel Bla Bla HOSTEL $

(☑800-500 8090, 8-909-899 6565; www.rnd.blablahostels.ru; Boshaya Sadovaya ul 65; dm R450-550, tw/d/tr R1200/1300/1400; ❇🛜) This brand new hostel features spacious, light-filled rooms, friendly management and a smack-dab central location. Dorm rooms (sleeping six to 10 people) have wooden bunk beds with privacy curtains and individual lamps, as well as lockers and the occasional piece of whimsical artwork. There is a comfy

common area and a super clean kitchen. Enter through the Fashion House (Дом Мод).

Yakor Hostel HOSTEL $

(Якорь Хостел; http://yakorhostel.ru; Turgenevskaya ul 80; dm/d R500/1400; 🅿❇🛜) On a quiet side street, this little hostel occupies an elegant 19th-century residential building, with elaborate mouldings, ceiling medallions and chandeliers bedecking the common space. The sleeping rooms are simpler, but immaculate, with wood bunks and lockers. Kitchen, wi-fi and parking are available.

★ Park City Rose BOUTIQUE HOTEL $$

(Гостиница Парк Сити; ☑288 8222; www.hotelparkcity.ru; Shaumyana ul 90; s R2900-4200, d R4100-4800; ❇🛜) Located one block south of the main drag, Park City Rose is a boutique hotel with 19 natty rooms and plenty of old-fashioned atmosphere. The rooms are uniquely decorated, but they all feature up-to-date amenities. Attentive service and central location make this under-the-radar spot one of the city's best midrange options.

Hotel Attaché HOTEL $$$

(Отель Атташе; ☑299 9888; www.hotel-attache.ru; pr Sokolova 19/22; r weekday R6400-6900, weekend R3800-4100) In a town where most hotels seem to be super-sized, the Attaché offers a delightfully intimate atmosphere, with 42 spacious and well-appointed rooms in an elegant 19th-century building. Soundproof windows, light-blocking shades and orthopedic mattresses ensure a good night's sleep. Note the substantial savings on weekends.

Don Plaza HOTEL $$$

(☑863-263 9052; www.don-plaza.ru; Bolshaya Sadovaya ul 115; s/d from R4900/5900; ❇@🛜) Now operated as a Hyatt Regency, this massive, remodelled, Soviet-style high-rise is one of several international business-class hotels in the city. As expected, its rooms are spacious, modern and well-equipped, also offering lovely city and river views. Prices include a generous breakfast.

✕ Eating

Bulochnaya No 5 BAKERY $

(Булочная Номер 5; Soborniy per 28; pastries R40-60; ⊙8am-9pm) It smells like heaven in this friendly little bakery and sweet shop, featuring loaves of freshly baked bread, piles of pastries and impressive sweet and savoury pies. It's worth sticking your nose in to get a whiff of the goodness.

Smetana
RUSSIAN, UKRAINIAN **$**

(Сметана; Bolshaya Sadovaya ul 80; mains R200-350, lunch R250; ☉10am-midnight Mon-Fri, from noon Sat & Sun; ✳🛜) Get your fix of *pelmeni* (Russian-style dumplings stuffed with meat) and *vareniki* (ravioli-like dumplings) and other Russian and Ukrainian favourites, all expertly prepared and presented. The bi-level setting is comfortable and cosy – reminiscent of a family home – with several different rooms to choose from. Very popular lunchtime spot.

Zolotoy Kolos
CAFE **$**

(Золотой колос; Bolshaya Sadovaya ul 43; dishes from R150; ☉8am-10pm) Mimicking the grand cafes of Old Europe, this sweet-treat haven is decked out with heavy drapes and chandeliers. It's a popular spot for families to grab a light lunch or to indulge in pastries, ice cream or dessert. Located just outside the gates of Gorky Park.

Shtefan Burger
BURGERS **$$**

(Штефан Бургер; www.shtefanburger.ru; Pushkinskaya ul 101; burgers R250-600; ☉noon-10pm; ✳🛜🌿) A speciality burger joint, named after the German chess whiz who supposedly invented the beefy sandwich. This cosy place offers a dozen unusual but tasty burgers (including fish, chicken and veggie options); three kinds of fried potatoes (thin-cut, thick-cut and wedge-cut); and two kinds of draught beer (light and dark). Everybody happy?

Schneider Weisse Brauhaus
RUSSIAN, GERMAN **$$**

(📋863-270 9242; www.kalinich.ru; Beregovaya ul 27; mains R400-800; ☉noon-midnight Sun-Thu, to 2am Fri & Sat) The interior of this German brewhouse offers an appealing blend of post-industrial chic and old-fashioned comfort. The menu ranges from hearty local dishes – many featuring local Don fish – to Bavarian specials straight off the grill. There are eight house beers on tap, which you might sample in the beer garden (of course).

Gavroche
INTERNATIONAL **$$$**

(Гаврош; 📋863-229 1169; Pushkinskaya ul 36; mains R600-900; ☉noon-10pm) This warm and welcoming wine bar offers a sophisticated menu with a French twist. Sample one of the delectable patés or steaming soups. The big leather booths are a comfy option, but in summertime it's hard to resist a seat on the breezy porch.

🍷 Drinking & Nightlife

8 Zeryon
CAFE

(8 Зерен; Pushkinskaya ul 158; ☉9am-10pm) At the intersection of two leafy pedestrian lanes, you couldn't find a greener, more peaceful setting for this delightful espresso bar. The interior is graced with big windows and lovely flower-painted walls, while there's also seating in a breezy outdoor pavilion. In addition to coffee, tea and fresh juices, there's a small selection of sandwiches and snacks.

Kraft Bar
CRAFT BEER

(Крафт Бар; ul Pushkinskaya 135/33; ☉noon-midnight Sun-Thu, to 2am Fri & Sat; 🛜) This little basement bar evokes a beer garden, while there is also seating on the shady pavement along Pushkinskaya ul. Take your pick from five house brews, two varieties of *medovukha* (honey ale) or a delicious homemade cider. A small menu of burgers, pizza and snacks is available to accompany your beverage of choice.

⭐ Entertainment

Rostov Musical Theatre
THEATRE

(Musykalny Teat; www.rostovopera.ru; Bolshaya Sadovaya ul 134; ☉ticket office 10am-7pm) This modern and notable theatre presents ballet and opera between September and June.

ℹ Getting There & Away

AIR

For the two-hour flight from Rostov to Moscow, Aeroflot (p680) has flights into Sheremetyevo (from R6500, six daily), while Rossiya Airlines (p680) flies into Vnukovo (from R5000, two daily). Rossiya also flies to St Petersburg (R8000, 2½ hours) once a day.

BOAT

Don Tour (p373) runs *teplokhody* (passenger boats) to Starocherkassk at 9am on Saturday and Sunday from May to October, returning to Rostov at 5pm (round-trip R740 to R790).

BUS

From the **bus station** (pr Siversa), buses go to Krasnodar (R600, three to five hours, hourly) and Volgograd (R1300, six hours, eight daily), as well as longer-distance buses to Astrakhan (R1650, 13 hours, one daily) and and Moscow (R1200 to R1500, 15 hours, four daily). Private express buses also serve these destinations.

TRAIN

Numerous trains pass through Rostov's **main train station** (pl Privokzalnaya), chugging north to Moscow (*kupe* R4200, 15 to 25 hours) and south to Sochi (*kupe* R2000 to R2500, 7½ to 12 hours) via Krasnodar (R1600 to R2800, three to five hours).

Elektrichki (suburban trains) also trundle to Krasnodar (3¼ hours, two daily) from the **local train station** (pr Siversa), 200m south of the main train station.

ⓘ Getting Around

Buses 7 and 1 and *marshrutka* 7A shuttle between the airport and the train station via Bolshaya Sadovaya ul (25 minutes).

Starocherkasskaya
Старочеркасская

☑ 863 / POP 5500 / ⊘ MOSCOW

Founded in 1593, flood-prone Starocherkasskaya was the Don Cossack capital until the early 18th century. Once a fortified town of 20,000, it's now a farming village with a main street restored to near-19th-century appearance. There are a few historic sights of note, including one fantastic church. But mostly it's a quiet town with an old-Russia atmosphere that offers a real contrast to the hustle and bustle of the modern cities.

That said, it's not so quiet on the last Sunday of the month (May to September), when the village hosts boisterous Cossack fairs, with much singing, dancing, horse riding and merrymaking. There are also annual Maslenitsa celebrations here, with pancakes and traditional games galore, when village residents prepare for the Great Lent fast and to greet the coming spring.

◉ Sights

Ataman Palace   MUSEUM
(Атаманский дворец; ul Pochtovaya 7; adult/child R170/130; ⊘9am-5pm) Once the living quarters of the Cossack chiefs, the Ataman Palace now houses an exhibition that traces the development of Don Cossack culture from the 16th century to the present day. There are some great artefacts, including an impressive 400-year-old sundial and plenty of antique Cossack weapons. Household items, clothing and artwork are also on display. Upstairs is a diorama of Starocherkasskaya, with an accompanying multimedia show (in Russian) about the town's history.

Adjacent to the palace is the 1761 **Church of Our Lady of the Don**, which was the private church of the Cossack chiefs.

Resurrection Cathedral   CHURCH
(Воскресенский собор; ul Sovetskaya) At the eastern end of ul Sovetskaya, the Resurrection Cathedral contains a soaring golden iconostasis, a baroque chandelier and an unusual floor of metal tiles. Peter the Great took a special interest in the church, and even helped lay the altar brickwork when he visited in 1709. The adjacent bell tower provides a bird's-eye panorama. Women should wear headscarves inside the church.

✖ Eating

Cafe Starocherkassk   CAFE $$
(Кафе Старочеркасск; ul Begovaya 8; mains R250-500; ⊘10am-10pm) Set in attractive, leafy grounds, this friendly cafe is a perfect spot to pause for lunch or to wait for your bus. Traditional soups, salads and snacks are on the menu, as are several kinds of bottled beer and Zhiguli on tap.

The cafe also has one of the only proper toilets in town, available for restaurant guests only. That in and of itself is worth the price of a beer.

ⓘ Getting There & Away

The most pleasant way to get to Starocherkasskaya is on a boat tour, run by Don Tour (p373) from Rostov. These typically run on Saturday and Sunday, from May to early October, setting off from Rostov at 9am and returning at 5pm (R740 to R790). Otherwise, it's *marshrutka* 151 (R65, one hour, hourly) from pl Karla Marksa in Rostov. Buses depart Rostov at the top of the hour; the last return service is at 5.45pm.

Krasnodar   Краснодар
☑ 861 / POP 745,000 / ⊘ MOSCOW

When Catherine the Great travelled south to tour the lands conquered from the Turks, her lover Potemkin had cheerful facades erected along her route. The goal was to hide the mud-splattered hovels that made up the newly founded city bearing her name, Yekaterinodar ('Catherine's Gift').

It's been a long time since Krasnodar has needed those facades. Today, its lively centre boasts pleasant streets lined with shops, cafes and restaurants. Tsarist-era buildings give parts of the city an elegant, European appearance that have earned it the sobriquet 'Little Paris'. There isn't a great deal to do in the city, but it's delightful for a short visit.

The road from Rostov-on-Don feeds into the northern end of Krasnaya ul, Krasnodar's

RUSSIAN CAUCASUS

2km-long leafy colonnade of a main street. Train and bus stations are about 2km to the southeast, just north of the Kuban River, which snakes around the city's southern and western flanks.

◎ Sights & Activities

★ Felitsyn Museum
MUSEUM

(Музей Фелицына; www.felicina.ru; Gimnazicheskaya ul 67; adult/child R250/120, special exhibits R100-200; ⊙10am-6pm Tue-Sun) This is an excellent little regional museum, located a few steps from Krasnaya ul. Exhibits feature some impressive archaeological finds; Cossack history and the Russian Civil War are also well covered. If you made it to Krasnodar, this is it.

Kovalenko Art Museum
MUSEUM

(www.kovalenomuseum.ru; Krasnaya ul 13; adult/child R250/120; ⊙10am-6pm Tue-Sun, to 9pm Thu) The region's oldest art museum, the Kovalenko's collections span the ages, from 'Old Rus' to post-Soviet periods. The building – the historic Shardonov house – is a work of art in itself.

Statue of Catherine the Great
MONUMENT

(cnr Postovaya ul & Krasnaya ul) An elaborate statue of Catherine the Great – with lute-strumming Cossacks and Potemkin at her heels – lords over an attractive park at the southern end of Krasnaya ul. There are fine old buildings in the side streets east of here.

Dog Capital Sculpture
MONUMENT

(ul Mira 35) This unusual sculpture, on the corner of central ul Krasnaya, features two elegantly dressed dogs out for a stroll. It was inspired by a quip by famed Soviet-era poet Vladimir Mayakovsky, who dubbed Krasnodar a 'canine capital' due to the number of dogs in the city.

Museum of the Weapons of Victory
MUSEUM

(Музей оружия Победы; ul Krasina 2; ⊙indoor exhibit 10am-5.30pm Wed-Sun, outdoor exhibit 24hr) FREE Located by the river in Victory Park (Парк имени 30-летия Победы; Beregovaya ul; ⊙24hr) FREE, this open-air museum's display of WWII tanks and rocket launchers conjures up images of Soviet-era military parades. Kids love to clamber all over the tanks. There's also a small indoor exhibit highlighting local contributions to the WWII victory.

Riverboats
CRUISE

(Теплоходы; ☑861-211 1156; Kubanskaya nab 39; adult/child R250; ⊙4-10pm Mon-Fri, noon-10pm Sat & Sun) Cruise along the Kuban River in riverboat 'Kuban' or 'Don'. The one-hour tour departs from the Kubanskaya nab (on the east side of the river) and goes to Victory Park (p376) and back.

⊨ Sleeping

Resting Rooms
HOSTEL $

(Komnaty Otdykha; ☑861-214 7344; Vokzalnaya pl; dm/s/d R1100/1500/2200) On the 3rd floor of the train station, the 'resting rooms' are basic but immaculate. It's a fine option if your stay is short.

Hotel Platan
HOTEL $$

(Гостиница Платан; ☑861-268 3007; www.platanhotel.ru/platan; ul Postovaya 41; s/d from R2800/3300, renovated s/d from R3100/3600; ☻❋ 🖥) This hotel feels like fairly standard post-Soviet fare, with functional rooms that vary according to their most recent renovation. In short, you get what you pay for; but even the cheapest are satisfactory. The location is convenient to the river and the Catherine the Great monument, one of Krasnodar's stand-out sights.

Hilton Garden Inn
HOTEL $$$

(☑861-210 2030; www.hilton.ru; Krasnaya ul 25/2; r from R5900; P ❋ @ 🖥) From the outside, it looks like a Soviet-era building – and it is, but inside, it's been completely revamped with marble and glass. Sleek rooms feature comfy mattresses, large work areas and contemporary furnishings.

Hotel Intourist
HOTEL $$$

(Гостиница Интурист; ☑861-268 5200; www.int-krd.ru; Krasnaya ul 109; s/d from R4000/4500; ❋ @ 🖥 ☝) This Soviet-era high-rise has been refurbished, now boasting bright, comfortable rooms with oversized windows and sleek bathrooms. For the most part, it feels like a modern, business-class hotel, despite the old-fashioned nomenclature. Friendly reception staff speak English and can assist with all travel arrangements.

✗ Eating

Krasnodar has no shortage of eateries, many of which are lined up along Krasnaya ul. Self-caterers should head to the central Sennoy Bazaar (ul Budyonnogo 129; ⊙7am-6pm) or the Kooperativny Market (cnr ul Golgolya & Krasnoarmeyskaya ul; ⊙7am-6pm) for rows of fresh fruit, pickled vegetables and dairy products.

Many Pelmeny　　　RUSSIAN, EUROPEAN **$**

(МэниПельмени; Krasnaya ul 33; mains R200-400; ◎10am-11pm) It's no secret what they do best at this cosy basement restaurant. You'll find more than a dozen varieties of the delicious dumpling, along with soups and salads and fresh-drawn beer. In summer months, there is seating in an enclosed patio.

LuboCoffee　　　CAFE **$**

(ЛюбоКофе; Krasnaya ul 68; mains R200-400; ◎8am-10pm; 🛜) This bright cafe has big armchairs and even bigger windows overlooking Krasnaya ul. The menu is pretty wide-ranging – soups, sandwiches, *pelmeni*, pizza, pasta. The warm welcome and free wi-fi make it a great place to spend a few hours if you are waiting for an onwards train. (Pay no attention to that international coffee chain next door.)

Yoburg　　　BURGERS **$$**

(Ёбург; Krasnaya ul 42; burgers R250-400; ◎10am-10pm; 🛜) This hipster burger joint is all about the irony, from the surprising burger options to the imagery on the wall (Bert and Ernie packing heat, for example). There are more burgers on the menu than seats in the joint.

La Cabaña　　　CAUCASIAN, RUSSIAN **$$**

(Ла Кабанья; Kubanskaya nab 39; mains R200-400; ◎11am-1am) This pleasant riverside cafe is a perfect perch for draining a few beers and watching the Kuban River pass patiently by. The menu features tasty shashlyk and salads, as well as other standard Russian fare. Take your pick from the stylish dining room or the breezy open-air tent.

🍷 Drinking & Nightlife

Pitcher Pub　　　BAR

(Питчер Паб; Krasnaya ul 68-70; ◎noon-midnight Sun-Thu, to 2am Fri & Sat; 🛜) Craft beer has arrived in the Russian provinces. Sample some of the local brews, such as Rose Bud (scented not with roses but with hibiscus), crafted right here in Krasnodar.

Coffee Biblioteka　　　CAFE

(Библиотека Кофе; ul Gogolya 66; ◎9am-midnight) When we asked about the availability of wi-fi at this stylish cafe, the barista answered, 'We have a somewhat different concept...books.' Bibliophiles will be blissful in this book-filled setting (though we didn't find any titles in English). Coffee drinks are delish, as are the small selection of sweets and sandwiches.

ℹ️ Information

There are ATMs along Krasnaya ul and in several hotel lobbies.

Main Post Office (Rashpilevskaya ul 58)

ℹ️ Getting There & Away

Krasnodar's **airport** (www.basel.aero) is 15km east of town. There are regular direct flights to Adler (from R2500), Moscow (from R4000) and St Petersburg (from R6000), as well as Antalya in Turkey, Erevan in Armenia, and Tashkent in Uzbekistan. Take trolleybus 7 or bus 1 to the airport from the train station (around 50 minutes).

From the Krasnodar **train station** (pl Privokzalnaya), trains go north to Rostov-on-Don (seat/*kupe* R712/1100, four to six hours) and on to Moscow (from R3300, 19 hours), or south to Sochi (seat/*kupe* R613/1534, four to six hours) and on to Adler.

The **bus station** (pl Privokzalnaya) also has services to Rostov-on-Don (from R550, four to six hours, six daily).

A combined daily train, ferry, bus service (R820,12 hours) takes passengers to Russia's newly annexed Crimea territory during the summer months. At the time of research, tickets were only available at Russian Railways ticket offices in Anapa or Krasnodar, not online.

BLACK SEA COAST

A narrow coastal strip edges the Black Sea, from where rolling hills ascend fairly rapidly into mountains in the southeast and low uplands in the northwest. This is the Black Sea Coast (Побережье Чёрного моря), Russia's sole seaside playground (until the Kremlin's 2014 annexation of Crimea). A long summer from June to October gives rise to pleasant weather, plenty of sunshine and a warm sea. Several resort towns dot the sometimes-rugged coast, the best known being Sochi, host city for the 2014 Winter Olympics.

Besides the grey and pebbly beaches in Sochi and nearby Adler, the region offers terrific walking in the Greater Caucasus foothills. Inland, Krasnaya Polyana is a once-sleepy mountain village that was transformed at great expense into the venue for Olympic ski and snowboard events. A new high-speed railway line, built especially for the Olympics, whisks passengers along the Black Sea coastline to Krasnaya Polyana from Sochi's main train station.

Sochi   Сочи

📞 862 / POP 389,900 / ⊘ MOSCOW

Gateway to the optimistically named 'Russian Riviera', Sochi is a Black Sea resort with a lively boardwalk and glorious sunsets. In summer, coastline nightclubs pump out booming baselines from dusk till dawn. Away from the embankment, magnolia- and cypress-filled parks provide a fine setting for strolling. And just outside of town, the Agura Valley offers easily accessible hiking amid waterfalls and sublime views.

While the sea is warm and the climate subtropical (among Russia's warmest destinations in winter), Sochi's beaches are disappointingly rocky and grey. You might find (imported) finer white sand at some private beaches in the summer months. In any case, the peak beach-going season (May to September) sees substantially higher prices.

In recent years, Sochi has become most famous as the host city for the 2014 Winter Olympics (even though the events were actually held at the neighbouring resorts of Adler and Krasnaya Polyana).

Sochi

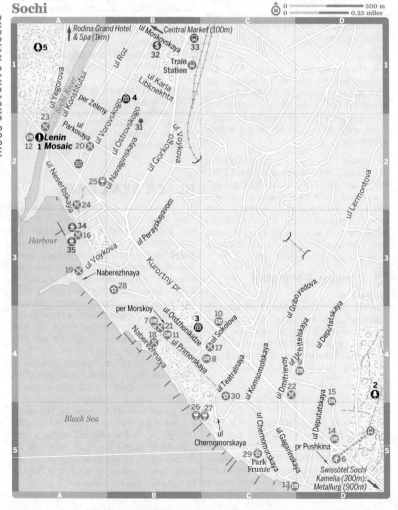

History

Sochi began life as a holiday resort in the final decades of the 19th century, when wealthy Russians came here to enjoy the sun and take spa treatments. Its development accelerated under Soviet authorities in the 1920s, when they drained the city's malaria-infested swamps and established a nature reserve.

It was during Stalin's reign that Sochi really flourished. Throughout the 1930s, a series of sanatoriums were constructed on the Black Sea coast to provide heavily subsidised holidays to Soviet workers. A typical holiday would have been a month at the sanatorium related to one's profession, such as the Metallurg (still open for business in today's capitalist Russia) for metal workers. In 1937, Stalin had his very own dacha built in the verdant hills around the city.

In the second half of the 20th century, Sochi continued to vie with Crimea as the Soviet Union's number-one holiday resort. The city's distinctive train station and sea port were constructed in the 1960s, and Sochi served as the backdrop to the immensely popular Soviet comedy, Бриллиантовая рука (Diamond Arm).

With the dissolution of the Soviet Union and the opening of Russia's borders, Sochi lost much of its appeal, as Russian holidaymakers opted en masse for package holidays on the beaches of Turkey and other previously forbidden shores. Sochi continued to attract crowds, but it was a resort on the decline – at least until the economic infusion spurred by the 2014 Winter Olympics.

◎ Sights & Activities

No more than 10m wide in most areas, Sochi's narrow and stony beaches are dressed up with artificial trees, sunbathing loungers, awnings and private changing pavilions. The main beaches are along Naberezhnaya and in front of Park Rivera. More private and secluded beaches, including some nude beaches, extend south from the city for around 160km. To access these beaches, simply hop on the Krasnaya Polyana–bound high-speed train from Sochi's main railway station. Get off at the Matsesta, Khosta or Izvestiya stations and wander down the coastline.

The snow-capped mountains behind Sochi are visible only from a sea cruise, which may carry the bonus of seeing dolphins. One- to two-hour cruises (R400 to R1000 per person) aboard a variety of vessels (yachts, passenger boats, catamarans, speedboats) leave throughout the day from the sea terminal (p384).

SOCHI'S OLYMPIC LEGACY

In 2007 Sochi was chosen by the International Olympic Committee as host for the 2014 Winter Olympics. It was a decision that left many scratching their heads in puzzlement. Not only is Sochi better known for palm trees than snow, the city is also within striking distance of the separatist insurgency that devastated nearby Chechnya. Never mind that its creaking infrastructure was far from Olympic standard.

Eager to prove that Russia is a powerful, modern country that can compete on the world stage, the government spent billions in preparation for the big event. Spending soared from an initial estimate of $12 billion to a reported $51 billion – making the Games by far the most expensive Olympics in history. In addition to building stadiums and new hotels, Russia also invested in dozens of infrastructure projects, including new roads, power stations, sewage systems, an upgraded airport and a high-speed rail to connect Krasnaya Polyana with Sochi and Adler. Authorities expressed their hope that the Games would transform Sochi into 'an international-level mega-resort'.

Post-Olympics, the new resort facilities are attracting a steady stream of visitors who are curious to experience the well-known summer sun and newly famous winter facilities. According to International Olympic Committee and the on-line Tourism Review, the years following the Olympic games have seen a significant increase in tourism, mostly by Russians. But it remains to be seen if the increase will be enough to amount to a pay-off on Russia's massive investment.

In any case, 'international-level mega-resort' is still quite a way off, as it's a largely Russian clientele enjoying the world-class facilities. (Not great for the economy, but not bad for travellers.)

For a series of photographs and essays about the selection of Sochi as an Olympic site, check out the Sochi Project (www.thesochiproject.com).

★ **Lenin Mosaic** PUBLIC ART
(Мозаика Ленина; Kurortny pr) How about this sparkling, red, 8m-high head shot of Ilyich as a backdrop for your holiday photos? This beauty was unveiled in 1980 to mark the 110th anniversary of the birth of the father of the Bolshevik Revolution.

Arboretum PARK
(Дендрарий; ☎862-297 5117; Kurortny pr; adult/child R270/120, cable car R500/260; ☉ park 8am-8pm, cable car 9am-8pm Tue-Sun & 11am-8pm Mon) On the southeastern edge of town, Sochi's lovely arboretum is lush with more than 1500 species of trees and shrubs, including numerous species of palm. It's a relaxing place to wander for a while. For a scenic overview, take the **cable car** (Канатная Дорога Дендрарий; adult/child R250/120) to the top and walk back down.

Park Rivera PARK
(Парк Ривьера; Kurortny pr; ☉ 10am-1am) Park Rivera is a small but lively greenscape that's criss-crossed with walking paths and dotted with games and kiddie rides. It's a pleasant place for a stroll, especially if you have kids in tow. Some of the palm trees here were planted by Soviet and Russian cosmonauts.

Museum of Sochi History MUSEUM
(Музей истории города-курорта Сочи; ☎862-264 2326; ul Vorovskogo 54; adult/child R100/50; ☉9am-5.30pm) Here's a smallish museum that delves into Sochi's archaeological history, its maritime roots, its role in WWII and other aspects of its social history. What shines is the space display, with the *Soyuz 9* capsule that returned to earth in June 1970 after 18 days in orbit. On board was a local lad, engineer Sevastyanov, and his pilot, Nikoliev.

Art Museum MUSEUM
(Художественный музей; ☎862-262 2947; Kurortny pr 51; adult/child R200/100; ☉10am-5.30pm Tue-Sun) In the middle of a leafy park, the Art Museum resides in a classical building that's a work of art in itself. The permanent collection includes age-old icons and paintings from the 19th to 21st centuries, as well as coins and weapons from the 1st century AD.

✦ Festivals & Events

Beer Festival BEER
The holiday season starts in late May with a weekend beer festival on Naberezhnaya.

Kinotavr Film Festival FILM
(www.kinotavr.ru) The week-long Kinotavr Film Festival in June attracts many big Russian film stars and the occasional foreign actor. Screenings inside the Winter Theatre incur a charge, but screenings outside are free.

🛏 Sleeping

Accommodation prices in Sochi rocketed before and during the Olympics. Nowadays, they are mostly in line with other Russian regional destinations, although rates increase by 25% to 50% between May and August. In any season, rates are more affordable in nearby Adler.

For an immersive cultural experience, adventurous travellers might consider a stay in a seaside sanatorium. One week is the typical minimum.

Riverskiy Hostel HOSTEL $
(Ривьерский хостел; ☑ 8-938-454 2054; www.sochivisit.com; Riverskiy per 3; dm R550-600, d R2200; ☺ 🛜) This friendly new hostel occupies a choice spot just south of Park Rivera, not far from the sea. Two- and six-bed dorm rooms are fitted with new beds, lockers and whimsical murals on the walls. Guests share the common kitchen and two bathrooms (which seem insufficient). No smoking, no alcohol.

Hostel Lermontov HOSTEL $
(Хостел Лермонтов; ☑ 8-918-208 0107; www.hostel-lermontov.ru; ul Lermontava 3; dm R500; 🛜) Here's a sweet retreat for budget travellers. In a quiet residential neighbourhood, this is a tiny hostel upstairs from an interior design shop. In addition to the two- and six-bed dorms, there's a communal kitchen and a charming garden. The whole place is filled with knick-knacks and love. It's a 15-minute walk to the beach.

Sochi Breeze Spa Hotel SPA HOTEL $$
(Сочи Бриз Спа Отель; ☑ 862-266 3800; www.sochibreeze.ru; Kurortny pr 72; s/d from R4100/4500; ☺ ❄ 🛜 🏊) The spa at Sochi Breeze includes a Russian *banya* (hot bath), Finnish sauna and Turkish bath, plus four pools (of varying temperatures) for soaking, swimming or taking a quick plunge. Soothe your sore muscles after spending the day skiing, hiking or strolling the seaside promenade. Rooms are adequate and service is friendly. It's a 10-minute walk to the beach.

Metallurg SANATORIUM $$
(Металлург; ☑ 8-800-200 2114, 862-267 2603; www.metallurg-sochi.ru; Kurortny pr 92; r per person incl meals from R3000; 🛜 🏊) The grand neoclassical edifice belies the simplicity of the rooms within. This former sanatorium of metallurgy workers offers a slew of medical services, in addition to sand, sea, sport and swimming pool.

Rodina Grand Hotel & Spa HOTEL $$$
(Гранд Отель и СПА Родина; ☑ 862-253 9000; www.grandhotelrodina.ru; Vinogradnaya ul 33; r from R42,000; ℗ ❄ 🛜 🏊) This ultra-swanky hotel – just north of Park Rivera – is the crème de la crème of high-end hotels in Sochi. Forty rooms and 20 villas are fitted with every comfort, from designer furniture to luxury linens. The property includes gorgeous gardens and a private beach.

The property features five different eating options, from a rooftop terrace with views of the Black Sea coast to the Black Magnolia evening restaurant, with its well-stocked wine cellar.

Sanremo BOUTIQUE HOTEL $$$
(Сан-Ремо; ☑ 862-227 0888; www.sanremo-apartments.ru; Chernomorskaya ul 13; apt from R11,000; ❄ 🛜 🏊) We dig the Sanremo for its intimate atmosphere (29 fabulous rooms), prime beachfront location and groovy restaurant-lounge at sea level. The minimalist rooms are spacious and modern, with enormous windows looking out to sea. They have access to a wide shared balcony with lounge chairs, but it's just a few steps to the sand.

A perfect spot for sundowners, the lounge downstairs has indoor and outdoor seating, a tantalising menu of seafood and an overall atmosphere of irrepressible coolness.

Villa Anna CASTLE $$$
(Вилла Анна; ☑ 862-240 4830; www.villa-anna-hotel.ru; Kurortny pr 72/7; s/d R4650/5000; ❄ 🛜) Here's your chance to sleep in a 16th-century Scottish castle. (Ahem.) This place is over the top, with a drawbridge over the koi pond moat and armoured knights guarding the entrance. In keeping with the theme, the 30 guest rooms have thick carpets, heavy drapes and solid wood furniture. The *banya* complex is particularly atmospheric. Don't leave without trying to pull Excalibur out of the rock in the garden.

Swissôtel Sochi Kamelia HOTEL $$$
(Swissôtel Сочи Камелия; ☑ 862-296 8801; www.swissotel.com/hotels/sochi-kamelia; Kurortny pr 89; r from R12,900; ℗ ☺ 🛜 🏊) Another luxury hotel built with the Winter Olympics

in mind, Swissotel Kamelia is tucked away from the centre of town, heading southeast along Kurortny pr. Located in a park overlooking the Black Sea, the spacious rooms are tasteful to a tee, with modern decor and wide balconies. If you're not facing the sea, you're missing out.

Bounty

BOUTIQUE HOTEL $$$

(☑ 862-262 2808; www.bounty-sochi.ru; Primorskaya ul 4b; r R5000-9000) The Bounty is a gem for its small size and personal service. The traditionally decorated rooms lack pizazz, but they are comfortable enough. The place is a block from the beach.

Marins Park Hotel

HOTEL $$$

(Маринс Парк Отель; ☑ 271 3000; www.park-hotel-sochi.ru; per Morskoy 2; r R4400-5600; ✳ @ 🛜 ☒) Step through the glass doors and into the marble lobby, sprinkled with shops. Here you'll find efficient English-speaking service and attractive, fairly priced accommodation. The understated rooms are decorated in light pastels and blonde-wood trim, with big windows welcoming in the light. Located in a quiet area just a block from the seafront.

Chernomorye Sanatorium

SANATORIUM $$$

(Черноморье Санаторий; ☑ 8-988-235 8400; www.chernomorye-rzd.ru; ul Ordzhonikidze 27; r per person incl meals R10,700; ✳ 🛜 ☒) With a convenient central location and an impressive modern facility, the sanitorium of the Russian railway system is one of the best in the area. In addition to the luxurious rooms, there are indoor and outdoor swimming pools, tennis courts and fitness centre, as well as a *banya* and sauna.

Hotel Magnolia

HOTEL $$$

(Гостиница Магнолия; ☑ 862-262 0166; www.sochi-magnolia.ru; Kurortny pr 50; s/d from R4700/5100; ✳ 🛜) Named after the flowering trees fronting the complex, the hotel has 126 brightly renovated rooms with modern floral prints and Ikea-style furniture. The location is smack-dab in the middle of town, though it's a 10-minute walk to the beach.

✖ Eating

Open-air restaurants line the seaside walkway, known as the Naberezhnaya. This is a good place to sample local Black Sea seafood (including oyster, mussels and pike perch) and Kuban cuisine. For self-catering, visit the colourful **Central Market** (Центральный рынок; Moskovskaya ul; ⊘ 6am-6pm) or the large **Perekrestok** (cnr ul Uchitelskaya &

Kurortny pr; ⊘ 24hr) supermarket in the centre of town.

Frapp

BELGIAN $

(www.instagram.com/frapp_sochi; ul Vorovskogo 5; waffles R245-325; ⊘ 9am-9pm) There's not much to the menu at this tiny cafe, but you don't need much – just a choice selection of sweet and savoury waffles, fresh juices and Viennese coffee. Pick a table in the cosy interior or on the shady porch. Service is super friendly.

Burgman

BURGERS $

(www.burgmansochi.ru; ul Ordzhonikidze 26a; burgers R330-600; ⊘ noon-midnight) Here's your friendly neighbourhood burger joint, touting farm-fresh ingredients and 18 different takes on the ever-popular sandwich. Besides your traditional beef patties, you'll find a veggie burger, a turkey burger, a crab cake and even a shrimp burger (no, we don't mean to imply that it's puny). Soups, salads and beers round out the menu.

Marinad

EUROPEAN, RUSSIAN $

(Маринад; Morskoy per 3; mains R200-500; ⊘ 10am-midnight; 🛜 🍴 ☒ 👶) Set in a gracious former residence, the restaurant comprises a series of intimate salons (and a lovely porch). Dine on traditional Russian fare, including *skoblyanki* (tasty, hardy meals prepared in an iron skillet). There's a delightful children's play area, so bring the little ones.

Chyo? Kharcho!

CAUCASIAN $$

(www.che-harcho.ru; Primorskaya ul 3/10; mains R240-600; ⊘ noon-midnight) This wide, welcoming terrace claims the best shashlyk on the Naberezhnaya, in addition to the namesake *kharcho* (lamb stew) and other Georgian specialities. It's an exceedingly pleasant place to quaff a beer and watch the action on the boardwalk and the beach beyond.

Brigantina

RUSSIAN, FRENCH $$

(Бригантина; Neserbskaya ul 3; mains R500-1000; ⊘ 8am-11pm) This pleasant French-owned restaurant enjoys a breezy location overlooking the harbour, with outdoor tables and a big menu of seafood and grilled meats. Mussels and bouillabaisse are among the highlights.

Sinbad

MIDDLE EASTERN $$

(www.facebook.com/rest.sinbad.sochi; ul Yegorava 2; mains R400-800; ⊘ 10am-11pm; 🍴) Opposite the entrance to Park Rivera, this busy restaurant is a lively place for Middle Eastern fare. The kebabs take a central place on the menu, but there's also hummus, lentil soup and other vegetarian goodness.

Stary Bazar   CAUCASIAN, EUROPEAN **$$**
(Старый Базар; ☑ 862-239 2919; Neserbskaya ul 4; mains R300-700; ⊘ 11am-midnight) Surrounded by greenery overlooking a small park, Stary Bazar is another established Sochi restaurant that continues to pack them in. And for good reason – the place offers a delightfully kitschy country-inn setting that is perfect for sampling the satisfying menu of Russian and Georgian food.

Dok   SEAFOOD **$$$**
(Док; ☑ 8-928-445 2929; www.facebook.com/dok.bar.sochi; ul Voykova 1, prichal 2; mains R600-1200; ⊘ noon-midnight) If you prefer your oysters on the half shell, this sophisticated little harbourside raw bar is for you. You'll fine varieties from the Far East and the White Sea, as well as the smaller guys from local Black Sea waters. The menu also features a few other seafood dishes and a good wine list.

SOCHI EXCURSIONS

Stalin's Dacha

This **retreat** (Дача Сталина; Kurortny pr 120; tours R300; ⊘ 10am-6pm) at Zelenaya Roscha, is a fascinating place, built specifically to accommodate a small, private and paranoid man. Tours are in Russian but some of the patriotic guides speak a little English. You'll get to see Stalin's private rooms (with some original furniture), the movie theatre where he checked every film before public release, and his billiards room where he played only those he could beat or who were wily enough to lose. The Stalin portraits on the walls were added after his death. The other paintings are all reproductions, as Stalin believed that artwork belonged to the people and therefore should hang in a museum. The depth of the water in the swimming pool (just 1.5m), the height of the stair treads, and most of the furniture were specially built to accommodate Stalin's small stature (165cm).

From Sochi take any Adler-bound bus and get off at the Zelenaya Roscha stop. Enter through the gates of the sanitorium and walk about 1km uphill to the dacha.

Sochi National Park

East of Sochi centre, the sprawling **Sochi National Park** (Сочинский национальный парк; www.sochinp.ru; R170; ⊘ 10am-6pm Oct-Apr, to 9pm May-Sep) traverses the Agura valley, offering scenic easy-to-access hiking, with rewarding views of nearby mountains and waterfalls. Popular routes lead to the lookout tower atop **Mt Bolshoy Akhun** or to the evocatively named **Eagle Cliffs** (Орлиные Скалы). Pick up an Agura Valley trail map at the park entrance.

Near the park entrance **Salkhino** (Салхино; ☑ 862-238 9111; Агурское ущелье ул 1; mains R400-800) is a suitably rustic Caucasian restaurant. They do a popular *khashlama* (Caucasian-spiced lamb stew), among many other dishes. There are Kuban dry reds on the wine list, along with Georgian and French vintages.

From Sochi or Adler, take bus 124 or 125 to the Sputnik Hotel skyscraper. From here the entrance is a 1km walk. Follow the road along Agura River until you get to Salkhino restaurant and the entrance beyond. Alternatively, it's a 30-minute walk from Zelenaya Roscha.

Mt Bolshoy Akhun is also serviced by an 11km road, which makes it a popular organised tour from Sochi. A 5½-hour excursion costs around R1500 and includes a stop at the Agura waterfalls.

Vorontsovskaya Cave

About 40km south from central Sochi, this chain of **caves** (Воронцовская Пещера; ☑ 441-1175; adult/child R350/200; ⊘ 10am-6pm May-Sep, shorter hours Oct-Apr) is a popular and worthwhile excursion. Some 12km of the cave system is mapped, but tourists have access to 500m of illuminated passages. Some of the rooms are quite spectacular, decorated with stalactites and stalagmites. To get here hire a taxi (about R3000) or join a tour (R700). It gets cold inside, so dress accordingly.

🍷 Drinking & Nightlife

Try the English-language www.sochicity-guide.com website for club and bar listings. Or just stroll along the Naberezhnaya and feel which way the wind is blowing.

Sea Zone   COCKTAIL BAR
(📋 233 6011; http://seazone.lrgsochi.ru; Primorskaya ul 17; ⊙ 10am-10pm; 📶) Just steps from the sand, Sea Zone is an enticingly upscale venue to relax in and savour the sunset. The covered terrace is tastefully furnished with dark wicker furniture and neutral-toned linens, or you can take a seat in the open air for fresh sea breezes. There's a short menu (including a raw bar) to accompany the cocktails.

Cabaret Mayak   GAY
(Кабаре Маяк; www.clubmayak.com; Navaginskaya ul 3; cover R300-500; ⊙ 7pm-7am) Perhaps Russia's most famous gay club, thanks to the massive media attention received during the 2014 Sochi Olympics, Club Mayak is now in a new location near the train station. Inside, drag queens and other performers continue to strut their stuff. Face control keeps out the uncool, so make sure you look your best.

Stargorod   BREWERY
(Старгород; 📋 862-227 0757; www.stargorod. net; Primorskaya ul 19; ⊙ 11am-1am; 📶) Below the Winter Theatre, this large Czech-run brewery offers great views of the Black Sea alongside its own beers and grilled meats. The fried and flavoured dark bread makes a great accompaniment for the house brews.

☆ Entertainment

Festival Concert Hall   LIVE MUSIC
(Фестивальный концертный зал; 📋 reception 262 4777, tickets 862-262 2941; www.festival-sochi. ru; ul Ordzhonikidze 5; tickets R350-1500; ⊙ box office 1-8pm) Many of Russia's top music acts play in Sochi – most at this massive hall with its front open to the sea embankment below.

Winter Theatre   THEATRE
(Зимний театр, Zimny Teatr; 📋 862-262 9616; Teatralnaya pl; ⊙ booking office 10am-7pm) Built in a majestic imperial style, this massive, colonnaded building would add grace to any world capital. Opera, ballet and drama are presented here.

Summer Theatre   THEATRE
(Летний театр, Letny Teatr; Chyornomorskaya ul 11, Park Frunze) True to its name, this architec-turally striking, neoclassical theatre stages open-air concerts and drama performances during the summer.

ℹ️ Information

Post Office (ul Vorovskogo 1/2)

TAVS (ТАВС; 📋 862-264 0526; www.sochitavs.ru; Navaginskaya ul 16; ⊙ 8am-8pm) Efficient air and train ticketing agency.

Uralsib Bank (Moskovskaya ul 5) 24hr ATM.

ℹ️ Getting There & Away

AIR

Sochi's **airport** (http://sochi-airport.com) is at Adler, 25km away. Many airlines fly to Moscow, including Aeroflot (from R5500). In summer there are flights to most other major Russian cities.

BOAT

The **sea terminal** (Морской вокзал; Ul Voykova 1) has various information kiosks with posted departures.

Twice a week in season, the hydrofoil **Comet** (📋 8-918-409 1296; expressbatumi@mail.ru; ul Neserbskaya 5; adult/child R5500/2500; ⊙ May-Oct) makes the five-hour trip between Sochi and Batumi, Georgia. The ride can be very rough and is highly dependent on weather. At the time of research, the route is open only for Georgians, Russians and other CIS nationals.

BUS

From the **bus station** (Автовокзал; ul Gorkogo 56a), there is a daily service to Kislovodsk (R800, 18 hours), which also calls at Krasnodar and Pyatigorsk. The faster service (13 hours) originates in Adler and stops at Mamayka station in Sochi.

TRAIN

The Sochi **train station** (ul Gorkogo) was revamped for the Olympics and is looking fabulous. There are services to Adler (35 minutes, R174, frequent) and Krasnaya Polyana (R254, 1¼ hours, six daily). The regular *elektrichki* stop frequently at beaches and coastal towns along their route, the fast *(skory)* ones less so.

Heading north, trains stop at Krasnodar (seat/ *kupe* R815/1455, four to eight hours, frequent) and Rostov-on-Don (*kupe* from R1500, seven to 11 hours, frequent) en route to Moscow. There are many trains to Moscow, but two are significantly faster (*kupe* R7100, 23 hours, twice daily), and there's one relatively fast train to St Petersburg (R7790, 37½ hours, departs 6.08pm).

Train 644 to Kislovodsk (kupe R3112, 13½ hours, daily) goes via Mineralnye Vody and Pyatigorsk.

ℹ️ Getting Around

From the bus station take *marshrutka* or bus 105 (R50 to R85, 40 minutes, every 20 minutes) to the airport in Adler. There are less frequent trains to the airport (R176, 43 minutes). A taxi costs from about R600 to R1000.

Adler   Адлер

🖉 862 / POP 76,500 / ⊘ MOSCOW

Despite a grand overhaul of its transport infrastructure for the 2014 Winter Olympics, the Black Sea resort of Adler lacks the nouveau riche affluence and attitude of Sochi, which is 30km to the north. Traditionally a popular destination for lower-income Russian holidaymakers, prices for lodging and food are slightly lower here.

Like other nearby resort towns, the main action is along the promenade (nonsmoking since the Olympics), where you'll find a wide variety of cafes, a funfair and souvenir stalls. If you're lucky, you'll spot dolphins frolicking in the Black Sea.

🅞 Sights

Sochi Park   AMUSEMENT PARK
(Сочи Парк; 🖉 8-800-100 3339; www.sochi-park.ru; Olimpisky pr 21; adult/child R1980/1600; ⊘10am-9pm May, 10am-10pm Jun-Aug; 🚃 Olimpisky Park) Located in the former Olympic park, this sprawling funfair is sometimes called Russian Disneyland, with 20 'European-standard' rides (including Russia's highest and fastest roller coaster). There are also hands-on activities and adventures for kids, as well as family-friendly entertainment, such as puppet shows, circus performances and a lights-and-fountains display. Take the train to Olimpisky Park station or take *marshrutka* 124 from Sochi's train station (R50). The castle hotel Bogatyr is also on-site.

Discovery World Aquarium   AQUARIUM
(Океанариум; www.sochiaquarium.com; Ul Lenina 219; adult/child R700/350; ⊘10am-6pm) If you're not swimming among the fish, or eating the fish, you might considering paying a visit to the fish in the Discovery World Aquarium, which is a reasonably entertaining rainy-day outing. The highlight is the 44m 'tunnel', which allows you to walk right through the reef and be surrounded by sea creatures on all sides. In addition to the 13 ocean aquariums, there's a fresh-water exhibit, complete with waterfall.

🛏️ Sleeping

There are many smallish hotels along the seaside promenade, which is a short walk from the bus station. In season, it's also common for individuals to rent private rooms. Talk to homeowners hanging out in the train station, or just stroll the streets and look for signs that say 'сдается' (rooms for rent).

Arriva Hotel   HOTEL $$
(🖉862-240 4582, 8-962-885 1859; www.arrivas-ochi.com; ul Prosveshcheniya 25a; r R3500-4500; ❄️🛜) This newish option is small and friendly, offering excellent value right on the seafront. The rooms are spacious and stylish, in a Gothic sort of way. Big windows let in plenty of light and sea breezes, while the balconies facing the water offer sunset views.

Hotel Prichal   HOTEL $$
(Гостиница Причал; 🖉8-988-404 4110, 862-240 4110; www.adler-prichal.ru; ul Prosveshcheniya 7; d R3500-5000; ⊖❄️🛜) Rooms at the Hotel Prichal are pretty simple – but who needs fancy when the place is filled with sunlight, fresh sea air and truly positive vibes. The Prichal is a pebble's throw from the Black Sea, so you'll enjoy waking up to the sound of gently (or otherwise) breaking waves. Breakfast included.

Adelphia   HOTEL $$
(Адельфия; 🖉8-918-606 6824, 8-988-404 4110; www.hotel-adelphia-adler.ru; ul Prosveshcheniya 13; s R2400-3600, d R3400-5000; ❄️🛜) Thirty metres from the beach, Adelphia occupies a striking building with an unusual curved edifice. The 44 rooms are comfortable, if a little formal for resort accommodation. There are fine views from the terrace and from some rooms, as well as a spa and an in-house *banya* (R2500).

AC   BOUTIQUE HOTEL $$$
(🖉862-241 0122; www.ac-hotel.ru; ul Prosveshcheniya 36; d R4500-5500; ⊖❄️@) This sleek-looking six-storey hotel has 40 sizeable rooms with clean lines, soft tones and contemporary style. It's on the east side of ul Prosyshcheniya (away from the water), but guests in the upper-floor rooms still enjoy sea views from their balconies. There's a cafe, restaurant and spa, and excellent service all around.

Radisson Blu Resort   HOTEL $$$
(🖉862-296 8100; www.radissonblu.com; ul Golubaya 1a; r R8000-12,000; ⊖❄️@🛜🏊) One

of several hotels built for the 2014 Winter Olympics, the Radisson Blu Resort sits a short distance from the former Olympic Park on the Adler coastline. Rooms are spacious and boast good views of either the Caucasus mountains or the Black Sea. It's pricey, but bargains are available off-season.

✖ Eating

Dozens of cafes, bars and restaurants line the lively promenade along the waterfront.

Café Radost   RUSSIAN $
(Кафе Радость; ul Karla Marksa 2; shashlyk R140-230; ⊘ 10am-2am) Just a few steps away from the seaside promenade, there is a festive, open-air joint serving up cold beer and sizzling shashlyk.

Café Fregat   RUSSIAN, INTERNATIONAL $$
(Кафе Фрегат; ul Karla Marksa; mains R250-500; ⊘ 10am-midnight) A vast restaurant with various dining rooms surrounding an inner courtyard. Here, tables surround a gurgling fountain and live music plays on most nights. Big menu of Western and Russian standards.

Mayak   EUROPEAN, RUSSIAN $$
(Маяк; ul Prosveshcheniya 35; mains R250-750; ⊘ 11am-midnight) Take your pick from the cosy interior, the palm-sheltered courtyard, or the tables right on the pavement overlooking the promenade. They are all attractive settings to sample Mayak's tempting grilled fish and meats (or pizza, if you prefer).

Despite the misleading address, it's located in the middle of the promenade next to the namesake lighthouse.

Royal Fish   SEAFOOD $$$
(☑ 8-928-458 9988; www.royalfish-sochi.ru; Bestuzhava per; mains R700-1200; ⊘ 10am-1am; 🛜) Tucked away in the far southern corner of the seaside promenade, this classy restaurant offers a good wine list and plenty of local seafood choices, including a raw bar with Black Sea oysters. Other enticing options include vichyssoise with smoked salmon, mussels doused in garlic sauce and salmon fillet served on a hot stone plate.

ⓘ Getting There & Away

The main bus stop is near the **central market** (Центральный рынок; ul Lenina), a 1km walk to the hotel- and restaurant-lined seaside promenade. Pick up frequent buses and *marshrutky* to Sochi (R50, 40 minutes) here or opposite the revamped **train station** (ul Lenina), which is an inconvenient 3km north of the bus station.

The train goes to Krasnaya Polyana (R190, 40 minutes, seven daily) or Sochi (R176, 35 minutes, 20 daily). Long-distance trains also connect Adler to Sochi, Krasnodar, Rostov-on-Don and Moscow.

A taxi from the airport or train station to the seaside area should cost around R400. You can take a taxi all the way to Sochi for about R1000.

Krasnaya Polyana
Красная Поляна

☑ 862 / POPULATION 4600 / ELEVATION 560M / ⊘ MOSCOW

A scenic road passing through a deep, narrow canyon leads up from Adler to Krasnaya Polyana (Red Valley), Russia's newly built ski mecca that hosted the 2014 Winter Olympics ski events. The scenery here is spectacular, with snow-capped mountains looming above three world-class ski resorts containing kilometres of high-quality pistes.

Krasnaya Polyana is actually the name of a sleepy village about 40km east of Adler, but most of the action takes place at the ski resorts further east. The undoubted jewel in the Olympic crown here is the Roza Khutor Alpine Resort (p387), which hosted the Olympics downhill skiing events and today offers phenomenal skiing and snowboarding to the general public. The area's highest mountain, Roza Pik, towers over a story-book village that is lined up along the Mzymta River. It's also a wonderful destination for hiking, shopping, strolling around town and gawking at the jaw-dropping scenery. Other excellent resorts and facilities dot the road between Krasnaya Polyana and Roza Khutor.

🏃 Activities

Skiing and snowboarding are the obvious attractions here. But the resorts are doing their best to make Krasnaya Polnaya a year-round destination, offering hiking, horseback riding and river rafting (a very tame version) on the Mzymta River.

The 2687m summit of **Mt Fisht** (Гора Фишт) is a splendid trek, if you have three or four days to spare. From Solokhay, a rough road leads 20km to the trailhead. From the trailhead it's 14km to stunning alpine Khmelnovskogo Lake, where you can camp in view of the surreal lunar landscape and spires of Mt Fisht. You'll need to go with a guide from a company such as **Masterskaya Priklucheniy** (Мастерская Приключений; ☑ 8-928 292 0596; www.extreme-sochi.ru; Nab Panorama 3, Roza Khutor).

After a day spent skiing or hiking in the mountains, the warm Russian banya (bathhouse) makes a great spot to recover in.

Roza Khutor
SKIING, CABLE CAR

(Роза Хутор; ☑ 8-8622-419 222; www.rosaski.com; Alpika; ski pass from R1600, cable car R1350; ⊙9am-4pm) This world-class ski complex was the largest venue for the Sochi Winter Olympics. It consists of 18 modern lifts and almost 80km of piste catering for all levels of proficiency. For non-skiers (or out of season), it's worth taking a cable car to the top of the Rosa Peak plateau (2320m) to enjoy the stunning views of nearby snow-capped mountains. Even without hitting the slopes, it's possible to spend a half-day hanging out in the pleasant cafes and enjoying the magnificent views.

Gorki Gorod
SKIING, OUTDOORS

(Горки Город; ☑ 8-800-550 2020; www.gorkygorod.ru; Esto-Sadok; ski pass adult/child R1900/1300, cable car R300-1100, bike pass R700-900, adventure park R300-350, water park adult/child R1000/500; ⊙9am-6pm) Formerly known as Gornaya Karusel, this top-notch ski resort was constructed for the 2014 Winter Olympics ski-jumping events. Today it boasts 12 modern lifts and 30km of high-quality piste amid the rugged terrain of Mt Aibga. There are some memorable views of neighbouring mountains and countryside from three transfer levels at 960m, 1450m and 2200m above sea level.

The resort is a pretty great summertime playground as well, with 7km of mountain bike tracks and four hiking trails taking in forests, fields and waterfalls. The so-called Adventure Park is a ropes obstacle course, strung between the trees at 1460m. There's even an indoor water park (open year-round) with a glass-domed roof showing off mountain views.

Gazprom Mountain Resort
SKIING, HIKING

(Гранд Отель Поляна; ☑ 862-259 5052; www.polyanski.ru; Achipsinskaya ul 16, Esto-Sadok; ski lift ticket weekdays/weekends from R1200/1350, cable car from R400; ⊙9am-11pm) With two different base stations, Gazprom's plush resort has 14 lifts and 21km of ski trails that cover a range of difficulty levels. Although it's primarily a downhill mountain, some Olympic Nordic events were held atop its broad, gently sloping ridge. In summer, the cable cars are operational, offering excellent hiking in the surrounding countryside and spectacular views.

Bannaya Skazka
BANYA

(Банная Сказка; ☑ 8-928 852 2852; www.spa-bani.com; ul Olimpiyskaya 36, Roza Khutor; per person before/after 2pm R500/1000) Here's a welcome warm-up after a day on the slopes. This spa centre – part of the Fort Eureka hotel complex – includes two atmospheric *bani*, each with a plunge pool and rest area. Hardy souls may prefer to cool off in the cold rush of the on-site mountain stream. It's a few steps from the Roza Khutor train station.

British Banya
BANYA

(British-баня; ☑ 8-918 607 6611; www.british-banya.com; Kosmolsky per, Krasnaya Polyana; per 3hr for 1-3 people R15,000; ⊙9am-last visitor) In Krasnaya Polyana village, British Banya has a beautiful setting against a mountainous backdrop with a round dipping pool and two saunas – all beautifully designed in natural wood and stone. Massages and other treatments are available, plus good teas are on hand. Alcohol is prohibited.

SkyPark
ADVENTURE SPORTS

(☑ 800-100 4207; www.ajhackett.com; Krasnoflotskaya ul, Kazachiy brod; ⊙10am-6.30pm May-Sep, to 5pm Oct-Apr) The setting is certainly spectacular for Russia's first park for all things aerial, including bungee jumping, zip-lining and more. The park overlooks the greenery and waterfalls of Sochi National Park, with views to the peaks of the Caucasus. In addition to two bungee jumps, there are hanging bridges, two different rock-climbing routes and an aerial swing.

The centrepiece of the park is the 439m Skybridge, a swaying steel-cable bridge that stretches between two cliffs at a height of 207m. Look for it from the highway, as you drive from Krasnaya Polyana to Adler.

🛏 Sleeping

The majority of top-end hotels are clustered around the Roza Khutor and Gornaya Karusel ski resorts, while some cheaper options can be found in Krasnaya Polyana village. See www.rosaski.com for a full list of Roza Khutor accommodation options.

Valset Apartments
APARTMENT **$$**

(Апартаменты Valset; ☑ 8-800-200 0048; www.azimuthotels.com; Roza Khutor; apt from R4500; 🐾❄🛜) Stylish apartments in the heart of the Roza Khutor are an excellent alternative to expensive hotel rooms, especially if you prefer to self-cater on occasion. A range of options are available, from cosy studios to two-bedroom apartments. There's a playground for the kiddies and amazing mountain views from your balcony.

Bridge Mountain
HOTEL $$

(☎8-800-100 1435, 862-243 9735; ul Zaschitnikov Kavkaza 120/3, Krasnaya Polyana; capsules R1800, r R2000-2600; ❋☎) In Krasnaya Polyana village, this friendly, modern hotel is an excellent midrange option for travellers who do not intend to spend their holiday in their room. The most economical option is the 9-sq-metre 'capsule', which includes two single beds and not much else. Standard rooms are a more generous 33-sq-metres, but still pretty sparse (though comfortable and modern).

There is a restaurant on-site, as well as a spa, a *banya* and ski equipment rental. Prices increase during ski season.

Utomlyonnye Solntsem
HOTEL $$

(Утомленные солнцем; ☎8-918-309 5893; www.hotel-kraspol.ru; ul Michurina 5/1, Krasnaya Polyana; d summer/winter from R2000/4000; ☎) Named after the Oscar-winning film by director Nikita Mikhalkov (*Burnt by the Sun* in English), this midrange hotel has clean but basic rooms in Krasnaya Polyana village. The place has an anachronistic air about it, having not quite shed its Soviet mantle, but it's a decent option for the price. Breakfast is included.

Hotel Tatyana
HOTEL $$

(Гостиница Татьяна; ☎862-243 9111; www.tatyana-alpik.ru; Estonskaya ul 75, Esto-Sadok; r R1900-2400, ste R2800-4000; ❋☎) Just across the street from Gorki Gorod, this attractive property is one of the more affordable options in town. An open fireplace warms the lobby. (If that doesn't do the trick, there's also a *banya* for rent.) Rooms are a bit dated, but otherwise comfortable and colourful.

Grand Hotel Polyana
RESORT $$$

(Гранд Отель Поляна; ☎862-259 5595; www.grandhotelpolyana.ru; Achipsinskaya ul 16, Esto-Sadok; r summer/winter from R5000/8600; P❋☎☎) Offering Krasnaya Polyana's finest accommodation, Gazprom's sprawling 400-room resort has spacious, handsome rooms, decked with oil paintings on the wall and stocked with luxury linens and Bulgari bath products. Every sort of amenity is at guests' disposal, including indoor and outdoor pools, tennis courts, spa centres, restaurants and ski slopes right on the property. Prices include breakfast.

Sochi Marriott Krasnaya Polyana
HOTEL $$$

(Сочи Марриотт Красная Поляна; ☎8-8622 354 392; www.marriott.com; Nab Vremena Goda 1, Esto-Sadok; r summer/winter from R6700/10,200; P❋@☎☎) This colossal top-end hotel at the foot of the Gorki Gorod ski lifts might belong to a major European chain, but its imposing facade is best described as nouveau-Soviet. Inside, however, things are much better, with spacious, comfortable rooms, as you would expect from Marriott. The views are fabulous, as are the spa facilities. Off-season deals abound.

Azimut Freestyle Hotel
HOTEL $$$

(☎8-800-200 0048, 862-243 1335; www.azimuthotels.com; Naberezhnaya Polyanka 4, Roza Khutor; s/d in summer from R3500/4100, in winter from R7500/8100; ☐❋☎) This stylish hotel is an excellent base for your outdoor adventure, with modern comfortable rooms, friendly service and fabulous mountain and river views. It's particular popular among the young, sporty set. Coming from Roza Khutor train station, it's the first hotel on the left bank. Discounts are available for advanced online booking.

✖ Eating

Aside from a decent selection of restaurants and cafes in and around the resorts, all the major hotels also have their own restaurants.

Perekrestok
SUPERMARKET $

(Перекрёсток; Nab Lavanda 2, Roza Khutor; ☉10am-10pm) Self-caterers will find everything they need on the 1st floor of this chain supermarket near Gorki Gorod.

★ Vershina 2200
RUSSIAN, EUROPEAN $$

(Вершина 2200; https://gorkygorod.ru/vershina_2200; Gorki Gorod; mains R800-1500; ☉10am-6pm) Sup a warming soup as you sit by the toasty fire and watch the snow fall on the ski slopes outside. Located at 2200m (the highest point in Gorki Gorod), this classy two-floor restaurant has fantastic views and serves a surprisingly wide mixture of European and Russian food.

Chyo? Kharcho!
CAUCASIAN $$

(Чё? Харчо!; www.che-harcho.ru; ul Olimpiskaya 37, Roza Khutor; mains R450-800) This popular restaurant serves generous portions of Caucasian dishes, including *kharcho,* the spicy Georgian soup that inspired its unusual name ('Huh? Kharcho!' in English). Also offers pizza among all the *khachapuri* and shashlyk. Indoor and outdoor seating and live music in the evenings. Find it right next to the Roza Khutor ski lifts.

Vysota 2320
CAFE $$

(Высота 2320; Roza Pik plateau; mains R600-1200; ⊘10am-5pm) Located high atop Roza Peak, the aptly named 'Altitude 2320' is the perfect place to kick back after skiing and snowboarding. The floor to ceiling windows yield a fabulous panorama all around: the Black Sea is visible from here on on a clear day. There's nothing too surprising on the menu, but the staples are artfully prepared and presented.

Modus
ITALIAN $$

(Модус; Nab Panorama 3, Roza Khutor; pizzas R500-800; ⊘10am-11pm Mon-Fri, to midnight Sat & Sun) Modus is a cool and casual pizzeria with a trendy vibe – but not too trendy. The warm, wooden interior is decked out with all manner of mismatched chairs, comfy couches and eclectic artwork, creating a very welcoming atmosphere indeed. Pizzas range from traditional (Margarita) to not-so-traditional (Barbecue), so take your pick!

Trikoni
RUSSIAN, EUROPEAN $$

(Трикони; www.trikoni.ru; ul Michurina 1, Krasnaya Polyana; mains R400-800; ⊘11am-11pm; 🛜🍸) Just up the road from Utomlyonnye Solntsem in Krasnaya Polyana village, Trikoni is an old-fashioned country inn with a menu full of Russian and Italian favourites. It's hearty, filling fare, that's sure to satisfy after a day on the slopes. In summer, take a seat on the deck with mountain views.

🛍 Shopping

Souvenir stalls and shops in all three Krasnaya Polyana ski resorts sell rather-large hairy Caucasian hats called *papakha*, tacky souvenirs, homemade wine, pickles and honey.

Krasnaya Polyana
Tasting Complex
FOOD & DRINKS

(Дегустационный комплекс 'Красная Поляна'; www.balzamsochi.ru; Nab Panorama 2, Roza Khutor; ⊘10am-9pm) Step inside this little shop to sample the local liqueurs, balsams and wines – many of which are infused with mountain herbs, fruit and honey from Krasnaya Polyana and nearby Abkhazia.

ⓘ Information

There are ATMs at all top-end hotels and at the ski resort base stations.

Emergency Services (☎243 0422)

Tourist Information Office (Туристический информационный центр; ☎259 5052; Achipsinskaya ul 16, Esto-Sadok; ⊘9am-6pm) The tourist information office is next to the Gorki Gorod ski lifts. Helpful, English-speaking staff can organise hiking and other activities in the summer months.

Ski-hire shops abound at both ski areas and in Krasnaya Polyana village.

ⓘ Getting There & Away

Krasnaya Polyana is approximately 40km east of Adler along the Mzymta River. There are two train stations in the resort area: **Esto-Sadok** (Эсто-Садок вокзал), near Krasnaya Polyana village; and **Roza Khutor** (p387), further east, near the resort of the same name. Comfortable trains from Sochi (via Adler) make the 1¼-hour journey six times a day (R233).

From the Sochi bus station, take bus or *marshrutka* 105, which goes to Krasnaya Polyana, stopping at all the resorts (R50 to R100, one to two hours, frequent). You can also pick up this bus at the Adler airport.

ⓘ Getting Around

From Roza Khutor train station, walk about 1km west along the river to reach the ski resort base station. Gorki Gorod and Gazprom Mountain Resort are both about 3km west of the train station, but the roads are not really pedestrian friendly. It's best to take a taxi (R400) or hop on bus 105. If you're staying at one of these resorts, hotel staff can arrange a transfer from Sochi or Adler.

MINERAL WATER SPAS

The central Caucasus rises from the steppe in an intriguing landscape studded with dead volcanoes and spouting mineral springs. The curative powers of the springs have attracted unhealthy, hypochondriac or just holiday-minded Russians since the late 18th century.

Today the healthy outnumber the ailing in the spas, sanatoriums and hotels scattered across the region known as Kavkazskie Mineralnye Vody (Caucasian Mineral Waters, Минеральные Воды). The parks and elegant spa buildings recall the 19th century, when fashionable society trekked from Moscow and St Petersburg to see, be seen and look for a spouse.

Many of the 130-plus springs have, however, fizzled out from lack of maintenance. Those that remain feed fountains in drinking galleries and provide the elixir for sanatorium treatments of ailing bodies.

Pyatigorsk and Kislovodsk are the main resorts. The transport hub, Mineralnye Vody, lacks mineral spas of its own, despite the name.

Mineralnye Vody
Минеральные Воды

'Minvody' is the main air-transport hub not only for Caucasian Mineral Waters but also for skiing and hiking around Mt Elbrus and Dombay. If you arrive late and need a bed, the train station resting rooms (Komnaty Otdikha; ☑ 86531-47 380; Mineralnye Vody Train Station, ul XXII Partsezda; r per 12/24 hr R620/1100) offer clean, affordable accommodation; otherwise Pyatigorsk is only a 30-minute drive or one-hour train journey away.

❶ Getting There & Away

During ski season, *marshrutky* await planes arriving at Minvody airport and shuttle groups of people straight to the Dombay and Elbrus ski areas (per person R600).

AIR

Mineralnye Vody Airport (Международный аэропорт Минеральные Воды; ☑ 87922-20 777; http://mvairport.ru) is 2km west of the centre on the M29 highway. Flights to Moscow and St Petersburg are frequent and there a few international connections, too.

BUS

The **bus station** (Автовокзал; Sovetskaya ul 97) is about 1.5km east of the airport with these services:

Kislovodsk R100, 1¼ hours, 12 daily
Krasnodar R985, 7½ hours, 12 daily
Nalchik R200, two hours, 15 daily
Rostov-on-Don R600, seven hours, four daily
Teberda R460, six hours, daily at 2.45pm

Bus 223 to Pyatigorsk (R65, 45 minutes) departs every 30 minutes from ul XXII Partsezda near the train station.

TAXI

Sample taxi prices from the airport: Pyatigorsk R600, Kislovodsk R800, Nalchik R1500, Terskol/Elbrus R2500 and Dombay R3000.

TRAIN

Minvody is on the main train line and thus well connected to points north and south. The centrally located **train station** (ul XXII Partsezda) picks up all trains heading to/from Pyatigorsk, Kislovodsk and Nalchik.

Elektrichki service Kislovodsk (R169, 1¾ hours) via Pyatigorsk (R69, 50 minutes) roughly every hour until 10pm. There are also *elektrichki* to Krasnodar (R1000, six hours, Wednesday, Friday and Sunday at 1.08pm) and Nalchik (R312, three hours, 8.48am and 2.26pm daily).

❶ Getting Around

Marshrutkya 11 links the airport and train station, passing by the bus station. A taxi between the airport and train station costs around R200.

Pyatigorsk
Пятигорск

☑ 8793 / POP 142,500 / ELEVATION 512M /
☺ MOSCOW

The five peaks of Mt Beshtau overlook Pyatigorsk – a name created from the Russian words for five and mountain. The town began life as Fort Konstantinovskaya in 1780 and quickly developed into a fashionable resort as it attracted Russian society to its spas and stately buildings. Checking into a sanatorium is still big business here. The most urbanised of the spa towns, it remains an attractive place to spend a few days with lovely walks in its parks, tree-lined streets and up central Mt Mashuk.

Prospekt Kirova runs west from Park Tsvetnik at the foot of Mt Mashuk through the town centre to the train station.

⊙ Sights

★**Mt Mashuk**　　　　　　MOUNTAIN
(гора Машук) There's a fantastic view of Pyatigorsk, and all the way to Mt Elbrus on good weather days, from the 993m summit of Mt Mashuk. You can reach here either by hiking up a tree-shaded road or – easier – riding the cable car (Канатка; http://kanatkakmw.ru; bul Gagarina; one way adult/child R210/50, return R360/100; ☺10am-9pm Sun-Thu, to 10pm Fri & Sat). The best views of Elbrus are early in the morning but it's also a lovely spot to come to for sunset.

If you're hoofing it, Mt Mashuk is about a 45-minute climb from the cable-car station. You can also rent bicycles (p394) next to the lower cable-car station.

★**Lermontov Museum**　　　　MUSEUM
(Государственный музей-заповедник М.Ю. Лермонтова; ☑ 8793-339 731; http://domiklermontova.ru; ul Lermontova 4; adult/child R200/100; ☺10am-6pm Wed-Sun) Many Pyatigorsk attractions revolve around larger-than-life writer, poet, painter, cavalry soldier, society beau and duellist Mikhail Lermontov.

Pyatigorsk

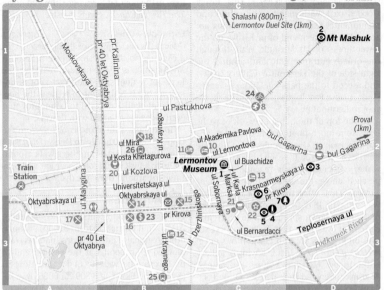

Shalashi (800m);
Lermontov Duel Site (1km)

RUSSIAN CAUCASUS PYATIGORSK

Pyatigorsk

Chief among them is this museum, a walled garden compound containing four cottages, including the pretty thatched one in which Lermontov lived during his final months. You can see original furniture, copies of Lermontov's poems, sketches and 19th-century trinkets.

Mt Beshtau   MOUNTAIN

(гора Бештау) Ask locals about hiking routes up and around this 1400m, five-peaked mountain that gives Pyatigorsk it's name. It's located a couple of kilometres northwest of the city, so you get a great view of the mountain from the top of Mt Mashuk.

Park Tsvetnik PARK

(Парк Цветник; ul Sobornaya) This lovely
wooded park with many architectural and
monumental features forms a 1km-long arc
around the eastern end of pr Kirova on the
lower slopes of Mt Mashuk. Walk through
the ornate entrance gate and around the
right side of the Lermontov Gallery (p394)
and ascend to the park via Diana's Grotto
(Грот Дианы; Park Tsvetnik), a favourite picnic
spot in Lermontov.

At the top of the hill, a network of paths
leads to a much-photographed bronze eagle (Бронзовый Орел) sculpture. Continue
northeast and you'll reach the Academic
Gallery (Академическая галерея; pr Kirova),
perched above the eastern terminus of pr
Kirova. This attractive classical building
was built in 1851 to house one of Pyatigorsk's best-known springs, No 16 (currently
closed). It was here that Pechorin first set
eyes on Princess Mary in Lermontov's novel
A Hero of Our Time. Inside a wing of gallery
is the Insect Museum (Музей Насекомых;
Academic Gallery; adult/child R100/50; ⊙10am-
9pm) housing a small collection of critters
(spiders, snakes, frogs) as well as a lovely
butterfly collection from around the globe.

Drinking Gallery NOTABLE BUILDING

(Питьевая Галерея; pr Kirova; ⊙7-10am, 11am-
3pm & 4-7pm) You can sample the local mineral water (small/large cups R2/5) here.
It tastes rather sulphurous, but the best
reasons for dropping in are the wonderful
mid-20th-century mosaics on the walls.

Proval HOT SPRINGS

(Провал; bul Gagarina; ⊙9am-5pm) FREE On
the south slope of Mt Mashuk, the Proval
natural spring lies hidden inside a cavern.
There is a religious icon on the wall inside.
Outside, a bronze statue of Ostap Bender,
the fictional fraudster who ran a ticket scam
here in the popular Soviet-era film and novel
The Twelve Chairs, greets guests.

Lermontov Duel Site HISTORIC SITE

(Место Дуэли Лермонтова; bul Gagarina) In
a clearing on the forested western flank of
Mt Mashuk is a monument marking the
Lermontov duel site. The exact spot is unknown, but it is thought to be near the nee-
dle-point obelisk devoted to Lermontov that
even today is bedecked with flowers.

To get here, ride marshrutka 16 from the
Upper Market to the Mesto Duely (Duel Site)
stop (five minutes). From there walk around
500m to a fork in the road, bear left and continue for around the same distance.

🏃 Activities

Full-day group excursions to Dombay,
Arkhyz and Elbrus (all from R1000) – among
other regional sightseeing destinations – are
hawked from booths at the eastern end of
pr Kirova; the website of Resort Bureau
(Курортное Бюро; ☑8-909 751 6006; www.ku-
rortnoeburo.ru; 1st flr, pr Kirova 27A; ⊙10am-8pm)
lists the tours in English, with prices. These
tours involve about eight hours of driving
and four hours on the ground at your destination. They also don't run every day (and
only if there are sufficient customers).

🛏 Sleeping

★Hostel Zhit' prosto Pyatigorsk HOSTEL $
(Хостел Жить просто Пятигорск; ☑8-988-108
8080; www.zhitprostohostel.ru; ul Yaklova 6A; dm/r
R450/1000; ❀❄🛜) A good location and
an international, arty vibe are both strong
points for this great new hostel. Dorms are
big, mixed and have a fun painting of a London bus on the side of the wooden cubicle

A HERO OF OUR TIME

The Caucasian Mineral Waters region is haunted by the Romantic writer Mikhail
Lermontov, whose tale 'Princess Mary', from his novel A Hero of Our Time, is set here. In
an uncanny echo of the novel's plot, Lermontov was killed in a duel at Pyatigorsk in 1841.

Lermontov was banished twice from his native St Petersburg to serve in the army in
Pyatigorsk: first, after blaming the tsarist authorities for the death in a duel of another
'troublesome' writer, Pushkin; and second, for himself duelling. Lermontov was challenged once again in Pyatigorsk for jesting about the clothes of one Major Martynov.
Firing first, Lermontov aimed into the air but was in return shot through the heart. Many
saw his death, like Pushkin's, as orchestrated by the authorities.

Many places in Kislovodsk and Pyatigorsk are linked to the man and his fiction, and a
visit to the superb Lermontov Museum (p390) in Pyatigorsk is essential.

bunk beds. There's a good communal kitchen, and washing machines.

Hostel Svoi
HOSTEL $

(Хостел Свои; ☑ 988 750 3800; www.hostel-pyatigorsk.ru; ul Krasnaya 5; dm/s/d R450/1100/1250; ⊕ ❄ ⊚) This clean, tidy hostel, on a quiet lane in the centre of town, sports a fresh colour scheme and shaggy rug-style blankets on the beds for those hankering after an Austin Powers moment. All rooms share bathrooms and there's free tea and coffee in the big kitchen-lounge with a balcony.

★ Bristol
HOTEL $$

(Бристоль; ☑ 8793-200 065; www.spahotel-bristol.ru; r from R3100; ⊕ ❄ ⊚ 🏊) The pair of armoured knights guarding the entrance to this hotel signal a note of old-world glamour, reinforced by motifs of antique maps in the decoration inside. Rooms are comfortable with modern facilities, and staff speak English.

There's a pleasant restaurant and separate bar (with some outdoor seating) in the hotel, which also has a spa and small indoor swimming pool.

Congress Hotel Intourist
HOTEL $$

(Конгресс-отель Интурист; ☑ 8793-349 249; www.hotel-intourist.ru; pl Lenina 13; s/d R2400/2900, renovated from R3000/3500; ⊕ ❄ ⊚) Pyatigorsk's biggest hotel, with 151 rooms, the partially refurbished Intourist is conveniently located for Mt Mashuk. The 'standard class' rooms hark back to the Brezhnev era, with their narrow beds and scuffed furnishings. Pricier renovated rooms are much more pleasant. All rooms have balconies, some with spectacular mountain views.

✗ Eating

Upper Market
MARKET $

(Верхний рынок, Verkhny Rynok; ul Levanevskogo; cheese per kilo from R350; ⊙ 7am-5pm; ☑) The ideal place to stock up on edibles for a picnic is this lively outdoor market. Vegetarians can find all kinds of salad and fruit items, as well as some local cheeses such as the stringy *chechil,* which comes in regular or smoked varieties, or the *brenza,* a soft white cheese with holes in it.

★ Shalashi
CAUCASIAN $$

(Шалаши; ☑ 8793-322 551; http://restoran-shalashi.ru; Lermontov Duel Site; mains R350-850; ⊙ 11am-1am; 🍴) This delightful Caucasian restaurant, surrounded by the forest 50m from the Lermontov duel site, has outdoor seating in round huts made

from branches. The house speciality is Azeri *sadzh* (a sizzling meat or fish dish served in a cast-iron pan with potatoes and onions).

Sakvoyazh
PIZZA $$

(Саквояж; ☑ 8793-392 555; pr Kirova 61; mains R310-990; ⊙ 10am-11pm Sun-Thu, to midnight Fri & Sat; 🍴) Apart from a wide range of tasty pizzas, this contemporary-styled restaurant serves several other dishes, including salads, steaks and pasta. There's also a kid's menu and a play area.

Art Café Nostalgia
RUSSIAN $$

(Арт Кафе Ностальжи; ☑ 8793-391 400; pr Kirova 56; mains R300-700; ⊙ 11am-midnight; 🍴 ☑) On restaurant-lined pr Kirova, Nostalgia has a pleasant outdoor terrace where you can dine on *pelmeni, pirozhki* (pies), trout, salmon and lots of other dishes, including vegetarian options.

Santa Fe
INTERNATIONAL $$

(Санта Фе; ☑ 8-928-267 3397; www.sf-cafe.ru; pr Kirova 69; mains R150-880; ⊙ 9am-midnight; 🍴) Stylish, with a huge menu (pastas, lasagne, steaks, sushi and over a dozen salads) and pleasant open-air tables. The ground-floor cafe has a hugely tempting display of cakes and pastries.

★ Daki
INTERNATIONAL $$$

(☑ 8-962-000 0000; www.daki-rest.com; 6th flr Arbat Shopping Centre, ul Oktyabrskaya 17; mains R500-2100; ⊙ noon-midnight; 🍴) The roof of a shopping mall is the location for this enormous restaurant, bar and nightclub with a huge outdoor terrace. The menu is big on seafood, steaks and sushi, all well prepared and presented. With live music on the central stage backed by an enormous screen, this clearly is the place for a major night out.

🍷 Drinking & Nightlife

★ Tet-a-Tet
CAFE

(☑ 8793-391 425; Kartinnaya Galareya, pr Kirova 23; ⊙ 11am-11pm) On the upper floor an attractive 19th-century building beside the entrance to Park Tsvetnik, this cafe, which doubles as an art gallery, serves a good range of drinks and sweet treats. Enjoy the breeze and leafy views from the wrap-around balcony seating.

Happy Coffee
CAFE

(Mikhailovskaya Galereya, bul Gagarina 2; ⊙ 10am-11pm) There's live music at 7.30pm most nights in this pleasant cafe, which occupies part of an 1848-vintage building. The arty interior design includes a mini paper airship hanging from the ceiling. The offerings of flavoured coffees, teas and desserts is impressive.

Tesla BAR
(☑8-962-428 8813; http://tesla-grill.net; ul Kozlova 28; ☺noon-1am) This stylish bar and restaurant is named after the Siberian-American inventor Nikola Tesla, whose image adorns the interior, along with naked light bulbs, LP players mounted on the walls like installation art, and other quirky touches. There's a separate covered verandah area out front for smokers and a good range of drinks and eats.

☆ Entertainment

Lermontov Gallery LIVE MUSIC
(Лермонтовская галерея; ☑8793-391 436; www.kursal.ru; Park Tsvetnik; tickets R200-500; ☺box office 10am-7pm) The striking light blue and beautifully proportioned Lermontov Gallery, built in 1901 in cast iron with stained-glass windows, is now a concert hall. It's well worth taking in a concert (both classical and popular music) at this architectural highlight.

ⓘ Information

Sberbank (Сбербанк; pr Kirova 59; ☺8.30am-6.15pm Mon-Fri, to 5.15pm Sat) Has ATMs.

Post Office (pr Kirova 52; ☺8am-8pm Mon-Fri, 9am-6pm Sat, 9am-2pm Sun)

ⓘ Getting There & Away

From the long-distance **bus station** (Avtovokzal; ☑8793-391 653; www.kmvavto.ru; ul Bunimovicha 34) there are numerous buses to Nalchik (R172, 1½ hours). The daily bus to Teberda (near Dombay) departs at 7.15am (R450, five hours).

An alternative way to Dombay is to take one of the regularly scheduled tour buses (one way from R1000).

The Pyatigorsk **train station** (☑8793-336 599; Privokzalnaya pl 1) has frequent *elektrichki* to both Kislovodsk (R101, one hour) and Mineralnye Vody (R69, 50 minutes).

ⓘ Getting Around

Trams 1, 3 and 5 (R19) connect the train station with the town centre along pr Kirova. *Marshrutky* depart from the train station and the **terminal** (ul Mira) opposite the Upper Market.

For taxis, call **Red Taxi** (☑8793-333 333, 8-919-733 3333; http://redtaxi.ru). A taxi to Mineralnye Vody airport (30 minutes) costs around R450.

Bicycles (bul Gagarina; per hour/day R150/700; ☺noon-8pm) can be rented from beside the lower cable car station.

Kislovodsk Кисловодск

☑8793 / POP 128,553 / ELEVATION 872M / ☺MOSCOW

This pleasant spa town has been a popular destination for Russian holidaymakers since the early 19th century, when the Romantic writers Mikhail Lermontov and Alexander Pushkin spent time in its verdant parks and rugged countryside.

The name means 'Sour Waters', but Kislovodsk has a decidedly sweet vibe. Despite the many tourists and sanatoriums scattered about, Kislovodsk remains relaxing to the core. The landscape is green, the many gardens well manicured, and the air, at nearly 1km above sea level, is crisp.

Pedestrianised Kurortny bul, running north–south from the post office to the Narzan Gallery, is Kislovodsk's main drag and spiritual nerve centre. The train station is just east of Kurortny bul up a smaller pedestrianised street, cobblestoned ul Karla Marksa. Kurortny Park spreads southeast from Narzan Gallery.

◉ Sights

Dozens of pleasant walking trails have been carved out of the lush, hilly landscape for the benefit of sanatorium-goers and visitors. Pick up a map of trails from kiosks behind the colonnade in Kurortny Park.

★ Kurortny Park NATURE RESERVE
(Курортный парк) Founded in 1823 and covering 1340 hectares, this hillside park is among the largest in Europe. It's riddled with walking trails past rivers, ponds, forests and formal gardens. The park ascends southeast from a plaza behind the semicircular **Colonnade** (Колоннада; pr Mira) to the peak of Mt Maloe Sedlo (Little Saddle; 1306m). There are several other entrances including the grand **Cascade Stairs** (Каскадная лестница; ul Volodarskogo 12).

It's a two- to three-hour hike from the base of the park to the so-called Olympic Complex (1200m), where you'll find the upper cable car terminal. On the way you'll pass various cafes, statues and other points of interest, including the luscious **Valley of Roses** (Долина роз; Kurortny Park). At 1065m you reach **Red Sun Hill** (Гора Красное солнышко; Kurortny Park), where, on a clear day, there are great panoramas of the yawning valleys and green plateaus of the surrounding countryside, including Mt Maloe Sedlo to the west and, on clear mornings, Mt Elbrus to the south.

Kislovodsk

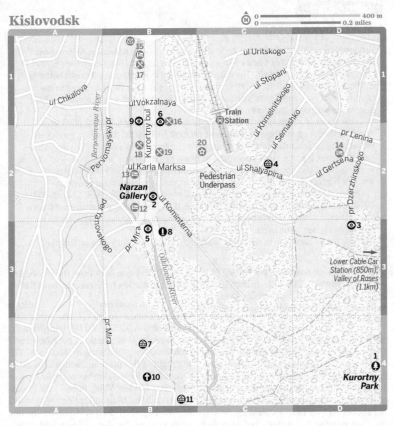

Kislovodsk

It's another 45-minute walk from the Olympic Complex to the summit of Mt Maloe Sedlo. Trails also lead to Mt Maly Dzhinal (1484m) and Mt Bolshoe Sedlo (1409m); Kislovodsk maps show all the walks, most of which are numbered and signed.

For a speedier ascent, you can ride the cable car. The **lower station** (канатная дорога;

ALIKONOVKA GORGE

Around 8km west of Kislovodsk is rugged **Alikonovka Gorge** (теснина Аликоновки). It's an attractive spot that trades on a legend about a boy who leapt from the nearby cliffs out of love for a local girl. The girl was supposed to leap too, but thought better of it. Those same craggy cliffs, shooting up from the gushing Alikonovka river, are now popular with rock climbers. There's pleasant walking here, too, and a natural spring where people come to drink the water.

In the midst of all this is **Hotel Zamok** (Гостиница Замок; ☑ 8-928-312 0003; www. zamok-kislovodsk.ru; ushchele reki Alikonovki; d R3500-5500; ❋ ☎), housed in a mock medieval castle. Standard rooms are modern and comfortable, but nothing out of the ordinary. However, the more expensive options boast beautiful beds and furniture, as well as working open fires. The hotel's Georgian **restaurant** (mains R300 to R750) has seats indoors in a baronial hall and the castle tower, as well as outside in wooden huts.

Opposite the hotel there's the more casual **Cafe Saklya** (Кафе Сакля; ☑ 8-928-312 0002; ushchele reki Alikonovki; mains R250-600; ⊙ 11am-11pm) serving Russian and Caucasian dishes in a rustic setting populated with a menagerie of stuffed animals (including a beer-drinking bear) and birds.

A taxi from Kislovodsk to the gorge is around R500 return, including waiting time.

☑ 8793-765 691; off Krepostnoy per, Kurotny Park; one way adult/child R200/120; ⊙ 10am-1pm & 2-5.30pm), close by the viewpoint over the Valley of Roses, is within 10 minutes' walk of the Cascade stairs.

★ **Narzan Gallery**　　　HOT SPRINGS
(Нарзанная Галерея; ☑ 8793-720 352; Kurortny bul 4C; cup/bottle of water R5/10; ⊙ 7-9am, 11am-2pm & 4-7pm) This graceful, well-preserved 1850s building recalls the spa town of Bath in England. Inside, the rich, carbonic Narzan Spring bubbles up inside a glass dome and spits out mineral-rich water – both hot and cold – into more than a dozen fountains. It doesn't taste that bad, and if you come here, you're obliged to have a cup, so drink up! Narzan means 'Drink of Brave Warriors' in Turkish.

Fountain　　　STREET
(Kurortny bul) An Italian company designed this circular fountain that performs a dramatic music and lights show (with even the occasional burst of fire!) every evening between 7.30pm and 10pm.

Ring Rock　　　NATURAL FEATURE
(Гора-Кольцо; off A157, Mirny; ⊙ rock 24hr, market 9am-6pm) This naturally formed archway, in a limestone cliff 10km north of central Kislovodsk, is an intriguing sight, despite the abundance of graffiti. At the base of the rock, and as good a reason to come here as any, is a market where vendors sell crochet shawls, woolly sock, sheepskin rugs and Caucasian hats made of felt and fur.

A taxi here and back from the city centre, including waiting time, costs around R400.

Yaroshenko Museum　　　MUSEUM
(Мемориальный музей-усадьба художника Н.А.Ярошенко; ☑ 8793-737 158; http://museum-yaroshenko.ru; ul Yaroshenko 1; per exhibit adult/child R100/free; ⊙ 10am-6pm Wed-Mon) The highlight of this museum, which is based in three attractive wooden houses in lovely gardens, is the 'White Villa' (Belaya Villa), housing a small but beautiful collection of works by Nikolai Yaroshenko (1846-98), a leading proponent of Russian realism and expert portrait painter, who settled in Kislovodsk in his latter years.

Yaroshenko's lovingly cared-for tomb is just outside nearby St Nicholas Cathedral. The museum has two entrances – one beside the cathedral and one from Kurortny Park.

St Nicholas Cathedral　　　CHURCH
(Свято-Никольский собор; ☑ 8793-730 717; http://jivonosniy-istochnik.ru; pr Mira 19) With five gold domes, this is a 1999 reconstruction of the original 19th-century orthodox cathedral destroyed during Soviet times in 1936. The interior decoration is dazzling.

Chaliapin Dacha Literary Museum　　　MUSEUM
(Музей 'Дача Шаляпина'; ☑ 8793-767 533; http://dacha-shalyapina.ru; ul Shalyapina; adult/child R100/free; ⊙ 10am-1pm & 2-6pm) The legendary Fyodor Chaliapin (1873–1938) lived in this palatial wood and stained-glass villa in 1917. Now a museum, it features paintings and photos of the Russian opera singer and

actor in various roles, plaster ceilings bursting with cherubs and fruit designs, and lovely glazed-tile chimneys. The museum also hosts classical-music concerts (R400) on Wednesdays and Fridays at 3pm.

Narzan Baths
NOTABLE BUILDING

(Нарзанные ванны; Kurortny bul 4) The Moorish exterior of the Narzan Baths, dating from 1904, is looking very handsome after a recent restoration. Unfortunately, the building has been closed for years and with interior restoration of the two swimming pools and 24 mineral baths ongoing, it's not clear when this building will again reopen.

Kislovodsk Museum of Local History "Fortress"
MUSEUM

(Кисловодский историко-краеведческий музей; ☑ 8793-737 039; www.museum-krepost.ru; per Mira 11; adult/child R150/75; ⊙ 10am-6pm) To secure Russia's new southern frontier, Catherine the Great built a line of forts along the Caucasus mountain range. Kislovodsk was one of them, and this local history museum occupies part of the remaining walls of that 1803 fort. Notable Russian writers, such as Alexander Pushkin, Leo Tolstoy and Mikhail Lermontov, were visitors to Kislovodsk, and you can see displays about them (all in Russian), as well as about Alexander Solzhenitsyn, who was born here.

Lermontov Monument
MONUMENT

(Памятник Лермонтову; Kurortny park) Near the Colonnade entrance to Kurortny Park is this multilevel monument to 19th-century writer Mikhail Lermontov. Caged in a grotto at ground level is an effigy of the red-eyed demon from Lermontov's famous poem, 'The Demon', believed to be his troubled alter ego.

☞ Tours

Excursion bureaus clustered on and around Kurortny bul sell trips to Dombay (R1200) and Arkhyz (R650), as well as a trip to Ring Rock and the local Honey Waterfalls. Contact the travel agency **KGBE** (Кисловодское Городское Бюро Экскурсий; ☑ 8793-767 420; www.kgbkavkaz.ru; pr Dzerzhinskogo 36; ⊙ 9am-6pm daily) for more trips.

🛏 Sleeping

Hostel Zhit' prosto
HOSTEL $

(☑ 8-988-708 3242; http://kslvd.zhitprostohostel. ru; ul Gertsena 3A; dm/r from R350/1200; 🛜) This colourfully decorated, modern hostel is a friendly place to stay with spacious dorms and pleasant private rooms that are good for groups or families. Not much English is spoken but the staff are friendly and helpful.

Hostel Outdoor
HOSTEL $

(☑ 928 307 3077; www.outdoor-hostel.ru; dm R350; 🛜) You can't fault the central location of this hostel, occupying part of the top floor a building next to the Drinking Gallery. The dorms are brightly painted and there are spotless large bathrooms and a kitchen area.

★ Grand Hotel
HOTEL $$

(Гранд Отель; ☑ 8793-733 119; www.grandhotel-kmv.ru; Kurortny bul 14; s/d incl breakfast from R3800/4000; ✹🛜) Pretty much living up to its name, this classy, perfectly located place offers friendly service and large, well-furnished rooms, complete with spacious bathrooms. Facilities include a sauna and the Vesna restaurant.

Pan Inter
HOTEL $$

(Гостиниица Пан Интер; ☑ 8793-728 877; www. hotel-paninter.ru; ul Kurortny 2B; s/d incl breakfast from R3500/4000; ✹🛜) Well-located Pan Inter has small but spotless, well-equipped rooms with a subdued colour scheme and shimmery fabrics. There's a small desk, stocked minibar and modern bathroom.

✗ Eating

Mimino
GEORGIAN $

(Мимино; ☑ 8793-722 288; http://mimino-kislovodsk.ru; Kurortny bul 6; mains R200-500; ⊙ 11am-11pm) This lively spot has an outdoor terrace set back from Kurortny bul. Start with piping-hot *khachapuri* and Georgian-style *solyanka* (a spicy soup) before moving onto sizzling kebabs.

Shokolad
INTERNATIONAL $

(Шоколад; ☑ 8-928-244 8006; Kurortny bul 19; mains R200-500; ⊙ 9am-10pm) Tired of shashlyk and *khachapuri*? Head to this modern, convivial cafe for good pizza, pasta, pastries, and a selection of tempting cakes.

★ 5642 Vsota
INTERNATIONAL $$

(5642 ВЫСОТА; ☑ 8-928-900 5642; www.novikovgroup.ru; Kurortny bul 13; mains R250-1000; ⊙ bakery cafe 9am-9pm, burger bar 11am-11pm, restaurant noon-midnight; 🛜🍴) Moscow's Novikov group ups the dining standards in Kislovodsk with this new three-part venture. An excellent bakery-cafe and burger bar (both decorated with murals by street artist Misha Most) flank the restaurant, with its open kitchen, appealing decor and mammoth menu featuring Adygean and Georgian cuisine.

The burger bar's veggie Greenpeace burger (R250) is an inspired touch and the luscious fruit tarts in the bakery are hard to resist.

★ **Barashka** CAUCASIAN $$
(Барашка; ☑8-962-493 9393; Kurortny bul 2B; mains R220-640; ☺11.30am-11pm; ☎🖉) Kudos to this convivial restaurant for its English menu and for tasty, well-presented food that matches the photos in that same menu. As well as traditional Caucasian dishes, such as the *khachipuri*, various shashlyk and stews, there are plenty of vegetarian options, too.

☆ Entertainment

Philharmonic Concert Hall CLASSICAL MUSIC
(Государственная Филармония На Кавказских Минеральных Водах; ☑8793-721 801; www.kursal.ru; ul Karla Marksa 3; tickets from R400) The North-Caucasus State Philharmonic play in this grand 1895 hall on a hill overlooking the railway station. Other popular music concerts with Russian singers and groups are also held here.

❶ Information

Main post office (Pervomayskiy pr 12; ☺8am-8pm Mon-Fri, 9am-6pm Sat, 9am-2pm Sun) There are ATMs here, too

❶ Getting There & Away

BUS
The **bus station** (Автовокзал г. Кисловодск; ☑879-375 7161; Promyshlennaya ul 4) is 6km north of the centre.

Frequent *marshrutky* and shared taxis leave from the train station for Pyatigorsk (R100, one hour) all day until late evening.

The easiest way to Dombay is on a regularly scheduled tour bus (R1200). Alternatively, head to Cherkessk and transfer there.

Other destinations include the following:
Arkhyz R469, five hours, one daily
Cherkessk R207, two hours, six daily
Krasnodar R984, 8½ hours, three daily
Nalchik R250, two hours, three daily

TRAIN
Trains depart from Kislovodsk's attractive **train station** (ul Vokzalnaya).
Mineralnye Vody R270, 1¾ hours, twice hourly (*elektrichka*)
Moscow *platskart/kupe* from R3200/R6500, 25 to 36 hours, three daily (3C express at 7.58pm)

Pyatigorsk R101, one hour, hourly (*elektrichka*)
Rostov-on-Don 1st/2nd class R2611/1120, eight hours, two daily (*elektrichka*)
Adler/Sochi *platskart/kupe* R2000/3500, 14½ hours, daily at 5.50pm
St Petersburg *platskart/kupe* R4350/7200, 50 hours, daily

Passenger trains also pass through Pyatigorsk and Roston-on-Don on their way to Adler/Sochi and St Petersburg.

CENTRAL CAUCASUS

Most visitors to the Russian Caucasus have their sights set firmly on the awesome Greater Caucasus mountains, in the central Caucasus (Центральный Кавказ), Europe's highest peaks by a considerable margin. There are 200 peaks over 4000m, 30 over 4500m and seven over 5000m, including the granddaddy, Mt Elbrus (5642m). Mont Blanc, the highest in Western Europe at 4807m, is exceeded by 15 Caucasus peaks.

But the statistics speak nothing of the savage beauty of these mountains, where smooth green foothills morph with brutal assertiveness into a virtually impenetrable wall of rock spires, glaciers and daunting cliffs rising hundreds of metres into the air.

The Greater Caucasus mountains are an adventure lover's playground. The two places most visited by foreigners for wonderful skiing, hiking and climbing are Dombay and Elbrus, but you can also organise some awesome adventures in Arkhyz and Nalchik.

Dombay & Teberda
Домбай и Теберда

☑DOMBAY 87872, TEBERDA 87879 / POP DOMBAY 657, TEBERDA 9058 / ELEVATION DOMBAY 1600M, TEBERDA 1280M / ☺MOSCOW

Even those well travelled in the world's most stunning wilderness areas can only gape in awe when they first set eyes on Dombay. Wedged into a box canyon at the confluence of three raging mountain rivers, the resort town is surrounded by a soaring crown of jagged, Matterhorn-like peaks of rock and ice, festooned with glaciers and gushing waterfalls.

So great is Dombay's natural majesty that the locals seemingly gave up on the town itself. Frankly, it's an eyesore, dishevelled and dominated by concrete hotels and abandoned Soviet-era complexes. Fortunately, it takes only a brisk walk or ride to put all that behind you. Local operators will do their best to make sure you see the best scenery – on foot, skis, horseback or by jeep or taxi – both here and in the larger town of Teberda, 22.5km northeast of Dombay, beside the Teberda river.

Dombay and its surrounding mountains lie within the Teberdinsky State Natural Biosphere Reserve. Three *ushchelie* (deep valleys) watered by glacier-fed torrents – Alibek from the west, Amanauz from the south and Dombay-Ulgen from the east – meet in the village with the Mussa-Achitara ridge rising to the east. Winding ul Karachaevskaya is Dombay's main street – you'll find most hotels, restaurants and other facilities along or shortly off it.

◉ Sights & Activities

The main activities are skiing in the winter and hiking and horse riding in the summer. Many local guides and outdoor adventure activity operators hang out near Sberbank on ul Karachaevskaya.

Teberdinsky State
Natural Biosphere Reserve   NATURE RESERVE
(Тебердинский государственный биосферный заповедник; ☑87879-51 326; http://teberda.org.ru; per Badukskiy 1, Teberda; R60; ☺9am-1pm & 2-6pm) This park has a small museum with stuffed animals and info on wildlife and geology as well as a mini zoo with deer, foxes, wolves and other local fauna.

You can arrange guides for trekking and horse riding here as well as follow trekking trails.

☺ Day Hiking
Many routes require a border permit and additionally may require a nature reserve pass (R300, payable at the guard post at the entry to the hike). It's a good idea to hire a guide, while some hikes, including Lake Turie in the Alibek Valley, require some mountaineering experience, as they may involve crossing glaciers and torrential rivers. There's also a bear population.

★ Mussa-Achitara Ridge   HIKING, SKIING
(Хребет Мусса-Ачитара) The 3200m-high Mussa-Achitara (Horse Thief) Ridge provides excellent skiing in winter and wonderful hiking in summer. Whatever time of year you come up here some truly memorable views of snow-capped mountains await.

Chyortova Melnitsa   HIKING
(Чертова Мельница) No border permit is needed to follow this 3km hike beside the Amanauz River to the 'Devil's Mill', a waterfall with good views of the Amanauz Glacier.

Head south out of town past the Dombay housing area and pick up the trail along the river. After negotiating a slippery stream crossing (icy through June) the path dissipates. Head uphill through the woods until the trail materialises again and follow it to the viewpoint.

Chuchkhur Waterfalls   HIKING
(Чучхурский водопад) It's a scenic, relatively easy 6km (two-hour) walk from the start of the first chairlift to two fine waterfalls on the Chuchkhur River. First, follow the vehicle track and then branch across the Russkaya polyana clearing and continue to the first set of waterfalls, the most impressive of which is 12m high.

Twenty minutes downstream from these falls, a 2km path forks south up Severny (North) Ptysh Valley to another waterfall.

Alibek Valley   HIKING
You don't need a border permit to follow this roughly 15km trail to Lake Turie, passing Alibek Glacier and the dramatic Alibek Falls, but hiring a guide to lead the way is a good idea.

Find the start by following the dirt road behind Snezhinka hotel for 6km up Alibek Valley to a mountaineers' hostel, passing a climbers' cemetery after 2km. From the hostel the trail ascends about two hours to the lake.

Baduksky Lakes   HIKING
(Третье Бадукское озеро; Terberda; R300; ☺8am-6pm) No border pass is needed to follow this trail from the Teberda River to these three glacial moraine lakes at 1971m, 1992m and 2000m. The walk starts from the suspension bridge over the river: don't leave here after 1pm, as you won't make it back in time before the bridge is closed.

☺ Lakes
There are several pretty lakes in the area that make for a fine swim on a warm summer day. The easiest to access is Kara-Kel Lake (Озеро Кара-Кёль; Teberda) just off the main road passing through Teberda; you can reach it by taxi or *mashrutka*. Also accessible by taxi is Tumanlykel Lake (Озеро Туманлыкель), around 7km northeast of Dombay.

WORTH A TRIP

GUM-BASHI PASS

One of the most scenic drives in the Southern Caucasus is over the **Gumbashi Pass** (Перевал Гум-баши; A157). This 95km road links Kislovodsk in the east and Karachaevsk in the west and is a great route for getting to or from Dombay. If the weather cooperates, you'll have sublime views of Mt Elbrus and the Greater Caucasus chain. There are a couple of cafes and several viewing spots near top of the pass, plus a rudimentary ski field with drag lifts in winter. You're sure to see Karachay herding their horses and cattle, too. A taxi between Kislovodsk and Dombay costs R3000.

Skiing

The ski season runs from late November until early May. Trails drop an eye-popping 1400 vertical metres to the valley floor. There is bowl skiing up above the treeline, as well as some mogul and glade runs for experts, and plenty of intermediate terrain. If going off piste, take a local guide.

The two cable cars and several chairlifts are run by different companies so you cannot buy a lift pass that covers all options. The **new cable car** (87879-58 005; http://dombai-kd.ru; ul Novaya Kanatnaya Doroga; cable car only adult/child R500/300, plus 1chairlift R850/300, plus 2chairlifts R1050/630; 9am-4.30pm Mon-Fri, 8.30am-5pm Sat & Sun) and chairlifts provide the best all-in-one-ticket, covering the route from the village to 3200m in three stages. The **old cable car** (Маятниковая Канатная Дорога; adult/child R400/200, per chairlifts on mountain R250; 8am-5pm) will get you up to 2270m from where you'll have to pay separately for two old chairlifts to reach 3012m.

Most hotels and several rental shops around town and on the mountain hire out skis and snowboards (R500 per day).

Sleeping

Rates double or triple in the ski season. It's also possible to rent private rooms or flats from the women who gather near the cable cars every morning.

Snezhnaya Koroleva HOTEL $
(Снежная Королева; 8-918-911 3332, 87872-58 370; http://snezhnaya-koroleva-dombai.ru; ul Karachaevskaya 39 & 41; d from R1500;)

These comfortable and good-value rooms have ample space to accommodate both you and your ski equipment. The hotel is split across two neighbouring buildings and includes a *banya* (R1500 per hour) and small swimming pool.

★ **Vershina Apartments** APARTMENT $$
(Апартаменты Вершина; 8-926-836 0064; www.apart-vershina.com; ul Karachaeveskaya 60, Dombay; 1/2-bedroom apt from R3000/5000;) Great value for money, these spacious modern apartments offer all mod cons, including heated flooring, fully equipped kitchens and washing machines. All have balconies with great views, there's a cafe on the ground floor for meals and, in summer, a rooftop pool.

★ **Andersen** HOTEL $$
(Андерсен; 8-992-009 0909; ul Alanskaya 7; r incl breakfast R2000-5000;) Dombay's most stylish hotel (with a whimsical interior design vaguely influenced by fairy tales) offers comfortable, contemporary furnished rooms and an excellent restaurant where at least one of the staff members speaks good English. It's popular with well-heeled Russian urbanites.

Grand Hotel HOTEL $$
(Гранд Отель; 8-928-923 8888; ul Karachaevskaya 62; d from R2500;) This central hotel has modern rooms with red-wood furniture, attractive bedspreads and efficient service. It's so close to the new cable-car station that from some upper rooms you can almost reach out and touch skiers as they ascend the ridge. Many other lower rooms lack views owing to new buildings surrounding the hotel.

Hotel Snezhinka HOTEL $$
(Гостиница Снежинка; 87879-58 279; http://snezhinka-hotel.ru; ul Karachaevskaya 121; r from R2000;) Follow Dombay's main road through the village to find the 'Snowflake' hotel. Rooms are clean and pleasant enough, especially if you go for the pricier *lyux* (suite) ones. There's a small tank of colourful fish in the lobby, a gnome in the garden and a big outdoor pool open from June to September (as well as a small indoor pool year round).

Hotel Snezhny Bars HOTEL $$
(Отель Снежный Барс; 87879-58 813; www.bar-shotel.ru; Dombay; s/d incl breakfast R2700/3000;) Snezhny Bars has nicely appointed rooms with red-wood furniture, comfy queen-sized beds and balconies with views. Upper-price rooms add even more space to

the equation. Follow ul Karichaevskaya after the cable-car station near Grand Hotel and take the third turning on the right.

Tarelka
CHALET $$$

(Тарелка; ☑ 800-555 4431; Mussa-Achitara Ridge; chalet R9400) One of the most unusual accommodation options in Russia is this vintage 'portable' ski chalet. Looking like a flying saucer that has landed in the heights of the Dombay mountains, it sleeps up to eight people at an altitude of 2400m.

You need to book the whole chalet, which is cosy, with a shower, toilet and small kitchen space. Open only between October and April, it's very popular with skiers and snowboarders, so book well in advance.

To learn more about these Futuro House pods, designed by the Finnish Architect Matti Suuronen, see www.thefuturohouse.com.

✘ Eating

Most locals belong to the Karachay ethnic minority and are Muslim, so it's their non-pork cuisine that is most easily found here. Look out for *sokhta* (a mammoth, sausage-like creation stuffed with minced liver and rice) and *dzhyorme* (a smaller sausage) as well as the ubiquitous *khichiny* (flat breads typically stuffed with meat or cheese).

★ Kafe Vstrecha
CAUCASIAN

(☑ 8-928-912 7703; Mussa-Achitara Ridge; mains R250; ⊙ 10am-5pm, May-Nov, 8am-5pm Dec-Apr) Given its location – beside the second chairlift station high above Dombay – the food here is very reasonably priced. There's a good selection of soups, salads and shashlyk, big steaming *manti* (steam palm-sized dumplings) and freshly made flat breads *khichiny* – with spectacular views thrown in for free from the outdoor seating.

Cafe Alibek
CAUCASIAN $$

(Кафе Алибек; ☑ 8-928-030 4033; ul Karachaevskaya 107; mains R300-600; ⊙ 9am-11pm Dec-Apr, 10am-10pm May-Nov) Enjoy the views of the nearby mountains at this cafe with a threadbare stuffed bear in the courtyard and friendly service. The tasty Caucasian dishes come in generous portions.

Café Kristall
RUSSIAN $$

(Кафе Кристалл; ul Karachaevskaya 103; meals R250-350; ⊙ 9am-midnight) As well as the usual Russian dishes and shashlyk this place specialises in Karachay cuisine, including various sausages. Specify weight (in grams) to avoid a hefty meal (and bill). Seating is

outside, on a covered balcony overlooking the gushing river, or in the dining room.

🔒 Shopping

Market stalls around the village and chairlift stations sell wool shawls, felt Georgian-style hats, woolly rugs and caps and bags of herbal 'mountain tea'.

ℹ Information

Dombai Info (www.dombai.info) Outdated on hotels and the like, but with some nonperishable information and photographs.

Sberbank (Сбербанк; ul Karachaevskaya 105; ⊙ 9am-noon & 1-3pm Mon-Fri) Currency exchange and ATM. There's also an ATM outside Vershina Apartments.

Rescue Service (Спасательная Служба; ☑ 87872-58 138; ⊙ 24hr) Emergency help, plus guiding and/or advice on more technical hikes and climbs.

ℹ Getting There & Away

All *marshrutky* originate at the **Ekspress grocery** (Экспресс) in the southwest of town. The schedule is displayed in the shop window. The *marshrutky* also pick up passengers outside Vershina Apartments. Destinations include Cherkessk (R225, 3½ hours, daily at 8am and 11am) and Karachaevsk (R120, two hours, four daily).

All buses pass through Teberda (R45, 25 minutes) and Karachaevsk.

For Arkhyz, the fastest route is to take the *marshrutka* to Zelenchuk (R180, 2½ hours, departing 9am), where you can catch an onward *marshrutka* or taxi (from R600) to Arkhyz.

RUSSIAN CAUCASUS DOMBAY & TEBERDA

ℹ BORDER PERMITS

Unfortunately, if you show up to Dombay or Teberda without a proper *propusk* (permit), your hiking prospects will be limited and you'll not be able to see much beyond the villages themselves. Foreigners require border permits for anywhere other than the village environs and the Mussa-Achitara Ridge. Permit processing through the FMS office (Отделение Управления Федеральной Миграционной Службы; ☑ 87879-22 260; Kyrdzhieva ul 1, Karachaevsk; ⊙ 9am-5pm Mon-Fri) is generally painless, but can take up to 60 days. Set the wheels in motion by contacting a local tour agency at least three months before your visit.

In ski season, frequent *marshrutky* shuttle people straight to Minvody airport (R700 per person).

A more expensive method of arriving is on a tour bus from Pyatigorsk or Kislovodsk (around R1200). Best of all is to hire a taxi to drive you over the Gum-bashi Pass (p400).

Taxis (ul Karachaevskaya) and 4WD to hire for day trips and transfers in and around Dombay wait opposite Sberbank.

Arkhyz   Архыз

☑ 87878 / POP 505 / ELEVATION 1450M / ☉ MOSCOW

Famed throughout Russia for its mineral water, Arkhyz is a small, scruffy but not unattractive village surrounded by some of the most beautiful mountain scenery in the Caucasus. The fast-flowing Bolshoy Zelenchuk River flows through the village, where you'll also find a souvenir market at the main crossroad. Around 8km down the road into the heart of the majestic mountains is the new Arkhyz ski resort with fast gondolas rising up from the 'Romantik' and 'Lunnaya polyana' areas.

🏃 Activities

The speedy gondola at the Arkhyz Resort (p48) runs year round to whisk you up to 2240m for spectacular views of the Greater Caucasus mountains. During the ski season there are also two chairlifts (one with its base at Romantik and one at Lunnaya polyana) covering some 15km of groomed trails to suit all grades of skier.

There's night skiing (adult/child R900/500) on Friday and Saturday and you can rent all your gear for around R1500 from the main service centre.

Talk to guides in Dombay or Pyatigorsk about the many treks around here. For major expeditions into the mountains you'll need a border permit – check well in advance with guides about this.

Rafting (☑ 8-928-389 4846; Krasnaya Skala, ul Beregovaya 4; R500 per person; ☉ May-Sep) and horse riding can be easily arranged.

🛏 Sleeping

★ **Pansionat Energetik**   HOTEL **$$**
(Пансионат Энергетик; ☑ 8-928-393 8777, 8-903-415 3087; www.arkhyz.com; ul Beregovaya 2; r incl breakfast from R1500; 🔊) Superbly maintained with some quirky retro interior design touches, the Energetik offers spacious rooms, all with balconies overlooking the rushing Bolshoy Zelenchuk River

and nearby mountains. Wi-fi works best in the lobby and the set two-course meals in the *stolovaya* (cafeteria; lunch/dinner R300/250) are a bargain.

Bicycles are available for rent (R200/800 per hour/day) and the staff can also hook you up with trekking guides.

Vertikal   HOTEL **$$**
(Вертикаль; ☑ 8-928-027 9962; http://arkhyz-vertical.ru; Turisticheskaya derevnya Romantik; s/d incl breakfast R2560/3200; 🌐🔊) So close to the gondola you could almost lean out of your bedroom window and touch it, the Vertikal offers the classiest accommodation at Arkhyz Resort. Rooms have modern furnishings and some contemporary art to liven up the walls. Facilities include a restaurant, a kids' playroom and a sauna.

Romantik   HOTEL **$$**
(Романтик; ☑ 8-909-493 2079; http://hotelromantik.ru; Turisticheskaya derevnya Romantik; s/d incl breakfast from R2700/4300; 🔊) At the base of Arkhyz ski resort, this modern hotel offers comfortable, functional rooms, as well as friendly staff. Rooms are split across two buildings with Romantic 1 being slightly more pricey than Romantic 2. Facilities include a billiard room, a kids' play area and a *banya* (R950 per hour).

🍴 Eating

There are plenty of eating options at the resort, with the largest restaurant **Tramplin 1650** (☑ 8-963-282 9990; Turisticheskaya derevnya Romantik; mains R450-550; ☉ noon-midnight; 🔊) also acting as the main après-ski venue during the winter season. Dining in Arkhyz village is basic, limited to simple cafes serving Russian and Caucasian dishes.

❶ Getting There & Away

All *marshrutky* pause at the tiny bus station in the centre of Arkhyz village before continuing on to terminate at Arkhyz Resort. During the ski season there are many more services, but year round you can expect the following daily services:

Pyatigorsk (R500; six hours) Leaves Arkhyz Resort at 2.30pm and Arkhyz village at 2.45pm, passing through Cherkessk and the airport, bus station and train station in Mineralnye Vody.

Kislovodsk (R430; five hours) Leaves Arkhyz Resort at 1.18pm and Arkhyz village at 1.30pm, and passes through Cherkessk.

For Dombay, catch the 10am *marshrutka* to Teberda (R300, 3½ hours) and transfer there or catch a taxi (R500).

Nalchik Нальчик

⬚ 8662 / POP 240,200 / ELEVATION 550M /
⬚ MOSCOW

The pleasant, traffic-prone capital of the Kabardino-Balkaria Republic straddles the rise of the steppes to the foothills of the Caucasus. Most visitors come through on their way to or from Mt Elbrus, but if you have some time to spare, there are a few things worth seeing, including a lush central park, an interesting museum and a chance for a side trip to the spectacular Cherek Valley.

In 2005 at least 14 people were killed and over 100 injured in fighting after Islamic militants took several government buildings. The last, much smaller-scale attack was in 2011, and currently Nalchik is a peaceful, busy commercial hub. You'll notice some increased security at the airport, train station and on the roads but there's little to worry about while visiting.

Two parallel main streets, pr Lenina and pr Shogentsukova, run southwest through the city centre from the train station on Osetinskaya ul. The airport and long-distance bus station are around 5km northeast of the centre, while the vast Central Park stretches down the city's southwest corner.

◎ Sights

Central Park PARK
(Центральный Парк Культуры И Отдыха) The large Central Park of Culture and Recreation (to give it its full name) offers forest lushness, small green lakes with paddle boats, an amusement park and the scenic Nalchik River, where locals take a dip to cool off on hot days. To get there, walk or jump on *marshrutka* 1 or 17 heading west along pr Shogentsukova.

Inside the park is a **chairlift** (Канатная дорога; Central Park; R200; ⊗9am-6.30pm), which ascends over a small lake to the hilltop **Restaurant Sosruko** (Ресторан Сосруко; ⬚8662-272 0070; off Profsoyuznaya ul; mains R250-850; ⊗11am-7pm May-Oct), an intriguing building designed as the head of local hero Sosruko with an outstretched arm and hand holding a flame. There are excellent views out to the nearby mountains from here.

**Kabardino-Balkaria
National Museum** MUSEUM
(Национальный музей Кабардино-Балкарской республики; ⬚8662-773 942; http://museum-kbrglav.ru; ul Gorkogo 62; adult/child R150/free; ⊗10am-6pm Tue-Sun) Local natural and man-made history is covered at this reasonably interesting museum. Labels are in Russian, but it's mainly a place for visual appreciation, with a good 3D topographical map of the mountains, colourful WWII propaganda posters, and art exhibits (some contemporary).

🏃 Activities

★**Elbrus Elevation** ADVENTURE
(⬚8-938-693 1514; http://elbruselevation.com) This new Nalchik-based adventure tour agency is a joint venture between American Shannon and Karbadian Zaur. Apart from climbs up Elbrus and ski tours at Dombay and Arkhyz, they also have great itineraries into the Cherek Valley including hiking or cycling. Among other activities they can arrange in the region are paragliding, ziplining and caving.

RUSSIAN CAUCASUS NALCHIK

DON'T MISS

EARLY CHRISTIAN SITES OF THE CENTRAL CAUCASUS

Some of the earliest Christian sites in Russia are to be found in the central Caucasus, where the medieval state of Alania once flourished. In Nizhny Arkhyz, an archaeological preserve surrounds the three **Zelenchuksky Churches** (Зеленчукский храм; Nizhny Arkhyz), originally built of stone in the 10th century and still in use today. A modern replica of a Byzantine stone chapel marks the spot on the main road from where pilgrims climb metal stairs to view **Lik Khrista** (Лик Христа; Nizhny Arkhyz), an ancient rock painting of the face of Christ, also known as the Arkhyz Saviour.

Around 7km north of Karachayevsk, on the way to or from Dombay, a dirt road leads uphill from the Ossetian village below to the early 10th-century **Shoana Church** (Шоанинский храм; im Kosta Khetagurov; ⊗9am-6pm). This remarkable stone building is perched on the edge of a cliff high above the Kuban River, providing spectacular views of the surrounding mountains.

Aushiger Hot Spring
HOT SPRINGS

(Аушигер Горячий бассейн; ☑ 8-928-081 9110; Aushiger Village; adult/child R100/50; ⊙ 7am-9pm) This large open-air swimming pool, 31km southeast of Nalchik, is filled with naturally warm water from the local hot spring. Locals swear by its medicinal properties. It's best experienced in the winter when you can sit in the warm pool surrounded by snow. *Marshrutky* (R50) leave for here from Nalchik's Zeleniy Bus Station (p405), or take a taxi (R500).

🛏 Sleeping

RGK Trek
HOTEL $$

(РГК Трек; ☑ 8662-720 612; www.trek.web-box.ru; Gorodskoy Park; r incl breakfast from R2600; ✳ 🛜) Beside the river flowing down the east side of Central Park, this attractive hotel and restaurant complex has spacious rooms with queen-size beds, sparkling modern bathrooms (some with Jacuzzi baths) and big windows to take in the surrounding greenery.

Hotel Rossiya
HOTEL $$

(Гостиница Россия; ☑ 8662-775 378; www.hotelrussia07.ru; pr Lenina 32; s/tw incl breakfast R2000/2500; ✳ 🛜) In the middle of town, opposite the musical theatre, the five-storey Rossiya has small but nicely renovated rooms with parquet floors, narrow single beds and big windows. The reception staff speak a little English.

Sindica
SPA HOTEL $$

(Синдика; ☑ 8662-492 626; http://spahotelsindica.ru; s/d from R3000/3500; ⊖🛜▣) Quite a way south of the city centre, but still within walking distance of the vast central park, is this reasonable, large Soviet-era hotel that's undergone some upgrading. The standard rooms bear the hallmark of regimes past but facilities get better the more you pay.

✖ Eating

Tameris
TURKISH $

(Тамерис; ☑ 8662-401 721; www.tameris.ru; pr Kuliyeva 3; mains R140-200; ⊙ 9am-10pm) Not far from Nalchik's soccer stadium, this pleasant modern cafe offers a selection of dishes from Turkey, as the owners once lived there. Also on the photo-menu are Russian and Kabardian food, as well as some delicious cakes.

Central Market
MARKET $

(Центральный рынок; ul Tolstogo 94; ⊙ 9am-6pm Tue-Sun) Browse the aisles of fruit, vegetables, cheeses and fresh-baked flat bread

to the ubiquitous strains of *lezginka* dance music in the central market, an ideal place for putting together a picnic.

Arabic Home
MIDDLE EASTERN $$

(Арабик Хоум; ☑ 8662-776 499; http://arabic-home.ru; ul Lenina 52; mains R250-400; ⊙ noon-midnight) If you can't face another *khachapuri*, head to stylish Arabic Home. Relax on a comfy sofa or take a window seat with a view of central Nalchik as you enjoy freshly made hummus and tasty falafel.

🛍 Shopping

Balkarskiy Market
MARKET

(Балкарский Рынок; off Kanukoeva; ⊙ 8am-3pm) Also known as the 'wool market', this is the place to shop for local products made from wool and fur, such as shawls, blankets, rugs and spectacularly shaggy hats. You're sure to find bear skins and stuffed animal heads here, too. The riverside location and shashyk stands make it a good place for an alfresco lunch.

Adyge Une
ARTS & CRAFTS

(Адыгэ Унэ; ☑ 8662-426 171; pr Lenina 49; ⊙ 9am-7pm) This excellent souvenir shop specialises in local Karabardian and Circassian items including fur hats, traditional clothing, pottery and beautifully wrought Dagestani silver jewellery.

ℹ Information

UFMS (УФМС по Кабардино-Балкарской Республике; ☑ 8662-777 536; ul Nogmova 64; ⊙ 9am-6pm Mon-Fri) You can secure border permits here – though the wait time is currently 60 days. It's easier to do so in advance through a travel agent in the Elbrus area.

ℹ Getting There & Away

From **Nalchik Airport** (☑ 8662-913 204; http://nalchik-airport.ru; ul Kabardinskaya 195) there's at least a daily connection to Moscow's Vnukovo airport, as well as three flights a week to Istanbul and twice a week to Antalya in Turkey.

Buses from long-distance **bus station No 1** (Автовокзал № 1; ul Gagarina 124) serve Mineralnye Vody (R250, two hours, eight daily), Pyatigorsk (R172, 1½ hours, 12 daily), Kislovodsk (R250, 2½ hours, four daily) and Terskol (R250, three hours, five daily). Another option to Terskol is to take a *marshrutka* to Tyrnyauz (R200, two hours) and transfer to a Terskol-bound *marshrutka* or taxi there.

From the **train station** (ul Osetinskaya 132A) there are *elektrichki* to Mineralnye Vody (R250, three hours, three daily). The Moscow-Nalchik trains 61/62 (*platskart/kupe* from R4555/7715,

36 hours) pass through Rostov-on-Don (*platskart/kupe* from R2190/3581, 11 hours).

❶ Getting Around

Mashrutky depart from **Zeleniy Bus Station** (Зеленый Автовокзал; ul Pacheva 54) for local destinations, including Aushiger hot springs.

Elbrus Area   Приэльбрусье

📳 86638 / ELEVATION 2085M (TERSKOL) /
🕑 MOSCOW

Mt Elbrus rises imperiously on a northern spur of the Caucasus ridge at the end of the Baksan Valley. Surrounding it, and flanking the valley, are mountains that are lower in height but equally awe-inspiring.

Most visitors come for the challenge of climbing Europe's highest peak, but there are dozens of fantastic, less-strenuous hikes in the area, and you can ski year-round on the higher reaches of Elbrus. If you're happy to pass on such activities, it's a pleasure to simply ride the cable cars and chairlifts, taking in the fresh air and stunning alpine views.

Mt Elbrus and its surrounding peaks and main resort villages all lie within the vast **Prielbrusye National Park** (Национальный парк Приэльбрусье), which has its office in the village of Elbrus, lower down the Baksan valley.

Closer to the mountains, you'll first hit the bustling ski village of **Cheget** (Чегет), at the base of Mt Cheget. Next is **Terskol** (Терскол), the ramshackle administrative hub. About 3km beyond Terskol the valley ends at **Azau** (Азау) where cable cars rise up Mt Elbrus.

◉ Sights & Activities

Skiing

The piste skiing on Elbrus is generally easier than on nearby Cheget, with terrain to suit all levels. The skiing beneath the lower cable-car station is good for beginners; there's also a kids' ski park next to the gondola base station. The uppermost cable car and chairlifts service a few steep and challenging runs for experts.

Year-round skiing is possible between Mir and Garabashi stations. From here snowcats bring advanced skiers a couple of hundred metres further up to the Diesel Hut, from where there are opportunities for off-piste skiing. These run regularly in the peak ski season (R1000 per person), but must be arranged in advance at other times – check with a local agency such as Elbrus Adventures (p407).

An all-day ski pass for the gondola costs R2100. Gear can be hired at most hotels or at numerous ski shops in Azau, Terskol and Cheget.

RUSSIAN CAUCASUS ELBRUS AREA

WORTH A TRIP

CHEREK VALLEY & UPPER BALKARIA

The Balkar are one of the two main ethnic groups of Karbadino-Balkaria. In 1944 all the Balkar, along with other Caucasus people, were banished to Central Asia, falsely accused of collaborating with the Nazis. When allowed to return in 1957, the new village of **Upper Balkaria** (Верхняя Балкария), 58km south of Nalchik, was established. This replaced 18 older villages, the ruins of which now dot the upper reaches of the spectacularly scenic Cherek Valley.

Aim for the restaurant **Tau El** (Тау Эль; ☑ 8-928-707 2393; www.facebook.com/HCTauel; ul Taulyeva, Verkhnyaya Balkariya; mains R150-270; ☺ 9am-10pm), which serves delicious shashlyk, salads and the buttery *khichiny* (flat breads stuffed with meat or cheese). This wooden complex, set on the Cherek Balkarsky River, faces the ruins of the largest of the abandoned villages. In their attractive grounds is a re-creation of what the old stone village homes looked like, as well as a small hotel with excellent rooms (R2000), should you decide to stay overnight and explore more of the area. There's a suspension bridge across the river here, providing access to the ruined village, which also has one of the most intact watch towers in the valley.

A journey into the Cherek Valley can be combined with visits to the Aushiger Hot Spring and the Blue Lakes (Голубые озёра; Babugent). You could charter a taxi for the day in Nalchik, or arrange a tour with Elbrus Elevation, with the option of cycling or hiking around 2km of the 125-year-old road into the valley, with vertigo-inducing views down the steep, narrow gorge.

Mt Cheget MOUNTAIN

(Гора Чегет) Expert skiers relish the moguls, steeps and glades offered by this ski area on the south side of the Baksan Valley. The piste occupies the lower reaches of 3461m Mt Cheget (Mt Donguz-Orunbashi).

Riding the **chairlift** (Cheget; round-trip R700, all-day pass R1200; ⊙chairlift 1 9am-4pm, chairlift 2 9.30am-3.30pm) up to 3040m, the raw majesty of the surrounding mountains is quickly revealed. To the west are the smooth, milky-white twin humps of Mt Elbrus, to the east the jagged peaks and near-vertical sides of 4454m Mt Donguz-Orun (Mt Donguzorun-Cheget-karabashi), with a distinctive glacier shaped like the number seven plastered to its side.

Cable Cars & Chairlifts

Even hardcore climbers will take one or more of the cable cars part way up Mt Elbrus. For general sightseers, they are a must.

The original way up is the **Elbrus Cable Car** (Azau; Krurozor station R500, Mir station R800, chair lift R200; ⊙9am-4pm) which transports around 30 people at a time in two stages to Mir station at 3450m. You can then ride a separate chairlift that goes up to 3680m. The system is cheaper and slower than the new **Elbrus Gondola** (Azau; Mir station adult/child R950/500, Garabashi station adult/child R1350/750; ⊙9am-4pm). With the opening of Garabashi station at 3847m, this is not only the most elevated cable car in Russia but also in Europe. This is as close as you'll get to to Elbrus' summit without climbing and the stunning mountain range views are certainly worth it.

Both the cable cars and the gondola run year-round except at times of maintenance during late autumn and spring, when they typically close one day a week.

Tour buses start arriving at 10am from July to August, and the queues at the base and mid-stations can be brutal – waits of up to two hours are common at weekends.

Hiking

A couple of easy, two- to three-hour walks start on the dirt road that climbs out of Terskol opposite the mosque and towards the white obelisk commemorating WWII losses. The dirt road's right fork leads up the Terskol Valley to a dramatic view of Mt Elbrus behind the hanging **Terskol Glacier**, dripping over a cliff edge. The left fork follows a 4WD track to an observatory (Международная обсерватория Пик Терскол; Terskol), with wonderful views across the Baksan Valley to Mt Cheget, Mt

Donguzorun and Mt Kogutanbashi (3819m). Neither of these routes require permits.

From the top of Cheget's lower chairlift, it's about a one-hour walk around the side of the mountain to **Donguz-Orunkel Lake** (озеро Донгуз-Орункел). Check conditions before starting off (snow cover on the ground is likely until July) and enquire whether you might need a border permit.

The situation with regards to permits is changeable. Check locally on the latest requirements before you set out and be sure to carry your passport.

Any walks towards the Georgian border do require a border permit. It's easiest to arrange permits in advance through a tour operator. Contact them at least 60 days before you plan to visit.

Tours

The best agencies are either active tour leaders or providers of specialist services for climbers, skiers and hikers. Most also offer 'light' packages for independent travellers, which include accommodation and logistical support, but no active tour guiding. English-, German- and French-speaking guides are usually readily available. Agencies can also help with visa and border-permit logistics and arrange guided climbs and treks of other mountains in the region.

As well as the following St Petersburg–based Wild Russia (p195) organises climbs of Elbrus using the less crowded northern route.

Viktor Yanchenko ADVENTURE

(☑8-928-225 4623; www.alpindustria-tour.ru) German-speaking, Pyatigorsk-based Viktor has climbed Elbrus over 200 times. He also speaks a little English and works with other experienced guides as the local rep for Alpindustria Tours, a major Russian tour company and outdoor outfitters with a shop in Azau.

Go-Elbrus ADVENTURE

(☑8-928-915 6753; www.go-elbrus.com) The German-Balkar couple in charge here are accomplished free skiers and mountaineers. Highly recommended for backcountry skiing trips, ski touring, ice climbing, Elbrus climbs and more creative ascents if you're looking for a private guide rather than a large tour.

Pilgrim Tours ADVENTURE

(Pilgrim-Tours-Бюро путешествий; ☑86638-495-660 3501; www.pilgrim-tours.com; Hotel Semerka, Cheget) This Moscow-based outfit is

MT ELBRUS

The two peaks of **Mt Elbrus** (Гора Эльбрус) – the western at 5642m and eastern at 5621m – bulge nearly 1000m above anything else in the vicinity. This volcanic cone has upper slopes reputedly coated in ice up to 200m thick; numerous glaciers grind down its flanks and several rivers start here. Although many come to climb or ski the mountain, cable cars carrying passengers as high as 3847m make it easygoing for those who just wish to admire the view.

The name 'Elbrus', meaning 'Two Heads', comes from Persian. In Balkar it's 'Mingi-Tau' (meaning 'thousands', ie very big mountain). The first (unconfirmed) climb was in 1829 by a Russian expedition with Khillar Khachirov, a lone Karachay hunter hired as a guide, apparently reaching the peak on his own. The lower eastern peak was officially climbed on 31 July 1868 and the western peak on 28 July 1874, both by British expeditions. For propaganda purposes in Soviet times, there were mass ascents involving hundreds of climbers. A telephone cable was even taken to the top so Comrade Stalin could share the news.

Climbing Elbrus

The climb on Elbrus is not technically difficult, but it's harder than, say, Mt Kilimanjaro, with which it is often compared. Climbing experience on ice is advisable, and a good degree of fitness is paramount.

The climbing season is between late May and October with July and August being the busiest months. Whatever the time of year, you don't want to take this mountain lightly. As on any 5500m-plus peak, clear weather can quickly turn into thick fog or worse. On average, about 10 people perish on Mt Elbrus each year. Do the sensible thing and take a guide.

The climb itself takes just one long day, but most climbers require at least seven days of training and altitude acclimatisation before attempting the summit. Climbers typically spend a few days in Terskol or Azau before taking the lifts up to spend a few nights on the mountain for further acclimatisation.

The actual climb starts around 4am from one of two points: the **Diesel Hut** (p409) (also called Priyut 11) at 4130m, from where it's a 10- to 12-hour hike to the summit; or the **Pastukhov Rocks** at 4700m, from where it's a seven- to eight-hour hike. Both are accessible by snowcat from the Barrels. Most people start from Pastukhov Rocks.

Ascents above 3700m require a permit. These must be applied for in advance from the **Elbrus Area National Park Office** (☑ 86638-78 620; http://elbruspark.com; ul Lesnaya 2, Elbrus; ⊙9am-6pm Mon-Fri). Tour operators or local guides can also arrange these for you.

A useful website for further information is www.elbrus.net.

a large, efficient company that leads Elbrus climbs. Their local office is in Cheget.

Geographic Bureau　　　ADVENTURE
(☑8-812-230 5794; www.geographicbureau.com) With nearly 30 years of experience, this St Petersburg–based tour company offers a range of Elbrus-related tours of between eight and 14 days, including ski tours and an intriguing Elbrus circuit.

Elbrus Adventures　　　ADVENTURE
(☑8-800-775 6709; http://elbrusadventures.ru; Azau; ⊙9am-6pm) The office for this efficient tour company is next to the cable car. They can arrange pretty much all you need in Elbrus, from equipment rentals and guides to accommodation. They are also the sole agent for LEAPrus 3912 (p410).

Mountain Guide　　　ADVENTURE
(☑8-906-433 3557; http://mountainguides.pro; beneath Alamat Hotel, Terskol) Krasnodar-based Sergey Baranov is the chief guide at this mountaineering agency, which has plenty of experience running climbing tours of Elbrus.

🛏 Sleeping & Eating

Expect to pay double to triple summer rates during the peak ski season (late December to early May). Also book well in advance for accommodation during July and August.

🛏 Cheget　　　Чегет

With a clutch of small hotels, slope-side cafes, market stalls and even an après-ski bar, Cheget is a more attractive proposition than Terskol, especially during the ski season.

Hotel Laguna
HOTEL **$$**

(Отель Лагуна; ☑ 86638-71 651; www.elbruslaguna.ru; Cheget; r from R3000; ☎) The most pleasant hotel in Cheget offers a good range of nicely decorated rooms and plenty of facilities including a laundry (R300), nice sauna and plunge pool (R1500 per hour) and the option of adding breakfast (R300) and dinner (R600) to your night's stay

Povorot
HOTEL **$$**

(Поворот; ☑ 86638-71 663; www.povorot.ru; Cheget; s/d incl breakfast from R3000/3500; ☎) This well-run hotel with English-speaking staff is popular with those who come to climb Mt Elbrus or hike in the area. Nicely furnished rooms have beautiful views of the surrounding countryside and amenities include a sauna and billiards. The hotel can also arrange permits, provide guides and airport transfers.

Nakra
HOTEL **$$**

(Накра; ☑ 86638-71 297, 8-928-930 6681; www.nakrahotel.ru; Cheget; s/d from R1500/2000; ☎) This stylish four-storey hotel has big, bright rooms and plenty of storage space for ski and snowboard equipment. It also has a good cafe, a sauna and a small plunge pool. Friendly staff can provide tips on hiking and arrange transfers to Nalchik and Min Vody.

Cafe Ai
RUSSIAN **$**

(Кафе Ай; Mt Cheget; mains R250-650; ⊙9am-3pm) This friendly cafe at the first chairlift stop on Mt Cheget serves tasty Russian and Caucasian dishes, as well as homemade wine (R100 a glass) and souvenir T-shirts. Look out for notices advertising guide services on the wall as you come in.

Kapitan Pit
BAR

(Капитан Питъ; ⊙4pm-midnight) The balcony in view of the ski mountain and Mt Donguzorun is a prime place to sink suds après-ski. They occasionally have live music.

🛏 Terskol
Терскол

Terskol may not be pretty, but it has a good selection of accommodation and its central location allows for relatively easy exploration of both Cheget and Azau.

★ Black Point Hostel
HOSTEL **$**

(☑8-928 722 2432; www.facebook.com/Blackpoint-hostel-104067390100529; Terskol; dm/s/d from R500/1800/2400; ⊜☎) Surrounded by pine trees, this black-painted wooden hostel has a hip, relaxed vibe with both spacious dorms and private rooms (a couple of luxury ones in a separate building were in the works when we visited). It's a breath of fresh air for the Elbrus accommodation scene and a great place to meet young climbers and skiers.

Hotel Salam
HOTEL **$**

(Отель Салам; ☑86638-71 471; www.salam-terskol.ru; Terskol; d from R800; ☎) On the main road in the centre of Terksol, this good-value hotel may not look much from the outside, but inside the rooms are comfy and cosy and improve on space and design the more you pay.

★ Kupol
RUSSIAN **$**

(Кафе Купол; ☑8-938-080 0243; http://cupolelbrus.com; mains R270-350; ⊙9am-11pm; ☎) Popular with climbers, this cafe is housed in a metallic cupola-shaped building and is decorated with photos from both Elbrus and Everest expeditions. Their minced-beef Elbrus cutlet (surrounded by a boiled-egg mince and with a deep fried potato coating) is tasty and calling out for Instagram.

Cafe Elbrusiya
RUSSIAN **$$**

(Кафе Эльбрусия; ☑08-967-422 5646; www.elbrus07.ru; Terskol; mains R220-400; ⊙8am-9.30pm) Squaddies from the nearby military base favour this place for its sizzling platters of beef and potatoes covered in melted cheese and enormous pizzas (big enough for two). The menu also has a wider than average range of salads, soups and breakfast items (served until noon).

The attached hotel was under renovation when we last dropped by. There's also an ATM outside.

🛏 Azau
Азау

Azau has a good range of accommodation with many new hotels. It's a better choice for intermediate skiers who want to be closer to Elbrus' groomed slopes. Elbrus climbers also usually end up here for a night or two before moving up to the accommodation above 3000m.

★ Azau Star Hotel
HOTEL

(☑08-964-032 6942; www.azaustar.ru; Azau; d incl breakfast from R4000; ❄☎▩) Azau's fanciest hotel offers high-standard, European ski-chalet-style rooms with balconies. The luxury VIP rooms come with spectacular valley views from the bathtubs! Service and facilities are excellent and include a *banya*

SOUTHEAST CAUCASUS

Why does Lonely Planet not cover these areas?

While the security situation in Chechnya, Dagestan, Ingushetia and North Ossetia has improved, the region remains volatile, and government advisories continue to warn against travel here. Poverty and corruption have created a fertile recruiting ground for Islamic extremists and shoot-outs between security forces and militants are not uncommon. It's worth keeping this in perspective, though. Violent incidents, when they do occur, rarely involve tourists.

In Chechnya, the most notorious of the republics, former rebel fighter Ramzan Kadyrov has brought about an uneasy peace for his Kremlin masters. Both Kadyrov and his feared personal army have been accused of torture and murder, as well as other human rights violations, most recently the persecution of LGBT Chechens. Elements of Islamic law are very much in force.

What Is There to See?

Adventure and cultural tours into the region are being organised by local expert guides such as Caucasus Explorer (☑ 8-499-653 9019; https://caucasus-explorer.com).

Dagestan, with a population made up of over 100 different ethnic groups, offers the 2000-year-old town of Derbent, listed as a Unesco World Heritage Site and graced by a magnificent ancient fortress. Other highlights include mountain villages such Rakhata, Gunib, Kubachi and Gotatl (the latter two famous for silverware), the sandy Caspian beaches and the 262m Sarykum dune, the highest in Europe.

Grozny, Chechnya's resurrected capital, boast modern skyscrapers that have locals comparing it to Dubai. You can also witness *zikrs* (sufi rituals) here.

Ingushetia is a spectacular hiking destination with medieval clan towers standing amid the graceful mountain landscape. The Ingush castle of Vovnushki rises from a steep cliffs on both sides of a narrow gorge. However, you will need to secure a border zone permit to access much of this area.

North Ossetian villages offer curious pagan rituals involving pies and sacred beer. Worthwhile destinations include the striking rock fortress of Dzivgis, medieval settlements in the Mamison valley, and a 'city of the dead' amid dramatic mountain scenery near the village of Dargavs.

Further Information

Human Rights Watch (www.hrw.org) remains a vocal defender of people's right to live without fear in the Caucasus.

(free for guests to use in the mornings), ice rink in winter and climbing wall in summer.

Free Ride HOTEL $
(☑ 86638-71 260; hotelfreeride@yandex.ru; Azau; s/d R800/1600; ⊙ cafe 8am-11pm) A great budget choice that's next door to Azau's old cable car base station, Free Ride offers attractive modern rooms as well as a lively cafe and bar serving a good range of Russian and Caucasus dishes. Take a peak at the upstairs dining room covered in evocative old black-and-white photos of the local Balkar people.

Shakherezada Hotel HOTEL $$
(Гостиница Шахерезада; ☑ 08-962-653 1575, 86638-71 327; www.shaherezada-km.ru; r from R2000; ☎) Offering big comfortable beds and highly patterned Middle Eastern–style furnishings, this is one of Azau's quirkier accommodation choices. It's steps from the new gondola up the mountain.

Mt Elbrus

No frills mountain huts and refuges on Mt Elbrus at or above 3800m include the Barrels (Бочки; dm R1000) and Diesel Hut (Дизель-Хат; dm R1000). Climbers use them as a base for acclimatisation before heading to the summit. Some operators have their own dedicated huts while spaces at others are limited, particularly in the high season for climbing during July and August, and should be booked via an agency. Be prepared for possibly sleepless nights as your head pounds from the lack oxygen.

★ **LEAPrus 3912**   HOTEL **$$$**

(☑ 8-800-775 6709; http://elbrusadventures.ru; dm incl full board R7500; ☎) For a touch of luxury at 3912m, LEAPrus is worth splashing out on. There are 12 bunks in two barrel pods with a third pod for the dining room and a separate (heated) toilet block (but no shower). Other perks include electricity, wifi, satellite TV, three decent meals, a guitar and out-this-world views.

🛍 Shopping

7 Summits Club   SPORTS & OUTDOORS

(Клуб 7 Вершин; ☑ 86638-71 717; info@7versh-in-elbrus.ru; Cheget; ⊙ 9am-7pm) Just after the turn-off to Cheget on the way to Terskol, this well-stocked shop rents all manner of mountaineering and hiking gear.

Elbrus Rental   SPORTS & OUTDOORS

(☑ 8-988-934 2644; http://elbrusrental.com; beneath Alamat Hotel, Terskol; ⊙ 9am-9pm) All your equipment needs for climbing or skiing on Elbrus and other surrounding mountains are satisfied here. The gear is high quality and new. Also here is the local office for the Mountain Guide (p407) tour agency.

ℹ Information

Beware of avalanches which hit the area with varying ferocity every few years or so – they are the cause of all the crooked trees you might see.

There are ATMs outside **Pansionat Cheget** (Пансионат Чегет; ☑ 08-928-693 9723; Cheget; Ⓟ ☎) in Cheget, Hotel Elbrusiya (p408) in

Terskol, and next to the Elbrus Gondola (p406) in Azau.

Elbrus (www.elbrus.net) Website with maps and practical information.

Post Office (Terskol; ⊙ 8am-6pm Mon-Fri, until 5pm Sat)

Rescue Service (☑ 86638-71 489; Terskol; ⊙ 24hr) Check in here before setting out for hikes. Look for the letters 'МЧС' on a fence near the Bayramuk cafe, a block west of the mosque.

For visas and border permits, go through one of the tour companies.

ℹ Getting There & Away

Marshrutky run to Nalchik from Terskol (R250, three hours) at 8am, 8.30am, 9.30am and 12.30pm. Alternatively, take a taxi (R1000) to Tyrnyauz and then a frequent *marshrutka* to Nalchik (R200). Taxis to and from Min Vody cost around R4000, to Nalchik R3000.

Arrange with tour operators running out of Kislovodsk and Pyatigorsk to use their excursions as a means of getting to and from Elbrus. Buses leave from beside the military base in Terskol. They do not pass through Cheget proper but only by the access road.

ℹ Getting Around

A taxi costs R200 from Terskol to Azau. Between Terskol and Cheget it's about 20 minutes' walk. In the ski season plenty of *marshrutky* and free shuttles operate between Cheget and Azau. Otherwise, walk or hitch a ride.

The Urals

Best Places to Eat

➜ Grill Taverna Montenegro (p417)

➜ Expedicia Restaurant (p417)

➜ Rosy Jane (p425)

➜ Nigora (p425)

➜ Azyk-Tulek (p430)

➜ Pashtet (p425)

Best Places to Stay

➜ Hotel Tsentralny (p424)

➜ Red Star Hostel (p424)

➜ Ecopark Zyuratkul (p431)

➜ Eva Hotel (p416)

Why Go?

Marking the border between Europe and Asia, the Ural Mountains (Урал) stretch from the Kara Sea in the north to Kazakhstan in the south. Modest in scale, they nevertheless proved to be rich in resources, and when Russia stumbled onto this Aladdin's cave full of lustrous treasures many centuries ago, the mineral riches filled the coffers and allowed Russia to expand into Siberia beyond.

Today Yekaterinburg, the largest of the region's towns, is a bustling centre and offers a base for exploring less-visited towns. Perm is a vibrant city home to some strong cultural attractions. Kungur has a spectacular ice cave, while the countryside offers hiking, cycling, rafting and horse riding. The conifer forest of the Sinegorye (Blue Mountains) makes the gently sloped ranges of the southern Ural Mountains look like frozen blue waves. Lake Turgoyak and two national parks are accessed from stations along the Ufa–Chelyabinsk railway.

When to Go
Yekaterinburg

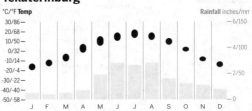

Dec–Feb Best for winter sports and culture.

Late Apr–May Fewer travellers in spring means little advance booking is needed.

Jun & Jul Street life, summer festivals and hiking can be enjoyed.

The Urals Highlights

1 Kungur Ice Cave (p418) Experiencing ice and a moment of pitch darkness.

2 Zyuratkul National Park (p430) Hiking into the mountain range or strolling the shoreline of Lake Zyuratkul.

3 Perm-36 (p416) Visiting the former labour camp and haunting Gulag memorial.

4 PERMM (p414) Making sense of the modern at this museum of contemporary art in Perm.

5 Church upon the Blood (p420) Tracing the historical contours of the murder of Russia's last tsar and his family in Yekaterinburg.

6 Nevyansk History and Architecture Museum (p427) Taking an excursion to the top of Nevyansk's Leaning Tower for spectacular views.

7 Capova Cave (p427) Admiring its ancient rock drawings.

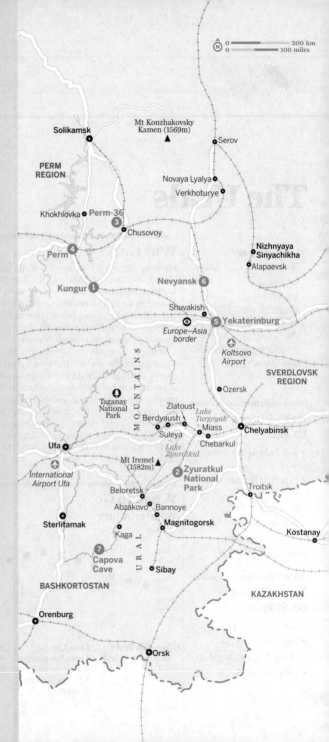

History

The Ural Mountains, running north to south and stretching from the Arctic ice to the Central Asian steppe, are one of the world's oldest mountain chains, the geological consequence of a colossal continental collision that occurred over 300 million years ago. Today the range marks the borderline of these once separate landmasses – Europe and Asia.

Before the arrival of Slavs, the region was populated by Uralic tribes, whose contemporary descendants include the Khanty and Mansi peoples of Western Siberia as well as the Finns and Hungarians of central Europe.

Slavic Expansion

In the 16th century, the rising Muscovite principality won a series of strategic battles against its tribal foes that finally opened the way for eastward expansion. Russian settlement of the Ural Mountains was led by monks, merchants and Cossacks.

Russia gained control over the lands between Moscow and the Ural Mountains through the work of St Stephan, the bishop of Perm, who built a string of monasteries and converted the native tribes. Seeking to exploit the natural wealth of the taiga (northern pine), pioneering merchants followed the clergy. They set up markets next to the monasteries, erecting great churches with their profits from the fur trade. Industrial families such as the Demidovs and Stroganovs began establishing factories in the region.

Industrial Expansion

The discovery of mineral wealth in the Ural Mountains during the reign of Peter the Great led to the first large-scale Russian settlements. Yekaterinburg, founded in 1723 and named for the Empress Catherine I (Yekaterina), wife of Peter the Great, emerged as the region's economic centre. Rich deposits of coal, iron ore and precious stones gave rise to a mining industry, including science and engineering institutes. By the early 19th century the region's metals industry supplied nearly all the iron produced in Russia and exported to European markets. The Statue of Liberty in New York and the roof on London's Houses of Parliament were made from copper and iron from the Ural Mountains.

In 1917 the Russian empire was consumed by the outbreak of revolution and civil war. Red revolutionaries and White loyalists fought back-and-forth battles across the Ural Mountains. Yekaterinburg became the site of one of history's most notorious political murders when Tsar Nicholas, Tsaritsa Alexandra and their children were shot in the middle of the night and disposed of in an abandoned mine.

The region figured prominently in the Soviet Union's successful industrialisation drive in the 1930s. Some of the world's largest steelworks and industrial complexes were built there, including Uralmash in Sverdlovsk (modern-day Yekaterinburg), and in Magnitogorsk in Chelyabinsk.

During WWII more than 700 factories were relocated to the region, beyond the reach of the advancing Nazis. The Ural Mountains became a centre of Soviet weapons manufacturing: Kalashnikov rifles from Izhevsk, T-34 tanks from Nizhny Tagil and the quaintly named 'Katyusha' (Katya) rockets from Chelyabinsk. During the Cold War, secret cities, identified only by number, were constructed in the region to house the military nuclear and biochemical industries.

The Urals after Communism

In the late Soviet period, a Urals-bred construction engineer turned anticommunist crusader was instrumental in toppling the Soviet system. Boris Yeltsin had gained a reputation as the energetic and populist-leaning communist governor of Sverdlovsk when the reform-minded Mikhail Gorbachev first introduced him to the national political stage, a move that Gorbachev would soon regret.

In his political fights against the old Soviet order and the neocommunists of the post-Soviet transition, the region provided Yeltsin with strong support. Despite the hardships that radical economic reform inflicted on the heavily subsidised industrial sector, the region remained a strong power base for Yeltsin.

As elsewhere in Russia, the postcommunist transition in the Ural Mountains did not go according to the early optimistic plans. The region suffered the severe collapse of its manufacturing and agricultural sectors. Public employees went without wages. Rocket scientists became taxi drivers. Mafia turf wars were waged over the right to 'protect' the nascent private business sector.

Today the region has recovered to become an economic powerhouse in Russia, and the main town of Yekaterinburg is the most economically dynamic and politically liberal town in the Urals.

Perm Пермь

☑ 342 / POP 1.05 MILLION / ⊘ MOSCOW +2HR

The word 'Perm' once meant a mysterious Finno-Ugric land encompassing most of the northwestern Ural Mountains that was colonised by Russians since the early medieval ages. But the city is relatively new, founded by the lieutenants of Peter I in 1723.

It is believed that Chekhov used Perm as the inspiration for the town his Three Sisters were so desperate to leave, and Boris Pasternak sent his Doctor Zhivago to a city clearly resembling Perm.

Located on the Kama River, Perm has long welcomed passers-by from various regions. Consequently, today's Perm is a cultural hotpot; the residents are welcoming and many of them speak English.

Perm has some interesting museums and cultural attractions, and is also the base from which to visit a great wooden architecture museum, located in Khokhlovka; the famous ice cave in Kungur; and a grim reminder of Soviet-era political persecution – the Perm-36 labour camp.

◉ Sights

Perm was one of the first cities in Russia to introduce the tourist line concept and has two tourist trails, both around 5km in length with signposts in English. The green line tracks the main architectural sights, while the red line has more of a romantic focus, with local life and love stories interlaced into the city's history. The Tourist Information Center (p418) has a free, multilingual *Green Line* booklet for self-guided city walks.

There are a number of good museums in town and every third Wednesday of the month entrance to most of them is free.

★ Museum of Contemporary Art PERMM
MUSEUM

(Музей современного искусства PERMM; ☑ 342-254 3552; www.permm.ru; bul Gagarin 24; R150; ⊘ noon-9pm Tue-Sun) This museum was opened in 2009 with the aid of gallery dealer Marat Gelman. At that time it was housed in the historic Perm River Station Hall. It moved in 2014 and today continues to play a pivotal role in the Perm contemporary-arts scene, with changing exhibits that attract a diverse crowd.

Museum of Perm Prehistory
MUSEUM

(Музей пермских древностей; ☑ 342-212 5657; www.museum.perm.ru/filiali/muzey-permskih-drevnostey; ul Sibirskaya 15; R120; ⊘ 10am-7pm Fri-Sun, Tue & Wed, noon-9pm Thu) The archaeological collection here encompasses over 2000 antiques, many from the Perm region. The highlight is a skeleton exhibit, where visitors will find a number of original and replica skeletons of dinosaurs and animals from prehistoric times. There is a big focus on the Permian period and animals unique to the area. Many of the explanations are in English.

Perm State Art Gallery
GALLERY

(Пермская Государственная Художественная Галерея; ☑ 342-212 2395; www.permartmuseum.ru; pr Komsomolsky 4; R120; ⊘ 10am-7pm Tue, Wed, Fri & Sat, noon-9pm Thu, 11am-7pm Sun) Housed in the grand Cathedral of Christ Transfiguration on the banks of the Kama, the Perm State Art Gallery is renowned for its collection of Permian wooden sculpture. Take trolleybus 1 to the stop Galereya, or trolleybus 5 to the stop Sovetskya, or trams 3, 4, 7 and 11 to the stop Tsum.

The brightly coloured figures are a product of an uneasy compromise between Christian missionaries and the native Finno-Ugric population.The Finno-Ugric population closely identified the Christian saints these sculptures depict with their ancient gods and treated them as such by smearing their lips with the blood of sacrificed animals.

Perm Regional Museum
MUSEUM

(Пермский Краеведческий Музей; www.museum.perm.ru; ul Monastyrskaya 11; R130; ⊘ 10am-7pm Tue, Wed & Fri-Sun, noon-9pm Thu) Located inside the imposing Meshkov House, this regional museum only gets really interesting when you see the small collection of intricate metal castings of the 'Perm animal style' used in the shamanistic practices of ancient Finno-Ugric Permians.

☈ Activities

★ Evrasia
ADVENTURE

(☑ 342-249 8222; www.permtours.com; ul Timiryazeva 50; ⊘ 10am-7pm Mon-Fri) Perm's oldest tourism company specialises in custom-made tours of Perm and beyond, with options spanning everything from city and Perm-36 tours to outdoor rafting, cycling and hiking trips. English-, German-, Italian- and Spanish-speaking guides are available by request and service from the Evrasia team is impeccable. The Evrasia office stocks maps and the *Green Line* booklet.

Perm

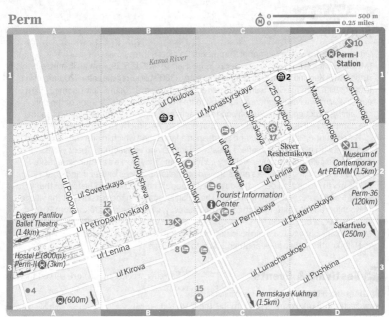

Kama River

THE URALS PERM

Perm

◎ Sights
1 Museum of Perm Prehistory	C2
2 Perm Regional Museum	C1
3 Perm State Art Gallery	B1

✦ Activities, Courses & Tours
4 Krasnov	A3
Permturist	(see 8)

🛏 Sleeping
5 Eva Hotel	C2
6 Hotel Astor	C2
7 Hotel Prikamye	C3
8 Hotel Ural	B3
9 Vicont Hotel	C2

⊗ Eating
10 Expedicia Restaurant	D1
11 Grill Taverna Montenegro	D2
12 Mishka Food	B2
13 Pelmennaya No 2	B3
14 Sister's Bar	C2

🍷 Drinking & Nightlife
15 Molotov Bar & Beer Shop	C3
16 Old Moose Pub	B2

✪ Entertainment
17 Tchaikovsky Theatre of Opera & Ballet	C2

ⓘ Transport
Aviakassa	(see 8)
Railways Booking Office	(see 8)

Krasnov ADVENTURE
(Краснов; ☏ 342-238 3520; www.uraltourism.ru; ul Borchaninova 4; ⊙10am-6.30pm Mon-Fri, by arrangement Sat) Offers active and adventure tourism such as rafting or cross-country skiing in the Urals, beginner Russian courses, river cruises and many more activities. The Russian version of the website has a wider and sometimes less expensive choice.

Permturist ADVENTURE
(Пермтурист; ☏ 342-218 6999; www.turizm-ural.ru; Hotel Ural, office 219, ul Lenina 58; ⊙10am-7pm Mon-Fri, by arrangement Sat) Located inside the Hotel Ural, Permturist organises excursions in Russian and English such as to the Kungur Ice Cave, as well as city tours in Perm.

PERM-36

Officially known as the Memorial Complex of Political Repressions, **Perm-36** (Мемориальный комплекс политических репрессий; ☑ 342-212 6129; www.itk36-museum.ru; derevnya Kuchino, Perm Krai; strict regime entry R300, special regime entry R200, excursion R100; ⊙ 9am-6pm Tue-Sun, tours in Russian at 10am, 11.30am, 1.30pm & 3pm), some 125km east of Perm, was a labour camp for dissidents from 1946 to 1987. It's one of the only remaining intact gulags in Russia and today acts as a museum, with exhibitions about the camp as well as changing displays that don't relate directly to life in the gulag.

It's a haunting site, isolated and set deep in a landscape which in summer is verdant and filled with birdsong. Countless artists, scientists and intellectuals spent years in the cold, damp cells here, many in solitary confinement. They worked at mundane tasks such as assembling fasteners and survived on measly portions of bread and gruel.

It's worth hiring a guide for the day to learn about the regimes and history of the gulag – and to get you there and back. The gulag is located in the outskirts of the village of Kuchino, about 25km from the town of Chusovoy, which itself is 100km from Perm. You can take a bus bound for Chusovoy or Lysva, get off at Tyomnaya (R200, two hours) station, walk back to the main road and backtrack to the Kuchino turn-off (also leading to (Makhnutino), then walk another 2.5km to the village.

⭐ Festivals & Events

⭐ **Diaghilev Festival**　　　PERFORMING ARTS
(www.diaghilevfest.ru) Perm is said to be the third ballet mecca, following Moscow and St Petersburg. Every two years the Diaghilev Festival (named after the famous Russian ballet star Sergey Diaghilev) attracts arts fans with its rich ballet and opera program.

Kamwa Festival　　　CULTURAL
(www.kamwa.ru) The annual 'ethno-futuristic' Kamwa Festival held in summer in Perm and Khokhlovka brings together ancient ethno-Ugric traditions and modern art, music and fashion. Dates vary considerably each year – see the website.

🛏 Sleeping

Hostel P　　　HOSTEL $
(☑ 342-214 7847; www.permhostel.ru; ul Lenina 67; dm R400-700; ✳🛜) Nine clean and pleasant rooms make up this friendly hostel, located close to Perm-II railway station, about 15 minutes' walk to the centre of town. There's a bright kitchen where guests can cook their own food as well as laundry facilities (for an additional fee).

⭐ **Eva Hotel**　　　BOUTIQUE HOTEL $$
(☑ 342-212 5858; www.eva-hotel.ru; ul Permskaya 63/1; incl breakfast s R3100-3800, d R3500-4200; P✳🛜🐾) Located in the centre of town on a quiet street, Eva Hotel is a delightful boutique stay with just 10 light-filled rooms. Staff are courteous and tasty breakfasts (changing weekly menu) are served in your room.

Vicont Hotel　　　BOUTIQUE HOTEL $$
(☑ 342-215 5670; www.hotelvicont.ru; ul Sovetskaya 40; incl breakfast s 3200-5000, d R3600-5300; ⊖✳🛜) A pleasant boutique hotel located close to all the city attractions, Vicont Hotel has nine double rooms, with continental breakfasts served in-room or in the on-site cafe.

Hotel Ural　　　HOTEL $$$
(Гостиница Урал; ☑ 342-218 6262; www.hotel-ural.com; ul Lenina 58; incl breakfast s R2700-7200, d R3600-12,400; ⊖@🛜) This one-time Soviet monolith rising up in the heart of the city has adapted to the age and boasts a shimmering, high-tech lobby and modern, reasonably sized rooms.

Hotel Prikamye　　　HOTEL $$$
(Отель Прикамье; ☑ 342-219 0840; www.prikamie-hotel.ru; pr Komsomolsky 27; incl breakfast s R3300-4600, d R3800-5300, ste R5600; ⊖🛜) Nicely spruced-up rooms in this former Soviet eyesore make Prikamye a very decent option. Deals are better if you book well ahead on the web.

Hotel Astor　　　HOTEL $$$
(Гостиница Астор; ☑ 342-212 2212; www.astorhotel.ru; ul Petropavlovskaya 40; incl breakfast s R3800-4300, d R4600-5600; ⊖✳🛜) 🐾 Spotless white dominates this hotel's colour scheme. It's a favourite among business travellers, and rooms are low-allergy.

Eating

Pelmennaya No 2
RUSSIAN $

(Пельменная No. 2; ☑342-212 3895; ul Lenina 47; pelmeni R160-340) Designed to depict a typical Russian *dacha*, Pelmennya No 2 is where the masses come for *pelmeni*. There's a wide selection of famous Russian dumplings, with everything from chicken to pork to fish. Pelmennya No 1 – part of the same chain and located a few blocks from the city centre – is a quieter option.

Sister's Bar
CAFE $

(☑342-259 2515; ul Lenina 54a; mains R240-440; ⊙11am-midnight Sun-Thu, to 1am Fri & Sat) Sisters Alaya and Ksenia opened this cafe in 2013 wanting to break away from their corporate jobs. The sisters enjoy Cantonese cuisine and food from the Basque region of Spain, so they serve a selection of dishes that are a bit of a mishmash. The indoor space is light and airy and there's a balcony that fills up in summer.

Mishka Food
CAFE $

(☑342-203 0352; ul Osinskaya 19; mains R160-380; ⊙10am-10pm; 🖥) Craving poached eggs? At Mishka Food there's a decent selection of modern cafe breakfast items available until 4pm. Breakfast, lunch or dinner, all the options are based on seasonal ingredients and look ever so pretty – make your decision by checking out mishka.food on Instagram.

Permskaya Kukhnya
RUSSIAN $$

(Пермская Кухня; ☑342-244 1355; ul Gazety Zvezda 75; mains R219-369; ⊙11am-11pm; ❄🖥☑) You can try Bashkir, Tatar, Russian and Finno-Ugric cuisine at this quirky and newly refurbished restaurant-museum. The manager is passionate about sharing his love for regional cuisine and might pop over to see what you think of the (sometimes) unusual menu offerings. Try the green soup – it's made from an endemic wild herb that only grows in the region.

Sakartvelo
GEORGIAN $$

(Сакартвело; ☑342-206 2929; www.sakartvelo-perm.ru; ul Maksima Gorkogo 58; mains R350-900; ⊙11am-midnight Sun-Fri, to 2am Sat; 🖥☑) This excellent Georgian restaurant makes good use of chilli in its dishes, including the excellent Tbilisi salad, a borsch with a chilli edge, and a good variety of shashlyk (meat kebab), served in a lavish but homely interior. There's a second location on ul Monastyrskya 12a.

★Expedicia Restaurant
RUSSIAN $$$

(Ресторан Экспедиция; ☑342-205 5975; www.expedicia-perm.ru; ul Monastyrskaya 3a; mains R570-1680, business lunches from R350; ⊙noon-last guest leaves daily; ❄) If you're happy to splash out you'll find spectacular northern Russian cuisine served here, with wild game and local fish dishes highly recommended. There's also a *banya*, a hotel and a gift shop for those who want to stay awhile.

Grill Taverna Montenegro
BALKAN $$$

(Гриль-Таверна Монтенегро; ☑342-212 1231; ul Maxima Gorkogo 28; mains R450-1960; ⊙noon-midnight Mon-Sat, 1pm-10pm Sun; 🖥) The trompe l'œil village fresco downstairs, upstairs pseudo-portico and outdoor terrace lend nice touches to this excellent restaurant. The Kalmyk lamb kebab is superbly grilled.

🍺 Drinking & Nightlife

★Molotov Bar & Beer Shop
BREWERY

(☑342-243 0326; ul Lunacharskogo 62b; ⊙6-11pm Tue-Thu, 5pm-1am Fri & Sat, to 11pm Sun) Molotov Brewery has been making its own Russian craft beers since 2012 – and in 2016 it opened a bar, which fills up with a beer-loving crowd most nights. The changing menu includes local and Russian beers, with at least five from Perm on sale at any one time. Usual pub fare, such as pizzas and burgers, is available.

Old Moose Pub
PUB

(☑342-203 2014; pr Komsomolsky 14; ⊙2pm-1am Sun-Thu, to 3am Fri & Sat) Owner Illya set out to open a pub that served the best international beers in town. He succeeded and today attracts a diverse crowd with his wide selection of predominantly Belgian, English, Czech and German beers, both draft and bottled. There are two more locations in the city, with the same huge list of beer variants.

☆ Entertainment

Evgeny Panfilov Ballet Theatre
BALLET

(Балет Евгения Панфилова; ☑342-271 6101; www.balletpanfilov.ru; ul Petropavlovskaya 185) A wide range of dance performances are held here, some quite unique and memorable – such as performances by the 'Eugene Panfilov Ballet of the Fat' group. Ticket prices are usually in the R200 to R500 range.

Tchaikovsky Theatre of Opera & Ballet
THEATRE

(Театр оперы и балета Чайковского; ☑ticket office 342-212 3087; www.arabesque.permonline.

ru; ul Petropavlovskaya 25; ⊘ ticket office 10am-2pm & 3-7pm) Performances by students of one of Russia's top ballet schools. Prices range from about R100 to R1000, depending on seat and performance.

ⓘ Information

Main Post Office (ul Lenina 28; ⊘ 8am-10pm Mon-Fri, 9am-6pm Sat & Sun)

Tourist Information Center (Туристский информационный центр; ☑ 342-241 1080; www.visitperm.ru; ul Lenina 39; ⊘ 9am-7pm Mon-Fri, 10am-6pm Sat & Sun) The Perm Region Tourist Centre has a wealth of information about Perm city and Perm region. There are plenty of information booklets in English and English-speaking staff members are happy to help with any queries. They are also responsive to emails and it is generally one of the most helpful tourist centres in the country.

ⓘ Getting There & Away

Inside the Hotel Ural you will find a **railways booking office** (☑ 342-233 0203; ⊘ 8am-7pm Mon-Fri, to 6pm Sat & Sun) and an **Aviakassa** (☑ 342-233 2509; ⊘ 8.30am-8pm Mon-Fri, 10am-5pm Sat & Sun).

AIR

Several airlines fly to Moscow (from R4400, two hours, frequent).

BOAT

The river station (Речной вокзал) is at the eastern end of ul Monastyrskaya, in front of Perm-I station. Boats do short tours of the Kama in the navigation season. Evrasia (p414) and Permturist (p415) can organise tours.

BUS

From the **bus station** (Автовокзал; ☑ 342-236 4434; www.avperm.ru; ul Revolyutsii 68) numerous buses go to Kungur (R258, 1¼ hours); there are frequent buses to Khokhlovka (R118, 1½ hours) and two daily buses to Ufa (R1300, 11½ hours). Buses to Kazan depart every two days, with some additional serves Friday and Saturday (R1500, 12 hours).

TRAIN

Perm-II, the city's major train station, 3km southwest of the centre, is on the trans-Siberian route. Many trains travel the route to/from Moscow, including all of the trans-Siberian *firmeny* (premium, long-distance) trains. If you're on a tighter budget, many cheaper trains do the route from R1890. Heading east, the next major stop on the trans-Siberian route is Yekaterinburg (*platskart/kupe* R1000/1444, six hours). For Kazan (R1300, 19 hours) the most direct route is with an inconvenient change in Izhevsk. Buses

can be better. Note that some trains depart from the *gornozavodskoe napravlenie* (mining track) on the north side of Perm-II, as opposed to the *glavnoe napravlenie* (main track). Trains to the east never depart from the mining track, only those to the north and west.

ⓘ Getting Around

Bus 42 and *marshrutka* (fixed-route minibus) 1t go between the bus station and the airport. Trolleybus 5 connects Perm-II station with Hotel Ural, tram 7 connects Perm-II with the corner of ul Lenina and ul Maksima Gorkogo via ul Petropavlovskaya, and tram 11 connects ul Maxima Gorkogo with the central market (about 400m from the bus station) via ul Petropavlovskaya and ul Borchaninova.

Kungur   Кунгур

☑ 34271 / POP 66,000 / ⊘ MOSCOW +2HR

Kungur's main attraction is the frozen magic of its ice cave (Кунгурская ледяная пещера; ☑ 342-716 2602; www.kungurcave.ru; Filippovka village, Kungur rayon; guided tour R600-700, with laser show R700-800, private tour R1500; ⊘ 10am-4pm, extended hours in summer). The network of caves stretches for more than 5km, although only about 1.5km are accessible. The ancient Finno-Ugric inhabitants of the region believed the cave to be the home of an underground creature, and the grottoes are adorned with ice formations and frozen lakes, although these are best seen in winter as most grottoes have minimal ice at other times.

The Ice Cave is about 5km out of town and you can enter only on guided tours. Bring warm clothes. The cost of the tour includes admission to a small museum on the site with displays of rocks and fossils.

The town itself is a little rundown and belies a skyline graced by a multitude of pretty church cupolas, including the 18th-century Tikhvinskaya Church in the centre and the Transfiguration Church on the other bank of the Sylva.

The beautiful countryside surrounding Kungur is great for outdoor sports, and bicycles as well as rafts, canoes and cross-country skis can be hired inexpensively at Stalagmit.

🛏 Sleeping & Eating

Stalagmit Tourist Complex   HOTEL $ (☑ 342-716 2602; www.hotel.kungurcave.ru; Kunger Cave; incl breakfast s R800-2000, d R1400-3000; ⊖ ⊛ 🖾 ≋) This popular complex is close to the cave entrance and offers excellent rooms with their own bathroom (the cheaper ones don't have fridges and TV). Take bus 9 from the train station to the last stop.

Hotel Iren
HOTEL $$

(Гостиница Ирень; ☑ 342-713 2270; www.hotel. kungur.ru; ul Lenina 30; r without bathroom R830-1830, incl breakfast s R1300-1800, d R2200-2500; ☺☏) In the centre of town, Hotel Iren is good value, but it doesn't have a lift. Even the rooms without bathrooms are pleasant enough, and the shared toilets and showers are very clean.

Tri Medvedya
RUSSIAN $

(Три медведя; ☑ 342-713 6739; ul Vorovskaya 5; mains from R200; ☺noon-2am Sun-Thu, to 3am Sat & Sun; ☏) Across the bridge in the centre of town, the riverside cafe-disco Tri Medvedya has very decent food. Helpful staff can order a taxi for you back to the bus and train stations.

❶ Getting There & Around

Located on the Trans-Siberian route, Kungur is served from Perm by frequent intercity trains (R400 to R670, 1½ hours), suburban trains (R175, 2¼ hours, four daily) and trains to/from Yekaterinburg (R463 to R1358, four hours). Bus is the best option from Perm, however, with departures every one to two hours; the most convenient leaves Perm at 8.25am or 9.25am and returns from Kungur at 6.40pm or 7.55pm (R214, 2½ hours). Buses to Ufa (R840, one daily) depart at 10am.

In Kungur, the bus and train stations are located alongside each other. Bus 9 (every one to two hours) plies the route between Hotel Iren, the train and bus stations, and the Stalagmit complex.

Yekaterinburg
Екатеринбург

☑ 343 / POP 1.5 MILLION / ☺ MOSCOW +2HR

Gem rush, miners' mythology, the execution of the Romanovs, the rise of Russia's first president, Boris Yeltsin, and gangster feuds of the 1990s – Yekaterinburg is not only Russia's fourth-largest city, it's like a piece of conceptual art with a fascinating historical subtext.

Bustling but less than startling on the outside, the political capital of the Ural Mountains is overflowing with history and culture, while its economic growth is manifested in a thriving restaurant scene and, as in many other regional capitals, in atrociously trafficked avenues.

With one of the best international airports in Russia and quite a few agencies experienced in dealing with foreign travellers, Yekaterinburg is a good base camp for exploring the Ural Mountains.

KHOKHLOVKA

For a day trip from Perm, travel some 45km north to this village where you'll find an impressive **Architectural-Eth-nographic Museum** (Архитектурно-этнографический музей; http://heritage. perm.ru/hohlovka/; R120; ☺10am-6pm, closed last Mon in month). Its impressive collection of wooden buildings includes two churches dating from the turn of the 18th century. Most of the structures are from the 19th or early 20th centuries, including an old firehouse, a salt-production facility and a Khanty izba (traditional wooden cottage).

A few buses a day serve Khokhlovka (Хохловка) from Perm (R118, 1½ hours), the best departing Perm at 9.55am and returning from Khokhlovka at 4.30pm.

History

Yekaterinburg was founded as a factory-fort in 1723 as part of Peter the Great's push to exploit the Ural region's mineral riches. The city was named after two Catherines: Peter's wife (later Empress Catherine I), and the Russian patron saint of mining.

The city is notorious, however, for being the place where the Bolsheviks murdered Tsar Nicholas II and his family in July 1918. Six years later, the town was renamed Sverdlovsk, after Yakov Sverdlov, a leading Bolshevik who was Vladimir Lenin's right-hand man until his death in the flu epidemic of 1919. The region still bears Sverdlov's name.

WWII turned Sverdlovsk into a major industrial centre, as hundreds of factories were transferred here from vulnerable areas west of the Ural Mountains. The city was closed to foreigners until 1990 because of its many defence plants.

During the late 1970s a civil engineering graduate of the local university, Boris Yeltsin, began to make his political mark, rising to become regional Communist Party boss before being promoted to Moscow in 1985. Several years later he was standing on a tank in Moscow as the leading figure in defending the country against a putsch by old-guard communists. He became the Russian Federation's first president in June 1991.

That year Yekaterinburg took back its original name. After suffering economic depression and Mafia lawlessness in the early

Yekaterinburg

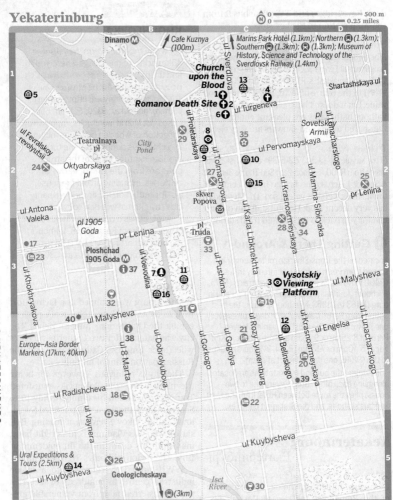

1990s, the city has boomed in recent years. Yekaterinburg is one of the very few cities in Russia governed by a mayor, Yevgeny Roizman, not from a party loyal to the kremlin.

◉ Sights

Each summer from May, after the snow has cleared, Yekaterinburg paints a red line on the footpath to guide visitors past major sights. It's marked on the tourist office (p426) city map. There's also a second walking route available for English speakers. There's no line painted anywhere for this one; instead, visitors are advised to go to izi.

travel and download the English-language audioguide.

★**Romanov Death Site**   CHURCH, MEMORIAL
(Место убийства Романовых; ul Karla Lib-knekhta & ul Tolmachyova 34; ☺ dawn-dusk) The massive Byzantine-style **Church upon the Blood** (Храм на Крови; ☎ 343-371 6168; www.hram-na-krovi.cerkov.ru) dominates this site where Tsar Nicholas II, his wife and children were murdered by Bolsheviks on the night of 16 July 1918. Nearby, the pretty wooden **Chapel of the Revered Martyr Grand Princess Yelizaveta Fyodorovna** (Часовня в честь великой княгини Елизаветы и

Yekaterinburg

инокини Варвары; ul Tolmachyova 34b; ⊙8am-6pm Mon-Fri) honours the imperial family's great-aunt and faithful friend.

The executions took place in the basement of a local engineer's house, known as Dom Ipatyeva (named for its owner, Nikolai Ipatyev). During the Soviet period, the building housed a local museum of atheism, but it was demolished in 1977 by then governor Boris Yeltsin, who feared it would attract monarchist sympathisers, and for many years the site was a vacant block marked by a small cross and the wooden chapel to Grand Princess Yelizaveta Fyodorovna. Yelizaveta Fyodorovna was a pious nun who met an even worse end than the other Romanovs when she was thrown down a mine shaft, poisoned with gas and buried.

★ **Vysotskiy**
Viewing Platform   NOTABLE BUILDING
(Высоцкий небоскрёб; ☑ 343-378 4646; www.visotsky-e.ru; ul Malysheva 51, fl 52; viewing platform R250-300, museum free; ⊙noon-10pm Mon-Fri, 10am-10pm Sat & Sun) Take the lift up

52 floors to the viewing platform for one of Russia's best urban panoramas. Children under 15 must be accompanied by an adult. The name of the tower is a pun on the Russian word for 'high' and the name of the singer Vladimir Vysotsky. A small museum is dedicated to 'Russia's raspy Dylan' here.

Yekaterinbrug History Museum   MUSEUM
(Музей истории Екатеринбурга; ☑ 343-371 2111; www.m-i-e.ru; ul Karla Libknekhta 26; R200; ⊙10am-6pm Mon-Thu, to 8pm Fri, 11am-6pm Sat & Sun) One of the more contemporary museums in town, most of the focus is on Yekaterinburg through the 18th and 19th centuries. Most exhibits are captioned in English and there are plenty of interactive displays.

Ascension Church   CHURCH
(Храм Вознесения Господня; www.voznesenka.cerkov.ru; ul Klary Tsetkin 11; ⊙dawn-dusk) The restored late-18th-century Ascension Church is the oldest in Yekaterinburg and rises moodily alongside parkland perfect for a stroll.

Military Technology Museum MUSEUM
(☎343-684 6784, 343-684 7218; www.museum.
elem.ru; ul Aleksandra Kozitsyna 2, Verkhnyaya
Pyshma; exhibition hall R100, outdoor exhibition
free; ☺10am-6pm Wed-Sun) This vast indoor
and open-air collection of tanks and armoured vehicles is located on the northern
outskirts of Yekaterinburg in Verkhnyaya
Pyshma. It's one of the largest of its kind in
the world, with an extensive range of large
military tanks and helicopters located outdoors, and smaller military craft and retro
automobiles on display indoors.

Take bus 111 or *marshrutky* 111 or 111a
from stop 'Kinotsentr Zarya' (at 'Uralmash'
metro station) to 'Zavodskaya'.

**Museum of Architecture
and Design** MUSEUM
(Музей истории архитектуры и дизайна;
☎343-372 0654; www.museumarch.com; ul Gorkogo 4a; R200; ☺11am-7pm Wed-Sat) Situated on
Istorichesky skver (Historical Sq), this museum is located on the grounds where the first
ironworks was established in Yekaterinburg
in 1723. In recent years the museum has had
an overhaul, and today the former 19th-
century factory and mint building houses a
fascinating collection of miniature buildings
depicting various historical eras throughout
Yekaterinburg's history.

Boris Yeltsin Presidential Center MUSEUM
(Президентский центр Бориса Ельцина;
☎495-729 5463; www.yeltsincenter.ru/yeltsin-
presidential-center; ul Borisa Eltsina 3; R200; ☺mu-
seum 10am-9pm Tue-Sun) Traffic was stopped
the day the Boris Yeltsin Presidential Center
was opened in 2015. The mammoth site includes a museum, a conference centre, an
art gallery and a bookshop, although it's the
museum that is of most interest to visitors.
The museum depicts the former Russian
prime minister's life through seven interactive zones designed to represent seven historical days during his ruling.

Most of the exhibit descriptions in the
museum are in Russian, but there is an
audioguide available for English-speakers.
There are a number of tours that visitors can
book, and although these are only available
in Russian now, there are plans to introduce
English-speaking options eventually.

Urals Military History Museum MUSEUM
(Уральский государственный военно-
исторический музей; ☎343-246 5080; http://
ugvim.ru; ul Krylova 2a; R180; ☺10am-8pm Wed, to
6pm Thu, to 5pm Fri-Sun) Worthwhile for buffs,

this military museum has two halls, one
dedicated to the Urals Volunteer Tank Corp.
Entry price is for both halls, but you can pay
and visit only one if you wish. In the yard is
a collection of tanks and planes.

Yekaterinburg

Museum of Fine Arts MUSEUM
(Екатеринбургский музей изобразительных
искусств; ☎343-371 0626; www.emii.ru; ul Vo-
evodina 5; R250; ☺11am-8pm Tue-Thu, to 7pm
Fri-Sun) The star exhibit of the Museum of
Fine Arts is its elaborate Kasli Iron Pavilion,
which won prizes in the 1900 Paris Expo.
The museum has a good collection of icons,
paintings and decorative art.

Nevyansk Icon Museum MUSEUM
(Музей Невянская икона; ☎343-220 6650; ul
Engelsa 15; R150; ☺11am-8pm Wed-Sun) FREE
Excellent icons from the 17th to the 20th
centuries, from the local Nevyansk school.

Literary Quarter AREA
(☎343-371 0300; www.ompu.ur.ru) Located
north of skver Popova, the Literary Quarter
features restored wooden houses, some of
them now museums about celebrated local
writers such as Dmitry Mamina-Sibiryak
and Pavel Bazhov; a full list of museums is
on the website.

Istorichesky Skver PARK
The prettiest and most lively part of Yekaterinburg in summer is the landscaped parkland
alongside the City Pond (Gorodskoy prud),
where pr Lenina crosses a small dam. This
was where Yekaterinburg began back in 1723.

**Metenkov House-Museum
of Photography** MUSEUM
(Фотографический музей Дом Метенкова;
☎343-371 0637; ul Karla Libknekhta 36; R150;
☺noon-8pm Tue-Sun) All the exhibitions are
temporary, but you'll always find a room
dedicated to Metenkov and his work here.
Other exhibition spaces usually feature
works from art residency participants
and various other photos, often dedicated
to Yekaterinburg and its history. Downstairs there's a photography shop that sells
old-fashioned cameras and souvenirs.

**Museum of History,
Science and Technology
of the Sverdlovsk Railway** MUSEUM
(Музей истории, науки и техники
Свердловской железной дороги; ☎343-358
4222; www.volzd.ru/museum-ekaterinburg.html; ul
Vokzalnaya 14; R100; ☺10am-6pm Tue-Sat) Rail-

way buffs will enjoy the good collection here, housed in and around the old train station, dating from 1881. Exhibits highlight the history of the railroad in the Urals, including a re-creation of the office of the Soviet-era railway director.

Ural Geological Museum MUSEUM
(Уральский геологический музей; ☑ 343-257 2547; http://ugm.ursmu.ru; ul Kuybysheva 39; R100; ☺ 11am-7pm Mon-Fri, to 5pm Sat & Sun) Over 500 minerals from the Ural Mountains region and a collection of meteorites can be seen here.

Literary-Memorial House-Museum Reshetnikov MUSEUM
(Литературно-мемориальный дом-музей Решетникова; ☑ 343-371 4526; ul Proletarskaya 6; R70; ☺ 10am-7pm Tue & Fri, 11am-8pm Wed & Thu, 11am-7pm Sat & Sun) Situated squarely in the literary quarter of Yekaterinburg, this museum re-creates some aspects of life in Reshetnikov's time, with a big focus on postal work since the author's father was a postman. Several sheds in the yard contain a blacksmith's workshop (complete with a blacksmith) and a small but interesting collection of 19th-century sleds and carriages.

Rastorguev-Kharitonov Mansion HISTORIC BUILDING
(Усадьба Расторгуев-Харитонова; ul Karla Libknekhta 44) Situated across the road from the site where the Romanov family was executed, this mansion dates from the late 18th and early 19th centuries and was one of the most significant buildings of the era. Today people come to admire the pretty angular facade and relax in the pleasant park behind it.

🏃 Activities & Tours

Ekaterinburg Guide Centre ADVENTURE
(Екатеринбургский центр гидов; ☑ 343-384 0048; www.ekaterinburgguide.com; office 12, pr Lenina 52/1; ☺ 10am-6pm Mon-Fri) Organises English-language tours of the city and trips into the countryside, including Nevyansk, Tobolsk and Nizhnyaya Sinyachikha, as well as winter activities and summer hiking and rafting expeditions. Day trips cost anything between R1800 and R8800, depending on destination and numbers. It also books hotel and hostel accommodation, often at discount rates.

The centre can also take you to the historic but hard-to-reach Verkhoturye. If taking the seven-hour tour to Nevyansk and the nearby old potters' village of Tavolgi, ask to stop on the way at the village of Kunary, where a local blacksmith has turned his wooden *izba* into a masterpiece of naive art.

Ural Expeditions & Tours ADVENTURE
(☑ 961-762 2863; http://welcome-ural.ru; office 4, ul Baumana 6; ☺ 11am-5pm Mon-Fri) This group of geologists who graduated from the Sverdlovsk Mining Institute leads trekking, rafting and horse-riding trips to all parts of the Ural Mountains, including Taganay and Zyuratkul National Parks. English-speaking guides.

THE URALS YEKATERINBURG

WORTH A TRIP

EUROPE–ASIA BORDER

The Ural Mountains have numerous monuments marking the border between Europe and Asia. Interestingly, the border was thought to be the Don River by the Ancient Greeks, but Yekaterinburg's founder Vasily Tatishchev drew it at the Ural Mountains in the mid-18th century, based on ideas of the day.

One of the more historic monuments is located 40km west of Yekaterinburg near Pervouralsk. It was erected in 1837 to commemorate a visit by Tsar Alexander II, who drank wine there and inadvertently began a favourite pastime of locals – drinking a glass in Europe and another glass in Asia (as if you needed an excuse!). To reach the monument, take a taxi (about R1000 return if you order in advance) to Pervouralsk. Expect to pay another R200 per hour for the driver to wait. Very frequent bus 150 leaves from the Severny bus station to Pervouralsk (R97; platform 9).

The city has erected a new border marker, more conveniently located just 17km out of Yekaterinburg and looking a little like a mini Eiffel Tower. This one is more kitsch, but a taxi will take you out there for about R600 return, with an hour at the monument.

Expect to pay R3600 to R4000 as an individual (less in groups) with reliable outfits such as Ekaterinburg Guide Centre or Yekaterinburg For You (p424).

Yekaterinburg For You

TOURS

(☑ 912-280 0870; www.yekaterinburg4u.ru) Experienced guide and journalist Luba Suslyakova offers a range of city and regional tours, including Nevyansk and the pottery town of Tavolgi, winter dog sledding, and the eclectic Mafia Tour, which takes visitors into the graveyards where Yekaterinburg's rival 'Uralmash' and 'Central' gangsters of the 1990s rest in peace.

🛏 Sleeping

⭐ Red Star Hostel

HOSTEL $

(☑ 343-383 5684; www.redstarhostel.ru; ul Gorkogo 65; 6-12-bed dm R290-650, d R1600; ⊖ 🛜) This excellent hostel opened in 2014 and has quickly established itself as a comfortable, very professionally run place, with 44 beds divided among male, female and mixed dorms, and a double with a large bed. It can do registration. Take trolleybus 1 or 9 from the train station to stop Kuybsheva.

⭐ Hotel Chekhov

BOUTIQUE HOTEL $$

(☑ 343-282 9737; http://chekhov-hotel.ru; ul 8 Marta 32; incl breakfast s R4500-5500, d R5000-6000; ⊖ 🛜) Hotel Chekhov offers modern, stylishly furnished rooms which make good use of exposed brick in a historic building. Take bus 23 from the train station to TRTs Grinvich.

Tenet Hotel

BUSINESS HOTEL $$

(☑ 343-385 8582; www.tenethotel.ru; ul Khokhryakova 1a; d incl breakfast R3500-9000; ⊖ 🛜 @ 🛜) Opened in 2016, this hotel is conveniently located in the centre of town and attracts a mostly business crowd. The design is contemporary with nods to the city's history through black-and-white photographs spread throughout the building. The restaurant, too, draws on this concept, with old classic Russian dishes vamped up with a modern twist.

Live Hotel

HOSTEL $$

(☑ 343-239 6969; www.live-ekb.ru; ul Krasnoarmeyskaya 72; dm/r from R600/R2600; ⊖ 🛜 @ 🛜) A newcomer to Yekaterinburg, this large and modern complex includes a hotel, a hostel, a communal work space and a conference centre. Rooms in both the hostel and hotel are clean and comfortable, with pops of colour freshening up the design.

Marins Park Hotel

HOTEL $$

(Маринс Парк Отель; ☑ 343-228 0000; www.sv-hotel.ru; ul Chelyuskintsev 106; incl breakfast s R2300-3200, d R3100-4000; ⊖ 🛜 🛜) Marins Park has successfully reinvented itself as a modern congress hotel; all rooms are small, and while renovation in the cheaper ones is simply a coat of pastel paint, others have been thoroughly updated. It has two enormous advantages: it's right across the road from the train station, and it does your laundry same-day for free.

⭐ Hotel Tsentralny

HISTORIC HOTEL $$$

(Отель Центральный; ☑ 343-350 1004; www.hotelcentr.ru; ul Malysheva 74; incl breakfast s R2300-5000, d R3500-7000; ⊖ 🛜) Opened in 1928, this historic hotel is housed in a grand art nouveau building in the heart of town and has seen its fair share of celebrity guests. It has 98 excellent business-class and standard rooms and eating and nightlife options are never far away. Trolleybuses 1 and 9 are among the many going to the hotel from the train station.

The hotel also acts as a museum, with photo displays on floors three to five. Guests and visitors can book a historical excursion through the hotel grounds, which costs R200 and takes approximately 30 minutes.

Novotel Yekaterinburg Centre

HOTEL $$$

(☑ 343-253 5383; www.novotel.com; ul Engelsa 7; incl breakfast s R5900-7700, d R6900-8100, ste R11,000; ⊖ 🛜 🛜) This excellent four-star chain hotel in the centre has variable rates and good deals online. Rooms are clean and comfortable and service always comes with a smile. The easiest way from the station is trolleybus 1 or 9 to ul Rozy Lyuksemburg stop.

🍴 Eating

Ul 8 Marta between pr Lenina and ul Malysheva has plenty of eating and drinking options, and ul Vaynera, which is partly pedestrian only, has a moderate choice of eateries. Whatever your food preference, there's lots of choice, spanning everything from local fare to international cuisine to modern cafe nosh.

Pelmeni Club

RUSSIAN $

(Пельмени Клаб; ☑ 343-271 3330; www.pelmeni-club.ru; ul Krasnoarmeyskaya 2; mains R190-470; 🛜) There's a great variety of *pelmeni* here, but what makes this restaurant stand out is the fact that you can learn to make your own. There is a second location on ul Lunacharskogo 82.

Nigora
UZBEK **$**

(Нигора; ☑343-295 1417; http://nigora.ru; ul Kuybysheva 55; mains R200; ☺noon-midnight) Yekaterinburg has several of these inexpensive Uzbek restaurants, all with young staff attired in Uzbek caps serving delicious Uzbek specialities. *Manti* (steamed, palm-sized dumplings), soups, sausages and shashlyk feature on the menu, including a very worthy lamb shashlyk. There are two other Nigora locations in town.

Stolle
CAFE **$**

(Штолле; ☑343-253 8005; ul Gorkogo 7a; pirogi R45-290; ☺10am-10pm Sun-Thu, to midnight Fri & Sat; ☑) Stolle specialises in sweet and savoury Russian *pirozhki* (pies), which you can buy by weight at the counter for takeaway or enjoy here in a relaxed atmosphere. There are three more locations in the city.

★Pashtet
RUSSIAN **$$**

(☑343-228 0059; www.rest-pashtet.ru; ul Tolmacheva 23; mains R390-1550, business lunches R400; ☺11am-11pm Sun-Thu, to midnight Fri & Sat; ☎) Reinvented Russian classics served in rooms designed to depict a traditional Russian summer *dacha*. Both the food and wine menus are extensive and the restaurant's house-made pâtés (pashtet in Russian) are definitely worth trying.

Cafe Kuznya
RUSSIAN **$$**

(Кафе Кузня; ☑343-286 2925; www.gorn66.ru; ul Melkovskaya 3; mains R215-625; ☺noon-11pm; ☎☑) A fascinating cafe with wooden interiors crafted by one woodwork artist and his students – Alexander Andreevich Lysyakov. The menu spans all the Russian classics with no surprises.

Khmeli Suneli
GEORGIAN **$$**

(Хмели Сунели; ☑343-350 6318; www.hmeli.ru; pr Lenina 69/10; mains R450; ☺noon-midnight Sun-Thu, to 2am Fri & Sat,; ☎) This large Georgian restaurant has a relaxed feel and is currently the best of its ilk in Yekaterinburg, serving a large range of soups, salads, fish and red-meat dishes and delicious shashlyk.

Cafe-Museum Demidov
RUSSIAN **$$**

(☑343-371 7344; www.demidov-ural.ru; ul Fevralskoy revolyutsii 9; mains R510-1200) A quirky cafe-museum spread over two storyes, where guests are encouraged to touch the random

collection of exhibits. The food is simple Russian fare; there are no elaborate descriptions and the meals come presented as if grandma was serving at home.

Shoko Kofeyniya
CAFE **$$**

(Шоко кофейня; ☑343-380 6600; www.shoko-coffee.ru; ul Malysheva 74; mains R290-450; ☺8am-2am Mon-Fri, 6am-2am Sat, to midnight Sun; ☎) This upmarket cafe is the pick of the crop among the cluster of bars and eateries located in and alongside the Hotel Tsentralny building. It has lighter dishes and a small selection of mains, but the desserts are the highlight. The hours are useful for chilling out late at night.

Vertikal
INTERNATIONAL **$$$**

(Вертикаль; ☑343-200 5151; www.vertical51.ru; ul Malysheva 51, fl 51; mains R320-2000; ☺noon-midnight Sun-Thu, to 2am Fri & Sat; ✳) Located on the 51st floor of the Vysotsky tower, Vertikal offers a formal, upmarket experience of pan-European dishes and some steaks, and its trump card: sensational views over town. Reserve ahead.

🍷 Drinking & Nightlife

★New Bar
BAR

(☑953-058 4455; www.new-bar.ru; ul 8 Marta 8; ☺6pm-6am; ☎) Relaxed art-scene cafe and cocktail bar on the top floor of Mytny Dvor mall. One storey below the same company restaurant serves Russian soul food and has a decent cocktail list. The restaurant is open noon to midnight daily.

Rosy Jane
PUB

(☑343-317 1855; www.rosyjane.ru; pr Lenina 32/34; ☺7am-6am Mon-Thu, to 7am Fri, 9am-7am Sat, to 6am Sun; ☎) This English-style pub aims at the New Russian drinking and eating crowd, who grace the bar and perch at polished wood tables gourmandising on steak and other very well-prepared Russian and international dishes (mains R550 to R1900). Steaks are top of the range. It serves decent breakfasts too, for early-risers or those still out from the night before. Entry is off ul Gorkogo.

Dr Scotch
PUB

(☑343-371 4363; www.doctorscotch.ru; ul Malysheva 56a; ☺noon-2am) Doc Scotch is one of the liveliest pubs in town and has the advantage of being very central. Expect lots of wood in the interior and even more beer.

Ben Hall PUB
(343-251 6368; www.benhall.ru; ul Narodnoy Voli 65; mains R250-950; ☺ noon-2am Sun-Thu, to 4am Fri & Sat) This popular pub hosts local rock bands and pop DJs at weekends, its owner being a well-known musician. Trams 15 and 27 from Operny Teatr or along pr Lenina to Tsirk (Цирк) drop you close by.

☆ Entertainment

Philharmonic CLASSICAL MUSIC
(Филармония; ☑ tickets 343-371 4682; www.sgaf.ru; ul Karla Libknekhta 38; tickets from R200) Yekaterinburg's top venue for the classical performing arts often hosts visiting directors and soloists, as well as regular performances by the acclaimed Ural Mountains academic orchestra.

Opera & Ballet Theatre OPERA, BALLET
(Театр оперы и балета; ☑ tickets 343-350 8057; www.uralopera.ru; pr Lenina 46a; tickets from R150) This ornate baroque theatre is a lovely place to see the Russian classics at a high standard.

Shopping

Grinvich MALL
(343-222 2525; www.grinvich.com; ul 8 Marta 46; ☺ 10am-10pm) This enormous shopping complex near the ul Vaynera pedestrian zone is an oasis away from the traffic.

ℹ Information

Main Post Office (Почтамт; pr Lenina 39; ☺ 8am-10pm Mon-Fri, 9am-6pm Sat & Sun)
Sverdlovsk Region Centre of Tourism (Центр развития туризма Свердловской области; ☑ 343-350 0525; www.gotoural.com; ul 8 Marta 13, 2 fl) Helpful city office with English-speaking staff. There are maps and brochures about Yekaterinburg as well as the whole Sverdlovsk Region.
Tourist Information Service (TIS; ☑ 343-222 2445; www.its.ekburg.ru; ul 8 Marta 21; ☺ 10am-7pm Mon-Fri, 11am-4pm Sat & Sun) Helpful official city tourist office, with free maps of town showing the Red Line walking trail to major sights.
Tourist Information Service (☑ 343-222 2445; www.its.ekburg.ru; terminal b, fl 2; ☺ 10am-7pm Mon-Fri) Airport branch of the city tourist office.

ℹ Getting There & Away

AIR

The main airport is **Koltsovo** (☑ 800-100 0333; www.koltsovo.ru), 15km southeast of the city centre. Frequent services include Moscow, Novosibirsk, Krasnoyarsk, Irkutsk, Khabarovsk, Ufa, St Petersburg, Samara, Vladivostok and a host of Black Sea hubs. International services include Frankfurt am Main (Germany), Beijing (China), Prague (Czech Republic) and Astana (Kazakhstan). **Aeroflot** (☑ 343-356 5570; www.aeroflot.ru; ul Belinskogo 41; ☺ 9am-7pm Mon-Fri) has offices here.

BUS

The **main bus station** (Южный автовокзал; Yuzhny avtovokzal; ☑ 343-257 1260; www.autovokzal.org) is 3km south of the city centre, but most buses also stop at the **Northern Bus Station** (Северный автовокзал; severny avtovokzal; ul Vokzalnaya 15a), conveniently located by the train station. Here you can catch frequent buses to Chelyabinsk (R550, four hours) and Alapaevsk (R380, three hours, five daily). There is also a bus station at Koltsovo airport serving destinations in the Sverdlovsk region and Chelyabinsk (R550, 3½ hours, frequent). Touts sell tickets for minibuses to Chelyabinsk (R700, 2½ hours, about every hour) at the main bus station.

TRAIN

Yekaterinburg – sometimes still called 'Sverdlovsk' on timetables – is a major rail junction with connections to all stops on the trans-Siberian route. All trains to Moscow stop at either Perm (R800, 5½ hours) or Kazan (R1180, 14½ hours). Frequent trains to/from Moscow include the Ural (R1700 to R3777, 26 hours, every couple of days) via Kazan. Heading east, the next major stops are Omsk (R1380, 14 hours) and Novosibirsk (R2134, 22 hours). You can buy tickets at outlets throughout the city, including the convenient **Railway & Air Kassa** (ЖД и Авиа кассы; ☑ 343-371 0400; www.bilet-vsegda.ru; ul Malysheva 31d; ☺ 24hr).

ℹ Getting Around

Bus 1 links the Sverdlovsk-Passazhirskaya train station and Koltsovo airport (one hour) from 6.30am to 11.30pm. Bus 039 goes from the airport to metro pl 1905 Goda. *Marshrutka* 39 goes to metro Geologicheskaya.

Many trolleybuses such as 1, 3 and 9 and *marshrutky* (pay on board) run along ul Sverdlova/ul Karla Libknekhta between the train station and pr Lenina. Marshrutka 21 connects the train station with pl 1905 Goda, continuing along ul 8 Marta to the Grinvich shopping centre. Bus 024 runs along ul 8 Marta to the Northern Bus Station alongside the train station. Trams 13, 15 and 18 cover long stretches of pr Lenina.

A single metro line runs between the northeastern suburbs and the city centre, with stops at the train station (Uralskaya), pl 1905 Goda and ul Kuybysheva near the synagogue (Geologicheskaya).

Around Yekaterinburg

Ganina Yama   Ганина Яма

**Monastery of
the Holy Martyrs**   CHRISTIAN SITE

(☑ 343-217 9146) After the Romanov family
was shot in the cellar of Dom Ipatyeva, their
bodies were discarded in the depths of the
forests of Ganina Yama, 16km northeast of
Yekaterinburg. In their honour, the Orthodox Church has built the exquisite Monastery of the Holy Martyrs at this pilgrimage
site. Expect to pay around R3600 to R4200
as an individual (less in groups) on tours
conducted by Ekaterinburg Guide Centre
(p423).

The nearest train station to Ganina Yama
is Shuvakish, served by *elektrichki* (suburban trains; R56, 30 minutes, every one to
two hours) from the central station. Buses
from the Northern Bus Station (Severny)
run out here at 3.30pm Saturday and 10am
Sunday (platform 11), returning at 8pm Saturday and 11.30am Sunday.

Nevyansk   Невья́нск

The small town of Nevyansk is in the heart
of the former patrimony of the Demidovs, a
family of industrialists who effectively controlled much of the Ural Mountains and
who received Peter I's blessing to develop
the region. At their most decadent stage,
they bought the Italian feudal title of Count
San-Donato.

**Nevyansk History and
Architecture Museum**   MUSEUM

(☑ excursion booking 343-564 4509; http://muse-
um-nev.ru; pl Revolyutsii 2; museum R70, Nevyansk
tower excursion per group of 1-5 people R1500;
⊙ 9am-6.30pm Tue-Sun, excursions from 10am)
The Nevyansk Leaning Tower is an impressive structure flanked by an equally impressive Saviour-Transfiguration Cathedral. The
worthwhile excursions (in Russian) into the
tower are the only ways to climb up for the
fantastic views unless you can latch onto a
group. *Elektrichka* (R142, 2½ hours, nine
daily) – some of them express trains (1½
hours) – run to Nevyansk, most bound for
Nizhny Tagil.

Byngi   HOMESTAY **$$**

(☑ 8-922 158 2183, in Germany Oct-Apr +49 (0)421-
40 89 66 60; www.semken.eu; ul Frunse 25, in Byn-
gi; s/d incl full board €80/125; ⊙ May-Sep) Seven
kilometres from Nevyansk, the lovely Byngi
is the perfect place to experience Russian
life in an Old Believers' village. Here an en-
trepreneurial German and his Russian wife
have converted an *izba* (log house) into a
guesthouse in the main building and erected
four summer yurts in the yard.

Elektrichka (R142, 1½ to 2½ hours, nine
daily) serve Nevyansk.

Excursions are available, and on a visit
you will be very much integrated eclectically
into local life in and around the village.

THE URALS AROUND YEKATERINBURG

WORTH A TRIP

CAPOVA CAVE

Located on the banks of the Belaya River in Burzyansky district, Capova Cave (Shul-
gan-Tash; ☑ 937-840 9840; www.capova.ru/www.shulgan-tash.ru; R360 standard excursion,
R4000 for excursion to see the real drawings; ⊙ 9am-7pm, excursions 10am-5pm) is a lime-
stone cave most famous for its ancient rock drawings from the Paleolithic era. There are
over 170 of these ancient images – most of them at least 18,000 years old and some up
to 36,400 years old.

A standard excursion (R360) includes entry to the first hall of the cave where you
can see high-quality photos of the ancient drawings. With advance notice and a hefty
fee (R4000), it is possible to visit halls two and three where the real drawings are found,
although there is talk of eventually discontinuing this option to better preserve the art.

The area is also famous for the traditional art of beekeeping. Wild bees live in the
hollows of trees and the Bashkir people climb the trees to extract the honey, which is
interesting to watch.

Capova Cave is located approximately 400km from the Ufa. Take the bus from Dvorec
Molodezhi on ul 50 let Oktyabrya 21 (R600, daily at 5pm, in summer 10am and 5pm).
From the small town of Starosubkhangulovo to the cave it's about 35km and is easiest by
flagging down a local taxi or hitchhiking.

Nizhnyaya Sinyachikha
Нижняя Синячиха

The village of Nizhnyaya Sinyachikha, about 150km northeast of Yekaterinburg and 12km north of Alapaevsk, is home to an excellent open-air **Architecture Museum** (Нижнесинячихинский музей-заповедник; ☑ 343-467 5118; http://нс-музей.рф/; ul Pervomaiskaya 20; excursions R250-400; ☺10am-5pm) of traditional Siberian log buildings, featuring displays of period furniture and domestic articles. Excursions of the museum are in Russian only, but you can wander around the grounds without a guide. While in town, visit the **stone cathedral**, which houses a good collection of regional folk art. This impressive ensemble of art and architecture was gathered from around the Ural Mountains and recompiled by the single-handed efforts of Ivan Samoylov, an enthusiastic local historian.

Five buses a day go to Alapaevsk (R297, three hours) from Yekaterinburg (Yuzhny Avtovokzal). Take a **taxi** (☑912-037 3924) from Alpaevsk to Nizhnyaya Sinyachikha and back (one way R250 to R300).

Ufa
Уфа

☑347 / POP 1.13 MILLION / ☺ MOSCOW +2HR

Ufa is the capital of the autonomous republic of Bashkortostan (Республика Башкортостан), home of the Bashkirs, a Muslim Turkic people who dominated most of the southern Ural Mountains before Russian colonisation. Although they're only a third of the republic's population, you can hear their lispy language spoken on the streets of Ufa, in rural areas and on the radio. Substantial hydrocarbon reserves have turned Bashkortostan into something of an oil khanate.

Ufa has a few interesting sights and you can spend a pleasant day walking through the streets exploring. Beyond Ufa village life dances to a different beat. In districts such as Ishambai, Baimak, Abzilil, Kugarchinski and Zianchurinski, all accessible by road, locals welcome travellers into their homes and share their food and their stories. All you need is a sense of adventure...and perhaps some Russian or Bashkir language skills.

⊙ Sights

★**Park Vatan** CULTURAL CENTRE
(Парк Ватан; ☑347-266 1960; www.parkvatan.ru; ☺noon-9pm) Park Vatan is a unique collection of boutique shops and arts-exhibition spaces housed in traditional yurts. Visitors can purchase delicacies such as local honey, drink local tea, and learn about the Republic of Bashkortostan as they move from yurt to yurt.

Bashkortostan National Museum MUSEUM
(Национальный музей Башкортостана; ☑347-272 1250; www.museumrb.ru; ul Sovetskaya 14; R150; ☺11am-6pm Tue-Fri & Sun, noon-8pm Sat) Housed in a renovated art-nouveau building, this museum is spread over two floors with thousands of exhibits spanning culture, ethnography, history and the natural environment. The exhibits on Bashkir history, including examples of yurt life, are the most interesting; all descriptions are in Russian. Walk a few minutes south along ul Lenina from the Trading Arcade to ul Pushkina.

SHIHANY MOUNTAINS

These ancient mountains hold deep meaning to the local people, who want to increase visitor numbers so that businesses realise their worth and don't destroy them for their limestone.

Today there are three peaks remaining (there were four but a factory business demolished one) and they are said to be some of the oldest mountains in the world, at around 285 million years of age.

Interestingly, they are composed of tiny coral rocks, demonstrating that this area was once deep under the sea. Today you can hike up the mountains and easily come across the coral rocks, some of which still have seashell fossils engraved onto them. Afterwards, it's worth taking a stroll around the local village **Urman Bishkazak**.

To get to Shihany Mountains, take a bus from Yuzhny Bus Station in Ufa to Sterlitamak (R300, 1½ hours, hourly), then take a taxi to the mountains (R250 to R300, 20 minutes; call ☑347-333 3222). Alternatively you can book a tour with In Ethnos.

Nesterov Art Gallery
GALLERY

(Картинная Галерея Нестерова; ☎347-272 1385; www.museum-nesterov.ru; ul Gogolya 27; R100; ◐10am-6.30pm Tue-Fri, noon-8.30pm Sat, 10am-6.30pm Sun) This small but interesting gallery contains a fabulous collection of over 100 artworks by Ufa native Mikhail Nesterov and 50 paintings by Ukrainian futurist David Burlyuk, which he left in a Bashkir village when escaping from the Red Army during the Civil War. It's located two blocks west of ul Lenina, on the corner of ul Pushkina.

Trading Arcade
HISTORIC BUILDING

(☎347-298 1058; www.gostinka.com; ul Verkhnetorgovaya 'ploshchad' 1; ◐10am-9pm) The focus of appealing ul Lenina is the 19th-century Trading Arcade, set back from the street. Behind the renovated facade is a luxuriously marble-lined shopping mall full of boutiques, cafes and shops selling local Bashkir honey. Take any *marshrutka* (fixed route minibus) going to the stop Gostinny Dvor (Гостиный двор).

🏃 Activities & Tours

Tengri
ADVENTURE SPORTS

(Тенгри; ☎347-088 9976; www.tengri.ru; office 309, 3rd fl, pr Oktyabrya 31; ◐9am-8pm Mon-Fri, 11am-4pm Sat) Offers a wide range of inexpensive adventure trips in the southern Urals. Horse riding, rafting and hiking are just some of the options.

In Ethnos
TOURS

(☎+793 7332 3422; www.inethnos.com; ul Mendeleeva 104; ◐9am-7pm) Offers a range of day tours from Ufa, the highlight of which is a visit to Shikhany Mountains – the oldest mountains in the world, about an hour's drive out of Ufa.

✦ Festivals & Events

International Festival of Arts
CULTURAL

(www.heartofeurasia.ru; ul Zaki Validi 2) A five-day cultural festival executed over two amphitheatres with a big focus on music and dance. Check the website for dates.

🛏 Sleeping

Hostel Afrika
HOSTEL $

(Хостел Африка; ☎927-236 2099; www.ufahostel.ru; ul Zapototskogo 10; 4-10 bed dm R450-1500; ◉🛜) This hostel run by a Russian couple is used to putting up foreigners. Rooms are bright and there's a communal kitchen. It doesn't do registrations. Bus 74 runs here to the stop Park im Yakutova (Парк им. Якутова) from the train station.

Hotel Azimut
HOTEL $$

(☎347-235 9000; www.azimuthotels.com; pr Oktyabya 81; s/d incl breakfast from R2300/3500; ◉✳@🛜) Located 5km from the central area, Azimut is a comfortable, contemporary hotel with good connections to the centre and train station. Two excellent places are very close by: the restaurant Burzhuika and the live-music pub Rock's Cafe (p430). Take buses or *marshrutky* 226, 249 or 290 from the centre or 74 from the train station to stop 'Gossovet' (Госсовет).

Hotel Bashkiria
HOTEL $$$

(Гостиница Башкирия; ☎347-279 0000; www.gkbashkortostan.ru; ul Lenina 25-29; s/d incl breakfast from R4900/6200; ✳@🛜🏊) Recently renovated, Hotel Bashkiria offers a comfortable and convenient stay in the centre of town.

Hotel Agidel
HOTEL $$$

(Гостиница Агидель; ☎347-272 5680; www.agidelhotel.ru; ul Lenina 16; incl breakfast s R2500, d R3900-8000; ◉✳🛜) Rooms are comfortable, tastefully furnished and fully renovated in this centrally located hotel almost opposite Gostinny Dvor.

🍴 Eating & Drinking

Pishka
CAFE $

(Пышка; ☎347-216 1615; www.pishka.ru; ul Revolyutsionnaya 32; meals R200; ◐9am-9pm Mon-Sat, to 8pm Sun) This branch of the Pishka chain serves classic Bashkir dishes such as *belish* (meat pie) and *tukmas* (chicken broth). Also try one of the pastries from the bakery section. Take any bus or *marshrutka* from the centre to the stop TK Tsentralny (ТК Центральный).

Ashhana Neneyka
BASHKIR $

(Ашхана Нэнэйка; ☎347-216 5535; pr Oktyabrya 4/2b; mains R125-330; ◐noon-11pm) Good-value, local cuisine the way a Bashkir grandma would make it. Try the horse-meat momo if you dare. There are two more locations in Ufa.

Burzhuika
INTERNATIONAL, RUSSIAN $$

(Буржуйка; ☎347-257 2585; www.burzhuynka.com; pr Oktyabrya 79/1; 2/3 courses R290/R340; ◐noon-midnight Sun-Thu, to 2am Fri & Sat; 🛜🚬) Ufa's hippest location for dinner, drinks or a hookah is located near the Hotel Azimut. The food is excellent and served in well-sized portions. Take buses or *marshrutky* 226, 249 or 290 from the centre or 74 from the train station to stop 'Gossovet' (Госсовет).

★ **Azyk-Tulek**   BASHKIR $$$
(Азык-Тулек; ☑ 347-216 2168; ul Karla Marksa 3b; mains R640-1090; ☺ noon-11.45pm Sun-Thu, to 2am Fri & Sat) An imaginative and modern take on Bashkir cuisine makes this one of the best dining choices in town. All dishes are beautifully presented and service comes with a smile. The entrée menu is particularity interesting and the wine list is extensive.

Coffee-Time   CAFE
(Кофе-Тайм; ☑ 347-272 0435; ul Oktyabrskoy Revolyutsii 3; coffee from R90; ☺ 24hr; 🛜) One of Ufa's most popular spots for a coffee break, with jazz music, B&W photos and fashionable young folk.

☆ Entertainment

★ **Ufa Jazz Club**   JAZZ
(Уфимский джаз клуб; ☑ 347-223 0100; www.jazzclubufa.com; ul let SSSR 50; performances R70, mains R210-490; ☺ 9am-midnight Mon-Fri, 11am-midnight Sat & Sun) It's worth venturing out of the centre of town for a night of soulful music, and Ufa Jazz Club delivers. Live-music performances include local jazz bands as well as international bands and artists.

Bashkir State Opera and Ballet Theatre   THEATRE
(Башкирский государственный театр оперы и балета; ☑ tickets 347-273 8472; www.bashopera.ru; ul Lenina 5/1; performances R150-650; ☺ ticket office 9am-7.30pm) A beautiful, historical theatre popular with locals and travellers alike. It's also the theatre where Rudolf Nureyev took his first steps.

Rock's Cafe   LIVE MUSIC
(☑ 347-292 7927; www.rockscafe.ru; pr Oktyabrya 79/1, set back from street; free except for larger acts; ☺ 7pm-2am Thu & Sun, to 6pm Fri & Sat) Not to be missed for live gigs, Rock's lives up to its name with local and national acts.

Lights of Ufa   LIVE MUSIC
(Огни Уфы; ☑ 347-290 8690; www.ogni-ufa.ru; ul 50 let Oktyabrya 19; ☺ noon-2am; 🛜) Concert hall, disco, sports bar and microbrewery in one. From ul Lenina, take any bus north to 'Dom Pechati'.

ⓘ Information

Post Office (Почтамт; ul Lenina 28; internet per hr R39; ☺ 8am-10pm Mon-Fri, 9am-6pm Sat & Sun, internet 8am-5pm Mon-Thu, to 4pm Fri) Internet left from the entrance.

Tourist Information Centre i-UFA
(Туристический информационный центр i-UFA; ☑ 347-272 7788; www.i-ufa.com; ul 50 let Oktyabrya; ☺ 9am-8pm Mon-Fri, 10am-6pm Sat & Sun) English-speaking staff work at this tourist centre.

Pick up the *Ufa City Transport Map* (Схема городского транспорта Уфы; R43) from the **Belaya Reka Dom Knigi** (☑ 347-273 4085; ul Lenina 24; ☺ 9.30am-9pm Mon-Fri, 10am-8pm Sat & Sun) bookshop, which has all routes (with a few inaccuracies) and stops and doubles as a useful street map.

ⓘ Getting There & Away

The train station is 2km north of the centre at the end of ul Karla Marksa. There are daily trains to Moscow (R1437 to R2672, 27 hours) some via Samara (R750 to R1645, 8½ hours). Trains also go to Ulyanovsk (R1100, 14 hours) in the west and Chelyabinsk (R715 to R999, 9½ hours) in the east. There is an overnight service to Magnitogorsk (R602, nine hours). Air and train tickets are available from **Sputnik Yulgash** (Спутник Юлгаш; ☑ 347-273 8666; www.sputnik-ufa.ru; ul Tsyurupy 93; ☺ 9am-8pm Mon-Fri, 11am-5pm Sat), including a daily flight to Kazan.

ⓘ Getting Around

The handy if convoluted bus 101 route snakes between the train station (climb the high steps outside to the top) and the airport, via Yuzhny Vokzal bus station and Gostinny Dvor on ul Lenina.

Ufa to Chelyabinsk

The area west of Chelyabinsk is called *Sinegorye* (Blue Mountains). Unlike its Australian namesake, it is conifer not eucalyptus forest that makes the low, gently sloped ranges of the southern Ural Mountains look like frozen blue waves. Also blue are the large placid lakes between the mountains, of which the most lauded are Lakes Turgoyak and Zyuratkul. The lakes and two national parks are accessed from stations along the Ufa–Chelyabinsk railway.

Zyuratkul National Park

The very remote and quietly beautiful **Zyuratkul National Park** (Национальный парк Зюраткуль; ☑ 351-613 2033; www.zuratkul.ru, headquarters in Satka; park levy per day R40) is a great place for hiking, climbing the Zyuratkul range, swimming in a lake, going to a banya (hot bath) and sleeping in a log house. If you stay on the lake, you may wake up and feel rather like Henry Thoreau at Walden Pond.

The national park is dominated by several forest-covered ranges and Lake Zyuratkul, which translates from Bashkir as 'heart lake'. This is best observed from the Zyuratkul range nearby – an easy four-hour hike along a boardwalk through the forest and then along the mostly well-marked mountain path, though the *kurum* (path of loose rocks) at the top can be challenging in wet weather. Access is through the wooden arch on the main road, 100m before the lake and about a 10-minute walk back from Ecopark Zyuratkul.

🛏 Sleeping

Zyuratkul National Park Guesthouses   CAMPGROUND $
(☑ 351-613 2183; www.zuratkul.ru; 4-/10-bed cottages R2000/5500) Zyuratkul National Park guesthouses are a 10-minute walk along the main road curving around the lake shore from the settlement around Ecopark Zyuratkul. Staff can also organise overnight guided expeditions into the park.

Ecopark Zyuratkul   HOTEL, RESORT $$
(☑8-922 716 1944; www.eco-zuratkul.com; Lake Zyuratkul; r without bathroom R2800, cottages

sleeping 4/5/7 R12,000/15,000/21,000) This resort consists of cottages and a simple hotel. Stays of less than two nights cost about 20% more. You'll find yourself in a realm of manicured lawns, asphalt paths, tennis courts, large modern cottages and a restaurant, but it is a well-run and friendly resort that offers a wide range of activities, including expeditions into the wilderness.

Taganay National Park

Dramatically set in a lake-filled valley, the town of Zlatoust (285km from Ufa) serves as the gateway to Taganay National Park (Национальный парк Таганай; ☑ 351-366 3433; www.taganay.org) one of the most popular hiking, mountain biking and rafting getaways in the Ural Mountains.

🛏 Sleeping

Taganai Travel Turbaza   LODGE $
(☑ 351-366 3433; Pushkinsky Poselok, Zlatoust; camping R150, 4-/6-bed cottages R1500/2000) Located at the Taganay National Park's entrance, with spartan cottages and *banya* on the premises. Organise stays through Taganay Park Headquarters (p432).

ℹ GETTING TO ZYURATKUL

Getting to Zyuratkul National Park takes a little planning. Coming from Chelyabinsk, catch the bus to Satka and then a taxi to Zyuratkul. Travelling from west to east, get off the train at Berdyaush, take a taxi to Zyuratkul and then a taxi either back to Satka for the Chelyabinsk bus or to Berdyaush for the train.

Trains to Berdyaush

The main way from Ufa or Chelyabinsk into Zyuratkul National Park is by long-distance train to Berdyaush (Ufa R574, 5½ hours; from Chelyabinsk, seat: R376 to R539, 3¾ hours). The town of Suleya (west of Berdyaush) is also an option.

Marshrutky Between Berdyaush & Satka

Almost hourly minibuses daily leave Berdyaush from the bus station (near the train station) and leave Satka from the main bus station (40 minutes).

Buses Between Satka & Chelyabinsk

At least four buses go daily to/from Chelyabinsk Severny bus station (R495, four hours).

Taxis to Lake Zyuratkul

There are no *marshrutky* (fixed route minibuses) or buses to the lake, so you need to take a taxi – the best springboard is Berdyaush, but Satka (off the main line) is also good. Taxis from either cost roughly R1500 and take about an hour.

Satka taxi companies (☑351-614 3444, 904-814 4114) Book an hour or more ahead for taxis to the lake.

Ecopark Zyuratkul This tourist base can book taxis for you (one way R1000 all up).

Hotel Bellmont HOTEL $$
(Гостиница Бельмонт; ☑ 351-365 5700; www.
bellmont.ru; ul Taganayskaya 194a, Zlatoust; s
R1800-3500, d R2990-4100, ste R5200; ☏) A
good business-class option in Zlatoust with
sauna and beauty treatments.

ⓘ Information

Taganay Park Headquarters (Национальный
парк Таганай; ☑ 351-366 3433; www.
taganay.org; ul Shishkina 3a, Zlatoust) The
headquarters is located on the other side of
Zlatoust from the national park and reached
by *marshrutka* 33. The park administration can
organise a stay at one of the *kordony* (forest
lodges) inside the national park and at Taganai
Travel Turbaza (p431).

ⓘ Getting There & Around

Zlatoust is served by long-distance trains from
Ufa on the Ufa–Chelyabinsk route (R610, 6½
hours) and frequent *elektrichki* or long-distance
trains from Chelyabinsk (from R380 to R460,
three hours).

The park entrance is located on the outskirts
of Zlatoust, reached from the train station by
marshrutka 33. From its final stop, take the road
leading towards the forest to a signposted turn.

Chelyabinsk Челябинск

☑ 351 / POP 1.2 MILLION / ⊘ MOSCOW +2HR

Industrial and earthy, Chelyabinsk would at
first glance seem to be a place best visited as
a springboard rather than as a destination
in itself, but dig beneath surface and you'll
find a pleasant place to explore. The city
has broad avenues, numerous green spaces,
and a few interesting museums, with exhi-
bitions spanning everything from modern
arts to historical artifacts. One of the most
interesting of these is the meteor remnants
(Chelyabinsk made headlines as the closest
city to the site of a 2013 meteor explosion)
displayed at the Chelyabinsk State Museum
of Local History.

Beyond the city, the lakes and small
towns of the region are pleasant to visit,
so it's worth taking the time to stay in this
oft-overlooked and underrated city to get a
taste of everyday Ural Mountains life.

◎ Sights

Ulitsa Kirova STREET
(ul Kirova) Chelyabinsk's highlight is stroll-
ing down the cobblestone pedestrian-only
ul Kirova, where shops, cafes and life-sized

bronze statues of local personalities dot the
street.

**Chelyabinsk State
Museum of Local History** MUSEUM
(Государственный исторический музей
Южного Урала; ☑ 351-263 0832; www.chel-
museum.ru; ul Truda 100; Russian/foreigner
R350/400; ⊙10am-7pm Tue-Fri, 11am-8pm Sat,
11am-7pm Sun) The modern Chelyabinsk
State Museum of Local History uses natural
light well to create an attractive exhibition
space, a space that is home to over 300,000
artifacts. The highlight is the fragment of
meteorite, discovered in the region after the
2013 explosion that took place not far from
the city.

The exhibits about the region's prehisto-
ry and fauna and flora are also very worth-
while, as are the displays about Russians
living in the Urals through time. Some ex-
planations are in English

Chelyabinsk Region Art Museum GALLERY
(Музей изобразительных искусств; ☑ 351-266
3817; www.chelmusart.ru; ul Truda 92a, pl Revolyut-
sii 1; Russian/foreigner R170/400; ⊙ 11am-7pm Tue,
Wed & Fri-Sun, 12pm-8pm Thu) The museum is
spread across two locations and contains a
small and moderately interesting collection
of European and Russian paintings and
earthenware.The two complexes also house
changing exhibitions.

🛏 Sleeping

Yuzhny Ural HOTEL $
(☑ 351-247 4510; www.hotel74.ru/ural/; pr Lenina
52; incl breakfast s/d without bathroom R850/1600,
r R3500; ☷☏) The higher-priced rooms in
this hotel are shoddy and poor value for
money, but the rooms without bathrooms –
though in even worse shape – are a safe,
cheap option in town. The central location
is a big plus. Take any transport going to pl
Revolyutsii.

★**Congress Hotel Malakhit** HOTEL $$
(Конгресс-отель Малахит; ☑ 351-245 0575;
www.hotel74.ru/malahit/; ul Truda 153; incl breakfast s R2300-3900, d R3500-4800; ☷✳@☏)
This hotel has reinvented itself as a spa
hotel with sauna, small sauna pool and
treatments. Rooms are modern and clean,
at rates often considerably less than its
formal prices. Malakhit houses **Mirage**, a
lively disco and karoake bar. Take bus 18 or
tram 3 or 5 from the train station to stop
Operny Teatr.

LAKE TURGOYAK

Although it's not as isolated or as beautiful as some other lakes in the region, Lake Turgoyak (http://turgoyak.com), near the factory town of Miass, is surrounded by mountains and provides a tranquil getaway for the locals of Chelyabinsk.

Club-Hotel Golden Beach (Клуб-отель Золотой пляж; ☑ 351-329 8091; www.goldenbeach. ru; weekday/weekend s R4100/5800, d R5100/6300; ☺✿✸) is one of the prime resorts on the lake, popular with Russian holiday-makers when the sun comes out. Golden Beach can organise boat trips to **St Vera's Island**, the location of an ancient site abandoned about 9000 years ago and later used by Old Believers in the 19th century. Excursions last two hours, including the 30-minute each-way trip, and take in monoliths and small caves.

Taxi Miass (☑ 351-328-4949) takes you from Miass to Golden Beach hotel for about R400 to R500 (no other transport goes there). Miass can be reached by long-distance trains and regular *elektrichka* (R280, two hours) from Chelyabinsk.

Parkcity HOTEL **$$$**
(☑ 351-731 2222; www.parkcityhotel.ru; ul Lesopark-ovaya 6; incl breakfast s R4500-5500, d R5500-6400, ste R7000-9000; ☺✿@✸) This hotel has friendly, efficient staff and, as well as the usual business facilities, bicycles for hire. Mini-standard rooms for singles cost R2900, and other discounts are available. *Marshrutky* 3 and 86 run here from pl Revolyutsy.

✗ Eating

Brothers EUROPEAN, ASIAN **$**
(☑ 351-264 2446; ul Kirova 110; mains R80-320; ⊙ noon-midnight; ✸) Two brothers opened this cafe in 2016, wanting to create a space where customers could enjoy healthy clean food with a dose of fun. Food options span soups, Asian-inspired salads and stir-fries and grills and the coffee is decent. They also run fun events suitable for solo travellers, including dance performances, and English-speaking classes combined with Xbox games.

White Millery BAKERY **$**
(Белая мельница; ☑ 351-782 6591; ul Kirova 92; 0.5kg bread from R30; ⊙ 8am-8pm Mon-Fri, 9am-9pm Sat & Sun; ✎) Owner-baker Katarina makes some of the best bread in town and her specialty is unleavened bread. You'll also find spices, honey and the shop's own line of cosmetics in the neatly presented space.

★ Uralskiye Pelmeni RUSSIAN **$$**
(☑ 351-265 9591; pr Lenina 66a; pelmeni R255-R595, mains R295-R895; ⊙ 9am-midnight Mon-Thu, to 2am Fri, noon-2am Sat, to midnight Sun; ✿✸) When Russians first crossed the Urals, they were a tribe of porridge-eaters, but through the encounter with Asian tribes they found something that changed their cuisine forever – *pelmeni* (Russian-style ravioli). This two-storey restaurant-cum-disco (often heaving with golden oldies) is all about *pelmeni*, with plenty of fillings – such as rabbit, goose and eel – to choose from.

Meet.Point INTERNATIONAL, SUSHI **$$**
(www.mega74.ru; ul Kirova 143; bento lunches R200-R320, mains R230-R550; ⊙ 11am-5am Sun-Thu, to 6am Fri-Sat; ✸✎▮) As well as a small selection of Russian and international mains, this cafe, bar, restaurant and – later in the evening – dance space and karaoke hall serves Japanese cuisine, pizza, various international dishes and specialises in grilled meats. It has a children's play area and hookah-smoking area.

Tsyplyata Tabaka GEORGIAN, UZBEK **$$**
(Цыплята табака; ☑ 351-266 1485; www.ct-chel. ru; ul Kirova 139; mains R300-950; ⊙ 11am-12pm; ✿✸▮) One of the oldest restaurants in town, Tsyplyata Tabaka is all about chicken tabaka, a Georgian specialty consisting of a whole pan-fried chicken. The wide-ranging menu also spans Russian favourites, with plenty of meat, poultry and seafood dishes on offer. In the summertime the terrace is a lovely spot to sit and watch the world go by.

🍷 Drinking & Nightlife

Maximilians PUB
(☑ 351-220 3510; www.maximilians.ru/chel; ul Truda 183; ⊙ 12pm-2am Sun-Thu, to 5am Fri & Sat) The Chelyabinsk branch of this popular chain of Bavarian-style pubs serves filling, hearty fare (business lunches R190 to R290, mains R460 to R930) with its own brews and has live music and a dance space. Trolleybuses 17 and 10 run here from pl Revolyutsii to stop 'Molniya'.

EASTERN BASHKORTOSTAN

Magnitogorsk is a highly industrial city best used as a jumping-off point for exploring eastern Bashkortostan and the southern Ural Mountains, a region where picture-perfect birch groves and large blue lakes fill depressions between gentle grass-covered hills and the mountain ranges.

The region is a favourite locally for rafting, horse riding and skiing. It has recently seen growth in camping and basic accommodation sites, including the option to stay in traditional Bashkiran wooden homes and yurts such as at **Etnotur Irandik** (Этнотур Ирандык; ☑ 927-343 7341; www.halalholiday.ru; Mustaevo village, Baimaksky district; full board R700) about 20km from the town of Sibay.

Turbaza Malinovka (☑ 347-224 6306, 347-924 3064; www.go-ural.com/malinovka; s/d from R800/1600),10km from Beloretsk (R400 by taxi; call ☑ 347-922 4155) under the Malinovaya (Raspberry) mountain, has several log houses sleeping up to about 17 people, plus a two-to-four-person dacha. There's a sauna on site and it offers a range of tours, including two-horse rides, jeep tours, rafting and hiking.

The resort **Abzakovo Bungalo Club** (☑ 347-927 3918; Proezd Gorny 8; s/d incl breakfast from R1600/2000; ☻) has skiing in winter months and is located 20km along the road towards Ufa from Lake Bannoyeis.

Getting There & Away

Magnitogorsk–Ufa Daily train service (*kupe* from R600, 9½ hours)

Magnitogorsk–Chelyabinsk Buses every 30 minutes (R740, five hours, every hour)

Magnitogorsk–Bannoye *Marshrutky* from train station (R60, 40 minutes, frequent)

Magnitogorsk–Beloretsk Hourly buses (R170, 1½ hours, two hourly), via Novoabzakovo station

Ufa–Beloretsk The nightly Ufa–Sibay train calls at Beloretsk at 6.10am local time (R420, six hours)

Nu i Che Art Pub   BAR
(Ну и Чё Art Pub; ☑ 351-222 0238; www.monopoly74.ru; ul Truda 105; ☺10pm-5am Sun-Thu, to 8am Fri & Sat) Part of the larger 'Monopoly' complex (it includes the restaurant and live venue Lunny Svet at ul Kirova 82), Art Pub is the pub-disco arm attracting a good mix from young to late 30s.

ℹ Information

Post Office (☑ 351-266 0125; ul Kirova 161; ☺8am-10pm Mon-Fri, 9am-6pm Sat & Sun)

ℹ Getting There & Away

Sputnik (Спутник; ☑ 351-265 1377; www.sputnik74.ru; pr Lenina 61b; ☺9am-7pm Mon-Fri, 10am-4pm Sat, 11am-3pm Sun) sells rail and air tickets.

Buses depart from the Severny Bus Station to Yekaterinburg (R550, four hours) and Magnitogorsk (R740, five hours, every hour). Touts sell tickets for minibuses to Yekaterinburg (R700, 2½ hours, about every hour) in front of the Severny Bus Station.

Trains go daily to Moscow (from R2500, 35 hours), via Ufa (R900, 9½ hours) and Samara (R1224, 19 hours). Trains 146 and 39 run on odd and even days respectively via Yekaterinburg to St Petersburg (*kupe* R4590, two days). Heading east, most trains cut through Kazakhstan (separate visa required). There are one to three daily trains to the capital, Astana (*kupe* R3723, 22 hours).

Several fast trains run daily to Yekaterinburg (R643, five hours).

ℹ Getting Around

The train station is on ul Svobody, 2.5km south of the centre. Bus 18 and trams 3 and 5 connect the train station with pl Revolyutsii in the centre and run north along ul Tsvillinga to Operny Teatr, near the bottom of ul Kirova. Trams 7 and 8 go to pl Revolyutsii from the train station.

Bus 1 runs to the airport from the train station. **Taxi** (☑ 351-737 3737) services are generally reliable, although don't expect too much chit-chatter from the drivers.

Western Siberia

Best Places to Eat

➡ Puppen Haus (p448)

➡ Romanov Restaurant (p443)

➡ Chum Restaurant-Museum (p440)

➡ Chaynaya Sinyukha (p467)

➡ La Maison (p448)

Best Places to Stay

➡ FunKey Hostel (p445)

➡ Gostinitsa na Starom Meste (p464)

➡ Kochenik Camping Ground (p472)

➡ Gogol Hotel (p451)

➡ DoubleTree by Hilton (p447)

Why Go?

Heading east from the Urals, the influence and reach of Moscow noticeably begins to wane as one enters Western Siberia (Западная Сибирь). Unforgiving winters and a history of Gulag camps give the region a bad rap. The reality is much different. Western Siberia opens its arms to visitors and has plenty to offer the passing traveller. Expect contrasts and extremes, from glaciated mountains to underground cafes, fine art museums to gentle forest rambles. For the international visitor there's no getting away from the fact that Western Siberia is not the easiest place in which to travel. Visitors need a willingness to rough it, and outside the big cities it helps to be able to speak at least rudimentary Russian. But those who make the effort will be rewarded with an insight into the Siberian way of life and – perhaps more importantly – receive a dose of the locals' legendary hospitality.

When to Go
Novosibirsk

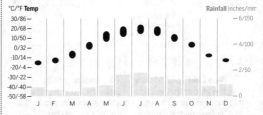

May Grand WWII Victory Day celebrations in Novosibirsk, wildflowers blooming in Altai.

Jul–Sep Bustling street scene in cities, trekking season in Altai.

Dec–Jan Tramp through Tomsk's winter wonderland and greet the New Year, Russian style.

History

Siberia's early Altai people were conceivably progenitors of the Inuit-Arctic cultures and of the Mongol-Turkic groups, which expanded in westbound waves with Attila, Chinggis (Genghis) Khaan and Timur (Tamerlane). The name Siberia comes from Sibir, a Turkic khanate and successor-state to the Golden Horde that ruled the region following Timur's 1395 invasion.

From 1563, Sibir started raiding what were then Russia's easternmost flanks. A Volga brigand called Yermak Timofeevich was sent to counter-attack. Though he had only 840 Cossack fighters, the prospect of battle seemed better than the tsar's death sentence that hung over him. With the unfair advantage of firearms, the tiny Cossack force managed to conquer Tyumen in 1580, turning Yermak into a Russian hero. Two

WESTERN SIBERIA

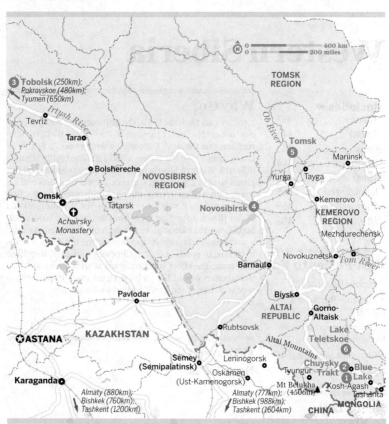

Western Siberia Highlights

1 Blue Lake (p472) Hiking over the glacier that leads to this sublime and oft-frozen lake halfway up the daunting Mt Aktru.

2 Chuysky Trakt (p470) Feeling Russia fade away and Central Asia come into play as you drive one of Russia's most spectacular roads.

3 Tobolsk (p440) Exploring Siberia's old capital with its glorious snow-white Kremlin and old town.

4 Novosibirsk (p444) Taking time out in Siberia's new capital with its bustling bars and creative museums.

5 Tomsk (p450) Taking a stroll through the Oxford of Siberia with its picturesque wooden homes and green-fingered gardens.

6 Lake Teletskoe (p467) Taking the slow boat down the placid lake waters that are Western Siberia's answer to Lake Baikal.

years later Yermak occupied Sibir's capital Isker, near today's Tobolsk. Russia's extraordinary eastward expansion had begun.

Initially, small Cossack units would set up an *ostrog* (fortress) at key river junctions. Local tribes would then be compelled to supply Muscovite fur traders, and villages slowly developed. Full-blown colonisation only started during the chaotic Time of Troubles (1606–13) as Russian peasants fled east in great numbers, bringing with them the diseases and alcohol that would subsequently decimate the native population. Meanwhile, settler numbers were swollen by exiled prisoners, and Old Believers seeking religious sanctuary. The construction of the first railways across Siberia in the late 19th century transformed the area. Many of today's cities, such as Novosibirsk in 1893, were founded as the rail lines stretched east.

After the October Revolution of 1917, anti-Bolshevik resistance briefly found a home in Western Siberia, and Omsk was the centre of Admiral Kolchak's White Russia from 1918 to 1919. As the USSR grew into a superpower, the area saw more than its fair share of Stalin's notorious Gulag camps. Nonetheless, unforced colonisation continued apace as patriotic workers and volunteer labourers undertook grandiose engineering projects, such as the construction of Novokuznetsk, virtually from scratch.

Since the USSR's collapse in 1991, some settlements built with Soviet disregard for economic logic have withered into gloomy virtual ghost towns. In contrast, discoveries of vast oil and gas deposits have led to booms in now-flashy but once remote cities like Tyumen.

Tyumen   Тюмень

📞 3452 / POP 581,000 / ⊘ MOSCOW +2HR

Founded in 1586, Tyumen was the first Russian settlement in Siberia. These days the city is the youthful, business-oriented capital of a vast, oil-rich *oblast* (region) stretching all the way to the Yamal and Gydansk peninsula on the Arctic Kara Sea. Don't let mention of oil-hungry businesspeople leave you thinking that this is a dull, money-focused city though. The city has a buzzing street life in summer and a couple of worthwhile sights that, taken together, will keep you entertained for a day or so. Tyumen is also the stepping stone to the gorgeous old town of Tobolsk, a few hours' bus or train ride away.

◉ Sights

If the weather is good, the best way to experience the city is by taking a stroll in the popular central City Park (Городской Парк; ul Lenina), or by walking along the riverside promenade.

★ Riverside Promenade   AREA
(Набережная) Tyumen's sleek riverside promenade runs northwest from the centre almost all the way to Trinity Monastery. The promenade offers great views of the Voznesensko Georgievskiy Church (Вознесенско-Георгиевский храм; Beregovaya ul) reflected in the Tura River from the opposite (east) bank. Lovers Bridge (Мост влюблённых; ul Kommunisticheskaya) leads over to the east bank, where you can explore curiously twisted old wooden houses along tree-lined Beregovaya ul (notably No. 73 and 53).

★ Trinity Monastery   MONASTERY
(Троицкий монастырь; ul Kommunisticheskaya 10) Riverside Trinity Monastery is undoubtedly Tyumen's most appealing architectural complex. Its kremlin-style crenellated outer wall is pierced by a single gate tower. Behind, gold domes top the striking Troitsky Church in the centre of the courtyard and, next to the black-turreted main gate, the 1727 Peter & Paul Church. In summer the flower beds of the complex burst with colour. The monastery is a pleasant 30-minute walk northwest from the city centre.

CORPSE OF HONOUR

Vladimir Lenin himself paid a visit to Tyumen – in 1941. Yes, he was already dead. The Soviets evacuated his body (just the body – his brain remained in Moscow) to Tyumen to keep it safe from the invading Germans. The body was kept under a veil of secrecy in the Selskhoz Academy (Сельсхоз Академия; ul Respubliki 7), an attractive early-20th-century brick building that still stands today, before being shipped back to Moscow in 1945. Throughout it all, the citizens of Tyumen remained blissfully unaware of the presence of a distinguished guest in their midst. Indeed, until after the war, few Russians had any idea the corpse had ever been transferred out of its mausoleum on Red Square!

WESTERN SIBERIA TYUMEN

Tyumen

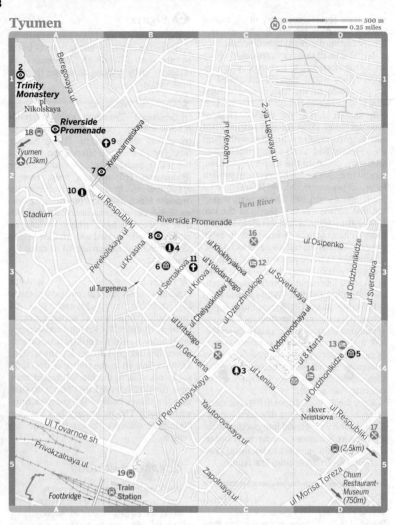

Fine Arts Museum
MUSEUM

(Музей изобразительного искусства; ☎ 3452-468 071; http://museum-72.ru; ul Ordzhonikidze 47; permenant collection free, temporary exhibition R150-200; ⊙ 10am-6pm Tue-Sun) **FREE** The Fine Arts Museum has several rotating and permanent exhibits ranging from ornate window frames saved from the city's old wooden houses to tiny, intricately carved bone figures produced by Siberian artists. While it's certainly one of the better galleries in Siberia, it gets expensive if you want to see all of the exhibits.

House-Museum of 19th- & 20th-Century History
MUSEUM

(Музей истории дома XIX-XX вв; ☎ 3452-464 963; ul Respubliki 18; R200; ⊙ 10am-6pm Wed-Sun) This museum contains artefacts from Tyumen's past and is housed in the city's finest carved cottage. The best way to experience the museum is by taking one of the museum guides whose stories will really bring the place alive. However, most guides only speak Russian or a smattering of English.

Znamensky Cathedral
CHURCH

(Знаменский собор; ul Semakova 13) With its voluptuously curved baroque towers, the

Tyumen

1786 Znamensky Cathedral is the most memorable of a dozen 'old' churches that have recently come back to life following years of neglect.

Civil War Monument MONUMENT
(Монумент в честь Гражданской войны; ul Respubliki) To the right of Selskhoz Academy (Сельсхоз Академия), this monument is dedicated to locals who died during battles against the Western-backed White Army immediately after the 1917 Bolshevik revolution.

WWII Monument MONUMENT
(ul Kommunisticheskaya) This unusual WWII monument features a Soviet woman piercing the heart of a winged reptilian creature. The embodiment of evil, we assume.

🛏 Sleeping

Muesli Mini Hotel HOSTEL $
(☑ 3452-464 191; ul Respubliki 49; dm from R800; ⊝❄☎) The dazzlingly bright primary colours this central hostel is painted in could liven up even the dullest Siberian day. It has tightly packed four- and eight-bed single-sex dorms, helpful staff who speak some English, and shared bathrooms (single sex) with glass-door showers, which is kind of odd!

Hotel Vostok HOTEL $$
(Гостиница Восток; ☑ 3452-686 111; www.vostok-tmn.ru; ul Respubliki 159; r incl breakfast from R3000; ⊝@☎) This former Soviet monstrosity has seen a massive facelift (inside, at least) and now boasts modern and, dare we say it, quite stylish and comfortable rooms, albeit still with Soviet dimensions (ie small). Some of the staff speak English. It's two easy bus stops from the centre along ul Respubliki.

Business Hotel Eurasia HOTEL $$$
(Бизнес-отель Евразия; ☑ 3452-222 000; www.eurasiahotel.ru; ul Sovetskaya 20; s/d incl breakfast from R5100/5800; ⊝❄☎) While not overloaded with character, it covers business travellers' needs with well-appointed rooms, a decent restaurant and a fitness centre. But the best part is that everything in the minibar is free of charge and no, that doesn't mean there's just water in the minibar!

Double Tree by Hilton BUSINESS HOTEL $$$
(☑ 3452-494 040; http://doubletree3.hilton.com; ul Ordzhonikidze 46; d incl breakfast from R4500; ⊝❄☎) If you're in the market for a state-of-the-art business hotel with ample facilities, you won't go wrong at this Hilton offering, which has calming colour schemes, wonderfully comfortable beds, black-out curtains (all too rare in Russia) and service that can't be faulted. Great value.

🍴 Eating

Schaste GEORGIAN $$
(Счастье; ☑ 3452-666 111; http://happyrest.ru; ul Respubliki 65, Kalinka Trade Centre; mains R300-700; ⊙11.45am-1am; ☎) Funky, glass-fishbowl-shaped restaurant and bar with leafy plants and bicycles mounted on the walls. There's a menu of Russian, international and some Georgian specialities such as fried *suluguni* (Georgian cheese), *kharcho* (beef stew) and *khinkali* (dumplings). If you're travelling with children they are sure to enjoy the kids play area inside a train carriage.

In Da USA AMERICAN $$
(Ин Да Юса; ☑ 3452-070755; http://indausa.ru; ul Chelyuskintsev 10; mains R300-450; ⊙noon-2am Sun-Thu, noon-6am Fri & Sat; ☎) In Da USA

is, naturally, festooned with Americana and serves Tyumen's best burgers along with Tex-Mex and a host of bar appetisers. It becomes a club famous for table-top dancing at weekends as well as live music and disco-coloured cocktails with sexy names.

Malina Bar CAFE **$$**
(Малина Бар; ul Pervomayskaya 18; meals R200-600; ⊙24hr; 🛜) The city slicker Malina Bar has a huge menu of Russian and European food, overly fluffy cakes, filling breakfasts, real coffee, fast wi-fi and cosy seating in grand leather couches. Upstairs is sister Italian restaurant-steak house **Berlusconi** (mains R300-1200; ⊙11am-3am Mon-Thu, 11am-6am Fri-Sat).

★**Chum Restaurant-Museum** RUSSIAN **$$$**
(Ресторан-музей Чум; ☑3452-621 660; http://maxim-rest.ru; str Maligina 59/12; mains R600-900; ⊙11am-2am) Inside a faux Siberian hunters cabin lined with furs and skis, this unusual restaurant specalises in the cuisine of northern Siberia. Dishes include salted fish, elk, reindeer tongues and wild boar. However, whereas the average Siberian hunter probably just munches on a great hunk of meat, here the dishes are given a totally modern touch and presented with arty flamboyance.

ⓘ Information

City maps and bus-route plans are sold at newspaper kiosks in the train station and throughout the city.
Main Post Office (Почтамт; ul Respubliki 56; ⊙8am-10pm Mon-Fri, 9am-6pm Sat & Sun)

ⓘ Getting There & Away

AIR
Tyumen's **Roshchino Airport** is 13km west of the centre. S7 and Aeroflot are among airlines with daily flights to Moscow (three hours), while regional carrier **Yamal Airlines** (http://yamal.aero) serves Novosibirsk (two hours, daily) and arctic hubs Novy Urengoy (daily) and Salekhard (daily) among many other destinations in Tyumen Oblast and beyond. Note that foreigners usually need a special permit to visit most Arctic Circle destinations. A second regional carrier, **UTAir** (www.utair.ru), serves Khanty-Mansiysk among other remote destinations in Tyumen Oblast.

BUS
From the **bus station** (ul Permyakova), 3km east of the centre, buses to Tobolsk (R580, four hours, seven daily) travel via Rasputin's home town of Pokrovskoe (R250, 1½ hours).

TRAIN
Several day and overnight trains go to Omsk (*platskart/kupe* R1708/2538, 8½ hours, 10.19pm) and points east along the Trans-Siberian main line, and dozens of westbound trains serve Yekaterinburg and beyond.

There are many daily trains to Tobolsk (from R600, 3½ hours). If you're looking to explore the Arctic, trains continue beyond Tobolsk all the way to Novy Urgenoy (at least twice daily). Other useful trains serve Barnaul (R3141/4056, 29 hours, daily at 4.41am) and Tomsk (R3423/4942, 23 hours, even-numbered days at 6.52am).

ⓘ Getting Around

To get to Roshchino Airport, 13km west of the centre, catch *marshrutka* 35 or bus 141 anywhere along ul Respubliki (30 minutes). Taxis from the city centre cost R300 if ordered by phone through your hotel.

From the train station, bus 27 serves Hotel Vostok and passes near the bus station – hop off at the Krosno stop, and cross ul Respubliki. Several other bus lines also link the train station with the city centre. Buses also run from the eastern end of ul Lunacharskogo up and down ul Respubliki to the city centre. Taxis around town cost R200.

Tobolsk Тобольск

☑3456 / POP 100,000 / ⊙ MOSCOW +2HR
Once Siberia's capital, Tobolsk is one of the region's most historic cities and one of the nation's most beautiful, sporting a magnificent snow-white kremlin and a charmingly decrepit old town. Tobolsk is off the Trans-Siberian main line but is well worth the short diversion from Tyumen.

The centre of the Russian colonisation of Siberia, Tobolsk was founded in 1587. Its strategic importance started to wane in the 1760s, when the new Great Siberian Trakt (post road) took a more southerly route. However, until the early 20th century it remained significant as a centre for both learning and exile. Involuntary guests included Fyodor Dostoevsky en route to exile in Omsk, and deposed Tsar Nicholas II and his family, who spent several months here in 1917 before being taken to Yekaterinburg and executed.

Buses from the inconvenient train station give visitors a dismal first impression. Tobolsk's glories begin 3km further south around the splendid kremlin. Immediately beyond and below the kremlin, the old town sinks into the Irtysh's boggy floodplain.

⊙ Sights

★ **Kremlin** HISTORIC BUILDING
(⊙ grounds 8am-8pm) The centrepiece of the tower-studded, white-walled, 18th-century kremlin is the glorious 1686 **St Sofia Cathedral** (Софийский собор; Krasnaya pl 2). Less eye-catching from the outside, but with splendid arched ceiling murals, is the **Intercession Cathedral** (Покровский собор; kremlin). Between the two is a 1799 **bell tower** (kremlin), built for the Uglich bell, which famously signalled a revolt against Tsar Boris Godunov. The Kremlin prison is now the **Castle Prison Museum** (Тюремный замок; ☎ 3456-222 776; www.tiamz.ru; Krasnaya pl 5; R300; ⊙ 10am-6pm Tue-Sun), where you can

Tobolsk

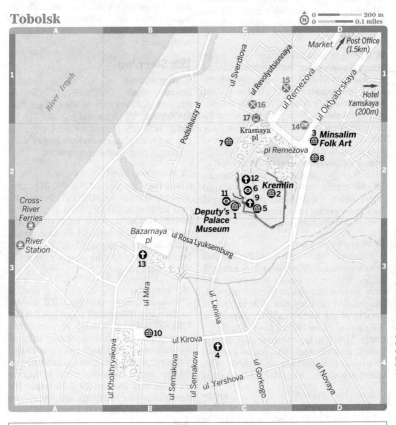

WESTERN SIBERIA TOBOLSK

Tobolsk

get a sense of the grim life behind bars in both Tsarist and Soviet times.

The elegant **Arkhiereysky Mansion** (Архиерейский Дом; kremlin) was closed for renovations when we visited and will eventually reopen as an Orthodox history museum.

Wooden stairs lead beneath the kremlin's **Pryamskoy Vzvoz** (Прямской Взвоз) (gatehouse) to the wonderfully dilapidated old town full of weather-beaten churches and angled wooden homes sinking between muddy lanes.

★ **Deputy's Palace Museum**   MUSEUM
(Дворец наместника; www.tiamz.ru; Krasnaya pl 1; admission R600; ⊙10am-6pm Tue-Sun) Tobolsk's best museum, and indeed one of the best museums in Siberia, occupies a beautiful 18th-century former administration on the southwestern edge of the Kremlin. The Romanovs called in here during their brief stint in Tobolsk in 1917, and a section of this remarkably modern museum is devoted to their time in Tobolsk. Tactile multimedia exhibits profile the characters who shaped Siberia before the Bolshevik revolution, and hometown heroes such as Dmitry Mendeleyev, who created the first periodic table.

★ **Minsalim Folk Art**   GALLERY
(Мастерская Минсалим; ☑3456-246 993; www.minsalim.ru; ul Oktyabrskaya 2; ⊙9am-6pm) FREE Minsalim is a master bone-carver who turns mammoth tusks and antler fragments into detailed figurines related to myths and legends of the local brand of shamanism. With a long mustache and flowing mane, eccentric Minsalim is something of a shaman himself, and will gladly lead you on a tour of his workshop behind the gallery (phone in advance). His son and some staff speak English.

Gubernsky Museum   MUSEUM
(Губернский музей; www.tiamz.ru; ul Oktyabrskaya 1; R200; ⊙10am-6pm Tue-Sun) Built in 1887 for the 300th anniversary of the founding of Tobolsk, the Gubernsky Museum has displays on the history of Tobolsk, a hugely impressive and near-complete mammoth skeleton and a display of bone carvings.

Archangel Mikhail Church   CHURCH
(Церковь Архангела Михаила; ul Lenina 24) The attractive Archangel Mikhail Church has a colourfully restored interior. The character of Tatiana Larina in Pushkin's epic *Eugene Onegin* is said to have been modelled on Natalya Fonvizina, a Decembrist wife who prayed here.

Zachary & Elisabeth Church   CHURCH
(Церковь Захария и Елизаветы; Bazarnaya pl 8) The 1759 Zachary & Elisabeth Church, with its soaring black-tipped spires, is extremely photogenic.

Kornilov Mansion   MUSEUM
(Дом Корнилова; ul Mira 9) The grand Kornilov Mansion, named after a 19th-century statesman and philanthropist, is closed while being converted into a museum dedicated to the Romanovs, but is still worth a look for its lavish exterior.

🛏 Sleeping

Resting Rooms   HOSTEL $
(komnaty otdykha; ☑3456-62 522; train station; dm 12/24hr from R600/800, s/d from R1400/2000; 🛜) Clean and friendly. The location is utterly impractical for visiting the city, but ideal if you're arriving late or waiting for an early-morning connection.

★ **Hotel Yamskaya**   HOTEL $$
(Гостиница Ямская; ☑3456-226 177; yamskaya-tobolsk@mail.ru; ul Bolshaya Sibirskaya 40; r incl breakfast R3300; 🛜) With cosy rooms, friendly service, a perfect location near the kremlin, and a warm and inviting overall atmosphere, this 12-room hotel borders on boutique. The prices are extremely reasonable for what you get.

★ **Hotel Sibir**   HOTEL $$
(Гостиница Сибирь; ☑3456-220 901; www.hotel-siberia.com; pl Remezova 1; s/d incl breakfast from R2100/3900; 🛜) Sibir's rooms are comfortable, spacious and festooned with fading old photos, dark wood furnishings and old-fashioned wallpaper, which gives it an enjoyably historical vibe. Another huge plus is that it's the closest to the kremlin of all Tobolsk's hotels. The breakfast is tasty and filling and the in-house restaurant is reliably good. A good-value spot.

🍴 Eating

While Tobolsk has seen a modest tourist boom in recent years, there is still no restaurant scene to speak of.

Kofeynya u Ershova   CAFE $
(Кофейня у Ершова; ☑3456-246 808; ul Remezova 7; mains R150-450; ⊙10am-11pm) An easy stop near the kremlin for relatively quick and cheap Russian eats – think lunch standards such as *bishteks* (Russian-style hamburger), *solyanka* (pickled vegetables and potato soup) and stuffed *bliny* (pancackes). Portions

tend to be on the small side so if you're hungry it might be worth ordering two dishes.

Ladeyny
RUSSIAN $$

(Ладейный; ☑ 3456-222 111; ul Revolutsionnaya 2; mains R250-500; ⏰ 11am-2am; 🛜) This place is a revolution as far as Tobolsk is concerned, an extra-large Siberian *izba* (wood house) that simply feels warm and welcoming. Specialities include Siberian fish and homemade *pelmeni* (ravioli) and *varenyky* (dumplings). Nights sometimes bring live music. The English menu is extremely rare for these parts.

★ Romanov Restaurant
RUSSIAN $$$

(Ресторан Романов; ☑ 3456-399 139; ul Microrayon 1, Hotel Slavyanskaya; mains R1000-1500; ⏰ noon-10pm) Housed in the Hotel Slavyanskaya, the very refined Romanov restaurant is in a class above everything else in Tobolsk. Dress sharp and tuck into a menu that features succulent 19th-century Russian dishes. Also has a family portrait of Russia's last tsar and his family on the ceiling and even today it can count ex-Presidents among its clientele.

ⓘ Information

Post Office (Почта; Komsomolsky pr 42; ⏰ 8am-6pm)

ⓘ Getting There & Away

There are frequent trains to Tyumen (from R600, four hours).

Train 125 trundles to Novosibirsk on odd-numbered days at 9.21am (from R4696, 24 hours) via Omsk, while the 115 is a late-night option to Omsk on odd-numbered days (*platskart/kupe* R2598/3197, 13¼ hours, 1.26am).

Buses are another option to Tyumen (R580, four hours) via Pokrovskoe (R300, 2½ hours), Rasputin's home village. Eight buses per day to various destinations pass through nearby Abalak, site of an interesting monastery.

In the warm months ferries leave from the **river station** and cruise the Irtysh north to Salekhard (1st-/2nd-/3rd-class R3000/1200/900, five days, about six monthly) via Khanty-Mansiysk (two days), and south to Omsk (R2200/1000/850, three days, about three monthly).

ⓘ Getting Around

Bus 4 and *marshrutka* (fixed-route minibus) 20 link the train station, new town and kremlin. Taxis to/from the station cost around R250.

There are small ferry boats criss-crossing back and forth over the River Irtysh throughout daylight hours and into the early evening. They leave from just north of the river station and further south.

Omsk   Омск

☑ 3812 / POP 1.15 MILLION / ⏰ MOSCOW +3HR

With its modest sights hidden behind busy roads and endless kilometres of drab concrete, this big industrial city is not worth a special detour. However, you may find it a convenient stopover to break up long journeys.

If you're looking to kill some time, the **Fine Arts Museum** (☑ 3812-200 047; www.vrubel.ru; ul Lenina 3; R150; ⏰ 10am-7pm Tue-Sun) displays a lot of fussy decorative arts. The rectilinear 1862 building was built as the Siberian governor's mansion and hosted passing tsars. In 1918–19, however, the building was home to Admiral Kolchak's counter-revolutionary government and was the heart of White Russia before the Reds eventually claimed the city.

Cross the bridge at ul Lenina, continue north and you'll pass several parks and notable buildings, including the ornate **Drama Theatre** (Омский театр драмы; www.omsk-drama.ru; ul Lenina 8a) built in the early 20th century, and the massive turquoise-and-gold domed **Assumption Cathedra** (Успенский собор; Sobornaya pl)l rebuilt after the collapse of the USSR.

🛏 Sleeping & Eating

Resting Rooms
HOSTEL $

(komnaty otdykha; ☑ 3812-442 347; train station; 12/24hr from R900/1600) Spacious and with en suites, these are some of the best train station rooms we've seen in Siberia.

Hotel Mayak
BUSINESS HOTEL $$$

(Гостиница Маяк; ☑ 3812-330 303; www.hotel-mayak.ru; ul Lermontova 2; s/tw incl breakfast R3400/4800; ⊕❄🛜) In the eye-catching rounded end of the vaguely ship-shaped art-deco river station, the Mayak has small, modish rooms with artistic lines and good bathrooms. Popular with Western business travellers. Friendly staff and an impressive breakfast buffet.

★ Lapshichnaya
Noodle Shop
VIETNAMESE $$

(Little Flower in Big Window; ☑ 3812-208 028; ul Lenina 20; ⏰ 11am-11pm) The fresh, healthy and slightly spiced soups and curries of Southeast Asia are a rare treat in Siberia, so it's worth making a special effort to eat at this light, bright and modern noodle bar. We particularly enjoyed the beef in a spicy soya sauce.

Tamada GEORGIAN $$

(Тамада; ☎ 3812-200 127; ul Gagarina 3; meals R450-800; ⊙ 10am-midnight; 🍴) It won't just be the food you remember at this Georgian restaurant. The setting, in a bizarre cave-like basement filled with fake ponds and palm trees, will live long in the memory too. The *khachapuri* (bread baked with cheese filling) and *lobiyo* (spicy red beans stewed in vegetables) are recommended. It's just off ul Lenina.

ℹ Information

K2 Adventures (www.adventuretravel.ru) Igor Fedyaev is the guru of adventure travel in Western Siberia. English-speaking, affable and responsive, he specialises in mountaineering expeditions in Altai and elsewhere, but can arrange just about any tour you want around Omsk or elsewhere in the region.

Post Office (Почтамт; ul Gertsena 1; ⊙ 8am-10pm Mon-Fri, 9am-6pm Sat & Sun)

ℹ Getting There & Away

Omsk is on the Trans-Siberian main line, which means numerous connections both east toward Novosibirsk (*platskart/kupe* from R1622/2700, about 7½ hours) and west toward Yekaterinburg. Destinations off the main line served from Omsk include Abakan (R3183/5412, 30 hours, daily), Barnaul (R2924/3549, 16 hours, one or two daily), Tomsk (R3167/4391, 14 hours, even-numbered days) and Tobolsk (R3547/4382, 12 hours, odd-numbered days at 8.30pm, even-numbered days at 10.16am).

An *elektrichka* (suburban train) serves Novosibirsk Tuesday, Thursday and Sunday at 2.55pm (1st-/2nd-/3rd-class R1623/1287/711, 6¾ hours).

ℹ Getting Around

The main streets, Ul Lenina and pr Marksa, run parallel to each other through the centre of town and cross the Om River just north of central pl Lenina. From the train station, trolleybus 4 and bus 69 are among many options that go to the centre along pr Marksa.

Novosibirsk Новосибирск

☎ 383 / POP 1.5 MILLION / ⊙ MOSCOW +4HR

Novosibirsk might be Russia's third-largest city, but you wouldn't know it. The city centre is compact and – thanks to lots of parks and tree-lined avenues – it has a quiet, green-fingered air to it, which makes it an ideal city for strolling about. And there's a lot here worth strolling for, including a slew of quirky museums and monuments, some impressive galleries, a good theatre and entertainment scene and some memorable places to eat. All this means it's hard not to like Novosibirsk and, sitting as it does on the main rail line, it makes a worthwhile Trans-Siberian pit stop. You can also jump off from here to architecturally splendid Tomsk, some 4½ hours away by bus.

Novosibirsk grew up in the 1890s around the Ob River bridge built for the Trans-Siberian Railway, and the city is festooned with original examples of the wood-lace architecture that prevailed at the time before the Soviets took over and started chucking concrete everywhere. Named Novo-Nikolaevsk until 1925 for the last tsar, it grew rapidly into Siberia's biggest metropolis, a key industrial and transport centre exploiting coalfields to the east and mineral deposits in the Urals.

Despite its daunting scale, Novosibirsk has a manageable centre focused on pl Lenina. The city's main axis, Krasny pr, runs through this square linking most points of interest.

◎ Sights

★ N.K. Rerikh Museum MUSEUM

(Музей Н.К. Рериха; www.sibro.ru; ul Kommunisticheskaya 38; R200, free every 2nd Sat; ⊙ 11am-7pm Fri-Mon & Wed, 1-8pm Thu) This museum is dedicated to the works and life of the painter Nikolai Rerikh (Nicholas Roerick), beloved in these parts because of his life-long passion for Altai. While the many paintings on display are reproductions, they provide a thorough synopsis of his life's work, and you can buy affordable prints in the excellent gift shop.

Rerikh was also a writer, a philosopher, a scientist, an archaeologist, a statesman – and a traveller. An epic five-year expedition around Central Asia (including Altai) and the Himalayas in the 1920s provided fodder for many of his paintings and philosophies. That journey is explored in depth here, making the museum an inspiring spot for modern-day vagabonds. Incredibly, the expedition traversed 35 mountain passes of more than 14,000ft! There is a 15-minute movie in English on the artist's life, and rooms dedicated to the works of his wife and two sons – talented artists, writers and/or thinkers in their own right.

If you can, try to time your visit to the museum to coincide with one of the beautiful classical music concerts (free with entry) on 3rd floor at 3pm every Thursday and on the second Saturday of each month.

★Novosibirsk State
History Museum   MUSEUM
(Краеведческий музей; Krasny pr 23; R200;
⊘10am-6pm Wed-Fri, 11am-7pm Sat-Sun) In an
elegant mansion, the State History Museum
has recently re-opened after renovations and
is now by far the best museum in Novosibirsk. The well-thought-out collection traces
the history of Siberia and Novosibirsk from
birth up to today. The highlights are the displays on nomadic life and shamanism (in the
basement). The regular temporary exhibitions are a more hit-and-miss affair and can
include anything from collections of posh
frocks to delicate-faced dolls and puppets.

★Alexander Nevsky Cathedral   CHURCH
(Собор Александра Невского; Krasny pr 1a)
The 1898 Alexander Nevsky Cathedral is a
red-brick Byzantine-style building with gilded domes and colourful murals. The cathedral was originally built as a monument in
honour of Tsar Alexander III who had initi-
ated the construction of Novosibirsk. It was
shut by the Soviet authorities in 1937 and
only re-opened in 1989.

Cathedral of the Ascension   CHURCH
(Вознесенский собор; ul Sovetskaya 91) The
gold-domed 1914 Cathedral of the Ascension
has a wonderful, colourful interior with a
soaring central space that's unexpected giv-
en its fairly squat exterior appearance.

USSR Museum   MUSEUM
(Музей СССР; ☑383-223 0266; ul Gorkogo 16;
R200; ⊘noon-6pm Tue-Sat) While the collection of '70s Soviet bric-a-brac in this museum
isn't particularly original, you get free rein
over the place, which means photo opps
galore. Dress yourself up (don't worry, it's
allowed!) as a Soviet apparatchik, country
dyevushka (girl) or Great Patriotic War soldier and snap away. The museum is housed
within a ramshackle wooden building.

State Art Museum   MUSEUM
(Художественный музей; Krasny pr 5; R200;
⊘noon-8pm Tue-Fri, 1-9pm Sat & Sun) The highlight is the museum's collection of 65 original
paintings by Nikolai Rerikh on the 2nd floor,
mostly mountainscapes from the celebrated
drifter's time in the Himalayas. The 2nd floor
also has a room of 17th-century European
(mostly Dutch) masters, a collection of icons
and several rooms dedicated to 18th-to-19th-
century Russian art. The 3rd floor has some
wonderful pieces from the Soviet era.

Chapel of St Nicholas   CHURCH
(Часовня Святителя Николая; Krasny pr) The
pretty Chapel of St Nicholas was said to mark
the geographical centre of Russia when it was
built in 1915. Demolished in the 1930s, it was
rebuilt in 1993 for Novosibirsk's centenary. Today it is an oasis of calm in the bustling city.

Monument to First Traffic Light   MONUMENT
(cnr ul Serebrennikovskaya & ul Sibrevkoma) This
humorous monument portraying a stumpy
little man staring up at a bendy traffic light
is based at the rumoured site of the city's first
ever traffic light. It's worth a quick diversion
if you're in the southern part of town.

🏃 Activities & Tours

Altair-Tur   TOURS
(Альтаир-Тур; ☑383-212 5115; www.altairtour.
ru; ul Sovetskaya 65, Novosibirsk; ⊘10am-7pm
Mon-Fri, to 5pm Sat) Very well-regarded,
fast-responding and English-speaking tour
company specialising in the Altai region
(but also most parts of Russia). It can organise anything from a car and driver through
to full-blown mountaineering expeditions
up the highest peaks in Altai. Happy to provide the required paperwork for visas.

Sibir Altai   TOUR
(☑383-299 0403; http://sibalt.ru; ul Chelyuskintsev 36, Novosibirsk; ⊘10am-6pm Mon-Fri, 11am-
3pm Sat) Packages Altai trips for local tourists, sold through numerous regional travel
agencies. Minimal English.

Tour Academy   TOURS
(☑383-204 8664; http://touracademy.ru; Bolshe-
vistskaya 101) Aimed primarily at a domestic
market, this experienced agency organises
hiking, rafting and even children's camps in
the Altai region as well as Sheregesh.

🛏 Sleeping

The best hotels and hostels book out fast,
especially from May to October: book ahead.

★FunKey Hostel   HOSTEL $
(☑383-263 6503; www.funhostel.ru; ul Frunze
5/2; dm R490-700, d R1700; ☕❄🛜) 'Funkey'
indeed. It backs up its quirky name with
one of Siberia's most creative hostel spaces.
Bright colours and eye-catching photos en-
liven walls, extra-tall bunk beds penetrate
soaring ceilings and guests kick back in a
delightfully wide-open kitchen and common
area. Staff are helpful, traveller savvy and

Novosibirsk

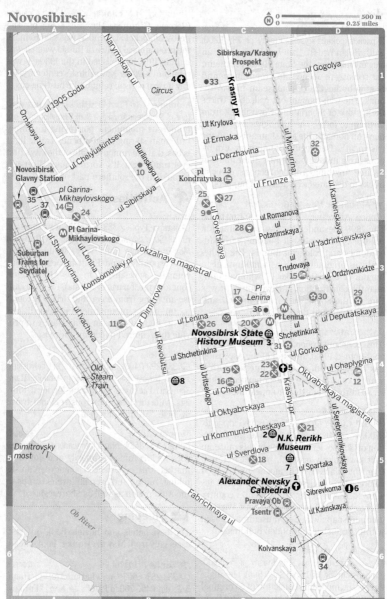

speak good English. Easily the best hostel in town.

Provence Hostel   HOSTEL $
(Хостел Прованс; ul Chaplygina 45; dm R650-700, d R2200; @ 🛜) Occupying the 2nd floor of an attractive century-old brick building, the Provence is a large hostel and one that comes across as a little more 'grown-up' than the town's other hostels. Gone are the chalk graffiti walls so common at the competition and in are subtle whites and a hint of the

Novosibirsk

Mediterranean. Capable, English-speaking staff. The kicker is the lack of much in the way of a communal lounge area.

Azimut Hotel Siberia HOTEL $$
(☑ 383-217 6970; www.azimuthotels.com; ul Lenina 21; s/d incl breakfast from R2750/2904; ☻❈☎) Big changes have been afoot at this large former Soviet-era hotel. It's been given a good revamp and the rooms (though remaining Soviet size challenged) are clean, plain, quiet and functional. The staff are very efficient and the included breakfast is a veritable feast. A very good deal.

Marins Park Hotel Novosibirsk HOTEL $$
(Конгресс-Гостиница Новосибирск; ☑ 383-364 0101; www.hotel-novosibirsk.ru; Vokzalnaya magistral 1; r incl breakfast from R2500; ☻❈@☎) Boasting awesome views of the city centre from its upper floors, this formerly glum Soviet-era tower has been transformed into a plush modern hotel with fantastic service and prime rooms. The live python in a huge cage beside the reception desk is a novel touch. Great weekend and online deals are often available.

★ **DoubleTree by Hilton** HOTEL $$$
(☑ 383-223 0100; www.novosibirsk.doubletreebyhilton.com; ul Kamenskaya 7/1; s/d incl breakfast weekday from R10,300/11,400, weekend from R5300/6400; ☻❈@☎☀) Has all the amenities you would expect, highlighted by luscious beds, mood lighting, ginormous plasma TVs, rain showers and (separate) extra-long bathtubs, although we'd like to see a bit more space in the standard rooms. Online booking can sometimes mean big discounts. The service is unusually good.

Novosibirsk Marriott Hotel BUSINESS HOTEL $$$
(☑ 383-230 0300; www.mariott.com; ul Ordzhonikidze 31; incl breakfast r Mon-Fri from R9751, Sat & Sun R7100; ☻❈☎☀) Architecturally speaking, the city's new Marriott Hotel, opposite the opera theatre, and in a pleasingly renovated old building with huge windows, blends nicely into the townscape. The decor is fairly cookie-cutter-luxury business class, though it's undeniably comfortable and well-run.

✖ Eating

Vilka-Lozhka CAFE $
(ul Frunze 2; meals R150-250; ☻9am-10pm; ☎) This upmarket *stolovaya* (cafeteria) is popular for a reason – hip and cool with groovy tunes and piping-hot Russian staples like *bliny* (pancakes) and borsch at dirt-cheap prices. It even has beer on tap. Good place for a simple and fun meal.

Shashlikoff
RUSSIAN **$**

(www.shashlikoff.com; Krasny pr 17; mains R250-300; ⊙9am-1am; 🖃) This popular chain is fantastic value. Its signature shashlyk (kebabs) come in meat and fish varieties, accompanied by a full complement of Russian soups and salads, and washed down with home-brewed beer (from R85). There's another branch opposite the train station (www.shashlikoff.com; Vokzalnaya magistral 1; mains R250-300; ⊙9am-1am; 🖃).

★ Park Cafe
INTERNATIONAL **$$**

(☑383-310 9070; www.parkcafensk.com; Kransy Prospekt 25/1; mains R400-800; ⊙7.30am-1am Mon-Fri, 9am-1am Sat & Sun) Bulbous lights, arty fairy colours, shelves of books and beautifully created and presented dishes mean that this very central restaurant has a loyal local fan club. After you've finished tucking into one of their yummy soups, salads, fish cakes or some delicately prepared macarons, take a walk through the pretty neighbouring park.

Goodman Steak House
STEAK **$$**

(☑383-289 2525; ul Sovetskaya 5; mains R540-720; ⊙noon-midnight) There's a busy, British-style pub atmosphere at the Goodman Steak House. Although plenty of people stop by after work for just a beer, it's renowned for having some of the best steaks in the city, as well as other pub favourites like chicken curry and homemade sausages.

Baranzhar
CENTRAL ASIAN **$$**

(☑383-209 0902; www.baranjar.ru; ul Sovetskaya 18; mains R300-550; ⊙noon-midnight; 🖃) With a warm, relaxed atmosphere and a creatively decorated dining room, it's no wonder that this central restaurant, which serves up an exotic flavour of Central Asia (although there's a fair few Russian staples as well), is currently one of Novosibirsk's favourites. The emphasis here is on kebabs, but the stuffed eggplant starter is delicious.

Tiflis
GEORGIAN **$$**

(Тифлис; ☑383-222 8181; www.tiflisnsk.ru; ul Sovetskaya 65; mains R400-600; ⊙11am-11pm; 🖃) This atmospheric tavern-cavern down in a basement offers the most authentic Georgian cuisine in town. The filling and delicious *khachapuri po-adzharski* (Georgian cheese bread with a raw egg swimming in the middle) is well worth a try. There's an English menu and the staff speak good English and will happily give menu suggestions.

Trattoria la Trenta
ITALIAN **$$**

(☑383-223 9291; http://latrenta.ru; ul Uritsekogo 9; pizzas around R440, mains R350-500; ⊙noon-11pm Sun-Thu, noon-midnight Fri & Sat; ⊛) You could almost imagine this cute little trattoria has been magically transported straight from a honey-coloured Tuscany village to big old Novosibirsk. The walls are lined in paintings and dried pasta and there's a shaded terrace for summer evenings. The menu lists all the Italian classics, but also includes a few local touches such as black buckwheat pizza bases. There's a reasonable wine list and the staff are warm and smiley.

★ Puppen Haus
RUSSIAN **$$$**

(☑383-251 0303; www.puppenhaus-resto.ru; ul Chaplygin 65/1; full meal around R2000; ⊙noon-midnight) The Puppen Haus (Puppet House), which specialises in refined traditional Siberian dishes, is both eccentric and divine. It consists of numerous little dining rooms and alcoves crammed with stony-eyed wooden puppets. The food is as memorable as the setting and if you've never tried elk steaks, Kamchatka lobster or – get this – boiled bear (!) then now is the chance. Advance bookings are wise in the evening.

★ La Maison
EUROPEAN **$$$**

(☑383-209 0010; ul Sovetskaya 25; mains R600-1500; ⊙10am-midnight) In a beautiful former theatre dating to 1908, this is Novosibirsk's most sumptuous restaurant. The French- and Russian-leaning menu features quail, rabbit, rack of lamb and octopus along with upmarket versions of *solyanka* (soup from pickled vegetables and potato) and other Russian country faves. Also has an extensive wine list and rich desserts such as millefeuille.

🍷 Drinking & Nightlife

★ Friends Cocktail Bar
BAR

(Krasny pr 22; ⊙6pm-6am) With bearded bartenders whipping up some of Siberia's best (and strongest) cocktails and a convivial crowd, this is unquestionably Novosibirsk's best spot to warm up for a night out. Indeed you may elect to not go anywhere else. Reliably action-packed on weekdays as well as weekends, and you can eat at equally trendy People's Bar & Grill (Krasny pr 22; mains R350-800; ⊙24hr) in the same building.

Truba
BAR

(Труба; www.vk.com/truba_nsk; ul Frunze 2; ⊙7pm till late; 🖃) It bills itself as a jazz bar but the line-up runs the gamut from jazz and blues to trash rock and grunge. Whatever is playing, this underground institution is well worth checking out.

Rock City CLUB
(Рок Сити; ☑383-227 0108; www.rockcity.ru; Krasny pr 37; cover R150-350) Everything from Latin dancing to DJs to heavy-rock concerts. Thursday is ladies' night and Tuesdays feature two-for-one cocktails.

☆ Entertainment

★ **Brodyachaya Sobaka** LIVE MUSIC
(Бродячая Собака; ☑383-218 8070; www.sobaka.su; Kamenskaya ul 32; ⊙5pm-1am Sun-Thu, 5pm-3am Fri & Sat; ☎) Weekends usually see live music performing at this grungy cabaret bar, while weekdays bring all manner of performing arts and other events ranging from clowns to quiz nights. Check the website for the schedule. To find it look for the discreet rust-red carved metal sign and then head down the stairs to the basement.

★ **Opera & Ballet Theatre** THEATRE
(Театр оперы и балета; ☑383-222 6040; http://novat.nsk.ru; Krasny pr 36; tickets R500-5000; ⊙Oct-Jun, most shows at 6.30pm) For classical culture don't miss an evening at this gigantic silver-domed theatre. Built in 1945, it's the largest theatre in Russia – bigger even than Moscow's Bolshoi. The grand interior alone makes performances here one of the city's highlights. Ticket prices depend on seats and performances.

Philharmonia CLASSICAL MUSIC
(Филармония; ☑383-223 4141; www.philharmonia-nsk.ru; Krasny pr 32; tickets R200-1500; ⊙most shows 7pm) Classical music concerts as well as a little jazz and other musical strains.

Spartak Stadium SPECTATOR SPORT
(Стадион Спартак; http://fc-sibir.ru; ul Frunze 15; tickets R100-300) This 12,500-capacity venue is the home of local football team Sibir. Games are usually played on Saturday or Sunday.

ℹ Information

Main Post Office (Главпочтамт; ul Sovetskaya 33; ⊙8am-10pm Mon-Fri, 9am-6pm Sat & Sun)

ℹ Getting There & Away

Novosibirsk is well connected by plane, train and road to the rest of Russia and it makes a logical stop on the Trans-Siberian. The well-located **Central Travel Bureau** (Центральное Бюро путешествий; Krasny pr 25; ⊙9am-8pm) is one of dozens of places to buy rail and air tickets, and also sells bus tickets (commission R100 to R200). Another such place is **Aviakassa** (Авиакасса; ul Gogolya 3; ⊙8.30am-8pm).

RAIL TRANSPORT FROM NOVOSIBIRSK
Trains from Novosibirsk

DESTINATION	MAIN TRAIN (FREQUENCY & DEPARTURE TIME)	FARE (PLATSKART/KUPE)	TIME (HR)
Abakan	68 (daily, 2.50am)	R2270/3121	23
Almaty	301 (odd-numbered days, 4.48pm)	R4297/5948	41
Barnaul	601 (daily, 6.12pm), 391 (odd-numbered days, 2.34pm)	R862/1754	5
Biysk	601 (daily, 8.03pm)	R1034/2888	9½
Novokuznetsk	105 (even-numbered days, 9.20pm), 118 (odd-numbered days, 8.45pm)	R1200/1936	8
Severobaikalsk	92 (even-numbered days, 4.49pm)	R3090/6794	40
Tobolsk	117 (odd-numbered days, 1.04am)	R4300/6400	21¾
Tomsk	38 (odd-numbered days, 3.36am), 392 (odd-numbered days, 12.37am)	from R638	5½

Suburban Trains From Novosibirsk

DESTINATION	SCHEDULE	FARE (R)	TIME (HR)
Novokuznetsk	daily except Wed, 2.40pm	2nd-1st-class R789/1048	6
Omsk	Mon, Wed, Fri, 2.55pm	2nd-1st-class R1622/2485	6¾

AIR

Novosibirsk's **Tolmachyovo Airport** (www.
tolmachevo.ru), 30km west of the city, is well-
connected to Moscow (four hours) and various
other domestic destinations. International destinations served by direct flights from Novosibirsk
include Beijing, several cities in Central Asia,
plus seasonal flights to destinations in Thailand,
Turkey and Greece.

BUS

From the **bus station** (Автовокзал; www.
nsk-avtovokzal.ru; Krasny pr 4) buses depart
every hour or so for Barnaul (R500, four hours)
and Tomsk (R740, 4½ hours). For roughly double
the price, shared taxis shave at least an hour or
more off those times but can take a while to fill
up. Taxi drivers stand outside the station trying
to entice customers.

TRAIN

The city's huge main train station, **Novosibirsk
Glavny** (ul Shamshurina 43), sits right on the
Trans-Siberian main line and there are plentiful
trains west to Moscow (48 to 55 hours) via
Omsk, Tyumen and Yekaterinburg, and east to
Irkutsk and beyond via Krasnoyarsk. For Tobolsk
you might be better off transferring in Tyumen.
For Tomsk the bus is a better option.

ⓘ Getting Around

From the bus station, bus 111z (111з) goes to Tolmachyovo airport every 30 minutes from 4am to
10.30pm, stopping at the **bus stop** by the train
station on the way. Allow an hour to get there
(more during Novosibirsk's infamous rush hour).
A taxi to the airport costs R800 (30 minutes, or
one hour during rush hour). Going the other way
drivers will often ask for R1200.

The metro has a major north–south line
running beneath Krasny pr and across the river
to ul Studencheskaya and pl Karla Marksa. For
the main train station you'll need metro stop
Ploshchad Garina-Mikhaylovskogo, which is on
a second three-stop line that intersects with the
major line at Sibirskaya/Krasny Prospekt.

Generally, buses and **marshrutky** (ul Shamshurina; 🛜) (minibuses) are handier than the
metro within the centre. Buses 8, 21 and 37
link the train station with the river station via pl
Lenina, Krasny pr and the bus station.

Tomsk Томск

📞 3822 / POP 524,000 / 🕐 MOSCOW +4HR

Magnificent in snow, but fun to be in at any
time of the year, the university city of Tomsk
boasts numerous examples of fine wooden
buildings and has an animated cafe and art
scene. The city has enjoyed the reputation as
the 'cultural capital of Siberia' since the 1960s,

when artists, writers and theatre and film directors were invited to take up residence here.

One of Siberia's oldest cities, Tomsk was
founded in 1604 and was a major trade
outpost before the founding of Novosibirsk
(then Novo-Nikolaevsk) and the subsequent
relocation of the Trans-Siberian Railway line.
With a huge and grand university, this is
above all a city of learning, and today around
one in every five residents is a student –
hence the youthful, intellectual atmosphere.

⊙ Sights

★ Memorial Museum   MUSEUM

(Мемориальный музей 'Следственная тюрьма
НКВД'; pr Lenina 44; R50, camera R100, tours in
Russian/English R200/400; ⊙10am-6pm) The
gloomy basement of this former NKVD (pro-
to-KGB) building is now a museum dedicated
to the unspeakable horrors that took place
here. Look for the Gulag map, the system of
Soviet labour camps depicted as a mass of red
dots across the territory of the former USSR.

Prisoners who passed through here included Gulag chronicler Eufrosinia Kers-
novskaya and the family of the purged Kazakh writer Akhmet Baytursinuli. Outside
the museum are two monuments to victims
of Stalinist repression – the larger to local
victims, the second to Poles slaughtered by
Uncle Joe and his cronies.

Tours are recommended, but for an English-
language one they should be booked in advance. If you go alone and don't read Russian,
you'll miss out on a lot; but, as they say, 'A picture is worth a thousand words', and the pictures on display here are just screaming out.

★ University & Siberian
Botanical Gardens   HISTORIC BUILDING

(Томский Государственный Университет;
📞 3822-529 816; greenhouses R250; ⊙greenhous-
es 10am-noon & 1-3pm Tue, Thu & Sat) The classically colonnaded main buildings of the university lie in resplendently leafy grounds, giving Tomsk the sobriquet 'Oxford of Siberia'.
Most of the buildings themselves are closed
to the public, but the grounds are open to all.
However, the Siberian Botanical Gardens,
at the southern edge of the grounds, are the
real highlight of a visit. The exterior gardens
contain samples of many Siberian plant species while the enormous greenhouses (guided tour only) get all tropical and steamy.

Ploshchad Lenina   HISTORIC SITE

Central pl Lenina isn't really a square so
much as a jumbled collection of beautifully

restored historic buildings interspersed with banal Soviet concrete lumps. The frustrated Lenin statue (pl Lenina), now relegated to a traffic circle, points at the ugly concrete of the Drama Theatre (p454), apparently demanding 'build more like that one'. Fortunately, nobody's listening. Topped with a golden angel, in a second circle beside Lenin, is the Iverskaya Chapel (Иверская часовня; pr Lenina; ⊙10am-6pm), whose celebrated icon is dubbed 'Tomsk's Spiritual Gateway'.

The drama theatre is flanked by the splendid 1784 Epiphany Cathedral (Богоявленский собор; pl Lenina 7), the former trading arches (Гостиный Двор; ul Lenina), and the elegant 1802 Hotel Magistrat (p451).

Tomsk Regional Museum
MUSEUM

(Краеведческий музей; ☑ 3822-512 935; www. tomskmuseum.ru; pr Lenina 75; R200; ⊙10am-6pm Tue-Sun) Housed in the splendid Atashev Palace, this modest museum has a 2500-year-old bear amulet and an interesting exhibit on the Great Tea Trail. But it's the building, commissioned in 1842 by the gold-mining entrepreneur Ivan Atashev, that's the main attraction. It was once used as a church, hence the incongruous steeple tower and wonderful organ hall.

Resurrection Hill
HISTORIC SITE

This dimple-sized hill was the location of Tomsk's original fortress, and the replica of its central wooden *spasskaya bashnya* (savior's tower), which stands here today, was built in 2004 for the city's 400th anniversary celebrations. Next to the tower, the Tomsk Historical Museum (Исторический музей Томска; Resurection Hill; museum/temporary exhibitions/ viewing tower R60/80/50; ⊙10am-7pm Tue-Sun) has spouted its own wooden observation tower; try to spot the seven historic churches from the top. The stone just outside the museum entrance marks the founding of the city.

Also up on Resurrection Hill is a pretty Catholic Church (ul Bakunina 4) dating to 1883.

WWII Memorial
MONUMENT

A Tomsk landmark, this moving mother-and-son monument is at the very southern end of pr Lenina. The beautiful birch-tree park (Лагерный сад) is a local favourite for strolls, not least for its views across the Tom River.

Tomsk Art Museum
MUSEUM

(Художественный музей; ☑ 3822-514 106; http://artmuseumtomsk.ru/page/1; per Nakhanovicha 3; R150; ⊙10am-6pm Tue-Sun) Well worth popping into for its wide range of perma-

nent and temporary exhibits. The highlight is the collection of 19th- and early 20th-century Russian art, and there's a small exhibit of 12th- to 13th-century religious icons.

Tours

Tomskturist
TOURS

(Томсктурист; ☑ 3822-532 121; www.tomskturist. ru; ul Belinskogo 15, Hotel Sputnik; ⊙9am-7pm Mon-Fri, 11am-4pm Sat) Tomskturist can arrange two-hour walking tours of the city, with English-, French- and German-speaking guides, although the price (R4500) makes this more of a group option. Can also help sort out Altai border-zone permits, arrange regional excursions and sell plane and train tickets. The offices are inside the Hotel Sputnik.

Sleeping

Hotel Siberia
HISTORIC HOTEL $$

(Гостиница Сибирь; ☑ 3822-527 225; www.ho-telsibir.tomsk.ru; pr Lenina 91; s/d/ste incl breakfast from R3500/4500/5000; ⊛🖙) This centrally located old hotel is popular, despite its largely unimaginative singles and doubles. It does, however, offer great suites with real fireplaces for R5500. Dinner is available on top of complimentary breakfast for R600 extra, but you'd be better off eating elsewhere.

Bon Apart Hotel
HOTEL $$

(☑ 3822-534 655; www.bon-apart.ru; ul Gertsena 1a; s/d incl breakfast from R4700/5900; 🖙) The large rooms here have comfortable, good-sized beds and polished tile bathrooms, but are otherwise very plain. The walk-in rates (quoted here) aren't worth bothering with – by booking online you'll likely pay 60% less, which makes the place more tempting.

★ Gogol Hotel
BOUTIQUE HOTEL $$$

(☑ 3822-909 709; http://gogolhotel.ru; ul Gogol 36a; s/d with breakfast from R3600/4800; ⊛🌐🖙) Bordering on boutique, this classy 19-room property has quickly become Tomsk's most sought-after address. Rooms are spacious, with muted grey tones, and the walls are emblazoned with photos of old Tomsk. You can swim in the king-sized beds and the breakfast is fantastic.

Hotel Magistrat
HISTORIC HOTEL $$$

(Гостиница Магистрат; ☑ 3822-511 111; www. magistrathotel.com; pl Lenina 15; s/d incl breakfast from R6900/8900; 🌐🖙) Dating back to 1802, this hotel has an air of gravitas – on the outside. Inside, there's lots of marble and a bit too much self-importance. The position,

WESTERN SIBERIA TOMSK

Tomsk

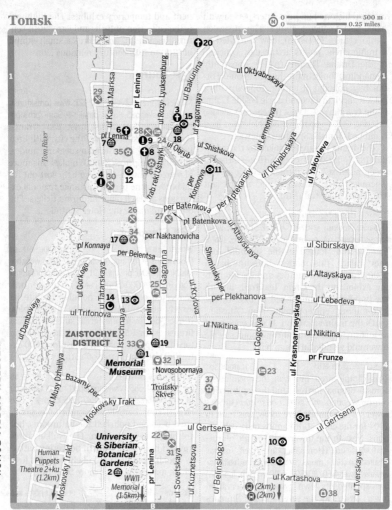

though, is prime and the rooms are truly enormous – a real rarity in Russia. No lift.

🍴 Eating

Bulanzhe CAFE **$**
(Буланже; pr Lenina 80; mains R200-350; ☺10am-11pm; 🛜📶) Fantastic cafe – bright and cheery with an exciting menu of international food, fresh salads, great coffee and a wide tea selection. The Belgian waffles are highly recommended. It's a place to chat and chew rather than work on a laptop.

Obzhorni Ryad RUSSIAN **$**
(Обжорный ряд; ul Gertsena 1, Bon Apart Hotel; mains R200-250; ☺11am-10pm; 🛜) For penny-pinchers in search of good-value Russian fare, look no further than this *stolovaya* (cafeteria), whose name translates to Guzzler's Row. Travelling children will appreciate the in-house play centre – and parents will appreciate the five minutes peace, it brings them. It's inside the Bon Apart Hotel.

⭐ Marle Bua ITALIAN **$$**
(📞3822-998 888; www.marlebua.ru; pl Lenina 11; mains R260-500; ☺8am-midnight Mon-Fri, 11am-

Tomsk

2am Sat, 11am-midnight Sun) For over 150 years this basement restaurant has been keeping the tummies of Tomsk full. In its latest incarnation it's an Italian restaurant and grill. As you'd expect from a place with such maturity, they know what they are doing in the kitchen, with dishes such as rabbit ragout, pasta and pizza. Service is smart and prices are low, considering the quality of food.

Vechny Zov   RUSSIAN **$$**
(Вечный Зов; ☑ 3822-528 167; www.vechzov. tomsk.ru; ul Sovetskaya 47; mains R200-800; ☺ noon-2am; 🛜) Named after a popular Soviet TV serial, this is the place to sample Siberian specialities like *stroganina* (frozen raw *chyr*, a white fish common in Arctic rivers, *muk-sun* (an Ob River white fish) and, perhaps morally questionable, bear meat. Carnivores can even go for a four-meat (bear, deer, pork, beef) *pelmeni* (Russian-style dumplings stuffed with meat). It boasts a mock Siberian ranch outside and a cosy antique-filled home feel inside.

Coffee House Leto Café   CAFE **$$**
(Кофейная Лето; ul Gagarina 2; meals R300-500; ☺ 8am-10pm; 🖉) A trippy, yellow vegetarian and glutton-free cafe decorated like a circus with kites and glass mobiles. The menu features food with hard-to-get (in Siberia) ingredients such as pumpkin, pesto and real feta cheese. Also has proper ground coffee.

★**Reka 827**   SEAFOOD **$$$**
(☑ 3822-902 020; www.reka827.ru; ul Kooperativnyy 2; mains R700-900; ☺ noon-midnight Sun-Thu, noon-1am Fri & Sat) If it's summer, sit out on one of the sun loungers on the deck of this sophisticated restaurant and eat great seafood while watching the locals swim in the river below. The fish dishes here are prepared with verve, which means you can look forward to tastes such as whole fried octopus and little fishy tapas-style dishes.

★**Slavyansky Bazar**   RUSSIAN **$$$**
(Славянский Базар; ☑ 3822-515 553; pl Lenina 10; mains R500-1200; ☺ noon-midnight Mon-Thu & Sun, noon-2am Fri & Sat; 🛜) Slavyansky Bazar, Tomsk's fanciest restaurant, is housed in a 19th-century building with an interior like something from a period drama. Chekhov ate at an earlier incarnation of this establishment in 1890. The food was one of the few things he liked about the city and if he

WOODEN HERITAGE ARCHITECTURE

Much of Tomsk's appeal lies in its well-preserved late-19th- and early-20th-century 'wooden-lace' architecture – carved windows and tracery on old log and timber houses. There are a few streets to home in on if touring the city on foot.

Ul Tatarskaya has perhaps the richest concentration of such houses. It's reached via the steps beside a lovely old house at **prospekt Lenina 56** (пр Ленина 56). The best examples are on the block north of ul Trifonova, where you'll also find the modest **Red Mosque** (Красная Мечеть; ul Tatarskaya 22), which dates from 1904. Over on the east side of pr Lenina, **ul Gagarina** is similarly endowed with graceful heritage houses.

A few blocks east of ul Belinskogo, near the corner of ul Krasnoarmeyskaya and ul Gertsena, look out for the spired, bright-turquoise **Russian-German House** (Российско-Немецкий Дом; ul Krasnoarmeyskaya 71), built in 1904; the late 19th-century **Dragon House** (Дом Дракона; ul Krasnoarmeyskaya 68) which is home to a clinic; and the fan-gabled early-20th-century **Peacock House** (Дом Павлина; ul Krasnoarmeyskaya 67a). **Ul Dzerzhinskogo**, one block east of ul Krasnoarmeyskaya, is worth a wander as well.

Other streets worth strolling are **per Kononova** – look for **No 2** (per Kononova 2), where the doomed communist mastermind Sergei Kirov lodged in 1905 – and nearby **ul Shishkova**. Finally, if you walk from Resurrection Hill (p451) to the **Voznesenskaya church** (Вознесенская церковь; ul Oktyabrsky Vzvoz 10), you will find yourself on a delightful, quiet road lined with timber log houses and lots of trees and plants.

ate here today, he would still approve. Expect refined takes on classic Russian dishes.

🍷 Drinking & Nightlife

⭐ Underground Jazz Café
BAR

(☎ 3822-516 319; www.jazzcafe.tomsk.ru; pr Lenina 46; cover charge weekends R250-400; ☺ 6pm-midnight; 🛜) A hip and literally underground basement with live jazz, including frequent US guests, most weekends. Also has an extensive drinks and food menu and old black-and-white films play in the background.

Sibirsky Pub
PUB

(Сибирский Паб; pl Novosobornaya 2; Guinness pints R360; ☺ 1pm-1am; 🛜) Siberia's first Irish pub was founded over a century ago by a certain Mr Crawley, an Anglo-Egyptian albino who'd gotten stuck in Tomsk after touring with a circus freak show. There are less freaks today, but as compensation there is live music at weekends.

☆ Entertainment

⭐ Human Puppets
Theatre 2+ku
PUPPET THEATRE

(Театр живых кукол 2+ку; ☎ 3822-420 486; www.2ky.tomsk.ru; Yuzhniy per 29; tickets R200-500) Housed in a quaint log cabin near the WWII memorial (take ul Savinykh all the way down until you can go no further), this one-man, homey 'robotic puppet' theatre is a real experience, and one you don't need

to understand Russian to appreciate. Check the website for performance details.

Philharmonia
CONCERT VENUE

(Филармония; ☎ 3822-515 186; http://bkz.tomsk.ru; pl Lenina 1) Classical music and great big-band jazz. Hosts the Tomsk International Jazz Festival in the first week of June.

Aelita Theatre
THEATRE

(Театр Аэлита; ☎ 3822-514 436; www.aelita.tom.ru; pr Lenina 78) Eclectic offerings, from rock concerts to Indian dance to experimental plays.

Drama Theatre
THEATRE

(Драматический театр; ☎ 3822-906 837; www.tomskdrama.ru; pl Lenina 4) The drama theatre might be housed in a huge ugly slab of concrete on pl Lenina, but the performances are far from ugly.

Organ Hall
CLASSICAL MUSIC

(pr Lenina 75; tickets R200-500; ☺ concerts 7pm, noon on Sun) Beautiful organ concerts are held several times a month upstairs in the Atashev Palace. The acoustics are brilliant.

Trud Stadium
STADIUM

(ul Belinskogo 15/1) Home stadium of local football side **Tom Tomsk** (Томь Томск ФК; tickets from R300). There's a shop selling Tomsk scarves and T-shirts. It's open 11am to 7pm Monday to Friday, and on weekends on home match days.

🛍 Shopping

Dzerzhinskogo Market   MARKET
(Дзержинского рынок; ul Dzerzhinskogo) This market sprawls for a full block south of ul Kartashova, providing photo opps as well as fuel in the form of local fruits and nuts.

ℹ Information

Main Post Office (Почтамт; pr Lenina 95; ⊙ 8am-10pm Mon-Fri, 9am-6pm Sat & Sun) Stamps, but no postcards of Tomsk (find postcards in most museums).

ℹ Getting There & Away

AIR

Bogashevo Airport (www.tomskairport.ru), 22km southeast of Tomsk, has several daily flights to Moscow plus a few seasonal charters. The choice is much wider from Novosibirsk.

BUS

For Novosibirsk, buses (R740, 4½ hours, every hour) depart from the central **bus station** (Автовокзал; https://avtovokzal.tomsk.ru), which is right next to the main train station. Buses also serve Abakan (R1950, 17 hours, four weekly) and Novokuznetsk (R912, seven hours, two daily Monday to Saturday, one daily Sunday).

TRAIN

From Tomsk I (main) train station, there's a train on even-numbered days to Barnaul (*platskart/ kupe* R1100/2000, 15½ hours, 9.20pm) via Novosibirsk. There are trains on odd-numbered days to Novokuznetsk (R1100/1530, 12½ hours, 7.33pm) and Moscow (R7350/11,060, 56 hours), and a train every 4th day to Vladivostok.

For more frequent connections east (towards Irkutsk) and west (towards Novosibirsk), take an *elektrichka* (suburban train) to Taiga (R112, two hours, 9.06am and 4.15pm) or a bus to Yurga (R210, two hours, four daily); most main-line Trans-Siberian trains stop at both stations. *Elektrichki* from Taiga to Tomsk depart at 7.07am and 4.15pm.

ℹ Getting Around

The bus station and Tomsk 1 (main) train station sit together about 2km southeast of the centre. Good maps are available in the train station and at street kiosks. A taxi to the city centre is around R150.

Buses 4, 12 and 12a run from pl Lenina to the train station via pr Lenina and pr Kirova. Hop on and off trolleybuses 1 and 3, or bus 17, which all go along pr Lenina.

Tomsk's antiquated and atmospheric trams are a great way to take a cheap (R15) city tour. Tram 2 runs the length of ul Sovetskaya before connecting with the train station via pr Kirova. Tram 1 trundles all the way to the city's northern outskirts via ul Sovetskaya and ul Bolshaya Podgornaya.

Novokuznetsk Новокузнецк

📞 3843 / POP 563,000 / ⊙ MOSCOW +4HR

Novokuznetsk, the largest city in the industrial Kemerovo region, boasts a well-laid-out centre and some impressive Soviet-era monuments. However, if you come here, chances are you're heading somewhere else – the city makes a convenient stopover point between Abakan and Biysk when overlanding between Tuva and Altai, and is also the jumping-off point to snowboarder haven Sheregesh.

Despite being used mainly as an overnight transit town the city isn't without its charms. There's a large central park that has a carnival atmosphere on summer weekends and a few low-key sights.

Founded on the right bank of the Tom River in 1618, the frequently enlarged Kuznetsk Fortress became one of the most important guardians of imperial Russia's southeastern frontier. The city's left (west) bank, named Stalinsk until 1961, was constructed almost from scratch by Soviet 'shockworkers' (superproductive workers) in the 1930s and is now the city centre. Novokuznetsk's metal plants, which supply 70% of Russia's train tracks, are mainly responsible for Novokuznetsk being one of the five most polluted cities in Russia, according to government figures.

Pr Metallurgov stretches north from the train station to the main drag, ul Kirova. The Tom River is a couple of kilometres east along ul Kirova. Maps are available in a kiosk inside the train station.

◉ Sights

Kuznetsk Fortress   HISTORIC SITE
(Кузнецкая крепость; 📞 3843-360 100; http:// kuzn-krepost.ru; Krepostnoy proezd 1; R20, plus per museum R100; ⊙ museums 9.30am-5.30pm Mon-Fri, 10am-5pm Sat & Sun) The restored stone ramparts of the Kuznetsk Fortress are massive and topped with cannons, but represent only 20% of their 1810 extent. Kids ride ponies around the attractive grounds, concerts are held and there are couple of modest museums that you can pop into – the archaeology museum, which contains mammoth tusks and old stone tools, is probably the most interesting.

The fortress is in the old part of town on the right (east) bank of the Tom River. To get here take frequent bus 5 from outside the bus station and get off at the first stop over the bridge (15 minutes). It's a 15-minute walk up the hill to the fortress via the beautiful 1792 Transfiguration Cathedral (Преображенский собор; ul Vodopadnaya 18).

Park Gagarina
PARK

(pr Metallurgov) If you only have a couple of hours to kill, take a stroll though this oasis of green just north of the train station. It contains a bust of a jolly-looking Yury Gagarin, a mothballed planetarium and the constructivist (and now empty) Kommunar Theatre (Кинотеатр Коммунар; pr Metalurgov 18), which once housed Siberia's first audio cinema. Just north of the theatre, two reverential statues of Soviet-era metalworkers guard pleasant Mettalurgists' Garden (Park Gagarina).

In the summer there's always plenty of life in the park with lots of cultural events, concerts and get-togethers taking place. Most of the city seems to come for an evening walk here at such times.

Former Soviet Builders Club
HISTORIC BUILDING

(ul Ordzhonikidzye 23) Guarded by two statues of Soviet workers, wielding a hammer and a plasterer's board, the one-time cement workers' club is now used as a cultural centre.

🛏 Sleeping & Eating

Bardin Hotel & Health
SPA HOTEL $$

(☑ 3843-357 200; www.bardinhotel.ru; ul Ordzhonikidze 32; s/d incl breakfast from R1920/2220; ❂✳🛜🏊) A 10-minute stroll west of the city centre, the Bardin is a new business hotel and spa that leaves any other place to stay in Novokuznetsk in the shade. Crisp rooms with lots of beige tints, an indoor pool, a health centre and, on top of all that, the chefs at the in-house restaurant will keep you well fed.

Hotel Novokuznetsk
HOTEL $$

(Гостиница Новокузнецк; ☑ 3843-465 155; www.novokuznetskaya.com; ul Kirova 53; s/d incl breakfast & dinner from R3200/4200; @🛜) It's 1977 all over again at this massive, echoey throw back to the Soviet era. Fortunately, though, the rooms have been somewhat renovated and brightened up. It's now just those gloomy corridors that need a face lift... Rates include breakfast and dinner, but frankly you might prefer to eat dinner elsewhere.

Pechki-Lavochki
RUSSIAN $

(Печки-Лавочки; ul Kirova 21a; mains R200-400; ❂9am-8pm) Traditional Russian food served in a rustic setting by waitresses dressed as peasants. The chain is named after a 1972 Soviet road film. It's next to a pharmacy on the city's main intersection (ul Kirova and pr Metalurgov).

🛈 Information

Main Post Office (pr Metallurgov 21; ❂8am-10pm Mon-Fri, 9am-6pm Sat & Sun)

🛈 Getting There & Away

There are a few flights a day from Novokuznetsk's Spichenkovo Airport to Moscow (four hours). To get to the airport, take bus or marshrutka (fixed-route minibus) 160 from the train station.

The elektrichka (suburban train) to Novosibirsk leaves at 7.05am every day except Wednesday (2nd-1st-class R721/940, six hours). There are one or two slower regular trains to Novosibirsk per day as well, including an overnight option on odd-numbered days. Trains run daily to Abakan (platskart/kupe R900/1700, nine hours, 9.20pm), and on even-numbered days to Tomsk (R1050/2010, 12 hours, 5.24pm).

There's a snail-slow elektrichka to Tashtagol (jumping-off point to Sheregesh) on odd-numbered days at 5.10am (from R136, five hours); the bus is a much better option.

From the **bus station** (Автовокзал), right next to the train station, there are hourly buses to Tashtagol (R290, 3½ hours). Shared taxis are an option to Tashtagol in the ski season (about R750, two hours). Buses also serve Barnaul (R800, seven hours, three daily), Biysk (R500, 5¼ hours, five daily), Krasnoyarsk (R1425, 14½ hours, 6.40pm), Novosibirsk (R1100, eight hours, four daily) and Tomsk (R912, seven hours, two daily).

Sheregesh   Шерегеш

☑ 3843 / POP 10,170 / ⓘ MOSCOW +4HR

Isolated and tiny Sheregesh is a mining village that has become the focus of a booming snowboarding and skiing scene in recent years. Those who make it here are rewarded with some of the most prolific snowfall in Russia, fairly uncrowded slopes and a raucous après-ski scene that would put many European resorts to shame. Out of season, Sheregesh has a lot less to offer, although you could use it as a base for day walks around the mountain ridges and through the forests. The journey here is an added bonus, winding through tiny villages and deserted country roads in view of the Gorniya Shoriya mountains.

🏃 Activities

Off-season, you can hike up the ski mountain and then along the mountain ridge which extends for some way before dropping back down to the resort again. Allow a half-day for such a walk. There are plenty of other walking opportunities on the surrounding hills and forests but in most cases it's a bit of a DIY adventure. Good-quality **mountain bikes** can be rented (from R300 per day) from Ays Club (p457) to explore Sheregesh village or to seek out more rugged terrain in the hills (ask the knowledgeable folks at Ays).

Sheregesh Ski Resort   SNOW SPORTS
(www.sheregesh.ru; gondolas R200, chairlifts per ride R100-150; ⊙ 9.30am-5pm) The ski resort sprawls over Zelyonaya (Green) Mountain (1257m), which is reputed to get Russia's finest powder. There are 17 ski runs served by three gondolas and several chairlifts. The slopes close around late April, but a few lifts stay open in the off-season to bring tourists up the mountain for spectacular views of the village and the surrounding taiga. Ski and snowboard rental is widely available at the base of the mountain from R300 per hour including boots.

The lifts are run by several different operators, which means you pay by the ride (around R100) instead of by the day, but it ends up being a fantastic value no matter how many runs you take.

Off-piste *rattrak* (snowcat) skiing is another option, and continues into July (although you'll be hard-pressed to rent equipment after April). Snowcats gather skiiers near the top of the main gondola and proceed up to the unusual 'Verbluda (Camel) Rocks'. Three hours of riding costs R500 per person – a bargain.

Snowmobiles also make the trip to Verbluda Rocks (R800 for the half-hour round-trip journey). With the wind in your face as you speed through the snow, it's hard not to feel a little like James Bond. Hold on tight! The trip lasts about half an hour, with time for photos and clambering about on the rocks.

🛏 Sleeping

The vast majority of hotels are based around the mountain. Prices listed are for ski-season weekdays; rates rise substantially on weekends in the ski season, and drop in the off-season. Note that outside of the ski season many places are closed and even those that are open have something of a closed atmosphere to them!

★ Ays Club   HOSTEL $
(Айс Клуб; ☑ 8-800-500 0489; www.ays-club.ru; dm R900, d from R2500; ❄ 🐾 🛏) Hip and funky, Ays is a self-contained party zone – a hostel,

a pumping basement nightclub ('Bunker'), a cafe and the Clever Irish pub rolled into one. The cheap dorms make it an obvious choice for young snowboarders on a budget, while the stylish, spacious private rooms will appeal to young-at-heart midrange travellers. One of the first hotels you'll come across as you approach the mountain and one of the few places open year-round.

Shorhotel   HOTEL $
(☑ 8-960-922 6084; ul Gagarina 27a; s/d R1100/1500; 🐾) In Sheregesh town rather than on the ski slopes, the small, family-run Shorhotel offers exceptional value for money with big, bright and quiet rooms, some of which have flowery photo murals on the walls. The downstairs cafe serves simple snacks and pancakes. It's a five-minute taxi ride to the ski lifts (R150).

Olga   HOTEL $$
(Ольга; ☑ 3843-900 222; www.olgahotel.ru; d from R3300; ❄ 🐾 🛏) One of the biggest hotels in the area and as close to the ski lifts and nightlife as you can get, Olga's is a typical large, ski-resort hotel – in other words it's an uninspired block of dark but comfortable rooms with lots of on-site facilities. Next door, an ice rink is attached to its Beer Gesh restaurant.

Berloga   HOTEL $$$
(Берлога; ☑ 3843-900 222; www.berlogahotel.ru; d from R5200; ❄ 🐾 🛏) This four-storey hotel describes itself as the 'cosiest place' in town and while other establishments might beg to differ, there's no denying the Berloga's attention to detail. Good-quality rooms, some with great views, as well as a swimming pool and a decent restaurant, make this an option worth considering.

🍴 Eating & Drinking

There are several eateries at the top and base of the mountain for lunch, plus plenty of shashlyk (meat kebab) and other open-air snacks available. Breakfast and dinner are typically taken in your hotel. While you are in Sheregesh, be sure to try the local wild leek. Local women sell it by the roadside for around R25 a bag. Known locally as *kabla*, and *cheremsha* in Russian, its distinctive garlicky taste is one you won't forget in a hurry!

Yurta   CENTRAL ASIAN $$
(mains R200-500) Hearty Central Asian fare served in an oversized heated yurt at the main base area.

★ **Grelka** BAR

(mains R300-400; ⊙noon-11pm) Right at the main base area, Grelka is the après-ski place. Convivial atmosphere, pub grub and competent bartenders serving a wide range of local and imported beers. When it warms up, the party moves out to the patio – it's a party you don't want to miss. Grelka is also the brains behind Sheregesh's infamous 'Bikini Ride', an annual event held during 'Grelka Fest' that owns the world record for the most people (around 500) in swimwear on the slopes at one time (women and men).

Clever PUB

(Ays Laska Hotel; Guiness pints R320) This cleverly named Irish pub is a fine place for a pint of Guinness or a round of après-ski shooters. There's another branch in the Ays Club (p457).

ℹ Orientation

For most visitors Sheregesh means the ski resort with its collection of resort hotels, restaurants and bars. The actual town of Sheregesh is a couple of kilometres down the slope from the resort and is a thoroughly uninspiring place.

ℹ Information

There are plenty of ATMs both in the town and at the base of the slopes, including in most hotels. Most have a R5000 per transaction restriction on foreign bank cards.

Sheregesh.ru (www.sheregesh.ru) has plenty of information on the scene at Sheregesh.

ℹ Getting There & Away

Bus 101 connects Sheregesh with the village of Tashtagol every 30 minutes from 6.45am to 11.30pm (R30, 30 minutes). A taxi from Sheregesh to Tashtagol should cost R450 to the town of Sheregesh and R600 to a hotel in the resort itself. There are hourly buses until 7pm from Tashtagol to Novokuznetsk (R296, 3½ hours).

In the ski season, Ays-Club and a few other resorts run fun buses directly from Novosibirsk to their respective properties on the slopes – contact **Ays-Club** (p457) for details.

There is no public transport to Altai. A taxi to Gorno-Altaisk (3½ hours) or Artybash (three hours) from Sheregesh will set you back about R5000. The road to Altai is partially unsealed but passable year-round and the journey is a beautiful one taking in wildflower meadows, dark forests and deep lakes.

Sheregesh's main **bus stop** is in the middle of town at the corner of ul Yubileynaya and ul Dzerzhinskogo. A taxi from the main bus stop to the slopes costs a flat R150.

ALTAI

Greater Altai (Алтай), bordering on Kazakhstan, China and Mongolia, consists of the Altai Territory and the Altai Republic. The Altai Territory, while pleasant enough, is most noteworthy as a gateway to the wonders of the unforgettable Altai Republic. This sprawling and sparsely populated region is home to over 7000 lakes, snow-capped mountains – including Siberia's highest peak (Mt Belukha, 4506m), shadowy forests, gurgling rivers, bears, wolves and even the ghost-like snow leopard. There are fabulous opportunities for hiking and mountain exploration, but often only for those organised enough to arrange the necessary permits two months in advance. The Altai Republic has long been regarded as an area of spiritual and occult significance, and Russian philosopher and painter Nikolai Rerikh (Nicholas Roerich) visited the region in the early 20th century in an attempt to locate the entrance to Shambala, the mythical enlightened land of Tibetan Buddhism. He failed, but you might not...

Gorno-Altaisk, the capital of the Altai Republic, is the logical jumping-off point for most of Altai's attractions. Be sure to get your visa registered here before heading onwards. Also note that if you plan to do any trekking in the high peaks of southern Altai, you'll need a border permit. If you are heading to Ust-Koksa or beyond (including Tyungur), you will also need a border permit. If you are heading to Mongolia, you will not need a permit as long as you don't venture off the M52 highway (aka the Chuysky Trakt).

Altai Culture

Asiatic ethnic-Altai people constitute around 30% of the Altai Republic's 200,000-strong population, and a vastly lower proportion in the heavily Russianised Altai Territory. Despite strong animist undercurrents, most Altai are nominally Christian and villages aren't visually distinct, though some rural Altai homes still incorporate an *ail* (yurt-like traditional dwellings). In the Altai language, 'hello' is *yakhshler,* 'thank you' (very much) is *(dyan) biyan/biyan bolzyn* and 'beautiful' is *charash*. Altai tea is served milky: add a bran-rich flour called *talkan* and it becomes a sort of porridge.

Some of the Altai Republic's 5% ethnic Kazakhs are still nomadic herders living in traditional felt yurts, notably around Kosh-Agach. Most Kazakhs are Muslims who are keen on *kumiss* (fermented mare's milk)

ALTAI'S STONE IDOLS

Altai is famous for its standing stone idols. Known locally as *kameniy babi* ('stone wenches', confusingly, given their masculine forms), the best were carved in human form with moustaches, shown holding a cup that symbolically housed the soul of the dead. There are also many groups of animal-shaped petroglyphs (rock drawings) of debatable origin. These may be fascinating but most are so faint that you might miss the scratches even when you're staring right at them.

but don't generally drink vodka and, consequently, Kazakh settlements have lower rates of violence than Altai ones.

Trekking in Altai

Trekking among Altai's snow-crested mountaintops is one of Western Siberia's main attractions, but it requires considerable preparation: compared to Nepal or New Zealand, hiking here requires a high degree of self-sufficiency. Not even the most popular trails have villages, signs or teahouses. Sadly, guides and packhorses usually aren't easy to arrange quickly in situ, except perhaps in Tyungur or Chemal. For many of the more interesting hikes complicated-to-obtain Border Zone permits are required for foreign trekkers and this puts most people off. However, there are a couple of interesting walking options open to anyone.

Tour companies, several of which are based in Novosibirsk and Barnaul, can help by prearranging various adventure, hiking, rafting or relaxation packages. Consider using them in July and August to book accommodation (especially if you want the luxury of a sit-down toilet) as demand very often outstrips supply during summer. Only a select few agencies have the English skills to deal with foreigners.

For maps, try the Dom Knigi shops in any big city, which sporadically stock 1:200,000 Altai sheets.

Barnaul
Барнаул

📞 3852 / POP 612,000 / ⏱ MOSCOW +4HR

The capital of the Altai Territory, Barnaul is a large, prosperous and buzzing industrial city and has been so almost since its foundation in 1730 as Ust-Barnaulskaya. While it's hardly a tourist hot spot, it offers just enough cafes and museums to keep you amused between transport connections. The main drag is pr Lenina, which runs 8km northwest from the river station.

⊙ Sights & Activities

Rapacious redevelopment has destroyed much of Barnaul's older architecture. Nonetheless, centuries-old remnants are dotted between the shopping malls. A few splendid examples include those at ulitsa Korolenko 96, ulitsa Pushkina 80 and ulitsa Polzunova 31 and ulitsa Polzunova 48.

★ Altai Arts, Literature & Culture Museum
MUSEUM

(Музей истории, литературы, искусства и культуры Алтая; http://gmilika22.ru; ul Tolstogo 2; R30; ⊙ 10am-6pm Tue-Sat) The impressively eclectic – not to mention good-value – Altai Arts, Literature & Culture Museum occupies a restored, furnished 1850s mansion. There are some fine icons, Rerikh sketches and a collection of Iron Age relics including the re-created tomb of a horseman complete with his trusty (though, at the moment of its sacrifice, probably rather annoyed) steed.

★ War History Museum
MUSEUM

(Музей истории войны; Komsomolsky pr 73b; ⊙ 9.30am-5.30pm Tue-Sat) FREE In an old brick house, the War History Museum is simple and all in Russian but the moving understatement of its Afghanistan and Chechnya memorials is particularly affecting.

War Memorial
MONUMENT

Near the train station in pl Pobedy, the War Memorial consists of a statue of a grieving mother with her lost son, an eternal flame and a very long list of the names of those who died too young.

Lenin the Toreador
MONUMENT

This unique Lenin monument sees the revolutionary apparently dressed up as a bullfighter.

Pokrovsky Church
CHURCH

(Покровский собор; ul Nikitina 135-7) This bulbous-domed brick building is the most appealing of the city's many churches and has a fine, gilded interior.

Regional Museum
MUSEUM

(Краеведческий музей; www.agkm.ru; ul Polzunova 46; R50; ⊙ 9.30am-5.30pm Tue-Wed & Fri-Sun, 11am-7pm Thu) Founded in 1823, the reasonably interesting Regional Museum is Siberia's

Altai Republic

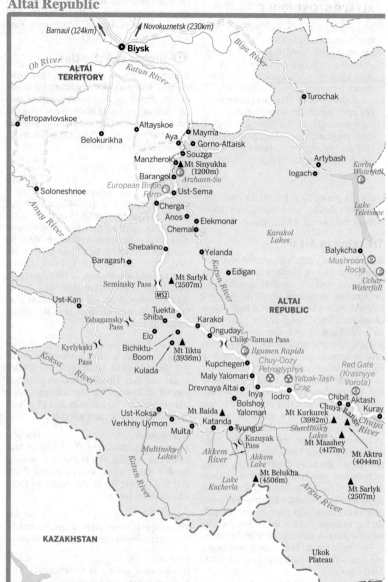

Barnaul (124km)
Novokuznetsk (230km)
Biysk
Ob River
ALTAI TERRITORY
Katun River
Biya River
Turochak
Petropavlovskoe
Altayskoe
Mayma
Belokurikha
Aya
Gorno-Altaisk
Artybash
Manzherok
Souzga
Iogach
Korbu Waterfall
Mt Sinyukha (1200m)
Arzhaan-Su
Barangol
European Bison Farm
Ust-Sema
Solonshnoe
Anuy River
Cherga
Anos
Elekmonar
Chemal
Karakol Lakes
Lake Teletskoe
Shebalino
Yelanda
Balykcha
Baragash
Mushroom Rocks
Edigan
Seminsky Pass
Mt Sarlyk (2507m)
M52
Katun River
ALTAI REPUBLIC
Uchar Waterfall
Ust-Kan
Tuekta
Yabagansky Pass
Shiba
Karakol
Elo
Onguday
Chike-Taman Pass
Kyrlyksky Pass
Bichiktu-Boom
Mt Iiktu (3936m)
Ilgumen Rapids
Chuy-Oozy Petroglyphs
Red Gate (Krasnye Vorota)
Kulada
Kupchegen
Yalbak-Tash Crag
Koksa River
Maly Yaloman
Drevnaya Altai
Inya
Iodro
Chibit
Aktash
Ust-Koksa
Mt Baida
Bolshoy Yaloman
Mt Kurkurek (3982m)
Chuya Range
Kuray
Verkhny Uymon
Katanda
Tyungur
Shavlinsky Lakes
Chuya River
Multa
Kuzuyak Pass
Mt Maashey (4177m)
Multinsky Lakes
Akkem River
Akkem Lake
Mt Aktru (4044m)
Katun River
Lake Kucherla
Mt Belukha (4506m)
Argut River
Mt Sarlyk (2507m)
KAZAKHSTAN
Ukok Plateau

oldest. Top exhibits include intriguing models of various 18th-century industrial processes.

FSB Headquarters
NOTABLE BUILDING

(Штаб ФСБ; pr Lenina 30) The city's Federal Security Services (FSB) headquarters is worth a peek. The bearded dude in the courtyard is Felix Dzerzhinsky, Cheka (KGB and FSB forerunner) founder. A much larger monument to Iron Felix was torn down in Moscow as the USSR imploded, and he is a very uncommon face indeed in modern Russia.

KHAKASSIA
REPUBLIC

TUVA
REPUBLIC

Chulyshman River

Balyktuyul

Ulagan

Bashkaus River

Lake Julunkul

M52 Kuray Steppe

Ortolyk

Mt Saylyugem (3411m) ▲

Kosh-Agach Kokorya M52

Chuy Steppe Mt Tapduayr (3305m) ▲

Tashanta

Chuysky Trakt ⊗

Kyzyl Uuy

M52

*Ulgii (40km);
Mugur-Aksy
(490km)*

MONGOLIA

0 ——— 100 km
0 ——— 50 miles

Ak Tur TOUR

(☑ 3852-659 407; www.aktour.ru; Ultra Business Centre, pr Lenina 10; ⊘ 10am-7pm Mon-Sat) Offers Altai rafting, road trips and mountain expeditions. Some English spoken.

🛏 Sleeping

★Hostel Arbuz HOSTEL $

(Хостел Арбуз; ☑ 3852-778 956; www.hostelarbuz.com; ul Severo-Zapadnaya 48d; dm R350-400, s/d R500/1000; ⊜@🛜) The rooms and dorms here might be small, but this is still one of the better hostels in southwest Siberia. The shared bathrooms are unusually impressive (love the green under-sink lighting) and the cafe and overall vibe is bright and optimistic. And how can you not like the watermelon theme? The drawback is its distance from the city centre.

To get there take any bus northwest along ul Lenina, hop off at No 134 (two stops beyond the railroad tracks), walk three minutes west and look for it in the courtyard.

★Hotel Altai HISTORIC HOTEL $$

(Гостиница Алтай; ☑ 3852-639 247; www.hotel-altay22.ru; pr Lenina 24; s/d incl breakfast R2200/3200; ⊜🛜) In an early 1940s building with elements of artdeco to it, this solid midrange hotel has heaps of old-fashioned charm including a grand, sweeping staircase, polished wooden floorboards and large rooms – some of which have sofas and armchairs. Do try and get a room facing away from the noisy main road.

Hotel Central BUSINESS HOTEL $$

(Гостиница Центральная; ☑ 3852-367 100; www.hotelcentral.ru; pr Lenina 57; d incl breakfast from R3500; ⊜❋🛜) Recently overhauled, this former Soviet landmark hotel now offers dashing rooms in dark hues. As with almost every former Soviet pile, the rooms are small but they've kitted them out in such a manner as to make the most of the available space. All up there's great bang for your buck to be had here.

Hotel Barnaul HOTEL $$

(Гостиница Барнаул; ☑ 3852-201 600; www.barnaulhotel.ru; pl Pobedy 3; incl breakfast s from R2450, tw from R3000, d from R3500; ❋@🛜) This thoroughly modernised 12-storey block near the train station is exactly what you would expect from a former Soviet hulk – clean and efficient, but with small beds and bathrooms. The kicker is that if you check in after midnight, the next night is free. It's probably the most popular hotel in Barnaul and, despite its size, is often full.

Hotel Sibir BUSINESS HOTEL $$$

(Гостиница Сибирь; ☑ 3852-624 200; www.siberia-hotel.ru; Sotsialistichesky pr 116; d from

WESTERN SIBERIA BARNAUL

Barnaul

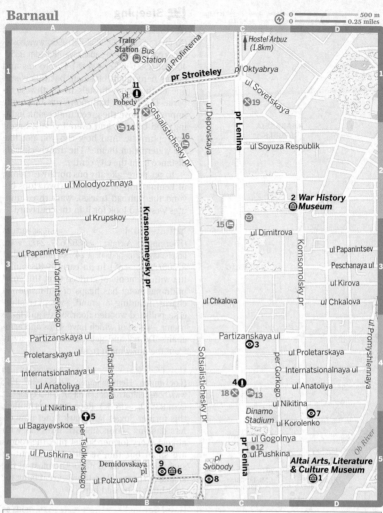

0 — 500 m
0 — 0.25 miles

WESTERN SIBERIA BARNAUL

Barnaul

◎ Top Sights
1 Altai Arts, Literature & Culture
Museum..D5
2 War History Museum................................D2

◎ Sights
3 FSB Headquarters......................................C4
4 Lenin the Toreador....................................C4
5 Pokrovsky Church......................................A5
6 Regional Museum......................................B5
7 Ulitsa Korolenko 96...................................D5
8 Ulitsa Polzunova 31...................................C5
9 Ulitsa Polzunova 48...................................B5
10 Ulitsa Pushkina 80....................................B5
11 War Memorial..B1

✪ Activities, Courses & Tours
12 Ak Tur...C5

🛏 Sleeping
13 Hotel Altai...C4
14 Hotel Barnaul...B2
15 Hotel Central..C3
16 Hotel Sibir..B2

✗ Eating
17 Gastro Pub 13..B1
18 Mozarella..C4
19 Velvet...C1

R5800; ⊜✳️🛜) This smart business hotel is built almost to international standards. It has a plum position, large subtly toned rooms, a prime breakfast buffet and decent sound proofing (needed because it fronts a main road). However, compared to most hotels in the region it's overpriced.

🍴 Eating

⭐ Velvet
RUSSIAN $$

(📋 3852-610 061; www.velvet-rest.ru; pr Lenina 80; mains R500-700; ⊙10am-midnight) Dress smart and come braced for one of Siberia's culinary highlights. Velvet, which lives inside an imposing slate grey building, holds the mantle of best restaurant in Barnaul. Using their magic the chefs here turn Russian and European classics into dishes worthy of an art gallery.

Gastro Pub 13
INTERNATIONAL $$

(📋 3852-624 313; pl Pobedy 1; mains R400-600; ⊙noon-2am) With its dark shadows and neon lighting, this place might look a lot like a nightclub from the outside, but with assured and artistic cooking, it's actually one of the better places to eat in Barnaul. Expect steaks, kebabs and other meaty dishes. It's in the same block as the cinema.

Mozarella
ITALIAN $$

(Hato & Dato; 📋 3852-353 931; www.hatodato.ru; pr Lenina 21a; mains R290-350; ⊙11am-noon) Delicious risottos, pastas and meat and fish dishes are served up at this cosy restaurant that's cheap, but doesn't skimp on food quality.

ⓘ Information

Main Post Office (Почтамт; pr Lenina 54; ⊙8am-8pm Mon-Fri, to 6pm Sat & Sun)

ⓘ Getting There & Away

Moscow (4½ hours, three daily) is the only regularly served destination served from Barnaul's airport.

There's a train to Tomsk (*platskart/kupe* R1100/2380, 12 hours, 6.12pm) via Novosibirsk (R845/1776, six hours) on odd-numbered days. There's one or two trains every night to Omsk (R1965/3549, 16 hours), some of which continue to Moscow. There's a train every fourth day to Novokuznetsk but the bus is much more convenient. Transfer in Novosibirsk for Krasnoyarsk and points east on the Trans-Siberian main line.

Elektrichki (suburban trains) to Biysk depart daily at 9am and 6.22pm (2nd-/1st-class R197/259, three hours).

Shared taxis can get you to Novosibirsk in 2½ hours (R1000) and to Biysk in 1½ hours (R600) but you may have to wait awhile for them to fill up. The road to Novosibirsk is busy, fast and dangerous. For much of its length it's single lane each way, meaning frequent hairy encounters with oncoming traffic. Shared taxis gather outside the train and bus station.

BUS

Barnaul's large and modern **bus station** (Автовокзал) is right next door to the train station and only a couple of minutes walk from the city centre. Electronic information signs give all departure times (in Russian).

DESTINATION	FARE	TIME (HR)	FREQUENCY
Biysk	R314	2½	hourly
Chemal	R1100	6½	2 daily
Gorno-Altaisk	R600	4	12 daily
Onguday	R780	8	10.45am
Novokuznetsk	R800	7	3 daily
Novosibirsk	R500	4½	hourly
Tomsk	R950	9	2 daily

ⓘ Getting Around

From pl Pobedy near the train station, buses 19 and 110 head northeast on pr Stroiteley, take a right on pr Lenina and continue to the **river station** (Речной Вокзал) at the terminus of pr Lenina. Buses 17, 57 and 60 link the river station with Demidovskaya pl, then run the length of Krasnoarmeysky pr to pl Pobedy before rejoining pr Lenina at pl Oktyabrya.

An atmospheric, clanky old tram line runs in a north–south direction through the centre of the city and other lines connect the suburbs.

Biysk
Бийск

📋 3854 / POP 210,000 / ⊙ MOSCOW +4HR

Friendly Biysk, 160km southeast of Barnaul, is not worth a special detour but its old town merits a wander if you are passing through en route to or from the Altai Mountains, for which it's the nearest railhead.

One of only three cities created on the orders of Peter the Great (the others were Moscow and St Petersburg!), Biysk was founded in 1709 at the junction of the Biya and Katun Rivers, but was quickly burnt down by the Dzhungarian Mongols. Biysk was reestablished 20km to the east in 1718. Unfortunately, nothing remains from this period. Most of the well-preserved architecture of the historic centre dates from the late 1800s.

⊙ Sights

Central Biysk is nothing special, so if you just have a few hours make a beeline for the **old town**. From the train station, buses 6, 10, 17 and 21 are among those that get you there via Krasnoarmeyskaya ul (15 minutes) and return via ul Lenina – the city's parallel central thoroughfares. You'll know you're there when you see the **Lenin Statue** in front of the City Court at ul Lenina 149. It might be the only Lenin in Russia dressed in a real Siberian *shanka-ushanka* (winter fur hat with ear flaps).

Start your walking tour at the beautiful **City Theatre** (Бийский городской драматический театр; www.biyskdrama.ucoz.ru; ul Sovetskaya 25), built in 1916, from which it's about a 30-minute walk northeast along scenic **ul Sovetskaya** to pl Garkavogo via the city's **War Memorial**, with its eternal flame; blue-domed late-19th-century **Assumption Church** (Успенская церковь; Sovetskaya ul 13) and the **City Garden**. There's an eye-catching **statue of Peter the Great** astride a horse in pl Garkavogo.

★ **Regional Museum**   MUSEUM
(Краеведческий музей; www.museum.ru/M1345; ul Lenina 134; R100; ⊙ 9am-5pm Wed-Sun) Housed in a wonderfully dilapidated 1912 merchant's house with original art nouveau fittings, this fine museum is home to standing stone idols, petroglyphs and a weathered old shaman's coat that locals consider lucky and so pop coins into the display case. Everything is written in Russian but one member of staff speaks French and will gleefully give French speakers a (very) detailed tour.

⊨ Sleeping & Eating

★ **Gostinitsa na Starom Meste**   HOTEL **$$**
(Гостиница на Старом Месте; ☑ 8-963-577 8450; www.na-starom-meste.ru; ul Sovetskaya 24; s/d incl breakfast from R2000/3000; ❀❊☎) For those few people who come to Biysk specifically to see the sights, 'Hotel in an Old Place', opposite an 1882 brick building in the middle of the quiet old town, is clearly, and quite rightly, the place to be. An extremely tasteful and understated boutique hotel. The roomy singles are especially good value.

★ **Na Starom Meste**   RUSSIAN **$$**
(☑ 8-963-577 8450; www.na-starom-meste.ru; ul Sovetskaya 22, Gostinitsa Na Starom; mains R500-600; ⊙ noon-midnight) With rich-smelling, exposed wooden roof beams, heavy wood tables and chairs and waitresses dressed as Russian peasants, this welcoming and cosy restaurant attached to the Gostinitsa Na Starom hotel has something of a beer-hall feel. The food consists of large portions of sizzlers, kebabs, steaks, soups and salads all prepared with the eye of a cooking craftsman.

Café Randevu   RUSSIAN **$$**
(Кафе Рандеву; Sovetskaya ul 4; mains R250-500; ⊙ 11am-2am) Behind a beautifully renovated old-town facade, this midrange cafe serves decent food and beer in a pleasant atmosphere.

⊙ Information

Post Office (Sovetskaya ul 34; ⊙ 8am-8pm Mon-Fri, 9am-6pm Sat, 9am-2pm Sun)

⊙ ALTAI BORDER ZONES

The Altai Republic's border zones with China, Kazakhstan and Mongolia have been under the control of the FSB (formerly the KGB) since 2006. Foreigners are required to submit an permit application to enter these areas. It affects anyone straying off the Chuysky Trakt between Kosh-Agach and the Mongolian border (you do not need the permit in the town or if sticking to the highway); and anyone travelling further south than, and including, Ust-Koksa.

Applications should be made in Russian and must be submitted by fax to the **FSB office** (ФСБ; Федеральная служба безопасности; ☑ 38822-48 261; pr Kommunistichesky 94) in Gorno-Altaisk several weeks before your journey (the entire process generally takes at least two months). The application should include passport details (everything, including where and when issued and expiry date), planned route, purpose of journey and home address. When the permit is ready, you must swing through Gorno-Altaisk to pick it up before travelling onward.

Needless to say, this is infinitely easier if you use the services of a travel agency. Travel agencies outside of Western Siberia are unlikely to be able to do this for you. Two local, English-speaking, companies who can help with this are Altair-Tur (p445) in Novosibirsk and K2 Adventures (p444) in Omsk. The likely penalty for travelling in a border zone without a permit is a stiff fine and expulsion from the country.

❶ Getting There & Away

The No 602 train trundles daily to Novosibirsk (*platskart/kupe* R632/1150, 9½ hours) via Barnaul. There are also trains to Krasnoyarsk (even-numbered days), Moscow (even-numbered days) and Almaty (odd-numbered days).

Elektrichki to Barnaul depart at 7.26am and 5.34pm (2nd-/1st-class R256/348, three hours).

BUSES FROM BIYSK

The bus station is 3.5km west of the city centre and next to the train station.

DESTINATION	FARE	TIME (HR)	FREQUENCY
Artybash	R486	4	2 daily
Barnaul	R314	2½	hourly
Gorno-Altaisk	R298	1¾	every 90 minutes
Novokuznetsk	R500	5¼	5 daily
Novosibirsk	R500 to R800	6	hourly

Gorno-Altaisk
Горно - Алтайск

☑ 38822 / POP 60,000 / ⊘ MOSCOW +4HR

Gorno-Altaisk, the capital of the Altai Republic, was founded in 1830 and immediately saw an influx of missionaries eager to convert local pagan tribes. Today it's a somewhat bland mixture of Soviet-era buildings and newer development running through an attractive valley. For travellers, it's a convenient jumping-off point for more far-flung bits of Altai, and it's a required stop for those heading to the Mt Belukha area or other Altai border zones.

⊙ Sights

If you have a day or two to kill in Gorno-Altaisk, why not go for a hike? The city has two single-lift ski slopes that make for nice climbs in the warmer months. Take any bus along the city's seemingly interminable main street, Kommunistichesky pr, and you'll see the them – there's one a couple blocks east of central pl Lenina.

★ A.V. Anokhin
National Museum of Altai   MUSEUM

(Национальный музей Республики Алтай имени А.В. Анохина; ☑ 38822-47 773; ul Choros-Gurkina 46; R250; ⊘ 11am-7pm Wed, Fri & Sat, 11am-8pm Thu, 11am-6pm Sun) This well-put-together museum offers a good introduction to Altai culture with a range of ethnographic exhibits, wildlife displays and local art and artefacts, including a room dedicated to the Altai landscape painter Grigory Choros-Gurkin. It also houses a stuffed collection of the local wildlife including a snow leopard and an interesting display on prehistoric life in the region (complete with mannequins living in the most sterile looking cave you've ever seen).

Svyato-Makarevsky Church   CHURCH

(Свято-Макарьевский храм; pr Kommunistichesky 146) Completed in 2006, this attractive wooden church boasts a wonderfully photographic backdrop of rolling lush hills.

🛏 Sleeping & Eating

★ Igman   HOTEL $$

(Игман; ☑ 38822-47 242; www.igman04.ru; ul Choros-Gurkina 71; r without bathroom R1000, d from R2300; ❀ 🛜) At the rear of the bus station, Igman is by far the best place to stay in town. Perfect location, good service and spacious rooms at reasonable prices – what's not to like? The cheaper rooms share clean bathrooms. Wi-fi is spotty.

Grillman   STEAK $$

(☑ 8-923-667 7719; ul Choros-Gurkina 39; mains R350-600; ⊘ noon-11pm) Hidden away in the basement of a shopping mall is Gorno-Altaisk's best restaurant. As the name suggests it's all about big hunks of meat here and whether you go for a steak or a kebab it's all unusually well cooked with only the best cuts being used. The owner speaks English and will give advice on what to order.

Travellers Coffee   CAFE $$

(pr Kommunistichesky 26; mains R200-350; ⊘ 8am-11pm; 🛜) This blossoming travel-themed Siberian chain is a welcome addition to Gorno-Altaisk's staid food scene. Well-priced breakfasts, the best coffee in the republic, Russian staples and light bites.

❶ Information

There's a **post office** (Почта; Kommunistichesky pr 61; ⊘ 9am-8pm Mon-Sat) next to the bus station.

Good city maps are available at street kiosks.

Apply at the **FSB Office** (p464) for border-zone permits. It's two bus stops west of the bus station, just over the Mayma River.

❶ Getting There & Away

Gorno-Altaisk's airport is out on the Chuysky Trakt in Mayma, 10km west of the centre. S7 has three weekly flights to Novosibirsk and daily flights to Moscow.

There's no railway but a **booth** (☉9am-7pm Mon-Fri, 10am-4pm Sat) within the **bus station** (pr Kommunistichesky) sells train tickets.

Buses are the main form of transport around here. In addition to public buses (p466), private *marshrutki* (in the form of 15-seat Gazelle vans) serve more remote destinations. There are two Gazelle departures every morning to Kosh-Agach (R550, 7½ hours, 8.30am and 10.30am) from the bus station. Pricier and quicker shared taxis sometimes make morning trips too.

❶ Getting Around

From central Gorno-Altaisk virtually all east-bound city buses take Kommunistichesky pr past the bus station, FSB building, Federal Migration Service office and market.

Lake Manzherok
Озеро Манжерок

☏ 38844 / ⊕ MOSCOW +4HR

The riverside lodges in and around peaceful Manzherok, 20km south of Aya, are an outdoorsy alternative to staying in Gorno-Altaisk.

Manzherok also has a burgeoning ski scene on **Mt Sinyukha** near Lake Manzherok in the nearby village of Ozernoe (Озерное). The top of the mountain affords marvelous panoramas of Lake Manzherok and the surrounding countryside from a **viewing platform**. You can also dress up like a Mongolian warrior or pose with an eagle for photos, if that's your thing.

Developers are eying Manzherok as the next Sheregesh, and plan to open hectares of new terrain and install up to 40 lifts over the next few years. At the time of research there was hectic building activity taking place at the foot of the mountain as new ski lodges were being built.

◉ Sights & Activities

One lift operates year-round (adult/child R400/250). The ride up the mountain covers almost 2.5km and takes 25 minutes. If you're feeling spry, you can walk up for free.

There's also a small climbing wall and tree canopy walkway close to the ski lift at the bottom of the mountain.

To get to the ski area from the centre of Manzherok, walk 1.5km south on the Chuysky Trakt and take a left at the sign to Ozeroe (at km473). Proceed 800m to a T-junction in Ozernoe, turn left and look for the ski area. It's a big old walk from the town centre, so hunt around for a taxi.

European Bison Farm　WILDLIFE RESERVE
(☏8-913-998 9991; km511; R250; ☉7am-2pm) A herd of two dozen European bison live in a semiwild status as they range across the meadows and forests of this 'farm'. European bison were hunted to extinction in the wild in the early 20th-century but today, thanks to ventures like this one, which breeds stock for re-introduction elsewhere, they are making a gradual comeback. A visit involves a short 'safari' to find the bison and an explanatory talk (in Russian only).

It's half an hour's drive south of Manzherok along the Chuysky Trakt. To get here you really need your own transport.

BUSES FROM GORNO-ALTAISK

DESTINATION	FARE	TIME (HR)	FREQUENCY
Aktash	R530	5½	7.15am, 10am
Artybash	R400	4	11.55am, 5.20pm
Barnaul	R600	4	12 daily
Biysk	R298	1¾	every 90 mins
Chemal	R300	2¼	3-4 daily
Novosibirsk	R1100	8	4 daily
Onguday	R250	3½	2.25pm
Tyungur	R850	9	8.20am, 1.45pm (summer)
Ulagan	R625	6	7.15am
Ust-Koksa	R1000	8	8.20am, 1.45pm (summer) & 9.40pm

ⓘ REGISTERING YOUR VISA IN GORNO-ALTAISK

It's not strictly necessary, but if you are travelling in the Altai Republic, you should pay attention to making sure your visa is properly registered. Technically the rules are the same as elsewhere: you only need to register if you are staying in one district for more than seven business days. But the local authorities tend not to be aware of this, and might demand to see a valid registration and/or a *khodataystvo* – a document from whoever sponsored your visa, listing where in Altai you'll be visiting (secure one of these before departing).

We advise the following:

➡ If you'll be staying in Altai for less than seven business days, it should suffice to get one registration in the usual way from a hotel in Gorno-Altaisk or elsewhere.

➡ If you'll be roaming around more than one district in Altai for *more* than seven business days, then it's a good idea to go to the **Federal Migration Service** (ФМС; Федеральная Миграционная Служба; ☑ 38822-61 546; top fl, Kommunistichesky pr 109; ☺ 9am-12.45pm & 2-6pm Mon-Fri) in Gorno-Altaisk to register your visa for your entire stay in Altai. It's four bus stops west of the bus station, roughly opposite the pretty wooden church at Kommunistichesky pr 146.

➡ If you'll be staying in Altai for more than seven business days but will be staying in a single district, then it should suffice to register upon arrival in that district – at the local FMS office, the post office or a hotel.

🛏 Sleeping & Eating

The best accommodation is on the river a few kilometres north or south of town.

Dva Medveda HOTEL **$**
(Два медведя; ☑ 8-923-707 7558; www.dvamedvedya.ru; Chuysky Trakt, 477.5km; 2-person tents/d from R1000/1400; 🛜) Great-value log cabins set in attractive grounds on the Katun River 6km south of Manzherok. Also offers excursions. The name translates as 'Two Bears' – although you won't see even one.

★Vityaz CABIN **$$**
(Витязь; ☑ 8-905-986 8768; Chuysky Trakt, 476.5km; tents R600, log cabins from R2500) The idyllic Vityaz, 5km south of Manzherok, has cosy log cabins right on the Katun River where it will just be you, the trees, the river and a couple of pet geese. The owner is lovely and there's a cafe selling simple snacky-type meals.

Turkompleks Manzherok LODGE **$$**
(Туркомплекс Манжерок; ☑ 38844-28 399; www.mangerok-altai.ru; Chuysky Trakt, km469; dm/s/d from R600/1400/1800; 🛜) This well-organised holiday complex just north of Manzherok sits behind a mock-Cossack stockade in a riverbank pine grove. The cheaper rooms have toilets but share showers. There's a man-made beach if you want to splash around in the Katun, mountain bikes for rent (R150/600 per hour/day) and there's a fleet of white-water rafts.

★Chaynaya Sinyukha UZBEK **$$**
(Чайная Синюха; Chuysky Trakt, 471.5k; meals R150-250; ☺ 9am-9pm) The freshly prepared Uzbek cuisine here is some of the best food in Altai, and well worth stopping for if heading south on the Chuysky Trakt. The *manti* (Uzbek dumplings), dusted with paprika, are particularly good, and the piping-hot *non* (Uzbek flat bread, or *lavash*) is right out of the *tandir* (clay oven). Has healthy salads too.

ⓘ Information

There's a **Sberbank** ATM (Сбербанк; Chuysky Trakt, 471km) near the post office.
Post Office (Chuysky Trakt, km471; ☺ 9am-5pm Mon-Fri)

ⓘ Getting There & Away

From Gorno-Altaisk, take a Chemal-bound bus to Manzherok or a taxi (R900).

Lake Teletskoe & Artybash
Озеро Телецкое и Артыбаш

☑ 38843 / POP 4500 / ☺ MOSCOW +4HR

Deep, delightful Lake Teletskoe is Altai's serene answer to Lake Baikal, a great place simply to relax and catch your breath. It's also Altai's largest lake. Ridge after forested ridge unfolds as you scuttle along on one of the myriad little pleasure boats that buzz out of Artybash village, the lake's charming tourist hub.

Lake Teletskoe drains into the Biya River at its westernmost nose. Artybash is on the right (north) bank, connected by bridge to little Iogach village, the main population centre and bus stop, on the left bank.

◎ Sights & Activities

Boat tours are the main activity, naturally. Besides the popular trip to Korbu Waterfall, you can jump on a hydrofoil to the **Altyn Tour** camp at the southern end of the lake, some 78km away (R1500 per person, eight hours return). Most boats leave from the main pier. The lake freezes over in winter and the village transforms into a winter wonderland, with snowmobiles the vehicle of choice.

Guesthouses and tour agencies around the bridge also offer **trekking** (R800 per person), **fishing, horseback-riding** and **rafting** on the Biya River.

Korbu Waterfall
WATERFALL

From June to September, there are many daily lake trips (R800 per person) to Korbu Waterfall. You have a choice between fast, noisy hydrofoils (four hours return) and larger, slower-paced craft (six to eight hours return). The falls are hardly memorable but the journey is very beautiful despite the blaring commentary. Along the way you'll pass by several other waterfalls and natural sights.

⌫ Sleeping & Eating

Many places open in peak season only; reservations are highly advisable in July and August. Prices drop by up to 50% outside the peak season.

Every second house in Artybash seems to have rooms or huts to rent. Prices start from R800. Many places demand minimum groups of three or more guests. Look for signs marked 'Сдаю Дом' and 'Сдаётся Дом' (house for rent). Hotel distances given are from the bridge.

Usadba Stary Zamok
CABIN $$

(Усадьба Старый замок; ☑ 38843-27 660; www.zamoktel.ru; km1.4; d from R3000) This sweetly kitsch little 'castle' has more of a log-cabin feel, with woody, fragrant rooms – some with lake views – opening to shared terraces. The onsite *stolovaya* (open 9am to 9pm in season) is fantastic value and has outdoor seating right on the lake. Jump in the cold lake then hit the *banya* (hot bath; R500 per hour).

Hotel Artybash
HOTEL $$

(Гостиница Артыбаш; ☑ 8-961-709 4242; www.artybash.com; d from R3230; ⊜🛜) The most modern hotel in the area, the Artybash has pretty uninspiring rooms, but some have great views of the Biya River. There's friendly English-speaking staff, and a good restaurant that offers Altai specialities such as *maral* (wild deer) among a bevvy of Russian staples. It's 300m before the bridge.

🛍 Shopping

Souvenir Shops
SOUVENIRS

(⊘8am-8pm) The souvenir shops around the start of the bridge sell all manner of interesting items, from Altai honey (R100 a small jar), Altai pop and traditional music, maps, 500mL bottles of deer blood (pure R1100 pure, cut with cow blood R300), Altai T-shirts and Altai instruments such as jew's harps (*kamys* in the local dialect, *vargan* in Russian; R300) and *ocarina* (yurt-shaped flutes).

ⓘ Information

Sberbank (Сбербанк; ⊘9.30am-noon & 2-3.30pm Mon-Sat) Next to the bridge on the logach side. Has an ATM.

ⓘ Getting There & Away

Buses to Gorno-Altaisk leave from a bus stop in front of the Zolotoe Ozera Cafe at the end of the bridge on the logach side of the river at 8.20am and 3.20pm (R400, four hours). For taxis to Sheregesh (R5000), ask around at any cafe or tour company.

Chemal
Чемал

☑38841 / POP 9400 / ⊘ MOSCOW +4HR

At the attractive junction of the Chemal and Katun Rivers, ever-expanding Chemal is hugely popular with Russian tourists in summer. They come for the white-water rafting, zip-lines, walking and, most importantly, the partying. For a foreign tourist Chemal is less appealing as a destination, but it still makes for a fun day or overnight trip from Gorno-Altaisk, 95km north, or Manzherok. If you want to continue south to Kosh-Agach and the high Altai mountains, you'll first need to backtrack to Ust-Sema on the Chuysky Trakt.

◎ Sights

In summer tour companies in town and around Varota Sartikpayev Gorge have stalls offering rafting trips on the Katun River from R500 per hour. The rafting is fairly tame.

Varota Sartikpayev Gorge   PARK

The tourist action in Chemal revolves around this canyon near the confluence of the Katun and Chemal Rivers. Despite power lines and summer crowds, views remain very pretty. Around the dam you can make 15m bungee jumps (adult/student R400/300) into the frothing outpour waters or fly over the waters on several short ziplines (*kanatnaya doroga;* R300 per ride). Both attractions impose 'fines' on anyone who backs out at the last second!

The area around the gorge occupies an important place in Altai mythology – the white pieces of cloth tied to trees here and elsewhere in the region are part of the Altai people's tradition of honouring their ancestors. However, by and large the only religion practised here today is one devoted to the god of tourism and tack.

To get to the gorge from the Ioanno Bogoslavski Chapel, walk about 15 minutes south along a narrow but well-trodden footpath high above the Katun until you emerge behind a small 1935 dam backed by souvenir stalls and open-air cafes selling Uzbek food, beer and traditional Altai tea.

After throwing yourself off cliffs and zipping over rivers you can return to Chemal via a different route. Cross the Chemal River near the zip-line via a footbridge, veer left, and look for a 4WD track heading up the hill directly in front of you to the east. It's a straightforward 45-minute hike to the top of the hill, from where there are fine views of Chemal and its surrounding mountains, valleys and rivers. Descend the way you came and return home via the inconspicuous amusement park near the reservoir at the base of the hill.

Altaysky Tsentr   MUSEUM

(ul Beshpekskaya 6; R100) From the centre of town walk about 500m south along central ul Pchyolkina, past small Park Pobedy, then turn right toward the river at the signpost to find the wonderful Altaysky Tsentr. This comprises three Altai-style wooden *ail*-huts with pointed metal roofs. The centrepiece is the traditional 'home' *ail*, with traditional clothing, kitchen instruments, furniture and other Altai knick-knacks (check out the cool grass-fueled lighter, ignited with a rock!).

The other huts contain a library and some of Choros-Gurkin's ethnographic works.

Adding flavour to a visit here is the eccentric hostess, Tansya Petrovna Bardina, who will regale you with stories of her late husband, the museum's founder, and will insist on taking photos of you from various vantage points within the museum. Good fun even if you don't understand Russian. Opening hours are whenever Tansya Petrovna is around to give you a (mandatory) tour.

Ioanno Bogoslavski Chapel   CHURCH

(⊙9am-7pm) On the northern edge of the Varota Sartikpayev Gorge, a wobbly footbridge leads across a stunning canyon to a craggy island in the Katun River on which is perched the tiny wooden Ioanno Bogoslavski Chapel, rebuilt in 2001 to the original 1849 design. Beside it, the rock miraculously shaped like a Madonna-and-child sculpture is supposedly natural.

🛏 Sleeping & Eating

As in the Lake Teletskoe area, locals rent out cottages or their own homes (from R1000 per person). Look for the ubiquitous 'Сдаётся Дом' (house for rent) signs. Just north of Chemal, the village of Elekmonar sprawls for 5km along the Katun River and is similarly endowed with myriad basic home- and hutstays along central ul Sovetskaya.

The food scene in Chemal is extremely limited, as most visitors self-cater from several well-stocked supermarkets on ul Pchyolkina. You'll find plenty of kiosks selling *chebureki* (greasy meat-filled turnovers), *plov* (meat and rice) and other Central Asian snacks near the tourist sights.

Royal Comfort   RESORT $$

(☏8-913-096 0000; www.royalcomfort88.ru; r from R2300, cabins from R5000; ☺❋🛜🏊) Large resort-style complex with spacious but dated rooms that have a gorgeous line in pink shower curtains. There are also some more appealing wooden cabins raised on stilts, perfect for families and groups. Lots of facilities and a bit of a party atmosphere. The owner speaks some English.

Maryin Ostrov Eco Resort   RESORT $$$

(☏8-800-222 0104; http://marin-ostrov.ru; ul Uozhanskaya 58; d from R15,600; ☺🛜🏊) The most exclusive (and yes, okay, expensive) address in the region, many of the beautiful cottages here have natural features such as jagged boulders built into them, and all have slick, modern decoration and all the facilities you could hope for, including a superb spa and pool complex. Oddly, they're not keen on potential guests turning up without a booking.

Areda 2-3
RESORT $$$

(☑3882-294 074; gk-areda@mail.ru; cabins/r from R5000/7000; ⊜ 🛜 ⛱) Delightfully situated several kilometres southeast of Chemal, down a narrow wooded country lane and beside a twisting, bubbling river, the Areda 2-3 has overly grandiose rooms or more appealing riverside cabins. However, whichever option you go for it's kind of overpriced.

Opta
CENTRAL ASIAN $

(mains around R200; ☉9am-9pm) This sky-blue open-air cafe and yurt serves traditional and tasty Altai and Central Asian dishes that will start to make Mongolia seem awfully close. It's at the southern end of town just where the road forks off for the gorges.

ℹ Information

Sberbank (Сбербанк; ul Sovetskaya; ☉9am-4pm Mon-Fri) Next to the bus station and with an ATM.

ℹ Getting There & Away

There are three or four trips a day to Gorno-Altaisk (R300, 2¼ hours) via Manzherok, with the 7.40am bus continuing on to Novosibirsk (R1600, nine hours). Additional trips to Barnaul (3pm) and Novosibirsk (11am) do not stop in Gorno-Altaisk, but do pass by nearby Mayma on the Chuysky Trakt.

If heading south along the Chuysky Trakt, you should arrange in advance to be picked up by private *marshrutka* (fixed-route minibus) in Manzherok (km471) or Ust-Sema (km499).

Chuysky Trakt
Чуйский тракт

The Chuysky Trakt (M52) is a sealed highway that runs 966km from Novosibirsk all the way to the Mongolian border. By far the most interesting stretch – which makes it one of Russia's great drives – runs for about 450km south from Mayma to Kosh-Agach in southern Altai. Frothy rivers, harrowing passes, craggy cliffs, rolling steppe, austere desert landscapes and – the *coup de grâce* – the mighty 4000m mountains of the Chuya range make this one ride you'll never forget.

Plenty of public and private *marshrutky* (fixed-route minibuses) ply the route between Gorno-Altaisk and Kosh-Agach (approximately seven hours). A ticket costs just R550, making this one of life's better cheap thrills. Ask your driver for a seat in the front. If you want to stop (and you will want to), you'll have to hire a private car. We recommend hiring a taxi for three or four days in order to get the most out of the area (taxi drivers in Gorno-Altaisk will request at least R5000 a day).

The Route

After following the Katun River south from Aya for about 150km out of Mayma, you'll start climbing up to the **Seminsky Pass**, at 1715m the highest point on the entire Chuysky Trakt. Don't let that statistic excite you too much though. The climb up to the pass is very gentle and if there wasn't a sign to inform you that you'd arrived, you'd probably just race on over. If you do stop though, you'll find snack and souvenir kiosks up here

---

WORTH A TRIP

AYA

There is a booming tourist scene south of Mayma concentrated around the wobbly, disused wooden bridge at km455 of the Chuysky Trakt. Access is via a new bridge (at km459) over the Katun River – cross this bridge to the other side then backtrack to the old bridge, where you'll find a gaggle of thumping nightclubs in the summer months. If you're stuck in Gorno-Altaisk and looking for a night out, this is where you should head to. Outside peak season it's pretty much dead.

Many agencies around the wooden bridge offer **rafting trips** (R500 per hour) and horse rides at short notice: handy if you haven't reserved anything more adventurous. Stalls sell jars of natural honey for around R400 and *sera*, a traditional Siberian 'chewing gum' made from cedar tree resin. There are also numerous outdoor cafes serving the usual shashlyk and beer. There are numerous accommodation options along the river here, but unless you want to party, we recommend heading 30km upstream to Manzherok for a more tranquil getaway. From Gorno-Altaisk, Chemal-bound buses are the best way to get to Aya, or take a taxi (R500).

along with a winter sports training centre and, rising gradually to the east, bleak and bald **Mt Sarlyk** (2507m). If you're looking for a relatively easy and easy-to-access climb in central Altai, Mt Sarlyk is your answer.

The road descends through Tuekta (km611) and Onguday (km634), then starts climbing again up to the beautiful, serpentine **Chike-Taman Pass** (km663). The pass acquired its name, which means 'flat sole' in Altai, before the Chuysky Trakt was built. The old road was so steep that locals believed you could see the bottom of the shoe of the person walking ahead of you. Today the pass is a more gradual affair, but from near the top (take the path behind the souvenir stands) you can still see the old road, which remains open to off-road vehicles. As with the Seminsky Pass there are a number of snack shops and souvenir stands here, some of which sell morally questionable bear and wolf paws turned into key rings and such like.

The pass descends through **Kupchegen** (km674), with *aily* (yurt-like traditional Altai dwellings) in almost every yard and the scenery rapidly starts to become more impressive. At km684 you rejoin the Katun River, last seen in Ust-Sema, and at km689 you get your first view of the high Altai mountains as the snow-capped Northern Chuya range comes into view. Next up is **Maly Yaloman** (km696), which sits in a cliff-ringed curl of river and has a microclimate allowing local villagers to grow pears, cherries and apples. Indeed, Altai is known for its myriad microclimates, and as you drive the length of the Chuysky Trakt you'll be amazed how dramatically the landscape changes with every bend in the road.

When you enter **Inya** (km703), be sure to keep your eyes open for what may be the most dramatically placed and memorable Lenin statue in Russia. At km712.5, picnic tables and prayer flags tempt you to stop for wonderful views of the meeting of the Chuya and Katun Rivers far below. Just beside the slip road for the simple Chuy-Oozy cafe at km714.2, very lightly scored road-side petroglyphs depict little antelope figures. But the big sight here, if you can spot it, is the legendary 'rock face' on the left bank of the Katun. If you can't make out its 'features', pop into the cafe and check out the helpful drawing hanging on a wall. Then go out and have another look. All should now be clear!

Some 3km before the tiny settlement of **Iodro**, on the left-hand side, stands a stone idol with a well-preserved and somewhat haunting face. There's another petroglyph group at Yalbak Tash crag, a five-minute walk north of km721. The road then snakes scenically through the Chuya Canyon. At km761, look up to the right for a glimpse of a waterfall crashing out of the hills. At km782 you enter **Chibit**, where there's an enticing camp on the river with partial views of the snow-capped Mt Aktru (4044m) and Mt Kurkurek (3982m).

Clouds permitting, the best views on the whole Chuysky Trakt are between Aktash (km790) and Kosh-Agach (km889). A few hundred metres beyond km796 is a small, sulphurous and electric blue geyser lake (p472). From km801 to km811 the Northern Chuyas are right in your face and you'll want to stop the car as much as possible for photos. Beyond this you begin to traverse the vast and desolate Kuray and Chuy Steppes, with distant panoramas of perennially snow-topped peaks. The Kuray Steppe regularly hosts Russia's paragliding championships. The cold and bleak village of **Kuray** is home to the Altai National Park office and is the launch pad for assaults on Mt Aktru.

The road leading to Kosh-Agach sees the greenery start to die out, and the scenery gradually transforms into something resembling a lunar landscape.

Onguday   Онгудай

📞 38845 / POP 5100 / ⊙ MOSCOW +4HR

Translating literally as '10 gods' (for the 10 surrounding peaks), this large village isn't especially appealing but it makes a good base for several excursions to the north of town.

The central and basic **Kok Boru Hotel** (Гостиница Кок-бору; 📞 3884-521 196; ul Erzu-masheva 8; r without bathroom R800; 🛜), which has an English-speaking receptionist and good-sized rooms, seems to attract all manner of interesting characters.

As the first major stop south of Gorno-Altaisk on the Chuysky Trakt, Onguday is relatively well-connected, with several bus and *marshrutka* trips daily to Gorno-Altaisk (R300). If heading south, have your hotel book a south-bound *marshrutka*, as most passing vehicles will be full.

Chibit   Чибит

📞 38846 / ⊙ MOSCOW +4HR

A pretty riverside village hemmed by forest peaks and partial views of the snow peaks beyond, Chibit has very few facilities for passing tourists, yet still makes a pleasant base amid the most dramatic part of the Chuysky Trakt.

TREKKING TO THE BLUE LAKE

While a disappointing amount of Altai is out of bounds to foreign tourists without the correct – and hard to obtain – permits, one place you can visit with fairly minimal effort is the Blue Lake halfway up the side of the spectacular frozen world of Mt Aktru (4044m).

The mountain lies within the protected Altai National Park and is only the highest of a knot of glaciated peaks surrounded by almost pristine conifer forest. The walk to the small, often frozen, turquoise-tinged lake, set inside a barren bowl of scree slopes, takes around six hours return. The route is fairly clearly waymarked as it wends its way through stunning old-growth forest and then up the edge of the massive glacier that drips off the side of Aktru before crossing a barren ridge and down to the lake. The walk itself is generally not too taxing and is remarkable for the changes of scenery in such a short distance.

Under certain weather conditions it's actually possible to walk up and over the glacier to get to the lake without the use of crampons and ropes. However, this should really only be attempted if you are with a knowledgeable guide who is aware of the glacier's many moods. Between mid-June and mid-August there are likely to be plenty of other people walking to the lake and a guide isn't strictly needed (though avoid walking on the glacier). However, these are not just high mountains, they're high mountains in Siberia, which means the weather can change here very, very fast. Even in summer it can go from baking sunshine one moment to a snow storm the next. It's vital to come prepared with very warm and waterproof clothing as well as supplies to see you through the night if you get stuck by the weather. So, while a guide isn't obligatory, it's certainly a very sensible idea. Unfortunately none are available in the vicinity of the mountains. Contact a respected local trekking company in advance; Altair-Tur (p445) is recommended.

The base for the ascent to the lake is the bleak roadside village of Kuray. From here you need to get a 'taxi' (think more along the lines of a tank than a saloon car) for the gruelling 32km drive along an absolutely dreadful mud track to a parking and camping area under the trees (allow up to two hours for the drive). The smallest vehicle, which will hold four passengers, costs R7000 return. Vehicles often wait by the edge of Kuray village, but if not there's a very helpful, English-speaking information office (Kuray; ☺9am-8pm) also on the edge of the village and they will call a taxi for you (do not even consider attempting the drive in your own car).

The lake can only be reached between late May and September.

The one good place to stay in town is the riverside **Kochenik camping ground and hotel** (☑8-903-990 6901; Km781; cabins/d R1400/3000; ☎) with simple wooden tent-shaped cabins (shared bathrooms) and a fewer posher, self-contained rooms. There's a small cafe where breakfast is available (R250) and evening meals can be prepared with advance notice. Otherwise fire up the barbecue and make your own. Staff can advise on walks in the Altai region. There's no direct public transport that begins or ends its journey in Chibit. If you're reliant on public transport, flag down a passing *marshrutka*.

Aktash   Акташ

☑ 38846 / POP 3400 / ☺ MOSCOW +4HR

This rundown and isolated village, whose name means 'white stone' in the Altai language, commands a dramatic area of craggy valleys. It could make a base for mountain adventures in the lovely Northern Chuya

Range with its challenging mountaineering on **Mt Aktru** (4044m; permit required) and **Mt Maashey** (4177m; permit required) or for trekking to the **Shavlinsky Lakes** (permit required) or the Blue Lake (no permit required) halfway up Mt Aktru. For all but the Blue Lake a guide is required as well as full expedition equipment, none of which you will find in Aktash, so arrange those in advance, along with your border permit, from a qualified tour company.

Cyclists taking on the glorious journey east to Tuva via Ulagan might find themselves in Aktash for a night (going beyond Ulagan requires a border permit).

◉ Sights

★ **Geyser Lake**   GEYSER

(km796.5) One of the more unusual sights along the Chusky Trakt is this sublime turquoise blue sulfur lake and geyser. This is no Yellowstone-style geyser erupting forth in drama; but it's a subtle charmer. Indiscreet bubbles mingle with black silt in the blue lake waters to form slow changing patterns in the lake floor. It's especially colourful and beautiful when the sun shines on it and the waters positively glow. The lake is a few minutes' drive south of Aktash just after km796 (look for the wooden sign). From here it's a five-minute walk along a rickety wooden walkway.

🛏 Sleeping

Yiot Hotel
HOTEL $

(☑ 8-913-029 3419; ul Pushkina 1; s/tw R400/800) The simple Yiot Hotel is located in a wood house just off central ul Mokhova.

Rasul Hotel
HOTEL $$

(Гостиница Расул; ☑ 8-913-992 3344; www. vk.com/rasulhotels; Chuysky Trakt; r from R2300; ⊜ 🛜) The flashiest hotel in town by a long shot is the often booked-out Rasul Hotel, easily spotted on the left as you enter town from the north.

ℹ Getting There & Away

A petrol station on the Chuysky Trakt on the south edge of town serves as the bus station. The daily public *marshrutka* to Gorno-Altaisk leaves at 7am (R530, 5½ hours), or catch the Ulagan–Gorno public *marshrutka* when it passes through at 1pm (booking required). Aktash to Kosh-Agach by taxi costs at least R1500.

Kosh-Agach
Кош Агач

☑ 38842 / POP 5500 / ⊘ MOSCOW +4HR

Kosh-Agach means 'last tree' in Kazakh, but that tree appears to have died long ago. Some 50km from the Russia–Mongolia border, Kosh-Agach is the driest inhabited place in the Russian Federation, with average rainfalls of under 150mm.

The town has a strange, end-of-the-world feeling about it, with its shanty-type homes petering out into magical flat steppe where free-range camels roam. When the dusty air clears, the nearby mountains appear from nowhere like apparitions. Russians are in the minority here, with Kazakhs and Altai making up something like 90% of the population.

Kosh-Agach is divided roughly in half by an often dried-up river (great bird watching when it is full, though). The centre of town is southwest of the river, with the two main streets – parallel ul Sovetskaya and ul Kooperativnaya – both intersecting with the Chuysky Trakt near the Khazret Osman Mosque.

◉ Sights & Activities

Kosh-Agach is the logical base for climbs in the Southern Chuya range, which tops out at Mt Maashey (4177m), and there are various other excursions available to those with the proper paperwork, including multiday expeditions to the remote and wind-battered highlands of the Ukok plateau, which is hard up against the Kazakhstan border and only recently opened to foreign tourists. Contact a specialist agency if you want to visit.

If you head out of town towards Mongolia, you'll come across Kosh-Agach's large Soviet-era welcome sign, which depicts three stern officials (one Slav, one Kazakh and one Altai) standing next to a hammer and sickle. The northern entrance of town is marked by statues of a yak, a camel and an eagle. Well worth a look, if only for the great photo opps.

🛏 Sleeping & Eating

Along ul Kooperativnaya you'll find several reasonably stocked grocery stores, a *stolovaya* (cafeteria) and some simple cafes serving mainly Central Asian fare.

★ Hotel Tsentralnaya
GUESTHOUSE $

(☑ 8-913-690 8428; ul Kooperativnaya 31; s/d/tr without bathroom R700/1200/1650; 🛜) There's exceptional value to be found at this homely guesthouse at the far western end of the main drag. The rooms are comfortable, if time-worn, and it's very friendly.

Zarya Hotel
GUESTHOUSE $

(☑ 8-913-698 5208; ul Kommunalnaya 71; r from R800; 🛜) Popular with bikers on a budget because of its central location just off the Chuysky Trakt and its nice kitchen. The rooms are basic, although some do have queen beds for couples and the owner is a charmer. There's a *banya* (hot bath) for guest use (R800).

Rasul Hotel
HOTEL $$

(Гостиница Расул; ☑ 8-913-991 3344; www. vk.com/rasulhotels; ul Novochuyskaya 72a; s/tw R1150/2300; ⊜ 🛜) This hotel, just off the Chuysky Trakt on the northeast side of the river, brings a lick of style to down-at-heel Kosh-Agach with its big, bright rooms. The downside of staying here is that no breakfast is provided and it's a really long walk to the town centre and somewhere to eat.

Yulduz
CENTRAL ASIAN $

(ul Voyskavaya, Chuysky Trakt 14; mains R150-250; ⊘ 11am-11pm) South of the centre on the Chuysky Trakt, Kazakh-run Yulduz is

UST-KOKSA, TYUNGUR & MT BELUKHA

The holy grail for many mountaineers visiting Altai is **Mt Belukha** (4506m), Siberia's highest peak. This is no peak for amateurs, but recreational hikers can hike around Belukha's base, which has some of the the best scenery Altai has to offer.

The catch, of course, is accessibility. Foreigners need to apply for a border permit (which takes around two months to issue), a time-consuming and expensive process that puts many visitors off – and indeed prevented us from conducting direct research of the area. If you plan in advance, however, you will not be disappointed.

The jumping-off point for treks is the small village of **Tyungur**, which sits in an appealing valley about 60km southeast of Ust-Koksa. One popular trek is the two- to three-day hike to stunning **Akkem Lake** at the foot of Mt Belukha. For a shorter trek that will give you a glimpse of the sacred peak, take a long day hike from Tyungur part-way up **Mt Baida**. Full-blown ascents of Belukha (grade 3A to 5A) are only for experienced mountaineers. Rafting and horse-trekking can also be organised out of Tyungur or Ust-Koksa.

For anything beyond a day hike, be aware that you're heading for real wilderness. Any hiking around Belukha will require a good degree of fitness and a guide and/or backcountry navigation experience. Choose only tour companies with extensive experience in the area. All of the following can organise one- to 12-day hikes in the area, although only Turbaza Vysotnik and K2 are qualified to lead full Belukha ascents.

K2 Adventures (p444) Based in Omsk, owner Igor Federov has years of mountaineering experience in the region.

Turbaza Vysotnik (☑ 8-981-273 9444; www.belukha.ru; ul Zarechnaya 7, Ust-Koksa) Offers almost anything you might need for mountaineering or treks into the wilderness.

Portal Beluha (☑ 8-913-998 0700; http://beluha.net; ul Naberezhnaya 55, Ust-Koksa) Based in Ust-Koksa and has plenty of regional experience.

If driving from Gorno-Altaisk, take the Chuysky Trakt as far as Tuekta, just north of Onguday. From Tuekta a sealed road runs due west to Ust-Kan, then south to Ust-Koksa. From Gorno-Altaisk a daily public *marshrutka* (fixed-route minibus) departs to Tyungur at 8.20am, with an additional trip at 1.45pm in the summer (R1000, nine hours). Additionally, there's an overnight trip from Barnaul to Ust-Koksa via Biysk and Gorno-Altaisk.

reputed to have the best *laghman* (thick noodle soup) in all of Altai along with *manti* (steamed, palm-sized dumplings) and its specialty Kazan Kebab (lamb), all homemade and fresh. Well worth the longish walk considering the town's other dismal options.

ⓘ Information

Visitors to Kosh-Agach do not need border permits as long as they remain in town. However you'll need one if you plan to venture off the Chuysky Trakt and into the steppe.

Federal Migration Service (Федеральная Миграционная Служба; ФМС; ul Kooperativnaya 28a; ⊙ 9am-5pm) No reason to be paranoid but the friendly folks here do check with hotels to make sure foreign guests are registered, and may ask for your *khodataystvo* (document from visa sponsor listing places to be visited) if they feel something is amiss.

There are several banks with functional ATMs on and around ul Kooperativnaya.

Post Office (ul Kooperativnaya 50; ⊙ 9am-6pm Mon-Fri, to 2pm Sat)

ⓘ Getting There & Away

There are no public *marshrutki* to Gorno-Altaisk but private *marshrutka* (Gazelle) 590 runs at least two daily trips (R550, 7½ hours, 8.30am and 10.30am), departing from opposite Hotel Tsentralnaya. Book a day in advance through your hotel to ensure a spot.

Shared taxis collect passengers at a stand opposite ul Sovetskaya 55 and head to Gorno-Altaisk (seat/whole taxi R800/5000); these can take a while to fill up so if you're in a hurry consider buying any empty seats. A private taxi from here to Aktash costs R1500; to the Mongolian border costs R900. For the rough ride from the border to Olgii, the nearest Mongolian settlement, you'll have to hire a UAZ (Russian 4WD) on the Mongolian side for a couple of hundred dollars.

Coming in from Mongolia you're unlikely to find transport quickly at the border. One option is to call a hotel in Kosh-Agach to send a taxi for you.

Note that the Mongolia–Russia border is closed on Sundays.

Eastern Siberia

Best Places to Eat

➡ 0.75 please (p483)

➡ Kochevnik (p512)

➡ Food & Bar 114 (p487)

➡ Orda (p532)

➡ Khozyain Taygi (p483)

Best Places to Stay

➡ Aldyn Bulak Yurt Hotel (p495)

➡ Belka Hostel (p517)

➡ Hovel Hostel (p482)

➡ Mergen Bator (p531)

➡ Nikita's Homestead (p520)

Why Go?

Endless ice-bound winters, kiln-hot summers, a history of imperial exile and Stalinist savagery – Eastern Siberia (Восточная Сибирь) isn't an obvious holiday destination, but there's much more to this vast region than blood-craving mosquitoes and blizzard-lost Gulag camps. Focus is given to the map by glorious Baikal, the world's deepest lake. Only Siberia could possess such a phenomenon with its crystal waters, mind-boggling stats and long list of outlandish endemic species. The lake presents a major obstacle to the Trans-Siberian Railway, which cradles Siberia in a string of intriguing cities such as architecturally grand Irkutsk, exotically Asian Ulan-Ude and youthful Krasnoyarsk.

But the trick to enjoying Eastern Siberia is in escaping the cities – hit the Great Baikal Trail, go hunting for Tuvan standing stones or seek out far-flung Buddhist temples in Buryatiya – the possibilities are almost as endless as the immense sweep of geography they occupy.

When to Go
Irkutsk

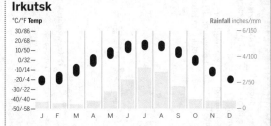

Mar Do a spot of ice fishing on Lake Baikal when the Siberian winter turns its surface hard as steel.

Jul Get on down at Shushenskoe's Mir Sibiri International Music Festival.

Sep Watch larch trees around Lake Baikal turn a fiery yellow during the brief autumn.

Eastern Siberia Highlights

1 Kyzyl (p493) Marvelling at ancient Scythian gold at the National Museum, and the uncanny sounds a human voice can make during Tuvan throat singing.

2 Lake Baikal (p504) Trekking, cycling or hitching a lift across the frozen lake.

3 Irkutsk (p505) Wandering boulevards of haughty 19th-century architecture in the

city once known as the 'Paris of Siberia'.

4 Ivolginsk (Ivolga) Datsan (p534) Meditating with monks at this and many other revived

Buddhist monasteries around the region.

5 Frolikha Adventure Coastline Trail (p501) Stepping out on Siberia's most

exhilarating long-distance hiking routes.

6 Circumbaikal Railway (p522) Taking a turn around Baikal's rocky southern shore.

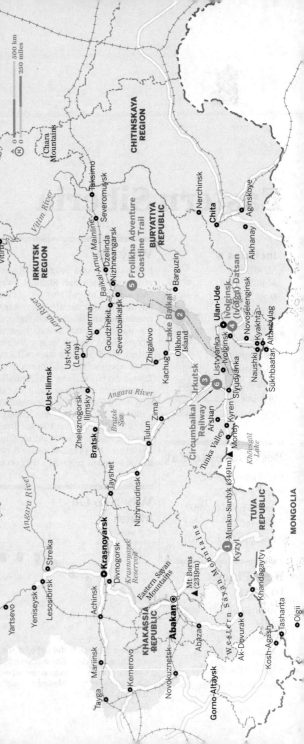

History

For century after tranquil prehistoric century, Eastern Siberia's indigenous peoples, such as the Evenki (Tungusi) north of Lake Baikal and the Kets of the Yenisey River, lived a peaceful existence in harmony with nature, harvesting game and berries in the thick taiga, fishing the rivers and building their *chumy* (tepees), largely oblivious of the outside world. In the south, horse-riding nomads of the Scythian culture (700 BC–AD 300) thrived in what is now Tuva, leaving behind fields of standing stones and circular *kurgany* (burial mounds) packed with intricately fashioned gold.

Gradually, however, Mongol-Turkic tribes began their expansion north and west, led by fearsome leaders such as Attila the Hun. The Buryats filtered north from Mongolia during the 11th and 12th centuries to assimilate local peoples and become the dominant ethnic group in Eastern Siberia. In the early 13th century, Chinggis (Genghis) Khaan united Mongol tribes across the region and went on to conquer China. Subsequent khans would sweep west across the steppe to sack the great cities of European Russia.

Enter the Russians

With a firm foothold in Western Siberia, small Cossack units began arriving further east in the early 17th century, establishing an *ostrog* (fortress) at river confluence positions such as Krasnoyarsk (1628), Ulan-Ude (1666, originally Verkhneudinsk) and Irkutsk (1651). Traders from European Russia followed and pressed indigenous peoples into supplying sable pelts at bargain prices (a tax called the *yasak*). The Buryats put up some resistance to the European invaders, but were no match for the Russian firearms.

European peasants were the next group to make the treacherous journey from the west, followed by banished prisoners and Old Believers after the religious rift of 1653; the original defensive forts burst into ramshackle timber towns. Other Siberian settlers included the influential Decembrists, who'd failed to pull off a coup in 1825, and political prisoners from the uprisings in Russian-occupied Poland. The end of serfdom in 1861 brought a tsunami of land-hungry peasants escaping the cramped conditions of European Russia.

In the 18th century, Tibetan Buddhism arrived in Buryat settlements east of Lake Baikal and was successfully superimposed onto existing shamanist beliefs. The western Buryats were never converted and shamanism still dominates west of the lake.

The Impact of the Railroads

Siberia's fur-based economy rapidly diversified and the discovery of gold further encouraged colonisation. Trade with China brought considerable wealth following the treaties of Nerchinsk in 1689 and Kyakhta in 1728. Lucrative tea caravans continued trudging the Siberian post road until put out of business by the Suez Canal and the Trans-Siberian Railway. The railway instantly changed the fortunes of cities, most notably Kyakhta on the border with Mongolia. Once one of the richest towns in all Russia, it plunged into provincial obscurity when the tea trade dried up. In the early 20th century the newly finished line brought yet another influx of Russian settlers.

Following the 1917 Bolshevik revolution and the outbreak of the Russian Civil War, Siberia declared itself firmly in the White camp under Admiral Kolchak. After much fierce fighting along the Trans-Siberian Railway, Red forces finally took the region in 1919. Kolchak was arrested and executed in Irkutsk in 1920, and the last shots of the civil war were fired in Tuva. From 1920 to 1922 Eastern Siberia was nominally independent, with the pro-Lenin Far Eastern Republic centred on Chita.

As the USSR stabilised and Stalin's infamous Gulag camps were created, Siberia reverted to its old role as a land of banishment. Nonetheless, unforced colonisation continued apace, especially after WWII when much heavy industry was shifted east for strategic security. Prisoners, volunteers and Soviets seeking higher pay (the so-called 'long rouble') for working in the east arrived to construct dams and transport infrastructure. The greatest of these projects was the ill-conceived Baikalo-Amurskaya Magistral (BAM) railway stretching over 4200km from Tayshet to Sovetskaya Gavan on the Pacific coast.

Post-Soviet Siberia

Since the end of the USSR in 1991, many towns and villages away from the economic beaten track (such as along the BAM and the Yenisey River) have deteriorated into virtual ghost towns. Others, such as Krasnoyarsk and Irkutsk, have benefited from Russia's new-found economic strength on the back of high oil and gas prices. Lake Baikal is attracting more tourists than ever, and Moscow has declared certain areas on its shores special economic zones slated for development. Having weathered the world economic downturn comparatively well, things are better across the region than they have ever been. But with this recent prosperity have come concerns about Siberia's ecologically sensitive habitats and the effects industry and mass tourism may be having on them. Eastern Siberia's Russian cities are firmly behind a now confidently authoritarian President Putin (who has a soft spot for certain locations in the region), but the self-governing Buryats, Khakass and Tuvans worry about the Kremlin's increasingly centralising tendencies.

KRASNOYARSK TERRITORY & KHAKASSIA

Vast and beautiful, the Greenland-shaped Krasnoyarsk Territory (Красноярский Край) stretches all the way from the Arctic islands of Severnaya Zemlya to a mountainous tip at Mt Borus. Its capital is Krasnoyarsk, a buzzing, forward-looking metropolis and a popular stop for travellers riding the Trans-Siberian Railway. Attached to it in the south is the autonomous republic of Khakassia – the land of snow-capped peaks, lake-dotted taiga and sparsely populated steppe grasslands. The native Khakass people are descendants of Turkic nomads, closely related to the Kyrgyz, but these days they are vastly outnumbered by Russians.

Like culturally similar Altai, the steppes of Khakassia and southern Krasnoyarsk Territory were a cradle of Siberian civilisation. Standing stones and *kurgany* pock the landscape; many are more than 3000 years old, though the most visually impressive date from the Turkic period (6th to 12th centuries). The Khyagas (Yenisey Kyrgyz) empire, from which the name Khakassia is derived, ruled much of Central Asia and central Siberia from around AD 840 until its golden age ended abriptly with the arrival of Chinggis Khan and company.

Russian trappers and Cossacks started moving into the northern, forested part of Krasnoyarsk Territory from the 15th century, building forts and imposing duties on indigenous fur hunters. The colonisation was spurred by the construction of the Great Siberian Trakt, a road connecting Siberia to European Russia. Colonists were supplemented by people exiled from all over the empire, most notably from Poland. By the beginning of the 20th century, the territory was largely populated by ethnic Russians, with the shamanist Khakass people largely Christianised and integrated into Russian society.

Krasnoyarsk   Красноярск

📞 391 / POP 1.08 MILLION / ⏰ MOSCOW +4HR

Orderly and affluent, Krasnoyarsk reflects in the blueish-grey surface of the mind-bogglingly wide Yenisey River, which marks the border between the swampy west and the mountainous east of Siberia. Uniquely, the million-strong city boasts a hugely popular national park located within city boundaries. The other prominent urban feature is unfortunately a giant aluminium plant, which contributes to some serious air pollution in the centre. With outstanding museums, a lively restaurant scene and some exquisite timber mansions popping up here and there amid the Soviet-era concrete, Krasnoyarsk is an agreeable place to break the long journey between Tomsk (612km west) and Lake Baikal.

◉ Sights

Dotted about Krasnoyarsk are some very fine wooden houses, notably ul Lenina 88 and 67 and ul Karla Marksa 118. There are also many art nouveau facades such as pr Mira 76, ul Lenina 62 and ul Parizhskoy Kommuny 13.

★ **Stolby Nature Reserve**   NATURE RESERVE
(www.stolby.ru) FREE Russia's most visited national park is located right across the river from Krasnoyarsk's city centre. Its highlight is the fingers of volcanic rock called **stolby** poking above gently sloping wooded mountains. To reach the most spectacular of them (as well as the newly opened visitors centre), follow the track (7km long) near Hotel Snezhnaya Dolina (bus 50). Alternatively, you can take the year-round **chairlift** (Фуникулёр; R250) at Bobrovy Log Ski Resort and hike about the same distance through the park.

New paths and steps mean going it alone is not the daredevil experience it once was, but English-language tours with SibTour-Guide (p482) are a much more pleasant and entertaining affair. Be aware that infected ticks are dangerous between May and July, and tick protection or predeparture encephalitis jabs are essential at this time.

★ **Ploshchad Mira**   MUSEUM
(Площадь Мира; 📞 212 4663; www.mira1.ru; pl Mira 1; adult/child R150/70; ⏰ 11am-7pm Tue, Wed & Fri-Sun) Krasnoyarsk's Lenin museum was opened on the occasion of the October Revolution's 70th anniversary in 1987, only to see the entire communist system collapse four years later. But, in a true revolutionary spirit, it has reinvented itself as a beautifully eclectic

Southern Krasnoyarsk Territory, Khakassia and Tuva

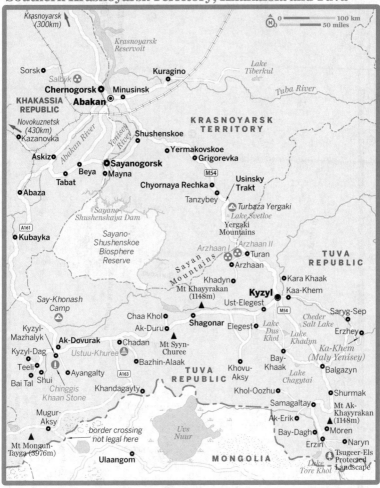

art venue that fuses elements of the original communist-era exhibitions with top-quality contemporary art and photography. An installation dedicated to Afghan and Chechen wars, mixing naive art with photographs and personal belongings, is especially poignant.

Ploshchad Mira also serves as the venue of Krasnoyarsk's art biennale, held in 2018 and 2020. The museum's old library has now been converted into what Russians call 'open space' – a wi-fi hotspot lounge, where you can comfortably spend time checking emails, reading a book or chatting with friends over a cup of coffee. Called Okna, it also runs lectures and public discussions.

Regional Museum MUSEUM
(Краеведческий музей; www.kkkm.ru; ul Dubrovinskogo 84; R150; ⊙10am-6pm Tue-Sun) Housed in an attractive 1912 art nouveau Egyptian temple, this is one of Siberia's better museums. Arranged around a Cossack explorer's ship, surprisingly well-presented exhibitions across the two floors examine every facet of the region's past, from Cossacks and gentlemen explorers to the Tunguska explosion, local fauna, prerevolution institutions and religious art.

Highlights include the 20th-century 'nostalgia' section on the upper level and the 4m-tall mammoth skeleton looking like

Krasnoyarsk

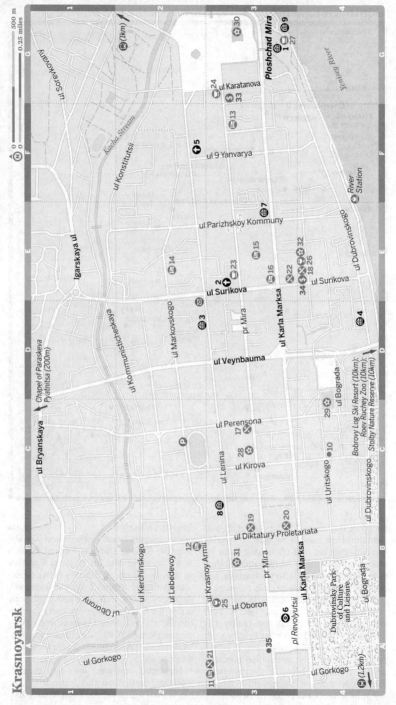

ul Sorevnovaniy

ul Konstitutsii

Kacha Stream

Igarskaya ul

Chapel of Paraskeva Pyatnitsa (200m)

ul Bryanskaya

ul Kommunisticheskaya

ul Markovskogo

ul Veynbauma

pr Mira

ul Surikova

ul 9 Yanvarya

ul Parizhskoy Kommuny

ul Karatanova

Ploshchad Mira

Yenisey River

River Station

ul Dubrovinskogo

ul Karla Marksa

ul Surikova

ul Lenina

ul Perensona

ul Kirova

ul Uritskogo

ul Bograda

ul Dubrovinskogo

ul Bograda

ul Diktatury Proletariata

pr Mira

ul Karla Marksa

ul Krasnoy Armii

ul Lebedevoy

ul Kerchinskogo

ul Oborony

ul Oboron

pl Revolyutsii

ul Gorkogo

ul Gorkogo

Dubrovinsky Park of Culture and Leisure

Bobrovy Log Ski Resort (10km); Roev Ruchey Zoo (10km); Stolby Nature Reserve (10km)

(1km)

(1.2km)

500 m
0.25 miles

something straight off a Hollywood museum movie set. There are touch-screen games for kids and a decent cafe to look forward to at the end.

Literature Museum MUSEUM
(Литературный музей; www.kkkm.ru/filialy-muzeya/literaturnyj-muzej; ul Lenina 66; R100; ⊙10am-6pm Tue-Sun) Occupying a glorious 1911 merchant's mansion, this wonderfully restored museum highlights various aspects of Siberian life that inspired authors who wrote about it – from cold and gloom to multicoloured gems and shaman dances. Of special note is the exhibit dedicated to Agafya Lykova, a member of the famous Old Believer hermit family.

Surikov Art Museum MUSEUM
(Художественный музей Сурикова; ul Parizhskoy Kommuny 20; R150; ⊙10am-6pm Tue, Wed & Fri-Sun, 1-9pm Thu) The cute Surikov Art Museum displays works by Russian 19th-century artist Ivan Surikov and his contemporaries. Its affiliate at **ul Mira 12** houses a small but impressive collection of Russian vanguard art, including Kandinsky, Malevich and Rodchenko.

Intercession Cathedral CHURCH
(Покровский собор; ul Surikova) This pleasingly small old church dating from 1795 has an interior of unusually glossed and intricately moulded stucco framing haloed saints.

SV Nikolai MUSEUM
(Святой Николай; R70; ⊙10am-8pm Tue-Sun) Permanently docked below Ploshchad Mira art centre is the SV *Nikolai*, the ship that transported future revolution leader Vladimir Lenin to exile in Shushenskoe in 1897 and the future Tsar Nikolai II across the Yenisey in 1891.

Chapel of Paraskeva Pyatnitsa NOTABLE BUILDING
(Часовня Параскевы Пятницы; top of Karaulnaya Hill) For some spectacular city views, climb Karaulnaya Hill (there's no bus) to the little chapel that features on the Russian 10-rouble banknote (now slowly being replaced with a coin). It was designed in 1855 by Konstantin Thon, the architect behind Moscow's Christ the Saviour Cathedral. At midday a deafening one-gun salute is fired from just below the chapel.

Roev Ruchey Zoo ZOO
(Зоопарк Роев ручей; www.roev.ru; adult/child R300/100; ⊙9am-9pm) Take bus 50 or 50A to this animal-friendly zoo near the Bobrovy Log Ski Resort to see numerous Siberian species.

Revolution Square SQUARE
(pl Revolyutsii) The city's vast central square showcases Soviet-era architectural classics in all their Stalinist glory – complete with colonnaded government buildings and a

statue of Lenin, who extends one hand as if inviting visitors for a stroll in **Dubrovinsky Park of Culture and Leisure**, another compulsory element of any Soviet city. Untouched by Moscow-style gentrification, the park is dotted with tacky 1990s funfair attractions and abuts in pleasantly revamped Levobereznaya nab – a riverside promenade, which is great for both walks and cycling.

A Ferris wheel is useful for photographers keen to snap a winning shot of the Yenisey and the foothills of Sayan mountains beyond it.

Resurrection Church   CHURCH
(Благовещенская церковь; ul 9 Yanvarya) The top-heavy but elegant Resurrection Church (1804–22) was decapitated in the 1930s but given a new tower in 1998–99. Its icon-filled interior billows with incense.

Surikov Museum-Estate   MUSEUM
(Музей-усадьба Сурикова; www.surikov-dom. com; ul Lenina 98; R200; ⊙10am-6pm Tue-Sun) The Surikov Museum-Estate preserves the house, sheds and vegetable patch of 19th-century painter Vasily Surikov (1848–1916). The heavy-gated garden forms a refreshing oasis of rural Siberia right in the city centre. More of Surikov's work is on show at the old-school Surikov Art Museum (p481).

🏃 Activities

Bobrovy Log Ski Resort   SNOW SPORTS
(Лыжный курорт Бобровый Лог; www.bobrovylog.ru; ul Sibirskaya 92; ski pass per hour/day R350/1300, ski hire from R450) Below the Stolby the slap and swish of skis and snowboards can be heard at the Bobrovy Log Ski Resort. Snow cannons keep the slopes going well into May, and in the summer months the Roedelbahn (a kind of downhill forest roller coaster), a pool and regular sports events keep the fun level high.

Cable car provides access to Stolby Nature Reserve (p478) observation point and hiking trails. The resort is also the location of one of the city's finest restaurants (p483). To get here, catch bus 37 that runs from the train station direct to the resort via pr Mira and Predmostnaya pl. An Uber ride from the centre costs R140.

👉 Tours

SibTourGuide   TOURS
(☑391-251 654, 8-913-534 2654; www.sibtourguide.com) Experienced tour guide Anatoly Brewhanov offers personalised hiking trips

into the Stolby, imaginative tours around Krasnoyarsk and general travel assistance. He also provides authentic 'rural experiences' at his dacha (summer country house), organises cruises along the Yenisey and leads trips to the site of the Tunguska Event, all while maintaining an info-packed website.

His great apartment hostel is sadly no more, but he was eyeing the possibility of launching a new accommodation project at the time of research.

Sayan Ring   TOURS
(☑391-223 1231; www.sayanring.com; ul Uritskogo 117, office 2-01; ⊙10am-7pm Mon-Fri) Agency specialising in Tuva and Khakassia tours.

🎉 Festivals & Events

Zelyony Festival   MUSIC
(Зелёный фестиваль; http://gorodprima.ru; ⊙Jun) Usually held in June on Tatyshev island, this giant picnic celebrates modern art and street food in addition to lots of good music.

🛏 Sleeping

⭐**Hovel Hostel**   HOSTEL $
(Хостел Ховел; ☑8-929-309 4020; www.hovel24. ru; ul Lenina 52 (enter from ul Markovskogo); dm/d without bathroom from R400/1400, q R2200; ☜) A sparkling oasis for budget travellers who have made it all the way here through Siberia's snowy wilderness, this boutique hostel features a large kitchen, a common area with comfy couches, and a range of rooms from dorms and cosy doubles to an airy two-level studio, ideal for a family with children.

⭐**Iris**   BOUTIQUE HOTEL $$
(Ирис; ☑391-227 2292; www.iris-apart-hotel.ru; pr Mira 37; s/d R3600/4000; ☜) Housed in a 19th-century former religious school for girls, the romantic French theme and impeccable personal service set the Iris apart from most Siberian hotels. The 10 rooms are done out in soothing beiges and light browns but the *pièces de résistance* here are the two romantic design suites, all period wallpaper, belle époque furniture and mock chateau elements.

Dom Neo   HOTEL $$
(Дом Нэо; ☑391-223 9360; www.dom-hotel24. ru/hotel/neo; ul Krasnoy Armii 10 str 5; r from R2800; ❖☜) Definitely the brightest-coloured building in central Krasnoyarsk, this progressive hotel achieves an optimal value for money ratio by cutting out optional amenities, such as minibars, and focusing entirely on the essentials – the bed, the bathroom

and the light. Everything is sparkling new and designed in a futuristic style. A filling set-menu breakfast is an extra R350 at Cafe Benedikt downstairs.

Hotel Oktyabrskaya
HOTEL $$$

(Гостиница Октябрьская; ☑ 391-223 0808; www.hoteloctober.ru; pr Mira 15; s/d from R3800/4200; ☎) Comfortable and professionally run with rooms approximating Western standards, albeit without air-conditioning. Satellite TV includes Western channels and some English is spoken. The trendy lobby area has a stylish juice bar. Includes breakfast.

Dom Hotel
HOTEL $$$

(☑ 391-290 6666; www.dom-hotel24.ru; ul Krasnoy Armii 16a; s/d from R4200/5900; @☎) Centred around a rather characterless courtyard, the 81 light-filled rooms at Krasnoyarsk's top business hotel are immaculately maintained and have become a firm favourite among foreigners looking for Western comforts. Staff are courteous and there is an inexpensive on-site restaurant. Breakfast costs extra.

Soft Hotel
HOTEL $$$

(☑ 391-228 2700; www.softhotel.ru; ul Surikova 16; s/d from R3900/4600; ❄☎) With its European business-standard facilities, waxy antique-style furniture, 21st-century bathrooms (with bidets!) and high-flying ceilings, taking the soft option might be the way to go now in Krasnoyarsk. Efficient service and good value for money – only the views and the nonbuffet breakfast disappoint slightly.

✖ Eating

Vinegret Bufet
CAFETERIA $

(Буфет Винегрет; ☑ 391-2311 989; https://vk.com/vinegretbufet; ul Surikova 12; mains R100-150; ☺10am-10pm) A vast and modern rustic-themed cafeteria, Vinegret lures white-collar workers with a large salad bar and a grill station. Pancakes with a variety of fillings make a good breakfast option.

★ 0.75 please
RUSSIAN $$

(☑ 391-215 2913; www.facebook.com/075please; pr Mira 86; mains R480-640; ☺noon-2am) This gem is two in one – a wine bar and an Arctic-themed restaurant that upgrades traditional Siberian staples to near-Michelin levels. *Nelma stroganina* (a kind of frozen ceviche) quite literally melts in your mouth. Reindeer steak with cheese and pear makes a star duo with homemade chokeberry liquor. Crème brûlée with sea buckthorn sorbet is nothing short of Elysian.

Bar Bulgakov
FUSION $$

(Бар Булгаков; ☑ 391-272 8778; http://barbulgakov.ru; ul Surikova 12; mains R250-700; ☺noon-2am; ☎♫) This delightfully bizarre space decorated with Soviet vanguard art and presided over by a Soviet-era female rower statue that holds a giant fork instead of an oar is best for late-night alcohol-infused dinners. The inventive fusion menu is permeated with Caucasian motifs and includes such wondrous concoctions as lamb and aubergine stew cooked in a clay pot with a rye bread cap.

A great set-menu lunch served from noon till 4pm costs R370.

Mike & Molly
ITALIAN $$

(www.mikeandmollycafe.ru; ul Diktatury Proletariata 32a; mains R200-500; ☺11am-midnight) The stylishly unassuming interior of this Italian job suggests the focus is firmly on the food, and that assumption would be right. Possibly Krasnoyarsk's best lasagnes, pastas, salads and proper starters land promptly on your table as you kick back on the black-cloth wall sofas with a glass of Chianti.

Svinya i Biser
EASTERN EUROPEAN $$

(Свинья и бисер; ☑ 391-290 4040; http://bellinigroup.ru/rest/pig-and-beads; ul Krasnoy Armii 16a; mains R250-600; ☺7am-1am) Its wood-rich interior strives to convey the ambience of old Europe. The menu at 'Pig & Beads' is carnivore concerto grosso, with pork playing the first violin. Sausages, shashlyks (meat kebabs), burgers, steaks, schnitzels – the menu seems to cover every method of preparing meat. Excellent buffet breakfasts are served from 7am (R450).

Shiv Ganga
INDIAN $$

(Шив ганга; ☑ 391-293 0064; https://vk.com/shivgangacafe; ul Diktatury Proletariata 28; mains R320-470; ☺11am-11pm) A small eatery run by actual Indians (rather than Russian esotericists, as often happens) comes as a pleasant surprise, especially for vegetarians. Inevitable problems with getting authentic spices does affect the taste of curries, but the overall quality is impressive.

Khozyain Taygi
RUSSIAN $$$

(Хозяин Тайги; ☑ 391-256 8649; www.bobrovylog.ru; ul Sibirskaya 92; mains R560-1100; ☺noon-midnight) Siberian taiga, in the form of Stolby Nature Reserve (p478), begins right outside this refined restaurant, entirely dedicated to the kind of food one can catch or forage in the world's largest forest. A sample menu could include mousse made of, well, moose for starters, *nelma* (Arctic salmon) as second course and terrific frozen red whortleberries mixed with cedar nut for dessert.

🍷 Drinking & Nightlife

⭐ Chaynaya Yurta   TEAHOUSE
(Чайная юрта; ☑ 391-297 6037; https://vk.com/yurtea; pl Mira 1; ☺ noon-midnight) Literally a yurt occupying a prime riverside spot next to the city's best museum, this place celebrates the tea culture of Siberian nomads. Try Orlan Sagaan tea, which contains the *sagaan-dalya* (a ubiquitous East Siberian herb rhododendron) or Tuvan tea with *talgan* (barley flour), milk and butter. The food menu is equally exotic.

Kofeynya Kultura   COFFEE
(Кофейня Культура; https://vk.com/culture_krsk; pr Mira 56; ☺ 8am-10pm) As the name suggests, this is a den of coffee nerds who see the dark brew as an agent of cultural revolution and who perpetually experiment with brewing techniques and equipment. Besides that, it is a pleasant modern environment to spend some time in the company of a friend or a gadget.

Tovarishch   CRAFT BEER
(Comrade; ☑ 8-913-836 5949; https://vk.com/clubtkbkrsk; ul Oborony 2a; ☺ 1pm-midnight) A few dozen brands of Russian and international beers, both draft and bottled, are on offer in this dim-lit bar with crypto-Maoist subtext ciphered in the decor. Zolotoy Yarlyk lager and Black Jack stout are among the most popular brews.

Zalech na Dno v Gamburg   BEER HALL
(Lying Low in Hamburg; ☑ 391-286 3355; http://berrywoodfamily.pl/blog/zalech-na-dno-v-gamburg; ul Surikova 12 k6; ☺ noon-2am) A vast vaulted cellar contains a German *biergarten* with a Siberian twist. There is a good dozen German, Czech and Belgian beers on tap, which you can top up with wurst and sauerkraut, or – more experimentally – with *suguday* (frozen raw fish with onion) served in a jar.

Krem   CAFE
(☑ 391-258 1538; pr Mira 10; ☺ 24hr; 🛜) One of Krasnoyarsk's classiest coffee houses has black-and-white photography, dark-wood furniture, a belt-stretching dessert menu and reasonably priced lattes and espressos.

☆ Entertainment

Dom Kino   CINEMA
(Дом кино; ☑ 391-227 2637; www.filmshouse.ru; pr Mira 88) A place to watch sophisticated arthouse cinema, often shown in the original language, with Russian subtitles.

Mod's Bar   LIVE MUSIC
(http://themodsbar.ru; ul Aviatorov 19; ☺ 6pm-morning) This new and smarter-than-usual nightlife venue, located inside Grand Hall Siberia in Vzlyotka area (east of the centre), runs DJ and live-music events, as well as dance and art performances during weekends. Thursday karaoke night features a live band that can smooth out even the lousiest singing.

Burton Bar   LIVE MUSIC
(☑ 391-214 0224; https://vk.com/burtonbar; ul Televizornaya 1 str 26) A far-flung indie rock and 'intellectual hip-hop' (whatever that is!) venue run by fans of the film director Tim Burton.

Opera-Ballet Theatre   THEATRE
(Театр оперы и балета; ☑ 391-227 8697; www.opera.krasnoyarsk.ru; ul Perensona 2) The architecturally nondescript Opera-Ballet Theatre has daily performances of productions such as *Carmen*, *Swan Lake* and *Romeo and Juliet* starting in the early evening, October to June.

Rock-Jazz Kafe   LIVE MUSIC
(Рок-Джаз Кафе; ☑ 391-252 3305; https://vk.com/rockjazzcafe; ul Surikova 12; ☺ 4pm-6am Tue-Sun) This dark venue showcases live bands around an upturned motorcycle from 10pm most days.

Philharmonia   LIVE MUSIC
(Филармония; ☑ 391-227 4930; www.krasfil.ru; pl Mira 2b) The Philharmonia has three concert halls showcasing folk, jazz and classical music.

Puppet Theatre   PUPPET THEATRE
(☑ 391-211 3000; www.puppet24.ru; ul Lenina 119) Classic Russian puppet shows such as *Chuk i Gek*, *Doktor Aybolit* and *Goldilocks* for kids and adults alike.

ⓘ Orientation

The city centre's grid layout, which makes Krasnoyarsk look a bit like American cities, is easy to navigate. The zoo, ski resort and Stolby Nature Reserve are over 10km west along the Yenisey's south bank.

ℹ️ Information

Rosbank (pr Mira 7; ⊘ 9am-6pm Mon-Thu, 9am-4.45pm Fri) Currency exchange and 24-hour indoor ATM.

Sberbank (Сбербанк; ul Surikova 15; ⊘ 10am-7pm Mon-Sat) Currency-exchange window and ATM.

Post Office (ul Lenina 62; ⊘ 8am-8pm Mon-Fri, 9am-6pm Sat)

Prospekt Mira (https://prmira.ru) is a Russian-only online publication that covers upcoming cultural events.

ℹ️ Getting There & Away

AIR

A new sparkling **Yemelyanovo Airport** (🗗 391-255 5999; www.yemelyanovo.ru) terminal was about to open at the time of writing. Services to almost anywhere in Siberia and the rest of Russia are available. International destinations include Bangkok and several Chinese airports.

TSAVS (ЦАВС; www.krascavs.ru; ul Mira 112; ⊘ 8am-8pm) is a centrally located one-stop shop for all bus, train and air tickets. Krasnoyarsk has the following flight connections:

Irkutsk from R8000, two daily
Kyzyl from R7700, four weekly
Moscow from R7500, up to seven daily
Novosibirsk from R5600, two daily

BOAT

Every few days in summer, passenger boats from Krasnoyarsk's spired **river station** (Речной вокзал) ply the Yenisey to Dudinka (1989km, 4½ to five days) but foreigners may not proceed beyond Igarka. SibTourGuide (p482) can arrange tickets.

BUS

The main **bus station** (Автовокзал; www.kras-avtovokzal.ru; ul Aerovokzalnaya 22) is to the northeast of the city centre and is best reached by Buses 49, 24 and 53 from ul Karla Marksa. Destinations:

Abakan R920, five hours, frequent
Kyzyl R1800, 14 hours, three daily
Tomsk R1300, 11 hours, daily
Yeniseysk R800, seven hours, 10 daily

TRAIN

TSAVS is the most central booking office, though the station itself is relatively central and often queue-free. Krasnoyarsk has the following rail connections:

Abakan platskart/kupe R1800/R2150, 11½ hours, one daily
Irkutsk platskart R1600, kupe R3300 to R5800, 18 hours, up to nine daily

Moscow platskart R7200, kupe R11,000 to R15,000, 64 hours, up to seven daily
Novosibirsk platskart R2000, kupe R2600 to R4000, 12 hours, up to 11 daily
Severobaikalsk platskart/kupe R3250/R6700, 27 to 35 hours, three daily
Tomsk platskart/kupe R1900/3250, 18 hours, every other day

ℹ️ Getting Around

There is no public transport between the airport and the city, except for rare and inconvenient buses stopping on the way between Cheremshanka and Krasnoyarsk bus station (one hour, R82, four to six daily). Taxis charge between R600 and R1000 for the ride into town.

Within the city centre, almost all public transport runs eastbound along ul Karla Marksa or pr Mira, returning westbound on ul Lenina. Frequent, if slow, trolleybus 7 trundles from the train station through the city centre via ul Karla Marksa. Useful bus 50 starts beyond the zoo, passes the Turbaza Yenisey and comes through the centre of town.

All major taxi app services – Gett, Uber, Yandex Taxi and Maxim – are represented. A typical Uber ride within the centre costs R80.

Divnogorsk & Ovsyanka
Дивногорск и Овсянка

From Krasnoyarsk, a popular day trip by bus follows the Yenisey River 27km to Divnogorsk town through a wide, wooded canyon. Some 5km beyond Divnogorsk's jetty is a vast 90m-high **dam**. Turbine-room visits are not permitted, but if you're lucky you might see ships being lifted by a technologically impressive inclined plane to the huge Krasnoyarsk Sea behind. A few kilometres beyond you can observe ice fishing from December to March or, in the summer, boats and yachts can be hired.

The Krasnoyarsk–Divnogorsk road has a panoramic overlook point at km23 and passes quaint Ovsyanka village. From the main road walk 100m (crossing the train tracks) to Ovsyanka's cute wooden **St Inokent Chapel** (ul Shchetinkina, Ovsyanka) then 50m right to find the **house-museum** (ul Shchetinkina 26, Ovsyanka; R100; ⊘ 10am-6pm Tue-Sun) of famous local writer Victor Astafiev, who died in 2001. Directly opposite in Astafiev's grandma's cottage-compound is the more interesting **Last Bow Museum** (ul Shchetinkina 35, Ovsyanka; R100; ⊘ 10am-6pm Tue-Sun) giving a taste of rural Siberian life.

Regular *marshrutky* (R100) leave from Krasnoyarsk's bus station. Ask the *marshrutka* driver to drop you off at Ovsyanka, 30km away from Krasnoyarsk. SibTourGuide (p482) in Krasnoyarsk offers various tailored excursions in English or will include the Divnogorsk loop as part of its 'Ten-Rouble Tour'.

Abakan Абакан

📞 3902 / POP 167,500 / ⊘ MOSCOW +4HR

Founded as a foothold *ostrog* (Cossack fort) in 1675, Abakan remained overshadowed until the 1930s by neighbouring Minusinsk, once the region's centre of European civilisation. With the tables now firmly turned, today the Khakass capital is a leafy, rapidly modernising place with a handful of undemanding sights and a population that will be (perhaps pleasantly) surprised to see you. Probably not worth a special trip on its own, Abakan does serve as a handy base for trips into Sayan mountains and Tuva.

◉ Sights

Khakassia National Museum   MUSEUM
(Хакасский национальный краеведческий музей; http://nhkm.ru; ul Pushkina 96; R200; ⊘10am-6pm Tue-Sun) The highlight at the National Museum is the atmospherically low-lit hall containing a striking exhibition dedicated to Khakassia's wealth of standing stones. Curators have erected a kind of mini Stonehenge in the middle of the space, with the walls around lined in 2000-year-old stone fragments – altogether a surprisingly impressive effort. A clearly underfunded collection of random period furniture, shaggy shamanic bric-a-brac and dubious art makes up the rest of the museum.

Railway Museum   MUSEUM
(Музей Истории Красноярской железной дороги; Station concourse; ⊘1-4.45pm Mon-Fri) FREE Worth visiting just to experience a Siberian attraction that doesn't charge admission. Train buffs will find the scale model of Abakan station in 1925, the collection of period railway uniforms and the various oversize chunks of obsolete equipment suitably captivating. Some display cases have been designed to resemble old carriage windows – similar also in that they're bolted firmly shut.

🛏 Sleeping

Lucomoria Hostel   HOSTEL $
(📞3902-397 069; www.lucomoria.ru/hostels/abakan; ul Torosova 12, apt 31h; dm from R350, d

with shared bathroom from R900) A renowned Tomsk hostel has planted its clone inside an apartment block near the airport, 3km from the centre. Rarely full, dorms accommodate a maximum of six guests who can enjoy a degree of privacy by pulling down green curtains on their bunk beds. That, along with a small kitchen and common area, gives the place a sufficiently homey feel.

Guest House on Likhacheva   GUESTHOUSE $$
(Гостевой дом на Лихачёва; 📞8-961-896 7989; www.lihacheva-abakan.otelic.ru; ul Akademika Likhacheva 1v; s/d incl breakfast R1900/2500; ❄🌐❄) This glass structure looks like an alien spacecraft amid the uninspiring suburbia on the outskirts of Abakan. The interior is even more unusual. Large rooms have pebble tile floors and black wallpaper, which subdues the light flooding in through panoramic windows. A sauna and a small pool are free of charge. A taxi to the centre costs R140.

Persona   HOTEL $$
(Персона; 📞3902-357 005; www.persona-abakan.ru; Sovetskaya ul 33; ⊘s/d R2500/3100; ❄🌐) Convenient for the bus station and close to a nice park, this modern if slightly bland facility has large rooms decorated in all shades of beige and sparkling bathrooms with human-size bathtubs. Breakfast, which needs to be ordered the night before, is served in a German-themed cellar restaurant.

Hotel Abakan   HOTEL $$
(Гостиница Абакан; 📞3902-203 025; www.abakan-hotel.ru; pr Lenina 59; r incl breakfast from R2600; 🌐) There's a bamboozling array of room categories at what was Abakan's first hotel, from the five unrenovated 'third class' pits to the 19 fully renovated, almost Western-standard doubles and beyond. The Soviet past pops up here and there but is slowly being smothered in fluffy white towels and dressing gowns. Big discounts on weekends.

Aziya Business Hotel   HOTEL $$$
(📞3902-215 777; http://asia-hotel.ru; ul Kirova 114 str 1; s/d incl breakfast from R3700/4800; ❄🌐) Abakan's slickest sleeping option is this top-notch business hotel with large and tastefully furnished rooms and two sophisticated restaurants on the premises. It's a short walk from central streets.

Chalpan   HOTEL $$$
(Чалпан; 📞3902-215 302; www.chalpan.ru; proyezd Shchorsa 5a; s/d R3780/4300; 🌐❄;

WORTH A TRIP

YENISEYSK

Easily reachable by bus, historic Yeniseysk (Енисейск) makes an engaging excursion off the Trans-Sib from Krasnoyarsk, 340km away. Now being spruced up for its 400-year anniversary (due in 2019), it was once Russia's great fur-trading capital, with world-famous 18th-century August trade fairs (recently revived for tourists), and 10 grand churches punctuating its skyline. Eclipsed by Krasnoyarsk despite a burst of gold-rush prosperity in the 1860s, the town is now a drowsy backwater with an unexpectedly good **Regional Museum** (ul Lenina 106; R100; ⊘9am-5pm Mon-Sat), some faded commercial grandeur along ul Lenina and many old houses; over 70 are considered architectural monuments. Most appealing of the surviving churches are the walled 1731 **Spaso-Preobrazhensky Monastery** (ul Raboche-Krestyanskaya 105) and the **Assumption Church** (Uspenskaya tserkov; ul Raboche-Krestyanskaya 116) with its unusual metal floor and splendid antique icons.

To reach Yeniseysk, take a bus (R620, seven hours, 10 daily) from Krasnoyarsk's bus station. The journey time makes a day trip impossible so organise accommodation beforehand through SibTourGuide (p482) in Krasnoyarsk.

From mid-June to early October, passenger ships slip along the Yenisey River from Krasnoyarsk to Dudinka in the Arctic Circle (4½ days) via Yeniseysk (17 hours) and Igarka (three days and two to seven hours). There are three to four sailings per week, most departing early morning. Returning upstream, journeys take 50% longer so most independent travellers choose to fly back to Krasnoyarsk. Foreigners are not allowed beyond Igarka, as Dudinka and nearby Norilsk are 'closed' towns. Contact SibTourGuide in Krasnoyarsk for timetables, tickets and round-trip tours.

One of the loveliest hotels in Abakan, the purpose-built Chalpan is colourful but not gaudy, with imaginatively designed rooms, flashy bathrooms, free tea and coffee in the rooms, a sauna, a pool (!), simple pricing and breakfast. It's well worth enduring the walk along pr Lenina and the staff's slightly indifferent attitude.

✕ Eating

Stolichny Supermarket　SUPERMARKET
(Супермаркет Столичный; ul Chertygasheva 108; ⊘8am-11pm) For picnickers and self-caterers, the self-service Stolichny Supermarket is the city centre's best-stocked grocery.

Georgian Pastry from USSR　GEORGIAN $
(Грузинская выпечка из СССР; ☑8-923-350 0005; ul Shchetinkina 32; pastry R80-150; ⊘8am-10pm) Not terribly authentic (perhaps the unnecessary Soviet nostalgia ingredient is to blame), but still quite tasty *khachapuri* along with other, less iconic Georgian bread and molten-cheese concoctions are a good reason to drop by this bakery and stock up for long train or bus journeys out of Abakan.

Vilka-Lozhka　EASTERN EUROPEAN $
(Вилка-ложка; ☑3902-214 261; ul Vyatkina 13; mains R90-120; ⊘9am-9pm) *Chebureki* (Tatar-styled pastry with meat and cheese filling) is the main draw in this slick modern *stolovaya* (canteen), which also serves standard Russian home-style fare to youthful clientele.

⭐**Food & Bar 114**　ASIAN $$
(☑3902-306 039; www.asia-hotel.ru/food-bar-114/; ul Kirova 114/1; mains R340-510; ⊘noon-midnight; 🛜) With its imaginative Asian-themed menu, this ain't your usual hotel restaurant. Turkish pea and quinoa salads provide relief to those suffering under Siberia's carnivore dictatorship. You can also go full Khakassian by ordering *potkhi* (warm sour cream dip) for starters, followed by *myun* lamb soup, *khan* blood sausage and *irben* tea with thyme, cream and honey.

Mama Roma　ITALIAN $$
(☑3902-223 122; www.abakan.mamaroma.ru; pr Lenina 59; mains R230-520; ⊘7am-midnight) A reliable source of quality pizzas, pastas and other Apennine fare, this chain restaurant occupies a prime location in the centre of Abakan. It is also about the best breakfast option in town.

Prosto　GASTROPUB $$
(Просто; ☑3902-397 704; ul Shchetinkina 32; mains R250-350; ⊘11am-midnight) Tasty European food and local craft beer come together in this tiny new gastrobar. The super-tender lamb fillet with vegetables is our fave.

🍷 Drinking & Nightlife

Travel Coffee
COFFEE

(www.instagram.com/travelcoffeeabakan; pr Leni-na 63; ⊙ 8am-10pm Mon-Fri, from 9am Sat & Sun) Surfboards that greet you at the entrance perhaps embody the ultimate travel dream one might conceive in a place that can't be further removed from the nearest ocean. Great hot chocolate and cocoa, as well as unusual guest drinks such as birch tree sap, on top of competently prepared coffee standards.

Kotofey
CAFE

(Котофей; cnr ul Yarygina & Sovetskaya ul; ⊙ 9am-midnight Mon-Fri, from 11am Sat & Sun) Unusually big-windowed corner cafe with frilly lace curtains, proper European-style cafe chairs, the odd leathery bench and decent brews.

ℹ️ Information

Main Post Office (ul Shchetinkina 20; ⊙ 8am-10pm Mon-Fri, 9am-6pm Sat & Sun)

ℹ️ Getting There & Away

AIR

Abakan's old-fashioned little **airport** (www.abakan-airport.ru) is 4km northwest of the city centre. There are flights to Moscow (R15,000, two daily) and Novosibirsk (R4800, four weekly). Buy tickets from the train station **Aviakassa** (☎ 3902-239 170; ⊙ 8am-5pm Mon-Fri) or **TSAVS** (Билетные кассы ЦАВС; ☎ 3902-223 736; www.krascavs.ru; ul Chertygasheva 106; ⊙ 8am-8pm).

BUS

Abakan's fairly well-regimented **bus station** (Автовокзал; ul Shevchenko) has connections to the following destinations:
Krasnoyarsk R920, 6½ to nine hours, hourly
Kyzyl R850, 6½ hours, at least two daily
Minusinsk R55, 25 to 40 minutes, frequent

Sayanogorsk R180, two hours, frequent
Shushenskoe R175, 1½ hours, hourly

TRAIN

Abakan has the following rail connections:
Krasnoyarsk *platskart/kupe* R1800/2150, 11½ hours, daily
Moscow *platskart/kupe* R8000/10,000, three days and three hours, daily
Novokuznetsk *platskart/kupe* R1300/2300, nine hours, daily
Novosibirsk *platskart/kupe* R2600/3200, 22 hours, daily

ℹ️ Getting Around

Maxim and Gett taxi apps work well in the city; a typical ride costs R80.

Around Abakan

Minusinsk   Минусинск

☎ 39132 / POP 68,300 / ⊙ MOSCOW +4HR
Minusinsk's scattering of partly derelict 18th- and 19th-century buildings offers more architectural interest than Abakan, and its grand, crumbling mansions and timber dwellings come as a pleasant surprise. Virtually abandoned during the communist decades, Minusinsk's old town is located across the protoka Minusinskaya waterway from the communist dystopia of the new town, 25km east of Abakan.

👁️ Sights

Martyanov Museum
MUSEUM

(☎ 39132-22 297; http://музей-мартьянова.рф; ul Martyanova 6; R80; ⊙ 10am-6pm) Filling three distinct buildings, the countless halls crammed with local taxidermy, Bronze and Iron Age finds, Tuvan and Khakass standing stones, traditional stringed instruments and shaggy shaman costumes just keep on coming at this admirable repository of the

---

ℹ️ ONWARDS TO KYZYL

With the new railroad to Kyzyl on hold, road is the only way to get in and out of Tuva. Although you can catch a regular bus from the bus station, it is often more convenient to use transport services operating from the far southeastern corner of the square in front of Abakan's train station. The ticket kiosk for the official minibus service (R1300, around five hours) is close to the departure point; departures are at 7.50am, 3.30pm and 7pm daily but it's a good idea to buy a ticket at least a day in advance. Shared taxis asking around R1500 per seat do the trip slightly faster. The best time to catch a ride is early morning when train 124 (Krasnoyarsk–Abakan) pulls in. At other times of day you could wait several hours for the vehicle to fill up. Sayan Ring (p482) in Krasnoyarsk also offers prearranged transfers, but these are only cost-effective for groups.

region's past. Away from the obvious prehistoric highlights, more off-beat exhibitions look at the construction of 1970s new Minusinsk and ethnic minorities from Europe that colonised Khakassia in the 19th century.

Allow around two hours to see everything and don't even think of veering off from the prescribed tour route. The museum has two other small branches in town, the **Decembrist Museum** (☑ 39132-206 44; ul Oborony 59; R40; ☺ 9am-6pm Mon-Fri) and **Krzyzanovsky & Starkov Flat Museum** (ul Oktyabrskaya 73; R40; ☺ 9am-5pm Mon-Wed & Fri, 10am-5pm Thu).

Saviour's Cathedral CHURCH
(Spassky Sobor; ul Komsomolskaya 10) This elegant 1803 church is across the square from the superb Martyanov Museum.

🛏 Sleeping & Eating

Hotel Amyl HOTEL **$$**
(Гостиница Амыл; ☑ 39132-20 106; www.hotelamil.ru; ul Lenina 74; r R1000-2500) The town's only decent digs reside in the fading grandeur of a 19th-century palace, half a block southeast of the Martyanov Museum. The 24 rooms range from basic to oddly characterful with comfy sofas, real potted plants and lots of carved wood. There's a tiny weekday-only *zakusochnaya* (pub-cafe) and useful town maps are sold in reception.

Blin.com RUSSIAN **$**
(www.cafe-blin.com; ul Krasnykh Partizan 16; crepes R60-120; ☺ 10am-8pm) A convenient pit stop in the centre of Minusinsk, this crêperie churns out pancakes with dozens of meaty, veg and sweet fillings.

ⓘ Getting There & Away

To get here from Abakan, take bus or *marshrutka* 120 (R50, 30 to 40 minutes) direct to old-town Minusinsk. These leave from the left-hand side of the bus station. Buy tickets from the small ticket booth nearby. Catch returning services from opposite the cathedral.

Shushenskoe Шушенское

☑ 39139 / POP 16,850 / ☺ MOSCOW +4HR

As every Soviet schoolkid was once taught, leafy Shushenskoe played host to Lenin for three years of (relatively comfortable) exile. For the 1970 centenary of Lenin's birth, a two-block area of the village centre was reconstructed to look as it had in 1870. These well-kept 'old' Siberian houses now form the **Shushenskoe Ethnographic Museum**

SALBYK

This Stonehenge-sized remnant of a 'royal' *kurgan* is Siberia's most impressive ring of **standing stones**. Excavated in 1956, it's in open fields, 5.6km down unsurfaced tracks south of km38 on the Chernogorsk–Sorsk road. About 2km before Salbyk (Салбык) notice the large, grassy dome of the unexcavated **'Princess' kurgan** it once resembled. Taxis from Abakan ask at least R2000 return. Admission to the site is R50.

(www.shush.ru; ul Novaya 1; adult/child R300/100; ☺ 10am-6pm). Many are convincingly furnished, and in summer costumed craftsmen sit around carving spoons. It's gently interesting, but as all trips are guided (in Russian) the visit can drag and you're locked into spending over 1½ hours seeing everything. You might also want to swing by **Peter & Paul Church** (Церковь Петра и Павла; ul Novaya; ☺ 10am-3pm), where in 1898 Lenin was married.

Around 25,000 music fans make camp in Shushenskoe during the annual **Mir Sibiri** (www.festmir.ru/en; ☺ Jul), previously known as the Sayan Ring Festival. The three-day-long folk-music bash attracts ensembles from across Siberia and the occasional overseas act.

🛏 Sleeping & Eating

Novaya Derevnya HOTEL **$$$**
(Новая деревня; ☑ 8-983-618 2210, 39139-34 433; www.shush.ru/nevderev; ul Novaya 1; d R4500-5500) You can get yourself exiled like Lenin in tidy 19th-century log houses that form a part of the Shushenskoe Ethnographic Museum.

Kofeynya Sadko CAFE **$**
(Кофейня Садко; ☑ 39139-37 199; ul Pervomayskaya 1; mains R200-300; ☺ 11am-midnight Sun-Thu, to 2am Fri & Sat) The only place in town for a sit-down meal is the unexpectedly bright Kofeynya Sadko, opposite the church, where petite portions of flavoursome food arrive on trendy square plates. As virtually the only source of sustenance for visitors, it's often crammed to the gills.

ⓘ Information

The **post office** (Polukoltsevaya ul 5; ☺ 8am-1pm & 2-8pm Mon-Fri, 9am-6pm Sat) offers internet and telephone connections, and sells rail and air tickets.

WORTH A TRIP

USINSKY TRAKT

Built between 1914 and 1917, the Usinsky Trakt (Усинский Тракт; now the M54 federal highway) is the main road between Minusinsk and Kyzyl in Tuva. Until the Kuragino–Kyzyl railway is completed (if it ever is), this narrow but smooth ribbon of asphalt through the Yergaki Mountains will remain essentially the only route in and out of Tuva for people and goods, most notably Tuva's much-valued coal and other precious minerals.

Around two hours out of Abakan, the road skirts the modest historical township of Yermakovskoe and passes the fruit-growing villages of Grigoryevka and Chyornaya Rechka before climbing into pretty birch-wood foothills. After a shashlyk (kebab) stop in Tanzybey (km560), the route climbs more steeply.

A truly magnificent view of the crazy, rough-cut Yergaki range knocks you breathless just before km598, and illustrates just why its Turkic name means 'fingers'. Dramatically impressive views continue to km601 and resume between km609 and km612. Expect heavy snowfalls here as late as early June.

A roadside cross (km603-04) marks the spot where former Krasnoyarsk governor Alexander Lebed (who negotiated an end to the first Chechen War in 1996) died in 2002 when his helicopter snagged power lines. Walk 1.5km up the steep track towards the radar station above for fabulous views from the ridge.

Seven kilometres further along the route, **Yergaki Ski Resort** (http://ergaki.com) is a year-round holiday destination popular with Krasnoyarsk and Abakan urbanites.

As the track descends, the scenery morphs through wooded river valleys into Tuva's panoramic roller-coaster grasslands. There's a police checkpoint at Shivilig (km703), but the first real settlement the road bisects within Tuva is Turan, a ramshackle village of old wooden homes largely inhabited by ethnic Russians. A road barrelling west just before the village heads towards Arzhaan through Tuva's spectacular Valley of the Kings. From Turan the road scales one final mountain pass before hurtling down into Kyzyl.

ⓘ Getting There & Away

Buses serve Abakan (R185, 1½ hours, eight daily) and Krasnoyarsk (R1200, 10½ hours, four daily). While waiting for buses, take time to admire the bus station's spectacular chunk of socialist realism: a gigantic collage celebrating the USSR's achievements, now partially obscured by kiosks.

Sayanogorsk Саяногорск

☏ 39042 / POP 48,300 / ⊘ MOSCOW +4HR

Purpose-built to accommodate hydroelectric workers, tidy Sayanogorsk serves as a gateway to Sayano-Shushenskaya Dam, located 36km south near the town's outlying neighbourhood of Cheryomushki. Sitting at the foothills of Sayany mountains, Sayanogorsk is in fact several *mikrorayony* districts scattered around the Yenisey valley. Snowy peaks rise majestically from the yellow steppe as you drive from Abakan. There are popular hiking routes and a modern ski resort in the area.

Communism, Lenin famously said, is the Soviet government plus the electrification of the entire country. Abbreviated as GOELRO, the plan to make electric power available in every corner of Russia was inspired by his Bolshevik friend, electrical engineer Gleb Krzyżanowski, who had spent a few years exiled in Minusinsk. HG Wells, who interviewed Lenin in 1920, dubbed him 'the Kremlin dreamer', being convinced that the plan was utterly utopian. A couple of decades later, all major rivers in Russia were dammed and what Russians know as 'Ilyich lamps' lit up in every household.

A 1970s tribute to that utopian spirit and the most visually striking of Soviet hydroelectric projects, Sayano-Shushenskaya Dam is symbolically located near both Lenin's and Krzyżanowski's places of exile.

◉ Sights

Sayano-Shushenskaya Dam DAM

(Саяно-Шушенская ГЭС; www.sshges.rushydro.ru/hpp/sshges) Completed in 1985, this stunning feat of engineering blocks a beautiful forested canyon cut through the Sayan mountains by the mighty Yenisey. At 242m, the dam is the world's 17th tallest, and the hydropower station is the world's ninth in production capacity. The six bronze figures that comprise the striking monument to Sayano-Shushenskaya Dam builders stand at a prime observation point about 500m from the dam. A gigantic water discharge facility is built into the rock on the other side of the river.

The dam is fresh from a thorough reconstruction that followed the 2009 catastrophe caused by a turbine breakdown, which killed 75 people trapped in the flooded machine hall.

🏃 Activities

Cheryomushki is the gateway to a section of **Shushensky Bor National Park** (admission R30), centred around the Borus range, a popular hiking destination for local adventure tourists. Sayanogorsk taxis can bring you to Talovka visitors centre, from where trails lead to a couple of nice lakes, waterfalls and a mountain pass with a view of Borus. From Cheryomushki, it is a 3km walk along a trail that starts at the end of the bridge across the Yenisey. English-speaking **Maria Zavorina** (Мария Заворина; ☑ 8-903-077 9647; https://vk.com/sayan_turism; treks per group R2000-3000), who works in the park, guides four- to six-hour treks to the main park sights. Many people come here to climb the Borus range, which requires overnighting in the valley below.

The popular **Gladenkaya Ski Resort** (Горнолыжный комплекс Гладенькая; ☑ 8-923-393 3300; http://ski-gladenkaya.ru/ski.html; Babik valley), 18km from Sayanogorsk, frequently hosts national skiing competitions. The signposted turn to Gladenkaya comes at Mayna, halfway between the bus station and Cheryomushki.

🛏 Sleeping & Eating

Hotel Sayanogorsk   HOTEL $$$
(Отель Саяногорск; ☑ 39042-61144; http://sayan-hotel.ru; mkr Tsentralny 50; s/d from R3600/4200; ❄ 🛜 ⊠) A funky piece of architecture, this triangular-shaped hotel has modern rooms with large comfy beds and attic-like reclining ceiling. There is a restaurant and a spa with a sauna and a small pool on the premises.

Cafe Toronto   INTERNATIONAL $$
(Кафе Торонто; ☑ 39042-68 088; mkr Internatsionaly 23a; mains R200-400) This grill restaurant is reputed to be the most decent eatery in Sayanogorsk. It's about 800m from the bus station – walk north on ul Yarygina and turn into Pionerskaya. What Canada has to do with it remains a mystery.

ℹ Getting There & Away

Marshrutka buses 2 and 2A ply the route between Sayanogorsk and Vtoraya Terrasa bus stop, from which it is a 5km walk along the river to the power station. If you are lucky, you may get a free ride on an infrequent tram that takes workers from Vtoraya Terrasa to an observation square under the dam. A taxi from the bus station to the observation point costs at least R1000 return (including wait) or R500 one way.

Buses to/from Abakan run every 30 minutes (one hour, R180). There are four services to Shushenskoe daily (1½ hours, R170), the most convenient departure times being 11.10am and 2.30pm.

TUVA

Nominally independent before WWII, fascinating Tuva (Тува in Russian, Тыва in Tuvan) is culturally similar to neighbouring Mongolia but with an international cult following all its own. Philatelists remember Tannu Tuva's curiously shaped 1930s postage stamps. World-music aficionados are mesmerised by Tuvan throat singers. And millions of armchair travellers read Ralph Leighton's *Tuva or Bust!,* a nontravel book telling how irrepressible Nobel Prize–winning physicist Richard Feynman failed to reach Soviet-era Kyzyl despite years of trying. With forests, mountains, lakes and vast undulating waves of beautiful, barely populated steppe, Tuva's a place you'll long remember.

History

Controlled from the 6th century by a succession of Turkic empires, in the 1750s Tuva became an outpost of China, against whose rule the much-celebrated Aldan Maadyr (60 Martyrs) rebelled in 1885. Tibetan Buddhism took root during the 19th century, co-existing with older shamanist beliefs; by the late 1920s one man in 15 in Tuva was a lama.

With the Chinese distracted by a revolution in 1911, Russia stirred up a separatist movement and took Tuva 'under protection' in 1914. The effects of Russia's October Revolution took two years to reach Tuva, climaxing in 1921 when the region was a last bolthole of the retreating White Russians, swiftly ejected into Mongolia by 'Red Partisans'. Tuva's prize was renewed independence as the Tuvan Agrarian Republic (Tyva Arat Respublik, TAR), better known to philatelists as Tannu Tuva. However, to communist Russia's chagrin, Prime Minister Donduk's government dared to declare Buddhism the state religion and favoured reunification with Mongolia. Russia's riposte was to install a dependable communist, Solchak Toka, as prime minister, and later to force Tuvans to write their language in the Cyrillic alphabet, creating a cultural divide with Mongolia.

Having 'voluntarily' helped Russia during WWII, Tuva's 'reward' was incorporation into the USSR. Russian immigration increased, Buddhism and shamanism were repressed, and the seminomadic Tuvans were collectivised; many Tuvans slaughtered their animals in preference to handing them over. When the Soviet Union collapsed in 1991, Tuva was one of only two republics (the other being Chechnya) that looked to secede. Many Russians left for the motherland and most still regard Tuva as a hostile place, with one notable exception – President Putin, who has made several trips to the region, one of which involved his (in)famous bare-chested photo shoot.

Tuvan Culture

Of the republic's 308,000 people, over two-thirds are ethnic Tuvans; they are Buddhist-shamanist by religion, Mongolian by cultural heritage and Turkic by language. Tuvan Cyrillic has a range of exotic extra vowels and most place names have different Russian and Tuvan variants.

Colourful *khuresh* is a form of Tuvan wrestling similar to Japanese sumo but without the ring, the formality or the huge bellies. Multiple heats (rounds) run simultaneously, each judged by a pair of referees, flamboyantly dressed in national costume. They'll occasionally slap the posteriors of fighters who seem not to be making sufficient effort. Tuvans also love Mongolian-style long-distance horse races but are most widely famed for their *khöömei* throat singers. *Khöömei* is both a general term and the name of a specific style in which low and whistling tones, all from a single throat, somehow harmonise with one another. The troll-like *kargyraa* style sounds like singing through a prolonged burp. *Sygyt* is reminiscent of a wine glass being rung by a wet finger: quaintly odd if you hear a recording but truly astonishing when you hear it coming out of a human mouth. Accompanying instruments often include a Jew's harp, a bowed two-stringed *igil* or a three-stringed *doshpular* (Tuvan banjo). Rhythms often remind listeners of horses galloping across the steppe.

The biggest throat-singing ensembles are all-star Chirgilchin, inventive Alash (www.alashensemble.com), Kaigal-ool's Huun Huur Tu, ethno-rock band Yat-Kha (www.yat-kha.ru), Khögzhümchü and the girl band Tuva Kyzy (www.tyvakyzy.com). Many members of these bands also perform with the Tuvan National Orchestra. Until his untimely death in 2013, Kongar-ol Ondar was the best-known throat singer outside Tuva. He collaborated with Frank Zappa and worked on the soundtrack for the Oscar-nominated film *Genghis Blues*.

Learning *khöömei* has become surprisingly popular among foreigners in recent years; arranging lessons is now much simpler than it once was.

Tuvan Food

Almost every rural household keeps a vat of *khoitpak* (fermented sour mare's milk), which tastes like ginger beer with a sediment of finely chopped brie. *Khoitpak* is drunk as is or distilled into alcoholic *araka*. Roast *dalgan* (a cereal, similar to Altai's bran-rich *talkan*) can be added to your salted milky tea or eaten with *oreme* (sour cream). Local cheeses include stringy *byshtag* and rock-hard Kazakh-style *kurut* balls.

Tuvans are said to have learned from Chinggis Khaan a special way to kill their sheep without wasting any of the animal's blood. Collected with miscellaneous offal in a handy intestine, this blood makes up the local delicacy *khan* sausage. Beyond Kyzyl, truck stops, *pelmeni* (meat ravioli) steamers and temperamental but incredibly cheap village *stolovye* (canteens) are your best hopes for a hot meal unless you're staying with families. Kyzyl residents often take their own supplies when travelling to the provinces.

★ Festivals & Events

Ask at the Centre for Tuvan Culture about local festivals, as reliable information is usually impossible to find anywhere else.

Shagaa   CULTURAL
(☺Feb) Tuvan New Year (February) is the biggest festival of the year, with *sangalyr* (purification ceremonies), including a huge spring cleaning, gift giving, visits to relatives and temple rituals.

Khöömei Symposium   CULTURAL
(☺Jun) An erratically held, though possibly now-annual event for enthusiasts, anthropologists and musicologists (and anyone else interested) including lectures, talks, demonstrations, competitions and performances, all with a throat-singing theme.

Ustuu Khuree   MUSIC
(www.ustuhure.ru; ☺Jul) Large world-music festival held in and around the Ustuu Khuree temple near Chadan in western Tuva.

VALLEY OF THE KINGS

This broad grassy vale (Долина царей) begins a few kilometres beyond a turning off the M54 highway north of Turan. It's famous in archaeological circles for its pancake-shaped Scythian *kurgany* (burial mounds) named after the village of Arzhaan at the end of the paved road. These have produced the most significant archaeological finds ever made in Tuva, now displayed in Kyzyl's National Museum.

The first roadside *kurgan* is **Arzhaan II**, which lies opposite shimmering Ak Khol (White Lake). During excavations in 2001 archaeologists unearthed some magnificent artefacts in several graves dating from the 7th century BC. Less well maintained, **Arzhaan I**, a little further along the road, is the largest *kurgan* in Tuva. A dig in the early 1970s turned up thousands of gold and silver artefacts plus the graves of two Scythian VIPs, 16 servants and 160 horses, but today only a large disc of clacking stones remains. The valley holds an amazing 700 burial sites and eight large *kurgany* await the archaeologist's trowel. However, digs are unpopular with villagers and shamans who believe the spirits should be left undisturbed.

Naadym   CULTURAL
(Jul/Aug) Tuva's most dramatic festival is Naadym, usually held in and around Kyzyl in the summer months. Vastly less touristy than the Mongolian equivalent, Naadym is a good opportunity to hear *khöömei* concerts, watch horse races and see *khuresh* wrestling in the flesh.

Dangers & Annoyances

Meeting locals is the key to experiencing Tuva, but be aware that Tuvans are notorious for their reaction to alcohol, becoming disproportionately aggressive, even among friends. Although the situation is improving, travellers should still take extra care wherever they travel in Tuva, making sure to steer well clear of drunks and avoid drinking vodka with local 'friends'. Wandering Kyzyl's streets after dark without local company is also not recommended.

Information

Friends of Tuva (www.fotuva.org) A useful collection of information about the republic.
VisitTuva (www.visittuva.ru) Official tourism site.

Kyzyl   Кызыл

39422 / POP 112,700 / MOSCOW +4HR
Fancifully located at the 'centre of Asia', the Tuvan capital is where the vast majority of travellers begin their exploration of this captivating republic. Although the city's Soviet-era concrete lacks any architectural charm, in recent years the purpose-built National Museum and the superb cultural centre have provided attractive focus for those interested in the country's mesmerising traditions.

The key to enjoying Kyzyl (and all of Tuva) is contacting tour companies and Kyzyl-based English-speaking helpers well in advance – up to two months ahead if you're planning to go anywhere near the Mongolian border, an area for which special permits are needed.

Sights

★ **National Museum**   MUSEUM
(Национальный музей; www.museum.tuva.ru; ul Titova 30; R300; 10am-6pm Wed-Sun) One of Tuva's 'must sees', the National Museum's huge modern home contains the usual arrangements of stuffed animals, WWII artefacts and dusty minerals, as well as more impressive halls dedicated to shamanism, Buddhist art and traditional Tuvan sports. However, all of this is just a teasing appetiser before the main course: a single, atmospherically lit and well-guarded room containing kilograms of Scythian gold jewellery, unearthed at Arzhaan I in the Valley of the Kings.

The 3000-year-old gold pieces, which can only be seen on a 40-minute Russian-language guided tour (interpreters available or bring your own), are exquisitely displayed against dark-blue felt and seem to illuminate the room with their ancient gleam. Look out for the 1.5kg solid-gold torque, never removed by the Scythian emperor, and thousands of millimetrically fashioned sequins, the likes of which modern-day jewellers claim not to have the skills or tools to reproduce.

Centre for Tuvan Culture   ARTS CENTRE
(Центр традиционной тувинской культуры/ Тыва ундезин культура тову; 39422-23 571; cnr ul Internatsionalnaya & ul Lenina) The

attractive two-storey timber building of the Centre for Tuvan Culture was founded in 2012 by legendary Tuvan musician Kongar-ol Ondar, who was its first director until his untimely death in 2013. The government-funded institution brings together all of Tuva's ensembles, the amazing National Orchestra, traditional costume-makers, metal-workers and sculptors in a single one-stop shop and makes accessing the extraordinary culture of Tuva much simpler than before.

On the ground floor there's a 150-seat **concert hall**, venue for the monthly concert given by one of Tuva's ensembles and decorated in motifs inspired by the Scythian gold in the National Museum. The basement hosts rehearsal rooms belonging to the different ensembles, and upstairs is the large studio used by the **Tuvan National Orchestra** (www.tuvanorchestra.ru) – between 10am and 2pm most weekdays, tourists are welcome to sit in on their rehearsal sessions.

Kyzyl

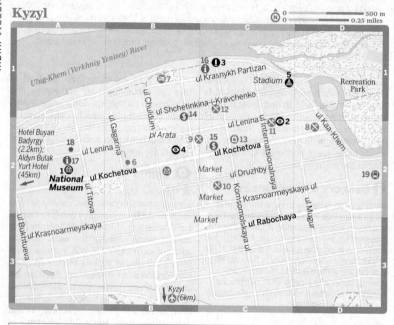

Just along the corridor is the **International Scientific Centre of Khöömei**.

The current director, Igor Koshkendey, speaks English and is keen to see more tourists coming to the centre. Through him, his staff and members of the National Orchestra, it's possible to access any aspect of Tuvan culture, find out about events and even arrange throat-singing lessons.

Centre of Asia Monument MONUMENT
(Памятник "Центр Азии"; Yenisey Embankment; ⊙7am-11pm) If you take a map of the world, cut out Asia and balance the continent on a pin, the centre of gravity would be Kyzyl. Well, only if you've used the utterly obscure Gall's stereographic projection. However, that doesn't stop the city from perpetuating the 'Centre of Asia' idea first posited by a mysterious 19th-century English eccentric and now marked with a monument standing in the middle of a manicured park that looks at the confluence of the two Yeniseys.

The creator of the monument, Buryat sculptor Dashi Namdakov, whose Chinggis (Genghis) Khaan sculpture stands near London's Marble Arch, drove inspiration from the Skythian gold finds, now housed at the Tuvan National Museum. The equestrian monument depicts a Skythian prince and his Amazon-like wife, who were put to rest with all their gold in a burial mound north of Kyzyl.

National Theatre THEATRE
(☑39422-11 566; ul Lenina 33) This Tibetan-styled white building with oriental wooden flourishes is the city's most architecturally distinctive structure.

Tsechenling Datsan BUDDHIST TEMPLE
(Буддийский храм Цеченлинг; ul Shchetinkina-Kravchenko 1) Brightly coloured prayer flags flutter in the breeze outside this white pagoda-style Buddhist temple, but it's disappointingly plain inside. There's a basic canteen and a Buddhist souvenir shop in the grounds.

☈ Activities & Tours

Evgeny Saryglar COURSE
(ana-saryglar@yandex.ru) Gives throat-singing and *igil* lessons. Have a few introductory sessions via Skype before you arrive.

Tsentr Asii TOURS
(Центр Азии; ☑39422-32 326; Hotel Odugen, ul Krasnykh Partizan 36; ⊙9am-6pm) Helpful agency that can arrange air tickets and vehicle transfers.

Alash Travel TOURS
(Алаш-Трэвел; ☑39422-21 850; alash@tuva.ru; ul Kochetova 60/12) Alash offers full-scale rafting and climbing expeditions, and can arrange horse-riding trips between Tuva and Altai. There is, unfortunately, a lack of English speakers in the office.

☐ Sleeping

With a couple of notable exceptions, Kyzyl's limited range of hotels is not much to throat sing about. They're also habitually full, so for a much jollier experience try to arrange a homestay (around R2000) through one of Kyzyl's helpers or tour companies, or stay in an apartment. High-end travellers should be able to check out the new four-star hotel Ene-Say: its construction was reaching the final stage when we visited.

★ Aldyn Bulak Yurt Hotel YURT $$
(☑39422-20 628; km45 Kyzyl–Ak-Dovurak Rd; per yurt R2500-5000, dm tepee/yurt R300/650; ❅) Cupped by bare hills at an attractively sacred site by the Yenisey River, the luxury yurts at this upmarket complex have flushing toilets, air-conditioning, hot showers and underfloor heating, while a more authentic experience is provided by basic yurts and tepees. Book through the Tourist Information Centre (p496). The huge yurt restaurant offers the best Tuvan food you'll taste anywhere in the republic.

Start the day with a climb up to the viewing points for spectacular vistas from the cliffs above the swirling river before paying your respects at the nearby *ovaa* (shamanist holy site) dedicated to *khöömei*. The site is 45km west of Kyzyl, clearly signposted off the main Kyzyl–Ak-Dovurak road. The hotel offers prearranged transfers from Kyzyl for a symbolic R100. It's remote, so there's no wi-fi.

Hotel Odugen HOTEL $$
(Гостиница Одуген; ☑39422-32 518; ul Krasnykh Partizan 36; s/tw R2300/4000) In a peaceful location by the Yenisey, this rapidly renovating hotel offers 28 en-suite rooms of varying standards. Whatever you choose, make sure you get one of the rooms with a balcony, from where there are spectacular river and mountain views. One of Kyzyl's best bars and a decent terrace cafe are also on the premises.

Hotel Buyan Badyrgy HOTEL $$$
(Гостиница Буян Бадыргы; ☑39422-56 420; www.badyrgy.ru; ul Moskovskaya 1; s/d from R2000/4000; ❅☎) Kyzyl's most comfortable

sleep is a R100 taxi ride from the city centre (or a short trip on airport-bound *marshrutka* 1A). The 37 standard rooms are clean and often smartly fitted out, but some bathrooms could do with an update. The price-to-quality ratio makes this a traveller favourite and a preferable choice to Kyzyl's hit-and-miss central hotels.

✖ Eating & Drinking

Note that no alcohol is on sale from shops after 7pm, in attempt to curb drunkenness and brawling.

Coffee Man
CAFE $
(ul Kochetova 2; mains R100-250; ⊙10am-11pm) Once the place to get a cuppa joe in Kyzyl, Coffee Man is now just another cafe, but one with filling pancakes and an English menu.

Vostorg
FAST FOOD $
(Восторг; ul Shchetinkina-Kravchenko 35; mains R40-90; ⊙8am-11pm) Perched above a supermarket of the same name, Kyzyl's best cheap eat is a plasticky no-frills self-service cafeteria where cash-strapped students and office workers fill up for a few roubles on generous platefuls of *pelmeni*, bliny, meatballs, *plov* (meat and rice), pork roast and *golubtsi* (cabbage rolls stuffed with rice and meat). Fresh doughnuts and pastries make this a decent breakfast spot.

Tos-Karak
RUSSIAN $$
(Тос-Карак; ul Lenina; R300-500; ⊙11am-11pm) Full range of meat- and intestine-heavy nomad dishes, along with salads and other vegetarian options, in this yurt restaurant frequented by throat singers from the nearby Centre of Tuvan Culture.

Subedey
RUSSIAN $$
(Субедей; ul Druzhby 149; mains R400-600; ⊙10am-1am; ✳) If your palate craves gastronomic adventure, head to this oversize Mongolian yurt in the market area for some authentic Tuvan cooking. *Khoorgan khoy edi* is fried mutton, *dalgan usken bydaa* is Tuvan noodle soup and there are milk-based desserts, *khoitpak* (fermented milk) and *araka* (milk vodka) to finish off. The first half of the menu features more European-style mains.

Fusion
INTERNATIONAL $$
(Кафе Фьюжн; www.kyzylcafe.ru; ul Tuvinskikh Dobrovoltsev 13; mains R200-400; ⊙noon-midnight; ✳ 🛜) If you just wanna hang out with your wireless-enabled device over a brew (of the bean or hop variety) in an unchallengingly stylish, faux-cosmo setting, Fusion is the place to install yourself. The pizza and sushi contain no intestines, the Russian fashion TV no politics and the service is competent if slow.

🛍 Shopping

Shever
GIFTS & SOUVENIRS
(Шевер; Komsomolskaya ul 23a; ⊙10am-6pm Mon-Fri, to 4pm Sat) Souvenir and craft shop selling top-quality handmade items such as small pieces of sculpture made from a soft stone called agalmatolite, silver jewellery from Ak-Dovurak, Jew's harps, 'I've-been-to-Tuva' T-shirts and handy city maps.

ℹ Information

ATMs are now plentiful in Kyzyl; changing currencies other than euros and dollars could be tricky.

Rosbank (Росбанк; ul Tuvinskikh Dobrovoltsev 10; ⊙9am-6pm Mon-Fri) Twenty-four-hour ATM accepting almost every kind of card.

Sberbank (Сбербанк; ul Kochetova 34a; ⊙8.30am-7pm Mon-Fri, 11am-4pm Sat) Exchange counter and ATM inside.

Post Office (ul Kochetova 53; ⊙8am-10pm Mon-Fri, 9am-6pm Sat & Sun) Has an internet room.

Sai-Khonash Travel (📱8-923-383 7109, 8-923-542 6566; https://saixonash.wordpress.com/) Tuva National Orchestra musician Evgeny Saryglar and his wife Anay-Khaak run an excellent yurt camp in a difficult-to-access part of western Tuva. They can also pretty much tailor a trip around Tuva for you. There is no office, just write to them or call. English and French are spoken.

Tourist Information Centre (http://visittuva.ru; Centre of Asia; ⊙9am-1pm & 2-6pm Mon-Fri) In theory (we visited shortly after it was opened), this slick government-run office with young enthusiastic staff should be your first point of call in Tuva, since they can put you in touch with tourist service providers anywhere in the republic and pretty much tailor your trip. There's a nice cafe and an art gallery on the premises, inside Centre of Asia.

Tourist Yurt (www.visittuva.ru; National Museum grounds; ⊙Jun-Aug) Summer-only yurt in the grounds of the National Museum. English-speaking staff can assist with accommodation and transport, and also distribute free maps and leaflets.

ℹ Getting There & Away

Opinions differ on whether the railway line to Kuragino will ever be completed. Even if it is, there's some confusion as to whether passenger services will run on the line. No developments are expected for some years, or at least until an investor is found.

EXPERIENCING KHÖÖMEI

Without doubt, Tuva's great draw is throat singing, aka *khöömei*. If you're interested in seeing a performance, by far the best place to start is the spanking-new Centre for Tuvan Culture (p493), a two-storey timber building opened in late 2011 on the site of the old museum. The current director, Igor Koshkendey, who speaks English, is the first point of contact at the centre.

For a more hands-on experience, take a throat-singing or *doshpular* (Tuvan banjo) lesson with National Orchestra member Evgeny Saryglar, who is also always in the know about upcoming *khöömei* performances in Kyzyl and beyond.

AIR

Kyzyl's shockingly up-to-date but sorely underexploited airport handles flights to Krasnoyarsk (daily) and a handy service to Irkutsk (three weekly). Moscow flights were suspended again in 2013 and don't look like making a return any time soon. *Marshrutka* 1A will get you to the airport.

Aziya-99 (Азия-99; ☑ 39422-22 214; www.asia99.ru; ul Lenina 58; ☺ 8am-7pm Mon-Fri, 9am-6pm Sat & Sun), opposite the National Museum, sells air tickets for all flights, including services departing from Abakan and Krasnoyarsk.

BUS

For the spectacularly scenic drive to Abakan, unofficial minibuses (R1300, five hours) leave when full from near the bus station. Official buses leave at least twice a day from within the bus station compound (R850, six hours).

Abakan-bound shared taxis and others heading to destinations within Tuva congregate in and around the chaotic car park behind Hotel Mongulek, but you'd be well advised to prearrange private transfers (along with accommodation) to places such as Ak-Dovurak and destinations south along the M54.

Around Kyzyl

On the Yenisey's northern bank, multiple springs gurgle straight from the rocks amid totem poles and trees heavy with prayer flags at cliff-side **Bobry Istochnik** (Beaver Spring). This popular barbecue and picnic spot with picturesque Kyzyl views can only be reached by taxi (at least R1000).

The giant **Kadarchy Herder Statue** surveys the city from a bare hill, five minutes' drive from Kyzyl's southernmost edge. Beyond, prayer flags photogenically deck the **Tos Bulak Spring**, which is the closest *arzhaan* (sacred spring) to the capital. To get a taste for the steppe, consider the relatively easy excursion to mirage-like **Cheder Salt Lake**, 42km away. The popular but slightly ramshackle

lakeside **Cheder Health Spa** (☑ 39422-644 47) has basic en-suite rooms, but book well ahead as the summer months see hundreds of locals invade this remote location to take mud cures and cool off in the briny waters.

Isolated amid endless grassy steppe 65km from Kyzyl, **Lake Dus Khol** is crowded with comically mud-blackened vacationers; its waters are so salty that you float Dead Sea style. Larger **Lake Khadyn** nearby is great for summer swimming and camping, though the water is still too salty to drink or use for cooking. To reach both, turn off the M54 at the km840 marker and head 20km along sandy, unsurfaced access tracks; arrange a prepaid private transfer with a Kyzyl agency if you don't fancy putting yourself at the mercy of local taxi drivers.

Following the Ka-Khem (Maly Yenisey) River southeast of Kyzyl, the steppe gives way to agricultural greenery around low-rise **Saryg-Sep**, beyond which an appallingly rutted road continues through woodland to the pretty Old Believers' village of **Erzhey**. Despite the extraordinary inaccessibility, there are several bungalow-hotels and hunting lodges en route and beyond. Kyzyl-based agencies organise trips to Old Believers' villages – check with the Tourist Information Centre.

Western Tuva
Западная Тува

The spectacularly picturesque and virtually traffic-free grassland routes that connect lonely settlements in the sparsely populated west of the republic are lined with sacred mountains, nomads' yurts and newly raised stupas. The area is likely to start getting more visitors after Russia and Mongolia complete the reconstruction of the Khandagaity–Borsho border crossing, so it can be used by everyone, not only nationals of the two countries.

The route looping round to Abakan from Tuva via Askiz is scenically varied, often beautiful and mesmerisingly vast in scale, though the Chinggis Khaan stone near Ak-Dovurak is virtually the only real 'sight'. While independent travel is feasible, you'll see a lot more in Tuva's west in the company of a local or a guide hired in Kyzyl. The Sayan Ring (p482) agency in Krasnoyarsk comes this way. The Yenisey federal highway (R257), which begins in Krasnoyarsk, is now being extended from Kyzyl to the border.

👁 Sights

Regional Museum   MUSEUM
(Culture Centre, ul Khomushku Vasily 23; admission by donation; ⊙on request) Delicately etched ancient stonework is the star attraction at this museum in Kyzyl-Mazhalyk, alongside an independence-era newspaper printed in the Tuvan Latin script, a mock-up of a yurt and figures sculpted in a kind of soapstone, a tradition practised in the area since Scythian times.

🛏 Sleeping

Say-Khonash Yurt Camp   YURT $$$
(☑8-923-383 7109, 8-923-542 6566; www.saixonash.wordpress.com; full board R1500) Located 55km north of Ak-Dovurak, the Say-Khonash Yurt Camp is the quintessential nomadic experience and brings visitors as close to the authentic rural lifestyle as they're ever likely to get without having to acquire Tuvan in-laws first. The six traditionally furnished yurts sleeping 12 are surrounded by real nomads' dwellings and their assorted animals in a jaw-slackeningly remote location few would ever chance upon.

The English-speaking owners (Evgeny and Anay-Khaak) and their extended family give masterclasses in felt production, yurt construction, traditional sheep butchery and Tuvan music, as well as organising multiday horse-riding and hiking trips to fantastically off-the-map locations.

No road, never mind public transport, goes anywhere near this place, so transfers from Kyzyl (or Abakan/Krasnoyarsk) must be arranged in advance with Sai-Khonash Travel (p496).

Kyzyl to Mongolian Border

Some 80km out of Kyzyl, dramatic Mt Khayyrakan (1148m), a spiky ridge blessed by the 14th Dalai Lama in 1992, comes into view but isn't reached until km107. Climb towards the stupa at the base of the mountain from the roadside cafe where buses make a brief stop. The small town of Chadan (Chadaana) is attractively dotted with wooden cottages and there's an appealing little museum. Apart from being the birthplace of Russia's current minister of defence, Sergei Shoygu, the town is most

---

HERO PROJECT OF THE CENTURY

The BAM is an astonishing victory of belief over adversity (and economic reason). This 'other' trans-Siberian line runs from Tayshet (417km east of Krasnoyarsk) around the top of Lake Baikal to Sovetskaya Gavan on the Pacific coast. It was begun in the 1930s to access the timber and minerals of the Lena Basin, and work stopped during WWII. Indeed, the tracks were stripped altogether and reused to lay a relief line to the besieged city of Stalingrad (now Volgograd).

Work effectively started all over again in 1974 when the existing Trans-Siberian Railway was felt to be vulnerable to attack by a potentially hostile China. The route, cut through nameless landscapes of virgin taiga and blasted through anonymous mountains, was built by patriotic volunteers and the BAM was labelled 'Hero Project of the Century' to encourage young people from across the Soviet Union to come and do their bit. But as cynicism began replacing enthusiasm in the late Brezhnev years, 'project of the century' turned into an ironic expression meaning a project that takes eternity to be completed. Building on permafrost pushed the cost of the project to US$25 billion, some 50 times more than the original Trans-Siberian Railway.

New 'BAM towns' grew with the railway, often populated by builders who decided to stay on. However, the line's opening in 1991 coincided with the collapse of the centrally planned USSR and the region's bright Soviet future never materialised. While Bratsk and Severobaikalsk survived, many other smaller, lonely settlements became virtual ghost towns. Today only a handful of passenger trains a day use the line.

famous as Tuva's former spiritual centre; the once-great **Ustuu Khuree Temple** 6km south of Chadan was utterly devastated in the Soviet era but has since been rebuilt and now hosts a large annual **music festival** in mid-July, embracing everything from *khöömei* to grunge rock. Participants camp in tents and yurts. Ak-Dovurak and Kyzyl-Mazhalyk are another hour's drive west. Beyond Chadan, the Yenisey federal highway turns to **Khandagayty**, the location of a major checkpoint on the Mongolian border.

WESTERN BAM

The official start of the 3100km-long Baikal–Amur Mainline (Baikalo-Amurskaya Magistral, BAM) is Tayshet, Siberia's busiest railway junction and a former Gulag town. From there the BAM crosses almost virgin territory that is more impressively mountainous than anything along the Trans-Siberian main line. Most travellers' top BAM stop is Severobaikalsk, an almost-tourist-ready hub for visiting Baikal's stunning north, with thermal mini spas nestling amid dramatic nameless peaks.

Tayshet Тайшет

📞 39563 / POP 35,500 / ⊘ MOSCOW +5HR

All Siberian roads, or railway lines at least, lead to Tayshet, a major rail junction where the Trans-Siberian, BAM and Tayshet–Abakan line collide. A child of the Trans-Sib, Tayshet had a difficult upbringing as the Gulag capital of Eastern Siberia. Between the late 1930s and the mid-1960s, numerous camps and prison colonies occupied bits of town, with everyone from 39,000 Japanese prisoners of war to well-known Moscow intellectuals passing through at various points. Not much remains of the camps today except for a few rows of prisoner-built wooden houses.

Taishet is now becoming known as the gateway to fascinating Tofalaria – an excruciatingly remote land inhabited by Tofy, Russia's smallest ethnic group.

⦿ Sights

Apart from the museum, Tayshet's other main sight is its modernised **railway station**, where a huge L-series loco stands beached to the right of the building and an Italian-built **water tower** rises in architectural incongruity behind. A pretty macabre **Lenin monument** next to the station features the communist leader's gold-painted head placed on a podium made of reflective black stone.

Museum MUSEUM

(ul Kalinina 1, Biryusinsk; R100; ⊘ 9am-6pm Mon-Sat) Leaving Tayshet's dusty/muddy streets and loco whistles, an interesting excursion is to neighbouring **Biryusinsk**, once a prosperous timber-processing town on the Trans-Sib. The local museum has some interesting rural knick-knacks, old samovars, a mock-up of a Siberian *izba* (log house) and a 1950s Soviet nostalgia section. The graves of Lithuanian exiles lie in the cemetery nearby. Biryusinsk is an R31 *marshrutka* ride from in front of Tayshet station.

Regional Museum MUSEUM

(ul Lenina 115; R20; ⊘ 10am-6pm Tue-Sat) To learn more about the town's (dark) past visit the Regional Museum, where easily musterable local historians are desperate to tell foreigners their story. There are also some exhibits belonging to Tofalaria.

🛏 Sleeping & Eating

Igor Shalygin HOMESTAY $$

(📞 8-924-716 4004; www.facebook.com/pg/Trans-sib-baikal-transit-319120791457041; per person R1000) The best reason to get off at Taishet is Igor Shalygin, an English- and German-speaking travel enthusiast who runs a cosy homestay in the old town, particularly popular with motorcycle overlanders. He can take you out to various beauty spots, romantically lost bits of the Trans-Sib and the old *trakt*, and give you a taste of authentic rural Siberian life.

The latter includes a superb *banya* (bathhouse), where the host performs the role of steam and twig master. In summer, Shalygin runs boat trips on the placid Biryusa River. In winter, when the river turns into an ice road, he can set up a trip to the reindeer herders and hunters of Tofalaria.

Kofeynya Paris COFFEE

(Taishet railway station; ⊘ 9am-1am) This surprisingly metropolitan cafe inside the train station serves good coffee and snacks till the last night train is gone.

Bratsk Братск

📞 3953 / POP 234,150 / ⊘ MOSCOW +5HR

Unless you're a fan of BAM or hydroelectric projects, Bratsk is perhaps not worth leaving the 'comfort' of your carriage bunk, though it does neatly break up the journey from both Irkutsk and Krasnoyarsk to Severobaikalsk. The city's raison d'être is a gigantic dam (GES), which drowned the original historic town in the 1960s. New Bratsk is an unnavigable and heavily polluted necklace of disconnected concrete 'subcities' and belching industrial zones, with the spirit-crushingly dull Tsentralny area at its heart.

○ Sights

Angara Village
MUSEUM

(www.bratskmuseum.ru; ul Komsomolskaya; R150; ◷10am-4.30pm Wed-Sun) Some 12km from Tsentralny, this impressive open-air ethnographic museum contains a rare 17th-century wooden watchtower and buildings rescued from submerged old Bratsk. A series of shaman sites and Evenki *chumy* (tepee-shaped conical dwellings) lie in the woods behind. Take a taxi or arrange a visit through Taiga Tours.

Bratsk Dam
LANDMARK

(Братская ГЭС; www.irkutskenergo.ru) A ferro-concrete symbol of the USSR's efforts to harness the might of Siberia's natural assets, between 1967 and 1971 the Bratsk hydroelectric power station was the world's largest single electricity producer. Slung between high cliffs and somehow holding back the mammoth Bratsk Sea – no one can deny it's a striking spectacle, especially from the window of BAM trains that pass right across the top.

Take any *marshrutka* from Tsentralny to Gidrostroitel, the closest slab of Bratsk to the dam. The only way to access the turbine rooms is through a local tour agency.

☞ Tours

Taiga Tours
TOURS

(☏3953-416 513; www.taiga-tours.ru; 2nd fl, Hotel Taiga; ◷10am-6pm Mon-Fri) Permits and guides to visit the dam's turbine rooms.

⌖ Sleeping & Eating

Hotel Shvedka
HOTEL $

(Гостиница Шведка; ☏8-902-179 0580; www.hotel-shvedka.ru; ul Mira 25; s/d from R1050/1400; 🛜) Rooms here range from battered and cheap to almost design standard. Ask to see which you're getting before you commit. Breakfast is extra and is taken in the hotel's own cafe.

Vremena Goda
HOTEL $$

(Времена года; ☏3953-414 777; www.hotel-bratsk.ru; ul Podbelskogo 12; d from R3500) The city's most elegant hotel occupies an Alpine-styled wooden chalet with tastefully designed rooms, where the smell of natural wood all but suppresses the industrial odours that prevail outside. Paper-thin walls mean you can eavesdrop on neighbours' Skype calls and stay informed about the rest of their activities.

Amrita
VEGETARIAN $

(☏3953-454 097; www.amritacentr.ru; ul Pionerskaya 5; mains R80-120; ◷noon-7pm; 🥗) In a gloomy macho town like Bratsk, this tidy vegetarian cafeteria comes as a pleasant surprise. Admittedly the lentil soup and samosas have lost any signs of their Indian roots, but perhaps it is the beginning of Siberia's own vegetarian cooking style.

Rock Garret
EASTERN EUROPEAN $$

(Рок Гаррет; ☏3953-411 417; www.cherdak-bratsk.ru; ul Mira 43; mains R300-400; ◷10am-2am) A restaurant, a pub and a rock-music venue – this all-in-one place is about the best option for an evening out in Bratsk. The menu is a carnivore's delight with a few Siberian elements, such as moose cutlets. Home-brewed lager, as well as English and Belgian ales, are on tap.

❶ Getting There & Away

For Tsentralny, get off BAM trains at the Anzyobi (Анзеби) station and transfer by bus or *elektrichka* (suburban train). Bratsk has the following rail connections:

Irkutsk *platskart/kupe* R2500/2650, 16½ to 18½ hours, daily

Krasnoyarsk *platskart/kupe* R2000/2100, 12½ hours, up to four daily

Moscow *platskart/kupe* R8350/10,000, three days and three hours, one or two daily

Severobaikalsk *platskart/kupe* R2100/2300, 14 to 17 hours, up to four daily

Irkutsk can also be reached by Western-standard coach (R1100, 10½ hours) from the Tsentralny bus station (ul Yuzhnaya) and summer hydrofoil from a river station in southeast Tsentralny. Check VSRP (☏3952-287 115; www.vsrp.ru) for details of the latter.

Severobaikalsk
Северобайкальск

☏30130, 30139 / POP 23,900 / ◷MOSCOW +5HR

Founded as a shack camp for railway workers in the mid-1970s, Severobaikalsk has grown into the most engaging halt on the BAM, where travellers vacate stuffy railway compartments to stretch legs in the taiga or cool off in Lake Baikal. The town itself is a grid of soulless, earthquake-proof apartment blocks with little in between, but the mountainscape and nameless wildernesses backing the lake quickly lure hikers and adventurers away from the concrete. They discover a land more remote, less peopled and generally more spectacular than Baikal's south, a place where lazy bears and reindeer-herding Evenki still rule in timeless peace, despite the best efforts of *Homo sovieticus*.

◉ Sights

Railway Station NOTABLE BUILDING
(pr 60 let SSSR; ⊙ 5am-midnight) The epicentre of SB's world is a striking construction with a nostalgically stranded steam locomotive standing guard to the right. The sweeping architectural design of the brave-new-world station resembles a ski jump, but it's really meant to look like a ship. As with the rest of Severobaikalsk, it was designed by architects from Leningrad, who tried to convey the sense of both places being united by the nautical theme.

An overhead bridge to the right of the station leads across the tracks towards a scenic clifftop trail that skirts the coast.

BAM Museum MUSEUM
(Музей БАМа; per Proletarsky 5; R50; ⊙ 10am-1pm & 2-6pm Tue-Sat) Having moved into larger premises, the town's friendly museum has exhibits on BAM railway history (workers' medals, grainy black-and-white photos, 'old' BAM tickets), some Buryat artefacts and a few mammoth bones. An adjacent room houses an **art gallery** where local artists display their works. There is also a souvenir shop that peddles shaman drums amid kitschy bric-a-brac.

God's Mother of Kazan Cathedral CHURCH
(ul Mira 10) A strange sight in a town built by Komsomol (Youth Communist League) enthusiasts, the town's new Orthodox church sports two impressive onion domes in gleaming gold and a monster chandelier inside. It stands just beyond the town's grey-concrete **war memorial**.

🏃 Activities

Severobaikalsk is the base for trekking expeditions along the Great Baikal Trail on the ice in winter. These, along with visits to Evenki reindeer herders, can be organised with the help of local tourist agencies and hotel owners.

Seismic activity in the northern Baikal area shakes free lots of thermal springs, around which tiny spas have sprouted. These are great places to soothe aching muscles after days of contortion in your BAM carriage bunk, though facilities are pretty basic. Costs are low for accommodation, food and bathing.

**Frolikha Adventure
Coastline Trail** TREKKING
Part of the Great Baikal Trail, this incredible, relatively demanding 100km adventure trekking route runs between the delta of the Verkhnyaya Angara River and the spa hamlet of Khakusy on Baikal's eastern shore. You'll need a boat to find the start of the trail at the mouth of the river, from where it takes eight days to reach Khakusy via countless lonely capes and bays, wild camping by the lake all the way.

Exhilarating river crossings (including a biggie – the River Frolikha), deserted beaches and show-stopping Baikal vistas punctuate the trail, and from Ayaya Bay a there-back hike to remote Lake Frolikha beckons.

For more information and trail maps, contact Severobaikalsk tour agencies, the Baikal Trail Hostel or Dresden-based Baikalplan.

Khakusy Spa SPA
(www.hakusy.com) To land at this idyllically isolated hot-spring *turbaza* (holiday camp) requires permits in summer (available through Severobaikalsk tour companies and hotels), but these are waived in February and March, when it takes about an hour to drive across the ice from Severobaikalsk. Bathing is fun in the snow and frozen steam creates curious ice patterns on the wooden spa buildings.

In summer, make sure you book the ferry well in advance as it's a popular trip among Russian holidaymakers. An alternative way to reach Khakusy is along the 100km Frolikha Adventure Coastline Trail.

👉 Tours

Severobaikalsk has a surprising number of agencies and individuals that can arrange accommodation and backcountry excursions.

Rashit Yakhin/BAM Tour TOURS
(☑ 8-914-833 1646, 30139-21 560; www.gobaikal.com; ul Oktyabrya 16/2) This experienced full-time travel-fixer, guide and ex-BAM worker suffered an immobilising stroke in the mid-1990s, rendering his spoken English somewhat hard to follow. Nonetheless, Rashit is quick to reply to emails and able to set ice-cycling and skiing trips on Baikal in winter

as well as catamaran trips in summer. Dacha (private summer cottage) visits are also on offer.

Maryasov Family
TOURS

(☑8-908-597 5988, 8-924-391 4514; www.baikaltrail.ru) The English-speaking family of Yevgeny Maryasov, a cofounder of the Great Baikal Trail, runs a homestay, information centre and tourism association as well as organising guided treks to Baikalskoe and Lake Frolikha, seal-spotting trips to Ayaya Bay and fascinating trips to the camps of Evenki reindeer herders.

Ecoland
TOURS

(☑8-902-162 1623, 30130-36 191; www.ecoland-tour.ru) This award-winning tour agency specialises in horse-riding trips, Baikal boat excursions and trekking.

🛏 Sleeping

Dad's House
HOSTEL $

(Папин дом; ☑8-983-430 9817, 8-950-060 7343; azubina@mail.ru; ul Promyshlennaya 17; dm R750) A pretty little cottage in an unpretty industrial neighbourhood, not far from the centre, this new hostel has eight bunk beds and offers sumptuous breakfasts for an extra R250.

Baikal Trail Hostel
HOMESTAY $

(☑8-924-779 2805, 8-924-391 4514, 30130-23 860; www.baikaltrailhostel.com; ul Studencheskaya 12, apt 16; tr per person R900; @🖥) Run by the younger generation of the Maryasov family in their own flat, SB's original hostel is now reduced to a three-bed homestay. Kitchen, washing machine and a communal climbing wall are at visitors' disposal. It's one of the best places in town to arrange backcountry treks and trips into the wilds around the northern end of Lake Baikal.

★ Zolotaya Rybka
GUESTHOUSE $$

(Золотая Рыбка; ☑30130-21 134; www.baikalgoldenfish.ru; ul Sibirskaya 14; d from R2300; 🖥) Well signposted from ul Olkhonskaya, SB's best guesthouse maintains immaculate and imaginatively designed rooms in three buildings providing glimpses of Lake Baikal through the trees. There are spotless toilets and showers throughout, guests have access to kitchens and a cook prepares a restaurant-standard breakfast on request (R300 extra). Owner offers trips to Evenki reindeer herders.

Dom u Baikala
GUESTHOUSE $$

(Дом у Байкала; ☑30130-239 50, 8-950-119 7380; www.baikal-kruiz.narod.ru; pr Neptunsky 3; d with/without bathroom R2600/2200; 🖥) Located in the pleasant lakeside residential area of Severobaikalsk, this cottage contains several clean and well-equipped if uninspiring rooms. The English-speaking owner runs tours of main northern Baikal attractions.

Hotel Olymp
HOTEL $$

(Гостиница Олимп; ☑30130-23 980; www.hotelolymp.ru; ul Poligrafistov 2b; s/d from R2200/2600, with shared bathroom from R1200/1500; 🖥) Severobaikalsk's smartest sleep has spotless, cool, airy rooms, though the plumbing could be more professionally screwed down. For this price you might expect breakfast and free wi-fi – you get neither.

✕ Eating

For quick and cheap eats – *pozi* (dumplings), shashlyk, *plov* and beer – try makeshift Buryat and Kyrgyz eateries in the shop row east of the station on pr 60 let SSSR.

Bar Bison
GRILL $$

(☑8-950-399 9359; www.vk.com/bizonsbk; Leningradsky pr 8; mains R200-600; ⊙11am-1am) There are all kinds of shashlyk and other grilled meat in this little restaurant-bar located in what looks like a construction site cabin by the town's market. Local Tikhonov & Sons beer is on tap. Gets a little rowdy on weekends.

Rialto
ITALIAN $$

(☑8-924-652 4151; ul Studencheskaya 8; mains R200-600; ⊙9am-9pm Mon-Thu, 10am-10pm Fri-Sun) Pizzas, pastas and really good coffee served in a pleasant Italianesque premises, decorated with pictures of Venice and Rome. Sometimes closes for banquets on the weekend.

🛍 Shopping

Market
MARKET

(Gorodskoy Rynok) Baikal fish, smoked and sundried, cedar pine nuts, *sagaan-dalya* and other local herbs – you'll find all of this in the town's small but bustling market located in the heart of town.

ℹ Information

There are ATMs at the railway station, in the Zheleznodorozhnik Culture Centre and at the Leningradsky pr branch of the VIST Supermarket.

Baikalplan (www.baikalplan.de)

Post Office (Почта; Leningradsky pr 6; ⊙9am-2pm & 3-7pm Mon-Fri, 9am-2pm Sat)

Warm North of Baikal (www.privet-baikal. ru; Leningradsky pr 5; ☺10am-6pm) The local tourism association has turned the town's library into an informal hospitality centre, where – in theory – someone should always be available to help travellers with accommodation and local tours. It also runs an English-language website with tons of information and listings.

❶ Getting There & Away

AIR

With hydrofoil services from Irkutsk and Olkhon suspended, two weekly flights from Irkutsk (R3750) and Ulan-Ude (R6500) operated by Angara airline provide the only fast option of getting into and out of Severobaikalsk.

BUS

Marshrutky cluster outside Severobaikalsk's train station and run to the following destinations:

Baikalskoe R70, 45 minutes, two daily
Goudzhekit R120, 45 minutes, three daily
Nizhneangarsk Airport R50, 50 minutes, half-hourly

TRAIN

Severobaikalsk has the following rail connections:

Bratsk *platskart/kupe* R2100/3700, 14 to 16 hours, three daily
Irkutsk *platskart/kupe* R3800/7000, 38 hours, daily
Krasnoyarsk *platskart/kupe* R3300/5600, 28 hours, three daily
Moscow *platskart/kupe* R9300/10,080, three days 18 hours, one or two daily
Tynda *platskart/kupe* R3000/3200, 26 hours, daily

❶ Getting Around

Taxi drivers charge a standard fare of R80 before 10pm and R100 during the night for trips anywhere around town. **Taxi Milent** (☑30130-255 33) is a very reliable service.

Around Severobaikalsk

Nizhneangarsk   Нижнеангарск

Until the BAM clunked into town, Nizhneangarsk had led an isolated existence for over 300 years, cobbling together its long streets of wooden houses and harvesting Baikal's rich *omul* (a type of fish) stocks. If truth be told, not much changed when the railway arrived, but despite the appearance of now larger Severobaikalsk 30km away,

the 5km-long village remains the administrative centre of northern Baikal.

The **Regional Museum** (ul Pobedy 37; R100; ☺10am-6pm Mon-Fri) chases the history of the region back to the 17th century and includes several Evenki exhibits. The museum often hosts performances by the local Evenki folklore collective **Sinilga**, which can be arranged through the Maryasov family (p502) in Severobaikalsk.

To the east of the town, a long spit of land known as **Yarki Island** caps the most northerly point of Lake Baikal and keeps powerful currents and waves out of the fragile habitat of the Verkhnyaya Angara delta. You can walk along its length.

Scenic low-altitude flights cross Lake Baikal to Irkutsk and Ulan-Ude when weather conditions allow.

Marshrutky (R70, 50 minutes) from Severobaikalsk run every 30 minutes along ul Pobedy then continue along the coast road (ul Rabochaya) to the airport.

Baikalskoe   Байкальское

This timeless little fishing village of log-built houses 45km south of Severobaikalsk has a jaw-droppingly picturesque lakeside location backed by wooded hills and snow-dusted peaks. Your first stop should be the small, informal **school museum** (R100; ☺10am-4pm). The only other sight is the wooden **Church of St Inokent**, which strikes a scenic lakeside pose.

Most visitors come to Baikalskoe on a day trip from Severobaikalsk, but if you do want to stay the night, arrange a homestay through tour agencies and fixers in Severobaikalsk. The Maryasov family in Severobaikalsk can put you up in the house of **Gertrude Freimane**, a Latvian deportee, who cooks excellent wild berry cakes. There's no cafe in the village, just a couple of shops selling basic foodstuffs.

Marshrutky (R100, 45 minutes) leave from outside Severobaikalsk train station every day early in the morning and in the early evening, returning an hour or so later.

A section of the Great Baikal Trail heads north from the fishing port 20 minutes up a cliff-side path towards the radio mast atop cape Ludar, from which there are particularly superb views looking back towards the village. Beyond that, Baikalskoe's shamanic **petroglyphs** hide in awkward-to-reach cliff-side locations and can only be found with the help of a knowledgeable local. The well-maintained trail continues another 18 scenic kilometres through beautiful cedar and spruce forests and past photogenic **Boguchan Island** to chilly **Lake Slyudyanskoe**, next to which stands the small **Echo turbaza** (holiday camp) – book through the Maryasov family.

The hike makes for a rewarding day trip and, with the path hugging the lake most of the way, there's little chance of getting lost. From the Echo *turbaza* head along a dirt track through the forest to the Severobaikalsk–Baikalskoe road to hitch a lift, or pre-arrange transport back to Severobaikalsk. Alternatively, some hikers tackle the day the other way round, catching the morning *marshrutka* to Echo *turbaza* then timing the hike to make the evening *marshrutka* back to Severobaikalsk.

LAKE BAIKAL

One of the world's oldest geographical features (formed 25 to 30 million years ago), magnificent Lake Baikal (Озеро Байкал) is the highlight of Eastern Siberia. Summer travellers enjoy gob-smacking vistas across waters of the deepest blue to soaring mountain ranges on the opposite shore; rarer winter visitors marvel at its powder-white surface, frozen steel-hard and scored with ice roads. Whether they swim in it, drink its water, skirt its southern tip by train, cycle or dog sled over it in winter or just admire it from 2000km of shoreline, most agree that Siberia doesn't get better than this.

Banana-shaped Baikal is 636km from north to south and up to 1637m deep, making it the world's deepest lake, containing nearly one-fifth of the planet's unfrozen fresh water. Despite some environmental concerns, it's pure enough to drink in most places but use

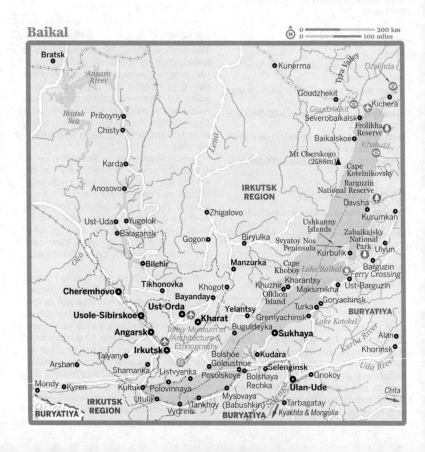

Baikal

common sense. Fed by 300 rivers, it's drained by just one, the Angara near Listvyanka.

Foreign tourists typically visit Baikal from Listvyanka via Irkutsk, but approaching via Ulan-Ude (for eastern Baikal) produces more beach fun and Severobaikalsk (on the BAM railway) is best for accessing wilderness trekking routes. Choosing well is important, as there's no round-lake road and the northern reaches are in effect cut off by land from the southern shores. Not even the Great Baikal Trail will create a complete loop, as some stretches of shoreline are just too remote. Hydrofoil connections are limited to summer services in the south plus the Irkutsk–Olkhon–Nizhneangarsk run. Inexplicably, there are virtually no scheduled boat services linking the east and west shores.

Note that the beautiful inland Tunka and Barguzin Valleys are accessed via Baikal towns.

Irkutsk Иркутск

☑ 3952 / POP 602,000 / ✪ MOSCOW +5HR

The de facto capital of Eastern Siberia, pleasantly historic Irkutsk is by far the most popular stop on the Trans-Siberian Railway between Moscow and all points east. With Lake Baikal a mere 70km away, the city is the best base from which to strike out for the western shoreline. Amid the 19th-century architecture, revived churches, classy eateries and numerous hostels, plentiful English-speaking agencies can help you plan anything from a winter trek across the lake's ice to a short walking tour through the city.

In recent years Irkutsk has seen something of a tourist boom, spawning a municipally funded information centre, detailed city maps planted at strategic points and a handful of freshly conceived museums, as well as the blockbuster 130 Kvartal project, an entire neighbourhood given over to typical Siberian timber buildings housing new restaurants, bars, cafes and the odd museum.

History

Founded in 1661 as a Cossack garrison to extract the fur tax from the indigenous Buryats, Irkutsk was the springboard for 18th-century expeditions to the far north and east, including Alaska – then known as 'Irkutsk's American district'.

As Eastern Siberia's trading and administrative centre, Irkutsk dispatched Siberian furs and ivory to Mongolia, Tibet and China in exchange for silk and tea. Constructed mostly of local timber, three-quarters of the city burnt down in the disastrous blaze of 1879. However, profits from the 1880s Lena Basin gold rush swiftly rebuilt the city's most important edifices in brick and stone.

Known as the 'Paris of Siberia', Irkutsk did not welcome news of the October Revolution. The city's well-to-do merchants only succumbed to the red tide in 1920, with the capture and execution of White Army commander Admiral Kolchak, whose controversial statue was re-erected in 2004. Soviet-era planning saw Irkutsk develop as the sprawling industrial and scientific centre that it remains today.

◉ Sights

Irkutsk's centre can be easily explored on foot – you'll only need to hop aboard a bus or *marshrutka* to see the Angara Dam and the Znamensky Monastery.

Volkonsky House-Museum MUSEUM
(Дом-музей Волконского; ☑ 3952-207 532; per Volkonskogo 10; R200, with Trubetskoy House-Museum R300; ✪ 10am-6pm Tue-Sun) The duck-egg-blue and white home of Decembrist Count Sergei Volkonsky, whose wife Maria Volkonskaya cuts the main figure in Christine Sutherland's unputdownable book *The Princess of Siberia,* is a small mansion set in a scruffy courtyard with stables, a barn and servant quarters. Renovated in the late 1980s, the house is now a museum telling the story of the family's exile in Irkutsk.

In the decade leading up to the Volkonskys' return to St Petersburg in 1856, the house was the epicentre of Irkutsk cultural life, with balls, musical soirées and parties attended by wealthy merchants and high-ranking local officials. A tour of the building, with its big ceramic stoves and original staircases, takes visitors from the family dining room, where governor Muravyov-Amursky once feasted on fruit and veg grown by Volkonsky himself in the garden out back, to the upstairs photo exhibition including portraits of Maria and other women who romantically followed their husbands and lovers into exile.

Emotionally charged items on show include Maria's pyramidal piano, a browsable book of images collected by fellow Decembrist wife Ekaterina Trubetskaya of the various places the Decembrists were imprisoned, and Maria's music box sent from Italy by her sister-in-law.

Irkutsk

Znamensky Monastery   MONASTERY
(ul Rabochego Shtaba) **FREE** Stranded on the wrong side of a thundering roundabout, the 1762 Znamensky Monastery is 1.9km northeast of Skver Kirova. Echoing with mellifluous plainsong, the wonderful interior has muralled vaulting, a towering iconostasis and a gold sarcophagus holding the miraculous relics of Siberian missionary St Inokent. Celebrity graves outside include the nautically themed tomb of Grigory Shelekhov, the man who claimed Alaska for Russia,

and a much humbler headstone belonging to Decembrist wife Ekaterina Trubetskaya (directly in front of you as you enter).

White Russian commander Admiral Kolchak was executed by Bolsheviks near the spot where his statue was controversially erected in November 2004 at the entrance to the monastery grounds; the plinth is exaggeratedly high enough to prevent diehard communists from committing acts of vandalism.

Trolleybus 3 trundles this way.

Kazansky Church (800m)

29

ul Oktyabrskoy Revolyutsii

3

60

12

ul Dekabrskikh Sobyty

ul Dzerzhinskogo

13

47

5

53 59

ul Sennaya

57

ul Engelsa

ul Karla Libknekhta

ul Utkina

Yamskaya ul

ul Sofia Perovskoy

ul Partizanskaya

ul Baikalskaya

30

Podgornaya ul

ul Neiskogo

Sovetskaya ul

*Usadba
Sukacheva (550m);
Hotel Zvezda (2km);
International
Irkutsk (4km)*

Central
Recreation
Park

52

ul Baikalskaya

24

*Hydrofoil Station (5km);
Baikal Business Centre (5km);
Angara Dam (5km)*

*Modul
(200m)*

130 Kvartal   AREA
(130th Block; btw uls Sedova & 3 lyulya) What does a city boasting some of Siberia's most impressive original timber architecture do to improve the visitor experience? Yes, that's right, recreate an entire quarter of yet more wooden buildings, some transported here from other locations, some fake. The unromantically named 130 Kvartal south of the Raising of the Cross Church is nonetheless a pleasant place to stroll, packed with restaurants, cafes and commercial museums, and culminating in Eastern Siberia's

only real 21st-century (and quite impressive) shopping mall.

Guarding the entrance to this timber theme park is a monster bronze *babr*, the mythical beast that features on Irkutsk's municipal coat of arms. The spot has become a popular place to have that 'I've been to Irkutsk' photo taken.

Trubetskoy House-Museum   MUSEUM
(Дом-музей Трубецкого; ul Dzerzhinskogo 64; R200, with Volkonsky House-Museum R300; ⊙10am-6pm Wed-Mon) Irkutsk's second Decembrist house-museum emerged from a recent renovation with English-language information, touchscreens and tinkling background music. This pleasingly symmetrical mini mansion was actually built for the daughter of Decembrist Sergei Trubetskoy – the original Trubetskoy house near the Znamensky Monastery burnt down in 1908. The lower level tells the Decembrists' story, from failed coup to arrival in Irkutsk, while the upper floor displays personal items belonging to Ekaterina Trubetskaya, Trubetskoy's French wife who died in Irkutsk.

Usadba Sukacheva   MUSEUM
(www.sukachoff.ru; ul Dekabrskikh Sobyty 112; R150; ⊙10am-6pm Tue, Wed & Fri-Sun, noon-8pm Thu) A small park on the edge of the historical centre contains a smattering of beautiful lacewood buildings and arbours. These house exhibitions dedicated to the family of 19th-century benefactor Vladimir Sukachev, who lived here until the October Revolution. The collection includes period furniture and paintings by old Spanish and Dutch masters. Perhaps the most touching bit is the recreated 'winter garden' – an indoor greenhouse filled with exotic tropical plants.

Sculpture Gallery   GALLERY
(Галерея скульптуры; ☎3952-487 054; www.museum.irk.ru; ul Sverdlova 16; R50; ⊙10am-6pm Tue-Sun) Opened in 2016, this lovely gallery puts in the spotlight Russian and Soviet sculpture previously kept in the city's main art museum and private collections, but the true highlights here are the whimsical creations of modern artists working with multicoloured Siberian gems.

Bronshteyn Gallery   GALLERY
(Галерея Бронштейна; ☎3952-209 208; www.vbgallery.ru; ul Oktyabrskoy Revolyutsii 3; adult/child R150/50; ⊙11am-8pm) A large and sparkling new modern art venue that most prominently features a collection of Dashi

Irkutsk

Namdakov's sculptures inspired by Buddhist prayer dolls used by Buryats. Also clearly inspired by Dalí. Very competently curated temporary exhibitions of local artists.

Statue of Tsar Alexander III MONUMENT
(Памятник Александру III) Adorning the Angara embankment, a recast statue of Alexander III (a copy of the 1904 original) has the only tsar ever to visit Siberia looking as though he's holding an invisible balloon on a string.

Raising of the Cross Church CHURCH
(Krestovozdvizhenskaya tserkov; ul Sedova 1) The 1758 baroque Raising of the Cross Church has a fine interior of gilt-edged icons and examples of intricate brickwork in a rounded

style that's unique to Irkutsk and the Selenga Delta village of Posolskoe.

Saviour's Church CHURCH
(Спасская церковь; www.spashram.irk.ru; ul Sukhe-Batora 2) Constructed in 1706, this is the oldest stone-built church in Eastern Siberia and has remnants of the original murals on its facade. Until the late 1990s it housed a museum, hence the rather bare interior.

Regional Museum MUSEUM
(Краеведческий музей; ☑ 3952-333 449; www.museum.irkutsk.ru; ul Karla Marksa 2; R200; ☺ 10am-7pm Tue-Sun) Irkutsk's rapidly ageing Regional Museum occupies a fancy 1880s brick building that formerly housed the Siberian Geographical Society, a club of Victorian-style gentlemen explorers. The highlights here are

the downstairs ethnographical exhibitions and the nostalgic display of 20th-century junk upstairs, as well as the small gift shop selling birch-bark boxes, jewellery made from Baikal minerals and other interesting souvenirs.

Bogoyavlensky Cathedral   CHURCH
(Богоявленский собор; ul Sukhe-Batora 1a) This fairy-tale ensemble of mini onion domes atop restored salmon, white and green towers first appeared on the Irkutsk skyline in 1718, but during the Soviet decades they served as a dormitory and a bakery. The interior is a fragrant riot of aureoled Byzantine saints with no surface left plain.

Sukachev Regional Art Museum   MUSEUM
(Иркутский областной художественный музей имени В. П. Сукачёва; www.museum.irk.ru; ul Lenina 5; R150; ☉10am-6pm Tue-Sun) The grand old art museum has a valuable though poorly lit collection ranging from Mongolian *thangkas* (Tibetan Buddhist religious paintings) to Russian Impressionist canvases. However, the main reason for coming here may be to see a top-notch temporary show (extra charge).

Museum of City Life   MUSEUM
(ul Dekabrskikh Sobyty 77; R120; ☉10am-6pm Thu-Tue) This small museum filling six rooms of a former merchant's house illustrates just why 19th-century Irkutsk was nicknamed the 'Paris of Siberia'. Changing exhibitions of everyday and decorative items such as lamps, dolls, tableware and porcelain are donated free of charge by the people of Irkutsk and are displayed against a background of period wallpaper, elegant double doors and high ceilings. The ticket is also valid for the tiny Tea Museum above the tourist office opposite.

City History Museum   MUSEUM
(www.history.irk.ru; ul Frank-Kamenetskogo 16a; R120; ☉10am-6pm Thu-Tue) Despite its palatial 19th-century home (built by wealthy merchant Sibiryakov in 1884), what should be Irkutsk's main repository of the past is in fact a rather limited exhibition on the city's history with absolutely nothing in English. Highlights include some interesting pre-Russian wooden yurts and tepees, a model of the Kazansky Church, some fascinating blown-up photos of 19th-century Irkutsk, and a 20th-century section with bric-a-brac from the Revolution up to the late 1990s.

Angara Dam   LANDMARK
Some 6km southeast of the centre, the 1956 Angara Dam is 2km long. Its construction raised Lake Baikal by up to 1m and caused environmental problems, most notably the silencing of the so-called singing sands on Baikal's eastern shore. The dam itself is hardly an attraction but moored nearby is the Angara icebreaker (www.angara.gavailer.ru; ul Marshala Zhukova 36a; R150; ☉10am-9pm).

Originally imported in kit form from Newcastle-upon-Tyne to carry Trans-Siberian Railway passengers across Lake Baikal (the trains went on her bigger sister ship *Baikal*, sunk during the Russian Civil War), this icebreaker is now a less-than-inspiring museum reached by a permanent gangway. Trolleybuses 3, 5, 7 and 8 head this way.

Kazansky Church   CHURCH
(ul Barrikad 34) The gigantic Kazansky Church is a theme-park-esque confection of salmon-pink walls and fluoro turquoise domes topped with gold baubled crosses. Get off tram 4 two stops northeast of the bus station.

🏃 Activities

Basninskiye Bani   BATHHOUSE
(☑3952-722 832; http://basninskiebani.ru; ul Sverdlova 35; before/after 4pm R900/1100; ☉noon-11pm Mon-Fri, 10am-11pm Sat & Sun) Come to this renovated bathhouse to steam off railway slime and fatigue. There are separate departments for men and women, to enjoy Turkish hammam in addition to traditional Russian *banya*. Foam massage is available in both departments.

Baikal Adventure   ADVENTURE SPORTS
(☑8-902-768 0505; www.baikal-adventure.com) Energetic agency specialising in adventurous trekking, biking, climbing and caving trips and full-blown expeditions.

Baikal Secrets   TREKKING
(☑8-914-949 1462; www.baikalsecrets.com) English-speaking Ivan and Yekaterina run summer and winter trekking tours on Baikal and in Tunka Valley.

👉 Tours

Local tour companies are useful not only for organising excursions but also for booking hotels and most kinds of tickets. All of Irkutsk's hostels can arrange Baikal tours.

Baikaler   TOURS
(☑3952-336 240, 8-908-663 3142; www.baikaler.com) Imaginative Jack Sheremetoff speaks very good English and is well tuned to

budget-traveller needs. Original personalised tours, two great hostels and a friendly welcome.

Denis Sobnakov
TOURS

(http://baikaltour.net) Sharing his time between Irkutsk and Ulan-Ude, one of Siberia's best guides offers tours to Olkhon and the southwestern shores of Baikal, as well as elsewhere around the region. Contact by email.

BaikalComplex
TOURS

(☑ 3952-461 557; www.baikalcomplex.com) Well-organised operation offering Lake Baikal accommodation and trips tailored for international travellers.

Baikalinfo
TOURS

(☑ 3952-707 012; www.baikalinfo.ru) Baikal tours as well as transfers, hikes and fishing trips.

BaikalExplorer
TOURS

(☑ 8-902-560 2440; www.baikalex.com) Baikal cruises, fishing and diving trips, treks in Tunka Valley.

Green Express
TOURS

(☑ 3952-734 400; www.greenexpress.ru) Professional outfit specialising in outdoor activities.

🛏 Sleeping

Irkutsk is struggling to catch up with the ever-increasing flow of Chinese and Russian tourists. Hostels are mushrooming, but there is a serious shortage of quality midrange options, so try to book in advance, especially if you are travelling during the high summer season or in February and March.

★ Baikaler Hostel
HOSTEL $

(☑ 3952-336 240; www.baikaler.com; ul Lenina 9, apt 11; dm R600, d with shared bathroom R1500; ❄ @ 🛜) Experienced tour guide Jack Sheremetoff had a super-central apartment hostel in Irkutsk long before the word even entered the Russian language. Despite competition, the city's original backpacker haven is still *the* place to meet travellers and organise trips. The spotless, air-conditioned dorms are spacious, but beds are limited so book ahead. The entrance is at the rear of the building.

Trans-Sib Hostel
HOSTEL $

(☑ 8-904-118 0652; www.irkutsk-hostel.com; per Sportivniy 9a, apt 8; dm/d from R750/1000; @ 🛜) Well-established, cosy backpacker hostel around a 10-minute walk from the train station offering a kitchen, washing machine,

a high bathroom-to-bed ratio and one of the best ranges of owner-led tours in town. Rates include a light breakfast.

52°17' Travel Center
HOSTEL $

(☑ 3952-725 217; https://5217.co; ul Gryaznova 15a; dm/tw R700/1800) The stated goal of opening sister hostels in every major city of the world is yet to be achieved, so for now this hyper-ambitious project is confined to a section of a quaint wooden cottage and has just one dorm sleeping 10. But it's a cosy place run by avid travellers, who also offer a variety of Baikal tours.

Best Hostel
HOSTEL $

(☑ 3952-242 091; www.hostel-irkutsk.com; ul Karla Marksa 41; dm R65-850, d R1700-4000) Yet to live up to its immodest self-description, this airy modern place stands out in the long list of Irkutsk's claustrophobic converted-flat hostels. Orthopaedic mattresses and a large, well-equipped kitchen area are among other virtues.

Hostel Katyusha
HOSTEL $

(☑ 8-914-899 9011; www.katyusha.club; ul Timiryazeva 6; dm from R450, d R1800) Freshly opened when we visited, this brightly coloured hostel occupies a new building and has lots of common space, unlike its labyrinthine competitors in Irkutsk old town. Breakfast is available for an extra R150.

Rolling Stones Hostel
HOSTEL $

(☑ 8-950-050 2888; www.vk.com/hostelrs; ul Karla Libknekhta 6; dm R600, d with/without bathroom R2400/1600; 🛜) This fashionably designed (think lots of wood and bare brick surfaces), if slightly cavernous, hostel is run by two young travel enthusiasts, who can help with trips to Baikal and elsewhere in the region. Bunk beds with orthopaedic mattresses are built in the manner of pigeon holes, so you can hide in your private little world protected from outside views.

Admiral Hostel
HOSTEL $

(☑ 8-902-560 2440; www.irkutskhotel.irk.ru; ul Cheremkhovsky 6, apt 1; dm R500-600, d with shared bathroom R1500-1600; @ 🛜) With its Kolchak-inspired name, this cosy 13-bed apartment hostel has become well-established digs for Trans-Siberian wanderers. The lower bunks sport privacy curtains, staff sell bus tickets to Olkhon Island, there's a free (light) breakfast and you can even get your washing done. Enter from the rear of the building.

Modul
HOTEL $$

(☑ 8-950-055 5519; ul Trilissera 57; s/d from R1800/2400) Not your honeymoon dream, but a budget hotel that goes an extra mile to compensate for cheap decor and drab surroundings. Smallish rooms are clean and come with a little dining table, lots of kitchenware, a kettle and a fridge. The wooden barracks-style building is tucked in the courtyard of a high-rise apartment block, a short walk from the centre.

Hotel Yevropa
HOTEL $$

(Гостиница Европа; ☑ 3952-291 515; www.europehotel.ru; ul Baikalskaya 69; s/d from R3600/4300; ✳ 🔊) Behind nine Doric columns, immaculate rooms are realistically priced at this gleaming four-star favourite. Reception staff speak English and the Western-style breakfast is reportedly the best in town.

Hotel Sayen
HOTEL $$$

(☑ 3952-500 000; www.sayen.ru; ul Karla Marksa 13b; r from R9300; ✳ 🔊) Described by some as the finest luxury sleep east of the Urals, this very central Japanese hotel gets rave reviews and justifiably so. The 24 rooms enjoy design-mag decor, big baths and gadgets galore, going beyond the standards of many Western hotels. Twenty-four-hour room service, two pricey restaurants and a celebrated Japanese spa provide additional ways to lighten your wallet of roubles.

Kupechesky Dvor
HOTEL $$$

(☑ 3952-797 000; www.kupecheskyhotel.ru; ul Sedova 10; d/tw R5400/6200; 🔊) Rising high above the 130 Kvartal, this professionally run, freshly minted timber hotel mixes traditional wooden architecture with boldly contemporary design features. The 14 rooms come with big colour-swirl carpets, retro light switches, revolving TV towers and some of the best bathrooms in the city. The English-speaking service is top-drawer and breakfast in the tiny reception area is included.

Marussia
BOUTIQUE HOTEL $$$

(☑ 3952-500 252; www.marussiahotel.ru; ul Sedova 12; s/d R4900/5600; 🔊) This timber-built 14-room boutique hotel in the 130 Kvartal has an unpretentious feel with a brown-beige colour scheme and stripped wooden floors sporting rustic rugs but with 21st-century bathrooms. Breakfast is taken in the hotel's first-rate cafe and receptionists speak your lingo.

Hotel Viktoria
HOTEL $$$

(☑ 3952-986 808; www.victoryhotel.ru; ul Bogdana Khmelnitskogo 1; s R3600-4000; d R4200-4600; ✳ @ 🔊) Just a few steps off ul Karla Marksa, the 30 rooms at this purpose-built tower hotel remain stylish and unfrumpy despite the antique-style furniture and flowery wall coverings. If you've been in Russia a while, the courteous staff, baths in every room and online booking could feel almost eccentric. Lower rates from September through to May.

BAIKAL'S ENVIRONMENTAL ISSUES

Home to an estimated 60,000 nerpa seals as well as hundreds of endemic species, Lake Baikal is beautiful, pristine and drinkably pure in most areas. As it holds an astonishing 80% of Russia's fresh water, environmentalists are keen to keep things that way. In the 1960s, despite the pressures of the Soviet system, it was the building of Baikal's first (and only) lakeside industrial plant that galvanised Russia's first major green movement. That plant, the Baikalsk Pulp and Paper Mill, was a major polluter of the lake until it closed in 2013.

But the ecosystem extends beyond the lake itself. Another challenge includes polluted inflows from the Selenga River, which carries much of Mongolia's untreated waste into the lake. The most contentious of recent worries is the US$16 billion Eastern Siberia oil pipeline which runs from Tayshet to the Pacific coast. Completed in 2009, the route deliberately loops north, avoiding the lakeshore itself. But with a potential 1.6 million barrels of oil flowing daily across the lake's northern water catchment area, an area highly prone to seismic activity, environmentalists fear that a quake-cracked pipeline could gush crude into Baikal's feedwaters.

For more information, see the websites of regional ecogroups Baikal Wave (http://baikalwave.blogspot.co.uk), Baikal Watch (www.earthisland.org/baikal) and the wonderful Baikal Web World (www.bww.irk.ru), which has lots about the wildlife, history and legends of the lake.

Hotel Zvezda
HOTEL $$$

(☎3952-540 000; www.zvezdahotel.ru; ul Yadrint-seva 1ж; s/d from R4500/5500; ❄�🗪) Within a Swiss chalet–style building, the 64 rooms here are modern and comfortable, service is pleasant and English is spoken, though you'd expect little less for these room rates. Its atmospheric restaurant specialises in game and exotic meats.

🍴 Eating

Slata
SUPERMARKET

(Слата; ul Karla Marksa 21; ⊙24hr) Supermarkets are surprisingly rare in central Irkutsk so this centrally located, open-all-hours store is a godsend. Stocks a lot of ready-to-eat meals (meatballs, steaks, salads), ideal for long train journeys.

Poznaya na Lenina
BURYAT $

(ul Lenina 25; mains R120-180; ⊙9am-11pm) With a stylishly dark interior and Buryat-themed modern paintings on the walls, this otherwise unpretentious cheapie is possibly the best place to sample *pozy* (R40 per person) and other Buryat-Mongolian fare in the city. The picture menu helps to break the language barrier.

Baikal Love Cafe
BURYAT $

(☎8-964-112 3181; www.instagram.com/baikall-ove_irkutsk; ul Lenina 32; mains R150-250; ⊙10am-10pm) For a quick introduction to native Siberians' food, check out this little eatery that serves Buryat *buuzy* dumplings, *bukhlyor* meat broth and *suguday* (Siberian version of ceviche) as well as Russian bliny pancakes and Central Asian noodle dishes. You'll be confronted by a bear skin hanging on the wall as you enter – because Siberia.

New Zealand Pies
PASTRIES $

(☎3952-940 054; https://vk.com/nzpies; ul Sverdlova 8; pies R80; ⊙8am-8pm) Blown into central Eurasia by Pacific winds (along with myriad secondhand Japanese cars), this tiny joint churns out delicious pies with unusual fillings, from Pacific salmon and giblets in sour cream sauce to strawberries and cherries. Something worth stocking up on before boarding your Trans-Siberian train.

Mamochka
CAFE $

(Мамочка; ul Karla Marksa 41; mains R80-100; ⊙10am-9pm) With its menu of imaginative salads, filling soups and (almost) healthy mains, this is no ordinary point-and-eat canteen. Swab the decks with a Slovak lager then

sit back and admire the interior, a mishmash of old newspapers and Soviet bric-a-brac.

Govinda
VEGETARIAN $

(☎3952-933 101; 2nd fl, ul Furye 4; mains R50-100; ⊙11am-8pm; ❄🖉) Irkutsk's only meat-free restaurant is a small self-service affair with a half-hearted Indian theme and a menu of soya sausages, basmati rice, spicy soups, mild curries, quorn chilli con carne, imaginative desserts and whole plantations of tea.

★Kochevnik
MONGOLIAN $$

(Кочевник; ☎3952-200 459; http://ресторан-кочевник.рф/; ul Gorkogo 19; mains R300-1200; ⊙11am-midnight) Take your taste buds to the Mongolian steppe for some yurt-size portions of mutton, lamb and steak as well as filling soups and *buuzy* dumplings, sluiced down with a bottle from the decent foreign wine list. Smiley service, a picture menu, low prices and an exotically curtained summer terrace make this one of the most agreeable places to dine in town.

★Rassolnik
RUSSIAN $$

(www.rassolnik.su; 130 Kvartal, ul 3 lyulya 3; mains R300-700; ⊙noon-midnight) Arguably the best eating addition in the 130 Kvartal, this retro restaurant serves up a 100% Soviet-era menu (think upmarket *pelmeni, okroshka, shchi, kvas* and grandmother's pickles) in a plush Stalinist banqueting hall bedecked in nostalgia-inducing knick-knackery. Classic Soviet-era films are projected onto one wall, the menu is designed like a 1960s scrapbook and waiting staff are dressed for the occasion.

La Boulangerie & Patisserie
BAKERY $$

(☎3952-432 339; ul Karla Marksa 41/1; set menu breakfast R350; ⊙9am-noon) This is the kind of place Siberia's earliest Francophones, the Decembrists, must have dreamed would emerge in Irkutsk one day. Believe us, no freshly baked croissant feels more invigorating than the one consumed straight after disembarking from a train in the middle of Siberia. A variety of breakfast sets is on offer, including a not fully authentic Full English.

Mamay
ASIAN $$

(Мамай; ☎3952-500 560; https://vk.com/mamai_club; 130 Kvartal, ul Sedova 16; mains R350-550; ⊙noon-1am) Like a nomad galloping through the steppe, the menu of this large modern restaurant carries goodies poached from all over Asia, from authentic tom yum and East Asian noodles to Siberian specialities,

SOMETHING FISHY

No trip to Baikal is complete without tasting **omul**, a distant relative of salmon that's delicious when freshly hot-smoked. There are over 50 other varieties of Baikal fish, including perch, black grayling, ugly frilly-nosed bullheads and tasty *sig* (lake herring). While the lake isn't Russia's greatest place for anglers, from February to April it offers the unusual spectacle of **ice fishing**. There are two forms: individuals with immense patience dangle miniature hooked lines through Inuit-style ice holes; elsewhere, especially in shallow waters, whole teams of villagers string long, thin nets beneath the ice and pull out *omul* by the hundred.

You can get beneath the ice yourself with Irkutsk-based scuba-diving outfit **Baikal Tek** (www.baikaldiving.ru). But the lake's greatest divers are the unique **nerpa seals**. Indigenous to Lake Baikal, they are the only seal in the world to spend its entire existence in a freshwater environment. They thrive in many locations on the lake's shore, but usually (and wisely) stay away from human populations.

like *muksun* (white Arctic fish) fillet and Mongolian lamb grilled on charcoal.

Design Bar INTERNATIONAL $$
(📞 3952-403 399; www.facebook.com/ilove-designbar; ul Karla Marksa 40; mains R400-500; ⊘noon-midnight) On the 2nd floor of a large interior design store and decorated with a multitude of red Chinese lamps, this intimate eatery-cum-bar serves inventive fusion food as well as cocktails. A great place for lunch (set menu R300 to R350), though getting a table is sometimes tricky.

Belaruskaya Gleba BELARUSIAN $$
(📞 3952-705 701; www.belaruskayagleba.ru; ul Karla Marksa 26a; mains R400-550; ⊘noon-11pm) The lengthy menu may apply to Guinness World Records as the longest list of meat and potato combinations, but that's what Belarusian cuisine is largely about. Folksy interior design and oom-pah-pah music are meant to carry you away to the good old Eastern Europe that celebrated calories instead of rejecting them with a scornful face.

Gastobar Kamchatka FUSION $$
(Гастробар Камчатка; 📞 3952-969 696; https://vk.com/kamchatkairk; 130 Kvartal, ul 3 Iyulya 9; mains R300-500) This casual eatery has a bit of everything from everywhere, with the actual Kamchatka peninsula represented by *kizhuch* (Pacific salmon) steak served with Thai salad. You can also have *khachapuri* (Georgian cheese pastry) and excellent cottage cheese buns with condensed milk. Pop music blared from loudspeakers is a tad annoying.

Paradnaya BURGERS $$
(Парадная; 📞 3952-958 980; www.instagram.com/restobar_paradnaya; Kievskaya ul 1; mains R350-450; ⊘noon-11pm) A gastropub with comfy leather couches, Paradnaya serves gourmet burgers and salads to its hispter clientele. Perfect for beer-fuelled chats with friends and travel companions.

Figaro ITALIAN $$
(www.figaro-resto.com; ul Karla Marksa 22; mains R700-1200; ⊘8am-midnight) It's pretty obvious from the outside that Figaro is no ordinary Siberian eatery. The glass-fronted dining space peppered with works of art and graced with unpretentiously stylish laid tables fills daily with diners downing award-winning pastas, seafood platters and meat dishes including lamb, wild boar and duck prepared by real Western European chefs.

Dom Rybaka SEAFOOD $$$
(Дом рыбака; 📞 3952-484 000; ul Partizanskaya 47; mains R400-1100; ⊘noon-midnight) You might have already been introduced to Siberian fish, but for fundamental ichthyology head to this upmarket restaurant on the outskirts of the old town. *Nelma, chir, taymen* and a dozen other fish varieties are served fried, stewed, grilled, as well as fresh – in the form of *suguday,* the Siberian version of ceviche. No English menu.

🍷 Drinking & Nightlife

⭐ **Belaya Vorona** CAFE
(Белая ворона; ul Karla Marksa 37; ⊘9am-10pm Mon-Fri, 10am-11pm Sat & Sun; 📶) Disciples of the bean should definitely head to the 'White Crow', a relaxing cellar-based coffee hangout hiding from view in the cellar of a flower shop on the main drag. A funky soundtrack provides background for caffeine or a late breakfast as you catch up on emails or wish

LOCAL KNOWLEDGE

THE GREAT BAIKAL TRAIL

Inspired largely by the Tahoe Rim Trail (a hiking path encircling Lake Tahoe in California and Nevada), a small band of enthusiasts began work in summer 2003 on the first section of what was grandly named the Great Baikal Trail (GBT; in Russian, Bolshaya Baikalskaya Tropa, BBT). Every summer since has seen hundreds of volunteers flock to Lake Baikal's pebbly shores to bring the GBT organisation's stated aim – the creation of a 2000km-long network of trails encircling the whole of Lake Baikal – closer to fruition. This ambition may still be a far-off dream, but the GBT is nonetheless the first such trail system in all Russia.

These rudimentary bits of infrastructure, the GBT organisation hopes, will attract more low-impact tourists to the region, thus encouraging eco-friendly businesses to flourish and providing an alternative to industrial and mass tourism development. Volunteers and local activists are also involved in raising awareness of environmental issues among local people, visiting schools and fundraising. Nomination as a finalist in *National Geographic*'s 2008 Geotourism Challenge is arguably the GBT's greatest achievement to date and greatly raised its profile in the world of ecotourism.

Many Baikal explorers simply enjoy trekking the 540km of trails created thus far, but every year young and old from around the world join work crews for a few enjoyable weeks of clearing pathways, cutting steps, creating markers and cobbling together footbridges. Those eager to volunteer should visit the GBT website (www.greatbaikaltrail. org) for more details.

Even if you don't intend to hike all the way to Bolshie Koty (20km away), hitting the trail is one of the best things to do in Listvyanka. To access it from the embankment, walk up ul Gudina (look out for Nerpinarium) until it becomes a dirt track that goes parallel to a little stream.

As you ascend, the trail will eventually bring you to an observation point with magnificent views of Baikal. From there, it starts descending to the shore, along which the rest of the route continues. For a full-length guided trek, contact Baikaler (p509) in Irkutsk.

you could read the Cyrillic paperbacks in the small book exchange.

Brasserie BBB PUB

(https://vk.com/brasseriebbbirk; ul Karla Marksa 41/1; ⊙9am-midnight) Belgian Benoit de With ended his career as beer plant manager and set up this great beer place. It has its own beer (cheap) and dozens of kinds of Belgian and other international beers. Belgian and French food is good, but expensive. Quiz shows and football broadcasts are both regular features.

Castro Cafe CAFE

(https://vk.com/castrocafe; 130 Kvartal, ul 3 Iyulya 7; ⊙8.30am-11pm) This place is cleverly divided into two areas – the downstairs bar for those who want a quick cup of brew, and a brightly coloured upstairs lounge zone with comfy couches and cushions.

Engineria Coffee COFFEE

(Инженерия кофе; ☑3952-580 404; https:// vk.com/engineeriacoffee; ul Karla Libknekhta 2; ⊙8am-8pm) These guys are nerdishly serious about the brew and if you share their passion, you can spend half an hour talking

about percolate, immersion and AeroPress in barely comprehensible industry slang. But the bottom line is they just make great coffee.

Library Bar BAR

(☑3952-926 925; ul Kalandarashvili 9; ⊙6pm-3am) Russian literary celebrities stare at you from every wall, so after a few pints of Smolensk craft beer or a selection of great cocktails, you might be treating Mayakovsky as your buddy. But you can find better company than dead poets as the place is located next to three popular hostels, so English-speaking travellers are in no short supply.

Kwak Inn BEER HALL

(☑3952-201 141; http://kwakinn.ru; Kievskaya ul 2; ⊙noon-1am) There is a bit of an American-diner feel about this supposedly Belgian place that belongs to Estonians. But crucially, it has a very good vibe, with friendly service and indeed lots of Belgian beer on tap.

Cheshskaya Pivovarnya PUB

(Чешская пивоварня; ul Krasnogvardeyskaya 29; ⊙5pm-2am Tue-Thu, from 4pm Fri & Sat, to midnight Sun & Mon) You'll smell this place before you see it as Irkutsk's unpretentious microbrewery-pub creates its own Pilsner Urquell lager, pumping out a pungent hop aroma in the process.

Bierhaus
PUB

(☑3952-550 555; www.bier-haus.ru; ul Gryaznova 1; ⊘noon-2am Mon-Thu, to 4am Fri & Sat, to midnight Sun; ⊛) Upmarket Bavarian-style *bierstube* (beer hall with heavy wooden furniture) serving Newcastle Brown and Guinness as well as German beers and sausages. Enter from ul Karla Marksa.

Lenin Street Coffee
CAFE

(ul Lenina 9; ⊘8.30am-9pm; ⊛) Simple, no-nonsense coffee place with a Western feel and pricey drinks. Good central place to hang out and surf the web.

☆ Entertainment

Benzin
LIVE MUSIC

(Бензин; ☑3952-204 205; https://vk.com/club-benzin; ul Fridrikha Engelsa 8b) A slick entertainment centre with four bars, frequent live gigs and DJ parties.

Rock'n'Roll Pub
LIVE MUSIC

(www.vk.com/rocknrollpub; Kievskaya ul 24) Head to this cheap no-frills pub and diner to check what Siberian and indie music are about.

Philharmonic Hall
LIVE MUSIC

(Филармония; ☑3952-242 968; www.filarmoniya.irk.ru; ul Dzerzhinskogo 2) Historic building staging regular children's shows and musical programs from jazz to classical.

Aistyonok Puppet Theatre
PUPPET THEATRE

(Театр кукол Аистёнок; ☑3952-205 825; www.aistenok-irkutsk.ru; ul Baikalskaya 32) Marionette shows for the kiddies.

🛍 Shopping

Central Market
MARKET

(☑3952-667 545; ul Chekhova 22; ⊘8am-7pm) Very central indeed, Irkutsk's well-maintained and perfectly authentic market is the place to stock up on cedar nuts, taiga herbs and Siberian fish, notably the famous Baikal *omul*, which can be packed in hermetic cellophane for transportation by air.

Karibu
CLOTHING

(ul Timiryazeva 34; ⊘10am-7pm Mon-Sat, noon-5pm Sun) Tiny shop selling beautifully furry *unty* (traditional deerskin cowboy boots) made on-site and typically costing around R10,000. Some English spoken.

Prodalit
BOOKS

(Продалитъ; ul Furye 8; ⊘10am-7pm Mon-Fri, to 6pm Sat & Sun) This large bookstore on the 2nd floor of a small shopping centre sells regional and city maps, Baikal- and Irkutsk-themed coffee-table books and Lonely Planet guides in Russian.

ℹ Information

Post Office (ul Karla Marksa 28; ⊘8am-8pm Mon-Fri, 9am-6pm Sat & Sun)

Tourist Office (☑3952-205 018; www.irkvisit.info; ul Dekabrskikh Sobyty 77; ⊘9am-8pm; ⊛) Municipally funded tourist office with English-speaking staff, free wi-fi, free city maps and lots of well-produced brochures and booklets on Irkutsk and Lake Baikal. Between June and August staff are posted at strategic points around the city handing out info.

www.irk.ru Local city info.

www.irkutsk.org Bags of information on every aspect of the city.

ℹ Getting There & Away

AIR

Irkutsk's antiquated little 'international' **airport** (www.iktport.ru) is handily placed near the city centre. Foreign destinations include Bangkok, Beijing, Seoul, Tokyo and Ulaanbaatar. Direct flights to Germany were scrapped in 2011 but might restart in the coming years.

For Moscow, there are direct flights with S7 Airlines, Aeroflot and some dodgier airlines (from R15,000, three daily). Iraero provides a crucial link to Kyzyl in Tuva (R4700, two weekly), though Antonov-24 planes are not for the faint-hearted.

Irkutsk also enjoys direct air links to dozens of other domestic destinations, with tickets for all services sold through the convenient **Central Air Agency** (Центральная авиакасса; ☑3952-500 703; http://ikt.moyreys.ru; ul Gorkogo 29; ⊘8am-7pm).

BOAT

In summer hydrofoils buzz along the Angara River to Listvyanka and up Lake Baikal to Bolshie Koty, Olkhon Island, Ust-Barguzin and Nizhneangarsk. Departures are from the **Raketa Hydrofoil Station** (Речной вокзал; Prichal Raketa) beyond the Angara Dam in Solnechny Mikro-Rayon, two minutes' walk from bus 16 stop 'Raketa'. Timetables are posted by the quay. Services in the other direction to Bratsk leave from a separate jetty in the city centre.

All services are operated by **VSRP** (☑3952-287 115; www.vsrp.ru). Check the English-language website for all times and prices.

BUS

From the partially renovated **bus station** (https://avtovokzal-on-line.ru; ul Oktyabrskoy Revolyutsii; ⊙ 5.30am-8pm), book tickets at least a day ahead in summer for Arshan (R400, four to five hours, two daily), Listvyanka (R110, 1¼ hours, hourly) via Taltsy (R90), Bratsk (R1050, 11 hours, eight daily) and Ust-Kut (on the BAM railway; R1800, 16 hours). The station has a left-luggage office.

Minibuses to Ulan-Ude (R1000, seven hours) and Slyudyanka (R200, two hours) depart throughout the day from the train station forecourt, where you can also catch a minibus to Arshan, if more convenient.

TRAIN

Irkutsk has the following rail connections:

Beijing kupe R18,200, 70 hours, twice weekly

Chita platskart/kupe from R2600/2900, 16 hours to 20 hours, up to six daily

Khabarovsk platskart/kupe R6600/10,000, 57 to 65 hours, two daily

Krasnoyarsk platskart/kupe from R2600/4600, 18 hours, up to nine daily

Moscow platskart/kupe from R13,000/R16,000, three days and three hours to five days and 18 hours, up to seven daily

Severobaikalsk platskart/kupe R3800/R5600, 34 hours, daily

Slyudyanka elektrichka R180, four hours, four daily

Ulaanbaatar kupe R7200, 27 hours, daily

Ulan-Ude platskart R1600, kupe R1900 to R2300, 6½ hours to 8½ hours, up to nine daily

Vladivostok platskart/kupe R5350/10,700, 72 hours, three daily

ⓘ Getting Around

Within the central area, walking is usually the best idea as one-way systems make bus routes confusing.

Frequent trolleybus 4 and bus/marshrutka 20, 80, 90 and countless others connect the city centre with the airport. A taxi to/from the airport costs around R110 with Gett or Maxim.

From the train station, trams 1, 2 and 4A run to ul Lenina and ul Timiryazeva, 4A continuing on to the bus station. Tram 4 links the central market with the bus station.

Gett and Maxim taxi app services are available. A typical fare for a ride in the centre is R90.

Listvyanka   Листвянка

♪ 3952 / POP 1970 / ⊙ MOSCOW +5HR

As the closest lakeside village to Irkutsk, Listvyanka – aka the 'Baikal Riviera' – is the touristy spot where most travellers go to dunk their toes in Baikal's pure waters. Having picked at *omul*, admired the hazy views of the Khamar Daban mountains on the opposite shore and huffed their way from one end of the village to the other, most are on a *marshrutka* back to Irkutsk late afternoon. But there's more to Listvyanka: stay longer to hike the Great Baikal Trail, discover more about the lake at the Baikal Museum and chill out at one of Siberia's most eco-friendly sleeps.

If you're looking for beach fun, the eastern shore (Buryatiya) is the place to build sandcastles. However, what the Buryat shore doesn't have is Listvyanka's range of activities: from short boat trips to diving and jet-skiing in the summer and ice mountain biking to lake treks and ice sculpting in the winter.

◉ Sights

Sourcing a map at Irkutsk's tourist office before you set off will save a lot of hunting.

Chersky Rock   NATURAL FEATURE
Listvyanka's best viewpoint, overlooking the source of the Angara, is named after Jan Czerski, a 19th-century Polish gentleman explorer. It is best accessed via the cable car of the mediocre Eastland ski resort (R300 return). To reach the resort, take a taxi or walk uphill along the road that starts near Baikal Museum.

As a young man, Czerski was exiled to Siberia for taking part in the 1863 uprising against the Russian Empire. Despite a complete lack of formal education, he grew to become one of Russia's most celebrated geographers and explorers of Siberia.

Retro Park   GARDENS
(ul Kulikova 62b; R100) This garden near the St Nicholas Church is full of wacky sculpture pieces fashioned from old Soviet-era cars and motorbikes. You can check out a few samples attached to the railings on the embankment so you know what to expect before heading there. To find the Retro Park, follow the signs on ul Kulikova.

Baikal Museum   MUSEUM
(www.bm.isc.irk.ru; ul Akademicheskaya 1, Rogatka; R310, minisub R500; ⊙ 9am-7pm, to 9pm 15 May-15 Sep) One of only three museums in the world dedicated solely to a lake, this sometimes overly scientific institution examines the science of Baikal from all angles. Pass quickly by the gruesomely discoloured fish samples and seal embryos in formaldehyde to the

tanks containing two frolicsome nerpa seals and the various Baikal fish that you may later encounter on restaurant menus.

Another attraction is a minisub simulator, which takes you deep down into Baikal's nippy waters. Adjoining the building is a park containing over 400 species of plants, some rare or endangered.

St Nicholas Church   CHURCH
(ul Kulikova 90) Listvyanka's small mid-19th-century timber church is dedicated to St Nicholas, who supposedly saved its merchant sponsor from a Baikal shipwreck.

🏃 Activities

Baikal Dog Sledding Centre   DOG SLEDDING
(☑8-983-412 2694, 8-914-940 4474; http://baikalsled.blogspot.ru; ul Kulikova 136a) From December to March the centre offers thrilling dog sledding on forest tracks. All kinds of tours are available, from 5km tasters to multi-day trans-Baikal ice expeditions costing tens of thousands of roubles. Some English spoken. Book through Baikaler (p509) in Irkutsk.

🛌 Sleeping

Many Irkutsk tour agents and even some hostels and hotels have their own guesthouse or homestay in Listvyanka. For turn-up-and-hope homestays, the best street to try first is ul Chapaeva.

★ Belka Hostel   HOSTEL $
(☑8-952-626 1251; www.baikaler.com; ul Chapaeva 77a; dm/tw R600/1500; @) 🏄 This purpose-built hostel located at the far end of ul Chapaeva provides top-notch digs for backpacker prices, leaving Listvyanka's other flat-footed accommodation in its green dust. From the energy-saving light bulbs and basalt-foam insulation to the solar-heated water and solar-generated electricity, owner Jack Sheremetoff has crafted a low-impact haven with lots of personal touches.

Start the day with a bit of sun worship on the yoga deck and breakfast on the forest-facing chill-out area; end it with a scramble up the mini climbing wall and a scrub-down in the *banya* before snuggling up in a handmade timber bed (no bunks) in an en-suite dorm. Two guest kitchens, 24-hour reception and many other features you won't find anywhere else. Booking well ahead is essential.

No fibre-optic cable laid in this part of Listvyanka, so sadly no wi-fi.

Derevenka   HOTEL $$
(☑8-914-877 5599; www.baikal-derevenka.ru; ul Gornaya 1; s/d from R1500/2000, tent pitch R200; ☎) On a ridge behind the shore road, cute little wooden huts (named after Baikal's winds) with stove-heaters, private toilets and hot water (but shared showers) offer Listvyanka's most appealing semibudget choice. Behind the complex is Listvyanka's only official camp site. Rates include breakfast.

Gavan Baikala   GUESTHOUSE $$
(☑3952-500 620; www.gavanbaykal.com; ul Gudina 84; d/q R3000/4500) This chalet-styled log house has a large common balcony with a distant view of the lake, and pine-scented rooms with soft mattresses and good shower cabins. Breakfast is served in the Chekhovian dining room. Conveniently located on the road leading up to the Great Baikal Trail.

Baikal Chalet   GUESTHOUSE $$
(☑8-914 895 1961, 3952-462 244; www.baikalcomplex.com; ul Gudina 75; tw R3200) The 13 comfortable twin rooms in this timber guesthouse around 800m back from the lake are a good deal. Its sister guesthouse in Bolshie Koty offers similar rates and standards. Breakfast included.

Priboy   HOTEL $$
(☑3952-496 725; http://hotel-priboy.ru; upper fl, ul Gorkogo 101; r from R3500) Spitting distance from the lake in the port area, this glass-and-steel hunk of incongruity has seen renovation in recent years, rendering the four lake-view rooms some of the best deals in town. The other 15 chambers are less spectacular but rates include breakfast taken in the downstairs cafe.

Dream of Baikal Hotel   HOTEL $$
(☑3952-496 888; www.dreamofbaikal.ru; ul Gorkogo 105; s R3500-5500, d R3800-5600; ☎) Set just an endemic species' throw from Baikal's lulling waves/crumbly ice, this newish, clumsily named, purpose-built hotel by the market is a step up from Listvyanka's usual timber guesthouses. Rooms bedecked in generous drapery are packed with faux-antique furniture. The reception works 24 hours, apart from when the receptionist dozes off just after lunch.

U Ozera   HOTEL $$$
(У Озера; ☑3952-496 777; www.listvjanka-baikal.ru; Irkutsk Hwy km3; d R4000-5000, cottages R5500; ☎) Just 10m from the shoreline, it's not surprising that all nine rooms (doubles only) at this small hotel have wonderful lake

WORTH A TRIP

TALTSY MUSEUM OF ARCHITECTURE & ETHNOGRAPHY

About 47km southeast of Irkutsk, 23km before Listvyanka, **Taltsy Museum of Architecture & Ethnography** (Архитектурно-этнографический музей Тальцы; http://talci-irkutsk.ru; R250; ☺10am-5pm, to 4pm in winter) is an impressive outdoor collection of old Siberian buildings set in a delightful riverside forest. Amid the renovated farmsteads are two chapels, a church, a watermill, some Evenki graves and the eye-catching 17th-century Iliminsk Ostrog watchtower. Listvyanka–Irkutsk buses and *marshrutky* stop on request at Taltsy's entrance (look out for the roadside 'Музей' sign), and the ticket booth is a minute's walk through the forest.

views. Rooms are a little too intimate but have balconies where you can stretch out. The cottages sleeping two lack the views but offer more space. Located between Krestovka and Rogatka.

Krestovaya pad   HOTEL $$$
(☏3952-496 863; www.krestovayapad.ru; ul Gornaya 14a; tw & d from R6500; ☏) This stylishly upmarket complex, with very comfortable international-standard pine-clad rooms, dominates the hillside above Krestovka.

Hotel Mayak   HOTEL $$$
(Отель Маяк; ☏3952-496 910; www.mayakhotel.ru; ul Gorkogo 85a; r from R4000; ☏) There were once (now mothballed) plans to transform Listvyanka and other villages on the shores of Lake Baikal into purpose-built resorts with plasticky upmarket hotels like the 'Lighthouse'. The village's most in-your-face hotel has Western-standard rooms, a good restaurant and an unbeatable location near the hydrofoil quay.

✖ Eating

Near the port, the large fish and souvenir market is the best place to buy smoked *omul* and is surrounded by greasy spoons offering cheap *plov* and shashlyk.

Café Podlemore   CAFE $
(ul Gorkogo 31; mains R200-300; ☺9am-midnight) The Podlemore has porridge and oven-fresh pastries, but rather flummoxed serving staff. Early opening makes it a popular breakfast halt.

Listvyanka Club   RUSSIAN $$
(☏3952-496 739; ul Sudzilovskogo 2; mains R300-500; ☺10am-11pm) This new airy lakeside place focuses on Baikal fish, with *omul* cooked in cedar seed juice (Russians call it cedar milk), bringing together the two most iconic local staples. There is also an ample list of meat dishes, including a good variety of homemade *pelmeni* dumplings.

Proshly Vek   RUSSIAN $$
(Прошлый век; ul Lazo 1; meals R460-700; ☺noon-midnight) Listvyanka's most characterful eatery has a nautical theme, a fish-heavy menu and Baikal views. The upper floor is filled with fascinating old junk, which you can admire while tucking into *omul* done any which way you please.

Berg House   RUSSIAN $$
(ul Gorkogo 59; mains R400-500; ☺11am-2am; ☏) Between the Mayak Hotel and the post office, this Anglophone-friendly cafe has understatedly laid picnic tables, pleasant service, large portions of fish and meat, as well as draft beer.

❶ Orientation

The village extends 4.5km from Rogatka at the mouth of the Angara to the market area. A single road skirts the shore, with three valleys running inland where most of Listvyanka's characterful timber dwellings and accommodation options are located. There's no public transport, which can mean some very long walks.

❶ Information

ATMs can be found in the Mayak and Priboy hotels.
Post Office (ul Gorkogo 49; ☺8am-1pm & 2-8pm Mon-Fri, 9am-6pm Sat)
Tourist Office (☏3952-656 099; hydrofoil quay; ☺10am-6pm) Located at the *marshrutka* terminus (there are several imposters), this surprisingly useful office hands out free maps as well as providing bus, ferry and hydrofoil timetables and offering imaginative Baikal boat trips. Bike rental available.

❶ Getting There & Away

Hourly *marshrutky* (R120, luggage R50, 1¼ hours) leave for Irkutsk from outside the tourist office (where tickets are bought). The last service departs at 9pm.

From mid-May to late September, hydrofoils stop at Listvyanka between Irkutsk and Bolshie Koty three times a day.

A tiny, battered car ferry lumbers across the never-frozen Angara River mouth to Port Baikal from Rogatka four times a day mid-May to mid-October, and just twice a day in the winter months.

Contact VSRP (☑3952-287 115; www.vsrp.ru) in Irkutsk for details of all these boat services.

Port Baikal Порт Байкал

☑3952 / POP 1960 / ☉ MOSCOW +5HR

You'd be excused for dismissing Port Baikal as a rusty semi-industrial eyesore when seen from Listvyanka across the unbridged mouth of the Angara River. But it has a melancholic appeal, with a pretty train station teleported here from somewhere in Central Europe and a port where derelict vessels are laid to rest. A kilometre southwest of the port, Baranchiki is a ramshackle 'real' village with lots of unkempt but authentic Siberian cottages and a couple of accommodation options. Awkward ferry connections mean that Port Baikal remains largely uncommercialised, lacking Listvyanka's attractions but also its crowds. It's thus popular with more meditative visitors, but the main draw is that it's both the beginning and terminus of the Circumbaikal Railway.

From 1900 to 1904 the Trans-Siberian Railway tracks from Irkutsk came to an abrupt halt at Port Baikal. They continued on Lake Baikal's far eastern shore at Mysovaya (Babushkin), and the watery gap was plugged by ice-breaking steamships, including the *Angara*, now restored and on view in Irkutsk. Later, the tracks were pushed south and around the lake. This Circumbaikal line required so many impressive tunnels and bridges that it earned the nickname 'The Tsar's Jewelled Buckle'. With the damming of the Angara River in the 1950s, the original Irkutsk–Port Baikal section was submerged and replaced with an Irkutsk–Kultuk shortcut (today's Trans-Siberian). That left poor little Port Baikal to wither away at the dead end of a rarely used but incredibly scenic branch line.

◎ Sights

Museum of Circum-Baikal Railway MUSEUM

(Port Baikal railway station; R30; ☉opens by request) Housed inside the nicely restored train station, this new and informative exhibition tells the story of Circumbaikal Railway. Toy train buffs will be delighted by the vintage scaled models of main tunnels.

☐ Sleeping & Eating

U Starogo Mayaka HOTEL $$

(☑3952-643 994, 3952-645 915; dm R800, d from R2200) Not too busy with its main occupation, Port Baikal's pretty railway station is part-timing as a hotel. Clean and bland in an almost nostalgically Soviet way, the rooms on the station's 2nd floor are perfect for spending a night, if you are late for the last ferry to Listvyanka.

Fort Baikal GUESTHOUSE $$

(☑3952-242 415, 8-908-668 73 91; www.fortbaikal.ru; Shcholka pad; cabins per person R1200; ☒) Around 2km away from Port Baikal and geared primarily for domestic tourists, this modern *turbaza* has summer-only rustic log houses with funky wooden fixtures, traditional wooden stoves and authentic samovars. Mountain bikes and horses available for hire. Staff can pick you up at the port, if you let them know in advance.

ⓘ Getting There & Away

The ferry to Rogatka (R62) near Listvyanka's Baikal Museum runs five times daily between mid-June and mid-September (at 8.15am, 11.15am, 4.15pm, 6.15pm and 8.15pm), but less frequently out of season and only twice in winter. Check the schedule beforehand. From mid-June to August there are direct hydrofoils to/from Irkutsk. All services are operated by VSRP (p515).

One or two trains a day come via the slow Circumbaikal route from Slyudyanka.

Olkhon Island Остров Ольхон

POP 1670 / ☉ MOSCOW +5HR

Halfway up Lake Baikal's western shore and reached by a short ferry journey from Sakhyurta (aka MRS), the serenely beautiful Olkhon Island is a wonderful place from which to view the lake and relax during a tour of Siberia. Considered one of five global poles of shamanic energy by the Buryat people, the 72km-long island's 'capital' is the unlovely village of Khuzhir (Хужир), which has seen quite a serious tourist boom over the last few years, improbably triggered by a song about Baikal winning a TV contest in China.

◎ Sights & Activities

Escaping Khuzhir's dusty, dung-splattered streets is the key to enjoying Olkhon. Every morning tours (from R900 per person) leave from Khuzhir's guesthouses to the north and south of the island, the most popular a seven-hour bounce in a UAZ minivan to dramatic **Cape Khoboy** at Olkhon's very northern tip, where Baikal seals sometimes bask.

Driver-guides cook fish soup for lunch over an open fire, but few speak any English. Between January and March, UAZ vans drive at least half the way on ice roads around the island. See the Nikita's Homestead website (www.olkhon.info) for details of this and other excursions (boat and even airplane trips are on offer in summer). Otherwise, rent a bike and strike out on your own.

In winter, bikes with studded tyres, as well as skates, are available for hire at Nikita's, but take all food and water with you as there's none outside Khuzhir.

Shaman Rocks   LANDMARK

The unmistakable Shaman Rocks are neither huge nor spectacular, but they have become the archetypal Baikal vista found on postcards and travel-guide covers. A long strip of sandy beach lines the Maloe More (Little Sea) east of the rocks.

Museum   MUSEUM

(ul Pervomayskaya 24; R100; ⊘10am-6pm) Khuzhir's small museum displays a random mix of stuffed animals, Soviet-era junk, local art and the personal possessions of its founder, Nikolai Revyakin, a teacher for five decades at the school next door.

🛏 Sleeping & Eating

Khuzhir has an ever-growing range of places to stay, though the vast majority of independent travellers bunk down at Nikita's Homestead. If all 50 rooms at Nikita's are full, staff can arrange homestays costing around R850, with meals taken at the Homestead canteen. Booking ahead anywhere in Khuzhir is only necessary during July and August.

★Nikita's Homestead   GUESTHOUSE $

(⊘8-914-895 7865; www.olkhon.info; ul Kirpichnaya 8; r incl breakfast & dinner with/without bathroom from R2200/1800; ⊘reception 8am-11pm) Occupying a sizeable chunk of Khuzhir, this intricately carved timber complex has grown (and continues to grow) into one of Siberia's top traveller hang-outs. The basic rooms in myriad shapes and sizes are attractively decorated with petroglyphs and other ethnic finery and heated by wood-burning stoves – but only a select

few have showers (put your name down for the *banya*).

The organic meals are served two times a day in the large canteen near reception and two other (paid) eateries stand behind. There's a small cycle-hire centre and a packed schedule of excursions and activities. Note there is no alcohol for sale at Nikita's and consumption on the premises is frowned upon.

U Olgi   GUESTHOUSE $

(⊘8-908-661 9015; ul Lesnaya 3-1; full board per person R1300) This well-liked option has nine rooms, three in a typical village house and six in a purpose-built, pine-fragrant building opposite. New showers and flushing toilets plus scrumptious Siberian fare cooked by Olga herself make this a winner every time. Book through Baikaler (p509) in Irkutsk.

Solnechnaya   GUESTHOUSE $

(Солнечная; ⊘3952-683 216; www.olkhon.com; ul Solnechnaya 14; half-board per person R1300-1600; @) A pleasant place to stay offering a good range of activities. Accommodation is in two-storey cabins and tiny single-room shacks with verandahs. Enter from ul Solnechnaya or from near the relay station at the top of the hill.

Voskresenie   GUESTHOUSE $$$

(Воскресенье; ⊘8-904-117 7526; olhonsng@gmail.com; ul Pushkina 16; r R4200) The owners, a former Soviet table-tennis champion and his polyglot wife, indulge in interior design passion, as you will immediately notice when you move into one of only four individually designed rooms that sleep up to three people. Newer ones display a significant progress in both skill and material supply.

The incredibly nice and well-informed hosts also run a cute coffee shop in the premises.

Baikal View   RESORT $$$

(⊘8-983-698 9460; www.baikalview.com; ul Rossiyskaya 17; s/d incl breakfast from R9000/9850) Looking from the outside like a research station in Antarctica, this upmarket establishment has rooms with laconic Scandinavian-style interior design featuring many light-coloured wooden surfaces. In summer there is an outdoor swimming pool. Available all year is a nice restaurant and spa that offers bath treatment in a *taban-arhan* wooden barrel.

BOLSHIE KOTY

Tiny and roadless, this serene Baikal village (Большие Коты) is what the great Siberian escape is all about. But things weren't always this quiet: in the 19th century Koty experienced a mini gold rush and boasted soap and candle factories, a glassworks, churches and a school. Today all that's long over, leaving Irkutsk bourgeoisie to assemble their lakeside dachas in peace.

A section of the Great Baikal Trail runs between Koty and Listvyanka, a fabulous full- or half-day hike (around 20km). Take plenty of food (drink from the lake) as there's none en route.

Two-day guided treks from Listvyanka to Bolshie Koty with **Baikaler** (p509) cost R7000 person (provided there are at least two people to form a group), including accommodation and food.

The only other way to reach Bolshie Koty (unless you hike from Listvyanka) is aboard one of the three hydrofoils a day from Irkutsk (via Listvyanka). Check **VSRP**(☑ 3952-287 115; www.vsrp.ru) for times and ticket prices. Winter ice roads briefly unite the village with the outside world.

Three minutes' walk from the hydrofoil quay is the **Lesnaya 7 Hostel** (☑ 8-904-118 7275; www.lesnaya7.com; ul Lesnaya 7; dm R700; ☺ summer only; @).

ℹ️ Information

There's no ATM on the island, so you'll need to bring enough cash to cover your stay.

ℹ️ Getting There & Away

The simplest way to reach Olkhon is aboard the *marshrutka* that leaves Irkutsk's hostels around 8.30am (R800). Many other services run in July and August but can be impossible to track down in Irkutsk.

With a little warning, agencies or hostels can usually find you a ride in a private car to/from Irkutsk (5½ hours) for R2500 per seat, R10,000 for the whole car. Prices include the short ferry ride to/from MRS – from mid-January to March an ice road replaces the ferry. When ice is partly formed or partly melted, the island is completely cut off for motor vehicles, but there is an ad hoc minihovercraft service operated by locals.

In summer a hydrofoil service operates from Irkutsk to Olkhon, dropping passengers near the ferry terminal, from where it's possible to hitch a paid lift into Khuzhir. See VSRP (p515) for times and prices.

Slyudyanka Слюдянка

☑ 39544 / POP 18,240 / ☺ MOSCOW +5HR

The lakeside railway town of Slyudyanka provides a grittier alternative to Listvyanka for those eager to get up close to Lake Baikal's waves/groaning ice and the Trans-Siberian Railway, which hugs the lake's pebbly shore either side of town. Most alight from a train at the glittering, solid-marble train station, which is a mere five-minute walk from Lake Baikal.

👁️ Sights & Activities

A rather strenuous trail heads up **Pik Cherskogo** (aka Mt Chersky) along the former post road to Mongolia, which formed a part of the Silk Route. Turbaza Pik Cherskogo provides accommodation at the top of the mountain, but book in advance.

The annual **Peak Chersky race**, usually held around 20 August, involves participants running either a section of or the entire 44km distance to the top. Inquire at Delight or Slyudyanka Hostel about dates and participation.

A popular picnic excursion is to **Cape Shaman**, an easy 4km stroll north towards Kultuk along Baikal's gravelly shore. Owners of the Slyudyanka Hostel run guided trips there and to the former marble and mica (*slyud* in Russian, hence the town's name) mines southeast of the town.

Baikal Mineral Museum   MUSEUM
(ul Slyudyanaya 36; R300; ☺ 10am-7pm) Geology buffs should consider heading to the privately run Baikal Mineral Museum, which claims to exhibit every mineral known to man.

East Siberian Railway Museum   MUSEUM
(ul Zheleznodorozhnaya 22; R100; ☺ 8am-noon & 1-5pm Mon-Fri) Amid the nearby railway repair sheds and admin buildings you'll find this fascinating little museum housed in an ornate wooden building set back from ul Zheleznodorozhnaya. There are exhibitions on the Circumbaikal Railway, the history of Slyudyanka and Lake Baikal, plus heaps of railway paraphernalia.

CIRCUMBAIKAL RAILWAY

Excruciatingly slow train ride or a great social event? Opinions are mixed, but taking one of the four-per-week Slyudyanka–Port Baikal trains along the scenic, lake-hugging Circumbaikal Railway remains a popular tourist activity. The most picturesque sections of the route are the valley, pebble beach and headland at Polovinnaya (around halfway), and the bridge area at km149. Note that most trains *from* Port Baikal travel by night and so are useless for sightseeing. Another thing to remember: if you travel outside summer season, you won't be able to catch a ferry to Listvyanka when you arrive in Port Baikal, so you'll have to overnight there. In summer, the last ferry departs at 8.45pm, so you'll be all right even if your Matanya train arrives late.

The old stone tunnels, cliff cuttings and bridges are an attraction even for non-train-buffs who might drive alongside sections of the route on winter ice roads from Kultuk. Hiking the entire route or just sections of the peaceful track is also popular, and walking a couple of kilometres from Port Baikal leads to some pleasant, if litter-marred, beaches. Or get off an Irkutsk–Slyudyanka *elektrichka* at Temnaya Pad three hours into the journey and hike down the stream valley for about an hour. You should emerge at km149 on the Circumbaikal track, from where you can continue by train to Port Baikal if you time things well.

At the time of research, Matanya trains departed from a side platform at Slyudyanka I station at 1.20pm on Monday, Thursday, Friday and Sunday – check timetables carefully. An additional but more expensive tourist train direct from Irkutsk departs at 8.20am on Wednesday and Saturday, reaching Slyudyanka at 10.30am. Except in high summer season, Matanya trains arrive in Port Baikal in the evening after the last ferry for Listvyanka has departed, so organising accommodation in advance is advisable.

An expensive alternative to Matanya is the retro-train tour run by Tu-tu Baikal (☑ 3952-500 849; http://tutubaikal.tilda.ws; ul Stepana Razina 26, Irkutsk; tour with/without Baikal view seat R5000/4500). An early-20th-century steamer pulls modern comfortable carriages, departing from Irkutsk train station twice a week at 8am and reaching Port Baikal in the evening. From there, people are ferried back to Irkutsk. Make sure you pay R500 extra for a Baikal view seat, otherwise the trip may turn into a disappointment.

Yet another, fun way of exploring the Circumbaikal Railway is by high-speed boat, which takes people from Listvyanka to Polovinnaya, where it stops for a picnic before returning back. Tours run by Krugobaikalsky Ekspress (☑ 3952-202 973; www.krugobaikalka.ru; bul Gagarina 68g, Irkutsk; tours adult/child R4700/4000) include transfers to/from Ikrutsk.

🛏 Sleeping & Eating

Self-catering is your best bet in Slyudyanka, unless you are staying at Delight, where every meal is a feast.

Slyudyanka Hostel   HOSTEL $
(☑ 8-902-576 7344, 39544-53 198; www.hostel-s.com; ul Shkolnaya 10, apt 7; dm R600; @) Six-bed hostel-homestay at the southern end of town providing a great opportunity to experience small-town Siberian family life. A fully equipped kitchen, heaps of outdoorsy tours and hikes, and evenings of authentic Baikal hospitality await for those who make the effort to find the place. It's a 20-minute walk, five-minute *marshrutka* ride (No 1) or R120 taxi journey along ul Parizhskoy Komuny. Booking ahead is pretty much essential.

Turbaza Pik Cherskogo   HOSTEL $
(☑ 8-902-543 6795; https://vk.com/turbazapik; tent pitch/dm R150/500) For the brave and intrepid who have made it all the way to the top of Chersky Peak, spartan dorms equipped with a gas cooker are available as an alternative to carrying a tent, but book in advance. Water is in very short supply, so a garden shower comes at extra charge – cold/hot water R100/200 per bucket.

Delight   HOMESTAY $$
(☑ 8-902-178 1788; rufenok@gmail.com; ul Kapotina 14; r R1800) Trekking and cycling enthusiasts Rufina and Yevgeny run this cosy and well-equipped homestay with just two rooms and a large shared bathroom, which contains a Trans-Siberian traveller's ultimate delight – a full-sized bathtub. For a small extra fee, Rufina cooks excellent din-

ners as well as breakfasts that by far surpass most served in multistarred hotels.

English-speaking Yevgeny is a wealth of info on Chersky Peak and Tunka Valley hikes, Munku-Sardyk climbs and ice treks on Baikal.

❶ Getting There & Away

Elektrichki (R70, four daily) from Irkutsk take three hours to arrive at Slyudyanka 1 station; ordinary passenger trains (*platskart* R850, up to eight daily) take just two hours. Slyudyanka is also the usual starting point for the Circumbaikal Railway trip. From the bus station *marshrutky* run to Irkutsk (R190, two hours, every 30 minutes). For Arshan, change at nearby Kultuk, reachable by local *marshrutka* (R36, 20 minutes).

Arshan & Tunka Valley

Аршан и Тункинская долина

📋 30156 / POP 2600 / ⊙ MOSCOW +5HR

Backed by the dramatic, cloud-wreathed peaks of the Eastern Sayan Mountains, the once-drowsy Buryat spa village of Arshan has been rudely awoken from its slumber in recent years. The fast-flowing Kyngyrga River still murmurs with ice-cold water from elevated valleys above the village, the prayer wheels still twirl at the tranquil little Buddhist temples and cows still blunder through the streets, but Russian-style tourism has intruded into the idyllic scene, bringing 24-hour *banya,* cut-price vodka, pounding stereos and grisly service in its wake. But despite this, Arshan is still the best base in the Tunka Valley from which to strike out into the mountains, with some superb hikes accessible on foot from the village.

◉ Sights & Activities

Arshan in Buryat means 'natural spring' and it's the pleasantly sweet, health-giving mineral water that most Russians come for. The huge Sayany Spa (closed after going bankrupt) stands at the entrance to the village on the main street (ul Traktovaya), which then fires itself 2km straight towards the mountains. Opposite the spa grounds, the **Dechen Ravzhalin Datsan** has two sparkling new prayer wheels, a miniature stupa and a dazzlingly colourful interior. From here ul Traktovaya then climbs in a parade of shops, derelict Soviet architecture and plasticky cafes and guesthouses towards the bus station, after which it swerves west to the sprawling

Kurort Arshan resort, where you can sample the water for free at a well-maintained well room, known as *byuvet.* Head up the stream from here to access the mountain footpaths or cross the river and walk 20 minutes through the forest to the diminutive **Bodkhi Dkharma Datsan**, set in an idyllic mountain-backed glade.

Arshan is a popular destination for trekkers, but even popular trails are virtually unmarked, which makes hiking on your own quite problematic. What anyone can safely do is explore the mouth of **Kyngyrga River canyon**. To reach it, walk through the Mongolian market, then climb white stairs, leading into Kurort Arshan park. From there, a forested trail runs along the precipice above the narrowing river valley. You'll finally reach wooden stairs descending to the first in a long cascade of Kyngyrga waterfalls. From the top of the stairs, a steeply ascending trail leads to an observation point with breathtaking views of both the canyon and the Tunka Valley. Think well before venturing anywhere beyond that point, as you are entering a challenging and sometimes dangerous terrain.

Arshan's most popular hike is the ascent of the 2412m-tall **Peak of Love**, towering above the village. Locals often dismiss it as 'an easy hike that anyone can do'. Don't believe them. Although you don't need special training or equipment, it is a physically demanding three- to five-hour ascent along a largely unmarked trail in mountains that are famous for sudden rainstorms or snowfalls. You'll need about the same time to walk back. If you really want to do it, stick with Russians who know the trail, or – even better – prearrange a guided hike with travel agencies in Irkutsk. The trail begins behind a quarry at the far end of Kurort Arshan.

Mongolian Market   MARKET
(⊙dusk-dawn) Traders bring Mongolian herbs, spices, clothes and leather items from across the nearby border to this colourful makeshift market that stretches for a few hundred metres along the Kyngyrga valley inside the territory of Kurort Arshan.

🛏 Sleeping & Eating

Even late at night locals line the bottom end of ul Traktovaya like hitchhikers, brandishing their 'Жильё' (rooms) signs in hope. These sometimes turn out to be unacceptably basic homestays from R500 per bed – check standards before committing. There is also about a dozen of professionally run *pensions*, typically located in large log houses. These are better booked in advance.

Eateries are thin on the ground, as most visitors prebook full board in their guesthouses. Some of the cafes at the top of ul Traktovaya are truly dire.

Yasnaya Polyana
GUESTHOUSE $

(Ясная Поляна; ☑8-904-114 7808; ul Traktovaya 109; s/d R350/700; ☺Jun-Sep) A friendly local English teacher runs this compound of 10 pine cottages, each containing two beds, a table, a stove ring and sometimes a kettle. Otherwise, things are pretty basic with a sun-heated shower (best in the evenings) and outdoor washing facilities.

Take the second left on entering the village (ul Traktovaya 99), then continue to the large unmarked green gate on your left.

Arshansky Bor
GUESTHOUSE $

(Аршанский бор; ☑8-924-399 5444; http://ar-shanbor.ru; ul Bratyev Domshevikh 44; dm from R500) This unmarked pink building was the best budget choice in Arshan at the time of

research. Rooms are dim and spartan, and facilities display the pressures of mass occupation, but there's a large kitchen, a common room and a barbecue area.

Maryina Roshcha
HOTEL $$

(Марьина Роща; ☑8-950-091 4771; www.mros-ha.com; ul Traktovaya 95; s/d incl breakfast from R1800/2300) Twenty years ago, you could only find such folksy timber mansions, known as *terem*, in illustrated fairy-tale books, but now *terem*-styled hotels are popping up everywhere. This one comes with a fully fledged farm that has rabbits, chickens and a vegetable garden. Included in the price, a hearty breakfast features some of its own produce.

Tuyana
HOTEL $$

(Туяна; ☑8-950-050 0569; www.tuyana.net; ul Lermontova 2; r from R2500) A cluster of modern timber houses with tidy, well-equipped rooms. There is a kitchen for self-caterers. The owner can advise on Peak of Love treks, but he only speaks Russian.

WORTH A TRIP

EXCURSIONS FROM ARSHAN

From the turn-off for Arshan it's just 9km along the Tunka Valley road to the village of **Zhemchug** (Жемчуг) where, for around R200, you can wallow in a series of hot pools that leave a chalky-green residue on skin and clothes.

Around 25km further along the road, the valley's unkempt, low-rise little 'capital' **Kyren** (Кырен) is home to the **Tunka National Park HQ** (☑30147-41 301; www.tunkapark.ru; Kyren, ul Lenina 130). Its small onion-topped church adds foreground to the photogenic alpine backdrop.

The little spa resort of **Nilova Pustyn**, some 30km further, is the starting point for a popular northbound trek to **Shumak**, a beautiful area of grass-covered mountains with over a hundred thermal springs scattered around the valley. The trek takes around three to four days to complete and goes through uninhabited mountain terrain. A number of agencies in Irkutsk, including Baikaler (p509), offer treks to Shumak, but these need to be arrange far in advance, as they require long preparations. The valley is home to the rather comfortable **Turbaza Shumak** (☑3952-534 000; http://shumak.ru; r from R1600), where one can rest after the hike, taking full advantage of numerous thermal pools in the vicinity. Staff can arrange expensive weekly helicopter transfers to/from Irkutsk (one way/return R14,000/17,000).

The valley road ends at **Mondy** (Монды) near **Munku-Sardyk** (3491m), the highest mountain in Eastern Siberia and the scene of an annual mass ascent (in May) marking the beginning of the climbing season. From the nearby Mongolian border post a road runs 21km to appealing Khövsgöl Lake, Baikal's little sister. Sadly, the crossing is only open for Russian and Mongolian nationals. The area around Mondy is a part of the border exclusion zone, which requires a special permit to visit that needs to be applied for two months in advance.

Some 190km west beyond Mondy the dumbfoundingly far-flung Oka region has been dubbed 'Tibet in miniature'. The 'capital' **Orlik** (Орлик) is the obvious place to arrange treks and horse-riding trips into some seriously isolated backcountry. The Oka River is also becoming popular with rafters.

Monetny Dvor GUESTHOUSE $$
(Монетный Двор; ☑8-904-115 6390, 8-950-077 3332; ul Traktovaya 89; s/d R1150/1800) Timber-built 24-bed guesthouse with rooms in a main building and three two-storey cottages. Cycle hire available.

Zakusochnaya Khamar Daban CAFETERIA $
(Закусочная Хамар Дабан; ul Traktovaya; mains R100-230; ☉10am-1am; ✾) Located opposite the Sayan Sanatorium, this pleasant canteen serves up a large menu of Buryat comfort food, including *boukhlyor* (lamb broth), *buuzy, khushuur* (fried dumplings) and *chebureki* (juicy Tatar meat and cheese pastry). The handwritten menu can be a challenge.

❶ Getting There & Away

The miniature bus station near the top of ul Traktovaya has the village's only ATM, plus left-luggage lockers. Tickets to Ulan-Ude are sold at the Arshan spa's own *avtokassa* across the square from the bus station. Arshan has the following bus and *marshrutka* connections:

Irkutsk R400, three to six daily

Kultuk (for Slyudyanka) R220 two hours, one or two daily

Ulan-Ude (via Kyren) R800, 11 hours, four daily

Eastern Baikal

Backed by the snow-capped Khamar-Daban mountains in the south and providing a gateway to the dramatic Barguzin Valley in the north, the eastern coast of Baikal is no less interesting than its western, which gets the bulk of visitors. That said, it is popular with local urbanites, from both Irkutsk and Ulan-Ude, so guesthouses or *turbazy* holiday camps can be found anywhere along the coast. There's plenty to do, from skiing or surfing in the south to birdwatching in the delta of the Selenga River and some serious hiking on Svyatoy Nos peninsula.

Selenga Delta

Some 300 waterways feed Lake Baikal, but none compare in size and volume to the Selenga River. One of only 80 rivers around the world to form a delta, the Selenga dumps its load of sand (and pollution from Mongolia) on Baikal's eastern shore in a huge fan of islands, reed beds and shallow channels measuring 35km across. Over 200 bird species draw spotters from all over the world; motorboat trips can be arranged through Ulan-Ude agencies.

Between birdwatching sessions many bed down in the village of Posolskoe, immediately south of the delta, where the Western-standard **Sofiya Hotel** (☑8-914-638 9521; full pension R1800) shares a lakeside location right beside a beautifully renovated monastery. Posolskoe is also the venue of regular watersports competitions, usually held in August, and ice boat races held in March. Sergei Klimov (p531) is the best person to contact, if you are interested in watching or participating.

Immediately north of the delta, a road bound for Zarechye passes several classic Baikal villages of unpainted log houses with sea-blue window shutters. The popular sandy beach at Enkhaluk fills up with Ulan-Ude residents in the hot months. **Baikalskaya Solianka** (☑8-902-565 3951, 3012-297 499; http://baikalmix.ru/; ul Lesnaya 17, Novy Enkhaluk; d/q with full board from R6000/10,000, yurts per person with full board from R1400) is a funky-looking and popular place to stay. Around 10km further on, the **Zagza thermal spring** (R200; ☉9am-9pm) provides a welcome alternative to Baikal's icy waters. A couple of kilometres beyond it, at Sukhaya, there is a good Buryat restaurant that also has rooms.

SOUTH OF THE SELENGA

East of Slyudyanka, the Trans-Siberian Railway and the parallel motorway skirt the coast up to Selenga Delta, where they both take a sharp turn east towards Ulan-Ude. Here, the snow-peaked Khamar-Daban Mountains rise steeply from the lake shore, leaving just a narrow strip of flat alluvial plain dotted with villages, where Irkutsk residents buy holiday homes to escape the city on hot summer weekends.

There are plenty of accommodation options, all of which are primarily geared to domestic tourists. Russians rave about **Ryzhaya Sova** (Рыжая сова, Red Owl; ☑8-914-006 4407; https://vk.com/copper_owl; ul Mira 15, Mangutay; per person from R750) at Mangutay (19km from Slyudyanka) and **Baikal Yeti** (☑8-904-150 0000; www.baikalyeti.com; ul Beregovaya 12, Utulik; dm/s/d from R500/1200/2000) in Utulik (32km from Slyudyanka).

Further north, 6km from Utulik, the unlovely **Baikalsk** is home to the now defunct Baikal Pulp and Paper Plant, which once was the lake's main polluter. However, it's swarming with visitors in winter, thanks to **Sobolinaya Gora** (Соболиная гора; www.baikalski.com) ski resort, which has been tested and approved by one avid skier, Vladimir Putin.

More adventurous skiers head to **Mamay Mountain**, near Vydrino, at the border of Irkutsk Region and Buryatiya. It has turned into a mecca for off-piste skiers, thanks to the efforts of Extreme Sports Federation, an informal group of adventure sports fans led by Sergei Klimov (p531) and based in Ulan-Ude. He is the best person to contact for details on access and conditions.

NORTH OF THE SELENGA

Access to the coast is across a forested pass from Ulan-Ude via tiny **Baturino** village, with its elegantly renovated Sretenskaya Church.

After around 2½ hours' drive, the newly paved road first meets Lake Baikal at pretty little **Gremyachinsk** (Гремячинск), a popular trip out of Ulan-Ude for hurried Trans-Siberian travellers with a day to spare. Located here is the good value **Baykalskaya Riviera** (☑8-983-531 2313; http://baikalriviera.ru; ul Lesnaya 36, Gremyachinsk; summer cabins s/d incl breakfast R1800/2400, with full board R2800/4400, standard incl breakfast s/d R4200/4600, with full board R5200/6600). The only fully fledged resort in the whole of Baikal, it offers simple, tastefully decorated summer-only wooden cabins and hotel-style accommodation year-round. Buses stop at a roadside cafe from which Gremyachinsk's sandy but litter-strewn beach is a 15-minute walk up ul Komsomolskaya. *Marshrutky* back to Ulan-Ude are often full so consider prebooking your return.

Approximately 5km from Gremyachinsk, at least 10 large tourist camps are strung around **Lake Kotokel**, whose thermal springs keep it warm year-round. At the northern end of the lake rises **Monastyrsky Island**, once home to an isolated hermitage and a church.

The main road offers surprisingly few Baikal views until the fishing port of **Turka**, from where there are pleasant walks to several secluded bays in either direction. Bigger **Goryachinsk** (Горячинск), around 3km from the lake, is centred on a typically institutional hot-springs *kurort* (spa) with cheap cottage homestays in the surrounding village.

Further north through the uninhabited taiga lies the quaint little fishing hamlet of **Maksimikha** (Максимиха), where picturesque Baikal beaches stretch northwest. From here the blacktop bends before zipping through the forest to Ust-Barguzin.

Ust-Barguzin   Усть-Баргузин

Low-rise Ust-Barguzin has sandy streets of traditional log homes with blue-and-white carved window frames. These are most attractive towards the northern end of the main street, ul Lenina, where it reaches the Barguzin River ferry. From here, views are magical towards the high-ridged peaks of the Svyatoy Nos Peninsula. Travelling in this remote area would be hard if not for the eminent Alelsander Beketov, who runs **Beketov Homestay** (☑30131-91 574; per Bolnichny 9; full board per person R1550, tent pitch R100) and **Banya Museum** (⊙by appointment only).

Daily *marshrutky* from Ust-Barguzin to to Ulan-Ude (R430 to R510, five hours) run twice a day and will pick you up from your accommodation if you book ahead. In July and August a daily hydrofoil links Ust-Barguzin with Irkutsk and Khuzhir on Olkhon Island; check out VSRP (p515) for details. In February and March the ice drive across Lake Baikal to Severobaikalsk takes around five hours.

Buy tickets ahead for Ulan-Ude–Barguzin *marshrutky* (R700, seven hours, three daily) and services to Kurumkan (R900, nine hours, two daily). From Barguzin public transport to Ust-Barguzin, Uro and Kurumkan is rare, though there's usually at least one service early morning and in the afternoon. Hitchhike or arrange a tour through the Beketovs in Ust-Barguzin.

Svyatoy Nos Peninsula

Rising almost vertically out of shimmering waters, dramatic Svyatoy Nos is one of Lake Baikal's most impressive features. It's within the mostly impenetrable **Zabaikalsky National Park** and joined to Ust-Barguzin by a muddy 20km sandbar that's possible but painful to drive along (there's also a toll). Guides can be hired at the **national park offices** (per Bolnichny 9, Ust-Barguzin) in Ust-Barguzin for all-day trek-climbs to the top of the peninsula, more than 1800m above Lake Baikal. The views from the summit are truly awe-inspiring.

Nerpa seals are particularly abundant off the peninsula's west coast around the **Ushkanny Islands**, accessible by charter boat from Ust-Barguzin. Contact Alexander Beketov at the national park headquarters. Prices begin at around R6000.

Barguzin & The Barguzin Valley

The road north from Ust-Barguzin emerges from thick forests at Barguzin, a low-rise town of wooden cottages that dates back to 1648. Walking from the bus station, you can see its handful of dilapidated historic buildings in about 20 minutes by heading along ul Krasnoarmeyskaya past the cursorily renovated old church to pl Lenina. Opposite the quaint little post office, the wooden-colonnaded Former Uezdny Bank (ul Krasnoarmeyskaya 54, Barguzin) was once the grand home of Decembrist Mikhail Kyukhelbeker. Other exiles to make a home in Barguzin were Jews from Poland and European Russia who arrived here in the 1830s and 1860s. The last signs of the Jewish community can be seen in the crumbling old cemetery (a block northeast of the church), where crooked Hebrew-inscribed graves stand to the left and Orthodox headstones, including that of Decembrist Mikhail Kyukhelbeker, to the right. Hidden in the village school and difficult to access, the small museum (☑8-924-391 3126; https://vk.com/muzej_barguzin; ul Kalinina 51a, Barguzin; R100) has some interesting Decembrist-related exhibits as well as the usual dusty rocks and mammoth bones.

Barguzin's real interest is as a launch pad for visiting the stunningly beautiful Barguzin Valley as it opens out into wide lake-dotted grassland, gloriously edged by a vast Toblerone of mountain peaks. These are most accessibly viewed across the meandering river plain from Uro village. Similarly inspiring panoramas continue for miles towards the idyllic village of Suvo, overshadowed by rock towers of the Suvo Saxony (Suvinskaya Saksoniya), so-called for its similarity to rock formations on the Czech–Saxony border. A few kilometres beyond Suvo, the roadside Bukhe Shulun (Byk), a huge boulder resembling a bull's hoof, is considered to have miraculous powers. Heading north you'll pass through widely scattered, old-fashioned villages where horse carts and sleighs outnumber cars. Way up on the valley's mountainous west side, Kurumkan (411km northeast of Ulan-Ude) has a small but photogenic peak-backed *datsan* (Buddhist temple). The valley tapers to a point 50km north of Kurumkan at Alla, where a tiny *kurort* (spa) can accommodate guests in the summer months.

SOUTHERN BURYATIYA & ZABAIKALSKY TERRITORY

Scenically magnificent, southern Buryatiya crouches on the Mongolian border like a cartographic crab squeezing Lake Baikal with its right pincer. Buryatiya Republic's vibrant capital, Ulan-Ude, is surrounded by hilly steppe dotted with lakes and crisscrossed by many rivers and streams. This is the heartland of the Buryats – relatives of Mongolians who have been strongly Russified over centuries, but still retained much of their culture (especially food!) as well as Buddhist and animist traditions.

The vast, sparsely populated Zabaikalsky Territory (Забайкальский край) stretches as far east as the wild Chara Mountains on the BAM railway, but in its more accessible southern reaches it's most interesting for the capital (Chita) and Buryat-populated areas to the south.

For the predeparture lowdown, check out Buryatiya's official English-language tourism website (www.visitburyatia.ru) and the government website (http://egov-buryatia.ru/eng/), which has English-language tourist information.

Buryat Culture

Indigenous ethnic Buryats are a Mongol people who comprise around 30% of Buryatiya's population, as well as 65% of the former Agin-Buryat Autonomous District southeast of Chita. Culturally there are two main Buryat groups. During the 19th century, forest-dwelling western Buryats retained their shamanic animist beliefs, while eastern Buryats from the southern steppes mostly converted to Tibetan Buddhism, maintaining a thick layer of local superstition. Although virtually every Buryat *datsan* was systematically destroyed during the communists' antireligious mania in the 1930s, today Buryat Buddhism is thriving. Many *datsany* have been rebuilt and seminaries for training Buddhist monks now operate at Ivolga and Aginskoe.

The Buryat language is Turkic, though very different from Tuvan and Altai. Dialects vary considerably between regions but almost everyone speaks decent, if heavily accented, Russian. Mongolians claim some Buryat dialects resemble their medieval tongue.

Ulan-Ude Улан-Удэ

📍 3012 / POP 414,000 / ⊘ MOSCOW +5HR

With its smiley Asian features, cosy city centre and fascinating Mongol-Buddhist culture, the Buryat capital is one of Eastern Siberia's most likeable cities. Quietly busy, welcoming and, after Siberia's Russian cities, refreshingly exotic, it's a pleasant place to base yourself for day trips to Buddhist temples and flits to eastern Lake Baikal's gently shelving beaches, easily reachable by bus. For some travellers UU is also a taster for what's to come in Mongolia.

Founded as a Cossack *ostrog* (fort) called Udinsk (later Verkhneudinsk) in 1666, the city prospered as a major stop on the tea-caravan route from China via Troitskosavsk (now Kyakhta). Renamed Ulan-Ude in 1934, it was a closed city until the 1980s due to its secret military plants (there are still mysterious blank spaces on city maps).

⊙ Sights

You can take in pretty much all that matters in Ulan-Ude by walking down ul Lenina from pl Sovetov to Odigitria Cathedral. The newly pedestrianised part of the route, locally known as Arbat (after its Moscow equivalent), features a statue of Russian writer Anton Chekhov, who spent one night here and noted in his diary that Ulan-Ude is a 'pleasant little town'. He didn't elaborate any further.

Lenin Head   MONUMENT

(pl Sovetov) Ulan-Ude's main square is entirely dominated by the world's largest Lenin head that creates an ensemble with the grey constructivist government building behind it. The 7.7m-high bronze bonce was installed in 1970 to celebrate Lenin's 100th birthday. Oddly, UU's bird population never seems to streak Lenin's bald scalp with their offerings – out of respect for the great man's achievements, bark diehard communists (but perhaps due to the barely visible antibird spikes, groan the rest).

Rinpoche Bagsha Datsan   BUDDHIST TEMPLE

(www.yelo-rinpoche.ru; ul Iya Dzerzhinskaya) Roosting high above the city's far north, the inside of this new and unexpectedly modern Tibetan temple looks like a kind of Buddhist-themed bus terminal, though the 6m-high gilt Buddha is pretty impressive. However, the real show-stealer here is the panoramic view, the smog-hazed city ringed by rumpled dust-bare peaks.

Take *marshrutka* 97 from outside the Hotel Baikal Plaza on pl Sovetov to the last stop (right by the temple entrance).

If you catch the monks doing their thing with drums, cymbals and chanting, the atmosphere can be electric. An extra feature is the circular walk around the temple featuring pavilions with grotesque, man-size representations of the Chinese signs of the zodiac.

Ulitsa Sobornaya   STREET

(Соборная улица; ul Sobornaya (Linkhovoina)) The pedestrianised street abutting Odigitria Cathedral preserves the spirit and the wooden lace architecture of the old downtown, populated by merchants and intelligentsia. Original inhabitants suffered badly from Bolshevik violence. A grim reminder of those violent times is the white stone building at the cathedral end of the street, which housed the NKVD – Stalin's secret police, responsible for torture and mass executions. You'll find a touching **monument to the victims of oppression** at the other end of the street.

Tragedy and comedy often walk hand in hand, as evidenced by the hilarious gilded statues on top of a house that stands right in front of the sombre monument. The house contains **Lev Bardanov art gallery**, the brainchild of a local businessman, and the statues depict four of his favourite local cultural figures. Locals say the collection is no less eccentric, but the gallery had still not been opened for the public, when we hung around.

Ethnographic Museum   MUSEUM

(www.ethnomuseum03.ru; Verkhnyaya Berezovka; R200; ⊘ 9am-5.30pm Wed-Fri, 10am-6.30pm Sat & Sun) In a forest clearing 6km from central Ulan-Ude, this outdoor collection of local architecture plus some reconstructed burial mounds and the odd stone totem is worth the trip. It's divided into seven areas, each devoted to a different nationality, tribe or ethnic group. There are Hun-era standing stones, Evenki *chumy*, traditional Buryat yurts, timber European town houses and a whole strip of Old Believers' homesteads, all brimming with period furniture and inhabited by costumed 'locals' giving craft demonstrations.

Marshrutka 37 from outside the Hotel Baikal Plaza on pl Sovetov passes within 1km and drivers are used to detouring to drop off tourists.

Opera & Ballet Theatre
THEATRE

(Бурятский государственный академический театр оперы и балета; ☎ 3012-213 600; www. uuopera.ru; ul Lenina 51) UU's striking Stalinist-era theatre reopened after lengthy renovation in 2011 (the first performance was for a group of foreign tourists from the luxury Golden Eagle train). Visitors cannot fail to be impressed by the level of craftsmanship inside, though some might be slightly surprised at the new lick of paint and rub of polish given to all the Soviet symbols, including a couple of smirking Stalins. The trademark performance is *Angara* – a ballet inspired by Buryat folklore and traditional music.

Ulan-Ude City Museum
MUSEUM

(www.uumuseum.ru; ul Lenina 26; R60; ⊙9am-6pm) Occupying the merchant's house where imperial heir Nicholas II stayed in 1891, this small but progressive museum has exhibits examining Verkhneudinsk's role in the tea and fur trades, the huge fairs that took place at the trading arches and several other aspects of the city's past.

Odigitria Cathedral
CHURCH

(ul Lenina 2) Built between 1741 and 1785, UU's largest church was also the first stone structure to appear in the city. Used as a museum store from 1929 until the fall of communism, its exterior has been renovated in a chalky white and the domes are once again tipped with gold, but the interiors are plain whitewash, awaiting their Byzantine decoration.

Geological Museum
MUSEUM

(Геологический музей Бурятии; ul Lenina 59; ⊙11am-5pm Mon-Fri) **FREE** This museum displays rocks, crystals and ores from the shores of Lake Baikal as well as art (for sale) made using multihued grit, sand and pebbles.

Khangalov Museum of Buryat History
MUSEUM

(Музей истории Бурятии им. М. Н. Хангалова; Profsoyuznaya ul 29; per exhibition R100-160; ⊙10am-6pm Tue-Sun) Housed in a badly ageing Soviet-era structure, the historical museum has rotating exhibitions dedicated to Buddhism, shamanism and traditional costumes. The 'Buryat timeline' history exhibition on the 2nd floor is mostly photographs, but at least there are English signs. Tickets to each exhibition are sold separately.

🏃 Activities & Tours

Ulan-Ude has several agencies happy to sell you Buryatiya and Baikal tours. English is often spoken.

★ Baikal Naran Tour
TOURS

(☎ 3012-215 097; www.baikalnaran.com; Office 105, Hotel Buryatiya, ul Kommunisticheskaya 47a) There's nothing director Sesegma (aka Svetlana) can't arrange for travellers in Buryatiya. An award-winning tour company and by far the best folks to approach if you want to see the republic's more remote corners, Old Believers' villages, the Selenga Delta, the Barguzin Valley and the region's Buddhist and shamanist heritage.

Denis Sobnakov
TOURS

(☎ 8-950-391 6325; www.burtour.com; ul Lenina 63) English-speaking Denis and his deputy Ivan run the city's best hostel as well as fun-packed walking tours of UU and many other Buryatiya-wide trips, including those to famous *datsany*, Old Believers' villages and beauty spots on Baikal. He has also started guiding groups along the entire Trans-Siberian route and in European Russia.

Andrey Suknev
VOLUNTEERING

(☎ 8-902-564 2678; www.facebook.com/andrey. suknev) The man who conceived the idea of the Great Baikal Trail has sadly closed his popular homestay hostel, but he is still someone to consult on GBT volunteer work in Buriyatiya, as well as on trips to Shumak in Tunka Valley.

Sergey Klimov
SKIING

(www.facebook.com/sergey.klimov.7146) The head of Buryatiya's rather informal Extreme Sports Federation is the person to ask about off-piste skiing and accommodation at Mamay Mountain.

MorinTur
TOURS

(☎ 3012-443 647; www.morintour.com; Hotel Sagaan Morin, ul Gagarina 25) Focuses on east Baikal, offering various ice and fishing adventures, a horse-sledge trip, seal watching, rafting in the Barguzin Valley and climbing on Svyatoy Nos (Holy Nose) Peninsula.

🛏 Sleeping

UU's hotel scene is improving, with new midrange places filling the gap between high-end hotels and hostels. The city doesn't suffer from very high occupancy, except in the summer months when booking ahead is advisable.

Ulan-Ude

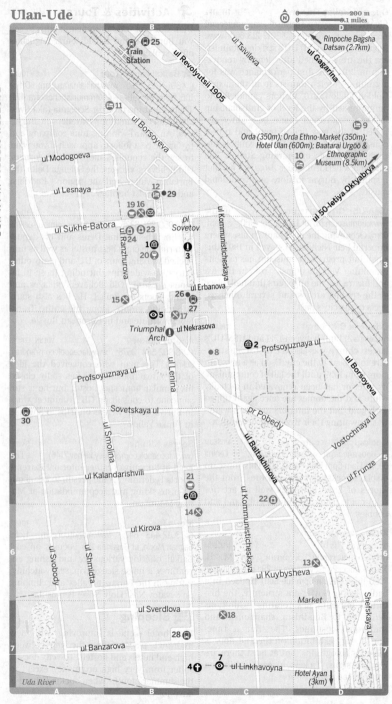

200 m
0.1 miles

Rinpoche Bagsha
Datsan (2.7km)

ul Tsivileva

ul Gagarina

ul Revolyutsii 1905

Train
Station

25

11

ul Borsoyeva

9

Orda (350m); Orda Ethno-Market (350m);
Hotel Ulan (600m); Baataraï Urgöö &
Ethnographic
Museum (8.5km)

10

ul Modogoeva

ul Lesnaya

12

29

ul 50-letiya Oktyabrya

19 16

pl
Sovetov

ul Kommunisticheskaya

ul Sukhe-Batora

24

23

1

3

ul Ranzhurova

20

ul Erbanova

15

26

27

5

17

Triumphal
Arch

ul Nekrasova

2

Profsoyuznaya ul

8

ul Borsoyeva

Profsoyuznaya ul

ul Lenina

Sovetskaya ul

pr Pobedy

30

ul Smolina

Vostochnaya ul

ul Kalandarishvili

21

ul Baltakhinova

6

22

ul Frunze

14

ul Kommunisticheskaya

ul Kirova

ul Svobody

ul Shmidta

13

Shefskaya ul

ul Kuybysheva

ul Sverdlova

Market

18

28

ul Banzarova

4

7

ul Linkhavoyna

Hotel Ayan
(3km)

Uda River

Ulan-Ude

★ **Ulan-Ude Travellers House**   HOSTEL **$**
(☑ 8-950-391 6325; www.uuhostel.com; ul Lenina 63, apt 18; dm R500-650; ☜) So central is this high-ceilinged apartment hostel, you might even catch a glimpse of Lenin's conk from one of the windows. The 14 beds are divided between two spacious, ethnically themed dorms (Russian and Buryat), there's a small kitchen where a free light breakfast is laid out daily, and heaps of UU information is pasted on the walls.

There's also a washing machine for guests to use. The exceptionally friendly owner, Denis Sobnakov, is in and out of town these days, but the place runs like a well-oiled machine and his staff are just as helpful in setting up trips to Baikal and around Buryatiya.

Hotel Ulan   HOTEL **$$**
(☑ 3012-551 110; ul 50-letiya Oktyabrya 32; s/d R1400/2100) This tiny hotel, with 10 comfortable rooms on the 1st floor of a Soviet apartment block (entrance at the back of the building), is good value for money. The location is not central, but a short tram ride from the main square. Receptionists put on funny folk costumes when they serve breakfast in your room in the morning.

Hotel Shumak   HOTEL **$$**
(☑ 8-902-160 8181; http://гостиницашумак.рф/; ul Revolyutsii 1905 goda 32; s/d R2000/2300)

Sleeping on a comfy bed amid a wood-dominated interior, you may very well forget it's just another apartment-block hotel in a not-so-pretty location. But being so close to both the train station and the centre makes it good value for money.

Hotel Ayan   HOTEL **$$**
(Отель Аян; ☑ 3012-415 141; www.ayanhotel.ru; ul Babushkina 164; s/d R850/1700; ❄☜) The inconvenient location 2km south of the city centre is more than recompensed by pristine international-standard rooms, some with air-conditioning. The cheapest singles are a good deal and every room has its own water heater. There's also a tiny cafe should you get peckish from all the stair climbing you'll do here – incredibly, this six-storey new-build has no lift.

A taxi from the train station costs around R170 or arrange a R300 private transfer with the hotel.

Mergen Bator   HOTEL **$$$**
(Отель Мэргэн Батор; ☑ 3012-200 002; www.mergen-bator.ru; ul Borsoyeva 19b; tw/d R6200/7000; ❄☜) UU's only 21st-century hotel is a swish pad indeed and completely on a par with any Western four-star establishment. From the trendy retro-veneered corridors to the commendably equipped fitness centre, the modern-as-tomorrow

bathrooms to the impeccable service, this place is worth splashing out on. Breakfast is included and can be served in your room free of charge.

Hotel Sagaan Morin
HOTEL $$$

(Отель Сагаан Морин; ☏ 3012-444 019; www.sagaan-morin.ru; ul Gagarina 25; s/d from R3800/4800; 🕾) The gleaming 17-storey, 89-room 'White Horse' offers spacious, crisply designed, almost understated rooms, lots of amenities and a 14th-floor restaurant (Panorama) with look-while-you-eat city vistas.

🍴 Eating

Ul Kommunisticheskaya, ul Sverdlova and the surrounding streets are packed with (sometimes very) basic dumpling canteens. For a fascinating insight into traditional Buryat life, Baikal Naran Tour can arrange dinner in a yurt with a local family out in the suburbs of Ulan-Ude.

Shenekhenskiye Buuzy
BURYAT $

(☏ 8-902-565 2862; www.vk.com/shenexen; ul Sverdlova 20; mains R120-200; ⊙ 8.30am-8pm) This heritage wooden *izba* painted in a rather psychedelic shade of green is a local institution run by Buryats who have been returning from Chinese exile in recent decades. They are widely considered as keepers of the *buuzy* golden standard. Order at the counter telling how many dumplings you want. Korean fern salad is our preferred side dish.

Shashlykoff
GRILL $

(Шашлыкофф; ☏ 3012-222 288; http://shashlikoff.com; ul Lenina 52; mains R200-250; ⊙ 10am-3am) A nationwide chain run by a national culinary show celebrity, Shashlykoff wins the battle for the hearts and stomachs of young Buryatians with the simple barbecue+beer formula, with homemade brew going as cheap as R73 per pint. The place is always heaving and getting a table can be challenging at dinner time.

Myasoroob
BURGERS $

(Мясоруб; ☏ 8-983-438 5386; www.facebook.com/myasoroob03; ul Sukhe-Batora 7; burgers R250-350; ⊙ 11am-11pm) Lumbersexual butchers seduce Buryatiya with nine kinds of gourmet burgers, craft beer and their trademark ginger *mors* (berry drink). A nice place for a quick lunch in the company of gadget-wielding hipsters.

Orda
BURYAT $$

(Орда; ☏ 3012-403 838; www.orda03.ru; ul Pushkina 4a; mains R500-1300; ⊙ noon-2am) An aspiring centre of Buryat cultural renaissance, the 'Horde' elevates coarse nomad cuisine to haute levels. Yes, it is largely meat with more meat and some onions, but the chef knows how to make lamb and even horse meat pieces as tender as spring artichokes. Frequent dinnertime concerts by famous Buryat musicians, including throat-singing artists, cost an extra R500 to R1000.

Modern Nomads
MONGOLIAN $$

(ul Ranzhurova 1; mains R400-700; ⊙ 11am-11pm) Clean-cut and very popular Mongolian place, good for a quick snack and a beer or for a full-blown dinner splurge costing thousands. Meat features heavily on the menu, but there are many veggie-friendly salads and other dishes with a contemporary twist to choose from, too.

Baatarai Urgöö
BURYAT $$

(www.baikalkhan.ru; Barguzinsky Trakt, Verkhnyaya Berezovka; mains R300-450; ⊙ 11am-11pm; 🕾) This yurt complex in the Verkhnyaya Berezovka suburb is a great lunch spot after a visit to the Ethnographical Museum. Take a seat in the main tent and give your taste buds the Buryat treatment in the form of *buuzy* (meat-filled dumplings), *bukhuler* (meat broth) and a glass of *airag* (fermented mare's milk). Take *marshrutka* 37 from pl Sovetov to the yurt stop.

Intalia
ITALIAN $$

(Инталия; ☏ 3012-210 204; https://vk.com/club69737023; ul Lenina 24b; mains R300-500; ⊙ 11am-11pm) Hidden in a quiet courtyard off the main pedestrian drag, this lovely trattoria treats visitors to competently cooked, if standard, Italian fare as well as juicy steaks.

Chay Khana
UZBEK $$

(Чай Хана; Evropa Business Centre, ul Baltakhinova; mains R250-590; ⊙ 11am-midnight Mon-Thu, to 2am Fri, 1pm-2am Sat, to midnight Sun) This high-perched Uzbek restaurant has a triangular cushion-scattered dining space, trendy oriental fabrics and a menu of exotic *plov*, grilled meats and imaginative salads. But it's the spectacular views of UU and the Selenga valley that are the real showstopper here, best enjoyed from the summer terrace. Take the lift to the 9th floor, then the stairs.

The business centre building is nicknamed 'the toilet' – you'll soon see why.

🍷 Drinking & Nightlife

Bar 12
BAR

(12th fl, Mergen Bator Hotel, Ul Borsoyeva 19b; ⊙24hr) Capping off the Mergen Bator hotel, this bar probably offers the best views of any in Russia: the entire Buryat capital and the surrounding mountainscape is laid out dramatically below you. The bar's party piece is to rotate through 360 degrees every 30 minutes, meaning you see the entire panorama without leaving your seat.

Macondo Coffee & Store
COFFEE

(ul Lenina 26) A bric-a-brac shop attached to the city museum comes with a hobbit-sized coffee bar that provides a welcome respite from dust, railway slime and instant coffee. It also brews by far the best latte this side of Khamar-Daban. Note the Gabriel García Márquez reference in the name.

Bisquit
CAFE

(Бисквит; ul Sukhe-Batora 7; ⊙11am-midnight) A stylish coffee-shop-cum-bar with bare brick walls and leather couches serves as coffee ambassador to Asian tea lands. Food is also available. A giant mirror at the entrance is handy for morning arrivals to examine damage after days on the train.

Churchill
PUB

(Черчилль; www.pubchurchill.ru; ul Lenina 55; ⊙noon-2am) A bekilted Scottish piper (well, a bagpiping dummy at least) greets you at the door of this relatively upmarket British-themed pub. The Brit paraphernalia extends throughout the two stylishly finished halls, the food is tasty and there's an international draught beer menu at central London prices.

🛍 Shopping

Zam
GIFTS & SOUVENIRS

(Зам; www.vk.com/zamspace; ul Sukhe-Batora, 16a; ⊙10am-7pm) This sparkling new shop doubles as a Buryat culture centre that runs lectures and masterclasses in traditional crafts. Goods include stylish jewellery by local artists, folk-themed clothes, locally produced leather bags and shoes. A little coffee bar attached to the counter comes as a bonus.

Orda Ethno-Market
ARTS & CRAFTS

(☑3012-441 001; http://ordagallery.ru/; ul Pushkina 4a; ⊙10am-7pm) Sometimes moving, sometimes kitschy modern Buryat art, clothes and souvenirs. Buddhist-themed metal sculpture contains some of the most striking items.

Dombo
GIFTS & SOUVENIRS

(Домбо; www.facebook.com/dombo.buryatia; ul Sukhe-Batora 16a; ⊙10am-1pm & 2-6.30pm Mon-Sat) Elegant artisanal ceramics by Ayuna Dorzhieva, who fuses Buryat motifs with modern art.

Central Market
MARKET

(ul Baltakhinova; ⊙9am-8pm) Tidy, Soviet-era market selling unusual local produce such as pine nuts, reindeer meat, buckthorn juice, *salo* (raw pig fat) and seasonal fruit and veg. At the back of the building are several stores offering *unty,* beautifully decorated reindeer skin boots. Prices start from around R12,000 a pair.

ℹ Orientation

UU's small city centre is divided into two districts, the communist-era upper city centred around pl Sovetov and the Lenin Head; and the riverside former merchant quarter, half of which still serves as the commercial hub extending from the 19th-century trading rows (pl Revolutsii). Dusty streets of crooked timber dwellings make up the other half.

ℹ Information

Handy ATMs can be found in the Buryatiya hotel and at the train station.

Post Office (ul Lenina 61; ⊙8am-10pm Mon-Fri, 9am-6pm Sat & Sun; 🖅)

Tourism Portal (www.uutravel.ru) Official tourism website with a smattering of interesting information in English.

Visit Buryatia (☑3012-210 332; www.visit-buryatia.ru) Official tourist board, which runs a summertime-only yurt-based information office on pl Sovetov.

ℹ Getting There & Away

AIR

UU's **Baikal Airport** (www.airportbaikal.ru), 11km from the city centre, handles surprisingly few flights. Buy tickets at the **Central Ticket Office** (ul Erbanova 14; ⊙9am-7pm) or **S7 Airlines** (ul Lenina 63; ⊙9am-7pm). Ulan-Ude has the following flight connections:

Irkutsk R3400, five weekly

Moscow R16,000, at least two daily

BUS

Ulan-Ude's **Selenga bus station** (Автовокзал Селенга; http://03bus.ru; ul Sovetskaya 1) is a tiny but user-friendly affair located to the west of pl Sovetov. Buy all tickets at least a day in advance. The useful Russian-language website http://03bus.ru updates schedules and prices

> ### ℹ️ ULAN-UDE TO ULAANBAATAR
>
> With flights between the two capitals once again grounded, there are just two ways to travel from Ulan-Ude to Ulaanbaatar, Mongolia. The least comfortable way is by Trans-Mongolian train, which takes between 15 and 23 hours to complete the 657km trip. A much cheaper and convenient way to go is to hop aboard the daily coach (R1500, 10 hours), which leaves from the main bus station in Ulan-Ude. Tickets can be bought from Baikal Naran Tour (p530) and the Ulan-Ude Travellers House (p531).

for destinations all over Buryatiya. The city has the following connections:

Arshan R800, 11 hours, four daily

Barguzin R660, seven hours, three daily

Kurumkan R800, nine hours, daily

Ust-Barguzin R530, six hours, twice daily

Additional *marshrutky* to Irkutsk (R1000, eight hours) and Chita (R1430, seven hours) run from the train station forecourt, departing throughout the day when full.

Minibuses run from pl Banzarova to **Ivolga** (pl Banzarova), where you can change for Ivolginsky *datsan*.

TRAIN

When travelling to Irkutsk, take a day train for superb views of Lake Baikal.

Ulan-Ude has the following rail connections:

Beijing *kupe* R15,000 to R19,000, 43 hours to 61 hours, two weekly

Chita *platskart/kupe* R1800/R2600, 10 to 12 hours, up to six daily

Irkutsk *platskart/kupe* R1600/R2500, seven to nine hours, up to nine daily

Ulaanbaatar *kupe* R4900, 15 or 23 hours, daily

ℹ️ Getting Around

From pl Sovetov *marshrutky* 28, 55 and 77 run a few times hourly to the airport, while *marshrutka* 37 passes the hippodrome, the Ethnographic Museum and Baatarai Urgöö restaurant. *Marshrutka* 97 climbs to the Rinpoche Bagsha Datsan.

Around Ulan-Ude

You could spend a week making day trips out of Ulan-Ude with Buddhist temples, Old Believers' villages and forgotten border settlements to explore. The main routes south are the scenic Ulan-Ude–Kyakhta road, which hugs the Selenga River for much of the way, and the Trans-Mongolian Railway, which crosses the border at the unremarkable railway town of Naushki. Note that both Naushki and Kyakhta are officially off limits to foreigners as they fall within the border zone. Permits to visit these places should be arranged through UU agencies at least two months before you travel.

All destinations around Ulan-Ude are served by *marshrutky* leaving from Ulan-Ude bus station. *Marshrutky* for Ivolginsk depart from pl Banzarova.

◉ Sights

Ivolginsk (Ivolga) Datsan   TEMPLE
(Иволгинский дацан; ⊙ premises dawn-dusk, temples 8am-5pm) The confident epicentre of Russian Buddhism owes its existence to none other than Josef Stalin, who reversed the Bolshevik policy of destroying temples and allowed it to be built, in a plot of marshy land 35km from Ulan-Ude, in gratitude to the Buryats for their sacrifices during WWII. The first temple was a modest affair, but today the *datsan* has grown large and is expanding fast. Pilgrims and tourists flock here on half-day trips from the Buryat capital.

The Ivolginsky *datsan* was one of only two working Buddhist temples in Soviet days (the other was at Aginskoe); most of what you see today has been built in the last two decades. A clockwise walk around the complex takes in countless monastery faculties, administrative buildings, monks' quarters and temples, but the most elaborate of all is the **Itygel Khambin Temple** honouring the 12th Khambo Lama, whose body was exhumed in 2002. To general astonishment, seven decades after his death his flesh had still not decomposed. Some 'experts' have even attested that the corpse's hair is still growing, albeit extraordinarily slowly. The body is displayed six times a year, attracting pilgrims from across the Buddhist world.

To reach the monastery, first take *marshrutka* 130 (R45, 40 minutes, four hourly) from pl Banzarova to the last stop in uninteresting Ivolga. There, another *marshrutka* (R25, no number, just a picture of the monastery or the word Дацан pasted to the front windscreen) waits to shuttle visitors the last few kilometres to the monastery compound. Otherwise contact agencies in Ulan-Ude, which offer private transfers and tours with well-informed guides.

The daily Gunrig Khural Ritual, which is said to protect participants from bad re-incarnations and black magic, is held at 9am.

Tamchinsky Datsan   TEMPLE

(Тамчинский дацан) First founded in 1741, this was Buryatiya's first Buddhist monastery and the mother ship of Russian Buddhism for two centuries. The original complex, 160km south of Ulan-Ude, was destroyed in the 1930s and the modern reconstruction is small scale and surrounded by the slowly dying village of Gus-inoe Ozero (30km south of Gusinoozersk). View the newly renovated former school of philosophy, test out the amazing acoustics of the main temple and chat with the mobile-phone-toting head lama who, for a donation, may let you camp in the grounds and eat in the small refectory.

To get there, take the 7.24am Naushki train from Ulan-Ude (four hours) and alight at Gusinoe Ozero. A train runs back to Ul-an-Ude late afternoon or you could hitch a lift to Gusinoozersk at the opposite end of the lake, from where there are regular *mar-shrutky* back to Ulan-Ude.

Atsagatsky Datsan   TEMPLE

(Ацагатский дацан) Once the centre of Bury-at Buddhist scholarship with an important scriptorium, this *datsan* was completely de-stroyed in the 1930s, but has crawled back to life since the fall of communism. The tiny on-site **Ayvan Darzhiev Museum** com-memorates the Atsagat monk who became a key counsellor to the 13th Dalai Lama. Pho-togenically gaudy, the little monastery sits on a lonely grassy knoll and is set back from km54 of the old Chita road – unfortunately there is no convenient public transport. A tour from Ulan-Ude will cost around R6000 for up to three people.

CHITA

📱 3022 / POP 329,400 / ⊙ MOSCOW +6HR

Of all Eastern Siberia's major cities, Chita (Чита) is the least prepared for visitors. Lit-erally put on the map by the noble-blood-ed Decembrists, one of whom designed its street-grid layout, today there's noth-ing aristocratic about this regional capital where Soviet symbols still embellish Sta-linist facades, shaven-headed conscripts guard pillared military headquarters and Chinese cross-border peddlers lug mon-ster bales past a well-tended Lenin statue.

Non-Chinese foreigners are still a rarity here; tourism is a thing that happens elsewhere.

Echoes of the Decembrist chapter in Chi-ta's history make the city just worth visit-ing, and a number of attractive old timber merchants' houses grace its arrow-straight streets. It's also the jumping-off point for important Buddhist sights in the south of Zabaikalsky Territory.

History

Founded in 1653, Chita developed as a rough-and-tumble silver-mining centre un-til it was force-fed a dose of urban culture in 1827 by the arrival of more than 80 exiled Decembrist gentlemen-rebels – or more pre-cisely, by the arrival of their wives and lovers who followed, setting up homes on what became known as ul Damskaya (Women's St). That's now the southern end of ul Stol-yarova, where sadly only a handful of rotting wooden cottages remains amid soulless con-crete apartment towers.

As gateway to the new East Chinese Rail-way, Chita boomed in the early 20th century, despite flirting with socialism. Following the excitement of 1905, socialists set up a 'Chita

WORTH A TRIP

NOVOSELENGINSK

Stockades and wooden houses on broad dust-blown roads give this small, 19th-century town of ten thousand souls (Новоселенгинск) a memorable 'Wild East' feel. The town's top attrac-tion is its **Decembrist Museum** (ul Lenina 53; R50; ⊙10am-6pm Wed-Sun), which tells the story of noble exiles who ended up here.

Walk a couple of kilometres east of the museum through the town towards the Selenga River to see the isolated ruins of the whitewashed **Spassky Church** on the grassy far bank; this is all that remains of Selenginsk, the original set-tlement, which was abandoned around 1800 due to frequent floods. You'll also find an unremarkable **obelisk** com-memorating Martha Cowie, the wife of a Scottish missionary who spent 22 years here translating the Bible into Mongolian and trying (wholly unsuccessfully) to wean the Buryats off Buddhism.

Marshrutky make the scenic trip from Ulan-Ude (R 200, 1½ hours, two daily).

Republic', which was brutally crushed within a year. After the 'real' revolutions of 1917, history gets even more exciting and complex. Bolsheviks took over, then lost control to Japanese forces who possibly intercepted part of Admiral Kolchak's famous 'gold train' before retreating east. By 1920 Chita was the capital of the short-lived Far Eastern Republic, a nominally independent, pro-Lenin buffer state whose parliament stood at ul Anokhina 63. The republic was absorbed into Soviet Russia in December 1922 once the Japanese had withdrawn from Russia's east coast. Closed and secretive for much of the Soviet era, today Chita is still very much a military city and once again flooded with Chinese traders.

⊙ Sights

★ **Decembrist Museum**   MUSEUM
(Музей Декабристов; www.museums75.ru/chitadekabr.htm; ul Selenginskaya; R130; ⊙ 10am-6pm Tue-Sun) If you're on the Decembrist trail through Siberia, this small but comprehensive museum is one of the best. It's housed in the 18th-century **Archangel Michael log church**, an unexpected sight amid the neighbourhood's shambolic apartment blocks. Inextricably linked to the Decembrist story, this was where they came to pray, where Annenkov married his French mistress Pauline Geuble and where the Volkonskys buried their daughter Sofia. Signs are in Russian only, but an English-language audio guide is available for R70.

WORTH A TRIP

OLD BELIEVERS' VILLAGES

To the south of Ulan-Ude lie several relatively accessible Old Believers' villages, most notably **Tarbagatay** (50km south), with its whitewashed church and small museum, and nearby **Desyatnikovo**. Turn up unannounced in these places and you'll see precious little; visits involving lots of colourful costumed singing, deliciously hearty homemade food and detailed explanations of the Old Believers' traditions and way of life must be prearranged through Ulan-Ude agencies. Otherwise you could try contacting **Semeyskie** (☑ 30146-56 160, 8-924-653 9501; www.starovery-pro.ru; ul Pushkina 2, Tarbagatay), the Old Believers' organisation that arranges visits, directly.

The ground-level exhibition begins with the names of all the Decembrists picked out in gold on a green background, followed by interesting items such as the original imperial order sentencing the noble rebels to banishment in Siberia and oils showing their leaders' executions. The 2nd floor looks at the wives who followed their menfolk into the Nerchinsk silver mines and the fates of all the Decembrists once they were allowed to settle where they pleased. Some of them lived long enough to feature as elderly, but rather stylish and optimistic-looking gentlemen, in black-and-white photographs displayed at the end of the exhibition.

Kuznetsov Regional Museum   MUSEUM
(Забайкальский краевой краеведческий музей им. А.К. Кузнецова; ☑ 3022-260 315; www.museums75.ru/museum.htm; ul Babushkina 113; R140; ⊙ 10am-5.45pm Tue-Sun) The unexpectedly lively Kuznetsov Regional Museum has been around since 1895 and the imposing mansion it currently occupies was purpose-built to house it in 1914. The inevitable stuffed animals fill the 1st floor, but it is the collection of Buddhist art and exhibitions dedicated to indigenous Siberians and Russian settlers, both located in the 2nd floor, that attract most visitors. An interesting and politically neutral exhibition telling the gruesome story of Russian Civil War fratricide was added in 2017.

Kazansky Cathedral   CHURCH
(Казанский кафедральный собор; train station forecourt) The train station reflected in its gilt onion domes, Chita's bright turquoise cathedral is the city's most impressive building, though inside it's lamentably plain. The original pre-Stalin cathedral stood on the main square, right on the spot where Lenin now fingers his lapels.

House of Officers   ARCHITECTURE
(ul Lenina 88) Striking gilded statues of soldiers adorn this landmark building that defines Chita as a military stronghold on the border with China. Walk through an archway to find yourself in **ODORA Park**, dotted with vintage military hardware.

Datsan   BUDDHIST TEMPLE
(ul Bogomyagkova 72; ⊙ 24hr) Chita's main Buddhist temple lies just outside the centre, a 15-minute walk or R150 taxi ride along Bogomyagkova from where it meets ul Babushkina. It's a recently built affair, but well kept and with all its prayer wheels, butter

THE DECEMBRIST WOMEN

Having patently failed to topple tsarist autocracy in December 1825, many prominent 'Decembrist' gentlemen revolutionaries were exiled to Siberia. They're popularly credited with bringing civilisation to the rough-edged local pioneer-convict population. Yet the real heroes were their womenfolk, who cobbled together the vast sleigh/carriage fares to get themselves to Siberia.

And that was just the start. Pauline Annenkova, the French mistress of one aristocratic prisoner, spent so long awaiting permission to see her lover in Chita that she had time to set up a fashionable dressmakers' shop in Irkutsk. By constantly surveying the prisoners' conditions, the women eventually shamed guards into reducing the brutality of the jail regimes, while their food parcels meant that Decembrists had more hope of surviving the minimal rations of their imprisonment. The Decembrist women came to form a core of civil society and introduced 'European standards of behaviour'. As conditions eventually eased, this formed the basis for a liberal Siberian aristocracy, especially in Chita and Irkutsk,where some Decembrists stayed on even after their formal banishment came to an end.

lamps and yin-yang drums firmly in place. The tranquil grounds are home to a tiny *buuzy* joint.

👉 Tours

Lanta TOURS
(Ланта; ☏ 3022-353 639; www.lanta-chita.ru; ul Leningradskaya 56; ☉ 9am-7pm Mon-Fri) Runs limited tours of Chita and Zabaikalsky Region. No English spoken.

Sunmar TOURS
(☏ 8-914-808 2020; www.turpomiru.com; mikrorayon Tsarsky 8; ☉ 10am-6pm) Tours of Alkhanay National Park and Khahatay ice caves; rafting trips. Some Chinese spoken, but no English.

🛏 Sleeping

Chita has little budget accommodation and homestays are nonexistent. Hotels are often full, meaning many travellers who fail to book ahead often have no choice but to check into top-end hotels.

Gostinny Dom GUESTHOUSE $$
(Гостинный дом; ☏ 8-914-521 7829; http://gostiniy-dom-chita.hoteloj.ru; ul Kirpichno-Zavodskaya 31a; d/tr from R1800/2300; 🛜) This log house on the outskirts of Chita has developed a bit of a following with the international biker crowd, particularly Korean and Japanese overlanders. That's partly because the owner is an avid motorcyclist, but more importantly because the place is both quiet and comfortable, perhaps the best value for money in Chita.

No breakfasts served, but there is a kitchen, equipped with a multicooker and a microwave for self-caterers. The centre can be reached by taxi for R130 or by *marshrutka* 21 for R22.

Hotel Arkadia HOTEL $$
(Гостиница Аркадия; ☏ 3022-352 636; www.arkadiyachita.ru; ul Lenina 120; s/d from R2450/3800; 🛜) Chita's best deal has well-kept rooms, clean bathrooms, online booking, efficient staff and no-fuss visa registration. Often offers very good rates on popular booking websites.

Hotel Zabaikale HOTEL $$
(Гостиница Забайкалье; ☏ 3022-359 819; www.zabhotel.ru; ul Leningradskaya 36; s R1650-3100, d from R3680; 🛜) Unbeatably located overlooking the main square, the cheaper renovated rooms at this huge complex are a fairly good deal. The hotel has a huge range of facilities including an air and rail ticket office, a spa, a children's playroom and a gym.

Hotel Vizit HOTEL $$$
(Гостиница Визит; ☏ 3022-356 945; www.chitahotelvizit.ru; ul Lenina 93; s/tw R3400/6400; ❄🛜) Occupying the 5th floor of a smoked-glass tower at the busy intersection of ul Lenina and ul Profsoyuznaya, this is Chita's best luxury offering with relaxing en-suite rooms, English-speaking receptionists and sparkling bathrooms. Some doubles have baths and the air-con provides relief from Chita's superheated summers.

Hotel Montblanc
HOTEL $$$

(☎ 3022-356 945; www.montblanc.eldonet.ru; ul Kostyushko-Grigorovicha 5; r from R4900; ❄ ☎) A block away from the main square, this purpose-built business hotel has immaculately snazzy rooms, though at these prices the plumbing could be a touch more professional. The buffet breakfast is served in the Ukraine-themed restaurant and check-out time at reception provides an opportunity to witness just how badly Russian and Chinese businessmen can behave.

✖ Eating & Drinking

Eating out ain't high on the list of things to enjoy in Chita, but despite the lack of choice and unimaginative menus, you won't go hungry.

Privoz
CAFETERIA $

(Привозъ; ul Lenina 93; canteen mains R90-250; ☺10am-midnight Sun-Wed, to 1am Thu-Sat) This clean and modern Odessa-themed service canteen serves well-cooked standard Russian fare and features a WWI machine gun on display in the middle of the premises.

Shchastye
INTERNATIONAL $$

(Счастье; ☎ 3022-507 808; http://happiness75. ru; ul Lenina 93, 2nd fl; mains R380-580, set-menu lunch R350; ☺1pm-11pm) Happiness (as the name translates) is when you find this oasis of whiteness and neatness in the middle of a scruffy Siberian city. Soviet-style redneck patrons who inhabit this dollhouse of a place add a comic edge to the picture. The globalist menu includes several kinds of tasty shashlyk and a mean tom yum.

OUT OF CHITA

If you find yourself in Chita, you are already well off the trodden path, but if you want to explore this wild corner of Siberia even more deeply, here are some ideas for you.

Around 270km from Chita lies **Nerchinsk**. Anyone with a knowledge of Russian history will be familiar with that name. The 1689 Treaty of Nerchinsk, recognising Russia's claims to the trans-Baikal region, was signed here and 130 years later the Decembrists were sent to work the silver mines around the village.

The only visitable attraction in Nerchinsk is the **Butin Palace Museum** (ul Sovetskaya 83, Nerchinsk; R100; ☺10am-1pm & 2-5.30pm Tue-Sat). Mikhail Butin, the local silver baron, built himself this impressive crenellated palace, furnished with what were then claimed to be the world's largest mirrors. He'd bought the mirrors at the 1878 World Fair in Paris and miraculously managed to ship them unscathed all the way to Nerchinsk via the China Sea and up the Amur River.

To reach Nerchinsk, take any train from Chita to Priiskovaya (*platskart/kupe* R900/1200, six hours) on the trans-Siberian main line, 10km from Nerchinsk. Change there onto local *marshrutky*.

There is also a fair amount of important Buddhist sights in the areas south of Chita that are predominantly populated by ethnic Buryats. Set just 2km from the 'holy' Onon River, **Tsugol Datsan** is surely the most memorable Buddhist temple in Russia. Located in the village of Tsugol, the almost 200-year-old building is extremely photogenic, with gilded Mongolian script-panels, wooden upper facades and tip-tilted roofs on each of its three storeys. Getting to/from Tsugol is a pain – it lies 13km from Olovyannaya, reachable by a single morning bus from Chita. From Olovyannaya take a taxi (at least R500, more if asked to wait) or hike along the river.

Directly south of Chita, **Alkhanay National Park** combines Buddhist history with natural beauty. Its rocky terrain with many streams and little waterfalls contains numerous objects of religious veneration so important they warranted a visit by the Dalai Lama in 1991. Reachable from Chita via Duldurga, 12km away, the park provides rather spartan accommodation in log cabins. Popular with Chita residents, the park is often closed due to bad weather conditions or forest fire. Its website (http://alkhana.ru) runs regular updates.

Travel agencies in Chita organise tours to these and other attractions in the vicinity, but they have little experience dealing with Western travellers.

Mama Roma
ITALIAN **$$**

(www.mamaroma.ru; ul Lermontova 9; mains R280-500; ⊘11am-10pm) Chequered tablecloths, glass divides, an English menu (!) and pleasant staff make this chain pizzeria an unexpectedly welcoming experience near the train station.

Harat's Pub
PUB

(ul Leningradskaya 15a; ⊘noon-2am) Savour the slightly surreal experience of sipping a pint of Newcastle Brown in an Irish pub in Chita, while pondering just where the owners got all those Celtic flags, old US number plates and imitation Tiffany lamps. Friendly service.

Shokoladnitsa
CAFE

(ul Leningradskaya 36; ⊘9am-midnight; 🛜) This Europeanly stylish peaceful oasis of a cafe is good for people-watching from the big windows while sipping coffee or tea and making full use of the free wi-fi.

🛍 Shopping

Zabaikalsky Khudozhestvenny Salon
GIFTS & SOUVENIRS

(Забайкальский художественный салон; ul Lenina 56; ⊘10am-7pm Mon-Fri, to 6pm Sat, 11am-6pm Sun) This huge shop stocks every perceivable souvenir from across the entire Russian Federation, from Buryat dolls to Kostroma linen, Dzhgel plates to Chita fridge magnets. Local artists' work and the owner's photography also available.

🛈 Information

VTB Bank (ВТБ Банк; ul Amurskaya 41; ⊘9am-6pm Mon-Fri) Has ATMs and currency-exchange window.

Main Post Office (ul Butina 37; ⊘8am-10pm Mon-Fri, 9am-6pm Sat & Sun) Quaintly spired wooden building on pl Lenina.

🛈 Getting There & Away

AIR

Kadala Airport (www.aerochita.ru) is 15km west of central Chita. Take bus 40

🛈 TICK WARNING

The encephalitis and Lyme disease threat is often underestimated in Siberia (both Western and Eastern). The ticks (*kleshchi*) that spread these nasty diseases are alarmingly plentiful from late April to September. The threat is worst in the taiga (mountain pine), especially in Altai, but ticks have even been found in city parks. Don't panic, but do cover up and be vigilant. Good antitick sprays and creams are available in big cities. It's best to stock up before you arrive in the region. Tick-borne diseases can also be transmitted through milk, so make sure you boil any bought fresh from local farmers.

or *marshrutka* 12 or 14. **AviaEkspress** (АвиаЭкспресс; 📞 3022-450 505; www.aviaexpress.ru; ul Lenina 55; ⊘8am-10pm) sells tickets for all flights, including the twice-daily service to Moscow (R16,800).

BUS

The only two services you're likely to need are the *marshrutky* to Aginskoe (R400, two hours, five daily) and the long-distance minivans to Ulan-Ude (R1100, seven hours). Both leave from a stop on the train station forecourt.

TRAIN

Chita has the following rail connections:

Beijing *kupe* R16,700, 53 hours, weekly

Blagoveshchensk *platskart/kupe* 3850/R5200, 38 hours, two daily

Khabarovsk *platskart/kupe* R4900/6500, 43½ hours, two daily

Tynda *platskart/kupe* R3100/5000, 27 hours, every other day

Ulan-Ude *platskart/kupe* R1800/R2500, 10 to 12 hours, up to six daily

Zabaikalsk *platskart/kupe* R1500/2600, 12 hours, daily

Russian Far East

Best Places to Eat

➡ Kvartira 30 (p557)

➡ Muscat Whale (p549)

➡ Zuma (p558)

➡ Chochur Muran (p570)

➡ Kvartira na Prospekte (p569)

Best Places to Stay

➡ Khabarovsk City Boutique Hotel (p548)

➡ Izba Hostel (p556)

➡ Hotel Golden House (p572)

➡ Hotel Parus (p548)

➡ Hotel Bira (p544)

Why Go?

Russia's distant end of the line, the wild wild east feels likes its own entity. 'Moscow is far' runs the local mantra, and trade and transport connections with its Asian neighbours are growing fast.

Kamchatka, the vast mountainous peninsula at the end of Russia, is the star of the show with smoking volcanoes, hot springs and snow-capped peaks to rival any on earth. Elsewhere the region is not as scenically spectacular, but does boast two charming cities in Vladivostok and Khabarovsk, the exceptional engineering feat of the BAM railway (the travel nerd's alternative to the Trans-Siberian), the vast wildernesses of Sakha, old Gulag camps, Cossack fort towns and entire cities raised on stilts over permafrost.

Many travellers skip the Far East entirely, cutting south from Lake Baikal to China – but that's all the better for those who make it here. Elbow room is definitely not in short supply.

When to Go

Vladivostok

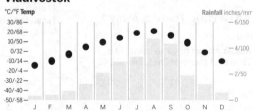

Feb & Mar Still the season for snowy delights, only not dark or slushy.

Jun Essentially midspring, with all the beauty and daylight that entails (plus mozzies).

Jul & Aug The best months to visit Kamchatka, with largely warm and clear days.

History

The Far East is Russia's own version of the wild west, where hardened Cossacks in the early 17th century – and young Soviets (and Gulag camp prisoners) in the 20th – came to exploit the region's untapped natural resources, such as gold in Kolyma, the diamonds of Sakha and oil off Sakhalin. The region was officially just a big chunk of Siberia until the Soviets anointed it a separate administrative

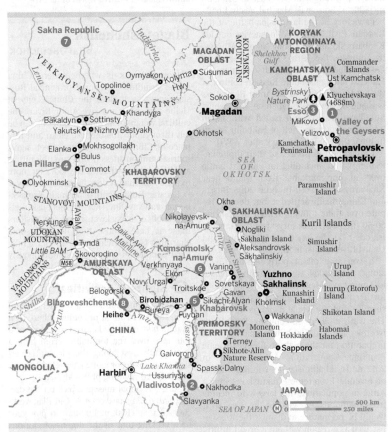

Russian Far East Highlights

❶ Valley of the Geysers (p588) Spending a day exploring some of Kamchatka's most stunning scenery by helicopter.

❷ Vladivostok (p551) Discovering the Russian Far East's most interesting and cosmopolitan city.

❸ Esso (p589) Hiking through gorgeous alpine scenery followed by a soak in a geothermal pool in Kamchatka's most accessible village.

❹ Lena Pillars (p571) Taking a cruise along the vast Lena River to see this magnificent natural phenomenon.

❺ Khabarovsk (p544) Enjoying a scenic riverside stroll, admiring grand architecture and joining in the nightlife of this student town.

❻ Komsomolsk-na-Amure (p562) Riding the extraordinary BAM railway to this charming and friendly Soviet outpost.

❼ Sakha Republic (p565) Escaping the modern world for the reindeer-filled, lake-strewn landscapes of vast, empty Yakutia.

❽ Blagoveshchensk (p542) Taking in exquisite tsarist buildings by the Amur River in this old Russian frontier town.

entity in the 1920s. Geographers still consider most of the Far East part of Siberia. Yet it has always felt more distant, more challenging, more godforsaken than points west.

Locally, much ado is made of Anton Chekhov's trip through the Far East to Sakhalin in 1890; of Bolshevik Marshal Vasily Blyukher's victory in the last major battle of the Russian Civil War at Volochaevka outside Khabarovsk; and of Count Nikolai Muravyov-Amursky, the 19th-century governor of Eastern Siberia who did much to open up the Far East and consolidate Russian control of the left (north) bank of the Amur River. Less is made of the Russo-Japanese War, which humiliated Russia and ended with Japan taking the southern half of Sakhalin Island in 1905; the USSR got it back after WWII.

China and the USSR had their diplomatic bumps too, including an outright battle over an unremarkable river island near Khabarovsk in 1969. In June 2005 Russia and China finally settled a four-decade dispute over their 4300km border by splitting 50-50 the Bolshoy Ussurysky and Tarabarov Islands near the junction of the Amur and Ussuri Rivers, outside Khabarovsk.

If you stop off at purpose-built towns along the Baikal-Amur Mainline (Baikalo-Amurskaya Magistral; BAM), or make it further north to Magadan, it's tempting to surmise that the whole region is in decline. The truth is far more complex. Busy Vladivostok saw a R600-billion makeover in preparation for the high-profile Asia-Pacific Economic Cooperation (APEC) summit in 2012, and Sakhalin Island is running wild in oil revenue. Even remote Yakutsk is seeing a surge in population, due largely to income from diamonds and gold in the area, so it would be premature to dismiss the Russian Far East as a region without a bright future.

EASTERN TRANS-SIBERIAN

Most travellers who make it this far east stick within this region, which extends along the final 40 hours or so of railroad that runs through anonymous villages north of the Chinese border, over the Amur River to lively Khabarovsk, and south through Primorsky Territory, ending at regional capital Vladivostok, the Far East's dynamic, enjoyable hub.

Natural attractions are generally more rewarding further north, but Khabarovsk and Vladivostok remain popular with travellers and are well set up for people on all budgets, while friendly Blagoveshchensk has the region's most impressive tsarist architecture, and Birobidzhan, with its patina of Jewish culture, is in a bizarre world of its own.

Blagoveshchensk
Благовещенск

📞 4162 / POP 225,000 / ⊘ MOSCOW +6HR

Blagoveshchensk is where modern China comes grinding up against provincial Russia, facing as it does the Chinese city of Heihe across the massive Amur River. The cultural weight of its giant neighbour can be felt throughout this modest, clean and tidy place – Chinese restaurants, street signs, tourists and business people are ubiquitous and it's fair to say that the city looks far more to the south than it does towards Moscow.

Located 110km south of the main Trans-Siberian railway line, Blagoveshchensk feels like a bit of a backwater and few visitors make it here. Those that do find some charming tsarist architecture and a friendly local population who seem simultaneously puzzled and delighted to have visitors.

⊙ Sights & Activities

A good starting point for a wander around is on the riverfront at pl Lenina, where teen skaters take over the Lenin statue steps and tots take over the fountains. From here a short walk west along the pleasant riverside promenade, or along parallel ul Lenina, takes you to yawning pl Pobedy.

At the regional museum, pick up the darling *Stary Blagoveshchensk* (Old Blagoveshchensk) map (R10, in Russian) to plot your own walking tour of the dozens of glorious tsarist-era buildings on shady backstreets around the centre. The most impressive buildings are on ul Lenina near the museum and on and around nearby pl Pobedy.

Anton Chekhov came through Blagoveshchensk during his epic trip through the Far East in 1890 (and headed straight to a Japanese prostitute, as recounted luridly in his later-published letters). A bust commemorating Chekhov's visit is on the facade of the lovely Institute of Geology and Wildlife Management building on pl Pobedy.

Amur Regional Museum   MUSEUM
(Амурский областной краеведческий музей; www.museumamur.org; ul Lenina 165; R300;

☻10am-6pm Tue, Wed & Fri, 10am-9pm Thu, 10am-7pm Sat & Sun) Housed in a former tsarist-era trading house and Soviet-era HQ for the Communist Youth League (Komsomol), this impressive museum has 26 halls containing plenty of interesting photos, 1940s record players and a meteor that fell to earth in 1991 near Tynda. Russian-history buffs will enjoy the model of the 17th-century Cossack fortress in nearby Albazin and a painting depicting the Manchurian invasion of the fort in 1685. Signage is in Russian only.

River Cruises
BOATING

(ul Amurskaya; per person R250) One-hour daytime and evening river cruises leave from a pier at the east end of ul Amurskaya from mid-May through September.

🛏 Sleeping

Green Hostel
HOSTEL $

(☎8-924-841 9008; www.green-hostels.ru; ul Ostrovskaya 65; dm R500-700; 🛜) This basic and not terribly friendly place has three dorm rooms with lino floors and a shared kitchen. It's just one block east of the bus station and centrally located. It's best to call ahead and let them know you're coming.

Hotel Gloria
HOTEL $$

(Гостиница Глория; www.hotelamur.com; ul Amurskaya 221; r from R3500; ❄🛜) Definitely one of the city's best options, this smart business hotel has large rooms, modern bathrooms and all the creature comforts you'd expect at the upper midrange level. Staff are friendly and efficient, and you're a short walk from the main sights.

Hotel Armenia
HOTEL $$

(Гостиница Армения; ☎4162-230 799; www.armeniablag.ru; ul Krasnoflotskaya 147; s/d incl breakfast from R2300/3800; ❄🛜) In an ideal location on the riverfront, the flashy Armenia has modern carpeted rooms in earthy hues, with flat-screen TVs and luxurious bathrooms. The best rooms have river views. There are several restaurants on-site, including a patio pizza spot and an overdecorated dining room serving excellent Armenian dishes.

Hotel Strannik
HOTEL $$

(Отель Странник; ☎4162-490 467; www.strannik-otel.ru; ul Teatralnaya 23; r from R3000; ❄🛜) This friendly hotel has a range of fairly eccentrically furnished rooms that are nevertheless very comfortable and clean. Downstairs there's a rather cool restaurant open throughout the day - be sure to behold the wonderfully over-the-top toilets if you visit. There's a 5% reduction if you book via their website.

🍴 Eating

SharLot Cafe
INTERNATIONAL $$

(ul Lenina 113; mains R250-650; ☻9am-midnight; 🛜) Low lit and even a little bit stylish, SharLot Cafe has numerous menus, though sadly none of them are currently in English. However, many of them come with photos, so it's easy enough to point at what you want. Dishes range from salads, soups and pasta to meat and fish grills and various desserts.

Kofinya na Bolshoi
CAFE $$

(Кофейня на Большой; ul Lenina 159; mains R350-750; ☻8am-1am; 🛜) Pleasant cafe with decent cappuccinos and a wide range of dishes including eggs and blini for breakfast, and risotto and pizzas for later on.

Mandarin
CHINESE $$

(Мандарин; ☎4162-331 751; ul 50 Let Oktyabrya 28; mains R400-800; ☻11am-midnight; 🛜) There are actually two Chinese restaurants sharing one kitchen here. Mandarin is the quieter and more sophisticated of the two and can be found around the back of the building. Panda, larger and noisier, is the better signposted and most visible from the main avenue.

ℹ Getting There & Away

Blagoveshchensk is 110km off the Trans-Siberian, reached via the branch line from Belogorsk. The **train station** (ЖД Вокзал; Statsionnaya ul) is 4km north of the river on ul 50 Let Oktyabrya, the main north–south artery. Take bus 30 (unless it's heading to 'mikro-rayon') from outside the station down ul 50 Let Oktyabrya to reach the centre.

Trains heading east backtrack to Belogorsk on their way to Khabarovsk (*kupe/platskartny* from R3700/3050, 13 hours, daily). Heading west, trains serve Chita (*kupe/platskartny* R4200/3500, 38 hours, even-numbered days) and Tynda (*kupe/platskartny* R3300/2800, 16¼ hours, odd-numbered days).

Additional options are available from Belogorsk to the north or Bureya to the east. *Marshrutky* connect Blagoveshchensk's **bus station** (автостанция; cnr ul 50 let Oktyabrya & ul Krasnoarmeyska) with the train stations in Belogorsk (R350, two hours, at least hourly from 7am to 7pm) and Bureya (R600, 3½ hours, three daily).

The **River Terminal** (Речной вокзал; ul Chaykovskogo 1) sends six daily boats to Heihe, China (return R1650, 15 minutes), from where there's an evening train to Harbin. You'll need a Chinese visa and a multiple-entry Russian visa if you plan to return.

Birobidzhan Биробиджан

📞 42622 / POP 74,500 / ⊘ MOSCOW +7HR

Quiet and shady, Birobidzhan is the rather unlikely capital of the Jewish Autonomous Region, a curious creation of Stalin designed to give Soviet Jews a homeland back in 1934 and which today remains the world's only officially Jewish territory outside Israel.

That the region failed to thrive is hardly surprising, given its swampy location, poor climate and the Stalin-sponsored anti-Semitism that characterised the dictator's later years. But somehow, despite having just a tiny number of Jews living here, Birobidzhan retains hints of its Jewish heritage and is a pleasant and unusual place to get off and wander around on your way along the Trans-Siberian.

The main streets ul Lenina and partially pedestrian ul Sholom-Aleykhema parallel the tracks just a five-minute walk south on ul Gorkogo from the train station. The Bira River is another five minutes along, where you'll find a pleasant sculpture-lined walkway with piped-in music and a popular town beach. Sights to see along the way include **Freud** (Биробиджанская еврейская религиозная община Фрейд; 📞 42622-41 531, 8-924-642 8731; ul Lenina 19; ⊘ 9am-5pm Mon-Fri), the Jewish culture central centre and synagogue. Call or ask around for Rabbi Roman Isakovich, who will give you a tour of the complex and talk about local history. The **Regional Museum** (Областной краеведческий музей; ul Lenina 25; R100; ⊘ 10am-6pm Wed-Fri, 9am-5pm Sat) has an excellent exhibit on the arrival of Jewish settlers to Birobidzhan in the 1930s, plus a mini diorama of the Volochaevka civil war battle.

For further reading, Masha Gessen's account of the Jewish Autonomous Region's history, *Where the Jews Aren't*, is highly recommended.

🛏 Sleeping & Eating

⭐ **Hotel Bira** HOTEL $$
(Гостиница Бира; 📞 42622-777 78; www.bira-hotel.ru; ul Sovetskaya 21; r from R2900; ❇ 🛜) Easily the pick of the hotels in Birobidzhan, the Bira is modern, with large and comfortable rooms with fridges and safes as well as the more standard appliances. There's a sauna and billiards room on-site, and the location is good.

Cafe Simkha JEWISH $$
(Кафе Симха; ul Lenina 19; mains R300-600; ⊘ 10am-11pm; 🛜) With its star of David light fittings and multiple types of hummus on the menu, Cafe Simkha is in it to win it as Birobidzhan's premier Jewish restaurant, even if much of its menu is Italian. It's also definitely the smartest place in town, bordering on the flouncy, but the food is tasty and good value.

Felicita CAFE $$
(ul Gorkogo 10; mains R250-750; ⊘ 10am-midnight; 🛜) A short stroll from the train station, Felicita is an attractive, Italian-themed cafe, with coffee, salads, light meals and pizzas.

ⓘ Getting There & Away

As a town on the Trans-Siberian, Birobidzhan is most commonly reached by train. It's just three hours from Khabarovsk or 10 hours from Blagoveshchensk. Coming from the west, you can easily stop off at Birobidzhan, have a look around and then grab a later train or bus for Khabarovsk.

While all Trans-Siberian trains stop at Birobidzhan **train station** (ЖД вокзал; Privokzalnaya pl), if you're heading to Khabarovsk, it's actually cheaper on the *elektrichka* (suburban train; R330, three hours, six daily).

You can also catch *marshrutky* to Khabarovsk (R350, three hours, hourly until 6pm) from the small **bus station** (автостанция) beside the train station.

Khabarovsk Хабаровск

📞 4212 / POP 607,000 / ⊘ MOSCOW +7HR

The Far East's most pleasant surprise, Khabarovsk boasts a dreamy riverside setting, vibrant nightlife, lots of greenery and boulevards lined with pretty tsarist-era buildings. It's something of a revelation if you're arriving on the train from Siberia to see such a thriving place after days of relentless taiga.

Khabarovsk's trump card is its well developed riverside park, which includes pleasant walkways through the trees, some lovely viewpoints and a popular town beach where people swim in the Amur River during the summer months.

It's hot in summer, but winter temperatures give it the unglamorous title of 'world's coldest city of over half a million people'. A dazzling display of ice sculptures occupy central pl Lenina from January until the spring thaw.

History

Khabarovsk was founded in 1858 as a military post by Eastern Siberia's governor-general, Count Nikolai Muravyov (later Muravyov-Amursky), during his campaign to take the Amur back from the Manchus.

It was named after the man who got the Russians into trouble with the Manchus in the first place, 17th-century Russian explorer Yerofey Khabarov, to whom a statue stands outside the train station today.

The Trans-Siberian Railway arrived from Vladivostok in 1897 and quickly heralded the development of Khabarovsk from a small town to a medium-sized city. During the Russian Civil War (1917–22), the town was occupied by Japanese troops. The final Bolshevik victory in the Far East was at Volochaevka, 45km west.

In 1969 Soviet and Chinese soldiers fought a bloody hand-to-hand battle over little Damansky Island in the Ussuri River. Since 1984, tensions have eased. Damansky and several other islands have been handed back to the Chinese.

◎ Sights

Walking is the main activity in Khabarovsk. Good spots are the fabulous **riverfront**, the busy main drag; ul Muravyova-Amurskogo with its impressive turn-of-the-20th-century architecture including the striking **Far Eastern State Research Library** (Дальневосточная государственная научная библиотека; ul Muravyova-Amurskogo 1), the mint-green **Tsentralny Gastronom** (ul Muravyova-Amurskogo 9) topped by a statue of Mercury and the former **House of Pioneers** (Дом пионеров; ul Muravyova-Amurskogo 17), now a 'palace of childhood creation'; and the green walkways that run up the middle of both Amursky bul and Ussuriysky bul, either side of ul Muravyova-Amurskogo.

Khabarovsk Regional Museum MUSEUM
(Хабаровский краевой музей; www.hkm.ru; ul Shevchenko 11; R350; ◎10am-6pm Tue-Sun) Located in an evocative 1894 red-brick building, this museum contains an excellent overview of Russian and Soviet history, despite not having a single word of non-Russian signage. Galleries take you decade by decade through the past with fascinating propaganda posters, old film clips, audio snippets, black-and-white photos (like the sad crowds gathered at the announcement of Stalin's demise) and rooms with period furnishings and accoutrements that give a taste of what life was like.

There's even a small section devoted to the Gulag (fitting, since the nearby prison population was bigger than the city's in the 1930s). Another section has garments, sleds and carvings of native peoples. The less in-triguing new building has a wing dedicated to the Amur River, with live fish in tanks and more stuffed animals.

Assumption Cathedral CATHEDRAL
(Градо-Хабаровский Успенский собор; Komsomolskaya pl) Built in 2002, this striking cathedral rose on the site of a far older church that was knocked down by Stalin during his antireligious campaigns.

Archaeology Museum MUSEUM
(Музей Археологии; ☑4212-24 177; ul Turgeneva 86; R250; ◎10am-6pm Tue-Sun) Undergoing a full renovation in 2017, this five-room museum displays tools and living essentials from early peoples. Pottery, animal skin huts, dugout canoes, a tiny model settlement and early hand tools are all normally here, though it was unclear how much of the exhibit would remain on display when the museum reopens.

Transfiguration Cathedral CATHEDRAL
(Спасо-Преображенский собор; ul Lenina) This highly impressive church's golden domes dazzle you from all over the city with its prime location overlooking the Amur River. The cathedral was built in the early 21st century and is the third tallest church in Russia, topping off at 96m. Inside there's one massive central iconostasis, but otherwise it's almost entirely bare.

Far Eastern Art Museum MUSEUM
(Дальневосточный художественный музей; ul Shevchenko 7; weekdays/weekend R250/300; ◎10am-6pm Tue-Sun) This smart and imposing building hosts a moderately interesting collection of local art, including religious icons, Japanese porcelain and 19th-century Russian paintings.

🏃 Activities & Tours

The most popular area tour offered by travel agents is to the interesting Nanai village of **Sikachi-Alyan**, where you can view the Sikachi-Alyan petroglyphs – stone carvings supposedly dating back 12,000 years. Hunting and fishing opportunities abound in the wild and woolly Khabarovsk region.

Amur River Cruise BOATING
(River boat landing; cruises from R500) Vital to Khabarovsk's rise, the Amur River can be seen on (at times rollicking) party boats. Cruises on the *Moskva-81* depart every two hours from 12.30pm to 12.30am, provided enough customers show up.

Khabarovsk

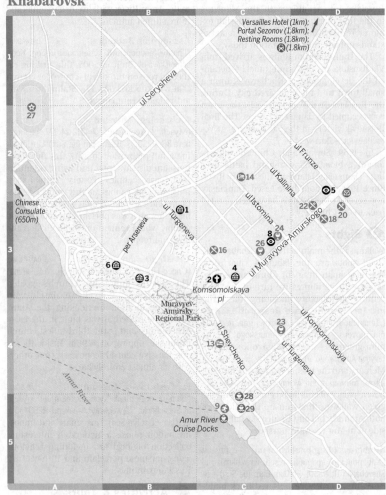

Versailles Hotel (1km);
Portal Sezonov (1.8km);
Resting Rooms (1.8km);
(1.8km)

ul Serysheva

ul Frunze

ul Kalinina

14

ul Istomina

5

22

18 20

ul Turgeneva

1

per Arseneva

8 24

16 26

6

3

2 4

Komsomolskaya
pl

Murayev-
Amursky
Regional Park

ul Shevchenko

23

ul Komsomolskaya

13

ul Turgeneva

ul Muravyova-Amurskogo

Chinese
Consulate
(650m)

Amur River

27

9 28
29

Amur River
Cruise Docks

RUSSIAN FAR EAST KHABAROVSK

Sergey Outfitter   TOURS

(Туристическая компания Вэлком; ☑ 4212-
735 990, 8-914-542 1331; www.sergoutfitter.com;
Office 1, ul Dzerzhinskogo 24) Burly Sergei Khro-
mykh is your man if you are looking to do
some hunting or fishing in the vast wilderness of Khabarovsk Territory or elsewhere
in the Far East. Call ahead to arrange for an
English-speaking guide.

Portal Sezonov   TOURS

(Портал Сезонов; ☑ 4212-389 288; www.
dvtravel.ru; ul Leningradskaya 58) Located in
the train station, the respected Portal Sezonov runs a wide range of tours, includ-

ing hiking and fishing trips, as well as city
tours. English-speaking guides available.

🛏 Sleeping

Kakadu Hostel   HOSTEL **$**

(☑ 4212-788 095; www.kakaduhostel.ru; entrance
1, ul Sheronova 10; dm R650, d with/without bathroom R2200/1600; ❋ ☎) This friendly and
colourful hostel has pleasant male and female dorms, cosy private rooms, helpful
staff and a clear sign visible from the main
road (other Russian hostels, please take
note!). There's a kitchen and communal

Khabarovsk

lounge, free laundry and English is spoken. Get directions before setting out.

From the airport take *marshrukta* 80 to the Volocvhayevskaya stop, while from the train station take trams 1, 2 or 6 to the Ussuriyskaya stop.

Like Hostel Khabarovsk   HOSTEL $
(Лайк Хостел Хабаровск; ☎8-924-403 4194; www.likehostels.ru; flat 20, entrance 2, ul Muravyova-Amurskogo 50; dm/s/d R590/1500/2000; ✲☎) This pleasant place has a fantastic location on the main avenue and is housed in a large apartment now divided into male

and female dorms and a couple of private rooms. There's a kitchen and small communal area, but no English. Enter the courtyard of the building from ul Sheronova, look for entrance 2 in the corner and dial '20'.

★**Hostel Valencia**   GUESTHOUSE $$
(☎8-914-172 7262; 3rd fl, ul Dzerzhinskogo 21a; s/d/tr/q with shared bathroom from R1600/1800/2400/2800; @☎) Named after the city where the owners lived for many years, this friendly eight-room guesthouse

INDIGENOUS GROUPS IN THE FAR EAST

Russia's rich cultural melting pot can seem utterly invisible if you only visit the main cities along the Trans-Siberian Railway. For a radically different perspective, it's worth getting off the beaten path, and learning a bit about the Far East's indigenous groups. A few starting points include the following:

Sakha Republic

Inhabiting a vast India-sized republic, the once-marginalised Sakha are today among the nation's most successful indigenous groups. Sakha (also known as Yakuts) have rich folk customs, including an oral storytelling tradition of great epic poems (some over 20,000 verses long), unique foods (like raw frozen fish, reindeer meat and fermented mare's milk) and a love for the *khomus* (mouth harp). Yakutsk is the gateway to it all, but if you want to visit a shaman or experience traditional life, you'll have to travel well beyond the city.

Kamchatka

The peninsula is home to a number of different groups, including the Even, the Itelmeni and the Koryak. Home to a mix of all three groups, the village of Esso is the best place to learn about the region's cultural diversity, particularly at the excellent Ethnographic Museum. Nomadic Even communities of reindeer herders inhabit hard-to-reach northern regions, though you can join the annual solstice celebration in Anavgay (near Esso) each June. Another Kamchatka event worth planning a trip around is the 1000km-long Beringia dog-sledding race, held in March each year.

Amur River Valley

Numbering around 12,000, the Nanai live on both the Russian and Chinese side of the Amur River. Like many other Far Eastern peoples, the Nanai have a deep respect for nature, and believe the spirit world inhabits most of the physical world around them. The most accessible community to visit is the village of Verkhnyaya Ekon near Komsomolsk-na-Amure.

has bright, attractively designed rooms that are kept sparkling clean. All rooms share bathrooms and toilets, but there's no kitchen and breakfast is not served. It remains a good deal though – find it in the last building in the yard, 75m back from the road.

Versailles Hotel HOTEL $$
(Гостиница Версаль; ☎4212-910 150; www.versal-hotel.net; Amursky bul 46a; s/d incl breakfast from R3200/3500; ❄@🛜) This cheerful hotel, an easy walk from the train station, has pleasant red-carpeted rooms with fridges and small sitting areas. It's set back from the street, fronted with lamp posts.

★**Khabarovsk City Boutique Hotel** BOUTIQUE HOTEL $$$
(Бутик-отель Хабаровск Сити; ☎4212-767 676; www.boutique-hotel.ru; ul Istomina 64; s/d incl breakfast from R3500/4500; ❄@🛜) Khabarovsk's most foreigner-friendly hotel has large, attractive rooms adorned with black-and-white photos from a bygone era. Throw in gorgeous bathrooms with rain showers, luxurious white bedspreads, a full complement of mod cons and a great location, and it's clear why this is an excellent pick.

★**Hotel Parus** HISTORIC HOTEL $$$
(Гостиничный комплекс Парус; ☎4212-335 555; www.hotel-parus.com; ul Shevchenko 5; s/d incl breakfast from R4950/6950; ❄@🛜) Part of a century-old brick building near the water, the 82-room Parus is definitely the smartest and most atmospheric top-end accommodation in Khabarovsk, with its chandeliers, iron staircase, riverside garden and reading room. Rooms are flouncy but sizeable and boast expensive Italian furniture and flat-screen TVs. Friendly, English-speaking service.

Amur Hotel HOTEL $$$
(Гостиница Амур; ☎4212-221 223; www.amurhotel.ru; ul Lenina 29; s/d incl breakfast from R4000/6000; ❄@🛜) Having undergone an impressive renovation, this one-time Soviet place has begun a new life as a stylish and (almost) boutique hotel with a low-lit, arty reception and a totally overhauled restaurant downstairs. The rooms are not as smart as the lobby might suggest, but they are comfy, clean and have ornate moulded ceilings.

Eating

Plantacia
CAFE $

(Плантация; ul Muravyova-Amurskogo 38; sandwiches R100-200; ⊙8am-midnight; 🔊) On Khabarovsk's main avenue, this reliable and great value subterranean spot serves good coffee, baked goods and sandwiches, making it an ideal breakfast or lunch place. You'll also find local chains Tempo Pizza and Papa Wok, Mama Pasta in the same basement, giving you plenty of culinary variety. It's popular with a young, student crowd.

★ Muscat Whale
ITALIAN $$

(Мускатный кит; ul Kalinina 82; mains R400-800; ⊙10am-11.30pm; 🔊) This gorgeous, chic yet pleasantly unfussy place is currently our top choice for a meal in Khabarovsk. The large and luminous space has white-tiled walls, painted brick and lots of wooden fittings, while its menu boasts wonderful fresh salads, scrumptious pizzas, innovative meat dishes and a huge dessert list.

Vdrova
PIZZA $$

(ВДрова; ul Muravyova-Amurskogo 15; mains R300-500; ⊙11am-midnight; 🔊) Vdrova comes with whimsically dressed Italian-style 'animators' who welcome you loudly, and sing, prance and shout throughout your meal in joyous waves of distraction perfect for anyone who doesn't have much to say to their dinner partner. The pizzas are some of the best in town though, and while many will hate the forced bonhomie, it can be a lot of fun.

Farsh
FUSION $$

(Фарш; ul Sheronova 72; mains R300-800; ⊙10am-midnight; 🔊) Another progressive place with an interesting and pleasingly unusual menu, Farsh dubs itself a gastrobar, but is really more of a fusion place with dishes such as Armenian tortillas filled with cheese, boiled pork salad with grapes in mustard sauce, and shrimp and squid wontons all on the menu. The stripped-down, white-painted walls give it a minimalist feel.

Satsivi
GEORGIAN $$

(Сациви; ul Frunze 53; mains R200-450; ⊙noon-midnight, until 2am Fri & Sat; 🔊🖊🍴) Fiercely popular and putting on a good show of being a traditional Georgian restaurant, despite its unhelpful location in a rather sterile business centre, Satsivi (named after a delicious chicken in walnut sauce dis) is a winner and boasts Khabarovsk's best Georgian cooking. The summer terrace is a great alternative to the rather dark main dining room.

Trattoria Semplice
ITALIAN $$

(☎4212-206 051; ul Pushkina 54; mains R300-500; ⊙11am-11.30pm; 🖊) White-painted plank walls, linen curtains and fresh-cut flowers brighten up this downstairs space near pl Lenina. The piping-hot thin-crust pizzas are among the city's best and even a small one can feed two (unless you're famished). Welcome is warm and friendly.

Chocolate
CAFE $$$

(ul Turgeneva 74; mains R500-1400; ⊙24hr; 🔊) A smart cafe favoured by Khabarovsk's upper middle class with a pricey menu of slick international dishes by day (fajitas, sautéed squid, smoked duck breast), it becomes a prime party spot after hours.

Drinking & Nightlife

★ Gatsby
LOUNGE

(☎4212-604 333; ul Istomina 49; ⊙noon-4am Mon-Thu, to 8am Fri & Sat, 5pm-4am Sun; 🔊) Handsomely designed Gatsby has a main-level restaurant and lounge (with good food from R300 to R800). Downstairs is a swanky bar in one room, with big comfy seats around a horseshoe-shaped bar, and a small dance floor with DJ in another room. It draws a stylish crowd, but the vibe overall is very welcoming.

Brozbar
CRAFT BEER

(Брозбар; ☎4212-204 230; ul Turgeneva 60; ⊙9am-midnight, until 2am Fri & Sat; 🔊) With its industrial feel, this new edition to Khabarovsk's busy bar scene is definitely on the edgier side atmosphere-wise (well, at least by local standards). It has a good range of local and international craft beers on sale as well as a full food menu.

Harat's
IRISH PUB

(www.harats.ru; ul Muravyova-Amurskogo 44; ⊙5pm-6am; 🔊) This traditionally decorated Irish-style pub has a good beer selection (with dozens on tap) and features live music regularly, with occasional cover charges (up to R300). It can be a lot of fun when it's full, but feels slightly eerie when empty due to all the slightly overdone Irish paraphernalia.

Harley Davidson Bar
BAR

(ul Komsomolskaya 88; ⊙24hr) Features nightly shows (rock or country bands, cabaret), 10 brews on tap, tattooed bartenders and a long wooden bar. Upstairs is a veranda bar with street views. Cover charge runs R300 on weekends, when it's absolutely packed with the cream of Khabarovsk's rocker youth.

☆ Entertainment

Theatre of Musical Comedy THEATRE
(Хабаровский краевой театр драмы и комедии; ☑ 4212-211 196; ul Karla Marksa 64; tickets R100-1200) Funny operettas run from November to April; big musical acts run from May to October. There's also the occasional ballet.

Platinum Arena ICE HOCKEY
(Платинум Арена; ☑ 4212-313502; www.platinum-arena.ru; ul Dikopoltseva 12) This is the home of Khabarovsk's ice hockey team, the Amur Tigers, a hot ticket from October to March.

Lenin Stadium FOOTBALL
(Стадион Ленина; Riverfront Sports Complex; tickets from R150) Home to Khabarovsk's first-division football team, SKA-Energiya.

🛍 Shopping

Tainy Remesla GIFTS & SOUVENIRS
(Тайны ремесла; ul Muravyova-Amurskogo 17; ⊙ 10am-7pm) This is the best souvenir shop in town, located in the old House of Pioneers building.

ℹ Information

Post Office (Почта; ul Muravyova-Amurskogo 28; ⊙ 8am-8pm Mon-Fri, 9am-6pm Sat & Sun)

ℹ Getting There & Away

AIR

Khabarovsk Novy Airport (☑ 4212-262 006; www.airkhv.ru) is 7km east of the train station; a taxi from the city centre costs around R300. This is the best connected airport in the Far East, with flights to cities throughout the region, as well as to many other large cities in Russia.

BOAT

Many companies at the **river terminal** (Речной вокзал; Ussuriysky bul; ⊙ 8am-7pm), such as **Sakhekspo** (Сахэкспо; ☑ 4212-656 668, 8-924-312 3019; 421624@mail.ru; Ussuriysky bul), offer morning and evening departures to Fuyuan, China (90 minutes), which cost R4500 including tour and overnight lodging.

BUS

The **bus station** (Автовокзал; ul Voronezh-skaya 19), 500m north of the train station (go by

TRANSPORT CONNECTIONS FROM KHABAROVSK

DESTINATION	MAIN TRAINS & FREQUENCY	RAIL PRICE (PLATSKART-NY/KUPE)	RAIL DURATION	AIRLINES	AIR PRICE (FROM R)	AIR DURATION & FREQUENCY
Beijing	N/A	N/A	N/A	Aurora	8200	3hr, Sun & Wed
Blagovesh-chensk	35 (daily)	R2100/3100	13½hr	Aurora	3000	2hr, 4 weekly
Irkutsk	1, 7, 43, 99, 133, 207 (2-3 daily)	from R6600/7600	58hr	Aeroflot, Ural Airlines, Ir Aero	10,000	3¾hr, daily
Komsomolsk	351 (daily), 667 (daily)	from R1300/2800	10hr	N/A	N/A	N/A
Magadan	N/A	N/A	N/A	Aurora	9900	2¾hr, daily
Moscow	1, 43, 99 (1-2 daily)	from R11, 300/20,600	5½ days	Aeroflot, Ros-siya Airlines	12,500	8hr, several daily
Neryungri	325 (daily)	R2700/4800	36hr	Yakutia Airlines	6200	2hr, Mon & Thu
Petropavlovsk-Kamchatsky	N/A	N/A	N/A	Aurora, Yaku-tia Airlines	9400	2½hr, daily
Seoul	N/A	N/A	N/A	Asiana, Aurora	12,500	3hr, daily
Vladivostok	2, 6, 8, 100, 202, 208, 352	from R1900/2100	11-15hr	Aurora, S7	2600	1¼hr, multiple daily
Yakutsk	N/A	N/A	N/A	Yakutia Airlines	12,950	2½hr, 4 weekly
Yuzhno-Sakhalinsk	N/A	N/A	N/A	Aurora, Yaku-tia Airlines	5900	2hr, 3 daily

tram or bus 4), sends nine buses daily to Komsomolsk (R600, 6½ hours) and hourly *marshrutky* to Birobidzhan (three hours, R350) until 6pm.

TRAIN

The full-service **train station** (ЖД вокзал; ul Leningradskaya) is lovely, with a supermarket nearby (to the left of the station when exiting). Note that almost all trains to Vladivostok are overnight.

It's also worth bearing in mind that the westbound/eastbound 1/2 Rossiya train between Moscow and Vladivostok (*platskart* from R17,300) is significantly more expensive than all other trains (*platskart* from R11,300), and only slightly faster (five days and 12 hours versus six days and three hours). The 7/8 train between Novosibirsk and Vladivostok is also relatively expensive.

For Birobidzhan, take any westbound train or a cheaper *elektrichka* (R330, three hours, six daily).

ⓘ Getting Around

From Khabarovsk's train station, about 3.5km northeast of the waterfront, bus 4 goes to Komsomolskaya pl (board opposite the station and head southeast) and trams 1 and 2 go near pl Lenina.

From the airport, 9km east of the centre, trolleybus 1 goes to Komsomolskaya pl along ul Muravyova-Amurskogo and bus 35 goes to the train station (25 minutes) and bus station. An official taxi to the centre from the airport is R500; usually R300 the other way. Trolleybuses and trams cost R22.

Vladivostok   Владивосток

☑ 423 / POP 606,000 / ⊙ MOSCOW + 7HR

The unofficial capital of the Russian Far East and one of Russia's most important commercial ports and naval bases, Vladivostok ('Master the East') is also a thoroughly charming city, with a gorgeous, hilly setting, striking architecture and numerous verdant islands and sandy bays along its Pacific coastline. Most notable of these is Golden Horn Bay (named for its likeness to Istanbul's), over which now soars a massive suspension bridge, one of two built in recent years that have hugely improved the city's lumbering Soviet-era infrastructure.

The rest of Russia slowly seems to be waking up to Vladivostok's potential as well. In 2016 St Petersburg's Mariinsky Theatre inaugurated its impressive glass and steel Primorsky Stage (p559), while the Hermitage Vladivostok (p554) is due to open in 2018. Vladivostok buzzes with cocktail bars,

---

ⓘ GETTING CHINESE VISAS IN THE FAR EAST

It's best to arrange Chinese visas in your home country, although foreigners with verve can attempt to obtain a Chinese visa on the road. In the Far East, only the **consulate** (☑ 4212-302 590; www.china-consulate.khb.ru/rus; Southern Bldg, Lenin Stadium 1; ⊙ 11am-1pm Mon, Wed & Fri) in Khabarovsk provides this service.

A one-month tourist visa for most costs from R2000 for five-day processing (expedited visas sometimes possible with a higher fee). Americans pay R9000 and Canadians pay R7300 (10-day processing only). You'll need a letter of invitation, application form and copies of your immigration card, latest hotel registration and Russian visa. All forms are in Russian, but travel agencies in Khabarovsk may be able to assist you with your application.

---

excellent restaurants and a renewed sense of purpose – don't miss the Far East's most dynamic and fast-paced city.

History

Founded in 1860, Vladivostok (meaning 'Master the East') became a naval base in 1872. Tsarevitch Nicholas (later Tsar Nicholas II) turned up in 1891 to inaugurate the new Trans-Siberian rail line. By the early 20th century, Vladivostok teemed with merchants, speculators and sailors of every nation in a manner more akin to Shanghai or Hong Kong than to Moscow. Koreans and Chinese, many of whom had built the city, accounted for four out of every five of its citizens.

After the fall of Port Arthur in the Russo-Japanese War of 1904–05, Vladivostok took on an even more crucial strategic role, and when the Bolsheviks seized power in European Russia, Japanese, Americans, French and English poured ashore here to support the tsarist counterattack. Vladivostok held out until 25 October 1922, when Soviet forces finally marched in and took control – it was the last city to fall.

In the years to follow, Stalin deported or shot most of the city's foreign population. Closed to foreigners from 1958 to 1992, Vladivostok opened up with a bang – literally (Mafia shoot-outs were a part of early business deals) – in the '90s, and quickly

Vladivostok

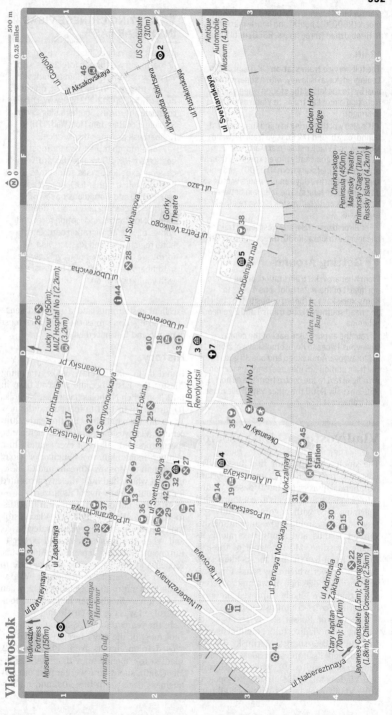

500 m
0.25 miles

US Consulate (310m)

Antique
Automobile
Museum (4.1km)

ul Gogolya

ul Aksakovskaya

ul Vsevoloda Sibirtseva

ul Pushkinskaya

ul Svetlanskaya

Golden Horn
Bridge

Cherkavskogo
Peninsula (450m);
Mariinsky Theatre
Primorsky Stage (1km);
Russky Island (4.2km)

ul Lazo

ul Sukhanova

Gorky
Theatre

ul Petra Velikogo

Korabelnaya nab

Golden Horn
Bay

ul Uborevicha

Lucky Tour (950m);
MUZ Hospital No 1 (2.2km);
(3.2km)

ul Uborevicha

Okeansky pr

Wharf No 1

pl Bortsov
Revolyutsii

ul Fontannaya

ul Aleutskaya

ul Semyonovskaya

ul Admirala Fokina

Okeansky pr

Train
Station

ul Svetlanskaya

ul Aleutskaya

pl
Vokzalnaya

ul Pogranichnaya

ul Posetskaya

ul Pervaya Morskaya

ul Zapadnaya

ul Tigrovaya

ul Batareynaya

Sportivnaya
Harbour

ul Naberezhnaya

ul Admirala
Zakharova

Stary Kapitan (1.5m); Pyongyang
(70m); Ra (1km)   Consulate
Japanese Consulate (1.8km); Chinese Consulate (2.5km)

ul Naberezhnaya

Vladivostok
Fortress
Museum (150m)

Amursky Gulf

Amursky Gulf

Vladivostok

established itself as the most prosperous and dynamic city in the Far East as trade and transport links with its Asian neighbours blossomed.

Vladivostok's infrastructure was torn asunder and rebuilt for the big APEC summit on Russky Island in 2012. The most eye-catching developments include two giant suspension bridges: one across Golden Horn Bay to the previously difficult-to-access Cherkavskogo Peninsula, the other spanning more than 4km to Russky Island across the Eastern Bosphorus Strait. A brand-new university campus opened there in 2012, and it's here that the city's break-neck development continues apace.

⊙ Sights

Vladivostok's sights are rather spread out, so be prepared to get to grips with the local public transport network or take plenty of taxis or tours. That said, the city centre is walkable.

⊙ Central Vladivostok

The main square in Vladivostok is port-side pl Bortsov Revolyutsii, where a massive new **cathedral** (Спасо-Преображенский кафедральный собор; pl Bortsov Revolyutsii) was under construction at the time of writing. The two main avenues are ul Aleutskaya and ul Svetlanskaya, which run perpendicular to one another and meet just west of pl Bortsov Revolyutsii. Ul Fokina (aka the Arbat) is a partially pedestrianised 'walking street' where locals stroll in the evening, running down to the cute Sportivnaya Harbour (p555), another lovely place to wander.

Arsenev Regional Museum   MUSEUM
(Приморский   Государственный Объединенный музей имени В. К. Арсеньева; 📋 423-241 3977; ul Svetlanskaya 20; R400; ⊙ 10am-7pm) This recently redone museum dates from 1890 and offers three floors of galleries, although sadly little in the way of English labelling. Exhibits delve into lo-

cal history, covering early explorers to the region, Vlad's vibrant Chinatown from the early 1900s, and civil war (with a short silent film playing across a broken screen). English-speaking guides are sometimes available for free tours.

Hermitage Vladivostok
MUSEUM

(www.hermitage.ru; ul Svetlanskaya 40) Due to open its local premises by 2018 in this gorgeous tsarist-era building in the centre of Vladivostok, the Hermitage is the latest big cultural institution to open a Far Eastern campus. Once complete, the fully renovated building will host temporary exhibits from the museum's vast collection in St Petersburg.

S-56 Submarine
MUSEUM

(Подводная лодка С-56; ☑ 423-221 6757; Korabelnaya nab; R100; ⊙ 9am-8pm) Perched near the waterfront, the S-56 submarine is worth a look. The first half is a ho-hum exhibit of badges and photos of men with badges (all in Russian). Keep going: towards the back you walk through an officers' lounge with a framed portrait of Stalin and then onto a bunk room with Christmas-coloured torpedoes. Outside, note the '14', marking the WWII sub's 'kills'.

Vladivostok Fortress Museum
MUSEUM

(Музей Владивостокская Крепость; ☑ 423-240 0896; ul Batareynaya 4a; R200; ⊙ 10am-6pm) On the site of an old artillery battery overlooking Sportivnaya Harbour, this museum has cannons outside, a six-room indoor exhibit of photos and many, many guns inside. There are thankfully English explanations, so it's quite accessible by Russian museum standards.

Primorsky Picture Gallery
GALLERY

(Приморская государственная картинная галерея; ul Aleutskaya 12; R250; ⊙ 11am-7pm Tue-Sun) Vladivostok's main art museum on Partizansky pr has long been under renovation and shows no sign of reopening any time soon. In the meantime, some of its decent collection can be seen at rotating temporary shows held at this annex.

Funicular
FUNICULAR

(Фуникулёр; ul Pushkinskaya; tickets R12; ⊙ 7am-8pm) Vladivostok's well-oiled funicular railway makes a fun 60-second ride up a 100m hill every few minutes unless the old girl is experiencing one of her frequent 'technical breaks'. At the top, cross ul Sukhanova via the underpass to a great lookout over the bay. It's next to a statue of Sts Cyril and Methodius (inventors of the Cyrillic alphabet) on the campus of DVGTU.

The base of the funicular is about a 15-minute walk from the centre.

◉ Outer Vladivostok

★ Zarya Centre for Contemporary Art
MUSEUM

(Центр современного искусства "Заря"; ☑ 423-231 7100; www.zaryavladivostok.ru; pr 100 let Vladivostoky 155; ⊙ noon-8pm Mon-Thu, 11am-10pm Fri-Sun) FREE The full renovation and repurposing of a former clothing factory into a giant creative complex containing offices, studios, cafes and work spaces is one of Vladivostok's most interesting recent developments. Visitors will be most interested in the excellent Zarya Centre for Contemporary Art, which is divided into two exhibition halls where top-notch temporary art and design exhibitions are held. Check out what's on via the website.

To get here from the centre, take bus 41 from outside Clover House (p557) or bus 31 from outside the train station (p560) to the stop Fabrika Zarya and then cross the road using the bridge.

Primorsky Oceanarium
AQUARIUM

(Приморский Океанариум; ☑ 423-223 9422; www.primocean.ru; ul Akademika Kasyanova 25; adult/child R700/400; ⊙ 10am-8pm Tue-Sun; 🔊) This massive new development on Russky Island is one of Vladivostok's planned key attractions and opened with great fanfare in 2016. It's a vast space in a remote, purpose-built building, and while it has all the potential to be a great traveller attraction, it actually had the feel of a place struggling on our last visit when the dolphinarium was closed, many tanks were empty and no food or drinks were available. Hopefully things will improve in time.

To get out here, jump on bus 15 from ul Aksakovskaya and get off at the last stop. A free shuttle bus will take you to the oceanarium's main entrance, or you can just walk the 500m yourself.

Russky Island
ISLAND

(Остров Русский) A fully militarised zone for most of the past 150 years, this big island just offshore has been reinvented as a business and academic centre (as home to the sprawling Far Eastern Federal University campus and the new Oceanarium). There's great tourism potential here, not least for some excellent beaches as you go deeper and deeper into the island and away from the city, but at the moment Russky Island is very much a DIY attraction.

Access to the island is by bus over the suspension bridge. Take a northbound bus 29 or bus 15 from Okeansky pr or ul Aksakovskaya (p560). The more-frequent bus 15 takes you to the DVFU campus, from which you can transfer to a minibus 29, which makes a loop, stopping in Rynda and other spots on the island. Rynda has a couple of resorts and the best beaches (just hop out when you see one you like). There are many forts on the island, including the **Voroshilov Battery** (Музей Ворошиловская батарея; R200; ⊗ 9am-5pm Wed-Sun).

Antique Automobile Museum   MUSEUM
(Музей автомотостарины; www.automotomuseum.vl.ru; ul Sakhalinskaya 2a; R200; ⊗10am-6pm Tue-Sun) If you're a bit of a car (or Soviet) nerd, the Antique Automobile Museum is an absolute classic. A room full of Soviet-mobiles (motorcycles too) from the 1930s to 1970s includes a 1948 M&M-green GAZ-20 'Pobeda' (Victory). Take bus 31 along ul Svetlanskaya and get off after it reaches the end of ul Borisenko.

Fort No 7   FORTRESS
(Форт No 7; R300; ⊗10am-6pm Tue-Sun) Of Vladivostok's multiple, numbered defensive forts, No 7 (14km north of the centre) gets our vote. It has 1.5km of tunnels, pretty much untouched since the last 400 soldiers stationed here left in 1923, although the NKVD later used it as an execution chamber. Take a taxi here.

Popov Island   ISLAND
(Остров Попова) Just beyond Russky Island, Popov Island is better regarded for its beaches and filled with many guesthouses and dachas. You'll probably need to stay overnight if you head out here, as there is only one boat per day (R100, 1½ hours), departing in the early evening from Vladivostok's Wharf No 1 (1-й Причал).

🏃 Activities

The **Sportivnaya Harbour** (Спортивная гавань) has a popular beach plus beer and shashlyk stands. You can hire paddle boats and rowboats here, and there's an amusement park just off the waterfront. Much of

the water facing Vladivostok is quite polluted, but it gets cleaner as you go north. Sunbathers can get on a northbound *elektrichka* and hop off at any beach that looks good – try Sedanka, where there are a few resorts with services. You'll find even better swimming on Popov Island or Russky Island.

Bridges of Vladivostok   CRUISE
(Мосты Владивостока; ☑423-299 9590; Wharf 30, Okeansky pr; R700-1000) This recommended outfit runs several daily cruises around the bays of Vladivostok. Departures at midday, 1pm and 2pm do an hour-long Bridges of Vladivostok tour, while a two-hour Sea Panorama tour leaves at 4.30pm, followed by a sunset cruise between 6.30pm and 8.30pm. All tours start and finish at Wharf 30.

Lotos Co   TOUR
(☑423-230 8025; www.lotosco.ru; ul Dalzavodskaya 1, office 303; ⊗10am-6pm Mon-Fri) Offers a comprehensive assortment of tours, including visits to Russky Island, Popov Island and nature trips to the Primorsky Territory (waterfall visits, river rafting). One unique tour it offers is a three-hour bus tour of the new campus of the Far East Federal University on Russky Island, which is not possible to do on your own.

☞ Tours

Lucky Tour   TOURS
(☑423-202 5070; www.luckytour.com; ul Moskovskaya 1; ⊗9.30am-6pm Mon-Fri) Lucky Tour has over 20 years' experience leading tours in the Primorsky region, and its guides know Vladivostok backwards. There are dozens of city tours designed for all types of travellers and interests. English is spoken.

Vladivostok Digger Club   TOURS
(Владивостокский диггер-клуб (ВДК); ☑423-255 2086; www.vladdig.org; office 303, ul Admirala Fokina 29a) This passionate outfit of fortress enthusiasts leads hour-long to full-day tours of Fort No 7, plus other forts, batteries and the tunnels that link them (some up to 3.5km long).

Dalintourist   TOURS
(Дальинтурист; ☑423-241 0903; www.dalintourist.ru; ul Admirala Fokina 8a; ⊗9am-7pm Mon-Fri, 10am-3pm Sat) Runs professional tours of the entire Primorsky region and can arrange English-speaking guides for Vladivostok city tours and beyond.

✪ Festivals & Events

V-Rox
MUSIC

(www.vrox.org/en; ☉ mid-Aug) The brainchild of local rock star Ilya Lagutenko of the famous Russian band Mumiy Troll, this massive rock festival is the biggest musical event in the Russian Far East. Held in mid-August, the four-day fest features some 70 different concerts around town (including in open-air venues), with performers from all over the world.

Pacific Meridian Film Festival
FILM

(Меридианы Тихого; www.pacificmeridianfest.ru; ☉ Sep) One of Russia's most important film festivals, the Pacific Meridian has been held in Vladivostok every year since 2003. Screenings take place at the Gorky Theatre in the centre of town, and for a week in early September the city overflows with Russian movie stars.

🛏 Sleeping

★ Izba Hostel
HOSTEL $

(Хостел Изба; ☎ 423-290 8508; www.izba-hostel.ru; ul Mordovtseva 3; dm R550-950, d from R2500; ☞) It's quite a leap to believe you're in a 'traditional Russian hostel' given Izba's location in a thoroughly Soviet tower block, but the charming staff at this brand-new place make an impressive effort to help you. With lots of wood and *matryoshka* patterns throughout, there's a great kitchen, a comfortable common area and spotless bathrooms. Location is also excellent.

The entrance is actually up a well-signed staircase on the ul Aleutskaya side of the building.

Gallery & More Guesthouse
HOSTEL $

(☎ 8-914-325 5060; www.galleryandmore.ru; ul Admirala Fokina 4b; dm R700, r from R1900; ☞) Enjoying a great location on the Arbat, this quirky and well-designed place combines an art gallery, cafe and small hostel. There's just one dorm with six beds, and several private rooms that are all extremely minimalist but rather funky and share bathrooms.

Mattress, Sailor & Albatross Hostel
HOSTEL $

(Хостел "Матрас, Матрос и Альбатрос"; ☎ 8-914-661 3836; www.mattresshostel.ru; ul Svetlanskaya 33/5; dm/s/d from R600/1300/2800; ☞) OK, so the name sounds much better in Russian, but this quirky place is a real winner for its superb location (in the trendy GUM courtyard, which is filled with bars, cafes and restaurants), its friendly staff and its new private rooms upstairs. The downside is the small kitchen and a lack of hang-out space – you'll have to go outside.

Vlad Marine Inn
HOSTEL $

(☎ 423-208 0280; www.vlad-marine.ru; ul Posetskaya 53; dm R700, d with/without private bathroom R2100/1700; ☞) In a cutely painted clapboard building on a hill in the centre of town, this inviting hostel has just five rooms, each with polished wood floors and ample natural light. Dorm beds have small individual flat-screen TVs, and the three doubles are pretty decent for the price. There's a basic kitchen for guests to use, but otherwise no food.

Optimum Hostel
HOSTEL $

(Barbados Hostel; ☎ 423-272 9111, 8-914-702 9111; www.hostel-optimum.ru; ul Aleutskaya 17; dm R600-800, d/tr R2200/2800; ❄ ☞) Set in a grand eight-storey 1930s building topped with statues and in a perfect central location, Optimum Hostel offers wood-floored dorm rooms, free laundry, English-speaking staff and a guest kitchen. Ring the 'Optimum' buzzer. Out of hours, go round the left to Barbados Hostel, in the same building, which is run by the same people and has a reception desk.

Do note that Barbados Hostel only has dorms, while Optimum also has private rooms, although they all share bathrooms. There's no air-con in Barbados.

Teplo
HOTEL $$

(☎ 423-290 9555; www.teplo-hotel.ru; ul Posetskaya 16; r from R2500; ❄ ☞) Teplo brings a dash of style to Vlad's lodging options with a lounge-like lobby (with sofas and table football), and a white-brick corridor leading back to the small but appealing rooms. Each is equipped with TV, fridge and half bath (shower and sink only). There's free laundry and a guest kitchen, and the location on a quiet but central street is excellent.

Hotel Moryak
HOTEL $$

(Гостиница Моряк; ☎ 423-249 9499; www.hotelm.ru; ul Posetskaya 38; s/d from R2500/2700; ❄ ☞) This grey-brick yct cheerful place has an endearing lobby with a stuffed sailor, the hotel namesake. The rooms are compact with thin walls (and mattresses) and *tiny* bathrooms. Threadbare *ekonom* rooms are quite worn, but overall they're a good deal given the hotel's central location.

Azimut Hotel
HOTEL $$$

(☎ 423-241 3500; www.azimuthotels.com; ul Naberezhnaya 10; s/d from R6600/8250; ❄ ☞) Formerly the Soviet-era Hotel Vladivostok, the Azimut group completely renovated this impressive hilltop property in 2015 and in doing so has led the charge to redevelop Vlad's rather unappealing beachfront. The vibe is sleek and stylish, with a fun approach to running a giant hotel. Highlights include an excellent restaurant, quiet rooms, professional staff and wonderful sea views.

Hotel Primorye HOTEL $$$

(Гостиница Приморье; ☑ 423-241 3040; www. hotelprimorye.ru; ul Posetskaya 20; s/d incl breakfast from R4900/5100; @ 🛜) Primorye has decent rooms with playful details such as funny artwork, though the design is rather dated and the beds are rock-hard. The best rooms are two-room suites with views of the warships in Golden Horn Bay. An enticing bakery and cafe adjoins the lobby, while there's also an excellent pizzeria next door.

Hotel Versailles HOTEL $$$

(Гостиница Версаль; ☑ 423-226 4201; www. hotel-versailles.ru; ul Svetlanskaya 10; s/d incl breakfast R6300/7300; 🛜) The Versailles does a decent job of recapturing the imperial grace of a century-old hotel that reopened in the '90s, despite some bizarre decorative pairings in the lobby (think '70s lounge seats and tsarist-style chandeliers). Quarters are spacious and have some wonderful furniture and lavish bathrooms.

Equator Hotel HOTEL $$$

(Гостиница Экватор; ☑ 423-241 1254; www. hotelequator.ru; ul Naberezhnaya 20; s/d from R3500/5500; 🛜) This old-school Soviet hotel has decent and clean midrange rooms that are fairly spacious but minimally equipped. Book an upper-floor even-numbered room for a sea view. It has an enviably central location overlooking the Sportivnaya Harbour.

✖ Eating

Vladivostok offers more culinary innovation and variety than anywhere else in Russia east of Moscow, and the dining here is likely to be a highlight of your visit. As a big port, fish and seafood dominate most menus, as do influences from nearby Korea and Japan. It's worth making dinner reservations for smarter places at the weekend.

Ne Riday CAFETERIA $

(Не Рыдай; ul Svetlanskaya 10; mains R60-130; ⊙9am-8pm; 🛜) This delightful cafeteria (whose name bizarrely means 'don't sob') is about as far from your Russian stereotyped *stolovaya* (canteen) as it's possible to get.

With a large range of Russian cooking on offer and a smart, sleek space with a chandelier set in a historic building, it makes for a superb-value lunch spot.

Five O'Clock CAFE $

(ul Admirala Folkina 6; snacks R50-200; ⊙8am-9pm Mon-Fri, 9am-9pm Sat, 11am-9pm Sun; 🖉) Russians so firmly believe that the British drink afternoon tea at 5pm each day that there's even a cafe named after this spurious assertion. The good news is that this much-loved local haunt on pedestrian ul Admirala Folkina serves muffins, cakes and quiche, all made fresh daily and sold for far less than you'll find elsewhere. Skip the coffee, though.

Clover House FAST FOOD, SUPERMARKET $

(ul Semyonovskaya 15; ⊙10am-9pm) A convenient mall housing a well-stocked supermarket with a deli, and a top-floor food court with incredible views.

Republic CAFETERIA $

(Республика; ul Aleutskaya 2; meals R200-350; ⊙9am-11pm Mon-Fri, 10am-11pm Sat & Sun; 🖉) This very pleasant and good value *stolovaya* draws a crowd of regulars with its tasty Russian dishes, home brew and funky interior. There's an on-site bar, and it makes a good alternative to eating in the station if you're waiting for a train.

★ Kvartira 30 EUROPEAN $$

(Квартира 30; ☑ 423-297 4483; ul Pologaya 65b; mains R400-600; ⊙noon-midnight; 🛜🖉) This fantastic treasure is hidden away in an extremely unlikely location amid a hilltop housing estate. Run by the charming Olga Gurskaya, who also uses the space to run cookery classes, Kvartira 30 offers some of the most interesting and innovative Russian food in the city: the aubergines marinated in lemon juice and chilli with toasted rye bread were a revelation.

With only five tables, it's a good idea to reserve for the evenings. Don't miss the *zefir* dessert, a kind of local marshmallow made from blueberries. To find it, it's best to start from Okeansky pr, where the entrance to the street is just a staircase through some trees that becomes a residential street. Head up the road and look for the yellow neoclassical building on the left: the restaurant is to the left-hand side of that.

★ Studio INTERNATIONAL $$

(☑ 423-255 2222; www.cafe-studio.ru; ul Svetlanskaya 18a; mains R300-900; ⊙24hr; 🛜🖉) In a courtyard in the heart of Vladivostok is this smart and appealing two-floor restaurant and lounge bar that attracts a young, well-heeled and in-the-know crowd. There's an enormous picture menu with everything from breakfasts and business lunches to seafood and pizzas; the elaborately gorgeous upstairs bar has to be seen to be believed.

★**Zuma** ASIAN **$$**
(Зума; ☑ 423-222 2666; ul Fontannaya 2; mains R300-1400; ⊙11am-2am Sun-Thu; 🛜🍴) A stylish but welcoming place, this two-floor restaurant-lounge is decked out in an elaborate but classy Angkor Wat–themed interior, replete with a massive black granite bar perfect for lingering with drinks. The real attraction here is the mouthwatering pan-Asian cooking (sushi, dumplings, stir-fries), plus creative salads, rack of lamb and a fabulous seafood selection.

★**Pyongyang** NORTH KOREAN **$$**
(Пхеньян; ul Verkhneportovaya 68b; mains R350-750; ⊙noon-midnight; 🍴) Staffed by waitresses from nearby North Korea who periodically break out into karaoke, this unique establishment is just strange enough to be considered a must-visit. You can pick from a photo menu of excellent food such as *bibimbap* (rice mixed with fried egg, sliced meat and other ingredients) and spicy fried pork with kimchi.

★**Food Like Food** RUSSIAN **$$**
(Еда как еда; ☑ 423-224 04674; ul Admirala Fokina 16; mains R400-1000; ⊙11am-midnight, until 2am Fri & Sat; 🛜) While it might sound like a fast food joint, this charming little white-painted basement restaurant is anything but. The menu takes in classical Russian cooking, but presents dishes with an original twist, such as aubergines in oyster sauce or salmon in green pea purée. Staff are exceptionally engaged and knowledgeable, and cute Russian knick-knacks adorn the walls.

Pizza M PIZZA **$$**
(Пицца М; ☑ 423-241 3430; ul Posetskaya 20; pizzas R300-650; ⊙24hr; 🛜🍴) Classier than its name might suggest, the M is one of Vlad's coolest hang-outs, with two unique rooms setting their style sights higher than the humble slice. The pizzas are available as thin or thick crust and are delicious. Delivery is also available.

Mauro Gianvanni PIZZA **$$**
(Мауро Джанванни; ☑ 423-222 0782; www.mauro-gianvanni.ru; ul Aleutskaya 21; mains R220-

700; ⊙noon-midnight Sun-Thu, until 2am Fri & Sat; 🍴) This little Italian-run brick-oven pizzeria has a modern interior and snappy service. The dozen-plus pizzas are crispy and arguably some of the best east of the Urals.

Supra GEORGIAN **$$**
(Супра; ☑ 423-227 7722; www.supravl.ru; ul Admirala Fokina 1b; mains R250-500; ⊙noon-midnight; 🍴) This bustling but charming spot has one of the best locations in town, meaning that it's always busy and you may well have to wait for a table. The traditionally clad staff work quickly in serving the various elements of a Georgian *supra* (feast) though, while the picture menu is huge and the realisation generally excellent.

Moloko & Myod INTERNATIONAL **$$**
(Молоко и Мёд; ul Sukhanova 6a; mains R400-750; ⊙10am-midnight Sun-Thu, to 2am Fri & Sat; 🛜🍴) A trendy spot with a popular street-side terrace, 'Milk & Honey' has fabulous daily brunch offerings, great coffee, dangerously good cocktails and a menu that includes *salade niçoise*, assorted tapas and seafood risotto. Blankets warm terrace dwellers on chilly evenings.

Brothers Bar & Grill INTERNATIONAL **$$$**
(☑ 423-257 7070; ul Bestuzheva 32; mains R400-1500; 🛜) This rather stylish steak and grill house is worth seeking out for its excellent food, English menu and convivial staff. There's a lovely summer terrace and top-notch cocktail bar in the backyard, while the main dining room is distinctly dark and moody. There's an impressive selection of steaks, seafood, pizza and even a whisky-glazed burger to delight in.

🍷 Drinking & Nightlife

★**Moonshine** COCKTAIL BAR
(ul Svetlanskaya 1/2; ⊙6pm-2am; 🛜) This exceptionally well-stocked and stylish place right by the seafront offers cocktails and a small but tantalising bar menu as well as wine by the glass. There's lots of exposed brickwork, distressed industrial fittings and rather love-it-or-hate-it lighting, but this is definitely a great spot to mix with Vladivostok's burgeoning creative classes.

★**Old Fashioned** COCKTAIL BAR
(☑ 432-279 1079; ul Petra Velikogo 4; ⊙noon-midnight, until 2am Fri & Sat; 🛜) This louche and fabulous cocktail lounge is a low-lit and beautifully set-out space, with a gorgeous wooden bar and gloriously comfortable sofas and

chairs to lounge in. There's a meaty restaurant attached, where diners eat inside a glass atrium outside – but it's by far best used as a place to nurse wonderful cocktails from the large list.

Ra
CLUB

(ul Nabarezhnaya 76; cover varies; ⊙1pm-5am) Where the cool kids can be found hanging out on the seafront boardwalk on summer evenings, this black-painted brick warehouse is a simple bar with a pool table facing the beach during the day, but come nightfall the space becomes the setting for all kinds of parties, including techno, house and gay nights.

Stary Kapitan
PUB

(Старый Капитан; ☑423-277 1077; www.oldcaptainpub.ru; Leitenanta Shmidta 17a; ⊙noon-1am Sun-Thu, to 3am Fri & Sat) Facing the marina, the Old Captain has an excellent selection of draft beers, such as German Weihenstephan. The delectable seafood dishes (pan-seared tiger prawns and scallops) and appetisers (salted herring with black bread toast) go nicely with the brews. Reserve on weekends, when there's live music.

Mumiy Troll
BAR

(Мумий Тролль; www.vvo.mumiytrollbar.com; ul Pogranichnaya 6; ⊙24hr) A fun and lively bar that draws a mix of locals and expats, rock-loving Mumiy Troll – set up by the nationally famous local band of the same name – has live acts most nights (from 10pm). There's rarely a cover, but guests must be 21 to enter.

Cuckoo Club
CLUB

(www.cuckooclub.ru; Okeansky pr 1a; cover R500-800; ⊙10pm-2am Mon-Thu, to 6am Fri & Sat) One of Vladivostok's fancier clubs, the dance floor here seethes at weekends and there's a lovely outdoor area that's the place to be seen in the summer months. Dress to impress to hurdle face control.

☆ Entertainment

Mariinsky Theatre
Primorsky Stage
CLASSICAL MUSIC

(Приморская сцена Мариинского театра; ☑423-240 6060; https://prim.mariinsky.ru; ul Fastovskaya 20; tickets R300-4000) This impressive new theatre is the Far Eastern stage of the venerable Mariinsky Theatre in St Petersburg and is the best place to see serious classical concerts, ballet and opera in the Russian Far East. The modern glass building contains both a big and small stage, as well as an outdoor summer stage.

Zabriskie Point
LIVE MUSIC

(Забриски Пойнт; ☑423-221 5715; ul Naberezhnaya 9a; cover R500-1000; ⊙9pm-5am Tue-Sun) Zabriskie is Vladivostok's main rock and jazz club, drawing an older crowd to view live music acts. It doubles as a nightclub with dancing after performances are finished for the night. There's great sound and plenty of character.

Philharmonic Hall
CLASSICAL MUSIC

(Филармония; ☑423-226 4022; www.primfil.ru; ul Svetlanskaya 15) Hosts classical music and jazz performances.

Stadium Dinamo
SPECTATOR SPORT

(Стадион Динамо; ul Pogranichnaya; tickets R200-400) The popular local football team, Luch-Energiya, plays games at this bayside stadium from April to November.

🛍 Shopping

GUM
GIFTS & SOUVENIRS

(ГУМ; ul Svetlanskaya 35; ⊙10am-8pm Mon-Sat, to 7pm Sun) This once deeply Soviet department store has undergone a recent full refurbishment and is now Vladivostok's best place to shop. It's also housed in the Far East's most elegant art deco building. You'll find traditional souvenirs on the 1st floor, as well as a range of restaurants, cafes and bars in its popular courtyard.

Flotsky Univermag
SPORTS & OUTDOORS

(Флотский универмаг; ul Svetlanskaya 11; ⊙10am-7pm Mon-Fri, to 6pm Sat & Sun) For unusual souvenir turf, follow the navy – this outfitter has those cute blue-and-white-striped navy undershirts and other navy and military gear, as well as useful travel gear such as torches, knives, maps and toothpaste. There are also all kinds of kitschy pro-Putin T-shirts.

ℹ Information

Currency-exchange desks and ATMs are all over town; you'll never have to worry about finding either.

City Hospital No 1 (Городская клиническая Больница №1; ☑423-245 2682; ul Sadovaya 22)

Post Office (Почта; ul Aleutskaya; ⊙8am-10pm Mon-Fri, 9am-6pm Sat & Sun) Offers postal services opposite the train station.

Primorsky Tourist Information Centre
(Туристско-информационный центр Приморского края; ☑423-240 7120; Hyundai Hotel, ul Semyonovskaya 29; ⊙9am-6pm Mon-Fri) Tucked inside the Hyundai Hotel in the centre of the city.

Tourist Information Desks At the airport and the train station.

www.tour.primorsky.ru Has information about the entire Primorsky Territory.

www.vladivostok-city.com Useful for pretrip city planning.

❶ Getting There & Away

Vladivostok is one of the Russian Far East's biggest transport hubs. In addition to serving as the terminus of the Trans-Siberian Railway, it has a large number of national and international flights, making getting here easy from almost anywhere in Russia and neighbouring countries.

AIR

Vladivostok has an excellent modern **airport** (Международный аэропорт Владивосток; ☑ 423-230 6909; www.vvo.aero; Artyom), located in Artyom (50km from the centre), with convenient, if irregular, rail access to the city.

BOAT

Vladivostok's ferry services depart from the **Marine Terminal** (Морской вокзал; Okeansky pr) in the centre of town. There is a weekly **Storm Marine** (☑ 423-230 2704; www.parom. su; office 124, Marine Terminal; ⊙ 9am-1pm & 2-6pm Mon-Fri) passenger-only ferry to Dong-hae in South Korea (from US$205 one way, 20 hours), which continues to Sakaiminato in Japan (from US$265 one way, 43 hours). It leaves Vladivostok at 2pm every Wednesday.

There is also a new weekly ferry, the Man Gyong Bong, to Rajin in North Korea run by **InvestStroyTrest** (ИнвестСтройТрест; ☑ 423-249 6560; www.rajin-investstroytrest.ru; Marine Port). This passenger and cargo ferry leaves Vladivostok each Friday at 8pm and returns to Vladivostok on Thursday at 7am (from R5300, eight hours). However, you will need a visa for North Korea to take this service.

BUS

Buses to Suifenhe, the border town with China, depart daily (except Sunday) at 6.20am

TRANSPORT CONNECTIONS FROM VLADIVOSTOK

DESTINATION	MAIN TRAINS & FREQUENCY	RAIL PRICE (R)	RAIL DURATION	AIRLINES	AIR PRICE (FROM R)	AIR DURATION & FREQUENCY
Beijing	N/A	N/A	N/A	Aeroflot, S7	6300	2½hr, Tue, Sat & Sun
Harbin	via Ussuriysk	from 13,500	N/A	Aurora, China Southern	4700	1¼hr, daily except Wed & Sat
Irkutsk	1, 7, 99, 207	*kupe* from 9200	70hr	S7, Ural Airlines, Ir Avia	13,800	4-6¼hr, daily except Mon & Thu
Khabarovsk	1, 5, 7, 99, 133, 201, 207, 351	*kupe* from 3400	11-15hr	Aurora, S7	3100	1¼hr, daily
Magadan	N/A	N/A	N/A	Yakutia Airlines	10,000	3hr, Tue & Fri
Moscow	1 (even-numbered days), 99 (even-numbered days)	*kupe* from 25,500	6 days	Aeroflot, Rossiya Airlines	13,000	9hr, 3-4 daily
Petropavlovsk-Kamchatsky	N/A	N/A	N/A	Ural Airlines, Aurora, S7, Yakutia Airlines	8700	3½hr, daily
Seoul	N/A	N/A	N/A	Aurora, S7, Korean Air	8700	2½hr, daily
Yakutsk	N/A	N/A	N/A	Yakutia Airlines	14,200	3hr, Wed & Sat
Yuzhno-Sakhalinsk	N/A	N/A	N/A	Aurora, S7	6500	2hr, daily

(R2850, four hours) from the **bus station** (автовокзал; ul Russkaya), 3km north of the centre. There are no buses all the way to Harbin, but you can pick up transport on the other side of the border. There are also frequent departures for other destinations in the region, though do be aware that some southbound destinations may be off limits to foreigners without a permit.

TRAIN

Vladivostok's magnificent art nouveau **train station** (ЖД вокзал Владивосток; pl Voksalnaya; ☺24hr) is located right in the centre of the city by the waterfront, and marks the terminus of the main Trans-Siberian railway line.

Save money by avoiding the No 1 Rossiya train to Moscow, which is massively overpriced due to its perceived prestige (in fact it's fairly similar to less excitingly named and numbered trains).

The Harbin train is a headache, with many stops and a long border check. Departures are early evening on Mondays and Thursdays, but the first night you only go as far as Ussuriysk, where they detach your car from the 351. You stay overnight in Ussuriysk and depart the next day for the border and Harbin. It's much quicker and easier to take a flight to Harbin. If you're headed to Beijing by train, you'll need to go to Harbin first and transfer there.

❶ Getting Around

TO/FROM THE AIRPORT

A speedy rail link, the plush Aeroexpress (50 minutes, R230) connects Vladivostok's train station with the airport. However, with just five trains daily, you'll be lucky if there's one leaving at a convenient time for your flight.

Bus and *marshrutka* 107 (R100 to R150) also connect the train station and airport, departing at least hourly throughout the day.

A taxi booth in the arrivals area charges R1500 for trips to the centre (45 minutes to one hour), and is the easiest way to connect to the city. A taxi from the city to the airport is around R1000.

LOCAL TRANSPORT

Much of Vladivostok's relatively compact centre can be covered on foot as long as you don't mind lots of steep ascents and descents.

Alternatively, buses are your best bet to get around. From in front of the train station, buses 23, 31 and 49 run north on ul Aleutskaya then swing east onto ul Svetlanskaya to the head of the bay. Bus 15 heads to the Primorsky Aquarium from the **ul Aksakovskaya bus stop**.

For trips of more than 5km, you'll save money ordering a taxi (most easily done using the apps Yandex Taxi or Taxi Maxim).

EASTERN BAM

The eastern half of the Baikal-Amur Mainline (Baikalo-Amurskaya Magistral; BAM), covering 2400km from Khani to Sovetskaya Gavan, is perhaps not as visually stimulating as the more mountainous western half, but is still mesmerising in its remoteness and sheer insistence on existing against all the odds.

The highlights of the eastern BAM are the BAM Museum in the unofficial BAM capital, Tynda, and the pastel-coloured pseudotsarist architecture of Komsomolsk-na-Amure, where you can also ski, visit Nanai villages or take a Gulag tour. There's not much between Tynda and Komsomolsk besides often lifeless trees, their roots severed by cruel permafrost below, and a slew of rather uninspired Soviet towns created to finish the railroad. Disembark only if you're searching for ghost towns or gold (prospecting is rife in this region). However, if you do get off, prepare to wait for up to a day for the next train.

A few links cut down to the Trans-Siberian. From Tynda, you can cut down to Skovorodino on the so-called Little BAM, built long before the BAM proper with slave labour in the 1930s. Other links south are at Novy Urgal and Komsomolsk, which both connect to Khabarovsk. The end of the line comes near Vanino, where you can catch a ferry across the Strait of Tartary to Sakhalin Island.

Tynda   Тында

📱 41656 / POP 35,500 / ☺ MOSCOW +6HR

The king of the BAM, Tynda is a nondescript town flanked by low-lying pine-covered hills. Many stop here, as it's a hub for trains between Severobaikalsk, Komsomolsk-na-Amure and, on the Little BAM, Blagoveshchensk to the south, or, on the in-progress AYaM (Amuro-Yakutskaya Mainline), Neryungri and Tommot to the north.

Don't expect quaint. Tynda's fully Soviet – there was nothing but a few shacks before BAM centralised its efforts here in 1974. Liven up your visit by arriving during a festival. The Bakaldin Festival rotates between several nearby Evenki villages in late May or early June, with traditional song, dance, reindeer rides and plenty of reindeer shashlyki and other native delicacies. March sees the Reindeer Hunter and Herder Festival.

⊙ Sights & Activities

Besides the plucky BAM Museum, about the only other thing worth checking out in Tynda is the dramatic sledgehammer-wielding **BAM Builders Monument** (Памятник строителям БАМа; ul Mokhortova) on ul Mokhortova, just south of central ul Krasnaya Presnaya, near its eastern end.

BAM Museum MUSEUM

(Музей истории Байкало-Амурской магистрали; http://muzbam.amur.muzkult.ru; ul Sportivnaya 22; R150; ⊙10am-2pm & 3-6pm Tue-Fri, to 7pm Sat) Tynda's pride and joy has four rooms of BAM relics and photos – sadly all devoid of English labelling – as well as exhibits on native Evenki culture, WWII, local art and regional wildlife. Don't miss the 9m-long 'barrel of Diogenes' parked in the yard, where many BAM workers lived during the railroad's construction. After crossing the pedestrian bridge from the train station, take the first left, continue 200m and turn right up Sportivnaya, where you'll soon see it on your left.

One section covers the Little BAM and the Gulag prisoners who built it in the 1930s. They lived (and died) in 24 BAM labour camps between Tynda and Bamovskaya, and some moving photos chronicle the extreme hardships these prisoners endured. Two rooms are dedicated to the big BAM, sections of which were built in the 1930s, 1940s and 1950s before Stalin died and the project was mothballed. A final display covers the period between its relaunch in 1974 and final completion in 1984.

Alexey Podprugin TOURS

(☑8-985-205 0365; bamland@mail.ru) Feisty adventurer Alexey Podprugin knows the wilderness surrounding Tynda well and can arrange kayaking, hiking and cross-country skiing trips. He doesn't speak English, so email him if you don't speak Russian.

🛏 Sleeping & Eating

Resting Rooms HOSTEL $

(Комнаты отдыха; ☑41656-73 297; train station, Zarechnaya ul; bed per 6/12/24hr from R650/990/1650) Comfy and clean dorm rooms in the train station. Shower available for nonguests (R150).

Hotel Yunost HOTEL $$

(Гостиница Юность; ☑41656-43 534; ul Krasnaya Presnaya 49; s/d from R3500/4000, s/d with shared bathroom R2000/3000; 🛜) Faded but fine option in centre; Dervla Murphy

recuperated here while writing *Through Siberia by Accident*. You can get wi-fi literally on one sofa in the lobby: it's free, but you might need a while to do anything. Staff don't speak English and regard foreigners with a pleasing amount of suspicion, which seems correct after such a long journey.

Piv Bar Teremok PIZZA $$

(Пив Бар Теремок; ul Krasnaya Presnaya 59a; mains R300-600; ⊙noon-midnight; 🛜) Serves up palatable pizzas, Drakon draft beer (from Khabarovsk) and has seating on an open-sided veranda. To find it, turn left at the eastern end of Krasnaya Presnaya, and walk up 50m.

ℹ Information

The train station has an ATM and left-luggage office (R140).

ℹ Getting There & Away

The **train station** (ЖД вокзал; Zarechnaya ul) – the city's most striking landmark – is across the Tynda River. A pedestrian bridge leads 1km north to ul Krasnaya Presnaya.

Train 75 heads via the BAM to Moscow (kupe/platskartny R20,800/10,000, five days) on even-numbered days, stopping in Severobaikalsk (kupe/platskartny R4600/2900, 27 hours), while trains 77, 97 and the 75 travelling in the other direction head to Novosibirsk (kupe/platskartny R11,600/6700, 67 hours), taking the Little BAM south on odd-numbered days to connect with the Trans-Siberian line at Skovorodino.

There are several daily departures to Neryungri, including the 325 (from R576, 5½ hours). Train 364 trundles to Komsomolsk daily (kupe/platskartny R5800/3000, 36 hours), and 325 heads daily to Khabarovsk at 2am via Skovorodino (kupe/platskartny R5500/3000, 28 hours).

Komsomolsk-na-Amure
Комсомольск-на-Амуре

☑4217 / POP 251,000 / ⊙ MOSCOW +7HR

After days of taiga and grey Soviet towns, Komsomolsk-na-Amure comes as a charming surprise with its attractive Stalin-era centre and pleasant Amur River setting. Built virtually from scratch in the 1930s as a vital cog in the Soviet Union's military industrial complex, Komsomolsk's name comes from the thousands of Communist Youth League volunteers who built the town alongside Gulag labourers.

Imitating the tsars, Stalin erected elaborate neoclassical buildings in the city centre and then festooned them with stars and statues of model Soviet citizens. Around town, factories sprouted up to produce ships, weapons, electricity and, most famously, Sukhoi (Su) fighter jets in a factory that still works today. Set along a few grand boulevards, the city is worth a night or more if you are getting on or off the BAM.

⊙ Sights & Activities

Just east of the river terminal is a **beach**, which is well attended on warm summer days.

Komsomolsk has a wealth of wonderful murals adorning the sides of apartment blocks and factories. Most were the creation of Khabarovsk-based artist Nikolai Dolbilkin, who lived here in the 1950s and '60s. Among the best are the double-triptych **WWII mosaic** (cnr pr Mira & alleya Truda) in the central grey *dom kultura* building near Sudostroitel Park (now inside a children's play space) and the **nauka (science) mosaic** (pr Lenina) at the Polytechnical Institute, a block east of Hotel Voskhod.

River Cruises   BOATING
(River Terminal; R300) On summer weekends, you can hop aboard 90-minute cruises along the Amur River. Boats depart at 3pm Saturday and Sunday as well as 7pm Thursday and Saturday. Buy tickets on board.

Municipal Museum
of Regional Studies   MUSEUM
(Городской краеведческий музей; www.kmsgkm.ru; cnr alleya Truda & ul Kirova; R250; ⊙9.30am-5pm Tue-Fri, 10am-5pm Sat & Sun) This proud town museum has several rooms of photos and artefacts showing how Komsomolsk rose from a pioneer camp in 1932 to an industrial Soviet city. It also contains some old fish-skin jackets and other Nanai artefacts. It's expensive for the sure-to-be-quick visit, even more so as there's no labelling in English.

WWII Memorial   MEMORIAL
(ul Dzherzhinskogo) Just northwest of the river terminal is the impressive WWII memorial, which features stoic faces chipped from stone, with nearby pillars marking the years of WWII.

Japanese POW Memorial   MONUMENT
(ul Ordzhonikidze) This small monument is dedicated to the memory of the Japanese prisoners of war who were forced to work building the BAM after WWII.

Komsomolsk-na-Amure

RUSSIAN FAR EAST KOMSOMOLSK-NA-AMURE

WORTH A TRIP

THE NATURE RESERVES OF PRIMORSKY TERRITORY

Vladivostok travel agents run a variety of city and regional tours, but they can be pricey when it comes to longer trips outside the city due to the large distances in Primorsky Territory.

Heading outside Vladivostok, the most interesting tour is probably to **Sikhote-Alin Nature Reserve** (Сихотэ-Алинский заповедник; ☑ 423-241 0033; http://russia.wcs.org), home to the World Conservation Society's Amur tiger project and a wonderfully wild slice of wilderness that's well worth taking the time to visit. Another option is visiting **Gaivoron** (Зоологический центр Биолого-почвенного института; ☑ 42352-74 249), 235km north of Vladivostok, where you can actually see a couple of Amur tigers held in captivity at the Russian Academy of Sciences biological research reserve. A third destination is the **Land of the Leopard National Park** (Национальный Парк Земля Леопарда; ☑ 423-201 2683; www.leopard-land.ru; Khasanskaya 6a, Barabash), an impressive reserve created in 2012 for the critically endangered Amur leopard. While the Amur leopard's rareness means you definitely won't see one in the wild, the landscape is gorgeous and your visit will help fund this critically important effort to save this gorgeous animal. Reckon on US$1200 for a six-day, five-night visit to any of the reserves organised by a Vladivostok travel agency and be aware that there are limited options to reduce either the cost or the time frame of such a trip.

☞ Tours

Nata Tour TOURS
(Ната-Тур; ☑ Mikhail 8-914-189 1784, Vladimir 8-914-177 3724; komsomolsknata@mail.ru; office 110, ul Vasyanina 12; ⊘ 10am-6pm Mon-Fri) These local experts arrange three- to five-hour 'Stalin tours' of the city's communist sites (including a Gulag camp) from R1300 per person; adventure tours involving fishing, rafting or skiing; and day trips and/or homestays at Verkhnyaya Ekon. Mikhail speaks English.

Other tours include white-water rafting trips that involve a train ride to Novy Urgal on the BAM. Slower one- to several-day floats can be done closer to Komsomolsk. Tours of the Yury Gagarin Aircraft Factory, where the Su jets are built, can also be arranged.

🛌 Sleeping

A pleasant alternative to a hotel is arranging a homestay through Nata Tour (p563) (R1000 per person including breakfast).

Resting Rooms HOSTEL $
(Комнаты отдыха; ☑ 4217-284 193; train station, pr Pervostroiteley; 12/24hr dm from R720/1100, s 12/24hr without bathroom R1040/1830) A clean and basic option inside the train station if you need a break from sleeping on trains.

★ **Biznestsentr** HOTEL $$
(Гостиничный комплекс Бизнес-центр; ☑ 4217-521 522; bc@etc.kna.ru; ul Dzerzhinskogo 3; s/d incl breakfast from R2000/2500; ❄🛜) Komsomolsk's most modern business-oriented hotel has bright, comfortably furnished rooms with modern bathrooms (including space-shuttle-like shower capsules). English-speaking receptionists are on hand too.

Hotel Voskhod HOTEL $$
(Гостиница Восход; ☑ 4217-535 131; www.hotel-voskhod.com; pr Pervostroiteley 31; s/d from R2200/2700; 🛜) A 10-minute walk from the train station, this eight-storey Soviet-era beast has decently renovated rooms and surprisingly friendly staff.

🍴 Eating

In the summer, you can feast on shashlyk (R200) and cold drinks along the riverfront overlooking the beach.

Kafema CAFE $
(Кафема; www.kafema.ru; Okyabrsky pr 39; pastries from R100; ⊘ 10am-8pm; 🛜) This place does the best coffee in town, and their passionate, well-trained baristas will even be able to sell you some of their delicious fresh beans to take with you on your travels. Cakes, pastries and other snacks are available.

Bistro RUSSIAN $
(Бистро; ul Lenina 19; mains R80-160; ⊘ 9am-10pm) Beside pl Lenina, this clean modern *stolovaya* serves tasty, affordable staples: baked dishes, roast meats and the usual beet- or potato salads are all on offer.

Shinok Pervach UKRAINIAN $$
(Шинок Первач; www.shinok-pervach.ru; ul Dzerzhinskogo 34; mains R300-900; ⊘ noon-3am; 🛜)

A local institution, Shinok Pervach is considered by locals to be the best restaurant in town. It serves up tasty grilled fish, roast meats and zingy salads (try the beetroot, walnut and prune for its subtle spice). The chunky wooden tables and circular dining room festooned maypole style with ribbons bestow a certain peasant chic to the place. Despite its address, it's actually located just off pr Internatsionalny.

❶ Getting There & Away

Despite its vast distance from everywhere, Komsomolsk has surprisingly good transport connections by rail, road, river and air to its distant neighbours elsewhere in the Far East.

AIR

Komsomolsk-na-Amur's small **airport** (Аэропорт Хурба) has flights on Aurora to Vladivostok each Wednesday and Friday (R3600, two hours).

BOAT

For a DIY adventure, head down the Amur River by hydrofoil to Nikolayevsk-na-Amure (from R4350, 11 hours). The boat departs three days a week from the **river terminal** (Речной вокзал) (currently on Monday, Wednesday and Friday mornings).

BUS

Local and long-distance buses leave from the **bus station** (автостанция; ☑ 4217-542 554; ⊙ 6am-10.30pm) near the river. Buses bound for Khabarovsk (from R640, six hours) leave every 90 minutes or so from 7am.

TRAIN

From Komsomolsk's pink **train station** (ЖД вокзал; pr Pervostroiteley), the excruciatingly slow 351 leaves daily for Vladivostok (*kupe/platskartny* R5500/2600, 25 hours). There are also two daily services (trains 351 and 667) to Khabarovsk (*kupe/platskartny* from R2300/1300, 10 hours).

On the BAM, the daily 363 heads west to Tynda (*kupe/platskartny* R5800/3000, 38 hours); to reach Severobaikalsk, change in Tynda. The daily train 351 heads east to Vanino (*kupe/platskartny* R2200/1400, 13 hours). The BAM's first/last stop, 'Sovetskaya Gavan-Sortirovka', 15 minutes east of Vanino, is not to be confused with the city of Sovetsakaya Gavan, an hour away from Vanino by bus.

❶ Getting Around

Within the city, handy tram 2 runs from the train station along ul Lenina and pr Mira to the river terminal (R20).

❶ FROM BAM TO SAKHALIN

BAM completists will end up in the grey Soviet port town of Vanino (actually the BAM ends 15 minutes beyond Vanino, in Sovetskaya Gavan-Sortirovka). From Vanino, there is a **Sakhalin Shipping Company** (SASCO; ☑ 42433-66 133, 42433-66 208; www.sasco.ru; ul Pobedy 18a, Kholmsk) ferry around three times a week leaving at varying times of day to Kholmsk on Sakhalin Island (tickets R1950 to R4200 depending on class, 18 hours). Do be aware that the two ferries working this route are very old, cramped and break down frequently. Despite this, your biggest obstacle is the unpredictable and fast-changing weather in the Strait of Tartary. Call the **ticket office** (SASCO; ☑ 42137-74 088; www.sasco.ru) in Vanino the day before to reserve a seat and to check the next day's ship is likely to sail, as it's far nicer to be stuck in Komsomolsk-na-Amure than Vanino.

SAKHA REPUBLIC & MAGADAN REGION

These two remote regions of Russia are locked in the grip of winter for over half the year and are both challenging but highly rewarding places to visit. Looming like a giant inverted iceberg north of the BAM line, the sprawl of the remote Sakha Republic (the country's largest region) takes time and effort to reach. Likewise, the smaller coastal Magadan Oblast is a chunk of wilderness that travel adventures are made of: a frozen and remote world of endless pine trees, vast rushing rivers and gold mines.

The most unrepentant dissidents (first Decembrists, then Bolsheviks and later anyone deemed by Stalin to be an 'enemy of the people') were exiled here in camps where escape was impossible due to the swamps, ice, bears and bug-infested forests spreading for hundreds of kilometres in each direction. Today both regions attract hardy explorers keen to see Russia's most wild and remote corners.

Yakutsk Якутск

☑ 4112 / POP 269,000 / ⊙ MOSCOW +6HR

Remote yet booming Yakutsk stands on stilts (the shifting permafrost causes buildings to collapse otherwise) and has its water

Yakutsk

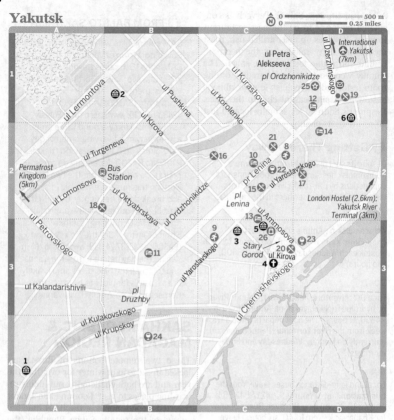

Yakutsk

◎ Sights

1 Archaeology & Ethnography Museum	A4
2 Khomus Museum	B1
Mammoth Museum	(see 1)
3 National Art Museum	C3
4 Transfiguration Church	C3
5 Treasury of the Sakha Republic	C3
6 Yakutsk Regional History Museum	D1

◎ Activities, Courses & Tours

7 Lena Tur Flot	D1
8 Visit Yakutia	C2
9 Yakutia Travel	C3

◎ Sleeping

10 Azimut Polar Star Hotel Yakutsk	C2
11 Bed & Breakfast Bravo	B3
12 Hotel Lena	D1
13 Hotel Tygyn Darkhan	C2
14 Mini-Hotel Prospect	D2

◎ Eating

15 Bon Ami	C2
16 Han Guk Kwan	C2
17 Khachapuri	D2
18 Kita Gava	A2
19 Kvartira na Prospekte	D1
20 Makhtal	C3
21 Stolovka Rublevka	C2
Tygyn Darkhan	(see 13)

◎ Drinking & Nightlife

22 Bar Onegin	C2
23 Dikaya Utka	D3
24 Evropa Klub	B4

◎ Entertainment

| 25 Sakha Theatre | D1 |

◎ Shopping

| 26 Kuday Bakhsy | C3 |

and gas delivered in giant overground pipes, the surreal, entangled sight of which might be its most enduring image to visitors.

With a long-awaited train link to the city still incomplete, it's pretty much cut off from the already remote Far East, and yet, unlike so many remote Russian cities out here, Yakutsk roars with optimism and gusto. New buildings are popping up all over the city and the population is rising, as the gold and diamond rush continues. Yakutsk is an excellent base for exploring the vast wilderness of Yakutia and has plenty to keep visitors entertained between forays into nature.

Brace yourself for extreme weather. It's hot and swarms with mosquitoes in summer and then utterly freezing in winter (January averages −40°C), a time of year nonetheless beloved by locals.

⊙ Sights

National Art Museum
MUSEUM

(Национальный Художественный Музей Республики Саха; ☑ 4112-335 274; www.sakha-museum.ru; ul Kirova 9; R150; ⊙10am-6pm Wed-Sun) If time is limited, don't miss this excellent museum, with Sakha-themed exhibits covering local craftmaking traditions (mammoth tusk carvings, reindeer boots, finely carved urns for *kumiss* – fermented mare's milk), landscape paintings and portraits. Look out for the captivating paintings of village life by Andrei Chikachev (born 1967), the most famous living Sakha artist.

Permafrost Kingdom
MUSEUM

(Царство вечной мерзлоты; Vilyusky trakt, km7; R500; ⊙9am-7pm) At Permafrost Kingdom, two neon-lit tunnels burrowed into a permanently frozen hill have been filled with dozens of fabulous, never-melting ice sculptures of local pagan gods and a host of more recognisable objects and characters – a sitting Buddha, a pharaoh, Ded Moroz (Russia's Santa Claus), a woolly mammoth and an icy interpretation of Picasso's *Guernica*. Silver coats and woolly boots are given out to keep you insulated.

Permafrost affects almost every aspect of life in Yakutsk, obstructing drainage, causing unstilted buildings to bow and then collapse, spontaneously chucking up mounds of earth, and emitting enough methane to possibly alter the earth's climate catastrophically. The Permafrost Kingdom is a great way to get up close and personal with this nebulous and omnipresent beast. In this subterranean permafrost zone, the temperature ranges from −7°C in summer to a balmy

(relative to outside temperatures) −20°C in winter. Indeed, caves adjacent to the kingdom are used for electricity-free cold storage in the warm months. This is by far Yakutsk's quirkiest attraction and makes for a great little excursion year-round. It's 13km west of Yakutsk's centre; buses 7 and 25 go here from pr Lenina, or a taxi is around R300.

Yakutsk Regional History Museum
MUSEUM

(Якутский государственный объединенный музей истории и культуры народов Севера; ☑ 4112- 425 174; pr Lenina 5/2; R300; ⊙10am-5pm Tue-Sun) A good place to delve deeper into Sakha culture, the this museum contains local minerals, information on the region's first Russian settlers and a mammoth skeleton alongside the standard Soviet natural history and WWII exhibits. Outside, there's a huge whale skeleton found in 1961, as well as the original museum building, a charming wooden structure full of traditional furnishings.

Transfiguration Church
CHURCH

(Преображенский собор) This mid-19th-century church with gorgeous golden domes in Yakutsk's old town is the city's most attractive.

Orto Doidu
ZOO

(Якутский зоопарк Орто Дойду; ☑ 4112-225 259; www.zoo.ykt.ru; Hangalassky ulus, Pokrovsky trakt, km50; R250; ⊙10am-7pm summer, 10am-5pm winter) This popular zoo is some distance from Yakutsk, but it's well worth the trouble of getting out here if you're interested in the fascinatingly hardy fauna of Yakutia and Arctic Russia. Among the collection you'll find polar bears, wolves, reindeer, elk, brown bears and even a golden eagle. To get here, take bus 202 from the bus station (R160, one hour). Buses leave at 9am, 11.30am, 2.30pm and 5pm.

Archaeology & Ethnography Museum
MUSEUM

(Музей Археологии и Этнографии, Музей Мамонта; ☑ 4112-361 647; UGU Bldg, ul Kulakovskogo 48; Mammoth/Ethnography Museum R200/150; ⊙10am-1pm & 2-5pm Tue-Fri, 11am-1pm & 2-4pm Sat) These two separately run museums are in the same building; sadly, neither enjoys the luxury of signage in English. On the bottom three floors you'll find one of the Far East's better displays on indigenous peoples, while the 4th floor gives an overview of mammoths in Sakha. See if they'll let you glimpse into the Mammoth Museum's refrigerated storage room, which is chock full of mammoth and woolly rhino bones.

Khomus Museum
MUSEUM

(Музей хомуса; ul Kirova 31; R250; ☺10am-1pm & 2-6pm Mon-Sat) *Khomus* (Jew's harps) play a big part in Sakha culture. Concerts occur year-round, when performers imitate natural sounds such as a horse neighing. The unexpected (and unfortunately soundtrack-free) Khomus Museum has a collection showcasing international Jew's harp heroes from present and past. Ask the welcoming staff for a demonstration.

Treasury of the Sakha Republic
MUSEUM

(Выставка Сокровищница Республики Саха; www.expo-gx.ru; ul Ammosova; R240; ☺tours 10am-4pm Mon-Fri) Pay a visit to this unique museum for a look at Yakutia's rich mineral wealth combined with fine craft traditions. You'll see exquisite carvings in mammoth tusks, tiny sculptures adorned with precious stones and a radiant 11-carat diamond. Admission is by 40-minute guided tour, which departs on the hour (except 1pm).

🏃 Activities

★ Visit Yakutia
TOURS

(☑8-924-765 9930, 4112-259 930; www.visityakutia.com; pr Lenina 17) This excellent outfit offers overland trips to Magadan, visits to reindeer herders, winter journeys to Oymyakon, Lena Pillar and Tiksi cruises, and a range of other outdoor activities including trekking, fishing, rafting and reindeer sledding. It's run by English-speaking Bolot Bochkarev.

Yakutia Travel
TOURS

(☑8-924-662 1144, 4112-351 144; www.yakutiatravel.com; office 66, ul Yaroslavsky 30/1) Experienced English-speaking staff can arrange Sakha wilderness tours, Lena Pillars boat trips, Oymyakon visits and plenty more. It also offers interesting ethnological trips to Sakha villages. An English-speaking guide is R1500 per day.

Lena Tur Flot
CRUISE

(Ленатурфлот; ☑4112-263 535; www.lenaturflot.ru; ul Dzerzhinskogo 2; 36hr cruise to Lena Pillars s/d cabin from R7500/12,000) Offers regular sailings from Yakutsk upriver to the Lena Pillars, as well as an epic 10-day cruise downriver to the Arctic Ocean town of Tiksi, for which you need special permission to visit.

Festivals & Events

Ysyakh
CULTURAL

One of Russia's better-kept secrets, the major Sakha festival of Ysyakh (tough to pronounce; try 'ehh-sekhh') is celebrated all over the Sakha Republic each year in June. The biggest event occurs in Us Khatyn field near the village of Zhetai, about 20km north of Yakutsk, on the first Saturday and Sunday after the summer solstice.

Don't miss the opening, at noon on Saturday, when hundreds of costumed performers, including Chinggis (Genghis) Khaan-like soldiers, reenact battles and people hand out free skewers of horsemeat and offer sips of horse milk.

Stands are filled by Sakha from across the republic, often set up around modern *irasa* (tepees); the rare foreigner is likely to be drawn in for horsemeat and *kumiss* (fermented mare's milk). The 'no alcohol' (other than mildly alcoholic *kumiss*) policy keeps things sober during the day, but it can't be guaranteed later on, when many locals come to greet the dawn – an all-night party for young and old. It's well worth planning your Yakutsk detour around this event, though be sure to book accommodation well in advance.

Packed buses head to/from the festival regularly from pr Lenina in Yakutsk (45 minutes).

🛌 Sleeping

London Hostel
HOSTEL $

(☑4112-210 031; bldg 2, ul B Chizhika 33b; dm/d R450/1500; 🛜) Despite its truly garish exterior (think Big Ben and the London Eye emblazoned onto the walls in photographic wallpaper), Yakutsk's first real hostel is a great deal that offers exactly what the traveller needs: two eight-bed dorms, two private rooms, shared toilets and showers, and a decent communal kitchen and lounge. From Lenina take bus 1 or 6 to the Aviagruppa stop.

★ Bed & Breakfast Bravo
GUESTHOUSE $$

(☑4112-405 111; www.bravo-hotel.ru; ul Ordzhonikidze 49, 9th fl, apt 64; s/d incl breakfast from R3500/4000; ❄🛜) Bravo is a little tricky to find and is not marked at all from the street. But once you get here, you'll find several apartments stitched together to form a spotless guesthouse boasting modern rooms outfitted with large flat-screen TVs, big windows, desks and excellent mattresses.

Go into the courtyard of 49 and turn right: the entrance is the second one. Ring buzzer number 64.

Hotel Ontario
GUESTHOUSE $$

(☑8-914-222 9030; hotelontario@bk.ru; ul Sergelyakhskoe, km13; s/d from R3200/3900; ❄🛜) Though it's far from the centre, pine-fringed

Hotel Ontario lets you wake to singing birds rather than honking horns. Rooms are small, modern and carpeted, but cosy with plank walls that smell of cedar. There's a restaurant on-site. It's a R250 taxi ride, or bus 25 stops nearby – get off at the Borisovka Pervaya stop.

Mini-Hotel Prospect
HOSTEL **$$**

(Мини-отель Проспект; ☑ 8-4112-423 118; flat 36, ul Lenina 11/1; s/d from R2000/3000; ☎) This very central, spotless budget option is effectively a self-service hostel. Three rooms share a bathroom and kitchen, but are otherwise totally independent. The owner, Lena, speaks some English and will meet you on arrival and give you a key. It's a great option if you want to be central without paying for a fancy hotel.

Hotel Tygyn Darkhan
HOTEL **$$$**

(Гостиница Тыгын Дархан; ☑ 4112-435 109; www.tygyn.ru; ul Ammosova 9; s/d incl breakfast from R5000/7950; ✳@☎☒) Just steps from pl Lenina and with the old town on its doorstep, TD's regular rooms follow a standard Soviet template, but are freshly updated and have modern bathrooms. Rates include use of the indoor pool, sauna and gym, and there's a popular restaurant on-site as well.

Azimut Polar Star Hotel Yakutsk
HOTEL **$$$**

(Azimut Отель Полярная Звезда Якутск; ☑ 4112-341 215; pr Lenina 24; s/d incl breakfast from R7800/9800; ✳@☎☒) Little appears to have changed at the top business hotel in town since the Azimut chain took over – the Polar Star remains a fairly ugly place with decent modern rooms reached by glass elevator. Service can be variable, but there's usually someone on hand who speaks a bit of English. Location is excellent.

Hotel Lena
HOTEL **$$$**

(Гостиница Лена; ☑ 4112-424 214; www.lena-hotel.ru; pr Lenina 8; s/d incl breakfast from R4500/6400; ☎) Fresh from a full refit in 2016, the Lena is looking good these days, even if it's impossible to truly disguise a Soviet hotel due to the small rooms and low ceilings. That said, it has a fantastic location and well-meaning staff, although there's way too much beige and brown in the new decor.

Eating

Stolovka Rublevka
CAFETERIA **$**

(Столовка Рублевка; ul Korolenko 2; meals R200-400; ☺9am-11pm; ☎) With leather armchairs

WORTH A TRIP

VERKHNAYA EKON

Tucked between the Amur River and bear-inhabited hills, this village (Верхняя Эконь) of 500 (of which half are Nanai) makes a fun day trip from Komsomolsk across the river. Its school has a small Nanai Museum with old shaman costumes and plenty of Nanai traditional pieces. It's possible to hike up the mountain. Three daily buses come from Komsomolsk (R50, one hour) but if you arrange for a taxi you can visit an eerie, unfinished 800m-long BAM tunnel at nearby Pivan village (north of the Amur Bridge), including pieces abandoned after WWII broke out.

and white brick walls, Rublevka is a surprisingly elegant *stolovaya* with a good selection of smoked fish, soups, dumplings, salads and cooked meat and fish plates. Great prices, too, and the advantage of not having to read a Russian menu.

Bon Ami
CAFE **$**

(ul Yaroslavskogo 22; desserts R80-280; ☺8.30am-8pm Mon-Fri, from 10am Sat & Sun) Pleasant cafe with frothy coffee drinks, buttery croissants and other temptations (cherry Danishes, apple strudel, honeycake, bliny). The takeaway shop is downstairs.

★ Kvartira na Prospekte
RUSSIAN **$$**

(Квартира на проспекте; pr Lenina 6/6; mains R400-900; ☺noon-midnight, until 2am Fri & Sat; ☎) This fun place makes a noble effort to resemble a babushka's living room, which is no mean feat since it moved to bigger premises and is now housed inside a thoroughly modern building. The menu remains excellent and inventive with dishes such as quinoa salad, couscous and Caesar salad with salmon.

★ Khachapuri
GEORGIAN **$$**

(Хачапури; ☑ 4112-261 601; www.vhachapuri.ru; ul Yaroslavskogo 13/2; mains R400-700; ☎) Georgia's culinary colonisation of even the farthest-flung parts of Russia continues apace, and this gorgeous place is easily one of Yakutsk's best dining options (should you tire of frozen fish). Attentive staff look after you in this bright and breezy place, with a pictorial *and* English menu, making navigating the Georgian dish names a breeze.

★Chochur Muran   RUSSIAN $$
(Чочур Муран; ☎8-924-661 6100; Vilyusky trakt, km7; meals R400-1600; ⊗noon-midnight; 🛜) In a Cossack-style lodge filled with antiques, Chochur Muran is an atmospheric and fun lunch stop if you are heading out to the nearby Permafrost Kingdom (p567). It's the best place around to try Sakha delicacies such as *stroganina* (frozen raw *chyr,* a white fish common in Arctic rivers), *zherebyatiny* (fillet of colt meat) and reindeer.

★Makhtal   YAKUT $$
(Махтал; ul Kirova 2; mains R350-1500; ⊗noon-1am; 🛜) In the old town, Makhtal is one of Yakutsk's most atmospheric options, with thick log walls adorned with traditional tapestries and handsomely attired waitstaff gliding about in broad-shouldered tunics and long flowing robes. Downstairs there's a cheap and informal cafeteria, while upstairs it's a Yakut feast with dishes including horse meat in caramel and *indigirka* (raw, frozen fish).

Han Guk Kwan   KOREAN $$
(Хан Гук Гван; LG Sakha Centre, ul Ordzhonikidze 36/1; mains R300-1100; ⊗noon-midnight) A large, airy and authentic Korean restaurant on the ground floor of one of Yakutsk's fanciest office buildings (look for the fabulous ornamental gates), Han Guk Kwan may have fairly surly waitstaff but the food is excellent and the R300 business lunch is great value.

Tygyn Darkhan   RUSSIAN $$
(Тыгын Дархан Ресторан; ☎4112-343 406; Hotel Tygyn Darkhan, ul Ammosova 9; mains R400-900; ⊗noon-3pm & 6-10pm; 🛜) Though the atmosphere is lacking, Tygyn Darkhan is *the* place to score Sakha specialities in the centre. Try *indigirka (*frozen raw *chyr* and onions – a bit like eating frozen fish in a ball of snow) and Darkhan *pelmeni* (horsemeat dumplings), washed down with a glass of *kumiss* and topped off with whipped cream and foxberries.

Kita Gava   JAPANESE $$
(Китагава; ul Oyunskogo 5; meals R500-1400; ⊗11am-1am; 🛜) The best place in town for sushi, Kita Gava is a buzzing place that serves up tasty sashimi platters, noodle soups and plump gyoza (dumplings). While not cheap, the food is good, the service fast and friendly, and the place buzzes with a young and well-heeled local crowd come evening.

🍷 Drinking & Nightlife

Dikaya Utka   PUB
(Дикая утка; ul Chernyshevskogo 20; ⊗noon-2am Mon-Fri, from 2pm Sat & Sun) A favourite of expats, the spacious wood-lined 'Wild Duck' is the go-to spot for refreshing brews, and there's decent pub grub on hand. There's live music on Friday and Saturday nights (cover R300; from 9pm). It's in the *stary gorod* (old city).

Evropa Klub   CLUB
(Европа Клуб; www.evropaklub.ru; pr Lenina 47; ⊗6pm-6am) The most popular club in the centre, Evropa is a five-storey complex with dance club, sports bar, bowling alley and, uh, strip club.

Bar Onegin   EUROPEAN
(Бар Онегин; pr Lenina 23; ⊗noon-2am; 🛜) Bar Onegin whips up tasty salads, sushi, pastas and grilled fish dishes (mains R350 to R650), but it mainly serves as a bar. It's a fairly stylish spot, with Pushkin-esque stencils on the wall and a chatty cocktail-sipping crowd at night.

☆ Entertainment

Sakha Theatre   THEATRE
(Саха Театр; ☎4112-341 331; pl Ordzhonikidze) A strikingly modern venue in the centre of the city that has theatre in Yakut and far more accessible traditional music performances.

🛍 Shopping

Kuday Bakhsy   GIFTS & SOUVENIRS
(Кудай Бахсы; ul Ammosova 3a; ⊗10am-7pm Mon-Fri, to 6pm Sat & Sun) In the old city, this is the best place in town to browse for crafts and souvenirs. You'll find mammoth tusk carvings, leather slippers, reindeer boots and gloves, embroidered dolls, Jew's harps, carved wooden bowls, paintings, knives, bizarre magnets and CDs of traditional music.

ℹ Information

There are plenty of ATMs around town, but particularly in the top-end hotels and all along pr Lenina.

Post Office (Почтамт; pl Ordzhonikidze; ⊗8am-8pm Mon-Fri, 9am-6pm Sat)

ℹ Getting There & Away

Passenger trains from Neryungri go as far north as Tommot in southern Sakha. The new Amuro-Yakutskaya Mainline (AYaM) passenger train will supposedly link Yakutsk with Tommot, Neryungri and Tynda, and thus the entire Russian rail

EXCURSIONS FROM YAKUTSK

Yakutsk's city limits can get a little grey and grubby at times, but things quickly get wild once you leave town. By just hiring a taxi (about R600 to R800 per hour), you can reach a couple of places; others involve boats.

Lena Pillars The area's most popular tour is the boat cruise to the 80km-long Lena Pillars (Lenskie Stolby), a 35-million-year-old stretch of Kimberly limestone on the edge of the Lena River, about 220km south of Yakutsk. Jagged spires and picturesque crumbling fronts (almost brick-like) look like ancient ruins if you squint. Many companies offer one- and two-day tours to the Lena Pillars. You can also book passage on a comfy 70-cabin ship for a 36- or 48-hour cruise offered by Lena Tur Flot (p568). Both tours include about five to eight hours at the pillars, a shaman ceremony and the chance to fish or swim. Meals cost extra. Boats leave from Yakutsk once or twice weekly from June to September and should be booked ahead through a travel agent or Lena Tur Flot.

Sottintsy Home to the **Druzhba Park Reserve** (Дружба Историко-Архитектурный Музей-Заповедник; ☑ 411-612 3171; Ust-Aldansky ulus; R200; ☉ 9am-6pm) – a collection of traditional dwellings – Sottintsy is about 60km north of Yakutsk on the opposite side of the Amur River. To get here take a bus to Kangalas and cross the Lena River by parom to Sottintsy; it's a 2km walk from the riverbank to the park.

Elanka Features a few rest houses, a small ethnographic museum and fishing on a peaceful patch of the Lena. It's a two-hour drive south via Mokhsogollakh.

Buotama River Between the Lena Pillars and Yakutsk, cutting west from the Lena, this narrow tree-lined river is popular for kayaking and rafting camping trips, where you can spot bear and fish in the wild. These start at about R8500 per person per day, not including meals.

Oymyakon This remote village 650km east of Yakutsk holds the record as the coldest inhabited spot on earth. Temperatures have been recorded as low as −71°C (in the nearby valleys they go down to −82°C). Oymyakon also has a breeding station for reindeer, horses and silver foxes. An annual Pole of Cold Festival, with reindeer races and (outdoor!) concerts, takes place here or in nearby Tomtor in late March. A one-week trip taking in Oymyakon and various other cold places organised by Yakutsk travel agencies runs to R104,000 per person for groups of three people, including transport by Russian UAZ jeeps.

network, though work is currently stalled on the project, with no completion date even mooted.

AIR

Yakutsk airport (Аэропорт Якутск; ☑ 4112-491 001; www.yks.aero), 7km northeast of the town centre, is well connected to most of Russia. Destinations include Moscow (six hours), Khabarovsk (2¾ hours), Vladivostok (3¼ hours), Novosibirsk (four hours) and Irkutsk (three hours), as well as Magadan (two hours) and numerous far-flung destinations in Sakha, including Neryungri (1¾ hours, daily except Sunday) and Tiksi (three hours, three weekly).

BOAT

Yakutsk remains an important port and dispatches ferries and cruise ships both up and down the giant Lena River during the summer months.

The most interesting ferry service is the four-day trip from Yakutsk to Tiksi, departing every 10 days between July and early September. The far shorter jaunt upriver to the Lena Pillars is one or two days and offers some lovely sights en route, including several hours to enjoy the pillars as well. Both services are offered by Lena Tur Flot (p568). Departures are from the **Yakutsk river terminal** (Речной вокзал; ul Novoportskaya 1), 2km northeast of the centre.

You can traverse the Lena by ferry (leaving from the terminal) to Nizhny Bestyakh on the opposite bank (R250, one hour). Departures are every 80 minutes from 7am to 6.20pm. Don't miss the last boat back at 7.40pm.

BUS & TAXI

Buses go from the Yakutsk **bus station** (Автовокзал; ul Oktyabrskaya 24) to relatively nearby points in Sakha. For overland journeys south to connect with the Russian railway network, it's more convenient to go by shared taxi to Tommot (R2000, about 10 to 14 hours) or Neryungri (R2800, 14 to 20 hours).

The rough UAZ journey to Neryungri crosses the Lena an hour south of Yakutsk in industrial

Mokhsogollakh. Most travel agencies can arrange this journey.

❶ Getting Around

A handy city bus is line 8 (R18), which goes past pr Lenina's hotels on its way between the river terminal and bus station. Bus 4 goes to the airport – catch it heading east on pr Lenina. Taxis charge around R150 for rides around the centre.

Magadan   Магадан

☑ 4132 / POP 92,000 / ⊙ MOSCOW +8HR

The centre of Stalin's unspeakably cruel Far Eastern Gulag system in the 1930s, Magadan is today an isolated but not unpleasant town on the Sea of Okhotsk. Despite its dark past, it boasts an attractive main avenue painted in pastels and has views of the surrounding countryside and snow-capped mountains in all directions. Magadan deals well with its terrible past by Russian standards, with a famous monument to the victims of the camps overlooking the town and a well-run museum that movingly details the prisoner experience.

Those who travel to Magadan today are usually business travellers brought here by the local gold mining and jewellery industries. The odd intrepid traveller and tour group also makes it here every now and then to check out the town and perhaps camp at the remnants of a remote Gulag camp, fish on the Arman River or go birdwatching or hiking.

◉ Sights & Activities

Mask of Sorrow   MONUMENT

(Маска скорби) Ernst Neizvestny's famous momument, erected in 1996, is the stark and brutalist concrete rendering of the suffering of the tens of thousands of political prisoners who passed through Kolyma's camps between the early 1930s and the late 1950s. Behind the giant mask made up of dozens of tiny faces kneels a weeping figure beneath a headless person on the cross. It's a deeply moving place, with good views across the town. A taxi here costs around R200 from the town centre.

Magadan Regional Museum   MUSEUM

(Магаданский областной краеведческий музей; ☑ 4132-651 148; www.magadanmuseum.ru; pr Karla Marksa 55; R100; ⊙ 10am-6pm Wed-Sun) As well as a standard and very detailed look at the lives of the local indigenous groups, this excellent museum displays a moving collection of artefacts from the Gulag camps, including a guard tower used in the Kolyma region. There's sadly no signage in English,

so non-Russians should call ahead to arrange a tour in English (R400 per small group).

Holy Trinity Cathedral   CATHEDRAL

(Свято-Троицкий кафедральный собор; Sobornaya pl; ⊙ 10am-3pm & 4-7pm) This striking gold-domed cathedral would catch your eye anywhere, but here, against a backdrop of grey apartment buildings, its beauty is instantly noticeable.

Kayur Travel   OUTDOORS

(Каюр Трэвел; ☑ 8-914-862 8920; www.kayur-travel.ru) This agency offers a whole range of tours into the wilderness of the Magadan region, including boat tours, skiing tours, ethnographic visits to indigenous peoples, fishing tours, hiking tours and snowmobile tours. Tours are conducted in Russian, but translators can be hired with notice.

🛏 Sleeping

★ Lucky Hostel   HOSTEL $

(☑ 4132-220 112; lucky-hostel@bk.ru; ul Kolymskoye Shosse 13; dm R600-750, d R2900; 🕸) Magadan's shiny new hostel has a giant sign, meaning that you won't be tramping around for ages trying to find it, as is often the way. Dorms are spick and span and sleep between four and eight, while the one private room has its own bathroom. There's a good guest kitchen and a washing machine to boot – what more do you need? Arriving by bus from the airport, ask to be let off at *tridtsat pyervy kvartal* (тридцать первый квартал).

VM Central Hotel   HOTEL $$

(ВМ Центральная гостиница; ☑ 4132-601 088; www.hotelvm.ru; pr Lenina 13; s/d incl breakfast from R3900/5200; 🕸) The lobby here is a study in Soviet exuberance and leads up to rooms that haven't had much done to them for decades. That said, they're perfectly comfortable and the staff here are remarkably friendly. Skip the breakfast, however.

★ Hotel Golden House   HOTEL $$$

(☑ 4132-201 111; www.hotel-goldenhouse.ru; ul Transportnaya 1; r/ste from R5000/9700; 🕸) The smartest option in town is this discreet but very warm and welcoming hotel on the 2nd floor of a business centre. It's not perfectly located, but the town centre is just a short walk away. Rooms are spacious, spotlessly clean and rather chic (if thoroughly beige), and there's a restaurant in the same building that serves all meals.

Magadan Hotel
HOTEL $$$

(Гостиница Магадан; ☎4132-604 557; www.
magadanhotel.ru; ul Proleterskaya 8; s/d incl
breakfast from R4200/6600; ☞) Almost
within bell-ringing distance of Magadan's
cathedral, this renovated Soviet hotel has
been given a very sophisticated and im-
pressive makeover. The lobby boasts both
artistically hung grass on the walls and a
stylish restaurant, and the rooms, while on
the small side, are immaculate. Welcome is
warm.

Eating & Drinking

As very little grows here, almost everything
you eat is flown in, making prices in shops
and restaurants a good deal higher than
what you'll pay on the 'mainland'.

Moskovskaya Ryumochnaya
RUSSIAN $$

(Московская Рюмочная; Proletarskaya ul 32;
mains R300-650; ⊙noon-midnight; ☞) Low
lighting, comfortable booth seating and
friendly staff make the 'Moscow Vodka Bar'
a great place for a meal. There's a big choice
from the large menu, including Russian favourites *pelmeni, vareniki* (boiled dumplings) and bliny, as well as a list of Magadan
specialities, pies, soups, steaks and a huge
range of vodka.

Torro Grill
STEAK $$$

(www.torrogrill.com; ul Pushkina 10; mains R600-
1550; ⊙noon-midnight; ☞) Pricey but definite-
ly one of the smartest places in town, this
large, upscale grill is easily one of Magadan's
best places for a meal or a drink. As well
as good steaks, they have a huge wine list,
burgers, salads, soups and lunch deals. It's
also one of the few places open late.

Alaska Beer Pub
PUB

(ul Dzerzhinskogo 26; ⊙noon-midnight; ☞) The
closest Magadan does to a charming bar is
this recently opened pub, a two-room es-
tablishment clad in timber and with cosy
booths to sit in and try various local and
imported brews.

ℹ Information

Visit Kolyma (Туристический
информационный центр Магаданской
области; ☎4132-651 587; http://visitkolyma.
ru/en-us; office 213, 2nd fl, Shkolny per 3) This
new office in an unlikely, unsigned location
opened in summer 2017 with the challenging
remit of encouraging tourism in the Kolyma
region.

ℹ Getting There & Around

Nearly all visitors arrive by plane at **Magadan
Sokol Airport** (Аэропорт Сокол Магадан;
☎4132-603 335; www.airport-magadan.ru;
Sokol), and there are daily flights to/from Mos-
cow and Khabarovsk and weekly connections to
Yakutsk, Petropavlovsk-Kamchatsky and Anadyr
(Chukotka) on Yakutia. The alternative to flying is
to take the intrepid overland route from Yakutsk
along the so-called road of bones (p575).

From the airport, bus 111 runs to Magadan's
bus station (Автовокзал; pr Lenina; R130,
50 minutes). Taxis run the route for R1500 to
R2000.

SAKHALIN

El Dorado for present-day businessfolk and
'hell' to Anton Chekhov, who famously passed
through in 1890 (not to mention the thou-
sands and thousands of prisoners shipped
here from the late 19th century), Sakhalin
(Сахалин) Island these days is defined by its
booming oil and gas hub, Yuzhno-Sakhalinsk.
But there's much more to this often beautiful
island, which is filled with a wild terrain of
forests, islands of seals, streams full of fish,
slopes for skiing and lots and lots of bears.
Relatively cheap flights can get you here, but
prepare to open the purse strings once you've
arrived: Sakhalin is no place for shoestringers.

The main 948km-long island is one of 59
(including the Kuril Islands) that make up
the Sakhalinskaya Oblast (Sakhalin Region).
Sakhalin's weather is – even locals will agree –
despicable. Winter is freezing and long, while
summer is humid and brief. August and Sep-
tember are the best months, mosquitoes not-
withstanding.

History

The first Japanese settlers came from Hok-
kaido in the early 1800s, attracted by marine
life so rich that one explorer wrote 'the water
looked as though it was boiling'. The island –
mistakenly named for an early map reference
to 'cliffs on the black river' ('Saghalien-An-
aghata' in Mongolian) – already had occu-
pants in the form of the Nivkhi, Oroki and
Aino peoples but, just as this didn't give pause
to the Japanese, the Russians were equally
heedless when they claimed Sakhalin in 1853.
Japan recogniseed Russian sovereignty in ex-
change for the rights to the Kuril Islands.

Japan restaked its claim on Sakhalin, seiz-
ing the island during the Russo-Japanese

War, and got to keep the southern half, which it called Karafuto, under the terms of the Treaty of Portsmouth (1905). In the final days of WWII, though, the Soviet Union staged a successful invasion, and Sakhalin became a highly militarised outpost of the Soviet empire, loaded with aircraft, missiles and guns.

In 1990 Muscovite governor Valentin Fyodorov vowed to create capitalism on the island. He privatised retail trade, but most people soon found themselves poorer. Fyodorov left, head down, in 1993. The demise of the USSR and the influx of thousands of oil-industry internationals succeeded where Fyodorov couldn't, and today Yuzhno-Sakhalinsk is one of the wealthiest cities in Russia.

Yuzhno-Sakhalinsk
Южно-Сахалинск

4242 / POP 193,600 / ⊙ MOSCOW +8HR

Yuzhno-Sakhalinsk is the prosperous and booming hub of Sakhalin Island, and a place changing fast as new office towers, hotels and apartment buildings shoot up all over the oil town's streets (which are still named after Lenin, Marx and other communists). Despite its firmly business atmosphere, Yuzhno is quite relaxed, with pleasant tree-lined sidewalks and looming mountains that you can ride chairlifts up and ski or climb down, and a couple of nods to its distant Japanese history. It's also a safe bet to say that you'll be one of the few tourists here, whenever it is you decide to travel.

◉ Sights

★ **Cathedral of the Nativity** CATHEDRAL
(Кафедральный Собор Рождества Христова; ul Gorkogo) This extraordinary new addition to Yuzhno-Sakhalinsk's otherwise ho-hum archi-

tectural ensemble is a staggeringly impressive golden-domed cathedral, which at 81m high is the tallest church in the Russian Far East. While the building was completed in 2016, it was still having its interior frescoes painted in 2017, and may not be fully complete for some time yet, although visitors are welcome.

Museum of Sakhalin Island:
A Book by AP Chekhov MUSEUM
(Музей книги А. П. Чехова Остров Сахалин; pr Mira 104; permanent/temporary collection R50/100; ⊙ 11am-6pm Tue-Sat) Based on Chekhov's seminal account of his few months working as a doctor on Sakhalin in the 1890s, this museum provides insight not only into life on Sakhalin in tsarist Russia but also into the life of the great playwright. More interesting than the untranslated Chekhov works are multimedia exhibits and lifesize models that give an idea of life on the island; there's even a recreated sleeping quarters for convicts (though you'll have to imagine the roaches and bedbugs).

A small gallery of temporary artwork is upstairs. The surrounding park has a few sculptures of Chekhov personages.

Sakhalin Regional Museum MUSEUM
(Сахалинский областной краеведческий музей; www.sakhalinmuseum.ru; Kommunistichesky pr 29; R100; ⊙ 11am-6pm Tue-Sun) The pagoda-roofed Sakhalin Regional Museum has a strong exhibit (sadly in Russian only) exploring the Japanese/Soviet overlap of the city's history, typified by the building itself, which served as the home of the Karafuto administration before the Soviets seized the island from the Japanese in 1945. The strong ethnographic section has some fascinating and unique Aino artefacts and photos from back before the original south Sakhalin inhabitants fled to Japan, plus bits on the Nivkhi and the rare Aleuts.

THE ROAD OF BONES

A dream for hardened adventurers, the infamous Kolyma Hwy – aka the 'road of bones', so named because of the countless Gulag labourers who froze to death building it – makes for a tough three- or four-day journey 2200km east to Magadan from Yakutsk. It's possible to negotiate a ride with a truck for the trip, or to hire 6WD vehicles going in either direction.

Visit Yakutia (p568) are specialists on the route and lead 10-day group tours in both the summer and winter months, as well as offering self-drive packages if you're not keen to do this seminal Russian overland journey with other travellers. Prices vary enormously depending on the numbers of people taking the tour and a dozen other factors, but this is definitely an adventure that will challenge even the hardiest Russia hands (not to mention your bank account). The route takes in the Verkhoyansk Mountains, Oymyakon, the world's coldest inhabited town, several former Gulag camps, the mining ghost town of Kadykchan, several working mining settlements and crosses countless rivers.

Yuzhno-Sakhalinsk

RUSSIAN FAR EAST YUZHNO-SAKHALINSK

Yuzhno-Sakhalinsk

THE KURILS

Spreading northeast of Japan, like stepping stones to Kamchatka, this gorgeous and rugged 56-island chain of 49 active volcanoes, azure-blue lagoons, steaming rivers and boiling lakes is one of the world's great adventures. The Kurils are part of the Pacific 'Ring of Fire' – the islands being the visible tips of an underwater volcanic mountain range. The rare visitors here are treated to dramatic landscapes, isolated coastal communities a world apart from the rest of Russia, and seas and skies brimming with marine and birdlife.

The three most populous islands, accessible by public boat and/or plane, are Kunashir, Iturup and Shikotan. You can attempt to visit these islands on your own, but secure permits first well in advance through a travel agent or from the border control office in Yuzhno-Sakhalinsk. Permits have become increasingly hard to get in recent years and you should begin planning your trip at least three months before you want to travel. Be prepared to get stuck for a few days because of storms and heavy fog. Late summer and early autumn provide the best chance of stable weather.

Aurora flies to Yuzhno-Kurilsk on Kunashir Island five times a week, and to Buravestnik, Iturup, four times per week. On the seas, **Sakhalin-Kurily** (Сахалин-Курилы; ☑ 4242-762 524; 'Fregat' office, 3rd fl, ul Kommunistichesky 21, Yuzhno-Sakhalinsk; ⊙ 10am-4pm) has a ferry that departs twice a week from Sakhalin to Kunashir, Shikotan, Iturup and back to Sakhalin. The entire loop takes up to two days. Omega Plus (p576) in Yuzhno-Sakhalinsk offers groups of four or more a seven-/eight-day tour to Kunashir or Iturup Island for R50,000 to R80,000 per person, including visa support. Transport is by public boat. Individuals can piggyback on these trips.

More northern islands, many of them uninhabited, can only be visited by private sea craft or on upmarket expeditions such as several 12- to 13-day cruises by **Heritage Expeditions** (www.heritage-expeditions.com). They offer a trip between Kamchatka and Sakhalin, and another from Sakhalin Island to Magadan; these typically happen in May and June (from US$8500 per person).

Art Museum
MUSEUM

(Художественный музей; ☑ 4242-723 643; ul Lenina 137; R70; ⊙ 10am-6pm Tue-Sun) This museum has a modest permanent collection of pre-Soviet Russian oil paintings and Korean and Japanese textiles upstairs, and changing exhibits downstairs. Best is getting inside the unique building, a former Japanese bank built in 1935.

🏃 Activities

The Kuril Islands qualify as trip-of-a-life-time material. Other tours offered by Yuzhno-Sakhalinsk travel agents include seal-infested Moneron Island off Sakhalin's southwest coast, plus shorter hops to points north, such as Tikhaya Bay, about 140km north of Yuzhno-Sakhalinsk (R3500 per person); and 1045m Chekhov Peak, a nice one-day climb in the Sakhalin Mountains not far from Yuzhno. Tikhaya Bay is possible as a DIY tour – just jump on any train heading north to Tikhy.

⭐ Gorny Vozdukh
SKIING

(Горный Воздух; ☑ 4242-511 110; www.ski-gv.ru; lift ticket summer R300, winter weekday/weekend R1300/1800) The 'Mountain Air' ski slope looms east of town on Yuzhno's biggest mountain. A chairlift runs all year (Friday to Sunday only in summer) and leads up the mountain – another heads down the back side. In winter it's hugely popular with skiers, while in summer hikers use the lifts to get a good start on some walking trails.

Omega Plus
OUTDOORS

(☑ 4242-723 410; www.omega-plus.ru; Office 347, 1st fl, Hotel Moneron, ul Kommunistichesky 86; ⊙ 9am-6pm Mon-Fri, 10am-3pm Sat) The travel agent in town most accustomed to handling foreigners, Omega Plus focuses on Japanese-heritage tours but also runs various area trips and week-long trips to the Kurils and Moneron Island. Ask for English-speaking Elena.

Sodruzhestvo
OUTDOORS

(Содружество; ☑ 4242-729 362; ul Komsomolskaya 192a; ⊙ 9am-6pm Mon-Fri) This well-established travel agency offers various trips to hard-to-reach parts of Sakhalin Island, including Chekhov Peak, various local lakes, some 19 different waterfalls and a volcano. It also offers themed tours of Yuzhno-Sakhalinsk, including ones centred on Chekhov and Japanese history.

Friends & Hikers
TRAVEL AGENCY

(Друзья & Походники; ☎8-914-755 4014; www. friendsandhikers.com; ⏰9am-6pm Mon-Fri) English-speaking Friends & Hikers runs a comprehensive range of hiking, fishing, kayaking, mountain-bike and boat tours in the summer, as well as ice-fishing, skiing, snowshoeing and snowmobile tours in the winter. English-speaking Ekaterina will help you plan your itinerary.

🛏 Sleeping

★ Hostel 65
HOSTEL **$**

(Хостел 65; ☎4242-774 409; www.hostel65.ru; ul Amurskaya 4; dm R800; 🛜) A well sign-posted Russian hostel – rivals, please take note – you'll find Hostel 65 centrally located on the ground floor of an apartment building. It has four sparkling-clean dorms, all with comfy wooden bunks and lockers, and there's a decent kitchen, a washing machine for guests and a friendly vibe, despite limited English.

Natalya Hotel
HOTEL **$$**

(Гостиница Наталья; ☎4242-464 949; www. natalyahotel.ru; ul Antona Buyukly 38; r/ste from R3600/5000; ✱🛜) This friendly business hotel offers bright, spacious rooms, with full kitchens (including stove and microwave). The rather dated furnishings might mean that it's a bit like visiting your aunt in Norilsk in 1993, but it's good value and staff are helpful. Breakfast is R400 extra. Entrance is in the back.

Lotus Hotel
HOTEL **$$**

(Гостиница Лотос; ☎4242-430 918; www.lotus-hotel.ru; ul Kurilskaya 41a; s/d incl breakfast from R2700/4000; ⊝✱🛜) On a peaceful street, the Lotus Hotel has clean and classically furnished rooms, with wood or parquet floors, natural light and a small desk. Pricier rooms feature an extra room, a kitchenette and small dining area. Excellent value, but some rooms are smoky and there's no lift.

Pacific Plaza Sakhalin
HOTEL **$$$**

(☎4242-455 000; www.sakhalinpacificplaza.ru; pr Mira 172; s/d incl breakfast from R5605/6372; ⊝✱@🛜) The Pacific Plaza is generally considered the top business hotel in town, and it's certainly the largest; an eight-floor green-and-grey blob of modernity with attractive carpeted rooms, lacquered wood furnishings and lots of creature comforts. There's good service, two eating spots (restaurant, lobby cafe) and a top-floor bar with a terrace open in summer.

Rubin Hotel
HOTEL **$$$**

(Гостиница Рубин; ☎4242-424 220; www.rubin-hotel.ru; ul Chekhova 85; s/d/ste incl breakfast from R4500/5000/5900; ✱🛜) Aimed primarily at longer-term visitors, but perfectly viable for a night or two, this is one of Yuzhno's most popular hotels. It looks like a polished Scandinavian motor inn – perfectly run, clean and welcoming. All rooms have kitchenettes, and include use of the gym and sauna. Breakfast is served in the popular Mishka Pub in the basement.

Gagarin Hotel
HOTEL **$$$**

(Гостиница Гагарин; ☎4242-498 400; www. gagarinhotel.ru; ul Komsomolskaya 133; s/d incl breakfast from R4500/5500; ⊝✱@🛜) A bit out of the way overlooking the namesake park, this pleasant business hotel capably fills the upper-midrange niche. Rooms are plush, with a modern design and sparkling bathrooms. There's also a sauna, for which guests enjoy a discount, and an excellent on-site restaurant, though breakfast is sadly lacklustre.

🍴 Eating & Drinking

Business lunches are naturally popular here – think R300 to R350. For shashlyk and beer tents head to **Gagarin Park** (Парк культуры и отдыха имени Ю. Гагарина; ⏰dawn-dusk).

Melnitsa
CAFE **$**

(Мельница; ul Lenina 171; pastries R50-100; ⏰8am-8pm Mon-Fri, from 10am Sat & Sun; 🛜) This is the most centrally located of this Sakhalin bakery chain where sticky Danishes, rich eclairs, sandwiches, coffee and tea are all on offer. It's a good breakfast spot and there's another usefully located branch on ul Sakhalinskaya (ul Sakhalinskaya 45; pastries R50-100; ⏰8am-8pm Mon-Fri, from 10am Sat & Sun; 🛜).

Supermarket Pervy
SUPERMARKET **$**

(Первый супермаркет; ul Lenina 219; ⏰7am-midnight) Good supermarket, with tempting bakery items and hot prepared dishes.

★ Nihon Mitai
JAPANESE **$$**

(☎4242-720 550; pr Pobedy 28b; mains R340-950; ⏰11am-11pm; 🅿) Yuzhno's favourite sushi spot is a bit out of the centre, but the very cool bamboo loft dining room is a great choice for soba noodles and ramen and picking from the sushi conveyor belt after 7pm. The ground floor has a small grocer with some Japanese products.

Marusya RUSSIAN $$
(Маруся; ul Lenina 219; mains R200-500; ⊗8am-midinight Mon-Fri, noon-midnight Sat & Sun; 🛜) A chic and friendly new addition to the city's eating options, Marusya is part contemporary riff on traditional Russian folk aesthetics and part acid trip with its vibrant and playful decor. Quality Russian staples are served cafeteria style until 4pm, after which it's table service only, transforming the space into something more refined and classy.

Cippolini ITALIAN $$
(SFERA Business Centre, ul Chekhova 78; mains R350-1400; ⊗11.30am-2.30pm & 6pm-midnight; 🛜🍴) This slick basement restaurant-bar has an extensive pub menu (including pizzas, pastas, seafood, steaks). Upstairs, stop in the cafe (open 8.30am to 5pm weekdays) for a coffee on the go. An expat fave.

Taj Mahal INDIAN $$
(📞4242-499 488; ul Antona Buyukly 38; mains R350-750; ⊗11.30am-10pm; 🛜🍴) Heavy inlaid wooden furniture and red tapestries set the stage for tasty chicken tikka masala, rich curries and fluffy naan bread at this expat favourite and contender for world's least likely location for an Indian restaurant.

Fursato JAPANESE $$
(Фурсато; ul Lenina 179; mains R500-1000; ⊗noon-11pm; 🛜🍴) With a picture menu, this popular Japanese spot serves up good but pricey sushi and sashimi platters, belly-filling *tonkatsu* (breaded pork cutlet), plus silky rich bowls of ramen, udon and soba noodles. The dining room may be a little low on atmosphere, but Fursato is one of the few places right in the centre of town.

★The Soho INTERNATIONAL $$$
(📞4242-391 888; www.sohocafe.ru; ul Kommunistichesky 31b; mains R500-2500; ⊗noon-1am; 🍴) Inside a small but fancy mall, this upscale minimalist place is unashamedly aimed at an international crowd, with English-speaking waitresses and an iPad menu that allows you to see each imaginative dish. These include gorgeously presented fare such as tuna carpaccio, lamb cutlets in a curry and coconut sauce, and roasted king crab with hollandaise.

Pak Degam KOREAN $$$
(Пак дэгам; 📞4242-241 080; www.pakdegam.ru; Kommunistichesky pr 31-6/1; barbecue sets R700-2600; ⊗noon-11pm; 🛜) This big and bustling Korean barbecue joint serves marinated meats in sets to be cooked at your table,

though there's a full pictorial English menu for nonbarbecue dishes if you're not feeling like playing chef. It's in an attractively furnished basement with lots of wood and comfortable booths, but also loud and invasive Russian pop.

Bar 133 INTERNATIONAL $$$
(Бар 133; ul Komsomolskaya 133; mains R600-2100; ⊗6pm-1am; 🛜) This friendly, cosy bar serves up some excellent food, and is popular with business travellers for whom the steep prices are of little concern. While it's possible to eat for a reasonable amount here, the best dishes, such as their rib-eye steak, filet mignon or lamb chops, are entirely worth the money.

Moosehead PUB
(ul Militseyskaya 8b; ⊗5pm-late Mon-Fri, from noon Sat, from 3pm Sun) Expats in the know head to this big dark-wood bar for cold beer and pub grub (mains R300 to R1000), famous seafood chowder and themed party nights.

ℹ️ Information

Tourist Information Centre (Туристско-информационный центр; 📞4242-306 080; www.gosakhalin.info; Kommunistichesky pr 18; 9am-6pm Mon-Fri) This very helpful and friendly tourist information centre is one of the best in the Far East, with excellent free maps and all sorts of excursions on sale, though sadly no English.

ℹ️ Getting There & Away

AIR

The **airport** (Аэропорт Южно-Сахалинск; 📞4242-788 311; www.airportus.ru; Khomutovo) is 8km south of the centre. Several airlines, including Aeroflot, Aurora and S7, fly regularly to Khabarovsk, Vladivostok, Novosibirsk, Moscow, Petropavlovsk-Kamchatsky and Blagoveshchensk. **Aeroflot** (📞toll free within Russia 8-800-444 5555; www.aeroflot.ru), Asiana and **S7** (📞toll free within Russia 8-800-700 0707; www.s7.ru) have three flights a week to Seoul, while **Aurora** (📞toll fre-e within Russia 8-800-250 4988; www.flyaurora.ru) has flights to Tokyo and Sapporo (two weekly). Aurora also has a weekly flight to Harbin.

BOAT

From June to September, once- or twice-weekly ferries run from Korsakov, 40km south of Yuzhno-Sakhalinsk, to Wakkanai on Hokkaido (from R8875, four hours). Book tickets at **Bi-Tomo** (Би-томо; 📞4242-726 889; www.bitomo.ru; ul Sakhalinskaya 1/1; ⊗9am-6pm Mon-Fri) or Omega Plus (p576).

Boats also run to the Kuril Islands and from the southern Sakhalin port of Kholmsk to Vanino on the mainland.

BUS

From the main bus stop outside the train station you can catch bus 56 for Kholmsk (R300, about 45 minutes) hourly from 8.45am to 9pm, bus 115 to Korsakov (R140, one hour) half-hourly or bus 111 to Aniva (about one hour).

TRAIN

From the train station, facing pl Lenina, the fastest train is the 1, which heads north at 10.42pm daily, stopping at Tiemovsk (*kupe* R3700, 9½ hours) and the end of the line, Nogliki (*kupe* R4400, 12 hours). The 2 train runs daily in the opposite direction. *Elektrichki* go to Bykov (daily, 1¾ hours) and Novo-derevenskya (two daily, 30 minutes).

❶ Getting Around

Bus 63 leaves for the airport, going east, from the bus stop on Kommunistichesky pr near ul Amurskaya (R20, 30 minutes). A taxi to/from the airport costs about R350.

Kamchatka

KAMCHATKA КАМЧАТКА

There are few places in the world that can enthral quite like Kamchatka, easily Russia's most scenically dramatic region. A vast volcanic peninsula that is almost entirely wilderness, Kamchatka is a place of extraordinary primal beauty, rushing rivers, hot springs and snow-capped peaks. Getting here takes time and effort, and exploring the region even more so, but few visitors leave anything other than awestruck.

Visitors to Kamchatka have traditionally been an intriguing mix of outdoorsy types and package tourists, both with deep pockets. Yet against all odds, Kamchatka has recently become viable for independent, relatively budget-conscious travellers.

The capital, Petropavlovsk-Kamchatsky, may be gritty, but it enjoys an incredible setting and has its share of easily accessible activities, including lift skiing into late May and some very doable volcano climbs. Kamchatka may not be a budget destination yet, but no longer is it strictly the domain of tycoons.

History

The man credited with the discovery of Kamchatka, in 1696, was the half-Cossack, half-Yakut adventurer Vladimir Atlasov, who, like most explorers of the time, was out to find new lands to plunder. He established two forts on the Kamchatka River that became bases for the Russian traders who followed.

The native Koryaks, Chukchi and Itelmeni warred with their new self-appointed overlords, but fared badly and their numbers were greatly diminished. Today, the remnants of the Chukchi nation inhabit the isolated northeast of Kamchatka, while the Koryaks live on the west coast of the peninsula with their territorial capital at Palana.

Kamchatka was long regarded as the least hospitable and remote place in the Russian Empire. In the 19th century, the peninsula became a useful base for exploring Alaska. When Alaska was sold off in 1867, Kamchatka might also have been up for grabs if the Americans had shown enough interest.

During the Cold War, Kamchatka was closed to all outsiders (Russians too) and took on a new strategic importance; foreign interest was definitely no longer welcome. It became a base for military airfields and early-warning radar systems, while the coastline sheltered parts of the Soviet Pacific Fleet.

❶ Getting Around

Locals are fond of repeating that on Kamchatka 'there are no roads, only directions'. You will have a hard time getting 'out there', where the bulk of Kamchatka's glory is (volcano bases, rivers, geysers), without an arranged 6WD truck or helicopter (or multiday hike). Regular bus connections go as far north as Esso and Ust-Kamchatsk. The cold months see winter roads (*zimniki*) open up that go further still, but of course the winter brings all kinds of other difficulties such as whiteouts and freezing temperatures.

HOW TO SEE KAMCHATKA

While it's getting easier than ever to visit Kamchatka on your own, limited infrastructure, permit requirements and risks like bear attacks and avalanches make preplanned tours mandatory for many places and highly advisable for others.

Tours

Many of Kamchatka's most famous sights, such as the Valley of the Geysers and Lake Kurilskoe, are only available by organised tour due to the need to charter a helicopter for the journey.

Plan ahead, especially in the months of July and August, otherwise days can be wasted scrambling for a guide to return from a trip or transport to be arranged from Petropavlovsk. Tours usually include everything – guides, transport, permits, hotels or tents to sleep in, sleeping bags and food. Most of the high-profile tours involve helicopter rides or 6WD/4WD transport.

Prices for the big day trips – Valley of the Geysers, Lake Kurilskoe and Mt Mutnovskaya – are set by the helicopter companies and tend to cost the same no matter which travel agency you use. Travel agencies pool clients for these tours. A day trip to the Valley of the Geysers costs R37,000 per person, including a one-hour helicopter ride each way, lunch and stops at Uzon Caldera and Zhupanova River.

Prices for longer tours cost anything from €2500 to €3500 depending on their length and how much time is spent in helicopters.

DIY with Guides

If you're wanting to get more 'out there' than Nalychevo or Esso, another option is simply hiring a local guide and going on a week-long or longer trek. Some travellers have done so to explore huge pockets of wilderness not featured here. The Visitor Centre (p587) or the Volcanoes of Kamchatka Park Office (p587) in Yelizovo are the best places to get a freelance guide.

DIY Without Guides

DIY travel is more difficult and comes with serious risks – especially if if you're looking to venture into the backcountry, where any misstep can be dangerous and you're best off having an experienced guide. A couple of local geologists were eaten by bears in 2008, by no means the first bear mauling in these parts. Winter travel eliminates the risk of bear attacks but creates new risks, such as days-long white-outs.

With those caveats established, the easiest fully DIY trips around Petropavlovsk include the hike up Mt Avachinskaya and trekking along the well-marked trails from Mt Avachinskaya to Nalychevo Valley. Another option is to head up to Esso, 10 hours north of Petropavlovsk by bus, where Bystrinsky Nature Park has an extensive network of well-marked and well-mapped trails.

Permits

As both a border region and a highly militarised zone, travel around Kamchatka involves a lot of permits; check on the latest rules before heading anywhere outside Petropavlovsk-Kamchatsky and Yelizovo. This is another reason why working with a travel agency is a good idea, as they'll be able to inform the local FSB office of your travel plans and ensure you won't get stopped from reaching your destination or get turned away once you arrive. Officially, you still need to register your intention to visit Esso even if you do nothing more than take the bus there and do a couple of small hikes. Although checks are infrequent, it's always much easier in Russia to follow the rules than break them. If you're on any form of guided tour, the travel agency will handle all of these permits for you.

The real workhorses of Kamchatka are its fleet of ageing helicopters, Mi-2 (capacity: six or eight people) and Mi-8 (capacity: 20 people), based at Yelizovo Airport. Used by volcanologists and travellers alike, the helicopters charge by time travelled in the air, and the fares are not cheap, necessitating group travel for most. Rides are exciting (and loud), with unbelievable views, windows you can open and room to roam about.

Kamchatka also has its own airline, **Petropavlovsk Kamchatsky Air Enterprise** (☑ 4152-300 660; http://aokap.ru; Yelizovo Airport), which does both scheduled and chartered forays to remote hamlets in the north part of the peninsula, such as Ossora, Palana and Tilichiki on the peninsula, and to Nikolskoye in the Commander Islands, known for its abundant wildlife and seal rookeries. Download the schedule from the website.

Petropavlovsk-Kamchatsky
Петропавловск-Камчатский

☑ 4152 / POP 181,000 / ⊙ MOSCOW +8HR

Anyone coming to experience the magical scenery and rugged beauty of Kamchatka will have to spend some time in the peninsula's sprawling capital, Petropavlovsk, and that's not necessarily a bad thing. Compared to the active volcanoes and geysers that bring travellers to Kamchatka, it's true that Petropavlovsk is a fairly workaday and architecturally uninteresting place. However it does have a magnificent setting on Avacha Bay and is overlooked by two giant volcanoes and surrounded by a long line of snow-capped mountains.

Though one of the oldest towns in the Far East, Petropavlovsk's seemingly endless main avenue is lined with mostly grim Soviet block housing, and there are just a smattering of historic buildings in the old town along the seafront. That said, locals are friendly and the glorious volcanoes are just a short drive, hike or helicopter journey away.

⊙ Sights

Petropavolvsk is a large, sprawling city that can't really be explored comfortably on foot, so get to know the buses, which plough the main drag from the bus station down to the old town. Locals talk about the various parts of town in terms of how far they are from the seafront, so the Avacha Hotel area is called 4km, the busy stretch of restaurants where ul Lukashevskogo meets pr 50 let Oktyabrya is called 6km and the area around the bus station is called 10km.

Trinity Cathedral
CHURCH

(Кафедральный Собор Святой Живоначальной Троицы; ul Vladivostokskaya 18) Petropavlovsk's largest and most impressive church is this golden-domed stunner, which sits on an outcrop from where it is visible from all over the city. Despite looking ancient, the church was built in the early 21st century, and still isn't complete as funds have dwindled. Still, from here there are great views of the bay.

Vulkanarium
MUSEUM

(Вулканариум; ☑ 8-963-832 0202; ul Klyuchevskaya 34; ⊙ 10am-8pm) This new museum was just about to open during our last visit to Kamchatka, and a quick peek inside as they were putting up the display revealed an impressive series of rooms with panels in English about the local volcanic clusters and their extraordinary, awesome powers. Definitely a good place to go before climbing one of the nearby giants.

Kamchatka Regional Museum
MUSEUM

(Камчатский краевой объединенный музей; ul Leninskaya 20; R120; ⊙ 10.30am-6pm Wed-Sun) Housed in an attractive half-timbered building overlooking the bay, this museum features an imaginative mix of relics and murals that outline Kamchatka's history, including a wide range of prehistoric weapons and tools, taxidermied animals, dioramas of nomadic herders, old cannonballs, weapons and flags. There's no signage in English, however, and so a visit without a guide can be frustrating.

Nikolskaya Hill
HILL

(Никольская сопка) Petropavlovsk's most charming spot for a walk, this thickly wooded hill is in the centre of the city between the harbour and the lake. There are numerous winding paths through the trees and some splendid views of Avacha Bay.

Lenin Statue
MONUMENT

(Памятник Ленина; pl Lenina) As Lenin statues go (and there are still around 1800 in Russia), this is an impressive one, with the revolutionary leader in a dramatic pose with his billowing coat tails flared dramatically to each side.

Mishennaya Hill
HILL

(Мишенная сопка) Wooded Mt Mishennaya (382m) offers an easy ascent with excellent views of town and Avacha Bay.

Beach
BEACH

Yes, there are beaches in Kamchatka too, and this one has gorgeous views of the bay and the distant snow-covered mountains, though

Petropavlovsk-Kamchatsky

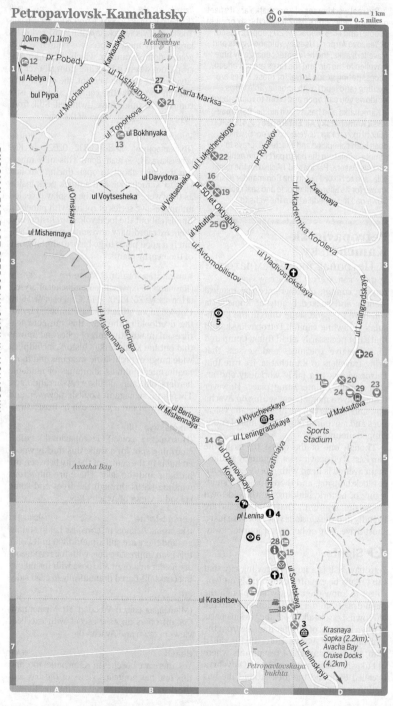

Petropavlovsk-Kamchatsky

it's unlikely you'll want to take a dip. There's a paved promenade and several benches for recumbent contemplation of the scene.

Alexander Nevsky Chapel   CHURCH
(Храм Александра Невского; ul Krasintsev) Originally built in 1857 to commemorate the victory over the British and the French in the Battle of Petropavlovsk, this wooden chapel was destroyed in 1937 during the antireligious campaigns under Stalin. It was rebuilt in 2007, and is now dwarfed by a newer and far larger church being built beside it.

🏃 Activities & Tours

Petropavlovsk has dozens of tour companies, so by all means shop around, but highly recommended agencies Explore Kamchatka, Kamchatintour and Lost World are all used to foreigners, speak English and reply promptly to emails. As well as offering everything from one-day to three-week tours, they all offer visa support and can help you charter helicopters, planes or 6WD vehicles. They are all run out of Petropavlovsk or nearby Yelizovo, where the helicopter pad and airport are both located.

Other popular tour activities include rafting, fishing trips, horse riding, dog sledding, snowmobiling, diving, surfing and heliskiing.

Kamchatintour   TOURS
(☑ 4152-201 010; www.kamchatintour.ru; 4th fl, Hotel Avacha, ul Leningradskaya 61; ⊙ 9am-7pm Mon-Fri, daily Jul & Aug) This is the most helpful Petropavlovsk agency we've found in terms of preplanning help and responsiveness. It can get you to its camp at Mt Avachinskaya on short notice, as well as organise a raft of other climbing, hiking and helicopter excursions.

Lost World   OUTDOORS
(☑ 4152-306 009, 24hr 8-622-810 177; www.travelkamchatka.com; ul Stellera 13a; ⊙ 9am-6pm Mon-Fri, daily in summer) This long-running operation has experienced guides (including outdoorsy volcanologists) who specialise in somewhat smaller groups and offer a range of tours focusing on bears, volcanoes, skiing, fishing, wilderness trekking and even dog sledding.

Krasnaya Sopka   SKIING
(Красная Сопка; ⊙ Nov-May) One of several ski areas within the city limits, this one is noteworthy for incredible views of Avacha Bay. T-bars take you up for R60 per run.

Avacha Bay Cruises   CRUISE
Petropavlovsk's stunningly beautiful bay, with volcanic Mt Vilyuchinsky (2173m) visible across the way on most days, is best appreciated on an Avacha Bay cruise. Standard three-hour cruises (per person R2200) take place most days in summer; book through

any travel agency. Better are the more sporadic six-hour tours that reach Starichkov Island, a haven for birdlife (from R4000 per person).

Snowave Surfschool Kamchatka
SURFING

([☎]8-924-792 5953; www.snowave-kamchatka. com) Since 2010 this intrepid gang of Russian surfers have been slowly promoting Kamchatka's world-class surf; they now run a well-attended annual surf camp on Khalaktirsky beach near Petropavlovsk during the brief surf season (June to October). In the winter months they swap surfing for snowboarding and head to the mountains.

🛏 Sleeping

Hostel 24
HOSTEL $

(Хостел 24; [☎] 4152-420 001; www.hostel24-kamchatka.ru; ul Sovetskaya 48; dm/tw R900/2900; [🛜]) Right in the centre of the city, Hostel 24 has clean dorms with wood floors and simple colour schemes, with four to 12 beds in each. A private twin is also available, as are laundry and a guest kitchen. It lacks atmosphere, but it's a great deal.

Hotel Avacha
HOTEL $

(Гостиница Авача; [☎] 4152-427 331; www. avachahotel.ru; ul Leningradskaya 61; dm R1800, s/d incl breakfast from R5400/7350; [@][🛜]) The rooms at Petropavlovsk's main business hotel are attractive enough but retain Soviet dimensions, especially the bathrooms. Budget travellers will be interested to know that there's a newly opened, surprisingly excellent hostel on the ground floor. There are two multibunk dorms, one for men and one for women, as well as a shared kitchen.

★ Nachalnik Kamchatki Mini Hotel
HOTEL $$

(Мини-отель Начальник Камчатки; [☎] 4152-346 500; www.nk-hotel.ru; ul Leningradskaya 14a; s/tw/d/ ste/cottage R3000/3500/4000/6000/12,500; [🛜]) A much-needed new midrange hotel, the 'Chief of Kamchatka' occupies a cute collection of buildings in the city centre, just a short stroll from the beach. Its nine rooms are well appointed and have folksy touches including a twin room designed as a Kamchatka-style wood cabin. The apartments on the top floor are excellent, with stylish bathrooms and city views.

Baza Po Priyomu Turistov
PENSION $$

(База по приёму туристов; [☎] 4152-420 591; ul Krasintsev 1; s/d R2250/2600) With a view of the city's docks, this place where sailors often put up offers much better value than most of Petropavlovsk's hotels. Rooms are small but clean, cosy and adequately furnished with rugs, TV and mini-fridge (although some bathrooms lack sinks, so you must brush your teeth in the shower). There's an 11pm curfew.

Hotel Edelveis
HOTEL $$

(Гостиница Эдельвейс; [☎] 4152-295 000; www. idelveis.com; pr Pobedy 27; s/d without bathroom R3300/4400, with bathroom R3900/5600; [🛜]) Although the bus station location isn't ideal, Edelveis deserves high marks for friendliness (some staff speak English) and its old-fashioned but comfy economy rooms and slicker standard rooms.

Hotel Geyser
HOTEL $$$

(Гостиница Гейзер; [☎] 4152-419 570; www.geyser-hotel.ru; ul Toporkova 10; s/d incl breakfast from R4500/6500; [@][🛜]) Rooms here have great views of Avacha Bay and are decently outfitted with flat-screen TV, desk and fridge. The fact that this is a Soviet-era hotel is well hidden, though some of the colour schemes might make you queasy. Aimed at groups travelling by bus, it's inconveniently located.

🍴 Eating

Bistro
CAFETERIA $

(Бистро; ul Sovetskaya 49; meals R150-250; [🕐]10am-8pm Mon-Sat, 11am-6pm Sun; [🛜]) This simple cafeteria in the centre of the city is a great option for a cheap meal while wandering around the old town. There's lots of choice and you don't have to worry about navigating a Russian menu.

Market
RUSSIAN $

(Рынок; pr 50 let Oktyabrya 16; [🕐]9am-8pm) This sprawling indoor market is a great spot for smoked fish, bread, cheese and vegetables, as well as nonfood items. It's a good place to stock up before a big trip into the wilderness.

★ San Marino
RUSSIAN $$

(Сан Марино; [☎] 4152-252 481; pr Karla Marksa 29/1; mains R400-800; [🕐]noon-1am; [🛜]) When you're just back from a hard trek, San Marino is Petropavlovsk's best splash for an excellent, exotic meal of Kamchatka crab, scallops, halibut and other delicacies. The entire place is lacy and flouncy, but don't let its severe uncoolness put you off. If you want to keep things economical, try the excellent-value business lunch (R400, noon to 4pm).

★ Da Vinci
ITALIAN $$

(Да Винчи; ☑ 4152-230 438; 4th fl, Parus Shopping Centre, pr 50 let Oktyabrya 16/1; mains R400-1000; ⊘ noon-midnight; ☎ ☑) Considered to have the best food in town by many locals, Da Vinci offers a full menu of Italian delicacies, including sumptuous risottos, crab ravioli, osso bucco and *vitello tonnato* (sliced veal in a creamy tuna sauce). The best wine list in town and attentive service from English-speaking waitstaff puts it over the edge.

Kyoto
JAPANESE $$

(Киото; ☑ 4152-337 722; ul Leninskaya 32; mains R300-600; ⊘ noon-midnight; ☎ ☑) Serving up good sushi, sashimi, ramen and other Japanese delights, this multiroom restaurant is friendly, fast and welcoming, with a picture menu and a kitchen that stays open later than most of the others on Petropavlovsk's seafront.

Korea House
KOREAN $$

(☑ 4152-421 193; ul Leninskaya 26; meals R400-1000; ⊘ 11am-10pm) On the hillside overlooking Avacha Bay just beyond the old town, this upscale Korean barbecue allows you to cook up your own meats tableside, as well as order soups and noodle dishes from the kitchen. Its seafood is also excellent and reservations are a good idea at the weekend.

Yamato
JAPANESE $$

(Ямато; ☑ 4152-267 700; ul Lukashevskogo 5; meals R400-800; ⊘ noon-midnight, until 3am Fri & Sat; ☎) Inside the Planeta Shopping Centre, Yamato serves delicious sushi in a low-lit setting with a dash of style (and a long fish-filled aquarium). It's rather dark, but service is friendly and fast. There's no sign visible from the street.

Milk Café
CAFE $$

(Милк Кафе; 3rd fl, Galant City Mall, ul Leningradskaya; mains R280-650; ⊘ 11am-8pm; ☎ ☑) The town's best pizzas are at this bright cafe, which also has healthy soups, salads and fondue, plus fine coffee and breakfasts. The menu has pictures in lieu of English.

🍷 Drinking & Nightlife

★ Kofeyko
COFFEE

(Кофейко; www.kofeiko.ru; Galant Plaza, ul Pogranichnaya 1/1; ⊘ 9am-8pm Mon-Sat, until 7pm Sun) Friendly barista Maksim, one of apparently just three trained coffee professionals on the Kamchatka Peninsula, runs this tiny little stand and shop, where he grinds one of over a dozen coffee types from around the world, and will craft you the perfect flat white or

double espresso. It's on the ground floor right ahead as you enter from ul Pogranichnaya.

Harat's Irish Pub
IRISH PUB

(www.harats.ru; ul Pogranichnaya 17; ⊘ noon-2am, until 4am Fri & Sat) There are a number of Harat's pubs in Russia, and we imagine that this one has comforted many a homesick traveller. There's a terrific range of brews on tap including Guinness, Magner's, London Porter and Oyster Stout. There's also a good photo menu of meaty pub food, including pork baked in Guinness, mussels in cream sauce and huge steaks (mains R350 to R1150).

Baraka
LOUNGE

(Барака; 4th fl, Parus Shopping Centre, pr 50 let Oktyabrya 16/1; ⊘ noon-5am; ☎) This swanky rooftop lounge has good views of the city, excellent cocktails and sushi, and is considered the best place in town to go dancing, with a large dance floor that gets packed at weekends.

🛍 Shopping

Alpindustriya
SPORTS & OUTDOORS

(Альпиндустрия; pr 50 let Oktyabrya 9/1; ⊘ 9am-9pm) This is a one-stop shop for all your outdoor gear and the perfect spot to pick up anything you may have forgotten before setting out into the wilderness. Prices are high, but they have pretty much anything you'll need.

ℹ Information

You can find ATMs fairly easily throughout the city, including in most hotels and shopping centres, such as **Planeta Shopping Centre** (ul Lukashevskogo 5), Parus and Galant City.

AS Lukashevskogo Hospital (Больница им. А.С. Лукашевского; ☑ 4152-120 610; www.kam-hospital.ru; ul Leningradskaya 114)

Hotel Petropavlovsk Medical Centre (☑ 4152-252 075; 2nd fl, pr Karla Marksa 31a; ⊘ 9am-8pm Mon-Fri)

Rescue Service (МЧС России; ☑ 4152-410 395; Khalaktyrskoye shosse 5; ⊘ 9am-6pm Mon-Fri) If you're travelling anywhere outside Petropavlovsk without the support of a travel agency, it's a very good idea to register your trip with the Emergency Situations Ministry. Should you have an accident or go missing, the ministry will have a head start in finding you.

Main Post Office (Главпочтамт; ul Leninskaya 60; ⊘ 8am-8pm Mon-Fri, 9am-6pm Sat, to 4pm Sun)

Tourist Office (Туристический информационный центр; ☑ 4152-307 330; www.visitkamchatka.ru; ul Leninskaya 62; ⊘ 9am-6pm Mon-Fri) You may not be lucky enough to catch the one English-speaking member of staff here, but this central office shows that Kamchatka is at least mildly interested in promoting tourism, and you'll be given a city map and a copy of *Kamchatka Explorer* magazine.

ℹ Getting There & Away

The only practical way to reach Petropavlovsk is by air. From the airport in Yelizovo, 30km northwest, there are at least daily flights to the following destinations:

Khabarovsk from R11,000, three hours

Moscow from R12,000, 8½ hours

Vladivostok from R10,500, 3½ hours

Be aware that flights during the peak July and August period can sell out, so it's a good idea to book ahead.

In the all-too-brief summer, **Yakutia Airlines** (☑ in Yakutsk 4112-491 299; www.yakutia.aero) flies between Petropavlovsk and Anchorage, Alaska. The 4½-hour flight runs on Saturdays between mid-July to mid-September. There are also connections to Novosibirsk, Magadan, Yuzhno-Sakhalinsk and Tokyo.

From the 10km bus station (Автостанция 10 км; pr Pobedy 28), buses depart daily at 9am to Esso (R1920, nine to 10 hours), and at 8am to Ust-Kamchatsk (R2440, 13 hours) via Klyuchi (R2100, 11 hours).

ℹ Getting Around

Petropavlovsk's 25km central avenue enters the city limits near the 10km bus station as pr Pobedy and changes its name 11 times as it snakes around bayside hills. Dozens of buses (R25) and *marshrutky* (R40) run along its length.

The 104 bus for the airport (R60, 35 minutes) departs from the centre of Petropavlovsk at the **4km bus station** (ul Pogranichnaya), which is also known as Старый рынок (КП). These buses then follow the main road out of town, stopping at each stop along the way, including the **10km bus station** (p586), before continuing to the airport and then Yelizovo's town centre. From the airport, take any bus signboarded '10km' from the Petropavlovsk stop across from the terminal. Taxis begin at around R700 depending on your negotiating skills.

Call ☑ 4152-460 160 for the best taxi rates around town or to Yelizovo and Paratunka.

Around Petropavlovsky-Kamchatsky

Mt Avachinskaya & Mt Koryakskaya

Two volcanoes near Petropavlovsk stand side by side 20km north of town (about 35km by road). The bigger and more forbidding one is Mt Koryakskaya (3456m), which takes experienced climbers two days to climb. The smaller one on the east is Mt Avachinskaya, generally included on tours and one of Kamchatka's 'easier' volcanoes to summit (about four to six hours up). Avachinskaya last erupted in 1991, but you can see it smoking daily.

A base-camp complex serves both volcanoes and sees a lot of action, including skiers and snowmobiles into early July; it gets quieter as you climb up. Just below Avachinskaya, the aptly named Camel Mountain is an easy one-hour climb, with lots of Siberian marmots on top and great views of Mt Koryakskaya.

Getting here is problematic. Snow blocks the final few kilometres of the rough access road through mid-July, which means you'll have to walk (or better yet, cross-country ski) the last bit, or hire Kamchatintour's (p583) snowcat. After mid-July you can get all the way to the base camp in a 4WD. The Visitor Centre in Yelizovo is the best place to find a driver. Freelance drivers charge R3000 to R4000 per car one way (R5000 to R6000 for round trip with wait time) to the base camp from Yelizovo; some can guide you up the mountain for an extra R2500 per group. Travel agencies might charge R6000 per car.

Kamchatintour has its own camp at the foot of Avachinskaya and offers a day trip out here for R5000 per person including lunch and snacks at the camp and a guide.

No permits are required to hike up Avachinskaya.

Nalychevo Nature Park

One of Kamchatka's most accessible attractions for hearty independent travellers is this nature park encompassing lovely Nalychevo Valley and the 12 volcanoes (four active) that surround it. A trail extends about 40km north from Mt Avachinskaya to the park's main base area, where there are many huts, camping spots, an information centre and, in summer, a handful of rangers who can point out hiking trails leading to hidden hot springs.

Camping is in designated areas or huts that vary wildly in quality. Before heading out, secure a park permit (R600), pick up a crude trail map and reserve a hut (per person R200 to R1000) at the park office in Yelizovo. GPS coordinates are also available. You might encounter foraging bears from June to September; the park office can brief you on proper precautions.

To get here, follow the instructions to Mt Avachinskaya, then walk. It's about a two-day hike from the Avachinskaya base camp to the park's main base area. You can exit the park via Pinachevo on the park's western boundary, but arrange to be picked up beforehand.

Yelizovo / Елизово

🗹 41531 / POP 39,500 / ⊙ MOSCOW +8HR

A good alternative base to Petropavlovsk, Yelizovo has some charm and the advantage of being right next to both the airport and the helipad, saving travellers hours of transit time if multiple forays into Kamchatka's wilderness are planned. There's a good visitor centre, some very pleasant accommodation and eating options, and the hot springs of nearby Paratunka to seal the deal.

The **Visitor Centre** (Туристский визит-центр; 🗹 8-900-444 0857, 8-962-472-110; 2nd fl, ul Ryabikov 1a; ⊙ 9am-1pm & 2-6pm Mon-Thu, 9am-1pm Fri), on the 2nd floor of the bus station, can point you in the direction of good hikes in the area, find you a trekking guide or help you join an organised tour. Likewise, visit the **Volcanoes of Kamchatka Park Office** (Природный парк Вуканы Камчатки; 🗹 41531-73 941, 41531-72 400; ul Zavoyko 33; ⊙ 9am-1pm & 2-6pm Mon-Fri) to get help planning and organising a visit to one of the four natural parks of Kamchatka administered under this umbrella organisation.

Yelizovo's small **Regional Museum** (Краеведческий Музей; 🗹 4152-64 161; ul Kruchiny 13; R50; ⊙ 10am-6pm Tue-Sat) has ethnographic exhibits, Russian weavings, local art and the requisite stuffed sables and marmots. **Golubaya Laguna** (Голубая Лагуна; ul Nevelskogo 6; R500; ⊙ 10am-midnight) is a large thermal pool with a restaurant and bar and plenty of space to relax.

Explore Kamchatka   TOURS

(🗹 8-962-280 7840; www.explorekamchatka.com; ul Bolshokova 41) This agency is run by an Alaskan who promotes alternative destinations and frequently helps visitors with unique requests (eg film crews seeking unique surfing spots). She's a mine of information for independent travellers and runs a great little **B&B** (🗹 8-984-163 9868; www.explorekamchatka.com; 41 Bolshako-va ul; r incl breakfast per person R3450; 🛜) 🍃.

🛏 Sleeping & Eating

Kamchatsky Stil' Hostel   HOSTEL $

(Хостел Камчатский Стиль; 🗹 8-951-290 6742, 8-962-281 8278; www.kamchatka-hostel.ru; ul Berin-ga 26; s/d/tr/q R1000/2300/3600/6800; 🛜) Run by the friendly Dima and Olga, this thoroughly local-style hostel inside a wooden house makes for a great introduction to Kamchatka, with cosy rooms and a shared kitchen.

Art Hotel   HOTEL $$

(Арт Отель Гостиница; 🗹 41531-71 443; www.arthotel-kamchatka.ru; ul Kruchiniy 3; s/d R4650/6000; 🛜) The Art Hotel is a cheerful though rather pricey place in the centre of town; some rooms have a private sauna and all are comfortable and spacious. There's a popular fish restaurant in the hotel, Fishery, which is also open to nonguests.

Stary Zamok   RUSSIAN $$

(Старый Замок; ul Zavoyko 123; mains R400-800; ⊙ noon-midnight Sun-Thu, noon-2am Fri & Sat) This old-school place is done out rather joylessly like a castle, but it has a full menu of calorific and meaty Russian dishes to warm up anyone after a day's hiking. It's south of the town centre; take bus 7 from the bus station and ask the driver to let you off at Stary Zamok.

Excellence   INTERNATIONAL $$$

(Meridian Trade Centre, ul Lenina 5a; mains R550-1000; ⊙ 11am-10pm, until midnight Fri & Sat; 🛜) Despite its rather uptight and precious appearance, Excellence boasts the most interesting menu in Yelizovo, serving everything from soups, potato pancakes and risotto to snails, which are accommodated under the heading 'unusual cuisine' on the menu. A good range of tasty breakfasts is served until noon daily.

ℹ Getting There & Around

Yelizovo Airport (Аэропорт Елизово; 🗹 4152-431 729; www.airport-pkc.ru) The peninsula's air traffic hub, with good domestic connections and flights to Japan and Korea. The 104 bus runs between Yelizovo's bus station, via the airport, to Petropavlovsk (R60, 40 minutes).

Avachinsky Heliport (Вертодром Авачинский; pr Izluchina) The helicopter hub for Kamchatka, this is where charter groups leave from on day trips to volcanoes and the Valley of the Geysers.

Frequent buses link Yelizovo's **bus station** (автостанция; ul Ryabikov 1a) with the airport (R23). Bus 7 connects the town centre to the south of town (R23), while bus 111 connects Yelizovo to Paratunka (R23).

Paratunka / Паратунка

Sprawled-out Paratunka, a hot-springs resort 25km south of Yelizovo, is a leafy and quiet place where locals love to come to relax in

HELISKIING & BACKCOUNTRY SKIING

Heliskiing tours of the mountains and volcanoes that make an arc around Petropavlovsk include unreal experiences such as skiing onto Pacific beaches or into Mt Mutnovskaya's fuming crater. Sky-high prices, however, deter most travellers.

Tours typically guarantee four days of skiing in a 10-day period to allow for weather inconsistencies – any wind or fog will ground you for the day. If the weather cooperates, you can pay (a lot) for extra days of heliskiing. Otherwise, the buffer days are spent snowcat skiing at the base of Mt Avachinskaya or at one of several small ski areas around town, trying out the hot springs, cruising around Avacha Bay or touring wild Pacific beaches. Conditions are most reliable in February and March.

The three main operators are **Vertikalny Mir** (☑ 8-903-740 0317; www.vertikalny-mir. com; Hotel Antarius, Paratunka), **Russian Heliboarding Club** (☑ 495-708 1555; www. helipro.ru) and Explore Kamchatka. Keep in mind that a massive avalanche swept away a helicopter and killed 10 people on a trip in 2010.

Backcountry skiing, such as trips into Nalychevo Valley, where there are also hot springs to splash in, is a cheaper alternative.

the various spas set up around hot-spring-fed swimming pools. It's bliss in the freezing winter months and a treat in summer as well. One of many, **Lesnaya** (Лесная; ☑ 4152-469 081; Paratunskoye shosse 25km; R1000; ☺ 10am-midnight) is surrounded by woods and has a sizable pool and a decent but pricey restaurant. It's on the left before reaching Paratunka (inform the bus driver where you're going). Another excellent option is Golubaya Laguna (p587), where there's a comfortable hotel and a restaurant and bar.

Paratunka is served by bus 111 from Petropavlovsk or 110 from Yelizovo (R45 to R60).

Valley of the Geysers
Долина Гейзеров

Kamchatka's most famous attractions lie 200km northeast of Petropavlovsk in the spectacular Valley of the Geysers (Dolina Geyzerov). Discovered in 1941, the 8km-long valley of a few dozen geysers cut through by the Geysernaya River is part of the protected Kronotsky Biosphere State Reserve.

Around 200 geothermal pressure valves sporadically blast steam, mud and water heavenward. The setting is exquisite and walking tours along a boardwalk take you past some of the more colourful and active geysers.

To get there you must travel by helicopter with a group on a day trip. Arrange through any travel agent: the price changes annually depending on fuel costs, but in 2017 it was R34,000 per person.

For an extra R3000 per person, the four- or five-hour trip can be extended with stops at Zhupanova River and Uzon Caldera, the remains of a 40,000-year-old volcano, now a 10km crater with steamy lakes.

Lake Kurilskoe
Озеро Курильское

Kamchatka's 'bear lake' – reached by helicopter – is so popular with the area's bears that, in August and September (when up to three million red salmon come to spawn), visitors can almost get tired of looking at them. The huge lake, formed by an eruption nearly 9000 years ago, is rimmed by volcanoes and home to a couple of lodges. The only trails in the area are bear trails. Don't wander alone: a Japanese photographer was eaten by a bear here in 2000.

Travel agents can set you up with a group flying out here on a day trip for R36,000 per person. Longer trips here are possible too; a 10-day bear/volcano odyssey that includes a few days around Lake Kurilskoe and a few days around Mt Mutnovskaya sells for around €3500 per person.

Mt Mutnovskaya
Гора Мутновская

Walking down into an active 4km-wide cone, past boiling mud pools and ice crevices cut by hot vapours of volcanic fumes, is like Frodo and Sam's last trek in *The Lord of the Rings*. Kamchatka volcanologists, who love all of Kamchatka's volcanoes, seem to hold Mt Mutnovskaya (2322m) in special regard – for studying, climbing or simply observing.

A wild road – handled by 6WD or good 4WD vehicles – reaches the base, but only after snows melt in mid-August (when some Petropavlovsk agencies offer day trips here). Otherwise, it's an expensive helicopter ride or an 8km to 15km hike (up to four hours one way, though not a difficult climb), depending on accessibility, to reach the cone, where you can hike (or ski) down past boiling mud pools.

It's particularly important to have a guide here. Weather can turn suddenly, and it's easy to get lost. Many tours climb the oval-shaped caldera of nearby Gorely (1829m). Base camps here are tent only.

Esso Эссо

📷 41542 / POP 2200 / ⊘ MOSCOW +8HR

The best destination for independent travellers in Kamchatka, Esso is set snug in a valley of green mountains, with a network of well-mapped hiking trails extending into the surrounding Bystrinsky Nature Park, plus hot-spring pools in town and rafting and horse-riding options nearby. It's a quiet, lovely place with the scent of pine, and locals who live in picturesque wooden cottages. Indeed, hardened Russia hands might find it hard to believe they're in Russia at all: it's all so clean, friendly and well cared for.

Evenki people migrated here 150 years ago from what is now the Sakha Republic, becoming the distinct Even people in the process. Here they met the local Itelmeni and Koryak people as well as Russians. Although Esso remains a mixed community, the nearby village of Anavgay is mostly Even.

◎ Sights

Ikar Lake LAKE

(Озеро Икар) A pleasant and easy hike along the Bystraya River and through some thick woods (where you may encounter bears: be sure to bring flares) will take you to this pristine lake surrounded by hills and distant snow-capped mountains. It's 9km from Esso to the lake, and it's well signed along the way.

Pioneer Hill MOUNTAIN

(Пионерская сопка) The giant hillside towering over Esso makes for a rather tough and sometimes inelegant scramble through the trees, but the views from the top over the valley are spectacular. The pathway begins near the Paramushir Tur (p590), and even though it's just 2km, it's quite an exhausting hike.

Ethnographic Museum MUSEUM

(Этнографический музей; ul Naberezhnaya 14a; R130; ⊙10am-1pm & 2-6pm Wed-Sun) You can find out much about the history of the area's peoples in this well-kept museum in a charming Cossack-style *izba* (wooden house) set beside the rushing river that flows through Esso. The museum contains some truly memorable old photos. There's a souvenir shop in a separate building.

🏃 Activities

You can hire mountain bikes at Altai (p590) guesthouse (per hour/day R200/600).

Most guesthouses can organise rafting Bystraya River (its name means 'fast', but don't expect white water). Most people just go for the day, but it's possible to do week-long trips with camping and salmon fishing. The price is R3000 per person per day, including all equipment. July to September is the best time to go.

Herds of 1000 to 2000 reindeer, managed by nomadic Evens, can be tracked down around Esso and Anavgay. They are reachable by helicopter in the warm months, and possibly by snowmobile during winter. An hour in a helicopter costs R150,000 in these parts. In late November there's a *zaboy* (slaughter) about 15km from Esso that's easier to reach.

Bystrinsky Nature Park HIKING

(Природный парк Быстринский; www.bystrinsky-park.com) The regional nature park that surrounds Esso, is a shining exception to the rule of neglected regional and national parks in Russia, and has well-marked trails, helpful staff and good facilities. Head to the Esso Visitor Centre for information on 11 spectacular hikes ranging from 2km to 42km in length.

Public Pool HOT SPRINGS

(⊙dawn-dusk) **FREE** Esso is so proud of its hot *istochniki* (springs) that in the 1950s a large public pool was built in the centre of the village for generations of locals to enjoy.

🎭 Festivals & Events

Neighbouring village Anavgay, located between Esso and the main road, holds a rollicking Even New Year festival during summer solstice in June, with plenty of dancing and singing into the wee hours.

🛏 Sleeping & Eating

Grushanka
GUESTHOUSE $

(Грушанка; ☎8-909-831 7813, 8-962-281 0101; Medvezhiy Ugol 5, Грушанка; r per person incl breakfast R950) Run by a friendly older couple, Grushanka gives a warm welcome. All-wood rooms have a cabin-like feel with pretty views of the countryside. There's a small hot pool facing the mountains in back.

Tri Medvedya
LODGE $

(Три Медведя; ☑8-902-461 5563; ul Zelenaya 19; r per person R1250) This two-storey wooden house has a mountain-lodge feel, with a fireplace, bearskin rugs and cocoon-like beds.

Altai
GUESTHOUSE $

(Алтай; ☑8-914-622 5454, 8-914-622 5455; ul Mostovaya 12a; s/d/tr from R1000/2000/3000; ☱) Near the bus stop, Altai is a gingerbread-like house with cosy but rather worn rooms that share a bathroom and a tiny hot pool. Many excursions offered including rafting trips, ski tours and visits to reindeer camps. Bicycle hire is available.

Sychey
GUESTHOUSE $

(Отель Домик Сычей; ☑8-914-622 9682; www.domikesso.ru; Naberezhnaya 5a; r per person R1000) Friendly Natalya runs this appealing little guesthouse on the manicured grounds of her green wooden house. There are two twin rooms downstairs and a large family room with four single beds upstairs. Each room has its own bathroom and kitchen, and both the decor and the atmosphere are very Russian.

★Paramushir Tur
HOTEL $$

(Парамушир Тур; ☑8-914 782 6008, 41542-21 442; www.paramushir.ru; ul 40 Let Pobedy 11; s/d/ cabin incl breakfast R4500/5600/7000; ☏☱) The only real hotel in town, the Paramushir Tur has spotlessly clean, comfortable rooms, helpful staff and is set in rather cutesy grounds at the base of Pioneer Hill. There's a great pool, sauna and barbecue area popular with weekenders, and the poolside cabins sleep three people. Pricey wi-fi is available.

Zarya
SUPERMARKET $

(Заря; ul Sovetskaya; ⊙9am-10pm) This is the best-stocked supermarket in town and the best place to get supplies for hikes. Fresh pies and rolls with fillings including meat, cabbage and egg make for good lunch fare.

Paramushir Tur Restaurant
RUSSIAN $$

(mains R400-850; ⊙8am-10pm) Inside the smartest hotel in town is Esso's only real restaurant. There's a big menu of traditional Russian cooking, including some particularly good meat and fish dishes. However, the atmosphere is rather lacking and you may well find yourself dining alone.

ℹ Information

There's an ATM at **Sberbank** (ul Sovetskaya 8; ⊙9.30am-4pm Mon-Fri); it's inside the bank itself and can only be used during working hours.

Esso Visitor Centre (☑41542-21 461; www.bystrinsky-park.com; ul Lenina 8; ⊙8.30am-12.30pm & 2-6pm Mon-Fri) This super helpful visitor centre in the middle of Esso can arrange park guides as well as 6WD charters. It offers extensive trail maps and has helpful English-speaking staff. Before you set off anywhere on your own, have the staff brief you on bear precautions and keep them apprised of your itinerary.

Attached to the visitor centre is a small museum (admission R50), where you can learn about the locally famous Beringia dogsled race. The centre also has info about traditional crafts in the area, and workshops where you can visit the artists.

ℹ Getting There & Away

The daily bus to Petropavlovsk (R1920, 10 hours) departs at 8am from the **bus station** (автостанция) in front of the green plank-wood ticket office.

Understand Russia

Russia Today

From its relations with the US, to its key involvement in conflicts in Syria and Ukraine, Russia is resurgent on the international stage. Front and centre is President Vladimir Putin, who, should he choose to run for re-election in 2018, appears unassailable despite opposition politician Alexey Navalny nipping at his heels. Whatever happens, you can be sure that little will be allowed to spoil the success of Russia's hosting of the 2018 FIFA World Cup.

Best on Film

Loveless (2017) Winner of the Jury Prize at the Cannes Film Festival in 2017, Andrei Zvyagintsev's follow-up to *Leviathan* is another subtle critique of contemporary Russian society.

My Perestroika (2010) Robin Hessman's film focuses on five Russians and the effect of the past 20 turbulent years on their lives.

Bolshoi Babylon (2015) Behind-the-scenes documentary exposing the violent rivalries in Russia's most famous ballet troupe.

Best in Print

Nothing Is True and Everything Is Possible: Adventures in Modern Russia (Peter Pomerantsev; 2014) Darkly entertaining tales of contemporary Russian life by TV producer Peter Pomerantsev.

The Last Man in Russia (Oliver Bullough; 2013) A spot-on portrait of modern Russia, told through the tumultuous and tragic life of an Orthodox priest.

Lost Cosmonaut and **Strange Telescopes** (Daniel Kalder; 2006 and 2009) Kalder's books explore some of Russia's quirkiest and least-visited locations.

Celebrating a Revolution?

Since Putin first came to power, the Kremlin has been searching for a national ideology that could replace that of communism under the Soviet Union. In 2016 the president named patriotism as that ideology, confirming many academics' and commentators' suspicions that the state had, in effect, hijacked the concept to serve its own agenda (ie keeping Putin in power). Russians are actively encouraged to have a sense of pride in their history through celebrations of the country's sacrifices and victories in WWII (known in Russia as the Great Patriotic War) and glorification of historical figures such as Ivan the Terrible and Vladimir the Great, both of whom have had recent public statues unveiled in their honour.

In historical terms, 2017 is a key date for Russia, being a century since the events that led to the creation of the Soviet Union. However, it is also a tricky celebration for the Kremlin to fully embrace since its root is one of revolution – an anathema to an administration keen to avoid any similar political upheavals. You don't have to look hard to see a confused response to the Soviet period across Russia and what it means for the modern country. One wonders what the embalmed Lenin in his bunker on Red Square would think about Russia's contemporary capitalist society that now surrounds him.

Complex International Relations

With his approval rating running around 84% at home, Russia's President Putin has been emboldened to follow a more aggressive international political agenda. There's the possibility that the Russians had a hand in the election of Donald Trump to the US presidency in 2016. There's its controversial military support for Syria's President Bashar al-Assad under the guise of keeping Islamic militants in check. And there's its military backing for separatists in eastern Ukraine where, three years on from Russia's annexation of Crimea, heavy fighting continues. In response to EU sanctions imposed on Russia because of that annexation, the Kremlin imposed its own embargo on certain EU agricultural products.

Putin Can Fix It

At the time of research, Putin had yet to confirm his candidacy for the 2018 presidential election. The Kremlin is known for pulling surprises, but few believe Putin is ready to relinquish control of the nation he has effectively ruled since 2000. The 64-year-old ex-KGB agent certainly appeared in command during an annual live national TV program in June 2017, during which he answered a selection from some 2.6 million questions raised by the public. The show – which could easily be called 'Putin Can Fix It' – saw the president promise to solve problems ranging from pot-holed streets and low wages to what to do with fired FBI director James Comey (offer him asylum in Russia, like Edward Snowden).

However, one problem that Putin is somewhat at a loss of how to fix is that of a growing opposition to his rule. In a change to the program's regular format, comments from social media scrolled across the screen, a fair few of them critical of the highly orchestrated event and of Putin himself. Days prior to the TV Q&A, tens of thousands of demonstrators had gathered in over 100 cities across Russia to march against corruption and Putin's regime. Along with a thousand other people, the protest's architect and Russia's leading opposition figure Alexey Navalny was arrested and sentenced to 25 days in jail.

The Problem with Navalny

Lawyer turned anticorruption crusader Navalny has been a thorn in Putin's side since 2008, when he started blogging about state graft. The 41-year-old emerged as an effective opposition leader during the parliamentary elections of 2011, when he urged his supporters not to vote for United Russia, which he dubbed the 'party of crooks and thieves'. Standing as a candidate in the Moscow mayoral elections of 2013, Navalny captured 27% of the vote despite a concerted attempt by the establishment to sideline him.

In the latest of several criminal prosecutions against him, Navalny was convicted of embezzlement in 2014. He claims this verdict, like those before it, is politically motivated; candidates with a criminal record are barred from standing for the presidency. Nevertheless, Navalny is determined to run, and has began campaigning across the country, taking his message as far afield as Siberia. Barred from national TV, Navalny – for all his team's internet and social media savvy – has a mountain to climb. Less than 50% of Russians know who he is, according to in-

POPULATION: **144.5 MILLION**

AREA: **17,098,242 SQ KM**

GDP: **US$1.326 TRILLION**

INFLATION: **4.1%**

if Russia were 100 people

81 would be Russian
4 would be Tatar
1 would be Ukrainian
1 would be Bashkir
1 would be Chuvash
12 would be other

belief systems
(% of population)

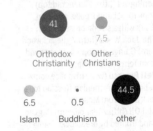

41 Orthodox Christianity
7.5 Other Christians
6.5 Islam
0.5 Buddhism
44.5 other

population per sq km

RUSSIA UK USA

✝ ≈ 8 people

Best on the Internet

Calvert Journal (www.calvertjournal.com) Best online guide to the creative and progressive side of Russia.

Russia! (http://readrussia.com) Sparky cultural and political features on all things Russian.

Russia in Global Affairs (http://eng.globalaffairs.ru) Features relating to Russian politics, economy and culture.

Russia Beyond the Headlines (www.rbth.com) News, views and cultural features.

Best Fiction

The Patriots (Sana Krasikov; 2017) An emotionally wrenching, multigenerational drama covering much of Russia's 20th- and early-21st-century history.

Day of the Oprichnik (Vladimir Sorokin; 2011) Dystopian drama set in Moscow in 2028 by one of Russia's most popular modern writers.

The Master and Margarita (Mikhail Bulgakov; 1967) A satirical masterpiece completed in 1940 just before the author's death.

Snowdrops (AD Miller; 2011) An edgy morality tale set in contemporary Russia.

Best in Music

Leningrad (http://leningrad.top) Punk rock, Latino, polka and Tom Waits with a strong brass section.

The Jack Wood (http://thejackwood.com) Garage-protopunk-blues band from Tomsk in Siberia.

Deti Picasso (www.myspace.com/detipicasso) Armenian-Russian folk-rock band from Moscow.

Alai Oli (http://alai-oli.com) Reggae band fronted by dreadlocked singer-songwriter Olga Markes.

Leonid Fedorov (www.leonidfedorov.ru) Semi-absurd poetry fused with acoustic guitars and hypnotic melodies.

dependent pollsters the Levada Center. Those that do know him are also likely to be aware of his strong nationalist views, which come with an unrepentant tinge of antimigrant rhetoric. This makes him a controversial figure that not all Russian liberals are in a hurry to support.

2018 World Cup

In June 2017 Russia held the Confederation Cup, a dress rehearsal for the FIFA 2018 World Cup. Antidiscrimination observers were present at all matches and referees had the chance to halt games if fans' abuse didn't cease after warnings. Russia is the first country in Eastern Europe to host the globe's most prestigious soccer championship, and national honour (not to mention Putin's reputation) is riding on the tournament's success. As with the 2014 Winter Olympics in Sochi, the chances of anything not going according to script are slim.

Transport upgrades including improved and new airports (Samara's Kurumoch International Airport, for example), better roads and speedier rail links are making it easier for travellers and football fans to get around Russia. However, the ongoing economic slowdown, mainly caused by the drop in crude oil prices, has caused the initial budget for improved infrastructure to be slashed by almost threefold to US$10 billion.

With a year to go, at the time of writing only five out of the 12 stadiums in 11 locations (Moscow, St Petersburg, Kaliningrad, Kazan, Nizhny Novgorod, Samara, Saransk, Rostov-on-Don, Sochi, Volgograd and Yekaterinburg) have been completed. Human Rights Watch have documented abuses at six stadium construction sites, including unpaid wages and hazardous working conditions that have led to deaths. This includes the decade-overdue Krestovsky Stadium in St Petersburg, where the budget has ballooned to as much as US$1.5 billion (the government claims US$700 million).

History

How Russia became the largest country on earth and modern-day superpower is an epic tale that puts *War and Peace* to shame for its cast of characters and dramatic events. The birth of the Russian state is usually identified with the founding of Novgorod in AD 862, although from the early 13th century until 1480 Russia was effectively a colony of the Mongols. The following 600 years have seen an ever-expanding nation ruled by tsars, commissars and presidents.

Formation of the Country

Russian Ancestors: Slavs & Vikings

There is some disagreement about where the Slavs originated, but in the first few centuries AD they expanded rapidly to the east, west and south from the vicinity of present-day northern Ukraine and southern Belarus. These Eastern Slavs were the ancestors of the Russians; they were still spreading eastward across the central Russian woodland belt in the 9th century. From the Western Slavs came the Poles, Czechs, Slovaks and others. The Southern Slavs became the Serbs, Croats, Slovenes and Bulgarians.

The Slavs' conversion to Christianity in the 9th and 10th centuries was accompanied by the introduction of an alphabet devised by Cyril, a Greek missionary (later St Cyril), which was simplified a few decades later by a fellow missionary, Methodius. The forerunner of Cyrillic, it was based on the Greek alphabet, with a dozen or so additional characters. The Bible was translated into the Southern Slav dialect, which became known as Church Slavonic and is the language of the Russian Orthodox Church's liturgy to this day.

The first Russian state developed out of the trade on river routes across Eastern Slavic areas – between the Baltic and Black Seas and, to a lesser extent, between the Baltic Sea and the Volga River. Vikings from Scandinavia – the Varangians, also called Varyagi by the Slavs – had been nosing east from the Baltic since the 6th century AD, trading and raiding for furs, slaves and amber, and coming into conflict with the Khazars and with Byzantium, the eastern centre of Christianity. To secure their hold on the trade routes, the Vikings made themselves masters of settlements

In line with common usage, we use directly transliterated names for pre-1700 rulers, anglicised names from Peter the Great until 1917, and again transliterated after that – thus Andrei Bogolyubov not Andrew, Vasily III not Basil; but Peter the Great not Pyotr, Catherine the Great not Yekaterina etc.

TIMELINE	c 30,000 BC	4th century AD	862
	Humans settle in many locations across what would become Russia's vast territory, including Sunghir near Vladimir and along the Aldan River in the Sakha Republic in the Russian Far East.	The Huns, a nomadic people from the Altai region, move into Eastern Europe. Under their leader Attila, their empire stretches from the Ural River to the Rhine.	The legendary Varangian (Scandinavian) Rurik of Jutland gains control of Staraya Ladoga and builds the Holmgard settlement near Novgorod. The infant version of Russia is born.

in key areas – places such as Novgorod, Smolensk, Staraya Ladoga and Kyiv (Kiev) in Ukraine. Though by no means united themselves, they created a loose confederation of city-states in the Eastern Slavic areas.

Kyivan Rus

In the 9th century, Rurik of Jutland founded the Rurik dynasty, the ruling family of the embryonic Russian state of Kyivan Rus and the dominant rulers in Eastern Slavic areas until the end of the 16th century. Kyivan Rus became a Christian state under Vladimir I, who also introduced the beginnings of a feudal structure to replace clan allegiances. However, some principalities – including Novgorod, Pskov and Vyatka (north of Kazan) – were ruled democratically by popular *vechi* (assemblies).

Kyiv's supremacy was broken by new invaders from the east – first the Pechenegs, then in 1093 the Polovtsy sacked the city. The European crusades from the late 11th century onward also cracked the Arab hold on southern Europe and the Mediterranean, reviving west–east trade routes and making Rus a commercial backwater.

Old Russian Fortresses

Staraya Ladoga

Smolensk

Pskov

Stary Izborsk

Rostov kremlin

The Rise of Rostov-Suzdal

The northern Rus principalities began breaking from Kyiv after about 1050. As Kyiv declined, the Russian population shifted northward and the fertile Rostov-Suzdal region northeast of Moscow began to be developed. Vladimir Monomakh of Kyiv founded the town of Vladimir there in 1108 and gave the Rostov-Suzdal principality to his son Yury Dolgoruky, who is credited with founding Moscow in 1147.

Rostov-Suzdal grew so rich and strong that Yury's son Andrei Bogolyubov tried to use his power to unite the Rus principalities. His troops took Kyiv in 1169, after which he declared Vladimir his capital, even though the church's headquarters remained in Kyiv until 1300. Rostov-Suzdal began to gear up for a challenge against the Bulgars' hold on the Volga–Ural Mountains region. The Bulgar people had originated further east several centuries before and had since converted to Islam. Their capital, Bolgar, was near modern Kazan, on the Volga.

Masha Holl's Life in Medieval Russia (http://medieval.mashaholl.com) abounds with intriguing details, such as the fact that surnames didn't exist in Russia for most of the Middle Ages.

The Golden Horde

Meanwhile, over in the east, a confederation of armies headed by the Mongolian warlord Chinggis (Genghis) Khaan (1167-1227) was busy subduing most of Asia, eventually crossing Russia into Europe to create history's largest land empire. In 1223 Chinggis' forces met the armies of the Russian princes and thrashed them at the Battle of Kalka River. This push into European Russia was cut short by the death of the warlord, but his grandson Batu Khaan returned in 1236 to finish the job, laying waste to Bolgar and Rostov-Suzdal, and annihilating most of the other Russian principalities,

1093–1108	1147	1169	1240
Vladimir Monomakh takes control of territory bounded by the Volga, Oka and Dvina Rivers, moves his capital to Suzdal and, in 1108, founds Vladimir, thus creating the Vladimir-Suzdal principality.	Vladimir's son Yury Dolgoruky builds a wooden fort, the forerunner of Moscow's Kremlin, and invites his allies to a banquet there; he's later considered the city's founder.	Yury's son Andrei Bogolyubov sacks Kyiv and moves his court to Vladimir, where he houses the Vladimir *Icon of the Mother of God* in the newly built Assumption Cathedral.	Alexander, Prince of Novgorod, aged 19, defeats the Swedes on the Neva River near present-day St Petersburg, thus earning himself the title 'Nevsky'.

including Kyiv, within four years. Novgorod was saved only by spring floods that prevented the invaders from crossing the marshes around the city.

Batu and his successors ruled the Golden Horde (one of the khanates into which Chinggis' empire had broken) from Saray on the Volga, near modern Volgograd. At its peak the Golden Horde's territory included most of Eastern Europe stretching from the banks of the Dnepr River in the west to deep into Siberia in the east and south to the Caucasus. The Horde's control over its subjects was indirect: although its armies raided them in traditional fashion if they grew uppity, it mainly used collaborative local princes to keep order, provide soldiers and collect taxes.

Alexander Nevsky & the Rise of Moscow

One such 'collaborator' was the Prince of Novgorod, Alexander Nevsky, a Russian hero (and later a saint of the Russian Church) for his resistance to German crusaders and Swedish invaders. In 1252 Batu Khaan put him on the throne as Grand Prince of Vladimir.

Nevsky and his successors acted as intermediaries between the Mongols and other Russian princes. With shrewd diplomacy, the princes of Moscow obtained and hung on to the title of grand prince from the early 14th century while other princes resumed their feuding. The church provided backing to Moscow by moving there from Vladimir in the 1320s and was in turn favoured with exemption from Mongol taxation.

With a new-found Russian confidence, Grand Prince Dmitry put Moscow at the head of a coalition of princes and took on the Mongols, defeating them in the battle of Kulikovo Pole on the Don River in 1380. The Mongols crushed this uprising in a three-year campaign but their days were numbered. Weakened by internal dissension, they fell at the end of the 14th century to the Turkic empire of Timur (Tamerlane), which was based in Samarkand (in present-day Uzbekistan). Yet the Russians, themselves divided as usual, remained vassals until 1480.

Ivan the Great

In 1478 Novgorod was first of the Great Russian principalities to be brought to heel by Ivan III. To secure his power in the city he installed a governor, deported the city's most influential families (thus pioneering a strategy that would be used with increasing severity by Russian rulers right up to Stalin) and ejected the Hanseatic merchants.

The exiles were replaced with Ivan's administrators, whose good performance was rewarded with temporary title to confiscated lands. This new approach to land tenure, called *pomestie* (estate), characterised Ivan's rule. Previously, the boyars (high-ranking nobles) had held land under a *votchina* (system of patrimony) giving them unlimited control and inheritance rights over their lands and the people on them. The freedom

Rus was the name of the dominant Kyivan Viking clan, but it wasn't until the 18th century that the term Russian or Great Russian came to be used exclusively for Eastern Slavs in the north, while those to the south or west were identified as Ukrainians or Belarusians.

In 2008 in a telephone poll conducted by the TV station Rossiya that involved over 50 million people, the medieval prince Alexander Nevsky took top place as the most famous Russian, followed by reformist Prime Minister Pyotr Stolypin, who was assassinated in 1911, and Stalin.

HISTORY FORMATION OF THE COUNTRY

1300	1328	1382	1389
As Kyiv loses its political and economic significance, the headquarters of the Russian Orthodox Church moves to Vladimir. In 1325 Metropolitan Peter moves the episcopal see to Moscow.	The Khan of the Golden Horde appoints Ivan I (Ivan the Moneybags) as Grand Prince of Vladimir with rights to collect taxes from other Russian principalities.	Led by the Khan Tokhtamysh, the Mongols invade again, slaughtering half of Moscow's population but allowing a supplicant Dmitry to remain Grand Prince of Vladimir.	Vasily I takes over his father Dmitry's titles on his death, without the weakened Khan's approval. He continues unifying the Russian lands and makes an alliance with Lithuania.

NOBLE TITLES

The title 'tsar', from the Latin *caesar*, was sometimes used by Ivan III in his diplomatic relations with the West. Ivan IV was the first ruler to be formally crowned 'Tsar of All Russia'. Peter the Great preferred emperor, though tsar remained in use. We usually use empress for a female ruler; a tsar's wife who does not become ruler is a *tsaritsa* (in English, tsarina). A tsar's son is a *tsarevitch* and his daughter a *tsarevna*. Boyars were feudal landholders who formed the early Russian aristocracy.

to shift allegiance to other princes had given them political clout, too. Now, with few alternative princes left, the influence of the boyars declined in favour of the new landholding civil servants. This increased central control spread to the lower levels of society with the growth of serfdom.

Ivan IV (the Terrible)

Ivan IV's marriage to Anastasia, from the Romanov boyar family, was a happy one – unlike the five that followed her death in 1560, a turning point in his life. Believing her to have been poisoned, Ivan instituted a reign of terror that earned him the sobriquet *grozny* (literally 'awesome' but commonly translated as 'terrible') and nearly destroyed all his earlier good works.

His subsequent career was indeed terrible, though he was admired for upholding Russian interests and tradition. His military victories helped transform Russia into the multiethnic, multireligious state it is today. However, his campaign against the Crimean Tatars nearly ended with the loss of Moscow, and a 24-year war with the Lithuanians, Poles, Swedes and Teutonic Knights to the west also failed to gain any territory for Russia.

Ivan's growing paranoia led him to launch a savage attack on Novgorod in 1570 that finally snuffed out that city's golden age. An argument about Ivan beating his son's wife (possibly causing her miscarriage) ended with the tsar accidentally killing his heir in 1581 with a blow to the head. Ivan himself died three years later during a game of chess. The later discovery of high amounts of mercury in his remains indicated that he died from poisoning – possibly by his own hand, as he had habitually used mercury to ease the pain of a fused spine.

The Time of Troubles

Ivan IV's official successor was his mentally enfeebled son Fyodor, who left the actual business of government to his brother-in-law, Boris Godunov, a skilled 'prime minister' who repaired much of the damage done by Ivan. Fyodor died childless in 1598, ending the 700-year Rurikid dynasty, and Boris ruled as tsar for seven more years.

Geoffrey Hosking's *Russia and the Russians* is a definitive one-volume trot through 1000 years of Russian history by a top scholar.

The story of Boris Godunov inspired both a play by Alexander Pushkin in 1831 and an opera by Modest Mussorgsky in 1869.

1425–62	1480	1505–33	1533
The 10-year-old Vasily II becomes Prince of Moscow. His long rule is plagued by civil war but also sees the collapse of the Golden Horde into smaller khanates.	Ivan III's armies face down those of the Tatars who come to extract tributes withheld by Muscovy for four years; this ends the Golden Horde's dominance of Russia.	Vasily III annexes the autonomous Russian provinces of Pskov and Ryazan, captures Smolensk from Lithuania and extends Moscow's influence south along the Volga towards Kazan.	Aged three, Ivan IV is proclaimed Grand Prince of Moscow when his father Vasily III dies. His mother acts as regent until she dies – possibly poisoned – in 1538.

Shortly after Boris's death, a Polish-backed Catholic pretender arrived on the scene claiming to be Dmitry, another son of Ivan the Terrible (who had in fact died in obscure circumstances in Uglich in 1591, possibly murdered on Boris Godunov's orders). This 'False Dmitry' gathered a huge ragtag army as he advanced on Moscow. Boris Godunov's son was lynched and the boyars acclaimed the pretender tsar.

Thus began the Time of Troubles (the Smuta), a spell of anarchy, dynastic chaos and foreign invasions. At its heart was a struggle between the boyars and central government (the tsar). Peace was restored in 1613 when 16-year-old Mikhail Romanov, a relative of Ivan IV's first wife, became tsar, the first of a new dynasty that was to rule until 1917.

The Romanov Dynasty

Peter the Great

Peter I, known as 'the Great' for his commanding 2.03m frame and his equally commanding victory over the Swedes, dragged Russia kicking and screaming into Europe and made the country a major world power.

Born to Tsar Alexey's second wife, Natalia, in 1672, Peter was an energetic and inquisitive youth who often visited Moscow's European district to learn about the West. Dutch and British ship captains in Arkhangelsk gave him navigation lessons on the White Sea.

Following his mother's death in 1694 and his half-brother Ivan's in 1696, Peter became Russia's sole ruler and embarked on a modernisation campaign, symbolised by his fact-finding mission to Europe in 1697–98. Travelling incognito under the name Peter Mikhailov, he learned about shipbuilding in Holland and met with fellow rulers in Prussia, the Netherlands, England, Austria and Poland. He also hired a thousand experts for service in Russia.

Peter's alliance with Prussia and Denmark led to the Great Northern War against Sweden (1700–21). The rout of Charles XII's forces at the Battle of Poltava (1709) heralded Russia's power and the collapse of the Swedish empire. The Treaty of Nystadt (1721) gave Peter control of the Gulf of Finland and the eastern shores of the Baltic Sea. In the midst of all this, in 1707, he put down another peasant rebellion, led by Don Cossack Kondraty Bulavin, and founded his new capital of St Petersburg in 1703.

Peter's Reforms

Peter's lasting legacy was mobilising Russian resources to compete on equal terms with the West. His territorial gains were small, but the strategic Baltic territories added ethnic variety, including a new upper class of German traders and administrators who formed the backbone of Russia's commercial and military expansion.

Russians often refer to the Mongol invaders as Tatars, when in fact the Tatars were simply one particularly powerful tribe that joined the Mongol bandwagon. The Tatars of Tatarstan actually descended from the Bulgars, who are distantly related to the Bulgarians of the Balkans.

HISTORY THE ROMANOV DYNASTY

Read all about Moscow's Kremlin – both the building and the notion of it as the seat of Russian power – in *Red Fortress: The Secret Heart of Russia's History* by Catherine Merridale, joint winner of the 2014 Wolfson History Prize.

1547	1552	1580	1598
The coronation of Ivan IV (whose military victories and fearsome temper later earn him the name Ivan the Terrible) sees the 16-year-old become 'Tsar of all the Russias'.	Ivan IV defeats the surviving Tatar khanates of Kazan and, four years later, Astrakhan, thus acquiring for Russia the entire Volga Region and a chunk of the Caspian Sea coast.	Yermak Timofeevich and his band of Cossack brigands capture Tyumen from the Turkic khanate Sibir and, two years later, take the capital, Isker, initiating Russia's expansion into Siberia.	Fyodor I dies without producing an heir, ending the 700-year-old Rurikid dynasty. Boris Godunov seizes the throne and proves a capable tsar, instituting educational and social reforms.

Vast sums of money were needed to build St Petersburg, pay a growing civil service, modernise the army and launch naval and commercial fleets. But money was scarce in an economy based on serf labour, so Peter slapped taxes on everything from coffins to beards, including an infamous 'Soul Tax' on all lower-class adult males. The lot of serfs worsened, as they bore the main tax burden.

Even the upper classes had to chip in: aristocrats could serve in either the army or the civil service, or lose their titles and land. Birth counted for little, with state servants being subject to Peter's Table of Ranks, a performance-based ladder of promotion, in which the upper grades conferred hereditary nobility. Some aristocrats lost all they had, while capable state employees of humble origin and thousands of foreigners became Russian nobles.

Female Rulers

Peter died in 1725 without naming a successor. His wife Catherine, a former servant and one-time mistress of the tsar's right-hand man Alexander Menshikov, became the first woman to rule Imperial Russia. In doing so, she blazed a path for other women, including her daughter Elizabeth and, later, Catherine the Great, who, between them, held on to the top job for the better part of 70 years.

Catherine left day-to-day administration of Russia to a governing body called the Supreme Privy Council, staffed by many of Peter's leading administrators. When the council elected Peter's niece Anna of Courland (a small principality in present-day Latvia) to the throne, with a contract stating that the council had the final say in policy decisions, Anna reacted by disbanding the council.

Anna ruled from 1730 to 1740, appointing a Baltic German baron, Ernst Johann von Bühren, to handle affairs of state. His name was Russified to Biron, but his heavy-handed, corrupt style came to symbolise the German influence on the royal family that had begun with Peter the Great.

During the reign of Peter's daughter, Elizabeth (1741–61), German influence waned and restrictions on the nobility were loosened. Some aristocrats began to dabble in manufacture and trade.

Catherine II (the Great)

Daughter of a German prince, Catherine came to Russia at the age of 15 to marry Empress Elizabeth's heir apparent, her nephew Peter III. Intelligent and ambitious, Catherine learned Russian, embraced the Orthodox Church and devoured the writings of European political philosophers.

Once empress, she embarked on a program of reforms, though she made it clear that she had no intention of limiting her own authority. A new legal code was drafted, the use of torture limited and religious toler-

Robert K Massie's *Peter the Great – His Life and World* is a good read about one of Russia's most influential rulers, and provides much detail about how he created St Petersburg.

Vincent Cronin's book *Catherine: Empress of All the Russias* paints a more sympathetic portrait than usual of a woman traditionally seen as a scheming, power-crazed sexpot.

1605	1606	1612	1613
Boris's son Fyodor II lasts just three months as tsar before he and his mother are assassinated on the arrival in Moscow of the first False Dmitry.	Vasily Shuysky plots against the False Dmitry, has him killed and becomes tsar until 1610, when he is, in turn, deposed and exiled to Warsaw.	A Russian militia led by Prince Dmitry Pozharsky retakes Moscow after three years of occupation by the Poles, a victory commemorated every 4 November by the Day of Unity.	Sixteen-year-old Mikhail Romanov, a relative of Ivan IV's first wife, is elected tsar by the Assembly of the Land (Zemsky Sobor), starting the Romanov dynasty.

ance supported. But any ideas she might have had of improving the lot of serfs went overboard with the violent peasant rebellion of 1773–74, led by the Don Cossack Yemelyan Pugachev, which spread from the Ural Mountains to the Caspian Sea and along the Volga. Hundreds of thousands of serfs responded to Pugachev's promises to end serfdom and taxation, but were beaten by famine and government armies. Pugachev was executed and Catherine put an end to Cossack autonomy.

In the cultural sphere, Catherine increased the number of schools and colleges and expanded publishing. Her vast collection of paintings forms the core of the present-day Hermitage collection. A critical elite gradually developed, alienated from most uneducated Russians, but also increasingly at odds with central authority – a 'split personality' common among future Russian radicals.

Read about the fascinating life of Grigory Potemkin, lover of Catherine the Great and mover and shaker in 18th-century Russia, in Simon Sebag Montefiore's *Prince of Princes: The Life of Potemkin*.

Territorial Gains

Catherine's reign saw major expansion at the expense of the weakened Ottoman Turks and Poles, engineered by her 'prime minister' and foremost lover Grigory Potemkin (Potyomkin). War with the Turks began in 1768, peaked with the naval victory at Çesme and ended with a 1774

RUSSIANS IN AMERICA

In 1648 the Cossack Semyon Dezhnev sailed round the northeastern corner of Asia, from the Pacific Ocean into the Arctic. Eighty years later Peter the Great commissioned Vitus Bering, a Danish officer in the Russian navy, to head the Great Northern Expedition, which was ostensibly a scientific survey of Kamchatka (claimed for the tsar in 1697 by the explorer Vladimir Atlasov) and the eastern seaboard. In reality the survey's aim was to expand Russia's Pacific sphere of influence as far south as Japan and across to North America.

On his second expedition Bering succeeded in discovering Alaska, landing in 1741. The Bering Strait separating Alaska from the Russian mainland is named after him. Unfortunately, on the return voyage his ship was wrecked off an island just 250km east of the Kamchatka coast. Bering died on the island and it, too, now carries his name.

Survivors of Bering's crew brought back reports of an abundance of foxes, fur seals and otters inhabiting the islands off the mainland, triggering a fresh wave of fur-inspired expansion. An Irkutsk trader, Grigory Shelekhov, landed on Kodiak Island (in present-day Alaska) in 1784 and, 15 years later, his successor founded Sitka (originally called New Archangel), the capital of Alaska until 1900.

Russia's early-19th-century attempts to gain more of a foothold on the west coast of America, which included visits by the imperial emissary Nikolai Rezanov to Spanish-controlled California in 1806, are documented with verve in *Glorious Misadventures* by Owen Matthews. It all came to naught and in 1867 Russia opted to sell all 1,518,800 sq km of its Alaskan territory to the US for $7.2 million.

1645	1667	1670–71	1676–82
Under the careful watch of boyar Boris Morozov, 16-year-old Aleksey I becomes tsar. During his reign Russia's territory expands to over 800 million hectares as the conquest of Siberia continues.	The war between Russia and Poland over modern-day Ukraine and Belarus ends with the Treaty of Andrusovo; Kyiv, Smolensk and lands east of the Dnepr remain under Russian control.	Cossack Stepan (Stenka) Razin leads an uprising in the Volga-Don region. His army of 200,000 seizes the entire lower Volga Basin before he is captured and executed in Red Square.	Fyodor III's keen intelligence lays the foundations for a more liberal attitude in the Russian court. Civil and military appointments start to be determined by merit rather than nobility.

THE COSSACKS

The word 'Cossack' (from the Turkic *kazak*, meaning free man, adventurer or horseman) was originally applied to residual Tatar groups and later to serfs, paupers and dropouts who fled south from Russia, Poland and Lithuania in the 15th century. They organised themselves into self-governing communities in the Don Basin, on the Dnepr River in Ukraine and in the southern Urals. Those in a given region (eg the Don Cossacks) were not just a tribe; the men constituted a *voysko* (army), within which each *stanitsa* (village-regiment) elected an *ataman* (leader).

Mindful of their skill as fighters, the Russian government treated the Cossacks carefully, offering autonomy in return for military service. Cossacks such as Yermak Timofeevich were the wedge that opened Siberia in the 17th century. By the 19th century there were a dozen Cossack armies from Ukraine to the Russian Far East and, as a group, they numbered 2.5 million people.

The Cossacks were not always cooperative with the Russian state. Three peasant uprisings in the Volga-Don region – 1670, 1707 and 1773 – were Cossack-led. After 1917 the Bolsheviks abolished Cossack institutions, though some cavalry units were revived in WWII. Since 1991 there has been a Cossack revival particularly in the Don region. Cossack regiments have been officially recognised, there is a presidential adviser on Cossacks and some Cossacks demand that the state recognise them as an ethnic group.

---

treaty giving Russia control of the north coast of the Black Sea, freedom of shipping through the Dardanelles to the Mediterranean and 'protectorship' of Christian interests in the Ottoman Empire – a pretext for later incursions into the Balkans. Crimea was annexed in 1783.

Poland had spent the previous century collapsing into a set of semi-independent units with a figurehead king in Warsaw. Catherine manipulated events with divide-and-rule tactics and even had another former lover, Stanislas Poniatowski, installed as king. Austria and Prussia proposed sharing Poland among the three powers – by 1795 the country had been carved up, ceasing to exist as an independent state until 1918. Eastern Poland and the Grand Duchy of Lithuania – roughly, present-day Lithuania, Belarus and western Ukraine – came under Russian rule.

> Benson Bobrick's book *East of the Sun* is a rollicking history of the conquest and settlement of Siberia and the Russian Far East, and is packed with gory details.

Alexander I

Catherine was succeeded by her son, Paul I. Often called the Russian Hamlet by Western scholars, he antagonised the gentry with attempts to reimpose compulsory state service and was killed in a coup in 1801.

Paul's son and successor was Catherine's favourite grandson, Alexander I, who had been trained by the best European tutors. He kicked off

1682	1689	1695	1703
Aleksey I's 10-year-old son Peter I becomes joint tsar with his chronically ill half-brother Ivan V. Ivan's elder sister Sophia, acting as regent, holds the real power.	Following a botched coup, Sophia enters a convent. Peter's mother, Natalia, becomes the power behind the throne. Her death in 1694 leaves her son as effective sole ruler.	Peter sends Russia's first navy down the Don River and captures the Black Sea port of Azov from the Crimean Tatars, vassals of the Ottoman Turks.	Peter I establishes the Peter and Paul Fortress on Zayachiy Island in the Neva River, thus founding Sankt Pieter Burkh (St Petersburg), named after his patron saint.

his reign with several reforms, including an expansion of the school system that brought education within reach of the lower middle classes. But he was soon preoccupied with the wars against Napoleon.

Under the Treaty of Tilsit in 1807, Alexander agreed to be Emperor of the East while Napoleon was declared Emperor of the West. This alliance, however, lasted only until 1810, when Russia's resumption of trade with England provoked the French leader to raise an army of 600,000 for an ill-fated march on Moscow.

Meanwhile Russia was expanding its territory on other fronts. The kingdom of Georgia united with Russia in 1801. After a war with Sweden (1807–09), Alexander became Grand Duke of Finland. Russia argued with Turkey over the Danube principalities of Bessarabia (covering modern Moldova and part of Ukraine) and Wallachia (now in Romania), taking Bessarabia in 1812. Persia ceded northern Azerbaijan a year later and Yerevan (in Armenia) in 1828.

The Road to Revolution
The Decembrists

Named after the month of their ill-fated and disorganised attempt to overthrow the new tsar, Nicholas I, the Decembrists were a body of reform-minded young army officers and upper-class nobles. The war against Napoleon and the subsequent four-month occupation of Paris exposed these officers to far more liberal ideas than existed in their homeland. On their return to Russia, they formed a couple of secret societies with the general aims of emancipating the serfs and introducing a constitutional monarchy. The officers' chance for action came with the unexpected death of Alexander on 19 November 1825.

Alexander's youngest brother, the militaristic Nicholas I, was due to be crowned on 26 December. On 14 December a group of officers led 3000 troops into St Petersburg's Senate Square, proclaiming their loyalty instead to Constantine, Alexander's elder brother. However, their leader, Prince Trubetskoy, suffering a last-minute change of heart, was a no-show along with other key figures. The revolt was quickly squashed by troops loyal to Nicholas.

Five of the Decembrists were executed and over 100 – mostly aristocrats and officers – were exiled to Siberia along with their families for terms of hard labour, mostly in rural parts of the Chita region. Pardoned by Tsar Alexander II in 1856, many of these exiles chose to stay on in Siberia, their presence having a marked effect on the educational and cultural life in their adopted towns.

The hit rock opera *Juno and Avos*, first performed in Moscow in 1981, is a Madame Butterfly–esque drama based on the tragic, real-life romance between Russian noble and adventurer Nikolai Rezanov and Conchita Arguello, the teenage daughter of the head of the Spanish mission in San Francisco.

The publication of nobleman Alexander Radishchev's *A Journey from St Petersburg to Moscow* (1790), a passionate attack on the institution of serfdom, enraged Catherine the Great. Radishchev's beliefs later inspired the Decembrist revolutionaries.

1712–14	1724	1728	1730
At the behest of Peter I, government institutions begin to move from Moscow, and St Petersburg assumes the administrative and ceremonial role as the Russian capital.	Catherine I (born Martha Elena Scowronska to lowly Latvian peasants), secretly betrothed to Peter I in 1707 and publicly married in 1712, is officially announced as Russia's co-ruler.	After the death of Peter I and two years of rule by his wife Catherine, his grandson Peter II shifts the Russian capital back to Moscow.	The direct male line of the Romanov dynasty ends with Peter II's death. His successor is Anna, Duchess of Courland, daughter of Peter the Great's half-brother and co-ruler, Ivan V.

The Crimean War

Nicholas I's reign (1825–55) was a time of stagnation and repression under a tsar who claimed: 'I do not rule Russia; 10,000 clerks do.' There were positive developments, however. The economy grew and grain exports increased. Nicholas detested serfdom, if only because he detested the serf-owning class. As a result, peasants on state lands, nearly half the total, were given title to the land and, in effect, freed.

In foreign policy, Nicholas' meddling in the Balkans was eventually to destroy Russian credibility in Europe. In 1854 Russian troops marched into the Ottoman provinces of Moldavia and Wallachia – ostensibly to protect Christian communities there. This was the spark for the Crimean War with the Ottoman Empire, Britain and France. At Sevastopol an Anglo-French-Turkish force besieged the Russian naval headquarters. Inept command on both sides led to a bloody, stalemated war.

in 1856 Alexander II, Nicholas' successor, accepted peace in Crimea on unfavourable terms. The war had revealed Russia's economic backwardness behind the post-1812 imperial glory and the time for reform had come.

Adam Zamoyski's book *1812: Napoleon's Fatal March on Moscow* is packed with graphic detail and individual stories that bring the famous defeat to life.

Revolutionary Movements

Abolition of serfdom in 1861 opened the way for a market economy and industrialisation. Railways and factories were built, and cities expanded as peasants left the land. Foreign investment in Russia grew during the 1880s and 1890s, but nothing was done to modernise farming, and very little to help peasants. By 1914, 85% of the Russian population was still rural, but their lot had barely improved in 50 years.

Peasants were angry at having to pay for land they considered theirs by right. Radical students, known as *narodniki* (populists), took to the countryside in the 1870s to rouse the peasants, but the students and the peasants were worlds apart and the campaign failed.

Other populists saw more value in cultivating revolution among the growing urban working class (the proletariat), while yet others turned to terrorism: one secret society, the People's Will, assassinated Alexander II with a bomb in 1881.

Not all opponents of tsarism were radical revolutionaries. Some moderates, well off and with much to lose from a revolution, called themselves liberals and advocated constitutional reform along Western European lines, with universal suffrage and a *duma* (national parliament). However, Alexander II refused to set up a representative assembly.

Discontent was sometimes directed at Jews and took the form of violent mass attacks (pogroms). At their height in the 1880s, these instances were often fanned by the authorities to divert social tension onto a convenient scapegoat.

Right up to the turn of the 20th century, Russia had serfs: peasants and servants who were tied to their master's estates. The value of those estates was determined not by their size or output but by the number of such indentured souls.

1732	1740	1741	1756
Empress Anna reverses the decision of Peter II and moves the capital to St Petersburg, presiding over the recommencement of the city's construction and development.	Twelve days before her death, Empress Anna adopts a two-month-old baby. He becomes Tsar Ivan VI, with his natural mother, Anna Leopoldovna of Mecklenburg, as regent.	Elizabeth, the second-oldest daughter of Peter I and Catherine I, seizes power in a bloodless coup. She creates the most luxurious court in Europe.	Russia takes on Prussia in the Seven Years' War that engulfs Europe; her armies are victorious at Battle of Gross-Jägersdorf in 1757, but hold off invading Königsberg.

THE IMPACT OF 1812

The inspiration most memorably for Tchaikovsky's *1812 Overture* and for the turn of events in Leo Tolstoy's epic novel *War and Peace*, the cultural impact of Napoleon's failed bid to conquer Russia endures today. But, according to Stephen Talty, author of *The Illustrious Dead: The Terrifying Story of How Typhus Killed Napoleon's Greatest Army*, if it hadn't been for a disease spread by lice, Napoleon's forces might have stood a far better chance of achieving their goal.

Vastly outnumbered, Russia's army retreated throughout the summer of 1812, scorching the earth in an attempt to deny the French sustenance and fighting some successful rearguard actions. However, it was the general filthiness of Poland and Lithuania that undermined the unwashed French troupes who began to succumb to typhus. By the time Napoleon reached Borodino, 130km outside Moscow, his army was down to around 100,000 men. The battle here was extremely bloody but inconclusive, with the Russians withdrawing in good order.

Before the month was out, Napoleon entered a deserted Moscow; the same day, the city began to burn down around him (by whose hand has never been established). Alexander ignored his overtures to negotiate. With winter coming and his supply lines overstretched, Napoleon was forced to retreat. His starving troops were picked off by Russian partisans. Only one in 20 made it back to the relative safety of Poland, and the Russians pursued them all the way to Paris.

Rise of Marxism

The more radical revolutionaries were genuinely surprised that there was no uprising after Alexander II's assassination. Most were rounded up and executed or exiled, and the reign of his son Alexander III was marked by repression of revolutionaries and liberals alike. Many revolutionaries fled abroad – including Georgy Plekhanov and Pavel Axelrod, founders of the Russian Social-Democratic Workers Party in 1883, and, in 1899, Vladimir Ulyanov, better known by his later pseudonym, Lenin.

Social democrats in Europe were being elected to parliaments and developing Marxism into 'parliamentary socialism', improving the lot of workers through legislation. But in Russia there was no parliament – and there was an active secret police, to boot. At a meeting of the Socialist International movement in London in 1903, Lenin stood for a violent overthrow of the government by a small, committed, well-organised party, while Plekhanov stood for mass membership and cooperation with other political forces.

Lenin won the vote through clever manoeuvring, and his faction came to be known as the Bolsheviks (meaning members of the majority); Plekhanov's faction became the Mensheviks (members of the minority). The

Ex-diplomat Sir Fitzroy Maclean wrote several entertaining, intelligent books on the country. *Holy Russia* is a good, short Russian history, while *All the Russias: The End of an Empire* covers the whole of the former USSR.

1761	1762	1768–74	1773
With Russian troops occupying Berlin, Prussia is saved only by Elizabeth's death and the ascension to the throne of her pro-German nephew, Peter III.	A coup led by a lover of Catherine II (Catherine the Great) ousts her husband Peter III. Catherine becomes empress and Peter is murdered shortly after.	Victories in the Russo-Turkish War, including the decisive Battle of Chesma, expand Russian control in southern Ukraine and give access to two ports on the Black Sea.	Yemelyan Pugachev, a Don Cossack, claims to be the overthrown Peter III and begins a violent peasant uprising, which is subsequently quelled by brute force.

Mensheviks actually outnumbered the Bolsheviks in the party, but Lenin clung to the name, for obvious reasons.

Russo-Japanese War

Nicholas II succeeded his father, Alexander III, in 1894. A weak tsar, who commanded less respect than his father, he was equally opposed to representative government.

The most serious blow to his position was a humiliating defeat by Japan when the two countries clashed over their respective 'spheres of influence' in the Far East – Russia's in Manchuria and Japan's in Korea. As in Crimea 50 years before, poor diplomacy led to war. In 1904 Japan attacked the Russian naval base at Port Arthur (near Dalian in present-day China).

The war continued on land and sea, with the ultimate disaster for Russia coming in May 1905, when the entire Baltic fleet, which had sailed halfway around the world to relieve Port Arthur, was sunk in the Tsushima Straits off Japan. In September 1905 Russia signed the Treaty of Portsmouth (New Hampshire), under the terms of which it gave up Port Arthur, Dalny and southern Sakhalin as well as any claims to Korea – but retained its preeminent position in Manchuria.

Despite all this, Siberia and the Russian Far East were prospering. From 1886 to 1911, the immigrant population leapt above eight million, thanks partly to ease of access via the new Trans-Siberian Railway. Most immigrants were peasants, who put Siberian agriculture at the head of the class in grain, stock and dairy farming. (Before the October Revolution, Europeans had Siberian butter on their tables.)

1905 Revolution

Unrest across Russia became widespread after the fall of Port Arthur. On 9 January 1905 a priest named Georgy Gapon led a crowd of 200,000 people to the Winter Palace in St Petersburg to petition the tsar for better working conditions. Singing 'God Save the Tsar', they were met by imperial guards, who opened fire and killed several hundred. This was Bloody Sunday.

Social democrat activists formed soviets (workers' councils) in St Petersburg and Moscow, which proved remarkably successful: the St Petersburg Soviet, led by Mensheviks under Leon Trotsky, declared a general strike, which brought the country to a standstill in October.

The tsar gave in and general elections were held in April 1906, creating a *duma* with a leftist majority that demanded further reforms. The tsar disbanded it. New elections in 1907 pushed the *duma* further to the left. It was again disbanded, and a new electoral law, limiting the vote to the upper classes and Orthodox Christians, ensured that the third and fourth *duma* were more cooperative with the tsar, who continued to choose the prime minister and cabinet.

A History of Russia by Nicholas Riasanovsky is one of the best single-volume versions of the whole Russian story through to the end of the Soviet Union.

Documents in Russian History (http://academic.shu.edu/russianhistory) is an online source of primary documents on Russia, including proclamations by the tsars and speeches by Lenin and Stalin.

1796	1801	1807	1810
Upon Catherine the Great's death, her son Paul I ascends the throne. One of his first acts as tsar is to decree that women can never again rule Russia.	Tsar Paul is murdered in his bedroom in the fortress-like Mikhaylovsky Castle. The coup places Alexander I on the throne; he vows to continue the reformist policies of his grandmother.	Following defeats at Austerlitz, north of Vienna, and then at Friedland, in Prussia, Alexander I signs the Treaty of Tilsit with Napoleon, uniting the two sides (in theory) against England.	Napoleon's armies make their ill-fated march on Moscow. Muscovites burn two-thirds of the capital rather than see it occupied by the French who are forced to retreat.

THE PRIEST OF SEX

Grigory Rasputin was born in the Siberian village of Pokrovskoe in 1869. Never a monk as is frequently supposed, Rasputin experienced a vision of the Virgin while working in the fields in his mid-20s and left Pokrovskoe to seek enlightenment. On his wanderings he came to believe, as did the contemporary Khlyst (Whip) sect, that sinning (especially through sex), then repenting, could bring people close to God.

In St Petersburg Rasputin's racy brand of redemption, along with his soothing talk, compassion and generosity, made him very popular with some aristocratic women. Eventually, he was summoned by Tsaritsa Alexandra and seemed able, thanks to some kind of hypnotic power, to halt the life-threatening bleeding of her haemophiliac son, Tsarevitch Alexey, the heir to the throne. Rasputin's influence on the imperial family grew to the point where he could make or break the careers of ministers and generals. He became increasingly unpopular and many scapegoated him for Russia's disastrous performance in WWI.

In 1916 Prince Felix Yusupov and others hatched an assassination plot. According to Yusupov's own account of the murderous affair, this proved to be easier said than done: Rasputin survived poisoning, several shots and a beating, all in one evening at St Petersburg's Yusupov Palace. Apparently he died only when drowned in a nearby river. However, a 2004 BBC documentary uncovered evidence that Rasputin actually died from bullet wounds, one of which was delivered by a British secret agent working in conjunction with the Russian plotters. For this fascinating version of events read Andrew Cook's *To Kill Rasputin*.

The capable prime minister Pyotr Stolypin abolished the hated redemption payments in the countryside. Enterprising peasants were now able to buy decent parcels of land, which could be worked efficiently; this led to the creation of a new class of *kulak* (wealthier peasant) and to a series of good harvests. It also made it easier for peasants to leave their villages, providing a mobile labour force for industry. Russia enjoyed unprecedented economic growth and radical activists lost their following.

Still, Stolypin was assassinated in 1911 and the tsarist regime again lost touch with the people. Nicholas became a puppet of his strong-willed, eccentric wife Alexandra, who herself fell under the spell of the Siberian mystic Rasputin.

Edmund Wilson's magnum opus, *To the Finland Station* (1940), is an authoritative account of the development of socialism and communism in Russia.

WWI & February Revolution

Russia's ties with the Balkans made it a main player in the world war that began there in 1914. The Russian campaign went badly from the start. Between 1915 and 1918 the theatre of war was mostly around Russia's western border and often on enemy territory. Much, if not most, of the fighting was with Austro-Hungarians in Galitsia (Halichina in Ukrainian), rather than with the Germans. The latter didn't make major advances into Russian territory until 1918, by which time an estimated two

1814	1817	1825	1853–56
Russian troops briefly occupy Paris after driving Napoleon back across Europe. A 'Holy Alliance' between Russia, Austria and Prussia is the outcome of the Congress of Vienna in 1815.	Alexander I's appointment of the brutal general Alexey Yermolov to subdue the fractious tribes of the Caucasus sows seeds of discontent that continue to have repercussions today.	Alexander I dies suddenly; reformers assemble in St Petersburg to protest the succession of Nicholas I. The new tsar brutally crushes the Decembrist Revolt, killing hundreds in the process.	Russia takes on an alliance of the British, French and the Ottoman Empire in the Crimean War, a conflict that includes the infamous Charge of the Light Brigade.

million Russian troops had been killed and Germany controlled Poland and much of the Baltic coast, Belarus and Ukraine.

The tsar responded to antiwar protests by disbanding the *duma* and assuming personal command in the field. At home, the disorganised government failed to introduce rationing, and in February 1917 in Petrograd (the new, 'less German' name for St Petersburg), discontent in the food queues turned to riots, kicking off the February Revolution. Soldiers and police mutinied, refusing to fire on demonstrators. A new Petrograd Soviet of Workers' and Soldiers' Deputies was formed on the 1905 model, and more sprang up elsewhere. The reconvened *duma* ignored an order to disband itself and set up a committee to assume government.

Now there were two alternative power bases in the capital. The soviet was a rallying and debating point for factory workers and soldiers; the *duma* committee attracted the educated and commercial elite. In February the two reached agreement on a provisional government that would demand the tsar's abdication. The tsar tried to return to Petrograd but was blocked by his own troops. On 1 March he abdicated.

The provisional government announced general elections for November 1917 and continued the war despite a collapse of discipline in the army and popular demands for peace. On 3 April Lenin and other exiled Bolsheviks returned to Petrograd. Though in the minority in the soviets, the Bolsheviks were organised and committed. They won over many with a demand for immediate 'peace, land and bread', and believed the soviets should seize power at once. But a series of violent mass demonstrations in July, inspired by the Bolsheviks, was in the end not fully backed by the soviets and was quelled. Lenin fled to Finland and Alexander Kerensky, a moderate Social Revolutionary, became prime minister.

October Revolution

In September the Russian military chief of staff General Kornilov sent cavalry to Petrograd to crush the soviets. Kerensky turned to the left for support against this insubordination, even courting the Bolsheviks, and defeated the counter-revolution. After this, public opinion favoured the Bolsheviks, who took control of the Petrograd Soviet (chaired by Trotsky, who had joined them) and, by extension, all the soviets in the land. Lenin decided it was time to seize power and returned from Finland in October.

During the night of 24 October 1917, Bolshevik workers and soldiers in Petrograd seized government buildings and communication centres, and arrested the provisional government, which was meeting in the Winter Palace. (Kerensky escaped, eventually dying in the US in 1970.) Soon after, a provisional government was formed, headed by Lenin, with Trotsky as commissar for foreign affairs and the Georgian Josef Stalin as commissar for nationalities, in charge of policy for all non-Russians in the former empire.

In 1909 Sergei Prokudin-Gorsky set out to shoot all of the 'lands and people living on Russian land' using his own colour photographic technique. View the stunning results at www.prokudin-gorsky.ru/collection.htm.

1855	1860	1861	1866
Nicholas I's successor, Alexander II, starts negotiations to end the Crimean War and realises reform is necessary if Russia is to remain a major European power.	The Treaty of Peking sees China cede to Japan all territory east of the Ussuri and as far south as the Korea border, including the newly established port of Vladivostok.	The emancipation of the serfs frees labour to feed the Russian industrial revolution. Workers flood into the capital, leading to overcrowding, poor sanitation, epidemics and societal discontent.	The revolutionary Dmitry Karakozov makes an unsuccessful attempt on the life of Alexander II, the first of several assassination bids; all student groups are banned at St Petersburg University.

Local soviets elsewhere in Russia seized power relatively easily, but the coup in Moscow took six days of fighting. The general elections scheduled for November went ahead with half of Russia's male population voting. Even though 55% chose Kerensky's rural socialist party and only 25% voted for the Bolsheviks, when the Founding Assembly met in January the Bolsheviks disbanded it after its first day in session, thus setting the antidemocratic tone for the coming decades.

Soviet Russia

Civil War

The Soviet government immediately redistributed land to those who worked it, signed an armistice with the Germans in December 1917, and set up its own secret police force, the Cheka. Trotsky, now military commissar, founded the Red Army in January 1918. In March the Bolshevik Party renamed itself the Communist Party and moved the capital to Moscow.

The murder of Nicholas II and his family in July 1918 was the prelude to a systematic program of arrest, torture and execution of anyone opposed to Soviet rule. Those hostile to the Bolsheviks, collectively termed 'Whites', had developed strongholds in the south and east of the country. But they lacked unity, including as they did tsarist stalwarts, landlord-killing social revolutionaries, Czech prisoners of war, Finnish partisans and Japanese troops. The Bolsheviks had the advantage of controlling the heart of Russia, including its war industry and communications. Full-scale civil war broke out in early 1918 and lasted until 1922 when the Red Army was victorious at Volochaevka, west of Khabarovsk.

By 1921 the Communist Party had firmly established one-party rule, thanks to the Red Army and the Cheka, which continued to eliminate opponents. Some opponents escaped, joining an estimated 1.5 million citizens in exile.

Robert Service has written celebrated biographies of Lenin, Stalin and Trotsky, as well as the *Penguin History of Modern Russia*, charting the country's history from Nicholas II to Putin.

War Communism

During the civil war, a system called War Communism subjected every aspect of society to the aim of victory. This meant sweeping nationalisation

---

THE SWITCH IN CALENDARS

Until 1918 Russian dates followed the Julian calendar, which lagged behind the Gregorian calendar (used by pretty much every other country in the world) by 13 days. The Soviet regime brought Russia into line by following 31 January 1918 with 14 February (skipping 1 to 13 February). This explains why, in Russian history, the revolution was on 25 October 1917 while in the West it occurred on 7 November 1917. The Julian calendar is still used in Russia by the Orthodox Church – Christmas Day is celebrated on 7 January instead of 25 December.

1867	1877–78	1881	1882
Debts from the Crimean War force Russia to sell gold-rich Alaska and the Aleutian Islands to the USA – their only supporter during the conflict – for US$7.2 million.	War against the Ottoman Empire results in the liberation of Bulgaria and annulment of the conditions of the Treaty of Paris of 1856 that ended the Crimean War.	Terrorists finally get Alexander II. St Petersburg's Church of the Saviour on Spilled Blood is built on the site of the assassination. Alexander III undoes many of his father's reforms.	Jews are subject to harsh legal restrictions in retribution for their alleged role in the assassination of Alexander II. A series of pogroms provokes Jewish migration from Russia.

in all economic sectors and strict administrative control by the Soviet government, which in turn was controlled by the Communist Party.

The Party itself was restructured to reflect Lenin's creed of 'democratic centralism', which held that Party decisions should be obeyed all the way down the line. A new political bureau, the Politburo, was created for Party decision-making, and a new secretariat supervised Party appointments, ensuring that only loyal members were given responsibility.

War Communism was also a form of social engineering to create a classless society. Many 'class enemies' were eliminated by execution or exile, with disastrous economic consequences. Forced food requisitions and hostility towards larger, more efficient farmers, combined with drought and a breakdown of infrastructure, led to the enormous famine of 1920–21, when between four and five million people died.

By turns anecdotal and specific, *A People's Tragedy: The Russian Revolution, 1891–1924* by erudite scholar Orlando Figes paints a vivid picture of this tumultuous period in Russian history.

The New Economic Policy

Under the New Economic Policy (NEP) adopted in 1921, the state continued to own the 'commanding heights' of the economy – large-scale industry, banks, transport – but allowed private enterprise to re-emerge. Farm output improved as *kulaks* (small-scale land owners) consolidated their holdings and employed landless peasants as wage earners. Farm surplus was sold to the cities in return for industrial products, giving rise to a new class of traders and small-scale industrialists called *nepmen*. By the late 1920s, agricultural and industrial production had reached prewar levels.

But the political tide was set the other way. At the 1921 Party congress, Lenin outlawed debate within the Party as 'factionalism', launching the first systematic purge among Party members. The Cheka was reorgan-

THE GULAG

From the 1920s onwards any new mines and factories were built in Central Asia and Siberia, which was resource-rich but thinly populated. A key labour force was provided by the network of concentration camps begun under Lenin and now called the Gulag, from the initial letters of Glavnoe Upravlenie Lagerey (Main Administration for Camps).

The Gulag's inmates – some of whose only 'offence' was to joke about Stalin or steal two spikelets of wheat from a *kolkhoz* field – cut trees, dug canals, laid railway tracks and worked in factories in remote areas, especially Siberia and the Russian Far East. A huge slice of the northeast was set aside exclusively for labour camps, and whole cities such as Komsomolsk-na-Amure and Magadan were developed as Gulag centres.

The Gulag population grew from 30,000 in 1928 to eight million in 1938. Overall at least 18 million people passed through the camp system; 90% of inmates died. The Gulag continued well after WWII; Boris Yeltsin announced the release of Russia's 'last 10' political prisoners from a camp near Perm in 1992.

1883	1886	1895	1896
The revolutionaries Georgy Plekhanov and Pavel Axelrod flee to Switzerland, adopt Marxism and found the Russian Social-Democratic Workers Party. One of their converts is Vladimir Lenin.	Alexander III authorises the building of 7500km of railroad across Siberia between Chelyabinsk and Vladivostok, laying the foundations for the Trans-Siberian Railway.	Lenin commands Russia's first Marxist cell in St Petersburg. He's arrested and sentenced to three years of exile in Shushenskoe where he marries Nadezhda Krupskaya in a church wedding.	Nicholas II's reign is marked by tragedy from the start when a stampede by crowds assembled in Moscow for his coronation results in over 1300 being trampled to death.

ised as the GPU (State Political Administration) in 1922, gaining much greater powers to operate outside the law.

Stalin vs Trotsky

In 1924, two years after suffering the first of a series of paralysing strokes, Lenin died. His embalmed remains were put on display in Moscow and a personality cult was built around him – all orchestrated by Stalin.

But Lenin had failed to name a successor and had expressed a low opinion of 'too rude' Stalin. The charismatic Trotsky, hero of the civil war and second only to Lenin as an architect of the revolution, wanted collectivisation of agriculture – an extension of War Communism – and worldwide revolution. He attacked Party 'bureaucrats' who wished to concentrate on socialism in the Soviet Union.

But even before Lenin's death, the powers that mattered in the Party and soviets had backed a three-man leadership of Zinoviev, Kamenev and Stalin, in which Stalin already pulled the strings. As Party general secretary, he controlled all appointments and had installed his supporters wherever it mattered. In 1927 he succeeded in getting Trotsky, his main rival, expelled.

Five-Year Plans & Farm Collectivisation

The first of Stalin's Five-Year Plans, announced in 1928, called for quadrupling the output of heavy industry, such as power stations, mines, steelworks and railways. Agriculture was to be collectivised to get the peasants to fulfil production quotas, which would feed the growing cities and provide food exports to pay for imported heavy machinery.

The forced collectivisation of agriculture destroyed the country's peasantry (still 80% of the population) as a class and as a way of life. Farmers were required to pool their land and resources into *kolkhozy* (collective farms), usually consisting of about 75 households and dozens of square kilometres in area, which became their collective property, in return for compulsory quotas of produce. These *kolkhozy* covered two-thirds of all farmland, supported by a network of Machine Tractor Stations that dispensed machinery and advice (political or otherwise).

Farmers who resisted – and most *kulaks* did, especially in Ukraine and the Volga and Don regions, which had the biggest grain surpluses – were killed or deported to labour camps in the millions. Farmers slaughtered their animals rather than hand them over, leading to the loss of half the national livestock. A drought and continued grain requisitions led to famine in the same three regions in 1932–33, in which millions more people perished. Ukrainians consider this famine, known as *golodomor*, a deliberate act of genocide against them while others say Stalin deliberately orchestrated this tragedy to wipe out opposition.

HISTORY SOVIET RUSSIA

Simon Sebag Montefiore has penned two highly revealing and entertaining books about Russia's most notorious 20th-century leader: *Stalin: The Court of the Red Czar* and *Young Stalin*.

1903	1904–05	1905	1906–07
The Russian Social-Democratic Workers Party splits into the radical Bolsheviks and the more conservative Mensheviks. The two factions coexist until 1912, when the Bolsheviks set up their own party.	In the Russo-Japanese War the Russians lose Port Arthur and see their fleet virtually annihilated. When Japan occupies Sakhalin Island, Russia is forced to sue for peace.	Hundreds of people are killed when troops fire on peaceful protestors presenting a petition to the tsar. Nicholas II is held responsible for the tragedy, dubbed Bloody Sunday.	Nicholas II allows elections for a *duma* (parliament) in 1906 and 1907. Both duma prove to be too left-wing for the tsar so he promptly dissolves them.

The Purges

Early camp inmates were often farmers caught up in collectivisation, but in the mid-1930s, following the assassination of Leningrad Communist Party boss Sergei Kirov, the terror shifted to Party members and other influential people not enthusiastic enough about Stalin. A series of show trials were held in Moscow, in which the charges ranged from murder plots and capitalist sympathies to Trotskyist conspiracies. The biggest such trial was in 1938 against 21 leading Bolsheviks, including Party theoretician Bukharin.

Throughout 1937 and 1938, the secret police (now called the NKVD, the People's Commissariat of Internal Affairs) took victims from their homes at night; most were never heard of again. In the non-Russian republics of the USSR, virtually the whole Party apparatus was eliminated on charges of 'bourgeois nationalism'. The bloody purge clawed its way into all sectors and levels of society – even 400 of the Red Army's 700 generals were shot. Its victims are thought to have totalled 8.5 million.

> Stalin once remarked that the death of one person was tragic, the death of a million 'a statistic': historians conservatively estimate that some 20 million Soviet citizens died as a result of his policies, purges and paranoia.

The German–Soviet Pact

In 1939 Russian offers of a security deal with the UK and France to counter Germany's possible invasion of Poland were met with a lukewarm reception. Under no illusions about Hitler's ultimate intentions, Stalin needed to buy time to prepare his country for war and saw a deal with the Germans as a route to making territorial gains in Poland.

On 23 August 1939 the Soviet and German foreign ministers, Molotov and Ribbentrop, signed a nonaggression pact. A secret protocol stated that any future rearrangement would divide Poland between them; Germany would have a free hand in Lithuania and the Soviet Union in Estonia, Latvia, Finland and Bessarabia, which had been lost to Romania in 1918.

Germany invaded Poland on 1 September; the UK and France declared war on Germany on 3 September. Stalin traded the Polish provinces of Warsaw and Lublin with Hitler for most of Lithuania and the Red Army marched into these territories less than three weeks later. The Soviet gains in Poland, many of which were areas inhabited by non-Polish speakers and had been under Russian control before WWI, were quickly incorporated into the Belarusian and Ukrainian republics of the USSR.

> *Stalingrad* by Antony Beevor is a superb book based on new access to long-secret archives and concentrates on the human cost of WWII.

The Great Patriotic War

'Operation Barbarossa', Hitler's secret plan for an invasion of the Soviet Union, began on 22 June 1941. Russia was better prepared, but the disorganised Red Army was no match for the German war machine, which advanced on three fronts. Within four months the Germans had overrun Minsk and Smolensk and were just outside Moscow. They had marched through the Baltic states and most of Ukraine and laid siege to Leningrad. Only an early, severe winter halted the advance.

1911	1912	1914	February 1917
Having survived court intrigues, including the wrath of Tsaritsa Alexandra for ordering Rasputin's expulsion from St Petersburg, reforming prime minister Pyotr Stolypin is assassinated while at the theatre in Kyiv.	The election of a fourth *duma* coincides with worker strikes. Even so, an exiled Lenin tells an audience in Switzerland that there will be no revolution in his lifetime.	WWI kicks off with an unprepared Russia invading Austrian Galicia and German Prussia and immediately suffering defeats. St Petersburg becomes the less Germanic-sounding Petrograd.	The February Revolution in Petrograd results in a soviet of Workers' and Soldiers' Deputies as well as a reconvened *duma*; Nicholas II abdicates on 1 March.

The Soviet commander, General Zhukov, used the winter to push the Germans back from Moscow. Leningrad held out – and continued to for 2¼ years, during which over half a million citizens died, mainly from starvation.

German atrocities against the local population stiffened resistance. Stalin appealed to old-fashioned patriotism and eased restrictions on the Church, ensuring that the whole country rallied to the cause with incredible endurance. Military goods supplied by the Allies through the northern ports of Murmansk and Arkhangelsk were invaluable in the early days of the war. All Soviet military industry was packed up, moved east of the Ural Mountains and worked by women and Gulag labour.

Stalingrad & the End of WWII

Lasting 199 days and claiming something in the order of 1.5 million lives, the Battle for Stalingrad was the longest, deadliest and strategically most decisive of WWII. By the end of 1943 the Red Army had driven the Germans out of most of the Soviet Union; it reached Berlin in April 1945.

The USSR's total losses, civilian and military, in WWII are thought to have numbered between 25 and 27 million. This compares to wartime deaths of between five and seven million for Germany, 400,000 for Britain and 330,000 for the USA.

Such sacrifices meant that the US and British leaders, Roosevelt and Churchill, were obliged to observe Stalin's wishes in the postwar settlement. At Tehran (November 1943) and Yalta (February 1945), the three agreed each to govern the areas they liberated until free elections could be held.

Soviet troops liberating Eastern Europe propped up local communist movements, which formed 'action committees' that either manipulated the elections or simply seized power when the results were unfavourable.

The Cold War

Control over Eastern Europe and postwar modernisation of industry, with the aid of German factories and engineers seized as war booty, made the Soviet Union one of the two major world powers. The first postwar Five-Year Plan was military and strategic (more heavy industry); consumer goods and agriculture remained low priorities.

A cold war was shaping up between the communist and capitalist worlds, and in the USSR the new demon became 'cosmopolitanism' – warm feelings towards the West. The first victims were the estimated two million Soviet citizens repatriated by the Allies in 1945 and 1946. Some were former prisoners of war or forced labourers taken by the Germans; others were refugees or people who had taken the chance of war to escape the USSR. They were sent straight to the Gulag in case their stay abroad had contaminated them. Party and government purges continued as Stalin's reign came to resemble that of Ivan the Terrible.

The Whisperers: Private Life in Stalin's Russia by Orlando Figes is an engrossing account of how ordinary people coped with the daily harsh realities of Soviet life.

Harrison Salisbury's The 900 Days: The Siege of Leningrad is the most thorough and harrowing account of the city's sufferings in WWII.

October 1917	March 1918	July 1918	1920
Lenin returns from Finland to lead the Bolshevik coup. Alexander Kerensky's moderate Socialist Party wins the November election, a result ignored by the Bolsheviks.	The Treaty of Brest-Litovsk marks Russia's formal exit from WWI and confirms the independence of Belarus, Finland, Ukraine and the Baltic states. The capital is moved to Moscow.	Having first been exiled to Tobolsk, Nicholas II, his immediate family and servants are murdered in Yekaterinburg as nationwide civil war between White and Red forces ensues.	Admiral Alexander Kolchak's White Army is defeated by the Red Army at Omsk. Kolchak retreats to Irkutsk where he's captured and shot. The civil war is over two years later.

WINNING THE SPACE RACE

The Space Race was the phrase used to sum up the Cold War rivalry between the US and the USSR to be the first to send rockets, satellites and people into outer space. Starting with both sides' efforts to develop rocket-delivered weapons during the 1940s, the competition really got going with Soviet advances in the late 1950s. The successful launch of satellite Sputnik I into orbit in 1957 was followed by Yury Gagarin's historic trip in 1961. Two years later Valentina Tereshkova became the first woman in space, and, in 1965, Alexey Leonov was the first person to perform a spacewalk.

NASA, the US space agency, desperate to regain the initiative, spent billions of dollars on its Apollo project, and managed to put men on the moon by the end of the 1960s. Some 40-odd years later, with the retirement of the US space shuttle Atlantis, the initiative is back with Russia's federal space agency Roscosmos, the only body now transferring space travellers – be they astronauts or cosmonauts – out to the International Space Station.

For more about the Space Race read *Red Moon Rising: Sputnik and the Rivalries that Ignited the Space Age* by Matthew Brzezinski.

The Khrushchev Thaw

With Stalin's death in 1953, power passed to a combined leadership of five Politburo members. One, Lavrenty Beria, the NKVD boss responsible under Stalin for millions of deaths, was secretly tried and shot (and the NKVD was reorganised as the KGB, the Committee for State Security, which was to remain firmly under Party control). In 1954 another of the Politburo members, Nikita Khrushchev, a pragmatic Ukrainian who had helped carry out 1930s purges, launched the Virgin Lands campaign, bringing vast tracts of Kazakhstan and Central Asia under cultivation. A series of good harvests did his reputation no harm.

During the 20th Party congress in 1956, Khrushchev made a 'secret speech' about crimes committed under Stalin. It was the beginning of de-Stalinisation (also known as the Thaw), marked by the release of millions of Gulag prisoners and a slightly more liberal political and intellectual climate. The congress also approved peaceful coexistence between communist and noncommunist regimes. The Soviet Union, Khrushchev argued, would soon triumph over the 'imperialists' by economic means. Despite the setback of the 1956 Hungarian rebellion, which was put down by Soviet troops, in 1957 he emerged the unchallenged leader of the USSR.

International Crises

A cautious détente between the USSR and the US in the late 1950s was undermined by a series of international crises. In 1961 Berlin was divided by the Wall to stop an exodus from East Germany. In 1962 the USSR

March 1921	March 1921	1922	1924
Sailors and soldiers at Kronstadt rebel against the Communists' increasingly dictatorial regime. The rebellion is brutally suppressed as debate with the Communist Party is outlawed.	The New Economic Policy (NEP), allowing limited private enterprise alongside state control of large-scale industry and infrastructure, is adopted by the 10th Party Congress and remains until 1927.	Lenin suffers a stroke. Josef Stalin is appointed Communist Party general secretary. The Union of Soviet Socialist Republics (USSR) is founded.	Lenin dies at 53 without designating a successor. Petrograd changes its name to Leningrad in his honour. Power is assumed by a triumvirate of Stalin, Lev Kamenev and Grigory Zinoviev.

supplied its Caribbean ally Cuba with defensive weapons, effectively stationing medium-range missiles with nuclear capability on the doorstep of the US. After some tense calling of bluff that brought the world to the brink of nuclear war, it withdrew the missiles.

A rift also opened between the Soviet Union and China, lasting roughly from 1960, when Krushchev withdrew Soviet advisers and economic assistance from the neighbouring country, to the death of Chairman Mao in 1976. During this period the two communist superpowers competed for the allegiance of newly independent Third World nations and came into conflict over areas in Central Asia and the Russian Far East that had been conquered by the tsars.

Khrushchev might have weathered such international problems if his domestic policies had been more successful. His attempts at reforming the communist system inevitably drew a backlash from more conservative members of the Party. In 1964, the Central Committee relieved Khrushchev of his posts because of 'advanced age and poor health'. He lived on in obscurity until dying of a heart attack in 1971.

The Brezhnev Stagnation

The new 'collective' leadership of Leonid Brezhnev (general secretary) and Alexey Kosygin (premier) soon devolved into a one-man show under conservative Brezhnev. Khrushchev's administrative reforms were rolled back and the economy stagnated, propped up only by the exploitation of huge Siberian oil and gas reserves.

As repression increased, the 'dissident' movement grew, along with *samizdat* (underground publications). Prison terms and forced labour did not seem to have the desired effect and, in 1972, the KGB chief, Yury Andropov, introduced new measures that included forced emigration and imprisonment in 'psychiatric institutions'.

Government and Party elites, known as *nomenklatura* (literally, 'list of nominees'), enjoyed lavish lifestyles, with access to goods that were unavailable to the average citizen. The ponderous, overcentralised economy, with its suffocating bureaucracy, was providing fewer and fewer improvements in general living standards. Corruption spread in the Party and a cynical malaise seeped through society. Brezhnev was rarely seen in public after his health declined in 1979.

Glasnost

Brezhnev's successor Yury Andropov replaced some officials with young technocrats and proposed campaigns against alcoholism (which was costing the economy dearly) and corruption, later carried out under Gorbachev. He also clamped down on dissidents and increased defence spending.

Red Plenty by Francis Spufford is an ingenious piece of writing – part novel, part social history – that focuses on real people and events from the 1950s to the late 1960s, when it briefly looked like the Soviet economic system was besting that of capitalist economies.

HISTORY SOVIET RUSSIA

Soviet Sites

Monument to the Heroic Defenders of Leningrad (St Petersburg)

Mamaev Kurgan (Volgograd)

Park Pobedy (Moscow)

Alyosha (Murmansk)

1928	1929	1932–33	1934
Stalin introduces the first 'Five-Year Plan', a program of centralised economic measures, including farm collectivisation and investment in heavy industry, designed to make the Soviet Union into a superpower.	Expelled from the Communist Party in 1927, Leon Trotsky goes into exile, ending up in Mexico, where an agent of Stalin wielding an ice pick finishes him off in 1940.	Famine kills millions as the forced collectivisation of farms slashes grain output and almost halves livestock. Agriculture does not reach precollectivisation levels until 1940.	Leningrad party boss Sergei Kirov is murdered as he leaves his office at the Smolny Institute. The assassination kicks off the Great Purges, ushering in Stalin's reign of terror.

Andropov died in February 1984, only 15 months after coming to power. Frail, 72-year-old Konstantin Chernenko, his successor, didn't even last that long. Mikhail Gorbachev, the next incumbent of the top job, understood that radically different policies were needed if the moribund Soviet Union was to survive.

The energetic 54-year-old launched an immediate turnover in the Politburo, bureaucracy and military, replacing many of the Brezhnevite 'old guard' with his own, younger supporters. 'Acceleration' in the economy and *glasnost* (openness) – first manifested in press criticism of poor economic management and past Party failings – were his initial slogans. Management initiative was encouraged, efficiency rewarded and bad practices were allowed to be criticised.

At his first meeting with Ronald Reagan in Geneva in 1985, Gorbachev suggested a 50% cut in long-range nuclear weaponry. By 1987 the two superpowers had agreed to remove all medium-range missiles from Europe, with other significant cuts in arms and troop numbers following. The 'new thinking' also put an end to Russia's military involvement in Afghanistan and led to improved relations with China.

Perestroika & Political Reform

In an effort to tackle the ingrained corruption of the Communist Party, *perestroika* (restructuring) combined limited private enterprise and private property, not unlike Lenin's NEP, with efforts to push decision-making and responsibility out towards the grass roots. New laws were enacted in both these fields in 1988, but their application, understandably, met resistance from the centralised bureaucracy.

The release at the end of 1986 of a famous dissident, Nobel Peace Prize winner Andrei Sakharov, from internal exile was the start of a general freeing of political prisoners. Religions were allowed to operate more freely.

In 1988 Gorbachev announced a new 'parliament', the Congress of People's Deputies, with two-thirds of its members to be elected directly by the people. A year later, the first elections for decades were held and the congress convened, to outspoken debate and national fascination. Though dominated by Party *apparatchiki* (members), the parliament also contained outspoken critics of the government such as Sakharov and Boris Yeltsin.

Sinatra Doctrine

Gorbachev sprang repeated surprises, including sudden purges of difficult opponents (such as the populist reformer Yeltsin), but the forces unleashed by his opening up of society grew impossible to control. From 1988 onward the reduced threat of repression and the experience of

---

Seventeen Moments in Soviet History (http://soviethistory.msu.edu) is a well-designed site that covers all the major events and social movements during the life of the USSR in fascinating detail.

1936–38	1939	1940	1941
At the Moscow show trials former senior Communist Party leaders are accused of conspiring to assassinate Stalin and other Soviet leaders, dismember the Soviet Union and restore capitalism.	When talks with Britain and France on a mutual defence treaty fail, Stalin signs a nonaggression pact with Germany, thus laying the ground for Poland's invasion and WWII.	Lithuania, Latvia and Estonia are incorporated into the USSR; along with Moldavia, they bring the total of SSRs up to its final number of 15.	Hitler invades Russia, beginning what is referred to in Russia as the Great Patriotic War. The Red Army is unprepared, and German forces advance rapidly across the country.

electing even semirepresentative assemblies spurred a growing clamour for independence in the Soviet satellite states.

One by one, the Eastern European countries threw off their Soviet puppet regimes in the autumn of 1989; the Berlin Wall fell on 9 November. The Brezhnev Doctrine, Gorbachev's spokesperson said, had given way to the 'Sinatra Doctrine': letting them do it *their* way. The formal reunification of Germany on 3 October 1990 marked the effective end of the Cold War.

In 1990 the three Baltic states of the USSR also declared (or, as they would have it, reaffirmed) their independence – an independence that, for the present, remained more theoretical than real. Before long, most other Soviet republics either followed suit or declared 'sovereignty' – the precedence of their own laws over the Soviet Union's. Gorbachev's proposal for an ill-defined new federal system for the Soviet Union won few friends.

Rise of Yeltsin

Also in 1990, Yeltsin won chairmanship of the parliament of the giant Russian Republic, which covered three-quarters of the USSR's area and contained more than half its population. Soon after coming to power, Gorbachev had promoted Yeltsin to head the Communist Party in Moscow, but had then dumped him in 1987–88 in the face of opposition to his reforms there from the Party's old guard. By that time, Yeltsin had already declared *perestroika* a failure, and these events produced a lasting personal enmity between the two men. Gorbachev increasingly struggled to hold together the radical reformers and the conservative old guard in the Party.

Once chosen as chairman of the Russian parliament, Yeltsin proceeded to jockey for power with Gorbachev. He seemed already to have concluded that real change was impossible not only under the Communist Party but also within a centrally controlled Soviet Union, the members of which were in any case showing severe centrifugal tendencies. Yeltsin resigned from the Communist Party and his parliament proclaimed the sovereignty of the Russian Republic.

Economic Collapse

In early 1990 Gorbachev persuaded the Communist Party to vote away its own constitutional monopoly on power, and parliament chose him for the newly created post of executive president, which further distanced the organs of government from the Party. But these events made little difference to the crisis into which the USSR was sliding, as what was left of the economy broke down and organised crime and black-marketeering boomed, profiting from a slackening of Soviet law and order.

Gorbachev's Nobel Peace Prize, awarded in the bleak winter of 1990–91 when fuel and food were disappearing from many shops, left the average

More than 20 years after the explosion at the Chornobyl nuclear station in Ukraine, Gorbachev wrote 'even more than my launch of *perestroika*, [Chornobyl] was perhaps the real cause of the collapse of the Soviet Union'.

1942	1944	1945	1947
Time magazine names Stalin Man of the Year, an accolade he'd previously received in 1939. Russia wins the Battle of Stalingrad at a cost of more than a million lives.	In January the 872-day blockade of Leningrad by the Germans is broken. Leningrad has suffered over a million casualties and is proclaimed a hero city.	The end of WWII sees the Soviet Union occupying the former Japanese territories of Sakhalin and the Kuril Islands, as well as much of Eastern Europe, leaving Berlin and Vienna divided cities.	US president Harry Truman initiates a policy of 'containment' of Soviet influence; a Cold War breaks out between the two rival superpowers that lasts until 1990.

Soviet citizen literally cold. The army, the security forces and the Party hardliners called with growing confidence for the restoration of law and order to save the country. Foreign Minister Eduard Shevardnadze, long one of Gorbachev's staunchest partners but now under constant old-guard sniping for 'losing Eastern Europe', resigned, warning of impending hardline dictatorship.

The August Coup

In June 1991 Yeltsin was voted president of the Russian Republic in the country's first-ever direct presidential elections. He demanded devolution of power from the Soviet Union to the republics and banned Communist Party cells from government offices and workplaces in Russia.

On 18 August 1991 the communist old guard attempted a coup but, in Moscow, Yeltsin escaped arrest and went to the White House, seat of the Russian parliament, to rally opposition. Crowds gathered outside the White House, persuaded some of the tank crews (who had been sent to disperse them) to switch sides, and started to build barricades. Yeltsin climbed on a tank to declare the coup illegal and call for a general strike. Troops disobeyed orders and refused to storm the White House.

The following day huge crowds opposed to the coup gathered in Moscow and Leningrad. Kazakhstan rejected the coup and Estonia declared full independence from the Soviet Union. On 21 August the tanks withdrew; the remaining coup leaders fled and were arrested.

End of the Soviet Union

Yeltsin responded by demanding control of all state property and banning the Communist Party in Russia. Gorbachev resigned as the USSR Party's leader the following day, ordering that the Party's property be transferred to the Soviet parliament.

Even before the coup, Gorbachev had been negotiating a last-ditch bid to save the Soviet Union with proposals for a looser union of independent states. In September the Soviet parliament abolished the centralised Soviet state, vesting power in three temporary governing bodies until a new union treaty could be signed. In the meantime Yeltsin was steadily transferring control over everything that mattered in Russia from Soviet hands into Russian ones.

On 8 December Yeltsin and the leaders of Ukraine and Belarus, meeting near Brest in Belarus, announced that the USSR no longer existed. They proclaimed a new Commonwealth of Independent States (CIS), a vague alliance of fully independent states with no central authority. Russia kicked the Soviet government out of the Kremlin on 19 December. Two days later eight more republics joined the CIS.

1948	1949	1950	1953
Allied forces occupying western zones of Germany unify their areas, leading to a year-long Soviet blockade of western Berlin. The result is the split of Germany into two states.	Having used espionage to kick-start its nuclear research program, the Soviet Union conducts its first nuclear weapon test (code name First Lightning) in August.	Following a two-month visit to Moscow, Mao and Stalin sign the Sino-Soviet Treaty of Friendship and Alliance, which includes a US$300 million low-interest loan from Russia to China.	In March Stalin suffers a fatal stroke. Lavrenty Beria takes charge, but in June is arrested, tried for treason and executed. Nikita Khrushchev becomes first secretary.

With the USSR dead, Gorbachev was a president without a country. He formally resigned on 25 December, the day the white, blue and red Russian flag replaced the Soviet red flag over the Kremlin.

The Yeltsin Years

Economic Reform & Regional Tensions

Even before Gorbachev's resignation, Yeltsin had announced plans to move to a free-market economy, appointing in November 1991 a reforming government to carry this out. State subsidies were to be phased out, prices freed, government spending cut, and state businesses, housing, land and agriculture privatised. Yeltsin became prime minister and defence minister, as well as president as an emergency measure.

With the economy already in chaos, all of Russia's nominally autonomous ethnic regions, some of them rich in natural resources, declared themselves independent republics, leading to fears that Russia might disintegrate as the USSR had just done. These worries were eventually defused, however, by three things: a 1992 treaty between the central government and the republics; a new constitution in 1993, which handed the other regions increased rights; and by changes in the tax system.

Some benefits of economic reform took hold during 1994 in a few big cities, notably Moscow and St Petersburg (the name to which Leningrad had reverted in 1991), where a market economy was taking root and an enterprise culture was developing among the younger generations.

Conflict with the Old Guard

Yeltsin's 'shock therapy' of economic reforms and plummeting international status put him on a collision course with the parliament, which was dominated by communists and nationalists. Organised crime was also steadily rising and corruption at all levels seemed more prevalent than before.

Yeltsin sacrificed key ministers and compromised on the pace of reform, but the parliament continued to issue resolutions contradicting his presidential decrees. In April 1993 a national referendum gave Yeltsin a big vote of confidence, both in his presidency and in his policies. He began framing a new constitution that would abolish the existing parliament and define more clearly the roles of president and legislature.

Finally, it came down to a trial of strength. In September 1993 Yeltsin dissolved the parliament, which in turn stripped him of all his powers. Yeltsin sent troops to blockade the White House, ordering the members to leave by 4 October. Many did, but on 2 and 3 October the National Salvation Front, an aggressive communist-nationalist group, attempted an insurrection, overwhelming the troops around the White House and attacking Moscow's Ostankino TV centre, where 62 people died. The next day troops stormed the White House, leaving at least 70 members of the public dead.

Yeltsin: A Life by Timothy J Colton casts a favourable light on the much-maligned former president, who led the destruction of Soviet Communism and the establishment of the Russian Federation.

1955	1956	1959	1962
In response to the US and Western Europe forming NATO, the Soviet Union gathers together the communist states of Central and Eastern Europe to sign the Warsaw Pact.	Soviet troops crush a Hungarian uprising. Khrushchev makes a 'Secret Speech' denouncing Stalin, thus commencing the de-Stalinisation of the Soviet Union, a period of economic reform and cultural thaw.	US vice president Richard Nixon's visit to Moscow is followed with a trip by Khrushchev to the US; he brings the idea of the self-service cafeteria back to the USSR.	US–Soviet relations take a turn for the worse during the Cuban Missile Crisis. Russia's climb-down in the Caribbean standoff deals a blow to Khrushchev's authority at home.

Reforming the Constitution

Russia's constitution was adopted by a national referendum in December 1993, the same month elections were held for a new two-house form of parliament. The name of the more influential lower house, the State Duma (Gosudarstvennaya Duma), consciously echoed tsarist Russia's parliaments.

The new constitution established a complex federal system of government made up of *oblasti* (regions), semiautonomous *respubliki* (republics), *kraya* (territories), autonomous *okruga* (districts), one autonomous region (the Jewish Autonomous Oblast) and the federal cities of Moscow, St Petersburg and Sevastopol. The republics have their own constitution and legislation; territories, regions, the federal cities and the autonomous districts and region have their own charter and legislation.

This structure is partly a hangover from the old Soviet system of nominally autonomous republics for many minority ethnic groups. Yeltsin struck deals with the republics, which largely pacified their demands for more autonomy, and in the new constitution awarded regions and territories much the same status as republics but declared that federal laws always took precedence over local ones.

One flaw of the constitution is that the president and the parliament can both make laws and effectively block each other's actions. In practice, the president can usually get his way through issuing presidential decrees. During Yeltsin's turbulent rule this happened often.

GOVERNING RUSSIA IN THE 21ST CENTURY

Russia's president is the head of state and has broad powers. He or she appoints the key government ministers, including the prime minister (who is effectively the deputy president), interior and defence ministers. The Duma has to approve the president's appointees. Presidential elections are held every six years.

The Duma's upper house, the Federation Council (Sovet Federatsii), has 170 seats occupied by two unelected representatives from each of Russia's administrative districts. Its primary purpose is to approve or reject laws proposed by the lower house, the State Duma, which oversees all legislation. Its 450 members are equally divided between representatives elected from single-member districts and those elected from party lists. This gives extra clout to the major parties and efforts to replace this system of representation with a purely proportional system have been shunned. Duma elections are held every four years in the December preceding the presidential elections.

In 2000 Putin started to recentralise power in the Kremlin by creating eight large federal districts, each with an appointed envoy. He also saw to it that the regions would have federally appointed governors. In March 2014 the Crimean Federal District was added following Russia's annexation of this area that for the previous 23 years had been part of Ukraine.

1964	1965	1972	1979
A coup against Khrushchev brings Leonid Brezhnev to power. Poet and future Nobel laureate Joseph Brodsky is labelled a 'social parasite' and sent into exile.	Oil begins to flow in Siberia as Prime Minister Alexey Kosygin tries to shift the Soviet economy over to light industry and producing consumer goods. His reforms are stymied by Brezhnev.	President Richard Nixon visits Moscow to sign the first Strategic Arms Limitation Treaty, restricting nuclear ballistic weapons and ushering in a period of détente between the two superpowers.	Russia invades Afghanistan to support its Marxist-Leninist regime against US-backed Islamic militants. The conflict drags on for nine years and is considered the Soviet Union's 'Vietnam'.

War in Chechnya

Yeltsin's foreign policy reflected the growing mood of conservative nationalism at home. The sudden demise of the Soviet Union had left many Russian citizens stranded in now potentially hostile countries. As the political tide turned against them, some of these Russians returned to the motherland. Under such circumstances the perceived need for a buffer zone between Russia and the outside world became a chief concern – and remains so.

Russian troops intervened in fighting in Tajikistan, Georgia and Moldova as UN-sanctioned peacekeepers, but also with the aim of strengthening Russia's hand in those regions, and by early 1995 Russian forces were stationed in all the other former republics except Estonia and Lithuania.

However, in the Muslim republic of Chechnya, which had declared independence from Russia in 1991, this policy proved particularly disastrous. Attempts to negotiate a settlement or have Chechnya's truculent leader Dzhokhar Dudayev deposed had stalled by the end of 1994.

Yeltsin ordered troops into Chechnya for what was meant to be a quick operation to restore Russian control. But the Chechens fought bitterly and by mid-1995 at least 25,000 people, mostly civilians, were dead, and the Russians had only just gained full control of the destroyed Chechen capital, Grozny. Dudayev was still holding out in southern Chechnya and guerrilla warfare continued. Yeltsin's popularity plummeted and, in the December 1995 elections, communists and nationalists won 45% of the Duma.

Rise of the Oligarchs

By early 1996, with presidential elections pending, Yeltsin was spending much time hidden away, suffering frequent bouts of various ill-defined sicknesses. When he was seen in public he often appeared confused and unstable. However, with the help of oligarchs such as media barons Boris Berezovsky and Vladimir Gusinsky, he was given a positive presentation on TV – the most powerful medium when it comes to persuading Russian voters.

In the July elections, Yeltsin easily defeated Communist leader Gennady Zyuganov. But by November he was in hospital undergoing quintuple heart-bypass surgery. While he recuperated, much of 1997 saw a series of financial shenanigans and deals that were power grabs by the various Russian billionaires and members of Yeltsin's inner circle known as 'the Family'. (Yeltsin himself would later come under investigation by Swiss and Russian authorities. However, following his resignation in 1999, Yeltsin was granted immunity from legal prosecution by his successor, Vladimir Putin.)

Economic Collapse & Recovery

By the spring of 1998 Russia was effectively bankrupt. Yeltsin tried to exert his authority by sacking the government for its bad economic management, but it was too late as foreign investors who had propped up Russia's econ-

Among the many rights enshrined in Russia's constitution are those to free trade and competition, private ownership of land and property, freedom of conscience and free movement in and out of the country. It also bans censorship, torture and the establishment of any official ideology.

To understand the conflicts in Chechnya, Anna Politkovskaya's *A Dirty War* and *Conversation with a Barbarian* by Paul Klebnikov are both worth reading. Politkovskaya and Klebnikov top the list of journalists killed in Russia in recent years.

HISTORY THE YELTSIN YEARS

1980	1982–84	1985	1989–90
Because of the invasion of Afghanistan, the US and 61 other nations boycott the Olympic Games held in Moscow. Four years later Soviet teams boycott the Los Angeles Olympics.	KGB supremo Yury Andropov is president for 15 months until his death in 1984. His successor, the doddering 72-year-old Konstantin Chernenko, hardly makes an impact before dying 13 months later.	Mikhail Gorbachev, 54, is elected general secretary of the Communist Party, the first Soviet leader to be born after the revolution. He institutes policies of *perestroika* and *glasnost*.	Gorbachev pulls Soviet troops from Afghanistan. He wins the Nobel Peace Prize in 1990, as Germany is reunited and Moscow relinquishes its increasingly enfeebled grip on Eastern European satellites.

The Oligarchs: Wealth and Power in the New Russia by David Hoffman gives a blow-by-blow account of the rise and sometimes fall of the 'robber barons' of modern Russia.

omy withdrew their capital. On 17 August the rouble was devalued, and in a repeat of scenes that had shaken the West during the Depression of 1929, many Russian banks faltered, leaving their depositors with nothing.

However, following the initial shock, the growing Russian middle class, mostly paid in untaxed cash dollars, suddenly realised that their salaries had increased threefold overnight (if counted in roubles) while prices largely remained the same. This led to a huge boom in consumer goods and services. Luxuries such as restaurants and fitness clubs, previously only for the rich, suddenly became available to many more people. The situation also provided a great opportunity for Russian consumer-goods producers: in 1999 imported products were rapidly replaced by high-quality local ones.

Moscow Bombings

In September 1999 a series of explosions rocked Moscow, virtually demolishing three apartment blocks and killing nearly 300 people. This unprecedented terrorism in the nation's capital fuelled unease and xenophobia, particularly against Chechens, who were popularly perceived as being responsible. An FSB (Federal Security Service, successor to the KGB) investigation concluded in 2002 that the bombings were masterminded by two non-Chechen Islamists – a view disputed by some, including the FSB operative Alexander Litvinenko, who would later be assassinated by lethal radiation poisoning in London in 2006.

The discovery of similar bombs in the city of Ryazan in September 1999, on top of Chechen incursions into Dagestan, was used by the Kremlin as a justification for launching air attacks on Grozny, the Chechen capital, sparking the second Chechen war. Amnesty International and the Council of Europe criticised both sides in the conflict for 'blatant and sustained' violations of international humanitarian law. Today the conflict has eased to a controllable simmer under the watch of the Kremlin-friendly Chechen president Ramzan Kadyrov.

The Putin Years

Rise of the Siloviki

Yeltsin's appointed successor, Vladimir Putin, swept to victory in the March 2000 presidential elections. The one-time KGB operative and FSB chief wasted no time in boosting military spending, re-establishing Kremlin control over the regions and cracking down on the critical media. Despite the increasingly bloody Chechen war, support for Putin remained solid, bearing out the president's own view – one that is frequently endorsed by a cross-section of Russians – that 'Russia needs a strong state power'.

Putin's cooperation with and support for the US-led assault on Afghanistan in the wake of 9/11 initially won him favour in the West. But doubts about the president's tough stance began to mount with the sub-

1991	1993	1994	1996
A failed coup in August against Gorbachev seals the end of the USSR. On Christmas Day, Gorbachev resigns and Boris Yeltsin takes charge as president of the Russian Federation.	In a clash of wills with the Russian parliament, Yeltsin sends in troops to deal with dissenters at Moscow's White House and Ostankino TV tower.	Russian troops invade the breakaway republic of Chechnya in December. In a brutal two-year campaign the Chechen capital, Grozny, is reduced to rubble and 300,000 people flee their homes.	Poor health doesn't stop Yeltsin from running for, and winning, a second term as president. His election is ensured by assistance from influential business oligarchs.

LAYING THE LAST TSAR TO REST

The disposal of bodies of the Romanovs at Ganina Yama in 1918 had been a bungled mess. Some bones were uncovered in 1976, but this discovery was kept secret until the remains were finally fully excavated in 1991. A year later the remains were conclusively identified as Tsar Nicholas II, his wife Tsaritsa Alexandra, three of their four daughters, the imperial doctor and three servants.

Missing were the remains of the imperial couple's only son, Tsarevitch Alexey, and one of their daughters, giving a new lease of life to theories that the youngest daughter, Anastasia, had somehow escaped. In 1994 an official Russian inquiry team pieced together the skulls found in the pit, badly damaged by rifle butts, hand grenades and acid. Using plaster models of the faces, DNA tests and dental records, they determined that the three daughters found were Olga, Tatyana – and Anastasia. The missing daughter was Maria, whose remains were unearthed in 2007 and formally identified along with those of her brother Alexey in 2008.

In mid-1998 the imperial remains were given a proper funeral at St Petersburg's SS Peter and Paul Cathedral, to lie alongside their predecessors dating back to Peter the Great. The Orthodox Church later canonised the tsar and his family as martyrs.

stantial death tolls of hostages that followed sieges at a Moscow theatre in October 2002 and at a school in Beslan in 2004.

Re-elected in 2004, Putin's power was consolidated as Russia's global status grew, in direct correlation to the money the country earned off natural gas and oil sales. Behind the scenes an alliance of ex-KGB/FSB operatives, law enforcers and bureaucrats, known as *siloviki* (power people), appeared to be taking control. The most prominent victims were oligarchs who either fled the country or, as in the case of one-time oil billionaire Mikhail Khodorkovsky, had their assets seized and, following trials widely regarded as unfair, sentenced to long stretches in prison.

Stoking Russian Nationalism

In 2005 the Kremlin, worried at the prospect of a Ukrainian-style Orange Revolution, supported the founding of the ultranationalist youth group Nashi (meaning Ours), a band of ardent Putin supporters who have been compared to Komsomol (the Soviet youth brigade) and the Hitler Youth.

Russian nationalism also came to the fore in relations with neighbouring Georgia and Ukraine. A six-day war broke out in August 2008 between Russia and Georgia over the breakaway regions of South Ossetia and Abkhazia, which Russia later recognised as independent countries. Russia's stated aim was not to allow Georgia and Ukraine to join NATO.

Threats by Russia's largest company, Gazprom, to cut off gas supplies to Ukraine in 2006 and 2008 because of unpaid bills also sent shudders

Night of Stone: Death and Memory in Twentieth-Century Russia by Catherine Merridale is an enthralling read, viewing the country's bleak recent history through the prisms of psychology and philosophy.

1999	2004	2005	2007
On New Year's Eve, in a move that catches everyone on the hop, Yeltsin resigns and entrusts the caretaker duties of president to his prime minister, Vladimir Putin.	Putin is re-elected. Russia's economy booms off the back of buoyant oil and gas prices. In September Chechen terrorists hold 1200 hostages at a school in Beslan, North Ossetia; there are 344 casualties.	China and Russia settle a post-WWII dispute over 2% of their 4300km common border. For the first time, the whole border between the two countries is legally defined.	The assassination of former FSB spy Alexander Litvinenko in London and closure of the British Council offices in St Petersburg and Yekaterinburg see UK–Russia relations reach a new low.

through much of Europe – a quarter of its gas comes from Gazprom and is piped through Ukraine.

Medvedev's Presidency

With no credible opponent, the March 2008 election of Dmitry Medvedev, a former chairman of Gazprom, as president was a forgone conclusion. Loyal to Putin ever since they worked together in the early 1990s for the St Petersburg government, 42-year-old Medvedev (the youngest Russian president so far) carried through his election promise of making Putin his prime minister.

At times during his presidency, Medvedev appeared to come out of the shadow of his predecessor. He sacked Moscow's long-serving mayor Yury Luzhkov in September 2010 and, a month later, struck a truce with NATO over a European missile defence shield. However, in August 2011, Putin said that he would run again for the presidency in 2012 and that Medvedev would be his chosen prime minister. Such political manoeuvring confirmed in the eyes of many that Putin had been pulling the strings behind a pliant Medvedev, biding his time until he could run again for the top job.

The Return of Putin

Russia's constitution has a two-consecutive term limit for presidents, but before the 2012 election changes were made to boost that term from four to six years. Hence when Putin was re-elected in March 2012 with over 60% of the vote, many people feared that they could conceivably be stuck with him with for another 12 years.

There's no doubting Putin's popularity; however, he and his party United Russia is far from universally loved, as proved by the tens of thousands who took to the streets of Moscow and other cities to protest the results of the national legislative elections of December 2011. The victory of United Russia was dogged by widespread allegations of vote-rigging and corruption.

United Russia's eventual tally was just under 50% of the vote, down from 64% in 2007, enough to give it a majority in parliament but no longer the two-thirds it needed to alter the constitution.

Releasing Prisoners & the Sochi Olympics

For thrashing out a couple of lines of their 'Punk Prayer' in Moscow's Cathedral of Christ the Saviour, three members of the female punk group Pussy Riot were jailed for two years in August 2012. The trial hit headlines around the world and brought condemnation on Russia for its approach to freedom of speech and human rights.

Pussy Riot members Maria Alyokhina and Nadezhda Tolokonnikova remained in jail until December 2013, when they were released in an amnesty celebrating the 20th anniversary of Russia's constitution.

I'm Going to Ruin Their Lives by Marc Bennetts, a Moscow-based Lonely Planet writer, offers a pacy, eyewitness account of Russia's recent protest movements.

Russia: A 1000-Year Chronicle of the Wild East by Martin Sixsmith presents an epic and very readable sweep of Russia's history. It is also a 50-part radio series for BBC Radio 4.

May 2008	August 2008	2009	2012
Former chairman of Gazprom Dmitry Medvedev succeeds Putin as Russia's third elected president. One of his first acts is to install his predecessor as prime minister.	Georgia makes military moves on the autonomous regions of South Ossetia and Abkhazia. A brief war with Russia follows and Georgia is forced to back down.	The global financial crisis hits Russia as the price of crude oil plummets. The economy begins to recover later in the year. US President Obama visits Moscow in July.	Putin is elected president for third time with over 60% of the vote, for an extended term of six years. Medvedev becomes the prime minister.

Among the 25,000 other people granted freedom was the former oligarch Mikhail Khodorkovsky, who had been incarcerated for a decade.

Tolokonnikova stated that she had been released only because of the approaching Winter Olympics Games in Sochi, which Putin did not want ruined. As the most expensive Olympics ever, with a budget of over US$51 billion, the sporting event was hyped as Russia's chance to turn around world opinion on the country. Was it money well spent? Well, Russia did top the medals table and the event was mostly hailed an organisational success.

However, the Olympics also acted as a lightning rod for disaffected Russians. The LGBT community protested the introduction of a controversial law banning the distribution of 'propaganda of nontraditional sexual relationships' and increased homophobia in the country. Environmentalists were angered by the detrimental effects of construction for the event.

Taking Back Crimea

Following months of violent street protests in Ukraine, in early 2014, Ukrainian President Viktor Yanukovych fled Kyiv for Moscow. With his administration deposed, and an interim government yet to establish its legitimacy across the country, Russian special troupes aided by local riot police began taking over government buildings and military facilities in Crimea. This peninsula on the north coast of the Black Sea had been transferred to Ukraine in 1954 by the Supreme Soviet as a symbolic gesture of the country's 300-year union with Russia. However, nearly 60% of its population are ethnic Russians and Russia's Black Sea Fleet had been based at Sevastapol since the 18th century, underlining the peninsula's key strategic value.

Only Crimean Tatars and a handful of Ukrainian activists voiced their disagreement at what was happening in Crimea, as the region's new Russia-backed government organised a 'referendum' on 16 March. The new leaders claimed that 97% 'voted' in favour of Crimea joining Russia; a few days later Moscow rubber-stamped the decision by incorporating the region into the Russian Federation. State Duma representative and Putin supporter Vyacheslav Nikonov justified the annexation by comparing it with the Cuban Missile Crisis in reverse, with Russia forced to defend its interests against an overly aggressive West. Detractors instead compared it with Hitler's move into the Sudetenland in 1938.

While the takeover of Crimea was largely peaceful, subsequent events in ethnic Russian–dominated areas of southern Ukraine have been the opposite. International sanctions were imposed on Russia following the shooting down over eastern Ukraine of Malaysian Airlines MH-17 in a suspected missile strike. In return, Russia issued its own sanctions against the West, leaving many to wonder if this was the start of another cold war.

Books on Putin

Putin's Russia (Anna Politkovskaya; 2007)

The Man Without a Face (Masha Gessen; 2010)

Mafia State (Luke Harding; 2011)

Fragile Empire (Ben Judah; 2013)

February 2014	March 2014	2016	2017
With a budget of over US$51 billion, the Winter Olympics transform Sochi and surroundings; Russia topsmedals table with a haul of 33.	Following a military intervention, Russia annexes Crimea, which had, since 1954, been a part of Ukraine; the international community refuses to recognise the move.	In parliamentary elections, United Russia increases its majority, with the remaining seats won by other pro-Putin parties. Key opposition figures, including Alexey Navalny, are barred from standing.	In March and June tens of thousands march on the streets to protest alleged corruption by the federal government in simultaneous demonstrations in many cities across Russia.

Russian People

Among the diverse people you might encounter in the world's biggest country are a Nenets reindeer herder in Siberia, a marketing executive in Moscow, an imam in Kazan or a Buddhist Buryat taxi driver in Ulan-Ude. Within the Russian Federation, one's 'nationality' refers to one's ethnicity rather than one's passport – and Russia has dozens of nationalities. Despite such enormous ethnic and cultural variation, there is much that Russian citizens have in common.

Demographic Trends

Over the last century Russia has gone from a country of peasants living in villages to a highly urban nation with close to three quarters of its 144.5 million population living in cities and towns. Rural communities are left to wither, with thousands of villages deserted or dying.

Russia is facing an alarming natural decline in its population, around 0.5% per year. It's estimated that by 2050 the population could have plummeted to 111 million, a 30% decrease on current figures. The main reasons for this are a high death rate, low birth rate, high rate of abortions and a low level of immigration.

Since 2011 the government has spent over a trillion roubles on projects to reverse this trend, including making large cash payouts to women who have more than two children, providing free land to families with three children or more, as well as increased child benefits and more affordable housing for young people. Harking back to a post-WWII Soviet policy, the government also resumed dishing out medals to 'heroic mothers' who have babies for Russia.

In 1920 Russia became the first country in the world to legalise abortion, and since then, it has remained the most popular form of birth control, with women allowed to terminate up to the 12th week of pregnancy. According to Russian news agency RIA Novosti, 1.2 million Russian women choose to terminate their pregnancies each year and 30,000 of them become sterile, many from the estimated 180,000 illegal abortions. In its investigation, the news agency also found several Moscow clinics offering discounts for abortions on International Women's Day.

In 2016 the government came under pressure to change the law when Patriarch Kirill, head of Russia's Christian Orthodox Church, signed a petition calling for a ban on abortion as well as on assisted reproduction and contraceptives with abortive effects.

Lifestyle

There can be a vast difference in the quality of life of urban and rural Russians. The modern developments of Moscow and other major cities are far from the norm, with many areas of the country seemingly little changed from the days of the USSR.

That said, some common features of contemporary life across Russia stand out, such as Soviet-era flats, dachas (summer country houses), education and weekly visits to the *banya* (bathhouse). Cohabitation remains

---

Russkiy Mir (www.russkiymir.ru) is a Russian government-sponsored organisation to preserve and promote the Russian language and culture throughout the world.

Moscow is Europe's largest city with a population of 12.4 million. Add in the city's unregistered residents and the real figure is likely as high as 18 million, according to experts. In contrast, 6400 villages disappeared between the 2002 and 2010 censuses, as their populations dwindled to zero.

less common than in the West, so when young couples get together, they get married just as often as not.

As the economy has improved so too has the average Russian's lifestyle, with more people than ever before owning a car, a computer and a mobile phone, and taking holidays abroad. The lives of Russian teenagers today couldn't be more different from those of their parents and grandparents, who within living memory endured shortages of all kinds of goods on top of the ideology of Soviet communism. It's not uncommon to come across young adults who have only the vaguest, if any, idea about Lenin or Stalin.

This is balanced against the memories of those who knew the former Soviet leaders only too well and are now suffering as the social safety net that the state once provided for them has been largely withdrawn.

Apartments & Dachas

For the vast majority of urban Russians, home is within a Soviet-vintage, drab, ugly housing complex. Many of these were built during the late 1950s and early 1960s when Khrushchev was in power, so are known as Khrushchevkas (or sometimes *khrushchoby,* for Khrushchev, and *trushchoby,* or slums). Meant to last just a couple of decades, they are very dilapidated on the outside, while the insides, though cramped, are invariably cosy and prettily decorated.

While there's usually a play area for kids in the middle of apartment blocks, they don't typically come with attached gardens. Instead, something like a third of Russian families have a small dacha. Often little more than a bare-bones hut (but sometimes quite luxurious), these retreats offer Russians refuge from city life, and as such figure prominently in the national psyche.

One of the most important aspects of dacha life is gardening. Families use this opportunity to grow all manner of vegetables and fruits to eat over the winter. Flowers also play an important part in creating the proper dacha ambience, and even among people who have no need to grow food, the contact with the soil provides an important balm for the Russian soul.

The Banya

For centuries, travellers to Russia have commented on the particular (and in many people's eyes, peculiar) traditions of the *banya,* which is somewhat like a bathhouse or sauna. To this day, Russians make it an important part of their week, and you can't say you've really been to Russia unless you've visited one.

The main element of the *banya* is the *parilka* (steam room). Here, rocks are heated by a furnace and water poured onto them using a long-handled ladle. Often a few drops of eucalyptus or pine oil (and sometimes even beer) are added to the water, creating a scent in the burst of scalding steam released into the room. After this, some people grab hold of a *venik* (a tied bundle of birch branches) and lightly beat themselves, or each other, with it. It does appear sadomasochistic, and there are theories tying the practice to other masochistic elements of Russian culture. Despite the mild sting, the effect is pleasant and cleansing: apparently, the birch leaves (or sometimes oak or, agonisingly, juniper branches) and their secretions help rid the skin of toxins.

The *banya* tradition is deeply ingrained in the Russian culture that emerged from the ancient Viking settlement of Novgorod, with the Kyivan Slavs making fun of their northern brothers for all that steamy whipping. In folk traditions, it has been customary for the bride and groom to take separate *bani* with their friends the night before the wedding, with

The results of studies carried out by the UN Development Programme in Russia (www.undp. ru/?iso=RU) covers issues such as poverty reduction, HIV/AIDS and democratic governance.

A scene in a *banya* kicks off the comedy *Irony of Fate* (*Ironiya Sudby ili s Legkim Parom,* 1975) directed by Eldar Ryazanov, a much-loved movie screened on TV every New Year's Eve.

BANYA RITUALS

Follow these tips to blend in with the locals at the *banya*:

➡ Bring a thermos of tea mixed with jam, spices and heaps of sugar. A few bottles of beer and some dried fish also do nicely, although at the better *bani*, food and drink are available.

➡ Strip down in the sex-segregated changing room, wishing '*Lyogkogo* (pronounced lyokh-ka-va) *para!*' to other bathers (meaning something like 'May your steam be easy!'), then head off into the *parilka*.

➡ After the birch-branch thrashing (best experienced lying down on a bench, with someone else administering the 'beating'), run outside and either plunge into the *basseyn* (ice-cold pool) or take a cold shower.

➡ Stagger back into the changing room, wishing fellow bathers '*S lyogkim parom!*' (Hope your steam was easy!).

➡ Wrap yourself in a sheet and discuss world issues before repeating the process – most *banya* aficionados go through the motions about five to 10 times over a two-hour period.

Best Bani

*Sanduny Baths
(Moscow)*

*Degtyarniye Baths
(St Petersburg)*

Helio Spa (Suzdal)

*Banya Museum
(Ust-Barguzin)*

*Basninskiye Bani
(Irkutsk)*

---

the *banya* itself the bridge to marriage. Husband and wife would also customarily bathe together after the ceremony, and midwives used to administer a steam bath to women during delivery. (It was not uncommon to give a hot birch minimassage to the newborn.) The *banya*, in short, is a place for physical and moral purification. For more about the design and health benefits of the *banya*, see http://russian-bath.com.

Education

From its beginning as an agrarian society in which literacy was limited to the few in the upper classes, the USSR achieved a literacy rate of 98% – among the best in the world. Russia continues to benefit from this legacy. Russian schools emphasise basics such as reading and mathematics, and the high literacy rate has been maintained. Many students go on to university and men can delay or avoid the compulsory national service by doing so.

Technical subjects such as science and mathematics are valued, and bright students are encouraged to specialise in a particular area from a young age. However, several studies have found that teachers are among the country's worst bribe-takers. Higher education is the most corrupt sphere, with bribes taken for admission to universities, exams and degrees.

Weddings

During any trip to Russia you can't help but notice the number of people getting hitched, particularly on Friday and Saturday when the registry offices (Zapis Aktov Grazhdanskogo Sostoyaniya, shortened to ZAGS) are open for business. Wedding parties are particularly conspicuous, as they tear around town in convoys of cars making lots of noise and having their photos taken at the official beauty and historical spots. A relatively new tradition (imported from Italy) is for a couple to place a lock inscribed with their names on a bridge and throw away the key into the river below.

Church weddings are fairly common; the Russian Orthodox variety go on for ages, especially for the best friends who have to hold crowns above the heads of the bride and the groom during the whole ceremony. For a marriage to be officially registered, though, all couples need to get a stamp in their passports at a ZAGS. Most ZAGS offices are drab

Russia has one of the highest rates of divorce of any country in the world, with one in every two marriages ending in legal separation.

Soviet buildings with a ceremonial hall designed like a modern Protestant church less the crucifix. There are also *dvortsy brakosochetaniy* (purpose-built wedding palaces) – a few are in actual old palaces of extraordinary elegance.

After the couple and two witnesses from both sides sign some papers, the bride and the groom exchange rings (which in the Orthodox tradition are worn on the right hand) and the registrar pronounces them husband and wife. The witnesses each wear a red sash around their shoulders with the word 'witness' written on it in golden letters. The groom's best man takes care of all tips and other payments, since it's traditional for the groom not to spend a single *kopek* (smallest unit of Russian currency) during the wedding. Another tradition is that the bride's mother does not attend the wedding ceremony, although she does go to the party.

Multiethnic Russia

Over 195 different ethnic groups are designated as nationalities in Russia – a result of the country's development through imperial expansion, forced movements and migration over many thousands of years. On paper, the USSR's divide-and-rule politics promoted awareness of ethnic 'national' identities. However, the drawing of ethnic boundaries was often arbitrary and designed to make each of the designated groups dependent on the Soviet state for their very identity.

With Sovietisation came a heavy dose of Slavic influence. Most native peoples have adopted Russian dress and diet, particularly those who live in the bigger towns and cities.

Tatars

Russia's biggest minority is the Tatars (3.9% of the population according to the 2010 census), who are descended from the Mongol-Tatar armies of Chinggis (Genghis) Khaan and his successors, and from earlier Hunnic, Turkic and Finno-Ugric settlers on the middle Volga. From around the 13th century, the Tatars started moving out of Siberia towards the European side of Russia, a process that sped up as Cossack forces conquered their way eastwards from the 16th century.

Today the Tatars are mostly Muslim, and about two million of them form nearly half the population of the Tatarstan Republic, the capital of

The Moscow-based human rights group SOVA Center (www.sova-center.ru) issues regular reports on racism and xenophobia in Russia. In 2016 they found that such attacks resulted in seven deaths and at least 69 injuries.

INTERACTING WITH LOCALS

Yes, some Russians can be miserable, uncooperative and guarded in their initial approach to strangers. However, with most people hospitality typically flows with extraordinary generosity. Visitors can find themselves regaled with stories, drowned in vodka and stuffed full of food. This can be especially true outside the big cities, where you'll meet locals determined to share everything they have with you, however meagre their resources.

There's a similar bipolarity in the Russian sense of humour. Unsmiling gloom and fatalistic melancholy remain archetypically Russian, but, as in Britain, this is often used as a foil to a deadpan, sarcastic humour. You'll also see this contradiction in Russians' attitudes towards their country. They love it deeply and will sing the praises of Mother Russia's great contributions to the arts and sciences, its long history and abundant physical attributes, then just as loudly point out its many failures.

The extreme side of this patriotism can manifest itself in an unpleasant streak of racism. Don't let it put you off, and take heart in the knowledge that as much as foreigners may be perplexed about the true nature of the Russian soul, the locals themselves still haven't got it figured out either. As the poet Fyodor Tyutchev (1803–73) said, 'You can't understand Russia with reason...you can only believe in her.'

which is Kazan. A couple more million or so Tatars live in other parts of Russia and the Commonwealth of Independent States (CIS).

Chuvash & Bashkirs

You'll encounter the Chuvash and Baskhir minority groups in the middle Volga region. The Chuvash, descendants of Turkic pre-Mongol settlers in the region, are mainly Orthodox Christian and form a majority (around 68% of the population) in the Chuvash Republic, immediately west of the Tatarstan Republic. The capital is Cheboksary (also known as Shupashkar).

The Muslim Bashkirs have Turkic roots. About half of them live in the Republic of Bashkortostan (capital: Ufa), where they are outnumbered by both Russians and Tatars. After the fall of Kazan in 1555, the Bashkirs 'voluntarily' aligned themselves with Russia. But various conflicts and rebellions subsequently broke out and it wasn't until the mid-18th century that Russian troops achieved full pacification of the area.

The BBC series *Russia – A Journey with Jonathan Dimbleby* is a revealing snapshot of a multifaceted country by one of the UK's top broadcasters.

Finno-Ugric Peoples

In central and Northern European Russia, there are several major groups of Finno-Ugric peoples, distant relatives of the Estonians, Hungarians and Finns:

➡ Orthodox or Muslim Mordvins, a quarter of whom live in the Republic of Mordovia (capital Saransk)

➡ Udmurts or Votyaks, predominantly Orthodox, two-thirds of whom live in Udmurtia (capital Izhevsk)

➡ Mari, with an animist/shamanist religion, nearly half of whom live in Mary-El (capital Yoshkar-Ola)

➡ Komi, who are Orthodox, most of whom live in the Komi Republic (capital Syktyvkar)

➡ Karelians, found in the Republic of Karelia, north of St Petersburg

➡ Sami, also known as Laps or Laplanders, mainly in the Kola Peninsula.

RACISM IN RUSSIA

Russia's constitution gives courts the power to ban groups inciting hatred or intolerant behaviour. Unfortunately, racist abuse and xenophobia remain a fact of life in this multiethnic nation. It's not uncommon to hear Central Asians and Caucasians referred to by the derogatory *churki* and *khachi*, Ukrainians *khokhly* and Jews *zhidy*. Even supposedly 'liberal' elements of Russian society can come out with shockingly racist remarks: anticorruption activist and opposition politician Alexey Navalny has frequently stated that half of all violent crimes in Russia are committed by immigrants – even though this figure is disputed.

Racial abuse of black African players in the nation's professional soccer leagues refuses to go away; in 2012 a petition from the largest fan group of Zenit, a St Petersburg-based team, demanded that the club exclude black players.

To their credit, Zenit enlisted a local ad agency to help change fans' attitudes. A clever cartoon video was created featuring the national Russian icon Pushkin – who had an Ethiopian great grandfather and was notably swarthy in skin colour.

Attitudes are broadening among younger and more affluent Russians as, for first time in the nation's history, large numbers of people are being exposed to life outside the country. Under communism people were rarely allowed to venture abroad – now they are doing so in droves. Today over 20 million Russians travel abroad each year, compared to 2.6 million in 1995. The result, apart from a fad for the exotic – whether it's Turkish pop music or *qalyans* (hookahs) in restaurants – is a greater tolerance and better understanding of other cultures.

Finno-Ugric people are also found in Asian Russia. The Khanty, also known as the Ostyak, were the first indigenous people encountered by 11th-century Novgorodian explorers as they came across the Ural Mountains. Along with the related Mansi or Voguls, many live in the swampy Khanty-Mansisk Autonomous District on the middle Ob River, north of Tobolsk.

Peoples of the Caucasus

The Russian northern Caucasus is a real ethnic jigsaw of at least 19 local nationalities including the Abaza and Adygeya (both also known as the Circassians), Chechens, Kabardians, Lezgians and Ossetians. Several of these peoples have been involved in ethnic conflicts in recent years.

Dagestan, which means 'mountain country' in Turkish, is an ethnographic wonder, populated by no fewer than 81 ethnic groups of different origins speaking 30 mostly endemic languages.

Together with the Dagestani, Ingush and other groups in the northwest Caucasus, Chechens are known in Russia by the common name *gortsy* (highlanders). Academic experts on the highly independent *gortsy* note how they continue to live by strict codes of honour and revenge, with clan-oriented blood feuds not uncommon even today. Most of the *gortsy* are Sunni Muslims, although the Salafist version of Islam has become popular in recent years.

Turkic peoples in the region include the Kumyk and Nogay in Dagestan, and the Karachay and Balkar in the western and central Caucasus.

Peoples of Siberia & the Russian Far East

More than 30 indigenous Siberian and Russian Far East peoples now make up less than 5% of the region's total population. The most numerous groups are the ethnic Mongol Buryats, the Yakuts or Sakha, Tuvans, Khakass and Altai. While each of these has a distinct Turkic-rooted language and their 'own' republic within the Russian Federation, only the Tuvans form a local majority.

Among the smaller groups are the Evenki, also called the Tungusi, spread widely but very thinly throughout Siberia. Related tribes include the Evens, scattered around the northeast but found mainly in Kamchatka, and the Nanai in the lower Amur River Basin; it's possible to visit some Nanai villages near Khabarovsk and Komosomolsk-na-Amure.

The Arctic hunter-herder Nenets, who number around 35,000, are the most numerous of the 25 'Peoples of the North'. Together with three smaller groups they are called the Samoyed, though the name is not very popular because it means 'self-eater' in Russian – a person who wears himself out physically and psychologically.

The Chukchi and Koryaks are the most numerous of six Palaeo-Siberian peoples of the far northeast, with languages that don't belong in any larger category. Their Stone Age forebears, who crossed the Bering Strait ice to the USA and Greenland, may also be remote ancestors of the Native Americans, Eskimos, Aleuts and the Oroks of Sakhalin Island.

Anna Reid's *The Shaman's Coat* is both a fascinating history of the major native peoples of Siberia and the Russian Far East and a lively travelogue.

The Smithsonian National Museum of Natural History (https://naturalhistory.si.edu/arctic/features/croads) in Washington, DC, provides a virtual exhibition on the native peoples of Siberia and Alaska.

RUSSIAN PEOPLE MULTIETHNIC RUSSIA

Religion

Russia adopted Christianity under Prince Vladimir of Kyiv in AD 988 after centuries of following animist beliefs. Since 1997 the Russian Orthodox Church (Russkaya Pravoslavnaya Tserkov) has been legally recognised as the leading faith and has resumed its prolific role in public life, just as it had in tsarist days. However, Russia is also a multiconfessional state with sizeable communities of Muslims, Buddhists and Jews and a constitution enshrining religious freedom.

Russian Orthodox Church

The religion's birth dates to AD 988 when Vladimir I adopted Christianity from Constantinople (Istanbul today), the eastern centre of Christianity in the Middle Ages. The Church flourished until 1653 when it was split by the reforms of Patriarch Nikon, who insisted, among other things, that the translation of the Bible be altered to conform with the Greek original and that the sign of the cross be made with three fingers, not two.

Those who refused to accept the reforms became known as Starovery (Old Believers) and were persecuted. Some fled to Siberia or remote parts of Central Asia, where small communities of followers survive. During a brief period in the late 18th century, when the followers were free from persecution, Old Believers also founded a community in Moscow which remains the most important in Russia.

Peter the Great replaced the self-governing patriarchate with a holy synod subordinate to the tsar, who effectively became head of the Church. When the Bolsheviks came to power Russia had over 50,000 churches. Atheism was vigorously promoted under Communist rule and Stalin attempted to wipe out religion altogether until 1941, when he decided the war effort needed the patriotism that the Church could stir up. Nikita Khrushchev renewed the attack in the 1950s, closing about 12,000 churches. By 1988 fewer than 7000 churches were active and many of the priests still allowed to practise were in the pay of the KGB.

Since the end of the Soviet Union, the Russian Orthodox Church has seen a huge revival. New churches have been built and many old churches and monasteries – which had been turned into museums, archive stores and even prisons – have been returned to Church hands and restored.

> Patriarch Kirill I of Moscow and All Russia is the head of the Church. The patriarch's residence is Moscow's Danilovsky Monastery, while the city's senior church is the Cathedral of Christ the Saviour. The Church's senior bishops bear the title 'metropolitan'.

Decor & Services

Churches are decorated with frescoes, mosaics and icons with the aim of conveying Christian teachings and assisting veneration. Different subjects are assigned traditional places in the church (the Last Judgement, for instance, appears on the western wall). The central focus is always an iconostasis (icon stand), often elaborately decorated. The iconostasis divides the main body of the church from the sanctuary, or altar area, at the eastern end, which is off limits to all but the priest.

Apart from some benches to the sides, there are no chairs or pews in Orthodox churches; people stand during services such as the Divine Liturgy (Bozhestvennaya Liturgia), lasting about two hours, which is held daily any time between 7am and 10am. Most churches also hold services at 5pm or 6pm daily. Some services include an *akafist,* a series of chants to the Virgin or saints.

Services are conducted not in Russian but 'Church Slavonic', the Southern Slavic dialect into which the Bible was first translated for Slavs. Paskha (Easter) is the focus of the Church year, with festive midnight services launching Easter Day.

Other Christian Churches

Russia has small numbers of Roman Catholics, and Lutheran and Baptist Protestants, mostly among the German, Polish and other non-Russian ethnic groups. Communities of Old Believers still survive in Siberia, where you may also encounter followers of Vissarion, considered by his followers to be a living modern-day Jesus.

According to a 2007 US government report on religious freedom, Russian courts have tried to use the 1997 religion law (asserting the Orthodox Church's leading role) to ban or impose restrictions on the Pentecostal Church, Jehovah's Witnesses and other minority Christian faiths.

Islam

Islam is Russia's second-most widely professed religion, believed to be practised by as many as 9.4 million people. Many more millions are Muslims by heritage. They are mainly found among the Tatar and Bashkir peoples and a few dozen of the Caucasian ethnic groups. Nearly all are Sunni Muslims, except for some Shi'a in Dagestan. Muslim Kazakhs, a small minority in southeast Altai, are the only long-term Islamic group east of Bashkortostan.

Muslim history in Russia goes back more than 1000 years. In the dying days of tsarist Russia, Muslims even had their own faction in the *duma* (parliament). The Islamic Cultural Centre of Russia, which includes a *madrasa* (college for Islamic learning), opened in Moscow in 1991.

Some Muslim peoples – notably the Chechens and Tatars – have been the most resistant of Russia's minorities to being brought within the Russian national fold since the fall of the Soviet Union, but this has been due as much to nationalism as to religion. In an apparent effort to ease tensions between the state and Muslim communities following the war in Chechnya, Russia became a member of the influential Organisation of Islamic Conferences in 2003.

Islam in Russia is fairly secularised – in predominantly Muslim areas you'll find women who are not veiled, for example, although many will wear headscarves; also, the Friday holy day is not a commercial holiday. Few local Muslims seriously abide by Islam's ban on drinking alcohol.

RELIGION OTHER CHRISTIAN CHURCHES

Just as in Catholic countries, children are traditionally named after saints as well as having a given name. Each saint has a 'saint's day' set in the Orthodox calendar. The day of one's namesake saint is celebrated like a second birthday.

If you are allowed into a working mosque, take off your shoes (and your socks, if they are dirty). Women should wear headscarves and dress modestly; men should also have their legs covered.

CHURCH-GOING RULES

➡ Working churches are open to everyone.

➡ As a visitor you should take care not to disturb any devotions or offend sensibilities.

➡ On entering a church, men bare their heads and women cover theirs.

➡ Shorts on men and miniskirts on women are considered inappropriate.

➡ Hands in pockets or crossed legs or arms may attract frowns.

➡ Photography is usually banned, especially during services; if in doubt, ask permission first.

Buddhism

There are around 1.5 million Buddhists in Russia. The Kalmyks – the largest ethnic group in the Republic of Kalmykia, northwest of the Caspian Sea – are traditionally members of the Gelugpa or 'Yellow Hat' sect of Tibetan Buddhism, whose spiritual leader is the Dalai Lama. They fled from wars in western Mongolia, where Buddhism had reached them not long before, to their present region in the 17th century.

The Gelugpa sect reached eastern Buryatiya and Tuva via Mongolia in the 18th century, but only really took root in the 19th century. As with other religions, Stalin did his best to wipe out Buddhism in the 1930s, destroying hundreds of *datsans* (Buddhist temples) and monasteries, and executing or exiling thousands of peaceable *lamas* (Buddhist priests).

Since 1950 Buddhism has been organised under a Buddhist Religious Board based at Ivolginsk. For more about Buddhism in Russia see http://buddhist.ru/eng.

Judaism

Jews, who are estimated to number around 186,000 people, are considered an ethnicity within Russia, as well as a religion. Most have been assimilated into Russian culture.

The largest communities are found in Moscow and St Petersburg, both of which have several historic working synagogues. There's also a small, conservative community of several thousand 'Mountain Jews' (Gorskie Yevrei) living mostly in the Caucasian cities of Nalchik, Pyatigorsk and Derbent. Siberia was once home to large numbers of Jews but now you'll only find noticeable communities in Yekaterinburg and the Jewish Autonomous Region – created during Stalin's era – centred on Birobidzhan.

There are two umbrella organisations of Russian Jewry. The Federation of Jewish Communities of the CIS supports the Italian-born Berl Lazar as chief rabbi – he is also a member of the Public Chamber of Russia, an oversight committee for government. The other is the Russian-Jewish Congress, which recognises Russian-born Adolf Shayevich as their chief rabbi; he's rabbi of the Moscow Choral Synagogue.

Beyond the Pale: The History of Jews in Russia (www.friends-partners.org/partners/beyond-the-pale) is an online version of an exhibition on Jewish history that has toured the country.

Animism & Shamanism

Many cultures, from the Finno-Ugric Mari and Udmurts to the nominally Buddhist Mongol Buryats, retain varying degrees of animism. This is often submerged beneath, or accepted in parallel with, other religions. Animism is a primal belief in the presence of spirits or spiritual qualities in objects of the natural world. Peaks and springs are especially revered and their spirits are thanked with token offerings. This explains (especially in Tuva and Altai) the coins, stone cairns, vodka bottles and abundant prayer ribbons that you'll commonly find around holy trees and mountain passes.

Buryat shaman Sarangerel's book Riding Windhorses is a great general introduction to shamanism.

Spiritual guidance is through a medium or shaman, a high priest, prophet and doctor in one. Animal skins, trance dances and a special type of drum are typical shamanic tools, though different shamans have different spiritual and medical gifts. Siberian museums exhibit many shamanic outfits. Krasnoyarsk's regional museum shows examples from many different tribal groups. Tuva is the most likely place to encounter practising shamans. There are shamanic school-clinics in Kyzyl, but, like visiting a doctor, you'll be expected to have a specific need and there will be fees for the consultation.

Performing Arts & Music

By late tsarist Russia the performing arts had evolved into grand and refined spectacles of ballet and opera created to entertain the nobility of St Petersburg and Moscow. These still delight audiences of all means around the world. But it's not all about the classical in Russian performing arts – rock and pop music are just as popular here as they are elsewhere; Chekhov's plays are staged alongside experimental theatre; and circus is revered as a great night's entertainment.

Dance

Birth of Russian Ballet

First brought to Russia under Tsar Alexey Mikhailovich in the 17th century, ballet in Russia evolved as an offshoot of French dance combined with Russian folk and peasant dance techniques. The result stunned Western Europeans when it was first taken on tour during the late 19th century.

The official beginnings of Russian ballet date to 1738 and the establishment of a school of dance in St Petersburg's Winter Palace, the precursor to the famed Vaganova School of Choreography, by French dance master Jean-Baptiste Landé. Moscow's Bolshoi Theatre dates from 1776. However, the true father of Russian ballet is considered to be Marius Petipa (1818–1910), the French dancer and choreographer who acted first as principal dancer, then premier ballet master, of the Imperial Theatre in St Petersburg. All told, he produced more than 60 full ballets (including Tchaikovsky's *Sleeping Beauty* and *Swan Lake*).

At the turn of the 20th century – Russian ballet's heyday – St Petersburg's Imperial School of Ballet rose to world prominence, producing a wealth of superstars including Vaslav Nijinsky, Anna Pavlova, Mathilda Kshesinskaya, George Balanchine and Michel Fokine. Sergei Diaghilev's Ballets Russes, formed in Paris in 1909 (with most of its members coming from the Imperial School of Ballet), took Europe by storm. The stage decor was painted by artists such as Alexander Benois.

For Ballet Lovers Only (www.for-ballet-lovers-only.com) has biographies of leading Bolshoi and Mariinsky dancers, both past and present, as well as a good links section if you want to learn more about Russian ballet.

Soviet Era to Modern Day

During Soviet rule, ballet enjoyed a privileged status, which allowed schools such as the Vaganova and companies like St Petersburg's Kirov (now the Mariinsky) and Moscow's Bolshoi to maintain lavish productions and high performance standards. At the Bolshoi, Yury Grigorovich emerged as the leading choreographer, with *Spartacus, Ivan the Terrible* and other successes that espoused Soviet moral and artistic values. Meanwhile, many of Soviet ballet's biggest stars emigrated or defected, including Rudolf Nureyev, Mikhail Baryshnikov and Natalia Makarova.

As the Soviet Union collapsed, artistic feuds at the Bolshoi between Grigorovich and his dancers, combined with a loss of state subsidies and the continued financial lure of the West to principal dancers, led to a crisis in the Russian ballet world. Grigorovich resigned in 1995, prompting dancers loyal to him to stage the Bolshoi's first-ever strike. The company ran through a series of artistic directors before finding stability and renewed acclaim under the dynamic direction of Alexey Ratmansky from 2004 to 2008. *Dreams of Japan* – one of the 20-plus ballets that Ratmansky has choreographed – was awarded a prestigious Golden Mask award in 1998. Under his direction the Bolshoi won Best Foreign Company in 2005 and 2007 from the prestigious Critics' Circle in London. In 2017 the Bolshoi and London's Royal Ballet debuted *Strapless*, their first coproduction.

Natasha's Dance: A Cultural History of Russia by Orlando Figes is an excellent book offering plenty of colourful anecdotes about great Russian writers, artists, composers and architects.

Scandals have dogged the Bolshoi in recent years. In 2011 the troupe's director Gennady Yanin was forced to step down following the release on the internet of erotic photos of him. In 2013 the former prima ballerina Anastasia Volochkova claimed that the Bolshoi was a 'giant brothel' with dancers forced to sleep with wealthy patrons. The same year Sergei Filin, the Bolshoi's artistic director, suffered damaged eyesight and a burned face in an acid attack orchestrated by Pavel Dmitrichenko, a dancer in the company.

In 2017 the Bolshoi was back in the headlines again following international shock at the last-minute cancellation of a new ballet based on the life of Rudolf Nureyev. The company's director general said the quality of the dancing was bad, but the rumour mill had it that the production's open portrayal of the dancer's homosexuality had fallen foul of a government that promotes conservative values.

Meanwhile in St Petersburg, charismatic Valery Gergiev is secure in his position at the Mariinsky, where he has been artistic director since 1988 and overall director since 1996. The ballet troupe reports to Yury Fateyev, who has pushed the dancers to embrace more than the classical repertoire for which they are most famous, staging ballets by George Balanchine and Jerome Robbins as well as Ratmansky, whose *Anna Karenina* (based on the Tolstoy novel) premiered in 2010.

Native Folk Dancing & Music

Traditional Russian folk dancing and music is still practised across the country, though your best chance of seeing it as a visitor is in cheesy shows in restaurants or at tourist-orientated extravaganzas such as **Feel Yourself Russian** (Map p184; ☑812-312 5500; www.folkshow.ru; ul Truda 4, Nikolayevsky Palace; ticket incl drinks & snacks R4900; ☺box office 11am-9pm, shows 7pm; Ⓜ Admiralteyskaya) in St Petersburg. Companies with solid reputations to watch out for include Igor Moiseyev Ballet (www.moiseyev. ru), the Ossipov Balalaika Orchestra (www.ossipovorchestra.ru/en) and the Pyatnitsky State Academic Russian Folk Choir, all offering repertoires with roots as old as Kyivan Rus, including heroic ballads and the familiar Slavic *trepak* (stamping folk dances).

The roots of Russian music lie in folk song and dance, and Orthodox Church chants. *Byliny* (epic folk songs of Russia's peasantry) preserved folk culture and lore through celebration of particular events such as great battles or harvests.

In Siberia and the Russian Far East, it's also possible to occasionally catch dance and music performances by native peoples. In the Altai, minstrels sing epic ballads, while in Tuva *khöömei* (throat singing) ranges from the ultradeep troll-warbling of *kargyraa* to the superhuman self-harmonising of *sygyt*.

Music

Classical, 19th Century

Mikhail Glinka (1804–57) is considered the father of Russian classical music; he was born in Smolensk, where an annual festival is held in his honour. As Russian composers (and other artists) struggled to find a national identity, several influential schools formed, from which some of Russia's most famous composers emerged. The Group of Five – Modest Mussorgsky, Nikolai Rimsky-Korsakov, Alexander Borodin, Cesar Kui and Mily Balakirev – believed a radical departure from traditional Western European composition necessary, and looked to *byliny* (epic folk songs) and folk music for themes. Their main opponent was Anton Rubinstein's conservatively rooted Russian Musical Society, which became the St Petersburg Conservatory in 1861, the first conservatory in Russia.

Triumphing in the middle ground was Pyotr Tchaikovsky (1840–93), who embraced Russian folklore and music as well as the disciplines of the Western European composers. The former lawyer first studied music at the St Petersburg Conservatory, but he later moved to Moscow to teach at the conservatory there. This was where all his major works were composed, including, in 1880, the magnificent *1812 Overture*.

Among his other famous pieces are the ballets *Swan Lake* (Lebedinoye Ozero), *Sleeping Beauty* (Spyashchaya Krasavitsa) and *The Nutcracker* (Shchelkunchik); the operas *Eugene Onegin* (Yevgeny Onegin) and *Queen of Spades* (Pikovaya Dama), both inspired by the works of Alexander Pushkin; and his final work, the *Pathétique* Symphony No 6. The romantic beauty of these pieces belies a tragic side to the composer, who led a tortured life as a closeted homosexual. The rumour mill has it that rather than dying of cholera, as reported, he committed suicide by poisoning himself following a 'trial' by his peers about his sexual behaviour.

Ken Russell's *The Music Lovers* is a feverishly sensational and at times hysterical biopic about Tchaikovsky. Richard Chamberlain plays the famously closeted composer and Glenda Jackson his entirely unsuitable wife, Nina.

Classical, 20th Century

Following in Tchaikovsky's romantic footsteps were Sergei Rachmaninov (1873–1943) and Igor Stravinsky (1882–1971) – who both fled Russia after the revolution. Stravinsky's *The Rite of Spring* – which created a furore at its first performance in Paris – and *The Firebird* were influenced by Russian folk music. Sergei Prokofiev (1891–1953), who also left Soviet Russia but returned in 1933, wrote the scores for Sergei Eisenstein's films *Alexander Nevsky* and *Ivan the Terrible,* the ballet *Romeo and Juliet,* and *Peter and the Wolf,* beloved of those who teach music to young children. He fell foul of the fickle Soviet authorities towards the end of his life and died on the same day as Stalin.

Dmitry Shostakovich (1906–75), who wrote brooding, bizarrely dissonant works, as well as accessible traditional classical music, was also alternately praised and condemned by the Soviet government. Despite initially not being to Stalin's liking, Shostakovich's Symphony No 7 – the *Leningrad* – brought him honour and international standing when it was performed by the Leningrad Philharmonic during the Siege of Leningrad. The authorities changed their minds again and banned his music in 1948, then 'rehabilitated' him after Stalin's death.

Progressive new music surfaced slowly in the post-Stalin era, with limited outside contact. Symphony No 1 by Alfred Schnittke (1934–98), probably the most important work of this major experimental modern Russian composer, had to be premiered by its champion, conductor Gennady Rozhdestvensky, in the provincial city of Gorky (now Nizhny Novgorod) in 1974. It was not played in Moscow until 1986.

Russian opera has produced many singing stars, from Fyodor Chaliapin in the early years of the 20th century to the current diva, soprano Anna Netrebko, who started as a cleaner at the Mariinsky and now commands the stages of top opera houses around the world.

Opera

Russian opera was born in St Petersburg when Mikhail Glinka's *A Life for the Tsar,* which merged traditional and Western influences, premiered on 9 December 1836. It told the story of peasant Ivan Susanin, who sacrifices himself to save Tsar Mikhail Romanov. He followed this with another folk-based opera, *Ruslan and Lyudmila* (1842), thus inaugurating the 'New Russian School' of composition.

Another pivotal moment in Russian opera was the 5 December 1890 premiere of Tchaikovsky's *Queen of Spades* at the Mariinsky. Adapted from a tale by Alexander Pushkin, the work surprised and invigorated the artistic community by successfully merging opera with topical social comment.

In March 2005 the Bolshoi premiered its first new opera in 26 years, *Rosenthal's Children* – with music by Leonid Desyatnikov and words by Vladimir Sorokin – to a hail of protests over its controversial plot about cloning. In 2006 the unconventional production of Tchaikovsky's *Eugene Onegin* by Bolshoi opera company's director Dmitry Tcherniakov split public opinion in Russia but wowed critics abroad.

Even so, contemporary opera in Russia continues to gain popularity. In 2012 Vasily Barkhatov produced four new operas written by Russian composers, in collaboration with the Laboratory of Contemporary Opera, an initiative of the Ministry of Culture. *Marevo* (Mirage), the first opera from Provmyza, a Nizhny Novgorod–based art collective, was nominated for the 2014 Innovation award in the visual-art category.

Rock & Pop

The Communist Party was no fan of pop music. Back in the 1960s, Vladimir Vysotsky (1938–80) was the dissident voice of the USSR, becoming a star despite being banned from TV, radio and major stages. Denied the chance to record or perform to big audiences, Russian rock groups were forced underground. By the 1970s – the Soviet hippie era – this genre of music had developed a huge following among a disaffected and distrustful youth. One of the most famous groups of this era is Mashina Vremeni (Time Machine), who formed in 1969 and are still going strong with the original lead vocalist Andrei Makarevich.

Although bands initially imitated their Western counterparts, by the 1980s there was a home-grown sound emerging. In Moscow, Leningrad (St Petersburg) and Yekaterinburg, in particular, many influential bands sprung up. Boris Grebenshikov and his band Akvarium (Aquarium) from Yekaterinburg caused a sensation wherever they performed; his folk rock and introspective lyrics became the emotional cry of a generation. At first, all of their music was circulated by illegal tapes known as *magizdat*, passed from listener to listener; concerts – known as *tusovka* (informal parties) – were held in remote halls or people's apartments in city suburbs, and just attending them could be risky. Other top bands of this era include DDT, Nautilus Pompilius and Bravo, whose lead singer Zhanna Aguzarova became Soviet rock's first female star.

Late Soviet rock's shining star, though, was Viktor Tsoy (1962–90), an ethnic Korean born in Leningrad, frontman of the group Kino; the band's classic album is 1988's *Gruppa Krovi* (Blood Group). Tsoy's early death in a car crash sealed his legendary status. Fans gather on the anniversary of his death (15 August) to this day and play his music. His grave, at the Bogoslovskogo Cemetery in St Petersburg, has been turned into a shrine, much like Jim Morrison's in Paris. There is also the 'Tsoy Wall', covered with Tsoy-related graffiti, on ul Arbat in Moscow.

Contemporary stars of the Russian rock scene include Mumiy Troll, formed by Vladivostok-born Ilya Lagutenko. The band regularly plays international festivals such as SXSW. Also gaining traction outside Russia is Tesla Boy, a synth-pop band led by Anton Sevidov. Roma Litvinov, aka Mujuice, is considered one of Russia's most innovative electronic musicians; his composition includes elements of jazz. Miron Fyodorov, better known by his stage name Oxxxymiron or Oxxxy, is a hugely successful hip-hop and rap artist with an English degree from Oxford University.

Theatre

Drama lover Catherine the Great set up the Imperial Theatre Administration and authorised the construction of Moscow's Bolshoi Theatre. During her reign Denis Fonvizin wrote *The Brigadier* (1769) and *The Minor* (1781), satirical comedies that are still performed today.

Music Festivals

Afisha Picnic (http://picnic.afisha.ru), Moscow

Sergei Kuryokhin International Festival (SKIF; https://www.facebook.com/pg/SKIFestival), St Petersburg

Usadba Jazz (www.usadba-jazz.ru), Moscow, St Petersburg

Alfa Future People (https://afp.ru), Nizhny Novgorod

V-ROX (http://vrox.org), Vladivostok

Directed by Alexey Uchitel, *Rock* (1988) is a revealing documentary about the Leningrad rock scene of the 1980s, featuring legends such as Boris Grebenshikov and Viktor Tsoy.

CIRCUS

While Western circuses grow smaller and become scarce, the Russian versions are still like those from childhood stories – prancing horses with acrobats on their backs, snarling lions and tigers, heart-stopping high-wire artists and hilarious clowns. They remain a highly popular form of entertainment.

The Russian circus tradition has roots in medieval travelling minstrels called *skomorokhi*, although the first modern-style circus (a performance within a ring) dates to the reign of Catherine the Great. The country's first permanent circus was established in St Petersburg in 1877, and in 1927 Moscow's School for Circus Arts became the world's first such training institution. Many cities still have their own troupes and most at least have an arena for visiting companies. Best known is Moscow's **Nikulin Circus** (p106).

In recent years, most major troupes have cleaned up their act with regard to the treatment of animals. At Moscow and St Petersburg circuses it is unlikely you will see animals treated cruelly or forced to perform degrading acts.

PERFORMING ARTS & MUSIC THEATRE

Nineteenth-century dramatists included Alexander Pushkin, whose drama *Boris Godunov* (1830) was later used as the libretto for the Mussorgsky Opera; Nikolai Gogol, whose tragic farce *The Government Inspector* (1836) was said to be a favourite play of Nicholas I; Alexander Griboedov, whose comedy satire *Woe from Wit* was a compulsory work in Russian literature lessons during the Soviet period; and Ivan Turgenev, whose languid *A Month in the Country* (1849) laid the way for the most famous Russian playwright of all: Anton Chekhov (1860–1904).

Chekhov's *The Seagull* (1896), *The Three Sisters* (1901), *The Cherry Orchard* (1904) and *Uncle Vanya* (1899), all of which take the angst of the provincial middle class as their theme, owed much of their success to their 'realist' productions at the Moscow Art Theatre by Konstantin Stanislavsky, which aimed to show life as it really was.

Theatre remained popular through the Soviet period, not least because it was one of the few areas of artistic life where a modicum of freedom of expression was permitted. Stalin famously said that although Mikhail Bulgakov's *White Guard* (1926) had been written by an enemy, it still deserved to be staged because of the author's outstanding talent. Bulgakov is perhaps the only person dubbed an enemy by Stalin and never persecuted. The avant-garde actor-director Vsevolod Meyerhold was not so fortunate.

Today both Moscow's and St Petersburg's theatre scenes are as lively as those in London and New York. Notable directors include Kama Gingkas, who works with the Moscow Art Theatre; Pyotr Fomenko, who heads up Moscow's Pyotr Fomenko Workshop Theatre; and Lev Dodin at the Maly Drama Theatre in St Petersburg. Dmitry Krymov, who began his career as a stage designer, heads up the Krymov Lab at Moscow's School of Dramatic Arts, where he crafts incredible, visually dramatic productions that have toured internationally. These include a version of Shakespeare's *A Midsummer Night's Dream* and *Opus No 7*, which in its two acts pays homage to the Jews lost in the Holocaust and the classical composer Shostakovich.

Oleg and Vladimir Presnyakov write plays and direct together under the joint name Presnyakov Brothers; they've been praised for their dramas' natural-sounding dialogue and sardonic wit. *Terrorism*, their best-known work, has been performed around the world.

Literature & Cinema

Some of the most vivid impressions of Russia have been shaped by the creative works of the country's writers and movie-makers. Although they really only got going in the 19th century, Russian writers wasted little time in carving out a prime place in the world of letters, producing towering classics in the fields of poetry and prose. In the process they have bagged five Nobel Prizes and frequently found themselves in conflict with the Russian establishment.

Literature

The Golden Age

The great collection of works produced during the 19th century has led to it being known as the 'Golden Age' of Russian literature. This was the time of the precocious and brilliant Alexander Pushkin (1799–1837), who penned the poems in verse *The Bronze Horseman* and *Eugene Onegin,* and Mikhail Lermontov (1814–41), author of *A Hero of Our Time.* Both were sent into exile by the authorities for their seditious writings; and both died young in duels, securing their romantic reputations for a country enthralled by doomed youthful heroes.

If you don't have the time or stamina for Tolstoy's *War and Peace,* then sample the master's work in his celebrated novellas *The Death of Ivan Ilyich* and *The Devil.*

Continuing the tradition of literary criticism of the powers that be was the novelist and playwright Nikolai Gogol (1809–52), whose novel *Dead Souls* exposed the widespread corruption in Russian society. Gogol created some of Russian literature's most memorable characters, including Akaky Akakievich, the tragicomic hero of *The Overcoat,* and Major Kovalyov, who chases his errant nose around St Petersburg when the shnozzle makes a break for it in the absurdist short story *The Nose.* His love of the surreal established a pattern in Russian literature that echoes through the works of Daniil Kharms, Mikhail Bulgakov and Viktor Pelevin in the next century.

More radical writers figured in the second half of the 19th century. In *Fathers and Sons,* by Ivan Turgenev (1818–83), the antihero Bazarov became a symbol for the antitsarist nihilist movement of the time. Before penning classics such as *Crime and Punishment* and *The Brothers Karamazov,* which deals with questions of morality, faith and salvation, Fyodor Dostoevsky (1821–81) fell foul of the authorities and was exiled for a decade from St Petersburg, first in Siberia and later in what is now Kazakhstan.

For a riveting account of Pushkin's fatal duel with French nobleman Georges d'Anthès and the events that preceded it, read Serena Vitale's *Pushkin's Button.*

Leo Tolstoy (1828–1910) sealed his reputation as one of Russia's greatest writers with his Napoleonic War saga *War and Peace,* and *Anna Karenina,* a tragedy about a woman who violates the rigid sexual code of her time. Such was his popularity that he was effectively protected from reprisals by the government, who did not approve of his unorthodox beliefs in Christian anarchy and pacifism.

The Silver Age

From the end of the 19th century until the early 1930s, the 'Silver Age' of Russian literature produced more towering talents. First came the rise of the symbolist movement in the Russian arts world. The outstanding figures of this time were philosopher Vladimir Solovyov (1853–1900); writer Andrei Bely (1880–1934), author of *Petersburg,* regarded by Vladimir Nabokov as one of the four greatest novels of the 20th century; and Maxim Gorky (1868–1936), who is considered to be the founder of socialist realism with his 1907 novel *Mother,* written during a Bolshevik Party fundraising trip in the US.

Alexander Blok (1880–1921) was a poet whose sympathy with the revolutions of 1905 and 1917 was praised by the Bolsheviks as an example of an established writer who had seen the light. His tragic poem 'The Twelve', published in 1918, shortly before his death, likens the Bolsheviks to the 12 Apostles who herald the new world. However, Blok soon grew deeply disenchanted with the revolution and in one of his last letters wrote that his Russia was devouring him.

Banned Writers & Nobel Prize Winners

The life of poet Anna Akhmatova (1889–1966) was filled with sorrow and loss – her family was imprisoned and killed, her friends exiled, tortured and arrested, her colleagues constantly hounded – but she refused to leave her beloved St Petersburg. Her verses depict the city with realism and monumentalism, particularly her epic *Poem Without a Hero.*

Another key poet of this age who also suffered for his art was Osip Mandelstam (1891–1938), who died in a Stalinist transit camp near Vladivostok. Akhmatova's and Mandelstam's lives are painfully recorded by Nadezhda Mandelstam in her autobiographical *Hope Against Hope.*

The work of the great satirist Mikhail Bulgakov (1891–1940), including *The Master and Margarita* and *Heart of a Dog,* was banned for years, as was the dark genius absurdist work of Daniil Kharms (1905–42). Kharms starved to death during the siege of Leningrad in 1942; it would be two decades later that his surreal stories and poems started to see the light of day and began to be circulated in the Soviet underground press.

Although best known abroad for his epic novel *Doctor Zhivago,* Boris Pasternak (1890–1960) is most celebrated in Russia for his poetry. *My Sister Life,* published in 1921, inspired many Russian poets thereafter. *Doctor Zhivago,* first published in an Italian translation in 1957, secured

The Last Station (2009), based on the novel by Jay Parini, is about the last year of Tolstoy's life. Christopher Plummer, who plays the writer, and Helen Mirren, playing his wife Sofya, were both nominated for Oscars.

PUSHKIN IS OUR EVERYTHING

The phrase 'Pushkin is our everything' – uttered by cultured Russians – provides the title for an insightful 2014 documentary (www.pushkinfilm.com) about the national bard by American writer and director Michael Beckelhimer. Today, it is rare to meet a Russian who cannot quote some Pushkin. However, for several years after the writer's untimely death in 1837 at age 38, following a duel fought over the honour of his wife, his works languished in relative obscurity.

Beckelhimer's documentary reveals how Pushkin's reputation was revived by 1880, when the first of what would be many statues of the nation's poet across Russia was unveiled in Moscow by the likes of Ivan Turgenev and Fyodor Dostoevsky. That status was enhanced and solidified in Russian consciousness during the Soviet era when, in 1937, Stalin orchestrated major centennial celebrations of the poet's death, emphasising his alleged atheism and his protocommunist politics (neither of which was entirely true).

Flat English translations of Pushkin's lyrical, witty and imaginative works, which range from classical odes and sonnets to short stories, plays and fairy tales, can often leave non-Russian speakers wondering what all the fuss is about. It is clear that Pushkin has had a strong influence on language spoken by Russians today. The enraptured Russians interviewed in the documentary talk of the lightness and beauty of Pushkin's words, and how they continue to resonate for them today, nine generations after they were first written.

him the Nobel Prize for Literature in 1958, but Pasternak turned it down, fearing that if he left Russia to accept the award he would not be allowed to return.

One writer who managed to keep in favour with the communist authorities was Mikhail Sholokhov (1905–84), with his sagas of revolution and war among the Don Cossacks – *And Quiet Flows the Don* and *The Don Flows Home to the Sea*. He won the Nobel Prize for Literature in 1965.

> Some notable Silver Age wordsmiths were the poet Velimir Khlebnikov and the poet and playwright Vladimir Mayakovsky, who, together with other futurists, issued the 1913 'Slap in the Face of Public Taste' manifesto urging fellow writers 'to throw Pushkin out of the steamship of modernity'.

Late Soviet Period Literature

The relaxing of state control over the arts during Khrushchev's time saw the emergence of poets such as Yevgeny Yevtushenko, who gained international fame in 1961 with *Babi Yar* (which denounced both Nazi and Russian anti-Semitism), as well as another Nobel Prize winner, Aleksandr Solzhenitsyn (1918–2008), who wrote mainly about life in the Gulag system.

Some believe the camp experience as related in *Kolyma Tales* by the great literary talent Varlam Shalamov (1907–82) is even more harrowing than that depicted by Solzhenitsyn. Also gaining critical praise was another former Kolyma inmate Eugenia Ginzburg (1904–77) for her memoir *Into the Whirlwind,* initially published abroad in 1967.

The fiercely talented poet Joseph Brodsky (1940–96), also a Nobel Prize winner, hailed from St Petersburg and was a protégé of poet Anna Akhmatova. In 1964 he was tried for 'social parasitism' and exiled to the north of Russia. However, after concerted international protests led by Jean-Paul Sartre, he returned to Leningrad in 1965, only to continue being a thorn in the side of the authorities. Like Solzhenitsyn, Brodsky was exiled to the US in 1972.

Preceding *glasnost* (openness) was native Siberian writer Valentin Rasputin, who is best known for his stories decrying the destruction of the land, spirit and traditions of the Russian people. His 1979 novel *Farewell to Matyora* is about a Siberian village flooded when a hydroelectric dam is built.

RUSSIA'S CONSCIENCE

Few writers' lives sum up the fickle nature of their relationship with the Russian state better than that of Aleksandr Solzhenitsyn (1918–2008). Persecuted and exiled by the Soviet Union, he returned to a country that considered him, in his latter years, both a crank and its conscience. Embraced by Vladimir Putin (whom Solzhenitsyn praised as 'a good dictator') for his nationalism, staunch belief in Russian Orthodoxy and hatred of the decadent West, the one-time dissident was given what amounted to a state funeral.

Decorated twice with medals for bravery during WWII, the young Solzhenitsyn first fell foul of the authorities in 1945 when he was arrested for anti-Stalin remarks found in letters to a friend. He subsequently served eight years in various camps and three more in enforced exile in Kazakhstan.

Khrushchev allowed the publication in 1962 of Solzhenitsyn's first novel, *One Day in the Life of Ivan Denisovich,* a short tale of Gulag life. The book sealed the writer's reputation and in 1970 he was awarded the Nobel Prize for Literature, although, like Boris Pasternak before him, he did not go to Sweden to receive it for fear that he would not be allowed to re-enter the USSR. Even so, he was exiled in 1974, when he went to the US. He finally returned to Russia in 1994.

To the end Solzhenitsyn remained a controversial figure. He was detested by many Gulag survivors, who accused him of collaborating with prison authorities. They looked suspiciously on Solzhenitsyn's ability to gain sole access to the archives that allowed him to write his best-known work, *The Gulag Archipelago,* which describes conditions at the camps on the Solovetsky Islands, even though he was never imprisoned there himself. In his final book, *200 Years Together,* about the history of Jews in Russia, he laid himself open to accusations of anti-Semitism.

Post-Soviet Literature

Recent years have witnessed a publishing boom, with the traditional Russian love of books as strong as ever. One of the most popular novelists is Grigol Chkhartishvili, who under his pen name Boris Akunin has authored an internationally successful series of historical detective novels, including *The Winter Queen* and *Turkish Gambit*, featuring the foppish Russian Sherlock Holmes, Erast Fandorin.

Viktor Yerofeyev's erotic novel *Russian Beauty* has been translated into 27 languages. Tatyana Tolstaya's *On the Golden Porch*, a collection of stories about big souls in little Moscow flats, made her an international name when it was published in the West in 1989. Her 2007 novel *The Slynx* is a dystopian fantasy set in a post-nuclear-holocaust world of mutant people, fearsome beasts and totalitarian rulers.

The prolific science fiction and pop-culture writer Viktor Pelevin has been compared to the great Mikhail Bulgakov. Several of his novels, including *The Yellow Arrow*, *The Sacred Book of the Werewolf* and *S.N.U.F.F.*, have also been widely translated. Vladimir Sorokin established his literary reputation abroad with his novels *The Queue* and *Ice*. In *Day of the Oprichnik*, he describes Russia in the year 2028 as a nationalist country ruled with an iron fist that has shut itself off from the West by building a wall.

Dmitry Bykov is one of the biggest names currently in Russian literary circles; he published a well-regarded biography of Boris Pasternak in 2007. His 2006 novel, *ZhD* (entitled *Living Souls* in its English translation), a satirical, anti-utopian, conspiracy-theory-laden tale of civil war set in near-future Russia, caused furious debate because of its Rus-phobic and anti-Semitic themes. Mikhail Shishkin has won all three of Russia's major literary awards. His books, including *Maidenhair* and *The Light and the Dark*, have been translated into English.

Cinema

The Propaganda Years

Even though there were a few Russian films made at the start of the 20th century, it was really under the Soviet system that this modern form of storytelling began to flourish. Lenin believed cinema to be the most important of all the arts and along with his Bolshevik colleagues saw the value of movies as propaganda.

Vast resources were pumped into studios to make historical dramas about Soviet and Russian victories such as Sergei Eisenstein's *Battleship Potemkin* (1925), a landmark of world cinema, and his *Alexander Nevsky* (1938), which contains one of cinema's great battle scenes. However, Eisenstein's *Ivan the Terrible* (1945), a discreet commentary on Stalinism, fell foul of state sponsors and was banned for many years.

The 1936 hit musical *Circus* was typical of the kind of propaganda movies were forced to carry at the height of Stalinism. The plot concerns an American circus artist hounded out of the US because she has a black baby; she finds both refuge and love, of course, in the Soviet Union. The lead actress, Lyubov Orlova, became the Soviet Union's biggest star of the time. She also headlined *Volga, Volga* (1938), another feel-good movie said to be Stalin's favourite film.

Taking Cinematic Risks

Of later Soviet directors, the dominant figure was Andrei Tarkovsky, whose films include *Andrei Rublyov* (1966), *Solaris* (1972) – the Russian answer to *2001: A Space Odyssey* – and *Stalker* (1979), which summed up the Leonid Brezhnev era pretty well, with its characters wandering,

LITERATURE & CINEMA CINEMA

Made into a movie by David Lean, Boris Pasternak's *Doctor Zhivago* is a richly philosophical novel spanning events from the dying days of tsarist Russia to the birth of the Soviet Union, offering personal insights into the revolution and the Russian Civil War along the way.

Mikhail Kalatozov's tragic WWII drama *The Cranes Are Flying* (1957), judged best film at Cannes in 1958, illuminates the sacrifices made by Russians during the Great Patriotic War.

puzzled, through a landscape of clanking trains, rusting metal and overgrown concrete. Tarkovsky died in exile in 1986.

Winning an Academy Award for best foreign-language film, *Moscow Doesn't Believe in Tears* (1980), directed by Vladimir Menshov, charts the course of three provincial gals who make Moscow their home from the 1950s to the 1970s. It's said that Ronald Reagan watched this kitchen-sink drama to get an idea of the Russian soul before his meetings with Gorbachev.

Glasnost brought new excitement in the film industry as film-makers were allowed to reassess Soviet life with unprecedented freedom and as audiences flocked to see previously banned films or the latest exposure of youth culture or Stalinism. Notable were Sergei Solovyov's avant-garde *ASSA* (1987), staring rock-god Viktor Tsoy and the artist Afrika (Sergei Bugaev), and Vasily Pichul's *Little Vera* (1989), for its frank portrayal of a family in chaos (exhausted wife, drunken husband, rebellious daughter) and its sexual content – mild by Western standards but startling to the Soviet audience.

Soviet cinema wasn't all doom, gloom and heavy propaganda. The romantic comedy *Irony of Fate* (1975) has a special place in all Russians' hearts, while a whole genre of 'Easterns' are epitomised by *White Sun of the Desert* (1969), a rollicking adventure set in Turkmenistan during the Russian Civil War of the 1920s. Still one of the top-selling DVDs in Russia, this cult movie is traditionally watched by cosmonauts before blast-off.

Post-Soviet Cinema

By the time Nikita Mikhalkov's *Burnt by the Sun* won the best foreign-language movie Oscar in 1994, Russian film production was suffering. Funding had dried up during the early 1990s, and audiences couldn't afford to go to the cinema anyway. The industry was back on track by the end of the decade though, with hits such as Alexy Balabanov's gangster drama *Brother* (1997) and Alexander Sokurov's *Molokh* (1999). Sokurov's ambitious *Russian Ark* was an international success in 2002, as was Andrei Zvyaginstev's moody thriller *The Return* the following year.

The glossy vampire thriller *Night Watch* (2004) struck box-office gold both at home and abroad, leading to an equally successful sequel, *Day Watch* (2006), and to Kazakhstan-born director Timur Bekmambetov being lured to Hollywood. *Stilyagi* (2008; entitled *Hipsters* for its international release) is a popular musical that casts a romantic eye on fashion-obsessed youths in 1950s Russia. Another international success, *How I Ended This Summer* (2010) is a tense thriller about the deadly clash of temperaments between an older and a younger scientist working on an isolated meteorological station off the coast of Chukotka.

Return of Censorship

Leviathan (2014), directed by Andrei Zvyagintsev, is a bleak tale of one man's struggle against official corruption in northern Russia. Even though it was nominated for an Oscar for best foreign-language movie and won awards at the Golden Globes and in Cannes, the movie initially struggled to secure a wide release across Russia's cinemas. All that changed after an estimated 1.5 million Russians downloaded the film illegally, prompting cinema chains to take a chance on a movie critical of the current regime.

Nine out of 10 movies made in Russia receive government financing. Although Putin has said he does not favour censorship, he has also said he is interested in Russian films that promote patriotism, and values such as a healthy lifestyle, spirituality, kindness and responsibility, along

The anthology *Today I Wrote Nothing: The Selected Writings of Daniil Kharms*, translated by Matvei Yankelevich, is worth dipping into to discover the bizarre works of this eccentric absurdist writer.

To find out more about contemporary Russian literature go to Read Russia (www.readrussia. org), which has various online resources and organises events to promote Russian writing.

Rossica is a glossy journal published by Academia Rossica (http:// academia-rossica. org). It features the works of top Russian contemporary writers and artists.

THE IMPACT OF SOCIALIST REALISM

In 1932 the Communist Party demanded socialist realism in art – a glorified depiction of communist values and the revolution in society. Henceforth, artists had the all-but-impossible task of conveying the Party line in their works, yet not falling foul of the notoriously fickle tastes of Stalin in the process.

The composer Dmitry Shostakovich, for example, was officially denounced twice (in 1936 and 1948) and suffered the banning of his compositions. Strongly opposed to socialist realism, theatre director Vsevolod Meyerhold had his theatre closed down; in 1939 he was imprisoned and later tortured and executed as a traitor. He was posthumously cleared of all charges in 1955.

Writers were particularly affected, including Vladimir Mayakovsky, who committed suicide, and the poet Anna Akhmatova, whose life was blighted by persecution and tragedy. Many, including Daniil Kharms, had their work driven underground, or were forced to smuggle their manuscripts out to the West for publication, as Boris Pasternak did for *Doctor Zhivago*.

---

with meeting the strategic goals of Russia. Such propaganda movies include the 3D war epic *Stalingrad*, a 2013 box-office smash in Russia.

Made with no government funding was Zvyagintsev's *Loveless*, which premiered at Cannes in 2017. It's another raw slice of contemporary Russian life that is unlikely to go down well with the authorities. Also attracting controversy is the costumed drama *Matilda*, directed by Alexey Uchitel, about Nicholas II's affair with Polish ballerina Mathilde Kschessinska. There have been calls for it to be banned since it is seen as disrespectful to the last tsar, who was canonised in 2000 by the Orthodox Church.

Russian Animation

Little known outside Russia is the country's great contribution to the art of animation. Two years before Disney's *Snow White*, stop-motion animation was used for *New Gulliver* (1935), a communist retelling of *Gulliver's Travels* featuring more than 3000 puppets. And rather than Disney's films, it was actually Lev Atamanov's beautiful *The Snow Queen* (1957), based on the Hans Christian Andersen story, that inspired young Hayao Miyazaki to become the master Japanese animator that he is today.

One of Russia's most respected animators today is Yury Norshteyn, whose masterpiece, *Hedgehog in the Mist* (1975), is philosophical and full of references to art and literature. The current master of the medium is Alexander Petrov, who paints in oil on glass sheets using his fingertips instead of brushes. He photographs one frame, modifies the picture with his fingers and photographs the next; this painstaking approach takes around a year of work to create just 10 minutes of film. *The Cow* (1989), his first solo work, displays Petrov's trademark montage sequences, in which objects, people and landscapes converge in a psychedelic swirl. Petrov won an Academy Award for *The Old Man and the Sea* (1999), based on the Hemingway novella. He was also nominated in 2007 for the dazzling *My Love,* an animated short set in prerevolutionary Russia.

The blog Animatsiya (http://niffiwan.livejournal.com) includes many clips from Russian animation films.

Held online for two weeks in April, T@ke Two (http://d2.rg.ru) is a festival of notable Russian films – features, documentaries and animations – released the previous year and screened with subtitles for free.

Architecture & Visual Art

From heavily detailed religious icons and onion-domed churches to statues of heroic workers and soaring Stalinist towers, Russian art and architecture has a distinctive style. In the post-Soviet world, architects and artists are pretty much free to do as they please. Visual artists, in particular, have done so with relish, both thumbing their noses at the past and present and embracing and rediscovering traditional Russian crafts and artistic inspiration.

Architecture

Until Soviet times most Russians lived in homes made of wood. The *izba* (single-storey log cottage) is still fairly common in the countryside, while some Siberian cities, notably Tomsk, retain fine timber town houses intricately decorated with 'wooden lace'. Stone and brick were usually the preserves of the Church, royalty and nobility.

Early Russian Churches

Early Russian architecture is best viewed in the country's most historic churches, in places such as Veliky Novgorod, Smolensk, Pskov and Vladimir-Suzdal. At their simplest, churches consisted of three aisles, each with an eastern apse (semicircular end), a dome or cupola over the central aisle next to the apse, and high vaulted roofs forming a crucifix shape centred on the dome.

Church architects developed the three-aisle pattern in the 11th and 12th centuries. Roofs then grew steeper to prevent the heavy northern snows collecting and crushing them, and windows grew narrower to keep the cold out. Pskov builders invented the little *kokoshnik* gable, which was semicircular or spade-shaped and usually found in rows supporting a dome or drum.

Where stone replaced brick, as in Vladimir's Assumption Cathedral, it was often carved into a glorious kaleidoscope of decorative images. Another Vladimir-Suzdal hallmark was the 'blind arcade', a wall decoration resembling a row of arches. The early church-citadel complexes required protection, and thus developed sturdy, fortress-style walls replete with fairy-tale towers – Russia's archetypal kremlins.

In the 16th century, the translation of the northern Russian wooden church features – such as the tent roof and the onion dome on a tall drum – into brick added up to a new, uniquely Russian architecture. St Basil's Cathedral, the Ivan the Great Bell Tower in the Moscow Kremlin and the Ascension Church at Kolomenskoe are three high points of this era.

In the 17th century builders in Moscow added tiers of *kokoshniki*, colourful tiles and brick patterning, to create jolly, merchant-financed churches. Mid-century, Patriarch Nikon outlawed such frippery, but elaboration returned later in the century with Western-influenced Moscow baroque, featuring ornate white detailing on redbrick walls.

Churches

Cathedral of St Sophia (Veliky Novgorod)

Trinity Cathedral (Pskov)

St Basil's Cathedral (Moscow)

Church of the Intercession on the Nerl (Bogolyubovo)

Baroque to Classicism

Mainstream baroque reached Russia as Peter the Great opened up the country to Western influences. As the focus was on his new capital, St Petersburg, he banned new stone construction elsewhere to ensure stone supplies. The great Italian architect Bartolomeo Rastrelli created an inspired series of rococo-style buildings for Empress Elizabeth. Three of the most brilliant were the Winter Palace and Smolny Cathedral, both in St Petersburg, and Catherine Palace at nearby Tsarskoe Selo.

Later in the 18th century, Catherine the Great turned away from rococo 'excess' towards Europe's new wave of classicism. This was an attempt to recreate the ambience of an idealised ancient Rome and Greece, with their mathematical proportions and rows of columns, pediments and domes. Catherine and her successors built waves of grand classical edifices in a bid to make St Petersburg the continent's most imposing capital. The simple classicism of Catherine's reign was exemplified by the Great Palace at Pavlovsk.

The grandiose Russian Empire–style was developed under Alexander I, highlighted in buildings such as the Admiralty and Kazan Cathedral in St Petersburg. St Isaac's Cathedral, built for Nicholas I, was the last big project of this wave of classicism in St Petersburg. Moscow abounds with Russian Empire–style buildings, as much of the city had to be rebuilt after the fire of 1812.

Revivals & Style Moderne

A series of architectural revivals, notably of early Russian styles, began in the late 19th century. The first pseudo-Russian phase produced the state department store GUM, the State History Museum and the Leningradsky *vokzal* (train station) in Moscow, and the Moskovsky *vokzal* and the Church of the Saviour on Spilled Blood in St Petersburg.

The early-20th-century neo-Russian movement brought a sturdy classical elegance to architecture across the nation, culminating in the extraordinary Kazansky vokzal in Moscow, which imitates no fewer than seven earlier styles. About the same time, Style Moderne, Russia's take on art nouveau, added wonderful curvaceous flourishes to many buildings right across Russia.

Wooden Buildings

Tomsk

Kizhi Museum Reserve

Vitoslavlitsy (Veliky Novgorod)

Nizhnyaya Sinya-chikha (Sverdlovsk Region)

Museum of Volga People's Architecture & Culture (Nizhny Novgorod)

FIGHTING TO PRESERVE THE PAST

In Russia it's down to national and local governments to decide what pieces of architecture warrant preservation. St Petersburg in particular spends millions of roubles on maintaining and renovating its stock of historic buildings. However, the pressure group Zhivoi Gorod (Living City; www.save-spb.ru) claims that the city is more interested in destruction, citing the demolition of hundreds of historically important buildings in recent years. However, citizen action in the city did manage to put the dampers on the controversial Okhta Tower, the planned headquarters of Gazprom. That project has now morphed into the Lakhta Tower, 9km from St Petersburg's historic centre.

The Moscow Architecture Preservation Society (MAPS; www.maps-moscow.com), a pressure group founded by architects, historians, heritage managers and journalists of various nationalities, has been fighting for several years to preserve the capital's architectural heritage. Its research shows more than 400 of the city's listed buildings have been demolished since 1989. Their efforts appear to be paying off, as previously threatened key 20th-century pieces of architecture including the constructivist apartment block Narkomfin, the Shukhov radio tower and Melnikov House have gained protection and are undergoing renovation.

Soviet Constructivism

The revolution gave rein to young constructivist architects, who rejected superficial decoration in favour of buildings whose appearance was a direct function of their uses and materials – a new architecture for a new society. They used glass and concrete in uncompromising geometric forms.

Konstantin Melnikov was probably the most famous constructivist and his own house off ul Arbat in Moscow is one of the most interesting examples of the style; the offices of Moscow news agencies *Pravda* and *Izvestia* are others. In the 1930s the constructivists were denounced, and a 400m-high design by perpetrators of yet another revival – monumental classicism – was chosen for Stalin's pet project, a Palace of Soviets in Moscow, which mercifully never got off the ground.

Stalin favoured neoclassical architecture, as it echoed ancient Athens. The dictator also liked architecture on a gigantic scale, underlining the might of the Soviet state. This style reached its apogee in the 'Seven Sisters', seven Gothic-style skyscrapers that sprouted around Moscow soon after WWII.

In 1955 Khrushchev condemned the 'excesses' of Stalin (who had died two years earlier) and disbanded the Soviet Academy of Architecture. After this, architects favoured a bland international modern style – constructivism without the spark, you might say – for prestigious buildings, while no style at all was evident in the drab blocks of cramped flats that sprouted countrywide.

Contemporary Architecture

Following the demise of the Soviet Union, architectural energies and civic funds initially went into the restoration of decayed churches and monasteries, as well as the rebuilding of structures such as Moscow's Cathedral of Christ the Saviour.

As far as contemporary domestic, commercial and cultural buildings are concerned, post-Soviet architects have not been kind to Russia. Featuring bright metals and mirrored glass, these buildings tend to be plopped down in the midst of otherwise unassuming vintage buildings, particularly in Moscow.

The oil-rich economy is producing some changes for the better and helping to fund interesting projects, especially in Moscow. Examples include the Garage Museum of Contemporary Art in Gorky Park, which was designed by Rem Koolhaas' OMA; the Moscow School of Management, a design by Adjaye Associates; the transformation of the GES2 power station by Renzo Piano into a new contemporary art centre for the V-A-C Foundation; and the gleaming towers of Moscow International Business Centre (Moscow City), which include Federation Towers. At the time of research this was the tallest building in Europe, but it is expected to soon be trumped by the Lakhta Centre in St Petersburg when it tops out at 462m.

Visual Art

Icons

Originally painted by monks as a spiritual exercise, icons are images intended to aid the veneration of the holy subjects they depict. Some believe that there are some icons that can grant luck and wishes, or even cause miracles.

The beginning of a distinct Russian icon tradition came when artists in Veliky Novgorod started to be influenced by local folk art in their representation of people, producing sharply outlined figures with softer faces and introducing lighter colours, including pale yellows and greens.

Style Moderne

Yaroslavsky vokzal (Moscow)

Vitebsky vokzal (St Petersburg)

Singer Building (St Petersburg)

Kupetz Eliseevs (St Petersburg)

Vyborg

Archi.ru (www. archi.ru) is an online resource that includes a daily digest of what's happening in the world of Russian architecture.

The earliest outstanding painter was Theophanes the Greek (Feofan Grek in Russian). He lived between 1340 and 1405, working in Byzantium, Novgorod and Moscow, and bringing a new delicacy and grace to the form. His finest works are in the Annunciation Cathedral of the Moscow Kremlin.

Andrei Rublyov, a monk at Sergiev Posad's Trinity Monastery of St Sergius and Moscow's Andronikov Monastery, was 20 years Theophanes' junior and the greatest Russian icon painter. His most famous work is the dreamy *Holy Trinity,* on display in Moscow's Tretyakov Gallery.

The layman Dionysius, the leading late-15th-century icon painter, elongated his figures and refined the use of colour. In the 16th century icons grew smaller and more crowded, their figures more realistic and Russian looking. In 17th-century Moscow, Simon Ushakov moved towards Western religious painting with the use of perspective and architectural backgrounds.

Peredvizhniki

The major artistic force of the 19th century was the Peredvizhniki (Wanderers), who saw art as a force for national awareness and social change. The movement gained its name from the touring exhibitions with which the artists widened their audience. It was patronised by the industrialists Savva Mamontov – whose Abramtsevo estate near Moscow became an artists colony – and brothers Pavel and Sergei Tretyakov (after whom the Tretyakov Gallery is named). The Peredvizhniki included Vasily Surikov, who painted vivid Russian historical scenes; Nicholas Ghe, with his biblical and historical scenes; the landscape painter Ivan Shishkin; and Ilya Repin, perhaps the best loved of all Russian artists. Repin's work ranged from social criticism (*Barge Haulers on the Volga*) through history (*Zaporizhsky Cossacks Writing a Letter to the Turkish Sultan*) to portraits of the famous.

Isaac Levitan, who revealed the beauty of the Russian landscape, was one of many others associated with the Peredvizhniki. The end-of-century genius Mikhail Vrubel, inspired by sparkling Byzantine and Venetian mosaics, also showed traces of Western influence.

The propaganda magazine *USSR in Construction* (1930–41) featured stunning design and photography by Nikolai Troshin, El Lisstsky, Alexander Rodchenko and Varvara Stepanova.

Modernism

Around the turn of the 20th century, the Mir Iskusstva (World of Art) movement in St Petersburg, led by Alexander Benois and Sergei Diaghilev under the motto 'art pure and unfettered', opened Russia to Western innovations such as Impressionism, art nouveau and symbolism. From about 1905, Russian art became a maelstrom of groups, styles and 'isms' as it absorbed decades of European change in just a few years, before it gave birth to its own avant-garde futurist movements.

Natalia Goncharova and Mikhail Larionov were at the centre of the Cézanne-influenced Jack of Diamonds group (with which Vasily Kandinsky was also associated) before developing neoprimitivism, based on popular arts and primitive icons.

In 1915 Kasimir Malevich announced the arrival of suprematism, declaring that his utterly abstract geometrical shapes – with the black square representing the ultimate 'zero form' – finally freed art from having to depict the material world and made it a doorway to higher realities.

Soviet-era Art

Futurists turned to the needs of the revolution – education, posters, banners – with enthusiasm, relishing the chance to act on their theories of how art shapes society. But at the end of the 1920s, formalist (abstract)

PERFORMANCE & PROTEST ART

Say what you like about contemporary artists in Russia, but don't accuse them of shying away from controversial subjects or putting their own safety, not to mention liberty, on the line for their art. More often than not, such art takes the form of performance.

Russia's most famous performance artist is Oleg Kulik, best known for taking on the persona of a dog as he crawled naked down Moscow's streets wearing a collar and lead. Along with Alexander Brener, who was jailed in 1997 for painting a green dollar sign on Malevich's painting *Suprematisme,* he is a key figure in the local 'actionism' movement.

Radical art collective Voina (War) made their name by filming live sex acts at Timiryazev State Biology Museum in Moscow and painting a 64m-tall penis on a drawbridge in St Petersburg in 2010; for that last stunt Voina won a R400,000 government-sponsored Innovatzia contemporary-art prize the following year. Among Voina's members are Pyotr Verzilov and his wife Nadezhda Tolokonnikova, who would go on to even greater notoriety as part of the feminist punk-rock collective Pussy Riot.

Grabbing recent headlines has been Petr Pavlensky who has stitched up his mouth and stood in front of St Petersburg's Kazan Cathedral; lain naked in front of the entrance to Saint Petersburg's Legislative Assembly wrapped in barbed wire; and, again naked, hammered a 20cm nail through his scrotum into Red Square. In November 2015, he set fire to the doors of Moscow's FSB office in a performance called 'Threat'. Pavlensky and his partner are currently in Paris seeking asylum following accusations of sexual assault in Russia, which they deny.

art fell out of favour; the Communist Party wanted socialist realism. Images of striving workers, heroic soldiers and inspiring leaders took over. Malevich ended up painting portraits (penetrating ones) and doing designs for Red Square parades.

After Stalin, an avant-garde 'conceptualist' underground was allowed to form. Ilya Kabakov painted, or sometimes just arranged, the debris of everyday life to show the gap between the promises and realities of Soviet existence. Erik Bulatov's 'Sots art' pointed to the devaluation of language by ironically reproducing Soviet slogans or depicting words disappearing over the horizon. In 1962 the authorities set up a show of such 'unofficial' art at the Moscow Manezh; Khrushchev called it 'dog shit' and sent it back underground. In the mid-1970s it resurfaced in the Moscow suburbs, only to be literally bulldozed back down.

A couple of good online resources for Russia's contemporary art scene are Art Guide (http://artguide.com) and The Art Newspaper Russia (www.theartnewspaper.ru), both of which include details of galleries and art shows in Moscow, St Petersburg and elsewhere.

Contemporary Art

In the immediate post-Soviet years, a lot of contemporary painters of note abandoned Russia for the West. Today, with increased economic prosperity, many of the most promising young artists are choosing to stay put. At specialist art galleries in Moscow and St Petersburg, you can find the latest works by Russians in and out of the motherland.

Artists to look out for include Siberian collective and satirists Blue Noses and the artist group AES+F (www.aes-group.org), whose multimedia work, such as *The Feast of Trimalchio,* reflects the lust for luxury in contemporary Russia. Also gaining international attention are Taus Makhacheva, whose work often involves questions of national identity and who is partly based in Makhachkala, Dagestan; and the site-specific installation artist Irina Korina. Both these artists represented Russia at the 2017 Venice Biennale.

Contemporary art galleries are booming from St Petersburg across to Vladivostok. Prestigious events to mark on your calendar include the Moscow Biennale of Contemporary Art (www.moscowbiennale.ru), Moscow Biennale for Young Russian Art (http://youngart.ru) and the Garage Triennial of Russian Contemporary Art, also held in Moscow.

Folk & Native Art

An amazing spectrum of richly decorated folk art has evolved in Russia. Perhaps most familiar are the intricately painted, enamelled wood boxes called *palekh*, after the village east of Moscow that's famous for them; and *finift*, luminous enamelled metal miniatures from Rostov-Veliky. From Gzhel, also east of Moscow, came glazed earthenware in the 18th century and its trademark blue-and-white porcelain in the 19th century. Gus-Khrustalny, south of Vladimir, maintains a glass-making tradition as old as Russia. Every region also has its own style of embroidery and some specialise in knitted and other fine fabrics.

The most common craft is woodcarving, represented by toys, distaffs (tools for hand-spinning flax) and gingerbread moulds in the museums, and in its most clichéd form by the nested *matryoshka* dolls. Surely the most familiar symbol of Russia, they actually only date from 1890. You'll also find the red, black and gold lacquered pine bowls called *khokhloma* overflowing from souvenir shops. Most uniquely Slavic are the 'gingerbread' houses of western and northern Russia and Siberia, with their carved window frames, lintels and trim. The art of carpentry flourished in 17th- and 18th-century houses and churches.

A revived interest in national traditions has recently brought good-quality craftwork into the open, and the process has been boosted by the restoration of churches and mosques and their artwork. There has also been a minor resurgence of woodcarving and bone carving. An even more popular craft is *beresta*, using birch bark to make containers and decorative objects, with colours varying according to the age and season of peeling. In Tuva, soapstone carving and traditional leather forming are also being rediscovered.

Holding the title of People's Artist of Russia, Ilya Glazunov (www.glazunov.ru) was a staunch defender of the Russian Orthodox cultural tradition which featured prominently in his work.

Food & Drink

Russia's glorious culinary heritage is enriched by influences from the Baltic to the Far East. The country's rich black soil provides an abundance of grains and vegetables used in a wonderful range of breads, salads, appetisers and soups that are the highlight of any Russian meal. Its waterways yield a unique range of fish and, as with any cold-climate country, there's a great love of fat-loaded dishes – Russia is no place to go on a diet!

Staples & Specialities

Breakfast

Typical *zavtrak* (breakfast) dishes include bliny (pancakes) with sweet or savoury fillings, various types of *kasha* (porridge) made from buckwheat or other grains, and *syrniki* (cottage-cheese fritters), delicious with jam, sugar and the universal Russian condiment, *smetana* (sour cream). *Khleb* (bread) is freshly baked and comes in a multitude of delicious varieties.

Appetisers & Salads

Whether as the preamble to a meal or something to nibble on between shots of vodka, *zakuski* (appetisers) are a big feature of Russian cuisine. They range from olives to bliny with mushrooms and from *tvorog* (cheese curd) to caviar, and include a multitude of inventive salads. Among the most popular recipes that you'll find on restaurant menus are *salat olivye* (chopped chicken or ham, potatoes, eggs, canned peas and other vegetables mixed with mayonnaise) and *selyodka pod shuboi* (literally 'herrings in fur coats'), a classic from the Soviet era that has slices of herring, beetroot and pickles covered in a creamy sauce.

Soups

No Russian meal is complete without soup, even in the summer when there are several refreshing cold varieties. The main ones to sample:

➡ borsch – this beetroot soup hails from Ukraine but is now synonymous with Russia. It can be served hot or cold and usually with *smetana* poured on top of it.

Russian Cookbooks

....

A Taste of Russia (Darra Goldstein)

Culinaria Russia (ed Marion Trutter)

....

The Russian Heritage Cookbook (Lynn Visson)

PURCHASING CAVIAR RESPONSIBLY

While nothing is as evocative of Russian imperial luxury as Beluga caviar, be aware that the sturgeon of the Caspian Sea are facing extinction due to the unsustainable and illegal plunder of their roe. If you do buy some black caviar, make a responsible purchase. Buy caviar only from shops (not on the street or at markets), in sealed jars (not loose) and, most importantly, make sure the jar or tin is sealed with a CITES (Convention on International Trade in Endangered Species) label, an international trade-control measure set up to reduce sturgeon poaching. Under Russian law, tourists are only permitted to export 250g of caviar per person.

For more information read *The Philosopher Fish* by ecojournalist Richard Adams Carey, a lively investigation into the life of the endangered sturgeon and the prized caviar it provides, and Vanora Bennett's lyrical *The Taste of Dreams*.

Some borsch is vegetarian (ask for *postny* borsch), but most is made with beef stock.

➡ *okroshka* – a cold soup made with chopped cucumber, potatoes, eggs, meat and herbs in a base of either *kvas* (fermented rye-bread water) or *kefir* (drinking yoghurt)

➡ *shchi* – there are vegetarian versions and ones with chicken, beef or lamb, but the base of this soup is always plenty of cabbage

➡ *solyanka* – a sometimes flavoursome concoction of pickled vegetables, meat and potato that used to be the staple winter food for the peasantry

➡ *ukha* – this classic recipe has four types of fish, herbs and a few vegetables in a transparent bouillon

Main Courses

Traditional Russian cuisine tends to be meaty and quite heavy. Popular dishes:

➡ *bef stroganov* – a beef, mushrooms and sour-cream dish said to have been invented in the mid 19th century by a French cook employed by the St Petersburg noble Alexander Stroganov

➡ *zharkoye* – hot pot; a meat stew served piping hot in a little jug

➡ *kotleta po kievsky* – chicken Kiev

➡ shashlyk – meat or fish kebabs

➡ *myaso po monastirsky* – beef topped with cheese is often relabelled *myaso po Sibirski* (Siberian meat)

➡ *pelmeni* – ravioli-like dumplings generally stuffed with pork or beef and served either heaped on a plate with sour cream, vinegar and butter, or in a stock soup; variations such as salmon or mushroom *pelmeni* are found on the menus of more chic restaurants

Central Asian–style dishes are also common, notably *plov* (fried rice with lamb and carrot) and *lagman* (noodles and meat in a soupy broth that gets spicier the further south you go). The range of fish and seafood is enormous, but common staples include *osyetrina* (sturgeon), *shchuka* (pike), *losos* or *syomga* (salmon), *treska* (chub) and *kalmar* (squid).

Desserts

The Russian sweet tooth is seriously sweet. Russians love *morozhenoye* (ice cream) with a passion: it's not unusual to see people gobbling dishfuls, even in the freezing cold. Gooey *torty* (cream cakes), often decorated in lurid colours, are also popular. *Pecheniye* (pastries) are eaten at tea time, in the traditional English style.

Regional Specialities

From the *koryushki* (freshwater smelt) that feature on menus in St Petersburg in late April to the mammoth king crabs of Kamchatka, Russia abounds with regional food specialities. As these two examples illustrate, different varieties of fish and seafood are always worth sampling. Try dried, salty *oblyoma* fish, found in the Volga, or Lake Baikal's delicious *omul,* a cousin of salmon and trout. The Russian Far East doesn't yield many specialist dishes but in the port of Vladivostok you can be sure of the freshness of seafood such as *kalmary* (calamari) and *grebeshki* (scallops).

Honey is used as an ingredient in several dishes and drinks in Western European Russia such as *vzbiten,* the decorated gingerbread made in Tula; a tea with herbs; and the alcoholic drink *medovukha* (honey ale). Cowberries, reindeer and elk meat are ingredients that figure in the cuisine of Northern European Russia. From this region, *lokhikeytto* is a

The Food and Cooking of Russia by Lesley Chamberlain, based on the author's research in the country during the late 1970s, is full of recipes as well as insights into what shaped Russian dining habits in the 20th century.

Russian chocolate and *konfetki* (sweets) are excellent and, with their colourful wrappings, make great presents. Local producers typically use more cocoa, so their chocolate is not as sweet as some non-Russian brands. Reputable manufacturers include Krasny Oktyabr (Red October) and Krupskoi.

deliciously creamy Karelian salmon and potato soup, ideally served with crispy croutons.

The tapestry of peoples and cultures along the Volga River yields several other specialities, such as the Finno-Ugric clear dumpling soup called *sup s klyutskami*. The *kasylyk* (dried-horsemeat sausage) and *zur balish* (meat pie) are both from Tatarstan, where *chek chek* (honey-drenched macaroni-shaped pieces of fried dough) are an essential part of any celebration.

In the Altai region of southern Siberia you can masticate on *sera*, a chewing gum made from cedar oil. While around the ski resort of Sheregesh, sample the wild leek with a distinctive garlicky taste known as *kabla* in the local language and *cheremsha* in Russian.

The Buddhist-influenced culinary traditions of the Republic of Kalmykia have brought the Tibetan-style buttery tea known as *dzhomba* to Europe. Further east in Buryatiya, and throughout the Russian Far East, you'll often encounter the steamed, palm-sized dumplings known as *manti, buuzy* and *pyan-se* (a peppery version). Two or three make a good, greasy meal. Siberia is most famous for its *pelmeni* (small ravioli dumplings) and you'll find local variations in all the major cities across the region.

Among the many Caucasus dishes you may come across are *sokhta* (a mammoth sausage stuffed with minced liver and rice), eaten around Dombay, and Kabardian food such as *zharuma* (fiery sausage stuffed with minced lamb, onion and spices), *gedlibzhe* (a spicy chicken dish) and *geshlubzhe*, a saucy bean dish that can be sampled around Nalchik. Delicious Ossetian *pirozhki* are pizza-like pies that come in *olibakh* (cheese), *sakharadzhin* (cheese and beet leaves) and *fidzhin* (meat) varieties.

Georgian Cuisine

Russian cuisine also borrows enormously from neighbouring countries, most obviously from those around the Caucasus, where shashlyk originated. In particular, the rich, spicy cuisine of the former Soviet republic of Georgia must be sampled while in Russia. Georgian meat and vegetable dishes use ground walnuts or walnut oil as an integral ingredient, yielding a distinctive rich, nutty flavour. Also characteristic of Georgian cuisine is the spice mixture *khmeli-suneli*, which combines coriander, garlic, chillies, pepper and savoury with a saffron substitute made from dried marigold petals.

Grilled meats are among the most beloved items on any Georgian menu. Herbs such as coriander, dill and parsley, and other ingredients such as scallions are often served fresh, with no preparation or sauce, as a palate-cleansing counterpoint to rich dishes. Grapes and pomegranates show up not only as desserts, but also as tart complements to roasted meats.

For vegetarians, Georgian eggplant dishes (notably garlic-laced *badrizhani nivrit*), *lobiyo* (spicy beans) and *khachapuri* (cheese bread) are a great blessing. *Khachapuri* comes in three main forms:

➡ flaky pastry squares (snack versions sold at markets)

➡ *khachapuri po-imeretinsk* – circles of fresh dough cooked with sour, salty *suluguni* cheese (sold in restaurants)

➡ *khachapuri po-adzharski* – topped with a raw egg in the crater (mix it quickly into the melted cheese; sold in restaurants)

Here are a few more Georgian favourites to get you started when faced with an incomprehensible menu:

➡ *basturma* – marinated, grilled meat; usually beef or lamb

➡ *bkhali* or *phkali* – a vegetable purée with herbs and walnuts, most often made with beetroot or spinach

Local Tastes

Filet korseta (horsemeat fillets), Sakha Republic

Susheny losey (dried elk), Sakha Republic

Chewy reindeer cartilage, Kamchatka

Khoitpak (fermented sour milk), Tuva

Please to the Table by Anya von Bremzen and John Welchman is nothing if not comprehensive, with more than 400 recipes from the Baltics, Central Asia and all points between, plus a wealth of background detail on Russian cuisine.

VEGETARIANS & VEGANS

Unless you're in one of the big cities or visiting during Lent, when many restaurants have special meat-free menus, Russia can be tough on vegetarians (and very tough on vegans). Main dishes are heavy on meat and poultry, vegetables are often boiled to death, and even the good vegetable and fish soups are usually made from meat stock.

If you're vegetarian, say so, early and often. You'll see a lot of cucumber and tomato salads, and – if so inclined – will develop an eagle eye for spotting *baklazhan* (eggplant) and dairy dishes. *Zakuski* (appetisers) include quite a lot of meatless ingredients such as eggs and mushrooms. Potatoes *(kartoshka, kartofel, pure)* are usually filed under 'garnish' not 'vegetable'.

Happy Cow (www.happycow.net) lists vegetarian restaurants across Russia's major cities.

⇒ *buglama* – beef or veal stew with tomatoes, dill and garlic

⇒ *chakhokhbili* – chicken slow-cooked with herbs and vegetables

⇒ *chikhirtmi* – lemony chicken soup

⇒ *dolmas* – vegetables (often tomatoes, eggplant or grape leaves) stuffed with beef

⇒ *kharcho* – thick, spicy rice and beef or lamb soup

⇒ *khinkali* – dumplings stuffed with lamb or a mixture of beef and pork

⇒ *lavash* – flat bread used to wrap cheese, tomatoes, herbs or meat

⇒ *pakhlava* – a walnut pastry similar to baklava, but made with sour-cream dough

⇒ *satsivi* – walnut, garlic and pomegranate paste, usually used as a chicken stuffing in cold starters

⇒ *shilaplavi* – rice pilaf, often with potatoes

Drinks

Spirits

Vodka, distilled from wheat, rye or, occasionally, potatoes, is the quintessential Russian alcohol. The word comes from *voda* (pronounced va-*da,* meaning 'water'). The classic recipe for vodka (a 40% alcohol-to-water mixture) was patented in 1894 by Dmitry Mendeleyev, the inventor of the periodic table. The drink's flavour derives from what's added after distillation, so as well as 'plain' vodka you'll find *klyukovka* (cranberry vodka), one of the most popular kinds), *pertsovka* (pepper vodka), *starka* (vodka flavoured with apple and pear leaves), *limonnaya* (lemon vodka) and *okhotnichya* (meaning 'hunter's vodka', with about a dozen ingredients, including peppers, juniper berries, ginger and cloves).

Among the hundreds of different brands for sale are famous ones such as Stolichnaya and Smirnoff, as well as those named after presidents (Putinka) and banks (Russian Standard). Better labels are Moskovskaya, Flagman, Gzhelka, and Zelonaya Marka (meaning 'Green Mark'), which was named after the Stalin-era government agency that regulated vodka quality. For more brands see www.russianvodka.com.

Russian brandy is called *konyak* and the finest come from the Caucasus. Winston Churchill reputedly preferred Armenian *konyak* over French Cognac, and although standards vary enormously, local five-star brandies are generally good.

Homemade moonshine is known as *samogon;* if you're at all in doubt about the alcohol's provenance, don't drink it – some of this stuff is highly poisonous.

'Drinking is the joy of the Rus. We cannot live without it.' With these words, Vladimir of Kyiv, the father of the Russian state, is said to have rejected abstinent Islam on his people's behalf in the 10th century.

DRINKING WATER

There's a huge market for bottled water, and since 2004 more than 2000 licences have been issued to providers; however, not all of it is as pure as it may seem. The Bottled Water Producers Union claim you're likely to be safer drinking water labelled *stolovaya* (purified tap water), which accounts for the vast majority of what's available, rather than *mineralnaya voda* (mineral water), which doesn't have to meet so many legal requirements for purity. One reliable brand of mineral water is Narzan.

For those concerned about both the environment and their health, boiling water and using a decent filter are sufficient if you want to drink what comes out of the tap.

Beer

Russians categorise beer by colour rather than fermentation process: light, red or semidark and dark. Light is more or less equivalent to lager and the last two are close to ales. The alcohol content of some stronger beers can be as high as 10%.

The local market leader is Baltika, based in St Petersburg and with 11 other breweries across the country, but there are scores of other palatable local brands and a fast growing sector of microbreweries producing craft beers.

Wine

Imported wine is widely available. Though the quality of some local bottles is improving, the Russian wine industry is notable mainly for its saccharine *polusladkoe* (semisweet) or *sladkoe* (sweet) dessert wines. Good *bryut* (very dry sparkling wine), *sukhoe* (dry) and *polusukhoe* (semidry) reds are readily found, but finding a palatable Russian dry white can be pretty tough. Locally produced sparkling wine Shampanskoye is cheap (around R300 a bottle) and popular even though it tastes nothing like champagne.

For more information about Russian wines, which are mainly produced in the North Caucasus, see Russian Wine Country (http://russianwinecountry.com).

Russian Beer Brands

Klinskoye Svetloe (lager)

Nevskoe Imperial (lager)

Yarpivo (pilsner)

Stary Melnik (lager)

Sibirskaya Korona (witbier)

Drinking Etiquette

➡ Breaking open a can or bottle of beer and drinking it while walking down the street or sitting in a park is pretty common.

➡ If you find yourself sharing a table at a bar or restaurant with locals, it's odds-on they'll press you to drink with them. Even people from distant tables, spotting foreigners, may be seized with hospitable urges.

➡ Vodka is drunk one shot at a time, neat of course, not sipped. This can be fun as you toast international friendship and so on, but vodka has a knack of creeping up on you from behind and the consequences can be appalling.

➡ It's traditional (and good sense) to eat a little something after each shot.

➡ Don't place an empty bottle on the table – it's considered polite to leave it on the floor.

➡ Refusing a drink can be very difficult, and Russians may continue to insist until they win you over. If you can't quite stand firm, take it in small gulps with copious thanks, while saying how you'd love to indulge but you have to be up early in the morning (or something similar).

➡ If you're really not in the mood, one sure-fire method of warding off all offers (as well as making people feel quite awful) is to say '*Ya alkogolik*' ('*Ya alkogolichka*' for women): 'I'm an alcoholic.'

Nonalcoholic Drinks

Russians make tea by brewing an extremely strong pot, pouring small shots of it into glasses, and topping the glasses up with hot water. This was traditionally done from the samovar, a metal urn with an inner tube filled with hot charcoal. Modern samovars have electric elements, like a kettle, which is actually what most Russians use to boil water for tea these days. Putting jam in tea instead of sugar is quite common for those who like to sweeten their drinks.

Chain-style cafes serving barista-style coffee are found all across Russia – cappuccino, espresso, latte and mocha are now as much a part of the average Russian lexicon as elsewhere.

The popular nonalcoholic beer *kvas* (fermented rye bread water) is made from bread and flavoured with ingredients that can include honey and horseradish. In summer, it's often dispensed on the street from big, wheeled tanks and is highly refreshing.

Sok can mean anything from fruit juice (usually in cartons rather than fresh) to heavily diluted fruit squash. *Mors,* made from all types of red berries, is a popular *sok. Napitok* means 'drink' – it's often a cheaper and weaker version of *sok,* maybe with some real fruit thrown in.

If you're buying milk away from big supermarkets, always check whether it's pasteurised. *Kefir* (yoghurt-like sour milk) is served as a breakfast drink – and is also recommended as a hangover cure. The Bashkirs, the Kazakhs of southernmost Altai, and the Sakha people drink *kumiss* (fermented mare's milk).

Restaurant.ru (http://en.resto-ran.ru) has listings and reviews for places to eat in Moscow and St Petersburg, as well as a recipe section.

Where to Eat & Drink

In general, a *kafe* is likely to be cheaper yet often more atmospherically cosy than a *restoran,* many of which are aimed at hosting weddings and banquets more than individual diners. A *kofeynya* is generally an upmarket cafe, though they often serve great meals too, as will a *pab* (upmarket pub with pricey imported beers) or *traktir* (tavern; often with 'traditional' Russian decor). A *zakusochnaya* can be anything from a pleasant cafe to a disreputable bar, but they usually sell cheap beer and have a limited food menu. Occasionally you'll come across *ryumochnaya,* dive bars specialising in vodka or *konyak* shots.

Increasingly common as you head east, a *buzznaya* is an unpretentious eatery serving Central Asian food and, most notably, *buuzy.* These are meat dumplings that you need to eat very carefully in order to avoid spraying yourself with boiling juices, as an embarrassed Mikhail Gorbachev famously did when visiting Ulan-Ude.

In old Soviet-era hotels and stations the *bufet* serves a range of simple snacks including *buterbrod* (open sandwiches). The *stolovaya* (canteen) is the common person's eatery, often located near stations or in public institutions such as universities. They are invariably cheap. Slide your tray along the counter and point to the food, and the staff will ladle it out. While unappealing, Soviet-style *stolovaya* can still be found, newer 'chic' versions serving very palatable food are also common in cities and towns.

In smaller towns the choice will be far narrower, perhaps limited to standard Russian meals such as *pelmeni* and *kotlety* (cutlets); in villages there may be no hot food available at all (though there's almost always DIY pot noodles available from kiosks and shops).

In *A Year of Russian Feasts,* Catherine Cheremeteff Jones recounts how Russia's finest dishes have been preserved and passed down through the feast days of the Russian Orthodox Church.

Quick Eats

There's plenty of fast food available from both local and international operations, supplemented by street kiosks, vans and cafes with tables. *Pitstsa* (pizza) and shashlyk (meat kebab) are common fare, as are bliny and *pelmeni.*

FOOD & DRINK WHERE TO EAT & DRINK

All large cities have Western-style supermarkets with a large range of Russian and imported goods. You'll generally have to leave all bags in a locker before entering. There are smaller food stores, called *kulinariya*, which sell ready-made food. Ubiquitous food-and-drink kiosks – generally located around parks and markets, on main streets and near train and bus stations – sell their poor-quality products but are handy and reasonably cheap.

Every sizeable town has a *rynok* (market), where locals sell spare produce from their dacha plots (check the market fringes), while bigger traders offload trucks full of fruit, vegetables, meat, dried goods and dairy products. Take your own shopping bag and go early in the morning for the liveliest scene and best selection; a certain amount of bargaining is acceptable, and it's a good idea to check prices with a trustworthy local first.

Homes, roadside vendors and well-stocked markets are your best bet for tasting the great range of wild mushrooms, *paporotniki* (fern tips), *shishki* (cedar nuts) and various soft fruits (red currants, raspberries) laboriously gathered by locals from the forest.

> It's common to find restaurants serving a three-course *biznes lunch* (set-menu lunch) from noon to 4pm, Monday to Friday, costing as little as R200 (R500 in Moscow and St Petersburg).

Ordering Food

It's always worth asking if a restaurant has an English-language menu. If not, even armed with a dictionary or a translation app on your phone, it may be difficult to decipher Russian menus (the different styles of printed Cyrillic are a challenge). Russian menus typically follow a standard form: first come *zakuski* (appetisers; often grouped into cold and hot dishes) followed by soups, sometimes listed under *pervye blyuda* (first courses). *Vtorye blyuda* (second courses; mains) are also known as *goryachiye blyuda* (hot courses). They can be divided into *firmenniye blyuda* (house specials; often listed at the front of the menu), *myasniye blyuda* (meat dishes), *ribniye blyuda* (fish dishes), *ptitsa blyuda* (poultry dishes) and *ovoshchniye blyuda* (vegetable dishes).

If the menu leaves you flummoxed, look at what the other diners are eating and point out what takes your fancy to the staff. Service charges are uncommon, except in the ritziest restaurants, but cover charges are frequent after 7pm, especially when there's live music (one would often gladly pay to stop the music). Check if there's a charge by asking, '*Vkhod platny?*' Leave around a 10% tip if the service has been good.

There is no charge for using the *garderob* (cloakroom) so do check in your coat before entering. Not doing so is considered extremely bad form.

> Most restaurant menus give the weight of portions as well as the price. In most cases, you'll be expected to choose an accompanying 'garnish' (priced separately) of *ris* (rice), potato or *grechka* (split buckwheat).

Celebrating with Food

Food and drink have long played a central role in many Russian celebrations from birthdays to religious holidays. It's traditional, for example, for wedding feasts to stretch on for hours (if not days in some villages) with all the participants generally getting legless.

The most important holiday for the Russian Orthodox Church is Paskha (Easter). Coming after the six-week fast of Lent, when meat and dairy products are forsworn, Easter dishes are rich, exemplified by the traditional cheesecake (also known as *paskha*) and the saffron-flavoured *kulich* (traditional, dome-shaped Easter bread). Together with brightly decorated boiled eggs, these are taken in baskets to church to be blessed during the Easter service.

Bliny are the food of choice during the week-long Maslenitsa (Butter Festival), which precedes Lent – it is the equivalent of Mardi Gras elsewhere.

Christmas (which is celebrated on 7 January in the Russian Orthodox calendar) is not as big a festival as New Year's Eve, which is celebrated

A GIFT TO YOUNG HOUSEWIVES

The most popular cookbook in 19th-century Russia was called *A Gift to Young House-wives*, a collection of favourite recipes and household-management tips. The author, Elena Molokhovets, a housewife herself, was dedicated to her 10 children, to the Orthodox Church and to her inexperienced 'female compatriots' who might need some assistance in keeping their homes running smoothly.

Reprinted 28 times between 1861 and 1914, Molokhovets' bestseller had new recipes and helpful hints added to each new edition. The last edition included thousands of recipes, as well as pointers on how to organise an efficient kitchen, set a proper table and clean a cast-iron pot.

Having gone out of print during the Soviet era, Molokhovets' 'gift' was bestowed upon contemporary readers when Joyce Toomre, a culinary historian, translated and reprinted this historical masterpiece. The 1992 version, *Classic Russian Cooking: Elena Molokhovets' A Gift to Young Housewives*, includes Toomre's detailed analysis of mealtimes, menus, ingredients and cooking techniques.

By Mara Vorhees

with a huge feast of *zakuski* and other traditional foods such as tangerines, Russian salads and *kholodets* (meat jelly). However, it is traditional to eat a sweet rice pudding called *kutya* at Christmas. The same dish is also left as an offering on graves during funerals.

Habits & Customs

It's traditional for Russians to eat a fairly heavy *obed* (early-afternoon meal; lunch) and a lighter *uzhin* (evening meal; supper). Entering some restaurants, you might feel like you're crashing a big party. Here, the purpose of eating out is less to taste exquisite food than to enjoy a whole evening of socialising and entertainment, with multiple courses, drinking and dancing. Dress is informal in all but top-end places.

While restaurants and cafes are common, dining out for the average Russian is not as commonplace as it is in many other countries – the choice of places to dine will be limited outside the main cities and towns. If you really want to experience Russia's famous hospitality – not to mention the best cuisine – never pass up the opportunity to eat at a Russian home. Be prepared to find tables groaning with food and hosts who will never be satisfied that you're full, no matter how much you eat or drink.

Eating with Kids

In all but the fanciest of restaurants children will be greeted with the warmest of welcomes. Some restaurants also have special children's rooms with toys. Kids' menus are uncommon, but you shouldn't have much problem getting the little ones to guzzle bliny or *bifshteks* – a Russian-style hamburger served without bread, and often topped with a fried egg. Make sure you check whether the milk is pasteurised – outside major cities it often isn't.

Landscape & Wildlife

As you'd expect for the world's largest country, spanning 13% of the globe, there's an enormous variety of terrain and wildlife in Russia. Mountains include Mt Elbrus (5642m), Europe's highest peak, and the highly active volcanoes of Kamchatka. Vegetative zones range from the frozen tundra in northern Siberia around the Arctic Circle to seemingly endless taiga (forest) and the fecund steppe (grasslands). Fauna boasts the rare Asian black bear and Amur tiger.

Lay of the Land

Urban development is concentrated mainly across Western European Russia and along the iron ribbon of tracks that constitute the Trans-Siberian Railway, thinning out in the frozen north and southern steppe.

Northern Russia is washed by the Barents, Kara, Laptev and East Siberian Seas. South of Finland, Russia opens on the Gulf of Finland, an inlet of the Baltic Sea; St Petersburg stands at the eastern end of this gulf.

East of Ukraine, the Russian Caucasus region commands stretches of the Black Sea and rugged, mountainous borders with Georgia and Azerbaijan. East of the Caucasus, Russia has an oil-rich stretch of Caspian Sea coast, north of which the Kazakhstan border runs up to the Ural Mountains.

Beyond the Urals, Asian Russia covers nearly 14 million sq km. Contrary to popular conception, only the western section of Asian Russia is actually called Siberia (Sibir). From the Amur regions in the south and the Sakha Republic (Yakutia) in the north, it becomes officially known as the Russian Far East (Dalny Vostok). The eastern seaboard is 15,500km long, giving Russia more 'Pacific Rim' than any other country.

Rivers & Lakes

Though none has the fame of the Nile or the Amazon, six of the world's 20 longest rivers are in Russia. Forming the China–Russia border, the east-flowing Amur (4416km) is nominally longest, along with the Lena (4400km), Yenisey (4090km), Irtysh (4245km) and Ob (3680km), all of which flow north across Siberia, ending up in the Arctic Ocean. In fact, if one were to measure the longest stretch including tributaries (as is frequently done with the Mississippi–Missouri in North America), the Ob–Irtysh would clock up 5410km, and the Angara–Yenisey a phenomenal 5550km. The latter may in fact be the world's longest river if Lake Baikal and the Selenga River (992km) are included, which directly feed into it. Lake Baikal itself is the world's deepest, holding nearly one-fifth of all the world's unfrozen fresh water.

Europe's longest river, the Volga (3690km), rises northwest of Moscow and flows via Kazan and Astrakhan into the Caspian Sea, the world's largest lake (371,800 sq km). Lake Onega (9600 sq km) and Lake Ladoga (18,390 sq km), both northeast of St Petersburg, are the biggest lakes in Europe.

Until the 20th century, boats on Russia's rivers offered the most important form of transport. Today, rivers are still economically important,

Wild Russia (www.
wild-russia.org) is
a website created
by the US-based
Center for
Russian Nature
Conservation,
which assists and
promotes nature
conservation
across Russia.

but mostly as sources of hydroelectric power, with dozens of major dams creating vast reservoirs. It's possible to visit Russia's largest hydroelectric dam at Sayano-Shushenskaya on the Yenisey near Sayanogorsk.

Vegetation & Wildlife

To grasp the full extent of Russia's enormous diversity of wildlife, it is useful to understand the country's major vegetative zones.

Tundra

Falling almost completely within the Arctic Circle, and extending from 60km to 420km south from the coast, the tundra is the most inhospitable of Russia's terrains. The ground is permanently frozen (in places recorded to a depth of 1450m) with whole strata of solid ice and just a thin, fragile carpet of delicate lichens, mosses, grasses and flowers lying on top. The few trees and bushes that manage to cling tenaciously to existence are stunted dwarfs, the permafrost refusing to yield to their roots. For nine months of the year the beleaguered greenery is also buried beneath thick snow. When the brief, warming summer comes, the permafrost prevents drainage and the tundra becomes a spongy wetland, pocked with lakes, pools and puddles.

Not surprisingly, wildlife has it hard on the tundra and there are few species that can survive its climate and desolation. Reindeer, however, have few problems and there are thought to be around four million in Russia's tundra regions. They can endure temperatures as low as -50°C and, like the camel, can store food reserves. Reindeer sustain themselves on lichen and grasses, in winter sniffing them out and pawing away the snow cover.

A similar diet sustains the lemming, a small, round, fat rodent fixed in the popular consciousness for its proclivity for launching itself en masse from clifftops. More amazing is its rate of reproduction. Lemmings can produce five or six litters annually, each comprising five or six young. The young in turn begin reproducing after only two months. With the lemming three-week gestation period, one pair could spawn close to 10,000 lemmings in a 12-month period. In reality, predators and insufficient food keep numbers down.

Other tundra mammals include the Arctic fox, a smaller, furrier cousin of the European fox and a big lemming fan, and the wolf, which, although it prefers the taiga, will range far and wide, drawn by the lure of reindeer meat. Make it as far as the Arctic coast and you could encounter seals, walruses (notably around Chukotka), polar bears and whales.

Taiga

Russia's taiga is the world's largest forest, covering about 5 million sq km (an area big enough to blanket the whole of India) and accounting for about 29% of the world's forest cover. Officially the taiga is the dense, moist subarctic coniferous forest that begins where the tundra ends and which is dominated by spruces and firs. When travelling through the depths of Siberia, two or three days can go by with nothing but the impenetrable and foreboding dark wall of the forest visible outside the train: 'Where it ends,' wrote Chekhov, 'only the migrating birds know.'

Though the conditions are less severe than in the Arctic region, it's still harsh and bitterly cold in winter. The trees commonly found here are pine, larch, spruce and fir. In the coldest (eastern) regions the deciduous larch predominates; by shedding its leaves it cuts down on water loss, and its shallow roots give it the best chance of survival in permafrost conditions.

Due to the permanent shade, the forest-floor vegetation isn't particularly dense (though it is wiry and spring-loaded, making it difficult for

Scenic Lakes
....
Baikal (Eastern Siberia)
....
Seliger (Tver Region)
....
Onega (Karelia)
....
Teletskoe (Altai)

Roger Took's *Running with Reindeer* is a vivid account of his travels in Russia's Kola Peninsula and the wildlife found there.

humans to move through), but there are a great variety of grasses, mosses, lichens, berries and mushrooms. These provide ample nourishment for the animals at the lower end of the food chain that, in turn, become food for others.

Among the wildlife that flourishes here are squirrels, chipmunks (which dine well on pine-cone seeds), voles, lemmings, polecats, foxes, wolverines and, less commonly now, the sable – a weasel-like creature whose luxuriant pelt played such a great role in the early exploration of Siberia.

The most common species of large mammal in the taiga is the elk, a large deer that can measure over 2m at the shoulder and weighs almost as much as a bear. The brown bear itself is also a Siberian inhabitant that you may come across, despite the Russian penchant for hunting it. Other taiga-abiding animals include deer, wolves, lynx and foxes.

Forest.ru (http://old.forest.ru), a site about Russian forests, their conservation and sustainable usage, has a lot of background and current information in English.

Steppe

From the latitudes of Voronezh and Saratov down into the Kuban area north of the Caucasus and all the way across southwestern Siberia stretch vast areas of flat or gently undulating grasslands know as steppe. Since much of this is on humus-rich *chernozem* (black earth), a large proportion is used to cultivate grain. Where soil is poorer, as in Tuva, the grasslands offer vast open expanses of sheep-mown wilderness, encouraging wildflowers and hikers.

The delta through which the Volga River enters the Caspian is, in contrast to the surrounding area, very rich in flora and fauna. Huge carpets of the pink or white Caspian lotus flower spread across the waters in summer, attracting over 200 species of birds in their millions. Wild boar and 30 other mammal species also roam the land.

The small saygak (a type of antelope), an ancient animal that once grazed all the way from Britain to Alaska, still roams the more arid steppe regions around the northern Caspian Sea. However, the species is under threat of extinction from hunting and the eradication of its traditional habitat.

The BBC website Nature Places (www.bbc.co.uk/nature/places/russia) has a series of short videos highlighting different aspects of Russia's amazing landscape and biodiversity.

Caucasus

The steppe gives way to mountainous regions in the Caucasus, a botanist's wonderland with 6000 highly varied plant species, including glorious wildflowers in summer. Among the animals of the Caucasus are the tur (a mountain goat), bezoar (wild goat), endangered mouflon (mountain sheep), chamois (an antelope), brown bear and reintroduced European bison. The lammergeier (bearded vulture), endangered griffon vulture, imperial eagle, peregrine falcon, goshawk and snowcock are among the Caucasus' most spectacular birds. Both types of vulture have been known to attack a live tur.

PUTIN & THE TIGERS

It's no secret that Vladimir Putin has a thing for tigers. In a publicity stunt in 2008, he was pictured fixing a tracking collar to a fully grown female Siberian tiger (also known as Amur tigers) after having shot her with a tranquilising dart. The same year, for his 56th birthday, Putin was presented with a two-month-old tiger cub: he later donated it to a zoo in Krasnodar Territory.

In November 2010, Putin hosted the International Tiger Conservation Forum in St Petersburg with the aim of doubling the number of tigers in the wild from 3200 to 7000 by 2022, the next Chinese Year of the Tiger. And in 2014, Putin was at it again, releasing three orphaned tigers into a remote part of the Amur Region. All this attention does appear to be helping, as the recorded number of tigers is slowly on the rise.

Kamchatka

The fantastic array of vegetation and wildlife in Kamchatka is a result of the geothermal bubbling, brewing and rumbling that goes on below the peninsula's surface, which manifests itself periodically in the eruption of one of around 30 active volcanoes. The minerals deposited by these eruptions have produced some incredibly fertile earth, which is capable of nurturing giant plants with accelerated growth rates. John Massey Stewart, in his book *The Nature of Russia*, gives the example of the drop-wort, normally just a small, unremarkable plant, which in Kamchatka can grow by as much as 10cm in 24 hours and reach a height of up to 4m. In the calderas (craters) of collapsed volcanoes, hot springs and thermal vents maintain a high temperature year-round, creating almost green-house-like conditions for plants. Waterfowl and all manner of animals make their way here to shelter from the worst of winter.

The volcanic ash also enriches the peninsula's rivers, leading to far greater spawnings of salmon than experienced anywhere else. And in thermally warmed pools the salmon also gain weight at a much higher rate. All of which is good news for the region's predatory mammals and large seabirds (and for local fisherfolk). The bears, in particular, benefit and the numerous Kamchatkan brown bears are the biggest of their species in Russia: a fully grown male stands at over 3m and weighs close to a tonne. Other well-fed fish-eaters are the peninsula's sea otters (a protected species), seals and the great sea eagle, one of the world's largest birds of prey, with a 2.5m wingspan. The coastline is favoured by birds, in particular, with over 200 recognised species including auks, tufted puffins and swans.

Ussuriland

Completely unique, Ussuriland is largely covered by a monsoon forest filled with an exotic array of flora and fauna, many species of which are found nowhere else in Russia. The topography is dominated by the Sikhote-Alin Range, which runs for more than 1000km in a spine parallel to the coast. Unlike the sparsely vegetated woodland floor of the taiga, the forests of Ussuriland have a lush undergrowth, with lianas and vines twined around trunks and draped from branches.

However, it's Ussuriland's animal life that arouses the most interest – not so much the wolves, sables or Asian black bears (tree-climbing, herbivorous cousins to the more common brown bears, also found here), as the Siberian or Amur tiger. The largest of all wild cats, the Siberian tiger can measure up to 3.5m in length. They prey on boar, though they've been observed to hunt and kill bears, livestock and even humans.

Ussuriland is also home to the Amur leopard, a big cat significantly rarer than the tiger, though less impressive and consequently less often mentioned. Around 30 of these leopards roam the lands bordering China and North Korea. Sadly, both the leopard and tiger are under threat from constant poaching by both Chinese and Russian hunters. For more about this beautiful animal see ALTA (Amur Leopard & Tiger Alliance; www.altaconservation.org).

State Nature Reserves

Russia has 102 official nature reserves (*zapovedniki*). First created in January 1917 (by the ill-fated Tsar Nicholas II), these are areas set aside to protect fauna and flora, often habitats of endangered or unique species. Visitor controls are very strict.

There are also 48 national parks (*natsionalniye parki*), ranging from the relatively tiny Bryansk Forest (122 sq km) on the border with Ukraine

The Russian Far East, A Reference Guide for Conservation and Development, edited by Josh Newell, gathers work by 90 specialists from Russia, the UK and the US on this fascinating chunk of the country.

A 2015 survey by the World Wildlife Fund found as many as 540 Amur tigers living in the Russian Far East, a significant increase over previous figures.

Novaya Zemlya, two islands that together cover 90,650 sq km, are a far-northern extension of the Ural Mountains in the Barents Sea. In October 1961 the USSR exploded the most powerful nuclear weapon ever tested here.

The Russian Geographical Society runs an annual media project (http://photo.rgo.ru) dedicated to the conservation of Russia's wild nature and fostering respect for the environment through the art of photography.

to the mammoth 88,000 sq km Russian Arctic made up of over 190 islands and, since the inclusion of Franz Josef Land in 2016, the nation's largest such reserve.

Other protected areas include 59 federal refuges, and 17 federal natural monuments. The government has plans for at least 18 new federally protected areas, including at least 11 national parks, and to expand some of the currently protected areas.

Some of these parks are open to visitors and, unlike in the old days when visitors' ramblings were strictly controlled, today you can sometimes hire the staff to show you around.

Environmental Issues

To commemorate the centenary of Russia's first nature reserve, President Putin officially decreed 2017 to be the 'Year of Ecology and Protected Areas'. Yet this is also a nation where fossil fuels rule. Oil, gas and coal produce 90% of Russia's energy, with nonfossil fuel energy sources barely getting a look in.

Environmental groups including Greenpeace Russia and the Norway-based NGO Bellona are highly critical of Russia's oil and gas industry expanding their operations in the country's delicate Arctic regions. In September 2013, the Russian navy intercepted Greenpeace's icebreaker *Arctic Sunrise* and towed it 320km to Murmansk, where the crew of 28 and two journalists on board were jailed for over two months on charges of piracy and hooliganism: they had been protesting oil exploration in the Barents Sea.

Few would dispute that Russia's delicate tundra and Arctic ecosystems have been destabilised by the construction of buildings, roads and railways and the extraction of underground resources. Of particular concern is the impact on the low-lying Yamal Peninsula at the mouth of the Ob, which contains some of the world's biggest gas reserves; parts of the peninsula have been crumbling into the sea as the permafrost melts near gas installations. However, Russian gas monopoly Gazprom claims continued development of the on- and offshore Yamal fields is 'crucial for securing Russia's gas production build-up' into the 21st century (see www.gazprom.com/about/production/projects/mega-yamal).

It's not just in the Arctic that new oil and gas fields are being developed: the Caspian and Baltic Seas and the Sea of Japan around Sakhalin and Kamchatka are also being drilled. Yet, according to Greenpeace Russia, there are almost no sea oil-spill and toxic-pollution prevention and response programs in the country – as demonstrated when an oil tanker sank in the Azov Sea in November 2007, spilling 1300 tonnes of fuel oil and 6100 tonnes of sulphur into the sea, affecting at least 20km of coastline.

Campaign groups such as Bellona have also claimed that environmental law was rewritten to accommodate illegal construction and waste dumping on previously protected lands during the construction phase of the 2014 Winter Olympics in Sochi, and that the area's drinking water was poisoned. When locals attempted to protest, they were harassed and jailed, such as environmentalist Evgeny Vitishko who served 22 months in a penal colony for his activism and was recognised as a prisoner of conscience by Amnesty International.

World Heritage Sites

Virgin Komi Forests, the Ural Mountains

Lake Baikal

Kamchatka's volcanoes

Altai Mountains

Western Caucasus

Curonian Spit

Central Sikhote-Alin Range

Lena Pillars

Survival Guide

Directory A–Z

Accommodation

B&Bs, Homestays & Serviced Apartments

European-style B&Bs are rare in Russia, but there are plenty of opportunities for staying in Russian homes. For an insight into how most Russians live, stay in an apartment-block flat, where apartments are usually rented as a whole but sometimes shared with the owners. Most of such options are listed on major home-sharing sites.

Moscow and St Petersburg have organisations specifically geared to accommodate foreign visitors in private flats at around €30 to €40 per person, normally with English-speaking hosts, breakfast and other services, such as excursions and extra meals.

Many travel agencies and tourism firms in these and other cities, as well as overseas, also offer homestays. The price will depend on things like how far the flat is from the city centre, whether the hosts speak English and whether any meals are provided. It's also worth checking whether a homestay or serviced apartment agency can provide visa support and registration and what the costs of this might be.

Camping

Camping in the wild is allowed, except in those areas signposted 'Не разбивать палатку' (No putting up of tents) and/or 'Не разжигать костры' (No campfires). Check with locals if you're in doubt.

Kempingi (organised camp sites) are rare and usually only open from June to September. Unlike Western camp sites, small wooden cabins often take up much of the space, leaving little room for tents. Some *kempingi* are in quite attractive woodland settings, but communal toilets and washrooms are often in poor condition and other facilities few.

Hostels

Increasingly common across Russia, particularly along the main Trans-Siberian route from St Petersburg to Vladivostok, Western-style hostels are a boon for budget (and other) travellers, as they not only offer affordable accommodation but also friendly and clued-up English-speaking staff. A dorm bed in a Moscow or St Petersburg hostel runs from R500 to R1000.

Hotels

Western-style hotels or international chains are represented in most regional capitals. A few hotels (usually budget ones) aren't registered for foreign guests or will only take you if you've already registered your visa, though these are fairly rare.

Most hotels have a range of rooms at widely differing prices – there's always a price list displayed (on the wall or in a menu-style booklet on the counter), which states the cost for every category. Staff are generally obliging about allowing guests to look around before checking in; ask *'Mozhno li posmotret nomer?'* (May I see the room?).

SLEEPING PRICE RANGES

The following price ranges are for high season and based on double rooms. Prices include private bathroom but exclude breakfast unless otherwise stated.

€ less than R1500 (less than R3000 in Moscow & St Petersburg)

€€ R1500–4000 (R3000–15,000 in Moscow & St Petersburg)

€€€ more than R4000 (more than R15,000 in Moscow & St Petersburg)

HOMESTAY AGENCIES

A number of agencies can arrange homestays, mainly in Moscow and St Petersburg, from as little as US$15 a day, but more commonly it's €30 to €60 depending on location and quality of accommodation. Some travel agencies can also make homestay arrangements.

International Homestay Agency (https:// homestayagency.com)

Host Families Association (HOFA; ☎7-911 766 5464; www.hofa.ru)

Worldwide Homestay (www.worldwidehomestay.com/ Russia.htm)

Not all hotels have genuine single rooms, and 'single' prices often refer to single occupancy of a double or twin room. Some hotels, mainly in the bottom and lower-middle ranges, have rooms for three or four people where the price per person is less than a single or double would be. Beds are typically single and where there is a double bed you'll generally pay somewhat more than for a similarly sized twin room.

Hot-water supplies are fairly reliable, but since hot water is supplied on a district basis, whole neighbourhoods can be without it for up to a month in summer, when the system is shut down for maintenance (the best hotels have their own hot-water systems).

A *lyuks* room is a suite, with a sitting room in addition to the bedroom and bathroom. A *polulyuks* is a somewhat less spacious suite.

In cities and towns, many midrange and top-end hotels catering to business people drop their prices at weekends. There can also be significant seasonal variations, with top prices kicking in over holiday periods, such as the first nine days of January and May.

PROCEDURES

When you check in most hotels will ask to see your passport – they may then keep it for anywhere up to 24 hours in order to register you with the authorities. Some budget and midrange hotels still operate a system where on each floor a *dezhurnaya* (floor lady) guards the keys for all the rooms in her little kingdom, and from whom you can arrange things like hot water to make tea.

Modern hotels generally have a check-out time, usually noon. However, some places charge by *sutki*, ie for a stay of 24 hours. Check which you've paid for before rushing to pack your bags. If you want to store your luggage somewhere safe for a late departure, arrange it with the *dezhurnaya* or front-desk staff.

Resting Rooms

Komnaty otdykha (resting rooms) are found at all major train stations and several of the smaller ones as well as at a few larger bus stations. Generally they have basic (but often quite clean) shared accommodation with communal sink and toilet. Some have showers but you'll often pay an extra fee to use them. Sometimes there are single and double rooms and, rarely, more luxurious ones with private bathrooms. The beds generally can be rented by the half-day (R50 to R1000) or 24-hour (R800 to R1700) period. Some will ask to see your train ticket before allowing you to stay.

Turbazy, Rest Houses & Sanatoriums

A *turbaza* is typically a no-frills holiday camp aimed at outdoor types. Basic accommodation is usually in spartan multiroom wooden bungalows or *domiky* (small huts). Don't expect indoor plumbing. In the Soviet era, *turbazy* were often owned by a factory or large company for use by its employees. Many became somewhat decrepit, but these days more and more are privatised and have been spruced up. At some, you can arrange boating, skiing, hiking or mountaineering.

Doma otdykha (rest houses) are similar to *turbazy*, though usually more luxurious. In peak seasons it's often essential to book through travel agencies in regional cities, as demand can be very high.

Sanatory (sanatoriums) have professional medical staff on hand to treat any illnesses you may have, design your diet and advise on correct rest. Most are ugly concrete eyesores in otherwise attractive rural or coastal settings. Sanatoriums can be spas, sea resorts (there are several good ones in Sochi and the Kaliningrad Region) or

BOOK YOUR STAY ONLINE

For more accommodation reviews by Lonely Planet authors, check out http://lonelyplanet.com/hotels/. You'll find independent reviews, as well as recommendations on the best places to stay. Best of all, you can book online.

VISITING MUSEUMS (& OTHER TOURIST ATTRACTIONS)

Some major attractions, such as Moscow's Kremlin, State History Museum and St Basil's, have ditched foreigner prices. All adults pay whatever the foreigner price used to be; all students, children and pensioners pay the low price. However, elsewhere, particularly in St Petersburg, foreigner prices rule. Higher foreigner fees are said to go towards preserving works of art and cultural treasures that might otherwise receive minimal state funding.

Moscow and St Petersburg apart, non-Russian labels, guides or catalogues in museums are fairly uncommon. If good English labelling is not available, you'll need to use a dictionary or language app to work out the precise details of what you're seeing – or be prepared to pay an additional fee for a guided tour.

Here are a few more things to keep in mind:

➡ Admittance typically stops one hour before the official closing time.

➡ If you wish to take photos or film a video, there will be a separate fee for this, typically an extra R100 for a still camera and R200 for video camera.

➡ Once a month many places close for a 'sanitary day', in theory to allow the place to be thoroughly cleaned. If you specially want to see a museum, it's always best to call ahead to check when it's open.

resorts where you can get some kind of nontraditional treatment (with *kumiss*, fermented mare's milk, for instance). They are mostly popular with locals.

Children

Families planning to travel to Russia with their children should have few problems, though there are some things to note.

Baby changing rooms are uncommon, and you wouldn't want to use many public toilets yourself, let alone change your baby's nappy in them. Head back to your hotel or to a modern cafe or fast-food outlet where the toilets, while typically small, should be clean. Nappies, powdered milk and baby food are widely available except in very rural areas.

There's no shortage of toyshops, but don't expect to find many, if any, English-language publications for kids. In Moscow and St Petersburg there several restaurants with play sections for kids.

Lonely Planet's *Travel with Children* contains useful advice on how to cope on the road and what to bring to make things go more smoothly.

Customs Regulations

➡ Searches beyond the perfunctory are quite rare, but clearing customs when you leave Russia by a land border can be lengthy.

➡ Visitors are allowed to bring in and take out up to US$10,000 (or its equivalent) in currency, and goods up to the value of €10,000, weighing less than 50kg, without making a customs declaration.

➡ Fill in a customs declaration form if you're bringing into Russia major equipment, antiques, artworks or musical instruments (including a guitar) that you plan to take out with you – get it stamped in the red channel of customs to avoid any problems leaving with the same goods.

➡ If you plan to export anything vaguely 'arty' – instruments, coins, jewellery, antiques, antiquarian manuscripts and books (older than 50 years) or art (also older than 50 years) – it should first be assessed by the **Ministry of Culture** (Министерство Культуры; Map p66; ☎499-391 4212; ul

Akademika Korolyova 21, bldg 1, office 505, 5th fl; ☺11am-5pm Mon-Fri; ⓜVDNKh); it is very difficult to export anything over 100 years old. Bring your item (or a photograph, if the item is large) and your receipt. If export is allowed, you'll be issued a receipt for tax paid, which you show to customs officers on your way out of the country.

Electricity

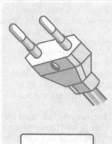

Type C
220V/50Hz

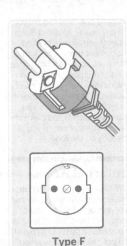

**Type F
230V/50Hz**

Embassies & Consulates

For a list of Russian embassies and consulates overseas see www.russianembassy.net. If you will be travelling in Russia for a long period of time (say a month or more), and particularly if you're heading to remote locations, it's wise to register with your embassy. This can be done over the phone or by email.

Australian Embassy
(Посольство Австралии; Map p78; ☑495-956 6070; www.russia.embassy.gov.au; Podkolokny per 10a/2; Ⓜ Kitay-Gorod)

Belarusian Embassy
(Посольство Белорусии; Map p78; ☑495-777 6644; www.embassybel.ru; ul Maroseyka 17/6; Ⓜ Kitay-Gorod)

Canadian Embassy
(Посольство Канады; Map p90; ☑495-925 6000; http://russia.gc.ca; Starokonyushenny per 23, Moscow; ⊘8.30am-5pm; Ⓜ Kropotkinskaya)

Chinese Embassy (Посольство Китая; Map p66; ☑consular 499-951 8436; http://ru.chinese embassy.org/rus; ul Druzhby 6,

Moscow; ⊘9am-noon Mon-Fri; Ⓜ Universitet)

Finnish Embassy (Посольство Финляндии; Map p90; ☑495-787 4174; www.finland.org.ru; Kropotkinsky per 15/17; ⊘9am-5pm; Ⓜ Park Kultury)

French Embassy (Посольство Франции; Map p94; ☑495-937 1500; www.ambafrance-ru.org; ul Bolshaya Yakimanka 45, Moscow; Ⓜ Oktyabrskaya)

German Embassy (Посольство Германии; Map p66; ☑495-937 9500; www.germania.diplo.de; Mosfilmovskaya ul 56, Moscow; ⊘9am-3pm; ☐119; Ⓜ Universitet)

Irish Embassy (Посольство Ирландии; Map p78; ☑495-937 5911; www.embassyofireland.ru; Grokholsky per 5; Ⓜ Prospekt Mira)

Japanese Embassy
(Посольство Японии; Map p78; ☑495-229 2550; www.ru.emb-japan.go.jp; Grokholsky per 27; Ⓜ Arbatskaya)

Latvian Embassy (Посольство Латвийской Республики; Map p78; ☑495-232 9760; www.mfa.gov.lv/en/moscow; ul Chaplygina 3; Ⓜ Chistye Prudy)

Lithuanian Embassy
(Посольство Литовской Республики; Map p86; ☑495-785 8605; http://ru.urm.lt; Borisoglebsky per 10; Ⓜ Arbatskaya)

Mongolian Embassy
(Посольство Монголии; Map p86; ☑495-690 4636; http://embassymongolia.ru; Borisoglebsky per 11; Ⓜ Arbatskaya)

Netherlands Embassy
(Посольство Королевства Нидерландов; Map p86; ☑495-797 2900; www.netherlands-embassy.ru; Kalashny per 6; Ⓜ Arbatskaya)

New Zealand Embassy (Map p86; ☑495-956 3579; www.nzembassy.com; Povarskaya ul 44, Moscow; Ⓜ Arbatskaya)

Norwegian Consulate (Map p180; ☑812-612 4100; Ligovsky pr 13-15; Ⓜ Pl Vosstaniya)

Polish Embassy (Map p86; ☑495-231 1500; http://moskwa.msz.gov.pl; ul Klimashkina 4; Ⓜ Belorusskaya)

UK Embassy (Посольство Великобритании; Map p90; ☑495-956 7200; www.gov.uk/government/world/russia; Smolenskaya nab 10, Moscow; ⊘9am-5pm; Ⓜ Smolenskaya)

Ukrainian Embassy
(Посольство Украины; Map p86; ☑495-629 3542, consular questions 495-629 9742; http://russia.mfa.gov.ua; Leontevsky per 18; Ⓜ Pushkinskaya)

US Embassy (Посольство США; Map p86; ☑495-728 5000; http://moscow.usembassy.gov; Bolshoy Devyatinsky per 8; Ⓜ Barrikadnaya)

Food

See the Food & Drink chapter (p652).

LGBT Travellers

➡ Russia is a conservative country and being gay is generally frowned upon. LGBT people face stigma,

---

EATING PRICE RANGES

The following price ranges refer to a standard main course.

€ less than R300 (less than R500 in Moscow and St Petersburg)

€€ R300–800 (around R500–1000 in Moscow and St Petersburg)

€€€ more than R800 (more than R1000 in Moscow and St Petersburg)

harassment and violence in their everyday lives.

➡ Homosexuality isn't illegal, but promoting it (and other LGBT lifestyles) is. What constitutes promotion is at the discretion of the authorities.

➡ There are active and relatively open gay and lesbian scenes in both Moscow and St Petersburg. Elsewhere, the gay scene tends to be underground.

➡ Visit http://english.gay.ru for information, good links and a resource for putting you in touch with personal guides for Moscow and St Petersburg.

➡ Coming Out (www.comingoutspb.com) is the site of a St Petersburg–based support organisation.

Health

Insurance

Good emergency medical treatment is not cheap in Russia, so take out a policy that covers you for the worst possible scenario, such as an accident requiring an emergency flight home.

Recommended Vaccinations

No vaccinations are required for travel to Russia, but the World Health Organization (WHO) recommends that all travellers should be covered for diphtheria, tetanus, measles, mumps, rubella and polio, regardless of their destination. Since most vaccines don't produce immunity until at least two weeks after they're given, visit a physician at least six weeks before departure.

Availability & Cost of Healthcare

Medical care is readily available across Russia, but the quality can vary enormously. The biggest cities and towns have the widest choice of places, with Moscow and St Petersburg well served by

sparkling international-style clinics that charge handsomely for their generally excellent and professional service: expect to pay around US$100 for an initial consultation. In remote areas doctors won't usually charge travellers, although it's recommended that you give them a present – such as chocolate, fancy alcohol or just money. In some cases, medical supplies required in a hospital may need to be bought from a pharmacy and nursing care may be limited.

Infectious Diseases

These include rabies, tick-borne encephalitis (a serious risk in rural Russia from May to July), HIV and AIDS, typhoid and hepatitis A. Consider having vaccinations before departure.

Environmental Hazards

It's unlikely you'll experience any environmental hazards, but if you do, it'll likely be to do with the climate or air pollution in the biggest cities only. Watch out for altitude sickness in the high mountains of the Caucasus, the Altai and Kamchatka; heat exhaustion and heat stroke or hypothermia and frostbite, depending on the season; stings or bites from insects, leeches and snakes.

Water Safety

While brushing your teeth with tap water is OK, assume that it isn't safe to drink. Stick to bottled water, boil water for 10 minutes, or use water purification tablets or a filter.

Insurance

We strongly recommend taking out travel insurance. Check the small print to see if the policy covers potentially dangerous sporting activities, such as diving or trekking. For medical treatment, some policies pay doctors or hospitals

directly but most require you to pay on the spot and claim later (keep all receipts and documentation). Check that the policy covers ambulances or an emergency flight home. Worldwide travel insurance is available at www.lonelyplanet.com/travel-insurance. You can buy, extend and claim online anytime – even if you're already on the road.

Internet Access

Wi-fi is common across Russia and usually access is free (or available for the cost of a cup of coffee). You may have to ask for a password (parol), to get online, and also input your mobile phone number. Sometimes this will need to be a Russian number (ie one starting with ☑+7); if you don't have one, ask a local if you can use their number.

If you don't have your own wi-fi-enabled device, it's probably easiest to get online in the business centres of hotels or at hostels that have a computer terminal.

Language Courses

English-language publications in Moscow and St Petersburg carry advertisements for Russian-language schools and tutors. The cost of formal coursework varies widely, but one-on-one tutoring can be a bargain – numerous professors and other highly skilled people are anxious to augment their incomes by teaching you Russian.

Another option for learning Russian is through one of the many international universities operating in Moscow and St Petersburg. These are usually affiliated with a school in either Britain or the USA. Or you could take a course through the **Eurolingua Institute** (www.eurolingua.com), which offers homestays combined with language courses.

DIRECTORY A–Z LEGAL MATTERS

Legal Matters

Avoid contact with the myriad types of police. It's not uncommon for them to bolster their incomes by extracting 'fines' from the unaware; you always have the right to insist to be taken to a police station (though we don't recommend this; if possible try to resolve the problem on the spot) or that the 'fine' be paid the legal way, through Sberbank. If you need police assistance (ie you've been the victim of a robbery or an assault), go to a station with a local for both language and moral support. Be persistent and patient.

If you are arrested, the police are obliged to inform your embassy or consulate immediately and allow you to communicate with it without delay. You can't count on the rules being followed, so be polite and respectful towards officials and hopefully things will go far more smoothly for you. In Russian, the phrase 'I'd like to call my embassy' is *'Pozhaluysta, ya khotel by pozvonit v posolstvo moyey strany'*.

Money

→ If prices are listed in US dollars or euros, you will still be presented with a final bill in roubles.

→ There are ATMs on every corner around the country these days; look out for signs that say *bankomat* (БАНКОМАТ).

→ Credit cards are commonly accepted in big cities, but don't expect to be able to use them in more off-the-beaten-track spots and rural areas.

→ Inform your bank or credit card provider of the dates you'll be travelling in Russia and using your card, to avoid a situation where the card is blocked.

Currency

The Russian currency is the rouble (рубль), abbreviated as 'р' in Russian or R in English. There are 100 *kopek*s in a rouble and these come in coin denominations of one (rarely seen), five, 10 and 50. Also issued in coins, roubles come in amounts of one, two, five and 10, with banknotes in values of 10, 50, 100, 200, 500, 1000, 2000 and 5000 roubles.

Credit Cards

Credit cards are commonly accepted, but don't rely on them outside of major cities and towns. Visa and Mastercard are the most widespread card types, while American Express can be problematic in some hotels and shops. Most sizeable cities have banks or exchange bureaux that will give you a cash advance on your credit card, but be prepared for paperwork in Russian.

Note that Western credit cards are not accepted in Russian-occupied Crimea, which officially is the territory of Ukraine, due to economic sanctions.

Exchanging Money

You'll usually get the best exchange rates for US dollars and Euros. British pounds are sometimes accepted in big cities, but the exchange rates are not so good; other currencies incur abysmal rates and are often virtually unchangeable.

Any currency you bring should be pristine: banks and exchange bureaux do not accept old, tatty bills with rips or tears. For US dollars, make certain they are the post-2006 designs printed with large offset portraits.

Carrying around wads of cash isn't the security problem you might imagine – nowadays, there are a lot of Russians with plenty more money on them than you. For security, though, divide your money into three or four stashes hidden out of view about your person.

Every town of any size will have at least one bank (most often Sberbank) or exchange office – be prepared to show your passport. Rates can vary from one establishment to the next (and are linked to how much cash you want to

---

PRACTICALITIES

Newspapers Main ones are government-owned *Rossiyskaya Gazeta*, the popular dailies *Izvestia* and *Komsomolskaya Pravda*, and the left-leaning daily *Trud*. *Novaya Gazeta* is known for its investigative journalism, as is the online news site *Meduza* (https://meduza.io)

TV Channel 1 (Pervy Kanal), NTV, Rossiya, Kultura, Sport 1, RenTV and the English-language Russia Today. Each region has a number of local channels, while in many hotels you'll have access to CNN and BBC World, plus several more satellite channels in English and other languages.

Radio Broken into three bands: AM, UKV (66MHz to 77MHz) and FM (100MHz to 107MHz). A Western-made FM radio usually won't go lower than 85MHz.

DVD Russian DVDs are region code 5.

Weights & Measures Russia uses the metric system.

change – larger amounts get better rates) so it's always worth shopping around.

Travellers Cheques

Travellers cheques are no longer a preferred method of carrying funds and will prove difficult to exchange in Russia.

Opening Hours

Banks 9am–6pm Monday to Friday, some open 9am–5pm Saturday

Bars and clubs noon–midnight Sunday to Thursday, to 6am Friday and Saturday

Cafes 9am–10pm

Post offices 8am–8pm or 9pm Monday to Friday, shorter hours Saturday and Sunday

Restaurants noon–midnight

Shops 10am–8pm

Supermarkets and food stores 24 hours

Photography

➡ Use judgment and discretion when taking photos of people. It's always better to ask first, and if the person doesn't want to be photographed, respect their privacy; older people can be uneasy about being photographed. In Russian, 'May I take a photograph of you?' is *Mozhno vas sfotografirovat?'*

➡ Be very careful about photographing stations, official-looking buildings and any type of military-security structure – if in doubt, put your camera away.

➡ Some museums and galleries forbid flash pictures, some ban all photography and most will charge you extra to snap away (typically R100). Some caretakers in historical buildings and churches will also charge you for the privilege of using a still or video camera.

Post

The Russian postal service is Pochta Rossia (www.pochta.ru). *Pochta* (ПОЧТАМТ) refers to any post office, *glavpochtamt* to a main post office and *mezhdunarodny glavpochtamt* to an international one.

Outward post is slow but fairly reliable; if you want to be certain, use registered post *(zakaznaya pochta)*. Airmail letters take two to three weeks from Moscow and St Petersburg to the UK, longer from other cities and three to four weeks to the US or Australasia. To send a postcard or letter up to 20g anywhere in the world by air costs R37.

In major cities you can usually find the services of at least one of the international

express carriers, such as FedEx or DHL.

Incoming mail is so unreliable that many companies, hotels and individuals use private services with addresses in Germany or Finland (a private carrier completes the mail's journey to its Russian destination). Other than this, your reliable options for receiving mail in Russia are nil: there's no poste restante, and embassies and consulates won't hold mail for transient visitors.

If sending mail to Russia or trying to receive it, note that addresses should be in reverse order: Russia (Россия), postal code (if known), city, street address, then name.

Public Holidays

In addition to the following official days, many businesses (but not restaurants, shops and museums) close for a week of bank holidays between 1 January and at least 8 January. Bank holidays are typically declared to merge national holidays with the nearest weekend.

New Year's Day 1 January

Russian Orthodox Christmas Day 7 January

Defender of the Fatherland Day 23 February

International Women's Day 8 March

International Labour Day/ Spring Festival 1 May

Victory Day 9 May

Russian Independence Day 12 June

Unity Day 4 November

Safe Travel

While Russia is a socially conservative and religious society, visitors will generally be able to travel safely.

➡ Don't leave any valuables or bags inside your car. Valuables lying around

RUSSIAN STREET NAMES

We use the Russian names of all streets and squares to help you when deciphering Cyrillic signs and asking locals the way. To save space, we use the following abbreviations.

ABBREVIATION	MEANING	SCRIPT	ENGLISH
bul	bulvar	бульвар	boulevard
nab	naberezhnaya	набережная	embankment
per	pereulok	переулок	side street
pl	ploshchad	площадь	square
pr	prospekt	проспект	avenue
sh	shosse	шоссе	road
ul	ulitsa	улица	street

hotel rooms also tempt providence.

➡ It's generally safe to leave your belongings unguarded when using the toilets on trains, but you'd be wise to get to know your fellow passengers first.

➡ Pickpockets and purse-snatchers operate in big cities and major towns. Keep your valuables close.

Scams

Be wary of officials, such as police (or people posing as police), asking to see your papers or tickets at stations – there's a small chance they will try to find something wrong with your documents and hold them to ransom. The only course of action is to remain calm and polite and stand your ground. Try to enlist the help of a passer-by to translate (or at least witness what is going on).

Dangerous Regions

Check with your government's foreign affairs ministry at home or your embassy in Russia for the latest danger zones. Although it's possible to travel in Northeast Caucasus (Dagestan, Chechnya and Ingushetia) these days, the area remains volatile. An Islamist insurgency is smouldering at all times and law-enforcement bodies are rarely concerned about sticking to the law.

In other parts of Russia, certain isolated villages suffer from the unpredictable side effects of chronic alcoholism, especially in western Tuva, where locals are frequently drunk and armed with knives.

In more remote areas of the country, specific natural hazards include bears and, from late May to July, potentially fatal tick-borne encephalitis (particularly in Siberia and Ussuriland in the Russian Far East). And, if trekking in Kamchatka, remember that many of those volcanoes are active.

GOVERNMENT TRAVEL ADVICE

The following government websites offer travel advisories and information on current hot spots.

Australian Department of Foreign Affairs (www.smartraveller.gov.au)

British Foreign Office (www.gov.uk/foreign-travel-advice)

Canadian Department of Foreign Affairs (www.dfait-maeci.gc.ca)

US State Department (http://travel.state.gov)

Border Zones & Restricted Areas

Official border crossings aside, Russia's borders are usually off-limits and care should be taken when approaching. Trekking in some border areas is allowed, but you will need to possess a permit, which although free can take at least 60 days to process. Being caught near borders without a permit could result in a large fine at best and deportation at worst. The same goes for Russia's closed cities (usually associated with the military in some way).

Then there are regulated areas (Зоны с регламентированным посещением для иностранных граждан), mainly wilderness zones scattered across the country, for which you need official permission from the FSB to enter. These are not obvious and rarely marked – if you are planning any serious back-country exploration, it's worth checking first what official permits you may need to avoid incurring fines or deportation.

Racism & Discrimination

Racism is a problem. Russian neo-Nazi and skinhead groups are violent and have been linked to many murders.

Although the statistics are much better than 10 years ago, attacks on Africans and Asians on city streets are not uncommon. Visitors of African, Middle Eastern and Asian descent should be aware that they may not always receive the warmest of welcomes, though Russian racism seems particularly focused toward Central Asians and people from the Caucasus.

Racist attitudes or statements can also come from highly educated Russians. Anti-Semitism, which was state-sponsored during Soviet times, is still easily stirred up by right-wing political parties.

It's a good idea to be vigilant on the streets around Hitler's birthday (20 April), when bands of right-wing thugs have been known to roam around spoiling for a fight with anyone who doesn't look Russian. Another potentially risky day is 2 August, when streets and parks are swarming with ex-paratroopers who celebrate their holiday with copious amounts of alcohol.

Widespread anti-American and anti-Western sentiments may sometimes create tense situations, though violence is unlikely.

Transport & Road Safety

Take care when crossing the road in large cities: some crazy drivers completely ignore traffic lights, while others tear off immediately when the lights change (which can be suddenly), leaving you stranded in the middle of the road. Many cars stop on the zebra these days, but some don't, so make sure all lanes are safe before crossing.

Telephone

The country code for Russia is ☑7.

Local calls from homes and most hotels are free. To make a long-distance call or to call a mobile from most phones, first dial ☑8, wait for a second dial tone, then dial the area code and phone number. To make an international call dial ☑8, wait for a second dial tone, then dial ☑10, then the country code etc. Some phones are for local calls only and won't give you that second dial tone.

To place an international call from a mobile phone, dial + and then the country code.

Mobile Phones

Major phone networks offering pay-as-you-go deals include Beeline, Megafon, MTS and Tele2.

Reception is available right along the Trans-Siberian Railway and increasingly in rural areas. MTS probably has the widest network, but also the worst reputation for customer service. We found Beeline to be pretty reliable.

To call a mobile phone from a landline, the line must be enabled to make paid (ie nonlocal) calls. SIMs and phone-call-credit top-up cards costing as little as R300 are available at mobile phone shops and kiosks across cities and towns as well as at airport arrival areas and train stations. Call prices are very low within local networks, but charges for roaming larger regions can mount up; cost-conscious locals switch SIM cards when crossing regional boundaries.

Topping up your credit can be done either via prepaid credit cards bought from kiosks or mobile phone shops or, more commonly, via paypoint machines found in shopping centres, underground passes, at metro and train stations. Choose your network, input your telephone number and the amount of credit you'd like, insert the cash and it's done, minus a 3% to 10% fee for the transaction. Confirmation of the top-up comes via a text message (in Russian) to your phone. You can also use the websites of mobile phone companies to top up your phone with a credit card.

Time

There are 11 time zones in Russia; the standard time is calculated from Moscow, which is GMT/UTC plus three hours year-round. In 2011, Russia abandoned the summer time switch, so the gap with European neighbours increases by an hour in winter. The following table is based on the summer time.

LOCATION	TIME
Moscow, St Petersburg, Kaliningrad	noon
Samara	1pm
Yekaterinburg & Tyumen	2pm
Novosibirsk	3pm
Krasnoyarsk & Tuva	4pm
Irkutsk & Ulan-Ude	5pm
Chita	6pm
Vladivostok & Sydney	7pm
Sakhalin region	8pm
Kamchatka	9pm
San Francisco	2am
New York	5am
London	10am
Paris & Berlin	11am
Riga, Kyiv, Helsinki & Minsk	noon

Toilets

➡ Pay toilets are identified by the words платный туалет (platny tualet). In any toilet, Ж (zhensky) stands for women's and M (muzhskoy) stands for men's.

➡ Public toilets are rare and can be dingy and uninviting. Toilets in major hotels, cafs or shopping centres are preferable.

➡ In all public toilets, the babushka you pay your R20 to can also provide miserly rations of toilet paper; it's always a good idea to carry your own.

Tourist Information

Official tourist offices are rare in Russia. Along the main trans-Siberian route, Western-style hostels are good sources of local info.

You're mainly dependent on hotel receptionists and administrators, service bureaus and travel firms for information. The latter two exist primarily to sell accommodation, excursions and transport – if you don't look like you want to book something, staff may or may not answer questions.

Travellers with Disabilities

Travellers with disabilities are not well catered for in Russia. Many footpaths are in poor condition and potentially hazardous and there is a lack of access ramps and lifts for wheelchairs. However, attitudes are enlightened and things are slowly changing. Major museums such as the Hermitage offer good access for those with disabilities. **Liberty** (Map p191; ☑812-232 8163; www.libertytour.ru; ul Polozova 12, Office 1; Ⓜ Petrogradskaya) is a tour agency specialising in wheelchair-accessible tours in St Petersburg.

Before setting off, get in touch with your national support organisation (preferably with the travel officer, if there is one).

TRAIN TIME

Right across Russia, timetables for long-distance trains are written according to Moscow time. The only exceptions are those for suburban services that run on local time – but not always, so double-check. Station clocks in most places are also set to Moscow time. We list how far ahead cities and towns are of Moscow time, eg Moscow +5hr, meaning five hours ahead of Moscow.

Nican (☑1300 655 535; www. nican.com.au)

Mare Nostrum (☑030-4502 6454; www.mare-nostrum.de)

Tourism For All (☑44-1539-726 111, 0845-124 9971; www. tourismforall.org.uk)

Accessible Journeys (☑1-610-521-0339, 1-800-846-4537; www.disabilitytravel.com)

Mobility International USA (☑1-541-343 1284; www. miusa.org)

Visas

If your trip into or out of Russia involves transit through, or a stay in, another country, such as Belarus, China or Kazakhstan, our advice is to arrange any necessary visa or visas in your home country before you enter Russia. For comprehensive information about visas see our Getting Your Visa chapter (p25).

Volunteering

Local enterprises, environmental groups and charities that are trying to improve Russia's environmental and social scorecard are usually on the lookout for volunteers. A good example is the Great Baikal Trail (www. greatbaikaltrail.org) helping to construct a hiking trail around Lake Baikal.

CCUSA (www.ccusa.com/ programs/campcounselors russia.aspx) This US-based organisation runs programs for those wanting to volunteer on Russian youth summer camps.

Go Overseas (www.gooverseas. com/volunteer-abroad/russia) Lists a range of opportunities, from working in hospitals to summer youth camps.

International Cultural Youth Exchange (www.icye.org) Offers a variety of volunteer projects, mostly in Samara.

Language Link Russia (http:// jobs.languagelink.ru) Volunteer to work at language centres across the country.

School of Russian & Asian Studies (http://students.sras. org/volunteer-opportunities-in-russia) US-based SRAS has complied an online list of volunteer opportunities in Russia.

World 4U (☑495-748 1748; www.world4u.ru) Russian volunteer association.

Women Travellers

Russian women are very independent and, in general, you won't attract attention by travelling alone. That said, it's not uncommon for a woman dining or drinking alone to be mistaken for a prostitute. Sexual harassment on the streets is rare, but a woman alone should certainly avoid ad hoc taxis at night – have one called for you from a reputable company.

Stereotyping of gender roles remains strong. Russian men will also typically rush to open doors for you, help you put on your coat and, on a date, act like a 'traditional' gentleman. (In return, they may be expecting you to act like a 'traditional' lady.)

Russian women tend to dress up and wear lots of make-up on nights out. If you wear casual gear, you may feel uncomfortable at a restaurant, a theatre or the ballet; in rural areas, wearing revealing clothing will probably attract unwanted attention.

Work

Bureaucracy makes getting a job or starting a business in Russia a hassle. It is wise to use a professional relocation firm to navigate the country's thicket of rules and regulations surrounding employment of foreigners. Good websites for expats are www. expat.ru and www.redtape. ru/forum.

Transport

GETTING THERE & AWAY

There are many routes into and out of Russia. Flights, cars and tours can be booked online at lonelyplanet.com/bookings.

Entering the Country

Unless you have a transit visa, you can enter the country on a one-way ticket. This means you have a great deal of flexibility once inside Russia to decide on the route you take when you leave.

Air

Airports

Moscow's **Sheremetyevo** (Шереметьево; ☑495-578 6565; www.svo.aero), **Domodedovo** (Домодедово; ☑495-933 6666; www.domodedovo.ru), **Vnukovo** (Внуково; ☑495-937 5555; www.vnukovo.ru) and Zhukovsky (http://zia.aero) airports, and St Peterburg's **Pulkovo International Airport** (LED; ☑812-337 3822; www.pulkovoairport.ru; Pulkovskoye sh) host the bulk of Russia's international flights.

Plenty of other cities have direct international connections, including Arkhangelsk, Irkutsk, Kaliningrad, Kazan, Khabarovsk, Krasnodar, Mineralnye Vody, Murmansk, Nalchik, Nizhny Novgorod, Novosibirsk, Perm, Yekaterinburg and Yuzhno-Sakhalinsk.

Land

Russia borders 14 countries. Popular land approaches include trains and buses from Central and Baltic European countries or on either the trans-Manchurian or trans-Mongolian train routes from China and Mongolia.

Border Crossings

Russia shares borders with Azerbaijan, Belarus, China, Estonia, Finland, Georgia, Kazakhstan, Latvia, Lithuania, Mongolia, North Korea, Norway, Poland and Ukraine. Before planning a journey into or out of Russia from any of these countries, check the visa situation for your nationality.

On trains, border crossings are a straightforward but drawn-out affair, with a steady stream of customs and ticket personnel scrutinising your passport and visa. If you're arriving by car or motorcycle, you'll need to show your vehicle registration and insurance papers, and your driving licence, passport and visa. These formalities are usually minimal for Western European citizens. On the Russian side, most cars are subjected to cursory inspection, with only a small percentage getting a thorough check.

CLIMATE CHANGE & TRAVEL

Every form of transport that relies on carbon-based fuel generates CO_2, the main cause of human-induced climate change. Modern travel is dependent on aeroplanes, which might use less fuel per kilometre per person than most cars but travel much greater distances. The altitude at which aircraft emit gases (including CO_2) and particles also contributes to their climate change impact. Many websites offer 'carbon calculators' that allow people to estimate the carbon emissions generated by their journey and, for those who wish to do so, to offset the impact of the greenhouse gases emitted with contributions to portfolios of climate-friendly initiatives throughout the world. Lonely Planet offsets the carbon footprint of all staff and author travel.

Azerbaijan

The main crossing is between Yarag-Kazmalyar in Dagestan and Samur in Azerbaijan. Take a shared taxi from Derbent to Yarag-Kazmalyar. You have to be in a vehicle to cross to border over the Samur River; *marshrutky* (fixed route minibuses) are the way to go. On the Azeri side take a shared taxi to Baku.

TRAIN

The direct Moscow–Baku train – *platzkart/kupe* (2nd/3rd class) R7080/9920; two days, three hours and 30 minutes; three weekly) – goes via Astrakhan, Makhachkala and Derbent.

Belarus

Russia and Belarus are members of a Customs Union, so there is no border control. That doesn't mean you can legally cross if you don't have both visas. Crossing without a visa is a criminal offence in both countries.

BUS

There are several daily between Minsk and Moscow (12 hours), but be aware of the potential problems with using the Russian–Belarus border.

CAR & MOTORCYCLE

Highway crossings between Russia and Belarus can't be used by the citizens of third countries. Non-Russian and Belarus passport holders travelling from the EU by road should use border crossings with Latvia or Estonia.

TRAIN

There are services to/from Kaliningrad, Moscow, Smolensk and St Petersburg, but be aware of the potential problems with using the Russian–Belarus border.

China

The road from Manzhouli to Zabaikalsk in the Chita Region is open to traffic; it's

RUSSIA–BELARUS BORDER PROBLEM

There are potentially serious implications for those transiting into Russia via Belarus on an international bus or train as you will not receive a Russian border stamp or an immigration form on entering the country. If you plan to exit Russia via a different route, this will be a problem and you could be fined.

We've not heard of any travellers running into serious difficulties but it would still be wise to make careful enquiries with visa authorities in both Belarus and Russia before you've confirmed your travel arrangements.

also possible to cross from Heihe to Blagoveshchensk using a ferry across the Amur River. A bus runs between Manzhouli and Zabaikalsk, but asking Russians for a ride is usually faster.

TRAIN

The classic way into Russia from China is along the trans-Mongolian and trans-Manchurian rail routes.

Vladivostok and Khabarovsk have other options for travelling overland to China.

Estonia

There are three border crossings, of which Narva is nearest to Tallinn. Conveniently for motorists, you can avoid queues by booking a time slot for your crossing from (but not into) Estonia for a small fee at www.estonianborder.eu.

There are daily trains between Tallinn and Moscow (*kupe* R5585, 15 hours, 30 minutes) and St Petersburg (R2855, seven hours and 20 minutes). By bus you can connect to/from Tallinn with St Petersburg (from €15, seven hours, seven daily) and Pskov (R1000, six hours, daily).

Finland

BUS

There are many daily buses between Helsinki and St Petersburg and Helsinki and Petrozavodsk, as well as three buses a week from Rovaniemi to Murmansk.

CAR & MOTORCYCLE

Highways cross at the Finnish border posts of Nuijamaa and Vaalimaa (Brusnichnoe and Torfyanovka, respectively, on the Russian side).

TRAIN

High-speed Allegro trains (from R3830, 3½ hours, four daily) connect St Petersburg and Helsinki. The daily 31/34 Leo Tolstoy service between Moscow and Helsinki (R6035, 14 hours and 20 minutes) also passes through St Petersburg (R4100, seven hours, 30 minutes).

Georgia

The Georgian Military Highway over the Greater Caucasus mountains provides a connection between Vladikavkaz in Russia and Tblisi in Georgia. It's possible to catch buses from Vladikavkaz to Lars where you'll need to arrange a taxi across the border itself to Kazbegi. As long as your papers are in order you should also be able to drive yourself between Russia and Georgia on this route; no border permit is required.

Kazakhstan

Roads into Kazakhstan head east from Astrakhan and south from Samara, Chelyabinsk, Orenburg and Omsk. There are buses (R1000, two daily, 11 hours) between Omsk and Astana, Kazakhstan's capital.

There are direct trains on even days between Moscow and Astana (*platzkartny/*

kupe R10,050/14,050, two days and six hours) in addition to services connecting Samara and Novosibirsk with Almaty.

Latvia
BUS
Rīga is connected by bus to Moscow (from €50, 15 hours, daily), St Petersburg (from €20, 11 hours, four daily), Pskov (€30, six hours, three daily) and Kaliningrad (from €20, eight hours, two daily).

CAR & MOTORCYCLE
The M9 Rīga–Moscow road crosses the border east of Zilupe (Latvia). Be prepared to lose a few hours at the border as checks are slow, especially on the Latvian side. The A212 road from Rīga leads to Pskov, crossing a corner of Estonia en route.

TRAIN
Overnight trains run between Rīga and Moscow (*platzkartny/kupe* R5400/9070, 16 hours, daily) and St Petersburg (*platzkartny/kupe* R3365/5985, 16 hours, daily).

Lithuania
BUS
From Kaliningrad there are services to Klaipėda (R500, four hours, three daily) and Vilnius (R850, six hours, two daily).

CAR & MOTORCYCLE
The border crossing points from Kaliningrad into Lithuania are Chernyshevskoye–Kibartay, Sovetsk–Panemune, Pogranichny–Ramoniškių and Morskoe–Nida.

TRAIN
Services link Vilnius with Kaliningrad (*platzkartny/kupe* R2120/3900, six hours, two to three daily) Moscow (*platzkartny/kupe* R5470/10,170, 14 hours, two daily) and St Petersburg (*platzkartny/kupe*

R5580/10,580, 17 hours, daily). The St Petersburg trains cross Latvia and the Moscow ones cross Belarus, for which you'll need a Belarus visa or transit visa.

Mongolia
BUS
There are direct buses between Ulaanbaatar and Ulan-Ude (R1100, 10 to 12 hours, daily).

CAR & MOTORCYCLE
It's possible to drive between Mongolia and Russia at the Tsagaanuur–Tashanta and Altanbulag–Kyakhta borders. Getting through these borders can be a very slow process; it helps to have written permission from a Mongolian embassy if you wish to bring a vehicle through.

TRAIN
Apart from the trans-Mongolian train connecting Moscow and Beijing, there's a direct train from Ulaanbaatar to Moscow (*kupe* R16,370, four days and two hours, twice weekly) as well as a service to and from Irkutsk (*kupe* R6445, 35 hours, daily).

North Korea
The only crossing of the 17km North Korea–Russia border is via trains going over the Friendship Bridge across the Tumen River. Only Russian and North Korean citizens can use this crossing. That said, back in 2008, a couple of Western tourists did manage to enter North Korea using this route – we do not recommend trying it.

Norway
BUS
There are minibus connections between Murmansk and Kirkenes (R1000, four to six hours, two daily).

CAR & MOTORCYCLE
The border crossing is at Storskog/Borisoglebsk on the Kirkenes–Murmansk road. As this is a sensitive border region, no stopping

is allowed along the Russian side of this road. Also non-Russian registered vehicles are barred from the Nikel–Zapolyarnye section of the M18 highway between 11pm and 7am and any time on Tuesday, Thursday or Saturday. On those days you will be diverted via Prirechniy, a longer drive involving a rough, unpaved section.

Poland
BUS
There are several daily buses between both Gdańsk and Olsztyn and Kaliningrad as well as daily buses to/from Warsaw (R1000, nine hours).

CAR & MOTORCYCLE
The main border crossing to/from Kaliningrad is at Bezledy/Bagrationovsk on the A195 highway. Queues here can be very long.

TRAIN
Warsaw is connected with Moscow (from R8730, 18 hours, daily). The Moscow trains enter Belarus near Brest, so you'll need a Belarus visa or transit visa.

Ukraine
The two countries were essentially at war with each other at the time of writing, but it was still possible to cross in both directions by vehicle or train, with the exception of rebel-held zones in southeastern Ukraine and Crimea. Note that crossing into the rebel-held zones or Crimea from the Russian side is a criminal offence under Ukrainian law. To enter Crimea from Ukraine, you need special permission from the Ukrainian authorities and you must return by the same route.

BUS
Several daily buses run between Moscow and Kyiv (from R1400, 15 to 17 hours) as well as Kharkiv (from R1100, 14 hours) and other major Ukrainian cities.

CAR & MOTORCYCLE

The main auto route between Kyiv and Moscow starts as the E93 (M20) north of Kyiv, but becomes the M3 when it branches off to the east some 50km south of Chernihiv. Kharkiv is connected to Moscow by the M2 road.

TRAIN

Trains from Kyiv to Moscow cross at the Ukrainian border town of Seredyna-Buda. Trains on this route include the following:

Moscow–Kyiv platzkartny/kupe R3735/6570, 12 to 13 hours, 30 minutes, six daily

Moscow–Lviv platzkartny/kupe R4980/8620, 23 hours, 45 minutes, daily via Kyiv

Moscow–Odesa kupe R8660, 23 hours, daily via Kyiv

St Petersburg–Kyiv platzkartny/kupe R4985/9020, 22 hours, 30 minutes, daily

UK & Western Europe

Travelling overland by train from the UK or Western Europe takes a minimum of two days and nights.

There are no direct trains from the UK to Russia. The cheapest route you can take is on the Eurostar (www.eurostar.com) to Brussels, and then via Cologne and Warsaw to Moscow. This journey passes through Minsk (Belarus), which may be problematic. All foreigners visiting Belarus need a visa, including those transiting by train – sort this out before arriving in Belarus. There may also be an issue crossing into Russia as you're unlikely to receive a visa stamp into the country or an immigration card.

To avoid such hassles consider taking the train to St Petersburg from Vilnius in Lithuania, which runs several times a week via Latvia. There are daily connections between Vilnius and Warsaw.

From Moscow and St Petersburg there are also regular direct international services to Berlin, Nice, Paris, Prague and Vienna (note all these services go via Belarus).

For European rail timetables check www.railfaneurope.net, which has links to all of Europe's national railways.

Sea

Passenger ferries routes include the following:

➡ Batumi (Georgia) to Sochi (serviced by hydrofoil; the route is open only for Georgians, Russians and other CIS nationals)

➡ Donghae (Korea) to Vladivostok

➡ Helsinki (Finland) to St Petersburg

➡ Sakaiminato (Japan) to Vladivostok

➡ Stockholm (Sweden) to St Petersburg

➡ Tallinn (Estonia) to St Petersburg

➡ Wakkanai (Japan) to Korsakov on Sakhalin

Tours

Trips to Moscow and St Petersburg are easily organised on your own. But for more complex itineraries, having an agency assist in booking transport and accommodation, securing guides, and helping with the visa paperwork is a good idea. For many outdoor activities, such as hiking or rafting, the services of an expert agency or guide are almost always required. Or you may choose to go the whole hog and have everything taken care of on a fully organised tour.

Agencies and tour companies can provide a range of travel services; most can also help arrange visas and transport tickets within Russia. Numerous, more locally based agencies can provide tours and excursions once you're in Russia. Many work in conjunction with overseas agencies, so if you go to them directly you'll usually pay less.

Australia

Eastern Europe/Russian Travel Centre (☎61-2-9262 1144; www.eetbtravel.com) This company specialises in tours to Russia and Eastern Europe. It has offices in Sydney, Australia, and Christchurch, New Zealand.

Passport Travel (☎61-3-9500 0444; www.travelcentre.com.au) This agency has plenty of experience organising trips to Russia including trans-Siberian itineraries.

Russian Gateway Tours (☎61-495 5109; www.russian-gateway.com.au) Operating since 1976, this company offers tours across the country, including to the disputed Crimean territory.

Sundowners Overland (☎61-3-9672 5386, 1300 133 457; www.sundownersoverland.com) Melbourne-based specialist in trans-Siberian packages and tours with nearly 50 years experience.

Travel Directors (☎61-8-9242 4200, 1300-856 661; www.traveldirectors.com.au) Upmarket trans-Siberian and Russian river cruise tour operator.

China

Monkeyshrine (☎852-2723 1376, 1-970-409 2880; www.monkeyshrine.com) Arranges all kinds of stopovers and homestay programs, and has a lot of experience in booking international trains for independent travellers.

Germany & Netherlands

Gleisnost (☎49-761-205 5130; www.gleisnost.de; Bertoldstraße 44, Freiburg) Knowledgeable agency arranging good-value trips on all trans-Siberian routes.

Lernidee Erlebnisreisen (☎49-30-786 0000; www.lernidee-reisen.de) Berlin-based agency specialising in trans-Siberian tours.

Pulexpress (☎030-887 1470; http://pulexpress.de) This Berlin-based agency is an official agent of the Russian Railways, with online booking and delivery.

Trans-Sputnik Nederland (☎020-797 9800; www. trans-sputnik.nl) Dutch agency specialising in organising tours on all trans-Siberian routes.

Japan

MO Tourist CIS Russian Centre (☎81-3-3432 7239; www. mo-tourist.co.jp) Can help arrange ferries and flights to Russia from Japan.

UK

Go Russia (☎44-20-3355 7717; www.justgorussia.co.uk) Cultural and adventure holiday specialist with trans-Siberian and cruise itineraries as well as other options.

GW Travel Ltd (☎44-161-928 9410; www.goldeneaglelux-urytrains.com) Organises luxury trans-Siberian tours on the *Golden Eagle* with en suite cabins, fine dining and first-class service.

IntoRussia (☎44-20-7603 5045; https://into-russia.co.uk) London-based team offering tours and tailor-made itineraries.

Real Russia (☎44-20-7100 7370; www.realrussia.co.uk) London-based firm specialising in Russian visas and travel.

Regent Holidays (☎44-20-3733 2907; www.regent-holidays. co.uk) Has over 40 years of experience organising travel and tours in Russia and its neighbours.

Russia Experience (☎1-8665 224308, 44-845 521 2910; www.trans-siberian.co.uk) Experienced and reliable operator with adventurous programs across the country.

Russia House (☎44-20-7403 9922; www.therussiahouse. co.uk) Agency experienced in dealing with corporate and business travel needs.

Russian National Tourist Office (☎44-131-661 7893, 44-20-985 1234; www.visitrus-sia.org.uk) Offers tours across Russia. It has offices in London and Edinburgh.

Scott's Tours (☎44-20-7383 5353; www.scottstours.co.uk)

Has experience arranging travel in Russia, China and Central Asia.

Steppes East (☎44-843-634 7901; www.steppestravel.co.uk) Organises generally high-end trips to Russia, Mongolia and China.

USA

Exeter International (☎1-800-633-1008, 1-813-251-5355; www.exeterinternational.com) Specialises in luxury tours to Russia.

Go To Russia Travel (☎1-888-263-0023, 1-404-827-0099; www.gotorussia.com) Offers tours and a full range of travel services. It has offices in Atlanta, San Francisco and Moscow.

Mir Corporation (☎1-206-624-7289, 1-800-424-7289; www. mircorp.com) Award-winning operation offering many different tours.

Ouzel Expeditions (☎1-800-825-8196, 1-907-783-2216; www.ouzel.com) Long-running specialist in fishing trips with destinations including Kamchatka.

Sokol Tours (☎1-724-935-5373; www.sokoltours.com) Tour options include train trips, Tuva and Kamchatka.

VisitRussia (☎812-309-5760, 495-505-6325; www.visitrussia. com) Can arrange package and customised tours; it has offices in Moscow and St Petersburg.

GETTING AROUND

Air

Major Russian airlines, including **Aeroflot** (☎495-223 5555, toll free in Russia 8-800 444 5555; www.aeroflot.com), **Rossiya** (☎8-495 139 7777, 8-800 444 5555; www.rossi-ya-airlines.com), **S7 Airlines** (☎495 783-0707, 8-800 700-0707; www.s7.ru), Ural Airlines (www.uralairlines.com), UTAir (www.utair.ru) and budget carrier Pobeda (www.pobeda. aero), have online booking, with the usual discounts for advance purchases. Otherwise, it's no problem buying a

ticket at ubiquitous *aviakassa* (ticket offices), which may be able to tell you about flights that you can't easily find out about online overseas. Online agencies specialising in Russian air tickets with English interfaces include **Anywayanyday** (☎8-800 775 7753; www.anywayanyday.com), **Pososhok.ru** (☎8-800 333 8118; www.pososhok.ru), One Two Trip! (www.onetwotrip. ru) and TicketsRU (www. tickets.ru).

Whenever you book airline tickets in Russia you'll need to show your passport and visa. Tickets can also be purchased at the airport right up to the departure of the flight and sometimes even if the city centre office says that the plane is full. Return fares are usually double the one-way fares.

It's a good idea to reconfirm your flight at least 24 hours before take-off, and check on the day of departure, too, as flights can be delayed, often for hours and with no or little explanation.

Airlines may bump you if you don't check in at least an hour before departure and can be very strict about charging for checked bags that are overweight, which generally means anything over 20kg. Pobeda is notoriously strict (as well as unpredictable and arbitrary) about baggage allowances and carry-on luggage.

Have your passport and ticket handy throughout the various security and ticket checks that can occur, right up until you find a seat. Some flights have assigned seats, others don't. On the latter, seating is a free-for-all.

Most internal flights in Moscow use either Domodedovo or Vnukovo airports; if you're connecting to Moscow's Sheremetyevo international airport, allow a few hours to cross town (at least three hours if you need to go by taxi, rather than train and metro). Small town airports offer facilities similar to the average bus shelter.

Boat

One of the most pleasant ways of travelling around Russia is by river. You can do this either by taking a cruise, which you can book directly with an operator or through agencies in Russia and overseas, or by using scheduled river passenger services. The season runs from late May through mid-October, but is shorter on some routes.

Moscow, St Petersburg & the Volga

There are numerous cruise boats plying the routes between Moscow and St Petersburg, many stopping at some of the Golden Ring cities on the way. Longer cruises to Northern European Russia and south along the Volga also originate in either of these cities. Some cruises are specifically aimed at foreign tourists.

Boat operators and agencies include the following:

Infoflot (☎7-989-611 4397; www.infoflot.com)

Mosturflot (☎495-221 7222; www.mosturflot.ru)

Orthodox Cruise Company (ОРТОДОКС; ☎499-943 8560; www.cruise.ru)

Rechflot (☎495-981 4555; www.rechflot.ru)

Rechturflot (☎495-646 8700; www.rtflot.ru)

Solnechny Parus (Map p180; ☎812-327 3525; www.solpar.ru; 2nd fl, Ligovsky pr 94A; Ⓜ Ligovsky Prospekt)

Viking Rivers Cruises (☎0800-319 6660; www.vikingriver-cruises.co.uk)

Vodohod (☎495-223 9604; www.bestrussiancruises.com)

Northern European Russia

Northern European Russia (including St Petersburg) is well served by various waterborne transport options. Apart from hydrofoil services along the Neva River and the Gulf of Finland from St Petersburg to Petrodvorets, there are also very popular cruises from St Petersburg to Valaam in Lake Ladoga, some continuing on to Lake Onega, Petrozavodsk and Kizhi. From Rabocheostrovsk you can take boats to the Solovetsky Islands.

Black Sea

Between June and September frequent hydrofoils connect the Black Sea ports of Novorossiysk, Anapa and Sochi.

Siberia & the Russian Far East

Siberia and the Russian Far East have a short navigation season (mid-June to September), with long-distance river transport limited to the Ob and Irtysh Rivers (Omsk–Tara–Tobolsk–Salekhard), the Lena (Ust-Kut–Lensk–Yakutsk) and the Yenisey (Krasnoyarsk–Yeniseysk–Igarka–Dudinka). You can also make one-day hops by hydrofoil along several sections of these rivers, along the Amur River (Komsomolsk–Nikolaevsk) and across Lake Baikal (Irkutsk–Olkhon–Severobaikalsk–Nizhneangarsk). Other Baikal services are limited to short hops around Irkutsk/Listvyanka and from Sakhyurta to Olkhon unless you charter a boat, most conveniently done in Listvyanka, Nizhneangarsk, Severobaikalsk or Ust-Barguzin. Irkutsk agencies can help.

Ferries from Vanino cross the Tatar Strait to Sakhalin,

AIRLINE SAFETY IN RUSSIA

Deadly lapses in Russian airline safety are frighteningly common. Hardly a year passes without a massive civil-aviation disaster. If you're worried about airline safety, the good news is that for many destinations in Russia, getting there by train or bus is practical and often preferable (if you have the time). But in some cases – where you're short of time or where your intended destination doesn't have reliable rail or road connections – you will have no choice but to take a flight.

Industry experts recommend taking the following factors into account when deciding whether an airline is safe to fly with in Russia:

➡ If there's a choice, stick to major airlines that are members of the International Air Transport Association (IATA) – these include Aeroflot, S7 and UTAir.

➡ A Class 1 Russian airport, which hosts more than seven million passengers per year, is much more likely to be safe to fly in and out of than a Class 5 airport, which serves less than 100,000 passengers a year.

➡ Fly with an airline that has regularly scheduled flights, not a charter. The accident rate for charter flights is about three times higher than for regular flights.

➡ Check https://aviation-safety.net or www.airlines-inform.com to see the number of accidents and incidents at an airport and to read traveller reviews.

but it can be murder trying to buy a ticket in the summer months. Although sailings are supposed to take place daily, in reality there is no set schedule. There are also irregular sailings from Korsakov, on Sakhalin, across to Yuzhno-Kurilsk in the Kuril Island chain (you'll need a permit for visiting the Kurils to make this voyage).

Out of Vladivostok there is a range of ferries to nearby islands and to beach resorts further south along the coast. For the truly adventurous with a month or so to spare, it may be possible to hitch a lift on one of the supply ships that sail out of Nakhodka and Vladivostok up to the Arctic Circle towns of Anadyr and Provideniya.

Beware that boat schedules can change radically from year to year (especially on Lake Baikal) and are only published infuriatingly near to the first sailing of each season.

Bus & Marshrutky

Long-distance buses tend to complement rather than compete with the rail network. They generally serve areas with no railway or routes on which trains are slow, infrequent or overloaded.

Most cities have an intercity bus station (автовокзал, *avtovokzal*). Tickets are sold at the station or on the bus. Fares are usually listed on the timetable and posted on a wall. Often you'll get a ticket with a seat assignment, either printed or scribbled on a till receipt. If you have luggage that needs to be stored in the bus baggage compartment, you may have to pay an extra fare, typically around 10% of the bus fare. Some bus stations may also apply a small fee for security measures.

Marshrutky (a Russian diminutive form of *marshrutnoye taksi*, meaning a fixed-route taxi) are minibuses that are often quicker than larger buses and rarely cost much more. Where roads are good and villages frequent, *marshrutky* can be twice as fast as buses and are well worth paying extra for.

Car & Motorcycle

Driving in Russia is not for the faint-hearted, but if you've a sense of humour, patience and a decent vehicle, it's an adventurous way to go. Both road quality and driving culture have improved a great deal in the last decade, so driving has become much more pleasant than before. There are also reliable car-hire companies.

The sheer number of vehicles and constant road improvements make traffic jams a largely unavoidable obstacle in the vicinities of Moscow, St Petersburg and other large cities. Russia's most popular navigation app, Yandex, monitors traffic jams in real time and sends you on the fastest route.

Bringing Your Own Vehicle

You'll need the following if bringing in your own vehicle to Russia:

➡ Your driving licence

➡ Your International Driving Permit (IDP)

➡ The vehicle's registration papers

➡ Third-party insurance valid in Russia (known as a 'green card')

➡ A customs declaration promising that you will take your vehicle with you when you leave

To minimise hassles, make sure you have all your documents translated into Russian. For more details see http://waytorussia.net/transport/international/car.html.

Driving Licence

You must be over 18 years of age to legally drive your own or a rented car or motorcycle in Russia. You'll also need to have a full driving licence and an International Driving Permit with a Russian translation of your licence, or a certified Russian translation of your full licence (you can certify translations at a Russian embassy or consulate).

Fuel

Western-style gas (petrol) stations are common. Petrol comes in four main grades and ranges from R30 to R40 per litre. Unleaded gas is available in major cities. *Dizel* (diesel) is also available for around R35 per litre. In the countryside, gas stations are usually not more than 70km apart, but you shouldn't rely on this.

Rental Cars & Car Sharing

Self-drive cars can be rented in all major Russian cities and some towns, too. Depending on where you're going, consider renting a car with a driver – they will at least know the state of local roads and be able to negotiate with traffic police should you be stopped.

Private cars sometimes operate as cabs over long distances and can be a great deal if there's a group of you to share the cost. Since they take the most direct route between cities, the savings in time can be considerable over slow trains and meandering buses. Typically you will find drivers offering this service outside bus terminals.

You'll need to negotiate a price with the driver. Look over their car and try to assess their sobriety before setting off. Note that you'll always have to pay return mileage if renting 'one way' and that many local drivers want to get home the same night, even if that's at 3am.

In addition, Blablacar.com sharing service is now widely used in Russia, but make sure you choose drivers with the best profile and reviews.

Road Conditions

Russian roads are a mixed bag – sometimes smooth, straight dual carriageways, sometimes pot-holed, narrow, winding and choked with the diesel fumes of slow, heavy vehicles.

Russian drivers use indicators far less than they should and like to overtake everything on the road – on the inside. They rarely switch on anything more than sidelights – and often not even those – until it's pitch black at night. Some say this is to avoid dazzling others, as, for some reason, dipping headlights is not common practice.

If an oncoming driver is flashing his headlights at you, this usually means to watch out for traffic police ahead.

Road Rules

➡ Drive on the right.

➡ Traffic coming from the right generally (but not always) has the right of way.

➡ Speed limits are generally 60km/h in towns and between 80km/h and 110km/h on highways.

➡ There may be a 90km/h zone, enforced by speed traps, as you leave a city.

➡ Children under 12 may not travel in the front seat; the use of seatbelts is mandatory.

➡ Motorcycle riders (and passengers) must wear crash helmets.

➡ The maximum legal blood-alcohol content is 0.03%, a rule that is strictly enforced. Police will first use a breathalyser test to check blood-alcohol levels. You have the legal right to insist on a blood test (which involves the police taking you to a hospital).

➡ Traffic lights that flicker green are about to change to yellow, then red. You will be pulled over if the police see you going through a yellow light, so drive cautiously.

The GIBDD

Russia's traffic police are officially called the GIBDD (ГИБДД standing for Государственная инспекция безопасности дорожного движения; www.gibdd.ru), but still known by their previous acronym: the GAI. The traffic cops are authorised to stop you, issue on-the-spot fines and, worst of all, shoot at your car if you refuse to pull over.

The GIBDD are notorious for hosting speed traps and finding ways to stop cars and collect 'fines' on the spot. Russian drivers often mount dashboard cameras in their cars to record what is going on, in a bid to stop corrupt policemen faking evidence or unfairly prosecuting them – you might want to do likewise! That said, their performance has improved a great deal in recent years, and unpleasant encounters with corrupt officers are less common.

For serious infractions, the GIBDD can confiscate your licence, which you'll have to retrieve from the main station. If your car is taken to a police parking lot, you should try to get it back as soon as possible, since you'll be charged a huge amount for each day that it's kept there.

Get the shield number of the arresting officer. By law, GIBDD officers are not allowed to take any money at all – fines should be paid via Sberbank. However, in reality Russian drivers normally pay the police approximately half the official fine, thus saving money and the time eaten up by Russian bureaucracy at the police station and the bank.

Hitching

Hitching is never entirely safe and we don't recommend it. Travellers who hitch should understand that they are taking a small but potentially serious risk.

That said, hitching in Russia is a common method of getting around, particularly in the countryside and remote areas not well served by public transport.

Rides are hailed by standing at the side of the road and flagging passing vehicles with a low, up-and-down wave (not an extended thumb). You are expected to pitch in for petrol; paying what would be the normal bus fare for a long-haul ride is considered appropriate.

Use common sense to keep safe. Avoid hitching at night. Women should exercise extreme caution. Avoid hitching alone and let someone know where you are planning to go.

Local Transport

Most cities have good public transport systems combining bus, trolleybus and tram; the biggest cities also have metro systems. Public transport is very cheap and easy to use, but you'll need to be able to decipher some Cyrillic. Taxis are plentiful.

Boat

In St Petersburg, Moscow and several other cities located on rivers, coasts, lakes or reservoirs, public ferries and water excursions give a different perspective.

Bus, Marshrutky, Trolleybus & Tram

Services are frequent in city centres but more erratic as you move out toward the edges. They can get jam-packed in the late afternoon or on poorly served routes.

A stop is usually marked by a roadside 'A' sign for buses, 'T' for trolleybuses, and ТРАМВАЙ or a 'T' hanging over the road for trams. The fare (R15 to R30) is usually paid to the conductor; if there is no conductor, pass the money to the driver. You will be charged extra if you have a large bag that takes up space.

Within most cities, *marshrutky* double up on official bus routes but are more frequent. They will also stop between official bus stops, which can save quite a walk.

Metro

The metro systems of Moscow and St Petersburg are excellent. There are smaller ones in Kazan, Nizhny Novgorod, Novosibirsk, Samara and Yekaterinburg.

Taxi

Normal yellow taxis, which could be hailed in the street and used meters, disappeared after the fall of Communism. The taxi situation was a pain until a few years ago, when phone apps, such as Gett and Yandex Taxi, made cabs much more affordable and easy to use. Download the various apps to your phone before or while in Russia.

Elsewhere, taxis are ordered by phone. If you need one, watch out for a taxi that has its phone number written on it. English-speaking operators are rare.

It's less common these days, but it's still possible to flag down a taxi, or just a random driver whose owner needs some extra cash, in the street. Check with locals to determine the average taxi fare in that city at the time of your visit; taxi prices around the country vary widely. Practise saying your destination and the amount you want to pay so that it comes out properly. Generally, the better your Russian, the lower the fare. If possible, let a Russian friend negotiate for you: they'll do better than you will.

To hail a taxi, stand at the side of the road, extend your arm and wait until something stops. When someone stops for you, state your destination and be prepared to negotiate the fare – fix this before getting in. If the driver's game, they will ask you to get in (*sadites*). Consider your safety before doing this.

RISKS & PRECAUTIONS

➡ Avoid taxis lurking outside foreign-run establishments, luxury hotels, railway stations and airports – they often charge far too much.

➡ Know your route: be familiar with how to get there and how long it should take.

➡ Never get into a taxi that has more than one person already in it, especially after dark.

➡ Keep your fare money in a separate pocket to avoid flashing large wads of cash.

➡ If you're staying at a private residence, have the taxi stop at the corner nearest your destination, not the exact address.

➡ Trust your instincts – if a driver looks creepy, take the next car.

Tours

Trips to Moscow and St Petersburg are easily organised on your own. But for more complex itineraries, having an agency assist in booking transport and accommodation, securing guides, and helping with the visa paperwork is a good idea. For many outdoor activities, such as hiking or rafting, the services of an expert agency or guide are almost always required. Or you may choose to go the whole hog and have everything taken care of on a fully organised tour.

Agencies and tour companies can provide a range of travel services; most can also help arrange visas and transport tickets within Russia. Numerous, more locally based agencies can provide tours and excursions once you're in Russia. Many work in conjunction with overseas agencies, so if you go to them directly you'll usually pay less.

Train

Trains run by **Russian Railways** (РЖД, RZD; ☑8-800 775 0000; www.rzd.ru) are generally comfortable and, depending on the class of travel, relatively inexpensive for the distances covered. The network is highly centralised, with Moscow, which has nine large train stations, as the main transfer hub. Given large distances, a vast majority of carriages are equipped with sleeping berths, while only newer and shorter-distance trains have seats.

A handful of high-speed services aside, trains are rarely speedy, but have a remarkable record for punctuality – if you're a minute late for your train, the chances are you'll be left standing on the platform. The fact that RZD managers have a large portion of their pay determined by the timeliness of their trains not only inspires promptness, but also results in the creation of generous schedules. You'll notice this when you find your train stationary for hours in the middle of nowhere only to suddenly start up and roll into the next station right on time.

Buying Tickets

There are a number of options for where to purchase tickets, including online from RZD. Bookings open 60 days before the date of departure. You'd be wise to buy well in advance over the busy summer months and holiday periods such as New Year and early May, when securing berths at short notice on certain trains can be difficult. Cheaper tickets for key trains on the busy Moscow–St Petersburg route can also be difficult to come by; keep your options flexible and you should be able to find something.

Even if you're told a particular service is sold out, it may still be possible to get on the train by speaking with the chief *provodnitsa*. Tell her your destination, offer the face ticket price first and move slowly upwards from there. You can usually come to some sort of agreement.

AT THE STATION

You will be confronted by several ticket windows. Some are special windows reserved exclusively for use by the elderly or infirm, heroes of the Great Patriotic War or members of the armed forces. All will have different operating hours and generally non-English-speaking staff.

The sensible option, especially if there are long queues, is to go to a service centre (сервисный центр), found at most major stations, where helpful staff can book your ticket for a small fee (typically around R200). They sometimes speak English.

Tickets for suburban trains are often sold at separate windows or from an automatic ticket machine (автомат). A table beside the machine tells you which price zone your destination is in.

AT TRAVEL AGENCIES & TICKET BUREAUX

In big cities and towns it's possible to buy tickets at special offices and some travel agencies away from the station.

ONLINE

You can buy tickets online directly from RZD. During the booking process, when asked to fill in 'Document Type' you should pick 'Foreign document' and then enter your passport number. Apart from the website, RZD now has a well-functioning mobile app, which allows you to purchase tickets within seconds. RZD has two types of electronic tickets:

e-tickets – These are coupons detailing your 14-digit order and 14-digit e-ticket numbers. Print them out and exchange for paper tickets at stations in Russia. Some stations have dedicated exchange points and/or self-service terminals; at all others you go to the regular booking windows.

e-registration – Only available for trains where you board at the initial station of the service, these are 'paperless' tickets; you'll still be sent an email confirmation but there's no need to exchange this for a regular ticket. You show the confirmation email and your passport to the *provodnitsa* on boarding the train.

Other online travel sites, such as tutu.ru (www.tutu.ru), also allow you to book tickets and can have the ticket delivered to your home or hotel, or allow you to pick it up at an agency or at the train station.

Long Distances

The regular long-distance service is a *skory poezd* (fast train). It rarely gets up enough speed to really merit the 'fast' label. The best *skory* trains often have names, eg the Rossiya (the Moscow to Vladivostok service). These 'name trains', or *firmeny poezda*, generally have cleaner, more modern cars and more convenient arrival and departure hours; they sometimes also have fewer stops, more 1st-class accommodation and restaurant cars.

The new modern trains that are being gradually introduced on the busiest routes are generally classified as *skorostnoy poezd* (high-speed train), but generally they go under their brand names. Servicing the Moscow–St Petersburg route, Sapsan trains are the Russian equivalent of German ICE or Italian Pendolino. The slower Lastochka and Strizh trains feel more like an average Western European suburban train.

A *passazhirskiy poezd* (passenger train) is an intercity train, found mostly on routes of 1000km or less. Journeys on these can take longer, as the trains clank

---

USEFUL RUSSIAN TERMS FOR BOAT TRAVEL

When buying tickets for a hydrofoil, avoid *ryad* (rows) one to three – spray will obscure your view, and although enclosed, you'll often get damp.

RUSSIAN	TRANSLITERATION	TRANSLATION
речной вокзал	*rechnoy vokzal*	river station
ракета, комета, заря	*raketa, kometa, zarya*	river-going hydrofoil
метеор	*meteor*	sea-going hydrofoil
теплоход	*teplokhod*	large passenger boat
катер	*kater*	smaller river or sea boat
корабль	*korabl*	generic word for large ship
лодка	*lodka*	small rowing boat
паром	*parom*	ferry
вверх	*vverkh*	upstream
вниз	*vniz*	downstream
туда	*tuda*	one way
туда и обратно	*tuda i obratno*	return

from one small town to the next. However, they are inexpensive and often well timed to allow an overnight sleep between neighbouring cities. Avoid trains numbered over 900. These are primarily baggage or postal services and are appallingly slow.

Short Distances

A *prigorodny poezd* (suburban train), commonly nicknamed an *elektrichka*, is a local service linking a city with its suburbs or nearby towns, or groups of adjacent towns – they are often useful for day trips, but can be fearfully crowded. There's no need to book ahead for these – just buy your ticket and go. In bigger stations there may be separate timetables, in addition to *prigorodny zal* (the usual name for ticket halls) and platforms, for these trains.

Timetables

Timetables are posted in stations and are revised twice a year. It's vital to note that the whole Russian rail network runs mostly on Moscow time, so timetables and station clocks from Kaliningrad to Vladivostok will be written in and set to Moscow time. Suburban rail services are the only general exception, which are usually listed in local time; it's best to check this.

Most stations have an information window; expect the attendant to speak only Russian and to give a bare minimum of information. Bigger stations will also have computerised terminals where you can check the timetable.

Online timetables are available on the RZD (http://pass.rzd.ru) website and at www.poezda.net.

Classes

Modern high-speed trains, such as Sapsan, have 1st- and 2nd-class carriages, and business class, which comes between the other two. The difference is in the seat comfort, legroom and on-board entertainment.

In all classes of carriage with sleeping accommodation, if you've not already paid for a pack of bed linen and face towels (called *postel*) in your ticket price, the *provodnik/provodnitsa* (male/female carriage attendant)

READING A TRAIN TIMETABLE

Russian train timetables vary from place to place but generally list a destination; number and category of train; frequency of service; and time of departure and arrival, in Moscow time unless otherwise noted. For services that originate somewhere else, you'll see a starting point and the final destination on the timetable. For example, when catching a train from Yekaterinburg to Irkutsk, the timetable may list Moscow as the origin and Irkutsk as the destination.

Number

Generally, the higher the Номер (*nomer*, number) of a train, the slower it is; anything over 900 is likely to be a mail train. High-speed trains, however, go under the numbers 151 through 198.

Category

➡ Скоростной (*Skorostnoy*, high-speed trains)

➡ Скорый (*Skory*, fast trains)

➡ Пассажирский (*Passazhirsky*, passenger trains)

➡ Почтово – багажный (*Pochtovo-bagazhny*, post-cargo trains)

➡ Пригородный (*Prigorodny*, suburban trains)

There may also be the name of the train, usually in quotation marks, eg 'Россия' ('Rossiya').

Frequency

➡ ежедневно (*yezhednevno*, daily; abbreviated еж)

➡ чётные (*chyotnye*, even-numbered dates; abbreviated ч)

➡ нечётные (*nechyotnye*, odd-numbered dates; abbreviated не)

➡ отменён (*otmenyon*, cancelled; abbreviated отмен)

Days of the week are listed usually as numbers (where 1 is Monday and 7 Sunday) or as abbreviations of the name of the day (Пон, Вт, Ср, Чт, Пт, Суб and Вск are, respectively, Monday to Sunday). Remember that time-zone differences can affect these days. So in Chita (Moscow +6hr) a train timetabled at 23.20 on Tuesday actually leaves at 5.20am on Wednesday. In

will offer it to you for a small charge, typically around R140. In 1st class the bed is usually made up already.

SPALNY VAGON (1ST CLASS)

The very top class – *myagky* (soft class) or *lyuks* – is only available on certain premium long-distance services. It offers a compartment sleeping up to two with an attached toilet and shower. There are between four and six compartments to each carriage.

Next down, and the most common type of 1st class, is SV (short for *spalny vagon*, or sleeping wagon). These compartments are the same size as 2nd class but have only two berths, so there's more room

and more privacy for double the cost. Toilets are shared.

All 1st-class compartments usually have TVs on which it's possible to watch videos or DVDs supplied by the *provodnitsa* for a small fee (there's nothing to stop you from bringing your own, although they'll need to work on a Russian DVD player).

KUPE (2ND CLASS)

The compartments in a *kupeyny* (2nd class, also called 'compartmentalised' carriage) – commonly shortened to *kupe* – are the standard accommodation on all long-distance trains. These carriages are divided into nine enclosed compartments, each with four reasonably comfortable berths, a fold-down table and just

enough room between the bunks to turn around.

In every carriage there's also one half-sized compartment with just two berths. This is usually occupied by the *provodnitsa* or reserved for railway employees; it's where you may end up if you do a deal directly with a *provodnitsa* for a train ticket.

PLATSKARTNY (3RD CLASS)

A reserved-place *platskartny* carriage, sometimes also called *zhyostky* ('hard class') and usually abbreviated to *platskart,* is a dorm carriage sleeping 54. The bunks are uncompartmentalised and are arranged in blocks of four down one side of the corridor and in pairs on the other, with the lower bunk on the latter

months with an odd number of days, two odd days follow one another (eg 31 May, 1 June). This throws out trains working on an alternate-day cycle so if travelling near the end of the month pay special attention to the hard-to-decipher footnotes on a timetable. For example, '27/V – 3/VI Ч' means that from 27 May to 3 June the train runs on even dates. On some trains, frequency depends on the time of year, in which case details are usually given in similar abbreviated small print: eg '27/VI – 31/VIII Ч; 1/IX – 25/VI 2, 5' means that from 27 June to 31 August the train runs on even dates, while from 1 September to 25 June it runs on Tuesday and Friday.

Arrival & Departure Times

Corresponding trains running in opposite directions on the same route may appear on the same line of the timetable. In this case you may find route entries such as время отправления с конечного пункта (*vremya otpravlenia s konechnogo punkta*), or the time of the return train leaves its station of origin. Train times are given in a 24-hour time format, and almost always in Moscow time (Московское время, *Moskovskoye vremya*). But suburban trains are usually marked in local time (местное время, *mestnoe vremya*). From here on it gets tricky (as though the rest wasn't), so don't confuse the following:

➡ время отправления (*vremya otpravleniya*) Time of departure

➡ время отправления с начального пункта(*vremya otpravleniya s nachalnogo punkta*) Time of departure from the train's starting point

➡ время прибытия (*vremya pribytiya*) Time of arrival at the station you're in

➡ время прибытия на конечный пункт (*vremya pribytiya v konechny punkt*) Time of arrival at the destination

➡ время в пути (*vremya v puti*) Duration of the journey

Distance

You may sometimes see the расстояние (*rasstoyaniye*) – distance in kilometres from the point of departure – on the timetable as well. These are rarely accurate and usually refer to the kilometre distance used to calculate the fare.

HOW TO BUY & READ YOUR TICKET

When buying a ticket in Russia, it's a good idea to arrive at the station or travel agency prepared. If you don't speak Russian, have someone who does write down the following information for you in Cyrillic:

⇒ How many tickets you require.

⇒ Your destination.

⇒ What class of ticket.

⇒ The preferred date of travel and time of day for departure.

Departure time
Always in Moscow time

Train number
The lower the number, the higher the standard and the price; the best trains are under 100. Odd-numbered trains head towards Moscow; even ones head east, away from the capital.

Train type

Carriage number and class
Л = two-bed SV
М = four-bed SV
К = kupe
П = platskartny
О = obshchiy

Departure date
Day and month

From/to

Bed number
If this is blank, the provodnitsa will allocate a bed on boarding

Passport number
With two-digit prefix for passport type and name of passenger

Total cost of ticket

Service charges
eg с бельём
(with bed linen)

РЖД 20
АСУ «ЭКСПРЕСС»
ПРО
ДО

ПОЕЗД   ОТПРАВЛЕНИЕ   ВАГОН

№ шифр | число | месяц | часы | мин. | № пип | Билет

109 МА   26 05 06 44   06 П   000942
ЕКАТЕРИНБ П-ПЕРМЬ 2 (2030000-2030
МЕСТА 050 % ФПК МОСКОВСКИЙ
ХК408063 1Т2 71 0903758 240511 17
000Р000878/ХЕЙВУД=ЭНТОНИ=ДЖЕЙМС
Н-668 . 2 РУБ В Т Ч.СТР.2 3. Р
СЕРВИС 92 2 В Т Ч НДС 14.06 РУБ
ВРЕМЯ ОТПР И ПРИБ МОСКОВСКОЕ

* 2 0 1 0 5 2 6 4 0 8 0 6 3 6 *

Also bring your passport; you'll be asked for it so that its number and your name can be printed on your ticket. The ticket and passport will be matched up by the provodnitsa (female carriage attendant) before you're allowed on the train – make sure the ticket-seller gets these details correct.

Tickets are printed by computer and come with a duplicate. Shortly after you've boarded the train the provodnitsa will come around and collect the tickets: sometimes they will take both copies and give you one back just before your final destination; often they will leave you with the copy. It will have been ripped slightly to show it's been used. Hang on to this ticket, especially if you're hopping on and off trains, since it provides evidence of how long you've been in a particular place and may prove useful if you're stopped by police.

Sometimes tickets are also sold with separate chits for insurance in the event of a fatal accident, or for bed linen and meals, but usually these prices appear on the ticket itself.

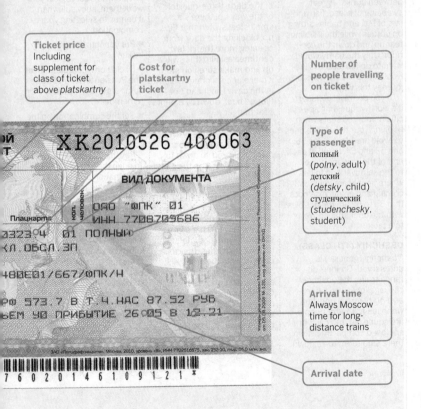

Ticket price
Including supplement for class of ticket above *platskartny*

Cost for platskartny ticket

Number of people travelling on ticket

Type of passenger
полный (*polny*, adult)
детский (*detsky*, child)
студенческий (*studenchesky*, student)

Arrival time
Always Moscow time for long-distance trains

Arrival date

side converting to a table and chairs during the day.

Despite the lack of privacy, *platskart* can be a favourite way to go. In summer, the lack of compartment walls means they don't become as stuffy as a *kupe*. Many travellers (women in particular) find *platskart* a better option than being cooped up with three (possibly drunken) Russian men. They are wonderful for meeting and getting to know ordinary Russians. *Platskart* tickets cost half to two-thirds the price of a 2nd-class berth.

On multiday journeys, however, some *platskart* carriages can begin to get messy, with clothing strung between bunks, a great swapping of bread, fish and jars of tea, and babies sitting on potties while their siblings tear up and down the corridor. Only the hardy would want to do Moscow to Vladivostok or a similar nonstop journey this way.

If you do travel *platskart*, it's worth requesting specific numbered seats when booking your ticket. The ones to avoid are 1 to 4, 33 to 38, and 53 and 54, found at each end of the carriage close to the samovar and toilets, where people are constantly coming and going. Also note that 39 to 52 are the doubles with the bunk that converts to a table.

OBSHCHIY (4TH CLASS)

Obshchiy (general) is unreserved. On long-distance trains the *obshchiy* carriage looks the same as a *platskartny* one, but when it's full, eight people are squeezed into each unenclosed compartment, so there's no room to lie down.

Suburban trains normally have only *obshchiy* class, which in this case means bench-type seating. On a few daytime-only intercity trains there are higher grade *obshchiy* carriages with more comfortable, reserved chairs.

Dangers & Annoyances

Make certain on all sleeper trains that your baggage is safely stowed, preferably in the steel bins beneath the lower bunks. In 1st- and 2nd-class compartments you can lock the door, but remember that it can be unlocked with a rather simple key; on the left side of the door, three-quarters of the way up, there's a small steel switch that flips up, blocking the door from opening more than a few centimetres. Flip this switch up and make sure you stuff a piece of cork or equivalent in the cavity so it can't be flipped back down by a bent coat hanger.

At station halts it's also a good idea to ask the *provodnitsa* to lock your compartment while you go down to stretch your legs on the platform. In cheaper *platskartny* carriages your unguarded possessions are often safer as there are more people around to keep watch.

Generally Russians love speaking with foreigners; on long train rides, they love drinking with them as well. Avoiding this is not always as easy as it would seem. Choose your drinking partners very carefully on trains and only drink from new bottles when you can watch the seal being broken.

Left Luggage

Many train stations have a left-luggage room (камера хранения, *kamera khranenia*) or left-luggage lockers (автоматические камеры хранения, *avtomaticheskiye kamery khranenia*). These are generally secure, but make sure you note down the room's opening and closing hours and, if in doubt, establish how long you can leave your stuff. Typical costs are around R200 per bag per day (according to size) or R200 per locker.

Here is how to work the left-luggage lockers (they're generally the same everywhere). Be suspicious of people who offer to help you work them, above all when it comes to selecting your combination.

➡ Put your stuff in an empty locker.

➡ Decide on a combination of one Russian letter and three numbers and write it down or remember it.

➡ Set the combination on the inside of the locker door.

➡ Close the locker.

➡ Pay the attendant the fee. To open the locker, set your combination on the outside of your locker door. Note that even though it seems as if the knobs on the outside of the door should correspond directly with those on the inside, the letter is always the left-most knob, followed by three numbers, on both the inside and the outside. After you've set your combination, wait a second or two for the electrical humming sound and then pull open the locker.

Language

Russian belongs to the Slavonic language family and is closely related to Belarusian and Ukrainian. It has more than 150 million speakers within the Russian Federation and is used as a second language in the former republics of the USSR, with a total number of speakers of more than 270 million people.

Russian is written in the Cyrillic alphabet (see the next page), and it's well worth the effort familiarising yourself with it so that you can read maps, timetables, menus and street signs. Otherwise, just read the coloured pronunciation guides given next to each Russian phrase in this chapter as if they were English, and you'll be understood. Most sounds are the same as in English, and the few differences in pronunciation are explained in the alphabet table. The stressed syllables are indicated with italics.

BASICS

Hello.	Здравствуйте.	zdrast·vuy·tye
Goodbye.	До свидания.	da svi·da·nya
Excuse me.	Простите.	pras·ti·tye
Sorry.	Извините.	iz·vi·ni·tye
Please.	Пожалуйста.	pa·zhal·sta
Thank you.	Спасибо.	spa·si·ba
You're welcome.	Пожалуйста.	pa·zhal·sta
Yes.	Да.	da
No.	Нет.	nyet

WANT MORE?

For in-depth language information and handy phrases, check out Lonely Planet's *Russian Phrasebook*. You'll find it at **shop.lonelyplanet.com**, or you can buy Lonely Planet's iPhone phrasebooks at the Apple App Store.

How are you?

| Как дела? | kak di·*la* |

Fine, thank you. And you?

| Хорошо, спасибо. | kha·ra·*sho* spa·*si*·ba |
| А у вас? | a u vas |

What's your name?

| Как вас зовут? | kak vas za·*vut* |

My name is ...

| Меня зовут ... | mi·*nya za*·vut ... |

Do you speak English?

| Вы говорите | vi ga·va·*ri*·tye |
| по-английски? | pa·an·*gli*·ski |

I don't understand.

| Я не понимаю. | ya nye pa·ni·*ma*·yu |

ACCOMMODATION

Where's a ...?	Где ...?	gdye ...
boarding house	пансионат	pan·si·a·*nat*
campsite	кемпинг	*kyem*·ping
hotel	отель	o·*tel*
youth hostel	хостел	*ho*·stel

Do you have a ... room?	У вас есть ...?	u vas yest' ...
single	одноместный номер	ad·na·*myest*·nih *no*·mir
double (one bed)		*no*·mir z
	двуспальной кроватью	dvu·*spal*'·noy kra·*va*·tyu
How much is it for ...?	Сколько стоит за ...?	*skol*'·ka *sto*·it za ...
a night	ночь	noch'
two people	двоих	dva·*ikh*

The ... isn't working.	... не работает.	... ne ra·*bo*·ta·yit
heating	Отопление	a·ta·*plye*·ni·ye
hot water	Горячая вода	ga·*rya*·cha·ya va·*da*
light	Свет	svyet

CYRILLIC ALPHABET

Cyrillic		Sound
А, а	a	as in 'father' (in a stressed syllable);
		as in 'ago' (in an unstressed syllable)
Б, б	b	as in 'but'
В, в	v	as in 'van'
Г, г	g	as in 'god'
Д, д	d	as in 'dog'
Е, е	ye	as in 'yet' (in a stressed syllable and at the end of a word);
	i	as in 'tin' (in an unstressed syllable)
Ё, ё	yo	as in 'yore' (often printed without dots)
Ж, ж	zh	as the 's' in 'measure'
З, з	z	as in 'zoo'
И, и	i	as the 'ee' in 'meet'
Й, й	y	as in 'boy' (not transliterated after ы or и)
К, к	k	as in 'kind'
Л, л	l	as in 'lamp'
М, м	m	as in 'mad'
Н, н	n	as in 'not'
О, о	o	as in 'more' (in a stressed syllable);
	a	as in 'hard' (in an unstressed syllable)
П, п	p	as in 'pig'
Р, р	r	as in 'rub' (rolled)
С, с	s	as in 'sing'
Т, т	t	as in 'ten'
У, у	u	as the 'oo' in 'fool'
Ф, ф	f	as in 'fan'
Х, х	kh	as the 'ch' in 'Bach'
Ц, ц	ts	as in 'bits'
Ч, ч	ch	as in 'chin'
Ш, ш	sh	as in 'shop'
Щ, щ	shch	as 'sh-ch' in 'fresh chips'
Ъ, ъ	–	'hard sign' meaning the preceding consonant is pronounced as it's written
Ы, ы	ih	as the 'y' in 'any'
Ь, ь	'	'soft sign' meaning the preceding consonant is pronounced like a faint y
Э, э	e	as in 'end'
Ю, ю	yu	as the 'u' in 'use'
Я, я	ya	as in 'yard' (in a stressed syllable);
	ye	as in 'yearn' (in an unstressed syllable)

DIRECTIONS

Where is ...?		
Где ...?		gdye ...

What's the address?

Какой адрес?		ka·*koy a*·dris

Could you write it down, please?

Запишите, пожалуйста.		za·pi·*shih*·tye pa·*zhal*·sta

Can you show me (on the map)?

Покажите мне, пожалуйста (на карте).		pa·ka·*zhih*·tye mnye pa·*zhal*·sta (na *kar*·tye)

Turn ...	Поверните ...	pa·vir·*ni*·tye ...
at the corner	за угол	za *u*·gal
at the traffic lights	на светофоре	na svi·ta·*fo*·rye
left	налево	na·*lye*·va
right	направо	na·*pra*·va

behind ...	за ...	za ...
far	далеко	da·li·*ko*
in front of ...	перед ...	*pye*·rit ...
near	близко	*blis*·ka
next to ...	рядом с ...	*rya*·dam s ...
opposite ...	напротив ...	na·*pro*·tif ...
straight ahead	прямо	*prya*·ma

EATING & DRINKING

I'd like to reserve a table for ...	Я бы хотел/ хотела заказать столик на ... (m/f)	ya bih khat·*yel*/ khat·*ye*·la za·ka·*zat' sto*·lik na ...
two people	двоих	dva·*ikh*
eight o'clock	восемь часов	*vo*·sim' chi·*sof*

What would you recommend?

Что вы рекомендуете?		shto vih ri·ka·min·*du*·it·ye

What's in that dish?

Что входит в это блюдо?		shto fkho·dit v e·ta *blyu*·da

That was delicious!

Было очень вкусно!		bih·la o·chin' *fkus*·na

Please bring the bill.

Принесите, пожалуйста счёт.		pri·ni·*sit*·ye pa·*zhal*·sta shot

I don't eat ...	Я не ем ...	ya nye yem ...
eggs	яйца	*yay*·tsa
fish	рыбу	*rih*·bu
poultry	птицу	*ptit*·su
red meat	мясо	*mya*·so

Key Words

bottle	бутылка	bu·*tihl*·ka
bowl	миска	*mis*·ka
breakfast	завтрак	*zaf*·trak
cold	холодный	kha·*lod*·nih
dinner	ужин	*u*·zhihn
dish	блюдо	*blyu*·da
fork	вилка	*vil*·ka
glass	стакан	sta·*kan*
hot (warm)	горячий	go·*rya*·chiy
knife	нож	nosh
lunch	обед	ab·*yet*
menu	меню	min·*yu*
plate	тарелка	tar·*yel*·ka
restaurant	ресторан	ris·ta·*ran*
spoon	ложка	*losh*·ka
with/without	с/без	s/byez

Meat & Fish

beef	говядина	gav·*ya*·di·na
caviar	икра	i·*kra*
chicken	курица	*ku*·rit·sa
duck	утка	*ut*·ka
fish	рыба	*rih*·ba
herring	сельдь	syelt'
lamb	баранина	ba·*ra*·ni·na
meat	мясо	*mya*·sa
oyster	устрица	*ust*·rit·sa
pork	свинина	svi·*ni*·na
prawn	креветка	kriv·*yet*·ka
salmon	лосось	la·*sauce*
turkey	индейка	ind·*yey*·ka
veal	телятина	til·*ya*·ti·na

Fruit & Vegetables

apple	яблоко	*yab*·la·ka
bean	фасоль	fa·*sol'*
cabbage	капуста	ka·*pu*·sta
capsicum	перец	*pye*·rits
carrot	морковь	mar·*kof'*
cauliflower	цветная капуста	tsvit·*na*·ya ka·*pu*·sta
cucumber	огурец	a·gur·*yets*
fruit	фрукты	*fruk*·tih
mushroom	гриб	grip
nut	орех	ar·*yekh*

onion	лук	luk
orange	апельсин	a·pil'·*sin*
peach	персик	*pyer*·sik
pear	груша	*gru*·sha
plum	слива	*sli*·va
potato	картошка	kar·*tosh*·ka
spinach	шпинат	shpi·*nat*
tomato	помидор	pa·mi·*dor*
vegetable	овощ	*o*·vash

Other

bread	хлеб	khlyep
cheese	сыр	sihr
egg	яйцо	yeyt·*so*
honey	мёд	myot
oil	масло	*mas*·la
pasta	паста	*pa*·sta
pepper	перец	*pye*·rits
rice	рис	ris
salt	соль	sol'
sugar	сахар	*sa*·khar
vinegar	уксус	*uk*·sus

Drinks

beer	пиво	*pi*·va
coffee	кофе	*kof*·ye
(orange) juice	(апельсиновый) сок	(a·pil'·*si*·na·vih) sok
milk	молоко	ma·la·*ko*
tea	чай	chey
(mineral) water	(минеральная) вода	(mi·ni·*ral'*·na·ya) va·*da*
wine	вино	vi·*no*

EMERGENCIES

Help! Помогите! pa·ma·*gi*·tye

Call ...! Вызовите ...! *vih*·za·vi·tye ...
  a doctor врача vra·*cha*
  the police полицию po·*li*·tsih·yu

Leave me alone!
проваливай! pro·*va*·li·vai

There's been an accident.
Произошёл pra·i·za·*shol*
несчастный случай. ne·*shas*·nih *slu*·chai

I'm lost.
Я заблудился/ ya za·blu·*dil*·sa/
заблудилась. (m/f) za·blu·*di*·las'

Where are the toilets?
Где здесь туалет? gdye zdyes' tu·al·*yet*

I'm ill.
Я болен/больна. (m/f) ya *bo*·lin/bal'·*na*

It hurts here.
Здесь болит. zdyes' ba·*lit*

I'm allergic to (antibiotics).
У меня алергия u min·*ya* a·lir·*gi*·ya
на (антибиотики). na (an·ti·bi·*o*·ti·ki)

SHOPPING & SERVICES

I need ...
Мне нужно ... mnye *nuzh*·na ...

I'm just looking.
Я просто смотрю. ya *pros*·ta smat·*ryu*

Can you show me?
Покажите, pa·ka·*zhih*·tye
пожалуйста? pa·*zhal*·sta

How much is it?
Сколько стоит? *skol'*·ka *sto*·it

That's too expensive.
Это очень дорого. e·ta o·chen'·*do*·ra·ga

There's a mistake in the bill.
Меня обсчитали. min·*ya* ap·shi·*ta*·li

bank	банк	bank
market	рынок	*rih*·nak
post office	почта	*poch*·ta
telephone office	телефонный пункт	ti·li·*fo*·nih punkt

Question Words		
What?	Что?	shto
When?	Когда?	kag·*da*
Where?	Где?	gdye
Which?	Какой?	ka·*koy*
Who?	Кто?	kto
Why?	Почему?	pa·chi·*mu*

TIME, DATES & NUMBERS

What time is it?
Который час? ka·*to*·rih chas

It's (10) o'clock.
(Десять) часов. (*dye*·sit') chi·*sof*

morning	утро	*ut*·ra
day	день	den
evening	вечер	*vye*·chir
yesterday	вчера	vchi·*ra*
today	сегодня	si·*vod*·nya
tomorrow	завтра	*zaft*·ra
Monday	понедельник	pa·ni·*dyel'*·nik
Tuesday	вторник	*ftor*·nik
Wednesday	среда	sri·*da*
Thursday	четверг	chit·*vyerk*
Friday	пятница	*pyat*·ni·tsa
Saturday	суббота	su·*bo*·ta
Sunday	воскресенье	vas·kri·*syen*·ye
January	январь	yan·*var'*
February	февраль	fiv·*ral'*
March	март	mart
April	апрель	ap·*ryel'*
May	май	mai
June	июнь	i·*yun'*
July	июль	i·*yul'*
August	август	*av*·gust
September	сентябрь	sin·*tyabr'*
October	октябрь	ak·*tyabr'*
November	ноябрь	na·*yabr'*
December	декабрь	di·*kabr'*
1	один	a·*din*
2	два	dva
3	три	tri
4	четыре	chi·*tih*·ri
5	пять	pyat'
6	шесть	shest'
7	семь	syem'
8	восемь	*vo*·sim'
9	девять	*dye*·vyat'
10	десять	*dye*·syat'
20	двадцать	*dva*·tsat'
30	тридцать	*tri*·tsat'
40	сорок	*so*·rak
50	пятьдесят	pi·dis·*yat*
60	шестдесят	shihs·dis·*yat*
70	семьдесят	*syem'*·dis·yat

80	восемьдесят	vo·sim'·di·sit
90	девяносто	di·vi·no·sta
100	сто	sto
1000	тысяча	tih·si·cha

TRANSPORT

Public Transport

A ... ticket (to Novgorod).	Билет ... (до Новгорода).	bil·yet ... (do nov·ga·rat·a)
one-way	в один конец	v a·din kan·yets
return	туда-обратно	tu·da ob·rat·no
bus	автобус	af·to·bus
train	поезд	po·ist
tram	трамвай	tram·vai
trolleybus	троллейбус	tra·lyey·bus
first	первый	pyer·vih
last	последний	pas·lyed·ni
platform	платформа	plat·for·ma
(bus) stop	остановка	a·sta·nof·ka
ticket	билет	bil·yet
Podorozhnik (SPB travel pass)	Подорожник	Pa·da·rozh·nik
ticket office	билетная касса	bil·yet·na·ya ka·sa
timetable	расписание	ras·pi·sa·ni·ye

When does it leave?
Когда отправляется? kag·da at·prav·lya·it·sa

How long does it take to get to ...?
Сколько времени нужно ехать до ...? skol'·ka vrye·mi·ni nuzh·na ye·khat' da ...

Does it stop at ...?
Поезд останавливается в ...? po·yist a·sta·nav·li·va·yit·sa v ...

Please stop here.
Остановитесь здесь, пожалуйста. a·sta·na·vit·yes' zdyes' pa·zhal·sta

Driving & Cycling

I'd like to hire a ...	Я бы хотел/ хотела взять ... напрокат. (m/f)	ya bih kha·tyel/ kha·tye·la vzyat' ... na pra·kat
4WD	машину с полным приводом	ma·shih·nu s pol·nihm pri·vo·dam
bicycle	велосипед	vi·la·si·pyet
car	машину	ma·shih·nu

To get by in Russian, mix and match these simple patterns with words of your choice:

When's (the next bus)?
Когда (будет следующий автобус)? kag·da (bu·dit slye·du·yu·shi af·to·bus)

Where's (the station)?
Где (станция)? gdye (stant·sih·ya)

Where can I (buy a padlock)?
Где можно (купить нависной замок)? gdye mozh·na (ku·pit' na·vis·noy za·mok)

Do you have (a map)?
Здесь есть (карте)? zdyes' yest' (kart·ye)

I'd like (the menu).
Я бы хотел/ хотела (меню). (m/f) ya bih khat·yel/ khat·ye·la (min·yu)

I'd like (to hire a car).
Я бы хотел/ хотела (взять машину). (m/f) ya bih khat·yel/ khat·ye·la (vzyat' ma·shih·nu)

Can I (come in)?
Можно (войти)? mozh·na (vey·ti)

Could you please (write it down)?
(Запишите), пожалуйста. (za·pi·shiht·ye) pa·zhal·sta

Do I need (a visa)?
Нужна ли (виза)? nuzh·na li (vi·za)

I need (assistance).
Мне нужна (помощь). mnye nuzh·na (po·mash)

motorbike	мотоцикл	ma·ta·tsikl
diesel	дизельное топливо	di·zil'·na·ye to·pli·va
regular	бензин номер 93	ben·zin no·mir di·vi·no·sta tri
unleaded	очищенный бензин	a·chi·shi·nih bin·zin

Is this the road to ...?
Эта дорога ведёт в ...? e·ta da·ro·ga vid·yot f ...

Where's a petrol station?
Где заправка? gdye za·praf·ka

Can I park here?
Здесь можно стоять? zdyes' mozh·na sta·yat'

I need a mechanic.
Мне нужен автомеханик. mnye nu·zhihn af·ta·mi·kha·nik

The car has broken down.
Машина сломалась. ma·shih·na sla·ma·las'

I have a flat tyre.
У меня лопнула шина. u min·ya lop·nu·la shih·na

I've run out of petrol.
У меня кончился бензин. u min·ya kon·chil·sa bin·zin

GLOSSARY

You may encounter some of the following terms and abbreviations during your travels in Russia.

aeroport – airport
ail – hexagonal or tepee-shaped yurt
apteka – pharmacy
arzhaan – Tuvan sacred spring
ataman – Cossack leader
aviakassa – air ticket office
avtobus – bus
avtostantsiya – bus stop
avtovokzal – bus terminal
AYaM – Amuro-Yakutskaya Magistral or Amur-Yakutsk Mainline

babushka – literally, 'grandmother', but used generally in Russian society for all old women
BAM – Baikalo-Amurskaya Magistral or Baikal-Amur Mainline, a trans-Siberian rail route
bankomat – automated teller machine (ATM)
banya – bathhouse
bashnya – tower
biblioteka – library
bifshteks – Russian-style hamburger
bilet – ticket
bolnitsa – hospital
bolshoy – big
boyar – high-ranking noble
bufet – snack bar selling cheap cold meats, boiled eggs, salads, bread, pastries etc
bukhta – bay
bulvar – boulevard
buterbrod – open sandwich
byliny – epic songs

chebureki – fried, meat-filled turnovers
chum – tepee-shaped tent made of birch bark
CIS (Commonwealth of Independent States) – an alliance (proclaimed in 1991) of independent states comprising the former USSR republics (less the three Baltic states); Sodruzhestvo Nezavisimykh Gosudarstv (SNG)

dacha – country cottage, summer house
datsan – Buddhist monastery
detsky – child's, children's
dezhurnaya – woman looking after a particular floor of a hotel
dolina – valley
dom – house
duma – parliament
dvorets – palace
dvorets kultury – literally, 'culture palace'; a meeting, social, entertainment, education centre, usually for a group such as railway workers, children etc

elektrichka – suburban train
etazh – floor (storey)

finift – luminous enamelled metal miniatures
firmeny poezda – trains with names (eg Rossiya); these are generally nicer trains
FSB (Federalnaya Sluzhba Bezopasnosti) – the Federal Security Service, the successor to the *KGB*

garderob – cloakroom
gastronom – speciality food shop
gavan – harbour
gazeta – newspaper
GIBDD (Gosudarsvennaya Inspektsiya po bezopasnosti dorozhnogo dvizheniya) – the State Automobile Inspectorate, aka the traffic police, still commonly known by their previous acronym GAI
glasnost – literally, 'openness'; the free-expression aspect of the Gorbachev reforms
glavpochtamt – main post office
gora – mountain
gorod – city, town
gostinitsa – hotel
gostiny dvor – trading arcade
Gulag (Glavnoe Upravlenie Lagerey) – Main Administration for Camps; the Soviet network of concentration camps

GUM (Gosudarstvenny Univermag) – State Department Store

igil – bowed, two-stringed Tuvan instrument
Intourist – old Soviet State Committee for Tourism, now privatised, split up and in competition with hundreds of other travel agencies
istochnik – mineral spring
izba – traditional, single-storey wooden cottage

kafe – café
kameny baba – standing stone idol
kamera khranenia – left-luggage office
kanal – canal
karta – map
kartofel, kartoshka – potatoes
kassa – ticket office, cashier's desk
kater – small ferry
kazak – Cossack
kempingi – organised camp sites; often have small cabins as well as tent sites
KGB (Komitet Gosudarstvennoy Bezopasnosti) – Committee of State Security
khachapuri – Georgian cheese bread
khleb – bread
khokhloma – red, black and gold lacquered pine bowls
khöömei – Tuvan throat singing
khram – church
khuresh – Tuvan style of wrestling
kino – cinema
kleshchi – ticks
kniga – book
kokoshniki – colourful gables and tiles laid in patterns
kolkhoz – collective farm
komnaty otdykha – resting rooms found at all major train stations and several smaller ones
kompot – fruit squash
Komsomol – Communist Youth League

kopek – the smallest, worthless unit of Russian currency

kordony – forest lodges, often found in national parks

korpus – building (ie one of several in a complex)

kray – territory

kremlin – a town's fortified stronghold

kulak – a peasant wealthy enough to own a farm, hire labour and engage in money lending

kupeyny, kupe – 2nd-class compartment on a train

kurgan – burial mound

kurort – spa

kvartira – flat, apartment

kvas – fermented rye bread water

lavra – senior monastery

lyux – a kind of hotel suite, with a sitting room in addition to bedroom and bathroom; a *polu-lyux* suite is the less spacious version

Mafia – anyone who has anything to do with crime, from genuine gangsters to victims of their protection rackets

magazin – shop

maly – small

manezh – riding school

marka – postage stamp or brand, trademark

marshrutka, marshrutnoye taksi – minibus that runs along a fixed route

matryoshka – set of painted wooden dolls within dolls

medovukha – honey ale (mead)

mestnoe vremya – local time

mezhdunarodny – international

mineralnaya voda – mineral water

monastyr – monastery

more – sea

morskoy vokzal – sea terminal

Moskovskoye vremya – Moscow time

most – bridge

muzey – museum; also some palaces, art galleries and non-working churches

muzhskoy – men's (toilet)

myagky – 1st-class train compartment

naberezhnaya – embankment

Nashi – Ours; ultranationalist youth group

nizhny – lower

nomenklatura – literally, 'list of nominees'; the old government and Communist Party elite

novy – new

novy russky – New Russians

obed – lunch

oblast – region

obshchiy – 4th-class place on a train

okruga – districts

omul – a cousin of salmon and trout, endemic to Lake Baikal

ostrog – fortress

ostrov – island

OVIR (Otdel Viz i Registratsii) – Department of Visas and Registration; now known under the acronym *PVU*, although outside Moscow OVIR is still likely to be in use

ozero – lake

palekh – enamelled wood boxes

parnyatnik – statue, monument

Paskha – Easter

passazhirsky poezd – inter-city stopping train

pelmeni – Russian-style ravioli stuffed with meat

perekhod – underground walkway

perestroika – literally, 're-structuring'; Mikhail Gorbachev's efforts to revive the Soviet economy

pereulok – lane, side street

pirozhki – savoury pies

platskartny, platskart – 3rd-class place on a train

ploshchad – square

pochta – post office

poezd – train

poliklinika – medical centre

polu-lyux – less spacious version of a *lyux*, a hotel suite

with a sitting room in addition to the bedroom and bathroom

polyana – glade, clearing

posolstvo – embassy

prichal – landing, pier

prigorodny poezd – suburban train

prigorodny zal – ticket hall

produkty – food store

proezd – passage

prokat – rental

propusk – permit, pass

prospekt – avenue

provodnik (m), provodnitsa (f) – carriage attendant on a train

PVU (Passportno-Vizovoye Upravleniye) – passport and visa department, formerly OVIR (an acronym which is still likely to be in use outside Moscow)

raketa – hydrofoil

rayon – district

rechnoy vokzal – river station

reka – river

remont, na remont – closed for repairs (a sign you see all too often)

restoran – restaurant

Rozhdestvo – Russian Orthodox Christmas

rynok – market

sad – garden

samovar – an urn used to heat water for tea

selo – village

sever – north

shawarma – grilled meat and salad wrapped in flat bread

shashlyk – meat kebab

shosse – highway

shtuka – piece (many items of produce are sold by the piece)

skory poezd – literally, 'fast train'; a long-distance train

sobor – cathedral

soviet – council

sovok – a contraction of *sovokopniy*, meaning communal person and referring to those who were born and lived during the Soviet period

spalny vagon – SV; 1st-class place on a train

spusk – descent, slope

Sputnik – former youth-travel arm of *Komsomol*; now just one of the bigger tourism agencies

stanitsa – Cossack village

stary – old

stolovaya – canteen, cafeteria

suvenir – souvenir

taiga – northern pine, fir, spruce and larch forest

taksofon – pay telephone

teatr – theatre

teatralnaya kassa – theatre ticket office

thangka – Buddhist religious paintings

traktir – tavern

tramvay – tram

tserkov – church

TsUM (Tsentralny Univermag) – name of a department store

tualet – toilet

tuda i obratno – literally, 'there and back'; return ticket

turbaza – tourist camp

ulitsa – street

univermag, universalny magazin – department store

ushchelie – gorge or valley

uzhin – supper

val – rampart

vareniki – dumplings with a variety of possible fillings

venik – tied bundle of birch branches

verkhny – upper

vkhod – way in, entrance

voda – water

vodny vokzal – ferry terminal

vokzal – station

vostok – east

vykhodnoy den – day off (Saturday, Sunday and holidays)

yantar – amber

yezhednevno – every day, daily

yug – south

yurt – nomad's portable, round tent-house made of felt or skins stretched over a collapsible frame of wood slats

zakaznaya – registered post

zakuski – appetisers

zal – hall, room

zaliv – gulf, bay

zamok – castle, fortress

zapad – west

zapovednik – special purpose (nature) reserve

zavtrak – breakfast

zhensky – women's (toilet)

zhetony – tokens (for metro etc)

Behind the Scenes

SEND US YOUR FEEDBACK

We love to hear from travellers – your comments keep us on our toes and help make our books better. Our well-travelled team reads every word on what you loved or loathed about this book. Although we cannot reply individually to your submissions, we always guarantee that your feedback goes straight to the appropriate authors, in time for the next edition. Each person who sends us information is thanked in the next edition – the most useful submissions are rewarded with a selection of digital PDF chapters.

Visit **lonelyplanet.com/contact** to submit your updates and suggestions or to ask for help. Our award-winning website also features inspirational travel stories, news and discussions.

Note: We may edit, reproduce and incorporate your comments in Lonely Planet products such as guidebooks, websites and digital products, so let us know if you don't want your comments reproduced or your name acknowledged. For a copy of our privacy policy visit lonelyplanet.com/privacy.

OUR READERS

Many thanks to the travellers who used the last edition and wrote to us with helpful hints, useful advice and interesting anecdotes:

Aleksandra Markovic, Alexander Shchepetkov, Álvaro Gómez-Meana & Jose-Carlos Elvira, Anders Blixt, Ariela Perelman, Benoit De Witte, Brian Burgoyne, Denis Umutvaev, Diego Tan, Grethe Mortensen, Helmut Lueders, Henning Rädlein, Julia Bruch, Julie Woods, Laura Fortey, Patrick Wierda, Sabine Walther, Sophie Hunter, Soren Poulsen, Steve Simpson

WRITER THANKS

Simon Richmond

Many thanks to my fellow author Regis and to Peter Kozyrev, Andrey and Sasha, Yegor Churakov, Vladimir Stolyarov, Dima Alimov, Konstantin Yurganov and Darina Gribova.

Mark Baker

I would like to thank all the friendly people who helped me along way down the Volga and around Kaliningrad. Special thanks to friends Alsu Kurmash, Andrey Grigoriev and his wife Alina, Julia Ziyatdinova and Ildar Gabidullin. Lubomir Hyska in Prague was especially helpful in sorting out my visas.

Marc Bennetts

Thanks to everyone who helped me out on my travels. Thanks also to Tanya and Masha for guarding

my ever-expanding record collection while I was away. And thanks to Brana for steering me through the system – again.

Stuart Butler

First and foremost – thank you to my ever-patient wife, Heather, and children, Jake and Grace, for putting up with everything while I worked on this project. Thank you also to Olga and Alexander of Altair Tur for visa papers and helping with the fab trek in Chuya Mountains. Also, thank you to (a different) Alexander for the driving and company along the Chuysky Trakt. Finally, thanks to Simon and Brana for encouragement.

Trent Holden & Kate Morgan

Huge thank you to DE Brana firstly for giving us the opportunity to travel back to Russia and research Western European Russia for Lonely Planet, and secondly for all of your assistance throughout the project. Big thank you goes to all of the amazing staff at the excellent Veliky Novgorod tourist information, as well as the tourist information office staff in Smolensk and Pskov for all of your assistance. We'd also like to thank our co-authors, in particular Leonid, for helpful tips and suggestions. And finally to all of the fantastic local people we met on our travels who made it such an enjoyable and fascinating trip.

Ali Lemer

Thanks to Jon Earle; Tara Kennaway; Dmitry Doronin, Ilaria Doronina & Babuskha Tamara; Gennady Gavrikov & Ilya Zlotnikov; Nikita and everyone in

Pereslavl-Zalessky's English Club; and to fellow authors Leonid Ragozin, Regis St Louis, Trent Holden, Kate Morgan, Simon Richmond, Mara Voorhees & Kira Tverskaya. Big thanks also to Brana Vladisavljevic, Tasmin Waby and Jane Atkin, and especially to all of the Lonely Planet eds and cartos who worked on this book.

Tom Masters

A huge thanks to all those who helped me in the Far East, but particularly to Anna Konevskaya at Kamchatintour, Martha Madson at Explore Kamchatka, Alexei Podprugin at Nata Tour, Aleksei Shein in Vladivostok, Masha Gessen, Sarah Weinknecht, Sergei Kromykh in Khabarovsk, Tolya Buzinsky, Bolot Bochkarev, Bogdan Chernov & Simon Patterson, as ever.

Leonid Ragozin

I would like to thank Anatoly Bryukhanov and Aleksey Makeyev for their invaluable help in Krasnoyarsk; Jack Sheremetoff and Denis Sobnakov for explaining Baikal and fun conversations; Igor Ozerov in Ulan-Ude for all his stories and a wonderful trip to the eastern coast; the charming Ilona Baikara for driving me around Tuva and as to the Saryglar family for making it happen; Igor Shalygin in Taishet for a superb and much-needed banya; Aleksandr Maryasov for helping out in Severobaikalsk. Finally, many huge thanks to my wife Maria Makeeva for helping out with the research, keeping me company on Olkhon and enduring my absence for the rest of the trip.

Regis St Louis

Many thanks to Tatiana and Vlad for the warm welcome in Petersburg; Peter Kozyrev for Chkalovsky knowledge and the late-night strolling seminar; Darina Gribova for the street art tour; Vladimir, Yegor and Natasha of Wild Russia for many local recommendations; and friend and fellow author Simon Richmond for his many helpful tips. Warm thanks to Cassandra and daughters Magdalena and Genevieve for all their support.

Mara Vorhees

Many thanks to my coauthors and resident Moscow experts Marc Bennetts and Leonid Ragozin. Always a pleasure to work with colleagues so insightful and well-informed. I also received useful information from Andrei Musiano and Sasha Serbina at Garage Museum of Contemporary Art and Dmitry Elovsky at Zaryadye Project, as well as Andrey Muchnik and Marina Dedozhdy. Unlimited thanks and love to мои самые любимые – Van, Shay and Jerry - for coming along for the adventure.

ACKNOWLEDGEMENTS

Climate map data adapted from Peel MC, Finlayson BL & McMahon TA (2007) 'Updated World Map of the Köppen-Geiger Climate Classification', Hydrology and Earth System Sciences, 11, 163344.

Moscow and St Petersburg Metro maps © Design by Art. Lebedev Studio

Illustrations p70-71 and p172-3 by Javier Zarracina

Cover photograph: Veliky Novgorod, Syntheticmessiah/Getty ©

THIS BOOK

This 8th edition of Lonely Planet's *Russia* guidebook was researched and written by Simon Richmond, Mark Baker, Marc Bennetts, Stuart Butler, Trent Holden, Ali Lemer, Tatyana Leonov, Tom Masters, Kate Morgan, Leonid Ragozin, Regis St Louis and Mara Vorhees. This guidebook was produced by the following:

Destination Editor Brana Vladisavljevic

Product Editors Heather Champion, Rachel Rawling

Senior Cartographers Valentina Kremenchutskaya, David Kemp

Book Designer Gwen Cotter

Assisting Editors Janet Austin, James Bainbridge, Judith Bamber, Michelle Bennett, Nigel Chin, Andrea Dobbin, Samantha Forge, Emma Gibbs, Victoria Harrison, Jennifer Hattam, Gabby Innes, Alex Knights, Anne Mason, Christopher Pitts, Sarah Reid, Fionnuala Twomey, Sam Wheeler

Assisting Cartographer Hunor Csutoros

Cover Researcher Naomi Parker

Thanks to Imogen Bannister, Joel Cotterell, Jane Grisman, James Hardy, Liz Heynes, Sandie Kestell, Genna Patterson, Wibowo Rusli, Jessica Ryan, Dianne Schallmeiner, Victoria Smith, Ross Taylor, Angela Tinson, Kira Tverskaya, Tony Wheeler

Index

<del>INDEX - G-K</del>

NOTES

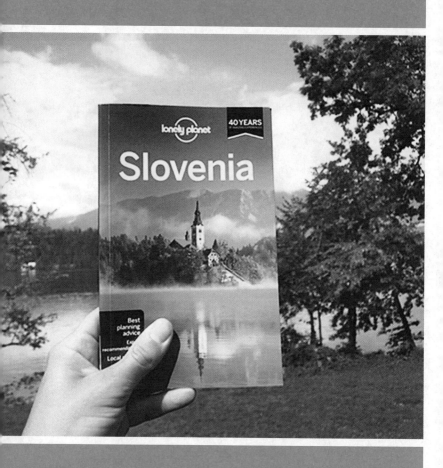

LONELY PLANET IN THE WILD

Send your 'Lonely Planet in the Wild' photos to social@lonelyplanet.com
We share the best on our Facebook page every week!

Map Legend

Sights

- Beach
- Bird Sanctuary
- Buddhist
- Castle/Palace
- Christian
- Confucian
- Hindu
- Islamic
- Jain
- Jewish
- Monument
- Museum/Gallery/Historic Building
- Ruin
- Shinto
- Sikh
- Taoist
- Winery/Vineyard
- Zoo/Wildlife Sanctuary
- Other Sight

Activities, Courses & Tours

- Bodysurfing
- Diving
- Canoeing/Kayaking
- Course/Tour
- Sento Hot Baths/Onsen
- Skiing
- Snorkelling
- Surfing
- Swimming/Pool
- Walking
- Windsurfing
- Other Activity

Sleeping

- Sleeping
- Camping
- Hut/Shelter

Eating

- Eating

Drinking & Nightlife

- Drinking & Nightlife
- Cafe

Entertainment

- Entertainment

Shopping

- Shopping

Information

- Bank
- Embassy/Consulate
- Hospital/Medical
- Internet
- Police
- Post Office
- Telephone
- Toilet
- Tourist Information
- Other Information

Geographic

- Beach
- Gate
- Hut/Shelter
- Lighthouse
- Lookout
- Mountain/Volcano
- Oasis
- Park
- Pass
- Picnic Area
- Waterfall

Population

- Capital (National)
- Capital (State/Province)
- City/Large Town
- Town/Village

Transport

- Airport
- Border crossing
- Bus
- Cable car/Funicular
- Cycling
- Ferry
- Metro station
- Monorail
- Parking
- Petrol station
- S-Bahn/Subway station
- Taxi
- T-bane/Tunnelbana station
- Train station/Railway
- Tram
- Tube station
- U-Bahn/Underground station
- Other Transport

Routes

- Tollway
- Freeway
- Primary
- Secondary
- Tertiary
- Lane
- Unsealed road
- Road under construction
- Plaza/Mall
- Steps
- Tunnel
- Pedestrian overpass
- Walking Tour
- Walking Tour detour
- Path/Walking Trail

Boundaries

- International
- State/Province
- Disputed
- Regional/Suburb
- Marine Park
- Cliff
- Wall

Hydrography

- River, Creek
- Intermittent River
- Canal
- Water
- Dry/Salt/Intermittent Lake
- Reef

Areas

- Airport/Runway
- Beach/Desert
- Cemetery (Christian)
- Cemetery (Other)
- Glacier
- Mudflat
- Park/Forest
- Sight (Building)
- Sportsground
- Swamp/Mangrove

Note: Not all symbols displayed above appear on the maps in this book

Regis St Louis

St Petersburg Regis grew up in a small town in the American Midwest – the kind of place that fuels big dreams of travel – and he developed an early fascination with foreign dialects and world cultures. He spent his formative years learning Russian and a handful of Romance languages, which served him well on journeys across much of the globe. Regis has contributed to more than 50 Lonely Planet titles, covering destinations across six continents. His travels have taken him from the mountains of Kamchatka to remote island villages in Melanesia, and to many grand urban landscapes. When not on the road, Regis lives in New Orleans.

Mara Vorhees

Russian Caucasus & Moscow Mara writes about food, travel and family fun around the world. Her work has been published by BBC Travel, *Boston Globe*, Delta Sky, *Vancouver Sun* and more. For Lonely Planet, she regularly writes about destinations in Central America and Eastern Europe, as well as New England, where she lives. She often travels with her twin boys in tow, earning her an expertise in family travel. Follow their adventures and misadventures at www.havetwinswilltravel.com.

on the beautiful beaches of Southwest France with his wife and two young children. His website is www.stuartbutlerjournalist.com.

Trent Holden
Western European Russia A Geelong-based writer, located just outside Melbourne, Trent has worked for Lonely Planet since 2005. He's covered 30-plus guidebooks across Asia, Africa and Australia. With a penchant for megacities, Trent's in his element when assigned to cover a nation's capital – the more chaotic the better – to unearth cool bars, art, street food and underground subculture. On the flipside he also writes books to idyllic tropical islands across Asia, in between going on safari to national parks in Africa and the subcontinent. When not travelling, Trent works as a freelance editor, reviewer and spends all his money catching live gigs. You can catch him on Twitter @hombreholden.

Ali Lemer
Golden Ring Ali has been working for Lonely Planet as a travel writer and editor since 2007. Besides authoring articles for lonelyplanet.com on Japan, Scotland and the US, she's written for several travel magazines and authored guidebooks on Bali, Hawaii and Russia; she also co-edited an anthology of personal narratives from migrant Australian authors called *Joyful Strains: Making Australia Home*. A native New Yorker, Ali has also lived and studied in Chicago, Prague, the UK and Melbourne, Australia, where she became naturalized several years ago. She currently resides in Brooklyn, NY.

Tatyana Leonov
The Urals Tatyana is a travel writer and editor based in Sydney, Australia when she's not on the road. She's written for *Lonely Planet Asia* magazine and lonelyplanet.com, as well as a heap of other magazines, newspapers and websites from around the world. Check out www.tatyanaleonov.com.au for more.

Tom Masters
Russian Far East Dreaming since he could walk of going to the most obscure places on earth, Tom has always had a taste for the unknown. This has led to a writing career that has taken him all over the world, including North Korea, the Arctic, Congo and Siberia. After graduating with a degree in Russian literature from the University of London, Tom went to work in Russia as a journalist at the *St Petersburg Times*. He now indulges his love of communist architecture by living on Karl-Marx-Allee in Berlin's Friedrichshain, but still returns regularly to the former Soviet Union for work. Tom can be found online at www.tommasters.net.

Kate Morgan
Western European Russia Having worked for Lonely Planet for over a decade now, Kate has been fortunate enough to cover plenty of ground working as a travel writer on destinations such as Shanghai, Japan, India, Russia, Zimbabwe, the Philippines and Phuket. She has done stints living in London, Paris and Osaka but these days is based in one of her favourite regions in the world – Victoria, Australia. In between travelling the world and writing about it, Kate enjoys spending time at home working as a freelance editor.

Leonid Ragozin
Moscow & Eastern Siberia Leonid studied beach dynamics at the Moscow State University, but for want of decent beaches in Russia, he switched to journalism and spent 12 years voyaging through different parts of the BBC, with a break for a four-year stint as a foreign correspondent for the Russian *Newsweek*. Leonid is currently a freelance journalist focusing largely on the conflict between Russia and Ukraine (both his Lonely Planet destinations), which prompted him to leave Moscow and find a new home in Rīga.

OUR STORY

A beat-up old car, a few dollars in the pocket and a sense of adventure. In 1972 that's all Tony and Maureen Wheeler needed for the trip of a lifetime – across Europe and Asia overland to Australia. It took several months, and at the end – broke but inspired – they sat at their kitchen table writing and stapling together their first travel guide, *Across Asia on the Cheap*. Within a week they'd sold 1500 copies. Lonely Planet was born.

Today, Lonely Planet has offices in Franklin, London, Melbourne, Oakland, Dublin, Beijing and Delhi, with more than 600 staff and writers. We share Tony's belief that 'a great guidebook should do three things: inform, educate and amuse'.

OUR WRITERS

Simon Richmond

Russian Caucasus & St Petersburg Journalist and photographer Simon has specialised as a travel writer since the early 1990s and first worked for Lonely Planet in 1999 on their Central Asia guide. He's long since stopped counting the number of guidebooks he's researched and written for the company, but countries covered including Australia, China, India, Iran, Japan, Korea, Malaysia, Mongolia, Myanmar (Burma), Russia, Singapore, South Africa and Turkey. For Lonely Planet's website he's penned features on topics from the world's best swimming pools to the joys of Urban Sketching – follow him on Instagram to see some of his photos and sketches.

Mark Baker

Kaliningrad Region & Volga Region Mark is a freelance travel writer with a penchant for offbeat stories and forgotten places. He's originally from the United States, but now makes his home in the Czech capital, Prague. He writes mainly on Eastern and Central Europe for Lonely Planet as well as other leading travel publishers, but finds real satisfaction in digging up stories in places that are too remote or quirky for the guides. Prior to becoming an author, he worked as a journalist for The Economist, Bloomberg News and Radio Free Europe, among other organisations. Instagram: @markbakerprague Twitter: @markbakerprague

Marc Bennetts

Northern European Russia Marc is a Moscow-based journalist and writer whose work has appeared in the UK's *Guardian* and *Times*, as well as other UK and US newspapers. He is the author of three books: *Football Dynamo* (Virgin, 2008) about Russia's football culture, *Kicking the Kremlin* (2014, Oneworld), about the anti-Putin protest movement and *I'm Going to Ruin Their Lives* (Oneworld, 2016), about how Putin has retailated. Marc has lived in Russia since 1997.

Stuart Butler

Western Siberia Stuart has been writing for Lonely Planet for a decade and during this time he's come eye to eye with gorillas in the Congolese jungles, met a man with horns on his head who could lie in fire, huffed and puffed over snowbound Himalayan mountain passes, interviewed a king who could turn into a tree and had his fortune told by a parrot. Oh, and he's met more than his fair share of self-proclaimed Gods. When not on the road for Lonely Planet he lives

OVER PAGE MORE WRITERS

Published by Lonely Planet Global Limited
CRN 554153
8th edition – March 2018
ISBN 978 1 78657 362 9
© Lonely Planet 2018 Photographs © as indicated 2018
10 9 8 7 6 5 4 3 2 1
Printed in China

Although the authors and Lonely Planet have taken all reasonable care in preparing this book, we make no warranty about the accuracy or completeness of its content and, to the maximum extent permitted, disclaim all liability arising from its use.

All rights reserved. No part of this publication may be copied, stored in a retrieval system, or transmitted in any form by any means, electronic, mechanical, recording or otherwise, except brief extracts for the purpose of review, and no part of this publication may be sold or hired, without the written permission of the publisher. Lonely Planet and the Lonely Planet logo are trademarks of Lonely Planet and are registered in the US Patent and Trademark Office and in other countries. Lonely Planet does not allow its name or logo to be appropriated by commercial establishments, such as retailers, restaurants or hotels. Please let us know of any misuses: lonelyplanet.com/ip.

Tuva

19 Throat singers zing and burp under upturned eaves, the yurts of nomads pimple the dust-bare grasslands, a hoard of Scythian gold gleams in the National Museum and a clipped Turkic tongue stutters on the dusty streets – this is Tuva (p491), a republic isolated from the rest of Russia by the Yergaki Mountains, where Slavic influence has all but faded. You'll long remember a tour of this incredible country, not least for its wildernesses peppered with petroglyph-etched standing stones and its unique traditional music. Below: Yurts near Kyzyl

Veliky Novgorod's Kremlin

20 In the town that considers itself Russia's birthplace stands one of the country's most impressive and picturesque stone fortresses. Within the grounds of the Kremlin (p258) rise the Byzantine 11th-century Cathedral of St Sophia and a 300-tonne sculpture celebrating 1000 years of Russian history. Climb the Kokui Tower for an overview of the complex, then enter the Novgorod State United Museum to see one of Russia's best collections of iconographic art. A pleasant park and riverside beach also fringe the magnificent brick walls.

Need to Know

For more information, see Survival Guide (p665)

Currency
Russian rouble (R)

Language
Russian

Visas
Required by all; apply at least a month in advance of your trip.

Money
Credit and debit cards accepted. ATMs plentiful. Euros or US dollars best currencies for exchange.

Mobile Phones
Prepaid SIM cards are readily available. International roaming possible.

Time
Moscow/St Petersburg (GMT/USC plus four hours)

When to Go

Dry climate
Warm to hot summers, cold/mild winters
Mild summers, cold winters
Mild summers, very cold winters
Cold climate

Kaliningrad
GO May–Sep

Moscow
GO May–Sep

Sochi
GO Jun–Nov

Irkutsk
GO Mar, Jun–Sep

Vladivostok
GO Jun–Oct

High Season
(Jun–Sep)

➡ Hot weather across most of the country.

➡ Peak season for Russians to go on holiday; all forms of transport should be booked in advance.

➡ Prices can rise in St Petersburg, particularly during White Nights in June and July.

Shoulder
(May & Oct)

➡ Late spring and early autumn see the country bathed in the fresh greenery or russet shades of the seasons.

➡ Good time for cultural events in cities and major parades on Victory Day (9 May).

Low Season
(Nov–Apr)

➡ Snow falls and temperatures plummet, creating the wintery Russia of the imagination.

➡ Best time for skiing (although resorts charge higher prices) and visiting museums and galleries.

Useful Websites

Lonely Planet (www.lonely
planet.com/russia) Destination
information, hotel bookings,
traveller forum and more.

Way to Russia (www.wayto
russia.net) Comprehensive
online travel guide.

Afisha (www.afisha.ru) Extensive restaurant, bar, museum
and event listings for all major
cities; in Russian only.

Moscow Expat Site (www.
expat.ru) Mine expat knowledge
of Russia.

English Russia (http://eng-
lishrussia.com) Russia-focused
blog with quirky images and
stories.

Important Numbers

Russia's country code	☏7
International access code	☏8
Fire	☏01
Police	☏02
Ambulance	☏03

Exchange Rates

Australia	A$1	R48
Canada	C$1	R48
Europe	€1	R70
Japan	¥100	R54
New Zealand	NZ$1	R45
UK	UK£1	R78
US	US$1	R60

For current exchange rates see
www.xe.com.

Daily Costs

**Budget:
Less than R1500**

➡ Dorm bed: R700–R800

➡ Café or street-stall meal:
R200–R500

➡ Travel on buses and metro:
R15–R50

**Midrange:
R1500–R4000**

➡ Double room in a midrange
hotel: R2000–R3000

➡ Two-course meal: R500–
R1000

➡ Museum entry fee: R100–
R400

➡ City-centre taxi ride: R200–
R300

**Top End:
More than R4000**

➡ Double room in a top-end
hotel: R5000-plus

➡ Two-course meal with wine:
R2000-plus

➡ Ballet tickets: R3500

➡ First-class train ticket (eg
Moscow–St Petersburg):
R7300

Opening Hours

Banks 9am–6pm Monday to
Friday, some open 9am–5pm
Saturday

Bars and Clubs noon–midnight
Sunday to Thursday, to 6am
Friday and Saturday

Cafes 9am–10pm

Post offices 8am–8pm or 9pm
Monday to Friday, shorter hours
Saturday and Sunday

Restaurants noon–midnight

Shops 10am–8pm

**Supermarkets and Food
stores** 24 hours

Arriving in Russia

**Sheremetyevo Airport
(Moscow)** Aeroexpress trains
(R500; 30 minutes) run to the
city every half-hour from 5am
to 12.30am. Taxis cost R2000 to
R2500 and take at least an hour.

Domodedovo Airport (Moscow)
Aeroexpress trains (R500; 45
minutes) run to the city every
half-hour between 6am and
11.30pm. Taxis cost R2000 to
R2500 and take at least an hour.

**Pulkovo Airport (St Peters-
burg)** Frequent buses (R36) run
to Moskovskaya metro station
(R45) for a total journey time
to the city centre of around 30
minutes. Taxis charge around
R1000 to the centre and can
take up to an hour depending
on traffic.

Getting Around

To check train times and make
bookings, go to the trip-planning
section of the RZD (Russian Railways; http://pass.rzd.ru) website.

Train The extensive network is
the best way of getting around,
with many comfortable overnight
services between far-flung cities.

Air Worth considering if you
need to speed up your travels
(with online tickets sometimes
cheaper than those for trains).
Only book airlines with solid
safety records.

Bus Useful for getting to
places not covered by the train.
Sometimes faster than local
elektrichka (suburban) train
services.

Car or taxi Sometimes the
only way to get to really remote
destinations.

For much more on
getting around,
see p680

First Time Russia

For more information, see Survival Guide (p665)

Checklist

➡ Make sure your passport is valid for at least six months beyond the expiry date of your visa.

➡ Arrange your visa.

➡ Check airline baggage restrictions.

➡ Check travel advisory websites.

➡ Tell banks and credit card providers your travel dates.

➡ Organise travel insurance.

What to Pack

➡ Good walking shoes – Russian cities are best explored on foot.

➡ Phrasebook, mini-dictionary or translation app.

➡ Earplugs and eye mask for napping on trains, noisy hotels and during long White Nights.

➡ A sense of humour and a bucketful of patience.

Top Tips for Your Trip

➡ Consider using a specialist travel agency to arrange visas, make key transport bookings and hire guides.

➡ Treat yourself to a stay at a business or luxury hotel over the weekend when many often drop their rates substantially to cover the shortfall in business customers. Big discounts can also be had on hotel rack rates when booked online.

➡ Rail tickets can be booked online or at stations 45 days in advance. There are discounts for online and advance bookings.

➡ Fixed-priced business lunches, common in cities, are a great deal and an ideal way to sample the cuisine at fancier restaurants.

➡ Schedule some time out of the big cities at rural or off-the-beaten track destinations to fully appreciate what is special about Russia.

What to Wear

Informal dress is generally fine. However, Russians do make an effort when they go to the theatre or a posh restaurant – you should do likewise if you want to fit in. If you're planning on exploring on foot, a comfortable pair of waterproof walking shoes will come in handy, as will an umbrella or rain jacket.

In winter, bundle up with several layers before going out and bring a long, windproof coat to stay nicely warm. Hats and coats are always removed on entering a museum or restaurant and left in the cloakroom.

Sleeping

For major cities and resorts it's a good idea to book a night or two in advance.

Hotels Range from unreconstructed edifices of the Soviet era to luxurious and contemporary.

Hostels Moscow and St Petersburg have rich pickings but you'll now also find many good ones in other major cities and towns.

B&B & homestays Not so common but worth searching out for a true experience of Russian hospitality.

Money

➡ If prices are listed in US dollars or euros, you will still be presented with a final bill in roubles.

➡ There are ATMs on every corner around the country these days; look out for signs that say *bankomat* (БАНКОМАТ).

➡ Credit cards are commonly accepted in big cities, but don't expect to be able to use them in more off-the-beaten-track spots and rural areas.

➡ Inform your bank or credit card provider of the dates you'll be travelling in Russia and using your card, to avoid a situation where the card is blocked.

For more information, see p671.

Bargaining

Prices are fixed in shops, but at souvenir markets, such as Izmailovo in Moscow, polite haggling over prices is a good idea.

Tipping

It is customary to tip in restaurants and cafes, but elsewhere it is optional. You are not expected to tip when you buy drinks from the bar.

Hotels Only in the most luxurious need you tip bellboys etc, and only if service is good.

Guides Around 10% of their daily rate; a small gift will also be appreciated.

Restaurants Leave around 10% if the service warrants it.

Taxis No need to tip as the fare is agreed either before you get in or it's metered.

Language

Russian is the common language, although dozens of other languages are spoken by ethnic minorities. It's relatively easy to find English speakers in the big cities, but not so easy in smaller towns and the countryside. Learning Cyrillic and a few key phrases will help you enormously in being able to decode street signs, menus and timetables. See Language (p691) for more info.

Is this Moscow or local time?
Это московское или местное время?
e·ta ma·skof·ska·ye i·li myes·na·ye vryem·ya

Russia has 11 time zones but the entire country's rail and air networks run on Moscow time. Ask if you're not certain what time zone your transport is running on.

I live in Moscow, I won't pay that much.
Я живу в Москве, я не буду платить так много.
ya zhih·vu v mask·vye ya nye bu·du pla·tit' tak mno·ga

Taxi drivers and market sellers sometimes try to charge foreigners more, so you may want to bargain in Russian.

Are you serving?
Вы обслуживаете? vih aps·lu·zhih·va·it·ye

It may be hard to attract the attention of workers in the service industry – if you want to get served, use this polite expression.

I don't drink alcohol.
Я не пью спиртного.
ya nye pyu spirt·no·va

Refusing a drink from generous locals can be very difficult, so if you're really not in the mood you'll need a firm, clear excuse.

5
May I have an official receipt, please?
Дайте мне официальную расписку, пожалуйста.
deyt·ye mnye a·fi·tsi·yal'·nu·yu ras·pis·ku pa·zhal·sta

Russian authorities might expect an unofficial payment to expedite their service, so always ask for an official receipt.

Etiquette

Russians are sticklers for formality. They're also rather superstitious. Follow these tips to avoid faux pas.

Visiting homes Shaking hands across the threshold is considered unlucky; wait until you're fully inside. Remove your shoes and coat on entering a house. Always bring a gift. If you give anyone flowers, make sure it's an odd number – even numbers for funerals.

Religion Women should cover their heads and bare shoulders when entering a church. In some monasteries and churches women are also required to wear a skirt – wraps are usually available at the door. Men should remove their hats in church and not wear shorts.

Eating & drinking Russians eat resting their wrists on the table edge, with fork in left hand and knife in the right. Vodka toasts are common at shared meals – it's rude to refuse to join in and traditional to eat a little something after each shot.

What's New

World Cup 2018

Host cities Moscow, St Petersburg, Sochi, Kazan, Saransk, Kaliningrad, Volgograd, Rostov-on-Don, Nizhny Novgorod, Yekaterinburg and Samara have all benefited from infrastructure improvements linked to the global soccer jamboree.

Park Zaryadye

Moscow's newest park offers four different microclimates (representing Russia's geographic zones), four museums and (eventually) an outdoor amphitheatre – check out the full plan at the pavilion. (p77)

New Holland

Closed to the public for nearly 300 years, the central St Petersburg island of New Holland has been reborn as a contemporary arts, culture and entertainment hub. (p185)

Gulag History Museum

Moscow's Gulag History Museum has a new R300-million home, which re-creates the bone-chilling conditions of the Soviet labour camps in which millions lived and died. (p81)

Museum of Russian Impressionism

This new, private museum showcases a little known and under-appreciated genre of art, using an impressive collection compiled by a billionaire-turned-art collector. (p87)

Arkhyz Resort

Fast modern gondolas whisk skiers and hikers up the slopes for a grandstand view across the Greater Caucasus mountains at Arkhyz Resort. (p48)

Garage Museum of Contemporary Art

Occupying a new, permanent home in Gorky Park's former Seasons of the Year restaurant building is Moscow's premier contemporary art museum Garage. (p92)

Boris Yeltsin Museum

Part of the swish Boris Yeltsin Presidential Center in Yekateriburg, this museum has an impressive and somewhat unusual collection of exhibits. (p422)

Zarya Centre for Contemporary Art

A former factory in Vladivostok, contemporary art is served up in exhibitions, films, lectures and other cool events. (p554)

Hermitage Vladivostok

Due to open in 2018, in a gorgeous tsarist-era building in the centre, is the Russian Far East branch of the famous St Petersburg art museum. (p554)

Georgievskaya Ulitsa

This re-created pedestrian-only street in the Golden Ring town of Vladimir conjours up Russia's past and is dotted with souvenir stores and whimsical bronze statues. (p127)

Nikola-Lenivets

The once abandoned village of Nikola-Lenivets, 220km southwest of Moscow, is now a huge open-air exhibition space dotted with gigantic installations made largely of wood. (p250)

For more recommendations and reviews, see lonelyplanet.com/russia

Plan Your Trip
Getting Your Visa

Save for a handful of exceptions, everyone needs a visa to visit Russia. Arranging one is generally straightforward but is likely to be time-consuming, bureaucratic and – depending on how quickly you need the visa – costly. Start the application process at least a month before your trip.

Starting the Process

For most travellers, a tourist visa (single- or double-entry), which is valid for a maximum of 30 days from the date of entry and is nonextendable, will be sufficient. If you plan on staying longer than a month, it's advisable to apply for a business visa – these are available as single-, double- or multiple-entry.

Whatever visa you go for, the process has three main stages: invitation, application and registration.

You may need separate permission for trips to sensitive border regions such as the Altai, Volga Delta, Caucasus and Tuva, which means the processing of your visa can take longer.

If your trip into or out of Russia involves transit through, or a stay in, another country, such as Belarus, China, Mongolia or Kazakhstan, our advice is to arrange any necessary visa or visas in your home country *before* you enter Russia.

Invitation

To obtain a visa, everyone needs an invitation, also known as 'visa support'. Hotels and hostels will usually issue anyone staying with them an invitation voucher free or for a small fee (typically around €20 to €30). If you are not staying in a hotel or hostel, you will need to buy an invitation – this can be done through most travel agents or via specialist visa agencies, also for around €20.

Visa Agencies

Action-visas.com www.action-visas.com

Comet Consular Services www.cometconsular.com

Express to Russia www.expresstorussia.com

IVDS www.ivds.de

Real Russia http://realrussia.co.uk

VisaCentral http://visacentral.com

VisaHQ.com http://russia.visahq.com

Way to Russia www.waytorussia.net

Main Visa Types

Tourist Valid for a maximum of 30 days, single- or double-entry, nonextendable.

Business Valid for three months, six months or one year (three years for US citizens); may or may not limit the number of entries.

Private On invitation from a Russian citizen, who provides your accommodation. Up to 90 days, single- or double-entry.

Transit By air for 72 hours, by train 10 days.

Russian Far East free e-visa Citizens of 18 countries can arrive without a visa for stays of up to 30 days, if entering via Vladivostok, Kamchatka or Sakhalin and staying only in the Russian Far East.

Application

Invitation voucher in hand, you can then apply for a visa. Wherever in the world you are applying, you can start by entering details in the online form of the Consular Department of the Russian Ministry of Foreign Affairs (https://visa.kdmid.ru/PetitionChoice.aspx).

Take care in answering the questions accurately on this form, including listing all the countries you have visited in the last 10 years and the dates of the visits – stamps in your passport will be checked against this information, and if there are anomalies you will likely have to restart the process. Keep a note of the unique identity number provided for your submitted form – if you have to make changes later, you will need this to access it without having to fill in the form from scratch again.

Russian embassies in many countries, including the UK, US, France and Germany, have contracted separate agencies to process the submission of visa applications and check everything is in order; these companies use online interfaces that direct the relevant information into the standard visa application form. In the UK, the agency is VFS.Global (http://ru.vfsglobal.co.uk), with offices in London and Edinburgh; in the US it's Invisa Logistic Services (http://ils-usa.com), with offices in Washington DC, New York, San Francisco, Houston and Seattle.

Consular offices apply different fees and slightly different application rules country by country. For example, at the time of writing, a pilot project to collect biometric data via fingerprinting was being run for visa applications in the UK, Denmark, Myanmar and Namibia. Avoid potential hassles by checking well in advance what these rules might be. Among the things that you will need are:

➡ A print-out of the invitation/visa support document.

➡ A passport-sized photograph for the application form.

➡ If you're self-employed, bank statements for the previous three months showing you have sufficient funds to cover your time in Russia.

➡ Details of your travel insurance.

The charge for the visa will depend on the type of visa applied for and how quickly you need it. We highly recommend applying for your visa in your home country rather than on the road. Trans-Mongolian travellers should note that unless you can prove you're a resident of China or Mongolia, attempting to get visas for Russia in Beijing and Ulaanbaatar can be a frustrating and ultimately fruitless exercise.

Registration

Every visitor to Russia should have their visa registered *within seven days of arrival,* excluding weekends and public holidays. The obligation to register is with the accommodating party – your hotel or hostel, or landlord, friend or family if you're staying in a private residence.

If you're staying at a hotel or hostel, the receptionist will register you for free. This will involve them photocopying every page of your passport. Once registered, you should receive a slip of paper confirming the dates you'll be staying at that particular accommodation. Keep this safe – there's a very small possibility that you may be asked by officials to show this to prove you've been registered (this is unlikely).

If staying in a homestay or rental apartment, you'll either need to make arrangements with the landlord or a friend to register you through the post office. See www.waytorussia.net/russianvisa/registration.html for how this can be done and for more details on the whole process.

Depending on how amenable your hotel or inviting agency is, you can request that they register you for longer than you'll actually be in one place. Otherwise, every time you move city or town and stay for more than seven days, it's necessary to go through the registration process again. There's no need to be overly paranoid about this, but the more thorough your registration record, the less chance you'll have of running into problems. Keep all transport tickets (especially if you spend

IMMIGRATION FORM

Immigration forms are produced electronically by passport control at airports. Take good care of your half of the completed form as you'll need it for registration and could face problems while travelling in Russia – and certainly will on leaving – if you can't produce it.

nights sleeping on trains) to prove to any overzealous police officers exactly when you arrived in a new place.

It's tempting to be lax about registration, and we've met many travellers who were and didn't experience any problems as a result of it; however, if you're travelling for a while in Russia, and particularly if you're visiting off-the-beaten-track places, it's worth making sure you are registered at each destination, since it's not uncommon to encounter cops hoping to catch tourists too hurried or disorganised to be able to explain long gaps in their registration.

Note that you will not be asked to show registration slips when leaving from international airports.

Visa Extensions & Changes

Any extensions or changes to your visa will be handled by Russia's Federal Migration Service (Federalnoy Migratsionnoy Slyzhby), which is often shortened to FMS. It's possible you'll hear the old acronyms PVU and OVIR used for this office as well.

Extensions are time-consuming and difficult; *tourist visas cannot be extended at all*. Avoid the need for an extension by arranging a longer visa than you might need. Note that many trains out of St Petersburg and Moscow to Eastern Europe cross the border after midnight, so make sure your visa is valid up to and including this day.

Types of Visa

In addition to the tourist visa, there are other types of useful visas.

Business

Available for three months, six months or one year (or three years for US citizens), and as single-, double- or multiple-entry visas, business visas are valid for up to 90 days of travel within any 180-day period. You don't actually need to be on business to apply for these visas (they're great for independent tourists with longer travel itineraries and flexible schedules), but to get one you must have a letter of invitation from a registered Russian company or organisation (these can be arranged via specialist visa agencies); a covering letter stating the purpose of your trip; and proof of sufficient funds to cover your visit.

Transit

For transit by air, a transit visa is usually valid for up to three days. For a non-stop Trans-Siberian Railway journey, it's valid for 10 days, giving westbound passengers a few days in Moscow; those heading east, however, are not allowed to linger in Moscow. Note that transit visas for train journeys are tricky to secure and are usually exactly the same price as a single-entry tourist visa (in the UK £70 for either, plus a service charge of £38.40).

Visa-Free Travel

Visa-free visits of up to 72 hours are available to tourists arriving at Russian ports including Kaliningrad, Korsakov, Novorossiysk, Sochi, St Petersburg, Vladivostok and Vyborg. You will need to enter and exit the city on a cruise or ferry such as that offered by St Peter Line or Saimaa Travel.

There is also a plan, yet to be executed at the time of research, for visa-free travel in the Russian Far East for citizens of 18 countries (not including the US, Canada or any EU nation). Electronic single-entry visas, valid for up to 30 days, will be issued directly at the Russian border in Vladivostok (and possibly up to a dozen other entry points across the region in the future).

If You Like...

Arts & Crafts

Russian Museum As well as having the country's best collection of works by native artists, this St Petersburg institution has a fantastic folk crafts section. (p164)

Flyonovo Crafts are still produced at the pretty riverside estate of late-19th-century art-lover Princess Maria Tenisheva, 18km southeast of Smolensk. (p247)

Novgorod State United Museum Within Veliky Novgorod's kremlin is an incredible collection of iconographic art spanning several centuries. (p259)

Izmaylovsky Market A bustling market for all kinds of handicrafts where you can also watch them being made or try your hand at making your own. (p116)

National Museum Marvel at 3000-year-old Scythian gold jewellery in Kyzyl, the capital of Tuva. (p493)

Yantarny The source of around 90% of the world's amber. Look for attractive amber bracelets, necklaces and pendants in Kaliningrad's shops. (p285)

Epic Journeys

Trans-Siberian Railway The 9289km trip from Moscow to Vladivostok is the big one to do. (p40)

Baikal-Amur Mainline (BAM) The 'other Trans-Sib' route takes you through very lonely parts of Siberia and the Russian Far East. (p41)

Chuysky Trakt Hop in a shared taxi or hire a car to travel the 600km route through dramatic Altai landscapes, including glimpses of snowy mountain peaks and vertigo-inducing canyons. (p470)

Neryungri to Yakutsk An iron butt is required for this full-day classic 4WD ride through the Sakha Republic.

Frolikha Adventure Coastline Trail Pushed through virgin territory by Great Baikal Trail volunteers, this 100km-long lakeside trail is an eight-day Siberian odyssey. (p501)

Golden Ring Circuit some of Russia's oldest and cutest towns on a loop that begins and ends in Moscow. (p125)

Imperial Grandeur

Catherine Palace The vast baroque centrepiece of Tsarskoe Selo is famed for its Amber Room, dazzling Great Hall and beautiful grounds. (p220)

Peterhof Gape at the Grand Cascade fronting Peter the Great's Gulf of Finland crash pad. (p217)

Yusupov Palace A canalside mansion offering a series of sumptuously decorated rooms culminating in a gilded mini-theatre. (p184)

Kolomenskoe Museum-Reserve An ancient royal country seat and Unesco World Heritage Site. (p104)

Tsaritsyno Palace The contemporary manifestation of the exotic summer home that Catherine the Great began but never finished. (p123)

Literary Titans

Anna Akhmatova Museum at the Fountain House Celebrating the life and times of the famous 20th-century St Petersburg–based poet. (p182)

Spasskoe-Lutovinovo The family home of Ivan Turgenev, surrounded by beautiful grounds, is a short trip from the literary town of Oryol. (p246)

Dostoevsky House Museum The author, famously associated with St Petersburg, lived for many years in this modest, riverside home in sleepy Staraya Russa. (p264)

Mikhailovskoe Stand in the shade of Pushkin's beloved oak tree on his family's estate near the small town of Pushkinskie Gory. (p269)

Lermontov Museum The 19th-century Romantic writer

lived in this thatched cottage in Pyatigorsk before meeting his death in a duel. (p390)

Yasnaya Polyana The estate where Leo Tolstoy was born, lived most of his life and is buried. (p237)

Majestic Landscapes

Dombay This Southern Caucasus resort town is encircled by jagged, Matterhorn-like peaks of rock and ice, festooned with glaciers and gushing waterfalls. (p398)

Kola Peninsula Spot the northern lights reflecting off snowbound forests and tundra in the Arctic wilderness. (p322)

Barguzin Valley Isolated, virtually uninhabited and hemmed by high peaks, this is one of the most stunning Siberian landscapes in which to go astray. (p527)

Kamchatka This Far East peninsula is studded with several dozen snow-capped volcanoes. (p579)

Volga Delta Where the mighty river explodes like a firecracker into myriad *raskaty* (channels). (p367)

Blue Lake No permit is needed to hike to the gorgeous lake halfway up the side of Mt Aktru (4044m) within Altai National Park. (p405)

Multicultural Encounters

Jewish Museum & Centre of Tolerance Constructivist architect Konstantin Melnikov's bus depot gets a thrilling makeover as one of the country's best museums. (p83)

Top: Hot springs, the Kurils (p578)

Bottom: Amber jewellery for sale, Kaliningrad

Tuva With its throat-singing, yurt-building, milk-fermenting traditions, this isolated republic in southern Siberia is a revelation. (p491)

Lovozero This dilapidated outpost is worth the trek for those wanting to come into contact with the reindeer-herding Sami (Lapp) people of the Kola Peninsula. (p315)

Elista The capital of Kalmykia is home to the only Buddhist national group within Europe. (p365)

Esso Make contact with Evenki and Even people in this pretty village in the hinterland of Kamchatka. (p589)

Kosh-Agach With a population made up almost entirely of ethnic Altai and Kazakhs, it's easy to forget you are still in Russia. (p473)

Off the Beaten Track

Zyuratkul National Park A remote and beautiful part of the Ural Mountains, with a lovely lake, hikes, log houses and a *banya* (bath house). (p430)

Teriberka Tourism is slowly taking off in this Sami village, one of the most picturesque spots in Arctic Russia. (p316)

Cherek Valley & Upper Balkaria Hike among the ruins of 18 Balkar villages in the spectacularly scenic Cherek Valley. (p405)

Shoana Church An early 10th-century Alanian church, claimed to be the oldest functioning chapel in the Russian Federation. (p403)

Solovetsky Islands Make a pilgrimage to these White Sea islands, home to one of Russia's best-known monasteries and also a former gulag camp. (p301)

The Kurils There are 49 active volcanoes in this Russian Far East chain of 56 islands, as well as beautiful lagoons, rivers and lakes. (p578)

Quirky Places & Experiences

Permafrost Kingdom A never-melting pod of elaborate ice sculptures in a cocoon of permafrost and neon. (p567)

Bunker-42 Cold War Museum A secret underground Cold War communications centre now open for exploration. (p84)

Sumarokovskaya Elk Farm Meet some friendly moose and drink their milk at this farm-cum-scientific institute outside Kostroma. (p141)

Dancing Forest Marvel at the twisting and turning pines, sculpted by the winds that whistle across the Kurshskaya Kosa National Park. (p289)

Chess City Sit on the 12 chairs of the Ostap Bender monument in this literary fantasy come to surreal life in Elista. (p366)

Religious Buildings

St Basil's Cathedral Easily the country's most famous church; its candy coloured domes and swirly spires face the Kremlin across Red Square. (p61)

Grand Choral Synagogue A lavish place of worship indicating the pivotal role played by Jews in imperial St Petersburg. (p187)

Ivolginsk (Ivolga) Datsan The centre of Russian Buddhism continues to expand into its dramatic setting. (p534)

Kul Sharif Mosque Dominating Kazan's World Heritage Site–listed kremlin is this enormous mosque named after the imam who died defending the city against Ivan the Terrible's troops. (p340)

Church of the Intercession on the Nerl Revered for its exemplary perfect proportions and beautiful setting. (p129)

Sergiev Posad Russia's holiest of holies, the beautiful Trinity Monastery of St Sergius. (p153)

Soviet Relics

Lenin's Mausoleum Soviet relics hardly come more authentic than the embalmed body of VI, a fixture of Red Square since 1924. (p76)

VDNKh This park offers grandiose pavilions, gilded statues and fabulous fountains originally built to glorify socialism's economic achievements. (p85)

Alyosha The ever-vigilant, utilitarian concrete statue keeps an eye on Murmansk's wind-whipped and splendidly hideous Soviet architecture. (p319)

Mamaev Kurgan An astounding 72m-tall statue of Mother Russia is the memorial to those who fell in the bloody Battle of Stalingrad. (p358)

Lenin Head Installed to celebrate the commie leader's 100th birthday, this gigantic bust dominates Ulan Ude's main square. (p529)

Lenin Mosaic Beautiful public art in Sochi created in 1980 to mark the 110th anniversary of the birth of the father of the Bolshevik Revolution. (p380)

Month by Month

TOP EVENTS

Easter, March/April

Victory Day, May

Sadko Festival, June

White Nights, June/July

Kamwa Festival, July

January

Much of Russia becomes snow- and ice-bound during this and subsequent winter months, but the weather rarely causes disruption to transport. Book transport tickets well in advance of the busy New Year period.

✹ Hyperborea Festival

This Karelian festival celebrates all that is wonderful about wintertime with parties, exhibitions, and an ice- and snow-sculpture competition that attracts entrants from across Russia and the world. The festival runs into February. (p296)

✹ Magic Ice of Siberia

Local and international teams compete for various prizes for their ice sculptures in the Siberian city of Krasnoyarsk in early January.

✹ Russian Orthodox Christmas (Rozhdestvo)

On Christmas Eve (6 January), the religious fast from morning to nightfall, after which they tuck in to a feast that includes roast duck and *kutya* (porridge). Special masses are held in churches at midnight.

February

In the depths of winter, the devout deny themselves meat, milk, alcohol and sex during Lent's 40-day pre-Easter fasting period. Many restaurants offer special Lenten menus.

✹ Butter Week (Maslenitsa)

The Russian for this Shrovetide festival comes from the word *masla* (butter). Folk shows and games celebrate the end of winter, with lots of pancake eating before Lent (pancakes were a pagan symbol of the sun).

✹ Defender of the Fatherland Day

This holiday on 23 February is celebrated with parades and processions in honour of veterans. Women also give small gifts to the men in their lives.

March

Lent continues. Come prepared for wet, cold weather.

✹ Festival of the North

A 10-day Arctic fun-fest replete with reindeer-sled races and snowmobile events. Kola's indigenous Sami (Lapp) people join the celebrations with displays of traditional culture. Kicks off in late March in Murmansk. (p321)

☆ Golden Mask Festival

This Moscow-based festival, usually held in late March and early April, involves two weeks of performances by Russia's premier drama, opera, dance and musical stars, culminating in a prestigious awards ceremony. (p96)

✹ Tibetan Buddhist New Year

A movable feast lasting 16 days, Tibetan Buddhist New Year (Tsagaalgan) celebrates the Lunar New Year and hence advances by about 10 days annually. It's mainly celebrated at family level in Buryatiya and Tuva, where it's known as Shagaa.

Women's Day

Celebrated on 8 March, this is like St Valentine's Day, with women getting presents of flowers, chocolates and the like, and a chance to rest up while men take care of the daily chores.

April

In Western European Russia, melting snow makes the streets a slushy mess. However, it's a great time to brave Siberia and the far north, where winter still rules but with less savage force.

Alexander Nevsky Festival

The second weekend in April sees this celebration in Veliky Novgorod honouring Russia's best-known prince. Members of historical clubs dress up as knights, engage in mock battle and storm the kremlin walls.

Easter (Paskha)

Easter Sunday begins with midnight services. Afterwards, people eat *kulich* (traditional dome-shaped bread) and *paskha* (cheesecake), and exchange painted wooden Easter eggs.

May

The long-awaited arrival of pleasant spring weather makes this one of the best months for travel. Between International Labour Day (1 May) and Victory Day (9 May), some offices and museums have limited hours as people take advantage of the holidays for extended R&R.

Cossack Fairs

Held in Starocherkassk on the last Sunday of the month from May to September, with much singing, dancing, horse-riding and merrymaking.

Glinka Festival

At the end of the month, the composer Mikhail Glinka is honoured in his home town of Smolensk with this weeklong festival of classical music that draws in top talent. (p251)

Victory Day

On 9 May, this Russian public holiday celebrates the end of WWII, which Russians call the Great Patriotic War. Big military parades in Moscow and St Petersburg are well worth attending. (p196)

June

A popular month for *den goroda* (city day), when towns celebrate their birthdays with parades and street festivals: Veliky Novgorod has one on 12 June and Tver on 25 June. The weather is hot, but be prepared for rain too.

International Platanov Festival

Voronezh hosts this ambitious weeklong jamboree of theatre, music and the arts (http://en.platonovfest.com) in memory of local talent Andrei Platanov, a banned Soviet-era writer.

Kinotavr Film Festival

Running for a week in early June, Sochi's Kinotavr Film Festival showcases more than a dozen feature-length Russian movies, with local film-makers and actors on hand. Open-air screenings too. (p381)

Moscow International Film Festival

Russia's premier film festival runs for eight days at the end of the month and includes retrospective and documentary cinema programmes as well as the usual awards. (p98)

Sabantuy

In the middle of June this holiday celebrated all over Tatarstan and beyond features horse races, *koresh* (wrestling matches) and joking competitions – although the humour may be lost in translation. (p343)

Sadko Festival

Held on the second weekend of June in Veliky Novgorod, this event includes Russian and international teams performing traditional folk art, dancing and singing. There's also a craft fair. (p261)

Uglich Versta

A few hundred bicyclists meet for three days of riding, singing and drinking during this annual cyclefest in the Golden Ring town of Uglich. Expect competitions, kids' events, entertainment and a bicycle parade.

White Nights

As days lengthen, Russia's cultural capital, St Petersburg, hosts a huge party made up of a variety of events, including a jampacked itinerary of shows at the Mariinsky Theatre

& Concert Hall. Events run until late July. (p196)

Ysyakh

Held around 21 June near Yakutsk, this celebration of Sakha culture includes the chance to sample traditional eats while watching local sports and spectacular costumed battle reenactments.

July

The best time to visit the Volga Delta is between late July and late September, when lotus flowers blossom. Russians head to the coast and their dachas (summer country houses) as the weather really heats up.

☆ Afisha Picnic

This one-day popular and rock music event (http://picnic.afisha.ru) is held in the Tsarist-era estate of Kolomenskoye on the banks of the Moscow River. It attracts a big international line-up.

El-Oiyn Festival

Held every two years on the first weekend of July, this 'folk games' festival gathers some 60,000 people for a celebration of Altai culture.

Kamwa Festival

The 'ethno-futuristic' Kamwa Festival, taking place in late July in Perm and Khokhlovka, brings together ancient ethno-Ugric traditions and modern culture. (p416)

☆ Mir Sibiri

Similar to the UK's Womad Festival, this large event floods the small Siberian town of Shushenskoe with almost 25,000 visitors. Tuvan throat singers usually steal the show. (p489)

Solovetsky Islands Herring Festival

Head to Solovki to get your hands on some of Russia's finest fish – literally, in the case of the bare-handed catch competition.

August

Train prices can spike during this hot month as many people take holidays. Book ahead if you want to travel on particular services along the trans-Siberian route.

Dzhangariada Festival

Held in late August or September, this Kalmyk cultural celebration takes place on the open steppe at a different location every year. It includes wrestling, archery contests and traditional singers.

Tuvan Naadym

Naadym offers four wild days of underpants-hoicking *khuresh* (Tuvan wrestling), stern-faced archery contests, gravity-defying feats of steppe horsemanship, lots of croaky throat singing and fireworks bursting over the Tuvan capital of Kyzyl. (p493)

October

Russia's brief, brilliantly colourful autumn is swiftly followed by the onset of winter – at the end of the month, come prepared for snow flurries and plummeting temperatures.

☆ Russian Grand Prix

The Formula 1 (www.formula1.com) caravan hits Sochi. The race takes place in the former Winter Olympic Park.

November

In the southern Caucasus you may be able to catch the swiftly fading colours of autumn, but here and elsewhere the weather is certainly getting colder as winter fast approaches.

Unity Day

Held on 4 November, this public holiday celebrates the expulsion of Polish forces from Moscow in 1612. There's usually a parade in Moscow's Red Square. Unity Day replaced a Soviet holiday to celebrate the 1917 October Revolution.

December

Short days and long nights keep people inside for most of this month. If you're prepared, it's the best time to see freshly snow-covered landscapes.

New Year's Eve

See out the old year with vodka and welcome in the new one with champagne while listening to the Kremlin chimes on TV.

Itineraries

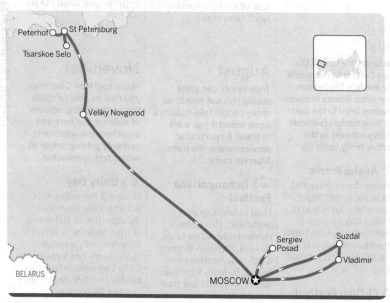

Peterhof ○ ○ St Petersburg
Tsarskoe Selo ○

○ Veliky Novgorod

BELARUS

Sergiev ○ Posad

Suzdal ○
○ Vladimir

MOSCOW ☆

2 WEEKS Russian Capitals

Start in **Moscow** where the Kremlin, Red Square, the Tretyakov Gallery, a performance at the Bolshoi Theatre and riding the grand metro system must all be factored into your schedule. Stretch your legs in the revamped Gorky Park and along the embankments by the Moscow River.

Save a few days for trips to the historic and serene Golden Ring towns of **Sergiev Posad**, **Suzdal** and **Vladimir**.

Break your journey between the two big cities at tourist-friendly **Veliky Novgorod**. It's home to an impressive riverside kremlin, ancient churches and a wonderful open-air museum of wooden architecture.

The historic heart of **St Petersburg** offers the incomparable Hermitage and Russian Museum, as well as the opportunity to cruise the city's rivers and canals. Enjoy some of Russia's top restaurants and bars, and attend first-rate performances at the Mariinsky and Mikhailovsky Theatres.

If you have the time, venture out to grand palaces set in beautifully landscaped grounds such as **Peterhof** and **Tsarskoe Selo**, easy half-day trips from the city.

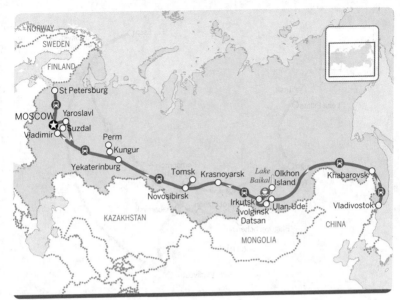

The Trans-Siberian Odyssey

Situated on a stunningly attractive natural harbour, the port of **Vladivostok** is worth a couple of days' sightseeing before boarding the train. An overnight journey west will take you to your first stop at **Khabarovsk**, a lively city with a lingering tsarist-era charm located on the banks of the Amur River.

Two more days down the line hop off the train at **Ulan-Ude**, the capital of Buryatiya, where Russian, Soviet and Mongolian cultures coexist; from here you can venture into the steppes to visit Russia's principal Buddhist monastery, **Ivolginsk (Ivolga) Datsan**.

The railway then skirts around the southern shores of magnificent **Lake Baikal**. Allow at least three days (preferably longer) to soak up the charms of this beautiful lake, basing yourself on beguiling **Olkhon Island**. Check out historic **Irkutsk** on the way to – or back from – the lake.

Flush with oil wealth, happening **Krasnoyarsk**, on the Yenisey River, affords the opportunity for scenic cruises along one of Siberia's most pleasant waterways. Siberia's capital of **Novosibirsk** offers big-city delights, including the gigantic Opera & Ballet Theatre. Detour slightly from the main Trans-Siberian Railway line to **Tomsk**, the 'cultural capital of Siberia', to hang with its lively student population and admire the city's treasure trove of wooden architecture.

Crossing the Urals into European Russia, spend a day or so in **Yekaterinburg**, a historic, bustling city well stocked with interesting museums and sites connected to the murder of the last tsar and his family. **Perm** is also doing an excellent job of reinventing itself as a cultural centre; use it as a base from which to make trips to an ice cave at **Kungur** and the Gulag labour camp Perm-36, preserved as a museum.

Finally, take a reviving break in the Golden Ring towns of **Yaroslavl** or **Vladimir**, which is also the access point for the idyllic village of **Suzdal**: all are stacked with beautiful, old onion-domed churches. You should then be fortified for the bustle of **Moscow** and **St Petersburg**.

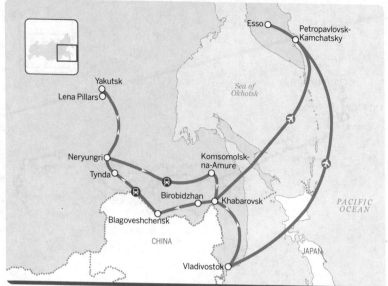

4 WEEKS Russian Far East circuit

Spend a few days in the booming capital of the region, the port of **Vladivostok**, taking in its beautiful location, thriving food and bar scene, great new arts centre and oceanarium, and constantly improving infrastructure. Next, head north to the attractive city of **Khabarovsk** by the Amur River, using this as a base for a side trip to **Birobidzhan**, the sleepy yet interesting capital of the Jewish Autonomous Region. Continue west to lively **Blagoveshchensk** with its splendid tsarist architecture (China is on the opposite bank of the Amur River).

An overnight train will transport you to **Tynda**, the main hub on the Baikal-Amur Mainline (BAM), which has a museum dedicated to this other Trans-Siberian rail route. Continue by train to **Neryungri**, where you have a choice: either fly or endure a very bumpy all-day ride in a Russian UAZ 4WD or van to **Yakutsk**, the extraordinary permafrost-bound capital of the Sakha Republic. In Yakutsk, visit the Permafrost Kingdom and Mammoth Museum. If it's the summer sailing season, cruise to the scenic **Lena Pillars** on the Lena River.

Backtrack to Neyrungri, reboard the BAM and take it through to the attractive city of **Komsomolsk-na-Amure**, built from scratch in the 1930s and decorated with some amazing Soviet-era mosaics.

Return by train to either Khabarovsk or Vladivostok, from where you can fly over the Seat of Okhotsk for a spectacular climax to the trip in Kamchatka. Be prepared to spend several days planning your outdoor adventures (and likely waiting for good weather) in the volcano-studded peninsula's capital, **Petropavlovsk-Kamchatsky**. Splash out on a helicopter tour to the amazing Valley of the Geysers, the bear hot spot of Lake Kurilskoe or the fuming caldera of Mt Mutnovskaya. Finally, make your way north to the lovely Evenki village of **Esso**, friendly to independent travellers with cheap guesthouses, public hot springs and well-mapped trails for trekking.

3 WEEKS Lakes of the Russian North

From **Moscow** follow the Volga River north to **Tver** where Catherine the Great used to pause on cross-country journeys. Make a side trip to serene **Lake Seliger**.

Top up on big-city culture and fun in **St Petersburg**, then take the train to **Petrozavodsk** to access Lake Ladoga and the island of **Valaam**, home to a beguiling working monastery. Return to Petrozavodsk, where you can board a hydrofoil that will zip you across Lake Onega to the island of **Kizhi**, an architectural reserve that includes the astounding Transfiguration Church, a symphony of wooden domes, gables and decoration.

The White Sea is the location of the **Solovetsky Islands**; the beautiful landscapes and monastery here were also the setting for some of the most brutal scenes in Solzhenitsyn's *The Gulag Archipelago*. More offbeat adventures, including top fishing sites, await in the **Kola Peninsula**.

Finish in **Murmansk** by checking out a decommissioned nuclear icebreaker and the giant concrete soldier *Alyosha*. In the summer, the sun never fully sets, while in winter you may witness the amazing northern lights.

3 WEEKS Volga Route to Astrakhan

Starting in **Moscow**, head east towards **Nizhny Novgorod** where the river can be viewed from above on a cable-car ride. Spend a day or so here enjoying the town's kremlin and museums. Consider making a day trip by hydrofoil to **Gorodets**, known for its folk arts.

The next major stop is the intriguing Tatarstan capital of **Kazan** with its World Heritage Site–listed kremlin that includes an enormous mosque and a small satellite branch of St Petersburg's Hermitage. The Volga continues to guide you south past Lenin's birthplace of **Ulyanovsk** and **Samara**, from where you can hike in the rocky Zhiguli Hills or search out the town's several offbeat design and cultural sights.

The 17-hour train journey to **Volgograd**, a city entirely rebuilt after Russia's bloodiest battle of WWII, is worth it to see the amazing 72m-tall statue of Mother Russia Mamaev Kurgan. The Volga spills into the Caspian Sea at **Astrakhan**, the jumping-off point for exploring the glorious natural attractions (including rare flamingos) of the Volga Delta; this is the home to the endangered sturgeon, the source of Beluga caviar.

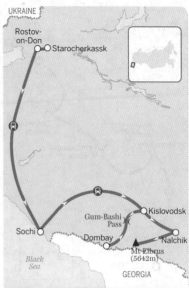

4 WEEKS — Siberia's Deep South

Begin in the oil-rich city of **Tyumen**, full of traditional architecture. Journey northeast to **Tobolsk**, whose splendid kremlin lords it over the Tobol and Irtysh Rivers; the last tsar and his family were exiled here before their fateful journey to Yekaterinburg.

Next, head south to **Barnaul**, the gateway to the mountainous Altai Republic. Here you can arrange a white-water rafting expedition or plan treks out to the pretty village of **Artybash** and beautiful **Lake Teletskoe**. Stop in **Gorno-Altaisk** to register your visa. Drive along the southern section of the panoramic **Chuysky Trakt**, a helter-skelter mountain road leading to yurt-dotted grasslands.

Return from the Chusky Trakt to **Biysk**, take a bus to **Novokuznetsk** and then a train to **Abakan** to arrange onward travel to Tuva. This remote and little-visited region, hard up against Mongolia – with which it shares several cultural similarities – is famed for its throat-singing nomads and mystical shamans. **Kyzyl** has a good National Museum and Cultural Centre and can be used as a base for expeditions to pretty villages and the vast Central Asian steppes.

3 WEEKS — Adventures in the Caucasus

The violence in parts of the Caucasus in recent decades has put off visitors, but this beautiful and multifaceted region of Russia is actually an amazing and, for the most part, safe place to travel, offering beaches, mountains and a fascinating mix of cultures.

Start in cosmopolitan **Rostov-on-Don**, where you can take a stroll or cruise along the Don River. Upriver it's worth making a day trip to the Cossack capital of **Starocherkassk**. Take an overnight train south to the coastal resort of **Sochi** to experience the glamour of the Russian Riviera as well as Stalin's extraordinary dacha. Next, head inland on another overnight train to the relaxing Mineral Waters spa town of **Kislovodsk**. Hire a taxi for a spectacular journey over the Gum-bashi Pass to the even more stunning mountain resort of **Dombay**. After a few days of hiking or skiing (depending on the season), hop on a series of *marshrutky* (fixed-route minibuses) via **Nalchik** to the big daddy of the Greater Caucasus range, **Mt Elbrus**. If you're planning to climb Europe's tallest peak, you'll need to set aside at least a week. If not, ride the cable cars up the mountain for out-of-this-world views.

Plan Your Trip

Great Train Journeys

One of the best ways to see Russia and connect with locals is to take a train journey. With nearly 85,300km of track, there's a fair chance that Russian Railways (RZD or РЖД) will have a service to suit your travel plans.

Tickets

Bookings & Costs

You can buy train tickets at stations and online – via RZD (https://pass.rzd.ru) or a host of other online travel agencies – up to 60 days in advance of your planned date of travel. Those selling tickets as agents for RZD will add their own charges to the basic fares. Note when booking that every train in Russia has two numbers: one for the eastbound service (even numbers) and one for the westbound (odd numbers).

RZD's fares vary by the class of carriage and/or berth or seat, season and demand for travel – expect to pay anything up to 20% more at peak travel times (eg early July to early August and around key holidays such as Easter and New Year). The inverse happens at slack times of the year, such as early January to March, when there are discounts on fares.

Children under five travel free if they share a berth/seat with an adult; otherwise, children under 10 pay a reduced fare for their own berth/seat.

Discounts are often available for online bookings and if you're prepared to take the upper bunks in *kupe* (2nd-class) carriages. It's also possible to have two grades of *kupe* fare, with or without meals.

Resources

Inspirational Books

The Big Red Train Ride (Eric Newby)

Through Siberia by Accident and **Silverland** (Dervla Murphy)

Trans-Siberian Railway (Anne and Olaf Meinhardt)

The Trans-Siberian Railway: A Traveller's Anthology (ed Deborah Manley)

To the Edge of the World: The Story of the Trans-Siberian Railway (Christian Wolmar)

Journey into the Mind's Eye (Lesley Blanch)

Useful Websites

RZD (Russian Railways; http://pass.rzd.ru) For bookings on the national rail network.

Man in Seat 61 (www.seat61.com) Up-to-date info and links.

Trans-Siberian Railway Web Encyclopedia (www.transsib.ru) Not updated, but still a mine of useful background info.

Trans-Siberian Railway Encyclopedia (https://trans-siberian-railway-encyclopedia.com) Download a copy of Robert Walker's ebook all about the various trans-Sib routes.

Ticket Classes

The five classes of ticket are:

➡ Мягкие (*myagky*; soft) 1st-class compartment sleeping two with its own toilet and shower; only available on certain *firmeny* (premium-class) services.

➡ CB (SV, standing for *spalny vagon*) Also 1st-class compartment sleeping two, but with shared toilets for the carriage.

➡ Купе (*kupe*) 2nd-class compartment sleeping four, with shared toilets for the carriage.

➡ Плацкарт (*platskart*) Dorm carriage with 54 berths; in the process of being phased out to replaced by double-decker carriages with private compartments.

➡ Общий (*obshchiy*) General or seating class, usually only for day trains.

Trans-Siberian Routes

Extending 9289km from Moscow to Vladivostok on the Pacific, and taking around six full days, the Trans-Siberian Railway is among the most famous of the world's great train journeys. Rolling out of Europe and into Asia, over vast swathes of taiga, steppe and desert, the Trans-Siberian – the world's longest single-service railway – makes all other train rides seem like once around the block with Thomas the Tank Engine.

Don't look for the Trans-Siberian Railway on a timetable, though. The term is used generically for three main lines and the numerous trains that run on them. For the first four days of travel out of Moscow's Yaroslavsky *vokzal* (station), the trans-Siberian, trans-Manchurian and trans-Mongolian routes all follow the same line, passing through Nizhny Novgorod on the way to Yekaterinburg in the Ural Mountains and then into Siberia.

Many travellers choose to break their journey at Irkutsk to visit Lake Baikal (we recommend you do), but otherwise, the three main services continue on round the southern tip of the lake to Ulan-Ude, another possible jumping-off point for Baikal. From here, trans-Siberian trains continue to Vladivostok, while the trans-Mongolian ones head south for the Mongolian border, Ulaanbaatar and Beijing. The trans-Manchurian service continues past Ulan-Ude to Chita, then turns southeast for Zabaikalsk on the Chinese border.

For details about the journey, read Lonely Planet's *Trans-Siberian Railway* guide.

Moscow to Vladivostok

The 1/2 *Rossiya* train is the premier Moscow–Vladivostok service, but tickets are more expensive; if you're stopping off along the route, it will be cheaper to use other trains. For comparison, a *kupe* berth for the whole journey on the 99/100 train, which also links Moscow and Vladivostok (via Yaroslavl), costs around R21,000 compared to R37,400 on the *Rossiya*.

If you'd prefer to skip Moscow in favour of St Petersburg as the start or finish of a trans-Siberian journey, the 71/72 *Demidovsky Express* between St Petersburg and Yekaterinburg is a recommended option.

And if you'd like to speed things up, there are also the high-speed *Strizh* trains connecting Moscow and Nizhny Novgorod in around three hours and 30 minutes.

Moscow to Ulaanbaatar & Beijing

The more popular of the two options running directly between Moscow and Beijing is the weekly 3/4 trans-Mongolian service, a Chinese train that travels via

---

BREAKING YOUR JOURNEY

There is no Russian rail pass. Hence, if you are travelling from, say, Moscow to Vladivostok, and plan on spending a night or two in Nizhny Novgorod and Irkutsk, you'll need three separate tickets: Moscow–Nizhny Novgorod, Nizhny Novgorod–Irkutsk and Irkutsk–Vladivostok.

If you're planning to frequently hop on and off trains and want to save some money along the way, it's a good idea to avoid the premium trains and go for the regular services, which offer the cheaper *platskart* (3rd-class) carriages. Most of these services are perfectly acceptable and take pretty much the same travelling time, point to point, as the premium trains.

SHE WHO MUST BE OBEYED

On any long-distance Russian train journey you'll soon learn who's in charge: the *provodnitsa*. Though sometimes male (*provodnik*), carriage attendants are usually women.

Apart from checking your ticket before boarding the train, doling out linen, and shaking you awake in the middle of the night when your train arrives, the job of the *provodnitsa* is to keep her carriage spick and span (most are very diligent about this) and to make sure the samovar is always fired up with hot water. They will have cups, plates and cutlery to borrow, if you need them, and can provide drinks and snacks for a small price.

On long journeys, the *provodnitsa* works in a team of two; one will be working while the other is resting.

Initially, a *provodnitsa* can come across as quite fearsome. Very few will speak any language other than Russian. All look as smart as sergeant majors in their RZD uniforms – and just as ready to knock you into shape if you step out of line! However, if you're polite and respectful to your *provodnitsa*, and bestow on her plenty of friendly smiles, chances are that she will do her best to make your journey a very pleasant one.

Ulaanbaatar and is the only one to offer deluxe carriages with showers.

If you're planning to stop off in Irkutsk, there's also the less fancy 361/362 service to/from Naushki, with through-carriages to/from Ulaanbaatar.

The weekly 19/20 *Vostok* trans-Manchurian service is a Russian train that crosses the border into China at Zabaikalsk, and passes through Harbin before terminating in Beijing seven days after its initial departure from Moscow.

The BAM: Tayshet to Sovetskaya Gavan

The alternative trans-Sib route is the Baikal-Amur Mainline (Baikalo-Amurskaya Magistral; BAM). It begins at Tayshet, 4515km east of Moscow, curls around the top of Lake Baikal, cuts through nonstop taiga, winds around snow-splattered mountains and burrows through endless tunnels on its way east to Sovetskaya Gavan on the Tatar Strait.

The BAM's prime attraction is the incredibly remote and utterly wild scenery viewed from the train window. As well as Lake Baikal's lovely northern lip, adventures on the BAM reach some very out-of-the-way places including Bratsk, Tynda and Komsomolsk-na-Amure.

Other Long-Distance Routes

Other intriguing services that link up far-flung corners of Russia and further afield include the 225/226 Murmansk–Adler train, a 76-hour service that connects the Arctic Circle city with the sun-kissed shores of the Black Sea. The train passes through Kem (jumping-off point for the Solovetsky Islands), Petrozavodsk (for access to Kizhi), Tver, Moscow, Voronezh, Rostov-on-Don and Sochi. If travelling this route in the winter months, apart from the glorious snow-blanketed wilderness (and little snowed-in villages pumping out chimney smoke), watch out for little ice-fishing 'cities' that pop up on wide frozen lakes and the occasional glimpse of villagers playing football on said icy expanses. Train breaks are always great for running out to buy huge smoked fish (including expensive smoked whole eels) from the babushkas on the platforms.

Even on short visits to the country it's possible to squeeze in one overnight train journey, the most popular one being between Moscow and St Petersburg. The high-speed, TGV-standard *Sapsan* trains may link the two metropolises in under four hours, but they lack the glamour and romance of climbing aboard premium overnight RZD services such as the *Krasnaya*

Strela (Red Arrow) or the private *Grand Express* (www.grandexpress.ru), which bills itself as a mobile hotel.

And if you really can't get enough of long-distance trains, the RZD network is just as connected to Europe's networks as it is to those of Asia's, offering direct services to, among other places, Berlin, Nice, Paris and Vienna. The Man in Seat Sixty-One (www.seat61.com) has full details.

On the Journey

There is nothing quite like the smell of a Russian train: coal smoke, coffee, garlic, sausage, sweat, vodka and dozens of other elements combine to form an aroma that's so distinctive it will be permanently etched in your sensual memory.

To calculate where you are while on a journey, keep an eye out for the small, black-and-white kilometre posts generally on the southern side of the track. These mark the distance to and from Moscow. In between each kilometre marker are smaller posts counting down roughly every 100m. The distances on train timetables don't always correspond to these marker posts (usually because the timetable distances are the ones used to calculate fares).

Luggage

Russians have a knack of making themselves totally at home on trains. This often means that they'll be travelling with plenty of luggage, causing inevitable juggling of the available space in all compartment classes.

In all but local trains there's a luggage bin underneath each lower berth that will hold a medium-sized backpack or small suitcase. There's also enough space beside the bin to squeeze in another medium-sized bag. Above the doorway (in 1st and 2nd classes) or over the upper bunks (in 3rd class) there's room to accommodate a couple more rucksacks.

Etiquette

➡ Sleeping compartments are mixed sex; when women indicate that they want to change clothing before going to bed or after getting up, men go out and loiter in the corridor.

➡ It's good manners to offer any food or drinks you bring to the fellow passengers in your compartment; Russians will always offer to share their food with you.

➡ Smoking is forbidden anywhere on the train and on the platforms.

➡ If service from the *provodnitsa* is especially good, a tip is a good way to show appreciation.

Toilets

Located at both ends of each carriage, toilets can be locked long before and after station stops (there's a timetable on the door). Except on a very few premium-service trains, there are no shower facilities – improvise with a sponge, flannel or short length of garden hose that you can attach to the tap for a dousing.

Food & Drink

Every sleeping carriage has a samovar filled with boiling water that's safe to drink and ideal for hot drinks, instant noodles or porridge.

The quality of food in dining cars varies. Rather than for eating, they become the place to hang out, drink beer and play cards, particularly on the long trans-Siberian trip. Note also on the trans-Mongolian and trans-Manchurian trains that the dining cars are changed at each border, so en route to Beijing you get Russian, Chinese and possibly Mongolian versions. Occasionally, between the Russian border and Ulaanbaatar there is no dining car.

A meal in a restaurant car can cost anything from R400 to R1000. If you don't fancy what's on offer, there's often a table of instant noodles, savoury snacks, chocolate, alcohol, juice and the like being peddled by staff. They sometimes make the rounds of the carriages, too, with a trolley of snacks and drinks. Prices are typically a little more than you'd pay at the kiosks or to the babushkas at the station halts.

Some tickets include a meal or snack; eg on the Sapsan services between Moscow and St Petersburg you'll be provided with an airline-style snack box or a full hot meal, depending on your class of ticket.

Shopping for supplies at the stations is part of the fun of any long-distance Russian train trip. The choice of items is often excellent, with fresh milk, ice cream, grilled chicken, boiled potatoes, home cooking such as *pelmeni* (Russian-style ravioli dumplings) or *pirozhki* (savoury pies), buckets of forest berries and smoked fish all on offer.

Plan Your Trip

Russian Adventures

Russia offers a thrilling and irresistible range of terrain for outdoor adventures. There are majestic mountains to climb and ski down, national parks and wilderness areas to hike through, and fast-flowing rivers for rafting and canoeing. Piloting a supersonic MiG fighter jet or training as a cosmonaut are also possible!

Preparing for your Adventure

While most specialist operators are professional, this is Russia, so be flexible, patient and prepared for things not to go as smoothly as you may hope. There will often also be a group of enthusiasts more than happy to share their knowledge and even equipment with a visitor; you might also be able to locate guides for trekking and other activities where detailed local knowledge is essential. Provide as much advance warning as possible; even if you can't hammer out all the details, give operators an idea of your interests.

Always check the safety equipment before you set out and make sure you know what's included in the quoted price. Also, make sure you have adequate insurance – many travel insurance policies have exclusions for risky activities, including skiing, diving and even trekking.

Boating, Canoeing & Rafting

Although the pollution of many rivers discourages numerous travellers from even getting near the water, the coasts offer many canoeing and kayaking possibilities.

Choose an Adventure

Inspiring Adventure Tales

Kolyma Diaries (Jacek Hugo-Bader; 2011) Hitch-hiking along the 2025km 'road of bones' from Magadan to Yakutsk.

River of No Reprieve (Jeffrey Tayler; 2006) Sailing an inflatable raft along the Lena River, from Lake Baikal to the Arctic Ocean.

A Siberian Winter's Tale (Helen Lloyd; http://helenstakeon.com) See photos and more of Helen's Siberian cycling adventure on her website.

Cycling Home from Siberia (Rob Lilwall; www.roblilwall.com) Rob's website features original blog posts and videos.

Consolations of the Forest (Sylvain Tesson; 2011) Living for six months as a hermit in a cabin beside Lake Baikal.

Top Adventures

Climbing mountains in the Caucasus

Hiking the Great Baikal Trail

Driving across Russia

Fishing for wild salmon in Kamchatka

Skiing in the Caucasus or at Sheregesh

The Altai region's pristine rivers are best for full-blown expedition-grade rafting, as well as easy, fun splashes possible on a 'turn up' basis. Kamchatka's Bystraya River is also recommended.

The Solovetsky Islands in Northern European Russia are an example of the remote and fascinating places that can be toured by boat during the summer.

The Volga Delta, with its fascinating flora and fauna, below Astrakhan, is an amazing place to explore by boat. In towns and parks with clean lakes, there are usually rowing boats available for rent during the warmer months. Moscow and St Petersburg have active yacht clubs. You can also arrange white-water rafting trips in Arkhyz and other locations in the central Caucasus.

California-based agency **Raft Siberia** (☎1-541-386-2271; www.raftsiberia.com) arranges rafting trips on the Katun, Chuya, Sayan Oka and Chatkal Rivers in Siberia. One of its founders, Vladimir Gavrilov, is the author of *Rivers of an Unknown Land: A Whitewater Guide to the Former Soviet Union,* the only English-language guidebook to include detailed information about rafting rivers in Russia.

Recommended Agencies

Kamchatintour (p583) One of the best agencies to organise rafting tours in Kamchatka.

Nata Tour (p563) White-water rafting trips and slower floats out of Komsomolsk-na-Amure.

Alash Travel (p495) Rafting adventures organised in Tuva.

MorinTur (p531) Rafting in the Barguzin Valley is one of the adventures on offer.

Wild Russia (p195) Yachting and kayaking on Lake Ladoga.

Team Gorky (p337) Canoe and rafting tours in the Nizhny Novgorod region.

Cycling

Russia's traffic-clogged cities are far from a cyclist's nirvana, but off-road cyclists will find plenty of challenging terrain. Rural Russians are quite fascinated with and friendly towards long-distance riders. Just make certain you have a bike designed for the harshest conditions and carry plenty of spare parts.

Bike rentals are available in Moscow, St Petersburg, Suzdal and Svetlogorsk among other locations.

For more online about cycling, see Towns.ru (www.towns.ru) which has reviews and pictures of charming off-the-beaten-path locations, many of which could be visited on a cycling tour. See also the website www.crazyguyonabike.com. The Moscow-based, non-profit social club **Russian Cycle Touring Club** (☎916-5822426; www.rctc.ru) runs tours each summer around the Golden Ring or between Moscow and St Petersburg.

Recommended Agencies

Moscow Bike Tours (p93) Cover more ground and see more sites on these pedalling tours around the capital.

Peterwalk Walking Tours (p195) Walking tours of St Petersburg, plus guided bike tours.

Team Gorky (p337) Cycling tours in the Nizhny Novgorod and along the Volga.

Elbrus Elevation (p403) Nalchik-based agency offering a great itinerary cycling into the Cherek Valley.

Diving

Those with the constitution of a walrus may fancy braving the frigid waters of Lake Baikal, the Baltic Sea to go diving – or even the Arctic Circle. A warmer alternative would be search out possibilities at the Black Sea coastal resorts.

Recommended Agencies

Arctic Circle PADI Dive Center (p314) Ice-diving trips in winter and regular diving in the summer off the Kola Peninsula.

Demersus (p285) Diving in Yantarny Lake, a former quarry in the Kaliningrad Region, with a depth of some 26m in places.

RuDive (Map p66; ☎495-925 7799; www.dive.ru; Suvorovskaya ul 19) Moscow dive centre that also organises trips to the White Sea and Lake Baikal.

Fishing

Serious anglers drool at the opportunity to fish the rivers, lakes and lagoons of the Kaliningrad Region, Northern European

DRIVING THE TRANS-SIBERIAN HIGHWAY

For intrepid souls, the challenge of driving across the vast expanse of Russia is irresistible. This is your chance to traverse some incredible landscapes (but also many, many kilometres of bland and boring views) and to come into contact with a wide range of locals.

Ewan McGregor and Charley Boorman wrote about their Russian road adventures in *Long Way Round* (www.longwayround.com); their round-the-world route took them from Volgograd all the way to Yakutsk and Magadan via Kazakhstan and Mongolia. The celebrity bikers had a camera crew and support team following them. For a more accurate view of what to expect, read *The Linger Longer* by brothers Chris and Simon Raven, who somehow coaxed a rusty Ford Sierra from the UK to Vladivostok; *One Steppe Beyond* by Thom Wheeler, which covers a similar journey in a VW camper van; *Travels in Siberia* by the humourist Ian Frazier, who was accompanied by two Russian guides on his 2001 drive from St Petersburg to Vladivostok in a Renault van; and *White Fever* by Jacek Hugo-Bader, who drives from Moscow to Vladivostok in the middle of winter.

Whatever your mode of transport, driving the 11,000km from St Petersburg to Vladivostok has become a more feasible proposition since the full black-top completion of the 2100km Amur Hwy, between Chita and Khabarovsk (previously the rockiest section of the road). Even so, it's worth heeding the words of President Vladimir Putin, who, in August 2011, drove a 350km stretch of the Amur Hwy in a bright-yellow Lada Kalina Sport, afterwards commenting: 'It is a dependable, modern farm road, but not the Autobahn.'

For more insight, read a feature by Tim McCready (www.timmccready.nz/travel) about his 14,000km road trip across Russia in 2015.

Russia, the Russian Far East and Siberia. Kamchatka is a particular draw, with steelhead fishing in the peninsula reckoned to be the best in the world.

Start saving up, though: organised fishing trips in Russia can be heart-stoppingly expensive. While it's possible to go it alone and just head off with rod and tackle, most regions had restrictions on fishing, so you'd be wise to at least check these out before departure. An interesting alternative is ice fishing for Lake Baikal's unique *omul* (a cousin of salmon).

Hooked: Fly Fishing Through Russia (titled *Reeling in Russia* in the US) by Fen Montaigne charts the former Moscow-based correspondent as he spends a revealing three months casting his rod in the country's largely polluted lakes and rivers.

Recommended Agencies

Sergey Outfitter (p546) Fish in the vast wilderness of Khabarovsk Territory.

Ouzel Expeditions (☑1-800-825-8196, 1-907-783-2216; www.ouzel.com) US-based specialist for wild salmon fishing trips to Kamchatka.

Megatest (Мегатест; Map p66; ☑499-126 9119; www.megatest.ru; kv 419, Cheremushkinsky proezd 5) Moscow-based agency focusing on fishing in the wilder parts of Russia.

Atlantic Salmon Reserve (p314) Fish this protected Kola Peninsula reserve for salmon, sea- and wild trout and Arctic char.

Arctic Land (p319) Arranges fishing trips out of Murmansk.

Flying, Skydiving & Paragliding

Several tour operators can arrange passenger flights in the supersonic MiG-29s that fly out of Nizhny Novgorod's Sokol Airbase to the edge of space, where you can view the curvature of the globe. **Incredible Adventures** (☑1-800-644-7382, 1-941-346-2603; www.incredible-adventures. com), a US-based operator, can also arrange flights in the L39 Albatross out of Vyazma Air Base, three hours south-west of Moscow. London-based **SkyandSpaceTravel.com** (☑44-20-3355 2245; www.

ADVENTURES IN SPACE

Once a highly classified community of cosmonauts and scientists, Zvezdny Gorodok (Star City), around 50km drive northeast of Moscow, is where those looking to blast off into outer space train for the experience. Since 2001 **Space Adventures** (☑1-703-524-7172; www.spaceadventures.com), a US-based company, has arranged for several billionaire civilians to achieve their dream of space flight by training here also.

While you don't need to be filthy rich to sign up for the programmes offered by Space Adventures, they are far from your everyday travel adventure, both in terms of cost and the amount of serious physical and mental commitment required. Cosmonaut training (US$89,500), for example, takes a week and includes a spacewalk mission simulation in a neutral buoyancy tank. The least costly deal is to train for a spacewalk (US$7650), which still includes visiting Star City, trying on an Orlan spacesuit, meeting with cosmonauts and chowing down at Star City's cafeteria.

Moscow-based **Space Tourism Ltd** (☑495-532 7717; www.bestrussiantour.com) can arrange similar tours to Star City, including zero-gravity flights from €5000. If you just want to visit Star City and have a look around, this is also possible. Tours of the technical area and museum can be arranged through **GCTC** (Yury Gagarin Russian Research & Test Cosmonauts Training Centre; ☑495-526 2612; www.gctc.su; Star City).

skyandspacetravel.com) and Moscow-based Space Tourism Ltd (p46), both authorised MiG agents, also organise trips to see the launch of the manned Soyuz spacecraft from the Baikonur Cosmodrome in Kazakhstan and a range of activities at Star City.

Helicopter sightseeing flights over St Petersburg can be arranged with **Baltic Airlines** (Map p191; ☑812-611 0956; www.maxibalttours.com; R5000; ☑11.30am-6pm Sat, Sun & holidays, May-Oct).

Tandem jumps and skydiving courses can be arranged at **Aerograd Kolomna** (☑495-790 1511; www.aerograd.ru; Korobcheevo Airfield, Kolomna), Russia's largest skydiving centre, 100km south of Moscow.

Paragliding is also popular in the Chegem Valley of the central Caucasus. Contact Elbrus Elevation (p403) in Nalchik, or Pyatigorsk-based Russian Mountain Holidays (https://russianmountainholidays.com) for details.

Hiking, Mountaineering & Rock Climbing

Serious hikers and climbers will have the Caucasus mountains topping their wish list, particularly the areas around Mt Elbrus, Dombay, Krasnaya Polyana and Mt Fisht. The Agura Valley is a prime location for rock climbing.

For any trekking in the Caucasus, check on the current situation and arrange any necessary permits at least three months in advance; this is best done through local agencies.

In the southern Ural Mountains, Zyuratkul National Park and Taganay National Park are beautiful places to hike. Siberia also harbours many equally fantastic hiking and mountaineering locations, principally the Altai region (again, you will need permits for most climbs in this area, including Mt Belukha) and around Lake Baikal, where you'll find the **Great Baikal Trail** (p514).

Kamchatka also has plentiful hiking and mountaineering possibilities, including the chance to climb active volcanoes, but you will need to hire guides to avoid danger.

Elsewhere, multiple national parks and state nature reserves exist, but don't expect them to have especially good facilities or even well-marked trails. For this reason, it's especially important to seek out local advice, information and even guides before setting off.

Safe Hiking Guidelines

Before embarking on a hike, consider the following:

● Be sure you're healthy and feel comfortable about hiking for a sustained period. The nearest village in Russia can be vastly further away than it would be in other countries.

● Get the best information you can about the physical and environmental conditions along your intended route. Russian 'trails' are generally nominal ideas rather than marked footpaths, so employing a guide is very wise.

● Walk only in regions, and on trails, within your realm of experience.

● Be prepared for severe and sudden changes in the weather and terrain; always take wet-weather gear.

● Pack essential survival gear, including emergency food rations and a leak-proof water bottle.

● If you can, find a hiking companion. At the very least, tell someone where you're going and refer to your compass frequently so you can find your way back.

● Unless you're planning a camping trip, start early so you can make it home before dark.

● Allow plenty of time.

● For longer routes, consider renting, or even buying (then later reselling) a packhorse.

Recommended Agencies

Masterskaya Priklucheniy (p386) Krasnaya Polyana–based outfitter offering rock-climbing trips in the Caucasus.

K2 Adventures (p444) Western Siberia agency specialising in mountaineering expeditions in Altai.

Elbrus Adventures (p407) Can arrange pretty much whatever you need to summit Elbrus.

Wild Russia (p195) Experienced outfitter leading climbs up Elbrus' less busy northern route.

Ak Tur (p461) Mountaineering expeditions in the Altai with this Barnaul-based agency.

Horse Riding

Many of the same areas that offer good hiking and mountaineering also offer horse-riding treks. Try Arkhyz, Dombay and Elbrus in the Caucasus, the Altai region, or around Lake Baikal and Kamchatka. There's also the famous Georgenburg Stud Farm (p286) in Chern-yakhovsk, where children can go horse riding.

Skiing & Winter Sports

The 2014 Winter Olympics in Sochi and Krasnaya Polyana put Russia on the radar of winter sports enthusiasts across the world.

Downhill ski slopes are scattered throughout the country, with the best ones in the Caucasus and mountainous areas of Siberia such as the Altai. You'll also find a couple in the Urals such as Abzakovo (www.abzakovo.com) and Magnitogorsk (www.ski-bannoe.ru).

Cross-country skiing is more common, attracting legions of enthusiasts during the long winters. Easily accessible for this type of skiing are the resorts **Krasnoe Ozero** (☑812-960 0960; www.krasnoeozero. ru; Korobitsyno) and **Tuutari Park** (☑812-380 5062; www.tyytari.spb.ru; Retselya 14; ◎5-10pm Mon-Fri, 10am-9pm Sat & Sun Dec-Mar), both near St Petersburg. Given the wealth of open space, you won't have a problem finding a place to hit the trail elsewhere. For off-piste adventures, try heli-skiing and back-country skiing in the Caucasus and Kamchatka.

For further details, go to World Snowboardguide.com (www.worldsnowboard-guide.com/resorts/russia) or Onboard.ru (https://onboard.ru).

Snowmobile safaris and activities such as cruises are also possible in the Russian Arctic.

UNUSUAL ADVENTURES

SkyPark (p387) Black Sea coast park for all things aerial, including bungee jumping and zip-lining.

Baikal Dog Sledding Centre (p517) Thrilling dog sledding on forest tracks around Listvyanka in winter.

Surf Siberia (http://surfsiberia.ru/ en) Ultimate surfing adventures in Kamchatka and the Russian Far East.

Ladoga Trophy Raid (www.ladoga-trophy.ru) An eight-day marathon around Lake Ladoga, starting and ending in St Petersburg.

Recommended Ski Resorts

Elbrus Gondola (p406) Terminating at 3847m, this gondola up Europe's highest peak allows year-round skiing.

Roza Khutor (p387) Ski the largest venue for the Sochi Winter Olympics, offering world-class facilities.

Gorki Gorod (p387) New resort with high-quality pistes amid the rugged terrain of Mt Aibga.

Arkhyz Resort (ВТРК Архыз; ☎800-100 5559; www.arhyz-resort.ru; Turisticheskaya derevnya Romantik 1; ski-lift pass adult/child R2000/1000, gondola only R700/350; ☺8.30am-6pm Sun-Thu, to 10pm Fri & Sat Dec-Mar, 8am-5pm Apr-Nov) Another brand-new resort in the Greater Caucasus.

Sheregesh Ski Resort (p457) Access the fine powder of Siberia via three gondolas and several chairlifts.

Bolshoy Vudyavr Ski Station (p313) Modern lifts are on offer at the best of Kirovsk's ski stations.

Recommended Agencies

Kola Travel (p314) An inspiring selection of Kola adventures as well as expeditions to Franz Josef Land.

VICAAR (☎812-572 1769; http://eng.norpolex. com) St Petersburg–based firm specialising in tours to the North Poles and Russian Arctic.

Pomor Tur (p309) Apply well in advance to secure official permission for icebreaker tours out of Arkhangelsk.

Nord Extreme Tour (p321) Snowmobile adventures run out Murmansk.

H4U (p314) Snowmobile trips to Mt Takhtarvum-chorr and picturesque Maly Vudyavr Lake in the Russian Arctic.

Regions at a Glance

When planning a trip to the largest country in the world, it's best to establish your travel priorities. The vast majority of visitors are going to want to spend time in Moscow and St Petersburg; both of these historic cities deliver the goods in terms of memorable sights and comfortable facilities, and function as bases for trips further afield to locations in Western European Russia or the Golden Ring. Siberia's splendid natural attractions are pretty irresistible but you're going to need time to see this vast area, which is more manageable when split into west and east regions. To get fully off the beaten track, head to the Russian Far East, Northern European Russia or the Caucasus.

Moscow

Art
History
Performing Arts

Glorious Galleries

The illustrious Tretyakov and Pushkin Galleries are only the beginning of the art in Moscow, where contemporary artists and their patrons are taking over former factories and warehouses to display their works.

Historical Landmarks

The Kremlin shows off the splendour of Muscovy's grand princes. St Basil's Cathedral recounts the defeat of the Tatars. And on Red Square, Lenin lies embalmed.

Theatre Scene

The city's classical performing arts are still among the best in the world. Nowadays, even the most traditional theatres are experimenting with innovative arrangements and cutting-edge choreographies.

p54

Golden Ring

Religious Art
Countryside
Villages

Churches & Icons

Admire the quintessentially Russian images of golden cupolas and white-washed monastery walls guarding stunning medieval frescoes and icons encased in richly decorated altars.

Country Roads

From Vladimir to Yaroslavl, drive or cycle the picturesque A113, which skirts through dark coniferous forests, sun-filled birch-tree groves and neat villages of brightly painted log houses and dilapidated churches.

Village Life

Wake up in a gingerbread cottage, plunge into the nearby lake or river, savour your breakfast bliny and take it easy for the day in a garden chair, with a book and a jar of freshly picked strawberries for company.

p125

50

PLAN YOUR TRIP REGIONS AT A GLANCE

St Petersburg

Palaces
History
Art

Imperial Splendour

Grand imperial palaces line the embankments of the Neva River, its tributaries and canals. Restoration over the past two decades has been painstaking – and the results are breathtaking.

Revolutionary Road

Everything about St Petersburg is revolutionary: from Peter the Great's determination to forge a new Russia by opening the country to the rest of Europe, to Lenin's leadership of a coup in 1917, which led to the creation of the world's first communist state.

Unrivalled Collections

The Hermitage collection is unrivalled. The Russian Museum groans under the weight of its unique collection of Russian paintings, from icons to the avant-garde.

p156

Western European Russia

Kremlins
Architecture
Literary Shrines

Mighty Fortresses

The formidable stone fortresses of early Rus trading towns such as Veliky Novgorod, Pskov and Smolensk stand today as majestic backdrops to historical explorations.

Mystical Churches

Enter the ancient monastery at Pechory or the icon-crammed cathedrals of Veliky Novgorod and Smolensk to witness the revival of Orthodox Christianity in the region where the religion originally took root.

Writers' Estates

The family estates of Pushkin, Turgenev and Tolstoy provide insight into the country life of the gentry in the 19th century. In Staraya Russa, Fyodor Dostoevsky's home looks just as he left it.

p232

Kaliningrad Region

History
Museums
Beaches

Historical Roots

A rebuilt Gothic cathedral and the city's gates and fortifications are fragments of the time when Kaliningrad was Königsberg in the kingdom of Prussia.

Fascinating Museums

Learn about maritime history at the Museum of the World Ocean and be dazzled by artworks carved from petrified tree resin at the Amber Museum.

Beautiful Beaches

Discover some of Russia's best beaches at Yantarny and Zelenogradsk and in the Kurshskaya Kosa National Park, where massive sand dunes and wind-sculpted pines are sandwiched between the Baltic and Curonian Lagoon.

p273

Northern European Russia

Outdoors
History
Museums

Great Outdoors

Each season offers its own adventures, from swimming with human 'walruses' in winter to summertime fishing for champion salmon in rugged yet pristine rivers.

Historical Architecture

From the wooden marvels of Kizhi and the haunting stone edifices of Solovki to the nautically inspired churches of landlocked Totma, the architectural landscape here is as worth traversing as the natural one.

Offbeat Museums

The mineral-heavy towns of the Kola region rock several highbrow geology repositories, offering unique glimpses into local life; and Arkhangelsk's WWII-centric museum is a destination in itself.

p291

Volga Region

Architecture
Landscapes
Food & Culture

Diverse Architecture

Historic kremlins overlook the Volga River in Nizhny Novgorod, Kazan and Astrakhan, and monumental Stalinist buildings rise up out of Volgograd, contrasted by simple cottages in towns.

Mighty Volga

The Volga has many different faces. The Samara Bend is perfect for hiking, and in the Volga Delta this magnificent river culminates in a spectacular wetland where boats are often the only mode of transport.

Culinary Culture

Tatar culture dominates Kazan and Astrakhan, where you can best sample Tatar cuisine. Buddhism and a very different culinary culture prevail in Kalmykia, and across the region you can try hearty Russian dishes.

p332

Russian Caucasus

Winter Sports
Outdoors
Scenery

Olympic Skiing

From Sochi, access the mountain resort of Krasnaya Polyana, which, thanks to the Olympics, has scores of memorable runs and an excellent assortment of cosy guesthouses and revitalising *bani* (hot baths) for when the day is done.

Terrific Trekking

The Caucasus are a magnet for adventure seekers. You can summit majestic Mt Elbrus – Europe's highest peak – or go on multi-day treks exploring some of Russia's most dramatic scenery.

Idyllic Scenery

Pretty mineral water towns such as Kislovodsk and Pyatigorsk, nestled in the Caucasus foothills, are idyllic settings for scenic walks in the surrounding hills.

p369

The Urals

Landscapes
Cities & Towns
Museums

Diverse Landscapes

The Ural Mountains may only be truly spectacular in the north, but they are a lush, picturesque getaway elsewhere – check out Lake Zyuratkul or the ice cave of Kungur.

Urban Life

Yekaterinburg, home to a good variety of museums, is the most famous of the region's cities. Chelyabinsk is idiosyncratic beneath its urban grit, and Perm is eccentric and different.

Gulag & Art

Contrast Perm-36, the once-horrific Gulag camp located outside the city, with the modern and contemporary art space PERMM, which offers up the shock of the new.

p411

Western Siberia

Outdoors
Winter Sports
Architecture

Magnificent Nature

The Altai Republic's snow-capped mountains and remote lakes make the region a playground for nature lovers. Tourism is massively underdeveloped here, though, so be prepared to rough it.

Skiing & Snowboarding

The Sheregesh ski resort may be rough around the edges, but at least you won't have to queue long for the lifts. It also enjoys a stunning location in the heart of the Siberian countryside.

Historic Buildings

Tobolsk, Siberia's old capital, sports a handsome kremlin and charmingly decrepit old town. In Siberia's 'cultural capital', Tomsk, it's easy to lose yourself in a wonderland of wooden mansions and log cabins.

p435

Eastern Siberia

Outdoors
Landscapes
Museums

Natural Playground

Whether you hike the Great Baikal Trail, discover the impenetrable taiga on horseback, click on skis for a bit of off-piste action or kayak Lake Baikal's sapphire waters, Eastern Siberia is outdoorsy bliss.

Stunning Vistas

Show-stopping vistas are ensured in Tuva's grasslands, Krasnoyarsk's Stolby Nature Reserve, the back country of the Barguzin Valley, and the snow-whipped Eastern Sayan Mountains.

Exceptional Museums

Be rendered speechless by the intricacy of Scythian gold, take a virtual submarine to Lake Baikal's murky depths, and peruse a mini Khakassian Stonehenge at the region's intriguing repositories of the past.

p475

Russian Far East

Mountains
Adventures
Indigenous Cultures

Magnificent Scenery

Kamchatka hogs the glory with its volcanoes, but Russia's entire eastern seaboard is a riot of old-growth taiga and icy peaks primed for adventure.

Extreme Adventure

In addition to anything mountain-related, you might hitch the Chukotka Hwy or drive a reindeer sled across the Arctic – you're only limited by your imagination (and bank balance) here.

Native People

The weak don't survive in the 'pole of cold', and so it is that the Far East's native inhabitants are among the world's hardiest. Journey to their villages, where they fish and herd reindeer, or celebrate the summer solstice with the Sakha at Yakutsk's Ysyakh.

p540

On the Road

Moscow

495, 496, 498, 499 / POP 12.5 MILLION

Best Places to Eat

➡ Delicatessen (p105)

➡ Café Pushkin (p108)

➡ Khachapuri (p107)

➡ Kitayskaya Gramota (p107)

➡ Lavka-Lavka (p105)

Best Places to Stay

➡ Hotel National (p101)

➡ Hotel de Paris (p101)

➡ Godzillas Hostel (p99)

➡ Loft Hostel 77 (p101)

➡ Bulgakov Mini-Hotel (p102)

Why Go?

The state becomes more authoritarian. International relations deteriorate. But Moscow (Москва) keeps getting cooler, more cosmopolitan and more creative. The capital is bursting with energy, as factories and warehouses are converted into art galleries and post-industrial nightclubs; parks are overrun with healthy, active, sporty types; and chefs experiment with their own interpretations of international cooking.

The ancient city has always been a haven for history buffs: the red-brick towers of the Kremlin occupy the founding site of Moscow; monuments and churches remember fallen heroes and victorious battles; and remains of the Soviet state are scattered all around. But now museums are broaching subjects long brushed under the carpet. The capital is even experiencing an unprecedented growth in birth rates. From artistry and history to recreation and procreation, Moscow is a cauldron of creativity.

When to Go
Moscow

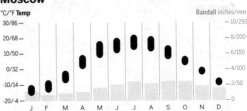

May – Jun Long daylight hours and mild temperatures entice Muscovites outdoors

Sep Moscow celebrates City Day, as the foliage turns the capital splendid autumnal shades.

Dec The snow-covered city hosts its premier cultural event, the December Nights Festival.

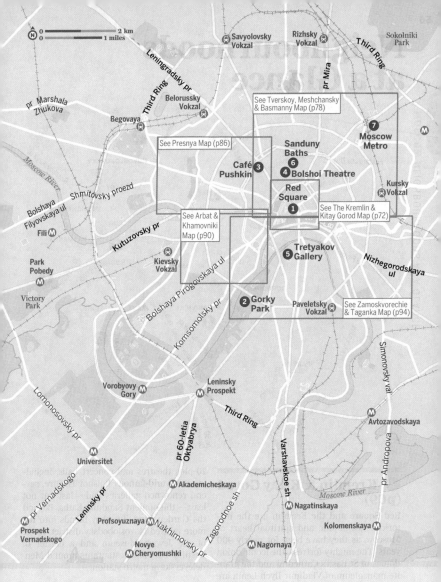

Moscow Highlights

1 Red Square (p69) Being awestruck by the Kremlin's tall towers and St Basil's on the city's central square.

2 Gorky Park (p64) Hanging out with Moscow's hipsters – riding bikes, admiring art, playing ping-pong or dancing under the stars.

3 Cafe Pushkin (p108) Splurging on a Russian feast amid faux-18th-century opulence.

4 Bolshoi Theatre (p113) Enjoying world-class ballet and opera at this historic theatre.

5 Tretyakov Gallery (p64) Ogling the icons, perusing the Peredvizhniki and contemplating avant-garde art

6 Sanduny Baths (p93) Steaming your cares away at this luxurious *banya*.

7 Moscow metro (p120) Travelling underground for a cheap history lesson and art exhibit all in one.

Neighbourhoods at a Glance

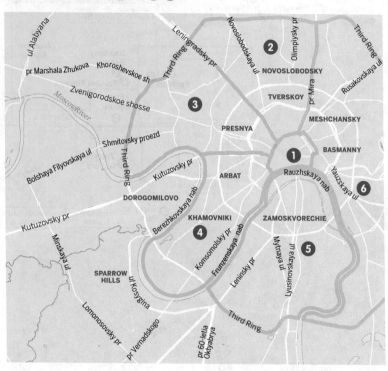

❶ Kremlin & Kitay Gorod (p69)

Red Square and the Kremlin are the historical, geographic and spiritual heart of Moscow, as they have been for nearly 900 years. The mighty fortress, the iconic onion domes of St Basil's Cathedral and the granite mausoleum of Vladimir Ilych Lenin are among the city's most important historical sights. The surrounding streets of Kitay Gorod are crammed with churches and old architecture. This is the starting point for any visit to Moscow.

❷ Tverskoy & Novoslobodsky (p77)

Moscow's busiest, swankiest and most commercialised district is also home to 20-plus theatres and concert halls, including the world-famous Bolshoi Theatre, several renowned galleries and – last but not least – the opulent Sanduny Baths. Beyond the Garden Ring, Tverskoy blends into the more relaxed Novoslobodsky district, home of the Jewish Museum and a cluster of bustling bars and restaurants around Mendeleyevskaya metro station.

❸ Meshchansky & Basmanny (p82)

Covering a large swathe of central Moscow, Meshchansky is markedly laid-back compared with its neighbouring districts. Here you'll find fewer offices, dominated as it is by prerevolutionary residential buildings. Beyond the Garden Ring, Basmanny is an area of 19th-century red-brick factories, now

ary sites, and more traditional venues such as the zoo (p85) and planetarium (p84). Presnya is also home to many of Moscow's top restaurants, including the highly lauded Cafe Pushkin (p108). The former textile factory at Tryokhgornaya (Трёхгорная Мануфактура; Map p86; www.trekhgorka.ru; Rochdelskaya ul 15; ⊙9.30am-8.30pm Mon-Sat, 10am-6pm Sun; Ⓜ Barrikadnaya) is fast becoming a centre for nightlife and dining.

⑤ Arbat & Khamovniki (p87)

The side-by-side districts of Arbat and Khamovniki are rich with culture. Moscow's most famous street, ul Arbat, is something of an art market, complete with portrait painters and soapbox poets, while the nearby streets are lined with museums and galleries, including the world-class Pushkin Museum of Fine Arts (p62). Khamovniki is home to the ancient Novodevichy Convent (p87) and Cemetery, as well as several unique newer museums. Further out, it's worth a trip to the south side of the Moscow River for certain key destinations, such as triumphant Park Pobedy (p93).

taken over by innovative postmodern galleries, cool cafes and digital startups. South of the Yauza, Taganskaya pl is a monster intersection that can be difficult to navigate, but the area is home to a few unusual sights, including Bunker-42 (p84) and the Museum of the Russian Icon (p83).

④ Presnya (p84)

The vast, diverse Presnya district spans the centuries, with a remarkable blend of building styes from the last three. The district's ample attractions include its impressive and varied architecture, several noteworthy liter-

⑥ Zamoskvorechie (p92)

With its low-rise buildings, quaint courtyards and multitude of onion domes, Zamoskvorechie is like a provincial Russian town that somehow ended up in central Moscow. The people responsible for the lingering old-world ambience are *kuptsy* (merchants) who populated the area until the 19th century and had completely different lifestyles and habits to the nobility living across the river. But modernity is very much present thanks to the ever-expanding gentrification belt that streches along the river, showcasing beautifully renovated parks, art spaces and hipster clusters filled with restaurants and bars.

TOP SIGHT
MOSCOW KREMLIN

The apex of Russian political power and once the centre of the Orthodox Church, the Kremlin is not only the kernel of Moscow but of the whole country. From here, autocratic tsars, communist dictators and modern-day presidents have done their best – and worst – for Russia. These red-brick walls and tent-roof towers enclose 800 years of artistic accomplishment, religious ceremony and political clout.

Entrance Towers & Around

The Kutafya Tower (Кутафья башня), which forms the main visitors' entrance today, stands apart from the Kremlin's west wall, at the end of a ramp over the Alexander Garden (Александровский сад; Ⓜ Aleksandrovsky Sad). Pass through the Kremlin walls beneath the 1495 Trinity Gate Tower (Троицкая башня); at 80m it's the tallest of the Kremlin's towers.

Immediately inside the Trinity Gate Tower, the lane to the right (south) passes the 17th-century Poteshny Palace (Потешный дворец), which housed the first Russian theatre and where Stalin later lived. The bombastic marble, glass and concrete State Kremlin Palace (Государственный Кремлёвский дворец; ☑ 495-620 7846; www.kremlinpalace.org/en), built between 1960 and 1961 for Communist Party congresses, is now home to the Kremlin Ballet.

Arsenal & Senate

North of the State Kremlin Palace is the 18th-century Arsenal (Арсенал), commissioned by Peter the Great to house workshops and depots for guns and weaponry. Now home to

DON'T MISS

➡ Assumption Cathedral

➡ Archangel Cathedral

➡ Annunciation Cathedral

➡ The Armoury

PRACTICALITIES

➡ Кремль

➡ Map p72

➡ ☑ 495-695 4146

➡ www.kreml.ru

➡ R500

➡ ⊙ 10am-5pm Fri-Wed, ticket office 9.30am-4.30pm Fri-Wed

➡ Ⓜ Aleksandrovsky Sad

the Kremlin Guard, the building is ringed with 800 captured Napoleonic cannons.

The offices of the president of Russia are in the yellow, triangular former Senate (Сенат) building, a fine 18th-century neoclassical edifice, east of the Arsenal.

Patriarch's Palace

Built for Patriarch Nikon mostly in the mid-17th century, the highlight of the Patriarch's Palace (Патриарший дворец) is the ceremonial Cross Hall (Крестовая палата), where the tsar's and ambassadorial feasts were held. From here you can access the five-domed Church of the Twelve Apostles (Церковь двенадцати апостолов), which has a gilded, wooden iconostasis and a collection of icons by leading 17th-century icon painters.

Assumption Cathedral

On the northern side of Sobornaya pl, the Assumption Cathedral (Успенский собор) is the focal church of prerevolutionary Russia and the burial place of most of the heads of the Russian Orthodox Church from the 1320s to 1700. If you have limited time, come straight here. The visitors entrance is at the western end.

Ivan the Great Bell Tower

With its two golden domes rising above the eastern side of Sobornaya pl, the Ivan the Great Bell Tower (Колокольня Ивана Великого; Map p72; R250; ☉10am-5pm Apr-Oct) is the Kremlin's tallest structure – a landmark visible from 30km away. Before the 20th century it was forbidden to build any higher in Moscow. Purchase a ticket to the architectural exhibit inside for a specifically timed admission to climb the 137 steps to the top for sweeping views.

Beside (not inside) the tower stands the world's biggest bell (Царь-колокол; Map p72), a 202-tonne monster that has never rung.

Archangel & Annunciation Cathedrals

The Archangel Cathedral (Архангельский собор) was for centuries the coronation, wedding and burial church of tsars. It was built by Ivan Kalita in 1333 to commemorate the end of the great famine, and dedicated to Archangel Michael, guardian of the Moscow princes.

The Annunciation Cathedral (Благовещенский собор), at the southwest corner of Sobornaya ploshchad, contains impressive murals in the gallery and an archaeology exhibit in the basement.

TICKETS TO THE KREMLIN

The main ticket office (Кассы музеев Кремля; Map p72; Alexander Garden; ☉9am-5pm Fri-Wed May-Sep, 9.30am-4.30pm Fri-Wed Oct-Apr; Ⓜ Aleksandrovsky Sad) is in Alexander Garden, next to the Kremlin wall. A ticket to the 'Architectural Ensemble of Sobornaya pl' covers entry to all five church-museums, as well as Patriarch's Palace. It does not include the Armoury, the Diamond Fund Exhibition or Ivan the Great Bell Tower, but you can and should buy those tickets here too. Tickets go on sale 45 minutes prior to each session; be at the ticket window when sales begin, as ticket numbers are limited.

Full-price tickets (but not children's tickets) for the churches and Armoury can be purchased in advance online – but you'll still have to pick them up at the ticket office.

Photography is not permitted inside the Armoury or any of the buildings on Sobornaya pl (Cathedral Sq).

Before entering the Kremlin, deposit large bags at the left-luggage office.

Great Kremlin & Armoury

The 700-room Great Kremlin Palace (Большой Кремлёвский дворец), built as an imperial residence between 1838 and 1849, is now an official residence of the Russian president, used for state visits and receptions. Apart from the Armoury (Оружейная палата; adult/child R700/free; ⊙ tours at 10am, noon, 2.30pm & 4.30pm Fri-Wed; Ⓜ Aleksandrovsky Sad), it's not open to the public.

Buy your time-specific ticket to the Armoury when you buy your ticket to the Kremlin. A one-hour audio guide is available to point out some of the collection's highlights. In Room 2, you'll find the renowned Easter eggs made by St Petersburg jeweller Fabergé.

If the Armoury hasn't sated your lust for bling, there are more in the separate Diamond Fund Exhibition (Алмазный фонд России; ☑ 495-629 2036; www.gokhran. ru; R500; ⊙ 10am-1pm & 2-5pm Fri-Wed). Security is super tight and you are not allowed to bring cameras, phones or bags of any sort.

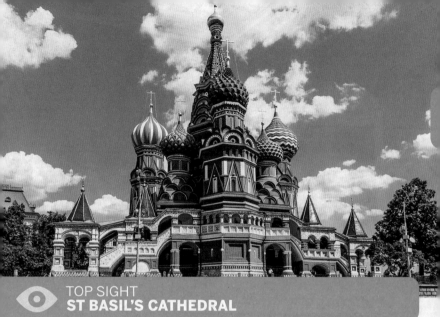

TOP SIGHT
ST BASIL'S CATHEDRAL

At the southern end of Red Square stands the icon of Russia: St Basil's Cathedral. This crazy confusion of colours, patterns and shapes is the culmination of a style that is unique to Russian architecture. In 1552 Ivan the Terrible captured the Tatar stronghold of Kazan on the Feast of Intercession. He commissioned this landmark church, officially the Intercession Cathedral, to commemorate the victory.

Created from 1555 to 1561, the cathedral's apparent anarchy of shapes hides a plan of nine main chapels. The tall, tent-roofed central tower houses the namesake Church of the Intercession of the Mother of God. The four biggest domes top four octagonal-towered chapels: the Church of Sts Cyprian & Justina, Church of the Holy Trinity, Church of the Icon of St Nicholas the Miracle Worker, and the Church of the Entry of the Lord into Jerusalem.

Legend has it that Ivan had the architects blinded so that they could never build anything comparable. Records show, however, that they were employed a quarter of a century later (four years after Ivan's death) to add an additional chapel.

Inside, the Church of St Vasily the Blessed, the northeastern chapel on the 1st floor, contains the canopy-covered crypt of its revered namesake saint. This 10th chapel – the only one at ground level – was added in 1588, after the saint's death. Look for the icon depicting St Vasily himself, with Red Square and the Kremlin in the background.

With white walls and a spiralling symbol of eternity painted in the vault, the light-filled Church of the Holy Trinity is a favourite. A 16th-century chandelier is suspended from the 20m ceiling. But the gem of the room is the unusual iconostasis.

DON'T MISS

➡ Church of St Vasily the Blessed

➡ Portals from the vestry to the central church

➡ Icon of the Old Testament Trinity

➡ Icon of the Life of St Alexander Nevsky

PRACTICALITIES

➡ Покровский собор, Храм Василия Блаженного

➡ Map p72

➡ adult/student R350/150

➡ ⊘ ticket office 11am-5pm Nov-Apr, to 6pm May-Oct

➡ Ⓜ Ploshchad Revolyutsii

TOP SIGHT
PUSHKIN MUSEUM OF FINE ARTS

Moscow's premier foreign-art museum is split over three branches, showing off a broad selection of European works, including masterpieces from ancient civilisations, the Italian Renaissance and the Dutch Golden Age, not to mention an incredible collection of Impressionist and post-Impressionist paintings in the 19th & 20th Century Art Gallery.

The main building will remain open until the completion of the new museum complex on ul Volkhonka. It is expected to open in 2019, when exhibits are likely to change locations.

The Ancient Civilization exhibits contain a surprisingly excellent collection, complete with ancient Egyptian weaponry, jewellery, ritual items and tombstones. The Greek and Italian Courts contain examples from the museum's original collection, which was made up of plaster-cast reproductions of Ancient and Renaissance masterpieces.

The 2nd floor is dominated by the 17th and 18th centuries. The highlight of the museum is the selection of Dutch masterpieces in rooms 9 through 11. Rembrandt is the star of the show, with many paintings on display, including his moving *Portrait of an Old Woman*. There is a separate gallery for the Rococo period, featuring some dreamy paintings by Boucher.

The separate 19th & 20th Century Art Gallery (www. arts-museum.ru; ul Volkhonka 14; adult/student R300/150; ⊙11am-7pm Tue-Sun, to 9pm Thu) contains a famed assemblage of Impressionist and post-Impressionist works, based on the collections of Moscow art patrons Sergei Shchukin and Ivan Morozov. The Museum of Private Collections (Музей личных коллекций; www.artprivatecollections.ru; ul Volkhonka 10; entry prices vary; ⊙noon-8pm Wed-Sun, to 9pm Thu) shows off complete collections donated by private individuals.

DON'T MISS

➡ Treasures of Troy

➡ Golden Age of Dutch Art

➡ Impressionist and post-Impressionist collections

PRACTICALITIES

➡ Музей изобразительных искусств им Пушкина

➡ Map p90

➡ ☎ 495-697 9578

➡ www.arts-museum.ru

➡ ul Volkhonka 12

➡ single/combined galleries R300/550

➡ ⊙11am-7pm Tue-Sun, to 9pm Thu

➡ Ⓜ Kropotkinskaya

◉ TOP SIGHT
STATE TRETYAKOV GALLERY MAIN BRANCH

The exotic boyar castle on a little lane in Zamoskvorechie contains the world's best collection of Russian icons and an outstanding collection of other pre-revolutionary Russian art. The building was designed by Viktor Vasnetsov between 1900 and 1905. The gallery started as the private collection of the 19th-century industrialist brothers Pavel and Sergei Tretyakov.

The tour of the gallery begins on the 2nd floor, where 18th- to 20th-century artists are exhibited. In the 1870s, daring artists started to use their medium to address social issues, thus founding the Peredvizhniki (Wanderers) movement. Artists to look out for include Vasily Perov (room 17), Ivan Kramskoi (room 20), Ivan Shishkin (room 25), Vasily Vereshchagin (room 27) and Nicholas Ge (room 31).

Ilya Repin (rooms 29 and 30) is perhaps the most beloved Russian realist painter. Mikhail Vrubel (rooms 32 to 34) was a Symbolist-era artist who defies classification.

Moving into the 20th century, artists such as Konstantin Korovin (room 43) and Pavel Kuznetsov (room 46) began to reject the rules of realism. Nikolai Rerikh (Nicholas Roerich) shows off his fantastical storytelling style in room 47.

Room 55 houses the Treasury, with its collection of metals, jewellery, embroidery and precious knickknacks. Icons are found in rooms 56 to 62. Andrei Rublyov's *Holy Trinity* (1420s) from Sergiev Posad, regarded as Russia's greatest icon, is in room 60.

Contemporary exhibits are housed in the Engineer's Building, next to the main building.

DON'T MISS

➡ Mikhail Vrubel's mural *The Princess of the Dream*

➡ *A Knight at the Crossroads* by Viktor Vasnetsov

➡ *Ivan the Terrible and his Son Ivan* by Ilya Repin

PRACTICALITIES

➡ Главный отдел Государственной Третьяковской галереи

➡ Map p94

➡ www.tretyakovgallery.ru

➡ Lavrushinsky per 10

➡ adult/child R500/200

➡ ⊘10am-6pm Tue, Wed & Sun, to 9pm Thu-Sat, last tickets 1hr before closing

➡ Ⓜ Tretyakovskaya

TOP SIGHT
GORKY PARK

Moscow's main city getaway is not your conventional expanse of nature preserved deep inside an urban jungle. Its mission is to mix leisure and culture in equal proportions. Designed in the 1920s by avant-garde architect Konstantin Melnikov as a piece of communist utopia, these days it showcases the enlightened transformation Moscow has undergone in recent years.

Activities include cycling, rollerblading, beach volleyball, extreme sports, table tennis and even pétanque. There are several bicycle- and skate-rental places around the park, with one conveniently located under the Andreyevsky pedestrian bridge. In winter, the ponds are flooded, turning the park into the city's biggest ice-skating rink (Парк Горького; ☑ 495-237 1266; ul Krymsky val; ◷ 10am-3pm & 5-11pm Tue-Sun; Ⓜ Park Kultury).

Head southwest along the river, past Andreyevsky Bridge, and you'll find yourself in Neskuchny Sad. Much less crowded than Gorky Park, full of shade, and criss-crossed by walking and cycling paths, it contains several sports facilities, including tennis courts, open-air table tennis and an open-air gym. Art objects pop up throughout the park as part of various exhibitions and festivals, but the Garage Museum of Contemporary Art plays the flagship role.

The open-air Pioner cinema shows films after dark, although almost all are in Russian. Its new competitor, Garage Screen, is located in front of Garage Museum of Contemporary Art.

The grand colonnaded arch that serves as the park's front entrance now contains a museum (Музей Парка Горького; ☑ 495-995 0020; ul Krymsky val 9, str 11; adult/student R300/150; Ⓜ Oktyabrskaya or Park Kultury), its exhibition largely comprised of old photographs and screens showing Soviet-era newsreels about the park. The hefty entrance fee offers access to the roof of the arch, from which there are sweeping views of the park and surrounds.

DON'T MISS

➡ Garage Museum of Contemporary Art

➡ Dancing under Andreyevsky Bridge

➡ View from the top of the arch that contains Gorky Park Museum

➡ Boules at Le Boule

PRACTICALITIES

➡ Парк Горького

➡ Map p94

➡ ◷ 24hr

➡ 🚇

➡ Ⓜ Oktyabrskaya

History

Moscow is first mentioned in the historic chronicles in 1147, when Prince Yury Dolgoruky invited his allies to a banquet: 'Come to me, brother, please come to Moscow'. It was Yury who ordered the construction of a moat-ringed wooden palisade on the hilltop, the first Kremlin. Traders and artisans set up just outside the Kremlin's walls turning Moscow into an economic as well as strategic centre.

Medieval Moscow

In the early half of the 13th century, the ferocious Golden Horde, a Mongol-led army of nomadic tribesmen, burned Moscow to the ground and killed its governor. The Golden Horde was mainly interested in tribute, and Moscow was conveniently situated to monitor the river trade and road traffic. As Moscow prospered, its political fortunes rose too. It soon surpassed Vladimir and Suzdal as the regional capital.

In the 1380 Battle of Kulikovo, Moscow's Grand Prince Dmitry defeated the Golden Horde on the banks of the Don River. He was thereafter immortalised as Dmitry Donskoy. From this time, Moscow acted as champion of the Russian cause.

Towards the end of the 15th century, Moscow emerged as an expanding autocratic state. Under the long reign of Grand Prince Ivan III (the Great), the eastern Slav principalities were consolidated into a single territorial entity. In 1480 Ivan's army faced down the Mongols at the Ugra River without a fight: the 200-year Mongol yoke was lifted.

Subsequently, Ivan III renovated the Kremlin, adding its brick walls and imposing watchtowers. Next to the Kremlin, traders and artisans congregated in Kitay Gorod, and a stone wall was erected around these commercial quarters. The city developed in concentric rings outward from this centre. As it emerged as a political capital, Moscow also took on the role of religious centre. In the mid-15th century, the Russian Orthodox Church was organised, independent of the Greek Church. Under Ivan IV (the Terrible), the city earned the nickname 'Gold-Domed Moscow' because of the multitude of monastery fortresses and magnificent churches constructed within them.

Imperial Moscow

In 1712, Peter the Great, who hated Moscow, announced the relocation of the capital to a swampland in the northwest that would become St Petersburg. Moscow fell into decline, later exacerbated by an outbreak of bubonic plague.

By the turn of the 19th century, Moscow had recovered from its gloom. By this time, the city hosted Russia's first university, museum and newspaper. Moscow's intellectual

MOSCOW IN ...

Two Days

Spend a day seeing what makes Moscow famous: St Basil's Cathedral, Lenin's Mausoleum and the Kremlin (including the bling in the Armoury). After lunch, stroll through Kitay Gorod discovering the countless 17th-century churches. Dine on trendy ul Petrovka, perhaps at Lavka-Lavka, then take in a show at the world-famous Bolshoi Theatre.

On your second day, admire the art and architecture at Novodevichy Convent, then head next door to the eponymous cemetery. Make your way into the Arbat district for an afternoon of art appreciation at the Pushkin Museum of Fine Arts or at one of the smaller niche galleries. In the evening, stroll along the Arbat enjoying the atmosphere of old Moscow.

Four Days

On your third day, get an early start to beat the crowds to the Tretyakov Gallery. Grab lunch at Mizandari at Red October. then stroll along Krymskaya naberezhnaya, where you can frolic in fountains and explore the outdoor art gallery at Art Muzeon. Then head across the street to Gorky Park for bicycle riding or boat paddling. Stay into the evening for drinking and dancing under the stars.

Reserve the morning on your last day for shopping at Izmaylovsky Market, crammed with souvenir stalls. On your way back to the centre, make a stop at Flakon and Khlebozavod No 9 or Winzavod to see the arty happenings in Moscow's former industrial spaces. Indulge in a farewell feast at Cafe Pushkin.

Greater Moscow

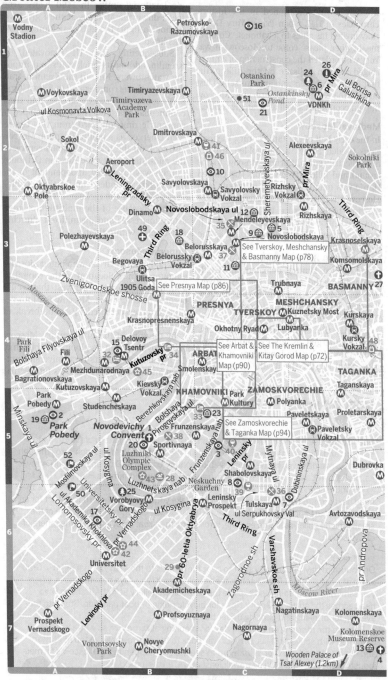

Ⓜ Vodny
Stadion

Petrovsko-
Razumovskaya

◉ 16

Ⓜ Voykovskaya

Ostankino
Park

24 26
🚇 Ⓜ 6 ⓜ pr Mira
ul Borisa
Galushkina

Timiryazevskaya Ⓜ

Timiryazeva
Academy
Park

● 51

*Ostankinsky
Pond*

21

VDNKh Ⓜ

Ⓜ Sokol

Dmitrovskaya Ⓜ

Alexeevskaya Ⓜ

Sokolniki
Park

Ⓜ Oktyabrskoe
Pole

Aeroport Ⓜ

🄼 41
🔒 46

🄼 10

Savyolovskaya
Ⓜ

Leningradsky
pr

Savyolovsky
Vokzal

Rizhsky
Vokzal

pr Mira

Rizhskaya Ⓜ

Ⓜ Dinamo

Novoslobodskaya ul

12 🏠

Sheremetyevskaya ul

Third Ring

Ⓜ Polezhayevskaya

49 ★
18 📷

35 🚇

Mendeleyevskaya
Ⓜ

9 Ⓜ 5
Novoslobodskaya
Ⓜ

Krasnoselskaya
Ⓜ

Belorusskaya Ⓜ

Belorussky
Vokzal

37 🏠

See Tverskoy, Meshchansky
& Basmanny Map (p78)

Komsomolskaya
Ⓜ

Begovaya Ⓜ

Ⓜ Ulitsa
1905 Goda

11 📷

Trubnaya Ⓜ

BASMANNY ✝ 27

Zvenigorodskoe shosse

See Presnya Map (p86)

MESHCHANSKY

Moscow River

PRESNYA

TVERSKOY Ⓜ Kuznetsky Most
Ⓜ

Kurskaya Ⓜ

Ⓜ Krasnopresnenskaya

Okhotny Ryad Ⓜ

Lubyanka
Ⓜ

Kursky
Vokzal 48

Park
Fili

15 Delovoy
🏠 Tsentr

See Arbat &
Khamovniki
Map (p90)

34 ★

See The Kremlin &
Kitay Gorod Map (p72)

Ⓜ Fili

32 🏠

Kutuzovsky pr

ARBAT Ⓜ

TAGANKA

Bolshaya Filyovskaya ul

Mezhdunarodnaya Ⓜ

45 ★

Smolenskay

ZAMOSKVORECHIE

Taganskaya
Ⓜ

Ⓜ Bagrationovskaya

Kievsky
Vokzal

KHAMOVNIKI

Park
Ⓜ Kultury

Polyanka Ⓜ

Kutuzovskaya Ⓜ

Berezhkovskaya nab

33 ⓜ 23

Paveletskaya
Ⓜ

Proletarskaya
Ⓜ

Park
Pobedy Ⓜ

Studencheskaya Ⓜ

Bolshaya
Pirogovskaya ul

Frunzenskaya nab

See Zamoskvorechie
& Taganka Map (p94)

Paveletsky
🚇 Vokzal

19 🏠 2

*Novodevichy
Convent* 1

38 ★

Frunzenskaya Ⓜ

20 🏠

Sportivnaya Ⓜ

Leninsky
pr

40 🚇

Mytnaya ul

Dubrovka
Ⓜ

52 🏠

Mosfilmovskaya ul

ul Kosygina

*Luzhniki
Olympic
Complex*

Shabolovskaya Ⓜ

Dubininskaya ul

50 🏠
17 🏠

Universitetsky pr

ul Akademika Khokhlova

Luzhnetskaya nab

43 ★ 28

25 🏠

Vorobyovy
Gory Ⓜ

*Neskuchny
Garden* 8

39

36 ✕
7

Avtozavodskaya
Ⓜ

pr Vernadskogo

44 ★
42

Lomonosovsky pr

ul Kosygina

Leninsky
Prospekt Ⓜ

Tulskaya Ⓜ

ul Serpukhovsky Val

Universitet Ⓜ

29

pr 60-letia Oktyabrya

Third Ring

Zagorodnoe sh

Moscow River

pr Andropova

Minskaya ul

Akademicheskaya
Ⓜ

Varshavskoe sh

Nagatinskaya
Ⓜ

Kolomenskaya
Ⓜ

Ⓜ Prospekt
Vernadskogo

Leninsky pr

Profsoyuznaya Ⓜ

Nagornaya
Ⓜ

Kolomenskoe
Museum Reserve
13 ✝ ⓜ

*Vorontsovsky
Park*

Novye
Ⓜ Cheryomushki

*Wooden Palace of
Tsar Alexey (1.2km)* ↘

4

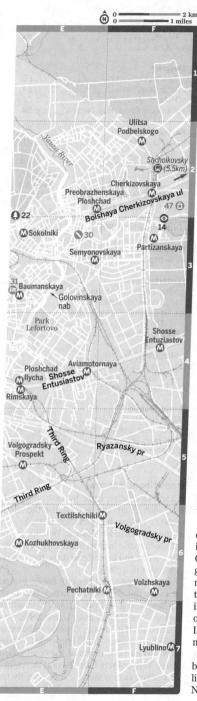

and literary scene gave rise to a nationalist-inspired Slavophile movement, which celebrated the cultural features of Russia that were distinctive from the West.

In the early 1800s Tsar Alexander I decided to resume trade with England, in violation of a treaty Russia had made with France. A furious Napoleon Bonaparte set out for Moscow with the largest military force the world had ever seen. The Russian army engaged the advancing French at the Battle of Borodino, 130km from Moscow. More than 100,000 soldiers lay dead at the end of this inconclusive one-day fight. Shortly thereafter, Napoleon entered a deserted Moscow. By some accounts, defiant Muscovites burned down their city rather than see it occupied. French soldiers tried to topple the formidable Kremlin, but its sturdy walls withstood their pummelling.

The city was swiftly rebuilt following Napoleon's final defeat. Monuments were erected to commemorate Russia's hard fought victory, including a Triumphal Arch and the grandiose Cathedral of Christ the Saviour. Meanwhile, the city's two outer defensive rings were replaced with the tree-lined Boulevard Ring and Garden Ring roads.

By midcentury, industry overtook commerce as the city's economic driving force. With a steady supply of cotton from Central Asia, Moscow became a leader in the textile industry, and was known as 'Calico Moscow'. By 1900, Moscow claimed more than one million inhabitants.

Red Moscow

The Bolshevik coup provoked a week of street fighting in Moscow, leaving more than 1000 dead. In 1918, fearing a German assault on St Petersburg, Lenin ordered that the capital return to Moscow.

In the 1930s Josef Stalin launched an industrial revolution, at the same time devising a comprehensive urban plan for Moscow. On paper, it appeared as a neatly organised garden city; unfortunately, it was implemented with a sledgehammer. Historic cathedrals and monuments were demolished, including landmarks such as the Cathedral of Christ the Saviour and Kazan Cathedral. In their place appeared the marble-bedecked metro and neo-Gothic skyscrapers.

When Hitler launched 'Operation Barbarossa' into Soviet territory in June 1941, Stalin was caught by surprise. By December the Nazis were just outside Moscow, within 30km

Greater Moscow

of the Kremlin, but an early winter halted the advance. In the Battle of Moscow, war hero General Zhukov staged a brilliant counteroffensive and saved the city from capture.

Stalin's successor, Nikita Khrushchev, a former mayor of Moscow, introduced wide-ranging reforms and promised to improve living conditions. Huge housing estates grew up round the city's outskirts. The expansion continued under Leonid Brezhnev. As the Soviet Union emerged as a military superpower, the aerospace, radio-electronics and nuclear weapons ministries operated factories and research laboratories in and around the capital. By 1980 the city's population surpassed eight million.

Transitional Moscow

Mikhail Gorbachev came to power in March 1985 with a mandate to revitalise the ailing socialist system; he promoted Boris Yeltsin as the new head of Moscow. Yeltsin's populist touch made him an instant success with Muscovites and he embraced the more open political atmosphere.

On 18 August 1991 the city awoke to find tanks in the streets. Gorbachev had been arrested and a self-proclaimed 'Committee for the State of Emergency in the USSR' proclaimed itself in charge. Crowds gathered at the White House to build barricades. Yeltsin, from atop a tank, declared the coup illegal. When KGB snipers didn't shoot, the coup – and Soviet communism – was over. By the year's end Boris Yeltsin had moved into the Kremlin.

The first years of transition were fraught with political conflict. In September 1993 Yeltsin issued a decree to shut down the Russian parliament. Events turned violent. The army intervened on the president's side and blasted the parliament into submission. In all, 145 people were killed and another 700 wounded – the worst single incident of bloodshed in the city since the Bolshevik takeover in 1917.

In 1992 Yury Luzhkov was appointed as Moscow's mayor by Yeltsin; he would go on to win three elections to the position while building himself and his family a commercial empire. The city government retained ownership of property in Moscow, giving Luzhkov's administration unprecedented control over would-be business ventures, and making him as much a CEO as a mayor.

While the rest of Russia struggled to survive the collapse of communism, Moscow quickly emerged as an enclave of affluence and dynamism. The new economy spawned a small group of 'New Russians', routinely derided and often envied for their garish displays of wealth.

In September 1999 a series of mysterious explosions in Moscow left more than 200 people dead. It was widely believed, although unproven, that Chechen terrorists were responsible for the bombings. This was the first of many terrorist attacks in the capital that were linked to the ongoing crisis in Chechnya, the worst of which was a siege of a Moscow theatre in 2002 that resulted in 120 deaths and hundreds of illnesses.

Millennium Moscow

In 2010, after 18 years in the job Luzhkov was replaced as Moscow mayor by Sergei Sobyanin, the former head of the presidential administration under Putin. Sobyanin promised a shift away from big business and huge construction projects to improving the city for regular-guy residents. To a large extent he has delivered as Moscow is gradually but noticeably becoming an easier, cleaner, more pleasant place to live.

While many Muscovites have lapped up the bread-and-circuses policies of the Putin-friendly city administration, not all are satisfied to sit back and accept politics as usual. In 2017, for the first time in years, a wave of anti-corruption protests took place in Moscow (and around the country). With the presidential election in 2018 – and Putin's certain participation – there are bound to be more. Still, most Muscovites are not in the mood for revolution.

Despite the conservative mood, Moscow has still managed to become one of Europe's coolest and most creative capitals. Gone are the days when the city was defined by New Russians' excessive displays of wealth. Nowadays, the capital's movers and shakers are the innovators – the artists, architects, designers and chefs – who are shaping the city's aesthetic and atmosphere.

⊙ Sights

◎ Kremlin & Kitay Gorod

★ **Red Square**   HISTORIC SITE

(Красная площадь; Map p72; Krasnaya pl; Ⓜ Ploshchad Revolyutsii) Immediately outside the Kremlin's northeastern wall is the celebrated Red Square, the 400m-by-150m area of cobblestones that is at the very heart of Moscow. Commanding the square from the southern end is St Basil's Cathedral (p61). This panorama never fails to send the heart aflutter, especially at night.

The word *krasnaya* in the name means 'red' now, but in old Russian it meant 'beautiful' and Krasnaya ploshchad lives up to this epithet. Furthermore, it evokes an incredible sense of import to stroll across the place where so much of Russian history has unfolded. Note that the square is often closed for various celebrations or their rehearsals, so allow some leeway in your schedule.

State History Museum   MUSEUM

(Государственный исторический музей; Map p72; www.shm.ru; Krasnaya pl 1; adult/student R350/100, audio guide R300; ⊙ ticket office 10am-5pm Wed, Thu, Sun & Mon, to 9pm Fri & Sat; Ⓜ Okhotny Ryad) At the northern end of Red Square, the State History Museum has an enormous collection covering Russian history from the time of the Stone Age. The building, dating from the late 19th century, is itself an attraction – each room is in the style of a different period or region, some with highly decorated walls echoing old Russian churches.

The exhibits about medieval Rus are excellent, with several rooms covering the Mongol invasions and the consolidation of the Russian state. The 2nd floor is dedicated to the Imperial period, with exhibits featuring personal items of the royals, furnishings and decoration from the palace interiors, and various artworks and documents from the

The Kremlin

A DAY AT THE KREMLIN

Only at the Kremlin can you see 800 years of Russian history and artistry in one day. Enter the ancient fortress through the Trinity Gate Tower and walk past the impressive Arsenal, ringed with cannons. Past the Patriarch's Palace, you'll find yourself surrounded by white-washed walls and golden domes. Your first stop is ❶ **Assumption Cathedral** with the solemn fresco over the doorway. As the most important church in prerevolutionary Russia, this 15th-century beauty was the burial site of the patriarchs. The ❷ **Ivan the Great Bell Tower** now contains a nifty multimedia exhibit on the architectural history of the Kremlin. The view from the top is worth the price of admission. The tower is flanked by the massive ❸ **Tsar Cannon & Bell**.

In the southeast corner, ❹ **Archangel Cathedral** has an elaborate interior, where three centuries of tsars and tsarinas are laid to rest. Your final stop on Sobornaya pl is ❺ **Annunciation Cathedral**, rich with frescoes and iconography.

Walk along the Great Kremlin Palace and enter the ❻ **Armoury** at the time designated on your ticket. After gawking at the goods, exit the Kremlin through Borovitsky Gate and stroll through the Alexander Garden to the ❼ **Tomb of the Unknown Soldier**.

TOP TIPS

➡ **Online Purchase** Full-price tickets to the Kremlin churches and the Armoury can be purchased in advance on the Kremlin website.

➡ **Lunch** There are no eating options. Plan to eat before you arrive or stash a snack.

EKATERINA BYKOVA/SHUTTERSTOCK ©

Assumption Cathedral
Once your eyes adjust to the colourful frescoes, the gilded fixtures and the iconography, try to locate *Saviour with the Angry Eye*, a 14th-century icon that is one of the oldest in the Kremlin.

Arsenal

BOROVITSKY TOWER

Use the entrance at Borovitsky Tower if you intend to skip the churches and visit only the Armoury or Diamond Fund.

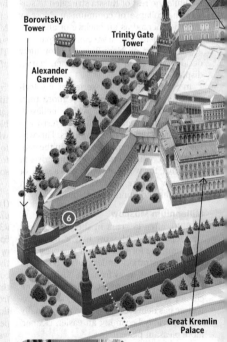

Borovitsky Tower

Trinity Gate Tower

Alexander Garden

Great Kremlin Palace

Armoury
Take advantage of the free audio guide to direct you to the most intriguing treasures of the Armoury, which is chock-full of precious metalworks and jewellery, armour and weapons, gowns and crowns, carriages and sledges.

DREAMER COMPANY/SHUTTERSTOCK ©

Tomb of the Unknown Soldier
Visit the Tomb of the Unknown Soldier honouring the heroes of the Great Patriotic War. Come at the top of the hour to see the solemn synchronicity of the changing of the guard.

TOWER TICKETS
Sessions at the Ivan the Great Bell Tower take place six or seven times a day, mid-May through September. Purchase tickets at the Kremlin ticket office 45 minutes before the session.

Ivan the Great Bell Tower
Check out the artistic electronic renderings of the Kremlin's history, then climb 137 steps to the belfry's upper gallery, where you will be rewarded with super, sweeping vistas of Sobornaya pl and beyond.

Patriarch's Palace

Moscow River

Tsar Cannon & Bell
Peer down the barrel of the monstrous Tsar Cannon and pose for a picture beside the oversized Tsar Bell, both of which are too big to serve their intended purpose.

Sobornaya pl

Annunciation Cathedral
Admire the artistic mastery of Russia's greatest icon painters – Theophanes the Greek and Andrei Rublyov – who are responsible for many of the icons in the deesis and festival rows of the iconostasis.

Archangel Cathedral
See the final resting place of princes and emperors who ruled Russia for more than 300 years, including the visionary Ivan the Great, the tortured Ivan the Terrible and the tragic Tsarevitch Dmitry.

The Kremlin & Kitay Gorod

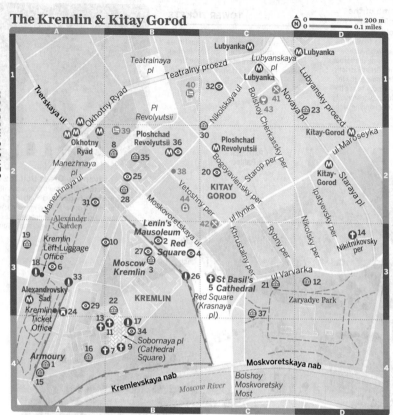

era. Specific rooms are dedicated to the rules of various tsars. An unexpected highlight is an exhibit addressing the expansion of the Russian Empire by examining the growing network of roads and how people travelled.

Saviour Gate Tower TOWER

(Спасская башня; Map p72) The Kremlin's 'official' exit onto Red Square is the stately red-brick Saviour Gate Tower. This gate – considered sacred – has been used for processions since tsarist times. The two white-stone plaques above the gate commemorate the tower's construction in 1491. The current clock was installed in the gate tower in the 1850s. Hauling 3m-long hands and weighing 25 tonnes, the clock takes up three of the tower's 10 levels. Its melodic chime sounds every 15 minutes across Red Square.

Church of the Trinity in Nikitniki CHURCH

(Церковь Троицы в Никитниках; Map p72; Ipatyevsky per; M Kitay-Gorod) Hidden between big government blocks, this little gem of a church is an exquisite example of Russian baroque. Built in the 1630s, its onion domes and tiers of red-and-white spade gables rise from a square tower. Its interior is covered with 1650s gospel frescoes by Simon Ushakov and others. A carved doorway leads into St Nikita the Martyr's Chapel, above the vault of the Nikitnikov merchant family, who were among the patrons who financed the church's construction.

Tomb of the Unknown Soldier MEMORIAL

(Могила неизвестного солдата; Map p72) The Tomb of the Unknown Soldier contains the remains of one soldier who died in December 1941 at Km41 of Leningradskoe sh – the nearest the Nazis came to Moscow. This is a kind of national pilgrimage spot, where newlyweds bring flowers and have their pictures taken. The inscription reads: 'Your name is unknown, your deeds immortal.' Every hour on the hour, the guards perform a perfectly

The Kremlin & Kitay Gorod

synchronised ceremony to change the guards on duty.

Polytechnical Museum MUSEUM
(Политехнический музей; Map p72; www.poly-mus.ru; Novaya pl 3/4; Ⓜ Lubyanka) Occupying the entire block of Novaya pl, this giant museum showcases the history of Russian science, technology and industry. Indeed, it has claimed to be the largest science museum in the world. The museum was closed for a long overdue renovation and update at the time of research, promising a 'fundamentally new museum and education centre' by 2018. In the meantime, a temporary exhibit has been set up at the VDNKh (p85).

War of 1812 Museum MUSEUM
(Музей отечественной войны 1812 года; Map p72; www.shm.ru; pl Revolyutsii 2; adult/child R350/150; ⊘10am-6pm Sun-Thu, to 9pm Fri & Sat, closed Mon Sep-May; Ⓜ Ploshchad Revolyutsii) Part Russian Revival, part neo-Renaissance, this red-brick beauty was built in the 1890s as the Moscow City Hall and later served as the Central Lenin Museum. It was converted into the War of 1812 Museum in honor of the war's 200-year anniversary. Artwork, documents, weapons and uniforms are all on display, with good multimedia exhibits offering a detailed depiction of the events and effects of the war.

Church of the Deposition of the Robe CHURCH
(Церковь Ризоположения; Map p72) This delicate single-domed church was built between 1484 and 1486 in exclusively Russian style. It was the private chapel of the heads of the Church, who tended to be highly suspicious of such people as Italian architects.

Synod Printing House HISTORIC BUILDING
(Печатный двор Синод; Map p72; Nikolskaya ul 15; Ⓜ Ploshchad Revolyutsii) Now housing the Russian State University for the Humanities, this elaborately decorated edifice is where Ivan Fyodorov reputedly produced Russia's first printed book, *The Apostle,* in 1563. You can see a statue (p76) of the man himself nearby. Spiralling Solomonic columns and Gothic windows frame the lion and unicorn, who are facing off in the centre of the facade.

Moscow Metro Map

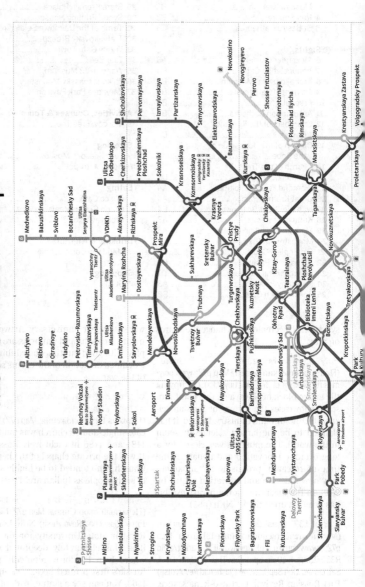

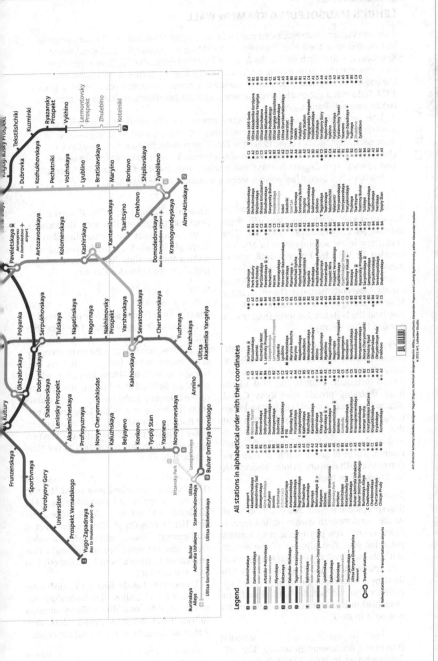

DON'T MISS

LENIN'S MAUSOLEUM & KREMLIN WALL

Although Vladimir Ilych requested that he be buried beside his mum in St Petersburg, he still lies in state at the foot of the Kremlin wall (Мавзолей Ленина; Map p72; www.lenin.ru; Krasnaya pl; ☉10am-1pm Tue-Thu, Sat & Sun; Ⓜ Ploshchad Revolyutsii) FREE, receiving visitors who come to pay their respects. Line up at the western corner of the square (near the entrance to Alexander Garden) to see the embalmed leader, who has been here since 1924. Note that photography is not allowed and stern guards ensure that all visitors remain respectful and silent.

After trooping past the embalmed figure, emerge from the mausoleum and inspect the Kremlin wall, where other communist heavy hitters are buried, including Lenin's successor Josef Stalin; Leonid Brezhnev; Felix Dzerzhinsky, the founder of the Cheka (forerunner of the KGB); respected Bolshevik Inessa Armand, rumored to have been Lenin's lover; Yury Gagarin, the first man in space; and John Reed, the American author of *Ten Days that Shook the World*, a first-hand account of the revolution.

Monastery of the Epiphany   MONASTERY
(Богоявленский монастырь; Map p72; Bogo-yavlensky per 2; Ⓜ Ploshchad Revolyutsii) This monastery is the second-oldest in Moscow, founded in 1296 by Prince Daniil, son of Alexander Nevsky. The current Epiphany Cathedral – with its tall, pink, gold-domed cupola – was constructed in the 1690s in the Moscow Baroque style. If you're lucky, you may hear the bells ringing forth from the old wooden belfry nearby.

Tretyakovsky Proezd   STREET
(Третьяковский проезд; Map p72; Ⓜ Teatralnaya) The gated walkway of Tretyakovsky proezd (originally built in the 1870s) leads from Teatralny proezd into Kitay Gorod. Nearby, you can see where archaeologists uncovered the 16th-century fortified wall that used to surround Kitay Gorod, as well as the foundations of the 1493 Trinity Church. There is also a statue of Ivan Fyodorov, the 16th-century printer responsible for Russia's first book.

Resurrection Gate   GATE
(Воскресенские ворота; Map p72; Krasnaya pl) At the northwestern corner of Red Square, Resurrection Gate provides a great vantage point for your first glimpse of the square. With its twin red towers topped by green tent spires, the original 1680 gateway was destroyed because Stalin thought it an impediment to the parades and demonstrations held in Red Square. This exact replica was built in 1995.

Vladimir I Statue   MONUMENT
(Памятник Владимиру Великому; Map p90; Borovitskaya pl) In 2016, Vladimir Putin unveiled a new monument dedicated to his namesake Vladimir I, ruler of Kyivan Rus from 980 to 1015. At 17m high, the massive statue towers over the surrounding Borovitskaya ploshchad. Vladimir is credited with uniting the fledgling Russian state and establishing the Orthodox Church.

Chambers of the Romanov Boyars   MUSEUM
(Палаты бояр Романовых; Map p72; www.shm.ru; ul Varvarka 10; Ⓜ Kitay-Gorod) This small but interesting museum is devoted to the lives of the Romanov family, who were mere boyars (nobles) before they became tsars. The house was built by Nikita Romanov, whose grandson Mikhail later became the first tsar of the 300-year Romanov dynasty. Exhibits show the house as it might have been when the Romanovs lived here in the 16th century. Enter from the rear of the building. The museum was closed for renovation at the time of research.

Old English Court   MUSEUM
(Палаты старого Английского двора; Map p72; www.mosmuseum.ru; ul Varvarka 4a; adult/child R200/100; ☉10am-6pm Tue, Wed & Fri-Sun, 11am-9pm Thu; Ⓜ Kitay-Gorod) This reconstructed 16th-century house, white with wooden roofs, was the residence of England's first emissaries to Russia (sent by Elizabeth I to Ivan the Terrible).

It also served as the base for English merchants, who were allowed to trade duty-free in exchange for providing military supplies to Ivan. Today, it houses a small exhibit dedicated to this early international exchange.

Archaeological Museum   MUSEUM
(Музей археологии Москвы; Map p72; www.mosmuseum.ru; Manezhnaya pl 1; adult/child

R300/150; ⊙10am-8pm Tue, Wed & Fri-Sun, 11am-9pm Thu; Ⓜ Okhotny Ryad) An excavation of Voskresensky Bridge (which used to span the Neglinnaya River at the foot of Tverskaya ul) uncovered coins, clothing and other artefacts from old Moscow. The museum displaying these treasures is situated in a 7m-deep underground pavilion that was formed during the excavation itself. The entrance is at the base of the Four Seasons Moscow hotel.

Manege Exhibition Centre GALLERY
(Выставочный центр Манеж; Map p72; http://moscowmanege.ru; Manezhnaya pl; exhibits R200-300; ⊙11am-8pm Tue-Sun; Ⓜ Biblioteka im Lenina) The long, low neoclassical building is Moscow Manege, a vast space that is used for art exhibitions and other events. In the works is a permanent exhibit dedicated to the iconic Soviet sculpture *Worker & Kolkhoz Woman,* on display at VDNKh (p85). Other events are wide-ranging, including exhibitions, concerts, poetry readings, film screenings and more.

Zaikonospassky Monastery MONASTERY
(Заиконоспасский монастырь; Map p72; Nikolskaya ul 7-9; Ⓜ Ploshchad Revolyutsii) This monastery was founded by Boris Godunov in 1600, although the church was built in 1660. The name means 'Behind the Icon Stall', a reference to the busy icon trade that once took place here. The now-functioning, multitiered **Saviour Church** is tucked into the courtyard away from the street.

◉ Tverskoy & Novoslobodsky

★**Hermitage Gardens** PARK
(Сады Эрмитажа; Map p78; www.mosgorsad.ru; ul Karetny Ryad 3; ⊙24hr; Ⓜ Pushkinskaya) FREE
All the things that have improved Moscow parks no end in recent years fill this small, charming garden to the brim. Today, it is possibly the most happening place in Moscow, where art, food and crafts festivals, and concerts, occur almost weekly, especially in summer. Apart from the welcoming lawns and benches, it boasts a large children's playground, a summer cinema and a cluster of food and crafts kiosks. Come here to unwind and mingle with the coolest Muscovites.

Museum of Soviet Arcade Machines MUSEUM
(Map p78; ☑495-628 4515; http://15kop.ru; ul Kuznetsky most 12; admission incl tour R450; ⊙11am-9pm; Ⓜ Kuznetsky Most) Growing up

---

DON'T MISS

PARK ZARYADYE

Opening in late 2017 and rolling out over 2018 is Park Zaryadye, Moscow's first major new park in 50 years. Occupying a prominent site along the Moscow River, wedged into historic Kitay Gorod and a short walk from Red Square, it has been designed by the New York firm Diller Scofidio & Renfro (DS&R).

The 13-hectare park will include four different areas representing Russia's geographic zones – tundra, steppe, forest and wetlands – flowing seemlessly into each other. The most anticipated feature, perhaps, is a sort of bridge to nowhere, which stretches out across Moskvoretskaya nab and over the Moscow River, then loops back to Zaryadye.

In addition to the parkland, Zaryadye will contain a vast outdoor amphitheatre and several new museums, built into the hillsides and showcasing Russia's natural resources and richness.

The centrepiece is the **Media Centre**, where visitors can watch aerial-view films on a 39m movie screen. In the Time Machine Room, the history of Russia unfolds on a 360-degree screen that surrounds the viewers. Other exhibits and videos show off various national parks and promote travel within Russia.

The **Zapavednaya Posolstvo** (Conservation Embassy) will be a state-of-the-art museum featuring a large terrarium and laboratory space, offering many educational programs. A separate **ice cave** – kept below freezing year-round – will feature the creations of Arctic ice artist Alexander Ponomarev.

The smaller Podzemniy Museum (Underground Museum) is an archaeological exhibition, showing off a piece of the old Kitay Gorod wall that was uncovered during excavation.

Finally, the **Zaryadye Park Pavilion** (Павильон парка "Зарядье"; Map p72; Moskvoretskaya ul) FREE serves as a museum of Park Zaryadye, providing an overview of the park and its development.

Tverskoy, Meshchansky & Basmanny

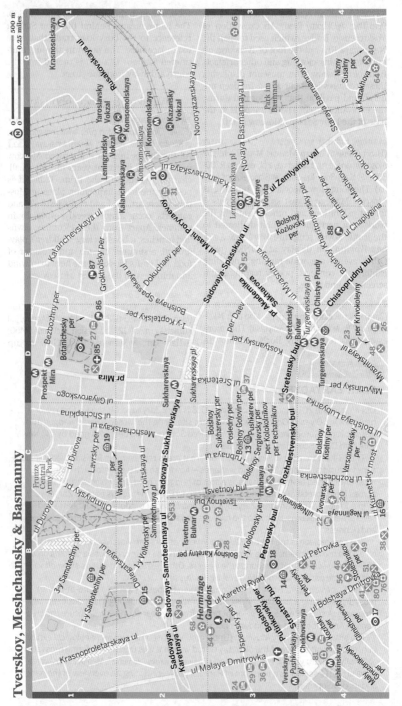

in the 1980s USSR was a peculiar, but not necessarily entirely bleak experience. Here is an example – a collection containing dozens of mostly functional Soviet arcade machines. At the entrance, visitors get a paper bag full of 15-kopek Soviet coins, which fire up these recreational dinosaurs that would look at home in the oldest episodes of Star Trek.

Central Museum of the
Armed Forces   MUSEUM

(Центральный музей Вооружённых Сил; Map p66; ☏495-681 6303; www.cmaf.ru; ul Sovetskoy Armii 2; adult/student R200/100; ☉10am-4.30pm Wed-Fri & Sun, to 6.30pm Sat; MDostoyevskaya) Covering the history of the Soviet and Russian military since 1917, this massive museum occupies 24 halls plus open-air exhibits. Over 800,000 military items, including uniforms, medals and weapons, are on display. Among the highlights are remainders of the American U2 spy plane (brought down in the Ural Mountains in 1960) and the victory flag raised over Berlin's Reichstag in 1945.

Glinka Museum
of Musical Culture   MUSEUM

(Музей музыкальной культуры Глинки; Map p66; ☏495-739 6226; www.glinka.museum; ul Fadeeva 4; admission R200; ☉noon-7pm Tue-Sun; MMayakovskaya) This musicologist's paradise boasts over 3000 instruments – handcrafted works of art – from the Caucasus and the Far East. Russia is very well represented – a 13th-century *gusli* (traditional instrument similar to a dulcimer) from Novgorod, skin drums from Yakutia, a *balalaika* (triangular instrument) by the master Semyon Nalimov – but you can also see such classic pieces as a violin made by Antonio Stradivari. Recordings accompany many of the rarer instruments, allowing visitors to experience their sound.

Church of the Nativity
of the Virgin in Putinki   CHURCH

(Церковь Рождества Богородицы в Путинках; Map p78; ul Malaya Dmitrovka 4; MPushkinskaya) When this church was completed in 1652, Patriarch Nikon responded by banning tent roofs like those featured here. Apparently, he considered such architecture too Russian, too secular and too far removed from the Church's Byzantine roots. Fortunately, the Church of the Nativity has survived to grace this corner near Pushkinskaya pl.

Tverskoy, Meshchansky & Basmanny

Moscow Museum of Modern Art MUSEUM
(Московский музей современного искусства; ММОМА; Map p78; www.mmoma.ru; ul Petrovka

25; adult/student R450/250, joint ticket for three venues R500/300; ⊗ noon-8pm Tue, Wed & Fri-Sun, 1-9pm Thu; Ⓜ Chekhovskaya) A pet project of the ubiquitous artist Zurab Tsereteli, this museum is housed in a classical 18th-century merchant's home, originally designed by Matvei Kazakov (architect of the Kremlin Senate). It is the perfect light-filled setting for an impressive collection of 20th-century paintings, sculptures and graphics, which include both Russian and foreign artists. The highlight is the collection of avant-garde art, with works by Chagall, Kandinsky and Malevich.

Museum of Decorative & Folk Art   MUSEUM

(Всероссийский музей декоративно-прикладного и народного искусства; Map p78; ☑ 495-609 0146; www.vmdpni.ru; Delegatskaya ul 3 & 5; adult/student R250/130; ☺ 10am-6pm Sun, Mon, Wed & Fri, to 9pm Thu, noon-8pm Sat; Ⓜ Tsvetnoy Bulvar) Just beyond the Garden Ring, this museum showcases centuries-old arts-and-crafts traditions from around Russia and the former Soviet republics. Of the 40,000 pieces in the collection, you might see *khokhloma* (laquered) woodwork from Nizhny Novgorod, including wooden toys and *matryoshky* (nested) dolls; baskets and other household items made from birch bark, a traditional Siberian technique; intricate embroidery and lacework from the north, as well as the ubiquitous Pavlov scarves; and playful Dymkovo pottery and Gzhel porcelain.

Gulag History Museum   MUSEUM

(Музей истории ГУЛАГа; Map p78; ☑ 495-621 7310; www.gmig.ru; 1-y Samotechny per 9 str 1; adult/student R300/150; ☺ 11am-6pm Tue, Wed & Fri, noon-8pm Thu; Ⓜ Dostoyevskaya) Stalin's genocide is a subject many Russians prefer to forget rather than reflect on, but this modern multimedia space serves as both a learning centre and a memorial to the millions who perished in concentration camps for 'enemies of the people'. The centrepiece display of objects handmade by prisoners is especially moving.

M'ARS Contemporary Art Centre   GALLERY

(Центр Современного Искусства М'АРС; Map p78; www.marsgallery.ru; Pushkarev per 5; R950-1300; ☺ 2-8pm Tue-Fri, noon-10pm Sat & Sun; Ⓜ Tsvetnoy Bulvar, Sukharevskaya) Founded by artists who were banned during the Soviet era, this gallery space includes 10 exhibit halls showing the work of top contemporary artists, as well as a cool cafe in the basement. The target audience here is people who invest in art – hence the high admission prices.

Detsky Mir   HISTORIC BUILDING

(Map p78; ☑ 495-777 8077; www.detmir.ru; Teatralny pr 5/1; ☺ 10am-10pm; ♿) **FREE** Dominated by the infamous KGB compound, Lubyanskaya ploshchad made adults shiver in Soviet times, but children dreamed of coming here, because another stately edifice in the square was filled with toys and goods intended entirely for them. Although the 1950s interior was lost in a 2008 reconstruction, it's worth visiting this children's department store to check out Soviet toy fashions at the **Museum of Childhood** and admire sweeping views of central Moscow from a rooftop observation point above it.

Contemporary History Museum   MUSEUM

(Музей современной истории России; Map p86; ☑ 495-699 6724; www.sovr.ru; Tverskaya ul

---

HOTEL METROPOL

The Hotel Metropol (p99) is among Moscow's finest examples of art nouveau architecture. The decorative panel on the hotel's central facade, facing Teatralny proezd, is based on a sketch by the artist Mikhail Vrubel. It depicts the legend of the Princess of Dreams, in which a troubadour falls in love with a kind and beautiful princess and travels across the seas to find her. He falls ill during the voyage and is near death when he finds his love. The princess embraces him, but he dies in her arms. Naturally, the princess reacts to his death by renouncing her worldly life. The ceramic panels were made at the pottery workshop at Savva Mamontov's estate in Abramtsevo (p121).

The ceramic work on the side of the hotel facing Teatralnaya pl is by the artist Alexander Golovin. The script was originally a quote from Nietzsche: 'Again the same story: when you build a house you notice that you have learned something'. During the Soviet era, these wise words were replaced with something more appropriate for the time: 'Only the dictatorship of the proletariat can liberate mankind from the oppression of capitalism'. Lenin, of course.

21; adult/student R250/100; ◷10am-6pm Tue-Sun; Ⓜ Pushkinskaya) Complete with stone lions, this opulent mansion was built to host the English Club – a venue favoured by Anglophile gentlemen and native Brits in tsarist times. After a stint as the Revolution Museum in the Soviet era, it now houses exhibitions that trace Russian history from the 1905 and 1917 revolutions up to present days.

Upper St Peter Monastery MONASTERY
(Петровский монастырь; Map p78; cnr ul Petrovka & Petrovsky bul; ◷8am-8pm; Ⓜ Chekhovskaya) The Upper St Peter Monastery was founded in the 1380s as part of an early defensive ring around Moscow. The main, onion-domed **Virgin of Bogolyubovo Church** dates from the late 17th century. The loveliest structure is the brick **Cathedral of Metropolitan Pyotr**, restored with a shingle roof. When Peter the Great ousted the Regent Sofia in 1690, his mother was so pleased she built him this church.

Dostoevsky House-Museum MUSEUM
(Дом-музей Достоевского; Map p66; ☏495-681 1085; ul Dostoevskogo 2; adult/student R150/50; ◷11am-5.30pm Tue & Fri-Sun, to 6.30pm Wed & Thu; Ⓜ Dostoyevskaya) Though this renowned Russian author is more closely associated with St Petersburg, Fyodor Dostoevsky was actually born in Moscow, where his family lived in a tiny apartment on the grounds of Marinsky Hospital. He lived here until the age of 16, when he went to St Petersburg to enter a military academy. The family's Moscow flat has been re-created according to descriptions written by Fyodor's brother.

Vasnetsov House-Museum MUSEUM
(Дом-музей Васнецова; Map p78; ☏495-681 1329; www.tretyakovgallery.ru; per Vasnetsova 13; adult/student R300/150; ◷10am-5pm Wed-Sun; Ⓜ Sukharevskaya) Viktor Vasnetsov was a Russian-revivalist painter, who drew inspiration from fairy tales and village mysticism. In 1894, he designed his own house in Moscow, which is now a museum. Fronted by a colourful gate, it is a charming home in neo-Russian style filled with the original wooden furniture, a tiled stove and many of the artist's paintings. The attic studio, where he once worked, is now adorned with paintings depicting Baba Yaga and other characters from Russian fairy tales.

Tverskaya ploshchad HISTORIC SITE
(Тверская площадь; Map p78) A statue of the founder of Moscow, Yury Dolgoruky, presides over this prominent square near the bottom of Tverskaya ul. So does Mayor Sergei Sobyanin, as the buffed-up five-storey building opposite is the Moscow mayor's office.

◉ Meshchansky & Basmanny

Aptekarsky Ogorod GARDENS
(Аптекарский огород; Map p78; www.hortus.ru; pr Mira 26; adult/student R/300/200; ◷10am-10pm May-Sep, to 5pm Oct-Apr; Ⓜ Prospekt Mira) Moscow's lovely botanic garden was established in 1706. Originally owned by the Moscow general hospital to grow herbs and other medicinal plants, its name translates, unsurprisngly, as Pharmacy Garden. Visitors can wander along the trails, enjoy an exhibition of ornamental plants and explore three greenhouses containing plants from more southernly climes.

Lubyanka HISTORIC BUILDING
(Лубянка; Map p78; Lubyanskaya pl; Ⓜ Lubyanka) Easily the most feared edifice in Russia, looming on the northeastern side of Lubyanskaya pl is the brain centre behind Stalin's genocidal purges and the network of concentration camps known as Gulag. The building came into life circa 1900 as the headquarters of an insurance company, but was taken over by the CheKa (Bolshevik secret police) in 1919 and remained in the hands of its successors – OGPU, NKVD, MGB and finally KGB. The building is not open to the public.

Sakharov Centre MUSEUM
(Map p94; ☏495-623 4401; www.sakharov-center.ru; ul Zemlyanoy val 57; ◷11am-7pm Tue-Sun; Ⓜ Chkalovskaya) FREE South of Kursky vokzal, by the Yauza River, is a small park with a two-storey house containing a human-rights centre named after Russia's most famous dissident. Inside is a museum recounting the life of Sakharov, the nuclear-physicist-turned-human-rights-advocate, detailing the years of repression in Russia and providing a history of the courage shown by the dissident movement. Free English-language tours are available on Wednesday, Friday and Saturday; book in advance.

Chistye Prudy PARK
(Чистые пруды; Map p78; Chistoprudny bul; Ⓜ Chistye Prudy) Clean Ponds is the lovely little pond that graces the Boulevard Ring at the ul Pokrovka intersection. The Boulevard Ring is always a prime location for

DON'T MISS

JEWISH MUSEUM & CENTRE OF TOLERANCE

Occupying a heritage garage, purpose-built to house a fleet of Leyland double-deckers that plied Moscow's streets in the 1920s, this vast museum (Еврейский музей и Центр толерантности; Map p66; ☑ 495-645 0550; www.jewish-museum.ru; ul Obraztsova 11 str 1A; adult/student R400/200; ☺ noon-10pm Sun-Thu, 10am-3pm Fri; Ⓜ Novoslobodskaya), filled with cutting-edge multimedia technology, tackles the uneasy subject of relations between Jews and the Russian state over the centuries. The exhibition relates the stories of pogroms, Jewish revolutionaries, the Holocaust and Soviet anti-Semitism in a calm and balanced manner. The somewhat limited collection of material exhibits is compensated for by the abundance of interactive video displays.

We especially like those that encourage visitors to search for answers to dilemmas faced by early 20th-century Jews – to stand up and fight, to emigrate or to assimilate and keep a low profile.

Russia's Jewish population was quite small until the 18th century, when the empire incorporated a vast chunk of Poland then inhabited by millions of Yiddish-speaking Jews. They were not allowed to move into Russia proper until the early 20th century – a policy that became known as the Pale of Settlement. This led to the perception of Jews as an ethnic, rather than religious group, which still lingers today.

strolling, but the quaint pond makes this a particularly desirable address. Paddleboats in summer and ice skating in winter are essential parts of the ambience. Buy a coffee, find a bench or sit on the grass, and watch the world go by.

Sokolniki PARK
(Сокольники; Map p66; ⓘ ; Ⓜ Sokolniki) FREE Changed beyond recognition in recent years, Sokolniki park is criss-crossed by cycling paths, and blends into a proper forest bordering on Losiny Ostrov national park (Национальный парк Лосиный остров). The area by the entrance (a short walk from Sokolniki metro station), centred on a fountain, is full of cool places to eat and welcoming benches. Further away, to the left of the entrance, is a funfair with rides and carousels. Another attraction is the Rosarium (Розариум), a manicured rose garden.

Museum of the Russian Icon MUSEUM
(Частный музей русской иконы; Map p94; www.russikona.ru; ul Goncharnaya 3; ☺ 11am-7pm Thu-Tue; Ⓜ Taganskaya) FREE This museum houses the private collection of Russian art patron Mikhail Abramov. He has personally amassed a collection of more than 4000 pieces of Russian and Eastern Christian art, including some 600 icons. The collection is unique in that it represents nearly all schools of Russian iconography. Highlights include Simon Ushakov's 17th-century depiction of the Virgin Odigitria and an icon of St Nikolai Mirlikiisky.

Novospassky Monastery MONASTERY
(Новоспасский монастырь; Map p94; ☎ 495-676 9570; www.spasnanovom.ru; Verkhny Novospassky proezd; ☺ 7am-7pm; Ⓜ Proletarskaya) F Novospassky Monastery, a 15th-century fort-monastery, is about 1km south of Taganskaya pl. The centrepiece of the monastery, the Transfiguration Cathedral, was built by the imperial Romanov family in the 1640s in imitation of the Kremlin's Assumption Cathedral. Frescoes depict the history of Christianity in Russia, while the Romanov family tree, which goes as far back as the Viking Prince Rurik, climbs one wall. The other church is the 1675 Intercession Church.

Choral Synagogue NOTABLE BUILDING
(Московская Хоральная Синагога; Map p78; Bolshoy Spasoglinishchevsky per 10; ☺ 9am-6pm; Ⓜ Kitay-Gorod) Construction of a synagogue was banned inside Kitay Gorod, so Moscow's oldest and most prominent synagogue was built just outside the city walls, not far from the Jewish settlement of Zaryadye. Construction started in 1881 but dragged on, due to roadblocks by the anti-Semitic tsarist government. It was finally completed in 1906 and was the only synagogue that continued to operate throughout the Soviet period, despite attempts to convert it into a workers' club.

Yelokhovsky Cathedral CHURCH
(Map p66; http://elohov.ru; Spartakovskaya ul 15; Ⓜ Baumanskaya) FREE Built between 1837 and 1845, the Church of the Epiphany in

Yelokhovo has been Moscow's senior Orthodox cathedral since 1943. With five domes in a Russian eclectic style, the cathedral is full of gilt and icons, not to mention worshippers kneeling, polishing and lighting candles. In the northern part is the tomb of St Nicholas the Miracle Worker.

Rublyov Museum of Early Russian Culture & Art MUSEUM
(Музей древнерусской культуры и искусства им Андрея Рублёва; Map p94; www.rublev-museum.ru; Andronevskaya pl 10; R250-400; ⊙11am-6pm Mon, Tue, Fri & Sat, 2-9pm Thu; Ⓜ Ploshchad Ilycha) On the grounds of Andronikov Monastery, the Rublyov Museum exhibits icons from days of yore and the present. Unfortunately, it does not include any work by its acclaimed namesake artist, though it is still worth visiting, not least for its romantic location. Andrei Rublyov, the master of icon painting, was a monk here in the 15th century. He is buried in the grounds, but no one knows quite where.

Bunker-42 Cold War Museum MUSEUM
(Map p94; ☑495-500 0554; www.bunker42.com; 5-y Kotelnichesky per 11; tours adult/student from R2200/1300; ⊙by appointment; Ⓜ Taganskaya) On a quiet side street near Taganskaya pl, a nondescript neoclassical building is the gateway to the secret Cold War–era communications centre. The facility was meant to serve as the communications headquarters in the event of a nuclear attack. As such, the building was just a shell, serving as an entryway to the 7000-sq-metre space 60m underground. Now in private hands, the facility has been converted into a sort of a museum dedicated to the Cold War.

Vysotsky Cultural Centre MUSEUM
(Культурный центр Высоцкого; Map p94; www.vysotsky.ru; Nizhny Tagansky tupik 3; R150; ⊙11am-6pm Tue & Wed, Fri-Sun; 1-9pm Thu; Ⓜ Taganskaya) Part museum, part performance space, part art exhibit, this cultural centre pays tribute to local legend Vladimir Vysotsky (1938–1980). Singer and songwriter, poet and actor, Vysotsky was one of the Soviet Union's most influential pop-culture figures, thanks mostly to the witty lyrics and social commentary in his songs. The permanent exhibit features a slew of photos and documents, as well as personal items, such as the bard's guitar.

⊙ Presnya

★ Mikhail Bulgakov Museum MUSEUM
(Музей Михаила Булгакова; Map p86; www.bulgakovmuseum.ru; Bolshaya Sadovaya ul 10; adult/child R150/50; ⊙noon-7pm Tue-Sun, 2-9pm Thu; Ⓜ Mayakovskaya) Author of *The Master and Margarita* and *Heart of a Dog*, Mikhail Bulgakov was a Soviet-era novelist who was labelled a counter-revolutionary and censored throughout his life. His most celebrated novels were published posthumously, earning him a sort of cult following in the late Soviet period. Bulgakov lived with his wife, Tatyana Lappa, in a flat in this block, which now houses an arts centre and theatre (Булгаковский Дом и Театр; Map p86; www.dombulgakova.ru; 1st fl, Bolshaya Sadovaya ul 10; ⊙1-11pm, to 1am Fri & Sat) on the ground floor, and a small museum in their actual flat.

★ Moscow Planetarium PLANETARIUM
(Московский планетарий; Map p86; www.planetarium-moscow.ru; Sadovaya-Kudrinskaya ul 5; Large Star Hall R550-750, Small Star Hall R100-200; ⊙10am-10pm Wed-Mon; Ⓜ Barrikadnaya) The planetarium has become one of the biggest and brightest stars on the Moscow museum circuit, now incorporating all kinds of high-tech gadgetry, interactive exhibits and educational programs. The centrepiece is the Large Star Hall (the biggest in Europe!), with its 25m silver dome roof, a landmark that is visible from the Garden Ring. Narration for the shows are available in multiple languages.

Narkomfin NOTABLE BUILDING
(Наркомфин; Map p86; Novinsky bul 25; Ⓜ Barrikadnaya) The model for Le Corbusier's Unité d'Habitation design principle, this architectural landmark was an early experiment in semicommunal living. Designed and built in the 1920s by Moisei Ginzburg and Ignatii Milinis, Narkomfin offered housing for members of the Commissariat of Finances. In line with constructivist ideals, communal space is maximised and individual space is minimised. Apartments have minute kitchens (or none at all) to encourage residents to eat in the communal dining room. Tours are available through Moscow ArchiGeek (p96).

Having been in a semiruinous state for many years, Narkomfin is finally slated for restoration – a three-year project beginning in late 2017. The architect overseeing the project is Alexey Ginzburg, grandson of the original architect, who intends to preserve and restore as much of the constructivist detail as possible. The apartments are likely to remain in private hands but the communal block is slated to house a cultural centre and museum that will hopefully be open to the public.

Museum of Oriental Art   MUSEUM

(Музей искусства народов востока; Map p86; ☑ 495-691 0212; www.orientmuseum.ru; Nikitsky bul 12a; R400; ⊙ 11am-8pm Tue-Sun; Ⓜ Arbatskaya) This impressive museum on the Boulevard Ring holds three floors of exhibits spanning the Asian continent. Of particular interest is the 1st floor, dedicated mostly to the Caucasus, Central Asia and North Asia (meaning the Russian republics of Cukotka, Yakutia and Priamurie). Several rooms on the 2nd floor are dedicated to Nikolai Rerikh, the Russian artist and explorer who spent several years travelling and painting in Asia.

Patriarch's Ponds   PARK

(Патриаршие пруды; Map p86; Bolshoy Patriarshy per; Ⓜ Mayakovskaya) Patriarch's Ponds hark back to Soviet days, when the parks were populated with children and *babushky*. Today you'll see grandmothers pushing strollers and lovers kissing on park benches. In summer, children romp on the swings, while winter sees them ice skating on the pond. The small park has a huge statue of 19th-century Russian writer Ivan Krylov, known to Russian children for his didactic tales.

Moscow Zoo   ZOO

(Московский зоопарк; Map p86; www.moscow-zoo.ru; Bolshaya Gruzinskaya ul 1; R500; ⊙ 10am-8pm Tue-Sun Apr-Sep, to 5pm Oct-Mar; ⊕; Ⓜ Barrikadnaya) Renovations in honour of the zoo's 150th anniversary are ongoing, but the place should be in great shape in coming years. Huge flocks of feathered friends populate the central ponds, making for a pleasant stroll for birdwatchers. For a new perspective on Moscow's nightlife, check out the nocturnal animal exhibit. Other highlights include the big cats (featuring Siberian tigers) and the polar bears. For more four-legged fun, follow the footbridge to see exhibits featuring animals from each continent.

> **WORTH A TRIP**
>
> #### VDNKh & OSTANKINO
>
> Palaces for workers! There is no better place to see this Soviet slogan put into practice than at **VDNKh** (Map p66; Ⓜ VDNKh), which stands for Exhibition of Achievements of the National Economy. Built in 1939, the place feels like a Stalinesque theme park, with palatial pavilions, each designed in its own unique style to represent all the Soviet republics and various industries, from geology to space exploration. A thorough reconstruction, under way at the time of writing, is expected to breathe new life into the area.
>
> Highlights include the **People's Friendship Fountain** surrounded by 16 gilded female figures dressed in ethnic costumes representing Soviet republics (the mysterious 16th figure stands for the Karelo-Finnish republic disbanded in 1956); the jaw-dropping **Stone Flower Fountain**, themed around Ural Mountains miners' mythology, and covered in semiprecious stones from the area; and the powerful **Worker & Kolkhoz Woman** (Map p66; ☑ 495-683 5640; http://moscowmanege.ru; R200; ⊙ noon-9pm Tue-Sun; Ⓜ VDNKh) monument designed by Vera Mukhina for the Soviet pavilion at 1937's Paris Expo.
>
> Approaching VDNKh from the metro, the soaring 100m titanium obelisk is a monument 'To the Conquerors of Space', built in 1964 to commemorate the launch of Sputnik. In its base is the **Cosmonautics Museum** (Map p66; www.kosmo-museum.ru; admission R250; ⊙ 11am-7pm Tue, Wed & Fri-Sun, to 9pm Thu; Ⓜ VDNKh), featuring cool space paraphernalia such as the first Soviet rocket engine and the moon rover Lunokhod. An inspiring collection of space-themed propaganda posters evokes the era of the space race.
>
> To the west is **Ostankino TV Tower** (Останкинская башня; Map p66; ☑ 8-800-100 5553; https://tvtower.ru; adult/child R1000/500; ⊙ 10am-10pm Mon-Thu, to 11pm Fri-Sun; Ⓜ VDNKh). The 337m-high observation deck offers 360-degree views and – horror! – a bit of glass floor. Admission is by guided tour, which take place hourly and must be booked in advance; bring your passport. There's a 40% discount on 10am and 11am tours during weekdays.

Presnya

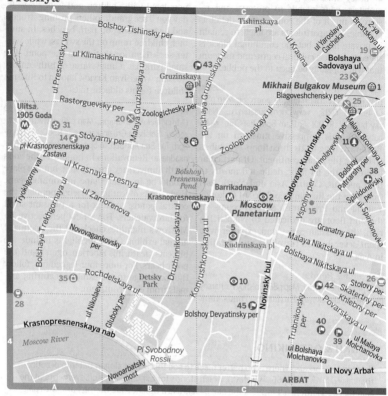

Ryabushinsky Mansion
MUSEUM

(Особняк Рябушинского; Map p86; Malaya Nikit-skaya ul 6/2; adult/student R400/150; ⊙11am-5.30pm Wed-Sun; ⓂPushkinskaya) Also known as the Gorky House-Museum, this fascinating 1906 art nouveau mansion was designed by architect Fyodor Shekhtel and gifted to celebrated author Maxim Gorky in 1931. The house is a visual fantasy with sculpted doorways, ceiling murals, stained glass, a carved stone staircase and exterior tilework. Besides the fantastic decor it contains many of Gorky's personal items, including his extensive library.

Moscow Museum of Modern Art Tverskoy
MUSEUM

(MMOMA; Map p86; www.mmoma.ru; Tverskoy bul 9; R150; ⊙noon-8pm; ⓂPushkinskaya) This small exhibition space, known as the 'Zurab Gallery', was formerly the studio of sculptor Zurab Tsereteli. As such, the space has seen many talented artists, musicians and writers among its guests. Nowadays it is an offshoot of the main MMOMA outlet on ul Petrovka (p80), and continues to host exhibitions, performances and cultural events. Be sure to check the website to see what's on, as the museum often closes between shows.

Moscow Museum of Modern Art Yermolayevsky
MUSEUM

(MMOMA; Map p86; www.mmoma.ru; Yermo-layevsky per 17; adult/student R250/100; ⊙noon-8pm; ⓂMayakovskaya) This handsome neo-classical building houses a branch of the main MMOMA on ul Petrovka (p80). Formerly the Moscow Union of Artists, it is now utilised for temporary exhibits of paintings, sculpture, photography and multimedia pieces. Be sure to check the website to see what's on, as the museum often closes between shows.

his final tortured months here. The rooms – now a small but captivating museum – are arranged as they were when Gogol lived in them. You can even see the fireplace where he famously threw his manuscript of *Dead Souls*.

Tsereteli Studio-Museum MUSEUM

(Музей-мастерская Зураба Церетели; Map p86; www.mmoma.ru; Bolshaya Gruzinskaya ul 15; adult/child R250/150; ☺noon-8pm Fri-Wed & 1-9pm Thu; ⊞; Ⓜ Belorusskaya) Moscow's most prolific artist has opened up his 'studio' as a space to exhibit his many masterpieces. You can't miss this place – whimsical characters adorn the front lawn. They give just a tiny hint of what's inside: a courtyard crammed with bigger-than-life bronze beauties and elaborate enamel work.

The highlight work is undoubtedly Putin in his judo costume, although the huge tile Moscow cityscapes are impressive. You'll also recognise some smaller-scale models of monuments that appear around town. Indoors, there are three floors of the master's sketches, paintings and enamel arts.

Moscow International Business Centre AREA

(Москва-сити; Map p66; Ⓜ Delovoi Tsentr) This strip along the Moscow River is the site of one of the capital's largest ongoing urban projects, also known as 'Moscow City'. Here, skyscrapers of glass and steel tower 20 stories over the rest of the city, shining like beacons to Moscow's wheeler-dealers and fortune-seekers. The 93-storey Tower East (Vostok) of the Federation complex is the tallest building in both Russia and Europe.

◉ Arbat & Khamovniki

★Novodevichy Convent CONVENT

(Новодевичий монастырь; Map p66; Novodevichy pr 1; adult/student R500/250, photos R300; ☺grounds 8am-8pm, museums 9am-5pm Wed-Mon; Ⓜ Sportivnaya) The Novodevichy Convent was founded in 1524 to celebrate the taking of Smolensk from Lithuania, an important step in Moscow's conquest of the old Kyivan Rus lands. The oldest and most dominant building on the grounds is the white Smolensk Cathedral, with a sumptuous interior covered in 16th-century frescoes. Novodevichy is a functioning monastery. Women are advised to cover their heads and shoulders when entering the churches, while men should wear long pants.

Museum of Russian Impressionism MUSEUM

(Map p66; www.rusimp.su; Bldg 11, Leningradsky pr 15; R250; ☺11am-8pm Fri-Tue, noon-9pm Wed-Thu; Ⓜ Belorusskaya) Few Russian artists embraced the Impressionist moniker, but many were influenced by the movement's style and techniques. At Moscow's newest art museum, billionaire art collector Boris Mint aims to educate and impress Muscovites (and visitors) about this important niche, at the same time showcasing his own collection, which includes works by the likes of Valenin Serov, Boris Kustodiev and Konstantin Korovin. The museum occupies part of the former Bolshevik chocolate factory – the sugar silo, to be exact. Sweet!

Gogol House MUSEUM

(Дом Гоголя; Map p86; www.domgogolya.ru; Nikitsky bul 7; R150; ☺noon-7pm Tue, Wed & Fri, 2-9pm Thu, noon-5pm Sat & Sun; Ⓜ Arbatskaya) The 19th-century writer Nikolai Gogol spent

Presnya

Novodevichy Cemetery CEMETERY
(Новодевичье кладбище; Map p66; Luzhnetsky pr 2; ⊙9am-5pm; MSportivnaya) FREE Adjacent to the Novodevichy Convent (p87), the Novodevichy Cemetery is one of Moscow's most prestigious resting places – a veritable who's who of Russian politics and culture. Here you will find the tombs of Bulgakov, Chekhov, Gogol, Mayakovsky, Prokofiev, Stanislavsky and Eisenstein, among many other Russian and Soviet cultural luminaries. The most recent notable addition to the cemetery is former President Boris Yeltsin, whose tomb is marked by an enormous Russian flag.

★**Cathedral of Christ the Saviour** CHURCH
(Храм Христа Спасителя; Map p90; www.xxc.ru; ul Volkhonka 15; ⊙1-5pm Mon, from 10am Tue-Sun; MKropotkinskaya) FREE This gargantuan cathedral was completed in 1997 – just in time to celebrate Moscow's 850th birthday. It is amazingly opulent, garishly grandiose and truly historic. The cathedral's sheer size and splendour guarantee its role as a love-it-or-hate-it landmark. Considering Stalin's plan for this site (a Palace of Soviets topped with a 100m statue of Lenin), Muscovites should at least be grateful they can admire the shiny domes of a church instead of the shiny dome of Ilyich's head.

Melnikov House NOTABLE BUILDING
(Дом Мельникова; Map p90; ☑495-697 8037; Krivoarbatsky per 10; ⊙courtyard 10am-7pm Mar-Oct, to 5pm Nov-Feb, house by appointment; MArbatskaya) The only private house built during the Soviet period, the home of Konstantin Melnikov stands as testament to the innovation of the Russian avant-garde. The architect created his unusual home from two interlocking cylinders – an ingenious design that employs no internal load-bearing wall. It was also experimental in its designation of living space, as the whole family slept in one room, divided by narrow wall screens.

DON'T MISS

FROM WORKERS' FACTORIES TO HIPSTER HANG-OUTS

Like the Bolsheviks a hundred years ago, Moscow hipsters are capturing one factory after another and redeveloping them, according to their tastes.

Flakon (Map p66; www.flacon.ru; ul Bolshaya Novodmitrovskaya 36; Ⓜ Dmitrovskaya) Arguably the most visually attractive of all the redeveloped industrial areas around Moscow, its mixture of brightly painted buildings and bare red brick resembling Portobello Rd in London. Once a glassware plant that produced bottles for the perfume industry, it is now home to dozens of funky shops and other businesses. Shopping for designer clothes and unusual souvenirs is the main reason for coming here.

Khlebozavod 9 The front entrance to this complex which was once a bread factory, is across the road from Flakon. Filling up with tenants at the time of writing, one of the early comers is **Svoboda** (Map p66; Novodmitrovskaya ul 1, str 9; ⊘ noon-11.30pm; Ⓜ Dmitrovskaya), a craft-beer and music venue.

Winzavod Center for Contemporary Art (Винзавод; Map p78; www.winzavod.ru; 4-y Syromyatnichesky per 1; Ⓜ Chkalovskaya) **FREE**. Formerly a wine-bottling factory, this post-industrial complex houses several art and photo galleries, as well as a few interesting gift shops and boutiques.

ArtPlay (Map p78; ☑ 495-620 0882; www.artplay.ru; ul Nizhny Syromyatnichesky per 10; ⊘ noon-8pm Tue-Sun; Ⓜ Chkalovskaya) **FREE** Occupying the former Manometer factory, this is home to firms specialising in urban planning and architectural design, as well as furniture showrooms and antique stores. Expect to see diverse and dynamic rotating exhibits.

Red October (Завод Красный Октябрь; Map p90; Bersenevskaya nab; Ⓜ Kropotkinskaya) **FREE** The former Red October chocolate factory is a defiant island of Russian modernity and European-ness filled with cool bars, restaurants and galleries including **Lumiere Brothers Photography Centre** (Map p90; www.lumiere.ru; Bolotnaya nab 3, bldg 1; R200-430; ⊘ noon-9pm Tue-Fri, to 10pm Sat & Sun). A huge power-station building here was under reconstruction at the time of writing, slated to open as another major modern art venue in 2019 under the name of GES-2.

Pushkin House-Museum MUSEUM
(Дом-музей Пушкина; Map p90; www.pushkin-museum.ru; ul Arbat 53; R300; ⊘ 10am-6pm Tue-Sun, noon-9pm Thu; Ⓜ Smolenskaya) After Alexander Pushkin married Natalia Goncharova at the nearby Church of the Grand Ascension, they moved to this charming blue house on the old Arbat. The museum provides some insight into the couple's home life, a source of much Russian romanticism. (The lovebirds are also featured in a statue across the street.) The ground floor contains a broader exhibit about Pushkin in Moscow.

Moscow Museum MUSEUM
(Музей Москвы; Map p90; www.mosmuseum.ru; Zubovsky bul 2; adult/student R200/100; ⊘ 10am-8pm Tue-Wed & Fri-Sun, 11am-9pm Thu; Ⓜ Park Kultury) The permanent history exhibit here demonstrates how the city has spread from its starting point at the Kremlin. It is heavy on artefacts from the 13th and 14th centuries, especially household items and weapons, although there is little information in English. More exciting, the museum has space to launch thought-provoking temporary exhibits, including artists' and other locals' perspectives on the city.

Tolstoy Estate-Museum MUSEUM
(Музей-усадьба Толстого 'Хамовники'; Map p66; www.tolstoymuseum.ru; ul Lva Tolstogo 21; adult/student R400/200; ⊘ 10am-6pm Tue, Wed & Fri-Sun, noon-8pm Thu; Ⓜ Park Kultury) Leo Tolstoy's winter home during the 1880s and 1890s now houses an interesting museum dedicated to the writer's home life. While it's not particularly opulent or large, the building is fitting for junior nobility – which Tolstoy was. Exhibits here demonstrate how Tolstoy lived, as opposed to his literary influences, which are explored at the **Tolstoy Literary Museum** (Литературный музей Толстого; Map p90; www.tolstoymuseum.ru; ul Prechistenka 11; adult/student R250/100; ⊘ noon-6pm Tue-Sun; Ⓜ Kropotkinskaya). See the salon where Sergei Rachmaninov and Nikolai Rimsky-Korsakov played piano, and the study where Tolstoy wove his epic tales.

MOSCOW SIGHTS

Arbat & Khamovniki

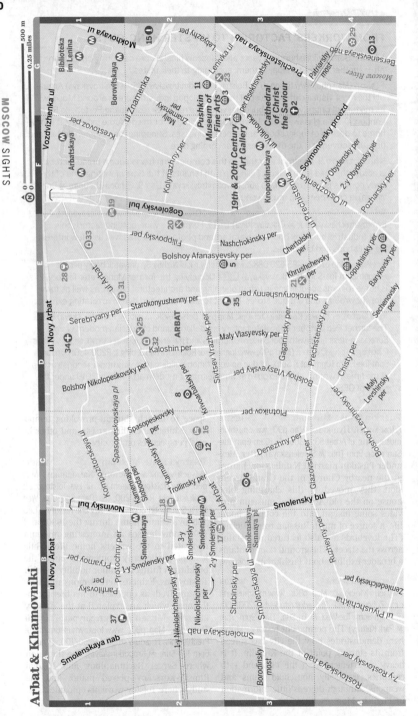

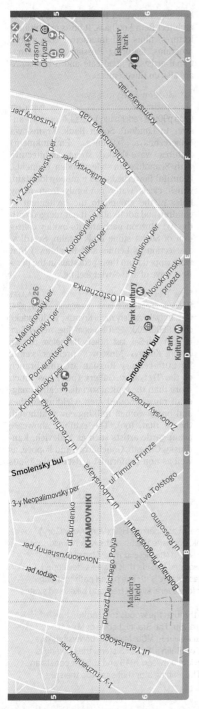

Burganov House MUSEUM

(Дом Бурганова; Map p90; ☎495-695 0429; www.burganov.ru; Bolshoy Afanasyevsky per 15; adult/child R150/100; ⊙11am-7pm Sat-Wed, noon-9pm Thu; M Kropotkinskaya) Part studio, part museum, the Burganov House is a unique venue in Moscow, where the craft goes on around you, as you peruse the sculptures and other artwork on display. Comprising several interconnected courtyards and houses, the works of surrealist sculptor Alexander Burganov are artfully displayed alongside pieces from the artist's private collection. The surrounding streets of the Arbat and Khamovniki districts also contain many examples of the artist's work.

Multimedia Art Museum   MUSEUM
(Мультимедиа Арт Музей; Map p90; www.mamm-mdf.ru; ul Ostozhenka 16; R500; ☺noon-9pm Tue-Sun; M Kropotkinskaya) This slick, modern gallery is home to an impressive photographic library and archives of contemporary and historic photography. The facility usually hosts several simultaneous exhibits, often featuring works by prominent photographers from the Soviet period, as well as contemporary artists. The complex also hosts several month-long festivals: Photobiennale and Fashion and Style in Photography (held in alternating years).

⊙ Zamoskvorechie

Garage Museum of
Contemporary Art   MUSEUM
(Map p94; ☑495-645 0520; www.garagemca.org; ul Krymsky val 9/32; adult/student R400/200; 11am-10pm; M Oktyabrskaya) The brainchild of Moscow art fairy Darya Zhukova, Garage is one of the capital's hottest modern-art venues. In mid-2015 the museum moved to spectacular new digs in Gorky Park – a derelict Soviet-era

building, renovated by the visionary Dutch architect Rem Koolhaas. It hosts exhibitions, lectures, films and interactive educational programs, featuring Russian and international artists. A good cafe and a bookstore are also on the premises.

Art Muzeon & Krymskaya
Naberezhnaya   PUBLIC ART
(Map p90; M Park Kultury) FREE Moscow's answer to London's South Bank, Krymskaya Naberezhnaya (Crimea Embankment) features wave-shaped street architecture with Scandinavian-style wooden elements, beautiful flowerbeds and a moody fountain, which ejects water randomly from many holes in the ground to the excitement of children and adults alike. It has merged with the Art Muzeon park and its motley collection of Soviet stone idols (Stalin, Sverdlov, a selection of Lenins and Brezhnevs) that were ripped from their pedestals in the post-1991 wave of anti-Soviet feeling.

New Tretyakov Gallery   GALLERY
(Новая Третьяковская галерея; Map p94; www.tretyakovgallery.ru; ul Krymsky val 10; adult/child R500/200; ☺10am-6pm Tue, Wed & Sun, to 9pm Thu-Sat, last tickets 1hr before closing; M Park Kultury) Moscow's premier venue for 20th-century Russian art, this branch of the Tretyakov Gallery (p64) has much more than the typical socialist realist images of muscle-bound men wielding scythes and busty women milking cows (although there's that, too). The exhibits showcase avant-garde artists such as Malevich, Kandinsky, Chagall, Goncharova and Popova, as well as non-conformist artists of the 1960s

---

WORTH A TRIP

SPARROW HILLS

The green hills in the south of Moscow are known as Sparrow Hills (Vorobyovy Gory). Running along the south side of the river bank, opposite the tip of the Khamovniki peninsula, is **Vorobyovy Gory Nature Preserve** (Воробьевы горы; Map p66; www.vorobyovy-gory.ru; M Vorobyovy Gory) FREE, a wooded hillside that is a less-developed, less-crowded extension of Gorky Park and Neskuchny Sad. The paved path that originates further north continues along the river for several kilometres, and bikes and skates are available to rent here.

Walking trails from the river bank wind up through the woods to a **lookout point**. From here, most of the city spreads out before you. The Stalinist spire of **Moscow State University** (Московский Государственный Университет; MGU; Map p66; Universitetskaya pl; M Universitet) towers over the square. One of Stalin's 'Seven Sisters', the building is the result of four years of hard labour by convicts between 1949 and 1953. It boasts an amazing 36 storeys and 33km of corridors. The shining star that sits atop the spire is supposed to weigh 12 tonnes.

and 1970s who refused to accept the official style.

In the same building, **Central House of Artists** (Центральный дом художника; ЦДХ; Map p94; www.cha.ru; admission R350; ⊙11am-7pm Tue-Sun; Ⓜ Oktyabrskaya), also known as **TsDkh**, is a huge exhibit space used for contemporary-art shows. A number of galleries are also housed here on a permanent basis.

Donskoy Monastery
MONASTERY

(Донской монастырь; Map p66; ☑ 495-952 1646; www.donskoi.org; Donskaya ul; Ⓜ Shabolovskaya) Moscow's youngest monastery, Donskoy was founded in 1591 as the home of the *Virgin of the Don* icon, now in the Tretyakov Gallery (p64). This icon is credited with the victory in the 1380 battle of Kulikovo; it's also said that, in 1591, the Tatar Khan Giri retreated without a fight after the icon showered him with burning arrows in a dream.

Danilov Monastery
MONASTERY

(Даниловский монастырь; Map p66; www.msdm.ru; ul Danilovsky val; ⊙7am-7pm; Ⓜ Tulskaya) **FREE** The headquarters of the Russian Orthodox Church stands behind white fortress walls. On holy days this place seethes with worshippers murmuring prayers, lighting candles and ladling holy water into jugs at the tiny chapel inside the gates. The Danilovsky Monastery was built in the late 13th century by Daniil, the first Prince of Moscow, as an outer city defence.

🏃 Activities

★ Sanduny Baths
BATHHOUSE

(Map p78; ☑ 495-782 1808; www.sanduny.ru; ul Neglinnaya 14; admission R1800-2800; ⊙8am-10pm Wed-Mon, second male top class 10am-midnight Tue-Fri, 8am-10pm Sat & Sun; Ⓜ Kuznetsky Most) Sanduny is the oldest and most luxurious *banya* (hot bath) in the city. The Gothic Room is a work of art with its rich woodcarving, while the main shower room has an aristocratic Roman feel to it. There are several classes, as on trains; regulars say that second male top class is actually better than the premium class.

Moscow Bike Tours
CYCLING

(☑8-916-970 1419; www.moscowbiketours.com; 2½hr tour US$40-60) Cover more ground and see more sights, while getting fresh air and a bit of exercise: that's a win-win-win! On the recommended 2½-hour bike tour, you'll enjoy magnificent views of Moscow from Krymskaya embankment, riding through

WORTH A TRIP

PARK POBEDY

The Great Patriotic War – as WWII is known in Russia – was a momentous event that is still vivid in the hearts, minds and memories of many Russian citizens. Magnificent **Park Pobedy** (Парк Победы; Map p66; www.poklonnaya-gora.ru; Kutuzovsky pr; ⊙dawn-dusk; ♿; Ⓜ Park Pobedy) **FREE** at Poklonnaya Hill is a huge memorial complex commemorating the sacrifice and celebrating the triumph of the war. Unveiled on the 50th anniversary of the victory, the park includes endless fountains, monuments and museums, as well as a memorial church, synagogue and mosque.

The park's centrepiece is the massive **Museum of the Great Patriotic War** (Центральный музей Великой Отечественной Войны; Map p66; www.poklonnayagora.ru; ul Bratiev Fonchenko 10; adult/child R300/200; ⊙10am-6pm Tue-Sun Nov-Mar, to 8pm Apr-Oct; Ⓜ Park Pobedy) with hundreds of exhibits, including dioramas of every major WWII battle the Russians fought in, as well as weapons, photographs, documents and other wartime memorabilia.

Gorky Park (p64) and all the way down to Sparrow Hills, before crossing into Khamovniki. Day and evening rides offered; extended tour available on weekends.

Moscow Free Tour
WALKING

(Map p72; ☑495-222 3466; www.moscowfreetour.com; Nikolskaya ul 4/5; guided walk free, paid tours from €31) Every day these enthusiastic ladies offer an informative, inspired 2½-hour guided walk around Red Square and Kitay Gorod – and it's completely free. It's so good that (they hope) you'll sign up for one of their excellent paid tours, covering the Kremlin, the Arbat and the Metro, or themes such as communist Moscow.

Moscow 360
WALKING

(☑8-985-447 8688; www.moscow360.org; tours per group from R2000) Paul is a private guide who offers excellent and entertaining walking tours in the centre, including the standards like a metro tour and a communist history tour. His speciality, however, is the AK-47 tour, which takes you to a shooting range to learn all about the infamous AK weapons and take a few shots yourself.

Zamoskvorechie & Taganka

1 km
0.5 miles

Gogolevsky bul
ul Znamenka
Bolshoy Znamensky per
Kropotkinskaya
Gagarinsky per
ul Prechistenka
ul Ostozhenka
ul Volkhonka

Bolshoy Afanasyevsky per
Starokonyushenny per

Kremlevskaya nab
Sofiyskaya nab
Bolshoy Kamenny most
Maly Moskvoretsky most
Moskvoretsky most
Bolotny Island
Repinsky skver
Bolotnaya nab

Bersenevsky per
Bersenevskaya nab
1-y Golutvinsky per
Yakimanskaya nab
Prechistenskaya nab
Pozharsky per
Zachatyevsky 1-y per

Korobeynikov per
Khilkov per

Moskvoretskaya nab
Rauzhskaya nab
Bolshoy Ustinsky most
Chugunny most
Komissariatsky most
ul Balchug

Kadashevskaya nab
Pyatnitskaya ul
Novokuznetskaya
Runovsky per
Ozerkovsky per
Sadovnicheskaya ul
Sadovnicheskaya nab
Ozerkovskaya nab

State Tretyakov Gallery Main Branch
3
Bolshoy Tolmachevsky per
ul Bolshaya Polyanka
18
Klimentovsky per
Tretyakovskaya
ul Bolshaya Ordynka
ul N A Ostrovskogo
Golikovsky per
Pyatnitsky per
ul Pyatnitskaya

Bolshaya Tatarskaya ul
ul Bakhrushina
Novokuznetskaya ul
2-y Novokuznetsky per
Tatarskaya ul

Polyanka
16
Bolshaya Yakimanka
1-y Kazachy per
Bolshaya Polyanka
Brodnikov per
Khvostov per
1-y Khvostov per
Spasonalivkovsky per
Pogorelsky per
Kazansky tupik
Kazansky per
2-y Montechikovsky per
Serpukhovskaya
Danilov Monastery (1.8km)

Oktyabrskaya
Zhitnaya ul
Dobryninskaya
30
Oktyabrskaya proezd
Apakova
Oktyabrskaya

Garage Museum of Contemporary Art
1
Donskoy Monastery (2.5km)
14
24
Pushkinskaya nab
Gorky Park
2
5
6
9
ul Krymsky val (Garden Ring)
Iskusstv Park
Maronovsky per
Krymsky most
Krymskaya nab
Moscow River

Valovaya ul
ul Zatsepa
Paveletskaya
25
Paveletsky Vokzal
Zatsepsky val
Stremyanny per

Kosmodamianskaya nab
Krasnokholmskaya nab
Bolshoy Krasnokholmsky most
Krasnokholmskaya nab
Zverev most
27
3-y Shlyuzovoy per
Shlyuzovaya nab
Shlyuzovoy most
Novospassky most
Kozhevnicheskaya ul

Moscow River
Kotelnicheskaya nab
7
8
23
Serebryanicheskaya nab
Ustinsky per
Bolshoy Ustinsky most

ul Nikoloyamskaya
ul Zemlyanoy val
ul Verkhnyaya Radishchevskaya
ul Goncharnaya
Verkhnaya Taganskaya per
13
Taganskaya
4
1-y Goncharny per
Taganskaya pl
Bolshaya Kommunisticheskaya ul
Nizhny Tagansky t
Nizhny Tagansky per

Polyaroslavskaya nab
12 F
Nikoloyamskaya nab
Kostomarovsky most
Androniyevskaya
ul Sergiya Radonezhskogo
11
Bibliotechnaya ul
Bolshoy Rogozhsky per
pl Abelmanovskaya Zastava
Nizhegorodskaya ul
Old Believers' Community (2km)
Shkolnaya ul
Bryansky per

Marksistskaya ul
10
Vorontsovskaya ul
Bolshie Kamenshchiki ul
Taganskaya
Tagansky Park
pl Krestyanskaya Zastava
Krestyanskaya pl
Proletarskaya
Krestyanskaya ul
3-y Krutitsky per
Sarinsky proezd
Saninsky proezd
Novospassky proezd
Novospassky most

Zamoskvorechie & Taganka

Kremlin Tour with Diana　　　　HISTORY
(☑ 8-965-150 0071; www.kremlintour.com) Diana Zalenskaya and her team offer private tours of the Kremlin (with or without the Armoury included). Recommended.

Luzhniki Aqua Complex　　　SWIMMING
(Аквакомплекс Лужники; Map p66; www.aqua-luzhniki.ru; Luzhnetskaya nab 24; per hr R1200-1500; ◷ 7am-11pm; Ⓜ Vorobyovy Gory) On the grounds of the Luzhniki Olympic Complex, the main venue for the 1980 Olympics, this aquatic facility includes a collection of swimming pools that are open year-round. There is a 50m lap pool and a kid-friendly recreational area, as well as table tennis, volleyball and a training room and sauna.

Krasnopresnkiye Bany　　BATHHOUSE
(Краснопресненские бани; Map p86; ☑ men's banya 495-255 5306, women's banya 495-253 8690; www.baninapresne.ru; Stolyarny per 7; R1400-1900; ◷ 8am-11pm; Ⓜ Ulitsa 1905 Goda) Lacking an old-fashioned, decadent atmosphere, this modern, clean, efficient place nonetheless provides a first-rate *banya* (hot-bath) experience. The facility has a Russian steam room, a Finnish sauna, a plunge pool and massage services.

Oliver Bikes　　　　　　　CYCLING
(Оливер Байкс; Map p94; ☑ 499-340 2609; www.bikerentalmoscow.com; Pyatnitskaya ul 3/4, str 2; per hr/day from R500/1200, tours per group R6000; ◷ 10am-11pm; Ⓜ Novokuznetskaya) Oliver rents all kinds of two-wheeled vehicles, including cruisers, mountain bikes, folding bikes and tandem bikes, all of which are in excellent condition. Its location is convenient for rides along the Moscow River. Oliver also offers weekend bike tours, but only occasionally in English.

☞ Tours

Remote Moscow　　　　　　TOURS
(http://remote-moscow.ru/eng; per person R2000; ◷ shows Thu-Sun) City tour meets theatre in this performance/quest, available in many places around the world, now including Moscow. The 90-minute walk takes participants through a series of interactions and encounters from the gates of a cemetery into the centre of the city. All you need to do is come to the starting point, put on headphones and follow the instructions.

Moscow Mania   TOURS

(www.mosmania.com; 2hr walk from R3500) This team of historians (with PhDs and everything) are passionate about their city and their subject. They have designed 50-plus tours on specialised topics – or they will customise one for you. Private tours for up to eight people.

Moscow ArchiGeek   TOURS

(Москва Глазами Инженера; ☑ 499-322 2325; www.archigeek.ru; tours from R1200) These architectural tours around Moscow hit some unusual destinations indeed, such as the modernist Chaika swimming pool or the clock tower of Kievsky vokzal (p119). Most are in Russian, but there are English-language tours to VDNKh (p85), Narkomfin (p84) and St Basil's Cathedral (p61). Also goes by the name 'Moscow Through the Eyes of an Engineer' (www.engineer-history.ru).

Patriarshy Dom Tours   TOURS

(Map p86; ☑ 495-795 0927; www.toursinrussia. com; Moscow School No 1239, Vspolny per 6; Moscow tours from US$22, day trips from US$65; Ⓜ Barrikadnaya) Provides a changing schedule of specialised tours of local museums, specific neighbourhoods and unusual themes, as well as out-of-town trips to the Golden Ring towns and other day-trip destinations. Occasionally takes groups inside the Great Kremlin Palace (p60), which is otherwise closed to the public. Pick up the monthly schedule at upscale hotels or view it online.

✨ Festivals & Events

Winter Festival   CULTURAL

An outdoor fun-fest for two weeks in December and January, for those with antifreeze in their veins. Admire the elaborate ice sculptures on Red Square, stand in a crowd of snowmen on ul Arbat and ride the troika at Izmailovsky Park.

Golden Mask Festival   THEATRE

(www.goldenmask.ru; ⊘ Mar-Apr) This festival involves two months of performances by Russia's premier drama, opera, dance and musical performers, culminating in a prestigious awards ceremony in April.

Chekhov International
Theatre Festival   THEATRE

(www.chekhovfest.ru) In odd-numbered years, theatre troupes descend on Moscow from all corners of the world for this renowned biennial festival. Drama and musical theatre performances are held at participating venues around town, from mid-May to mid-June.

🏃 City Walk
Metro Tour: Underground Art

START KOMSOMOLSKAYA
END PARK POBEDY
DISTANCE 18KM, ONE TO TWO HOURS

Every day, as many as seven million people ride the Moscow metro. What's more, this transport system marries function and form: many of the stations are marble-faced, frescoed, gilded works of art. Take this tour for an overview of Moscow's most interesting and impressive metro stations.

Start at ❶ **Komsomolskaya**, where the red line (Sokolnicheskaya liniya) intersects with the Ring line (Koltsevaya liniya). Both stations are named for the youth workers who helped with early construction. In the red line station, look for the Komsomol emblem at the top of the limestone pillars and the majolica-tile panel showing the volunteers hard at work.

From Komsomolskaya, proceed anti-clockwise around the Ring line, getting off at each stop along the way.

Originally named for the nearby MGU Botanical Garden, ❷ **Prospekt Mira** features elegant, white-porcelain depictions of figures planting trees, bringing in the harvest and generally living in harmony.

❸ **Novoslobodskaya** is enveloped in the art-nouveau artistry of 32 stained-glass panels. Six windows depict the so-called intellectual professions: architect, geographer, agronomist, engineer, artist and musician. At one end of the central hall is the mosaic *Peace in the Whole World*. The pair of white doves was a later addition to the mosaic, replacing a portrait of Stalin.

At ❹ **Belorusskaya** the ceiling mosaics celebrate the culture, economy and history of Russia's neighbour to the west. The 12 ceiling panels illustrate different aspects of their culture, while the floor pattern reproduces traditional Belarusian ornamentation.

Switch here to the green Zamoskvoretskaya line (where the Belarusian theme continues) and travel south.

❺ **Mayakovskaya** is the pièce de résistance of the Moscow metro. The

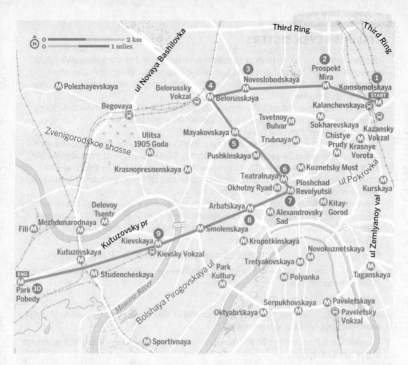

grand-prize winner at the 1938 World's Fair in New York has an art-deco central hall that's all pink rhodonite, with slender, steel columns. The inspiring, upward-looking mosaics on the ceiling depict *24 Hours in the Land of the Soviets*. This is also one of the deepest stations (33m), which allowed it to serve as an air-raid shelter during WWII.

The decor at ⑥ **Teatralnaya** follows a theatrical theme. The porcelain figures represent seven of the Soviet republics by wearing national dress and playing musical instruments from their homeland.

Change here to ⑦ **Ploshchad Revolyutsii** on line three (the dark-blue Arbatsko-Pokrovskaya line). This dramatic station is basically an underground sculpture gallery. The life-sized bronze statues represent the roles played by the people during the revolution and in the 'new world' that comes after. Heading up the escalators, the themes are: revolution, industry, agriculture, hunting, education, sport and child rearing. Touch the nose of the border guard's dog for good luck on exams. Take the dark-blue line heading west.

Shallow ⑧ **Arbatskaya** was damaged by a German bomb in 1941. The station was closed and a parallel line was built much deeper. Service was restored on the shallow line the following decade, which explains the existence of two Arbatskaya stations (and two Smolenskaya stations, for that matter) on two different lines.

At 250m, Arbatskaya is one of the longest stations. A braided moulding emphasises the arched ceiling, while red marble and detailed ornamentation give the whole station a baroque atmosphere.

At ⑨ **Kievskaya**, the elegant white-marble hall is adorned with a Kiyivan-style ornamental frieze, while the frescoed panels depict farmers in folk costume, giant vegetables and other aspects of the idyllic Ukrainian existence. The fresco at the end of the hall celebrates 300 years of Russian-Ukrainian cooperation. Ironic.

The newer ⑩ **Park Pobedy** opened after the complex at Poklonnaya Gora, which commemorated the 50th anniversary of the victory in the Great Patriotic War. Moscow's deepest metro station it has the longest escalators in the world. The enamel panels at either end of the hall (created by Zurab Tsereteli) depict the victories of 1812 and 1945.

From here you can return to the centre by retracing your ride on the dark-blue line.

STALIN'S SEVEN SISTERS

The foundations for seven large skyscrapers were laid in 1947 to mark Moscow's 800th anniversary. Stalin had decided that Moscow suffered from a 'skyscraper gap' when compared to the USA, and ordered the construction of these seven behemoths to jump-start the city's skyline.

One of the main architects, Vyacheslav Oltarzhevsky, had worked in New York during the skyscraper boom of the 1930s, and his experience proved essential. (Fortunately, he'd been released from the Gulag in time to help.)

In addition to the 'Seven Sisters' listed here, there were plans in place to build an eighth Stalinist skyscraper in Zaryadye (near Kitay Gorod). The historic district was razed in 1947 and a foundation was laid for a 32-storey tower. It did not get any further than that – for better and for worse – and the foundation was later used for the gargantuan Hotel Rossiya (demolished in 2006). This is now the site of the new **Park Zaryadye** (p77).

With their widely scattered locations, the towers provide a unique visual reference for Moscow. Their official name in Russia is *vysotky* (high-rise) as opposed to *neboskryob* (foreign skyscraper). They have been nicknamed variously the 'Seven Sisters', the 'wedding cakes', 'Stalin's sisters' and more.

Foreign Affairs Ministry (Map p90; Smolenskaya-Sennaya pl 32/34; Ⓜ Smolenskaya)

Hilton Moscow Leningradskaya (Гостиница Ленинградская; Map p78; Kalanchevskaya ul 21/40; Ⓜ Komsomolskaya)

Radisson Royal Hotel Ukraina (p102)

Kotelnicheskaya Apartment Block (Высотка на Котельнической набережной; Map p94; Kotelnicheskaya nab 17/1; Ⓜ Taganskaya)

Kudrinskaya Apartment Block (Высотка на Кудринской площади; Map p86; Kudrinskaya pl 1; Ⓜ Barrikadnaya)

Moscow State University (p92)

Transport Ministry (Высотка на площади Красных Ворот; Map p78; ul Sadovaya-Spasskaya; Ⓜ Krasnye Vorota)

Moscow International Film Festival FILM (www.moscowfilmfestival.ru) This 10-day event in June/July attracts filmmakers from the US and Europe, as well as the most promising Russian artists. Films are shown at theatres around the city.

City Day CULTURAL
City Day, or *den goroda* in Russian, celebrates Moscow's birthday on the first weekend in September. The day kicks off with a festive parade, followed by live music on Red Square and plenty of food, fireworks and fun.

Moscow Biennale of Contemporary Art ART
(www.moscowbiennale.ru) This month-long festival, held in odd-numbered years in September (and sometimes in different months), has played a key role in establishing the capital as an international centre for contemporary art. Venues around the city exhibit works by artists from around the world.

December Nights Festival ART, MUSIC
(www.arts-museum.ru) This prestigious annual festival in December is hosted at the Pushkin Museum of Fine Arts (p62), with a month of performances by high-profile musicians and accompanying art exhibits.

🛏 Sleeping

Hotels have become more affordable for foreigners, due to the weak rouble, but Moscow is still not a cheap place to sleep. The city is flush with international luxury hotels. A slew of good hostels have opened, and more midrange accommodation is now also appearing, usually in the form of 'mini-hotels'. Prices include the 18% value-added tax (VAT), but not the 5% sales tax, which is charged mainly at luxury hotels.

The following prices refer to a double room with a private bathroom. Breakfast is not included unless otherwise indicated.

€ less than R3000
€€ R3000–R15,000
€€€ more than R15,000

🛏 Kremlin & Kitay Gorod

⭐**Hotel Metropol**   HISTORIC HOTEL **$$**
(Map p72; ☑499-501 7800; www.metropol-mos-cow.ru; Teatralny proezd 1/4; r from R10,000; 😊❄🛜💂; Ⓜ Teatralnaya) Nothing short of an art nouveau masterpiece, the 1907 Metropol brings an artistic, historic touch to every nook and cranny, from the spectacular exterior to the grand lobby and the individually decorated (but small) rooms. The breakfast buffet (R2250) is quite an affair, with an extravagant feast served under the restaurant's gorgeous stained-glass ceiling.

Kitay-Gorod Hotel   HOTEL **$$**
(Отель Китай-Город; Map p78; ☑495-991 9971; www.otel-kg.ru; Lubyansky proezd 25; s R2900-6500, d R3700-8000; ❄🛜💂; Ⓜ Kitay-Gorod) A rare chance for budget-conscious travellers to stay this close to Red Square, with easy access to the metro and many nearby restaurants. Forty-six small but comfortable rooms are situated on two floors of this residential building. The location can be noisy: it's worth requesting air-con as you'll want to keep your windows closed. Prices are lower on weekends.

Four Seasons Moscow   HISTORIC HOTEL **$$$**
(Map p72; ☑499-277 7100; www.fourseasons.com; Okhotny ryad 2; r from R27,000; ❄🛜💂; Ⓜ Okhotny Ryad) Long a fixture on the Moscow skyline, the infamous Hotel Moskva was demolished in 2003, but Four Seasons reconstructed the old exterior, complete with architectural quirks. The updated interior, of course, is contemporary and classy, with over 200 luxurious rooms and suites, as well as a fancy spa and a glass-roofed swimming pool.

🛏 Tverskoy & Novoslobodsky

Bolshoi Hostel   HOSTEL **$**
(Map p78; ☑8-926-135 4687; www.hostelbolshoi.ru; ul Petrovskiye Linii 1; dm from R700; Ⓜ Trubnaya) It might be just a hostel – bunk beds, shared showers and all that – but the location is indeed five-star, amid boutiques, fancy restaurants and luxury hotels in the city's ritziest district. This new establishment, with circa 50 beds and a large kitchen area, occupies a former communal flat in a stately 19th-century residential building.

Godzillas Hostel   HOSTEL **$**
(Map p78; ☑495-699 4223; www.godzillashostel.com; Bolshoy Karetny per 6; dm R700-950, s/d R2200/2800; ❄@🛜; Ⓜ Tsvetnoy Bulvar) Tried and true, Godzillas is Moscow's best-known hostel, with dozens of beds spread out over four floors. The rooms come in various sizes, but they are all spacious and light-filled and painted in different colours. To cater to the many guests, there are bathroom facilities on each floor, three kitchens and a big living room with satellite TV.

Chocolate Hostel   HOSTEL **$**
(Map p78; ☑8-910-446 1778; www.chocohostel.com; Degtyarny per 15, apt 4; dm R600-700, tw/tr R2600/3300; @🛜; Ⓜ Pushkinskaya) Chocolate lovers rejoice – this charming hostel will soothe your craving. Bring your favourite brand from home for their collection. In return you'll get simple, friendly accommodation – colourfully painted rooms with metal furniture and old-style parquet floors. Bonus: bikes available for rent!

Golden Apple   BOUTIQUE HOTEL **$$**
(Map p78; ☑495-980 7000; www.goldenapple.ru; ul Malaya Dmitrovka 11; d from R5100; 😊❄🛜; Ⓜ Pushkinskaya) A classical edifice fronts the street, but the interior is sleek and sophisticated. The rooms are decorated in a minimalist, modern style – subdued whites and greys punctuated by contrasting coloured drapes and funky light fixtures. Comfort is paramount, with no skimping on luxuries such as heated bathroom floors and down-filled duvets.

Guest House Amelie   GUESTHOUSE **$$**
(Map p78; ☑495-650 1789; www.hotel-amelie.ru; Strastnoy bul 4, str 3, apt 17; r from R5000; 🛜; Ⓜ Chekhovskaya) Amelie benefits from its superb location right by Pushkinskaya ploshchad – it's unlikely you will find a room much cheaper than this in the vicinity, and it's a very nicely furnished room, too! On the downside, the hotel is a converted apartment, which means shared bathrooms and an unmarked entrance located on Kozitsky per.

Pushkin Hotel   HOTEL **$$**
(Отель Пушкин; Map p78; ☑495-201 0222; http://otel-pushkin.ru; Nastasyinsky per 5 1; r from R4500; ❄🛜; Ⓜ Pushkinskaya) Just off the eponymous square, this hotel strives to fuse 19th-century style with the modern perception of comfort. We'd call it plush, if not for the tiny, B&B-style reception area. There is a restaurant on the premises, but no need to use it since the area is packed with great places to eat and drink.

Hotel Savoy BOUTIQUE HOTEL $$$
(Отель Савой; Map p78; ☑ 495-620 8500; www.
savoy.ru; ul Rozhdestvenka 3; r from R13,000;
⊜❄ 🛜🛋; Ⓜ Lubyanka) Built in 1912, the Sa-
voy maintains an atmosphere of tsarist-era
privilege for its guests, and is more intimate
and affordable than other luxury hotels. All
rooms are equipped with marble bathrooms
and Italian fittings and furnishings. The
state-of-the-art health club includes a glass-
domed 20m swimming pool, complete with
geysers and cascades to refresh tired bodies.

🛏 Meshchansky & Basmanny

Fasol Hostel HOSTEL $
(Map p78; ☑ 495-240 9409; http://fasol.co;
Arkhangelsky per 11/16 str 3; dm from R900, d
with shared bathroom R3100; Ⓜ Chistye Prudy)
The entrance to this hostel, hidden in the
courtyards amid 19th-century apartment
blocks, looks unassuming. However, with
over 80 beds this popular and professionally
run place is a major league player. Dorms,
sleeping six to eight, are decorated with
psychedelic wall paintings; bunk beds come
with body-friendly mattresses, curtains and
individual lights, allowing guests to enjoy
full autonomy.

Comrade Hostel HOSTEL $
(Map p78; ☑ 499-709 8760; www.comradehostel.
com; ul Maroseyka 11; dm/s/d R750/2400/2900;
⊜ @🛜; Ⓜ Kitay-Gorod) It's hard to find this
tiny place – go into the courtyard and look
for entrance No 3, where you might spot
a computer-printed sign in the 3rd-floor
window. Inside is a great welcoming atmos-
phere, although the place is usually packed.
Ten to 12 beds are squeezed into the dorm
rooms, plus there are mattresses on the floor
if need be.

★ Brick Design Hotel BOUTIQUE HOTEL $$
(Map p78; ☑ 499-110 2470; www.brickhotel.ru; My-
asnitskaya ul 24/7 str 3/4; s/d from R6200/7100;
❄🛜; Ⓜ Chistye Prudy) Not only is this boutique hotel cosy, thoughtfully designed and
very centrally located, it also doubles as an
art gallery, with original works by Russian
20th-century conceptualist artists adorning
the walls. That's in addition to a very tasteful
combination of modern and antique furniture. Visitors also rave about the breakfast,
which comes fresh from farms near Moscow.

Garden Embassy HOTEL $$
(Map p78; ☑ 495-124 4095; http://ge-hotel.com;
Botanichesky per 5; s/d from R6200/6700; ❄🛜;

Ⓜ Prospekt Mira) In a street lined with foreign
embassies, this apartment hotel is indeed
an embassy of style, with large and fully
equipped apartments facing beautiful Apt-
ekarsky Ogorod. A calming respite from the
city.

**Hilton Moscow
Leningradskaya** HISTORIC HOTEL $$
(Map p78; ☑ 495-627 5550; www.hilton.ru/hotels/
hilton-moscow-leningradskaya; Kalanchevskaya
ul 21/40; d from R6500; ⊜❄🛜; Ⓜ Komsomolskaya) Occupying one of the iconic Stalinist
skyscrapers, the old Leningradskaya Hotel is
now part of the Hilton empire. The American chain has maintained the Soviet gran-
diosity in the lobby, but has updated the
rooms with contemporary design and state-
of-the-art amenities.

Sretenskaya Hotel HOTEL $$
(Сретенская гостиница; Map p78; ☑ 495-933
5544; www.hotel-sretenskaya.ru; ul Sretenka 15; s/d
from R4200/5200; ⊜❄@🛜; Ⓜ Sukharevskaya)
Special for its small size and friendly staff,
the Sretenskaya boasts a romantic Russian
atmosphere. Rooms have high ceilings and
tasteful, traditional decor. This place is par-
ticularly welcoming in winter, when you can
warm your bones in the sauna, or soak up
some sun in the tropical 'winter garden'.

Hotel Sverchkov 8 HOTEL $$
(Сверчков 8; Map p78; ☑ 495-625 4978;
www.sverchkov-8.ru; Sverchkov per 8; s/d from
R4200/4800; ⊜❄🛜; Ⓜ Chistye Prudy) This
tiny 11-room hotel in a graceful 19th-centu-
ry building is situated on a quiet residential
lane. The hallways are lined with plants, and
paintings by local artists adorn the walls.
Though rooms have old-style bathrooms
and faded furniture, this place is a rarity for
its intimacy and homely feel.

Elokhovsky Hotel HOTEL $$
(Отель Елоховский; Map p66; ☑ 495-632
2300; www.elohotel.ru; ul Spartakovskaya 24; s/d
R4500/5300; ❄🛜; Ⓜ Baumanskaya) Admit-
tedly not very central and occupying the
top floor of a shopping arcade, this hotel is
nevertheless about the best value for money
in Moscow. Rooms are painted in soothing
colours, complemented by cityscapes of the
world's major cities. The coffee machine in
the lobby is available 24 hours. Bauman-
skaya metro and Yelokhovsky Cathedral are
a stone's throw away.

SERVICED APARTMENTS

Some entrepreneurial Muscovites rent out apartments on a short-term basis. Flats are equipped with kitchens and laundry facilities and they almost always offer wi-fi access. The rental agency usually makes arrangements for the flat to be cleaned every day or every few days. Often, a good-sized flat is available for the price of a hotel room, or less. It is an ideal solution for families or travellers in a small group.

Prices for apartments start at around R5000 per night. Expect to pay more for fully renovated, Western-style apartments. Although there are usually discounts for longer stays, they are not significant, so these services are not ideal for long-term renters.

Moscow Suites (⌨ 495-233 6429; www.moscowsuites.ru; studios from US$100; ☎) Slick apartments in central locations on Tverskaya or Novy Arbat. Airport pick-up and visa support are included in the price.

Intermark Hospitality (⌨ 495-221 8922; www.intermarksa.ru; 1-/2-room apt from R5800/6800; ☎) Catering mostly to business travellers, Intermark offers four-star accommodation in the city centre.

Enjoy Moscow (⌨ 8-916-976 4807; www.enjoymoscow.com; apt from US$120; ☎) Has a range of apartments in the Tverskoy district. Apartments vary in size and decor, but the company provides responsive, reliable service.

HOFA (⌨ 8-911-766 5464; www.hofa.ru; s/d from €33/52, apt €44-67; ☎) Authentic (and affordable) stays in a Russian family's apartment (with or without the family).

Moscow4rent.com (⌨ 495-225 5405; www.moscow4rent.com; studios from US$83) Centrally located flats, with internet, satellite TV and unlimited international phone calls.

⌂ Presnya

★ Loft Hostel 77 HOSTEL $
(Map p86; ⌨ 499-110 4228; www.hostel-77.com; Bldg 3a, Maly Gnezdnikovsky per 9; dm R1000-1400; ☎; Ⓜ Pushkinskaya) This sweet spot offers stylish dorm rooms (if that's not an oxymoron), fully equipped with lockers, individual lights, orthopaedic mattresses and privacy curtains. Exposed brick walls and leather furniture create an attractive shabby-chic atmosphere. Multilingual staff and a super-central locale are added pluses. The only drawback is the lack of a kitchen, but the surrounding streets are packed with eateries.

High Level Hostel HOSTEL $
(Map p66; ⌨ +87-963-757 9533; www.hostelhl.ru; 43rd fl, bldg 2, Presnenskaya nab 6, Imperia Tower; dm R1500-1700; d R3800; ✳ ☎; Ⓜ Delovoy Tsentr) Located at 170m above the city, this place claims to be the world's first and only skyscraper hostel. This means incredible panoramic city view from the common area. Rooms are furnished with sturdy wooden bunks, desks and lockers. Service is excellent, with breakfast and laundry included in the price.

★ Hotel de Paris BOUTIQUE HOTEL $$
(Map p86; ⌨ 495-777 0052; www.cityhotelgroup.ru; Bldg 3, Bolshaya Bronnaya ul 23; d from R6800; Ⓟ ✳ ☎; Ⓜ Pushkinskaya) Steps from the hustle and bustle of Tverskaya, this is a delightfully stylish hotel tucked into a quiet courtyard off the Boulevard Ring. Situated on the lower floors, the rooms do not get much natural light, but they feature king-sized beds, whirlpool tubs and elegant design. Service is consistently friendly. Prices drop on weekends, offering terrific value.

Key Element Hotel HOTEL $$
(Отель Элемент; Map p86; ⌨ 495-988 0064; www.key-element.ru; Bldg 5, Bolshaya Nikitskaya ul 24/1; d R3800-4500; ✳ ☎; Ⓜ Arbatskaya) The location on trendy Bolshaya Nikitskaya is prime, and prices are unbeatable, so you'll forgive the side-street entrance and the fact that rooms can be rented by the hour. It's actually a perfectly respectable place, with spotless rooms, pleasant decor and helpful staff. The cheapest rooms are tiny, so unless you're travelling solo, you'll probably want to upgrade.

★ Hotel National HISTORIC HOTEL $$$
(Map p78; ⌨ 495-258 7000; www.national.ru; Mokhovaya ul 15/1; d with/without Kremlin views from R14,600/9700; ✳ ☎; Ⓜ Okhotny Ryad) Now operated by Starwood Resorts, this 1903 beauty occupies a prime location at the base of Tverskaya ul, just across from Alexander Garden. As such, some rooms have magnificent views

of the Kremlin (worth the extra roubles). Original artwork lines the walls and antique-style furnishings grace the premises. The rooms themselves are classically luxurious.

Arbat & Khamovniki

Jedi Hostel HOSTEL $
(Map p90; ☑ 929-681 0041; http://jedihostel.com; 4th fl, 2-y Smolensky per 1/4; dm/d from US$11/40; ✳ @ 🛜; Ⓜ Smolenskaya) This place exudes (and requires) good vibes, with its wacky and wonderful mural-painted walls and pillow-strewn 'lounge zone'. Dorm beds are actually little 'pods' with shades that ensure complete privacy. Lockers, kitchen and laundry facilities are available. Get the door code before you show up.

★ Bulgakov Mini-Hotel HOTEL $$
(Map p90; ☑ 495-229 8018; www.bulgakovhotel.com; ul Arbat 49; s/d from R3600/4000; ⊖ @ 🛜; Ⓜ Smolenskaya) The classy rooms, graced with high ceilings and *Master and Margarita*-inspired art, are as good as it gets in Moscow for this price, especially considering the primo location. The bathrooms are tiny but they are private. Enter the courtyard from Plotnikov per and use entrance No 2.

★ Hotel Grafskiy BOUTIQUE HOTEL $$
(Отель Графский; Map p66; ☑ 499-677 5727; www.grafskiyhotel.ru; Bldg 5, ul Lva Tolstogo 23; s R6000-8000, d R7700-9000; P ✳ 🛜; Ⓜ Park Kultury) Live next door to Leo Tolstoy (p89) at this new boutique hotel, in a building dating from 1866. Both service and style are simple

AIRPORT ACCOMMODATION

Recommended for transit travellers who need to crash between flights, both these hotels operate free shuttlebuses from their respective airports.

Aerotel Domodedovo (Аэротель Домодедово; ☑ 495-795 3868; www.airhotel.ru; Domodedovo airport; r R5200; P ✳ @ 🛜) Small but satisfactory rooms, plus a fitness centre and billiards room.

Atlanta Sheremetyevo Hotel (☑ 499-647 5947; www.atlanta-hotel.ru; 7 Severnaya ul, Sheremetyevsky; s/d R2500/3700; ⊖ ✳ 🛜) Friendly, small and convenient, the Atlanta is an anomaly in the airport world. Reduced rates are available for six- and 12-hour layovers.

but quite delightful. Some of the 38 rooms have exposed brick walls or loft-style ceilings. Outside the Garden Ring, this neighbourhood is still pretty lively, with a number of restaurants and bars in the immediate vicinity.

Mercure Arbat Hotel BOUTIQUE HOTEL $$
(Гостиница Меркурий Арбат; Map p90; ☑ 495-225 0025; www.mercure.com; Smolenskaya pl 6; r from R6200; ⊖ ✳ 🛜; Ⓜ Smolenskaya) We're charmed by this sweet and stylish hotel. Rooms are attractive and rather plush to boot. The most affordable ones have two twins or one queen-size bed, plus work space, flat-screen TVs and chic bathrooms with basin sinks. It's surprisingly quiet for its location right on the Garden Ring. Excellent value, especially on weekends.

★ Russo Balt Hotel BOUTIQUE HOTEL $$$
(Map p90; ☑ 495-645 3873; www.russo-balthotel.com; Gogolevsky bul 31; s R13,500-15,000, d R15,400-16,900; ✳ @ 🛜; Ⓜ Arbatskaya) With 15 rooms in an exquisite art deco building, the Russo Balt is as intimate and elegant as it gets in Moscow. Standard rooms are on the small side, but the whole place is beautifully decorated with period furnishings and original artwork, with the utmost attention to detail. Highly recommended.

Radisson Royal Hotel Ukraina HISTORIC HOTEL $$$
(Гостиница Украина; Map p66; ☑ 495-221 5555; www.radissonblu.com; Kutuzovsky pr 2/1; r from R11,700; ⊖ ✳ 🛜 🖾; Ⓜ Kievskaya) Housed in one of Stalin's 'Seven Sisters', this bombastic beauty sits majestically on the banks of the Moscow River facing the White House. It has retained its old-fashioned ostentation, with crystal chandeliers, polished marble and a ceiling fresco in the lobby. Heavy drapes, textured wallpaper and reproduction antiques give the guest rooms a similar atmosphere – with all the modern amenities.

Zamoskvorechie

Three Penguins HOSTEL $
(Три Пингвина; Map p94; ☑ 8-910-446 1778; www.3penguins.ru; Pyatnitskaya ul 20, str 2; dm/d R750/R2600; 🛜; Ⓜ Novokuznetskaya) This very small hostel is located in a converted flat with a comfy (we'd even say intimate) common area in the building best identified by Illarion cafe, just off Pyatnitskaya ul. Apart from the dorms, it features four doubles – two regular and two with bunk beds.

Troika

HOTEL **$$**

(Map p94; ☑ 495-204 2226; www.hoteltroyka. ru; Sadovnicheskaya ul 5; r from R4000; ☒; M Novokuznetskaya) This tourist hotel has a top-notch location across the bridge from Red Square, which makes it great value for money. All rooms are on the 1st floor of an 18th-century building with bare-brick walls and vaulted ceilings typical of that age.

Park Inn Sadu

HOTEL **$$**

(Map p94; ☑ 495-644 4844; www.parkinn.ru; ul Bolshaya Polyanka 17; s/d incl breakfast from R6500/7500; ☒☎; M Polyanka) This very regular branch of the Park Inn chain – think slightly impersonal, predictable comforts – boasts a prime location within walking distance of the Kremlin and the Red October cluster of bars and galleries. Prices fall to a jaw-dropping low in the middle of summer.

Na Kazachyem

HOTEL **$$**

(На Казачьем; Map p94; ☑ 495-745 2190; 1-y Kazachy per 4; s/d from R7600/8600; ☒☎☒; M Polyanka) Set in the historic heart of Zamoskvorechie, Na Kazachyem re-creates the atmosphere of an 18th-century estate. The light-filled atrium, bedecked with a crystal chandelier, and 15 classically decorated rooms provide a perfect setting for old-fashioned Russian hospitality. Reduced rates on weekends.

Ozerkovskaya Hotel

BOUTIQUE HOTEL **$$**

(Озерковская гостиница; Map p94; ☑ 495-783 5553; www.ozerkhotel.ru; Ozerkovskaya nab 50; s/d incl breakfast from R2900/3500; ☒☎; M Paveletskaya) This comfy, cosy hotel has only 27 rooms, including three that are tucked up under the mansard roof. The rooms are simply decorated, but parquet floors and comfortable queen-sized beds rank it above the standard post-Soviet fare. Add in attentive service and a central location (convenient for the express train to Domodedovo airport), and you've got an excellent-value accommodation option.

★Hotel Baltschug Kempinski

HISTORIC HOTEL **$$$**

(Балчуг Кемпински; Map p94; ☑ 495-287 2000; www.kempinski-moscow.com; ul Balchug 1; r with/ without view from R13,600/12,000; ☒☎☒; M Kitay-Gorod, Ploshchad Revolyutsii) If you want to wake up to views of the sun glinting off the Kremlin's golden domes, this luxurious property on the Moscow River is the place for you. It is a historic hotel, built in 1898, with 230 high-ceilinged rooms that are sophisticated and sumptuous in design.

Eating

In recent years Moscow has blossomed into a culinary capital. Foodies will be thrilled by the dining options, from old-fashioned *haute-russe* to contemporary 'author cuisine'. The ban on imported foodstuffs means that chefs are finding innovative ways to utilise local ingredients, rediscovering ancient cooking techniques and inventing new ones in the process. And Moscow diners are eating it up. Literally.

✗ Kremlin & Kitay Gorod

Stolovaya No 57

CAFETERIA **$**

(Столовая 57; Map p72; ☑ 495-620 3129; https:// gumrussia.com/shops/stolovaya-57; 3rd fl, GUM, Krasnaya pl 3; mains R200-300; ⊘10am-10pm; M Okhotny Ryad) Newly minted, this old-style cafeteria offers a nostalgic re-creation of dining in post-Stalinist Russia. The food is good – and cheap for such a fancy store. Meat cutlets and cold salads come highly recommended. This is a great place to try 'herring in a fur coat' (herring, beetroots, carrots and potatoes).

Grand Coffee Mania

CAFE **$$**

(Кофе мания; Map p72; ☑ 495-960 2295; www. coffeemania.ru; Mal Cherkassky per 2; breakfast R300-500, mains R500-1200; ⊘8am-midnight Mon-Thu, to 2am Fri, 10am-2am Sat, 10am-midnight Sun; ☒☎☒; M Lubyanka) This place has the same overpriced but appetising fare as other outlets of the ubiquitous chain, but the fabulous 'grand cafe' interior makes this one a special experience. Marble floors, art deco chandeliers and elaborate latticework evoke another era. Efficient service and excellent atmosphere.

Bosco Cafe

ITALIAN **$$$**

(Map p72; ☑ 495-620 3182; https://gumrussia.com/ cafe/bosco-cafe; GUM, Krasnaya pl 3; pasta R500-1000, mains R1200-2000; ⊘10am-10pm; M Ploshchad Revolyutsii) Sip a cappuccino in view of the Kremlin. Munch on lunch while the crowds line up at Lenin's Mausoleum. Enjoy an afternoon aperitif while admiring St Basil's domes. Service is lacking and the menu is overpriced, but this cafe on the 1st floor of the GUM mall is the only place to sit right on Red Square and marvel at its magnificence.

The menu is wide-ranging, so you don't have to spend a fortune. Reservations recommended for dinner.

Tverskoy & Novoslobodsky

Batoni
GEORGIAN **$**

(Map p66; ☑ 499-653 6530; www.batoni-kafe.ru; Novoslobodskaya ul 18; mains R300-600; ⊙11.30am-midnight; Ⓜ Mendeleyevskaya) Among myriad Georgian places in Moscow, Batoni is about the loveliest and the most scrupulous at sourcing all the right ingredients for century-old recipes. *Pkhali* (walnut paste) snacks, *khachapuri* (cheese bread) and lamb shashlyk kebabs are all up to Mt Kazbek-high standards. For a proper taste of Georgia, order a bottle Mukuzani or Kindzmarauli – the country's best reds.

Zupperia
INTERNATIONAL **$**

(Map p78; ☑ 915-391 8309; www.facebook.com/Zupperia; Sadovaya-Samotechnaya ul 20; soups & salads R300-400; ⊙8am-11pm; ☎; Ⓜ Tsvetnoy Bulvar) Designed to look like a transplant from some old-worldish European city, this unpretentious eatery is run by local celebrity chef Uilliam Lamberti. The minimalist menu includes soups, bruschettas and salads. At first glance, the place seems to consist of one long table, but there is more seating downstairs. Takeaway is available.

Lepim i Varim
RUSSIAN **$**

(Лепим и варим; Map p78; ☑ 8-985-688 9606; www.lepimivarim.ru; Stoleshnikov per 9, str 1; mains R220-350; ⊙10am-11pm) This cosy place touts itself as 'the most visited boutique' in the flashy Stoleshnikov per, but instead of Armani clothes it celebrates arguably the most vital item on any Russian menu – *pelmeni* (dumplings), as well as their relatives from all around the world. Perfectly shaped, the dumplings seem fit for a catwalk display in Milan and taste even better.

Rynok & Obshchepit Shouk
ISRAELI **$**

(Рынок и Общепит Шук; Map p66; ☑ 495-966 2501; www.facebook.com/rynokshuk; Veskovsky per 7; sandwiches R250-320; ⊙8am-11pm; Ⓜ Novoslobodskaya) This quirky place, a cross between a corner shop and a hip falafel joint, also makes top-quality *shawarma* (grilled meat and salad wrapped in flat bread) in the fashionably open kitchen. The shop section has a good selection of Israeli vegetable preserves, fruit and wine.

Tsvetnoy Food Court
INTERNATIONAL **$**

(Map p78; ☑ 495-737 7773; www.tsvetnoy.com; Tsvetnoy bul 15, str 1; tapas R100-400; ⊙noon-10pm; Ⓜ Tsvetnoy Bulvar) The two upper floors of Tsvetnoy Central Market shopping mall are filled with refined delis and cafes, some

---

WORTH A TRIP

KOLOMENSKOE MUSEUM-RESERVE

Set amid 4 sq km of picturesque parkland, on a bluff above a bend in the Moscow River, **Kolomenskoe** (Музей-заповедник "Коломенское"; Map p66; www.mgomz.com; ⊙grounds 8am-9pm; Ⓜ Kolomenskaya, Kashirskaya) **FREE** is an ancient royal country seat and a Unesco World Heritage Site. Shortly after its founding in the 14th century, the village became a favourite destination for the princes of Moscow. The royal estate is now an eclectic mix of churches and gates, as well as other buildings that were added to the complex over the years.

Outside the front gate, overlooking the river, rises Kolomenskoe's loveliest structure, the quintessentially Russian **Ascension Church** (Map p66; pr Andropova 39; ⊙10am-6pm Tue-Sun; Ⓜ Kolomenskaya). Built between 1530 and 1532 for Grand Prince Vasily III, it probably celebrated the birth of his heir, Ivan the Terrible. An important development in Russian architecture, it reproduced the shapes of wooden churches in brick for the first time.

In the mid-17th century, Tsar Alexey built a palace so fabulous it was dubbed 'the eighth wonder of the world'. This whimsical building was famous for its mishmash of tent-roofed towers and onion-shaped eaves, all crafted from wood and structured without a single nail. Unfortunately, this legendary building was demolished in 1768 by Catherine the Great. Some 230 years later, a kitschy gingerbread **replica** (Дворец царя Алексея Михайловича; pr Andropova 39; R400; ⊙10am-6pm Tue-Sun; Ⓜ Kashirskaya) was built on Kholomenskoes grounds.

Among the old wooden buildings on the grounds is **Peter the Great's cabin**, where he lived while supervising ship- and fort-building at Arkhangelsk. The cabin is surrounded by a re-creation of the tsar's orchards and gardens.

of them outstandingly good. Little snacks hailing from Basque Country in Spain have generated a bit of a cult following for Tapas & Pintxos, on the 5th floor. The Dagestani dumpling shop on the 6th floor makes for equally exciting culinary travel.

★**Delicatessen** INTERNATIONAL **$$**
(Деликатесы; Map p78; www.newdeli.ru; Sadovaya-Karetnaya ul 20; mains R500-800; ⊗ noon-midnight Tue-Sun; 🛜; M Tsvetnoy Bulvar) The affable and chatty owners of this place travel the world and experiment with the menu a lot, turning burgers, pizzas and pasta into artfully constructed objects of modern culinary art. The other source of joy is a cabinet filled with bottles of ripening fruity liquors, which may destroy your budget if consumed uncontrollably (a pointless warning, we know).

★**Lavka-Lavka** INTERNATIONAL **$$**
(Лавка-Лавка; Map p78; ☑ 8-903-115 5033; www.restoran.lavkalavka.com; ul Petrovka 21, str 2; mains R500-950; ⊗ noon-midnight Tue-Thu & Sun, to 1am Fri & Sat; 🛜 🖶; M Teatralnaya) 🍴 Welcome to the Russian Portlandia – all the food here is organic and hails from little farms where you may rest assured all the lambs and chickens lived a very happy life before being served to you on a plate. Irony aside, this is a great place to sample local food cooked in a funky improvisational style.

Fresh VEGETARIAN **$$**
(Свежий; Map p78; ☑ 8-965-278 9089; www.freshrestaurant.ru; ul Bolshaya Dmitrovka 11; mains R500-650; ⊗ 11am-11pm; 🛜 🖋; M Teatralnaya) Fresh out of Canada, this is the kind of vegetarian restaurant that people pour into not for lifestyle reasons, but because the modern, post-ethnic food and the escapist ambience are great. Definitely go for the smoothies. Vegans and rawists will not feel neglected.

Voronezh INTERNATIONAL **$$**
(Воронеж; Map p78; www.voronej.com; ul Bolshaya Dmitrovka 12/1, str 1; mains R300-720; ⊗ 9am-9pm; M Teatralnaya) Its darkened, scarlet-coloured interior makes this bistro look a bit like an oriental opium den, but it is in fact a carnivore temple, where patrons seem to fall into a deeply meditative state while munching on their burgers and excellent pastrami sandwiches. One of the best places for lunch in the city centre.

Golodny-Zloy FUSION **$$**
(Hangry; Map p78; ☑ 495-792 7105; http://perelmanpeople.com/restoran/golodnyy-zloy; Tsvetnoy

bul 2; mains R500-700; ⊗ noon-midnight Sun-Thu, to 2am Fri & Sat; 🛜; M Trubnaya) Filling up with white collars from the business centre above it, this trendsetting establishment combines unlikely ingredients and cooking methods with unfailingly excellent results – just try their smoked-mussel soup or dorado cooked with sorrel. Visual art is also involved, with each dish designed to entertain the eye as much as to please the stomach.

Seven EUROPEAN **$$**
(Map p78; ☑ 495-205 0277; Dmitrovsky per 7; mains R500-900; ⊗ 8am-11pm; M Teatralnaya) You'll find a pleasant mix of post-industrial and theatrical in this dimly lit space, where low-hanging chandeliers and comfortable chairs make for a long and enjoyable evening. The menu mirrors the city outside – inventively cosmopolitan with a sprinkle of Soviet nostalgia and a strong bias towards domestic meat and vegetable producers.

Technicum EUROPEAN **$$**
(Map p78; ☑ 495-230 0605; www.tehnikumbistro.ru; ul Bolshaya Dmitrovka 7/5, str 2; mains R480-650; ⊗ 9am-midnight; M Teatralnaya) Casual, friendly and focused on taste, rather than trying to impress with shocking exoticism, Technicum is one of the places that shape the modern outlook of Moscow's culinary scene. The laconic menu contains a short list of fish and meat dishes (note the outstanding mutton with aubergine) as well as soups, including an exemplary borsch served with Borodinsky rye bread.

★**Brasserie Most** FRENCH **$$$**
(Map p78; ☑ 495-660 0706; www.brasseriemost.ru; ul Kuznetsky most 6/3; mains R1000-3000; ⊗ 8am-midnight Mon-Fri, from 9am Sat & Sun; M Teatralnaya) Moscow's most venerated and erudite restaurateur Aleksander Rappoport shares his love for regional French cuisine in this classy and expensive place on Kuznetsky most. The menu is a grand gastrotour taking in seemingly every major area of France from Brittany to Alsace. Authenticity is religion here. If they say bouillabaisse, you can be sure it will taste exactly like Marseille's best.

Druzhba CHINESE **$$$**
(Дружба; Map p66; ☑ 499-973 1212; Novoslobodskaya ul 4; mains R700-1200; ⊗ 11am-11pm; 🖋; M Novoslobodskaya) Druzhba earns high marks for authenticity, and as far as Sichuan cuisine goes that means spicy. Chinese restaurants in Moscow are notorious for turning down their seasoning to appeal to Russian taste buds,

MOSCOW FOR CHILDREN

The Russian capital might not seem like an appealing destination for kids, but you'd be surprised. In Moscow, little people will find museums, parks, theatres and even restaurants that cater especially to them.

Sights & Activities

With over 100 parks and gardens, Moscow has plenty of space for children to let off steam. Many have playgrounds, while larger spaces such as Gorky Park (p64) and Vorobyovy Gory Nature Preserve (p92) rent bicycles, paddle boats and such. There are also plenty of kid-friendly museums, including places such as the **Experimentanium** (Экспериментаниум; Map p66; ☑ 495-789 3658; www.experimentanium.ru; ul Butyrskaya 46/2; adult/child R650/550; ☺ 9.30am-7pm Mon-Fri, 10am-8pm Sat & Sun; ⊕; Ⓜ Savyolovskaya) and Museum of Soviet Arcade Machines (p77).

Most sights and museums offer reduced-rate tickets for children up to 12 or 18 years of age. Kids younger than five are often free of charge. Look out for family tickets.

Eating

Many restaurants host 'children's parties' on Saturday and Sunday afternoons, offering toys, games, entertainment and supervision for kids while their parents eat.

Restaurants such as **Anderson for Pop** (Андерсон для Пап; Map p86; ☑ 499-753 1601; www.cafe-anderson.ru; Malaya Gruzinskaya ul 15/1; mains R390-620; ☺ 9am-11pm Mon-Fri, 10am-11pm Sat & Sun; ⊕; Ⓜ Barrikadnaya) and Professor Puf (p108) have dedicated play areas for children. At Elardzhi (p108), kids frolic in the courtyard with playground and petting zoo.

Entertainment

Children will see hundreds of puppets at the **Obraztsov Puppet Museum** (Театр и музей кукол Образцова; Map p78; ☑ 495-699 5373; www.puppet.ru; Sadovaya-Samotechnaya ul 3; ☺ box office 11am-2.30pm & 3.30-7pm; Ⓜ Tsvetnoy Bulvar), then see them come to life at the attached theatre.

Choose between two acclaimed circuses: **Bolshoi Circus on Vernadskogo** (Map p66; ☑ 495-930 0300; www.greatcircus.ru; pr Vernadskogo 7; tickets R600-3000; ☺ shows 7pm Wed, 1pm & 5pm Sat, 3pm Sun; ⊕; Ⓜ Universitet) and **Nikulin Circus on Tsvetnoy Bulvar** (Цирк Никулина на Цветном бульваре; Map p78; ☑ 495-625 8970; www.circusnikulin.ru; Tsvetnoy bul 13; tickets R400-2500; ☺ box office 11am-2pm & 3-7pm; Ⓜ Tsvetnoy Bulvar). The acrobatics will astound and amaze, while clowns and animal tricks will leave them laughing.

Local legend Natalya Sats founded the **Moscow Children's Musical Theatre** (Детский Музыкальный театр им. Н.И.Сац; Map p66; ☑ 495-120 2515; www.teatr-sats.ru; pr Vernadskogo 5; tickets R500-1500; ☺ box office noon-7pm; ⊕; Ⓜ Universitet) to entertain and educate children with song and dance.

Transport

The metro might be fun for young ones, but be careful during rush hour, when trains and platforms are packed. Both Lingo Taxi (p121) and Detskoe Taxi (p121) will look out for your children, offering smoke-free cars and child seats upon request.

---

but Druzhba is the exception, which explains why this place is often packed with Chinese patrons. The chicken with peppers gets red-hot reviews.

🍴 Meshchansky & Basmanny

★ **Dukhan Chito-Ra**   GEORGIAN **$**
(Map p78; ☑ 8-916-393 0030; www.chito-ra.ru; ul Kazakhova 10 str 2; mains R300-500; ☺ noon-11pm; Ⓜ Kurskaya) It's a blessing when one of the most revered Georgian eateries in town is also one of the cheapest. The object of worship here is *khinkali* – large, meat-filled dumplings – but the traditional veggie starters are also great. The rather inevitable downside is that the place is constantly busy and there is often a queue to get in.

★ Darbazi
GEORGIAN $$

(Map p94; ☑ 495-915 3632; www.darbazirest.ru; ul Nikoloyamskaya 16; mains R590-1500; ⊙ noon-midnight; ☜; Ⓜ Taganskaya) The vast majority of Georgian restaurants focus on the most popular, tried-and-true fare, such as shashlyk (meat kebabs) and *khinkali* (dumplings). This classy place goes far beyond these, listing less well-known delicacies with almost encyclopedic meticulousness. Our favourite is *chakapuli* (lamb cooked in white wine with tarragon) and *Megreli kharcho* (duck in walnut sauce).

★ Kitayskaya Gramota
CHINESE $$

(Китайская грамота; Map p78; ☑ 495-625 4757; http://chinagramota.ru/; ul Sretenka 1; mains R400-1200; ⊙ noon-midnight; Ⓜ Sretenskaya) Ignore the fact that the waiting staff are dressed as Mao's soldiers; this is the place to try outstanding Cantonese fare in an atmosphere echoing that of the opium war's decadence. A true culinary magician, the Chinese chef turns any ingredient – from hog paw to octopus to simple milk – into a mouth-watering delicacy.

Odessa-Mama
UKRAINIAN $$

(Map p78; ☑ 8-964-647 1110; www.cafeodessa.ru; per Krivokolenny 10 str 5; R400-800; ⊙ 10am-11pm Sun-Thu, to 2am Fri & Sat; Ⓜ Chistye Prudy) Come have to celebrate Odessa, affectionately called 'mama' by the residents of this port city. What mama cooks is a wild fusion of Jewish, Ukrainian and Balkan foods, with a strong emphasis on Black Sea fish. It's like island hopping – from *forshmak* (Jewish herring pate) to Ukrainian borsch and eventually to fried Odessa gobies.

Yuzhane
MODERN EUROPEAN $$

(Map p78; ☑ 495-926 1640; www.facebook.com/yuzhanemsk/; pr Akademika Sakharova 10; mains R450-1300; ⊙ noon-midnight; Ⓜ Krasnye Vorota) A carnivore stronghold, Yuzhane (which means 'the Southerners') gets its meat from the Kuban area in southern Russia, hence the name. The chef's philosophy is to utilise every bit of an animal's body, so in addition to juicy steaks, the menu features all kinds of by-products. The southern theme is backed by seafood and a wealth of vegetables, including meaty tomatoes.

Madam Galife
GEORGIAN $$

(Map p78; ☑ 495-775 2601; www.madamgalife.ru; Prospect Mira 26/1; mains R430-850; ⊙ noon-5am; ☜; Ⓜ Prospekt Mira) A brainchild of famous Georgian film director Rezo Gabriadze, this is much more than just another Caucasian restaurant. It faces the charming Aptekarsky Ogorod gardens for starters, and the interior design – combining naive art with antiques brought from Georgia – is superb. Food is a mixture of Georgian and European. To avoid disappointment, stick to the former.

✕ Presnya

★ Stolle
CAFE $

(Штолле; Map p86; www.stolle.ru; Bldg 1, Bolshaya Sadovaya ul 3; mains R200-400; ⊙ 8am-11pm; ✳☜♨; Ⓜ Mayakovskaya) The entire menu at Stolle is excellent, but the *pirozhki* (savoury pies) are irresistible. A 'stolle' is a traditional Saxon Christmas cake: the selection of sweets and savouries sits on the counter, fresh from the oven. It may be difficult to decide (mushroom or meat, apricot or apple?), but you really can't go wrong.

Volkonsky
BAKERY $

(Волконский; Map p86; www.wolkonsky.com; Bolshaya Sadovaya ul 2/46; mains R250-400, sweets from R100; ⊙ bakery 8am-11pm, cafe 24hr; ☜♨; Ⓜ Mayakovskaya) The queue often runs out the door, as loyal patrons wait their turn for the city's best freshly baked breads, pastries and pies. It's worth the wait, especially if you decide on a fruit-filled croissant or to-die-for olive bread. Next door there are big wooden tables where you can get large bowls of coffee or tea.

★ Twins
RUSSIAN $$

(Map p86; ☑ 495-695 4510; www.twinsmoscow.ru; Malaya Bronnaya ul 13; mains R650-1750; ☜; Ⓜ Tverskaya) Swoon-worthy identical-twin chefs Sergei and Ivan Berezutskiy bring their contrasting tastes and creative talents to this delightful restaurant. The brothers take a thoroughly modern approach to Russian cooking, with ingredients procured from all corners of the country. Seating is on the pleasant terrace or in the classy, kitschy dining room.

★ Khachapuri
GEORGIAN $$

(Хачапури; Map p86; ☑ 8-985-764 3118; www.hacha.ru; Bolshoy Gnezdnikovsky per 10; khachapuri R220-420, mains R430-690; ✳☜; Ⓜ Pushkinskaya) Unassuming, affordable and appetising, this urban cafe exemplifies what people love about Georgian culture: the warm hospitality and the freshly baked *khachapuri* (cheese bread). Aside from eight types of delicious *khachapuri*, there's also an array of soups, shashlyk (kebabs), *khinkali* (dumplings) and other Georgian favourites.

Gran Cafe Dr Zhivago
RUSSIAN $$

(Гранд Кафе Dr Живаго; Map p78; ☑499-922 0100; www.drzhivago.ru; Mokhovaya ul 15/1; mains R540-1200; ☺24hr; Ⓜ Okhotny Ryad) An excellent breakfast choice before visiting the Kremlin, this round-the-clock place mixes Soviet nostalgia with a great deal of mischievous irony in both design and food. The chef has upgraded the menu of a standard pioneer camp's canteen to near-haute-cuisine level, with masterfully cooked porridge, pancakes, *vareniki* (boiled dumplings, like ravioli) and cottage-cheese pies.

★ Cafe Pushkin
RUSSIAN $$$

(Кафе Пушкинъ; Map p86; ☑495-739 0033; www.cafe-pushkin.ru; Tverskoy bul 26a; business lunch R620-930, mains R1000-2500; ☺24hr; ❄☎; Ⓜ Pushkinskaya) The tsarina of *haute-russe* dining, offering an exquisite blend of Russian and French cuisines. Service and food are done to perfection. The lovely 19th-century building has a different atmosphere on each floor, including a richly decorated library and a pleasant rooftop cafe.

✕ Arbat & Khamovniki

★ Varenichnaya No 1
RUSSIAN $

(Map p90; www.varenichnaya.ru; ul Arbat 29; business lunch R290-340, mains R220-490; ☺10am-midnight; ☑☷; Ⓜ Arbatskaya) Retro Soviet is all the rage in Moscow, and this old-style restaurant does it right, with books lining the walls, old movies on the B&W TV, and Cold War–era prices. The menu features tasty, filling *vareniki* and *pelmeni* (Russian-style dumplings stuffed with meats), with sweet and savoury fillings. Bonus: an excellent house-made pickled veggie plate to make you pucker.

Usachevsky Market
MARKET $

(Map p66; ☑8-999-003 0030; www.usachevsky.ru; ul Usachyova 26; mains R200-600; ☺9am-9pm; Ⓜ Sportivnaya) An old market has been taken over by hipster foodies, who instantly filled the premises with little eateries serving Georgian, Uzbek, Italian, Israeli and you-name-it cuisine, as well as shops representing small-scale Russian food producers, such as Kostroma Cheese. It's a great place for lunch and shopping, if you happen to be nearby.

Professor Puf
RUSSIAN $

(Map p90; www.professorpuf.ru; Bldg 1, ul Volkhonka 9; breakfast R150-200, lunch R350-500; ☺8am-10pm Mon-Fri, from 10am Sat & Sun; ☎☑☷; Ⓜ Kropotkinskaya) A select menu of Russian classics shows off fresh ingredients, old-fashioned cooking methods and contemporary flare. Pleasant, efficient service and a super-central location make this a great option before or after a morning at the museum. Unfortunately named, but otherwise delightful, especially the house-made bread and pastries.

★ Elardzhi
GEORGIAN $$

(Эларджи; Map p90; ☑495-627 7897; www.ginza.ru; Gagarinsky per 15a; mains R600-800; ☺noon-midnight; ☷; Ⓜ Kropotkinskaya) Moscow's Georgian restaurants are all very tasty, but this one is also tasteful. You'll be charmed from the moment you enter the courtyard, where live rabbits and lambs greet all comers. Sink into a sofa in the romantic dining room or on the light-filled porch; then feast on delicacies, such as the namesake dish, *elarji* (cornmeal with Sulguni cheese).

★ Chemodan
RUSSIAN $$$

(Чемодан; Map p90; ☑495-695 3819; www.chemodan-msk.ru; Gogolevsky bul 25; mains R900-1950; ❄☑; Ⓜ Kropotkinskaya) A unique opportunity to sample Siberian cuisine (rare, that is, for those of us who don't frequent Siberia). The menu highlights game meat, regional seafood and wild fruits and berries (and pine cones). The dining room is decorated with old photos and antiques, creating a romantic atmosphere that any adventurer would be happy to return home to. Highly recommended.

✕ Zamoskvorechie

Mitzva Bar
ISRAELI

(Map p94; ☑495-532 4224; www.facebook.com/mitzva.msk; Pyatnitskaya ul 3/4, str 1; ☺3pm-3am; Ⓜ Novokuznetskaya) A baby of the recent Israeli food craze, this restaurant-cum-bar hides in an atmospheric vaulted cellar decorated with Judaic and Masonic symbols. The talented chef's wild imagination turns Jewish standards, such as gefilte fish (stuffed carp), into art objects fit for the fusion cuisine of the future. There are great cocktails, too.

★ Mizandari
GEORGIAN $

(Map p90; ☑8-903-263 9990; www.mizandari.ru; Bolotnaya nab 5, str 1; mains R300-500; ☺11am-11pm Sun-Thu, to midnight Fri & Sat; Ⓜ Kropotkinskaya) Georgian restaurants in Moscow tend to be either expensive or tacky. This small family-run place is neither. Come with friends and order a selection of appetizers, such as *pkhali* and *lobio* (both made of walnut paste), *khachapuri* (cheese bread) and *kharcho* (spicy lamb soup). Bless you if you can still accommodate a main course after all that!

AC/DC in Tbilisi   GEORGIAN $

(Map p66; ☑8-909-955 4043; www.facebook. com/acdcintbilisi; Gorky Park; mains R250-350; ☺10am-10pm; Ⓜ Oktyabrskaya) Burgers and Georgia (the one in the Caucasus) seem to inhabit parallel universes, but they get together in this summer-only Gorky Park kiosk. An otherwise very ordinary burger turns Georgian with the help of hot *adjika* sauce and *suluguni* cheese. The meatballs in *satsivi* (walnut, garlic and pomegranate paste) are another thing to try here.

★ Danilovsky Market   MARKET $$

(Map p66; www.danrinok.ru; Mytnaya ul 74; mains R400-600; ☺8am-8pm; Ⓜ Tulskaya) A showcase of the area's ongoing gentrification, this giant Soviet-era farmers' market is now largely about deli food cooked and served in myriad little eateries, including such gems as a Dagestani dumpling shop and a Vietnamese pho-soup kitchen. The market itself looks very orderly, if a tiny bit artificial, with uniformed vendors and thoughtfully designed premises.

Fedya, dich!   FUSION $$

(Федя, дичь!; Map p66; ☑8-916-747 0110; Mytnaya ul 74; mains R650-820; ☺11am-11pm; Ⓜ Tulskaya) Let's take a walk on the wild side of the Moscow food scene. This place gets fresh supplies of fish and game from faraway corners of Siberia. Sea of Japan oysters and Arctic fish tartare are fresh and delicious despite crossing eight time zones to land on your table; so are wild-boar cutlets and deer steaks with forest berries.

Syrovarnya   EASTERN EUROPEAN $$

(Map p90; ☑495-727 3880; www.novikovgroup.ru/ restaurants/syrovarnya; Bersenevsky per 2, str 1; mains R400-700; ☺noon-midnight Mon-Thu, 24hr Fri-Sun; Ⓜ Polyanka, Kropotkinskaya) Domestic cheese production is all the rage in Russia, which has banned cheese exports from the EU in retaliation for Western sanctions. This restaurant serves hearty, homey meals, most of which contain cheese produced right here – in a micro-creamery that you see first

COOK LIKE A LOCAL

If you love Russian food, you can learn to make it yourself. **Taste of Russia** (Map p78; ☑8-929-694 3797; www.tasterussia. ru; bldg 4, Kazarmenny per 3; 3hr course R3500, market tour R1500; Ⓜ Kurskaya) offers courses in English, as well as market tours, wine tastings and special children's classes. Cooking courses take place in the evening, when you prepare the meal, then eat it together.

thing after coming inside. A shop selling top-quality cheese is also on the premises.

Chugunny most   BISTRO $$

(Чугунный мост; Map p94; ☑495-959 4418; www.facebook.com/chugunniimost; Pyatnitskaya ul 6; mains R700-1000; ☺9am-midnight; Ⓜ Tretyakovskaya) This place illustrates the direction in which the entire Moscow restaurant scene seems to be heading – a bistro-cum-bar that would not be out of place in somewhere like Prenzlauer Berg, Berlin. The subdued, wood-dominated decor is almost therapeutic and the inventive, post-ethnic food makes you want to live or work in the vicinity, just so it can be your local.

The R550 set-lunch deal is about the best value for money in town. The place is a good breakfast choice, too.

★ Björn   SCANDINAVIAN $$$

(Map p94; ☑495-953 9059; http://bjorn.rest; Pyatnitskaya ul 3; mains R600-1200; Ⓜ Novokuznetskaya) A neat cluster of fir trees on a busy street hides a Nordic gem that deserves a saga to glorify its many virtues. This is not an 'ethnic' restaurant, but a presentation of futuristic Scandinavian cuisine straight out of a science fiction movie. From salads to desserts, every dish looks deceptively simple, visually perfect and 23rd century.

🍷 Drinking & Nightlife

Solo traveller looking for drinking buddies? Freaked out by face control? An organised pub crawl is a guaranteed way to meet fine folks from around the world, get into some cool clubs and discover Moscow's nightlife. The **City Pub Crawl** (www.citypubcrawl.ru; R1500) includes four clubs, four drinks and one band of very merry Moscow travellers. Dancing on the bar is also included.

Kremlin & Kitay Gorod

Mandarin Combustible   LOUNGE

(Map p72; ☑495-745 0700; Mal Cherkassky per 2; ◉noon-6am; ☎; Ⓜ Lubyanka) Dining, drinking and dancing are all on offer in this sexy space. There is a long menu of Pan Asian cuisine – as well as sushi, pasta, tapas and more – served all night long for Moscow's nonstop party people. Drinks are forgettable and service is slack, but everything (and everyone) looks fine – and sometimes that's what matters.

Tverskoy & Novoslobodsky

★**Noor / Electro**   BAR

(Map p86; ☑8-903-136 7686; www.noorbar.com; ul Tverskaya 23/12; ◉8pm-3am Mon-Wed, to 6am Thu-Sun; Ⓜ Pushkinskaya) There is little to say about this misleadingly unassuming bar, apart from the fact that everything in it is close to perfection. It has it all – prime location, convivial atmosphere, eclectic DJ music, friendly bartenders and superb drinks. Though declared 'the best' by various magazines on several occasions, it doesn't feel like they care.

32.05   CAFE

(Map p78; ☑905-703 3205; www.veranda3205.ru; ul Karetny Ryad 3; ◉11am-3am; Ⓜ Pushkinskaya) The biggest drinking and eating establishment in Hermitage Gardens, this verandah positioned at the back of the park's main building looks a bit like a greenhouse. In summer, tables (and patrons) spill out into the park, making it one of the city's best places for outdoor drinking. With its long bar and joyful atmosphere, the place also heaves in winter.

Enthusiast   BAR

(Энтузиаст; Map p78; Stoleshnikov per 7, str 5; ◉noon-11pm Sun-Thu, to 2am Fri & Sat; Ⓜ Teatralnaya) Scooter enthusiast, that is. But you don't have to be one in order to enjoy this superbly laid-back bar hidden at the far end of a fancifully shaped courtyard and disguised as a spare-parts shop. On a warm day, grab a beer or cider, settle into a beach chair and let harmony descend on you.

Meshchansky & Basmanny

★**Sisters Cafe**   CAFE

(Map p78; ☑495-623 0932; www.cafesisters.com; ul Pokrovka 6; ◉noon-11pm; ☎; Ⓜ Kitay-Gorod)

This cosy and quiet cafe-cum-bar has a distinct feminine touch about it – as if Chekhov's sisters have finally made their way to Moscow and started a new life here. Cheapish smoothies, lemonades and teas are on offer, but the wine and cocktail lists are equally impressive.

★**Ukuleleshnaya**   BAR

(Укулелешная; Map p78; ☑495-642 5726; www.uku-uku.ru; ul Pokrovka 17 str 1; ◉noon-midnight Sun-Thu, noon-4am Fri & Sat; Ⓜ Chistye Prudy) In its new location, this is now more of a bar than a musical instrument shop, although ukuleles still adorn the walls, prompting an occasional jam session. Craft beer prevails on the drinks list, but Ukuleleshnaya also serves experimental cocktails of its own invention. Live concerts happen regularly and resident Pomeranian Spitz Berseny (cute dog) presides over the resulting madness.

Chaynaya Vysota   TEAHOUSE

(Чайная высота; Map p78; http://cha108.ru/; ul Pokrovka 27 str 1; ☎; Ⓜ Chistye Prudy) Tearoom? Gelateria? This place looks more like an academic library of tea and ice cream, an impression enhanced by it sharing premises with a bookstore. The tea menu is an endless list of pu'ers and oolongs, while ice-cream flavours represent everything that grows in the former USSR – from gooseberry or fir-needle juice to chestnuts and Crimean rose petals.

Tsurtsum Cafe   CAFE

(Цурцум кафе; Map p78; 4-y Syromyatnichesky per 1 str 6; ◉10am-11pm) Synonymous with Winzavod (p89) art centre, where it is located, Tsurtsum is a watering hole where all the beasts of the post-industrial savannah at the back of Kursky vokzal gather to sit on the verandah and plot new start-ups, performances and revolutions. Great for people-watching and non-malicious, self-educating eavesdropping – if you speak Russian.

Solyanka   CAFE, CLUB

(Map p78; ☑8-903-745 1313; http://s-11.ru; ul Solyanka 11; ◉11am-6am; ☎; Ⓜ Kitay Gorod) Solyanka 11 is an historic 18th-century merchant's mansion that has been revamped into an edgy, arty club. Wide-plank floors, exposed brick walls, leather furniture and funky light fixtures transform the space. By day it's an excellent restaurant, serving contemporary, creative Russian and European food.

LGBT MOSCOW

There have been reports of police harassment around gay clubs and cruising areas in Moscow. Exercise extra caution around LGBT-specific venues (or avoid them) and you are unlikely to experience any problems. Moscow Pride has not taken place since it was banned by city courts (despite fines from the European Court of Human Rights in 2010).

All this said, Moscow is the most cosmopolitan of Russian cities, and the active gay and lesbian scene reflects this attitude. Newspapers such as the *Moscow Times* feature articles about gay and lesbian issues, as well as listings of gay and lesbian clubs. Gay. ru (http://english.gay.ru) is rather out-of-date, but still has good links and resources for getting in touch with personal guides.

Venues

Propaganda (Map p78; www.propagandamoscow.com; Bolshoy Zlatoustinsky per 7; ☉ noon-6am; ☎; Ⓜ Kitay-Gorod) This long-time favourite looks to be straight from the warehouse district, with exposed brick walls and pipe ceilings. It's a cafe by day, but at night they clear the dance floor and let the DJ do his stuff. This is a gay-friendly place, especially on Sunday nights.

Secret (Map p78; www.secret-club.ru; Nizhny Susalny per 7, Bldg 8; ☉ 11pm-6am; Ⓜ Kurskaya) The 'sliding scale' cover charge and cheap drinks attract a young, student crowd to this gay nightclub. The earlier you arrive, the cheaper the admission, but if you're a male aged 18 to 22, it's free any time. Two dance floors, plus live music or drag shows on weekends.

In the evening, the big bar room gets cleared of tables and the DJ spins hip-hop, techno and rave. The music usually starts at 11pm (and so does the face control).

Tsiferblat ANTICAFE
(Циферблат; Map p78; ☎ 8-962-964 6786; www. domnadereve.ziferblat.net; ul Pokrovka 12 str 1; 1st hour R180, subsequent hours R120; ☉ 8.30am-12am Mon-Thu, till 6am Fri, Sat, 10am-12am Sun; ☎; Ⓜ Kitay-Gorod) How often do you head to a cafe just because you need somewhere nice to spend some time in, not because you are desperate to get a coffee? Tsiferblat was the first establishment in Moscow that turned the idea of a coffee shop upside down. Here you pay for time, while coffee, as well as lemonade and cookies, are free.

They call it an 'anticafe'. Looking like an old flat, this place is good for chatting with friends or for fiddling with your gadgets, but it might be slightly too noisy if you need to do some real work. Enter at the back of the building, then walk to the 2nd floor.

🍷 Presnya

⭐**Time-Out Rooftop Bar** COCKTAIL BAR
(Map p86; http://hotelpeking.ru/timeout-roof-top-bar; 12th fl, Bolshaya Sadovaya ul 5; ☉ noon-2am Sun-Thu, to 6am Fri & Sat; Ⓜ Mayakovskaya) On the upper floors of the throwback Peking Hotel (Гостиница Пекин; Map p86;

☑ 495-650 0900; www.hotelpeking.ru; Bolshaya Sadovaya ul 5/1; r from R7600; ❄ ☎; Ⓜ Mayakovskaya), this trendy bar is nothing but 'now'. That includes the bartenders sporting plaid and their delicious concoctions, specially created for different times of the day. The decor is pretty impressive – particularly the spectacular city skyline view. A perfect place for sundowners (or sun-ups, if you last that long).

Art Lebedev Cafe Studio CAFE
(Кафе Студия Артемия Лебедева; Map p86; www.artlebedev.ru; Bolshaya Nikitskaya ul 35b; ☉ 8am-11pm Mon-Fri, from 10am Sat & Sun; ☎; Ⓜ Arbatskaya) Owned by design guru Artemy Lebedev, this tiny space invites an attractive arty crowd to sip fancy coffee drinks and exotic teas. Regulars love the house-made *kasha* (porridge) for breakfast and the shady terrace in summer months. Don't miss the shop downstairs.

Jagger BAR
(Map p86; www.jaggercity.ru; Bldg 30, Rochdel-skaya ul 15; ☉ noon-midnight Mon-Wed, to 6am Thu-Sat, 2pm-midnight Sun; Ⓜ Ulitsa 1905 Goda) Tucked into the courtyard in the old Tryokhgornaya (p57) manufacturing complex, Jagger is a super hot bar with a super cool vibe. Excellent cocktails, sharp clientele and laid-back atmosphere are characteristic of a new Moscow nightlife that is cosmopolitan

and cultured, not over-the-top outrageous. Still, you have to know where to look for this place. And you have to look good.

Coffee Mania
CAFE

(Кофемания; Map p86; www.coffeemania.ru; Bolshaya Nikitskaya ul 13, Moscow Conservatory; ☺24hr; ☎; Ⓜ Okhotny Ryad) A longtime popular place for the rich and beautiful to congregate, this friendly, informal cafe is beloved for its homemade soups, freshly squeezed juices and steaming (if overpriced) cappuccinos, not to mention its summer terrace overlooking the leafy courtyard of the Moscow Conservatory.

 Arbat & Khamovniki

Dom 12
WINE BAR

(Map p90; www.dom12cafe.ru; Mansurovsky per 12; ☺noon-6am; Ⓜ Park Kultury) Eclectic and atmospheric, Dom 12 may be the perfect place to attend an event or chat with friends over a glass of wine. The cosy interior is enhanced by natural materials, comfy chairs and low lighting. Besides the excellent wine list, the place offers poetry nights, lectures, concerts and dancing. Delightful!

Zhiguli Beer Hall
BREWERY

(Пивной зал Жигули; Map p90; www.zhiguli.su; ul Novy Arbat 11; beer R210-350; ☺10am-2am Sun-Thu, to 4am Fri & Sat; ☎; Ⓜ Arbatskaya) It's hard to classify this old-style *stolovaya* (cafeteria) that happens to brew great beer. The place

---

ⓘ FACE CONTROL

'Face control' is the common practice of denying entry to clubs and bars based on a person's appearance. It's not unusual for nightlife hot spots to try to create an illusion of exclusivity, but some Moscow clubs take the practice to a new level.

A few tips for avoiding rejection:

➡ Dress sharp. No shorts, sneakers or sportswear.

➡ Smile. Show the bouncer that you are going to enhance the atmosphere inside.

➡ Book a table (sometimes requires a table deposit).

➡ Speak English. Foreigners are not as special as they used to be, but they're still sort of special.

---

harks back to the Soviet years, when a popular *pivnaya* beer joint with the same name was a Novy Arbat institution. The minimalist decor and cafeteria-style service recalls the heyday, although it's been updated with big-screen TVs and a separate table-service dining room.

 Zamoskvorechie

★ Bar Strelka
CAFE, CLUB

(Map p90; www.barstrelka.com; Bersenevskaya nab 14/5, bldg 5a; ☺9am-midnight Mon-Thu, to 3am Fri, noon-3am Sat, noon-midnight Sun; ☎; Ⓜ Kropotkinskaya) Located just below the Patriarshy most, the bar-restaurant at the Strelka Institute (p115) is the ideal starting point for an evening in the Red October (p89) complex. The rooftop terrace has unbeatable Moscow River views, but the interior is equally cool in a shabby-chic sort of way. The bar menu is excellent and there is usually somebody tinkling the ivories.

★ Gipsy
CLUB, CAFE

(Map p90; www.bargipsy.ru; Bolotnaya nab 3/4; ☺6pm-1am Sun-Thu, 2pm-6am Fri & Sat) Euphoria reigns in this postmodern nomad camp of a bar with its strategic rooftop position on Red October (p89). The decor is bright-coloured kitsch, which among other oddities means fake palm trees and toilet doors covered with artificial fur. The DJ and live-music repertoires are aptly eclectic.

Le Boule
BAR

(Map p66; ☑495-518 8412; Gorky Park; ☺noon-midnight; ☎; Ⓜ Oktyabrskaya) The goatee and moustache factor is high in this hipster-ridden verandah bar that comes with a dozen pétanque lanes. Grab a pitcher of sangria or a pint of cider and have a go at what is arguably the most alcohol-compatible sport. Live bands often play on the verandah in the early evening.

Kusochki
BAR

(Pieces; Map p66; ☑495-114 5525; www.kusochki-cafe.ru; ul Shabolovka 63; ☺noon-midnight Sun-Thu, to 6am Fri & Sat; Ⓜ Shabolovskaya) This Shabolovka district local is an alcohol-infused version of the Mad Hatter's tea party with a hint of BDSM. It features waitresses dressed as paramedics and policewomen, cocktails served in drip bags and a table inside a prison cell, where you can handcuff your drinking buddies if that sounds like a fun thing to do. Extensive drinks list and good food.

MOJO
BAR

(Map p94; ☑ 495-999 0507; www.facebook.com/mojobarmoscow; ul Valovaya 26; ☺ 9am-midnight; Ⓜ Dobryninskaya) The name may not sound original, but these guys do get your mojo working! Their magic formula includes outstanding cocktails, classily understated design with subdued lights, great deli food, modern art on the walls and DJ music. The expat owners mingle and drink with patrons – sometimes so hard, they can't open shop on Sunday.

Underdog
CRAFT BEER

(Map p94; Klimentovsky per 12, str 14; ☺ 2pm-2am; Ⓜ Tretyakovskaya) This cosy little pub hidden away from the perpetually crowded Klimentovsky per has the melancholy of an Edward Hopper painting or a good road movie. The beer menu is an all-encompassing list of IPAs, APAs, lagers, krieks and whatnot – mostly produced at local microbreweries. Some Russian beers come with crazy names like Shaman Has Three Hands.

Parka
CRAFT BEER

(Map p94; ☑ 8-926-160 6313; www.facebook.com/parkacraft; Pyatnitskaya ul 22, str 1; ☺ 1pm-2am; Ⓜ Novokuznetskaya) 'Parka' is a *banya* (bathhouse) term, hence the sauna-like decor, and just like a proper *banya*, this a very relaxing place. The friendly bartenders let you try any beer before you commit to buying a pint; the brews, many with crazy Runglish names, are mostly local.

☆ Entertainment

The performing arts are one of Moscow's biggest attractions. Highly acclaimed, professional artists stage productions in elegant theatres around the city, most of which have been recently revamped and look marvellous.

Most theatres sell tickets online. Or, you can do it the old-fashioned way and buy tickets directly from the theatre box office or from a *teatralnaya kassa* (theatre kiosk), several of which are scattered about the city. Note, many venues are closed between late June and early September.

☆ Tverskoy & Novoslobodsky

★ Bolshoi Theatre
BALLET, OPERA

(Большой театр; Map p78; ☑ 495-455 5555; www.bolshoi.ru; Teatralnaya pl 1; tickets R100-12,000; ☺ closed Jul–mid-Sep; Ⓜ Teatralnaya) An evening at the Bolshoi is still one of Moscow's most romantic and entertaining options for a night on the town. The glittering six-tier auditorium has an electric atmosphere, evoking over 240 years of premier music and dance. Both the ballet and opera companies perform a range of Russian and foreign works here.

Stanislavsky Electrotheatre
ARTS CENTRE

(Map p86; ☑ 495-699 7224; http://electrotheatre.ru; ul Tverskaya 23; Ⓜ Pushkinskaya) Renowned performance artist Boris Yukhananov has revived this old theatre as Moscow's hottest venue for experimental performance and visual art. Dance, music, cinema and theatre form a sparkling cocktail of genres and there is not a day without something new, strange and exciting going on.

Novaya Opera
OPERA

(Новая опера; Map p78; ☑ 495-694 0868; www.novayaopera.ru; ul Karetny Ryad 3; ☺ box office noon-7.30pm; Ⓜ Tsvetnoy Bulvar) This theatre company was founded in 1991 by then-mayor Luzhkov and artistic director Evgeny Kolobov. Maestro Kolobov stated, 'we do not pretend to be innovators in this beautiful and complicated genre of opera'. As such, the 'New Opera' stages the old classics, and does it well. The gorgeous, modern opera house is set amid the Hermitage Gardens.

Moscow Art Theatre (MKhT)
THEATRE

(Московский художественный театр (MXAT); Map p78; www.mxat.ru; Kamergersky per 3; ☺ box office noon-7pm; Ⓜ Teatralnaya) Often called the most influential theatre in Europe, this is where method acting was founded over 100 years ago, by Stanislavsky and Nemirovich-Danchenko. Besides the theatre itself and an acting studio-school, a small museum about the theatre's history is also on-site.

☆ Meshchansky & Basmanny

Gogol Centre
THEATRE

(Гоголь-центр; Map p78; ☑ 499-262 9214; www.gogolcenter.com; ul Kazakhova 8; Ⓜ Kurskaya) One of the most talked-about theatres in Moscow is under constant political pressure due to the nonconformist position of its director Kirill Serebrennikov. Gogol Centre is a modern venue that hosts many musical and dance performances as well as cutting-edge drama. The latter is difficult to appreciate without knowing Russian.

New Ballet DANCE
(Map p78; ☑ 495-265 7510; www.newballet.ru; Novaya Basmannaya ul 25/2; ☺ box office 11am-7pm; Ⓜ Krasnye Vorota) If you can't stand to see another *Swan Lake*, you will be pleased to know that the New Ballet performs innovative contemporary dance. This performance art, called 'plastic ballet', incorporates elements of classical and modern dance, as well as pantomime and drama. The theatre is tiny, providing an up-close look at original, cutting-edge choreography.

Pirogi on Maroseyka LIVE MUSIC, CINEMA
(Map p78; https://pirogicafe.ru; ul Maroseyka 9/2; ☺ 24hr; ☎; Ⓜ Kitay-Gorod) If you have ever visited Pirogi's earlier incarnations, you might be surprised by the club's slick storefront. Inside, it's not dark and it's not grungy. Do not fear, however, as the crucial elements have not changed: decent food, affordable beer and movies and music every night, all of which draw the young, broke and beautiful.

☆ Presnya

**Spartak Stadium
(Otkrytie Arena)** SPECTATOR SPORT
(Стадион Спартак (Открытие Арена); ☑ 495-411 5200; www.otkritiearena.ru; Volokolamskoe shosse 67; Ⓜ Tushinskaya) Home to professional football club FC Spartak, this bizarre-looking arena – easy to recognise by the Spartak red-and-white on the exterior – was built for the 2018 World Cup (and expected to host the opening game). In addition to the 42,000-capacity stadium, the complex includes an indoor arena and extensive facilities for other sports.

Tchaikovsky Concert Hall CLASSICAL MUSIC
(Концертный зал имени Чайковского; Map p86; ☑ 495-232 0400; www.meloman.ru; Triumfalnaya pl 4/31; tickets R800-3000; ☺ concerts 7pm, closed Aug; Ⓜ Mayakovskaya) Home to the famous Moscow State Philharmonic (Moskovskaya Filharmonia), the capital's oldest symphony orchestra, Tchaikovsky Concert Hall was established in 1921. It's a huge auditorium, with seating for 1600 people.

Expect to hear the Russian classics, such as Stravinsky, Rachmaninov and Shostakovich, as well as other European favourites. Look out for children's concerts, jazz ensembles and other special performances.

**Moscow Tchaikovsky
Conservatory** CLASSICAL MUSIC
(Московская консерватория имени Чайковского; Map p86; ☑ box office 495-629 9401; www.mosconsv.ru; Bolshaya Nikitskaya ul 13; Ⓜ Okhotny Ryad) The country's largest music school, named for Tchaikovsky of course, has two venues, both of which host concerts, recitals and competitions. The Great Hall of the Conservatory is home to the **Moscow Symphony Orchestra** (MSO; www.moscowsymphony.ru), a low-budget but highly lauded orchestra under the direction of Vladimir Ziva.

Moscow English Theatre THEATRE
(MET; Map p86; ☑ 495-690 4658; www.moscowenglishtheatre.com; Bol Nikitskaya ul 19/13; Ⓜ Arbatskaya) Founded by English actor Jonathan Bex, the MET performs contemporary American and British plays for English-speaking audiences. The company's original production – the comedy *Educating Rita*, by Willy Russell – sold out five straight seasons. The repertoire has expanded to include drama and mystery. The MET performs at the Mayakovsky Theatre.

Sixteen Tons LIVE MUSIC
(Шестнадцать тонн; Map p86; ☑ 495-253 1550; www.16tons.ru; ul Presnensky val 6; cover R600-1200; ☺ 11am-6am; ☎; Ⓜ Ulitsa 1905 Goda) Downstairs, the brassy English pub-restaurant has an excellent house-brewed bitter. Upstairs, the club gets some of the best Russian bands that play in Moscow and an occasional first-rate or semi-obscure Western groups. Show times are subject to change so check the website for details.

☆ Arbat & Khamovniki

Luzhniki Stadium SPECTATOR SPORT
(Олимпийский Комплекс Лужники; Map p66; ☑ 495-780 0808; www.luzhniki.ru; Luzhnetskaya nab 24; Ⓜ Sportivnaya) This giant stadium (home to football club FC Torpedo) is the capital's largest, seating nearly 81,000 people. The stadium is part of the Luzhniki Olympic Complex, which was the chief venue for the 1980 Summer Olympics. In recent years, it underwent a major upgrade, in preparation for hosting the 2018 World Cup Final.

Pioner Cinema CINEMA
(Кинотеатр Пионер; Map p66; ☑ 499-240 5240; http://pioner-cinema.ru; Kutuzovsky pr 21; Ⓜ Kiyevskaya) Almost all of the films shown in

Russia are dubbed into the Russian language, but this cinema theatre is a pleasant exception. Apart from sticking with the original language, it screens festival and art-house films that you won't be able to see elsewhere.

☆ Zamoskvorechie

Moscow International House of Music CLASSICAL MUSIC
(Map p94; ☑ 495-730 1011; www.mmdm.ru; Kosmodemyanskaya nab 52/8; tickets R200-2000; Ⓜ Paveletskaya) This graceful, modern glass building has three halls, including Svetlanov Hall, which holds the largest organ in Russia. Needless to say, organ concerts held here are impressive. This is the usual venue for performances by the **National Philharmonic of Russia** (Национальный филармонический оркестр России; Map p94; ☑ 495-730 3778; www.nfor.ru), a privately financed, highly lauded, classical-music organisation. Founded in 1991, the symphony is directed and conducted by the esteemed Vladimir Spivakov.

Strelka Institute ARTS CENTRE
(Map p90; www.strelkainstitute.ru; Bersenevskaya nab 14/5; Ⓜ Kropotkinskaya or Polyanka) This institute is the focal point of the development at the Red October (p89) chocolate factory. Aside from the course offerings and the popular bar (p112), Strelka brings a healthy dose of contemporary culture to Moscow, hosting lectures, workshops, film screenings and concerts.

🔒 Shopping

News flash: Moscow is an expensive city. So don't come looking for bargains. Do come looking for creative and classy clothing and jewellery by local designers; an innovative art scene; high-quality handicrafts, linens, glassware and folk art; and unusual souvenirs that you won't find anywhere else.

Excellent shopping streets include the famous ul Arbat, crammed with souvenir stalls; swanky ul Petrovka, with its nearby pleasant pedestrian lanes; and charming Nikolskaya ul, terminating at the gated fashion fantasy world inside Tretyakovsky proezd.

The city's new contemporary-art centres house art galleries, as well as performance and studio space, clubs, cafes and other creative enterprises. Here, you can see the works of many artists under one roof (or at least in one block).

🔒 Kremlin & Kitay Gorod

GUM MALL
(ГУМ; Map p72; www.gum.ru; Krasnaya pl 3; ⊙ 10am-10pm; Ⓜ Ploshchad Revolyutsii) Behind its elaborate 240m-long facade on the northeastern side of Red Square, GUM is a bright, bustling shopping mall with hundreds of fancy stores and restaurants. With a skylight roof and three-level arcades, the spectacular interior was a revolutionary design when it was built in the 1890s, replacing the Upper Trading Rows that previously occupied this site.

🔒 Tverskoy & Novoslobodsky

★ Transylvania MUSIC
(Map p78; ☑ 495-629 8786; www.transylvania.ru; Tverskaya ul 6/1, bldg 5; ⊙ 11am-10pm; Ⓜ Teatralnaya) From the courtyard, look for the black metal door that leads down into this dungeon of a shop, which houses room after room of CDs, in every genre imaginable. If you are curious about the *russky* rock scene, this is where you can sample some songs.

★ Yekaterina FASHION & ACCESSORIES
(Екатерина; Map p78; www.mexa-ekaterina.ru; ul Bolshaya Dmitrovka 11; ⊙ 11am-9pm; Ⓜ Teatralnaya) One of Russia's oldest furriers, this place has been manufacturing *shapky* (fur hats) and *shuby* (fur coats) since 1912. While Yekaterina has always maintained a reputation for high-quality furs and leather, its designs are constantly changing and updating to stay on top of fashion trends.

Roomchik CLOTHING
(Map p78; ☑ 495-629 6241; http://roomchik.ru; ul Bolshaya Dmitrovka 9, entrance 2, fl 2; ⊙ noon-9pm) A showroom of a popular online shop, which focuses primarily on little-known Russian designer brands. Definitely a place to look for high-quality clothes that nobody else has.

Yeliseev Grocery FOOD & DRINKS
(Елисеевский магазин; Map p78; Tverskaya ul 14; ⊙ 8am-9pm Mon-Sat, 10am-6pm Sun; Ⓜ Pushkinskaya) Peek in here for a glimpse of pre-revolutionary grandeur, as the store is set in the former mansion of the successful merchant Yeliseev. It now houses an upscale market selling caviar and other delicacies. It's a great place to shop for souvenirs for your foodie friends back home.

WORTH A TRIP

IZMAYLOVO

Never mind the kitschy mock Kremlin that surrounds it, **Izmaylovsky Market** (Map p66; www.kremlin-izmailovo.com; Izmaylovskoye shosse 73; ⊙10am-8pm; Ⓜ Partizanskaya) is the ultimate place to shop for *matryoshka* dolls, military uniforms, icons, Soviet badges, and some real antiques. Huge and diverse, it is almost a theme park, with shops, cafes and a couple of not terribly exciting museums.

Serious antiquarians occupy the 2nd floor of the wooden trade row surrounding the palace, but for really good stuff you need to come here at an ungodly hour on Saturday morning and compete with pros from Moscow galleries. Keep in mind that Russia bans the export of any item older than 100 years. Feel free to negotiate, but don't expect vendors to come down more than 10%. This place is technically open every day, but many vendors come out only on weekends, when the selection is greater.

Tsvetnoy   SHOPPING CENTRE

(Map p78; ☑ 495-737 7773; Tsvetnoy bul 15, str 1; ⊙10am-10pm Mon-Sat, from 11am Sun; Ⓜ Tsvetnoy Bulvar) Of all shopping centres in central Moscow, this is the funkiest, with clothes and interior-design items from international and emerging Russian brands, a good bookstore and a great food court on the upper floor.

TsUM   DEPARTMENT STORE

(ЦУМ; Map p78; www.tsum.ru; ul Petrovka 2; Ⓜ Teatralnaya) TsUM stands for Tsentralny Universalny Magazin (Central Department Store). Built in 1909 as the Scottish-owned Muir & Merrilees, it was the first department store aimed at middle-class shoppers. These days it's filled with designer labels and luxury items.

Podarki vMeste s Vorovski   GIFTS & SOUVENIRS

(Подарки вМесте с Воровски; Map p78; www. facebook.com/svorovskim; Kuznetsky most 21/5; ⊙10am-9pm; Ⓜ Lubyanka) This sweet little boutique houses a cooperative of four designer gift producers. The rather cramped space is filled with hundreds of useful and useless (but pretty) items, including Galereyka's felt slippers and hats (some shaped as Soviet tanks) and Ptitsa Sinitsa's stylish ceramics with Eastern European folklore motifs.

🏠 Meshchansky & Basmanny

Mir Kino   MUSIC

(Мир кино; Map p78; ☑ 495 628 5145; ul Maroseyka 6/8 str 2; ⊙11am-9pm; Ⓜ Kitay-Gorod) This tiny shop that sells second-hand vinyl and CDs has a few shelves dedicated to Russian indie music from the 1980s to present. There is also a Korean dumpling shop in the same premises.

Naivno? Ochen!   HOMEWARES

(Наивно? Очень!; Map p66; ☑499-678 0162; www.orz-design.ru; ArtPlay, ul Nizhnyaya Syromyatnicheskaya 10; ⊙11am-10pm; Ⓜ Kurksaya) These folks do a great service selling souvenirs – cups, plates and T-shirts – themed on inspired and whimsical drawings produced by children with special needs. Proceeds go to charities that help them. It's a big deal for a country which lags far behind the West on that front.

Biblio-Globus   BOOKS

(Map p78; ☑ 495-781 1900; www.biblio-globus.ru; Myasnitskaya ul 6; ⊙9am-10pm Mon-Fri, 10am-9pm Sat & Sun; Ⓜ Lubyanka) Moscow's favourite bookshop is huge, with lots of souvenir books devoted to language, art and history, and a good selection of maps and travel guides. A user-friendly computerised catalogue will help you find what you're looking for. Just to prove that Russia's consumer culture can keep up with the best of them, there's a coffee shop on the ground floor.

Khokhlovka Original   CLOTHING

(Map p78; http://hhlvk.ru; Khokhlovsky per 7; ⊙noon-10pm; Ⓜ Kitay-Gorod) This is about the most clandestine fashion store we've ever reviewed. To get in, enter a graffiti-covered courtyard, then look for a small gap between two single-storey buildings on your left – the door is inside the tiny passage. The small showroom displays clothes and accessories produced by dozens of young (but often stellar) Russian designers.

Odensya Dlya Schastya   CLOTHING

(Оденься для счастья; Map p78; ul Pokrovka 31; ⊙11am-9pm; Ⓜ Kurskaya) This sweet boutique – encouraging shoppers to 'dress for happiness' – carries unique clothing by a few distinctive designers, including Moscow native Oleg Biryukov. The designer's eponymous label features refined styles with long, flowing lines and subdued, solid colours. The tastefulness and elegance exemplify the new direction of Russian fashion.

🔒 Presnya

Ponaroshku TOYS

(Понарошку; Map p86; www.ponaroshku.ru; Maly Palashevsky per 2/8; ⊙10.30am-8.30pm; Ⓜ Pushkinskaya) This tiny store is packed with books, games, plush animals and beautiful painted wooden toys. This is the place to find some souvenirs for the little people in your life.

Valentin Yudashkin
Boutique FASHION & ACCESSORIES

(Map p86; www.yudashkin.com; Bldg 1, Voznesenskiy per 6/3; ⊙10am-7pm; Ⓜ Kievskaya) The best-known Russian fashion designer is Valentin Yudashkin, whose classy clothes are on display at the Louvre and the Met, as well as the State History Museum in Moscow (look but don't touch!). If you wish to try something on, head to this swanky boutique, which seems like a museum but has many things that you can, in fact, buy.

🔒 Arbat & Khamovniki

Russian Embroidery
& Lace GIFTS & SOUVENIRS

(Русская вышивка и кружево; Map p90; ul Arbat 31; ⊙11am-8pm Mon-Sat, to 5pm Sun; Ⓜ Smolenskaya) Considering the lack of flashy signs and kitsch, it would be easy to miss this plain storefront on the Arbat. But inside there are treasures galore, from elegant tablecloths and napkins to delicate handmade sweaters and embroidered shirts.

Russkie Chasovye Traditsii JEWELLERY

(Русские часовые традиции; Map p90; www.smirs.com; ul Arbat 11; ⊙10am-9pm; Ⓜ Arbatskaya) If you're in the market for a fancy timepiece, pop into the Arbat outlet of 'Russian Watch Traditions'. On this touristy drag, these small shops carry exclusively Russian brands, including Aviator, Buran, Vostok, Poljot, Romanoff and Denissov.

Association of Artists
of the Decorative Arts GIFTS & SOUVENIRS

(Ассоциация художников декоративно-прикладного искусства; AHDI; Map p90; www.ahdi.ru; ul Arbat 21; ⊙11am-8pm; Ⓜ Arbatskaya) Look for the ceramic number plate and the small sign indicating the entrance to this 'exposition hall', which is actually a cluster of small shops, each showcasing arts and crafts by local artists. In addition to paintings and pottery, the most intriguing items

are the gorgeous knit sweaters, woolly coats and embroidered dresses – all handmade and unique.

🔒 Zamoskvorechie

Alyonka CHOCOLATE

(Map p90; www.shop.alenka.ru; Bersenevskaya nab 6, str 1; ⊙10am-8pm; Ⓜ Polyanka or Kropotkinskaya) Although the old Red October (p89) chocolate factory has long been converted into a hipster den, you can still sample the products of Russian chocolatiers at the shop located at the far end of the old factory. Alyonka is an iconic Soviet brand of chocolate candies with a picture of a rosy-cheeked peasant girl wearing a kerchief on the wrapper.

Gzhel Porcelain CERAMICS

(Map p94; http://farfor-gzhel.ru; Pyatnitskaya ul 10, str 1; ⊙10am-9pm) Gzhel porcelain, with its signature white-and-blue folkloric decor, is sold here.

❶ Information

DANGERS & ANNOYANCES

Moscow is mostly a safe city.

➡ As in any big city, be on guard against pickpockets, especially around train stations and in crowded metro cars.

➡ Always be cautious about taking taxis late at night, especially near bars and clubs. Never get into a car that already has two or more people in it.

➡ Always carry a photocopy of your passport and visa. If stopped by a member of the police force, it is perfectly acceptable to show a photocopy.

➡ Your biggest threat in Moscow is xenophobic or overly friendly drunks.

EMERGENCY

Tourist Helpline ☏ 800-220 0001/2
Universal Emergency Number ☏ 112

INTERNET ACCESS

➡ Almost all hotels and hostels offer wi-fi, as do many bars, restaurants and cafes. It isn't always free, but it is ubiquitous. There is also free wi-fi on the metro and at hot spots around the city.

➡ To use the free wi-fi, you will be obliged to register your phone number to obtain a pass code. Some services only accept Russian telephone numbers, in which case you may have to ask a local to use their number.

MEDIA

The weekly *Moscow Times* (www.themoscow
times.com) is the last remaining publication for
English-language news. It covers Russian and
international issues, as well as sport and entertainment. Find it at hotels and restaurants.

MEDICAL SERVICES

Hospitals

Both the International Clinic MEDSI and the European Medical Centre accept health insurance
from major international providers.

Botkin Hospital (Map p66; ☑ 495-945 0045;
www.mosgorzdrav.ru; 2-y Botkinsky proezd 5;
⊙ 24hr; Ⓜ Begovaya) The best Russian facility. From Begovaya metro station, walk 1km
northeast on Khoroshevskoe sh and Begovoy
pr. Turn left on Begovaya ul and continue to 2-y
Botkinsky proezd.

European Medical Centre (Map p86; ☑ 495-
933 6655; www.emcmos.ru; Spiridonevsky per
5; ⊙ 24hr; Ⓜ Mayakovskaya) Includes medical
and dental facilities, which are open around
the clock for emergencies. The staff speak 10
languages.

International Clinic MEDSI (Map p78; ☑ 495-
933 7700; https://medsi.ru; Grokholsky per 1;
⊙ 24hr; Ⓜ Pr Mira) Offers 24-hour emergency
service, consultations and a full range of
medical specialists, including paediatricians
and dentists. There is also an on-site pharmacy
with English-speaking staff.

Pharmacies

36.6 Arbat (Map p90; ul Novy Arbat 15;
⊙ 9am-10pm; Ⓜ Arbatskaya)

36.6 Basmanny (Map p78; ul Pokrovka 1/13;
⊙ 9am-9pm; Ⓜ Kitay-Gorod)

36.6 Tverskaya (Map p86; Tverskaya ul 25/9;
⊙ 24hr; Ⓜ Mayakovskaya)

36.6 Zamoskvorechie (Map p94; Klimentovsky
per 12; ⊙ 8am-10pm; Ⓜ Tretyakovskaya)

MONEY

➧ ATMs linked to international networks are all
over Moscow – look for bankomat (банкомат)
signs.

➧ Credit cards accepted by most hotels and
restaurants. Americans may have some difficulty if they do not have a 'chip and pin' credit
card. This is more of a problem at shops than at
hotels and restaurants.

➧ US dollars and euros are widely accepted at
exchange bureaus.

POST

Main Post Office (Map p78; Myasnitskaya ul
26; ⊙ 24hr; Ⓜ Chistye Prudy)

TELEPHONE

➧ There are now four area codes operating
within Moscow. Both ☑ 495 and ☑ 499 are
used in the city, while ☑ 496 and ☑ 498 are
used on the outskirts.

➧ For all calls within Russia (including within
Moscow), you must dial 8 plus the 10-digit
number including the area code.

TOURIST INFORMATION

Discover Moscow (https://um.mos.ru/en/dis-
cover-moscow) A comprehensive site organised
by the City of Moscow.

Tourist Hotline (☑ 8-800-220 0001, ☑ 8-800-
220 0002, ☑ 495-663 1393)

Kremlin Left-Luggage Office (Map p72; Alexander Garden; ⊙ 9am-6.30pm Fri-Wed)

❶ Getting There & Away

AIR

Most travellers arrive in Moscow by air, flying
into one of the city's four international airports:

Sheremetyevo (Шереметьево; ☑ 495-578
6565; www.svo.aero) 30km northwest of the
city centre, this is Moscow's busiest airport.
The Aeroexpress Train (p120) makes the
35-minute trip between Sheremetyevo (located
next to Terminal E) and Belorussky vokzal
every half-hour from 5.30am to 12.30am.

Domodedovo (Домодедово; ☑ 495-933 6666;
www.domodedovo.ru) About 48km south of the
city is the city's most efficient international airport. The Aeroexpress Train leaves Paveletsky
vokzal every half-hour between 6am and midnight for the 45-minute trip to Domodedovo.

Vnukovo (Внуково; ☑ 495-937 5555; www.
vnukovo.ru) About 30km southwest of the city
centre, this airport mostly has flights to/from
the Caucasus, Moldova and Kaliningrad, as well
as domestic flights and a smattering of flights
to Europe. The Aeroexpress Train makes the
35-minute run from Kievsky vokzal to Vnukovo
airport every hour from 6am to 11pm.

Zhukovsky (Жуковский; ☑ 495-228 9600;
http://zia.aero) Opened in 2016, Moscow's
fourth international airport is about 40km
southeast of the city. It mostly serves Central
Asian destinations, and is a hub for Ural Airlines.

BOAT

There are numerous cruise boats plying the
routes between Moscow and St Petersburg, most
stopping at Uglich, Yaroslavl, Goritsky Monastery, Kizhi and Mondrogy (near Lake Ladoga).
Ships are similar in quality and size, carrying
about 250 passengers.

BUS

Bus service may be useful for destinations that
are not served by train. The **central bus station**

(Центральный автовокзал, Щёлковский автовокзал; ☑ 499-748 8029; www.avtovokzaly.ru; Ⓜ Shchyolkovskaya), sometimes called Shchyolkovsky bus station, is located 8km east of the city centre. Long-distance buses travel to Ivanovo (R750, 5½ hours, eight daily), Kyiv (R1600, 16 hours, 3.45pm), Minsk (R1100, 12 hours, 6.40pm), Nizhny Novgorod (R900, six hours, three daily) via Vladimir (R400, 3½ hours), Plyos (R850, seven hours, 6pm) and Yuryev-Polsky (R450, four hours, four daily). It's advisable to book ahead, especially for travel on weekends.

CAR & MOTORCYCLE

Driving in and around Moscow is difficult, to say the least, due to massive traffic jams, challenging navigation and shortages of parking. That said, you may wish to hire a car if you are leaving the city, eg taking a day trip to sites around Moscow or driving around the Golden Ring.

TRAIN

Rail riders will arrive at one of Moscow's central train stations, all with easy access to the metro. Most taxi companies offer a fixed rate of R400 to R600 for a train station transfer.

Stations

Belarus Station (Белорусский вокзал; http://belorussky.dzvr.ru; Tverskaya Zastava pl; ☎; Ⓜ Belorusskaya) has trains to/from northern and central Europe, as well as suburban trains to/from the west, including Mozhaysk and Borodino. This is also where you'll catch the Aeroexpress Train to Sheremetyevo international airport.

Kazan Station (Казанский вокзал; http://kazansky.dzvr.ru; Komsomolskaya pl; ☎;

Ⓜ Komsomolskaya) has trains to/from Kazan and points southeast, as well as some trains to/from Vladimir, Nizhny Novgorod, the Ural Mountains and Siberia.

Kiev Station (Киевский вокзал; www.kievsky-vokzal.ru; Kievskaya pl; ☎; Ⓜ Kievskaya) serves Kyiv and western Ukraine, as well as points further west, such as Moldova, Slovakia, Hungary, Austria, Prague, Romania, Bulgaria, Croatia, Serbia and Greece. This is also where you'll catch the Aeroexpress Train to Vnukovo international airport.

Kursk Station (Курский вокзал; http://kursky.dzvr.ru; pl Kurskogo vokzala; Ⓜ Kurskaya) serves Oryol, Kursk, Krasnodar, Adler, the Caucasus, eastern Ukraine, Crimea, Georgia and Azerbaijan. It also has some trains to/from Rostov-on-Don, Vladimir, Nizhny Novgorod and Perm; and suburban trains to/from the east and south, including Chekhov and Tula.

Leningrad Station (Ленинградский вокзал; http://leningradsky.dzvr.ru; Komsomolskaya pl; ☎; Ⓜ Komsomolskaya) serves Tver, Novgorod, Pskov, St Petersburg, Vyborg, Murmansk, Estonia and Helsinki. Note that sometimes this station is referred to on timetables and tickets by its former name, Oktyabrsky (Октябрьский).

Pavelets Station (Павелецкий вокзал; http://paveletsky.dzvr.ru; Paveletskaya pl; Ⓜ Paveletskaya) serves points south, including the Volga region and Central Asia. This is also the departure/arrival point for the Aeroexpress Train to Domodedovo international airport.

Rīga Station (Рижский вокзал; http://rizhsky.dzvr.ru; Rizhskaya pl; Ⓜ Rizhskaya) serves Latvia, with suburban trains to/from the northwest, including Istra and Novoierusalimskaya.

TRAINS CONNECTING MOSCOW & ST PETERSBURG

All trains to St Petersburg depart from Leningrad Station (p119). Book your tickets at any train station or through your hotel. Alternatively, buy tickets online at the official site of the Russian railroad (www.rzd.ru).

Overnight

There are about a dozen overnight trains connecting the cities. Most depart between 10pm and 1am, arriving the following morning between 6am and 8am. On the more comfortable *firmeny* trains, a 1st-class *SV* ticket (two-person cabin) costs R5500 to R7000, while a 2nd-class *kupe* (four-person cabin) is R3000 to R4000.

Sample departure times and fares:

2 Krasnaya Strela 1st-/2nd-class R7000/3600, eight hours, 11.55pm

4 Ekspress 1st-/2nd-class R5300/3400, nine hours, 11.30pm

20 Megapolis 1st-/2nd-class R6300/3800, 8½ hours, 12.20am

54 Grand Express 1st-/2nd-class R6600/3840, nine hours, 11.40pm

Sapsan

Travelling at speeds of 200km/h Sapsan trains connect the cities in about four hours or less. Trains depart throughout the day. Comfortable seats cost R3500 to R4500.

Yaroslav Station (Ярославский вокзал; http://yaroslavsky.dzvr.ru; Komsomolskaya pl; 🛜; Ⓜ Komsomolskaya) The main station for Trans-Siberian trains, with services to Yaroslavl, Arkhangelsk, Vorkuta, the Russian Far East, Mongolia, China and North Korea; some trains to/from Vladimir, Nizhny Novgorod, Kostroma, Vologda, Perm, the Ural Mountains and Siberia, and suburban trains to/from the northeast, including Abramtsevo and Sergiev Posad.

ⓘ Getting Around

Most visitors won't need anything but Moscow's super-efficient metro system, which allows you to get to pretty much anywhere in the city without thinking about complicated bus or tram routes. Connecting to the metro, an overground railway ring line (Moscow Central Ring) circles the city, which may be useful for some sights on the outskirts.

TO/FROM THE AIRPORTS

The three main airports – not yet including Zhukovsky (p118) – are accessible by the convenient **Aeroexpress Train** (☑ 8-800-700 3377; www.aeroexpress.ru; airport one way R420; ☺ 6am–midnight) from the city centre; reduced rates are available for online purchases. Alternatively, order an official airport taxi from the dispatcher's desk in the terminal (R2000 to R2500 to the city centre). You can save some cash by booking in advance to take advantage of the fixed rates offered by most companies (usually from R1500 to R1800 to/from any airport). Driving times vary wildly depending on the traffic.

BICYCLE

There are more and more bicycles on the streets and pavements of Moscow. Cycling in the centre

---

ⓘ BIKE SHARE

Moscow's new bike-share program is VeloBike (www.velobike.ru), an innovative system designed to cut down on traffic and encourage healthier living in the capital. It started in 2013 and now offers some 2700 bicycles at 350 stations around the city.

➡ Go online to purchase a membership (R150 for a day, R600 for a month, plus deposit). Now you are ready to roll!

➡ Use your credit card to unlock a bike at any station, go for a ride, and return your bike to any station. The first 30 minutes incurs no additional charge, but after that you'll pay for use.

➡ The system is designed for transportation rather than recreation, so it's a good deal for short rides from point A to point B. For longer rides, you may be better off renting from Oliver Bikes (p95).

---

of Moscow is still a dangerous prospect, as the streets are overcrowded with fast-moving cars and nasty exhaust fumes.

That said, the city has launched a campaign to make the city safer for cyclists. As of 2016, there were some 250km of bike lanes, with plans for an additional 500km to be painted in coming years. There are a few parks and other off-road areas that are suitable for pleasure riding, including Gorky Park (p64), Vorobyovy Gory Nature Preserve (p92), Sokolniki (p83) and VDNKh (p85).

If you're nervous about navigating the streets on your own (or if you just want some company), Moscow Bike Tours (p93) are a great way to see the city by bicycle.

BOAT

For new perspectives on Moscow's neighbourhoods, fine views of the Kremlin, or just good, old-fashioned transport, a boat ride on the Moscow River is one of the city's highlights. **Capital Shipping Co** (ССК, Столичная Судоходная Компания; ☑ 495-225 6070; www.cck-ship.ru; adult/child 60min cruise R900/700, 2-day pass R2400/2000) offers a two-day pass, so you can get on and off wherever you wish.

BUS, TROLLEYBUS & TRAM

Buses, trolleybuses and trams might be necessary for reaching some sights away from the city centre. *Marshrutki* (private buses and minibuses) are particularly useful to reach some destinations on the outskirts of Moscow. Buses can also be useful for a few cross-town or radial routes that the metro misses. In particular, there are several buses that run around the Kremlin Ring (Mokhovaya ul, ul Okhotny Ryad, Teatralny pr, Staray pl), which is useful for the city centre.

If you don't have a ticket, you can buy one or several single-trip Ediny tickets from the driver for R55 per ticket.

METRO

The **Moscow Metro** (www.mosmetro.ru; per ride R55) is by far the easiest, quickest and cheapest way of getting around Moscow. Plus, many of the elegant stations are marble-faced, frescoed, gilded works of art. The 150-plus stations are marked outside by large 'M' signs.

Reliability The trains are generally reliable: you will rarely wait on a platform for more than three minutes. Nonetheless, they do get packed, especially during the city's rush hours.

Tickets Ediny and Troika cards are sold at ticket booths. Queues can be long, so it's useful (and slightly cheaper) to buy a multiple-ride ticket.

Maps & Signage Stations have maps of the system at the entrance and signs on each platform showing the destinations. The maps are generally in Cyrillic and Latin script, although the signs are usually only in Cyrillic. The carriages

ℹ CITY TRANSPORT TICKETS

Moscow has a unified ticketing system. All tickets are essentially smart cards that you must tap on the reader at the turnstiles before entering a metro station or on the bus.

Most convenient for short-term visitors is the red **Ediny** (Единый) ticket, which is good for all kinds of transport and available at metro stations. Depending on your time and logistics, you can choose between buying a ticket good for a single trip for R55, two trips for R110, 20 trips for R720, 40 trips for R1440 or 60 trips for R1700.

If you are staying in Moscow for more than a few days, it is recommended that you get a **Troika** (Тройка) top-up card, also available at metro stations. It works on all kinds of transport and gives a slightly cheaper rate than Ediny.

If your accommodation warrants taking a bus or tram to the nearest metro station, you may consider buying a **90 Minutes card** (single trip R65), which includes one metro ride and an unlimited number of bus/tram/trolleybus rides.

Another ticket type is **TAT**, which is only good for trams, buses and trolleybuses, but it is of little use for most visitors.

---

also have maps inside that show the stops for that line in both Roman and Cyrillic letters.

Transfers Interchange stations are linked by underground passages, indicated by *perekhod* signs, usually blue with a stick figure running up the stairs. Be aware that when two or more lines meet, the intersecting stations often (but not always) have different names.

Moscow Central Ring Operated by Russian Railways, the new ring line complements the existing metro system and is good for moving between such far-flung attractions as Izmaylovsky Market (p116), the **Botanical Gardens** (Map p66; www.gbsad.ru; Ⓜ Botanichesky Sad) and Moscow International Business Centre (p87).

TAXI

Taxi cabs are affordable. Unfortunately, you can't really flag down an official metered taxi in the street and most taxi drivers and dispatchers do not speak English.

These days, most people use mobile phone apps, such as **Yandex.Taxi** (Яндекс.Такси; https://taxi.yandex.com), to order a cab. This solves the language barrier issue to an extent, given that you know the precise departure and destination address. If you have the app, try to make sure it's easy to park where you are, otherwise the driver will start calling you and asking questions in Russian.

You can also order an official taxi by phone or book it online, or get a Russian-speaker to do this for you. Normally, the dispatcher will ring you back within a few minutes to provide a description and licence number of the car. Most companies will send a car within 30 minutes of your call. Some reliable companies offer online scheduling.

Detskoe Taxi (Детское Такси; ☑ 495-765 1180; www.detskoetaxi.ru) 'Children's Taxi' has smoke-free cars and car seats for your children.

Lingo Taxi (www.lingotaxi.com) Promises English-speaking drivers (and usually delivers).

New Yellow Taxi (Новое жёлтое такси; ☑ 495-940 8888; www.nyt.ru)

Taxi Blues (☑ 495-925 5115; www.taxi-blues.ru)

Unofficial Taxis

This is now less common, but in the past almost any car in Moscow could be a taxi if the price was right. In the centre, you can often still stick your arm out and someone will stop pretty soon.

➡ Many private cars cruise around as unofficial taxis, and other drivers will often take you if they're going in roughly the same direction.

➡ Expect to pay R300 to R500 for a ride around the city centre.

➡ Don't hesitate to wave on a car if you don't like the look of its occupants. As a general rule, it's best to avoid riding in cars that already have a passenger. Be particularly careful taking a taxi that is waiting outside a nightclub or bar.

AROUND MOSCOW

As you leave Moscow, the fast-paced modern capital fades from view and the slower-paced, old-fashioned countryside unfolds around you. The subtly changing landscape of the Moscow region (Подмосковье) is crossed by winding rivers and dotted with peasant villages – the classic provincial Russia immortalised by artists and writers over the centuries.

Country Estates

Abramtsevo   Абрамцево

Railway tycoon and art patron Savva Mamontov bought this lovely estate 45km north of Moscow in 1870. Here, he hosted

Around Moscow

Akhangelskoe   Архангельское

In 1810, the wealthy Prince Nikolai Yusupov purchased this grand palace on the outskirts of Moscow, and turned it into the spectacular **Arkhangelskoe Estate** (Музей-усадьба Архангельское; ☑ 495-561 9759; www.arkhangelskoe.ru; grounds R150, grounds & museum R400; ⊙ grounds 10am-8pm Wed-Sun, exhibits 10.30am-4.30pm Wed-Fri, 10am-6pm Sat & Sun). Now his palace displays the paintings, furniture, sculptures, glass, tapestries and porcelain that Yusupov accumulated over the years. In June, the estate is the exquisite setting for the popular **Usadba Jazz Festival** (☑ 499-248 3605; www.usadba-jazz.ru; tickets from R4000).

From Tushinskaya metro, take bus 541 or 549 or *marshrutka* (fixed-route minibus) 151 to Arkhangelskoe (R50, 30 minutes).

a whole slew of painters and musicians, including Ilya Repin, landscape artist Isaak Levitan, portraitist Valentin Serov and ceramicist Mikhail Vrubel, as well as opera singer Fyodor Chaliapin. Today the **Abramtsevo Estate Museum-Preserve** (Музей-заповедник Абрамцево; ☑ 496-543 2470; www.abramtsevo.net; Museynaya ul 1, Abramtsevo; grounds R60, buildings & grounds R400; ⊙ 10am-6pm Wed-Sun Apr-Sep, 10am-4pm Wed-Sun Oct-Mar) is a delightful retreat from Moscow or addition to a trip to nearby Sergiev Posad.

You can enter most of the buildings, some of which contain exhibits, if you buy the general admission ticket. The exception is the **Manor House** (Усадебный дом; adult/child R300/150), which requires a separate admission ticket. The prettiest building is the **Saviour Church 'Not Made by Hand'** (Храм Спаса Нерукотворного).

The best place to eat is **Cafe Abramtsevo** (Кафе Абрамцево; ☑ 8-915-177 3649; www.cafe-abramtsevo.ru; mains R340-640; ⊙ 10am-6pm) across the street and down the lane from the main entrance to the estate.

Suburban trains run every half-hour from Moscow's Yaroslavsky station (R250, 1¼ hours). Most – but not all – trains to Sergiev Posad or Alexandrov stop at Abramtsevo. There are also regular buses between Abramtsevo and Sergiev Posad (R50, 20 minutes).

From the train platform, follow the foot trail through the woods, straight across the fire road, through a residential community and down a rough set of stairs. Before reaching the highway, turn left to cross the bridge and continue up into the parking area. The 1km walk is not well signposted.

Peredelkino   Переделкино

Boris Pasternak – poet, author of *Doctor Zhivago* and winner of the 1958 Nobel Prize for Literature – lived for a long time on Moscow's southwestern outskirts, just 5km beyond the city's outer ring road, where there is now the **Pasternak House-Museum** (Дом-Музей Бориса Пастернака; ☑ 495-934 5175; www.pasternakmuseum.ru; ul Pavlenko 3, Peredelkino; adult/child R150/100; ⊙ 11am-6pm Tue-Sun). Run by his descendents, it's an authentic glimpse into the life of the writer.

Frequent suburban trains go from Moscow's Kiev Station to Peredelkino (R60, 25 minutes) on the line to Kaluga-II station. From Peredelkino station, follow the path west along the train tracks past the cemetery (where Pasternak is buried) and over the bridge. After about 400m, ul Pavlenko is on the right-hand side.

Gorki Leninskie Горки Ленинские

In Lenin's later years, he and his family spent time at the Morozov manor house, set on lovely wooded grounds, 32km southeast of the capital. The estate now houses a Lenin **museum** (Музей-заповедник "Горки Ленинские"; ☑ 495-548 9309; www.mgorki.ru; all exhibits R600; ⊙ 10am-7pm Wed-Sun May-Sep, 10am-4pm Wed-Sun Oct-Apr) and a re-creation of Lenin's Kremlin office and apartment, as well as his vintage Rolls-Royce.

Bus 439 (R62, 30 minutes) leaves every 90 minutes for the estate from the Domodedovskaya metro station in Moscow. From the bus stop, you have to walk about 1km through a residential neighbourhood to the museum grounds. By car, follow the M4 highway (Kashirskoe sh) to 11km beyond the MKAD ring road, then turn left to Gorki Leninskie. There is a cafe on the grounds.

Klin Клин

From 1885, composer Pyotr Tchaikovsky spent his summers in Klin, 75km northwest of Moscow. In a charming house on the edge of town, he wrote the *Nutcracker* and *Sleeping Beauty*, as well as his famous Pathétique Symphony No 6. After he died in 1893, the estate was converted into a museum (Дом-Музей Чайковского; ☎ 496-245 8196, 496-245 1050; www.tchaikovsky-house-museum.ru; ul Chaykovskogo 48, Klin; R500, audio guide R150, photography R200; ☉ 10am-5pm Fri-Tue). The house is maintained just as it was when Tchaikovsky lived here. You can peruse photographs and personal effects, but only special guests are allowed to play his grand piano. Occasional concerts are held in the concert hall here.

Suburban trains from Moscow's Leningrad Station run to Klin (R180, one to 1½ hours) throughout the day. Most of these continue to Tver (R150, 45 minutes to one hour). From the station, take *marshrutka* 5 to Tchaikovsky's estate.

Melikhovo Мелихово

'My estate's not much,' wrote playwright Anton Chekhov of his home at Melikhovo, south of Moscow, 'but the surroundings are magnificent'. Chekhov lived here from 1892 until 1899 and wrote some of his most celebrated plays, including *The Seagull* and *Uncle Vanya*. Today, the estate houses the museum (Музей-заповедник А.П. Чехова "Мелихово"; ☎ 8-916-484 7247; www.chekhovmuseum.com; adult/child R200/165; ☉ 10am-5pm Tue-Sun) dedicated to the playwright and his work. Theatre buffs should visit in May, when the museum hosts Melikhovo Spring, a week-long theatre festival.

Suburban trains (R180, 1½ hours) run frequently from Moscow's Kursk Station to Chekhov, 12km west of Melikhovo. Bus 25 makes the 20-minute journey between Chekhov and Melikhovo, with departures just about every hour.

Istra Истра

☎ 498 / POPULATION 35,100

In the 17th century, Nikon – the patriarch whose reforms drove the Old Believers from the Orthodox Church – decided to show one and all that Russia deserved to be the centre of the Christian world. He did this by building a little Holy City right at home, complete with its own Church of the Holy Sepulchre.

◉ Sights

New Jerusalem Monastery MONASTERY (Новоиерусалимский монастырь; www.n-jerusalem.ru; Sovietskaya ul 2; ☉ 10am-6pm Tue-Sun Jun-Aug, to 5pm Sep-May) FREE This grandiose complex was founded in 1656 near the picturesque Istra River (renamed the 'Jordan' by Patriarch Nikon). Unlike other Moscow monasteries, this one had no military use. The centrepiece is the Cathedral of the Resurrection (Воскресенский собор), modelled after Jerusalem's Church of the Holy Sepulchre. After years as a museum, the monastery is now in Orthodox hands and is looking quite spectacular after a recent renovation.

TSARITSYNO PALACE

On a wooded hill in far southeast Moscow, Tsaritsyno Palace (Музей-заповедник Царицыно; ☎ 495-355 4844; www.tsaritsyno-museum.ru; Great Palace & Khlebny Dom adult/student R350/100, all exhibition spaces R800; ☉ grounds 6am-midnight, exhibits 11am-6pm Tue-Fri, to 8pm Sat & Sun; Ⓜ Orekhovo) is a modern-day manifestation of the exotic summer home that Catherine the Great began in 1775, but never finished. For hundreds of years, the palace was little more than a shell, until the Russian government finally decided to finish it in 2007.

Nowadays, the Great Palace is a fantastical building that combines old Russian, Gothic, classical and Arabic styles. Inside, exhibits are dedicated to the history of Tsaritsyno, as well as the life of Catherine the Great. The extensive grounds include some other lovely buildings.

From Orekhovo metro station, walk towards the ponds past an open-air stage, where old folks gather to dance to 1960s tunes in summer, then turn right towards the palace.

New Jerusalem Museum MUSEUM
(Музей Новый Иерусалим; www.museum-new-jerusalem.ru; Novo-Ierusalimsckaya nab 1; exhibits each R200-500, all R650; ⊙10am-6pm Tue-Fri, to 8pm Sat, to 7pm Sun) The huge 'new' New Jerusalem Museum is a modern, state-of-the-art museum, located across the river from the eponymous monastery. Exhibits draw on the hundreds of thousands of items in the monastery collections, including weapons, icons and artwork from the 17th century to modern times. Highlights include personal items belonging to Patriarch Nikon, as well as 20th-century drawings and handicrafts from around the Moscow region.

❶ Getting There & Away

Suburban trains run from Moscow's Rizhsky *vokzal* to Istra (R145, 1½ hours, hourly), from where buses run to the Muzey stop by the New Jerusalem Monastery. The 20-minute walk from Istra train station is a pleasant alternative.

Borodino Бородино

In 1812 Napoleon invaded Russia, lured by the prospect of taking Moscow. For three months the Russians retreated, until on 26 August the two armies met in a bloody battle of attrition at the village of Borodino. In 15 hours, more than one third of each army was killed – over 100,000 soldiers in all. Europe would not again experience fighting as devastating as this until WWI. The French seemed to be the winners, as the Russians withdrew and abandoned Moscow. But Borodino was, in fact, the beginning of the end for Napoleon, who was soon in full, disastrous retreat.

Two hundred years later, the rural site presents a vivid history lesson. Start at the Borodino Museum (Музей-панорама 'Бородинская битва'; www.borodino.ru; adult/student R200/100; ⊙10am-6pm Tue-Sun May-Oct, 9am-5pm Tue-Sun Nov-Apr), which provides a useful overview, then spend the rest of the day exploring the 100-sq-km preserve. If you have your own car, you can see monuments marking the sites of the most ferocious fighting, as well as the headquarters of both the French and Russian armies. If you come by train, you'll probably be limited to the monuments along the road between the train station and the museum (which is many).

The rolling hills around Borodino and Semyonovskoe are largely undeveloped, due to their historic status. Facilities are extremely limited; if you forgot to pack your picnic, there's a small cafe (Арт-Кафе Бородино; mains R400-600) on the museum grounds serving Russian standards.

◉ Sights

Borodino Field HISTORIC SITE
(Бородинское поле; www.borodino.ru; museum & all exhibits R400) The entire battlefield – more than 100 sq km – is now part of the Borodino Field Museum-Preserve, its vast fields dotted with dozens of memorials to specific divisions and generals. The hilltop monument in front of Borodino Museum is Bagration's tomb (Могила Багратиона), the grave of Prince Bagration, a heroic Georgian infantry general who was mortally wounded in battle. The front line was roughly along the 4km road from Borodino train station to the museum: you'll see many monuments close to the road.

Further south, a concentration of monuments around Semyonovskoe marks the battle's most frenzied fighting. Here, Bagration's heroic Second Army, opposing far more numerous French forces, was virtually obliterated. Apparently, Russian commander Mikhail Kutuzov deliberately sacrificed Bagration's army to save his larger First Army, opposing lighter French forces in the northern part of the battlefield. Kutuzov's headquarters are marked by an obelisk in the village of Gorky. Another obelisk near Shevardino to the southwest, paid for in 1912 with French donations, marks Napoleon's camp.

The battle scene was re-created during WWII, when the Red Army confronted the Nazis on this very site. Memorials to this battle also dot the fields, and WWII trenches surround the monument to Bagration. Near the train station are two WWII mass graves.

❶ Getting There & Away

A suburban train leaves from Moscow's Belorussky station to Borodino (R255, 2½ hours) at 7.51am (with additional trains departing at 9.52am and 11.22am on weekends). There are return trains at 3.29pm and 8.22pm. It's a 4km walk from Borodino station through the battlefield to Borodino Museum.

Since the area is rural, visiting by car is more convenient and probably more rewarding. If driving from Moscow, stay on the M1 highway (Minskoe sh) until the Mozhaysk turn-off, 95km beyond the Moscow outer ring road. It's 5km north to Mozhaysk, then 13km west to Borodino village.

Golden Ring

Best Places to Eat

➡ Gostevaya Izba (p154)

➡ Traktir Popov Lug (p152)

➡ Chaynaya (p135)

➡ SupBerry (p149)

➡ Gostiny Dvor (p135)

➡ Restaurant Panorama (p130)

Best Places to Stay

➡ Skvorechnik (p140)

➡ Surikov Guest House (p134)

➡ Ioann Vasilyevich (p146)

➡ Art Hotel (p152)

➡ Volga-Volga (p137)

Why Go?

Touring the Golden Ring, a string of medieval towns northeast of Moscow, is like settling into the comforting arms of Mother Russia: it's a bucolic realm of whitewashed churches with golden onion domes, rippling meadows blanketed with flowers, and samovars bubbling away in colourful gingerbread cottages. In contrast to Moscow's cosmopolitan chaos, these ancient towns are a cultural salve for the Slavic soul: you'll find the spiritual heart of the Orthodox Church here, as well as historic architecture, religious art, traditional cooking and time-honoured handicrafts. Centuries ago this was the power core of eastern Kyivan Rus, but it declined as Moscow took political centre stage. Largely untouched by Soviet industrialisation, it now attracts flocks of Russian tourists searching for a lost idyll.

Wander through medieval monasteries. Cycle the countryside. Unwind in a *banya* (hot bath) after a meal of freshly caught fish and local ale. Whatever you do, grab this Golden Ring for yourself.

When to Go
Vladimir

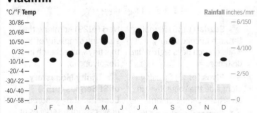

Late Jan The air is crisp, the snow is fleecy and a hot *banya* awaits.

Jun Fields are covered in wild-flowers – Russian nature never looks more beautiful.

Aug Thousands flock to the forests to pick mushrooms and wild berries.

Vladimir   Владимир

☑ 4922 / POP 345,380 / ⊕ MOSCOW

Founded at the dawn of the 12th century on a bluff over the Klyazma River, Vladimir became the cradle of Russian history when Prince Andrei Bogolyubsky moved his capital there from Kyiv in 1169. Thus began Vladimir's Golden Age, when many of the beautifully carved white-stone buildings for which the

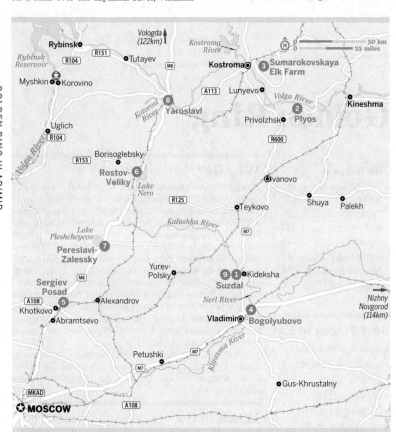

Golden Ring Highlights

① **Suzdal** (p130) Rambling through bucolic beauty while church bells sigh in the distance.

② **Plyos** (p136) Strolling alongside the Volga River in an artist's serene dream.

③ **Sumarokovskaya Elk Farm** (p141) Feeding carrots to elk and tasting their milk at this research farm.

④ **Church of the Intercession on the**

Nerl (p129) Admiring the stunning simplicity of this tiny white church in Bogolyubovo.

⑤ **Trinity Monastery of St Sergius** (p153) Contemplating sonorous prayers during services at Russia's holiest monastery.

⑥ **Rostov-Veliky** (p147) Dipping your toes in Lake Nero before watching the sun set over the pink walls of a 17th-century fortress.

⑦ **Traktir Popov Lug** (p152) Savouring traditional dishes at this farm-to-table tavern outside Pereslavl-Zalessky.

⑧ **Music & Time** (p144) Listening to antique gramophones and a symphony of bells at this Yaroslavl museum.

⑨ **Helio Spa** (p134) Steaming out your travel fatigue at a *banya* in Suzdal.

area is renowned were built by Bogolyubsky and his brother, Prince Vsevolod the Big Nest. After a Mongol invasion devastated the town in 1238, power shifted some 200km west to a minor settlement called Moscow. Though Vladimir eventually rebounded from the ruins, it would never regain its former glory.

Today this bustling city is the administrative centre of Vladimir Oblast. Although not as charmingly bucolic as nearby Suzdal, Vladimir's easy access from Moscow, its centrally located Unesco-listed sights and its stunning river-valley panoramas make it an ideal starting point for a Golden Ring tour.

◉ Sights

A two-hour self-guided walking tour (R350) with an English audio guide and a map of the city centre is available for hire at the small tourist information office (p130).

★ Assumption Cathedral   CHURCH
(Успенский собор; ☑ 4922-325 201; www.vladmuseum.ru; pl Sobornaya; adult/child R100/free; ⊙ visitors 1-4.45pm Tue-Sun) Set dramatically high above the Klyazma River, this simple but majestic piece of pre-Mongol architecture is the legacy of Prince Andrei Bogolyubsky, the man who began shifting power from Kyiv to Northeastern Rus (which eventually evolved into Muscovy). A white-stone version of Kyiv's brick Byzantine churches, the cathedral was constructed from 1158 to 1160, though it was rebuilt and expanded after a fire in 1185. It was added to Unesco's World Heritage List in 1992.

The seat of the Vladimir and Suzdal diocese, the cathedral has held services for its entire history except from 1927 to 1944. The cool, hushed interior is a riot of gold leaf – the baroque iconostasis was constructed with a donation from Catherine the Great. A few restored 12th-century murals of peacocks and prophets can be seen about halfway up the inner wall of the outer north aisle (originally an outside wall); the real treasures, though, are the Last Judgement frescoes by Andrei Rublyov and Daniil Chyorny, painted in 1408 in the central nave and inner south aisle (under the choir gallery toward the western end).

Comply with the standard church dress code (no shorts for men; covered head and long skirts for women) at all times, and be especially mindful of people's sensitivities outside the designated 'tourist time'. Tickets can be purchased at the small kiosk in the courtyard to the right of the cathedral.

★ Old Vladimir Museum   VIEWPOINT, MUSEUM
(Музей 'Старый Владимир'; www.vladmuseum.ru; ul Kozlov t; adult/child R100/free; ⊙ 10am-6pm Mon-Thu, to 8pm Fri-Sun) This red-brick former water tower contains a multistorey exhibit of everyday objects from Vladimir's history (no English signage); the display of old clocks and stopwatches is among the most interesting. But follow the curving staircase all the way up to find the real draw here: the observation deck, which offers magnificent 360-degree views of Vladimir, with the Klyazma River curling lazily off into the distance and gold church domes set against the surrounding blue sky and green fields.

Cathedral of St Dmitry   CHURCH
(Дмитриевский собор; www.vladmuseum.ru; Bolshaya Moskovskaya ul 60; adult/child R100/free; ⊙ 10am-6pm Mon-Thu, to 8pm Fri-Sun May-Sep, 11am-5pm Wed-Mon Oct-Apr) Built between 1193 and 1197, this exquisite, Unesco-listed white-stone cathedral represents the epitome of Russian stone carving. The attraction here is the cathedral's exterior walls, which are covered in an amazing profusion of images. At their top centre, the north, south and west walls all show King David bewitching birds and beasts with music.

Georgievskaya Ulitsa   STREET, VIEWPOINT
This pedestrian-only street curving southwest from the main strip was lovingly recreated in 2015 as a brick-paved thoroughfare from the old days, dotted with souvenir stores, whimsical bronze statues of 19th-century locals and working water pumps; at its far end is the former water tower (p127). It's a lovely place for a stroll – don't miss the broad viewing terraces at the eastern end, which offer stunning views of Assumption Cathedral (p127) (especially gorgeous floodlit at night)

History Museum   MUSEUM
(Исторический музей; ☑ 4922-322 284; Bolshaya Moskovskaya ul 64; adult/child R100/free; ⊙ 11am-6pm Mon-Thu, 10am-7pm Fri-Sun) This museum displays many remains and reproductions of the ornamentation from Vladimir's two cathedrals as part of an extensive exhibition covering the history of the town from Kyivan princes to the 1917 revolution. Particularly interesting are the artefacts upstairs, including a remarkable keyboard-less typewriter from 1905. The red-brick edifice was purpose-built in 1902.

GOLDEN RING VLADIMIR

Crystal, Lacquer Miniatures & Embroidery Museum MUSEUM
(Выставка хрусталя, лаковой миниатюры и вышивки; www.vladmuseum.ru; Dvoryanskaya ul 2; adult/child R100/free; ⊙11am-7pm Sun-Fri, to 9pm Sat) Housed in the former **Old Believers' Trinity Church** (1916), this museum features the crafts of Gus-Khrustalny and other nearby towns. The 1st floor displays a huge variety of crystal pieces (old and new), while upstairs is a collection of embroidered cloth and 19th-century lacquer boxes painted with scenes from Russian history. Keep an eye out for the particular-

ly detailed 10-piece *matryoshka* (nesting doll) that's over a century old. A basement shop has a decent selection of crystal for sale.

Golden Gate HISTORIC BUILDING, MUSEUM
(Золотые ворота; ☑ 4922-322 559; www.vladmuseum.ru; Bolshaya Moskovskaya ul 1; adult/child R100/free; ⊙9am-6pm) In the 1160s Andrei Bogolyubsky built five defensive gates to guard his city; only this former western entrance survives. It was later restored and expanded under Catherine the Great. Up the narrow stone staircase, a **military mu-**

Vladimir

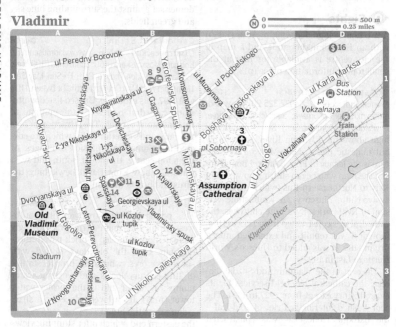

Vladimir

DON'T MISS

THE CHURCH OF PERFECTION

Tourists and pilgrims all flock to Bogolyubovo, just 12km northeast of Vladimir, for this perfect little jewel of a 12th-century church standing amid a flower-covered floodplain.

The **Church of the Intercession on the Nerl** (Церковь Покрова на Нерли; ⊙10am-6pm Tue-Sun) is the gold standard of Russian architecture. Apart from ideal proportions, its beauty lies in a brilliantly chosen waterside location (floods aside) and the sparing use of delicate carving.

Legend has it that Prince Andrei Bogolyubsky had the church built in memory of his favourite son, Izyaslav, who was killed in battle against the Bulgars. As with the **Cathedral of St Dmitry** (p127) in Vladimir, King David sits at the top of three facades, the birds and beasts entranced by his music. The interior has more carvings, including 20 pairs of lions. If the church is closed (from October to April the opening hours are more sporadic), try asking at the house behind.

To reach this famous church, take bus 152 (R20) from the Golden Gate or Sobornaya pl in Vladimir and get off by the massive, blue-domed Bogolyubsky Monastery, which contains remnants of Prince Andrei's palace. Walk past the monastery to Vokzalnaya ul, the first street on the right, and follow it down to the train station. Cross the pedestrian bridge over the railroad tracks and follow the stone path for 1km across the meadow. If driving, take the M7 east out of Vladimir until you get to the monastery, then turn right onto Vokzalnaya and park at the train station.

seum displays weapons and armour from the 1200s through WWII (plus a 1970s cosmonaut suit); the centrepiece is a slightly fusty diorama of Vladimir being ravaged by Mongols in 1238, set to flashing lights and dramatic narration (English version available upon request).

🛏 Sleeping

Vladimir's accommodation scene has expanded greatly in recent years, though given the proximity of the much more idyllic Suzdal, you may prefer to overnight there (unless you need to catch an early morning train to Moscow or Nizhny Novgorod).

Rus HOTEL **$$**
(Русь; ☑4922-322 736; www.rushotel33.ru; ul Gagarina 14; s/d incl breakfast from R3000/3600; ❋🔊) Occupying a large old house on a quiet corner just two blocks from Bolshaya Moskovskaya ul, this hotel offers nicely appointed and comfortable (if rather beige) rooms with extra towels and bathrobes. Reception staff are helpful and speak some English. Breakfast is included.

Nice Hostel HOSTEL **$**
(Найс Хостел; ☑4922-421 231, 8-902-888 5004; www.nicehostel33.ru; Manezhney t 1; dm/d from R510/1500; 🔊) This brand-new hostel won't win any design awards, but it's spotless and offers a free breakfast in the common kitchen. Dorm rooms (male-only, female-only and

mixed) have four, six or eight beds; five doubles are available (three with private bathrooms), as well as a four-bed family room (R2600). There's a washing machine and iron for guest use.

Voznesenskaya Sloboda HOTEL **$$$**
(Вознесенская слобода; ☑4922-325 494; www.vsloboda.ru; ul Voznesenskaya 14b; d R4800; 🅿❋🔊) Perched on a bluff with tremendous views of the valley, this hotel has one of the most scenic locations in the area. Outside is a quiet neighbourhood of old wooden cottages and villas dominated by the elegant Ascension Church, whose bells chime idyllically throughout the day. The new building's interior is tastefully designed to resemble art nouveau style c 1900.

🍴 Eating & Drinking

Salmon & Coffee INTERNATIONAL **$$**
(Лосось и кофе; www.losos-coffee.ru; Bolshaya Moskovskaya ul 19a; mains R340-790; ⊙11am-1am Sun-Thu, to 8am Fri & Sat; 🔊) Salmon is yet to be found in the Klyazma, and coffee is not exactly what medieval princes had for breakfast. But instead of hinting at the city's past, this DJ cafe serving Asian and European dishes aims for a cosmopolitan touch in an ancient town. Lots of dark wood, dim lights and magenta-coloured metal railings create a cool, intriguing atmosphere.

Piteyny Dom
Kuptsa Andreyeva
RUSSIAN $$

(Питейный дом Купца Андреева; ☑ 4922-326 545; www.andreevbeer.com/dom; Bolshaya Moskovskaya ul 16; mains R350-685; ⊙ 11am-midnight Sun-Wed, to 2am Thu-Sat; ☎) Merchant Andreyev's Liquor House, as the name translates, makes a half-hearted attempt to pass off as an old-world Russian *kabak* (pub), but its main virtues are the home-brewed beers on tap and hearty Russian meals, including all the classics – from *shchi* (cabbage soup) to bliny. Service can be slow, but the beer helps to make the time fly faster.

★ Restaurant Panorama
RUSSIAN $$$

(Ресторан Панорама; ☑ 4922-464 746; Bolshaya Moskovskaya ul 44b; mains R380-1260; ⊙ noon-midnight Sun-Thu, to 2am Fri & Sat) This upscale restaurant, hidden down a lane off the main street, offers perhaps the fanciest meal in town, with attentive service, an elegant atmosphere and – true to its name – great views over the river valley from your table. The menu features the usual salads, pasta and meat dishes, including a rabbit confit the restaurant insists is worth the wait.

★ Four Brewers Pub
CRAFT BEER

(Паб Четыре Пивовара; www.4brewers.ru; Bolshaya Moskovskaya ul 12; ⊙ 2pm-midnight Sun-Thu, to 2am Fri & Sat) This pocket-sized pub offers 20 brews on tap and dozens more in bottles – porter, IPA, stout, ale, you name it – all from the brewers' own vats or other Russian microbreweries, with such unforgettable names as 'Banana Kraken', 'Santa Muerte', 'Roksana and the Endless Universe' and (our personal favourite) 'Black Jesus, White Pepper'. Bartenders happily offer recommendations and free tastes.

Kofein
CAFE, COFFEE

(Кофеин; Gagarina ul 1; ⊙ 8.30am-11pm Sun-Thu, to midnight Fri & Sat; ☎) This smart cafe in the town centre offers a variety of delicious desserts and espresso-based coffees (as well as a full food menu). Vegans, rejoice – there's soy milk, too. Free wi-fi.

❶ Information

Russian Agricultural Bank (Россельхозбанк; Bolshaya Moskovskaya ul; ⊙ 9.30am-5.30pm Mon-Fri, ATM 24hr)

Sberbank (Сбербанк; Bolshaya Moskovskaya ul 27; ⊙ 9am-7pm Mon-Fri, to 5pm Sat, ATM 24hr) Has exchange facilities.

Post Office (ul Podbelskogo 2; ⊙ 8am-10pm) Also has an ATM.

Vladimir Tourist Information (☑ 4922-377 000; www.invladimir.ru/en; Sobornaya pl; ⊙ 10am-6pm Tue-Sun) Located in a small house on the western side of Sobornaya pl.

Vladimir Region Tourist Information (www.tourism33.ru)

❶ Getting There & Away

Vladimir is on the main trans-Siberian line between Moscow and Nizhny Novgorod and on a major highway leading to Kazan.

BUS

The bus is a poor option from Moscow or Nizhny Novgorod – the train is much faster and more reliable. Conveniently for those heading on to Suzdal, the bus station (автовокзал; Vokzalnaya pl) is right across from Vladimir's **train station**.

Buses run to Suzdal (R95, 45 minutes, several times per hour) and Yaroslavl (R610 to R699, five hours, 7.15am and 4.30pm).

TAXI

A one-way **taxi** (☑ 4922-555 555) to Suzdal costs approximately R600 (or download the Gett app from www.gett.com to order from your smartphone).

TRAIN

There are nine services a day from Moscow's Kursk Station (Kursky vokzal), with modern Strizh and slightly less comfortable Lastochka trains (R600 to R1600, 1¾ hours). Both of these continue to Nizhny Novgorod (Strizh R1000 to R1750, Lastochka R800, two hours).

All long-distance trains heading towards Tatarstan and Siberia also call at Vladimir.

❶ Getting Around

Trolleybus 5 from the train and bus stations runs along Bolshaya Moskovskaya ul.

Suzdal   Суздаль

☑ 49231 / POPULATION 10,535 / ⊙ MOSCOW

The sparkling diamond in the Golden Ring is undoubtedly Suzdal – if you have time for only one of these towns, this is the one to see. With rolling green fields carpeted with dandelions, a gentle river curling lazily through a historic town centre, sunlight bouncing off golden church domes and the sound of horse clops and church bells carrying softly through the air, you may feel like you've stumbled into a storybook Russia.

Suzdal served as a royal capital when Moscow was still a cluster of cowsheds, and was a major monastic centre and an important commercial hub for many years as well. But in 1864, local merchants failed to get the Trans-Siberian Railway built through here (it went to Vladimir instead). Suzdal was thus bypassed both by trains and 20th-century progress, preserving its idyllic character for future visitors.

◉ Sights

★**Saviour Monastery of St Euthymius** MONASTERY
(Спасо-Евфимиев монастырь; ☑ 49231-20 746; ul Lenina; adult/child R400/free; ⊙ 10am-7pm Sun-Thu, to 9pm Fri & Sat) Founded in the 14th century to protect the town's northern entrance, Suzdal's biggest monastery grew mighty in the 16th and 17th centuries after Vasily III, Ivan the Terrible and the noble Pozharsky family funded impressive new stone buildings and made large land and property acquisitions. It was girded with its great brick walls and towers in the 17th century.

Right at the entrance, the **Annunciation Gate Church** (Благовещенская надвратная церковь) houses an interesting exhibit on Dmitry Pozharsky (1578–1642), leader of the Russian army that drove the Polish invaders from Moscow in 1612.

A tall 16th- to 17th-century cathedral **bell tower** (Звонница) stands before the seven-domed **Cathedral of the Transfiguration of the Saviour** (Спасо-Преображенский собор); every hour on the hour from 11am to 5pm a short concert of chimes is played on its bells. The cathedral was built in the 1590s in 12th- to 13th-century Vladimir–Suzdal style. Inside, restoration has uncovered some bright 1689 frescoes by the school of Gury Nikitin from Kostroma. The tomb of Prince Dmitry Pozharsky is by the cathedral's east wall.

The 1525 **Assumption Refectory Church** (Успенская церковь), facing the bell tower, adjoins the old **Father Superior's chambers** (Палаты отца-игумена), which house a display of Russian icons and an excellent naive-art exhibition showcasing works by local amateur painters from the Soviet era.

The old **Monastery Dungeon** (Монастырская тюрьма), set up in 1764 for religious dissidents, is at the north end of the complex. It now houses a fascinating exhibit on the monastery's prison history, including displays of some of the better-known prisoners who stayed here. The Bolsheviks used

the monastery as a concentration camp after the 1917 revolution. During WWII, German and Italian officers captured in the Battle of Stalingrad were kept here.

To the northeast of the main cathedral group, the combined **Hospital Chambers & St Nicholas Church** (Больничные кельи и Никольская церковь) feature a rich collection of gold church treasures.

★**Kremlin** FORTRESS
(Кремль; ☑ 49231-21 624; www.vladmuseum.ru; ul Kremlyovskaya; joint ticket adult/child R350/free; ⊙ exhibitions 9am-6pm Sun-Thu, to 9pm Fri & Sat, grounds to 9pm) The grandfather of the Moscow Kremlin, this citadel was the 12th-century base of Prince Yury Dolgoruky, who ruled the vast northeastern part of Kyivan Rus (and, among other things, founded a small outpost that would eventually become the Russian capital). The 1.4km-long earthen ramparts of Suzdal's kremlin enclose a few streets of houses and a handful of churches, as well as the main cathedral group on Kremlyovskaya ul.

The Unesco-listed **Nativity of the Virgin Cathedral** (Церковь Казанской иконы Божьей Матери; adult/child R100/free; ⊙ 9am-7pm Sun-Thu, to 9pm Fri & Sat), its deep blue domes spangled with gold stars, was built in 1225 (only its richly carved lower section is original white stone, though, the rest being 16th-century brick). The inside is sumptuous, with 13th- and 17th-century frescoes and 13th-century damascene (gold on copper) west and south doors.

Within the kremlin, the **Archbishop's Chambers** (Архиерейские палаты) house the **Suzdal History Exhibition**, which includes the original 13th-century door from the cathedral, photos of its interior and a visit to the 18th-century **Cross Hall** (Крестовая палата), which was used for receptions. The tent-roofed 1635 kremlin **bell tower** (Звонница), directly across the yard from the cathedral, contains additional exhibits, including the 17th-century **Jordan Canopy** (Иорданская сень), the only one of its kind left in Russia; every January on Epiphany Day, this 28m-tall painted wooden structure would be placed over a cross-shaped hole in the ice on the Kamenka for the annual rite of blessing the river water.

To the southwest, between the cathedral and the river, is the 1766 **Nikolskaya Wooden Church** (Никольская деревянная церковь), which was moved to Suzdal from a nearby village in 1960. (Other rural wooden

Suzdal

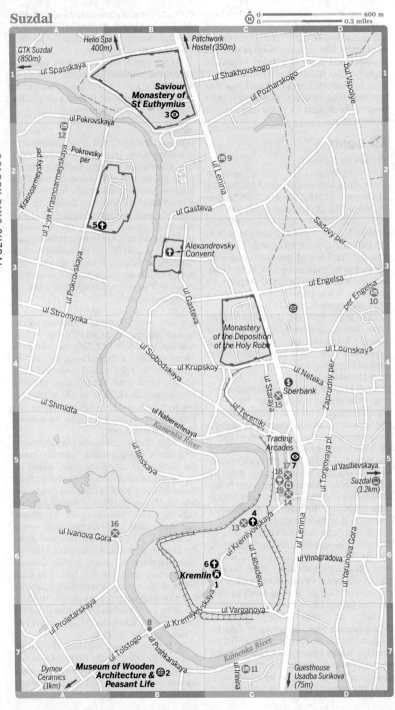

GOLDEN RING SUZDAL

N 0 ——————— 400 m
0 ——————— 0.2 miles

GTK Suzdal
(850m)

Helio Spa
400m

Patchwork
Hostel (350m)

ul Spasskaya

ul Shakhovskogo

ul Pozharskogo

bul Vspolye

**Saviour
Monastery of
St Euthymius**
3

ul Pokrovskaya

12

9

Pokrovsky
per

ul Lenina

Sadovy per

Krasnoarmeysky per

ul 1-ya Krasnoarmeyskaya

ul Gasteva

5

**Alexandrovsky
Convent**

ul Engelsa

per Engelsa

10

ul Pokrovskaya

ul Stromynka

ul Gasteva

**Monastery
of the Deposition
of the Holy Robe**

ul Lounskaya

ul Slobodskaya

ul Krupskoy

ul Neteka

ul Shmidta

ul Naberezhnaya

ul Teremki

ul Staraya

Sberbank

15

Zaprudny per

Kamenka River

ul Ilinskaya

**Trading
Arcades**

7

ul Vasilievskaya

Suzdal
(1.2km)

18

19

14

ul Torgovaya pl

16

ul Ivanova Gora

13

4

ul Kremlyovskaya

ul Lenina

6

Kremlin

1

ul Lebedeva

ul Vinogradova

ul Yarunova Gora

ul Proletarskaya

ul Varganova

8

ul Kremlyovskaya

ul Tolstogo

ul Pushkarskaya

Kamenka River

Dymov
Ceramics
(1km)

**Museum of Wooden
Architecture &
Peasant Life**
2

ul Trinina

11

Guesthouse
Usadba Surikova
(75m)

Suzdal

buildings were subsequently moved for preservation to the excellent Museum of Wooden Architecture & Peasant Life, across the river.)

If you don't want to see all of the exhibitions, you can pay for admission to the cathedral separately; to walk around the grounds only costs R50 (children get in free).

★ **Museum of Wooden**
Architecture & Peasant Life MUSEUM
(Музей деревянного зодчества и крестьянского быта; www.vladmuseum.ru; ul Pushkarskaya; adult/child R300/free; ⊙9am-7pm Sun-Thu, to 9pm Fri & Sat; 🚻) This open-air museum across the river from Suzdal's kremlin offers a fascinating glimpse into the traditional lives of rural folk in this area. Besides log houses, windmills, a barn, and lots of tools and handicrafts, its highlights are the 1756 Transfiguration Church

(Преображенская церковь) and the simpler 1776 Resurrection Church (Воскресенская церковь). There's a similar museum in Kostroma (p139), too.

A number of local artisans sell traditional crafts at a row of stalls set up on the left side of the site. They include Maria Frolova (Мария Фролова; ☎8-920-936 3063; www.frolmaster-nn.ru), whose beautiful pieces of filigree embroidery make lovely, unique gifts.

Church of the Assumption
of the Mother of God CHURCH
(Храм успения божией матери; ul Kremlyovskaya 8; ⊙8am-8pm) This small red church up the street from the kremlin (p131) features a beautiful icon of the Virgin Mary created by 16th-century artist Fyodor Zubov, as well as a large gold-and-glass coffin containing the relics of St Arseny (1550–1625), the Archbishop of Suzdal.

Holy Intercession Convent CONVENT
(Свято-Покровский монастырь; www.spokrovmon.ru; Pokrovskaya ul; ⊙7am-7pm) 🆓 It's a classic Suzdal picture: the whitewashed beauty of monastic walls surrounded by green meadows on the banks of the lazily meandering river. Inside are beds of brightly coloured flowers tended by the nuns, who live in wooden cottages left over from a rustic hotel built here when the convent was closed after the revolution (it was revived in 1992). Founded in 1364, this convent was originally a place of exile for the unwanted wives of tsars.

Torgovaya Ploshchad SQUARE
(Торговая Площадь) Suzdal's Torgovaya pl (Market Sq) is dominated by the pillared Trading Arcades (Торговые ряды; 1806–11) along its western side. There are several churches in the immediate vicinity, including the 1739 Kazan Church (Казанская церковь) and the 1720 Resurrection Church (Воскресенская церковь) right on the square; the latter's hours are irregular but if it's open you can take the precarious climb to the top of the bell tower to be rewarded with wonderful views of Suzdal's gold-domed skyline.

Across ul Lenina, the five-domed 1707 Tsar Constantine Church (Цареконстантиновская церковь) in the square's northeastern corner is a working church with an ornate interior; next door is the 1750 Church of Our Lady of Sorrows (Скорбященская церковь).

GOLDEN RING SUZDAL

🏃 Activities

The gentle hills and attractive countryside around Suzdal are ideal for cycling, with bicycles available for rent at many hotels, including **GTK Suzdal** (ГТК Суздаль; ☑ 49231-23 380, 49231-20 908; www.gtksuzdal.ru; ul Korovniki 45; ⊙ 10am-6pm). **Gnezdo Pekarya** (Гнездо пекаря), a small bakery on the river side of the **Trading Arcades**, also has a stand of bikes outside the shop with a price list in English.

Helio Spa   BATHHOUSE

(☑ 49231-23 939; www.suzdal.heliopark.ru; ul Korovniki 14) Cleanse body and soul with a visit to a Russian *banya*. Beautiful lakeside *bani* can be rented at Helio Park Hotel for R1600/1800 per hour on weekdays/weekends (minimum two hours) for up to six to eight people; attendant services, such as a gentle thrashing with *veniki* (birch branches), are available at extra cost. Advance booking is necessary.

Boat Trips   CRUISE

(☑ 8-916-423 2541; ul Pushkarskaya, at ul Tostogo; adult/child R350/free; ⊙ hourly noon-7pm) Once an hour a boat takes tourists on a 40-minute cruise up and down the Kamenka River, leaving from the bridge by the Museum of Wooden Architecture. It's a good chance to look at and take pictures of Suzdal's many monasteries and churches from a different perspective. Call to enquire about evening charters. Children under 10 ride for free.

Dymov Ceramics   ART

(Дымов керамика; ☑ 8-980-752 3555, 495-500 0173; www.dymovceramic.ru/en; Solnechnaya ul 7, Ivanovskoye; 👪) Traditional crafts are particularly popular in the Suzdal area; this well-regarded ceramics studio in a Suzdal suburb offers you a chance to take home your own creation, with one-hour classes in pottery and tile-making for kids and adults. See the website for pricing and details. Pressed for time? You can buy a piece from Dymov's **shop** (Дымов керамика; ☑ 49231-21 190; www.dymovceramic.ru/en; Trading Arcades, Torgovaya pl; ⊙ 10am-7pm).

🛏 Sleeping

Suzdal is a popular destination for both domestic and international tourists, which means there are plenty of accommodation choices around town, from vast holiday resorts to quaint two- or three-room guesthouses. You can save some money if you avoid staying over at weekends and holidays.

Patchwork Hostel   HOSTEL $

(☑ 8-930-831 3958; www.vk.com/hostel_patchwork; ul Gogolya 59; dm incl breakfast R600-700; 🅿🛜) With just two dorm rooms (a six-bed mixed and a four-bed women-only), this new hostel is pocket-sized but spotless, and a short walk from the St Euthymius Monastery. Thoughtful touches include free tea and coffee in the common room and USB charging ports at each bed. The staff speak excellent English, too. Bikes are available for rent.

★ Petrov Dom   GUESTHOUSE $$

(Петров дом; ☑ 8-919-025 6884; www.petrovdom.ru; per Engelsa 18; r from R2000; 🅿🛜) Vlad and Lena offer three nicely furnished rooms in their wooden dacha-style house with a lovely garden on a quiet side street. It's a great option for travellers with children. A sumptuous breakfast costs just R200; self-caterers can use the kitchen and garden grill. There's also a private *banya* built by Vlad himself, available for guest rental.

Note that per Engelsa is the street just south of ul Engelsa. There's no sign on the house; just look for the very large sun symbol on the front gates.

★ Surikov Guest House   GUESTHOUSE $$

(Гостевой дом Суриковых; ☑ 8-915-752 4950, 49231-21 568; ul Krasnoarmeyskaya 53; d incl breakfast R2500; 🅿🛜) This 11-room boutique guesthouse is positioned at a particularly picturesque bend of the Kamenka River across from the walls of the St Euthymius Monastery. It has modestly sized but comfortable rooms equipped with rustic-style furniture (some made by the owner himself) and a Russian restaurant (for guests only) on the 1st floor. Visitors rave about this place.

Guesthouse Usadba Surikova   B&B $$

(Гостиница Усадьба Сурикова; ☑ 8-920-910 7477; ul Lenina 35; r incl breakfast R2500; 🅿❄🛜🏊) This little B&B a few minutes' walk south of the kremlin is neat as a pin and cute as a button. Attentive host Alexander provides a filling, homemade breakfast each morning (including delicious Russian pancakes). Comfortable, spacious rooms come with mini-fridges.

Pushkarskaya Sloboda   RESORT $$$

(Пушкарская слобода; ☑ 49231-23 303; www.pushkarka.ru; ul Lenina 45; d from R4950; 🅿❄🛜🏊) This attractive riverside holiday village has everything you might want for a Russian idyll, including accommodation options in traditionally styled log cabins (from R7900). It has three restaurants (including a rustic country tavern and a formal dining room) and a spa centre with pool. The staff can also arrange all sorts of tours and classes around Suzdal.

Nikolayevsky Posad   RESORT $$$

(Николаевский посад; ☑ 49231-23 585; www.nposad.ru; ul Lenina 138; s/d from R4250/5500; P ✳ 🗣 ⚑) This large, manicured resort near the St Euthymius Monastery has comfortable, contemporary rooms and suites (as well as four- to eight-bed dorms, R1300) in two-storey buildings styled as old mansion houses. There's a nice restaurant and a 'hangover' cafe, plus a 25m pool, fitness centre, spa and children's play area. Bicycles are available for rent, too.

🍴 Eating & Drinking

Most of the good eating options are along ul Lenina and in the Trading Arcades on Torgovaya pl. The larger hotels also have restaurants.

★ Chaynaya   RUSSIAN $

(Чайная; www.tea-suzdal.ru; ul Kremlyovskaya 10g; mains R130-450; ☺ 10am-9pm) It's hidden behind a kitsch crafts market, but this place is a gem. Russian standards – bliny, *shchi*, mushroom dishes and pickles – are prominently represented, but it's all the unusual (and rather experimental) items on the menu that make Chaynaya so special. Red-buckwheat pancakes, anyone?

★ Gostiny Dvor   RUSSIAN $$

(Гостиный дворъ; ☑ 49231-021 190; www.suzdal-dvor.ru; Trading Arcades, Torgovaya pl; mains R450-550; ☺ 10am-10pm Mon-Thu, 9am-11pm Fri-Sun; 🗣 🍴) There are so many things to like about this place: eclectic decor of rustic antiques and warm wood; outside terrace tables offering river views; hearty Russian dishes (chicken, pike, *pelmeni* dumplings) prepared with modern flair; and friendly, attentive service, to start. Finish up with a tasting set of house-made *medovukha* (honey ale) while the kids amuse themselves in the playroom.

Salmon & Coffee   INTERNATIONAL $$

(Лосось и кофе; www.losos-coffee.ru; Trading Arcades, Torgovaya pl; mains R340-590; ☺ noon-11pm Mon-Thu, to midnight Fri, 11am-2am Sat, 11am-11pm Sun; 🗣) With its whitewashed wood interior and rustic-style decor, this rather quaint cafe on Torgovaya pl is one of the best places in town for an unhurried lunch or a cup of coffee. Despite the name, salmon is not really prominent on the menu, which includes inventive fusion European dishes and sushi.

Kharchevnya   RUSSIAN $$

(Харчевня; ☑ 49231-20 722; ul Lenina 73; R320-450; ☺ 9am-11pm) It's perhaps the most unassuming and unpretentious cafe in Suzdal, but it's also the best. The long menu covers all traditional Russian staples from *shchi* to bliny pancakes. Service is fast and friendly. The location is convenient for most attractions and hotels.

Kvasnaya Izba   RUSSIAN $$

(☑ 8-915-779 0577; www.kvasnaya-izba.ru; ul Pushkarskaya 51; meals R350-550; ☺ 10am-9pm; 🗣) This restaurant is slightly out of the way, but it's worth a bit of a walk if you'd like to sample all kinds of *kvas* – Russia's traditional drink made of fermented rye bread. Flavours on offer include apple, thyme and blackcurrant. You might just want some liquid refreshment, but the *kvas* goes equally well with the hearty Russian meals here.

Graf Suvorov & Mead-Tasting Hall   BEER HALL

(Граф Суворов и зал дегустаций; ☑ 8-905-734 5404, 49231-20 803; Trading Arcades, Torgovaya pl; tasting menu R300-500; ☺ 10am-6pm Mon-Fri, to 8pm Sat & Sun) Sit beneath vaulted ceilings and contemplate kitsch murals of Russian military hero Count Suvorov's exploits in the Alps as you make your way through a tasting set (10 samples) of the few dozen varieties of locally produced *medovukha*, a mildly alcoholic honey ale. Flavours also include berry and herb infusions. Located on the back (river) side of the Trading Arcades.

ℹ Information

Sberbank (Сбербанк; ul Lenina 73a; ☺ 8am-4.30pm Mon-Fri) Exchange office and ATM.

Post Office (Krasnaya pl 3; ☺ 8am-8pm Mon-Fri, to 6pm Sat, 9am-2pm Sun)

ℹ Getting There & Away

The **bus station** (Автовокзал; ☑ 49231-020 147; Vasilievskaya ul 44; ☺ 4.30am-8pm) is 2km east of the centre on Vasilievskaya ul. Some long-distance buses pass the central square on the way.

There is no bus service to Suzdal from Moscow; you'll need to take a train to Vladimir and then switch to a Suzdal-bound bus there. Buses run very regularly throughout the day to and from Vladimir (R95, 45 minutes).

For Plyos, take a bus to Ivanovo (R150, 1½ hours, hourly 8am to 7.30pm) and change there for service to Plyos (R173, two hours, 10 daily).

Plyos
Плёс

☑ 49339 / POP 2196 / ⊘ MOSCOW

One of the smallest Golden Ring destinations at just 3 sq km, Plyos is a tranquil town of old wooden houses and hilly streets winding down to the Volga, located halfway between Ivanovo and Kostroma. An early settlement here was destroyed by Mongols in 1238; Plyos was founded and fortified in 1410 by Prince Vasily I.

The town's historical renown stems from an artists' retreat in the late 19th century: Isaac Levitan, Russia's most celebrated landscape artist, painted its serenity when he lived here. More recent infamy is thanks to Milovka, Prime Minister Dmitry Medvedev's multibillion-rouble, 80-hectare country estate that anti-corruption activists say has a murky money trail. In 2016, politician and Putin opponent Alexey Navalny published a drone video that soars high above the property's 6m fence, showing the 19th-century manor buildings, guesthouses, staff hotel, private ski run, three helipads and a multi-tiered pool.

◉ Sights & Activities

The river embankment (Sovetskaya ul) is dotted with former mansions and other beautiful buildings that make for a lovely architecture walk, including the 1907 Novozhilova House – the only building in Plyos built in Style Moderne (Russia's take on art nouveau) – which once hosted visiting British royals Prince and Princess Michael of Kent, and the hillside, pistachio-green House of Seven Windows, with its front garden and wrought-iron fence.

Various sculptures are also placed alongside the river, including a cat, a picture frame overlooking the water and a woman in 19th-century dress.

Resurrection Hill
VIEWPOINT

(Воскресенская гора; ul Karla Marksa) For a bird's-eye view over Plyos, head up the hill from Torgovaya pl to the wooden stairs on the right. Climb to the top (there's a handy resting bench halfway up) and follow the path to the right, where you'll see a war memorial. A few steps beyond that is the (unfenced!) edge of the bluff, where you can look down over the Church of the Resurrection, the Volga and the villages on the other side.

Levitan House Museum
MUSEUM

(Дом-музей Левитана; ☑ 49339-43 478; www.ples-museum.ru; ul Lunachskogo 4; adult/child R120/60; ⊘ 10am-2pm & 3-5pm Tue-Sun) Art by famed Russian painter Isaac Levitan is displayed in the riverside house where he and painters Alexey Stepanov and Sofia Kuvshinnikova lived for three summers, from 1888 to 1890. Levitan produced some 200 works in Plyos, including some of his best. Various personal belongings, as well as paintings by Stepanov and Kuvshinnikova, are also on display. Outside across the street is a bust of the man himself.

Landscape Museum
MUSEUM

(Музей пейзажа; ☑ 8-930-347 6771; www.ples-museum.ru; ul Lunacharskogo 20; adult/student R80/40; ⊘ 10am-6pm Tue-Sun summer, to 5pm winter) The Plyos landscape has inspired many painters to capture it; many such works from the mid-19th to early-20th centuries hang in this museum, housed in a former mansion at the far eastern end of the embankment. Nearby is a bronze sculpture of a 19th-century woman looking out at the world through the empty frame of an easel.

Church of St Barbara
CHURCH

(Церковь Святой Варвары; Varvarinskaya ul) On a hillside with a commanding view of the Volga is this working church built in 1821 and restored to its former glory in the 1980s. Painter Isaac Levitan portrayed it in his masterwork *Evening: Golden Plyos* (1889), which hangs in the Tretyakov Gallery (p63) in Moscow.

Torgovaya Ploschad
SQUARE

(Торговая площадь) The oldest part of town is along the river, as evidenced by the ramparts of the old fort, which dates from 1410. Central Torgovaya pl (Market Sq) has long been the town's mercantile heart, with rows of trading stalls for commercial activity coming along the Volga (although these days they're much quieter). One of the town's oldest streets, tiny ul Kalashnaya (⊘ 10am-7pm), has been converted into two rows of stalls selling the usual souvenirs (*matryoshki* nesting dolls, woodcarvings, magnets etc).

Rising high above the square is the gorgeously refurbished Church of the Resurrection (Воскресенская Церковь; ul Lenina 2; ⊘ 9am-6pm). Walk south up Proyezdnoy per (away from the river) and follow the road around to the left for about 550m to get to the tent-roofed Assumption Cathedral (Успенский собор; 1699), one of artist Isaac Levitan's favourite painting subjects.

Boat Rides
CRUISE

(🚣 8-910-995 3208; Sovetskaya ul 43; adult/child R300/150, child under 7 free; ⏰ 11am-5pm) Cruises up and down the Volga, lasting approximately 45 to 50 minutes, can be taken from the 'Dana' berth on the embankment. The boat leaves every hour on the hour from 11am to 5pm. Commentary is in Russian.

🛏 Sleeping

Since Prime Minister Dmitry Medvedev made Plyos his favourite holiday spot, VIP holiday homes have sprung up around the tiny town – and greatly inflated the prices for other accommodation. Less expensive homestay options are available; check www.plyos.info for more information.

★ Volga-Volga
GUESTHOUSE $$$

(Волга-Волга; 📞 8-910-999 8822; www.volga-ples.ru; ul Spusk Gory Svobody 12b; s/d incl breakfast from R4000/4500; 🅿 📶) A large wooden building resembling a traditional Russian gingerbread cottage and perched on the slope of a deep ravine leading to the Volga, with individually themed rooms and a relaxed dacha (summer country house) atmosphere. Relax with a cup of tea by the beautifully tiled fireplace in the lounge. There's a *banya*, too.

Chastny Visit
GUESTHOUSE $$$

(Частный визит; 📞 8-920-343 2998, 8-901-191 9819; www.pless.ru; ul Gornaya Sloboda 7; d/ste from R9000/12,000; 🅿 ❄ 📶 📶 📶) Occupying a prime spot on the edge of a spectacular Volga-facing bluff, this sweet wooden cottage with country-style rooms filled with antiques – some with fantastic views – is run by a French–Russian couple. Prices, however, may damage your idyll. Breakfast is included and dinner is available at the (rather expensive) restaurant on the premises.

🍴 Eating & Drinking

Cast Iron Pot Restaurant
RUSSIAN $$

(Ресторан Чугунок; 📞 493-293 9812; Sovetskaya ul 35; mains R250-450; ⏰ noon-11pm Mon-Thu, to midnight Fri, 11am-midnight Sat, to 11pm Sun) Meat is on the menu at this little place in a red-brick house with large wooden shutters on the embankment – the restaurant specialises in steaks and grilled skewers (especially of lamb or veal). The friendly waiters are dressed in faux-traditional shirts, which lends the cafe's set-up some atmosphere. Save room for the apple strudel.

Dachnik
RUSSIAN $$

(Дачник; 📞 49339-432 07; Sovetskaya ul 39; mains R200-390; ⏰ 10am-10pm) A small place in a prime spot on the embankment that serves well-cooked traditional Russian food. The menu isn't large but it has some interesting choices, including local smoked bream and Uzbek pilaf with beef, as well as a few salads. For riverside dining, ask for seats in the restaurant's veranda across the road.

★ Plyos Beer House
BREWERY

(Плёсский Пивной Дом; 📞 8-920-673 1265; ul Yuryevskaya 4; ⏰ 11am-11pm; 📶) Marvel at the giant tree in the middle of the upstairs bar and snag the corner table for views of the Church of the Resurrection and the Volga – especially compelling at sunset. The brewery offers its own beers on tap, along with tasting flights of regional berry or herbal vodka 'infusions'. The menu features local game such as elk steak.

ℹ Information

There's a freestanding ATM kiosk (⏰ 24hr) on Sovetskaya ul, just down from the main square.
www.ples.ru Official city web portal.
www.plios.ru Has information on many of the town's classic buildings, as well as a self-guided walking tour.

ℹ Getting There & Away

Plyos is a 20km detour northeast from Privolzhsk on the main Golden Ring route; its remoteness and hilly topography make it best visited with your own wheels.

The **bus stop** (автостанция; 📞 info 49339-43 350; ul Gornaya Sloboda 33) is at the top of the hill heading into town. Travelling to/from Suzdal, change to a Plyos-bound bus at Ivanovo (R173, two hours, 10 daily). Heading from Plyos to Kostroma, take a taxi or catch the returning Ivanovo bus to Privolzhsk (30 minutes), where you can hop on one of the hourly transit buses plying the route between Ivanovo and Kostroma.

Kostroma
Кострома

📞 4942 / POPULATION 268,742 / ⏰ MOSCOW

The Volga flows lazily past the 18th-century neoclassical architecture of this modest-sized city, the northernmost on the Golden Ring circuit and one that played a crucial role in the advent of the Romanov dynasty that ruled Russia for over 300 years. Founded by Yury Dolgoruky in 1152, Kostroma developed as an important regional market town thanks to its location on the river; its former commercial glory is evidenced by the enormous Trading Arcades on Susaninskaya pl, the equally huge main square.

Its major sight, the Monastery of St Ipaty (p139), is across the Kostroma River to the west. A number of museums can be found in

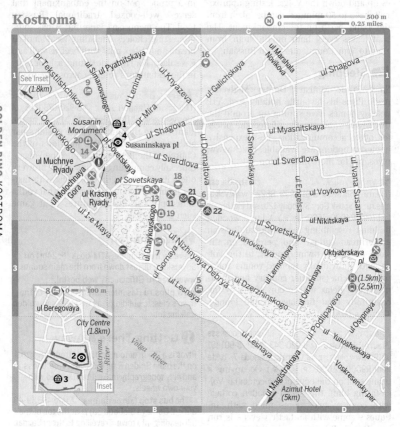

Kostroma

the area around Susaninskaya pl, the parks south of which are perfect for a riverside ramble. If you have an extra day, take a trip out to the countryside to see one of Russia's few elk farms (p141).

◎ Sights

Monastery of St Ipaty
MONASTERY

(Ипатьевский монастырь; ☑4942-312 589; www.ipatievsky-monastery.ru; Russian/foreigner R50/150, photography R100; ◎9am-5.30pm) Named after St Ipaty (Hypatios) of Gangara, this monastery at the confluence of the Volga and Kostroma Rivers was founded in the 1330s by Chet, a Tatar prince who converted to Christianity. In 1590 his descendant, Tsar Boris Godunov, built its Trinity Cathedral (Троицкий собор), which contains more than 80 old frescoes by a school of 17th-century Kostroma painters, as well as some 20th-century additions. (The fresco in the southern part of the sanctuary depicts Chet's baptism by St Ipaty.)

In 1613 the 17-year-old Mikhail Romanov, who had spent over a decade in exile as a political rival to the Godunovs, was living in the monastery when he was informed that he had been chosen to be Russia's next tsar. All successive Romanov tsars thus came here to visit the monastery's red-painted Romanov Chambers (Палаты бояр Романовых), located opposite the cathedral, which today contain a rather dull historic exhibition.

Much more interesting is the Refectory (Трапезная), which displays church treasures and old icons over two floors, as well as film footage of the last of the Romanovs, Tsar Nicholas II and his family, visiting Kostroma in 1913 for the big 300-year jubilee of their house. (The 400-year jubilee in 2013 turned out to be a fairly low-key event.) In a bizarre coincidence, the Romanov dynasty began in the Monastery of St Ipaty and met its end at Ipatyev House, the residence in Yekaterinburg where the family was executed in 1918.

The monastery is 2.5km west of the town centre. Take bus 14 from Susaninskaya pl and get off at the first stop across the river; it's a 650m walk southeast from there.

Museum of Wooden Architecture
MUSEUM

(Музей деревянного зодчества; ☑4942-373 872; www.kostrsloboda.ru; ul Prosveshcheniya 1b; adult/child R150/free; ◎10am-7pm May-Sep, 9am-5pm Oct-Apr) Essentially a large riverside park, this open-air museum comprises a large collection of old, rural wooden buildings moved here for preservation, including peasant families' houses, cleverly engineered windmills and churches – many built without nails. Some buildings display various artefacts of rural life, and the grounds (which are open an hour later than the exhibits) are pleasant for strolling, listening to the chirping of resident frogs and admiring the handiwork of the artists.

Guardhouse
HISTORIC BUILDING, MUSEUM

(Гауптвахта; www.kostromamuseum.ru/gauptvahta; ul Lenina 1/2; joint ticket adult/child R250/free; ◎11am-7pm) Constructed in 1826, this small guardhouse was originally a brig to hold arrested soldiers until trial. During the Soviet era it was used as offices for various institutions, including a library and a registry office. Today it belongs to the Kostroma Museum Reserve and houses three separate exhibits on military history, with displays of weapons and uniforms (from both Russia and other countries) from the medieval era to modern times.

Susaninskaya Ploshchad
SQUARE

(Сусанинская площадь) Picturesque Susaninskaya pl was built under Catherine the Great's patronage after a fire in 1773 (based on, as legend says, the shape of her fan) and nicely revamped for the Romanov dynasty's 400-year anniversary in 2013. Its immense Italianate Trading Arcades used to house hundreds of shops selling goods shipped along the Volga in its heyday, some of which are still represented in its street names (flour, tobacco, fish, spices and milk). Today it houses Kostroma's central market (Центральный рынок; Trading Arcades, ul Muchnye Ryady 1; ◎7am-7pm summer, 8am-6pm winter).

The Ivan Susanin Monument (Памятник Ивану Сусанину), standing in a small park between the arcades, celebrates a local hero who guided Polish soldiers hunting for Mikhail Romanov into a swamp – and to their deaths. (Ivan didn't survive, either.) His deed was lionized by Mikhail Glinka in the opera A Life for the Tsar.

The opposite side of the square features a manicured park with radiating paths and is graced by an imposing neoclassical Fire Tower (Пожарная каланча), built in 1827, and a former Guardhouse (p139).

🏃 Activities

Azimut Hotel Bathhouse
BATHHOUSE

(☑8-800-200 0048, 4942-390 505; ul Magistralnaya 40; 2hr bath rental for up to 6 people R2500;

5pm-3am) Right by the turn towards the centre on the main Yaroslavl road, this hotel is famous for its *banya* complex, which offers a dozen treatments (at extra cost), from traditional to slightly left field. Most involve quick shifts between boiling-hot and ice-cold tubs, and an attendant pummelling you with *veniki* – which feels way better than it might sound.

🛏 Sleeping

Whichever hotel you are staying at, if you're coming into town by bus, ask the driver to let you off at Oktyabrskaya pl once you cross the Volga – this will save you a big trek back into town from the bus station.

Hostel Academy — HOSTEL $

(Хостел Академия; ☎4942-496 165; www.achostel.com; ul Lesnaya 11a; dm incl breakfast R450-600; 🛜) Equipped with dorms sleeping four, six and eight, as well as twin and double rooms (R1400 to R1500), this friendly hostel occupies the 1st floor of a building on the Volga embankment; the large common room has a shared kitchen and a TV with game console. A washing machine is available for guest use.

Ya-Hotel — HOTEL $$

(Я-Отель; ☎8-910-955 5003, 4942-555 000; ya-hotel@mail.ru; ul Simanovskogo 5b; s/d incl breakfast R2600/3200; 🅿️❄️🛜) This very modern multi-floor hotel is one of Kostroma's newest, and the location down the street from Susaninskaya pl can't be beaten. There's 24-hour reception and an elevator to access upper floors. 'Comfort' double rooms (R3500) come with a kitchenette with microwave and mini-fridge. The entrance is on ul Pyatnitskaya.

★ Skvorechnik — B&B $$$

(Скворечник; ☎4942-222 122, 8-920-390 7077; www.artskvorechnik.ru; ul Chaykovskogo 17b; d/f incl breakfast from R3500/4000; 🛜🍽) At this 'Birdhouse' you may not want to leave the nest. Six artfully designed rooms are fitted with natural materials (wood, cotton, Kostroma linen), soothing pastels and tasteful quirks – we loved the hanging bouquet of lights over the platform bed in room 1. Breakfast is served in a family-friendly lounge with arty activities for the kids; babysitting services also available.

Old Street — HOTEL $$$

(☎4942-496 999; www.oldstreethotel.ru; ul Sovetskaya 10; s/d incl breakfast from R3700/4200; 🅿️❄️🛜) A heritage house on the main street has been transformed into a plush little hotel that gets rave reviews from guests. We counted seven pillows topping king-sized beds in tastefully designed modern rooms, which offer work desks, soft bathrobes and bathrooms with large tubs and heated floors. 'Comfort' rooms and suites (from R8500) also feature bidets and terraces.

Yablonevy Sad — RENTAL HOUSE $$$

(Apple Orchard; Яблоневый сад; ☎8-953-656 7513; ul Osoviakhima 6a; R7500; 🅿️🛜🍽) This stylishly designed, boutique *izba* (log house), which sleeps six to eight, is built around a tiled hearth and set in a garden. Three ensuite bedrooms with large beds and many tiny, artful details will make you feel like you've found a fairy-tale forest refuge. A sumptuous Russian breakfast (think porridge and thick pancakes with apples) is included.

🍴 Eating

To stock up on fresh garden produce and Caucasian *lavash* (flat bread), it's a good idea to head to the food stalls inside the central market (p139).

Izbushka — INTERNATIONAL $

(Избушка; ☎4942-222 221; pl Sovetskaya 4; mains R200-350; ⏰10am-midnight Sun-Thu, to 1am Fri & Sat; 🚻) Head upstairs to sink into a comfy chair at this airy, modern cafe with a chilled-out vibe. Options include Italian dishes, salads, Russian *vareniki* (boiled dumplings) and mains such as braised rabbit and fried perch. The cafe also serves beer, wine and cocktails, so you can linger awhile after dessert while the kids amuse themselves in the play area.

Pita Grill Street Food — LEBANESE, BURGERS $

(ul Muchnye Ryady 1; mains R90-150; ⏰9am-10pm) This new casual fast-food joint in the centre of town cooks up fresh *shawarma* (grilled meat and salad wrapped in flat bread), burgers and fries. Save room for a milkshake for dessert.

Horns & Hoofs — EUROPEAN $

(Рога и копыта; www.rogaikopita44.org; ul Sovetskaya 2; mains R250-385; h8.30am-10pm Sun-Thu, to midnight Fri & Sat) This frivolously decorated restaurant is inspired by the beloved Russian satire The Twelve Chairs (1928), in which a deathbed confession inspires a wild search across the country for hidden

SUMAROKOVSKAYA ELK FARM

One of the many bold experiments undertaken in the Soviet era was an attempt to domesticate European elk (*Alces alces;* known as 'moose' in North America) for meat or dairy farming. Elk milk has much more protein and fat than cows' milk and is considered good for ulcers.

To this end, the **Sumarokovskaya Elk Farm** (Сумароковская лосеферма; ✆ 4942-359 433; www.loseferma.ru; Sumarokovo; adult/child R150/100; ◷ 10am-3pm) was created in 1963 about 25km from Kostroma. Commercial elk farming never took off for a multitude of practical reasons, however; these days focus has shifted to breeding animals for areas where this iconic taiga (forest) creature is becoming extinct. The farm also regularly supplies milk to a local sanatorium, which uses it in medical treatment for gastrointestinal diseases.

The best time to visit is summer. In May you can see the newly born calves; in September they're released from their quarantine enclosures. Juvenile and adult elk wander contentedly in their summer paddocks; your tour guide will give you carrots to feed to the animals. The little shop has elk milk available to taste (R60) or purchase (R1200 per litre) from May to September – and, of course, a variety of elk-themed souvenirs year-round. (It's best to visit earlier in the day if you can.)

The farm makes for a pleasant half-day countryside trip if you have a car. From the centre of Kostroma, drive southeast along ul Sovetskaya, which becomes Kineshemskoye sh; continue past the bus station to Poddubnoye. Turn left at the sign for Ikonnikovo and continue just past the small hamlet of Gridino, where you'll see a signposted right turn onto an unsealed road (it's safe for cars); follow that 6km to the farm.

A return taxi from Kostroma with a one-hour wait will cost around R800. Public transport is tougher: take a Gushchino- or Sintsovo-bound bus (20 minutes, six daily) to the Spas stop in Gridino. From there, walk down the unsealed road for 6km.

In winter the whole elk population moves to temporary enclosures in nearby locations, so be sure to enquire with the farm before heading out there. Heavy snow often renders the access road impassable.

GOLDEN RING KOSTROMA

treasure. Wrought-iron furniture, B&W photos and waiters dressed as old-world chauffeurs set the atmosphere. There's a good selection of soups, salads and main dishes, as well as pastries and coffee drinks.

Hundertwasser   CAFE $
(www.restwow.ru; 2nd fl, Oktyabrskaya pl 3; mains R220-300; ◷ 8am-midnight Mon-Thu, to 1am Fri, 10am-1am Sat, 11am-midnight Sun; 🛜 🐾) Resembling a kaleidoscope, this large cafe evokes colour schemes and curving shapes favoured by Viennese vanguard architect Friedensreich Hundertwasser. Local youngsters come here to chat over a cup of coffee or a water pipe, or indulge in some all-day breakfast, fresh juices or smoothies. There's a kids' menu, too.

Honey, I'll Be Late   GASTROPUB, STEAK $$
(Дорогая, буду поздно; www.budupozdno.ru; ul Nizhnyaya Debrya 2/15, cnr ul Chaykovskogo; steaks R300-620; ◷ noon-2am Sun-Thu, to 6am Fri & Sat) With a burger called 'Tear Your Face', you know this is a place that takes meat se-

riously: the speciality is grilled steaks in a variety of cuts. Wash it down with craft beer (choose from dozens) or one of the signature cocktails. After one or two 'Long Islands a la Russe' you'll fully understand how this place got its name.

Not into steak? The restaurant also offers salads, soups, pastas and quesadillas (with a dairy-free vegan-cheese option). Head to the back to get a window booth overlooking the park. Water pipes are available, too.

Slaviansky   RUSSIAN $$
(Славянский; ✆ 4942-315 460; ul Molochnaya Gora 1; meals R250-700; ◷ noon-midnight Sun-Thu, to 2am Fri & Sat) With festive traditional decor, this popular restaurant is a great place for locally produced beer and various vodka-based liquors, with flavours ranging from cranberry to horseradish. Sumptuous meat dishes are broadly based on traditional Russian recipes, but service can be very slow. Bookings recommended.

🍸 Drinking & Nightlife

Traveler's Coffee COFFEE, CAFE
(Трэвэлерс Кофе; ☑8-953-642 8203; www.travel ers-coffee.com; ul Sovetskaya 17; ☺8am-midnight; 📶) A corporate coffee joint in the Starbucks mold, Traveler's offers cappuccinos and lattes for bleary-eyed souls in search of an espresso redemption (as well as breakfast dishes, salads, sandwiches and pastas). Soy milk is available. Also has branches in Yaroslavl.

Kamelot Cafe Bar BAR
(Камелот кафе бар; pl Sovetskaya 4; ☺11am-4am Sun-Thu, to 6am Fri & Sat) The swords and medieval sconces at this booth-filled bar-lounge are perhaps a bit over the top, but if you want to keep the party going late, it's open all night on weekends (and after a few drinks who cares about the decor anyway?). The bar also offers *nargilas* (water pipes) and a full food menu.

Dudki Bar BAR
(Дудки бар; ☑4942-300 003; www.dudkibar. ru; pr Mira 18; ☺noon-2am Sun-Thu, to 4am Fri & Sat; 📶) Local hipsters love this self-ironic bar, perhaps for the snug, oversized upholstered booths that make you feel like you've got your own little private corner of the universe. The bar has a full menu of mainly European and Asian dishes (mains R300 to R350). There's another branch (p147) in Yaroslavl.

🛍 Shopping

★ Art Polka ARTS & CRAFTS
(Арт Полка; ul Chayavskogo 9; ☺noon-8pm) 'Polka' means 'shelf' in Russian, and every shelf here contains handmade wares from a different local artist – it's like a miniature craft fair. You'll find everything from lucite-encased flower jewellery and woodcut badges to soaps and beard conditioner. There are chocolate truffles and iced gingerbread cookies, too. A great place to find presents for your friends back home.

ℹ Information

You'll find 24-hour ATMs dotted along major thoroughfares such as pr Mira and ul Sovetskaya.

Sberbank (Сбербанк; ul Sovetskaya 6; ☺8.30am-5.30pm Mon-Fri, 9am-3pm Sat, ATM 24hr) Next to the post office on ul Sovetskaya.

Post Office (ul Sovetskaya 79/73; ☺8am-8pm Mon-Fri, 9am-6pm Sat) On Oktyabrskaya pl.

Post Office (ul Sovetskaya 6; ☺8am-8pm Mon-Fri, 9am-6pm Sat, 9am-2pm Sun).

ℹ Getting There & Away

BUS

The **bus station** (Автовокзал Кострома) is 4.4km east of Susaninskaya pl on Kineshemskoye sh, the continuation of ul Sovetskaya. There are hourly services to Yaroslavl (R287, 1½ hours, hourly) and Ivanovo (R300 to R360, 2½ hours, hourly), which is where you'll need to transfer for Suzdal (R150, 1½ hours, five daily) and Nizhny Novgorod (R640, five hours, eight daily).

Heading to Plyos, take one of the hourly Ivanovo buses and change at Privolzhsk (R150 to R185, 1¼ hours). There are also direct services to Moscow (R1050, 6½ hours, seven daily).

TRAIN

The train station, **Kostroma Novaya** (Кострома-Новая; pl Shirokova 2), is 3.5km east of Susaninskaya pl. There are three daily suburban trains to/from Yaroslavl (R303, 2½ hours) and two long-distance trains to/from Yaroslavsky vokzal in Moscow (R1250 to R2350, 6½ hours), although these leave either very late or very early.

ℹ Getting Around

Buses 1, 2, 9, 14, 81 and 101 run between the bus station and Susaninskaya pl, along the full length of ul Sovetskaya. Trolleybus 2 runs between the train station and Susaninskaya pl. Each line costs R17 to ride.

You can also rent bicycles by the hour, day or week at **Bicycles for Rent** (Прокат велосипедов; ☑4942-301 552; www.vk.com/velovprokat; ul Gornaya 3; hr/day/week R150/700/3000; ☺1-10pm Mon-Fri, from 10am Sat & Sun).

Taxi Maxim (☑4942-666 666)

Yaroslavl Ярославль

☑4852 / POPULATION 595,200 / ☺ MOSCOW

Yaroslavl is the largest and oldest (founded 1010) city on the Golden Ring, a fact underscored by its place of honour on the Russian 1000-rouble note (including the 15-domed church of John the Baptist on the back). Embraced by two rivers, the mighty Volga and the smaller Kotorosl, Yaroslavl's centre is dotted with onion domes like no other place in Russia. This religious zeal dates back to the times of Kyivan Rus, when the town was founded by Prince Yaroslav to guard his realm's northeastern flank.

Most of the buildings gracing the quaint, Unesco-listed historic city centre were built by rich merchants in the 17th to 19th centuries, competing to out do one other in beautifying their city. Thankfully, much of that beauty has been unscathed by Soviet development.

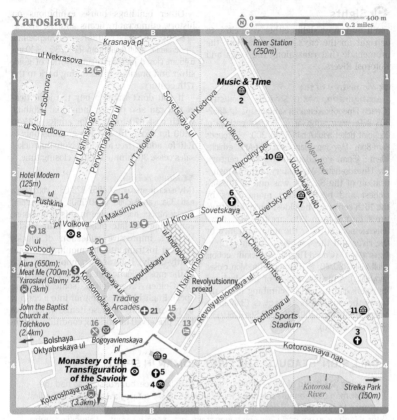

Yaroslavl

N 0 _____ 400 m
0 _____ 0.2 miles

Krasnaya pl

ul Nekrasova

12

ul Sobinova

ul Ustiinskogo

Music & Time
2

ul Sverdlova

Hotel Modern
(125m)

ul Pushkina

Pervomayskaya ul

ul Trefoleva

Sovetskaya ul

ul Kedrova

ul Volkova

River Station
(250m)

Narodny per

10

Volzhskaya nab

Volga River

17 *14*

ul Maksimova

19

ul Kirova

Sovetskaya pl

6

7

Sovetsky per

18

pl Volkova

8

ul Svobody

20

Pervomayskaya ul

Deputatskaya ul

ul Andropova

ul Nakhimsona

pl Chelyuskintsev

Aura (650m);
Meat Me (700m);
Yaroslavl Glavny
(3km)

22

Komsomolskaya ul

Revolyutsionny
proezd

Revolyutsionnaya ul

John the Baptist
Church at
Tolchkovo
(2.4km)

Trading
Arcades *21*

15

Pochtovaya ul

Sports
Stadium

11

16

13

3

Bolshaya
Oktyabrskaya ul

Bogoyavlenskaya
pl

Kotoroslnaya nab

Monastery of the
Transfiguration
of the Saviour

1 *9*

5

4

Kotoroslnaya nab
(3.3km)

Kotorosl
River

Strelka Park
(150m)

GOLDEN RING YAROSLAVL

⊙ Sights

You'll find most sights either very close to or right on the city's main attraction: the promenade that runs along the Volga and Kotorosl Rivers.

★ Monastery of the Transfiguration of the Saviour   MONASTERY

(Спасо-Преображенский монастырь; ☑ 4852-303 869; www.yarmp.yar.ru; Bogoyavlenskaya pl 25; joint ticket adult/child R700/300; ⊙ grounds 8am-8pm May-Sep, 9am-6pm Oct-Apr, exhibits 10am-5.45pm) Founded in the 12th century, the Unesco-listed Monastery of the Transfiguration of the Saviour was one of Russia's richest and best-fortified monasteries by the 16th century. The oldest surviving structures, dating from 1516, are the Holy Gate (святые ворота) near the main entrance by the river and the Cathedral of the Transfiguration (Спасо-Преображенский собор; adult/child R80/40; ⊙ 10am-6pm Thu-Mon, closed rainy days). A bird's-eye view of Yaroslavl and its rivers can be had by climbing up to the top of the cathedral's bell tower (Звонница; adult/child Mon-Fri R200/100, Sat & Sun R250/130; ⊙ 8.30am-7.30pm).

Other buildings house exhibitions on history, ethnography, icons and the Treasures of Yaroslavl Exhibition (Сокровища Ярославля; adult/child from R200/80; ⊙ 10am-5.45pm, closed Tue), featuring works of gold, silver and precious gems dating back to the 17th century.

If you don't want to buy the joint ticket you can also pay for individual exhibits, which cost R70 to R250 for adults (R35 to R100 for kids). To visit the grounds only is R40 for adults (free for kids). Note that ticket sales cease 30 minutes before closing time.

★ Music & Time   MUSEUM

(Музыка и время; ☑ 4852-328 637; Volzhskaya nab 33a; adult/child R250/150; ⊙ 10am-7pm) Every object has a voice in this little house containing the late magician John Mostoslavsky's impressive collection of clocks, musical instruments (harmoniums, a loud hurdy-gurdy), bells and gramophones – one of the most eclectic museum experiences in the Golden Ring. Guides (some of whom speak English) turn each tour into a concert by playing many of these items, which have been preserved in working condition. Down-

---

CALL SIGN 'SEAGULL': THE FIRST WOMAN IN SPACE

Everyone has heard of Yury Gagarin, the first man in space, but Russia also had the first woman cosmonaut: Valentina Tereshkova (b 1937), a Yaroslavl native and the first woman to orbit Earth. Raised in a village 30km from the city, and a textile worker at a local factory, in her early 20s she began training at a nearby amateur skydiving club. After Gagarin's successful 1961 flight, the chief of the Soviet space programme decided to send up a woman, too; due to her parachuting expertise Tereshkova was one of the five successful applicants (out of over 400) admitted to the women's cosmonaut corps.

After months of intense aeronautical training, including 120 parachute jumps, Tereshkova was selected to pilot the *Vostok* 6 flight, the final mission of the programme that had begun with Gagarin and *Vostok* 1. On 16 June 1963, the 26-year-old Tereshkova – call sign 'Chaika' (Seagull) – was sealed inside the small capsule and launched into orbit. All seemed to be going well until Tereshkova discovered a critical error in the capsule's flight program, which would have made the *Vostok* 6 unable to descend to Earth – instead, it would have eventually spun off into outer space forever. Fortunately, ground control was able to figure out and radio up a fix, and Tereshkova successfully returned to Earth – parachuting almost 7km to the ground and landing 230km southeast of Novosibirsk (a statue of a soaring, helmet-less Tereshkova marks the spot). She had spent almost three days in space, circling the planet 48 times; her photographs of the horizon would later help scientists identify layers of aerosol in the atmosphere.

After her flight, Tereshkova received countless international honours, including the Hero of the Soviet Union medal, the USSR's highest award. She went on to a long and prestigious political career (also earning a doctorate in engineering along the way) and today still serves as an elected official in the Duma, the lower house of the Russian legislature. A large plaque honouring Tereshkova can be seen just off Yaroslavl's pl Volkova, on the wall of ul Svobody 9.

stairs is a huge collection of hot irons from centuries past and other antique artefacts.

Yaroslavl Art Museum (Governor's House) MUSEUM

(Ярославский художественный музей (Губернаторский дом); ☑ 4852-303 504; www.artmuseum.yar.ru; Volzhskaya nab 23; joint ticket adult/child R200/free; ⊙ 10am-6pm Tue-Thu & Sat-Sun, noon-8pm Fri) The main branch of the city's art museum, housed in the restored former governors' mansion (built 1823), showcases two permanent exhibits on 18th- to 20th-century Russian art (individual or joint ticket available), with a large hall dedicated to Impressionist Konstantin Korovin; audio guides (R50) are available in English. Temporary exhibits – recent ones included art of the post-revolutionary 20th century – have their own admission prices.

Church of Elijah the Prophet CHURCH

(Церковь Ильи Пророка; ☑ 4852-304 072; www.yarmp.yar.ru; Sovetskaya pl 7; adult/child R100/50; ⊙ 8.30am-7pm May-Oct, by appointment Oct-Apr, closed rainy days) The exquisite church that dominates Sovetskaya pl was built by some prominent local fur dealers in 1650. It has some of the Golden Ring's brightest frescoes, done by the ubiquitous painter Gury Nikitin of Kostroma and his school, and detailed exterior tiles. The church is closed on rainy days to protect the frescoes from moisture.

John the Baptist Church at Tolchkovo CHURCH

(Церковь Иоанна Крестителя в Толчково; www.yarmp.yar.ru; 2-ya Zakotoroslnaya nab 69; adult/child R80/40; ⊙ 10am-5pm Wed-Sun May-Oct, closed rainy days) It's a shame that dingy industrial surroundings discourage most people from visiting Yaroslavl's largest and most unique church – you may recognise it from the 1000-rouble currency note. Protected by Unesco, the red-brick structure (built 1671–87) boasts a staggering 15 green-coloured cupolas and some of the most extensive series of frescoes in the Orthodox world. It's located on the southern bank of the Kotorosl, by the second bridge.

The church is a 3km (10-minute) car or taxi ride from the centre. By public transport from Bogoyavlenskaya pl, take a southbound *marshrutka* (fixed-route minibus) 87 or bus 19k for four stops, disembarking at the ul Karabulina stop. Walk back towards the bridge and turn left at the corner; walk north towards the river and then west to the church (about 500m).

Note that the church is closed on rainy days to protect the frescoes from moisture.

Yaroslavl Art Museum (Metropolitan Palace) GALLERY

(Ярославский художественный музей (Митрополичьи палаты); www.artmuseum.yar.ru; Volzhskaya nab 1; adult/family/child R110/180/free; ⊙ 10am-6pm Tue-Sun) The 17th-century former chambers of the metropolitan showcase icons and other religious art from the 13th to 18th centuries. Temporary exhibits have separate admission prices; a recent one featured women's fashion from 1890 to 1910.

History of Yaroslavl Museum MUSEUM

(Музей Истории Ярославля; ☑ 4852-304 175; http://mukmig.yaroslavl.ru; Volzhskaya nab 17; joint ticket adult/child R130/free; ⊙ 10am-6pm Wed-Mon) This museum is in a lovely house built in 1894 by a local merchant. The main exhibit recounts the history of Yaroslavl through many artefacts from the past 10 centuries; other rooms hold temporary exhibits, such as on the history of medicine in the city. A monument to victims of war and repression in the 20th century sits in the peaceful courtyard garden.

If you don't want to buy the joint ticket you can also pay R80 each for individual exhibits (free for kids).

Annunciation Cathedral CHURCH

(Успенский кафедральный собор; ☑ 4852-725 781; http://yar-uspenie.cerkov.ru; Kotoroslnaya nab 2/1; ⊙ 8am-7.30pm May-Sep, to 6pm Oct-Apr) FREE The city's main cathedral originally dated from 1215, but was blown up by the Bolsheviks in 1937. What you see now is a modern replica erected for Yaroslav's millennium celebrations in 2010. In front of it, a stone-slab monument marks the spot where Prince Yaroslav founded the city in 1010.

Past the cathedral, the new Strelka Park stretches right onto the tip of land between the Volga and the Kotorosl Rivers, where the Yaroslavl Millennium Monument was opened in 2010.

Ploshchad Volkova SQUARE

The massive gate-shaped Vlasyevskaya Watchtower (1659) combined with the Church of the Sign loom over this square named after Fyodor Volkov, who founded Russia's first professional theatre in 1750 in a Yaroslavl leather store. The beautiful neoclassical Volkov Theatre (1911) anchoring the north side of the square remains home to one of Russia's most renowned theatrical troupes.

🏃 Activities

River Station
CRUISE

(Речной вокзал; ☑4852-228 144; www.yarport. com; Volzhskaya nab 4) Summer services from the city's riverine gateway include a range of slow boats to local destinations. The best trip is to Tolga (R28, one hour, five daily), where you'll find a convent with lovely buildings from the 17th century.

🛌 Sleeping

City Hostel
HOSTEL $

(☑8-910-973 5263, 4852-727 782; www.yarcityhostel.ru; 2nd fl, ul Nekrasova 1/2; dm/f from R600/1600; ❋🛜) Modern and stylish – light-coloured wood abounds – this hostel is in brand-new digs in a quiet but central location. Accommodation is in bunk or twin beds in one of several en-suite rooms; a family room has a double bed and a bunk bed. There's a bright common kitchen with a free washing machine for guest use. No breakfast included.

★ Kuptsov Dom
BOUTIQUE HOTEL $$

(Купцовъ дом; ☑4852-207 788; www.kdhotel. ru; ul Trefoleva 21; s/d incl breakfast R3250/3850; 🅿❋🛜) A central location just off Volkov pl and elegantly decorated rooms with white furniture and light floral wallpaper make this new hotel in a historic building hard to beat for value. Helpful reception staff speak English, and a generous buffet breakfast is included. You can save some money by opting for one of the slightly cheaper attic rooms.

★ Ioann Vasilyevich
BOUTIQUE HOTEL $$

(Иоанн Васильевич; ☑4852-670 760; www.ivyar. ru; Revolyutsionnaya ul 34; s/d R2300/3600; ❋🛜) If you don't mind a Soviet spy or a medieval tsar staring at you from the wall when you wake, here's your chance to immerse yourself in Russian cinema. Each of the 27 comfortable rooms is themed around a different Russian film, with colour schemes, furniture and fixtures selected accordingly. There's a great restaurant on-site, too.

Hotel Modern
HOTEL $$

(☑4852-207 777; www.hotelmodern.ru; ul Pushkina 5; s/d incl breakfast R3200/3900; ❋🛜❋) With a central location in a heritage-listed building on a quiet street, and 14 modern and comfortable (even if somewhat bland) rooms, Hotel Modern offers great value and is an easy walking distance to the main commercial strips. Reception staff are warm and helpful and speak some English.

🍴 Eating

If you're on a budget, try the top-floor food court at the Aura shopping centre (Аура; ul Pobedy 41; ⊙10am-10pm; 🛜).

★ Buffet No 1
BUFFET $

(Буфет № 1; ☑4852-646 401; ul Nakhimsona 23/55; mains R100-250; ⊙8am-11pm; 🛜) With an art nouveau exterior and an upscale dining room, this self-serve buffet – which offers a large and inexpensive selection of tasty salads, omelettes, meat mains with side dishes, Italian pastas, Asian noodle dishes, and desserts – is a great place for a cheap meal in pleasant surrounds. Its location near most of the main sights is perfect, too.

Podbelka
RUSSIAN $

(Подбелка; ☑4852-593 053; Bolshaya Oktyabrskaya ul 28; mains R120-350; ⊙24hr) 'Podbelka' is how Yaroslavl's first Soviet *pelmennaya* (dumpling cafeteria), which occupied these premises in the 1920s, was colloquially known to the townsfolk. In its post-historical reincarnation it's a hip, all-night eatery serving traditional *pelmeni* and *vareniki* (Russian dumplings stuffed with meat or vegetables), along with many of their foreign cousins, such as Georgian *khinkali*.

Meat Me
MIDDLE EASTERN $

(3rd fl, Aura, ul Pobedy 41; mains R140-290; ⊙10am-10pm; 🛜) Meataholics can gorge on excellent pork or chicken kebabs on skewers, or doner kebabs wrapped in fresh *lavash* at this kiosk in the food court of the Aura shopping centre. There's also falafel, hummus, hot dogs and – oddly enough – Canadian poutine (chips topped with cheese curds and gravy).

Ioann Vasilyevich
RUSSIAN $$

(Иоанн Васильевич; ☑8-902-331 4707; www. ivyar.ru; Revolyutsionnaya ul 34; mains R340-580; ⊙24hr; 🛜) A large menu of tasty, artfully presented Russian favourites – such as Olivier salad, 'Herring in a Fur Coat', *pelmeni* dumplings, local perch and rabbit kidneys – features at this restaurant, which is decorated as if you're having dinner with its eponymous 16th-century tsar (aka Ivan the Terrible). A visit to the inventively designed toilets downstairs will give you a lift, too.

🍷 Drinking & Nightlife

★ Krapiva
CRAFT BEER

(Крапива; ul Kirova 10; ⊙noon-1am Sun-Thu, to 6am Fri & Sat) With more than 150 craft beers to choose from – 40 rotating on the taps and dozens more in bottles – whether you're a beer snob or a beer slob this Moscow import has something to your taste. Nondrinkers can choose from numerous artisanal soft drinks. Light wood, red brick and metal-drum bar tables give off a comfy sort of rustic-industrial vibe.

Dudki Bar PUB

(☑ 4852-330 933; www.dudkibar.ru; ul Sobinova 33; ⊗ noon-2am Sun-Thu, to 6am Fri & Sat; 🛜) One of the most happening places in town, this bar-restaurant really gets going on weekends. Brass instruments and pictures of dogs portrayed as aristocratic ancestors adorn the walls, with a large bar on the 2nd floor and a more intimate one downstairs. European and Asian dishes feature on the menu. There's another branch in Kostroma (p142).

Organic Coffee COFFEE, CAFE

(☑ 4852-731 947; 2nd fl, ul Kirova 13/31; ⊗ 8am-midnight; 🛜) This sizeable all-day cafe serves all manner of espresso-based coffees, iced or hot, as well as desserts and light meals (salads, pastas etc). The cafe also offers soy milk. There are two other branches around town, as well.

Anti-Cafe Samoye Vremya CAFE

(Самое время; ☑ 4852-286 644; www.samo-evremya76.ru; 2nd fl, ul Trefoleva 22; per min R2; ⊗ 10am-midnight Mon-Thu, to 2am Fri & Sat) Part of a nationwide trend, this 'anti-cafe' charges for the time you spend on the premises and provides coffee and great homemade cookies for free. You can lounge on a couch surfing the internet, play Xbox on a large screen in a dedicated room or make friends with young Russians who come along to play table games and chat.

ℹ Information

VTB24 Bank (ВТБ24 банк; Komsomolskaya ul 6; ⊗ 9am-8pm Mon-Fri, 10am-4pm Sat, ATM 24hr) Has a currency exchange desk.

Pharmacy (Аптека; ul Pervomayskaya 47; ⊗ 24hr)

Post Office (Komsomolskaya ul 22; ⊗ 8am-10pm Mon-Fri, 9am-6pm Sat & Sun)

ℹ Getting There & Away

BUS

The **bus station** (Ярославский автовокзал; www.yarbust.ru; Moskovsky pr 80a) is 3.3km south of the Kotorosl River. There are seven daily services to/from Moscow (R700, 4½ hours). Be-

tween those and the regional lines, you can also get to Rostov-Veliky (R130 to R250, one hour, frequent), Pereslavl-Zalessky (R310 to R400, two hours, 11 daily) and Sergiev Posad (R450 to R550, three hours, six daily).

Buses go to Kostroma (R287, two hours, nine daily) and Uglich (R293, three hours, 13 daily). There are also two buses daily for Suzdal (R517 to R592, 4½ hours, 9.35am and 4.20pm).

Some buses bound for Moscow and Uglich either depart from or stop at the main **train station** on the way.

TRAIN

The main train station is **Yaroslavl Glavny** (Ярославль-Главный; ul Svobody), about 3km west of the centre. There are 14 daily trains from Moscow's Yaroslavsky station bound for northern Russia and Siberia that stop at Yaroslavl (R545 to R886, four hours), with most calling at Rostov-Veliky or Sergiev Posad.

There are three daily trains (two on Thursdays) to/from Kostroma (R303, 2½ hours). Transit northbound trains continue to Vologda (R500 to R1475, four hours, 11 daily) and Arkhangelsk (R1846 to R2935, 16 hours, four daily). Eastbound trains go to Perm (R2422 to R3414, 19 hours, three daily) and beyond the Urals.

To get to the station from the centre, take *marshrutky* (minibus) 45, 76 or 81, or buses 6, 8, or 72.

ℹ Getting Around

From **Yaroslavl Glavny train station**, trolleybus 1 runs along ul Svobody to pl Volkova and on to Krasnaya pl. From the **bus station** trolleybus 5 or 9 goes to Bogoyavlenskaya pl. The fare is R20.

Maxim Taxi (☑ 4852-666 666)

Troika Taxi (☑ 4852-333 333)

Rostov-Veliky

Ростов-Великий

☑ 48536 / POP 30,943 / ⊗ MOSCOW

Coloured in the same delicate shade of pink as the sunsets they've been watching for hundreds of years, the impregnable walls and perfectly proportioned towers of Rostov-Veliky's kremlin rise magnificently above the shimmering Lake Nero.

First chronicled in the year 862, Rostov-Veliky was the original capital of the Kyivan princes who moved into the Finno-Ugric lands that would later become known as Muscovy and Russia. Today it's a sleepy, village-like town that wakes you up with the sound of roosters and gets eerily quiet when darkness falls.

◉ Sights & Activities

★ Rostov-Veliky Kremlin FORTRESS

(Ростовский кремль; ☑ 48536-61 502; www.rostmuseum.ru; ul Petrovicheva 1; joint ticket adult/child R600/free; ⊙ 10am-5.30pm Sun-Thu, to 8pm Fri & Sat) Rostov-Veliky's main attraction is unashamedly photogenic. Though founded in the 12th century, most of the buildings date to the 1670s and 1680s.

The five magnificent domes of the Assumption Cathedral (Успенский собор) dominate the kremlin from just outside its north wall. The oldest structure in Rostov-Veliky, it was completed in 1512; the belfry (Звонница; donation adult/child R100/50) was added in 1682. Each of its 15 bells has a name; the largest, weighing 32 tonnes, is called 'Sysoy'.

The west gate (the main entrance) and the north gate are straddled by the Gate-Church of St John the Divine (Надвратная церковь Иоанна Богослова) and the Gate-Church of the Resurrection (Надвратная церковь Воскресения), both of which are richly decorated with 17th-century frescoes. Enter these churches from the kremlin walls, which you can access from the stairs next to the north gate.

The metropolitan's private chapel, the Church of the Saviour-over-the-Galleries (Церковь Спаса-на-Сенях), contained within the metropolitan's house (Покои митрополита), has the most beautiful interior of all, covered in colourful frescoes. Other rooms in the house are filled with exhibits: the White Chamber (Белая палата) displays religious antiquities, while the Red Chamber (Красная палата) shows off beautiful, luminous pieces of *finift* (painted enamel miniatures), a Rostov artistic speciality.

If you don't want to buy the joint ticket, you can simply pay for individual exhibitions, which range from R50 to R200; to walk around the grounds only costs R50 (children get in free). Outside service hours, you can access the cathedral through the church shop on ul Karla Marksa.

Monastery of Saviour & St Jacob MONASTERY, VIEWPOINT

(ul Engelsa 44; ⊙ 9am-7pm) This restored monastery (originally founded in the late 14th century) is the sparkling-white fairy-tale apparition you'll see as you approach Rostov-Veliky by road or rail. English-language tours may be available from the tour office next to the gates, but the best reason to visit is to climb the wall on its lake side (donation R50) and up to the tower in the southwestern corner – you'll enjoy stupendous 360-degree views over the monastery, Lake Nero and Rostov.

Outside the gates you'll find locals selling smoked fish and souvenirs. The monastery is 2km southwest of the kremlin (p148); you can walk along the lake on ul Podozerka.

Boat Trips BOATING, CRUISE

(☑ 8-985-643 3084, 8-903-638 0133; ul Podozerka 35; tours per person R300, rental per hr R400; ⊙ May-Sep) For a different perspective on Rostov-Veliky, take a 45-minute cruise of Lake Nero. Boats leave from a pier on the lakefront to the southwest of the kremlin and pass the shoreside Monastery of Saviour & St Jacob as well as an island in the middle of the lake. You can also rent out rowboats and pedal boats to use yourself.

🛏 Sleeping & Eating

Rostov-Veliky is a popular weekend destination, so hotels here often charge lower prices on weeknights. Yaroslavl is only an hour away, though, and has many more – and better – sleeping options, so it may not be worth staying overnight here.

Khors GUESTHOUSE $

(Хорс; ☑ 8-962-209 0605, 48536-62 483; www.khors.org; ul Podozerka 31; d R1500, with shared bathroom R1000-1500; @ 🖹) This sprawling, eclectic lakeside complex has seven small rooms (available in summer) with very basic furniture and shared bathroom and kitchen, as well as a year-round en-suite double and apartment. The lack of luxury is made up for by the friendly artist-owners (who have their own gallery), the huge garden and the rooftop deck with swing chairs overlooking Lake Nero.

Russkoye Podvorye HOTEL $$

(Русское подворье; ☑ 48536-64 255; www.russkoe-podvorie.ru; ul Marshala Alexeyeva 9; d/tr from R1600/2800; ✳ 🖹 🖾) This hotel occupies an 18th-century arcaded merchant's house. Fairly modern rooms have spirit-lifting floral ornaments and comfy beds. Breakfasts are served in perhaps the best restaurant (Русское подворье; ☑ 48536-64 255; www.russkoe-podvorie.ru; ul Marshala Alexeyeva 9; mains R200-400, weekday lunch special R160; ⊙ 8am-11pm Sun-Thu, to midnight Fri & Sat) in town. You can splash out on larger suites with spa baths, and there's also a new sauna and small pool on-site.

NORTHERN VOLGA CIRCUIT

If you're intrigued by the idea of a trip through markedly less touristy and slightly desolate northern Russian towns and villages, take the following circuit route, starting in Yaroslavl. While doable by local buses, it's much better in a rented car – the roads are almost
empty and the scenery is captivating.

From Yaroslavl, regional road R151 goes northwest along the Volga River to **Tutayev**
(Тутаев; also known by its old name – Romanov-Borisoglebsk), 39km away. Disregard
the slightly drab environs on the embankment and look across the Volga: the view of its
far bank (which you can reach by ferry) is astonishingly idyllic, with quaint churches and
wooden houses scattered around green hills.

From Tutayev, it's 51km along the same road to **Rybinsk** (Рыбинск). This busy city has
a well-preserved historic centre and a beautiful Volga embankment graced by the towering edifice of the New Bread Exchange, built in the Russian revivalist style in 1912 (it now
houses an interesting regional museum). There are numerous hotels in Rybinsk; **YurLa**
(☑ 4855-289 063; http://en.yurla.ru; Volzhskaya nab 201; s/d incl breakfast from R2500/3000;
🅿 ❊ 🛜) offers good value and a convenient riverside location. **SupBerry** (Гастропаб
СупБерри; ☑ 485-555 0001; www.vk.com/supberry_cafe; ul Stoyalaya 16; mains R200-500;
🕙10am-11pm; 🛜) is a great, centrally located gastropub.

After Rybinsk, the route turns sharply southwest via the R104 towards **Myshkin**
(Мышкин), 47km away; at Korovino you'll need to take a **ferry** (Мышкинский паром; cars
R250, pedestrians free; 🕙 departs hourly, 6.30am-8.30pm) across the Volga. A small town of
wooden cottages, tiny Myshkin has for years been leveraging the pun in its name, which
contains the Russian word for 'mouse'. Unless you have a mighty mouse mania you can
skip the rather twee Museum of Mice – the eclectic (and packed) collection of artefacts
in the **history museum** (Музей истории города; ul Uglichskaya 19; adult/child R60/40;
🕙10am-5pm Tue-Sun) across the road is considerably more interesting.

Head south out of Myshkin on Lesnaya ul/78N, following the Volga 54km southwest to
Uglich (Углич) – the scene of an unsolved crime that changed Russian history. In 1591,
eight-year-old Prince Dmitry, the youngest son of Ivan the Terrible, died in rather suspicious circumstances. The official report was that he fell on a knife during an epileptic fit;
many believe, however, that he was killed on the orders of his foster father, Boris Godunov, to remove him from the line of succession.

Within the riverside **kremlin** (☑ 48532-53 678; www.uglmus.ru; ul Kreml, Uglich; adult/stu-
dent/child R350/300/100; 🕙9am-6pm summer, to 5pm winter), the 15th-century **Prince's
Chambers** house a historical exhibit on Dmitry's sad fate. The star-spangled **Church
of St Dmitry on the Blood** was built in 1692 on the spot where the body was found.
Its 300kg bell, which announced the boy's death, was banished for many years to the
Siberian town of Tobolsk (after Godunov ordered it to be publicly flogged and have its
'tongue' ripped out); it has since returned to its rightful location in Uglich. If you want
to spend the night, you can splash out on a room at the opulent **Volzhskaya Riviera**
(Волжская Ривьера; ☑ 48532-91 900; www.volga-hotel.com; Uspenskaya pl 8; r from R2290-
4370; 🅿 ❊ @ 🛜 ☒).

Head south from Uglich on R104, and then east on R153 for 70km, to reach **Borisoglebsky** (Борисоглебский), home of the astounding white fortress of the Rostov-Bori-
soglebsky Monastery, built in 1363. Continue east for another 22km to reach the town of
Rostov-Veliky (p147) and the M8 Moscow–Yaroslavl highway.

Dom na Pogrebakh   HISTORIC HOTEL **$$**
(Дом на погребах; ☑ 48536-61 244; www.domna
pogrebah.ru; d R2300-2500, with shared bathroom
from R1000; 🛜) Right inside the kremlin
near the east gate, this building dating from
the late 17th century has clean, wood-pan-
elled rooms with heavy doors and very basic
furniture – but if you can snag a room look-

ing out at the west gate the charming view
will make up for it. Room 15 is particularly
spacious, with newer furnishings and en-
suite bathroom.

⭐**Yaroslavna**   RESORT **$$$**
(Ярославна; ☑ 48536-67 002, 8-961-162 6986;
www.yaroslavna-nero.ru; Yaroslavskiy sh 1b, Lvy;

duplex d from R3900;   ) For a taste of country life, try this resort on Lake Nero 7km south of Rostov-Veliky. Pine-log cabins contain duplex doubles; the 'family' cottage (from R7500) sleeps six. All are decorated in rustic style and have kitchenettes. With a restaurant, pool, spa, *bani,* playground and activities including horse riding, boat rides and even minigolf, you may not want to leave.

Appetit   INTERNATIONAL **$$**
(Аппетит; 48536-64 404; Sobornaya pl 2; mains R280-430; 9am-9pm Sun-Thu, to 11pm Fri & Sat;) Hidden down a signed archway across from the kremlin is this cool little cafe with a chilled-out vibe and a large menu featuring Russian dishes, pizza, pastas, soups and salads (as well as omelettes and porridge for breakfast). Relax on couch seating inside or veranda seating outside (where there's also a little play area set up for the kids).

 Shopping

Dom Remyosel   GIFTS & SOUVENIRS
(Дом ремесел; 48536-67 223, 48536-64 452; www.domremesel.com; Tolstovskaya nab 16; 10am-6pm) This little crafts shop tucked away down a side street is perfect for browsing through gifts and souvenirs, handmade by local artists in a variety of styles: ceramics, woodcarvings, pillows, painted figurines and the like. The shop also offers classes in making dolls, clay whistles, bark shoes, Easter eggs and other traditional souvenirs (from R200 per person).

❶ Getting There & Away

The train station, which is called **Rostov Yaroslavsky** (Ростов-Ярославский; Privokzalnaya pl), is 2km north of the **kremlin**, off the M8. Buses leave from a kiosk just outside. Walking south along ul Lunacharskogo will take you to the centre of town.

Pereslavl-Zalessky
Переславль-Залесский

 48535 / POP 41,925 / MOSCOW
Another ancient lakeside town, Pereslavl-Zalessky is a popular dacha (summer country house) getaway for Muscovites. Its attractions are scattered around a large area, which makes it hard to explore without a car or a bicycle. But quiet and pretty spots are easily found once you escape from the main drag.

The town's main claim to fame is as the birthplace of 13th-century prince (and later Russian saint) Alexander Nevsky. Its earthen walls and the little Cathedral of the Transfiguration are as old as the town itself, founded in 1152 by Prince Yury Dolguruky. Lake Pleshcheyevo is also famous as the unlikely cradle of the Russian navy – thanks to a boat-loving teenager who went on to become Peter the Great.

Note that the main road that runs through town changes names several times along its length. North of the Trubezh River it's Rostovskaya ul; within the centre it's Sovetskaya ul; and south of the old kremlin walls it's ul Kardovskogo. Finally, south of Podgornaya it becomes Moskovskaya ul.

◉ Sights & Activities

A number of sights are located on and near Krasnaya pl (p152) in the centre of town, within the grassy hills that are what remain of the ancient kremlin; these can be reached on foot. The rest are spread out along the road that splits off from the main street at Goritsky Monastery (ul Podgornaya) and curls around the western shore of the lake. Depending on how far you want to go, if you don't have your own wheels a taxi ride is your best bet for these.

At the tourist information office (p153) you can rent out an audio guide (R300) in English or German with several self-guided walking-tour routes around town.

In warmer months Lake Pleshcheyevo is a popular site for water activities such as windsurfing, kitesurfing and stand-up paddleboarding (SUP). Local outfitter **Surf-Point** (8-915-985 6434; www.surf-point.ru; ul Petra I 43b, Veskovo; hire/training per hr SUP R400/1000, windsurfing R800/1900, kitesurfing R1500/2500) offers lessons and equipment rental.

★ Pereslavl Railway Museum   MUSEUM
(Переславский железнодорожный музей; 48535-49 479; www.kukushka.ru; Talitsy; adult/child R150/free; 10am-6pm Wed-Sun) A large collection of old locomotives, coaches, boxcars and other narrow-gauge railroad relics that once ran through this part of Russia (up to the middle of the 20th century) are displayed on tracks and inside a depot at this unique outdoor museum. Other interesting bits include a motorcar converted to run on rails and a recreated stationmaster's office, plus various train-themed souvenirs. Don't

miss a chance to ride under your own steam on the handcart (adult/child R150/free).

To get here by car, head west on Podgornaya ul from Pereslavl's main road (the same way as for the Botik Museum); continue 17km to Kupanskoye. Turn left at the blue sign that says 'Музей Паровозов 3km' (Museum of Steam Locomotives), bear right at the fork and continue on to the tiny village of Talitsy. You'll need to park at the free lot at the village entrance and walk the last 400m to the museum. Exact GPS coordinates can be found on the museum's website.

Note that the only toilet facilities at the museum are two old-fashioned outhouses.

★Goritsky Monastery   MONASTERY
(Горицкий монастырь; ☑ 48535-38 100; www.museumpereslavl.ru; Muzeyny per 4; joint ticket adult/child R450/200; ◷10am-6pm Tue-Sun May-Sep, to 5pm Oct-Apr) This large hilltop monastery 2.5km south of the centre was founded in the 14th century, though the oldest buildings today are the 17th-century gates, gate-church and belfry. Its centrepiece is the Assumption Cathedral, with its beautiful carved iconostasis, but don't miss a trip up to the top floor of the Church of the Epiphany's belfry (Колокольня Церкви Богоявления; Goritsky Monastery; adult/child R80/50) for terrific views over Pereslavl and Lake Pleshcheyevo. The other buildings hold various art and history exhibits.

There are also some good views towards town and the lake from a guard tower in the southern monastery wall, behind the Assumption Cathedral.

If you don't want to buy the joint ticket you can also pay for individual exhibits, which range from R40 to R160 for adults (free to R40 for kids); to walk around the grounds only costs R50 (children get in free).

If driving, head south on the main road, head up the hill past the turn-off to the Botik Museum, then take the first right turn and follow it west to the monastery.

★Assumption Cathedral   CHURCH
(Собор Успения; Goritsky Monastery; adult/child R80/60) Hearing your footsteps echoing in the gloom as you walk through this empty, unrestored cathedral (built 1744) within Goritsky Monastery makes it almost seem more sobering than an actual church service. The magnificent gilded iconostasis, completed in 1759, is populated with paintings of saints and religious scenes (a handy sign offers a key); along the doors at bottom is a carving of the Last Supper. Inside is also a display of old tombstones dating from the 16th to 18th centuries.

Peter's Sailboat Museum   MUSEUM
(Музей Ботик Петра I; ☑ 48535-62 116; www.museumpereslavl.ru; ul Petra I, Veskovo; joint ticket adult/child R180/100; ◷10am-6pm Tue-Sun May-Sep, to 5pm Oct-Apr) Lake Pleshcheyevo is where a 16-year-old Peter the Great developed his obsession with the sea while on holiday. He continued to study navigation and boatbuilding and by age 20 had built a 'toy flotilla' of more than 100 small ships in Pereslavl, which he took out on the lake for naval manoeuvres. His sailboat *Fortuna*, one of only two of these 17th-century vessels to survive, is on display at this museum complex dedicated to Peter's seafaring efforts.

The *Fortuna* occupies its own building on the hilltop site; several other 19th-century buildings (including a recently restored one known as the White Palace) feature interesting historical and art exhibits relating to the emperor. The tree-shaded grounds make for a pleasant stroll.

The site is 3.5km west of Pereslavl's main road on Podgornaya ul; driving south from the town centre, turn right at the sign for the museum. You can park at the somewhat tacky boat-themed tourist plaza across the road; note that you'll have to pay for admission to the grounds first (R20), then walk up to the White Palace to buy tickets for the other exhibits (R40 to R100) – or else you can just buy the joint ticket for access to everything. There's also a brochure in English available for R10.

Forty Martyrs' Church   CHURCH
(Сорокосвятская церковь; Levaya nab 165) Built in 1755, this lakeside church is named for the Forty Martyrs of Sebaste, a group of Roman soldiers who froze to death on a wintry lake in present-day Turkey rather than turn their backs on their Christian faith. It's not open to the public, but there's a beautiful (modern) tile-work rendition of the martyrs on the outer wall, and it's a lovely walk beside the Trubezh River down to the lake.

Cathedral of the
Transfiguration of the Saviour   CHURCH
(Спасо-Преображенский собор; ☑ 48535-31 910; www.museumpereslavl.ru; Krasnaya pl; adult/child R80/50; ◷10am-6pm May-Sep) At the northwestern end of Krasnaya pl, standing out against the background of the grassy remains of the ancient town walls, is

one of the oldest buildings in Russia: this brilliant-white limestone church with a single sea-green dome, was built from 1152 to 1157 for Prince Yury Dolgoruky and his court (and restored in 2015). The interior is cool and hushed thanks to the 1.5m-thick walls. Inside is a 19th-century marble icon-ostasis; sadly, the original 12th-century frescoes have not survived.

Radio Museum
MUSEUM

(Музей Радио; ☑48535-62 280; oldradio-gp@yandex.ru; Podgornaya ul 40; adult/child R150/50; ⏱10am-6pm Tue-Sun) Even if you can't understand Russian, if you love gadgets check out this two-storey museum packed with dozens of old radios, TV sets and film cameras, some of which are a century old. The radios, gleaming in polished wood cabinets with light-up dials, are particularly fetching – and many of them still work, as the couple who run the place will proudly display. Wait until you see the tiny TV screen ingeniously magnified by glycerine.

Krasnaya Ploschad
SQUARE

(Красная площадь; Sovetskaya ul) This grassy square off the main road is at the heart of what was once Prince Yury Dolgoruky's kremlin. At one end is the 1152 Cathedral of the Transfiguration of the Saviour; a bust of 13th-century prince Alexander Nevsky stands in front. Three additional churches across the square include the tent-roofed **Church of Peter the Metropolitan** (Церковь митрополита Петра; ul Sadovaya 5), built in 1585 and renovated in 1957, and the 18th-century twin churches fronting the road.

🛏 Sleeping

★ Art Hotel
APARTMENT $$

(Арт-Отель; ☑8-910-979 0706; art-hotel.pz@yandex.ru; Bolshaya Protechnaya ul 45; d incl breakfast R2800, 1-bedroom cottage R4000-4500; P❄☎❖) Double rooms and cottages are set amid flowering gardens with pet rabbits, with an on-site art gallery and *banya* (available at extra cost); interiors are all lovingly hand-decorated in bohemian style featuring original artwork by the owners, who also own Gallery Guest House. The larger two-bedroom cottage (from R10,000) has its own kitchenette and can sleep up to six people.

★ Gallery Guest House
B&B $$

(Гостевой Дом Галерея; ☑8-910-823 5232; www.gallery-hotel.info; Podgornaya ul 86; r incl breakfast from R2500; P❄❖) Each of the seven en-suite rooms at this lovely B&B are decorated in a different palette of warm hues, with natural-wood walls and hand-painted furniture. A delicious homemade breakfast is served in the sunny dining area. The common area doubles as a gallery, hung with paintings by local artists.

Albitsky Sad Motel
HOTEL $$

(Альбицкий сад; ☑48535-31 430; www.albitskisad.ru; ul Kardovskogo 21; s/d from R2500/3500; P❄❖) On the main road just south of the centre, 'Albitsky Garden' resembles an old manor house, with a flower-filled garden at the back. It offers 16 tastefully decorated rooms; the most recently refurbished ones are on the 2nd floor, with light colours and a cosy feel. 'Comfort'-level rooms have a mini-fridge. Breakfast is à la carte at the inviting restaurant.

🍴 Eating

Cafe Pirog & Borsch
RUSSIAN, CAFE $

(Кафе Пирогъ & борщъ; ul Kardovskogo 3; mains R120-200; ⏱10am-8pm Sun-Fri, to 9pm Sat; ☎) A colourful interior of traditional tiles puts this cheap and cheerful cafe a cut above. The menu features tasty classics such as *vareniki* (dumplings), soups, bliny and savoury pies (*pirozhki*), plus all-day breakfast. Look for the wooden house on the main road with orange trim and a small sign, just south of the old town walls. There's parking alongside.

★ Traktir Popov Lug
RUSSIAN $$

(Трактир Попов Луг; ☑48535-94 542, 8-920-659 0682; www.popovlug.ru; ul Podgornaya; mains R350-550; ⏱11am-11pm Sun-Mon, to midnight Fri & Sat) Step back in time at 'Popov Meadow', a large log building kitted out like a medieval Russian tavern. Feast on locally caught fish and venison or homemade sausages and cheese from the restaurant's own farm while folk musicians play traditional tunes. There's also a farm store on-site selling organic produce.

Monpansier Cafe Restaurant
RUSSIAN $$

(Кафе Монпансье; ☑8-901-195 7012, 48535-62 012; www.monpasie-pereslavl.com; Sovetskaya ul 10; mains R260-430; ⏱9am-11pm; ☎✍) Russian classics abound at this cosy central eatery decorated as if from Grandma's attic, although some European additions and seasonal specialties round out the menu nicely (there's a decent selection of vegetarian dishes, too). Terrace seating is available in summer. With some friends? Order the tea set and have your very own samovar brought to your table.

ℹ Information

There's a freestanding **Sberbank kiosk** (Rostovskaya ul 27; ⊙24hr) on the main street about 500m north of the river.

Post Office (ul Svobody 1a; ⊙8am-1pm & 2-8pm Mon-Fri, 9am-1pm & 2-6pm Sat)

Tourist Information Office (☑48535-31 832; www.tourismpereslavl.ru; ul Proezdnaya 1; ⊙9am-6pm; 🕾) The friendly staff here are eager to help. City maps cost R50.

ℹ Getting There & Away

Pereslavl-Zalessky is not on a train line, but buses travel frequently to Moscow (R550, 2¼ hours, six daily); they also stop at Sergiev Posad on the way (R300, 45 minutes). Others travel to Yaroslavl (R400, 2½ hours, 16 daily) via Rostov-Veliky (R250, 1¼ hours).

The **bus station** (Автовокзал; ul Moskovskaya 113) is 4km southwest of the Trubezh River in the centre of town.

ℹ Getting Around

Bus 1 runs up and down the main street from just south of the bus station; heading out from the centre you can catch it just north of the river.

Taxis wait at Narodnaya pl, on the west side of the main road just north of the river; you can also call directly.

888 Taxi (☑48535-30 888)

Taxi Troika (☑48535-26 333)

Sergiev Posad
Сергиев Посад

☑496 / POP 113,492 / ⊙ MOSCOW

Blue-and-gold cupolas offset by snow-white walls – this colour scheme lies at the heart of the Russian perception of divinity and Sergiev Posad's monastery is a textbook example. It doesn't get any holier than this in Russia, for the place was founded in 1340 by the country's most revered saint, St Sergius of Radonezh. Since the 14th century, pilgrims have been journeying here to pay homage to him.

Although the Bolsheviks closed the monastery, it was reopened following WWII as a museum, residence of the patriarch and a working monastery. The patriarch and the church's administrative centre moved to the Danilovsky Monastery in Moscow in 1988, but the Trinity Monastery of St Sergius remains one of the most important spiritual sites in Russia.

Pr Krasnoy Armii is the main street, running north to south through the town centre. The train and bus stations are on opposite corners of a wide square (Vokzalnaya pl) to the east of pr Krasnoy Armii; the monastery is about 1.5km north of there.

◉ Sights

★Trinity Monastery
of St Sergius   MONASTERY
(Свято-Троицкая Сергиева Лавра; ☑info 496-544 5334, tours 496-540 5721; www.stsl.ru; ⊙5am-9pm) ᴿᴿᴱᴱ In 1340 St Sergius of Radonezh founded this *lavra* (senior monastery), which soon became the spiritual centre of Russian Orthodoxy. St Sergius was credited with providing mystic support to Prince Dmitry Donskoy in his improbable victory over the Tatars in the Battle of Kulikovo in 1380. Soon after his death at the age of 78, Sergius was named Russia's patron saint.

Spruced up on the occasion of St Sergius' 700-year anniversary in 2014, the monastery is an active religious centre with a visible population of monks in residence. This mystical place is a window into the age-old belief system that has provided Russia with centuries of spiritual sustenance.

Built in 1423, the squat, gold-domed Trinity Cathedral (Троицкий собор) is the heart of the monastery, as well as its oldest surviving building. The tomb of St Sergius stands in the church's southeastern corner, where a memorial service for him goes on all day, every day. The icon-festooned interior, lit by oil lamps, is largely the work of the great medieval painter Andrei Rublyov and his students.

The star-spangled Cathedral of the Assumption (Успенский собор) was modelled on the cathedral of the same name in the Moscow Kremlin. It was finished in 1585 with money left by Ivan the Terrible in a fit of remorse for killing his son. To the left of the main entrance is the rectangular tomb of Boris Godunov, the only tsar not buried in the Moscow Kremlin or St Petersburg's SS Peter & Paul Cathedral. Another notable grave is that of St Innokenty, known as the 'apostle of America' for founding the Russian Orthodox community in Alaska.

Nearby, the resplendent Chapel-at-the-Well (Накладезная часовня) was built over a spring that is said to have appeared during the Polish siege of 1608–10, in the Time of

Troubles. The five-tier baroque **bell tower** (колокольня) – at 88.5m, the highest in Russia – took nearly 30 years to build (from 1741 to 1770), and once had 42 bells, the largest of which weighed 65 tonnes.

The **sacristy** (ризница), behind Trinity Cathedral, displays the monastery's extraordinarily rich **treasury**, bulging with 600 years of donations by the rich and powerful – tapestries, jewel-encrusted vestments, solid-gold chalices and more. At the time of research it was unavailable for tours due to restoration works, with no set date to reopen.

The huge block with the 'wallpaper' paint job is the **Refectory Church of St Sergius** (Трапезная церковь преподобного Сергия), so called because it was once a dining hall for pilgrims. Now it's the Assumption Cathedral's winter counterpart, holding morning services in cold weather. It's closed outside services, except for guided tours. The green building next door is the metropolitan's residence.

Toy Museum   MUSEUM
(Музей Игрушек; ☑ 496-540 4101; www.museumot.info; pr Krasnoy Armii 123; adult/child R200/100; ⊙ 10am-5pm Wed-Sun) The multiple changing exhibits feature toys from throughout Russian history and around the world; recent exhibits have included toys from the royal children of two centuries of the Romanov dynasty and toys with a naval theme. The museum has a particularly good collection of nesting dolls, as Sergiev Posad was the centre of *matryoshka* production before the revolution. Children under 3 are admitted for free.

🛏 Sleeping & Eating

Fox House Hostel   HOSTEL $
(Фокс Хаус хостел; ☑ 8-968-085 8300; fox househostel@gmail.com; 2nd fl, pr Krasnoy Armii 96; dm R500-600, d R1600; ⊛) This little hostel about 750km south of the monastery is very convenient for the train and bus stations. There are four- and six-bed dorms (one for women only) as well as private rooms, and a small common area with a kitchen and a long dining table. Some snacks, beer and pre-made food (eg pasta, salad) are available for purchase, too.

Old Hotel Lavra   HOTEL $$
(Старая гостиница Лавры; ☑ 496-549 9000; www.lavrahotel.ru; pr Krasnoy Armii 133; s/d from R2700/3100; ⊛) Built in 1822 as pilgrim accommodation, this massive monastery hotel

has been revived in its original capacity, with nothing to distract its supposedly puritan guests from prayer and contemplation – not even TV. But despite their blandness, rooms are modern and very clean. There's a vast restaurant on the premises. Unsurprisingly, alcohol is strictly banned throughout the complex. Breakfast is R200.

Varenichnaya No 9   DUMPLINGS $
(Вареничная No 9; ☑ 8-965-373 2732; ul Karla Marksa 3; dumplings R200-300; ⊙ 9am-10pm; ⊛ ⊘) The dining room is decorated like a classic library (shelves of old books, dark-leather couch seating and vintage Russian posters) at this satisfying dumpling cafe a block off the main street. The menu has sections for Russian, Asian and Italian dumplings, with several vegetarian options. Finish up with Turkish coffee or espresso and one of the monster-sized slices of cake.

⭐ **Gostevaya Izba**   RUSSIAN $$
(Гостевая Изба; ☑ 496-541 4343; www.sergiev-kanon.ru; Aptekarsky per 2; meals R350-850; ⊙ 10am-11pm; ⊘) Right by the monastery walls, this wonderful restaurant recreates classic dishes metropolitans of the past might have eaten outside fasting periods, such as apple-roasted duck breast with lingonberry sauce. Portions are ample and the food delicious. Try some *kvas* (fermented rye bread water), fireweed tea or Siberian malt lemonade straight from the monastery's own brewery.

Fortunately for vegetarians, the menu has a considerable fasting section, too.

🍷 Drinking & Nightlife

Bar Svoi   CRAFT BEER
(Бар Свои; ☑ 8-963-787 3289; www.svoi.bar; 1-ya Rybnaya ul 9/26; ⊙ noon-midnight Sun-Thu, to 4am Fri & Sat; ⊛) The best bar that we found in Sergiev Posad, with a selection of 20 rotating craft beers on draught (as well as Guinness for the purists). There's a decent menu of pub grub, too. The 2nd floor has booths and sometimes live music.

Popeye Coffee Bar   COFFEE
(www.coffeebarpopeye.ru; Vokzalnaya pl 1; ⊙ 6am-9pm Mon-Fri, from 9am Sat & Sun) This piccolo-sized coffee shop isn't much bigger than a large closet, but if you're travelling via bus or train it's the best place to find properly made espresso-based drinks (even flat whites) as soon as you get to town. Look for the corner

door immediately to the right of the McDonald's facing the train station.

Shopping

Gorod Masterov   ARTS & CRAFTS
(Город мастеров; ☑ 8-903-583 3160, 496-541 4130; www.city-of-craftsmen.ru; ul Karla Marksa 7; ⊙ 10am-7pm) Forget the carbon-copy *matryoshki* you see at tourist stalls everywhere – 'City of Craftsmen' sells beautiful hand-painted nesting dolls that are several cuts above, including sets of animals, old Russian kings and even astronauts. There are also carved wooden boxes and lovely Christmas ornaments. You can also take a class (R500) and paint your own *matryoshka* (advance booking required).

❶ Getting There & Away

Considering the horrendous traffic jams on the road approaches to Moscow, train is a much better way of getting to Sergiev Posad from the capital.

BUS

A suburban route, Bus 388 to Sergiev Posad (R200, 1½ hours) departs from Moscow's VDNKh metro station approximately every 15 minutes from 6.45am to 10.50pm.

Transit buses for Yaroslavl (R550, three hours) pass regularly; all these will take you to Pereslavl-Zalessky (R300, 45 minutes) and Rostov-Veliky (R400, two hours) if you can get a ticket. You can catch buses to Kostroma or Rybinsk from Yaroslavl. The **bus station** (Автовокзал; Vokzalnaya pl 49a) is about 370m east of pr Krasnoy Armii, opposite the train station.

TRAIN

The fastest transport option is the express commuter train that departs from Moscow's Yaroslavsky vokzal (R210 to R260, one hour); there are four daily during the week, three on weekends. Cheaper but slower *elektrichki* (R164, 1½ hours) depart a few times per hour throughout the day. The **train station** (Сергиев Посад; Vokzalnaya pl) is 400m east of pr Krasnoy Armii, opposite the bus station.

Since there are no direct trains to Pereslavl-Zalessky or Rostov-Veliky, you'll need to take a bus from Sergiev Posad.

❶ Getting Around

Numerous *marshrutky* run up and down pr Krasnoy Armii to and from pl Vokzalnaya; if you're heading back to the bus or train station, look for a bus with a sign saying на вокзал *(na vokzal;* 'to the station') in the window.

Taxi Standart (☑ 8-916-547 4444; www.taxi-standart.ru)

St Petersburg

☑ 812 / POP 5,281,579 / ⊘ MOSCOW

Best Places to Eat

➜ EM Restaurant (p204)

➜ Cococo (p202)

➜ Gräs x Madbaren (p202)

➜ Yat (p202)

➜ Duo Gastrobar (p202)

Best Places to Stay

➜ Baby Lemonade Hostel (p196)

➜ Soul Kitchen Hostel (p199)

➜ Alexander House (p199)

➜ Rossi Hotel (p197)

Why Go?

Beautiful, complex and imperious, with a hedonistic, creative temperament, St Petersburg (Санкт-Петербург)is the ultimate Russian diva. From her early days as an uninhabited swamp, the 300-year-old city has been nurtured by a succession of rulers, enduring practically everything that history and nature's harsh elements could throw at her. Constantly in need of repair but with a carefree party attitude, Piter (as she's known by locals) still seduces all who gaze upon her grand facades, glittering spires and gilded domes. Such an environment has inspired many of Russia's greatest artists, including Pushkin, Gogol, Dostoevsky, Rachmaninov, Tchaikovsky and Shostakovich.

When to Go
St Petersburg

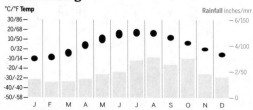

Mid-May–mid-Jul Visit during the White Nights, when the sun never truly sets.

May & Sep A great time to visit the city, avoiding the crowds of the peak months.

Nov–Jan Freezing, dark and blanketed in snow, winter in St Petersburg can still be magical.

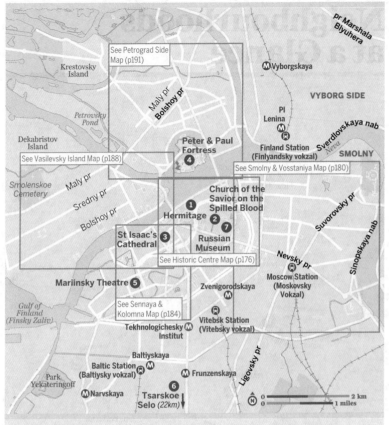

St Petersburg Highlights

1 Hermitage (p160) Spending a day (or more!) in one of the world's most unrivalled art collections.

2 Church of the Savior on the Spilled Blood (p170) Witnessing the amazing kaleidoscope of colours of this iconic church.

3 St Isaac's Cathedral (p166) Climbing the enormous dome for the best view over the imperial city.

4 Peter & Paul Fortress (p163) Paying your respects at the tombs of the Romanovs at the city's first major building.

5 Mariinsky Theatre (p210) Enjoying a ballet or opera at this historic theatre and its newer auditorium.

6 Tsarskoe Selo (p219) Heading out of town to see Catherine the Great's incredible summer palace.

7 Russian Museum (p164) Taking in the excellent collection of local art, from icons to the new.

History

It was Peter the Great's desire to make Russia a major European power that led to the founding of St Petersburg. At the start of the Great Northern War (1700–21), he captured the Swedish outposts on the Neva, and in 1703 he began the construction of his city with the Peter & Paul Fortress.

After Peter trounced the Swedes at Poltava in 1709, the city he named Sankt Pieter Burch (in Dutch style, after his namesake) really began to grow. In 1712 Peter moved the capital from Moscow to this still embryonic site, drafting in armies of peasants and Swedish prisoners of war to work as forced labour. Many died of disease and exhaustion, and St Petersburg is still known as 'a city built upon bones' to many Russians. Architects and artisans came to St Petersburg from all over Europe though, and by Peter's

Neighbourhoods at a Glance

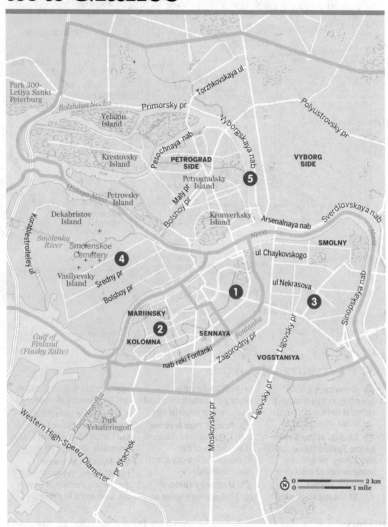

❶ Historic Heart (p167)

Radiating out from the golden spire of the Admiralty towards the Fontanka River, the Historic Heart has plenty of obvious attractions, such as the Hermitage, Russian Museum and the Church on the Spilled Blood, not to mention the city's most famous avenue: Nevsky Prospekt. There are also quirky gems like the Museum of Soviet Arcade Machines and a quartet of lovely parks. This is where you will be spending most of your time in St Petersburg, especially as the area is also blessed with excellent hotels, dining and drinking options.

② Smolny & Vosstaniya (p179)

This agglomeration of four districts (Smolny, Liteyny, Vosstaniya and Vladimirskaya) is also part of the city centre. The Smolny peninsula is a well-heeled residential district dominated by the Smolny Cathedral, while next-door Liteyny is centred on Liteyny pr, a commercial street between the Smolny and the Fontanka River. South of Nevsky pr are Vosstaniya and Vladimirskaya. Vosstaniya is the focus of St Petersburg's underground art and drinking scene, while the stunning Vladimirsky Cathedral, is a mercantile district full of shopping, markets and a clutch of quirky museums.

③ Sennaya & Kolomna (p184)

These two areas adjoin the Historic Heart and are almost as historic themselves. Sennaya is centred on Sennaya Pl (the Haymarket), a traditionally poor area that was immortalised in Dostoevsky's *Crime and Punishment* and has somehow retained its seedy, down-at-heel air despite a big attempt to redevelop it. Kolomna is the largest of seven islands and a quiet, rather out-of-the-way place, although one steeped in history and great beauty. It contains the world-famous Mariinsky Theatre and more canals and rivers than any other part of the city.

④ Vasilyevsky Island (p187)

The eastern edge of Vasilyevsky Island (or VO as it's usually shortened to) was originally designed to be the administrative heart of the city under Peter the Great. The plan was never carried out but there's still a concentration of historical sights there, including the Strelka (p188) and Kunstkamera (p187). The western side of the island is more industrial, but is also home to the fantastic Erarta Museum of Contemporary Art (p187). Transport fans will be thrilled by the opportunity to tour a couple of submarines and an icebreaker, and by museums devoted to trams and the metro.

⑤ Petrograd & Vyborg Sides (p190)

The Petrograd Side is a fascinating place that includes everything from the Peter and Paul Fortress to an impressive clutch of Style Moderne buildings lining its main drag. It also hosts a beautiful mosque, many interesting museums and huge swaths of parkland on the Kirov Islands, the city's largest green lung. The Vyborg Side is famous for its role in Soviet history and can be a little bleak. That said, a walk around the fascinating postindustrial landscape here will appeal to travellers who have palace fatigue, and a few interesting sights make the trip worthwhile.

TOP SIGHT
THE HERMITAGE

The Hermitage fully lives up to its sterling reputation. You can be absorbed by its treasures for days and still come out wanting more. The enormous collection (over three million items, only a fraction of which are on display in 360 rooms) almost amounts to a comprehensive history of Western European art.

History

Catherine the Great, one of the greatest art collectors of all time, began the collection. Nicholas I also greatly enriched it and opened the galleries to the public for the first time in 1852.

It was the post-revolutionary period that saw the collection increase threefold, as many valuable private collections were seized by the state, including those of the Stroganovs, Sheremetyevs and Yusupovs. In 1948 it incorporated the renowned collections of post-Impressionist and Impressionist paintings of Moscow industrialists Sergei Shchukin and Ivan Morozov.

Visiting the Hermitage

The State Hermitage consists of five linked buildings along riverside Dvortsovaya nab (rom west to east):

Winter Palace (Зимний дворец) This stunning mint-green, white and gold profusion of columns, windows and recesses, with its roof topped by rows of classical statues, was commissioned from Bartolomeo Rastrelli in 1754 by Empress Elizabeth. Catherine the Great and her successors had most of the interior remodelled in a classical style by 1837. It remained an imperial home until 1917,

DON'T MISS

➡ Rembrandt (Room 254)

➡ Great Church (Room 271)

➡ Treasure Gallery

➡ Peacock Clock (Room 204)

PRACTICALITIES

➡ Государственный Эрмитаж

➡ Map p176

➡ www.hermitagemuseum.org

➡ Dvortsovaya pl 2

➡ joint ticket R700

➡ ⏱ 10.30am-6pm Tue, Thu, Sat & Sun, to 9pm Wed & Fri

➡ Ⓜ Admiralteyskaya

though the last two tsars spent more time in other palaces.

Small Hermitage (Малый Эрмитаж; Map p176) Used by Catherine the Great as a retreat and to house the art collection started by Peter the Great, which she significantly expanded.

Great (Old) Hermitage (Большой (Старый) Эрмитаж; Map p176) This section of the museum (also known as the Large Hermitage) dates from the time of Catherine the Great. It mainly houses Italian Rennaissance art including works by Leonardo da Vinci, Raphael, Giorgione, Titian, Botticelli, Caravaggio and Tiepolo.

New Hermitage (Новый Эрмитаж; Map p176) Built for Nicholas II in 1852, to hold the growing art collection and as a museum for the public. Designed by German neoclassicist architect and painter von Klenze, the historically preserved rooms house the museum's collections of ancient art, European paintings, sculptures and decorative art.

Hermitage Theatre (Map p176; ☎ 812-408 1084; https://hermitagetheater.com; Dvortsovaya nab 32; online tickets from R8300) Designed by Giacomo Quarenghi, this intimate neo-classical auditorium was once the private theatre of the imperial family, and stands on the site of the original Winter Palace of Peter I.

The main public entrance is via the courtyard of the Winter Palace off Palace Sq.

Quick Tour

It would take days to fully do justice to the Hermitage's huge collection. If your time is limited, zone in on the following rooms:

Room 100 Ancient Egypt

Jordan Staircase Directly ahead when you pass through the main entrance inside the Winter Palace.

Rooms 175–98 Imperial state rooms and apartments, including the Malachite Hall, Nicholas Hall, Armorial Hall and Hall of St George.

Room 204 The Pavilion Hall.

Rooms 207–238 Italian art, 13th to 18th centuries.

Rooms 239–40 Spanish art, 16th to 18th centuries.

Rooms 245–47 Flemish art, 17th century.

Rooms 249–254 Dutch art, 17th century.

Room 271 Grand Church, the imperial family's cathedral.

Room 298–301 English art.

The Hermitage is a dynamic institution. Displays change, renovations continue, specific pieces go on tour, and temporary exhibitions occupy particular rooms, displacing whatever normally resides there, so be prepared for slight changes.

Organised Tours

Contact the excursions office (☑ 812-571 8446; ⊙ 11am-1pm & 2-4pm) to arrange a guided tour. These are one way to avoid queuing and, although they whiz round the main sections in about 1½ hours, at least they provide an introduction to the place in English, German or French. It's easy to 'lose' the group and stay on until closing time.

Also contact the excursions office if you plan to visit the Hermitage's Treasure Gallery (☑ 812-571 8446; www.hermitagemuseum.org; Winter Palace, Dvortsovaya pl; tour of Diamond or Golden Rooms R350). These two special collections, guarded behind vault doors, are open only by guided tour, for which you should either call ahead to reserve a place, or buy a ticket at the entrance. The Golden Rooms collection focuses on a hoard of fabulous Scythian and Greek gold and silver from the Caucasus, Crimea and Ukraine, dating from the 7th to 2nd centuries BC; the Diamond Rooms section has fabulous jewellery from Western Europe, and pieces from as far apart as China, India and Iran.

Other Branches

As much as you see in the museum, there's about 20 times more in its vaults, part of which you can visit at the Hermitage Storage Facility (p190). Other museum branches are the General Staff Building (p167; home to the Hermitage's amazing collection of Impressionist and post-Impressionist works), the Winter Palace of Peter I (Зимний дворец Петра Первого; Map p176; www.hermitagemuseum. org; Dvortsovaya nab 32; admission R150; ⊙ 10.30am-5pm Tue-Sat, 10am-4pm Sun; Ⓜ Admiralteyskaya), the Menshikov Palace (p189) on Vasilyevsky Island, and the Imperial Porcelain factory (www.ipm.ru; pr Obukhovsky Oborony 151; R300; ⊙ 10am-7pm Mon-Fri; Ⓜ Lomonosovskaya).

 TOP SIGHT
PETER & PAUL FORTRESS

Housing a cathedral, a former prison and various exhibitions, this large defensive fortress on Zayachy Island, founded in 1703, is the kernel from which St Petersburg grew and a must-see for history buffs. There are also panoramic views from the fortress walls.

The main entrance is across the **Ioannovsky Bridge** at the island's northeast end; there's also access via the **Kronwerk Bridge** (within walking distance of Sportivnaya metro station). Individual tickets are needed for each of the fortress's attractions – though a combined ticket gives access to Peter and Paul Cathedral, the Trubetskoy Bastion and three other sites.

All of Russia's prerevolutionary rulers from Peter the Great onwards (except Peter II and Ivan VI) are buried inside the **SS Peter & Paul Cathedral** (☉10am-7pm Mon, Tue & Thu-Sat, 11am-7pm Sun), which has a magnificent baroque interior. To ascend its 122.5m **bell tower** you'll have to join a guided tour (in Russian only), which happen several times a day.

Don't miss the **Commandant's House** (adult/student R200/120; ☉11am-6pm Mon & Thu-Sun, to 5pm Tue), which charts the history of the region from medieval times to 1918; or **Trubetskoy Bastion** (adult/student R200/120; ☉10am-7pm Thu-Mon, to 6pm Tue), where original cells are used for displays about former political prisoners, including Maxim Gorky, Leon Trotsky and Fyodor Dostoevsky.

A separate ticket gains you access to both the **Postern**, a 97.4m passage hidden in the fortress walls, and the **Neva Panorama** (adult/student R300/270; ☉10am-8pm Thu-Tue), a walkway atop the walls, which concludes at **Naryshkin Bastion**. Every day at noon a cannon is fired from here, a tradition dating back to Peter the Great's times.

DON'T MISS

➡ SS Peter & Paul Cathedral

➡ Trubetskoy Bastion

➡ Commandant's House

➡ Neva Panorama

➡ The beach

PRACTICALITIES

➡ Петропавловская крепость

➡ Map p191

➡ www.spbmuseum.ru

➡ grounds free, Peter & Paul Cathedral adult/child R450/250, combined ticket for 5 exhibitions R600/350

➡ ☉ grounds 8.30am-8pm, exhibitions 11am-6pm Mon & Thu-Sun, 10am-5pm Tue

➡ Ⓜ Gorkovskaya

ANTON_IVANOV/SHUTTERSTOCK ©

TOP SIGHT
RUSSIAN MUSEUM

Focusing solely on Russian art, from ancient church icons to 20th-century paintings, the Russian Museum's collection is magnificent and can easily be viewed in half a day or less. The collection is less overwhelming than that of the Hermitage, but the masterpieces nonetheless keep on coming as you tour the Mikhailovsky Palace and the attached Benois Wing.

Enter the Mikhailovsky Palace's lower floor to the right of the main facade. Pick up a museum map before ascending the magnificent main staircase to the 1st floor: this is where the chronological exhibits from the 10th century begin.

Galleries do close for restoration, and works are sometimes loaned out, so be prepared for slight changes to the following.

Mikhailovsky Palace, 2nd floor

Rooms 1–4 Work from the three major schools of Russian icon painting: Novgorod, Muscovy and Pskov.

Room 7 Sculpture of *Empress Anna with an Arab Boy*.

Room 11 The ornate White Hall, with period furniture by Rossi, is where Strauss and Berlioz performed concerts.

Room 14 Karl Bryullov's massive *Last Day of Pompeii* (1827–33), which was, in its time, the most famous Russian painting ever; there were queues for months to see it. Ivan Aivazovsky's seascapes also stand out, such as *The Wave*.

Room 15 Features a huge number of studies for Alexander Ivanov's most famous work, *The Appearance of Christ to the People*, which hangs in Moscow's Tretyakov Gallery.

DON'T MISS

➡ *The Wave* – Ivan Aivazovsky

➡ *Barge Haulers on the Volga* – Ilya Repin

➡ *Last Day of Pompeii* – Karl Bryullov

➡ *Portrait of the Poetess Anna Akhmatova* – Nathan Altman

PRACTICALITIES

➡ Русский музей

➡ Map p176

➡ ☎ 812-595 4248

➡ www.rusmuseum.ru

➡ Inzhenernaya ul 4

➡ adult/student R450/200

➡ ⊘ 10am-8pm Mon, 10am-6pm Wed & Fri-Sun, 1-9pm Thu

➡ Ⓜ Nevsky Prospekt

Mikhailovsky Palace, 1st floor

Rooms 23–26 The Wanderers (Peredvizhniki) and associated artists, including KA Savitsky's *To War* (Room 31); and Konstantin Makovsky (Room 25). Ghe's masterpiece, *Peter I Interrogating Tsarevich Alexey in Peterhof,* is usually in Room 26 along with other dark Ghe's works such as *The Last Supper.*

Room 28 Pause to take in the talent of Ukrainian artist Marie Bashkirtseff's striking portraits, such as *Umbrella* and the *Three Smiles* series.

Rooms 33–34 Works by Ilya Repin (1844–1930), probably Russia's best-loved artist. His masterpiece, *Barge Haulers on the Volga,* an unrivalled portrait of misery and enslavement in rural Russia, shows why the early Soviet authorities held him up as a model for the Socialist Realist painters to come.

Rooms 48 Mark Antokolsky's statues *Ivan the Terrible* and *Death of Socrates* flank a souvenir stand. From here, enter the Benois Wing to your right or continue straight for the Russian folk art galleries.

Room 54 Repin's enormous rendition of the *Ceremonial Sitting of the State Council on 7 May 1901, Marking the Centenary of Its Foundation.*

Benois Wing 2nd & 1st floors

Room 66 Works by the father of modern Russian art, Mikhail Vrubel, including *Epic Hero (Bogatyr).*

Rooms 67–71 Works by important early-20th-century painters Nikolai Sapunin, Mikhail Nesterov and Boris Kustodiev, whose *Merchant's Wife at Tea* is perhaps the most well-known picture here.

Room 72 Nathan Altman's famous cubist *Portrait of Anna Akhmatova.*

Room 75–76 Suprematism by Kasimir Malevich.

Rooms 77–78 Constructivist works by Alexander Lebedev and Alexander Rodchenko.

Rooms 79 Kuzma Petrov-Vodkin's *Portrait of Akhmatova* and *Mother of God.*

Rooms 80–81 Despite Stalin-era censorship, there are some interesting portraits of daily life here, such as Alexander Samokhvalov's *Militarised Komsomol.*

Rooms 82–86 Late Soviet art. Look for Alexei Sundukov's *Queue,* capturing the failed economy of the times, and Dmitry Zhilinsky's *The Artist's Family,* showing several generations of a family.

Rooms 87–94 From art nouveau–inspired pieces to Soviet-era textiles and porcelain.

To reach the 1st floor of the Benois Wing (following your tour of the museum's main collection), use the stairs down off Rooms 91 and 92.

Mikhailovsky Palace was designed by Carlo Rossi and built between 1819 and 1825. It was a gift for Grand Duke Mikhail (brother of Tsars Alexander I and Nicholas I) as compensation for missing out on the throne. Nicholas II opened it as a public gallery on 7 March 1898.

The Benois Wing houses pieces from the 20th century as well as temporary exhibitions. It was constructed between 1914 and 1919. It is accessible through an entrance on nab kanala Griboyedova and connected to the original palace.

OTHER BRANCHES

Permanent and temporary exhibitions by the Russian Museum are also held at the Marble Palace, the Mikhailovsky Castle (also known as the Engineer's Castle) and the Stroganov Palace. Combined tickets, available at each palace, cover entrance either to your choice of two the same day (adult/student R600/270) or to all four within a three-day period (R850/400).

ST PETERSBURG RUSSIAN MUSEUM

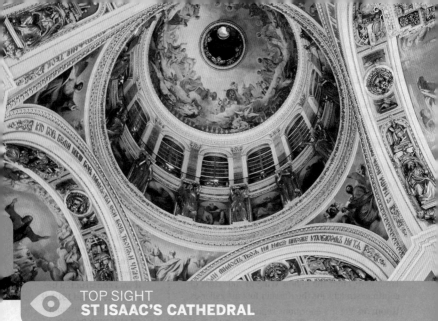

TOP SIGHT
ST ISAAC'S CATHEDRAL

The golden dome of St Isaac's Cathedral dominates the city's skyline. Its lavish interior is open as a museum, although services are held in the cathedral throughout the year. Most people bypass the museum to climb the 262 steps to the *kolonnada* (colonnade) around the drum of the dome, providing superb city views.

Named after St Isaac of Dalmatia, on whose feast day Peter the Great was born, this is one of the largest domed buildings in the world. French architect Auguste Montferrand began designing the cathedral in 1818. Due partly to technical issues, it took so long to build (until 1858) that Nicholas I was able to insist on an even more grandiose structure than Montferrand had originally planned. More than 100kg of gold leaf was used to cover the 21.8m-high dome alone, while the huge granite pillars on the building's facade each weigh over 120 tonnes. There's a statue of Montferrand holding a model of the cathedral on the west facade, although Nicholas I denied the architect his dying wish, to be buried here, considering it too high an honour for a mere artisan.

The cathedral's interior is lavishly decorated with 600 sq metres of mosaics, 16,000kg of malachite, 14 types of marble and an 816-sq-metre ceiling painting by Karl Bryullov. Look out for some hsitoric photographs of the cathedral, too.

Check the website for details of choral concerts that are occasionally held here. From May to October both the cathedral and colonnade are open until 10.30pm, and from 1 June to 20 August the colonnade stays open until 4.30am.

DON'T MISS

➡ The dome for amazing views

➡ The lavish interiors

➡ Display of historic photos

➡ Statue of Montferrand

PRACTICALITIES

➡ Исаакиевский собор

➡ Map p184

➡ ☎ 812-315 9732

➡ www.cathedral.ru

➡ Isaakievskaya pl

➡ cathedral adult/student R250/150, colonnade R150

➡ ☺ cathedral 10.30am-10.30pm Thu-Tue May-Sep, to 6pm Oct-Apr; colonnade 10.30am-10.30pm May-Oct, to 6pm Nov-Apr

➡ Ⓜ Admiralteyskaya

death in 1725 the city had a population of 40,000 and some 90% of Russia's foreign trade passed through it.

Between 1741 and 1825, during the reigns of Empress Elizabeth, Catherine the Great and Alexander I, St Petersburg became a cosmopolitan city with an imperial court of famed splendour. These monarchs commissioned glittering palaces, government buildings and grand churches.

Revolution & War

The emancipation of the serfs in 1861 and industrialisation, which peaked in the 1890s, brought a flood of workers into the city, leading to squalor, disease and festering discontent. St Petersburg became a hotbed of strikes and political violence, and was the hub of the 1905 revolution, sparked by 'Bloody Sunday' on 9 January 1905, when a strikers' march to petition the tsar in the Winter Palace was fired on by troops. In 1914, in a wave of patriotism at the start of WWI, the city's name was changed to the Russian-style Petrograd.

In 1917 the workers' protests turned into a general strike and troops mutinied, forcing the end of the monarchy in March and the establishment of a provisional government. Seven months later, Lenin's Bolshevik Party staged an audacious coup and the Soviet government came into being. Fearing a German attack on Petrograd, the new government moved the capital back to Moscow in March 1918.

Renamed Leningrad after Lenin's death in 1924, the city became a hub of Stalin's 1930s industrialisation program. By 1939 its population had grown to 3.1 million and it accounted for 11% of Soviet industrial output. Stalin feared the city as a rival power-base, however, and the 1934 assassination of the local communist chief Sergei Kirov at the Smolny Institute was the start of his 1930s Communist Party purge.

When Germany attacked the USSR in June 1941, its armies took only 2 1/2 months to reach Leningrad. It was the birthplace of Bolshevism, and Hitler swore to wipe the city from the face of the earth. His troops besieged the city in what would become the defining event of the 20th century for St Petersburg. Around a million people died from shelling, starvation and disease in what's often called the '900 Days' (actually 872). By comparison, the USA and UK suffered about 700,000 dead between them in total for the whole of WWII. Leningrad survived and, after the war, was proclaimed a 'hero city'.

St Petersburg Again

During the 1960s and '70s, Leningrad developed a reputation as a dissident's city with an artistic underground spearheaded by the poet Joseph Brodsky and, later, rock groups such as Akvarium. In 1989 Anatoly Sobchak, a reform-minded candidate, was elected mayor. Two years later, as the USSR crumbled, the city's citizens voted to bring back the name of St Petersburg (though the region around the city remains known as Leningradskaya Oblast).

In the anarchic post-Soviet years of the early 1990s, it often seemed like the local 'Mafia' were more in charge than the city's elected officials, who proved to be equally corrupt. Romanov ghosts returned to the city on 17 July 1998, when the remains of Tsar Nicholas II and some of his family were buried in the crypt at the SS Peter & Paul Cathedral within the fortress of the same name.

Five years later enormous sums were budgeted to spruce up the city for its tercentenary celebrations. Local boy made good Vladimir Putin didn't waste the opportunity to return to his birthplace and show it off to visiting heads of state and other dignitaries. The city still enjoys a prominent status in modern Russia today and is a favourite spot for summits and other governmental meetings.

⊙ Sights

◎ Historic Heart

★ **General Staff Building** MUSEUM

(Здание Главного штаба; Map p176; www.hermitagemuseum.org; Dvortsovaya pl 6-8; R300, incl main Hermitage museum & other buildings R700; ⊙10.30am-6pm Tue, Thu, Sat & Sun, to 9pm Wed & Fri; ⓂAdmiralteyskaya) The east wing of this magnificent building, wrapping around the south of Dvortsovaya pl and designed by Carlo Rossi in the 1820s, marries restored interiors with contemporary architecture to create a series of galleries displaying the Hermitage's amazing collection of Impressionist and post-Impressionist works. Contemporary art is here, too, often in temporary exhibitions by major artists.

Greater St Petersburg

0 — 1 miles
0 — 2 km

G — **F** — **E** — **D** — **C** — **B** — **A**

pl Shaumyana

Piskaryovsky pr

Sverdlovskaya nab

Smolnaya nab

Sinopskaya nab

Neva

VYBORG SIDE

SMOLNY

Kondratevsky pr

Polyustrovsky pr

ul Zhukova

Shpalernaya ul

Kirochnaya ul

ul Nekrasova

Lesnaya

Chugunnaya ul

Vyborgskaya

Bolshoy Sampsonievsky pr

Pl Lenina

Finland Station (Finlyandsky vokzal)

5

Liteyny pr

Nevsky pr

HISTORIC HEART

See Historic Centre Map (p176)

Neva

SENNAYA

See Petrograd Side Map (p191)

Kamennoostrovsky pr

See Sennaya & Kolomna Map (p184)

Chyornaya Rechka

PETROGRAD SIDE

MARIINSKY

3

7

Kamenny Island

Bolshaya al

Pesochnaya nab

Bolshoy pr

ul Savushkina

Hermitage Storage Facility

1

Staraya Derevnya

Primorsky pr

2

16

Krestovsky Island

Krestovsky pr

Petrovsky Island

VASILYEVSKY ISLAND

Sredny pr

Bolshoy pr

See Vasilevsky Island Map (p188)

Srednyaya Nevka

8

4

10

21

Rowing Canal

Malaya Neva

Dekabristov Island

ul Nalichnaya

Finsky Zaliv

Morskaya nab

Marine Facade Terminal

3

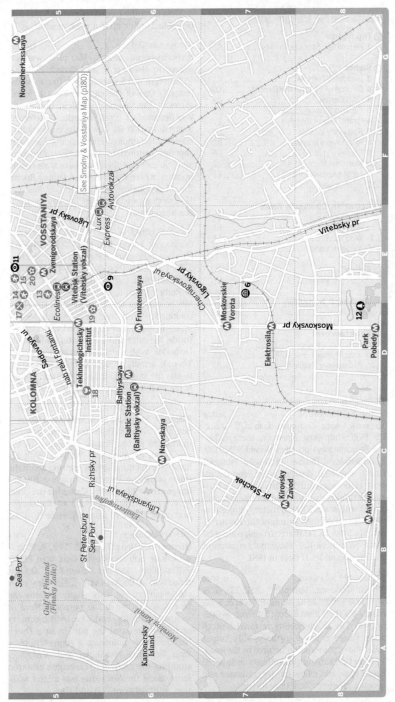

Greater St Petersburg

★ **Church of the Saviour
on the Spilled Blood** CHURCH
(Церковь Спаса на Крови; Map p176; ☎812-315 1636; http://eng.cathedral.ru/spasa_na_krovi/; Konyushennaya pl; adult/student R250/150; ☺10.30am-6pm Thu-Tue; Ⓜ Nevsky Prospekt) This five-domed dazzler is St Petersburg's most elaborate church with a classic Russian Orthodox exterior, and an interior decorated with some 7000 sq metres of mosaics. Officially called the Church of the Resurrection of Christ, its far more striking colloquial name references the assassination attempt on Tsar Alexander II here in 1881.

★ **Fabergé Museum** MUSEUM
(Музей Фаберже; Map p176; ☎812-333 2655; http://fabergemuseum.ru; nab reki Fontanki 21; R450, incl tour R600; ☺10am-8.45pm Sat-Thurs; Ⓜ Gostiny Dvor) The magnificently restored Shuvalovsky Palace is home to the world's largest collection of pieces manufactured by the jeweller Peter Carl Fabergé (including nine imperial Easter eggs) and fellow master craftsmen and -women of pre-revolutionary Russia.

Tickets for the guided tours (one hour) can be booked online up to a week in advance.

Stroganov Palace MUSEUM
(Строгановский дворец; Map p176; www.rusmuseum.ru; Nevsky pr 17; adult/student R300/150; ☺10am-6pm Wed & Fri-Mon, 1-9pm Thu; Ⓜ Nevsky Prospekt) One of the city's loveliest baroque exteriors, the salmon-pink Stroganov Palace was designed by court favourite Bartolomeo Rastrelli in 1753 for one of the city's leading aristocratic families. The building has been superbly restored by the Russian Museum, and you can visit the impressive state rooms upstairs, where the Arabesque Dining Room, the Mineralogical Study and the Rastrelli Hall, with its vast frieze ceiling, are the obvious highlights.

Kazan Cathedral CHURCH
(Казанский собор; Map p176; ☎812-314 4663; http://kazansky-spb.ru; Kazanskaya pl 2; ☺8.30am-7.30pm; Ⓜ Nevsky Prospekt) **FREE** This neoclassical cathedral, partly modelled on St Peter's in Rome, was commissioned by Tsar Paul before he was murdered in a coup. Its 111m-long colonnaded arms reach out towards Nevsky pr, encircling a garden studded with statues. Inside, the cathedral is dark and traditionally Orthodox, with a daunting 80m-high dome. There is usually a queue of believers waiting to kiss the icon of Our Lady of Kazan, a copy of one of Russia's most important icons.

Bronze Horseman MONUMENT
(Map p184; Senatskaya pl; Ⓜ Sadovaya) The most famous statue of Peter the Great was immortalised as the Bronze Horseman in the epic poem by Alexander Pushkin. With his horse (representing Russia) rearing above the snake of treason, Peter's enormous statue was sculpted over 12 years for Catherine the Great by Frenchman Etienne Falconet. Its inscription reads 'To Peter I from Catherine II – 1782'.

Summer Garden PARK
(Летний сад; Map p176; ☎812-314 0374; https://igardens.ru; nab reki Moyki; tours from R1200; ☺10am-10pm May-Sep, 10am-8pm Oct-Mar, closed Apr; Ⓜ Gostiny Dvor) **FREE** The city's oldest park, these leafy, shady gardens can be entered either at the northern Neva or southern Moyka end. Early-18th-century architects designed the garden in a Dutch baroque style, following a geometric plan, with fountains, pavilions and sculptures studding the grounds. The ornate cast-iron fence along the Neva side was a later addition, built between 1771 and 1784.

Marble Palace
PALACE

(Мраморный дворец; Map p176; ☎ 812-595 4248; www.rusmuseum.ru; Millionnaya ul 5; adult/student R300/150; ⊙ 10am-6pm Mon, Wed & Fri-Sun, 1-9pm Thu; Ⓜ Nevsky Prospekt) This branch of the Russian Museum (p164) features temporary exhibitions of contemporary art and a permanent display of paintings from the Ludwig Museum in Cologne that includes works by Picasso, Warhol, Basquiat and Liechtenstein. The palace, designed by Antonio Rinaldi, gets its name from the 36 kinds of marble used in its construction. Highlights include the Gala Staircase, made of subtly changing grey Urals marble; and the impressive Marble Hall, with walls of lapis lazuli and marble in a range of colours from yellow to pink.

Mikhailovsky Castle
MUSEUM

(Михайловский замок; Map p176; ☎ 812-595 4248; www.rusmuseum.ru; Sadovaya ul 2; adult/student R300/150; ⊙ 10am-6pm Mon, Wed & Fri-Sun, 1-9pm Thu; Ⓜ Gostiny Dvor) A branch of the Russian Museum (p164), the castle is worth visiting for its temporary exhibits as well as a few finely restored state rooms, including the lavish burgundy and gilt throne room of Tsar Paul I's wife Maria Fyodorovna.

Mikhailovsky Garden
PARK

(Михайловский сад; Map p176; https://igardens.ru; ⊙ 10am-10pm May-Sep, 10am-8pm Oct-Mar, closed Apr; Ⓜ Nevsky Prospekt) FREE Administered by the Russian Museum, these 8.7-hectare gardens are lovely and offer an impressive perspective of Mikhailovsky Castle. They are famous for their Style Moderne wrought-iron fence and gates, a profusion of metallic blooms and flourishes that wrap around one side of the Church on the Spilled Blood.

Museum of Soviet Arcade Machines
MUSEUM

(Map p176; ☎ 812-740 0240; http://15kop.ru; Konyushennaya pl 2; adult/student R450/350; ⊙ 11am-8pm, until 9pm May-Sep; Ⓜ Nevsky Prospekt) Giving new meaning to 'back in the USSR', this 'museum' is sure to be one of the most entertaining ones you will visit in St Petersburg. Admission includes a stack of 15 kopek coins used to operate the 50-odd game machines in its collection, which date to the Brezhnev era.

Mars Field
PARK

(Марсово поле; Map p176; nab Lebyazhey kanavki; Ⓜ Nevsky Prospekt) Named after the Roman god of war and once the scene of 19th-century military parades, the grassy Mars Field is a popular spot for strollers, even though in the early 20th century it was used as a burial ground for victims and heroes of the revolution. At its centre, an eternal flame (Map p176) has been burning since 1957 in memory of the victims of all wars and revolutions in St Petersburg.

ST PETERSBURG SIGHTS

ST PETERSBURG IN ...

Two Days
On day one wander down Nevsky pr, dropping into the Church of the Saviour on the Spilled Blood and Kazan Cathedral. Also take in the view from atop St Isaac's Cathedral. After lunch visit the Yusupov Palace and New Holland. Spend the evening seeing a ballet or opera at the Mariinsky Theatre.

Devote day two to the wondrous Hermitage and its extraordinary collection, including the stellar impressionist collection in the General Staff Building on the other side of Palace Sq. When you leave, relax by taking a sightseeing cruise around the canals, followed by dinner at Cococo, enjoying contemporary takes on traditional Russian cuisine.

Four Days
On day three start at the Peter & Paul Fortress to see where the city began, and wander past the Mosque and take in the Style Modern architecture of Kamennoostrovsky pr. Wander across the bridge to Vasilevsky Island and see the Strelka, the fascinating Kunstkamera and then either the Menshikov Palace, for history fans, or the Erarta Museum of Contemporary Art, for art lovers.

Start day four travelling out to Pushkin (Tsarskoe Selo) for a visit to the extraordinary Catherine Palace, and then continue to nearby Pavlovsk for a walk in the gorgeous gardens. If you have time on returning to the city, make a tour of the superb Russian Museum. Top it all off with cocktails at one of St Petersburg's cosy bars such as Apotheke Bar.

The Hermitage

A HALF-DAY TOUR

Successfully navigating the State Hermitage Museum, with its four vast interconnecting buildings and around 360 rooms, is an art form in itself. Our half-day tour of the highlights can be done in four hours, or easily extended to a full day.

Once past ticket control start by ascending the grand ❶ **Jordan Staircase** to Neva Enfilade and Great Enfilade for the impressive staterooms, including the former throne room St George's Hall and the 1812 War Gallery (Room 197), and the Romanovs' private apartments. Admire the newly restored ❷ **Great Church** then make your way back to the Neva side of the building via the Western Gallery (Room 262) to find the splendid ❸ **Pavilion Hall** with its view onto the Hanging Garden and the gilded Peacock Clock, always a crowd pleaser.

Make your way along the series of smaller galleries in the Large Hermitage hung with Italian Renaissance art, including masterpieces by ❹ **Da Vinci** and ❺ **Caravaggio**. The Loggia of Raphael (Room 227) is also impressive. Linger a while in the galleries containing Spanish art before taking in the Dutch collection, the highlight of which is the hoard of ❻ **Rembrandt** canvases in Room 254.

Descend the Council Staircase (Room 206), noting the giant malachite vase, to the ground floor where the fantastic Egyptian collection awaits in Room 100 as well as the galleries of Greek and Roman Antiquities. If you have extra time, it's well worth booking tours to see the special exhibition in the ❼ **Gold Rooms** of the Treasure Gallery.

TOP TIPS

➡ Reserve tickets online to skip the long lines.

➡ Bring a sandwich and a bottle of water with you: the cafe isn't great.

➡ Wear comfortable shoes.

➡ Bear in mind the only cloakroom is before ticket control, so you can't go back and pick up a sweater.

Jordan Staircase
Originally designed by Rastrelli, in the 18th century this incredible white marble construction was known as the Ambassadorial Staircase because it was the way into the palace for official receptions.

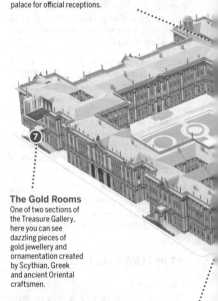

The Gold Rooms
One of two sections of the Treasure Gallery, here you can see dazzling pieces of gold jewellery and ornamentation created by Scythian, Greek and ancient Oriental craftsmen.

Great Church
This stunningly ornate church was the Romanovs' private place of worship and the venue for the marriage of the last tsar, Nicholas II, to Alexandra Feodorovna in 1895.

Rembrandt
A moving portrait of contrition and forgiveness, *Return of the Prodigal Son* (Room 254) depicts the biblical scene of a wayward son returning to his father.

Da Vinci
Along with the *Benois Madonna*, also here, *Madonna and Child (Madonna Litta*; Room 214) is one of just a handful of paintings known to be the work of Leonardo da Vinci.

St George's Hall

Hermitage Theatre

Pavilion Hall
Apart from the Peacock Clock, the Pavilion Hall also contains beautifully detailed mosaic tables made by Italian and Russian craftsmen in the mid-19th century.

Caravaggio
The Lute Player (Room 237) is the Hermitage's only Caravaggio, and a work that the master of light and shade described as the best piece he'd ever painted.

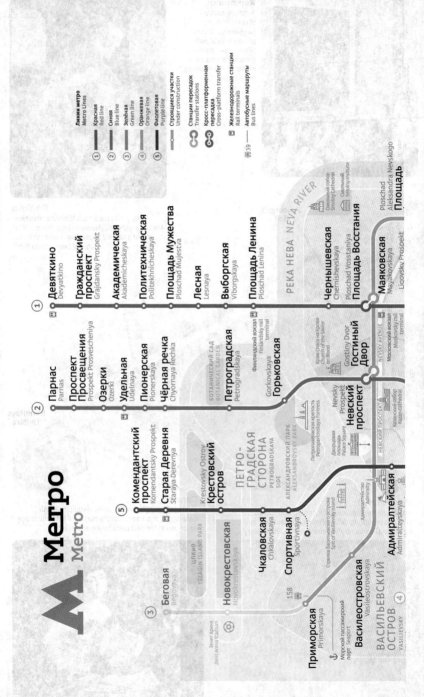

Метро
Metro

Линии метро
Metro Lines

- ① Красная — Red line
- ② Синяя — Blue line
- ③ Зелёная — Green line
- ④ Оранжевая — Orange line
- ⑤ Фиолетовая — Purple line

Строящиеся участки
Under construction

Станции пересадок
Transfer stations

Кросс-платформенная пересадка
Cross-platform transfer

Железнодорожные станции
Rail terminals

Автобусные маршруты
Bus lines

РЕКА НЕВА NEVA RIVER

① Линия 1
- Девяткино — Devyatkino
- Гражданский проспект — Grajdansky Prospekt
- Академическая — Akademicheskaya
- Политехническая — Politekhnicheskaya
- Площадь Мужества — Ploschad Mujestva
- Лесная — Lesnaya
- Выборгская — Viborgskaya
- Площадь Ленина — Ploschad Lenina
- Чернышевская — Chernishevskaya
- Площадь Восстания — Ploschad Vosstaniya
- Маяковская — Mayakovskaya
- Площадь Александра Невского — Ploschad Aleksandra Nevskogo

② Линия 2
- Парнас — Parnas
- Проспект Просвещения — Prospekt Prosvescheniya
- Озерки — Ozerki
- Удельная — Udelnaya
- Пионерская — Pionerskaya
- Чёрная речка — Chyornaya Rechka
- Петроградская — Petrogradskaya
- Горьковская — Gorkovskaya
- Невский проспект — Nevsky Prospekt

⑤ Линия 5
- Комендантский проспект — Komendantsky Prospekt
- Старая Деревня — Staraya Derevnya
- Крестовский остров — Krestovsky Ostrov
- Чкаловская — Chkalovskaya
- Спортивная — Sportivnaya
- Адмиралтейская — Admiralteyskaya

④ Линия 4
- Приморская — Primorskaya
- Василеостровская — Vasileostrovskaya

③ Линия 3
- Беговая — Begovaya
- Новокрестовская — Novokrestovskaya

БОТАНИЧЕСКИЙ САД
BOTANICAL GARDEN

Финляндский вокзал
Finlandsky rail terminal

Смольный собор
Smolny Cathedral
Smolny Institute

Храм Спас-на-Крови
Church of the Savior on Blood

Гостиный Двор
Gostiny Dvor

Московский вокзал
Moskovsky rail terminal

Казанский собор
Kazan Cathedral

Петропавловская крепость
Petropavlovskaya Fortress

Дворцовая площадь
Palace Square

Адмиралтейство
Admiralty

НЕВСКИЙ ПРОСПЕКТ
NEVSKY AVENUE

ПЕТРО-ГРАДСКАЯ СТОРОНА
PETROGRADSKAYA SIDE

АЛЕКСАНДРОВСКИЙ ПАРК
ALEKSANDROVSKY PARK

ЕЛАГИН ОСТРОВ ЦПКиО
YELAGIN ISLAND PARK

Стрелка Васильевского острова
Spit of Vasilievsky Island

ВАСИЛЬЕВСКИЙ ОСТРОВ
VASILYEVSKY ISLAND

Морской пассажирский порт Seaport

Зенит Арена
Zenit Arena Stadium

158

39

158

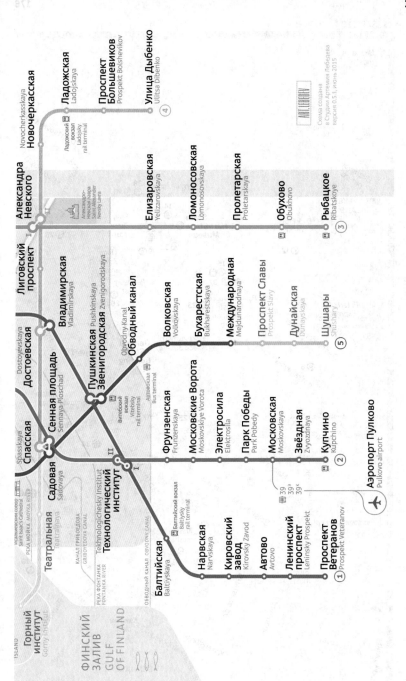

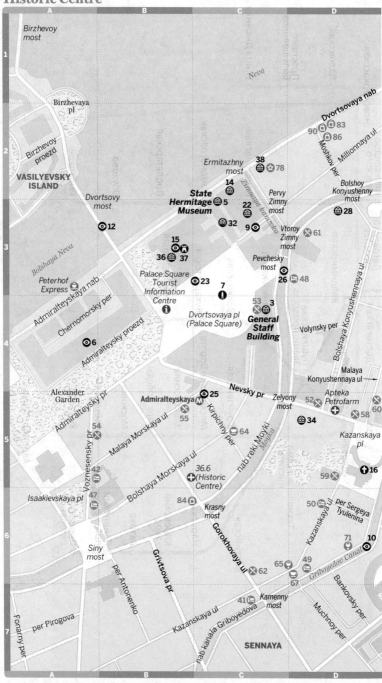

ST PETERSBURG

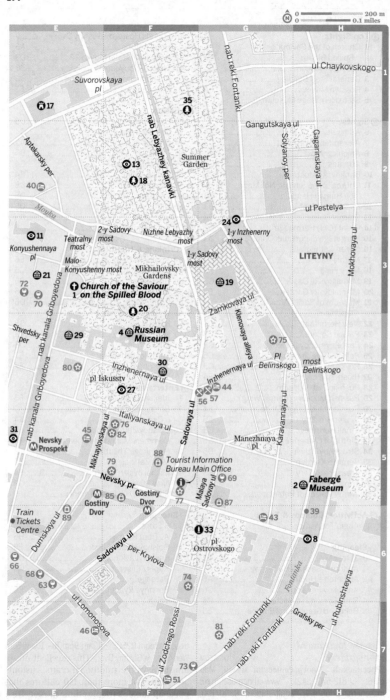

Historic Centre

**Russian Museum of
Ethnography**   MUSEUM
(Российский Этнографический музей; Map
p176; ☎812-570 5421; www.ethnomuseum.ru;
Inzhenernaya ul 4/1; adult/student R300/100,

treasure room R250; ☺10am-9pm Tue, 10am-6pm
Wed-Sun; Ⓜ Gostiny Dvor) This excellent museum displays the traditional crafts, customs
and beliefs of more than 150 cultures that
make up Russia's fragile ethnic mosaic. It's a

marvellous collection with particularly strong sections on the Jews of Russia, Transcaucasia and Central Asia, including rugs and two full-size yurts (nomads' portable tenthouses). Galleries are accessed either side of the magnificent 1000-sq-m Marble Hall, flanked by rows of pink Karelian-marble columns, in which events and concerts are held.

Admiralty ARCHITECTURE
(Адмиралтейство; Map p176; Admiralteysky proezd 1; Ⓜ Admiralteyskaya) The gilded spire of the Admiralty is a prime St Petersburg landmark, visible from Gorokhovaya ul, Voznesensky pr and Nevsky pr, as all of these roads radiate outwards from this central point. From 1711 to 1917, this spot was the headquarters of the Russian navy; now it houses the country's largest military naval college and is closed to the public.

◎ Smolny & Vosstaniya

★ Alexander Nevsky
Monastery MONASTERY
(Александро-Невская лавра; Map p180; www. lavra.spb.ru; Nevsky pr 179/2; cemetery R400, pantheon R150; ☉ grounds 6am-11pm in summer, 8am-9pm in winter, churches 6am-9pm, cemeteries 9.30am-6pm in summer, 11am-4pm in winter, pantheon 11am-5pm Tue, Wed & Fri-Sun; Ⓜ Ploshchad

Aleksandra Nevskogo) The Alexander Nevsky Monastery – named for the patron saint of St Petersburg – is the city's most ancient and eminent monastery. Peter the Great made a mistake when he founded the monastery on this spot at the far end of Nevsky pr, thinking wrongly that it was the site where Alexander of Novgorod had beaten the Swedes in 1240. Nonetheless, in 1797 the monastery became a *lavra*, the most senior grade of Russian Orthodox monasteries.

Today it is a working monastery that attracts the most devout believers – a revered and holy place – as well as the gravesite of some of Russia's most famous artistic figures. You can wander freely around most of the grounds, but you must buy tickets from the kiosk on your right after entering the main gates to enter the most important two graveyards.

Museum of the Defence &
Blockade of Leningrad MUSEUM
(Музей обороны и блокады Ленинграда; Map p180; www.blokadamus.ru; Solyarnoy per 9; R250, audio guide R300; ☉ 10am-6pm Thu-Mon, 12.30pm-8.30pm Wed; Ⓜ Chernyshevskaya) The grim but engrossing displays here contain donations from survivors, propaganda posters from the blockade period and many photos depicting life and death during the siege.

THE BRIDGES OF ST PETERSBURG

Some 342 bridges span St Petersburg's network of canals and waterways. It's quite a sight to witness the raising of the bridges (p214) over the Neva river during the navigation period. **Dvortsovy most** (Palace Bridge; Дворцовый мост; Map p176; Ⓜ Admiralteyskaya), beside the Winter Palace, is one of the most popular spots to watch this event as there is classical music broadcasting and a carnival atmosphere with street vendors and plenty of sightseeing boats bobbing in the Neva.

Some of the most charming bridges, though, are the smaller structures that span the canals around the city. Here are a few of our favourites:

Anichkov most (Аничков мост; Map p176) Features rearing horses at all four corners, symbolising humanity's struggle with, and taming of, nature.

Bankovsky most (Банковский мост; Map p176) Suspended by cables emerging from the mouths of golden-winged griffins. The name comes from the Assignment Bank (now a university), which stands on one side of the bridge.

Most Lomonosova (Мост Ломоносова; Map p168) Four Doric towers contain the mechanism that pulls up the moveable central section, allowing tall boats to pass along the Fontanka underneath.

Lviny most (Bridge of Four Lions; Map p184) This suspension bridge is supported by two pairs of regal lions.

Panteleymonovsky most (Пантелеймоновский мост; Map p176) At the confluence of the Moyka and the Fontanka, this beauty features lamp posts bedecked with the double-headed eagle and railings adorned with the coat of arms.

ST PETERSBURG SIGHTS

Smolny & Vosstaniya

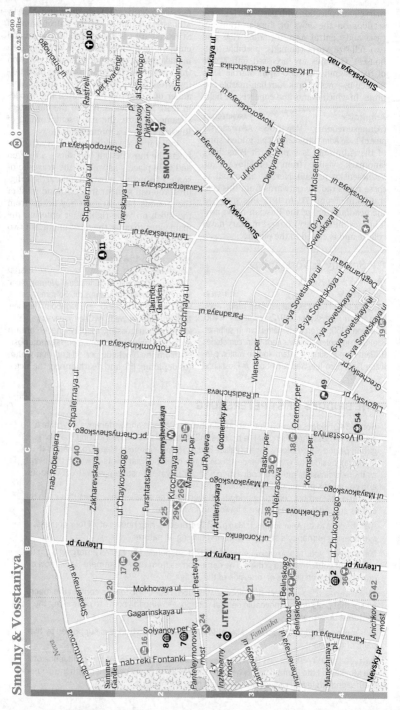

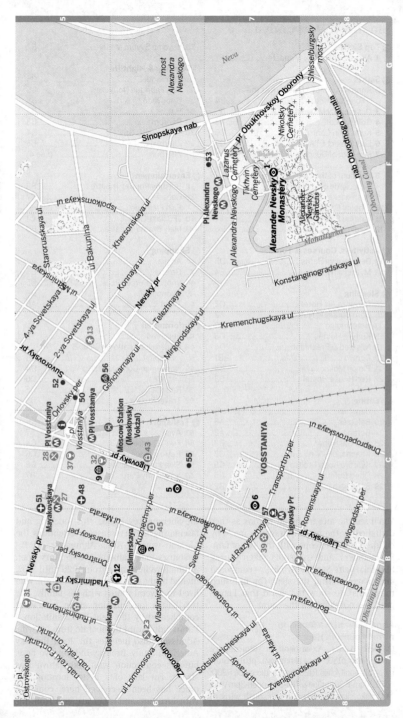

Smolny & Vosstaniya

You'll see the meagre bread rations as they dwindled by the month, drawings made by children trying to cope with the loss of family members, and snapshots taken during Shostakovich's Symphony No.9 – composed and played during the siege (by famished musicians), to show the world that Leningrad was not down for the count.

**Anna Akhmatova Museum
at the Fountain House** MUSEUM
(Музей Анны Ахматовой в Фонтанном Доме; Map p180; www.akhmatova.spb.ru; Liteyny pr 51; adult/child R120/free, audio guide R200; ◷10.30am-6.30pm Tue & Thu-Sun, noon-8pm Wed; ⓜMayakovskaya) Housed in the south wing of the Sheremetyev Palace, this touching and fascinating literary museum celebrates the life and work of Anna Akhmatova, St Petersburg's most famous 20th-century poet. Akhmatova lived here from 1926 until 1952, invited by the art scholar Nikolai Punin, who lived in several rooms with his family. The two had a long-running affair, somewhat complicated by the tight living situation – Punin didn't want to separate from his wife. Admission also includes the Josef Brodsky American Study. Brodsky did not live here, but his connection with Akhmatova was strong. For lack of a better location, his office has been re-created here, complete with furniture and other artifacts from his

adopted home in Massachusetts. Funds are currently being collected to open a Josef Brodsky Museum at the poet's former home a few blocks away on Liteyny pr.

When coming to the museum, be sure to enter from Liteyny pr, rather than from the Fontanka River, where the main palace entrance is, as it's not possible to reach the museum from there.

Dostoevsky Museum MUSEUM
(Литературно-мемориальный музей Ф.М. Достоевского; Map p180; www.md.spb.ru; Kuznechny per 5/2; adult/student R250/100, audio guide R250; ☺ 11am-6pm Tue-Sun, 1-8pm Wed; M Vladimirskaya) ✐ Fyodor Dostoevsky lived in flats all over the city (mostly in Sennaya), but his final residence is this 'memorial flat' where he lived from 1878 until he died in 1881. The apartment remains as it was when the Dostoevsky family lived here, including the study where he wrote *The Brothers Karamazov*, and the office of Anna Grigorievna, his wife, who recopied, edited and sold all of his books.

Lumiere Hall ARTS CENTRE
(Map p168; ☑ 8-812-407 1731; www.lumierehall.ru/spb; nab Obvodny kanala 74; R500; ☺ 11am-11pm; M Fruzenskaya) In a once industrial part of the city, Lumiere Hall hosts large-format multimedia exhibitions – basically massive 3D projections in a 360-degree space, with audio commentary on the works displayed and the artists behind the creations. Take a seat on beanbags and enjoy the show. Recent installations have included projections of paintings by Ivan Aivazovsky, Van Gogh and Gustav Klimt. It's a 1km walk from the metro station. Head up to the canal and turn right.

Tauride Palace & Gardens PARK
(Таврический дворец и сад; Map p180; ☺ 8am-8pm Aug-Mar, to 10pm May-Jul, closed Apr; M Chernyshevskaya) Catherine the Great had this baroque palace built in 1783 for Grigory Potemkin, a famed general and her companion for many years. Today it is home to the Commonwealth of Independent States and is closed to the public. The gardens, on the other hand, are open to all; once the romping grounds of the tsarina, they became a park for the people under the Soviets, and their facilities include a lake, several cafes and an entertainment centre.

Pushkinskaya 10 GALLERY
(Арт-Центр Пушкинская 10; Map p180; www.p-10.ru; Ligovsky pr 53; R500; ☺ 4-8pm Wed-Fri, noon-8pm Sat & Sun; M Ploshchad Vosstaniya) This now

legendary locale is a former apartment block – affectionately called by its street address despite the fact that the public entrance is actually on Ligovsky pr – that contains studio and gallery space, as well as music clubs Fish Fabrique (p210) and **Fabrique Nouvelle** (Map p180; www.fishfabrique.spb.ru; ☺ 3pm-late), plus an assortment of other shops and galleries. It offers a unique opportunity to hang out with local musicians and artists, who are always eager to talk about their work. One ticket gives admission to all the galleries.

Vladimirsky Cathedral CATHEDRAL
(Владимирский собор; Map p180; Vladimirsky pr 20; ☺ 8am-6pm, services 6pm daily; M Vladimirskaya) This fantastic, five-domed cathedral, ascribed to Domenico Trezzini, is the namesake of this neighbourhood. Incorporating both baroque and neoclassical elements, the cathedral was built in the 1760s, with Giacomo Quarenghi's neoclassical bell tower added later in the century. Over the centuries the congregation has included Dostoevsky, who lived around the corner. The cathedral was closed in 1932 and the Soviets turned it into an underwear factory, but in 1990 it was reconsecrated and resumed its originally intended function.

Museum of Decorative & Applied Arts MUSEUM
(Музей прикладного искусства; Map p180; ☑ 812-273 3258; www.spbghpa.ru; Solyanoy per 15; adult/student R300/150, excursion in Russian R2000; ☺ 11am-5pm Tue-Sat; M Chernyshevskaya) Also known as the Stieglitz Museum, this fascinating establishment is as beautiful as you would expect a decorative arts museum to be. An array of gorgeous objects is on display, from medieval furniture to 18th-century Russian tiled stoves and contemporary works by the students of the Applied Arts School (also housed here). This museum is less visited than some of its counterparts in the city, but the quiet atmosphere only adds to its appeal.

Kuryokhin Centre ARTS CENTRE
(Map p180; ☑ 812-322 4223; www.kuryokhin.net; 4th flr, Ligovsky pr 73; R100; ☺ 11am-9pm Mon-Sat; M Ploshchad Vosstaniya) Named after Sergey Kuryokhin (1954–96), a legend of the Russian contemporary arts and music scene, this is the temporary home of the arts centre until its new home on Vasilevsky Island is ready (late 2019). You can view some of the talented avant-garde artists work and those of his contemporaries including the

band Kino and performance artist Vladislav Mamyshev-Monroe, as well exhibitions of new works that push the artistic boundaries.

Smolny Cathedral
CHURCH

(Смольный собор; Map p180; ☑812-577 1421; pl Rastrelli 3/1; belltower adult/child R150/50; ⏱church 7am-8pm, bell-tower 10am-6pm; Ⓜ Chernyshevskaya) If baroque is your thing, then look no further than the sky-blue Smolny Cathedral, an unrivalled masterpiece of the genre that ranks among Bartolomeo Rastrelli's most amazing creations. The cathedral is the centrepiece of a convent mostly built to Rastrelli's designs between 1748 and 1757. His

inspiration was to combine baroque details with the forest of towers and onion domes typical of an old Russian monastery. You'll get a fascinating perspective over the church and city beyond from the 63m-high bell tower.

◉ Sennaya & Kolomna

★ Yusupov Palace
PALACE

(Юсуповский дворец; Map p184; ☑921-970 3038; www.yusupov-palace.ru; nab reki Moyki 94; adult/student incl audio guide R700/500, Rasputin tour adult/student R350/250; ⏱11am-6pm; Ⓜ Sadovaya) This spectacular palace on the Moyka River has some of the best 19th-century

Sennaya & Kolomna

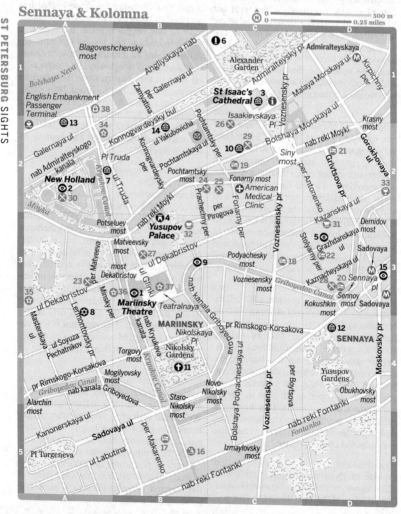

interiors in the city, in addition to a fascinating and gruesome history. The palace's last owner was the eccentric Prince Felix Yusupov, a high-society darling and at one time the richest man in Russia. Most notoriously, the palace is the place where Grigory Rasputin was murdered in 1916, and the basement where this now infamous plot unravelled can be visited as part of a guided tour.

★ **New Holland** ISLAND
(Новая Голландия; Map p184; www.newholland-sp.ru; nab Admiralteyskogo kanala; ⊙9am-10pm Mon-Thu, to 11pm Fri-Sun; Ⓜ Sadovaya) This triangular island was closed for the most part of the last three centuries, and has opened to the public in dazzling fashion. There's plenty going on here, with hundreds of events happening throughout the year. There are summertime concerts, art exhibitions, yoga classes and film screenings, plus restaurants, cafes and shops. You can also come to enjoy a bit of quiet on the grass – or on one of the pontoons floating in the pond.

Central Naval Museum MUSEUM
(Центральный военно-морской музей; Map p184; ☑812-303 8513; www.navalmuseum.ru; pl Truda; adult/student R600/400; ⊙11am-6pm Wed-Sun; Ⓜ Admiralteyskaya) Following a move to this beautifully repurposed building opposite the former shipyard of New Holland, the Central Naval Museum has moved into the 21st century and is now one of St Petersburg's best history museums. The superb, light-bathed building houses an enormous collection of models, paintings and other artefacts from three centuries of Russian naval history, including *botik,* the small boat known as the 'grandfather of the Russian navy' – stumbling across it in the late 17th century was Peter the Great's inspiration to create a Russian maritime force.

House of Music PALACE
(Дом музыки; Map p188; ☑812-400 1400; www.spdm.ru; nab reki Moyki 211; tours R350; Ⓜ Sadovaya) This fabulous and fully restored mansion on the Moyka River belonged to Grand Duke Alexey, the son of Alexander II. The wrought-iron-and-stone fence is one of its most stunning features, with the Grand Duke's monogram adorning the gates. Tours of the house usually take place once or twice a week, but the dates vary and tickets often sell out in advance, so check the website. Another way to visit the interior is to attend a concert here.

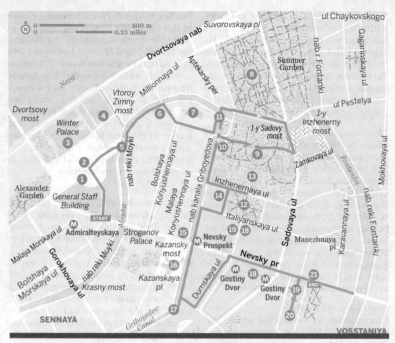

🏃 City Walk
Historic Heart

START DVORTSOVAYA PL
END KUPETZ ELISEEVS
LENGTH 2KM; THREE HOURS

Approach the magnificent ① **Palace Square** on Dvortsovaya pl, from Bolshaya Morskaya ul. Turning the corner from Nevsky pr, behold the ② **Alexander Column**, framed under the triumphal arch with the ③ **Winter Palace** (p160) as its backdrop. Turn right at the square's northeast corner to find the colossal ④ **Atlantes** holding aloft the portico of the New Hermitage.

At the Moyka River; cross to the eastern bank using the ⑤ **Pevchesky Most**. Head north along the river to the final residence of Russia's most celebrated poet, the ⑥ **Pushkin Flat-Museum**. Around the corner Konyushennaya pl is dominated by the 18th-century court stables. In this complex you can visit the ⑦ **Church of the Saviour Not Made by Human Hand** where Pushkin's funeral service was held.

Take a rest in either the ⑧ **Mars Field** (p171) or the shady ⑨ **Mikhailovsky Gardens** (p171). Revived, you'll be ready for the spectacular ⑩ **Church on the Spilled Blood** (p170). There's a view of the church from ⑪ **Teatralny most** at the intersection of the Moyka and Griboyedov Canal.

Detour off nab kanala Griboyedova to find a statue of Pushkin in ⑫ **pl Iskusstv**. The square is ringed by cultural institutions, including the ⑬ **Russian Museum** (p164) and ⑭ **Mikhailovsky Theatre** (p209).

At the junction of Nevsky pr and nab kanala Griboyedova admire the Style Moderne beauty ⑮ **Singer Building** (p213). It's a whimsical contrast to the formidable ⑯ **Kazan Cathedral** (p170) opposite. Behind the church, ⑰ **Bankovsky most** (p179) is the city's most picturesque and photographed bridge.

Head up Dumskaya ul to Nevsky pr and navigate the vaulted gallery surrounding the ⑱ **Bolshoy Gostiny Dvor** (p213), the 18th-century trading arcade. A short walk east along Nevsky pr is Ploshchad Ostrovskogo, a small park with an impressive ⑲ **statue of Catherine the Great** and a view the facade of the ⑳ **Alexandrinsky Theatre** (p209). Finish up at the grand food hall ㉑ **Kupetz Eliseevs** (p213).

Grand Choral Synagogue SYNAGOGUE

(Большая хоральная синагога; Map p184; ☑921-978 4464; www.eng.jewishpetersburg.ru; Lermontovsky pr 2; ☺10am-6pm Sun-Fri, services 10am Sat; Ⓜ Sadovaya) Designed by Vasily Stasov, the striking Grand Choral Synagogue opened in 1893 to provide a central place of worship for St Petersburg's growing Jewish community. Its lavishness (particularly notable in the 47m-high cupola and the decorative wedding chapel) indicates the pivotal role that Jews played in imperial St Petersburg. The synagogue was fully revamped in 2003. Visitors are welcome except on the Sabbath and other holy days. Men and married women should cover their heads upon entering.

Nikolsky Cathedral CATHEDRAL

(Никольский собор; Map p184; Nikolskaya pl 1/3; ☺9am-7pm; Ⓜ Sadovaya) Surrounded on two sides by canals, this ice-blue cathedral is one of the most picture-perfect in the city, beloved by locals for its baroque spires and golden domes. It was one of the few churches that still operated during the Soviet era, when organised religion was effectively banned.

Rumyantsev Mansion MUSEUM

(Особняк Румянцева; Map p184; www.spb-museum.ru; Angliyskaya nab 44; adult/student R200/100; ☺11am-6pm Thu-Mon, to 5pm Tue; Ⓜ Admiralteyskaya) History buffs should not miss this oft-overlooked but superb local museum. Part of the State Museum of the History of St Petersburg, the mansion contains an exhibition of 20th-century history, including displays devoted to the 1921 New Economic Policy (NEP), the industrialisation and development of the 1930s, and the Siege of Leningrad during WWII. Exhibitions are unusual in that they depict everyday life in the city during these historic periods. Each room has an explanatory panel in English.

Sennaya Ploshchad SQUARE

(Сенная площадь; Map p184; Ⓜ Sennaya Ploshchad) Immortalised by Dostoevsky, who lived all over the neighbourhood and set *Crime and Punishment* here, St Petersburg's Haymarket was once the city's filthy underbelly. Indeed, until a much-needed face-lift just over a decade ago, the square was overloaded with makeshift kiosks and market stalls, which made it a magnet for the homeless, beggars, pickpockets and drunks. These days, you'll have to look hard to find vestiges of its once insalubrious days.

Nabokov Museum MUSEUM

(Музей Набокова; Map p184; www.nabokov.museums.spbu.ru/En; Bolshaya Morskaya ul 47; ☺11am-6pm Tue-Fri, to 5pm Sat; Ⓜ Admiralteyskaya) FREE This 19th-century townhouse was the suitably grand childhood home of Vladimir Nabokov, infamous author of *Lolita* and arguably the most versatile of 20th century Russian writers. Here Nabokov lived with his wealthy family from his birth in 1899 until the revolution in 1917, when they left the country. Nabokov artefacts on display include family photographs, first editions of his books and parts of his extensive butterfly collection.

Railway Museum MUSEUM

(Музей железнодорожного транспорта; Map p184; www.cmzt.narod.ru; Sadovaya ul 50; adult/student Mon-Fri R300/150, Sat & Sun R400/200; ☺10.30am-5.30pm; Ⓜ Sadovaya) This museum near Sennaya pl is a must for train-set fans and modellers. It houses a collection of scale locomotives and model railway bridges, often made by the engineers who built the real ones. The oldest such collection in the world, the museum dates to 1809, 28 years before Russia had its first working train!

◉ Vasilyevsky Island

★Kunstkamera MUSEUM

(Кунсткамера; Map p188; ☑812-328 1412; www.kunstkamera.ru; Universitetskaya nab 3, entrance on Tamozhenny per; adult/child R300/100; ☺11am-7pm Tue-Sun; Ⓜ Admiralteyskaya) Also known as the Museum of Ethnology and Anthropology, this is the city's first museum, founded in 1714 by Peter himself. It is famous largely for its ghoulish collection of monstrosities, preserved 'freaks', two-headed mutant foetuses, deformed animals and odd body parts, all collected by Peter. While most rush to see these sad specimens, there are also interesting exhibitions on native peoples from around the world.

★Erarta Museum of Contemporary Art MUSEUM

(Музей современного искусства Эрарта; Map p188; ☑812-324 0809; www.erarta.com; 29-ya Liniya 2; adult/under 21yr R500/350; ☺10am-10pm Wed-Mon; Ⓜ Vasileostrovskaya) Erarta's superb hoard of 2300 pieces of Russian contemporary art trumps its somewhat far-flung location. Housed in an ingeniously converted neoclassical Stalinist building, the museum is spread over five floors, with the main galleries

Vasilevsky Island

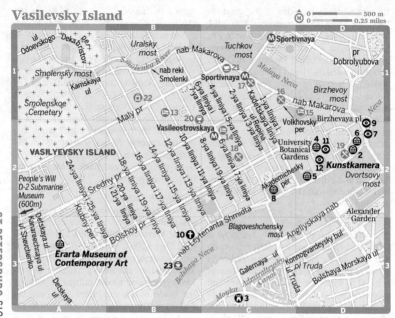

Vasilevsky Island

focused on the permanent collection. There are also installation spaces, plenty of temporary exhibitions, occasional shows, plus a good restaurant and gift shop.

Strelka　　　　　　　　　　　LANDMARK
(Map p188; Birzhevaya pl; Ⓜ Vasileostrovskaya) This eastern tip of Vasilyevsky Island is

where Peter the Great wanted his new city's administrative and intellectual centre to be. In fact, it became the focus of the city's maritime trade, symbolised by the colonnaded Customs House (now the Institute of Russian Literature) and the Old Stock Exchange. The Strelka is flanked by the pair of **Rostral Columns** (Ростральная колонна;

Map p188; Birzhevaya pl; Ⓜ Vasileostrovskaya), archetypal St Petersburg landmarks.

Museum of Zoology   MUSEUM

(Зоологический музей; Map p188; ☏ 812-328 0112; www.zin.ru; Universitetskaya nab 1; adult/student R250/150; ⊗ 11am-6pm Wed-Mon; Ⓜ Admiralteyskaya) One of the biggest and best of its kind in the world, the Museum of Zoology was founded in 1832 and has some amazing exhibits, including a vast blue whale skeleton that greets you in the first hall. The highlight is unquestionably the stuffed skin of a

44,000-year-old woolly mammoth thawed out of the Siberian ice in 1902. There are also skeletons of a further three mammoths, including two baby ones – all incredible finds.

Menshikov Palace   MUSEUM

(Государственный Эрмитаж-Дворец Меншикова; Map p188; ☏ 812-323 1112; www. hermitagemuseum.org; Universitetskaya nab 15; admission R300; ⊗ 10.30am-6pm Tue, Thu, Sat & Sun, to 9pm Wed & Fri; Ⓜ Vasileostrovskaya) The first stone building in the city, the Menshikov Palace was built to the grandiose tastes of Prince

CREATIVE CLUSTERS

Occupying either old buildings or former industrial complexes across the city are a series of 'creative clusters' that are home to a vibrant mix of artists, creative businesses, boutiques, bars and restaurants. The following are the best ones:

Loft Project ETAGI (Лофт проект ЭТАЖИ; Map p180; ☏ 812-458 5005; www.loftprojecteta-gi.ru; Ligovsky pr 74; rooftop R100; ⊗ 9am-11pm; Ⓜ Ligovsky Prospekt) This five-floor former bakery, which includes exhibition spaces, eye-catching shops, a hostel, a bar and a cafe, kicked off the creative cluster trend in 2007. In the yard, converted shipping containers house yet more pop-up clothing shops, record sellers, cafes and eateries whipping up affordable street food.

Taiga (Тайга; Map p176; http://taiga.space; Dvortsovaya nab 20; ⊗ 1-9pm; ☏; Ⓜ Admiralteyskaya) The warren of rooms in the ancient building near the Hermitage are worth exploring to find cool businesses ranging from a barber to fashion and books. **8 Store** (Map p176; ☏ 8-981-741 1880; http://8-store.ru; Dvortsovaya nab 20; ⊗ 1-9pm; Ⓜ Admiralteyskaya), a stylish boutique stacked with clothes and accessories by local designers, is one of the best. Also great for original design gifts and souvenirs is **Imenno Lavka** (Именно-лавка; Map p176; ☏ 8-921-581 0466; www.imenno-lavka.ru; TAIGA, Dvortsovaya nab 20; ⊗ 11am-7pm; Ⓜ Admiralteyskaya).

Golitsyn Loft (Map p180; nab reky Fontanky 20; Ⓜ Gostiny Dvor) This new epicentre of creativity on the Fontanka River offers the usual mix of businesses as well as a hostel with capsule-style bunks. Enter via the archway into a large courtyard, which is spread with outdoor eating and drinking spots in the summer, then head up any of the stairwells into the five buildings for a bit of urban exploration. On weekends the centre stages events, such as craft markets, concerts and film screenings.

Berthold Center (Бертгольд Центр; Map p184; www.vk.com/bertholdcentre; Grazhdanskaya ul 13; Ⓜ Sadovaya) A handful of shops, cafes and galleries spread around a former foundry. There's a courtyard in the centre of the complex that gathers a young, bohemian crowd – especially during special events and concerts (bands sometimes play on a rooftop just overlooking the courtyard).

Artmuza (Артмуза; Map p188; ☏ 812-313 4703; http://artmuza.spb.ru; 13-ya liniya 70-72; ⊗ 11am-10pm; Ⓜ Sportivnaya) With around 13,000 sq metres of space over several floors, this is one of St Petersburg's largest creative clusters. On the ground floor look out for the joint atelier of **Snega Gallery** and **Slavutnitsa** where designers specialise in making clothes and accessories based on traditional Russian costumes and patterns. Also come here to see exhibitions and theatre, and to the enjoy the view from its large rooftop terrace (where there's also a cafe).

Tkachi (Ткачи; Map p180; www.tkachi.com; nab Obvodnogo kanala 60; ⊗ 10am-10pm; Ⓜ Obvodny Kanal) In an otherwise derelict part of town, 'Weavers' is an impressive conversion of a warehouse into a 'creative space'. On the ground floor you'll find gifts, clothes, bikes and electronics, while the 5th floor is a huge exhibition space and restaurant.

Alexander Menshikov, Peter the Great's closest friend and the first governor of St Petersburg. It is now a branch of the Hermitage, and while only a relatively small part of the palace is open to visitors, its interiors are some of the oldest and best preserved in the city.

Twelve Colleges UNIVERSITY
(Двенадцать коллегий; Map p188; Mendeleevskaya liniya; M Vasileostrovskaya) Completed in 1744 and marked by a statue of scientist-poet Mikhail Lomonosov (1711–65), the 400m-long Twelve Colleges is one of St Petersburg's oldest buildings. It was originally meant for Peter's government ministries, but is now part of the university, which stretches out behind it. Within these walls populist philosopher Nikolai Chernyshevsky studied, Alexander Popov created some of the world's first radio waves and a young Vladimir Putin earned a degree in law.

This is also where Dmitry Mendeleev invented the periodic table of elements, and the building now contains the small **Mendeleev Museum** (Музей-Архив Санкт-Петербургского Университета Д.И.Менделеева; Map p188; ☑ 812-328 9744; Universitetskaya nab 7-9; ⏰ 11am-4pm Mon-Fri; M Vasileostrovskaya) FREE. Also of interest here is the **University Sculpture Garden** (Map p188; Universitetskaya nab 11; ⏰ 8am-5pm; M Admiralteyskaya) FREE, which can be accessed from the main entrance.

Temple of the Assumption CHURCH
(Храм Успения Пресвятой Богородицы; Map p188; ☑ 812-321 7473; http://spb.optina.ru; nab Leytenanta Shmidta 27/2; ⏰ 8am-8pm; M Vasileostrovskaya) FREE This stunning 1895 neo-Byzantine church was built by architect Vasily Kosyakov on the site of a former monastery. It was closed during the Soviet period, and in 1957 the building became the city's first – and very popular – year-round skating rink. The 7.7m, 861kg metal cross on the roof was only replaced in 1998. Following a wonderful renovation, the church is looking superb again; do go inside to see the murals and icons covering the interior.

Russian Academy of Fine Arts Museum MUSEUM
(Музей Академии Художеств; Map p188; ☑ 812-323 6496; www.nimrah.ru; Universitetskaya nab 17; R500, photos R500; ⏰ noon-8pm Wed, 11am-7pm Thu, Sat & Sun, 1-9pm Fri; M Vasileostrovskaya) Art-lovers should not bypass the museum of this time-tested institution, which contains work by academy students and faculty

dating back to its foundation in 1857. Two 3500-year-old sphinxes guard the entrance of this original location of the academy, where boys would live from the age of five until they graduated at age 15. It was an experiment to create a new species of human: the artist.

◉ Petrograd & Vyborg Sides

★**Hermitage Storage Facility** MUSEUM
(Реставрационно-хранительский центр Старая деревня; Map p168; ☑ 812-340 1026; www.hermitagemuseum.org; Zausadebnaya ul 37A; tours R550; ⏰ tours 11am, 1pm, 1.30pm & 3.30pm Wed-Sun; 🚻; M Staraya Derevnya) Guided tours of the Hermitage's state-of-the-art restoration and storage facility are highly recommended. This is not a formal exhibition as such, but the guides are knowledgeable and the examples chosen for display (paintings, furniture and carriages) are wonderful.

The storage facility is directly behind the big shopping centre opposite the metro station – look for the enormous golden-yellow glass facility decorated with shapes inspired by petroglyphs.

Museum of Political History MUSEUM
(Музей политической истории России; Map p191; ☑ 812-313 6163; www.polithistory.ru; ul Kuybysheva 4; adult/child R200/free, audio guide R200; ⏰ 10am-6pm Sat-Tue, 10am-8pm Wed & Fri, closed Thu; M Gorkovskaya) The elegant Style Moderne Kshesinskaya Palace (1904) is a highly appropriate location for this excellent museum – one of the city's best – covering Russian politics in detail up to contemporary times.

The palace, previously the home of Mathilda Kshesinskaya, famous ballet dancer and one-time lover of Nicholas II in his pre-tsar days, was briefly the headquarters of the Bolsheviks, and Lenin often gave speeches from the balcony.

Kirov Museum MUSEUM
(Музей Кирова; Map p191; www.kirovmuseum.ru; Kamennoostrovsky pr 26/28; adult/child R150/100; ⏰ 11am-6pm Thu-Tue; M Petrogradskaya) Leningrad party boss Sergei Kirov was one of the most powerful men in Russia in the early 1930s. His decidedly un-proletarian apartment is now a fascinating museum showing how the Bolshevik elite really lived: take a quick journey back to the days of Soviet glory, including choice examples of 1920s technology, such as the first-ever Soviet-produced type-

Petrograd Side

◎ Top Sights
1 Peter & Paul Fortress C4

◎ Sights
2 Artillery Museum.................................C4
3 Botanical Gardens D1
4 Commandant's House.........................C4
5 Cruiser Aurora....................................D3
6 Kirov Museum.....................................C2
7 Mosque...C3
8 Museum of Political History...............D3
9 Neva Panorama...................................C4
10 SS Peter & Paul Cathedral................C4
11 Trubetskoy Bastion...........................C4

✪ Activities, Courses & Tours
12 Baltic Airlines....................................B4
13 Liberty...B2

🛏 Sleeping
14 Sovremenik..C3
15 Tradition Hotel...................................B4

✗ Eating
16 Chekhov...C2
17 Koryushka..C4
18 Le Menu...B4
19 Lev y Ptichka.....................................B3
20 Paninaro..A2

☕ Drinking & Nightlife
21 Big Wine Freaks D1
22 Bolshoy Bar..B2
23 Double B...B3
24 Yasli...B3

✪ Entertainment
25 A2...C1
26 Hi-Hat...C1
27 Kamchatka B4

ⓘ Information
28 Raduga (Petrograd Side).....................B2

Vyborg

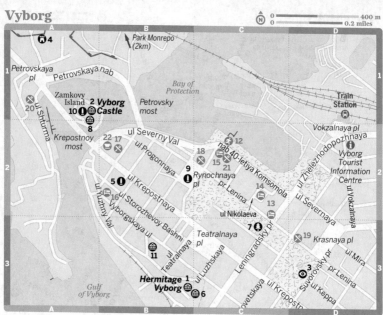

Vyborg

⊚ Top Sights

⊚ Sights

✪ Activities, Courses & Tours

⊟ Sleeping

⊗ Eating

⊙ Drinking & Nightlife

writer and a conspicuously noncommunist GE fridge, complete with plastic food inside.

Botanical Gardens   GARDENS
(Ботанический сад; Map p191; ☑ 812-372 5464; http://botsad-spb.com; ul Professora Popova 2; adult/child R300/200; ☺ grounds 10am-8pm Tue-Sun May-Sep; greenhouse 11am-4.30pm Tue-Sun year-round; ⓜ Petrogradskaya) On eastern Aptekarsky (Apothecary) Island, this was once a garden of medicinal plants – founded by Peter the Great himself in 1714 – that gave the island its name. Today the botanical gardens contain 26 greenhouses on a 22-hectare site. It is a lovely place to stroll around, and a fascinating place to visit – and not just for botanists.

Buddhist Temple   TEMPLE
(Буддистский Храм; Map p168; ☑ 981-755 9605; www.dazan.spb.ru; Primorsky pr 91; ☺ 10am-6pm Mon-Fri, to 7pm Sat & Sun; ⓜ Staraya Derevnya) Another in the city's collection of grand religious buildings is this beautiful functioning *datsan* (temple) where respectful visitors are welcome. The main prayer hall has lovely mosaic decoration and there's a cheap and

cheerful cafe in the basement. The temple was built between 1909 and 1915 at the instigation of Pyotr Badmaev, a Buddhist physician to Tsar Nicholas II.

Cruiser Aurora   MUSEUM

(Крейсер Аврора; Map p191; ☏812-230 8440; www.aurora.org.ru; Petrovskaya nab; adult/child R600/400; ☺11am-6pm Wed-Sun; ⚓; MGorkovskaya) Moored on the Bolshaya Nevka, the *Aurora* had a walk-on part in the Communist Revolution. On the night of 25 October 1917, its crew fired a blank round from the forward gun as a signal for the start of the assault on the Winter Palace. Restored and painted in pretty colours, it's a living museum that swarms with kids on weekends.

Artillery Museum   MUSEUM

(Музей Артиллерии; Map p191; ☏812-232 0296; www.artillery-museum.ru; Kroneverskaya nab; adult/student R400/250; ☺11am-6pm Wed-Sun; ⚓; MGorkovskaya) Housed in the fort's original arsenal, across the moat from the Peter & Paul Fortress, this fire-powered museum chronicles Russia's military history, with examples of weapons dating all the way back to the Stone Age. The centrepiece is Lenin's armoured car, which he rode in triumph from the Finland Station (Finlyandsky vokzal).

Mosque   MOSQUE

(Соборная мечеть; Map p191; ☏821-233 9819; http://dum-spb.ru/kontakty; Kronverksky pr 7; ☺7am-9pm; MGorkovskaya) This beautiful working mosque (built 1910–14) was modelled on Samarkand's Gur-e Amir Mausoleum. Its fluted azure dome and minarets are stunning and surprisingly prominent in the city's skyline. Outside of prayer times, if you are respectfully dressed (women should wear a head covering, men long trousers), you can walk through the gate at the northeast side and ask the guard for entry – the interior is equally lovely.

If you are allowed in, remove your shoes, do not talk and do not take photos.

🏃 Activities

★ Palace Bridge Wellness Club   SPA

(Map p188; ☏812-335 2214; www.pbwellnessclub.ru; Birzhevoy per 4A; before/after 4pm Mon-Fri R990/1390, 4hr/whole day Sat & Sun R1790/1990, children 3-12ye half-price, children under 3yr free; ☺gym, sauna & pool 7am-11pm, spa 10am-10pm; MSportivnaya) Attached to the Sokos Hotel Palace Bridge, there's a good gym and a variety of spa treatments here, but the highlights are the giant swimming pool (with jet fountains to massage tired backs) and the many styles of sauna (including Finnish and Russian) in which to steam away all your stresses.

Degtyarniye Baths   BATHHOUSE

(Дегтярные Бани; Map p180; ☏812-985 1983; www.d1a.ru; Degtyarnaya ul 1a; per hr R400-750, private banya R4500-17,500; ☺8.30am-10pm;

ST PETERSBURG ACTIVITIES

WORTH A TRIP

STREET ART MUSEUM

You won't regret making the effort to see the magnificent **Street Art Museum** (☏812-448 1593; http://streetartmuseum.ru; shosse Revolutsii 84, Okhta, entrance on Umansky per; adult/student R350/250; ☺noon-10pm Tue-Sun May-Sep; MPloshchad Lenina, then bus 137 or 530) set inside a former 11-hectare industrial site. You'll find a wide variety of formats, from huge murals covering walls to mixed-media installations set inside a former boiler-house. Every year, the exhibition changes, with top artists from around the globe invited to contribute on themes like Revolution (featured in 2017 on the 100-year anniversary of Russia's October Revolution), Migrants and Peace.

Intriguingly, parts of this industrial complex are still active, with workers at the laminated plastics factory SLOPAST surrounded by the encroaching artwork. Some of the workshops are decorated with epic works by the likes of top Russian streets artists Timothy Radya, Kirill Kto and Nikita Nomerz as well as the Spanish artist Escif. Before he died in 2013, Pasha 183 – frequently referred to as Russia's Banksy because of his anonymity – also contributed 'Walls Don't Sleep' a beautiful monochrome mural based on an image of Soviet factory workers.

Guided tours happen on weekends (at 1pm and 2pm); call ahead to ensure an English-speaking guide is on hand. The museum also hosts outdoor concerts and other big events. Check the website for the latest.

It's located in the industrial zone of Okhta, a 20-minute bus ride east of Ploshchad Lenina. Buses 28, 37 and 137 all go there.

Ⓜ Ploshchad Vosstaniya) These modern baths are divided up into men's and women's sections, or you can book private unisex *bani* (hot baths) of varying degrees of luxury (these accommodate up to 14 people). Prices are cheaper before 1pm on weekdays. Minimum charge of two hours.

Mytninskiye Bani   BATHHOUSE
(Мытнинские бани; Map p180; www.mybanya. spb.ru; ul Mytninskaya 17-19; per hr R200-350; ⊘8am-10pm Fri-Tue; Ⓜ Ploshchad Vosstaniya) Unique in the city, Mytninskiye Bani is heated by a wood furnace, just like the log-cabin bathhouses that are still found in the Rus-

---

WORTH A TRIP

SOVIET SOUTH

Sprawling southern St Petersburg was once planned to be the centre of Stalin's Leningrad, and it contains grand buildings, over-the-top monuments and sculpture-lined green spaces that celebrate now mostly forgotten figures of the past. You'll also see largely middle-class Russians and families, who've given new life to these marble-lined boulevards.

Moscow Triumphal Arch

Bristling with spears, shields and banners, this imposing 12-columned gate was built to celebrate victory in the 1828 Russo-Turkish War and once marked the southern entrance to the imperial capital. In 1936 the gates were dismantled under Stalin's order and were later used as anti-tank defences in WWII. They were restored in 1960.

Grand Market Rossiya

Russia in all its grit and glory – from the industrial sprawl of Magnitogorsk to the glittering domes of Moscow – is on full display at this vast **re-creation** (Map p168; ☑812-495 5465; www.grandmaket.ru; Tsvetochnaya ul 16; adult/child R480/280, audio-guide or binoculars R250; ⊘10am-8pm; Ⓜ Moskovskoe Vorota) of the motherland in miniature. One huge room contains mountains, cities, rivers and lakes, with lots of mechanised action that you can observe while strolling around.

Park Pobedy

This large green space gathers a cross-section of Petersburgers, including young families, teens and canoodling couples who stroll the leafy paths and enjoy the views over the ponds and flower gardens. Built to celebrate Russia's victory in WWII, the **park** (Map p168; Moskovsky pr; ⊘6am-midnight; Ⓜ Park Pobedy) is full of statues of Soviet war heroes, and has a beneficent depiction of Lenin interacting with small children.

Chesme Church

This striking red-and-white 18th-century Gothic **church** (Чесменская церковь; https:// chesma.spb.ru; ul Lensoveta 12; ⊘10am-7pm; Ⓜ Moskovskaya) commemorates the 1770 Battle of Chesme. This is where Catherine the Great was standing when news arrived of the victory over the Turks. The capricious monarch ordered a shrine be built to preserve this historic moment. It now seems particularly incongruous with its Stalinist surroundings.

House of the Soviets

Begun by Noi Trotsky in 1936, the bombastic **House of Soviets** (Дом советов; Moskovsky pr 212; Ⓜ Moskovskaya) was only finished after the war, by which time the architect had been purged. Nonetheless, this magnificently sinister building is a great example of Stalinist design, with its columns and bas-reliefs and an enormous frieze across the top.

Monument to the Heroic Defenders of Leningrad

Centred around a 48m-high obelisk, the **monument** (Монумент героическим защитникам Ленинграда; www.spbmuseum.ru; pl Pobedy; R200; ⊘10am-6pm Thu-Mon, until 5pm Tue; Ⓜ Moskovskaya), unveiled in 1975, symbolises the city's encirclement and eventual victory in WWII. On a lower level, flickering torches ring a very moving sculpture depicting the city's suffering. From there, you can enter an underground exhibition, which delves into the war and siege.

sian countryside. It's actually the oldest communal *banya* in the city, and in addition to a *parilka* (steam room) and plunge pool, the private 'lux' *banya* (R1000 to R2000 per hour) includes a swanky lounge area with leather furniture and a pool table.

Kazachiye Bani
BATHHOUSE

(Казачьи бани; Map p168; www.kazbani.ru; Bolshoy Kazachy per 11; per 2hr R100-300, private banya per hr R850-1700; ⊙8am-10pm Tue-Sun; ⓂPushkinskaya) Following a trend that is occurring throughout the city, the communal *banya* is something of an afterthought here. The majority of the venue is given over to very swanky, private *bani,* which are an excellent option for groups of up to 10 people. The cheaper communal *banya* is good value though.

★Piter Kayak
KAYAKING

(Map p184; ☑921-435 9457; http://piterkayak. com; nab Kryukova kanala 26; tours R1700-R2500; ⊙tours at 7am Tue-Sun Apr-Sep) Experienced kayaker Denis and his friendly young team lead these excellent early morning tours which last around four hours and cover 11km. The canals and rivers are at their quietest at this time and, unlike on regular boat tours, the slower pace allows you to admire the wonderful surroundings at your leisure.

Wild Russia
ADVENTURE SPORTS

(Map p168; ☑812-313 8030; www.wildrussia.spb. ru; office 224, nab reki Fontanki 59; ⓂGostiny Dvor) Yachting and kayaking on Lake Ladoga can be arranged through the friendly and capable guys at Wild Russia. They can also arrange many other outdoor activities including off-road biking, parachuting, quad biking and rock climbing outside the city.

☞ Tours

In a city as large as St Petersburg, a lot of travellers prefer to be shown around on a walking tour to kick things off. There are several excellent ones on offer, as well as bike tours and a hop-on, hop-off bus that can take you around the main sights of the centre. Viewing St Petersburg from a boat is an idyllic way to tour the city, and during the main tourist season (May to October) there are plenty of boats offering to help you do this. They are typically found at the Anichkov most landing on the Fontanka River, just off Nevsky pr; on the Neva outside the Hermitage and the Admiralty; beside the Kazan-

sky most over the Griboyedova Canal; and along the Moyka River at Nevsky pr.

★Peterwalk Walking Tours
WALKING

(☑812-943 1229; http://peterswalk.com; from R1320) Going for over 20 years, Peter Kozyrev's innovative and passionately led tours are highly recommended as a way to see the city with knowledgeable locals. The daily Original Peterswalk (R1320) is one of the favourites and leaves daily from the Julia Child Bistro (p204) at 10.30am from April to end of September. Other tours from around R2000.

★Sputnik Tours
WALKING

(☑499-110 5266; www.sputnik8.com; price varies) This online tour agency is one with a difference: they act as a market place for locals wanting to give their own unique tours of their own city. Browse, select a tour, register and pay a deposit and then you get given the contact number of the guide. A superb way to meet locals you'd never meet otherwise.

★Anglo Tourismo
BOATING

(Map p176; ☑8-921-989 4722; http://anglotourismo.com; 27 nab reki Fontanki; 1hr cruise adult/ student R1900/900; ⓂGostiny Dvor) There's a huge number of companies offering cruises all over the Historic Heart, all with similar prices and itineraries. Anglo Tourismo, however, is the only operator to run tours with commentary in English. Between May and September the schedule runs every 1½ hours between 11am and 6.30pm. From 1 June to 31 August there are also additional night cruises.

City Tour
BUS

(☑812-648 1228; https://citytourspb.ru; one day pass adult/child R700/300) The familiar red 'hop on, hop off' double-decker buses you'll see in most big cities in Europe (and beyond) are now well-established in St Petersburg. They offer a useful service for anyone unable to walk easily; buses run along Nevsky pr, passing the Hermitage, going over the Strelka, the Petrograd Side and then back to the historic centre.

Tickets are valid for as many trips in the time period as you like, and you can buy tickets when you board the bus. In summer months they also run a 'hop on, hop off' boat tour (one day bus and boat pass adult/ child R1400/700) around the main rivers and canals.

✯ Festivals & Events

Easter RELIGIOUS
(Paskha; ☉ Mar/Apr) Head to Kazan Cathedral to see Russia's most important religious festival in full Russian Orthodox style: the church (as well as many others around the city) is packed out.

Mariinsky Ballet Festival PERFORMING ARTS
(www.mariinsky.ru; ☉ Apr) The city's principal dance theatre hosts this week-long international ballet festival, where the cream of Russian ballet dancers showcase their talents.

Victory Day CELEBRATION
(☉ 9 May) St Petersburg celebrates not only the end of WWII in 1945 but also the breaking of the Nazi blockade. The highlight is a victory parade on Nevsky pr, culminating in soldiers marching on Dvortsovaya pl and fireworks over the Neva in the evening.

City Day FIESTA
(☉ 27 May) Laying flowers at the Monument to Peter I on Senate Square (Bronze Horseman) is a tradition on the city's official birthday. Mass celebrations are held throughout the city centre including brass bands, folk dancing and mass drunkenness.

Stars of the White Nights Festival MUSIC
(www.mariinsky.ru; ☉ late May–mid-Jul) Held at the Mariinsky, the Conservatoire and the Hermitage Theatre, this festival has become a huge draw and now lasts far longer than the White Nights (officially the last 10 days of June) after which it is named. You'll see ballet, opera and classical music concerts premiered and reprised.

Scarlet Sails FIREWORKS
(Алые паруса; http://parusaspb.ru; ☉ Jun) The highlight of the White Nights season, this one-night festival includes performing arts staged in Palace Square, and crowds of around one million lining the banks of the Neva for a spectacular fireworks display and to see a magnificent red-sail Swedish frigate float by.

Festival of Festivals FILM
(www.filmfest.ru; ☉ late Jun) This annual international film festival held at the Rodina cinema is a non-competitive showcase of the best Russian and world cinema.

Open Look/Russian Look DANCE
(www.open-look.org; ☉ Jul) Contemporary dance companies from around the world perform in the prestigious Open Look festival, with shows mainly at the Alexandrinsky's New Stage as well as a handful of other venues. It's immediately followed by Russian Look, which showcases the home-grown talent.

Usadba Jazz MUSIC
(http://usadba-jazz.com; ☉ Jul) The musical juggernaut that is Russia's largest open-air festival of jazz and all kinds of other improvised contemporary music makes its way to Yelagin Island.

SKIF PERFORMING ARTS
(www.kuryokhin.net; ☉ Sep) Dedicated to Sergey Kuryokhin (1954–96), a talented local musician, actor and all round creative, this long-running festival focuses on the experimental and cutting edge across a range of artistic disciplines including music, art and film.

Arts Square Winter Festival MUSIC
(www.artsquarewinterfest.ru; ☉ Dec) A musical highlight of the year, this festival at the Philharmonia takes different themes each year. Both classical and contemporary opera and orchestral works are staged.

🛏 Sleeping

Hotels in St Petersburg are fairly expensive, with a lack of good midrange places in the city centre. Though they do exist, they tend to get booked up well in advance (particularly during the summer months), so plan ahead if you want to stay in the historic heart.

It is essential to reserve at least a month in advance for accommodation during the White Nights (late May to early July).

The following price ranges refer to the cheapest room available during the high season (May to July).

€ less than R3000
€€ R3000–15,000
€€€ more than R15,000

Historic Heart

★ **Baby Lemonade Hostel** HOSTEL $
(Map p176; ☑ 812-570 7943; http://babylemonade.epoquehostels.com; Inzhenernaya ul 7; dm/d with shared bathroom from R600/2500, d from R3800; @ 🖥; Ⓜ Gostiny Dvor) The owner of Baby Lemonade is crazy about the 1960s and it shows in the pop-art, psychedelic design of this friendly, fun hostel with two pleasant, large dorms and a great kitchen and living room. However, it's worth splashing out for the boutique-hotel-

worthy private rooms that are in a separate flat with great rooftop views.

★ Friends Hostel
by Gostiny Dvor
HOTEL $$

(Map p176; ✆812-740-4720; www.en.friendsplace. ru/druzya-na-lomonosova; ul Lomonosva 3; r from R5200; @ 🛜; Ⓜ Gostiny Dvor) Sharing the top floor of a renovated historic building with a budget hotel, this is one of the best branches of the Friends chain. There are no dorms here and all the rooms have attached bathrooms, but the same cosy, quirky decorative charm is in place – complete with cuddly toys and flowery print curtains and linens.

★ Rachmaninov
Antique Hotel
BOUTIQUE HOTEL $$

(Map p176; ✆812-327 7466; www.hotelrachmaninov.com; Kazanskaya ul 5; s/d from R6300/7500; @ 🛜; Ⓜ Nevsky Prospekt) The long-established Rachmaninov still feels like a secret place for those in the know. Perfectly located and run by friendly staff, it's pleasantly old world, with hardwood floors and attractive Russian furnishings, particularly in the breakfast salon, which has a grand piano.

Pio on Griboyedov
HOTEL $$

(Map p176; ✆812-571 9476; http://hotelpio.ru; nab kanala Griboyedova 35, apt 5; s/d with shared bathroom from R3400/4000, s/d with private bathroom from R4500/5500; 🛜; Ⓜ Nevsky Prospekt) There are just six rooms here and three of them share bathrooms and toilets, but it is much more like staying in a large apartment than a hostel. The communal areas are very pleasant and the rooms are comfortable and clean. Even better is the friendly service, central location and big windows overlooking the canal.

3MostA
HOTEL $$

(Map p176; ✆812-611 1188; www.3mosta.com; nab reki Moyki 3a; s/d from R5000/9000; ❄🛜; Ⓜ Nevsky Prospekt) Near three bridges over the Moyka River, this 26-room property is surprisingly uncramped given its wonderful location. Even the standard rooms are of a good size with tasteful furniture, minibars and TVs. Some rooms have great views across to the Church on the Spilled Blood, and all guests have access to the roof for the panoramic experience.

Anichkov Pension
PENSION $$

(Map p176; ✆812-314 7059; www.anichkov. com; Apt 4, Nevsky pr 64; s/d/ste incl breakfast R5500/6000/10,000; ❄🛜; Ⓜ Gostiny Dvor)

ⓘ ACCOMMODATION AGENCIES

The following local agencies can help you with short-term accommodation:

HOFA (www.hofa.ru)

Intro by Irina (www.introbyirina.com)

Ostwest.com (p214)

On the 3rd floor of a handsome apartment building with an antique lift, this six-room pension takes its name from the nearby bridge. The standard rooms are fine, but the suites are well worth paying a little more for. The delightful breakfast room with a grand piano offers balcony views. Look for the entrance on Karavannaya ul.

★ Belmond
Grand Hotel Europe
HERITAGE HOTEL $$$

(Map p176; ✆812-329 6000; www.belmond.com/ grand-hotel-europe-st-petersburg; Mikhailovskaya ul 1/7; d from R26,500/31,270; ❄@🛜🏊; Ⓜ Nevsky Prospekt) Since 1830, when Carlo Rossi united three adjacent buildings with the grandiose facade we see today, little has been allowed to change in this heritage building. No two rooms are the same at this iconic hotel, but most are spacious and elegant in design. It's worth paying extra for the terrace rooms, which afford spectacular views across the city's rooftops.

★ Rossi Hotel
BOUTIQUE HOTEL $$$

(Map p176; ✆812-635 6333; www.rossihotels.com; nab reki Fontanki 55; s/d/ste from R9740/9830/15,230; ❄@🛜; Ⓜ Gostiny Dvor) Occupying a beautifully restored building on one of St Petersburg's prettiest squares, the Rossi's 65 rooms are all designed differently, but their brightness and moulded ceilings are uniform. Antique beds, super-sleek bathrooms, exposed brick walls and lots of cool designer touches create a great blend of old and new.

Hotel Astoria
HISTORIC HOTEL $$$

(Map p176; ✆812-494 5757; www.roccofortehotels.com; Bolshaya Morskaya ul 39; r/ste from R34,800/76,000; ❄@🛜🏊; Ⓜ Admiralteyskaya) What the Hotel Astoria has lost of its original Style Moderne decor, it more than compensates for in contemporary style and top-notch service. Little wonder it's beloved by visiting VIPs, from kings to rock stars. Rooms marry the hotel's heritage character with a more modern design, while the best

KIROVSKY ISLANDS

If you need a quick break from the city, these three outer delta islands (Кировские острова) on the Petrograd Side and an ideal place to head. Once marshy forests, the islands were granted to 18th- and 19th-century court favourites and developed into elegant playgrounds. Still mostly parkland, they are leafy venues for picnics, river sports and White Nights' cavorting, as well as home to St Petersburg's super rich.

Krestovsky Island (Крестовский остров Map p168; 🚇; Ⓜ Krestovsky Ostrov) The biggest of the three, Krestovsky consists mostly of the vast **Maritime Victory Park** (Приморский парк Победы; www.primparkpobedy.ru; Krestovsky pr), dotted with sports fields; at the far western end is the massive, 68,000-seat **Krestovsky Stadium**, (Стадион Крестовский) which will play a pivotal role in the 2018 FIFA World Cup. At the park's main entrance opposite the metro station you can rent bikes and in-line skates. Also here is **Divo Ostrov** (Диво-Остров; www.divo-ostrov.ru; rides R100-500; ⊙ noon-7pm) is a Disney-style amusement park with exciting fairgrrides that kids will adore.

Kamenny Island (Каменный Остров; Map p168; Ⓜ Chyornaya Rechka) Century-old dacha (country cottages) and mansions, inhabited by very wealthy locals, line the wooded lanes that twist their way around Kamenny (Stone) Island. Punctuated by a series of canals, lakes and ponds, Kameny is pleasant for strolling at any time of year. At its east end, the **Church of St John the Baptist** (Церковь Рождества Иоанна Предтечи; Kamennoostrovsky pr; ⊙ 9am-6pm), built in 1776–81, has been charmingly restored.

   Car-free **Yelagin Island** (Елагин остров; Map p168; www.elaginpark.org; ice skating per hr R200-300; ⊙ ice skating 11am-9pm; Ⓜ Krestovsky Ostrov) becomes a winter wonderland in colder temperatures, with sledding, cross-country skiing and ice skating. Skis and skates are available for hire. In summer months, it's a great place to rent in-line skates.

suites are sprinkled with antiques and have spectacular views onto St Isaac's Cathedral.

The same views – at a slightly lower price – are also available next door at its sister property, the **Angleterre Hotel** (Map p176; ☎ 812-494 5607; www.angleterrehotel.com; Malaya Morskaya ul 24; r/ste from R24,545/58,765; ✷ @ 🛜 ⛳; Ⓜ Admiralteyskaya), where guests can use the gym and pool.

Kempinski Hotel Moyka 22　　HOTEL $$$
(Map p176; ☎ 812-335 9111; www.kempinski. com; nab reki Moyki 22; r/ste with breakfast from R26,000/47,400; ✷ @ 🛜; Ⓜ Nevsky Prospekt) Practically on the doorstep of the Hermitage, this superb hotel has all the comforts you'd expect of an international luxury chain. Rooms have a stylish marine theme, with cherry-wood furniture and a handsome navy-blue-and-gold colour scheme. The 360-degree panorama from the rooftop **Belle View** restaurant and bar is unbeatable.

🛏 Smolny & Vosstaniya

Kultura Hostel　　HOSTEL $
(Map p180; ☎ 921-870 0177; http://kulturahostel. com; ul Vosstaniya 24; dm/r with shared bathroom from R550/3000; 🛜; Ⓜ Ploshchad Vosstaniya) Following the formula of other creative

clusters around town, this one, behind the post office on ul Vosstaniya, is also home to a hostel. In this case, some thought has been applied to the design of the rooms, each of which have colourful St Petersburg–themed designs on the walls. The location is cool, with boutiques, cafes and a bar on hand.

Red House Hostel　　HOSTEL $
(Map p180; ☎ 911-785 6488; www.redhousehostel. com; 2nd fl, ul Belinskogo 11; dm R550-700; 😊 🛜; Ⓜ Mayakovskaya) With its very desirable central location, the Red House Hostel is a fine choice. It's small, and rather cramped with six- to 12-bed dorms, but guests are made to feel right at home in this somewhat bohemian abode. There's a communal kitchen and a washing machine.

Hotel Indigo　　HOTEL $$
(Map p180; ☎ 812-454 5577; www.indigospb. com; ul Chaykovskogo 17, Smolny; r from R10,700; 😊 ✷ @ 🛜; Ⓜ Chernyshevskaya) A total overhaul of the original building – a prerevolutionary hotel in its day – paved the way for the sleek and stylish Hotel Indigo, a big step up from many St Petersburg offerings with its excellent service and handsomely designed guestrooms The incredible atrium makes even the

interior-facing rooms light-filled, and touches such as rain showers and free minibars in rooms are also very welcome.

Nils Bed & Breakfast
HOMESTAY $$

(Map p180; ☑812-923 0575; www.rentroom.ru; 5-ya Sovetskaya ul 21, Smolny; s R3850-4600, d R4900-5600; ☎; Ⓜ Ploshchad Vosstaniya) Nils Bed & Breakfast is an excellent option at a great price. Four spacious rooms share two modern bathrooms, as well as a beautiful light-filled common area and kitchen. Nils renovated this place himself, taking great care to preserve the mouldings, wooden floors and other architectural elements.

Pio on Mokhovaya
B&B $$

(Map p180; ☑812-273 3585; Mokhovaya ul 39, Smolny; s/d/tr/q incl breakfast R3500/4500/5400/6100; ☺☎; Ⓜ Chernyshevskaya) This lovely lodging is the second Pio property in Petersburg. It's very spacious, stylish and comfortable, as well as being child friendly, with family groups warmly welcomed and provided for. It's in a quiet, residential neighbourhood a short walk from the Historic Heart. There is also a Finnish sauna on-site. Call 10 on the intercom to be buzzed in.

Ognivo
GUESTHOUSE $$

(Map p180; ☑812-579 6295; www.ognivo-spb.com; ul Chaykovskogo 4; s/d from R4000/4800) Ognivo earns high marks for its attractive, well-maintained rooms and quiet location. There's a bit of whimsy to the design in some of the 15 rooms, with inner wooden shutters over the windows, bold wallpaper and wildly patterned tilework in the bathrooms – others have cast-iron chandeliers and wood-beamed ceilings for a more medieval look.

Demetra Art Hotel
BOUTIQUE HOTEL $$$

(Map p180; ☑812-640 0408; www.demetra-art-hotel.com; ul Vosstaniya 44; r R16,000-24,000, ste R36,000; ✳☎; Ⓜ Chernyshevskaya) In a grand art nouveau building dating from 1913, the Demetra Art Hotel has plush rooms with oak flooring, richly patterned drapes and duvets, and touches of artwork throughout (reproductions of works from the celebrated Erata Museum). Some rooms can be on the small side, though the top-notch service, stylish bar and restaurant, and great location add to the appeal.

Dom Boutique Hotel
HOTEL $$$

(Map p180; www.domboutiquehotel.uk; Gangutskaya ul 4; r R12,000-20,000; ✳☎; Ⓜ Cherny-

shevskaya) Just off the Fontanka River, this newish place has stylish rooms with king-sized beds, classy furniture and gilded antique-looking mirrors, plus sleek bathrooms with black subway tiles and brass fixtures. The common areas are fine spots to unwind, and there's a restaurant and bar on hand.

Sennaya & Kolomna

★ Soul Kitchen Hostel
HOSTEL $

(Map p184; ☑8-965-816 3470; www.soulkitchenhostel.com; nab reki Moyki 62/2, apt 9, Sennaya; dm R1500-2400, d R5700-9000; @☎; Ⓜ Admiralteyskaya) Soul Kitchen blends boho hipness and boutique-hotel comfort, scoring perfect 10s in many key categories: private rooms (chic), dorm beds (double-wide with privacy-protecting curtains), common areas and kitchen (all beautifully designed). The lounge is a fine place to hang out, with a record player, a big screen projector (for movie nights) and an artful design.

★ Alexander House
BOUTIQUE HOTEL $$

(Map p184; ☑812-334 3540; www.a-house.ru; nab kanala Kryukova 27, Kolomna; s/d/apt incl breakfast from R9000/12,200/14,600; ☺✳☎; Ⓜ Sadovaya) This historic building opposite the Nikolsky Cathedral dates back to 1826, and contains a beautifully designed guesthouse. Each of the 14 spacious rooms are named after a city (Kyoto, Marrakesh, Venice) and contain artwork and crafts from there. Beautifully polished floors, warm colours and beamed ceilings are common throughout. There's also a lovely fireplace-warmed lounge and a vine-laden courtyard, plus a guests-only restaurant.

★ Andrey & Sasha's Homestay
APARTMENT $$

(Map p176; ☑8-921-409 6701, 812-315 3330; asamatuga@mail.ru; nab kanala Griboyedova 51, Sennaya; r R5800-7300; ☎; Ⓜ Sadovaya) Energetic Italophiles Andrey and Sasha extend the warmest of welcomes to travellers lucky enough to rent out one of their three apartments (by the room or in its entirety). All are centrally located and eclectically decorated with lots of designer touches and an eye for beautiful furniture, tiles and mirrors. Bathrooms are shared, as are kitchen facilities.

Chao Mama
HOTEL $$

(Map p184; ☑812-570 0444; www.chaomama.ru; Grazhdanskaya ul 27; d R3600-7500; ✳☎; Ⓜ Sadovaya) In an excellent location, Chao

Mama has nine stylish rooms, each boasting a unique design, and offers excellent value for the money. The best rooms have small kitchenettes and ample natural light, while the 54-sq-metre Gagarin Room has two balconies and sleeps up to four. For something a little cosier, opt for the artfully designed Jacqueline, which also boasts a fireplace.

Hotel Gogol HOTEL $$
(Map p184; ☑ 812-571 1841; www.gogolhotel.com; nab kanala Griboyedova 69, Sennaya; s/d from R5100/6400; ☻ ❋ ⊕; Ⓜ Sadovaya) There's great value to be had at this centrally located hotel, a conversion of the house where the great writer Nikolai Gogol himself apparently once lived. The rooms are cosy and enjoy inoffensive decoration, with views of the canal or a quiet residential courtyard. Reception is on the 2nd floor, and there's a basement restaurant.

Zolotaya Seredina HOTEL $$
(Золотая Середина; Map p184; ☑ 931-592 6413; www.retrohotel.ru; Grazhdanskaya ul 16, Sennaya; s/d R2900/3400, with shared bathroom R2100/2500; ⊕; Ⓜ Sadovaya) Tucked into a quiet courtyard in the narrow streets north of Sennaya pl, this friendly little hotel is a great bargain. A few antiques are scattered around to justify its 'retro' claims, but most furniture and all facilities are quite modern, with a kitchen for guest use, as well as a washing machine.

Hotel Domina Prestige HOTEL $$$
(Map p184; ☑ 812-385 9900; www.dominarussia. com; nab Reki Moyki 99, Sennaya; r R9100-21,000; ☻ ❋ ⊕; Ⓜ Admiralteyskaya) This excellent property makes an immediate impression as its traditional Moyka embankment exterior gives way to a bright, modern and colourful atrium. Some of the decor is undoubtedly rather Russian in taste, but it's still stylish and fun. Rooms are comfortable and spacious, with extras such as coffee facilities and great bathrooms. There's also a sauna, gym and restaurant.

🏨 Vasilyevsky Island

Online Hostel HOSTEL $
(Map p188; ☑ 812-329 9594; http://online-hostel. com/; Apt 1, 6-ya liniya 27; dm/d incl breakfast from R800/2700; @ ⊕; Ⓜ Vasileostrovskaya) The pick of the hostels on Vasilyevsky Island couldn't have a more convenient location opposite the metro station. Dorms are pretty cramped

but there's a welcoming and colourful vibe to the place. Fun touches include an electronic keyboard and Xbox games to play in the lounge and kitchen area.

★ NasHotel HOTEL $$
(Map p188; ☑ 812-323 2231; www.nashotel.ru; 11-ya liniya 50; s/d from R9500/10,600; ❋ ⊕; Ⓜ Vasileostrovskaya) This spotless, smart and stylish hotel occupies a very tall, beautifully remodelled building with a striking exterior on this quiet side street. Its rooms are blazes of colours, complete with modern furnishings, garish art and great views from the higher floors. A nice perk are the free bicycles for guests to use to get around.

Sokos Hotel Palace Bridge BUSINESS HOTEL $$
(Map p188; ☑ 812-335 2200; www.sokoshotels. com; Birzhevoy per 4A; r from R10,900; ❋ @; Ⓜ Sportivnaya) This is the best of several hotels in the city run by Finnish chain Sokos because of its excellent spa and fitness centre with a wonderful large swimming pool and saunas. The rooms are large and a bit bland, but it's a quiet location and a popular spot with business travellers.

🏨 Petrograd & Vyborg Sides

Sovremenik HOTEL $
(Современник; Map p191; ☑ 812-312 9339; www. artefact-hotel.ru; ul Kronverskaya 1; dm/d/tr/q R790/2900/4300/4800; ❋ ⊕; Ⓜ Gorkovskaya) This small, cheerfully decorated mini-hotel has nine rooms tucked inside an apartment building a short stroll from Alexandrovsky Park. It's a colourful, somewhat whimsically decorated place, with repurposed bird cages, hats turned into lamps and bold artwork in some rooms. The friendly service and shared kitchen add to the appeal.

Tradition Hotel HOTEL $$
(Map p191; ☑ 812-405 8855; www.traditionhotel.ru; pr Dobrolyubova 2; r incl breakfast R9100-13,500; ❋ @ ⊕; Ⓜ Sportivnaya) This charming small hotel is a consistent traveller favourite due to its smiling, helpful staff who really go out of their way for guests. Its spacious, carpeted rooms are comfortable and well appointed with good-size bathrooms and a vaguely antique style.

🍴 Eating

There has never been a better time to eat out in St Petersburg. The range and quality of food available seem to increase year

ST PETERSBURG FOR CHILDREN

There are plenty of activities that children will love in St Petersburg, especially during the summer months when the whole city is something of an outdoor playground.

Top museums for children include the Museum of Zoology (p189), with thousands of stuffed animals (including several mammoths) on display; the Railway Museum (p187), where you can see a range of scale locomotives and model railway bridges; and the Central Naval Museum (p185) with its superb collection of model boats. Also sure to entrance kids and adults alike are the incredibly detailed scale models of early 18th century St Petersburg at **Petrovskaya Akvatoria** (Петровская Акватория; Map p176; ☑812-933 4152; www.peteraqua.ru; Malaya Morskaya ul 4/1; adult/child R400/200; ⊗10am-10pm; Ⓜ Admiralteyskaya) and the even more epic model village of Russia's greatest sights at Grand Maket (p194).

One of the best parks to take kids in the city is on New Holland (p185) where there's a great kid's playground, a wooden model of a frigate to climb around, a giant chess set and free pétanque (a form of boules). Amusement parks, boats and bikes for hire, and lots of open space make the Kirovsky Islands another great outdoors option.

Wonderful puppet shows can be seen at both the **Bolshoy Puppet Theatre** (Большой театр кукол; Map p180; www.puppets.ru; ul Nekrasova 10; tickets R350-600; Ⓜ Chernyshevskaya) and **Demmeni Marionette Theatre** (Map p176; ☑812-310 5879; www.demmeni.ru; Nevsky pr 52; ⊗tickets from R500; Ⓜ Gostiny Dvor). For traditional-style circus shows the historic **St Petersburg State Circus** (Map p176; ☑812-570 5198; www.circus.spb.ru; nab reki Fontanki 3; tickets R500-6000; Ⓜ Gostiny Dvor) can't be beat.

on year, making stereotypes about Russian food now seem like bizarre anachronisms. Petersburgers have well and truly caught the foodie bug, and while little of good quality is cheap in this town, the choice is now bigger than ever.

The following price ranges refer to the average cost of a main course.

€ less than R500
€€ R500–1000
€€€ more than R1000

🍴 Historic Heart

★**Zoom Café** EUROPEAN $
(Map p176; ☑812-612 1329; www.cafezoom.ru; Gorokhovaya ul 22; mains R350-550; ⊗9am-midnight Mon-Fri, from 11am Sat, from 1pm Sun; 🛜☑🚼; Ⓜ Nevsky Prospekt) A perennially popular cafe (expect to wait for a table at peak times) with a cosy feel and an interesting menu, ranging from Japanese-style chicken in teriyaki sauce to potato pancakes with salmon and cream cheese. Well-stocked bookshelves, a range of board games and adorable cuddly toys (each with its own name) encourage lingering.

Jack & Chan INTERNATIONAL $
(Map p176; ☑812-982 0535; http://jack-and-chan.com; Inzhenernaya ul 7; mains R350-420; ⊗11am-midnight Sun-Thu, until 2am Fri & Sat; 🛜; Ⓜ Gostiny Dvor) The restaurant name, a punning reference to Jackie Chan in Russian, neatly sums up the burger-meets-Asian menu at this fine and stylish casual diner. Try the sweet-and-sour fish and the prawn-and-avocado salad with glass noodles.

Marketplace RUSSIAN, INTERNATIONAL $
(Map p176; http://market-place.me; Nevsky pr 24; mains R200-300; ⊗8am-5.30am; 🛜☑; Ⓜ Nevsky Prospekt) The most central branch of this mini-chain that brings a high-class polish to the self-serve canteen concept with many dishes cooked freshly on the spot to order. The hip design of the multi-level space is very appealing, making this a great spot to linger, especially if you indulge in one of the desserts or cocktails served on the 1st floor.

Ukrop VEGAN $
(Map p176; ☑812-946 3035; www.cafe-ukrop.ru; Malaya Konyushennaya ul 14; mains R280-360; ⊗9am-11pm; 🛜☑; Ⓜ Nevsky Prospekt) Proving veggie, vegan and raw food can be inventive and tasty as well as wholesome, Ukrop (meaning dill) also makes an effort with its bright and whimsical craft design, which includes swing seats and lots of natural materials. There are other branches on Vasilyevsky Island and ul Vosstaniya.

Cafe Hermitage INTERNATIONAL $

(Кафе Эрмитаж; Map p176; ☑812-703 7528; General Staff Builidng, 8 Dvortsovaya pl; mains R250-450; ☺11am-11pm Tue, Thu, Sat & Sun, until 8pm Wed & Fri; Ⓜ Admiralteyskaya) When the east wing of the General Staff Building was turned into a new branch of the Hermitage, they at least made sure it had a decent place to eat (unlike in the Winter Palace). It's a self-serve cafe for drinks, appealing sandwiches and hot dishes and can be visited whether or not you go into the museum itself.

Biblioteka INTERNATIONAL $

(Map p176; ☑812-244 1594; www.ilovenevsky.ru; Nevsky pr 20; mains R250-600; ☺8am-11pm Sun-Thu, to midnight Fri & Sat; ☎; Ⓜ Nevsky Prospekt) You could spend the better part of a day here. Ground floor is a waiter-service cafe where it's difficult to avoid being tempted by the cake and dessert display by the door; next up is a more formal restaurant; and on the top floor there's a multiroomed lounge bar (closed Monday and Tuesday) with live music and DJs until 1am on Friday and Saturday.

★Yat RUSSIAN $$

(Ять; Map p176; ☑812-957 0023; www.eatinyat. com; nab reki Moyki 16; mains R370-750; ☺11am-11pm; ☎🖶; Ⓜ Admiralteyskaya) Perfectly placed for eating near the Hermitage, this country-cottage-style restaurant has a very appealing menu of traditional dishes, presented with aplomb. The *shchi* (cabbage-based soup) is excellent, and there is also a

---

LOCAL KNOWLEDGE

LOCAL CHAINS

St Petersburg has a number of home-grown restaurant and cafe chains that are well worth knowing about as they provide cheap and reliable eating options all over town. Chief among these is the now international pie chain Stolle (Штолле; www.stolle.ru), a near-ubiquitous cafe where delicious, moist savoury and sweet pies are available to eat in and take away. Similar and equally numerous is the chain of bakery cafes Bulochnye F. Volcheka (Булочные Ф. Вольчека; www.fvolchek.ru). A couple of other chains to look out for are coffee-and-cake specialists Bushe (Буше; www. bushe.ru) and Baltic Bread (Балтийский Хлеб; www.baltic-bread.ru), which does good sandwiches and pastries.

---

tempting range of flavoured vodkas. There's a fab kids area with pet rabbits for them to feed.

★Gräs x Madbaren FUSION $$

(Map p176; ☑812-928 1818; http://grasmadbaren. com; ul Inzhenernaya 7; mains R420-550, tasting menu R2500; ☺1-11pm Sun-Thu, until 1am Fri & Sat; ☎; Ⓜ Gostiny Dvor) Anton Abrezov is the talented exec chef behind this Scandi-cool meets Russian locavore restaurant where you can sample dishes such as a delicious corned beef salad with black garlic and pickled vegetables or an upmarket twist on ramen noodles with succulent roast pork.

The connected cocktail bar Madbaren is equally inventive, offering libations such as Siberian Penicillin (horseradish vodka, pollen syrup and rhubarb).

★Gogol RUSSIAN $$

(Гоголь; Map p176; ☑812-312.6097; http://restaurant-gogol.ru; Malaya Morskaya ul 8; mains R350-690; ☺9am-3am; ☎; Ⓜ Admiralteyskaya) Like its sibling restaurant Chekov, Gogol whisks diners back to the genteel days of prerevolutionary Russian home dining. The menu comes in a novel, with chapters for each of the traditional courses. Salads, soups, dumplings and classics such as chicken Kiev are all very well done and served in charming, small dining rooms.

★Cococo RUSSIAN $$$

(Map p176; ☑812-418 2060; www.kokoko.spb.ru; Voznesensky pr 6; mains R650-1300; ☺7-11am, 2pm-1am; ☎; Ⓜ Admiralteyskaya) Cococo has charmed locals with its inventive approach to contemporary Russian cuisine. Your food is likely to arrive disguised as, say, a small bird's egg, a can of peas or a broken flower pot – all rather gimmicky, theatrical and fun. The best way to sample what it does is with its tasting menu (R2900). Bookings are advised.

🍴 Smolny & Vosstaniya

★Duo Gastrobar FUSION $

(Map p180; ☑812-994 5443; www.duobar.ru; ul Kirochnaya 8A; mains R350-500; ☺1pm-midnight; Ⓜ Chernyshevskaya) Boasting a minimalist Scandinavian design scheme, Duo Gastrobar has wowed diners with its outstanding cooking that showcases quality ingredients with global accents in delectable plates such as crab bruschetta, duck breast with smoked cheese and tomato, and rich French onion soup. There's an excellent wine list (over a dozen by the glass) as well.

Bekitzer
ISRAELI **$**

(Бекицер; Map p180; ☑812-926 4342; www.facebook.com/bktzr; ul Rubinshteyna 40; mains R180-450; ☉noon-6am Mon-Fri, from noon Sat & Sun; ☎🗷; Ⓜ Dostoyevskaya) Always crowded and spilling out into the street, this Israeli-themed eatery and drinking den lures hip and joyful people with its creative cocktails, Israeli Shiraz and the best falafel wraps this side of the Baltic sea. Other culinary temptations include sabich salad (with eggplant, egg, hummus and tahini), appetiser spreads with baba ghanoush and pitas, and rather imaginative matzah pizzas.

Khachapuri i Vino
GEORGIAN **$**

(Map p180; ☑812-273 6797; Mayokovskogo 56; mains R310-390; ☉noon-midnight; ☎🗷; Ⓜ Chernyshevskaya) This welcoming, warmly lit space serves outstanding Georgian fare. The recipes aren't overly complicated, and the fine ingredients speak for themselves in flavour-rich dishes like aubergine baked with *suluguni* (a type of cheese), pork dumplings, and tender lamb stew with coriander. Don't miss the excellent *khachapuri* (cheese bread), which comes in a dozen varieties and is whipped up by the bakers in front.

Obed Bufet
CAFETERIA **$**

(Обед Буфет; Map p180; 5th fl, Nevsky Centre, Nevsky pr 114; mains R250-380; ☉10am-11pm; ☎; Ⓜ Mayakovskaya) Just what St Petersburg needs: a well-organised, central and inviting cafeteria run by the city's most successful restaurant group. Here you'll find an extraordinary range of salads, soups, sandwiches, pizzas and meat dishes. There is even a 50% discount until noon and 30% after 9pm, making this a superb deal (come at 9pm for the latter, otherwise there will be no food left).

Botanika
VEGETARIAN **$**

(Ботаника; Map p180; ☑812-272 7091; www.cafebotanika.ru; ul Pestelya 7; mains R360-650; ☉11am-midnight; ☎🗷; Ⓜ Chernyshevskaya) This vegetarian charmer lives up to its green-minded name, with zesty fresh salads, veggie curries and ingredient-rich soups, plus a menu that takes in Russian, Indian and Italian dishes, all of which are handsomely executed. It's a friendly space, with plants and flower vases sprinkled about, and there's even a playroom and menu for the kids.

★ Schengen
INTERNATIONAL **$$**

(Шенген; Map p180; ☑812-922 1197; ul Kirochnaya 5; mains R480-850; ☉9am-midnight Mon-Fri, from 11am Sat & Sun; ☎; Ⓜ Chernyshevskaya) A breath of fresh air just off Liteyny pr, Schengen represents local aspirations to the wider world. The wide-ranging menu is packed with temptations, from tender halibut with tomatoes and zucchini to slow-cooked venison with parsnip cream and plums in red wine. It's served up in a cool and relaxing two-room space where efficient staff glide from table to table.

★ Banshiki
RUSSIAN **$$**

(Банщики; Map p180; ☑921-941 1744; www.banshiki.spb.ru; Degtyanaya 1; mains R500-1100; ☉11am-11pm; ☎; Ⓜ ploshad Vosstaniya) Although it opened in 2017, Banshiki has already earned a sterling reputation for its excellent Russian cuisine, serving up a huge variety of nostalgic dishes with a contemporary touch. Everything is made in house, from its refreshing *kvas* to dried meats and eight types of smoked fish. Don't overlook cherry *vareniki* (dumplings) with sour cream, oxtail ragout or the rich borscht.

Vsyo na Svyom Mestye
INTERNATIONAL **$$**

(Всё на Своём Месте; Map p180; ☑812-932 0256; Liteyny pr 7; mains R380-740; ☉noon-midnight) A hip little gastrobar with warm ambiance, tables made of converted sewing machines, and a record player providing the tunes. Stop in for creative market-fresh fare, which might include cod filet on cauliflower purée, ramen soup, or polenta with roast chicken and oyster mushrooms – all goes nicely with the craft brews and easy-going vibe.

✕ Sennaya & Kolomna

1818 Kafe and Bikes
INTERNATIONAL **$**

(Кафе и Велосипеды; Map p184; www.cafe1818.ru; ul Dekabristov 31; mains R240-420; ☉10am-11pm Mon-Fri, from 11am Sat & Sun; ☎🗷; Ⓜ Sadovaya) 🖉 Combining a love of bicycles and street food from around the globe, Kafe and Bikes serves up delicious cooking amid upbeat grooves, exposed bulbs and those slate grey walls so prevalent in St Petersburg. *Shawarmas*, wok-fried buckwheat noodles with vegetables, pizzas, *khachapuri* and *syriniki* (sweet cheese fritters) are all served up in a hurry by friendly staff.

ST PETERSBURG EATING

Co-op Garage
PIZZA $

(Map p168; www.cooperativegarage.com; Gorokhovaya 47; pizzas R260-390; ☺noon-midnight Sun-Thu, to 2am Fri & Sat; ☎♪) Tucked into an unmarked courtyard off Gorokhovaya, this sprawling restaurant and drinking den is the go-to spot for creatively topped thin-crust pizzas and craft beers. The industrial setting draws a chatty crowd of tatted-up hipsters and style mavens, with a mostly rock soundtrack playing in the background. On warm days you can take a table in the courtyard.

Volkonsky Deli
INTERNATIONAL $

(Map p184; www.newhollandsp.ru/en/foundry; nab Admiralteyskogo kanala; mains R280-450; ☺11am-10pm; ☎♪) The best place for a quick bite on New Holland Island is this buzzing little self-serve deli, which offers soups, salads, sandwiches and heavenly baked goods. On warm days the tables out front are the place to be.

★ Teplo
MODERN EUROPEAN $$

(Map p184; ☑812-570 1974; www.v-teple.ru; Bolshaya Morskaya ul 45; mains R360-940; ☺9am-midnight Mon-Fri, from 11am Sat & Sun; ✴☎♪; Ⓜ Admiralteyskaya) This much-feted, eclectic and original restaurant has got it all just right. The venue itself is a lot of fun to nose around, with multiple small rooms, nooks and crannies. Service is friendly and fast (when it's not too busy) and the peppy, inventive Italian-leaning menu has something for everyone. Reservations are usually required, so call ahead.

★ Severyanin
RUSSIAN $$

(Северянин; Map p184; ☑921-951 6396; www.severyanin.me; 18 Stolyarny per; mains R620-1300; ☺noon-midnight; ☎; Ⓜ Sennaya Ploshchad) An old-fashioned elegance prevails at Severyanin, one of the top choices for Russian cuisine near Sennaya ploshchad. Amid vintage wallpaper, mirrored armoires and tasseled lampshades, you might feel like you've stepped back a few decades. Start off with the excellent mushroom soup or borscht, before moving on to rabbit ragout in puff pastry or Baltic flounder with wine sauce.

Julia Child Bistro
INTERNATIONAL $$

(Map p184; ☑812-929 0797; Grazhdanskaya ul 27; mains R310-490; ☺9am-11pm Mon-Fri, from 10am Sat & Sun; ☎♪; Ⓜ Sadovaya) This neighbourhood charmer is a fine anytime spot, with good coffees, teas and snacks, plus creative thoughtfully prepared dishes like *kasha* (porridge) with mushrooms and feta for breakfast, or halibut with lemon cabbage and celery mousse later in the day. Kindly staff and a laid-back setting will make you want to stick around for a while.

Sadko
RUSSIAN $$

(Map p184; ☑812-903 2373; www.sadko-rst.ru; ul Glinki 2; mains R540-1200; ☺noon-1am; ♦; Ⓜ Sennaya Ploshchad) Serving all the Russian favourites, this impressive restaurant's decor combines traditional Zhostovo floral designs and Murano glass chandeliers amid vaulted ceilings and elegantly set tables. It's popular with theatregoers (reserve ahead in the high season), as it's an obvious pre- or post-Mariinsky dining option.

Idiot
RUSSIAN $$

(Map p184; ☑921-946 5173; www.idiot-spb.com/eng; nab reki Moyki 82; mains R300-1000, brunch R690; ☺11am-1am; ☎♪; Ⓜ Sennaya Ploshchad) Something of an expat favourite, the Idiot is a charming place that has been serving up high-quality Russian fare for years now. The friendly basement location is all about atmosphere, relaxation and fun (encouraged by the complimentary vodka coming with each meal). You can't go wrong here, whether opting for blini with caviar, grilled trout or *pelmeni* (Russian-style ravioli) with mushrooms and sour cream.

EM Restaurant
EUROPEAN $$$

(Map p184; ☑921-960 2177; http://emrestaurant.ru; nab reki Moyki 84; set menu R3500; ☺7-11pm Tue-Sun; ☎♪; Ⓜ Admiralteyskaya) Bookings are essential for this superb restaurant where the chefs calmly prepare seven beautifully presented courses in an open kitchen. Be prepared for such exotic elements as reindeer, smoked perch, red cabbage sorbet and fois gras coloured with squid ink. Individual food preferences can be catered to and every Sunday they work their culinary magic on a vegan menu.

Russian Vodka Room No 1
RUSSIAN $$$

(Map p184; ☑812-570 6420; www.vodkaroom.ru; Konnogvardeysky bul 4; mains R490-1530; ✴☎; Ⓜ Admiralteyskaya) This charming, welcoming place is the restaurant of the **Russian Vodka Museum** (Музей русской водки; Map p184; www.vodkamuseum.su; with/without tour R450/200, unguided/guided tasting tour R450/600; ☺noon-7pm), but it's good enough to be a destination in its own right. The interior enjoys a grand old-world dacha feel, as does the menu: rack of lamb in pomegranate sauce, whole fried Gatchina trout and Kamchatka crab with porcini mushrooms take you back to imperial tastes and tsarist opulence.

✖ Vasilyevsky Island

Khachapuri i Vino   CAUCASIAN $
(Хачапури и вино; Map p188; ☑ 8-911-174 9007; https://vk.com/hachapuriivino; Kadetskaya liniya 29; mains R300-500; ☑ 11.30am-midnight Sun-Thu, until 1am Fri & Sat; ☎; Ⓜ Vasileostrovskaya) Specialising in Adzhika cuisine from the Caucasus, this stylish place offers 10 types of *khachapuri*, the cheesy dough pies that are a bit like a thick-crust pizza. You can also sample *khinkali* (dumplings), Georgian wines and all-day breakfast dishes such as spicy scrambled eggs.

★Buter Brodsky   EUROPEAN $$
(Бутер Бродский; Map p188; ☑ 8-911-922 2606; https://vk.com/buterbrodskybar; nab Makarova 16; mains R260-780; ☑ noon-midnight; ☎; Ⓜ Sportivnaya) Shabby chic has never looked so good as it does at this cafe-bar dedicated to the poet Joseph Brodsky (the name is a pun on *buterbrod*, the Russian word for sandwich), a super-stylish addition to Vasilyevsky Island's eating and drinking scene. The menu runs from excellent *smørrebrød* (open sandwiches; from R260) to various set meals of salads and soup.

Pryanosti & Radosti   CAUCASIAN $$
(Пряности & Радости; Map p188; ☑ 812-640 1616; http://ginza.ru; 6-ya liniya 13; mains R550-1320; ☑ 10am-1am Mon-Thu, until 3am Fri-Sun; ☑ ⓘ; Ⓜ Vasileostrovskaya) If you're travelling with young children they will love this branch of the Ginza Project–run chain for its colourful, fun design that includes a children's room in the shape of a galleon, parrots in wall niches, an outdoor playground in summer and a real-life menagerie of animals, including a racoon, Clarissa the goat and two rabbits.

★Restoran   RUSSIAN $$$
(Ресторанъ; Map p188; ☑ 812-323 3031; Tamozhenny per 2; mains R700-2600; ☑ noon-11pm; ☎; Ⓜ Admiralteyskaya) Nearly 20 years on the scene and this excellent place is still going strong. Stylish and airily bright, Restoran is somehow formal and relaxed at the same time. The menu combines the best of *haute Russe* cuisine with enough modern flair to keep things interesting: try duck baked with apples or whole baked sterlet (a species of sturgeon) in white wine and herbs.

✖ Petrograd & Vyborg Sides

Le Menu   RUSSIAN $
(Map p191; http://le-menu.ru; Kronverksky pr 79; mains R320-570; ☑ 9am-11pm; ☎ ☑; Ⓜ Gorkovskaya) This smart cafe serves a good-value menu of thoughtfully prepared fish, meat and pasta dishes, along with a good

ST PETERSBURG EATING

DINE OR DRINK WITH A VIEW

Making the most of St Petersburg's architectural beauty are these top restaurants, cafes and bars with views:

Koryushka (Корюшка; Map p191; ☑ 812-640 1616; www.ginza.ru/spb/restaurant/korushka; Petropavlovskaya krepost 3, Zayachy Island; mains R650-2400; ☑ noon-1am; ☎ ⓘ; Ⓜ Gorkovskaya) Gaze across the Neva towards the Hermitage from this restaurant which serves lightly battered and fried smelt *(koryushka)*, a St Petersburg speciality.

Terrassa (Map p176; ☑ 812-640 1616; http://ginza.ru/spb/restaurant/terrassa; Kazanskaya ul 3a; mains R600-1000; ☑ 11am-1am, from noon Sat & Sun; ☎ ☑; Ⓜ Nevsky Prospekt) Splendid views from the terrace (only open in warmer months) of Kazan Cathedral.

Mansarda (Мансарда; Map p184; ☑ 812-946 4303; www.ginza.ru; ul Pochtamskaya 3; mains R590-1690; ☑ noon-1am; ❄ ☎; Ⓜ Admiralteyskaya) You can almost touch the dome of St Isaac's Cathedral from the nicest tables here (book in advance).

Solaris Lab (Map p184; www.facebook.com/solarislab11; per Pirogova 18, 4th fl; ☑ 1pm-midnight; Ⓜ Sadovaya) Cafe under a glass, semi-spherical dome with magnificent views over the russet rooftops to the glittering dome of St Isaac's.

Sky Bar (Map p168; Top fl, Hotel Azimut, Lermontovsky pr 43/1; ☑ 5pm-1am; ☎; Ⓜ Baltiyskaya) The top floor of the Soviet Era Azimut Hotel, one of the city's biggest eyesores, is also home to this aptly named bar with a bird's eye view of the city.

selection of vegetarian fare. The sophisticated setting encompasses wooden floorboards and chandeliers.

★**Chekhov** RUSSIAN $$
(Чехов; Map p191; ☎812-234 4511; http://restaurant-chekhov.ru; Petropavlovskaya ul 4; mains R550-890; ◷noon-11pm; ⓂPetrogradskaya) Despite a totally nondescript appearance from the street, this restaurant's charming interior perfectly recalls that of a 19th-century dacha and makes for a wonderful setting for a meal. The menu, hidden inside classic novels, features lovingly prepared dishes such as roasted venison with bilberry sauce or Murmansk sole with dill potatoes and stewed leeks.

Paninaro ITALIAN $$
(Map p191; Bolshaya Zelenina 28; mains R380-780; ◷9am-11.30pm Mon-Fri, from 11am Sat & Sun; ☑) Delightfully off the beaten path, Paninaro is a gem set inside one of the Petrogradky's most striking apartment buildings (don't miss the murals up top – visible on the opposite side of the street). Stop in for tasty house-made pastas topped with grilled vegetables, creative salads and pizzas, and refreshing cocktails.

Lev y Ptichka GEORGIAN $$
(Лев и Птичка; Map p191; ☎988-7069; Bolshoi pr 19; 🛜☑) Amid big fur hats, a lion *(lev)* mural, decorative wooden chandeliers and other curious design elements, this friendly spot has a loyal local following for its delicious and reasonably priced Georgian fare, including piping hot *khachapuri* fired up at the baker's oven in front. Plates are small and meant for sharing. Entrance is on ul Chaykino.

🍷 Drinking & Nightlife

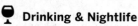

A city of midnight hedonists, St Petersburg has plenty of bars, pubs and cafes where you can enjoy a craft beer, an aritsan coffee or a strong cocktail at almost any time of day.

You can drink almost everywhere; even in smart restaurants you're generally welcome to come in and order just a beer, while the city's best cocktail bars are superb. The centre of the drinking scene is **Dumskaya ul** and **ul Lomonosova**, lined with dive bars and dance clubs and a sea of drunken revellers at the weekends.

🍷 Historic Heart

★**Mod Club** BAR, CLUB
(Map p176; www.modclub.info; nab kanala Griboyedova 7; cover R150-350; ◷6pm-6am; ⓂNevsky Prospekt) A popular spot for students and other indie types who appreciate the fun and friendly atmosphere and a cool mix of music both live and spun. Laid-back and great fun, this is a solid choice for a night out.

★**Coffee 22** CAFE
(Map p176; https://vk.com/coffeeat22; ul Kazanskaya 22; ◷8.30am-11pm Mon-Thu, until 1am Fri, 10am-1am Sat, 10am-11pm Sun; 🛜; ⓂNevsky Prospekt) In an area heavily saturated with hipster cafes, Coffee 22 – with its tattooed baristas and service staff, arty decor (piercing portrait of poet Jospeh Brodsky, a rustic wall of dried mosses) and fashion-forward customers – is perhaps the hippest of them all. Listen to its DJs via its mixcloud.com/coffee22 soundtrack.

SECRET BARS & RESTAURANTS

Secret 'speakeasy' style bars and restaurants where you'll need to call or email ahead for the password and directions are hip these days in St Petersburg. These are a couple we like:

Kvartira Kosti Kroitsa (Квартира Кости Кройца; Map p180; www.kreutzflat.com; 5th fl, apt 8, ul Marata 1, 921-651 7788; mains R450-730; ◷24hr; 🛜☑; ⓂMayakovskaya) A beautifully designed bourgeois hideaway, Kvartira Kosti comprises a stylish restaurant with views over Nevsky pr, a small handsomely designed bar, and a surprising tea salon tucked in the back, with stained glass skylight and elegant furnishings set amid a circular room. The menu features Asian-style noodle dishes, creative salads, risotto, fish and chips, and a full breakfast lineup.

Kabinet (Map p176; ☎8-911-921 1944; www.instagram.com/kabinet_bar; Malaya Sadovaya ul 8; ◷8am-6pm; ⓂGostiny Dvor) Bookings are essential for this speakeasy cocktail bar styled as a secret poker join and hidden beneath the Grill Brothers burger restaurant. It's a fun, sophisticated place with the waiters dealing sets of cards to determine your choice of cocktail.

★ Top Hops
CRAFT BEER

(Map p176; ☑ 8-966-757 0116; www.tophops.ru; nab reki Fontanki 55; ⊘ 4pm-1am Mon-Thu, 2pm-2am Fri-Sun; 🛜; Ⓜ Gostiny Dvor) One of the nicer craft-beer bars in town, this riverside space with friendly staff serves up a regularly changing menu of 20 beers on tap and scores more in bottles. The tasty Mexican snacks and food (go for nachos and chilli) go down exceptionally well while you sample your way through their range.

★ Borodabar
COCKTAIL BAR

(Map p176; ☑ 911 923 8940; www.facebook.com/Borodabar; Kazanskaya ul 11; ⊘ 5pm-2am Sun-Thu, to 6am Fri & Sat; 🛜; Ⓜ Nevsky Prospekt) Boroda means beard in Russian, and sure enough you'll see plenty of facial hair and tattoos in this hipster cocktail hang out. Never mind, as the mixologists really know their stuff – we can particularly recommend their smoked Old Fashioned, which is infused with tobacco smoke, and their colourful (and potent) range of shots.

★ Apotheke Bar
COCKTAIL BAR

(Map p176; ☑ 812-337 1535; http://hatgroup.ru/apotheke-bar; ul Lomonosova 1; ⊘ 8pm-6am Tue-Sun; Ⓜ Gostiny Dvor) The antithesis of the nearby dive bars, Apotheke is a calm, cosy cocoon for cocktail connoisseurs. Its slogan is 'think what you drink' so there's no official menu but a friendly young bartender, most likely in a white jacket and sporting a hipster moustache, to make suggestions or simply surprise you.

Piff Paff
BAR

(Map p176; ☑ 812-312 6227; http://pifpafhair.wixsite.com/pifpaf; nab kanala Griboyedova 31; ⊘ 10am-3am Sun-Thu, until 6am Fri & Sat; 🛜; Ⓜ Nevsky Prospekt) It's a happening bar, it serves a mean burger and there's a hairdressers at the back – should you fancy a new 'do' part-way through the night. Oh, and there's a fussball table, if conversation lags and you fancy a bit of hand-twisting action.

Tanzploshchadka
CLUB

(Танцплощадка; Map p176; www.tancplo.com; Konyushennaya pl 2a; ⊘ 8pm-6am Fri & Sat; Ⓜ Nevsky Prospket) Beloved by beautiful young things, this is the dance club of the moment with a shabby-chic indoor space beneath a lofty vaulted brick ceiling and plenty of outdoor space should it get too hot inside. Find it at the back, through the archway and courtyard complex south of Konyushennaya pl.

Bonch Cafe
CAFE

(Map p176; ☑ 812-740 7083; www.bonchcoffee.ru; Bolshaya Morskaya ul 16; ⊘ 8.30am-midnight Mon-Fri, from 10am Sat & Sun; 🛜; Ⓜ Admiralteyskaya) Coffee is brewed just the way you like it at this pleasantly designed cafe occupying a large corner space in a handy location. It's a great place for breakfast as well as late-night sweet treats as there's 30% off all desserts after 10pm.

🍷 Smolny & Vosstaniya

★ Hat
BAR

(Map p180; ul Belinskogo 9; ⊘ 7pm-5am; Ⓜ Gostiny Dvor) The wonderfully retro-feeling Hat is a serious spot for jazz and whiskey lovers, who come for the nightly live music and the cool cat crowd that makes this wonderfully designed bar feel like it's been transported out of 1950s Greenwich Village. A very welcome change of gear for St Petersburg's drinking options, but it can be extremely packed at weekends.

★ Union Bar & Grill
BAR

(Map p180; www.facebook.com/barunion; Liteyny pr 55; ⊘ 6pm-4am Sun-Thu, to 6am Fri & Sat; 🛜; Ⓜ Mayakovskaya) The Union is a glamorous and fun place, characterised by one enormous long wooden bar, low lighting and a New York feel. It's all rather adult, with a serious cocktail list and designer beers on tap. The hip 20- and 30-something crowd packs in on weekends to catch live bands, but it's generally quiet during the week.

There's good snack fare (burgers, hummus with pita, shawarma) from the grill in the back room, and a tiny rear patio for the smoking crowd.

★ Ziferblat
ANTICAFE

(Циферблат; Map p180; ☑ 981-180 7022; www.ziferblat.net; 2nd fl, Nevsky pr 81; per min R3, after first hr R2 per min; ⊘ 11am-midnight; 🛜; Ⓜ Ploshchad Vosstaniya) A charming multiroom 'free space' that has started a world-wide trend, Ziferblat is the original anti-cafe in St Petersburg. Coffee, tea, soft drinks and biscuits are included as you while away your time playing chess and other board games, reading, playing instruments (help yourself to the piano and guitar) or just hanging out with the arty young locals who frequent its cosy rooms.

The unsigned entrance is hard to find. Look for the big #81 sign on Nevsky pr, then find the door with buzzers just east of there. Ring Циферблат (labelled in Russian only).

★ **Redrum** BAR

(Map p180; ☑ 812-416 1126; www.facebook.com/ redrumbarspb; ul Nekrasova 26; ⏰ 4pm-1am Sun-Thu, to 3am Fri & Sat; Ⓜ Mayakovskaya) One of St Petersburg's best drinking dens, Redrum hits all the right notes. It has a cosy, white brick interior, a welcoming, easy-going crowd, and a stellar line-up of craft brews (some two dozen on tap). There's also good pub fare on hand to go with that creative line-up of Session Indian Pale Ales, sour ales, Berliner Weisse and porters.

Have a seat at the small circular bar and get ordering tips from the friendly bartenders, who will be happy to point you in the right direction.

★ **Commode** BAR

(Map p180; www.commode.club; ul Rubinshteyna 1, 2nd fl; per hr R180; ⏰ 4pm-2am Sun-Thu, to 6am Fri & Sat) Stopping in for drinks at Commode feels more like hanging out in an upper class friend's stylish apartment. After getting buzzed up, you can hang out in various high-ceilinged rooms, catch a small concert or poetry slam, browse books in the quasi-library room, play a round of table football, or chat with the easy-going crowd that have fallen for the place. Drink and snack prices are kept low (cocktails run R100 to R150), but you'll pay by the hour – not unlike an anticafe – for time spent at this so-called self-cost bar.

Griboyedov CLUB

(Грибоедов; Map p180; www.griboedovclub.ru; Voronezhskaya ul 2a; ⏰ noon-6am Mon-Fri, from 2pm Sat & Sun; 🛜; Ⓜ Ligovsky Prospekt) Griboyedov is hands-down the longest-standing and most respected music club in the city. Housed in a repurposed bomb shelter, this one was founded by local ska collective Dva Samolyota. It's a low-key bar in the early evening, gradually morphing into a dance club later in the night. Admission varies from free to upwards of R400, depending on who's playing or spinning.

Ziferburg ANTICAFE

(Map p180; nab reki Fontanki 20; per min R3; ⏰ 11am-midnight; Ⓜ Gostiny Dvor) Tucked inside the Golitsyn Loft, this is one of St Petersburg's loveliest spots to while away an afternoon. Elegant furnishings, huge windows and a piano in the corner set the scene. Like other anti-cafes, you'll pay by the minute, with drinks and cookies part of the deal. The price tops out at R540, meaning you won't pay more than that even if you spend all day here.

🍷 Sennaya & Kolomna

Stirka 40 BAR

(Стирка; Map p184; Kazanskaya ul 26; ⏰ 11am-midnight Sun-Thu, to 4am Fri & Sat; 🛜; Ⓜ Sennaya Ploshchad) This friendly joint, whose name means 'washing', has three washing machines, so you can drop off a load and have a few beers while you wait. A novel idea, though one few people seem to take advantage of. Its small and unassuming layout makes it a great place for a quiet drink with a cool young crowd.

Schumli CAFE

(Map p184; www.schumli.ru; Kazanskaya ul 40; ⏰ 9.30am-10pm Mon-Fri, from noon Sat & Sun; 🛜; Ⓜ Sennaya Ploshchad) With its large range of coffees, sumptuous selection of cakes and – best of all – freshly made Belgian waffles, this small but friendly cafe is a great place to regain flagging energy when wandering around the city. There's an upstairs dining room for full meals (mains R320 to R640), but coffee with a side of something sweet is the real reason to come.

🍷 Vasilyevsky Island

★ **Beer Boutique 1516** CRAFT BEER

(Пивной бутик 1516; Map p188; ☑ 812-328 6066; http://butik1516.ru; 9-ya liniya 55; ⏰ 3-10pm; Ⓜ Vasileostrovskaya) Your craft-beer cravings are sure to be satisfied at this bar-cum-bottle shop that has dedicated itself to the best of local and international ales. There's usually around 17 beers on tap and 300 or so in bottles to choose from – so it could be a long night.

★ **Radosti Kofe** CAFE

(Радости Кофе; Map p188; ☑ 812-925 7222; www.facebook.com/radosticoffee/; nab Makarova 28; ⏰ 8am-11pm; 🛜; Ⓜ Sportivnaya) A leafy, relaxed ambience and river views across to the Petrograd side make this a pleasant pit stop for coffee, other drinks and snacks while touring Vasilyevsky Island. They can make their drinks with soy, almond or hazelnut milk as well. The menu is available in English.

🍷 Petrograd & Vyborg Sides

Big Wine Freaks WINE BAR

(Map p191; ☑ 921-938 6063; Instrumentalnaya ul 3; ⏰ 6pm-1am Tue-Sat; 🛜) Boasting a stylish contemporary design, this aptly named place serves a good variety of wines from Europe

LGBT ST PETERSBURG

St Petersburg's LGBT nightlife is centred on the large and mainstream club **Central Station** (Map p176; ☎ 812-312 3600; http://centralstation.ru; ul Lomonosova 1/28; cover after midnight R100-300; ☉ 6pm-6am; Ⓜ Nevsky Prospekt) and the more alternative **Golubaya Ustritsa** (Map p176; ☎ 8-921-332 5161; www.boyster.ru; ul Lomonosova 1; ☉ 7pm-6am; Ⓜ Gostiny Dvor), a self-styled 'trash bar' that guarantees a raucous and cheap night out for anyone. Another option is the long-running Soviet-style club **Cabaret** (Кабаре; Map p180; www.cabarespb.ru; Razyezzhaya ul 43; cover R300-600; ☉ 11pm-6am Thu-Sat; Ⓜ Ligovsky Prospekt) where the 2.30am drag show at weekends is very popular.

There is a busy and growing LGBT scene, but it remains fairly discreet. Gay pride marches are routinely attacked by far right groups and the police often harass protesters. Coming Out (www.comingoutspb.com) is the site of a St Petersburg–based support organisation.

and the New World, plus tasty snacks to go with those tempranillos and chardonnays. Helpful staff – all trained sommeliers – can provide tips on what to order. There's live music, along the lines of acoustic jazz, on Wednesday nights from 8pm.

Double B
CAFE

(Даблби; Map p191; www.double-b.ru; Kronverksky pr; ☉ 8am-10pm Mon-Fri, from 10am Sat & Sun; Ⓜ Gorkovskaya) One of Petrograd Side's best coffee spots is this hip little cafe on busy Kronverksky pr. Staff can make you a perfect brew with all the essential gadgetry. A green and grey colour scheme, geometric designs, curious lamps and a big picture window make a fine setting for a bit of caffeinated daydreaming.

Yasli
BAR

(Ясли; Map p191; www.facebook.com/yaslibar; ul Markina 1; ☉ noon-midnight Sun-Thu, to 2am Fri & Sat; ☎; Ⓜ Gorkovskaya) Tucked down a narrow lane off busy Kronverksky, Yasli makes a fine retreat on chilly nights, with its excellent craft brews on tap and satisfying pub grub (like fish and chips). The setting channels a bit of Brooklyn chic with industrial fixtures and a hip but unpretentious crowd.

Bolshoy Bar
BAR

(Большой Бар; Map p191; ☉ 9am-1am Sun-Tue, to 4am Wed-Sat; ☎) A dapper boxcar-sized spot with old-time music and black-and-white films playing silently in the background, wryly named Bolshoi serves up good coffees by day and first-rate cocktails by night – though daytime drinking isn't discouraged. Slip into a comfy bar stool and order an aperol spritz from the talented but bristly barman.

⭐ Entertainment

The classical performing arts are one of the biggest draws in St Petersburg. Highly acclaimed professional artists stage productions in elegant theatres around the city, many of which have been recently revamped and look marvellous.

★ Alexandrinsky Theatre
THEATRE

(Map p176; ☎ 812-710 4103; www.alexandrinsky.ru; pl Ostrovskogo 2; tickets R900-6000; Ⓜ Gostiny Dvor) This magnificent venue is just one part of an immaculate architectural ensemble designed by Carlo Rossi. The theatre's interior oozes 19th-century elegance and style, and it's worth taking a peek even if you don't see a production here.

New Stage
PERFORMING ARTS

(Новая сцена; Map p176; ☎ 812-401 5341; http://alexandrinsky.ru; nab reki Fontanki 49a; Ⓜ Gostiny Dvor) The New Stage at Alexandrinsky, which opened in 2013, is a strikingly modern building for the historic city center but one that keeps a low profile due to the architect's ingenious use of glass and a secluded courtyard space. Come here to see contemporary dance, music, film, lectures and other events.

★ Mikhailovsky Theatre
PERFORMING ARTS

(Михайловский театр; Map p176; ☎ 812-595 4305; www.mikhailovsky.ru; pl Iskusstv 1; tickets R500-5000; Ⓜ Nevsky Prospekt) This illustrious stage delivers the Russian ballet or operatic experience, complete with multitiered theatre, frescoed ceiling and elaborate productions. Pl Iskusstv (Arts Sq) is a lovely setting for this respected venue, which is home to the State Academic Opera & Ballet Company.

MARIINSKY THEATRE

The **Mariinsky Theatre** (Мариинский театр; Map p184; ☑ 812-326 4141; www.mariinsky.ru; Teatralnaya pl 1; tickets R1200-6500; Ⓜ Sadovaya) has played a pivotal role in Russian ballet and opera ever since it was built in 1859 and remains one of Russia's most loved and respected cultural institutions. Its pretty green-and-white main building on aptly named Teatralnaya pl (Theatre Sq) is a must for any visitor wanting to see one of the world's great ballet and opera stages, while its newer second stage, the **Mariinsky II** (Мариинский II; Map p184; ☑ 812-326 4141; www.mariinsky.ru; ul Dekabristov 34; tickets R350-6000; ⊘ ticket office 11am-7pm; Ⓜ Sadovaya), is a state-of-the-art opera house for the 21st century.

The best way to experience these buildings is to see an opera or ballet. Outside performance times you can wander into the theatre's foyer and maybe peep into the lovely auditorium. Private tours are sometimes available – ask at the main ticket office if these are running during your visit.

Known as the Kirov Ballet during the Soviet era, the Mariinsky has an illustrious history, with troupe members including such ballet greats as Nijinsky, Nureyev, Pavlova and Baryshnikov. In recent years the company has been invigorated by the current Artistic and General Director Valery Gergiev. It is pretty certain that the Mariinsky Theatre will close at some point in 2018 or 2019 for a full (and, again, much needed) renovation, so visit the building's faded grandeur while you can.

Shostakovich Philharmonia CLASSICAL MUSIC
(Санкт-Петербургская филармония им. Д.Д.Шостаковича; Map p176; www.philharmonia.spb.ru; tickets R800-2500; Ⓜ Nevsky Prospekt) Under the artistic direction of world-famous conductor Yury Temirkanov, the Philharmonia represents the finest in orchestral music. The **Bolshoy Zal** (Большой зал; Map p176; ☑ 812-240-01-80; Mikhailovskaya ul 2; Ⓜ Nevsky Prospekt) is the venue for a full program of symphonic performances, while the nearby **Maly Zal** (Малый Зал; Map p176; ☑ 812-571 8333; Nevsky pr 30; Ⓜ Gostiny Dvor) hosts smaller ensembles. Both venues are used for numerous music festivals.

Cosmonaut LIVE MUSIC
(Космонавт; Map p168; www.cosmonavt.su; ul Bronnitskaya 24; tickets R300-800; ☎; Ⓜ Tekhnologichesky Institut) This fantastic conversion of a Soviet-era cinema in a rather nondescript part of town is a great venue for medium-sized concerts and a good place to see live acts in St Petersburg. There's air-conditioning, which is a godsend in summer, and a very comfortable VIP lounge upstairs, with seating throughout.

Fish Fabrique LIVE MUSIC
(Map p180; http://fishfabrique.ru; Ligovsky pr 53; ⊘ noon-4am daily, concerts from 8pm Thu-Sun; ☎; Ⓜ Ploshchad Vosstaniya) There are St Petersburg institutions and then there's Fish Fabrique, the museum of local boho life that has been going for over two decades. Here, in the dark underbelly of Pushkinskaya 10, artists, musicians and counter culturalists of all ages meet to drink beer and listen to music.

Maly Drama Theatre THEATRE
(Малый драматический театр; Map p180; www.mdt-dodin.ru; ul Rubinshteyna 18; Ⓜ Vladimirskaya) Also called the Theatre of Europe, the Maly is St Petersburg's most internationally celebrated theatre. Its director Lev Dodin is famed for his long version of Fyodor Dostoevsky's *The Devils,* as well as Anton Chekhov's *Play Without a Name,* both of which toured the world to great acclaim. It's also one of the few theatres that does (some) performances with subtitles.

Jazz Philharmonic Hall JAZZ
(Map p168; www.jazz-hall.com; Zagorodny pr 27; cover R1200-1500; ⊘ concerts 7pm or 8pm Wed-Sun; Ⓜ Vladimirskaya) Founded by legendary jazz violinist and composer David Goloshchokin, this venue represents the more traditional side of jazz. Two resident bands perform straight jazz and Dixieland in the big hall, which seats up to 200 people. The smaller Ellington Hall is used for occasional acoustic performances. Foreign guests also appear doing mainstream and modern jazz; check the website for details.

JFC Jazz Club JAZZ
(Map p180; ☑ 812-272 9850; www.jfc-club.spb.ru; Shpalernaya ul 33; cover R200-500; ⊘ 7-10pm;

Ⓜ Chernyshevskaya) Very small and very New York, this cool club is the best place in the city to hear modern, innovative jazz music, as well as blues, bluegrass and various other styles (see the website for a list of what's on). The space is tiny, so book a table online if you want to sit down.

Rimsky-Korsakov Conservatory CLASSICAL MUSIC

(Консерватория имени Н. А. Римского-Корсакова; Map p184; ☏ 812-312 2519; www.conservatory.ru; Teatralnaya pl 3; tickets R300-2000; Ⓜ Sadovaya) This illustrious music school was the first public music school in Russia. The Bolshoy Zal (Big Hall) on the 3rd floor is an excellent place to see performances by up-and-coming musicians throughout the academic year, while the Maly Zal (Small Hall) often hosts free concerts from present students and alumni; check when you're in town for what's on.

Mariinsky Concert Hall CLASSICAL MUSIC

(Мариинский концертный зал; Map p184; www.mariinsky.ru; ul Dekabristov 37; tickets R700-1800; ⊙ ticket office 11am-8pm; Ⓜ Sadovaya) Opened in 2007, this concert hall is a magnificent multifaceted creation. It manages to preserve the historic brick facade of the set and scenery warehouse that previously stood on this spot, while the modern main entrance, facing ul Dekabristov, is all tinted glass and angular lines, hardly hinting at the beautiful old building behind.

Hi-Hat LIVE PERFORMANCE

(Map p191; www.facebook.com/hihatrooftop; Aptekarsky pr 4; Ⓜ Petrogradskaya) On the rooftop of an art cluster near the Botanical Gardens, Hi-Hat hosts nights of live music, DJs and open-air film screenings. The creative line-up and open-air setting draws out style mavens and a party-minded crowd. The schedule is erratic, but events typically run from 5pm or 6pm to around 1am on Fridays and Saturdays (with the odd Sunday and Thursday happening). Check the website for the schedule.

A2 LIVE MUSIC

(Map p191; ☏ 812-333 0379; http://a2.fm; pr Medikov 3; tickets from R500; Ⓜ Petrogradskaya) With an outstanding sound system and an eclectic line-up of live music and DJs, A2 is one of the best venues for contemporary sounds in the city. It houses two concert halls (seating 1500 and 5000) and has a

staggering number of bars sprinkled about the complex.

Kamchatka CLUB

(Map p191; www.clubkamchatka.ru; ul Blokhina 15; cover R250-350; ⊙ 7pm-2am; Ⓜ Sportivnaya) A shrine to Viktor Tsoy, the late Soviet-era rocker who worked as caretaker of this former boilerhouse bunker with band mates from Kino. Music lovers flock here to light candles and watch a new generation thrash out their stuff. The line-up is varied and it's worth dropping by if only for a quick drink in this highly atmospheric place – find it tucked in a courtyard off the street.

Shopping

Historic Heart

★ Au Pont Rouge DEPARTMENT STORE

(Map p176; https://aupontrouge.ru; nab reki Moyki 73-79; ⊙ 10am-10pm; Ⓜ Admiralteyskaya) Dating from 1906-7 the one-time Esders and Scheefhaals department store has been beautifully restored and is one of the most glamorous places to shop in the city. This glorious Style Moderne building is now dubbed Au Pont Rouge after the **Krasny most** (Red Bridge) it stands beside. Inside you'll find choice fashions and accessories and top-notch souvenirs.

Perinnye Ryady ARTS & CRAFTS

(Перинные ряды, арт-центр; Map p176; ☏ 812-440 2028; http://artcenter.ru; Dumskaya ul 4; ⊙ 10am-8pm; Ⓜ Gostiny Dvor) Scores of arts-and-craft stores can be found in this arcade in the middle of Dumskaya ul, among them **Collection**, with a wide range of painted works, several by members of the Union of Artists of Russia, and **Pionersky Magazin**, specialising in Soviet-era memorabilia, where you're guaranteed to find a bust of Lenin and colourful propaganda and art posters.

Smolny & Vosstaniya

Phonoteka MUSIC

(Фонотека; Map p180; www.phonoteka.ru; ul Marata 28; ⊙ 10am-10pm; Ⓜ Mayakovskaya) This cool store will thrill anyone interested in music and cinema, as it sells a very cool range of vinyls from all eras (it's particularly strong on rare Soviet discs), a great selection of CDs from around the world and a discerning choice of film and documentary on DVD, making it an excellent place to buy Russian films.

Anglia
BOOKS

(Map p180; nab reki Fontanki 30; ⊙10am-8pm Mon-Fri, from 11am Sat, noon-7pm Sun; MGostiny Dvor) The city's only dedicated English-language bookshop has a good selection of contemporary literature, classics, dictionaries, history and travel writing – plus a dedicated section on Russia. It also hosts small art and photography displays, organises book readings and generally is a cornerstone of expat life in St Petersburg.

Imperial Porcelain
HOMEWARES

(Императорский Фарфор; Map p180; www.ipm.ru; Vladimirsky pr 7; ⊙10am-8pm; MVladimirskaya) This is one of many convenient city centre locations of the famous porcelain factory that once made tea sets for the Romanovs. If you're determined to get a bargain, head out to the **factory outlet** (Императорский Фарфор; www.ipm.ru; pr Obukhovsky Oborony 151; ⊙10am-8pm; MLomonosovskaya) where prices are a bit cheaper.

Galeria
SHOPPING CENTRE

(Галерея; Map p180; www.galeria.spb.ru; Ligovsky pr 30A; ⊙10am-11pm; MPloshchad Vosstaniya) This extraordinary place has rather changed everything for shopping in St Petersburg – there are probably as many shops here as elsewhere in the entire city centre. Spread over five floors, with around 300 shops (including H&M, Michael Kors, Marks & Spencer, Kiehl's and Zara), this really is a one-stop shop for pretty much all your shopping needs.

WORTH A TRIP

UDELNAYA FAIR

This weekend **market** (Удельная ярмарка; Skobolvesky pr, Vyborg Side; ⊙8am-5pm Sat & Sun; MUdelnaya) is a treasure trove of Soviet ephemera, prerevolutionary antiques, WWII artefacts and bonkers kitsch from all eras is truly worth travelling to see. Exit the metro station to the right and follow the crowds across the train tracks. Continue beyond the large permanent market, which is of very little interest, until you come to a huge area of independent stalls, all varying in quality and content.

Sennaya & Kolomna

Rediska
ARTS & CRAFTS

(Map p184; Grazhdanskaya ul 13, Berthold Centre; ⊙noon-10pm; MSadovaya) Near the courtyard of the Berthold Centre, this delightful shop has lots of eye-catching objects, much of it made in-house or produced by St Petersburg artisans. You'll find jewellery imprinted with famous paintings, whimsical wooden clocks, ceramics, tiny Konstructor kits (a kind of miniature Lego), artfully painted flasks, backpacks, sunglasses and handmade soaps, lotions and candles.

Northway
GIFTS & SOUVENIRS

(Map p184; Angliyskaya nab 36/2; ⊙9am-8pm; MAdmiralteyskaya) There is quite simply no bigger collection of *matryoshki* (nesting dolls), amber, fur and other Russian souvenir staples than that on offer at this very impressive and stylish shop right on the Neva embankment. Look no further for Russian gifts to take home.

ⓘ Information

DANGER & ANNOYANCES

➜ Foreigners tend to find Russians quite brusque and even unfriendly. Remember, this is a cultural thing, and try not to be offended by it. Russians take a while to warm up, but when they do they're exceptionally friendly.

➜ There is an ongoing epidemic of racist attacks in St Petersburg. If you look very obviously non-Russian, it's a good idea to avoid the suburbs and take taxis at night.

➜ Due to legislation criminalising the 'promotion of homosexuality' to minors, levels of homophobia are higher now than they have been for some time. Gay travellers are advised to remain discreet.

DISCOUNT CARDS

If you're a student, bring an International Student Identity Card (ISIC) to get discounts – cards issued by non-Russian universities will not always be accepted. The Hermitage is the blissful exception, where anyone with a student card from any country gets in for free. Senior citizens (usually anyone over the age of 60) are often also eligible for discounts, so bring your passport with you as proof of age.

The St Petersburg Card (https://petersburg-card.com) is sold online and by the St Petersburg Tourist Centre (p214). It gives a range of discounts on tours and sights such as the Hermitage, Peterhof and Tsarskoe Selo (the savings aren't huge) as well as acting as a stored-value card for public transport.

HISTORIC SHOPS OF NEVSKY PROSPEKT

Nikolai Gogol described it as 'Petersburg's universal channel of communication' in his story *Nevsky Prospekt*. Some 300 years on from its creation, little has changed. Nevsky remains the city's most famous street, running 4.7km from the Admiralty to the Alexandr Nevsky Monastery, from which it takes its name. Taking a stroll along it is an essential St Petersburg experience and particularly special at dusk as the low light casts shadows and picks out silhouettes from the elegant mix of architecture.

The inner 2.5km to Moscow Station (Moskovsky vokzal) is the city's prime shopping drag that pulses with street life. Here you'll find baroque palaces, churches in a range of denominations, all manner of entertainments and, above all, shops, some historic in their own right. These are the key ones not to miss:

Singer Building (Map p176; Nevsky pr 28; M Nevsky Prospekt) The former headquarters of the Singer sewing machine company, which opened a factory in the Russian capital in 1904, is one of St Petersburg's most gorgeous buildings. Its Style Modern architecture, designed by Pavel Suzor, and topped with a glass tower and scuplture, also housed the American consulate for a few years prior to WWI. It's possible to access the offices part of the building including the interior of the glass dome on a tour (R6000 for up to three people) organised with **Placemates** (925 845 3747; http://placemates.ru; prices vary).

Bolshoy Gostiny Dvor (Большой Гостиный Двор; Map p176; 812-630 5408; http://bgd.ru; Nevsky pr 35; 10am-10pm; M Gostiny Dvor) One of the world's first indoor shopping malls, the 'Big Merchant Yard' dates from between 1757 and 1785 and stretches 230m along Nevsky pr (its perimeter is more than 1km long). This Rastrelli creation is not as elaborate as some of his other work, finished as it was by Vallin de la Mothe in a more sober neoclassical style. At its height at the turn of the 20th century, Gostiny Dvor contained over 170 shops.

Passage (Пассаж; Map p176; 812-313 7400; http://passage.spb.ru; Nevsky pr 48; 10am-9pm; M Gostiny Dvor) Built between 1846 and 1848, this arcade has a glass roof spanning the entire block from Nevsky to Italiyanskaya ul. Dostoevsky wrote a story about a man who was swallowed by a crocodile in Passage, after a live crocodile was exhibited here in 1864. Look for the small exhibition on the 1st floor with historical photos and other items related to the arcade. The handsomely restored ground floor has several good souvenir and antique shops.

Kupetz Eliseevs (Map p176; 812-456 6666; www.kupetzeliseevs.ru; Nevsky pr 56; 10am-11pm; M Gostiny Dvor) This Style Moderne stunner is St Petersburg's most elegant grocery store. Built in 1904 as the flagship of the Eliseevs Brothers's highly successful chain of food emporiums, little expense or design flourish was spared in its construction. In recent years the building has been restored to its full grandeur with huge plate-glass windows providing glimpses into a dazzling interior of stained glass, chandeliers, polished brass and a giant pineapple palm. The building's exterior is no less lavish, graced with four allegorical sculptures representing industry, trade and commerce, art and science. The building also included a theatre, which is still functioning.

EMERGENCY

Ambulance 03
Fire Department 01
Police 02

INTERNET ACCESS

Internet access is excellent and practically universal. Nearly all hotels have free wireless internet. Many restaurants, cafes, bars and clubs also have wi-fi. You may have to ask for a password (*parol*) to get online, and also input your mobile phone number. Sometimes this will need to be a Russian number (ie one starting with 7); if you don't have one, ask a local if you can use their number.

MEDIA

There is no English-language newspaper but the free bimonthly **In Your Pocket** (www.inyourpocket.com) magazine is worth picking up for events listings and other background information.

MEDICAL SERVICES

Clinics

These private clinics have facilities of an international standard and are pricey, but generally accept major international insurance policies, including direct billing.

American Medical Clinic (Map p184; ☑812-740 2090; www.amclinic.ru; nab reki Moyki 78; ⊙24hr; Ⓜ Admiralteyskaya)

Euromed (Map p180; ☑812-327 0301; www.euromed.ru; Suvorovsky pr 60; ⊙24hr; Ⓜ Chernyshevskaya)

Medem International Clinic & Hospital (Map p180; ☑812-336 3333; www.medem.ru; ul Marata 6; ⊙24hr; Ⓜ Mayakovskaya)

Pharmacies

A chain of 24-hour pharmacies called **36.6 Pharmacy** (www.366.ru) has many branches around the city, including in the **Historic Centre** (Map p176; ☑812-324 2666; Gorokhovaya ul 16; ⊙9am-9pm Mon-Fri, 10am-9pm Sat & Sun; Ⓜ Admiralteskaya). Other convenient pharmacies include Raduga, with branches in the **Petrograd Side** (Радуга; Map p191; Bolshoy pr 62; ⊙9am-10pm Mon-Fri, from 10am Sat & Sun; Ⓜ Petrogradskaya) and **Smolny** (Map p180; ☑812-275 8189; Nevsky pr 98, Smolny; ⊙24hr; Ⓜ Mayakovskaya).

Apteka Petrofarm (Map p176; ☑812-571 3767; www.petropharm6.webapteka.ru; Nevsky pr 22-24; ⊙24hr)

MONEY

ATMs are everywhere and debit and credit cards are accepted in most places. Still, it's always a good idea to carry some cash.

POST

To send parcels home, head to the elegant **main post office** (Map p184; Pochtamtskaya ul 9; Ⓜ Admiralteyskaya). Smaller post offices may refuse to send parcels internationally; most importantly, your package is more likely to reach its destination if you send it from the main post office. You will need to provide a return address in St Petersburg – your hotel name will be fine.

TOILETS

Around nearly all metro stations and tourist attractions there's at least one blue Portaka-bin-type toilet staffed by an attendant who will charge around R35 for the honour of using it. There are also pay toilets in all main-line train stations and free ones in museums. As a general rule, it's far better to stop for a drink in a cafe or duck into a fancy hotel and use their cleaner facilities.

TOURIST INFORMATION

Tourist information is halfway decent in St Petersburg. In addition to the Tourist Information Bureau's **main office** (Map p176; ☑812-303 0555, 812-242 3909; http://eng.ispb.info; Sadovaya ul 14/52; ⊙10am-7pm Mon-Sat; Ⓜ Gostiny Dvor), just off Nevsky pr in the Historic Heart, there is an office in **Smolny** (Map p180; pl Vosstaniya; ⊙10am-7pm; Ⓜ Ploshchad Vosstaniya), and kiosks at **Palace Square** (Map p176; ☑931-326-5744; Dvortsovaya pl; ⊙10am-7pm; Ⓜ Admiralteyskaya), **St Isaac's Cathedral** (Map p184; Isaakievskaya pl; ⊙10am-7pm; Ⓜ Admiralteyskaya) and **Pulkovo Airport** (⊙9am-8pm).

TRAVEL AGENCIES

Ost-West (Map p180; ☑812-327 3416; www.ostwest.com; office 306, ul Vosstaniya 7; ⊙10am-6.30pm Mon-Fri; Ⓜ pl Vosstaniya)

Travel Russia (Map p180; ☑812-407 2015; www.travelrussia.su; Office 206, Suvorovsky Pr 2B; ⊙9am-7pm Mon-Fri; Ⓜ Ploshchad Vosstaniya)

ⓘ Getting There & Away

AIR

Most travellers arrive in St Petersburg at **Pulkovo International Airport** (LED; ☑812-337 3822; www.pulkovoairport.ru; Pulkovskoye sh), 23km south of the city. This terminal building, which opened in 2014, and is confusingly still referred to as Terminal 1, handles all domestic and international flights and is St Petersburg's only airport.

ⓘ RAISING THE BRIDGES

From mid-April until late November major bridges across the Neva rise roughly between 1.30am and 5am to allow ships to sail through the city. Check the timetable at www.razvodka-mostov.ru (in Russian only). Because of the new fixed suspension bridges on the Western High Speed Diameter highway across the mouth of the Neva you will not be stuck either side of the river when the bridges go up. Note also that between May and the end of November the M5 metro line shuttles every 20 minutes back and forth between Admiralteyskaya and Sportivnaya stations between 1am and 3am on Saturday and Sunday and the eve of public holidays, creating an easy way to get between the islands and the Historic Heart.

BOAT

Cruise ships dock at one of the following:

Marine Facade Terminal (Пассажирский Порт Санкт-Петербург Морской фасад; Map p168; ☑ 812-303 6740; www.portspb.ru; 1 Bereg Nevskoy gubi; Ⓜ Primorskaya)

Sea Port (Морской вокзал; Map p168; ☑ 812-337 2060; www.mvokzal.ru; pl Morskoy Slavy 1)

English Embankment Passenger Terminal (Map p184)

Lieutenant Schmidt Passenger Terminal (Map p188)

St Petersburg Sea Port (Морской порт Санкт-Петербурга; Map p168; www.seaport. spb.ru; Mezhevoy kanal 5)

River Passenger Terminal (Речной вокзал; ☑ 812-262 6321, 812-262 0239; Obukhovskoy Oborony pr 195; Ⓜ Proletarskaya)

You can buy ferry tickets for nearly all boats at the **Ferry Centre** (Паромный центр; Map p180; ☑ 812-327 3377; www.paromy.ru; ul Vosstaniya 19; ⊙ 10am-7pm Mon-Fri; Ⓜ Ploshchad Vosstaniya), a short walk from the Moscow Station. Alternatively, it's possible to buy ferry tickets in the Sea Port, as well as online through the ferry companies themselves.

BUS

St Petersburg's main bus station, **Avtovokzal** (Автобусный вокзал; Map p168; ☑ 812-766 5777; www.avokzal.ru; nab Obvodnogo kanala 36; Ⓜ Obvodny Kanal), has bus connections to cities all over western Russia, including Veliky Novgorod, but most travellers won't use it. If you do happen to arrive here, it's a short walk along the canal to the metro station Obvodny Kanal (Line 5).

Lux Express (Map p168; ☑ 812-441 3757; www.luxexpress.eu; nab Obvodnogo kanala 36; ⊙ 9am-9pm; Ⓜ Baltiyskaya) runs buses from both Avtovokzal and from outside the Baltic Station (Baltiysky vokzal). Its buses run to Tallinn (from R1950, seven daily, seven hours), Rīga (from R2275, four daily, 11 hours) and Helsinki (from R1650, three daily, 7½ hours).

Ecolines (Map p168; ☑ 812-409 9410; www. ecolines.ru; Podezdny per 3; ⊙ 8am-10pm; Ⓜ Pushkinskaya) runs daily buses from the **Vitebsk Station** (p217) to Tallinn (R1210, five daily, seven hours), Rīga (R2240, four daily; 11 hours), Minsk (R2130, three daily, 14 hours), Prague (R6130, two to three daily, 36 to 38 hours) and Berlin (R6840, two to three daily, 34 hours).

Transgold (☑ 812-995 0605; www.transgold. ru) run door-to-door *marshrutky* (minibuses) to and from Helsinki and other destinations in Finland from R1300.

CAR & MOTORCYCLE

The most convenient border crossing from Estonia when driving to St Petersburg is Narva. You can avoid queues by booking a time slot for your crossing from (but not into) Estonia for a small fee at www.estonianborder.eu.

Heading to the city from Finland, highways cross the Finnish border posts of Nuijamaa and Vaalimaa (Brusnichnoe and Torfyanovka, respectively, on the Russian side).

TRAIN

Buying train tickets in person can be done at any train station (even at a different terminus from where your train departs, although waiting time can be long if you buy them at a counter. Far quicker are the ticket machines, which all work in English and where you can usually pay in both cash and by credit card. Another option is the centrally located **Train Tickets Centre** (Кассы ЖД; Map p176; nab kanala Griboyedova 24; ⊙ 8am-8pm Mon-Sat, until 6pm Sun; Ⓜ Gostiny Dvor), where there are also ticket machines, which makes waiting in line unnecessary.

Stations

Trains from Helsinki arrive at the Finland Station (p217). From here you can connect to anywhere in the city by metro from the Ploshchad Lenina station (Line 1) on the square outside the station.

Some trains from the Leningradskaya Oblast and those from Helsinki to Moscow stop en route in St Petersburg at the **Ladoga Station** (Ladozhsky vokzal; Ладожский вокзал; http://lvspb. ru; Zanevsky pr 73; Ⓜ Ladozhskaya; Ladozhsky vokzal). It's served by the Ladozhskaya metro station (Line 4).

If you're arriving from Moscow, you'll come to the Moscow Station (p217; Moskovsky vokzal), in the centre of the city. There are two metro stations close by: pl Vosstaniya (Line 1) and Mayakovskaya (Line 3). To get here (you can enter both stations through one building) turn left outside the main entrance to the Moscow Station, and the exit is on one side of the building on Ligovsky pr.

Moscow

There are about 10 overnight trains travelling between St Petersburg and Moscow. Most depart between 10pm and 1am, arriving in the capital the following morning between 6am and 8am. On the more comfortable *firmeny* trains, such as the *Red Arrow* (Красная стрела) or *Grand Express* (ГРАНД ЭКСПРЕСС) a deluxe sleeping carriage is between R12,800 and R16,400, 1st-class compartment (two-person cabin) around R16,300, while a 2nd-class *kupe* (four-person cabin) is R2800. Less fancy trains offer 3rd-class *platzkartny* (dorm-style sleeping carriages) for R1570 and even sitting-only carriages for R890.

Sapsan high-speed trains travel at 200km/h to reach Moscow in around four hours. There are six to eight daily departures. Comfortable 2nd-class seats start at R1300, while super-spacious 1st-class seats run from R5000.

Elsewhere in Russia

St Petersburg has excellent connections to the rest of European Russia, with daily trains to Murmansk, Petrozavodsk, Kaliningrad, Nizhny Novgorod, Novgorod, Pskov and Yekaterinburg. Less frequent services connect the city to Arkhangelsk and Kazan. Southern Russia and Siberia are generally reached via Moscow, although there are some direct trains to the Black Sea coast from St Petersburg. However, be aware that these cut through Belarus, necessitating a transit visa for Belarus and a double entry visa.

Finland & Other International Destinations

From Helsinki there are four daily Allegro express trains that take you from the Finnish capital to St Petersburg in an impressive 3½ hours; see www.vr.fi for prices and timetables. Services in both directions stop at Vyborg.

St Petersburg is well connected by train to lots of cities throughout Eastern Europe, including Berlin, Budapest, Kaliningrad, Kyiv, Prague and Warsaw, but all trains pass through Belarus, for which you're required to hold a transit visa. The train to Smolensk in Russia also passes through Belarus.

ⓘ Getting Around

TO/FROM THE AIRPORT

An official taxi to the centre should cost between R800 and R1000; if you book one via an app, it's likely to be R700. Alternatively, take bus 39 (35 minutes) or 39A (20 minutes) to Moskovskaya metro station for R35, then take the metro from Moskovskaya (Line 2) all over the city for R45.

BICYCLE

Despite the local traffic being still in the learning stages about basic respect for cyclists, this is a great way to get around this huge and flat city.

➡ Some youth hostels and bike shops, such as **Rentbike** (Map p168; ☑ 812-981 0155; www.rentbike.org; Naberezhnaya fontanki 77; per hr/day from R100/500; ⊘10am-10pm; Ⓜ Sennaya Ploshchad) and **Skladnye Velosipedy** (Складные Велосипеды; Map p180; ☑ 812-748 1407; www.shulzbikes.ru; Goncharnaya ul 20; bike hire per day/24 hr R700/1000; ⊘11am-9pm), hire bikes for as little as R500 per day.

➡ If you're keen to do a lot of cycling, bring a helmet, bike lights and a good lock from home, as these are hard to come by.

➡ **Velogorod** (☑ 812-648 2100; http://spb.velogorod.org; ride/day pass R45/129) is a handy bike-sharing system with 56 stations across the city. You'll need to use the website or download their app to hire one of their bicycles.

BUS, MARSHRUTKA, TROLLEYBUS & TRAM

Buses and, particularly *marshrutky* (minibuses), are a very handy way to get around the city and they tend to cover routes that the metro doesn't, making them essential for certain parts of town. Most travellers find taking them a bit daunting, however, as there's little signage in English. On both buses and trolleybuses, you get on and then pay a conductor; the fare is R40. *Marshrutky* rates are usually posted on the inside of the bus near the driver.

Increasingly rare, trams are still useful in areas such as Kolomna and Vasilyevsky Island where there is little else available.

Useful routes include:

Tram 6 Great for travelling between areas north of the river without going through the centre: connects Vasilyevsky Island with the Petrograd Side and the Vyborg Side.

Trolleybus 7 Goes from Smolny along Nevsky pr, over the river, along the Strelka and to the Petrograd Side.

CAR

You can hire cars from the major international agencies such as **Avis** (Map p180; ☑ 812-600 1213; www.avisrussia.ru; pl Alexandra Nevskogo 2; ⊘9am-9pm; Ⓜ pl Alexandra Nevskogo) and **Hertz** (☑ 812-454 7099; www.hertz.ru; Pulkovskoe sh 41) as well as local operations to get around the city and further afield.

For something a little different, you can rent vintage cars, including retro Soviet models such as Chaikas and Volgas, from **Retro v Mode** (Ретро в моде; Map p180; ☑ 812-927 1837; www.retrovmode.ru; office 16, Korpus 6, Ligovsky pr 50; ⊘10am-1pm & 2-8pm). Rates start around R1500 per hour and they can also arrange drivers.

METRO

The St Petersburg **Metro** (☑ 800 350 1155; www.metro.spb.ru; ⊘6am-12.45am) is a very efficient five-lined system. The network of some 70 stations is most usefully employed for travelling long distances, especially connecting the suburbs to the city centre. New stations are being added and it's possible that the one at Teatralnaya, next to the Mariinsky Theatre, will be operational by 2020.

Look for signs with a big blue 'M' signifying the entrance to the metro. The flat fare for a trip is R45; you will have to buy an additional ticket if you are carrying a significant amount of baggage. If you wish to buy a single journey, ask for 'adin proyezd' and you will be given a zheton (token) to put in the machine.

If you are staying more than a day or two, however, it's worth buying a smart card (R60), which is good for multiple journeys to be used over the course of a fixed time period – for example, 10 trips in seven days for R355. Their main advantage is that you won't have to line up to buy tickets – the ticket counters can have very long lines during peak hours.

The metro system is fully signed in English, so it's quite easy to use, even for first-timers in Russia.

TAXI

Taxi apps, such as Gett and Yandex Taxi, are all the rage in St Petersburg and they've brought down the prices of taxis in general, while improving the service a great deal.

Aside from the apps, the best way to get a taxi is to order it by phone. Operators will usually not speak English, so unless you speak Russian, ask your hotel reception to call a taxi for you. It also remains possible to flag down a random car in the street and negotiate the price, keeping in mind all security caveats.

Peterburgskoe Taksi 068 (☑ 812-324 7777, in St Petersburg 068; www.taxi068.ru)

Taxi-4 (☑ 812-333 4333; www.taxi-4.ru)

Taxi Blues (Такси-Блюз; ☑ 812-321 8888; www.taxiblues.ru)

Taxi 6000000 (☑ 812-600 0000; http://6-000-000.ru) Has operators and drivers who speak English.

AROUND ST PETERSBURG

There are several grand imperial palaces and estates surrounding St Petersburg. Peterhof and the palace-park ensembles at Tsarskoe Selo and Pavlovsk are the best and a visit to St Petersburg is not complete without a trip to at least one of them. Be warned that at the height of summer the endless tourist crowds can be frustrating. Moreover, while Peterhof is the most impressive palace, it's overpriced for foreigners. Tsarskoe Selo is the best value-for-money day trip.

If your time is short, or you wish to avoid the long queues at the palaces, book yourself into a guided tour of Peterhof, Tsarskoe Selo or Pavlovsk with a travel agency, and make sure that they book your entry ticket for you. Peter's Walking Tours (p195) in St Petersburg can do this for you.

Peterhof   Петергоф

☑ 812 / POP 73,400

Hugging the Gulf of Finland, 29km west of St Petersburg, Peterhof – the 'Russian Versailles' – is a far cry from the original cabin Peter the Great had built here to oversee construction of the Kronshtadt naval base. Peter liked the place so much he built a villa, Monplaisir, here and then a whole series of palaces and ornate gardens. Peterhof was renamed Petrodvorets (Peter's Palace) in 1944 but has since reverted to its original name. The palace and buildings are surrounded by

---

HISTORIC RAILWAY STATIONS

As the birthplace of Russia's railway system, it's not surprising that St Petersburg has some grand stations. The oldest and most elegant is the **Vitebsk Station** (Vitebsky vokzal; Витебский вокзал; Zagorodny pr 52; Ⓜ Pushkinskaya), originally built in 1837 for the tsar's private train line to Tsarskoe Selo. The current building dates from 1904 and is partly graced with gorgeous Style Moderne interiors.

While you're at the **Moscow Station** (Moskovsky vokzal; Московский вокзал; www.moskovsky-vokzal.ru; Nevsky pr 85; Ⓜ Ploshchad Vosstaniya), look up at the expansive ceiling mural in the main entrance hall. There's also a striking giant bust of Peter the Great in the hall leading to the platforms.

The **Finland Station** (Finlyandsky vokzal; Финляндский вокзал; Map p168; pl Lenina 6; Ⓜ Ploshchad Lenina), rebuilt in the 1970s in rectilinear Soviet style, is where Lenin finally arrived in 1917 after 17 years in exile abroad. Here he gave his legendary speech from the top of an armoured car to a crowd who had heard of, but never seen the man. After fleeing a second time he again arrived here from Finland, this time disguised as a railway fireman, and the locomotive he rode in is displayed behind glass on the platform. Walk out onto the square that still bears Lenin's name and you'll see a marvellous statue of the man himself at the far end.

Around St Petersburg

Zelenogorsk
Repino
Penaty
Toksovo
Sestroretsk
Kotlin Island
Kronstadt
Gulf of Finland
St Petersburg
Lomonosov
Oranienbaum
Peterhof
Strelna
Neva
Ropsha
Detskoe Selo
Pushkin (Tsarskoe Selo)
Pavlovsk
Gatchina

0 — 10 km
0 — 5 miles

leafy gardens and a spectacular ensemble of gravity-powered fountains.

What you see today is largely a reconstruction, as Peterhof was a major casualty of WWII. Apart from the damage done by the Germans, the palace suffered the worst under Soviet bombing raids in December 1941 and January 1942, because Stalin was determined to thwart Hitler's plan of hosting a New Year's victory celebration here.

⊙ Sights

★ Lower Park
PARK

(Нижний парк; www.peterhofmuseum.ru; adult/student May-Oct R750/400, Nov-Apr free; ⊙9am-7pm) One of the greatest attractions outside of St Petersburg is the jaw-dropping collection of gilded fountains, statue-lined lanes, and picturesque canals that make up the Lower Park of Peterhof. Even if you'd rather not brave the crowds to visit the palace, it's still well worth a visit here, to see its over-the-top Grand Cascade (⊙11am-5pm Mon-Fri, to 6pm Sat & Sun May-Oct) and other water features, including trick fountains that douse unsuspecting visitors.

★ Grand Palace
PALACE

(Большой дворец; www.peterhofmuseum.ru; ul Razvodnaya; adult/student R700/400, audio guide

R600; ⊙10.30am-6pm Tue-Sun, closed last Tue of month) The Grand Palace is an imposing building, although with just 30-something rooms, it is not nearly as large as your typical tsarist palace. From the start of June to the end of September it is open to foreign tourists only between noon and 2pm, and again from 4.15pm to 5.45pm (to 7.45pm on Saturdays), due to guided tours being only in Russian at other times (it is quite possible to leave your group, however).

While Peter's palace was relatively modest, Rastrelli grossly enlarged the building for Empress Elizabeth. Later, Catherine the Great toned things down a little with a redecoration, although that's not really apparent from the glittering halls and art-filled galleries that are visible today. All the paintings, furniture and chandeliers are original, as everything was removed from the premises before the Germans arrived in WWII. The Chesme Hall is full of huge paintings of Russia's destruction of the Turkish fleet at Çesme in 1770. Other highlights include the exquisite East and West Chinese Cabinets, the Picture Hall and Peter's Study. The Throne Room is the biggest in the palace, with Peter's red velvet throne as centrepiece, while the Picture Hall lives up to its name, with hundreds of portraits crowding its walls.

After WWII, Peterhof was largely left in ruins. Hitler had intended to throw a party here when his plans to occupy the Astoria Hotel were thwarted. He drew up pompous invitations, which obviously incensed his Soviet foes. Stalin's response was to pre-empt any such celebration by bombing the estate himself, in the winter of 1941–42, so it is ironic but true that most of the damage at Peterhof occurred at the hands of the Soviets. What you see today is largely a reconstruction; the main palace was completely gutted and only a few of its walls were left standing.

Park Alexandria
PARK

(Парк Александрия; adult/student R300/200; ⊙9am-10pm) Even on summer weekends, the rambling and overgrown Park Alexandria is peaceful and practically empty. Built for Tsar Nicholas I (and named for his tsarina), these grounds offer a sweet retreat from the crowds. Originally named for Alexander Nevsky, the Gothic chapel (adult/student R300/200; ⊙10.30am-6pm Tue-Sun) was completed in 1834 as the private chapel of Nicholas I. Nearby is the cottage (Коттедж; adult/student R500/300; ⊙10.30am-6pm Tue-Sun) that was built around the same time as his summer residence.

🛏 Sleeping & Eating

New Peterhof Hotel
HOTEL $$

(☑ 812-319 1010; www.new-peterhof.com; Sankt Peterburgsky pr 34; s/d from R5000/5900; 📶 🖾) This impressive hotel complex has 150 rooms in an unusually designed building near Peterhof's Upper Garden. Rooms are modern and sleek with all the amenities you'd expect, and the best have photogenic views of the Peter and Paul Church.

Shtandart Restaurant
RUSSIAN $$

(Ресторан Штандарт; www.restaurantshtandart. spb.ru; Lower Park; mains R590-1300; ⊘ 11am-8pm) This large and upmarket restaurant overlooks the Gulf of Finland, just west of the boat dock, with plenty of seating both inside and out. It has a large and meaty menu full of filling but interesting Russian classics.

Grand Orangerie
RUSSIAN $$

(Lower Park; set menus R450-800; ⊘ 11am-8pm) This cafe in the orangery is a fine choice for lunch. It gets busy, though, so you may have to queue for a spot. It has a cafeteria-style counter where you can pick out your Russian classics; don't neglect the cake selection.

ℹ Getting There & Away

It's easy and cheap to reach Peterhof by bus or *marshrutka. Marshrutka* 300, 424 and 424A (R80) leave from outside the Avtovo metro station, while *marshrutka* 103 leaves from outside Leninsky Prospekt station. All pass through the town of Peterhof, immediately outside the palace. Tell the driver you want to go '*vo dvaryéts*' ('to the palace') and you'll be let off near the main entrance to the Upper Garden, on Sankt-Peterburgsky pr.

There's also a reasonably frequent suburban train (R60, 40 minutes) from Baltic Station (Baltiysky vokzal) to Novy Peterhof, from where you can walk (around 30 minutes), or take any bus except 357 to the fifth stop, which will take another 10 minutes.

From May to September, the **Peterhof Express** (Map p176; www.peterhof-express. com; single/return adult R800/1500, student R600/1000; ⊘ 10am-6pm) hydrofoil departs from the jetty in front of the Admiralty every 30 minutes from 9am. It's an expensive but highly enjoyable way to get to Peterhof, and you arrive right in front of the palace. The last hydrofoil leaves Peterhof at 7pm, and the trip takes 30 minutes.

Pushkin (Tsarskoe Selo)
Пушкин (Царское Село)

☑ 812 / POP 106,100

The grand imperial estate of Tsarskoe Selo in the town of Pushkin, 25km south of St Petersburg, is often combined on a day trip with the palace and sprawling park at Pavlovsk, 4km further south. It's a great combination, but start out early as there's lots to see: Pushkin can easily be a full-day trip in itself.

The railway that connects Pushkin and Pavlovsk with St Petersburg was Russia's first, opened in 1837 to carry the imperial family between here and the then capital. The town changed its name to Pushkin in 1937 after Russia's favourite poet, who studied here and whose school and dacha you can also visit. While the palace and park complex's name has reverted to Tsarskoe Selo (The Tsar's Village), the town remains proudly named for the national bard.

ℹ PETERHOF TICKETS & OPENING HOURS

Inexplicably, many museums within the Peterhof estate have different closing days, although all the buildings are open from Friday to Sunday. With the exception of the Grand Palace, most buildings are open only at weekends between October and April, and some are closed entirely out of season. In any case, it's extraordinarily expensive to see all the attractions from the inside, as they each charge separate hefty admission fees, plus an extra ticket to take photographs or videos – on top of which you're paying at least 75% more than locals. There are some joint tickets to several sights, which save you something, but sadly there's no general ticket available. Nearly all tours and posted information are in Russian, so it's worth investing in an information booklet, available at the kiosks near the entrances.

The lovely Upper Garden is free. Admission to the Lower Park is payable at the cash booths on the jetty and outside the gates leading to the Grand Cascade. There's no re-entering the park; if you leave the grounds, you'll have to purchase another ticket to get back in.

⊙ Sights

★ **Catherine Palace** PALACE
(Екатерининский дворец; www.tzar.ru; Sadovaya ul 7; adult/student R1000/350, audio guide R150; ☉10am-4.45pm Wed-Sun) The centrepiece of Tsarskoe Selo, created under Empresses Elizabeth and Catherine the Great between 1744 and 1796, is the vast baroque Catherine Palace, designed by Rastrelli and named after Peter the Great's second wife. The palace can only be visited by individuals between noon and 2pm, and 4pm and 4.45pm, otherwise it's reserved for pre-booked tour groups, such is its rightful popularity. The audio guide is well worth taking, as it gives detailed explanation of what you'll see in each room.

As at the Winter Palace, Catherine the Great had many of Rastrelli's original interiors remodelled in classical style. Most of the gaudy exterior and 20-odd rooms of the palace have been beautifully restored – compare them to the photographs of the devastation left by the Germans.

The interiors are superb, with highlights including the Great Hall, the Arabesque Hall, the baroque Cavalier's Dining Room, the White State Dining Room, the Crimson and Green Pilaster Rooms, the Portrait Hall and, of course, the world-famous Amber Room (p222). The panels used in the latter were a gift given to Peter the Great, but not put to any use until 1743 when Elizabeth decided to use them decoratively, after which they were ingeniously incorporated into the walls here. What you see is a reconstruction of the original that disappeared during WWII and is believed to have been destroyed.

★ **Catherine Park** PARK
(Екатерининский парк; May-Sep R120, Oct-Apr free; ☉9am-6pm) Around the Catherine Palace extends the lovely Catherine Park. The main entrance is on Sadovaya ul, next to the **Palace Chapel**. The park extends around the ornamental Great Pond and contains an array of interesting buildings, follies and pavilions.

Near the Catherine Palace, the **Cameron Gallery** (☉11am-6pm) normally has rotating exhibitions. Between the gallery and the palace, notice the south-pointing ramp that Cameron added for the ageing empress to walk down into the park.

OFF THE BEATEN TRACK

ORANIENBAUM

Oranienbaum (Ораниенбаум, Orange Tree), the palace of Peter the Great's right-hand man Alexander Menshikov is 5km down the coast from Peterhof. The buildings are part of the Unesco World Heritage Site, and provide a fine window into Russia's imperial past. The surrounding **park** (Музей-заповедник Ораниенбаум; www.peterhofmuseum.ru; ☉9am-8pm) FREE is worth a visit in its own right, with beautifully landscaped paths amid the lakes and greenery.

Menshikov's impressive **palace** (Большой Меншиковский Дворец; adult/student R400/250; ☉10.30am-6pm Wed-Mon) underwent a full restoration and reopened its state rooms in 2014. Most of the interiors are restorations of the 19th century ones, so reflect the taste of the various Romanovs who used the palace, rather than Menshikov himself, of whom there is no trace.

Among the other buildings in the park open to the public is the **Chinese Palace** (Китайский дворец; adult/student R500/300; ☉10.30am-6pm Tue-Sun). Built for Catherine the Great as her private residence at Oranienbaum, this over-the-top rococo palace, designed by Antonio Rinaldi, is distinctly un-Chinese looking and, in fact, gets its name from its chinoiserie interiors, which feature painted ceilings and fine inlaid-wood floors and walls.

Opposite Oranienbaum's main entrance, **Okhota** (Охота; Dvortsovy pr 65a; mains R480-1220; ☉noon-9pm Mon-Thu, to midnight Fri-Sun) serves up hearty fare in a traditional Russian environment. It's big on taxidermy for its hunting-themed decor.

Trains from St Petersburg's Baltic Station (Baltiysky vokzal) to Peterhof continues to Oranienbaum (R81, one hour). Get off at Lomonosov Station and walk diagonally across the little park in front, keep going up to the main road, turn right, pass the unmissable Archangel Michael Cathedral, and you'll reach the park entrance on your left. Alternatively you can take marshrutky 300, 424 or 424A to Lomonosov (R70) from outside metro Avtovo. Get off at the Archangel Michael Cathedral and follow the park perimeter to the left until you reach the entrance.

Pushkin

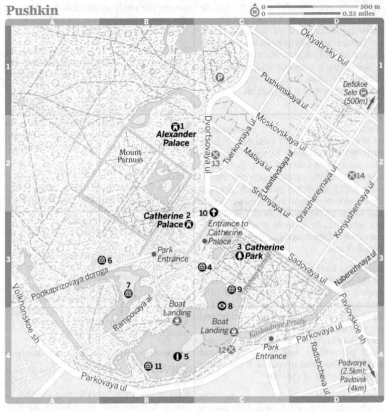

N 0 _____ 500 m
0 _____ 0.25 miles

Pushkin

The park's outer section focuses on the **Great Pond**. In summer you can take a ferry to the little island to visit the **Chesme Column** (adult/child R250/150; ◷11am-6pm May-Sep). Beside the pond, the blue baroque **Grotto Pavilion** (◷10am-5pm Fri-Wed) **FREE** houses temporary exhibitions in summer. A walk around the Great Pond will reveal other buildings that the royals built over the years, including the very incongruous-look-

ing **Turkish Bath** (R200; ◷11am-6pm Thu-Tue Jun-Sep), with its minaret-style tower, the wonderful Marble Bridge, the **Chinese Pavillon**, and a **Concert Hall** (tickets R500) isolated on an island, where concerts take place every Saturday at 5pm.

★**Alexander Palace** PALACE
(Александровский дворец; Dvortsovaya ul 2) The classical Alexander Palace, built by

Quarenghi between 1792 and 1796 for the future Alexander I, is surrounded by the charming Alexander Park. Nicholas II, the last Russian tsar, was its main tenant and he made it his residence for much of his reign.

The palace is currently undergoing renovation and is closed to the public, with completion due in 2018 at the earliest.

✖ Eating

White Rabbit
INTERNATIONAL $$

(ul Moskovskaya 22; mains R490-870; ⊘11am-11pm; 🐾) In the centre of town, this pub-like place serves decent fish and chips, savoury meat pies, pesto pasta and lots of other satisfying dishes in a comfy, easy-going environment. Sink into a leather booth, and warm up over a hot meal, followed by tea, while taking in traces of whimsical decor (White Rabbit pays homage to *Alice in Wonderland*).

Admiralty Restaurant
RUSSIAN $$

(📞812-465 3549; www.admiral.gutsait.ru; Parkovaya ul; mains R450-950; ⊘noon-11pm; 🐾) The best restaurant in Catherine Park is set in an elegant, brick-walled dining room and features reliably good dishes, including beef cheeks in wine sauce, leg of lamb, and homemade *pelmeni,* as well as risottos, pastas and other European selections. It lies on the southeast corner of the lake.

Solenya Varenya
RUSSIAN $$

(Соленья-Варенья; 📞8-812-465 2685; www.solenya-varenya.ru; Srednyaya ul 2; mains R350-850; ⊘10am-11pm; 🐾) Outside of Catherine Park, this elegant spot makes a fine setting for a traditional Russian meal. Bliny with mushrooms, cabbage soup, and grilled salmon are among the nicely executed dishes. You can also stop in for afternoon tea and snacks after palace viewing.

Daniel
INTERNATIONAL $$$

(Даниель; 📞812-466 9116; www.restaurant-daniel.ru; Srednyaya ul 2/3; mains R800-1850; ⊘11am-11pm; 🐾) Daniel offers a blow-out gastronomic feast within stumbling distance of the Catherine Palace. Swedish chef Eric Viedgård conjures culinary magic with his seasonally changing menu in an elegant contemporary space with heritage touches.

❶ Getting There & Away

From Moskovskaya metro station, take the exit marked 'Buses for the airport', and then pick up *marshrutka* 286, 299, 342 or K545 towards Pushkin (R40). These buses all continue to Pavlovsk (R50). Look for Пушкин or Дворец on the buses.

Suburban trains run from Vitebsk Station (Vitebsky vokzal) in St Petersburg, but they're infrequent except for weekends. For Pushkin, get off at Detskoe Selo (Детское село, R47, 30 minutes) and for Pavlovsk (R54, 40 minutes) at Pavlovsk Station (Павловск). From Detskoe Selo station, *marshrutky* (R25) frequently run the 500m or so to Tsarskoe Selo.

Pavlovsk
Павловск

📞812 / POP 16,200

Less visited than better known Pushkin to the east, Pavlovsk is nevertheless home to a stunning 18th-century royal palace and one of the finest green spaces in greater St Petersburg. It's well worth tacking on a visit here to explore the artfully designed interiors – and a small but first-rate collection of

---

THE MYSTERY OF THE AMBER ROOM

The original Amber Room was created from exquisitely engraved amber panels given to Peter the Great by King Friedrich Wilhelm I of Prussia in 1716. Rastrelli later combined the panels with gilded woodcarvings, mirrors, agate and jasper mosaics to decorate one of the rooms of the Catherine Palace. Plundered by the Nazis during WWII, the room's decorative panels were last exhibited in Königsberg's castle in 1941. Four years later, with the castle in ruins, the Amber Room was presumed destroyed. Or was it?

In 2004, as Putin and then German Chancellor Gerhardt Schröder presided over the opening of the new US$18 million Amber Room, restored largely with German funds, rumours about the original panels continued to swirl. There are those who believe that parts, if not all, of the original Amber Room remain hidden away (see www.amberroom.org). The mystery gained traction in February 2008 as attention focused on the possible contents of an artificial cavern discovered near the village of Deutschneudorf on Germany's border with the Czech Republic. Nothing conclusive has yet been unearthed here, though, so the mystery continues.

old-world masterpieces – followed by a stroll amid the verdure of Pavlovsk park.

Between 1781 and 1786, on orders from Catherine the Great, architect Charles Cameron designed the Great Palace in Pavlovsk. The palace was designated for Catherine's son Paul (hence the name, Pavlovsk), and it was his second wife, Maria Fyodorovna, who orchestrated the design of the interiors. It served as a royal residence until 1917. Ironically, the original palace burnt down two weeks after WWII when a careless Soviet soldier's cigarette set off German mines (the Soviets blamed the Germans). As at Tsarskoe Selo, its restoration is remarkable.

◎ Sights

Pavlovsk Great Palace   PALACE
(Большой Павловский дворец; www.pavlovsk-museum.ru; ul Sadovaya 20; adult/child R600/250; ◎ 10am-6pm, closed Tue, Fri & 1st Mon of month) 🚶 One of the most tragic and mysterious characters in the Romanov royal family, emperor Paul I was intensely disliked by his own courtiers, who eventually strangled him with a scarf. Whatever historians say about him, however, he had great taste, as displayed in this glorious palace, the finest rooms of which are on the middle floor of the central block.

Charles Cameron designed the round Italian Hall beneath the dome and the Grecian Hall to its west, though the lovely green fluted columns were added by his assistant Vincenzo Brenna. Flanking these are two private suites designed mainly by Brenna – Paul's along the north side of the block and Maria Fyodorovna's on the south.

The Hall of War of the military-obsessed Paul contrasts with Maria's Hall of Peace, decorated with musical instruments and flowers. On the middle floor of the south block are Paul's Throne Room and the Hall of the Maltese Knights of St John, of whom he was the Grand Master.

Pavlovsk Park   PARK
(Павловский парк; adult/child R150/100; ◎ 6am-9pm Sat-Thu, closed 1st Mon of month) You'll have to pay to enter the serene Pavlovsk Great Park just to access the palace, so it's worth exploring while you're here. Filled with rivers and ponds, tree-lined avenues, classical statues and hidden temples, it's a delightful place to get lost in. Highlights include the Rose Pavilion (Розовый павильон; Pavlovsk Park; adult/student R300/150; ◎ 11am-6pm Wed-Sun) and the Private Garden

(Собственный садик; Pavlovsk Park; adult/child R250/150; ◎ 11am-7pm), with its beautifully arranged flowerbeds and impressive sculpture of the Three Graces.

Bike hire (R300 per hour) is available in several locations around the park and is a great way to explore, as distances are great.

🍴 Eating

Podvorye   RUSSIAN $$$
(📞 812-454 5464; www.podvorye.ru; Filtrovskoye sh 16; mains R620-1450; ◎ noon-11pm) A short walk northeast of Pavlovsk train station, you'll find this traditional Russian log house on steroids. Huge portions of delicious Russian food are dished up, with a side-order of live Russian music and dancing.

❶ Getting There & Away

Trains and *marshrutky* running from St Petersburg to Pushkin continue to Pavlovsk. *Marshrutky* (R30) frequently shuttle between Pushkin and Pavlovsk; catch one from Pavolovskoe sh near the southeast corner of Catherine Park, and get off either at Pavlovsk Station Bus Stop (for entry to the park) or in front of Pavlovsk's palace.

Gatchina   Гатчина

📞 81371 / POP 93,000
Far less touristy than the other country palaces close to St Petersburg, Gatchina, 45km southwest of the city, can make for a very pleasant half-day trip. Gatchina is a busy and bustling town, which just happens to also host a tsarist palace and park.

◎ Sights

In the nearby town there are a couple of interesting churches. The baroque Pavlovsk Cathedral (Павловский собор; ul Sobornaya; ◎ 9am-7pm), at the end of the pedestrianised shopping street off the central pr 25 Oktyabrya, has a grandly restored interior with a soaring central dome. A short walk west is the Pokrovsky Cathedral (Покровский собор; Krasnaya ul; ◎ 9am-6pm), a red-brick building with bright blue domes.

Gatchina Great Palace   PALACE
(Большой Гатчинский дворец; www.gatchina-palace.ru/en; Krasnoarmeysky pr 1; adult/student R300/150, audio guide R200; ◎ 10am-6pm Tue-Sun, closed 1st Tue of month) Shaped in a graceful curve around a central turret, the Gatchina Great Palace certainly lives up to its name – its enormous (if surprisingly plain) facade is

quite a sight to behold, overlooking a vast parade ground and backing onto the huge landscaped grounds. Built by Rinaldi between 1766 and 1781 in an early classicism style for Catherine the Great's favourite Grigory Orlov, the palace curiously combines motifs of a medieval fortress with elements commonly seen in Russian imperial residences.

It's hard to call it beautiful, but there's no doubt that it's extremely impressive. After Orlov's death in 1783, Catherine the Great bought the palace from his heirs and gifted it to her son Paul, who redesigned the exterior between 1792 and 1798.

Inside, the 10 state rooms on the 2nd floor are impressive, including Paul I's throne room, hung with huge tapestries, and his wife Maria Fyodorovna's throne room, the walls of which are covered in paintings. Most impressive of all is the White Hall, a Rinaldi creation from the 1770s that was redone by Brenna in the 1790s. On the balcony is an impressive collection of sundials.

Admission covers entry to the palace and all three pavillions in the grounds.

Gatchina Park
PARK

(Гатчинский парк; ⊙ dawn-dusk) `FREE` Gatchina Park is more overgrown and romantic than the other palaces' parklands. The park has many winding paths through birch groves and across bridges to islands in the large White Lake. Look out for the frankly bizarre **Birch House** (Березовый домик; adult/student R50/20; ⊙ 10am-6pm Tue-Sun May-Sep), which was a present from Maria Fyodorovna to Paul I. With a rough facade made of birch logs, the interior is actually very refined, with a beautiful hardwood floor made from timber from around the world.

✕ Eating

There is a cafe in the Grand Palace and a couple of simple cafes in the grounds, but as the place was made for picnicking, your best bet is to bring your own lunch. If you haven't done so, however, there are a couple of decent options spread out along pedestrianised ul Sobornaya.

Kafe Piramida
RUSSIAN $

(Кафе Пирамида; ul Sobornaya 3a; mains R255-380; ⊙ 10am-11pm) Serving a wide range of traditional Russian dishes as well as pizza, plus delicious cakes and coffees, this cosy place is near the Pavlovsk Cathedral. It's poorly signposted, but is handily located just off pr 25 Oktyabrya.

Chasy
RUSSIAN $$

(Часы; http://cafe-watch.ru; ul Sobornaya 7; mains R450-980; ⊙ 10am-midnight) Hands-down Gatchina's best eatery, Chasy is a friendly spot for grilled meats and seafood, and sushi. It's also a fine afternoon spot for a pot of tea and dessert. Look for the clock over the entrance (more timepieces lie within).

ⓘ Getting There & Away

The quickest way to get to Gatchina is by bus. Bus K18, K18A and 431 (R100, 45 minutes) run this route from outside Moskovskaya metro station and stop right by the park. Bus 100 (R100, one hour) also runs regularly from Moskovskaya; buses wait outside the massive House of Soviets and stop just short of Gatchina Park. Tell the driver you want to go to the palace ('v dvaryéts') – the bus turns off before you get to the park.

There are trains to Gatchina Baltiysky (R102, one hour) from St Petersburg's Baltic Station (Baltiysky vokzal) every one to two hours. The train station is directly in front of the palace.

Kronshtadt
Кронштадт

📋 812 / POP 43,000

With its grand cathedral, waterfront parks and pretty canal-lined avenues, Kronstadt makes for a fascinating half-day visit. Aside from taking in one grand neo-Byzantine church and visiting a little-visited corner of greater St Petersburg, this is a fine place for seeing Russia's mighty naval centre, and getting an overview of the bay on a boat tour.

Within a year of founding St Petersburg, Peter – desirous of protecting his new Baltic toehold – started work on the fortress of Kronshtadt on Kotlin Island, 29km out in the Gulf of Finland. It's been a pivotal Soviet and Russian naval base ever since, and was closed to foreigners until 1996.

In 1921 the hungry and poor Red Army sailors stationed here organised an ill-fated mutiny against the Bolsheviks. They set up a Provisional Revolutionary Committee and drafted a resolution demanding, among other things, an end to Lenin's harsh War Communism. On 16 March 1921 the mutineers were defeated when 50,000 troops crossed the ice from Petrograd and massacred nearly the entire naval force. The sailors' stand wasn't entirely in vain as afterwards Lenin did scrap War Communism.

◉ Sights & Activities

Naval Cathedral
CHURCH

(Морской собор; Yakornaya pl; ⊙ 9am-6.30pm) Kronshtadt's key sight is the unusual and beautiful Naval Cathedral. Built between 1903 and 1913 to honour Russian naval muscle, this neo-Byzantine wonder stands on Yakornaya pl (Anchor Sq), where you'll also find an eternal flame for Kronshtadt's sailors, and the florid art nouveau monument of Admiral Makarov.

The cathedral underwent a thorough renovation for its centennial celebrations and is now looking breathtaking, both inside and out. Its 75m-high cupola is the highest point in town, and its enormous interior makes its use as a cinema during the Soviet period rather logical.

Reeperbahn
CRUISE

(☑ 821-382 0888; Middle Harbour; adult/student R550/400; ⊙ departures 1.30pm, 3.30pm & 5.30pm May-Sep) From the Middle Harbour beside Petrovsky Park, you can take cruises to various forts around the island, including Fort Konstantin. Several companies offer cruises, including Reeperbahn, with three daily departures in summer.

✖ Eating

Cafe Kashtan
RUSSIAN $

(Кафе Каштан; pr Lenina 25; mains R300-500; ⊙ 11am-11pm) The entrance to this charming little place is actually on ul Andreevskaya, a side-street of the main shopping street, pr Lenina. It's friendly and has a wide selection of pub fare as well as coffee and desserts like tiramisu.

Bolshaya Cherepakha
RUSSIAN $$

(Большая Черепаха; www.big-turtle.com; ul Karla Libknekhta 29; mains R400-750; ⊙ 11am-11pm) One of Kronshtadt's better restaurants, the 'Big Turtle' serves up salads, spaghetti with seafood, perch fillet with vegetables, and grilled meats. With decent beers on tap, it's also a fine spot for an afternoon drink. It's located a short stroll from the Naval Cathedral – cross the main bridge and continue up Roshalya, where you'll see it on the right.

ℹ Getting There & Away

Catch bus 101 to Kronshtadt from Staraya Derevnya metro station (R40, 40 minutes). Upon exiting the metro, turn hard left and then walk past the *marshrutky* and trams until you come to a second bus park where the 101 bus begins and ends its route. Alternatively take *marshrutka*

405 from Chyornaya Rechka station (R80, 40 minutes); exit the station to your left and cross the street to find the stop.

Vehicles heading back to St Petersburg depart from both sides of the large 'Dom Byta' on the corner of ul Grazhdanskaya and pr Lenina. From there it's about a 1km walk southeast to the Naval Cathedral.

With the completion of St Petersburg's ring road, it's now possible to reach Kronshtadt from Oranienbaum, meaning it's perfectly feasible to combine a trip here with a visit to one of the Tsarist palaces.

Leningrad Region
Ленинградская область

If you have more time, there are several other places in the Leningrad region that can be seen in a day trip or longer from St Petersburg. These including the charming old Finnish town of Vyborg, the sleepy village of Staraya Ladoga and the monastery town of Tikhvin.

Vyborg

☑ 81378 / POP 78,500 / TIME MOSCOW

This appealing Gulf of Finland provincial town is dominated by a medieval castle and peppered with beautiful Finnish art-nouveau buildings and romantic cobblestone streets. An important port and rail junction, Vyborg is 174km northwest of St Petersburg and just 30km from the Finnish border. It has just about enough to do to justify staying over, but is also an easy day trip from St Petersburg.

The border has jumped back and forth around Vyborg for most of its history. Peter the Great captured it from the Swedes in 1710. A century later it fell within autonomous Finland, and after the revolution Vyborg remained part of independent Finland. Since then the Finns have called it Viipuri. Stalin took Vyborg in 1939, lost it to the Finns during WWII, and on getting it back at the end of the war deported all the Finns. Today the Finns are back by the coachloads for sightseeing and carousing on the weekends.

◉ Sights

With the exception of Park Monrepo, all Vyborg's main sights are neatly arranged around a compact peninsula, making it an ideal town to explore on foot.

Apart from the castle, other relics of Vyborg's Swedish times are found in the squat

REPINO РЕПИНО

Come summer, Petersburgers stream out of the city to relax on the beaches to the north between Sestroretsk and Zelenogorsk on the Gulf of Finland. Between these two towns you'll find the village of Repino, 45km from St Petersburg. From 1918 to the end of WWII, this area was part of Finland and the village was known as Kuokkala. In 1948, back in Russian hands, the village was renamed in honour of its most famous resident, Ilya Repin.

Penaty (Пенаты; ☑ 812-432 0828; www.nimrah.ru; Primorskoe Shosse 411; adult/student R300/200; ⊙ museum 10.30am-6pm Wed-Sun, grounds 10.30am-8pm Wed-Mon), the artist's home in his later years, is preserved as a museum. Repin bought land here in 1899, named the estate after a Roman household god and designed the light-flooded house in an arts-and-crafts style. Several of Repin's paintings still hang on the walls and the furnishings have been left just as they were during his residence, which was up to his death in 1930. His grave, marked by a simple Russian Orthodox wooden cross, is in the surrounding park, along with a couple of wooden follies also designed by Repin.

While here also visit the nearby **Beach Laskovy** (Пляж Ласковый) and stop for a meal at either **Skazka** (☑ 812-432 1251; www.skazkarepino.ru; Primorskoe Shosse 415; mains R570-1490; ⊙ 11am-11pm; ☎), which has an attractive dining room with big picture windows and a terrace – both fine spots for enjoying its nicely executed dishes– or **Penaty** (Пенаты; ☑ 812-432 1125; Primorskoe Shosse 411A; mains R400-850; ⊙ 10am-10pm), which serves a good range of Russian dishes and offers a pleasant flower-trimmed terrace.

The easiest way to get to Repino is to take the frequent *marshrutky* 400 (R105, one hour) that leave from near Finland Station (Finlyandsky vokzal) – cross ul Komsomola, and look for the stop on the right side of pl Lenina. You can also catch bus 211 (R90, one hour) from beside Chyornya Rechka metro station. Be sure to tell the driver that you want to get out at Penaty.

Round Tower (Map p192; pl Rynochnaya), which now houses a restaurant; the remains of the 15th-century **Town Hall** (Башня Ратуши; Map p192; ul Vyborgskaya 15), with its distinctive white tower crowned with what resembles a giant metallic wizard's hat; and the **Clock Tower** (Часовая башня; Map p192; ul Krepostnaya 5), dating to 1490.

★**Vyborg Castle**   HISTORIC BUILDING
(Выборгский замок; Map p192; Zamkovy Island; grounds free, museum R100; ⊙ grounds 9am-7pm daily, exhibitions 10am-6pm) Rising stoutly from an islet in Vyborg Bay, this castle was built by the Swedes in 1293 when they first captured Karelia from Novgorod. Most of it now consists of 16th-century alterations. The castle contains several exhibition halls, including a mildly diverting small **museum** (Map p192; R100; ⊙ 10am-6pm Tue-Sun) on local history, but the main attraction is climbing the many steps of whitewashed **St Olaf's Tower** (Map p192) for commanding views over the town (closed for renovations at time of research).

★**Hermitage Vyborg**   MUSEUM
(Эрмитаж Выборг; Map p192; ul Ladanova 1; adult/student R250/150; ⊙ 10am-6pm) Housed in a wing of a striking building designed by Finnish architect Uno Ulberg in 1930, this small museum hosts themed exhibitions that are curated from the Hermitage's massive collection and change every six months. The functional white building, which sits in the middle of an old defensive bastion, is shared with Vyborg's arts school, which also has a **gallery** (Map p192; ul Ladanova 1; ⊙ 10am-6pm Mon-Fri) FREE with regularly changing exhibitions.

Alvar Aalto Library   ARCHITECTURE
(Biblioteka Alvara Aalto; Map p192; ☑ 81378-24 937; www.aalto.vbgcity.ru/excursion_eng; pr Suvorova 4; guided tour in Russian/English R150/350; ⊙ 11am-7pm Mon-Fri year-round & noon-7pm Sat Sep-May) A must-see for architecture fans is the beautifully designed public library, one of Finnish architect Alvar Aalto's iconic designs. After years of restoration, the 1935 building looks lovelier than ever, with painstaking efforts to return it to Aalto's original vision. Handmade bronze-handled doors, circular skylights in the reading room, and elegant birchwood shelves are among the many features. It's still a working public library, open to all (though oddly, it lacks wi-fi). Call to book a guided tour in English.

Park Monrepo PARK
(Парк Монрепо; www.parkmonrepos.org; adult/
child R200/free; ⊙10am-9pm May-Sep, to 6pm
Oct-Apr) A lovely place to escape the world
for a few hours, if not most of the day, is
this 180-hectare park facing onto tranquil
Zashchitnaya Bay. It's laid out in a classical
style, with various pavilions, curved bridges,
arbours and sculptures. Bus 1 or 6 (R30, 15
minutes) will get you here from outside the
train and bus stations.

Anninskie Fortifications FORTRESS
(Аннинские укрепления; Map p192; Petrovskaya
ul) At the southern end of Tverdysh Island
is this double line of fortifications, built between 1730 and 1750 as protection against
the Swedes and named after Empress Anna
Ioanovna. Nearby, on a hill just above the
restaurant Russky Dvor, a handsome statue
of Peter the Great, erected on the bicente-
nary of the city's capture by Russia, surveys
the town.

Lenin & Esplanade Parks PARK
(Map p192) Explore these two central and
adjacent leafy parks, separated by Leningradsky pr, to find intriguing statutes and
carved trees. At the southern end of Lenin
Park is the Alvar Aalto Library (p226), designed by the famous Finnish architect in
1935 and, in the Esplanade Park, the Lutheran SS Peter & Paul Cathedral (Собор
святых апостолов Петра и Павла).

🏃 Activities

Boat Stand BOATING
(Map p192; nab 40-letiya Komsomola; boat hire
per hr R250-300; ⊙10am-10pm May-Sep) In the
warmer months, the best place to be is out
on the water, boating peacefully, with the
backdrop of old Vyborg ever at your side. A
handy boat stand near the centre of town
hires out rowboats and paddleboats and can
get you out on the water in a hurry.

Festival & Events
In July, the town hosts the ambitious five-
day Vyborg Intelligent Performance
(www.vkontakte.ru/vbgpromenade) arts festival, which includes live music, theatre and
lectures.

🛏 Sleeping
Vyborg has plenty of accommodation, but
the town can get busy on weekends with
boatloads of visiting Finns, so book ahead if

you plan to visit then. Rates at most places
usually include breakfast.

Vyborg Hostel HOSTEL $
(Map p192; ☑8-921-950 0201; www.vyborghos-
tel.ru; ul Vyborgskaya 4; dm R600-700, r R1500;
📶) Vyborg's hostel has bright, clean and
well-maintained rooms that are rather
lacking in charm. There's plenty of space,
lots of bathrooms, a communal kitchen and
bikes for hire, and the location couldn't be
better.

Letuchaya Mysh HOTEL $$
(Летучая мышь; Map p192; ☑81378-34 537;
www.bathotel.ru; ul Nikolaeva 3; s/d/apt with breakfast from R2500/2800/4600) This appealing
boutique-style hotel occupies a small, historic building just off pr Lenina. All rooms
have bathrooms and TVs, and there's a good
on-site restaurant. It's definitely the most
atmospheric place to stay in Vyborg, even if
it is overshadowed by a large Soviet block
of flats.

Victoria Hotel HOTEL $$
(Map p192; ☑8-81378 52 800; www.ibc-victoria.
com; nab 40-letiya Komsomola; s/d R5900/6250;
❄📶) An excellent new hotel overlooking
the waterfront, the Victoria has modern,
comfortably furnished rooms with quality
furnishings. The best rooms have scenic bay
views. There's also a sauna, fitness centre
and rooftop restaurant.

Apart-Hotel Ullberg APARTMENT $$
(Map p192; ☑81378-55 417; www.hotel-apart.ru;
Leningradsky pr 10; apt R3100-3800; 📶) This
well-located guesthouse overlooks Park
Lenina from its 4th-floor perch inside a
handsome 1915 building. It has five brightly
decorated, comfy rooms, all of which have
mini-kitchens.

🍴 Eating & Drinking

Café Respect CAFE $
(Кафе Респект; Map p192; ☑81378-34 007; ul
Podgornaya 10; mains R450-700; ⊙11am-8pm)
This cosy place, with only a few tables and
an old European feel, is found on a charming old street in the middle of the old town.
It only has a Russian menu, but offers the
usual range of dishes such as salads and
soups.

Champion PUB FOOD $
(Чемпион; Map p192; pr Lenina 10; mains R380-
790; ⊙11am-2am; 📶) This modern pub is full
of sporting paraphernalia and has plenty of

TVs screening sports and music videos. It's a good place for a cooling pint of Paulaner and a globe-trotting mix of international dishes (pastas, burgers, fried squid), for a meal or snack.

★ Russky Dvor RUSSIAN $$
(Русский Двор; Map p192; ☑ 81378-26 369; ul Shturma; meals R400-720; ☉ noon-midnight) The terrace overlooking the castle and town is an ideal spot to enjoy some traditional Russian dishes like venison with berry sauce. The chef cures his own salmon and you can drink their delicious homemade honey and horseradish *kvas* (fermented rye-bread water). The high-ceilinged castle-like interior is also impressive, though sometimes ruined by blaring Russian pop music.

Vkus EUROPEAN $$
(Вкус; Map p192; ☑ 81378-52 823; nab 40-letiya Komsomola; mains R430-1395; ☉ noon-midnight) On the top floor of the Victoria Hotel, Vkus serves up Italian fare like risotto, lasagna and caprese salad, as well as spicy rack of lamb and other filling plates. With wonderful views from the small outdoor deck, Vkus is a fine spot for a drink – though the coffee isn't up to par.

Round Tower Restaurant RUSSIAN $$
(Круглая башня; Map p192; Rynochnaya pl 1; mains R420-850; ☉ noon-midnight, to 2am Fri & Sat) On the top floor of a 16th-century tower, this atmospheric and long-running place is a reliable option for traditional Russian cuisine, although it can sometimes be booked out by tour groups.

Kafe Krendel CAFE
(Кофейня Крендель; Map p192; Severny Val 3; ☉ 9.30am-8.30pm) Near the Old Town Hall, Kafe Krendel is a charming little spot for coffee, pastries, quiche and desserts – including an excellent house-made carrot cake. In the summer, the tables on the square are a fine place to enjoy the relaxed vibe of Vyborg.

Central Market MARKET $$
(Центральный рынок; Map p192; Rynochnaya pl; ☉ 8am-6pm) Pull together supplies for a picnic from the Central Market just north of the Round Tower. From Thursdays to Sundays there's also a small craft market held on the square in front.

❶ Information

Vyborg Tourist Information Centre (Map p192; ☑ 905-210 5555; www.vyborg-info.ru; Vokzalnaya ul 13; ☉ 9am-5pm)

❶ Getting There & Away

The bus and train stations are opposite each other on Vokzalnaya pl.

BOAT

Saimaa Travel (www.saimaatravel.fi) arranges visa-free cruises (one/two days from €63/118 per person) from Lappeenranta in Finland to Vyborg.

BUS

Services to/from St Petersburg (R280, to/from either metro stations Devyatkino or Parnas) run every 20 minutes from 6.30am to 8pm. Theoretically, travel time is around 2¼ hours, but the traffic can lengthen this, so the train remains the best option.

TRAIN

Elektrichki (R301, 2½ hours, hourly) leave from St Petersburg's Finland Station (Finlyandsky vokzal): Of these, there are also a handful of express services (R331, 1¼ hours, four daily), or the far more expensive Helsinki-bound trains, which stop in Vyborg (R2236, one hour).

Staraya Ladoga

☑ 81363 / POP 3200 / TIME MOSCOW

Although you'd hardly guess it now, this tranquil village, 125km east of St Petersburg on the winding banks of the Volkhov River, lays claim to being Russia's first capital. The idea of this place being a 'capital' of anywhere is quite extraordinary, though, and today you'll find an ancient fortress, several churches and some prettily painted wooden cottages. It makes for a pleasant escape from St Petersburg, particularly in summer, when a swim in the river adds to the charm.

The town was known simply as Ladoga until 1704, when Peter the Great founded Novaya (New) Ladoga to the north as a transfer point for the materials arriving to build St Petersburg. Protected as a national reserve, the town's basic layout has remained virtually unchanged since the 12th century, give or take a few ugly Soviet blocks.

❍ Sights

Everything of interest lies along the main road that runs parallel to the river.

Staraya Ladoga Fortress　　　HISTORIC SITE
(Староладожская крепость; adult/child R150/
free; ⊙9am-5pm Mon-Fri, to 6pm Sat & Sun) Towards the southern end of the village, and
with an excellent view along the river, the
7m-thick walls and stout towers of this
fortress are slowly being rebuilt. Inside
the grounds you'll find the small stone **St
George's Church** (Георгиевская Церковь;
9am-6pm; ⊙May-Oct), only open May to October in order to protect the remains of the
delicate 12th-century frescoes still visible on
its walls, and the cute wooden **Church of
Dimitry Solun**.

The Vorotnaya Tower houses the good
**Historical-Architectural & Archaeologi-
cal Museum** (⊙9am-5pm Mon-Fri, to 6pm Sat
& Sun), which displays an interesting retrospective of the area's history, including a
scale model of how the fortress once looked
and items found on archaeological digs,
with English explanations.

Visiting this soulful old place and wandering around its crumbling ramparts is a
unique experience and you might feel you're
in a Tarkovsky film.

**Svyato-Uspensky Devichy
Monastery**　　　MONASTERY
(Свято-Успенский девичий монастырь; Volk-
hovsky pr; ⊙9am-6pm) The women's monastery on the main road in Staraya Ladoga is
a remarkably atmospheric place to wander.
The small brick church, with its 900-year-
old frescoes, is only open on weekends during summer; at other times you can visit the
grounds.

Nikolsky Monastery　　　MONASTERY
(Никольский монастырь; www.en.nikmonas.ru;
⊙9am-6pm) This attractive walled complex

dates to the 12th century and is still in the
process of being rebuilt following its de-
commissioning during the Soviet years. The
main church and bell tower now look quite
handsome. Nearby is a pontoon from which
you can swim in the river.

The monastery is located about 1km
south of Staraya Ladoga Fortress.

🛏 Sleeping & Eating

Staraya Ladoga Hotel　　　HOTEL $
(Отель Старая Ладога; ☑931-531 9043;
ul Sovetskaya 6; s/d with shared bathroom
R1700/2200; 🛜) The best overnight option
in Staraya Ladoga is this modest grey-
brick hotel, tucked down a lane north of
the Svyato-Uspensky Devichy Monastery.
Although it looks unpromising from the
outside, the rooms are fairly well maintained with sizeable windows overlooking
the surrounding greenery.

Mini-Hotel Ladya　　　BOUTIQUE HOTEL $
(Гостиница Ладья; ☑81363-49 555; Sovetskaya
3; r R2000-2500; 🛜) While not looking promising from the outside, this five-room hotel,
which shares the premises of the local clinic,
has pleasant, contemporary-styled rooms
and even a sauna. Only tea and coffee are
served, so you'll have to make your own
breakfast arrangements.

Knyaz Rurik　　　RUSSIAN $$
(Князь Рюрик; ul Kultury 7; mains R285-520;
⊙10am-9pm Sun-Thu, to 11pm Fri & Sat) Rurik's
family tree is painted across the brick wall of
this small, nicely designed restaurant, which
displays ye olde local shields as decoration.
Portions of mushroom soup, bliny, salad and
shashlyk are small but tasty.

RUSSIA'S ANCIENT CAPITAL

Just as the origins of Rus are continually debated, so is Staraya Ladoga's status as 'Rus-
sia's first capital'. Nevertheless, its age (historians have given 753 as the village's birth
date) and significance remain uncontested.

When the Scandinavian Viking Rurik, along with his relatives Truvor and Sineus, swept
into ancient Russia in 862, he built a wooden fortress on the Volkhov River and made this
his base. Rurik is depicted in a colourful mosaic on the side of the village school. Locals
also claim that one of the **tumuli** (Урочище Сопки) at the north end of the village is the
grave of Oleg, Rurik's successor.

Archaeological expeditions continue to uncover a wealth of information about the
town's past. In 1997 a second 9th-century fortress was discovered 2km outside the
village. Evidence of Byzantine influences in the frescoes of the village's 12th-century
churches point to the town as a cultural as well as historical and commercial crossroads.

❶ Getting There & Away

Elektrichki to Volkhov (the Volkhovstroy I station) depart from both St Petersburg's Moskovsky and Ladozhsky stations (R300, 2½ hours, 20 daily). From Volkhov, bus 23 (R48, 30 minutes, hourly) departs from the main bus stop outside the station towards Novaya Ladoga, passing through Staraya Ladoga. Get off when you see the fortress. A taxi from Volkhov costs R320.

Buses to and from Tikhvin also pass near the Yuzhkovo turn-off to the village, so you can combine a visit to both destinations. When you get off at Yuzhkovo, take a taxi (there are usually a couple hanging around to meet buses) to Staraya Ladoga (R250). It's also just as easy to take a train from Tikhvin to Volkhov.

Tikhvin   Тихвин

☑ 81367 / POP 57,900 / TIME MOSCOW

The highlight of this small, quiet town on the banks of the Tikhvinka River is a beautiful monastery established in 1560 by decree of Ivan the Terrible. There's been a community here since the 14th century, and for thousands of years before that the area formed part of the hereditary lands of the Finnic Veps (also known as Vepsians). Tikhvin is also the birthplace of Nikolai Rimsky-Korsakov, whose music was inspired by the local nature, folk tunes and religious ringing of bells.

◉ Sights

Tikhvin Monastery of the Mother of God   MONASTERY

(Тихвинский Богородичный Успенский Мужской Монастырь; www.tihvinskii-monastyr.ru; ul Tikhvinskaya 1; ⊙8am-8pm) Rising like a fairy tale across the Tabory pond, this complex is about a 1km walk from the train station straight along Sovetskaya ul. At its heart is the onion-domed **Assumption Cathedral**, established in 1510, and painted inside, and partially outside, with detailed frescoes. A famous icon of Mary and Jesus said to have been painted by the apostle Luke draws awed pilgrims from across Russia, particularly on 9 July, when a procession celebrates the return of the icon to Tikhvin.

The complex's nunnery, crowned by a five-spired belfry, is where Ivan the Terrible sent his fourth wife to be confined. Within the walls you'll also find several museums, including the **Tikhvin Historical Memorial & Architectural Museum** (ul Tikhvinskaya 1; adult/child R120/free; ⊙9am-5pm Tue-Sun),

which has interesting displays on the monastery's history and examples of its religious art dating back to the 16th century.

Rimsky-Korsakov House-Museum   MUSEUM

(Государственный Дом-музей Римского-Корсакова; ☑81369-51 509; ul Rimskogo-Korsakova 12; adult/child R110/free; ⊙10am-5pm Tue-Sun) This early-19th-century wooden house was the composer's childhood home until the age of 12. It became a museum in 1944, the centenary of Rimsky-Korsakov's birth, and the rooms have been reconstructed to look as they would have done when his family was living there. The charming guides will point out all the original features, including a Becker grand piano on which concerts are sometimes given (call for details).

There's a stone bust of the composer on a plinth in the small park next to the house. Opposite is the tiny **Church of All Saints Polkovaya** (Церковь Всех Святых "Полковая"), which also sometimes hosts concerts.

🛏 Sleeping & Eating

Hostel Nochlezhka   GUESTHOUSE $

(Хостел Ночлежка; ☑931-284 3404; ul Sovetskaya 3B; dm/s/d R600/1500/2000; ❋☎) A short stroll from the train station, this pleasant new option has a few small, simply furnished rooms and a facade that evokes the old countryside with its log cabin exterior. The best rooms have small balconies.

Podvorye   HOTEL $$

(Подворье; ☑81367-51 330; www.podworie.ru; ul Novgorodskaya 35; s/d with breakfast R2600/3200; ☎) The interior of this small hotel emulates a log house, with spacious clean rooms that are thickly carpeted. Its adjoining restaurant is the place in town for a meal, with a menu of mainly Russian dishes (R320 to R650).

Verizhitsa   HOTEL $$

(Верижица; ☑8-921-975 4433; www.verizhitsa.ru; Smolensky Shlyuz; d/q R5500/9900; ☎) This appealing complex of wooden log cabins (some of which accommodate up to six people) has a leafy forest setting 5km east of Tikhvin. The cabins are comfortable and there's a restaurant (mains R350 to R760) and traditional-style *banya* (extra fee), plus free bikes (and ping pong!) for guests. A taxi from Tikhvin costs around R250.

Chainaya   CAFE $

(Чайная; Tikhvin Monastery of the Mother of God; meals around R300; ⊙9am-8pm) In the monastery grounds, you'll find this simple canteen, serving delicious bliny, soups, fish rissoles, homemade *pelmeni* and *kvas*. In summer you can enjoy your refreshments on an outdoor terrace.

Istoriya RUSSIAN $$
(История; ul Sovetskaya 62; Mains R460-840; ☺noon-midnight) Restaurant 'History' boasts country charm on the inside, with heavy wooden tables and chairs and old photos of Tikhvin on the walls. The cooking is decent, with Russian classics like *pelmeni* and borscht, plus grilled fish and pastas made in-house.

It's located just before the turnoff to the monastery.

❶ Getting There & Away

The town is on the rail route to Vologda and Arkhangelsk, so you could break your journey to or from either of those destinations here.

Tikhvin's bus and train stations are opposite each other on Vokzalny per. Trains here leave from St Petersburg's Ladozhsky vokzal (*platskart/kupe* R670/1150, three to four hours, six daily). Bus 860 goes four times a day from St Petersburg's bus station to Tikhvin (R400, 4½ hours). The last departure from Tikhvin back to St Petersburg is around 5pm.

To travel to Staraya Ladoga, there is no direct service. By train you can travel from Tikhvin to Volkhov (1½ to two hours, from R550, eight daily), and hop on an onward bus (R48, 30 minutes) or taxi (R330) into town.

Western European Russia

Best Places to Eat

➡ Zavod Bar (p262)

➡ Pyotr Petrovich (p236)

➡ Rusakov (p268)

➡ Mamonts (p255)

➡ Tirol (p252)

Best Places to Stay

➡ Dvor Podznoeva (p268)

➡ Usadba (p251)

➡ Hotel 903 (p267)

➡ Amaks Staraya Russa (p264)

➡ Izborsk Park (p271)

Why Go?

This ancient, Arcadian region showcases Mother Russia at her most fertile: Tolstoy, Turgenev, Dostoevsky's *The Brothers Karamazov* and nothing less than the modern country itself were all born here. It's a lofty legacy and nowhere does Western European Russia (Западно – Европейская Россия) let you forget it. The imposing kremlins, soaring cathedrals and cultural treasures of cities such as Veliky Novgorod, Pskov and Smolensk bear stunning testament to golden eras. Budding writers flock to the area's wealth of literary estates – Staraya Russa, Spasskoe-Lutovinovo, Yasnaya Polyana and Pushkin's ancestral home, Mikhailovskoe – with high hopes there's something in the water; and character-filled smaller towns such as Yelets and Oryol are photogenic throwbacks to prerevolutionary Russia. Even the tiny, far-flung village of Stary Izborsk – a stone's throw from the Estonian border – claims a distinguished heritage: it's home to the oldest stone fortress in Russia.

When to Go
Smolensk

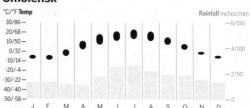

Apr–May The weather thaws and there are few tourists; Victory Day celebrations take place.

Jun–Aug The sun comes out and there are many summer events and festivals.

Dec–Mar Witness magnificent European bison in the wild at Orlovskoye Polesye National Park.

SOUTH OF MOSCOW

Tula   Тула

☎ 4872 / POPULATION 501,000 / ⊘ MOSCOW

A town centre graced by a picturesque kremlin, a fascinating industrial history reflected in several museums, and a considerable number of good restaurants and bars: there's much to recommend in Tula. The key attraction, though, is Yasnaya Polyana, Leo Tolstoy's country estate, where he wrote some of the 19th century's great Russian novels; it's just south of the city.

WESTERN EUROPEAN RUSSIA TULA

Western European Russia Highlights

① Yasnaya Polyana (p237) Returning to rural 19th-century Russia at the leafy estate and final resting place of Leo Tolstoy.

② Stary Izborsk (p270) Exploring the country's oldest stone fortress and getting a taste of Russian rural life while staying at a country guesthouse.

③ Assumption Cathedral (p247) Admiring Smolensk's stunning cathedral and going on a museum crawl in the hilly Hero City.

④ Veliky Novgorod (p257) Exploring a magnificent kremlin, ancient churches and monasteries in this tourist-friendly town.

⑤ Oryol (p242) Acquainting yourself with Russia's literary talent in the city's house-museums, and taking a day trip to Spasskoe-Lutovinovo, Turgenev's lovely country estate.

⑥ Yelets (p238) Admiring the beautifully decorated churches and pastel-coloured wooden buildings.

Tula

N 0 ——————— 500 m
   0 ——————— 0.25 miles

ul Liteynaya

ul Arsenalnaya

ul Oktyabrskaya

per Ryazhsky

ul Galkina

ul Ryazhskaya

yl Gorkogo

21

ul Lunacharskogo

ul Demidovskaya

Upa River

nab Dreyera

per Oruzheyny

per Oruzheyny

Yasnaya
Polyana
Tour Office

ul Demidovskaya plotina

**Arms 1
Museum**

ul Dreyera

ul Mosina

ul Soyfera

ul Leytezena

ul Kominterna

ul Lenina

ul Sovetskaya

ul Metallistov

Hotel
Moskva (900m);
Moskovsky
(900m)

22

pr Krasnoarmeysky

18

ul Soyuznaya

15

**Tula
Kremlin**

2

ul Klary Tsetkin

per Denisovsky

5

ul Bratyev Zhabrovykh

6
10

ul Khalturina

ul Revolyutsii

ul Demonstratsii

pl
Lenina

11

ul Mendeleevskaya

ul Dzerzhinskaya

ul Engelsa

per Tsentralny

ul Sovetskaya

13

ul Kaminskogo

ul Pushkinskaya

14

ul Turgenevskaya

ul Zhukovskogo

ul Pionerskaya

ul Pushkinskaya

20

ul Bundurina

ul Svobody

4

ul Engelsa

12

ul Koletvinova

ul Staronikitskaya

17

ul Pervomayskaya

16

7

pr Lenina

9

ul Gogolevskaya

ul Lva Tolstogo

ul Oboronnaya

19

ul Budennogo

ul Petra Alekseeva

**Tula Regional
Arts Museum**

3

8

(900m);
Hotel Tula
(1km)

ul Timiryazeva

ul Mikheeva

ul Kaulya

Tula

◉ Sights

★ **Tula Kremlin**   HISTORIC BUILDING
(Тульский кремль; ul Mendeleevskaya 10; admission kremlin R150, kremlin & ramparts R200; ☺9am-5pm Tue-Sun) This restored stone fortress, first constructed out of wood in the early 16th century, is home to the stunning 18th-century **Assumption Cathedral** (Успенский собор). The kremlin's grounds are entered through the green-domed **Odoyevskikh Vorog Tower**. Climb up to the **ramparts** to view the insides of some of the other eight towers punctuating the walls.

★ **Arms Museum**   MUSEUM
(Музей Оружия; www.museum-arms.ru; ul Oktyabrskaya 2; R350; ☺10am-6pm Mon-Thu, to 8pm Fri & Sat) Tula has been a weapons manufacturing centre for centuries, a legacy celebrated at this fantastically kitted-out new building that houses an impressive collection of metal weaponry and armoury dating back to medieval times. It's impossible not to appreciate the delicate skill and artistry applied to some of the weapons. The museum also has a branch within the **Tula kremlin**; you can buy a combination ticket that gives access to both (R550). There are some impressive missile tanks and military vehicles on display out front.

★ **Tula Regional Arts Museum**   MUSEUM
(Музей изобразительных искусств; ul Engelsa 64; R170; ☺10am-6pm Tue-Sun) This exceptional gallery charts a course from gilded icons and late-15th-century European paintings through to fascinating pieces of socialist realism from the 20th century, including animat-

ed porcelain figurines of heroic workers and explorers. The exquisite collection includes works by Russian artists such as Ivanov, Shishkin and Repin, as well as furniture and classical marble statues.

Tula Necropolis   HISTORIC SITE
(Тульский некрополь; www.tiam-tula.ru; ul Lva Tolstogo 79; museum R40; ☺museum 9am-6pm Mon-Fri) Set over 50 hectares, photography buffs will love this huge, gorgeously creepy graveyard, with hundreds of telegenic tombstones slowly being devoured by forest. There's a small museum attached, but the most fun comes from poking around in the wonderfully peaceful grounds, which are free to enter. To get here enter via ul Lva Tolstogo, where there is the beautiful white baroque 18th-century **All Saints Cathedral**.

Tolstoy Statue   MONUMENT
(Central Park) Local wags have it that the writer – celebrated here in a huge statue of him walking – was on his way to the vodka factory that was once housed in the nearby brick building. It's at the pr Lenina end of **Central Park** (Центральный парк Белоусова; ul Engelsa 66).

Antiquities Exhibition Centre   MUSEUM
(Музейно-выставочный центр Тульские древности; ☎4872-361 663; www.kulpole.ru; pr Lenina 47; admission from R80; ☺10am-6pm Sun-Fri, to 7pm Sat, closed last Wed of the month) In this interactive museum split between two buildings, kids will get a kick out of the Stone Age and Bronze Age finds from the Tula area, including arrowheads and fish hooks. English tours (R1000 per group) tell

WESTERN EUROPEAN RUSSIA TULA

the stories behind the collections. Have a go at pottery and blacksmithing, or sip tea and nibble gingerbread in a reconstructed 19th-century wooden Tula home.

Tula Samovar Museum
MUSEUM

(Музей Тульские самовары; www.samovar. museum-tula.ru; ul Mendeleevskaya 8; R100; ⏲10am-6pm Tue-Wed & Sun, to 8pm Thu-Sat) 'To take one's own samovar to Tula' is a Russian idiom coined by Anton Chekhov, denoting a pointless activity. Local production of this essential part of the Russian tea-making tradition was started in the late 18th century. This small museum showcases that history with a collection of samovars, including a replica of one that belonged to Stalin and a cute collection of mini-samovars. You can buy samovars here, although there's more choice in the kiosk in Tula's train station.

🛏 Sleeping

Zvezdnyi Hotel
HOTEL $

(☑4872-455 155; ul Kutuzova 100; d incl breakfast & welcome drink from R2500; ✳🔊🛁) While it may not be central, this is a great-value option in a residential area near a park. The comfy rooms are spacious, there's a filling buffet breakfast served in the next-door Loft Hotel (p236) and an attached Japanese restaurant. Staff are friendly and the *marshrutky* stop is right across the road (15 to 20 minutes to the city centre, R20).

Profit
HOTEL $$

(Профит; ☑4872-252 020; www.profit.mega tula.ru; ul Sovetskaya 59; s/d incl breakfast from R3500/4000; ✳@🔊) This mini-hotel on the 4th and 5th floors of a business centre has comfy modern rooms that you'll probably spend very little time in, given its proximity to the kremlin and other local attractions.

Loft Hotel
HOTEL $$

(☑4872-443 939; ul Kutuzova 100; d incl breakfast from R2700; ✳🔊🛁) This modern boutique-style hotel offers spacious rooms, a good buffet breakfast and exceptionally helpful English-speaking staff. It's a 15- to 20-minute bus ride into the city centre and the *marshrutky* stop is across the road.

Armenia
HOTEL $$

(Армения; ☑4872-250 600; www.ind-garnik.ru; ul Sovetskaya 47; s/d incl breakfast from R3400/4080; ✳🔊🛁) Part of a swish business and entertainment complex, this appealing hotel offers professional, English-speaking staff, some kremlin views (worth the upgrade) and spacious, well-furnished rooms. There's also a pool (free to guests from 7am to 11am), 24-hour sauna, restaurant serving Armenian and Russian dishes, and a billiards club.

Hotel & Garden
BOUTIQUE HOTEL $$$

(☑4872-710 002; www.11hotel.ru; pr Lenina 57; s/d incl breakfast R3900/4200; ✳🔊) While perhaps falling short of boutique aspirations, this charming, brown-brick English-style inn nevertheless makes for a good choice. Its modern motel-style rooms are smallish, yet comfortable, and lent a bit of class by vintage grand prix photography adorning the walls. It's centrally located, tucked away off the main drag in a lot behind Sovetskiy Sport, accessed via ul Lva Tolstogo.

🍴 Eating

Cafe Chocolate
CAFE $

(Кафе Шоколад; pr Lenina 31; dishes from R240, coffee from R120; ⏲10am-11pm; 🔊) Head upstairs, away from the street bustle, to this pleasant cafe with a European feel. Grab a slice of artfully designed cake and a coffee or cocktail for the perfect sightseeing break. There's a helpful picture menu of the light meals and snacks on offer, too.

★Pyotr Petrovich
RUSSIAN $$

(Пётр Петрович; ☑4872-717 400; http://petrpetrovich.ru; ul Pervomayskaya 13; mains R290-1100; ⏲noon-1am Sun-Thu, to 2am Fri & Sat; 🔊) Sitting pretty in an exquisitely restored mansion near the entrance to Central Park, this merry brasserie should not be missed by anyone with taste buds. With its own on-site brewery, dozens of sinful dishes, including homemade sausages (and ubiquitous lashings of cream sauce), famous desserts and a lively atmosphere, it's rightfully popular and gets predictably crowded.

Lisya Nora
RUSSIAN $$

(Лисья Нора; Foxy Burrow; ul Pervomayskaya 12; mains R340-550; ⏲noon-midnight) This woodsy little den comes across all hunters' lodge, with onion-bunch decor and stuffed talking points hanging on the walls. It's a popular hang out, and its menu is all about meat, sizzling plates of which are chomped down with homemade bread and domestic liqueurs with 'medicinal' properties. There's a 10% discount on meals ordered between noon and 4pm.

YASNAYA POLYANA

Located 14km south of central Tula, **Yasnaya Polyana** (Ясная Поляна; ☑4872-393 599; www.ypmuseum.ru; grounds R100, Tolstoy House guided tour in Russian R350; ⊙9am-5pm Tue-Sun) is billed as a 'typical Russian estate' of the late 19th century, which it is save for one important fact: this is where Leo Tolstoy, author of *War and Peace* and *Anna Karenina*, was born, lived most of his life and is buried. Beyond the addition of a few helpful signs, little has changed since that time.

Rooms in the modestly proportioned **Tolstoy House** have been kept just as they were at the time of the writer's death in 1910, with his writing desk and the bizarre child-sized chair he sat on to work, as well as books and furniture. You need to join a guided tour (in Russian) to enter the house; there are no English captions. For an English-language guided visit to the estate and surrounds, contact **Yasnaya Polyana Tour Office** (☑4872-393 599; tour@tolstoy.ru; ul Oktyabrskaya 14; ⊙9am-7pm Mon-Fri) in Tula (R5000 for up to 10 people, R5500 on weekends).

On the estate grounds close to Tolstoy House is the **Kuzminsky House**, an imaginatively designed exhibition covering Tolstoy's inspirations from 1851 to 1869, when he finished *War and Peace*. A short walk into the estate's shady forest is Tolstoy's **grave**. The actual grave is unmarked – as per the author's request – though signs point the way (in English).

From where the Tula bus stops on the main road, it's a 3.5km walk in the opposite direction from Yasnaya Polyana to reach **Kozlova Zaseka** (Козлова Засека; R30; ⊙9.30am-4.30pm Wed-Sun, closed last Wed of the month), the old-fashioned train station where Tolstoy set off for his final journey in 1910. It's now maintained as a one-room museum by a charming bunch of ladies. There's a short video showing footage of the writer at the station and arriving in Moscow.

Should you wish to stay near the estate there's the comfortable and cosy **Yasnaya Polyana Hotel,** (☑48751-76 146; www.yphotel.org; s/d R4200/4800; ❋☎) which also has a restaurant. Alternatively **Cafe Preshpekt** (Кафе Прешпект; meals R150-370; ⊙8am-8pm) across from the estate entrance, prepares dishes according to recipes by Tolstoy's wife, Sofia Andreevna.

From Tula, take *marshrutka* 114 or 117 (R20, 20 minutes) from anywhere along pr Lenina. Ask the driver to let you off at Yasnaya Polyana – it's a 2km walk from the main road to the estate. You can walk or catch a taxi from the estate to Kozlova Zaseka; from there, several buses stop outside the museum to get back to Tula.

Kremlin Tavern GEORGIAN $$
(☑4872-702 645; www.hinkalnaya-tula.ru; per Blagoveshchenskaya 2; mains R190-550; ⊙11am-11pm) The perfect lunch or dinner break after exploring the kremlin, this tavern is a comfy spot to feast on traditional Georgian cuisine – especially the bulging *khinkali* (dumplings) and *khachapuri* (cheese bread). To avoid losing all the juicy goodness from your *khinkali*, do as the locals do and hold it upside down by the stem with your hands and then bite and suck!

🍷 **Drinking & Nightlife**

★ **Restaurant-Brewery**

Augustine MICROBREWERY
(Ресторан-пивоварня Августин; ☑4872-318 899; www.augustine-beer.ru; ul Zhavoronkova 1a; ⊙noon-midnight Sun-Thu, to 2am Fri & Sat) Brewing all of its ales on-site, this gastropub is a must for craft-beer lovers. With some 15 types on offer, there's plenty to get through, from a range of IPAs and pale ales to Russian imperial stout and a heap of Belgian- and German-style pilsners and lagers. Some interesting varietals include a triple-black New Zealand IPA, Australian double IPA and a pumpkin ale.

Beerlin BAR
(pr Krasnoarmeysky 4; ⊙11am-11pm Sun-Thu, to 1am Fri & Sat; ☎) Work your way through the many fine cask-pumped ales (five/10 tasters for R380/760) from around Europe at this spacious bar and restaurant. With its wood-panelled walls, bar and furniture, it does a fine impersonation of a traditional English country pub.

Sovetskiy Sport SPORTS BAR
(Советский Спорт; pr Lenina 57; ⊙noon-midnight; ☎) This compact basement bar combines a bit of Soviet-era kitsch and propa-

ganda with a modern-day enthusiasm for televised sports; join the armchair athletes in front of one of the many flat screens. They do decent food here too.

☆ Entertainment

Drama Theatre THEATRE
(Тульский академический театр драмы; ☑ 4872-311 169; www.tuldramteatr.ru; pr Lenina 34a; tickets from R200) The drama, dance and opera staged here are well produced.

🔒 Shopping

Pryanik Museum & Shop FOOD
(Музей Тульский пряник; ul Oktyabrskaya 45b; ☺ 8am-8pm, museum 10am-4pm) Tula is renowned Russia-wide for its *pryaniki* (inscribed ginger cakes) and locals pack out this tiny bakery store-cum-cafe, stocking up on blocks of gingerbread in all shapes and sizes, filled with flavours from blueberry to lemon. The bakery has been churning them out since 1881. There's a small museum next door (R50) – check out the monster 16kg loaf!

Salden's Beer Shop FOOD & DRINKS
(www.saldens.ru; pr Krasnoarmeysky 22; ☺ 2-10pm Mon-Fri, from noon Sat & Sun) Tula's Salden's Brewery is one of provincial Russia's most respected craft-beer brewers and this tiny takeaway store is a great spot to pick up a couple of tasters. Fill up a 500mL or 1L plastic bottle from one of the taps or grab a bottle from the beer fridge.

ℹ Information

Post Office & Telephone Office (Почта и круглосуточный переговорный пункт; ☑ 4872-363 668; pr Lenina 33; ☺ 8am-10pm Mon-Fri, 9am-6pm Sat & Sun)
Tourist Information Centre (www.visittula. com; ☺ 10am-7pm Tue-Sun) This centre inside the kremlin can assist with info on Tula and they have an English map of the city and region.

ℹ Getting There & Away

BUS
From the **bus station** (pr Lenina), frequent services run to Moscow (R450, three hours), Oryol (R410, four hours, seven daily), Voronezh (R815, seven hours, three daily) and Yelets (R485, four hours, five daily).

Private minibuses (R320, three hours) connect regularly with various metro stations in Moscow, departing from the train and bus stations.

TRAIN
Both *elektrichki* (suburban trains) and normal trains run to Moscow (*platskart/kupe* R1056/2215, three hours, frequent) from the **Moskovsky train station** (ul Puteyskaya). Other services include Oryol (R1031/1770, 2½ hours, frequent) and Yelets (R1140/2003, 4½ hours, seven daily).

ℹ Getting Around

Buses and *marshrutky* (fixed-route minibuses, R20) run from the train station along pr Krasnoarmeysky to pl Lenina and then up pr Lenina – take the 4, 11, 30, 37 or 56. For the bus station, take trolleybus 5 from outside the train station.

Yelets Елец

☑ 47467 / POPULATION 108,400 / ☺ MOSCOW
On the tranquil Sosna River, sleepy Yelets stands out as one of the early Rus settlements to have retained some of its traditional character. The town centre is littered with large and small churches in various stages of disrepair and lined with pastel-coloured buildings and wooden cottages.

Founded in 1146 as a fortification against the Turkic invaders from the east, Yelets became a punching bag for the Mongol Tatars, who devastated it half a dozen times during the Middle Ages. The town became famous for its intricate lacemaking from the 18th century.

Yelets' centre is laid out in a grid, with ul Kommunarov connecting Hotel Yelets in the west with Ascension Cathedral in the east. Further east (downhill) lies the Sosna River.

◎ Sights

★ **Ascension Cathedral** CATHEDRAL
(Вознесенский собор; ul Pushkinskaya; ☺ services 8-11am & 5-7pm) Designed by Konstantin Ton (1794–1881), the genius behind Moscow's Cathedral of Christ the Saviour, the Kremlin Armoury and the Grand Kremlin Palace, this beautiful cathedral lords over Yelets from the foot of ul Kommunarov. Beneath the cathedral's gleaming golden dome, the eye-popping, multicoloured interior glitters with gilt-framed iconography stacked high on each wall.

At 74m in height (including the golden cross), this is one of the tallest cathedrals in Russia. Its looming glory is visible from almost anywhere in Yelets, but you can catch the best view from the bridge crossing the Sosna, just east of town.

House Museum of Yelets Lace
MUSEUM

(Дом-музей Елецкого кружева; ☑47467-27 506; www.elez-mezenat.ru; ul Oktyabrskaya 108; R60; ⊙by appointment) This quaint, bright-blue building contains an exquisite collection of Yelets lacework displayed in elegant surrounds. The 2nd floor has a collection of paintings by local artists. It's best to phone or email ahead for an appointment, though it may be open if you just pop by.

City Park
PARK

(Городской парк; ul Kommunarov) This park has a summertime Ferris wheel, a concert stage, amusement rides and a statue of writer Ivan Bunin. Next to the main entrance is the antique red-brick fire station; ask the firefighters if you can climb the observation tower for a bird's-eye view of the town's gilded cupolas.

Regional Museum
MUSEUM

(Городской краеведческий музей; ul Lenina 99; R60; ⊙9.30am-4.30pm Tue-Sat) Housed in a sweet black-and-white 19th-century building, this surprisingly diverse museum is worth visiting. Among the miscellany, you'll find a room of stuffed moose, bears and a wolf; woolly mammoth bones found in Yelets; a model of ancient Yelets; Soviet-era coins; artefacts from the region; and a replica of Pushkin's death mask.

Ivan Bunin Museum
MUSEUM

(Дом-музей Бунина; ul Maksima Gorkogo 16; R60; ⊙9.30am-4.30pm Tue-Sat) The writer, poet and 1933 Nobel laureate Ivan Bunin (1870–1953) spent some of his childhood in Yelets, studying at the town's gymnasium. This small museum chronicles his life and works. Check out the wallmap with pins marking the places he visited – Mogadishu, Sri Lanka and Spain, to name a few. No English captions.

Great Count's Church
CHURCH

(Великокняжеская церковь; ul Sovetskaya; ⊙9am-5pm) Built during the early 1900s, this inventive piece of religious architecture has distinctly modernist, art nouveau flair, with an exotically tiled interior of metallic hues. The cross on the top is made of crystal.

Vvedenskaya Church
CHURCH

(Введенская церковь; Vvedensky spusk) This jewel-box of a church stands near a cluster of photogenic late-17th- and early-18th-century wooden houses. Follow the road from the church to the bottom of the hill and check out a lovely riverside beach popular with sunbathing locals.

Khrennikov Museum
MUSEUM

(Дом-музей Хренникова; ☑47467-49 476; ul Mayakovskogo 16; R60; ⊙9am-4.30pm Wed-Sun) Successful Soviet composer Tikhon Khrennikov grew up and first studied music in this rust-red wooden house. Original furniture, photos and artefacts are on display. The documentation is also interesting as a history of Soviet aesthetics.

Znamensky Monastery
MONASTERY

(Знаменский монастырь; ul Slobodskaya 5; ⊙6am-10pm) There are fine views across town from this restored early-19th-century hilltop monastery. The white steeple and gold-domed church are easily recognisable from afar, and the interior is decorated with some seriously fabulous frescoes. The grounds are well tended with flower beds, a small aviary with peacocks, and an attractive wooden chapel. Look for the natural spring, beside a blue ablutions hall at the bottom of the hill near the steps.

🛏 Sleeping & Eating

Bazilik
HOTEL $$

(Базилик; ☑8-919-167 8110; www.basilik48.ru; ul Mira 88/17; s/d R1500/2500; 🛜) The Bazilik is a small guesthouse with basic but comfortable-enough rooms, a communal kitchen and a stellar location just 400m from the town centre (pl Lenina).

Hotel Grand Yelets
HOTEL $$$

(Отель Гранд Елец; ☑47467-61 050; www.grandelets.ru; ul Mayakovskogo, 5; r/deluxe from R5400/6000; ❄🛜) Offering a quiet location close to the Ascension Cathedral – with balcony views from some rooms – this grand, pale-yellow hotel looks historic but was actually built in 2016 and styled on an 18th-century palace, complete with chandeliers and decorative features. There's a karaoke room and restaurant on the ground floor.

Jem Cafe
CAFE $

(Кафе Джем; ul Sverdlova 17; mains R130-650; ⊙10am-10pm; 🛜) The Jem is a snuggly dark-wood cafe near the city centre with a summer terrace and lamp-lit interior. There's nothing unexpected on the menu (bliny, pasta, sandwiches, risotto) but it's all done well, as are the strong coffees (from R90) and deliciously thick hot chocolate.

Tomato
PIZZA $

(Помидор; ul Mira 113; pizza from R250; ⊙11am-11pm Mon-Fri, to midnight Sat & Sun; 🛜🅿) Yes it's a chain but, given the limited choice in Yelets, this branch, with an outdoor terrace overlooking pl Lenina, is not a bad option for generic but tasty pizzas and pastas, or just a drink. There's an indoor play area for children.

Stary Gorod
RUSSIAN $$

(Старый Город; ul Mira 100; meals R200-460; ⊙ 11am-4pm & 5pm-1am) The faux Greek statues, low lighting and heavy drapes are a little gaudy but this is the fanciest choice in town. There are plenty of Russian meals to choose from.

ⓘ Getting There & Away

BUS

There are two long-distance bus stations in Yelets: **Avtostantsiya-1** (ul Zadonskaya 47) is near the train station on the main highway (this is where Voronezh buses arrive and depart), while **Avtostantsiya-2** (sh Moskovskoye 3b) is 2.5km west of City Park off ul Kommunarov. Bus services from Avtostantsiya-2 include Moscow (R800, seven hours, frequent), Oryol (R320, 4½ hours, two daily), Voronezh (R232, 2½ hours, frequent) and Tula (R434, 4½ hours, four daily).

TRAIN

Trains travel from **Yelets station** (pl Privokzalnaya) to Moscow (*platskart/kupe* R1480/2072, seven to nine hours, 11 daily) and Tula (R1123/1448, 4½ hours, eight daily). The train station is about 3km southeast of the centre. To get from the station to the town centre, walk to the west end of the platform and cross the tracks to the bus stop.

Voronezh   Воронеж

📞 4732 / POPULATION 1,014,610 / ⊙ MOSCOW

A stop in this industry-focused metropolis can be useful to break up the long journey between Moscow and destinations in Ukraine or the Caucasus. There are some grand buildings worth a gander around pl Lenina and along pr Revolyutsii towards the impressive Annunciation Cathedral.

Following the development of a navy shipyard (the first in Russia) by Peter the Great in the late 1600s, Voronezh became the largest city in southern Russia and a major hub for agriculture and manufacturing. Between 1928 and 1934, it was the capital of the Central Black Earth Oblast, a huge expanse of western Russia noted for its good soil. Destroyed in WWII, the city is now back on track, with a renovated city centre, new developments sprouting every year and gentrification on its way in the form of hipster cafes and wine bars.

⊙ Sights

The streets of Voronezh are scattered with a miscellany of amusing bronze statues. Among others, there's the lucky kitten (touch its left paw and make a wish!); a 'therapeutic' chair said to imbue the sitter with positive energy; and a cute balalaika and accordion sitting casually near the more formal bust of a local composer.

IN Kramskoy Regional Fine Arts Museum
MUSEUM

(Воронежский областной художественный музей им. И.Н. Крамского; www.kramskoi.vzh.ru; pr Revolyutsii 18; adult/child R150/100; ⊙ 10am-6pm Wed, Thu, Sat & Sun, from 11am Fri) Reached through a passage leading into a courtyard, this excellent regional arts museum offers up a solid collection of Russian painting and sculpture, and Greek and Roman sculpture. Quality temporary exhibitions are held behind the main building.

Central Market
MARKET

(http://centr-rynokvrn.ru; ul Pushkinskaya, 8; ⊙ 7am-7pm Tue-Sat, to 4pm Mon, to 5pm Sun) A stroll around this modern glass-ceilinged food market is a good way to while away some time. Check out spices, fresh produce, Russian cakes, dairy and deli items, as well as fish and meat. There's also a hipster food truck selling burgers out front.

Oceanarium
AQUARIUM

(Воронежский океанариум; www.cityparkgrad.ru/entertaiment/oceanarium; Citypark Grad Shopping Centre, Voronezh-Moscow Hwy; adult/child from R550/250; ⊙ 2-9pm Mon, from 10am Tue-Sun) That one of Europe's largest aquariums can be found in a shopping centre in a landlocked town synonymous with Black Earth may seem a little odd, but you'll find the huge collection of marine life – and other animals from around the world – even more astounding. There are over 200 fish species, including tiger sharks (daily feeding shows), piranhas, seals, Humboldt penguins and creepy giant Japanese spider crabs. Buses run regularly from Voronezh: see the website for details. Prices increase by R100 on weekends.

Regional Museum
MUSEUM

(Краеведческий музей; ul Plekhanovskaya 29; admission R140; ⊙ 11am-6pm Wed, noon-8pm Thu, 10am-6pm Fri-Sun) Displays permanent exhibits on Peter the Great and the history of the region from before the Bronze Age up to the Soviet era.

Annunciation Cathedral CHURCH
(Благовещенский кафедральный собор; sad Pervomaisky; ☉7am-7pm) Russia's third-largest working church, this handsome 97m-high structure was built in Russo-Byzantine style in the late 19th century. Outside stands a statue of the early-18th-century cleric St Mitrofan surrounded by four angels. By contrast, the metal fence ringing the complex is decorated with Soviet-era symbols.

St Alexey of Akatov Women's Monastery CONVENT
(Алексеево-Акатов женский монастырь; ul Osvobozhdeniya Truda 1) This out-of-the-way restored nunnery, founded in 1674, is near the river on lovely grounds, which include a tiny graveyard surrounded by colourful, lopsided cottages. The interior of the church is covered entirely with frescoes. If you're lucky, you'll catch the nuns' choir in action.

Resurrection Church CHURCH
(Свято-Воскресенский храм; ul Ordzhonikidze 15) This attractive large green-domed church, a short walk east of pl Lenina, boasts a colourful fresco-covered interior that hosts regular choral services.

🛏 Sleeping

★ Hostel Krysha HOSTEL $
(Хостел Крыша; Roof Hostel; ☎4732-606 885; ul Revolyutsii 1905 Goda 31a; dm R500-690, d from R1100; ☏) With helpful, English-speaking staff, bright, clean rooms, a well-equipped kitchen, and a location within walking distance of the best of Voronezh, this sparkling hostel is a good bet. There is a choice of eight-bed or six-bed dorms (female or male only, no mixed) with lockers, or private doubles.

★ Art Hotel HOTEL $$$
(☎4732-399 299; www.arthotelv.ru; ul Dzerzhinskogo 5b; s/d incl breakfast from R4450/5500; ☏) Italian leather club chairs and furniture give the lobby here a classy atmosphere that extends to the pleasant, light-filled rooms. Helpful English-speaking staff, a communal sauna and an upmarket Italian restaurant, Portofino, round out the offering.

Petrovsky Passazh Hotel HOTEL $$$
(Отель Петровский Пассаж; ☎4732-556 070; www.petrohotel.ru; ul 20-ti Letiya VLKSM 54a; s/d from R3900/5600; ✴☏) Located above a shopping centre, this hotel has spacious rooms, modern furnishings, fast wi-fi and big flat-screen TVs. The owner here is a hunter, which accounts for the stuffed bear and wildcat in the corridors. Judging by the photos on the walls it looks to be popular with local celebs too. Staff speak English.

🍴 Eating

★ CoVok Sovetskoe Cafe RUSSIAN $
(ul Kukolkina 29; mains R150-430; ☉noon-midnight Sun-Thu, until 1am Fri & Sat; ☏) This nostalgic cafe recalls the days of the USSR, not with kitsch propaganda posters, but with cosy nooks, antiques, black-and-white TVs flickering on the walls and a witty menu highlighting the best of erstwhile Soviet republics such as Georgia (khinkali), Belorussia (potato pancakes), Uzbekistan (pilaf) and Ukraine (brisket, borsch). There's also an entire section devoted to salo (lard): what's not to love?

DJA + Go INTERNATIONAL $$
(☎4732-588 058; ul Nikitskaya 1; mains R250-600; ☉noon-11pm Mon-Thu & Sun, to 2am Fri & Sat; ☏) This chic wine bar and restaurant is located in a crumbling historic building. Big windows, high ceilings and an open kitchen set the mood for eyeballing the creatively presented dishes emerging from the kitchen. The menu is small but offers grilled fish dishes, pasta and filling salads. Pair with a good bottle of wine.

★ Garmoshka RUSSIAN $$$
(Гармошка; ☎4732-525759; www.cafe-garmoshka.ru; ul Karla Marxa 94; mains R380-880; ☉11am-11pm) Housed in a historic building, and done up like a wealthy merchant's home, Garmoshka is the fanciest night out in town. The atmospheric tone is traditional Russia, replete with antiques, a library filled with books of famous authors from the region, staff clad in traditional Russian dress and piano music filling the rooms. The menu is Russian classics, featuring exotic meats (including bear).

🍸 Drinking & Nightlife

★ Ptichka COFFEE
(ul Komissarzhevskoy 4; ☉9am-9pm Mon-Fri, 10am-10pm Sat & Sun; ☏) Hipster coffee has arrived in Voronezh; the tattooed baristas at this cute cafe are doing serious brews. Beans are sourced from Kenya, Burundi and Brazil, and you can have coffees (from R130) including AeroPress, pour-over, V60, espresso and an Australian lungo inspired by a barista world-champion from Melbourne.

Bar Duck BAR

(ul Plekhanovskaya 23; ☉ 6pm-6am) Find this cosy modern basement bar, its walls plastered with scrapbook cuttings (and a clientele just plastered), a few blocks northwest of pl Lenina, across from the central market (p240). It also does meals.

Brügger PUB

(ul Stepan Razin 36; ☉ noon-midnight Mon-Thu & Sun, to 2am Fri & Sat; 🛜) This corner tap room and brasserie comes with comfy armchair seating, exposed brick walls and a fantastic range of local craft beers on tap. Service is efficient and friendly and they'll happily give you some tastings at the bar. Pub food is on the menu (R150 to R560).

☆ Entertainment

Opera & Ballet Theatre THEATRE

(☑ 4732-553 927; http://theatre.vzh.ru; pl Lenina 7) Quality productions are mounted at this handsome classical-style theatre.

❶ Getting There & Away

AIR

The **airport** (www.aeroport-voronezh.ru; sh Zadonskoe) is 10km north of the centre along sh Zadonskoe, with several flights daily to Moscow's Domodedovo Airport (R3000, one hour).

BUS

The **bus station** (Moskovsky pr 17) is 3km northwest of pl Lenina, with services to Moscow (R877, eight to 11 hours), Saratov (R1051, 12 hours) and Volgograd (R1136, 11 hours). Six services a day run to Yelets (R231, three hours) and two daily to Oryol (R670, seven hours).

TRAIN

The main train station is **Voronezh 1** (pl Chernyakhovskogo), around 1.5km north of pl Lenina, with services to Moscow (platskart/kupe R1194/2493, 10½ hours, 10 daily), St Petersburg (R2283/3326, 24 hours, two daily) and Yelets (R788/1036, 5½ hours, four daily).

❶ Getting Around

From Voronezh 1 train station there are many marshrutky (R15, 10 to 15 minutes); to reach the city centre, look for those going to pl Lenina (Площадь Ленина). Some long-distance trains stop at Pridacha (Придача), about 10km outside the city. If you arrive there, follow the crowd 300m out of the station, where you'll find a car park full of marshrutky to whisk you into town; take the 104 for the city centre (R15). A taxi costs around R350.

To reach the city centre from the bus station, exit the station and catch bus 5A (R15), which runs along ul Plekhanovskaya.

Oryol   Орёл

☑ 4862 / POPULATION 318,136 / ☉ MOSCOW

With its attractive mix of historic buildings, riverside parks and red-and-yellow trams, Oryol (arr-yol) harks back to prerevolutionary Russia. It also has a more gritty face, featuring some classic brutalist Soviet architecture.

The town is most known for its literary legacy, with some 12 local writers – most notably Turgenev, Bunin and Leskov – and their work is remembered in several small house-museums. It's also the ideal base for visiting Ivan Turgenev's beautiful estate, Spasskoe-Lutovinovo (p246), and is the gateway to Orlovskoye Polesye National Park (p247).

A fortress is thought to have stood on the bluff overlooking the confluence of the Oka and Orlik Rivers since at least the 12th century. Legend has it that an eagle (oryol in Russian) alighted on the fortress, giving the settlement its name. The city reached its peak during the 19th century, when a surprising number of the gentry (19,000 out of a population of 32,000) lived here.

◉ Sights

Ivan Bunin Museum MUSEUM

(Музей Бунина; ☑ 4862-760 774; Georgevsky per 1; R50; ☉ 10am-5pm Sat-Thu) There's a good collection of photos and other documents relating to the Nobel Prize–winning writer (no English captions, however), plus a 'Paris Room' devoted to his years as an emigrant, including the bed in which he died. At the end of the one-hour tour (R500, in Russian), the guide flips on a tape player and Bunin himself reads one of his last poems, 'Solitude'.

Turgenev Museum MUSEUM

(Музей Тургенева; ☑ 4862-762 737; ul Turgeneva 11) Turgenev's estate, Spasskoe-Lutovinovo, may be the literary mecca around these parts, but not to be outdone, Oryol has this museum filled with old photos and notes written by the man. There are tributes to Turgenev throughout town, including a statue of him overlooking the Oka on Turgenevsky spusk, the sloping street off pl Lenina, and a bust in the public garden. The museum was under restoration at the time of research.

Oryol

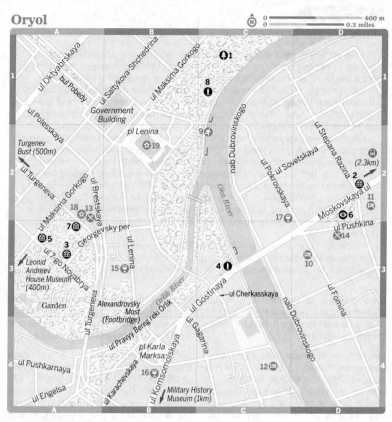

Oryol

Nikolai Leskov House Museum   MUSEUM
(Дом-музей Лескова; ☎ 4862-763 465; ul 7-go Noyabrya 24; R100; ◷ 10am-5pm Sat-Thu) Author and journalist Nikolai Leskov (1831–95), who wrote the book on which the opera *Lady Macbeth of Mtsensk* is based, is remembered at this museum. It's usually housed in a turquoise wooden mansion, but at the time of research this was under renovation and the museum had moved

KURSK

The biggest tank battle of WWII took place near Kursk (Курск) in July and August of 1943. A major turning point in the conflict, Russia's defeat of the Nazis signalled the beginning of the end for Hitler, who never launched another major attack on the Eastern Front.

Unsurprisingly, Kursk itself was thoroughly trashed, with little architecture left standing. The town today honours its history with museums and monuments that will be of interest mainly to history buffs. **Victory Memorial** (Мемориал Победы; Pobedy pr) dominates the northern entrance to the city. The soaring arch is surrounded by military paraphernalia including tanks and heavy artillery from WWII plus an eternal flame and a memorial to those who died on the submarine Kursk in 2000. The Regional Museum has plenty of displays and information on Kursk's part in WWII while the Young Defenders of the Motherland Museum tells the tragic stories of the children and teenagers who fought against fascism.

There are frequent trains to Kursk from Moscow (R1659/2680, five to seven hours), St Petersburg (R2681/3744, 17 hours) and all over the region, including Oryol (from R766/1165, 1¾ hours) and Tula (from R1050/1414, four hours). There are also plenty of minibuses during the day linking Kursk with Oryol (R314, 2½ hours) and Voronezh (R548, four hours).

Numerous buses, trams and *marshrutky* (R10) ply the route between the train station and Krasnaya pl in the centre. Bus 1 and tram 2 travel between the train station and the bus station. Taxis charge around R150 from either station to the town centre.

here. Displays, in Russian only, include photographs and personal items. Note his uncanny resemblance to Robert De Niro in the portrait on entry.

Leonid Andreev House Museum   MUSEUM
(Дом-музей Леонида Андреева; ul 2-a Push-karnaya 41; R100; ⊙10am-5pm) Inside this cottage, the birthplace of writer and dramatist Leonid Andreev, there is a beautiful piano and examples of Andreev's art and photography: he was an early Russian exponent of colour photography and his compositions are remarkable.

◉ Other Sights & Activities

Ivan The Terrible Monument   MONUMENT
(pl Bogoyavlenskaya) Unveiled in late 2016, Russia's first monument to the formidable 16th-century tsar, Ivan the Terrible, has caused plenty of controversy. Locals protested against the plans for months and the planned location was moved from a central square to a spot near the river. The city of Oryol was chosen as authorities believe Ivan founded the region, though this is debated by historians. The bronze monument has him sitting atop a horse carrying high the Orthodox cross.

Ploshchad Mira   SQUARE
(Площадь Мира) The southern end of 'Peace Square' is easily identified by its WWII **tank memorial**, one of the original involved in liberating Oryol from German occupation

in August 1943. Note the hammer-and-sickle symbols on the park benches. Opposite the square's northwest corner is the elegant **Dom Knigi** (ul Moskovskaya 17) building.

Military History Museum   MUSEUM
(Орловский военно-исторический музей; ☑4862-590 645; ul Normandiya-Neman 1; R70; ⊙9am-6pm) This detailed museum covers military history through the years, including the Napoleonic War, Russian Civil War, WWI and WWII, as well as more recent conflicts, such as in Afghanistan and Chechnya. Displays include military uniforms, photographs, paintings and epic 180-degree battle scene dioramas. There is a military tank and equipment out front.

City Park of Culture & Rest   PARK
(Городской парк культуры и отдыха; ul Maksima Gorkogo) There's an **amusement park** (аттракционы) at the northeastern end of this leafy riverside park and a **statue** of the Russian novelist, Ivan Turgenev. You can rent **rowing boats** (Прокат лодок; ⊙9am-9pm) during the warmer months.

🛏 Sleeping

Many of Oryol's hotels are stuck in a Soviet time warp, which – depending on your tastes – will either delight or appall with their austere rooms and long, creepy hallways, as well as poor plumbing in some cases.

★ **Retrotur**   HOTEL **$$**

(Гостиница Ретро-Тур; ☎4862-490 502; www.
retrotur-orel.ru; ul Levyy Bereg Reki Oki 15; s/d
from R2300/2800; ❋🖰) Sitting pretty on the
banks of the Oka River, this hotel is with-
in walking distance of the centre but offers
respite from the hubbub. Despite being close
to a traffic overpass, the spacious rooms are
quiet, with natural light and polished tim-
ber floors. Request a room with a view of the
river; room 7 is the pick. A good restaurant
(mains from R180) is attached.

Atlantida   HOTEL **$$**

(Атлантида; ☎4862-717 233; www.atlantida-hotel.
ru; ul Fomina 4a; s/d incl breakfast R3300/3700;
❋🖰) Overlook the nouveau-riche decorative
touches: this midsized hotel, restaurant and
business complex is a decent option right
near Peace Sq, and its 'ye olde' restaurant-bar
(theme: cashed-up woodsman) is lots of fun.

Hotel Oryol   HOTEL **$$$**

(Гостиница Орёл; ☎4862-550 525; www.orelho-
tel.ru; pl Mira 4; s/d from R3000/4200, lyux r from
R6400; ❋🖰) A touch of grandeur remains
in the distinguished exterior, public areas
and *lyux* (suite) rooms of this historic hotel
opposite Peace Sq. It's not quite as gilded in
the more affordable rooms, but they are airy
and comfortable.

✖ **Eating**

Kakhovka   GASTROPUB **$$**

(Каховка; ☎4862-445 363; ul Turgeneva 16; mains
R350-600; ⏰noon-midnight Sun-Thu, to 2am Fri &
Sat; 🖰) With its exposed light bulbs, bright
industrial decor and warehouse feel, Kak-
hovka could fit in comfortably somewhere
in Brooklyn. Chargrilled meats feature on
the menu along with burgers. Russian craft
beer fills the fridge and there is Belgian-style
beer on tap; otherwise opt for a good-quality
cocktail (great mocktail choices, too).

3 Etazh   EUROPEAN **$$**

(3 Этаж; ☎4862-544 130; https://3etaj.ru; 3rd fl,
ul Pushkina 6; pizzas R190-550; ⏰8am-midnight
Sun-Thu, from noon Fri & Sat; 🖰) Excellent thin-
crust pizzas, topped waffles and filling sand-
wiches are just the start of the great things
about this whimsical cafe. Vegetarians will
find some solace here, with actual meals de-
signed just for them.

Labirint   EUROPEAN **$$**

(Лабиринт; ☎4862-426 532; www.labirintclub.ru;
ul Pushkina 6; meals R390-650; ⏰noon-1am Sun-
Thu, to 2am Fri & Sat; 🖰) This appealing, upmarket cafe-lounge serves up excellent salads,
pastas and meat dishes such as shashlyk and
pork fillets, plus some vegetarian options,
including a no-meat version of steak tartare.

🍷 **Drinking & Nightlife**

Bridge Bar   PUB

(У моста; ☎4862-435 602; ul Lenina 13;
⏰noon-midnight; 🖰) Heading down pedestrianised ul Lenina away from pl Lenina, on
the right before you hit the bridge, you'll find
this cosy basement beer bar with stuffed animals on the wall and a flip-book menu of
Russian craft beer. The atmosphere is friendly and there's good pub food to fuel up on.

Bar Boris   SPORTS BAR

(Бар Борис; ☎4862-780 606; www.barboris.ru;
2nd fl, ul Pushkina 6; meals R320-690; ⏰4pm-4am
Mon-Fri, from noon Sat & Sun; 🖰) Boris' tiered,
polished wood parliament-style bench
seating, aimed at a cinema-sized sports TV
screen, is the ultimate in sports bars. The
long dark-wood bar, beers from around the
world and tasty food – bratwurst, quesadillas, schnitzels – are enticing enough, even if
you're not a sports fan. It's all to a soundtrack
of mostly punk, indie and rock music.

Chester Pub   PUB

(Честер Паб; ☎4862-543 054; http://chesterpub.
ru; ul Komsomolskaya 36; mains R350-700; 🖰)
Decorated with bulldog statuettes, Union
Jack flags and portraits of QEII and Churchill, this baronial-sized pub attempts to recreate a bit of England. Rounding out the picture is a tempting selection of their own beer
brewed on-site (from R90) and a wide-ranging
menu including several styles of sausage.

Pint House   PUB

(☎4862-490 007; ul Pokrovskaya 3; ⏰noon-2am;
🖰) When the weekend comes, this is Oryol's
premier party place, with quaffing crowds
going bonkers to live bands. The rest of the
time, it is a fairly distinguished watering
hole, with gentlemen's-lounge-style booths,
unfiltered house beers on the menu and infused vodkas. There's a fine pub-grub menu
with helpful pictures for ordering.

☆ **Entertainment**

Turgenev Theatre   THEATRE

(Орловский государственный академический
театр имени И.С. Тургенева; ☎4862-761 639;
pl Lenina) Hosts plays and concerts in a clever
modernist building – the facade mimics the
effect of a stage with the curtains drawn.

DON'T MISS

SPASSKOE-LUTOVINOVO

Surrounded by beautiful countryside, Spasskoe-Lutovinovo (Спасское-Лутовиново; www.spasskoye-lutovinovo.ru; guided tour main house R300, grounds only R70; ☉9am-5pm), 65km north of Oryol, is the family estate of Ivan Turgenev (1818–83), where the 19th-century novelist completed most of his novels, including his famous book, *Fathers and Sons*. The main house contains some original furniture, artworks collected by the writer, books and personal items. There's an icon hanging in Turgenev's study that was given to the family by Ivan the Terrible, and the chessboard is set ready to play (Turgenev was a masterful player).

To visit the main house you need to join a tour; it's best to arrange English-language tours (R1000) in advance.

Though he spent much of his life in Moscow, St Petersburg, Germany and France, Turgenev thought of Spasskoe-Lutovinovo as his home and returned here many times. He was also exiled here in 1852–3 as a result of his work *A Sportsman's Sketches*, which displeased the tsar.

Also on the grounds is the restored family church, which holds regular services, and there is a small literature museum (R100). The big oak tree planted as a sapling by Turgenev and the writer's 'exile house' are a short walk from the main house.

Take a *marshrutka* (fixed-route minibus) from Oryol to Mtsensk (R78, one hour, frequently), then switch at Mtsensk's bus station to a Spasskoe-Lutovinovo bus (R38, 30 minutes, hourly), or take a taxi (around R250). You can also organise a taxi from Oryol (approx R900 including an hour waiting time).

Teatr Russky Stil
THEATRE

(Муниципальный театр Русский стиль; ☏4862-762 024; http://rs-teatr.ru; ul Turgeneva 18) A fun, small-scale, occasionally experimental theatre that presents mostly comedies.

ⓘ Information

There's a tourist information office in town, but no English is spoken; refer to www.tourism-orel.ru for lots of handy info on Oryol as a literary city, plus links to various tour operators.

ⓘ Getting There & Away

BUS

The **bus station** (ul Avtovokzalnaya) is 4km to the south, with services to Moscow (from R600, six hours, three to four daily), Smolensk (from R880, seven hours, two to three daily), Tula (from R356, four hours, frequent), Voronezh (from R340, seven hours, two daily), Yelets (from R430, 4½ hours, two daily) and Kursk (from R314, 2½ hours, frequent).

TRAIN

The **train station** (pl Privokzalnaya) is around 2.5km north from central pl Mira.

Trains run to Moscow (*platskart/kupe* from R1283/1550, four to six hours, frequent), St Petersburg (from R2526/3200, 15 hours, two daily), Voronezh (from R1404/2385, 7½ hours, two daily) and Tula (R1031/1564, two hours, frequent).

ⓘ Getting Around

From the train station, tram 1 and trolleybus 3 stop near Ploshchad Mira (Peace Sq), convenient for Hotel Oryol and a few bars and restaurants. From the bus station, tram 1 or 3 and trolleybus 1 stop at the square.

Trolleybuses 4 and 6, which run along ul Turgeneva, also provide convenient access to the bus station. Trolleybus 5 to the train station runs along ul Maksima Gorkogo.

Taxis to the train or bus station from pl Lenina charge about R150.

NORTH & WEST OF MOSCOW

Smolensk
Смоленск

☏4812 / POPULATION 326,861 / ☉ MOSCOW

Set on the upper Dnepr River, this grand city offers 16th-century fortress walls and towers to explore, excellent architecture, onion-dome churches and well-landscaped parks. The highlight is the magnificent Assumption Cathedral sitting pretty on the hill, but art and music are also well represented in the hometown of composer Mikhail Glinka and 19th-century arts patron Princess Maria Tenisheva, whose estate of Flyonovo makes for an interesting side trip.

History

Smolensk was first mentioned in 863 as the capital of the Slavic Krivichi tribe. The town's auspicious setting gave it early control over trade routes between Moscow and the west, and between the Baltic and Black Seas. By the late 1100s, Smolensk was one of the strongest principalities in Eastern Europe.

As Muscovy and Lithuania vied for power in the 13th century, Smolensk was caught in the middle and was successively invaded from both sides. The battle between Russia and Napoleon's army outside Smolensk in 1812 (later immortalised in Tolstoy's *War and Peace*) is commemorated by a couple of monuments in town. Composer Mikhail Glinka, regarded as the founder of Russian classical music, grew up near Smolensk and performed frequently in the Nobles' Hall, facing what is now the Glinka Garden.

Almost 95% of Smolensk was destroyed in WWII, but was quickly rebuilt, often along original plans. It was later awarded the rare status of Hero City (город-герой).

☉ Sights

Information on many of Smolensk's galleries and museums can be found at www.smolensk-museum.ru (in Russian).

★ **Assumption Cathedral** CATHEDRAL
(Успенский кафедральный собор; ul Sobornaya Gora 5; ☉ 7am-8pm) Dominating the skyline is this huge green-and-white working cathedral topped by five silver domes. A church has stood here since 1101; this one was built in the late 17th and early 18th centuries.

Even more splendid within, its spectacular gilded and icon-encrusted interior so impressed Napoleon that, according to legend, he set a guard to stop his own men from vandalising the cathedral.

Immediately on your left as you enter, look for a small framed icon of the Virgin, richly encrusted with pearls drawn from the Dnepr around Smolensk. Further on, a cluster of candles marks a supposedly wonder-working icon of the Virgin. This is a 16th-century copy of the original, said to be by St Luke, which had been on this site since 1103 and was stolen in 1923.

★ **Art Gallery** GALLERY
(Художественная галерея; ☑ 4812-381 591; ul Kommunisticheskaya 4; R120; ☉ 10am-6pm Tue, Wed, Fri & Sun, 11am-7pm Thu & Sat) Housed in a beautiful building with wrought-iron staircases, this splendid collection includes pieces by luminaries such as Valentin Serov, Ilya Repin and Vasily Tropinin, as well as a good sampling of socialist realism, 14th-to-18th-century icons and European old masters. You'll also find portraits of Princess Maria Tenisheva, who created the Flyonovo (Флёново; p252) estate outside town. There are some English captions throughout.

Smolensk WWII Museum MUSEUM
(Смоленщина в годы Великой Отечественной войны 1941-1945 гг; ☑ 4812-383 119; ul Dzerzhinskogo 4a; adult/child R120/free; ☉ 10am-6pm Tue-Sun, closed last Tue of the month) This comprehensive museum covers WWII in the Smolensk area from the beginning of the war and occupation by the Nazis to the region's

---

OFF THE BEATEN TRACK

ORLOVSKOYE POLESYE NATIONAL PARK

This **national park** (☑ 9208-192 333; www.orlpolesie.ru; ☉ visitor centre 8am-noon & 1-5pm Mon-Fri), 85km northwest of Oryol, is a placid slice of taiga, with over 360 sq km of thick forest, lakes and wildflower-dotted grasslands. It's a fantastic spot for fishing, camping and walking, but this is more than your average nature getaway. The park is home to more than 500 European bison, which roam free under a special protection and breeding program. The well-managed park runs **bison tours** (R2000 per group, winter only), allowing visitors to observe the grand beasts feeding and playing.

Orlovskoye Polesye also houses an open-air **zoo**, a sacred spring and an ostrich farm. Outdoorsy types can trek along signposted ecotrails or take off on a rented bike, boat or horse. The website has full details of activities and accommodation options.

In theory it's possible to get here via public transport by catching a train to Bryansk and alighting at Khotynets, then catching a bus on to Zhudre village. You can also get a bus to Khotynets from Oryol. However, in reality having your own transport is the only real option.

Smolensk

N 0 _____ 500 m
0 _____ 0.25 miles

WESTERN EUROPEAN RUSSIA SMOLENSK

Vitebskoe sh

pl Privokzalnaya

Buses to Moscow

ul 12 let Oktyabrya

ul Belyaeva

ul Novomoskovskaya

🔂 13 ul Kashena

pl Kolkhoznaya

19 ul Zhelyabova

Bus Station

ul Zhelyabova

33

Dnepr River

ul Krasnoflotskaya Bolshaya

ul Soboleva

27 ul Studencheskaya

Shkolnaya ul

ul Bakunina 22

Assumption Cathedral

🔂 2

ul Bolshaya Sovetskaya

ul Nogina

ul Voykova

17

20

ul Dzerzhinskogo

ul Przhevalskogo

ul Kopenkova

ul Kozlova

3

10

11

8

ul Lenina

5 Lopatinsky Gardens

21

pl Lenina

6

7 26

31 ul Mayakovskogo

9 32

ul Tukhachevskogo

24

1 ul Kommunisticheskaya

Art Gallery

30

29

14

23

18

4

ul Glinki

12

15

28

pl Smirnova

25

16

ul Gagarina

ul Tenishevoy

ul Isakovskogo

ul Dzerzhinskogo

ul Oktyabrskoy Revolyutsii

Smolensk

liberation. Displays (captions in Russian) include weaponry, military uniforms, medals and original photos and documents, and there is a bunker diorama titled Birth of the Soviet Guard. Outside is a large collection of tanks, canons and aircraft that kids will delight in climbing on, as well as a trench bunker you can walk through.

History Museum   MUSEUM
(Исторический музей; ☎ 4812-383 862; ul Lenina 8; adult/child R100/free; ⊙10am-6pm Tue-Thu, Sat & Sun, to 5pm Fri) This gorgeous mustard-coloured building is home to a range of different galleries over two floors, covering natural and local history. Displays include medieval knight armory, a 26kg gold-plated bible and a wooly mammoth skeleton from Siberia (the tusks are a replica).

Fortress Walls & Around   HISTORIC SITE
(Крепостные стены и окрестности) Making a circuit of the restored city walls, long sections of which boast fine towers reminiscent of the Moscow Kremlin, is a pleasant way to pass a warm summer evening, with parks, various monuments and churches to be encountered along the way. Originally built between 1596 and 1602, the impressive 6.5km-long, 5.5m-thick, 15m-high walls had 38 towers, with 17 still standing.

Overlooking the Spartak Stadium, just outside the line of the walls on the west side of Lopatinsky Gardens, the Korolevsky Bastion (Королевский бастион) is a high earth rampart built by the Poles who captured Smolensk in 1611. It saw heavy fighting in 1654 and 1812.

Backing onto a longish southwest stretch of the walls, the Lopatinsky Gardens have the 26m-high cast-iron Monument to the 1812 Defenders (Памятник защитникам Смоленска 1812 г). At the foot of the walls southeast of Glinka Garden you'll find an eternal flame memorial (Мемориал Вечный огонь; Lopatisnky Gardens), plus another monument to the heroes of 1812 (Памятник героям 1812 г). The nearby, witch-hatted Thunder Tower (Громовая башня) offers city views and a small museum.

Glinka Garden   PARK
(Городской сад Глинки) At the east end of this shady garden with fountains, an 1885 statue of the composer Glinka is surrounded by a fence with excerpts from his opera *A Life for the Tsar* wrought into the iron. Opposite is the concert hall (p252) in which he performed. The north side of the garden is bordered by the expansive pl Lenina, where a statue of Vladimir Ilyich himself stands in front of the palatial city hall, once the House of Soviets.

NIKOLA-LENIVETS

Adopted by a group of architects and land artists more than 20 years ago, the once abandoned village of **Nikola-Lenivets** (http://nikola-lenivets.ru; ☑ 495 150 5475), 220km southwest of Moscow in the Kaluga region, is now a huge open-air exhibition space with gigantic installations made largely of wood and located along a circular route running through the forest. You could call it abstract architecture.

The centrepiece is the *Universal Mind*, a massive temple-like structure designed by one of the project's founders, Nikolay Polissky. Preceded by an avenue lined with wooden pillars, it's made of convoluted tree branches and resembles a giant human brain. Connecting the branches are metal plates, which catch the light of the setting sun, making the whole construction shine like a gold nugget.

In the adjacent field the *Gilded Calf*, by another Nikola-Lenivets founder, Vasily Shchetinin, resembles a caravelle or a bull – depending on the angle you're looking from. The artist mused over what the *Charging Bull* statue in New York's Wall Street would look like at the time of a financial meltdown, and imagined that the bull would turn into a new Noah's ark bringing people back from the sea of greed.

The village itself sits on the bank of the Ugra River, which leads into the dense forest of Ugra National Park. Thousands flock to Nikola-Lenivets for the annual **Archstoyanie** (http://arch.stoyanie.ru/) international festival in summer (dates vary), when new objects are presented.

You can buy maps and hire bicycles from the **reception office** at the main turn to the village. A windowless but airy wooden **hostel** offers several rooms, a penthouse and bunkbeds. There are also wooden **huts** and large **tents,** which can be booked for overnight stays. A modern cafe in the village is a good place to chill out, but for a great dining experience try **Ferma**, a nearby farm run by Sergey Morozov and his wife Anna. Their own garden produce is served as delicious soups and salads or with handmade pasta, and a selection of homemade drinks includes rhubarb *kompot* (a sweet soft drink) and *samogon* (traditional moonshine).

Your best bet for getting here is to hire a car in Moscow. Exit the city via Leninsky Prospekt, which becomes Kyiv highway. After about 100km, turn right to Medyn; from there, turn to Kondrovo and follow the signs to the village. The trip takes just over three hours, if you avoid the horrendous weekend traffic jams in Moscow. There's no public transport to Nikola-Lenivets, but you can get an *elektrichka* (suburban train) from Kievsky Vokzal in Moscow to Maloyaroslavets. Then book one of the drivers listed on Nikola-Lenivets' website (in Russian-only) or contact the reception office to get them to arrange it for you.

Smolensk Flax Museum MUSEUM
(Музей Смоленский лён; Nicholas Tower, ul Marshala Zhukova 6; R80; ⊙10am-6pm Tue-Thu, Sat & Sun, to 5pm Fri) Flax production developed from the Middle Ages as one of Smolensk's main industries, as the moderate climate sustained soil ideal for growing the plant. Exhibits here will give you some idea of how the process works (though no English captions) and of the lovely products and traditional clothing that can be made from the resulting cloth.

Trinity Monastery MONASTERY
(Свято-Троицкий женский монастырь; ul Bolshaya Sovetskaya 9) Much restoration work has been done on this charming, pink-walled convent, which also runs a small orphanage for girls. Donations are welcome.

Konenkov Sculpture Museum MUSEUM
(Музей скульптуры Коненкова; ☑ 4812-382 029; ul Mayakovskogo 7; R80; ⊙10am-6pm Tue-Thu, Sat & Sun, to 5pm Fri) Contains playful woodworks by Smolensk Oblast native Sergei Konenkov, otherwise known as the 'Russian Rodin'. The museum also has works by other noted Smolensk artists.

Dom Knigi ARCHITECTURE
(Дом Книги; ul Bolshaya Sovetskaya 12/1; ⊙10am-2pm & 3-6pm Mon-Fri, 10am-4pm Sun) This bookshop only sells Russian-language titles, but if you don't read Russian it's still a worthwhile stop to admire the beautiful blue baroque building.

Peter & Paul Church CHURCH
(Церковь Петра и Павла; ul Kashena 20) With obvious Byzantine influences, this red-brick

12th-century chapel (1146) is the oldest in the city and a local icon.

In the World of
Fairytales Museum
MUSEUM

(Музей В мире сказки; ☑ 4812-382 226; ul Lenina 15; adult/child R50/20; ☺ 10am-6pm Sun-Thu, to 5pm Fri; 🖼) One for the kids, where they've smashed the boring don't-touch rules. It's a small creative space with activities and interactive exhibits based on Russian fairy tales. Even scary-looking Baba Yaga is there. It has some great little wooden toys for sale.

✸ Festivals & Events

Glinka Festival
MUSIC

A showcase of Russian classical music that runs between the last week of May and the first week of June. It takes place in venues across town.

Shooting Stars
Fireworks Festival
FIREWORKS

Smolensk's skies erupt every July with artfully choreographed fireworks set to classical and live music.

🛏 Sleeping

Felix Hostel
HOSTEL $

(Феликс Хостел; ☑ 8-904-360 0032; www.felix-hotel.ru; ul Dzerzhinskogo 19; dm/d R500/1000; 🖲) Moments from some of the city's top attractions and across from Lopatinsky Gardens, Felix Hostel is small and nothing flash, but a great find. Dorms are clean and cheerful with solid bunks, TVs, lockers and shared bathrooms. There is a good communal kitchen and a couple of private double rooms. The manager speaks English.

There's no sign so it's tough to find; call before arriving as there's not always someone at reception.

Mini Hotel Na Avtovokzale
HOSTEL $

(☑ 4812-633 202; ul Kashena 13; dm/s/d with shared bathroom R500/800/1600) A surprisingly decent budget option, given it's at the bus station, this clean and functional hostel offers spacious, spick-and-span dorms. Private rooms are adequate for a night or two, and perfect for late arrivals coming via overnight bus or train. Management can be a little vague, however.

★ Respect Hotel
HOTEL $$

(Отель Респект; ☑ 4812-382 138; www.respect67.ru; ul Parizhskoy Komunny, 18; s/d incl breakfast from R2200/2500; ❄🖲) In a great location between the Assumption Cathedral and the city centre, this cosy hotel deserves some respect for its spacious, modern and sparkling clean rooms. Some rooms also overlook the peaceful garden, but walls are on the thin side so some neighbouring murmurings might be heard. Breakfast is served in the ground-floor cafe. Wi-fi can be patchy.

Smolenskhotel
HOTEL $$

(Гостиница; ☑ 4812-383 604; www.smolensk-hotel.ru; ul Lenina 2/1; s/d/studios incl breakfast R2970/3990/5980; 🖲) Set on the edge of Glinka Garden, this centrally located five-storey hotel is Soviet era meets old-world charm in the lobby. It has basic rooms, decked out in a lot of brown, with TV and fridge. Service is professional and efficient. Discounts are available for longer stays and groups.

★ Usadba
BOUTIQUE HOTEL $$$

(Усадьба; ☑ 4812-385 936; r incl breakfast R4000-10,000; ❄🖲) In a quiet residential area that's still close to the city centre, this cute boutique hotel offers 22 comfortable rooms with good facilities (room 5 has cathedral views). There's an attached restaurant, where breakfast and other meals are served, as well as a DVD library, pool and small traditional wooden sauna (R800 per hour before 4pm, R1000 per hour after 4pm).

✗ Eating

Russkiy Dvor
RUSSIAN $

(Русский Двор; www.pizzadomino.ru/Russkiy_Dvor; Glinka Garden; mains R80-200; ☺ 10am-11pm; 🖼) This place looks like a cross between St Basil's Cathedral and McDonald's inside. It's fast food, but the quality is surprisingly high, which may explain the long queues at lunchtime.

Samovar
RUSSIAN $

(Самовар; ul Lenina 14; pies from R90; ☺ 10am-10pm; 🖲) Perfect for a lunch break along ul Lenina, Samovar is an appealing self-serve restaurant specialising in traditional savoury and sweet pies. Sit up front and people-watch through the big windows or opt for the terrace in warmer weather.

Domino
EUROPEAN $

(Домино; www.pizzadomino.ru; ul Dzerzhinskogo 16; pizza from R80, mains R70-200; ☺ 24hr) Kitsch! Glorious kitsch! Even if peasant-on-acid decor isn't your thing, you'll still enjoy the fast-food offerings from this chain. The front and

WORTH A TRIP

FYLONOVO

In the late 19th and early 20th centuries, illustrious artists and musicians, including Stravinsky, Chaliapin, Vrubel and Serov, visited Flyonovo (Флёново), the pretty riverside estate of art lover Princess Maria Tenisheva, near Talashkino, 18km southeast of Smolensk. The visitors joined in applied-art workshops, which the princess organised for her peasants, and helped in building projects. The most striking result is the almost psychedelic decoration on the exterior of the brick **Holy Spirit Church** (Церковь Святого Духа), particularly the mural of Christ over the entrance, designed by well-known landscape painter Rerikh.

On the estate grounds is the ornately decorative wooden house **Teremok** (Изба Теремок; R80; ☉10am-5pm Tue-Sun, closed last Thu of the month), with its folk-art museum, while the interior of another large but simpler wooden building is the former arts school. The first headmaster of the school was SV Malutin, the inventor of the beloved *matryoshka* (nesting dolls). A smaller building (R80) sells crafts still produced here.

Take *marshrutka* 104 from Smolensk's bus station to Talashkino (R28, 20 minutes), from where it's a pleasant 2km walk to the estate. You can hop on the same *marshrutka* at pl Smirnova. The 130 often goes direct from Smolensk: ask at the station. It's possible to get a taxi from Smolensk for around R370 one-way and ask the driver to wait for the return.

side patios that open in summer are good for a drink. There are several Dominoes across town.

★Tirol RUSSIAN $$
(Тироль; ☑4812-385 851; ul Marshala Zhukova 9; mains R250-750; ☉noon-1am; ☎) You won't want to leave this charming, snug little den, done up like a babushka's house with old-style wallpaper, stuffed animals, figurine lamps and knickknacks. There's a hearty, soul-warming menu to match, featuring sausages and some delicious creamy soups.

Temnitsa RUSSIAN $$
(☑4812-244 999; www.temnitsa.ru; ul Studencheskaya 4; mains R490-1250) Set in the old castle walls, this charming restaurant has plenty of character, with stained-glass windows, a tiny fireplace, exposed-brick walls and lovely views of the Dnepr from its balcony. The menu features well-prepared traditional Russian dishes.

Saint Jacques FUSION $$
(Сен-Жак; ☑4812-242 444; www.san-jak.ru; Churilovskiy per 19; mains R320-1100; ☉11am-midnight Sun-Thu, to 2am Fri & Sat; ☎) Saint Jacques adds some ooh la la to the Smolensk dining scene. The St Petersburg chef doffs his beret ever so slightly to France with upmarket bouillabaisse and sturgeon steak with beurre blanc. There's also salmon ravioli, black fish burgers and goulash. Service is outstanding.

🍷 Drinking & Nightlife

Hagen in the Blonye BREWERY
(☑4812-387 612; http://hagen-blonie.ru; ul Kommunisticheskaya 6; ☉10am-11pm; ☎) Darkwood booths, plaid wallpaper and stained glass give this brewery bar-restaurant an inviting British gastropub feel. They brew their own German-style beer on-site and offer tasting paddles (four beers R100). The tea selection is a standout here, including an authentic masala chai, blooming-flower teas and alcoholic versions. Burgers, pizza and beer snacks are also available.

Dvoinoe Solntse TEAHOUSE
(Двойное Солнце; ☑4812-630 220; www.doublesun.ru; ul Barklaya-de-Tolli 7; ☉1pm-midnight) Taking a stab at re-creating a traditional Japanese teahouse, this place has floor seating, screens and low tables. An excellent range of tea is on offer (cup from R135). Food is also available, including sushi, and there is a store selling tea accessories.

☆ Entertainment

Glinka Concert Hall CLASSICAL MUSIC
(Концертный зал им. М. И. Глинки Смоленской государственной филармонии; ☑4812-32 984; www.smolensk-filarmonia.ru; ul Glinki 3; tickets from R400; ☉box office noon-7pm Tue-Sat, 1-6pm Sun) Attending a concert is the best way to get a look at the reconstructed hall where Mikhail Glinka once entertained Russian nobility and launched the history of secular classical music in Russia.

🔒 Shopping

Smolenskaya Izba
GIFTS & SOUVENIRS

(Художественная мастерская гончарного искусства-Смоленская Изба; ☑4812-407 404; www.km67.ru; ul Tukhachevskogo 5; ⊙10am-7pm) Not only does this great little place sell souvenirs and craftwork, the likes of which you won't find elsewhere, but it allows visitors to have a go at creating their own. Pottery, painting and doll-making workshops for groups and individuals are loads of fun: book before showing up.

Zadneprovsky Market
MARKET

(Заднепровский рынок; pl Kolkhoznaya; ⊙8am-6pm Tue-Sun, to 2pm Mon) Pick up fresh food and ogle the bustle at Smolensk's main market.

ℹ️ Information

Smolensk Travel
(☑4812-404 375; www.smolensk-travel.ru; ul Karl Marxa 12; ⊙10am-7pm Mon-Sat) The helpful staff here can assist with buying transport tickets and booking hotels. They also arrange English guided tours of the city and day trips in the region. English is spoken.

ℹ️ Getting There & Away

BUS

Buses to Moscow (from R700, six hours, nine daily) leave from outside the main train station and, less often, from the **bus station** (Автовокзал; ul Dzerzhinskogo). Other services include Pskov (R790, eight hours, two daily) and St Petersburg (from R1000, 10 to 14 hours, three daily).

TRAIN

From the **train station** (ul 12 let Oktyabrya) there are around 18 daily connections with Moscow (platskart/kupe from R977/2298, 5½ hours); trains to St Petersburg (R2215/2468, 15 hours) leave most days. International services run to Minsk, Warsaw, Prague and Vienna.

ℹ️ Getting Around

From the train and bus stations, you can take the bus, tram 4 (R17) or marshrutka 41 to the centre of town. Taxis to the centre cost around R150.

Tver
Тверь

☑4822 / POPULATION 408,852 / ⊙ MOSCOW

On the Volga, 150km northwest of Moscow, Tver dates back to the 12th century. After a fire levelled most of the town in 1763, the architect Pyotr Nikitin replanned Tver's centre on a three-ray system and built his patron, Catherine the Great, a 'road palace' to rest in on journeys between the then-Russian capital of St Petersburg and Moscow.

Picturesque 18th- and 19th-century townhouses and churches still line the main streets and riverbank, but the Soviet period was unkind to Tver. Not only was the town renamed Kalinin (after local Mikhail Kalinin, Stalin's puppet president during WWII), the authorities tore down the Cathedral of the Transfiguration of our Saviour in 1935 (one had stood on the same spot since the late 13th century) and converted the mosque into a cafe. The latter has since been returned to the Muslim community.

Tver is a good access point for historic Torzhok and Lake Seliger.

⊙ Sights & Activities

Art Gallery
GALLERY

(Тверская областная картинная галерея; ☑4822-342-561; www.gallery.tver.ru; ul Dmitry Donskoy 37; R100; ⊙11am-5pm Tue-Sun) This gallery is usually housed in Catherine the Great's 1775 Road Palace (which is being very slowly restored), but for now you'll find the collection in a less-imposing business centre just out of the town centre. There's a bit of everything here, from folk art and furniture to 14th-century icons and some impressive Soviet-era paintings.

Museum of Tver Life
MUSEUM

(Музей тверского быта; ☑4822-528 404; ul Gorkogo 19/14; R80; ⊙11am-5pm Wed-Sun) This museum is split across two adjacent houses: one is set up to display the life of wealthy merchants; the other (across the street in a crumbling building, entered around the back) has more general exhibits, including a reconstruction of a typical rural wooden dwelling, plus beautiful examples of embroidery and traditional costumes.

City Garden
PARK

(Городской сад; http://gorsad-tver.ru; ul Sovetskaya) On the grounds of what once was Tver's kremlin, this park has a **fun fair** (rides from R60) with a Ferris wheel and cafes, and often hosts live concerts on summer weekends. Part of the park lies on the north bank of the Volga, where a promenade provides lovely views of the old houses to the south. In summer, **excursion boats** (Экскурсионный причал; 45mins R250; ⊙11am-9pm) sail from the jetty.

Tver

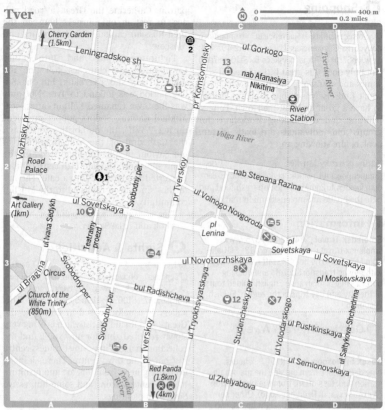

Tver

Church of the White Trinity CHURCH

(Церковь Белая Троица; pl Troitskaya) Amid a quaint neighbourhood of old wooden houses with carved eaves and window frames, west of the market on ul Bragina, you'll find Tver's oldest building, a stately stone church dating from 1564 that miraculously escaped the usual fate during the Soviet years. Women should cover their heads with a scarf before entering.

🛏 Sleeping

★ **Hostel Kalinin** HOSTEL $

(Хостел Калинин; ☎4822-609 060; www. kalininhostel.ru; ul Volnogo Novgoroda 19; dm from R500, d R1500; 🛜) Brightly painted rooms are comfortable and remarkably clean at this well-located hostel. Spacious dorms (mixed or female-only) come with lockers and individual lamps, and the fully equipped designer kitchen and common room are places you'll actually want to spend time. Reception is on hand 24/7. The entrance is tucked away at the rear, off the main street; best to call ahead.

★**Cherry Garden** HOTEL $$
(Вишневый сад; ☑ 4822-752 820; http://hotel-cherrygarden.ru; ul Chekhova 30; d from R2500; ❄️📶) What it lacks in central location, sweet Cherry Garden makes up for with everything else. Friendly staff go out of their way to help, there's a decent breakfast buffet and free wi-fi, and rooms are modern and comfortable; some have balconies and spa baths. It's a 10-minute taxi ride to the centre.

Hotel Volga HOTEL $$
(Гостиница Волга; ☑ 4822-348 123; www.volga-tver.ru; ul Zhelyabova 1; s/d from R3200/3800; 📶) Overlooking the Tmaka River, Hotel Volga is a good choice for friendly service and comfortable, if somewhat dated, rooms. Request a river-view room and note that standard rooms have no air-conditioning. There's a restaurant on the 2nd floor.

Gubernator Hotel HOTEL $$
(Отель Губернаторъ; ☑ 4822-579 909; www.gubernatorhotel.ru; ul Novotorzhskaya 15; s/d incl breakfast R3600/4000; 📶) This mega-central hotel is housed in a pure-white 18th-century building. The interior is equally attractive, with spacious, squeaky-clean rooms and friendly English-speaking staff. There's no lift but there is an attached restaurant (open 7am to 11pm).

✖️ Eating

★**Mamonts** EUROPEAN $$
(Мамонтс; ☑ 4822-415 107; http://mamonts-bar.com; ul Novotorzhskaya 18; mains R290-550; ⏱11am-midnight Sun-Thu, to 5am Fri & Sat) Mamonts is an elegantly hip spot where Tver's cool kids come to dine and sip cocktails before hitting the adjoining dance floor to DJs spinning tunes. The menu spans sushi, pastas, salads and a few Russian classics done with a twist and creatively presented. Service is friendly and unpretentious.

La Provincia INTERNATIONAL, RUSSIAN $$
(☑ 4822-631 031; http://laprovincia.fabula group.ru; bul Radishcheva 47; mains R380-730; ⏱noon-midnight) Hidden away in a quiet courtyard with an outdoor terrace, La Provincia is a cosy restaurant with comfy armchairs and lace-covered lamps. The menu offers Russian dishes – borsch, smoked fish

with sour cream – along with international cuisine, such as pasta carbonara, pork tenderloin and paella.

Manilov RUSSIAN $$
(Манилов; ☑ 4822-476 495; www.manilovkafe.ru; ul Sovetskaya 17; meals R130-400; ⏱10am-midnight Mon-Thu, to 11pm Sat & Sun) Step into a 19th-century-style parlour at this sweet restaurant with its entrance on Studenchesky per. Dig into traditional favourites such as borsch, *vareniki* (boiled dumplings) and chicken kiev, mop them up with homemade bread and sample the horseradish-flavoured spirit. Set lunches are available weekdays from noon to 3pm for R200.

🍷 Drinking & Nightlife

Red Panda CRAFT BEER
(Красная Панда; ☑ 4822-360 028; ul Sklizkova 44; ⏱4pm-midnight Sun-Thu, to 3am Fri & Sat; 📶) It might be a fair hike south from the town centre, but Red Panda is a great basement craft-beer bar with tasty food and a welcoming atmosphere. Ten Russian craft beers are on tap (0.5L from R180) plus there's good music, board games, pub grub, and indie films shown on Sunday nights. A taxi from the centre should cost around R180.

Mr Moose CRAFT BEER
(Мистер Лось; ☑ 4822-570 078; bul Radishcheva 33; ⏱noon-10pm) A tiny drink-in or takeaway craft-beer shop with around 15 Russian beers on tap (from R270) and a small selection of bottled beers. It's tucked away off the main street.

Citybar BAR
(ul Sovetskaya 14; ⏱8am-late Mon-Thu & Sun, to 6am Fri & Sat) With a ground-floor summer terrace and a mix of rooms and nooks on the second floor, this bar offers something for all tastes. Grab a velvet bar stool under the chandeliers and sip cocktails or opt for karaoke or catching a live band. DJs spin tunes on Friday and Saturday nights. Pizzas (R340 to R400) are available.

Kafe Vremya CAFE
(Кафе Время; nab Afanasiya Nikitina 36; ⏱2-11pm Mon-Thu, noon-midnight Fri-Sun) Set on the Volga River (opposite City Garden's Ferris wheel on the other side of the river) the popular Kafe Vremya (Cafe Time) is a great spot for a leisurely coffee and cake break, or a cold beer in summer, at the riverside outdoor tables. They also do meals.

Shopping

Beer Logic FOOD & DRINKS
(☑ 8-920-183 2451; https://vk.com/beerlogic; nab Afanasiya Nikitina 24; ☺ 3-10pm Mon, from noon Tue-Sun) Pop into this small takeaway shop by the river to get a plastic bottle filled with your choice of a range of Russian craft beer on tap (1L from R180). It also has a selection of bottled beers from around the globe. Though the riverside tempts, note that public drinking is not permitted.

ℹ Getting There & Away

The **train station** (ul Kominterna) is 4km south of the centre, with the **bus station** (ul Kominterna) 400m to its east. Cruise ships and other long-distance riverboats dock at the **river station** (Речной вокзал) on the north shore of the Volga.

Elektrichki (R370, three hours) stopping at Tver leave roughly every two hours from Moscow's Leningradsky station. Long-distance trains between Moscow and St Petersburg and between Moscow and Pskov also pause at Tver.

There are also buses (R456, three hours) to/from Moscow's Yaroslavsky and Leningradsky stations.

ℹ Getting Around

Tram 5 and *marshrutky* 3, 22 and 4 (R20) run from the bus and train stations up pr Chaykovskogo and pr Tverskoy to the town centre.

Torzhok Торжок

☑ 4822 / POPULATION 46, 700 / ☺ MOSCOW

Hugging the Tvertsa River, the church spire and domed skyline of Torzhok (Торжок) seems straight out of a Russian fairy tale. An easy day trip from Tver, or a pit stop en route to Ostashkov, Torzhok was once on the main road from St Petersburg to Moscow. Pushkin passed through several times on his travels.

☉ Sights

All-Russian Museum
of History and Ethnography MUSEUM
(Всероссийский историко-этнографический музей; www.viemusei.ru; ul Bakunina 6; adult/student R150/100; ☺ 10am-6pm Wed-Sun) Worthwhile museum covering the history of the region with some great dioramas of a living room and a picnic in a forest. Other displays include frescoes, religious relics and archaeological finds from the Upper Volga region.

Borisoglebsky Monastery MONASTERY
(Борисоглебский мужской монастырь; ul Staritskaya 7; bell tower R100, museum R50-150, grounds free; ☺ 10am-6pm) The oldest monastery complex in Tver Oblast still bustles with religious activity; visitors and pilgrims are welcome. The adjoining museum has exhibits on the history of the monastery

---

OFF THE BEATEN TRACK

OSTASHKOV & LAKE SELIGER

Ostashkov (Осташков и Озеро Селигер), 199km west of Tver, is the main base for exploring the lakes, waterways and islands around Lake Seliger. The resort town, sitting on a peninsula at the southern end of the lake, is a jumble of tumbledown wooden cottages, decaying Soviet-era apartment blocks and artfully crumbling churches, some of which are under repair.

The lake itself is delightful, best appreciated on a **boat excursion** (☑ 48235-51 568; www.seligerkruiz.ru; Leninsky pr 41; 3-5hr cruises adult/child from R700/400; ☺ Jun-Sep). Alternatively, relax by wandering along the town's promenades, lounging on the beaches, swimming in Seliger's clear, clean waters and climbing the bell tower of the handsome Trinity Cathedral, now the **regional museum** (☑ 48235-51 024; ul Volodarskogo 19; R50-80; ☺ 11am-5pm Wed-Sun), for a brilliant view of the surroundings.

There are several options along the lakefront with lovely views, of which **Orlovskaya Dom 1** (Орловская Дом 1; ☑ 8-910-830 0515; www.orlovskaja.ru; per Chaikin Bereg; r from R2000) is the standout. It's also possible to camp at the tip of the peninsula that juts out north of Ostashkov's monastery. Visit www.ostashkov.ru/rest for a list of options (in Russian), including lakeside cottages outside town.

Buses and minibuses (from R492, 4½ hours, 14 daily) connect Ostashkov with Tver; the buses run via Torzhok (R250, 2½ hours). Minibuses also head to and from Moscow (R730, six hours, at least three daily). While there's a train station in Ostashkov, there are no direct trains from Moscow, so buses are your best option to get here.

and Torzhok. You can climb to the top of the bell tower in summer for fine views of the city.

Archangel Michael   CHURCH

(Михайло-Архангельский храм; ⊙9am-5pm Mon-Fri, to 7pm Sat & Sun) Perched on a hill near the Borisoglebsky Monastery, this sky-blue-domed beauty has a stunningly decorated interior.

AS Pushkin Museum   MUSEUM

(Музей Пушкина; ul Dzerzhinskogo 71; R80; ⊙11am-5pm Wed-Sun) Housed in a grey-painted 18th-century wooden building, this museum contains various exhibits relating to Russia's ubiquitous Pushkin. On display you'll find antique furniture, clothing, books, doodles by the great man himself that evoke local 19th-century scenes, and replica drafts of his poems.

Goldwork Embroidery
Museum and Factory   MUSEUM

(Музей фабрики Торжокские золотошвеи; www.zolotoshveya.com; Kalinin sh 12; adult/child R80/20; ⊙9am-5pm Mon-Sat, to 3pm Sun) Torzhok is famous for its stunning gold-wire embroidery, found in artwork, insignia and royal clothing. There are exquisite displays at this museum, including Russian fashion over the years and embroidery of Stalin and the USSR; the attached shop sells superb crafts and clothing made on the premises.

🍽 Sleeping & Eating

Onix Hotel   HOTEL $$

(⊉4822-614 141; www.onix-hotels.ru/torzhok; ul Mednikovykh 4; s/d incl breakfast from R2000/2450; ✴🅿🛜) A short walk from the Borisoglebsky Monastery stands this welcoming hotel in a cream 18th-century building with neat and comfortable rooms. The helpful staff speak some English and there is a small exhibition in the lobby of archaeological artifacts found on the site. The attached restaurant (mains R250-650; ⊙8am-11pm) is a great spot for a meal.

Lira Cafe   CAFE $

(ul Dzerzhinskog 73; meals from R100; ⊙10am-8pm; 🛜) Lira is set in a lovely riverside park right by the Pushkin Museum, with white garden furniture scattered around in front. Light meals and snacks are on offer – it's known for its Pozharsky cutlet – along with the usual tea and coffee.

🛈 Getting There & Away

Buses connect Torzhok with Tver (R150, 1¾ hours, three to four per hour), as well as with Ostashkov.

Veliky Novgorod
Великий Новгород

⊉8162 / POPULATION MOSCOW / ⊙ MOSCOW

Veliky Novgorod (usually shortened to Novgorod) is a proud and beautiful city, billed as the 'Birthplace of Russia', and the most popular town in the Western European Russia region. It was here, in 862, that Prince Rurik proclaimed the modern Russian state – the Rurik dynasty went on to rule Russia for more than 750 years. The ancient settlement was a major centre for trade, literacy, democracy and the spread of Orthodoxy; its glorious Cathedral of St Sophia is the oldest church in Russia. Straddling the Volkhov River, this attractive, tourist-friendly destination is a popular weekend getaway for St Petersburg residents – to avoid the crowds, come during the week. Novgorod is also a good base for visiting Staraya Russa, Dostoevsky's hometown.

History

Much of Novgorod's early history is known through Norse sagas, as this was the first permanent settlement of the Varangian Norsemen who established the embryonic Russian state. By the 12th century the city was Russia's biggest: an independent quasi-democracy whose princes were hired and fired by an assembly of citizens, and whose strong, spare style of church architecture, icon painting and down-to-earth *byliny* (epic folk songs) would become distinct idioms.

Spared from the Mongol Tatars, who got bogged down in the surrounding swamps, Novgorod suffered most at the hands of other Russians: Ivan III of Moscow attacked and annexed it in 1477, and Ivan the Terrible's storm-troopers razed the city and slaughtered 60,000 people in a savage pogrom. The founding of St Petersburg finished it off as a trading centre.

🅞 Sights

There are scores of old churches and monasteries around town. The helpful tourist office (p263) can provide details of which ones are open either as museums or for services.

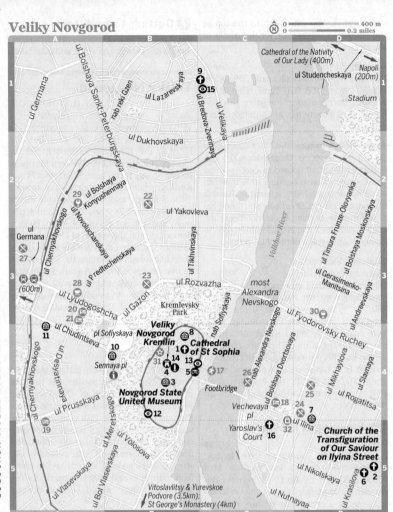

◎ Kremlin

On the west bank of the Volkhov River, and surrounded by a pleasant wooded park, the **kremlin** (◎6am-midnight) **FREE** is one of Russia's oldest. Originally called the Detinets (and still often referred to as such), the fortification dates to the 9th century, and was rebuilt with brick in the 14th century; this still stands today. The complex is worth seeing with a guide; arrange one through the tourist office. You can walk part of the **kremlin walls** (◎10am-2pm & 3-6pm Mon, Tue & Thu, to 8pm Fri-Sun) for views over

the complex and the city. **Boat tours** (1hr tour R500; ◎10am-9pm May-Oct) operate from the kremlin's pier.

★ **Cathedral of St Sophia**   CATHEDRAL
(Софийский собор; www.saintsofianovg.or-tox.ru; ◎8am-8pm, services 10am-noon daily & 6-8pm Tue, Wed & Fri-Sun) This is the oldest church in Russia (finished in 1050) and one of the country's oldest stone buildings. It's the kremlin's focal point and you couldn't miss it if you tried – its golden dome positively glows. St Sophia houses many icons dating from the 14th century, but none are

Veliky Novgorod

WESTERN EUROPEAN RUSSIA NOVGOROD

as important as that of Novgorod's patron saint, Our Lady of the Sign, which, the story goes, miraculously saved the city from destruction in 1170 after being struck by an arrow.

★ Novgorod State United Museum MUSEUM

(Новгородский государственный объединенный музей-заповедник; www.novgorodmuseum.ru; Kremlin 11; adult/student R200/150; ⏱10am-6pm Wed-Mon, closed last Thu of the month) Within the kremlin walls is this must-see museum that houses three strikingly comprehensive exhibitions covering the history of Veliky Novgorod, Russian woodcarving and Russian icons. The latter contains one of the world's largest collections of icons, with around 260 pieces placed in chronological order, allowing you to appreciate the progression of skills and techniques through the centuries. The English audio guide (R200) is recommended if you want to get the most out of a visit.

Downstairs in the history section (with minimal English signage), birch-bark manuscripts are displayed, some of them 800 years old. The letters, documents and drawings by people of all ages and social classes indicate that literacy was widespread in medieval Novgorod.

The woodcarving exhibits include everything from the mundane (kitchen utensils and furniture) to more elaborate religious objects.

Millennium of Russia Monument MONUMENT

(Памятник Тысячелетию России) This gargantuan 16m-high, 100-tonne sculpture was unveiled in 1862 on the 1000th anniversary of the Varangian Prince Rurik's arrival, a moment heralded as the start of Russian history. It depicts 127 figures captured in heavy bronze, including rulers, statesmen, artists, scholars and a few fortunate hangers-on.

The women at the top are Mother Russia and the Russian Orthodox Church. Around the middle, clockwise from the south, are Rurik, Prince Vladimir of Kyiv (who introduced Christianity), tsars Mikhail Romanov, Peter the Great and Ivan III, and Dmitry Donskoy trampling a Mongol Tatar. In the bottom band on the east side are nobles and rulers, including Catherine the Great with an armload of laurels for all her lovers. Alexander Nevsky and other military heroes are on the north side, and literary and artistic figures are on the west.

Belfry
NOTABLE BUILDING

(Звонница Софийского собора; adult/child R200/150; ☉10am-2pm & 3-6pm Thu-Tue Apr-Oct) The belfry, with its enormous steel bells, has a small bell museum and an observation platform providing good photo opps of the Cathedral of St Sophia (p258) on one side and fine views across the beach and river on the other. You can combine a visit with the kremlin wall walk (p258; combo ticket adult/child R300/150), though views are arguably good enough from the belfry.

Kokui Tower
NOTABLE BUILDING

(Башня Кокуй; adult/student R200/150; ☉noon-2.30pm & 3.30-8pm Tue, Wed & Fri-Sun Jun-Oct, closed last Wed of the month) The 41m-tall Kokui Tower was built in the 18th century, and a climb up its narrow stairs provides panoramic views across the kremlin complex and the city. It was closed indefinitely at the time of research as it was undergoing restoration.

Chamber of Facets
HISTORIC BUILDING

(Грановитая палата; adult/student R200/150) Part of a palace built in 1433, this Gothic chamber once housed Novgorod's Supreme Court and was the scene of many ceremonies and soirées, not all of them pleasant. Ivan the Terrible reputedly slaughtered tablefuls of noble guests right here, wrongly believing they were plotting against him. These days, you'll find religious artefacts, some fine ancient craftwork, and frescoes. The gorgeous interior, recently renovated, is worth the admission price alone.

◉ Yaroslavl's Court

Across a footbridge from the kremlin are the photogenic remnants of the 18th-century market arcade Yaroslavl's Court (Ярославово дворище). Beyond that is the market gatehouse, an array of churches sponsored by 13th-to-16th-century merchant guilds, and a 'road palace' built in the 18th century as a rest stop for Catherine the Great.

The 12th-century Kyiv-style **St Nicholas Cathedral** (Собор Святого Николая; adult/student R150/100; ☉10am-6pm Tue, Wed & Fri-Sun, closed last Fri of the month) is all that remains of the early palace complex of the Novgorod princes, from which Yaroslav's Court gets its name. Inside are church artefacts and temporary exhibitions of local interest. Downstairs you can see fragments from the church's original frescoes.

◉ Other Sights

★ Church of the Transfiguration of Our Saviour on Ilyina Street
CHURCH

(Церковь Преображения Господня Спасителя на улице Ильина; ul Ilina; adult/student R180/110; ☉10am-5pm Wed-Sun) This compact church is famous for housing the only surviving frescoes by legendary Byzantine painter Theophanes the Greek (1378) – they came close to extinction when the church served as a Nazi machine-gun nest. Restoration has exposed as much of the frescoes as possible, though they are still faint, and a small exhibit upstairs includes reproductions with explanations in Russian. The church closes on the last Thursday of the month and in wet weather.

Cathedral of Our Lady of the Sign
CATHEDRAL

(Знаменский собор; adult/student R150/100; ☉10am-5pm Thu-Mon, closed 1st Thu of the month) While the outside of this 17th-century Moscow-style complex has seen better days, the interior is festooned with frescoes painted by masters from Kostroma in the Golden Ring. The cathedral occasionally hosts choral concerts.

Centre of Musical Antiquities
MUSEUM

(Центр музыкальных древностей; ☎8162-635 019; www.centrpovetkina.ru; ul Ilina 9b; R200; ☉2-4pm Tue-Sun) This small but lovingly maintained museum houses a wonderful collection of traditional folk-music instruments specific to Novgorod and around, including replicas of instruments dating back to the 10th to 15th centuries and found during excavations. The centre hosts performances on weekends. To find it, follow ul Ilina away from the river and turn left into ul Mikhaylova and first left.

Fine Arts Museum
MUSEUM

(Музей изобразительных искусств; www.artmus.natm.ru; pl Sofiykaya 2; adult/student R300/150; ☉10am-6pm Tue, Wed & Fri-Sun, 1-9pm Thu, closed last Wed of the month) A strong provincial collection of paintings by 18th- and 19th-century Russian artists, as well as temporary shows. The 3rd floor features Novgorod artists.

Hall of Military Glory
MUSEUM

(Зал воинской славы; ul Chudintseva 11/62; R70; ☉10am-1pm & 2-5pm Tue-Sat) Novgorod boasts status as a City of Military Glory and has the museum to prove it. Wax statues and

WORTH A TRIP

ST GEORGE'S MONASTERY & VITOSLAVLITSY

Set amid peaceful marsh and lakelands a 15-minute bus ride south of the Veliky Novgorod town centre, these two sights make for a great excursion. Founded in 1030 by Yaroslav the Wise, the picturesque **St George's Monastery** (Свято-Юрьев мужской монастырь; www.georg.orthodoxy.ru; ⌚10am-8pm) FREE functions as a theological school. It features the heavily reconstructed **Cathedral of St George** and a clutch of 19th-century add-ons.

About 600m up the road **Vitoslavlitsy** (Витославлицы; www.novgorodmuseum.ru; adult/student R200/150; ⌚10am-8pm May-Aug, to 6pm Apr & Sep, to 5pm Oct-Mar) is an evocative open-air museum of 22 beautiful wooden peasant houses and churches, some dating back to the 16th century, and the highlight being the soaring **Church of the Nativity of Our Lady** (1531). What makes these buildings all the more remarkable is that they were all constructed without nails. There's a cafe on the grounds, plus a good souvenir shop and craft sellers.

Opposite Vitoslavlitsy is Yurevskoe Podvore (p262) a 16-room rustic log-cabin-style hotel. The restaurant prepares traditional Russian meals (R600 to R1000).

Catch bus 7 or 7A (R22 one way), which depart on the opposite side of the road from the tourist office.

bas-reliefs tell the stories of the city's heroism from ancient Rus to modern times.

Novgorod Regional Folk Arts Centre ARTS CENTRE
(Новгородский областной Дом народного творчества; ☎8162-739 626; www.dnt-folk.ru; ul Bredova-Zverinaya 14; ⌚9am-1pm & 1.30-5.30pm) You can participate in two-hour workshops (in Russian only) on producing Russian crafts at this arts centre on the grounds of the former 15th-century Zverin Monastery (Зверин-Покровский монастырь); book ahead at the tourist office (p263). There's also a small craft shop on-site.

Also on the monastery grounds is the tiny **Church of St Simeon** (Церковь Симеона Богоприимца; ul Bredova-Zverinaya; adult/student R150/100; ⌚10am-5pm Sat-Wed, closed 1st Mon of the month). The arts centre is on the right as you approach the grounds, and the church is around the corner past the military base.

Cathedral of the Nativity of Our Lady CHURCH
(Собор Рождества Богородицы Антониева монастыря; ul Studencheskaya; adult/student R150/100; ⌚10am-5pm Wed-Sun, closed 1st Wed of the month) Legend has it that St Anthony took just three days to sail down Europe's rivers from Italy to Novgorod on a rock in 1106. You can view the supposed boulder, which apparently has healing properties, at the entrance to this church on the grounds of the Antoniev Monastery.

Festivals & Events

See www.visitnovgorod.ru for a full list of annual events.

City Day CULTURAL
Concerts, processions and fairs celebrate the city's birthday during the second weekend in June.

Sadko Festival CULTURAL
Held over the second weekend of June, this celebration includes both Russian and international teams performing traditional folk art, dancing and singing. There's also a craft fair.

Kupala CULTURAL
Held on the banks of Lake Ilmen in early July, this traditional St John's Day celebration combines old pagan rites with Orthodox rituals. Events include music, dance, food and swimming in the lake.

Sleeping

Hostel Cruise Bolshaya Yel HOSTEL $
(Хостел Круиз – Большая Ель; ☎8162-772 283; www.cruisehotel.ru; ul Prusskaya 11; dm R600, d with/without private bathroom from R1500/1200; 📶) If you're looking for a hostel with bells and whistles, keep moving: this ain't your typical backpacker hang-out. Instead, expect a typically Soviet-style institutional set-up, but one that remains a decent, well-priced and clean budget option with an excellent location a brief stroll from the kremlin.

★ **Hotel Volkhov**　　　　　HOTEL **$$**
(Гостиница Волхов; ☎8162-225 500; www.
hotel-volkhov.ru; ul Predtechenskaya 24; s/d incl
breakfast from R2500/3700; @ 🖥) This cen-
trally located, modern hotel runs like a well-
oiled machine, with nicely furnished rooms,
pleasant English-speaking staff, laundry ser-
vice and free wi-fi. A sauna (from R800) is
available to guests. The breakfasts, offering a
choice of Continental, Russian or 'American',
are actually very good. There's an elegant
5th-floor bar-bistro overlooking the square
and a buzzing lobby cafe.

Hanza　　　　　HOTEL **$$**
(Отель Hanza; ☎8162-535 300; ul Dvortsovaya 1;
d from R2500 incl breakfast; ✳ 🖥) Hanza offers
functional and comfortable rooms in a quiet
yet central location near the river.

Hotel Akron　　　　　HOTEL **$$**
(Гостиница Акрон; ☎8162-736 908; www.
hotel-acron.ru; ul Predtechenskaya 24; s/d from
R2250/2800; 🖥) In a handy central location
close to the kremlin and the bus and train
stations, the Akron offers comfortable Soviet-
era rooms with modern bathroom, TV, wi-fi
and mini-fridge. Service is friendly and there's
an on-site cafe. Note: there is no lift.

Hotel Sadko　　　　　HOTEL **$$**
(Садко; ☎8162-663 004; www.hotel-sadko.ru;
ul Fyodorovsky Ruchey 16; s/d incl breakfast from
R2200/3200; 🖥) Though it's in a quiet part
of town, the Sadko – offering pleasant rooms
with mini-fridges – is within walking distance of Novgorod's major attractions. It has
an attached restaurant.

Yurevskoe Podvore　　　　　HOTEL **$$**
(Юрьевское Подворье; ☎8162-946 060; www.
tk-podvorie.ru; Yurevskoe sh 6a; d incl breakfast
from R3700; ✳ 🖥) Handy for the Vitoslavlitsy
(p261) museum, this rustic log-cabin-style
hotel has 16 charming rooms with a few
stuffed animals hanging around. The res-
taurant prepares traditional Russian meals
(R600 to R1000).

✕ Eating

Kolobok　　　　　CAFETERIA **$**
(Колобок; ul Bolshaya Moskovskaya 28; piroshki
& pastries from R30; ⏲8am-2pm & 2.30-8pm) A
Novgorodian institution, this Soviet throw-
back is no retro homage – this is the real
deal, with a communal coffee tank (for the
sweet-toothed only), trillion-kilojoule salads
and cheap, super-fresh pastries right from

the oven. The daily onslaught of students
and locals gives some clue as to this place's
popularity.

★ **Zavod Bar**　　　　　RUSSIAN **$$**
(☎8162-683 186; www.alkon.su; ul Germana 2;
mains R270-560; ⏲noon-midnight, to 2am Fri &
Sat; 🖥) Attached to the Alkon Distillery,
Zavod is a chic and cosy restaurant with
exposed brick, an open fire and great food.
Go for the homemade *pelmeni* filled with
fish and meats, or a sweeter strawberry and
cottage cheese option. Pair your meal with a
tasting set of the distillery's vodka or cranberry *nastoyka* (liqueur; three shots from
R390), which comes with a plate of vodka
snacks.

★ **Dom Berga**　　　　　RUSSIAN **$$**
(Дом Берга; ☎8162-948 838; www.domberga.
ru; ul Bolshaya Moskovskaya 24; cafe/restaurant
meals from R120/520; ⏲cafe 9am-9pm, restau-
rant noon-midnight) Enjoy expertly prepared
Russian dishes in this 19th-century former
merchant's home, with a choice between a
simple cafe out the back or a fancier res-
taurant in front. Be sure to try the honey
mead.

Na Korme　　　　　RUSSIAN **$$**
(На Корме; www.fregatflagman.ru; nab Aleksandra
Nevskogo, 22/1; meals R300-1300; ⏲noon-mid-
night Mon-Thu & Sun, to 2am Fri & Sat; 🖥) While
the idea of an old merchant's ship turned
restaurant on the river might seem a little
kitsch, Na Korme offers great views of the
kremlin dished up with Russian classics,
game meat (including moose bangers and
mash) and, of course, the obligatory pizza
and sushi options.

Derzhavny　　　　　RUSSIAN **$$**
(Державный; ☎8162-773 023; ul Gazon 5/2;
meals R180-550; ⏲10am-11pm Mon-Fri, noon-
2am Sat, noon-11pm Sun) Nudging up against
the kremlin complex, this cavernous place
evokes ye olde Novgorod, with faux fres-
coes on the ceiling and artefacts on the
walls. The menu is heavy on hearty Rus-
sian cuisine (*pelmeni*, bliny, soups) and
includes plenty of beautifully prepared
game meats; wild boar and bear feature. As
Derzhavny takes the slow-cooking concept
very literally: be prepared to wait for your
order at times.

Cafe Asia　　　　　INTERNATIONAL **$$**
(Кафе Азия; ☎8162-772 227; ul Yakovleva 22/1;
meals R220-800; ⏲noon-midnight) Japanese,

Uzbek and Russian cuisine, together at last! If miso soup, chicken pilaf and Russian salad combos sound like they'd float your boat, this place – with a decor that's part Russian-staid, part bellydancer-a-go-go – is for you. It all comes together nicely somehow, and Asia is a popular hang-out. Business lunches (noon to 4pm weekdays) are R210, and there is a helpful picture menu.

Napoli ITALIAN $$
(Наполи; ☑ 8162-603 095; www.napoli-restaurant.ru; ul Studencheskaya 21/43; mains R410-790, pizza 380-670; ⊘ noon-midnight; 🛜) A cosy and rustic Italian restaurant, Napoli bakes its pizzas in a brick oven and serves tasty delicacies such as veal osso bucco and a risotto with porcini and truffle oil.

🍷 Drinking & Nightlife

★ Samovar CRAFT BEER
(ul Fyodorovsky Ruchey 9/17; ⊘ 6-11pm Mon-Thu, to midnight Fri & Sat, 4-11pm Sun) Cool bohemian Samovar is a great spot to hang out, with an all-welcome atmosphere, good vinyl spinning, art on the red-painted walls and a range of Russian craft beer on tap.

Pivovarov BAR
(Пивоваровъ; ☑ 8162-607 477; ul Novoluchanskaya 26; ⊘ 1pm-1am; 🛜) Those seeking out local experiences – combined with cheap beer – should find this tiny dive-bar set in a residential apartment block. There's a number of local lagers on tap (from R65 for 500mL), which you can drink while watching local telly. There's also a range of smoked fish, meats and nuts to snack on.

All Ready CAFE
(☑ 8162-601 271; ul Lyudogoshcha 10; ⊘ 11am-midnight; 🛜) All Ready is a bright contemporary cafe with pot plants and comfy cushioned booths. Centrally located, it's a handy spot for a coffee or cocktail break. It also does light snacks and meals (pastas, burgers, salads and so on) from R90 to R320.

☆ Entertainment

Concert Hall CLASSICAL MUSIC
(Концертный зал Новгородской филармонии; ☑ 8162-772 777; http://philnov.ru; Kremlin 8; tickets from R200) Veliky Novgorod's Philharmonic Concert Hall often hosts live classical and popular music concerts; check the website for the schedule and ticket prices.

🛍 Shopping

Alkon Distillery FOOD & DRINKS
(www.alkon.su; ul Germana 2; ⊘ 10am-9pm) The Alkon distillery has been in operation for over 100 years, producing a range of infused vodka (honey, thyme, rosemary) and high-quality sadko vodka, along with traditional nastoyka cranberry liqueur. Pick up a couple of bottles here at their small shop (from R120). The website has info in English and there is an English handout in-store.

Na Torgu GIFTS & SOUVENIRS
(На Торгу; ☑ 8162-664 472; ul Ilina 2; ⊘ 10am-8pm) Small store selling Novgorod's best selection of local arts and craft souvenirs, including woolen hats, jewellery and *matryoshki*. It has an art gallery upstairs.

ℹ Information

Tourist Office (Туристский информационный центр-Красная Изба; ☑ 8162-773 074; www.visitnovgorod.ru; Sennaya pl 5; ⊘ 9.30am-6pm) One of the best tourist information centres in the country, this friendly English-speaking office provides helpful maps and local advice. City tours – on foot or bicycle – and excursions tailored to specific interests can be arranged. It even has a **24-hour tourist helpline** (☑ 8162-998 686). The comprehensive website is in English and other languages.

ℹ Getting There & Away

BUS
The **bus station** (Автовокзал; ul Oktyabryaskaya) is 1.5km northwest of the kremlin.

Bus services include St Petersburg (R330, four hours, frequent), Pskov (R580, 4½ hours, 8am and 4pm) and Staraya Russa (R200, 1¾ hours, frequent).

TRAIN
The **train station** (Новгород-на-Волхове; ul Oktyabryaskaya) is next to the bus station.

Elektrichki (suburban trains) run to St Petersburg's Moscow Station (R400, three hours, two daily). There's also a handy overnight train to Moscow (*platskart/kupe* R1622/2161, eight hours) leaving at 9.20pm, as well as a faster Moscow train (five hours, two daily) with a connection in Chudovo.

ℹ Getting Around

Buses 7 and 7A run from the bus and train stations to the kremlin and town centre; otherwise it's a 15-minute walk.

Staraya Russa Старая Русса

☑ 81652 / POPULATION 31,809 / ⊙ MOSCOW

Set along the tranquil Polist River, Staraya Russa retains the idyllic charm of the 19th century, when Dostoevsky wrote much of *The Brothers Karamazov* here. The town is the setting for the novel – visit the streets and churches the characters frequented and the home of Dostoevsky himself. There's also a handful of museums worth checking out.

The town, 100km southeast of Veliky Novgorod, can easily be visited for the day.

⊙ Sights

★ Dostoevsky House Museum MUSEUM

(Дом-музей Ф. М. Достоевского; ☑ 81652-21 477; http://russa.novgorod.ru/russa/fmdost.php; ul Dostoevskogo 42; adult/student R180/110; ⊙ 10am-6pm Tue-Sun, closed last Thu of the month) The author's family lived on the 1st floor of this riverside dacha, which contains many original pieces. Dostoevsky's bookcase is still stocked, and his desk has replicas from his mazelike drafts – you can see his doodles on the pages. An English-language handout available at the ticket office details the collection.

Kartinnaya Gallery GALLERY

(Картинная Галерея; pl Timura Frunze; adult/student R180/110; ⊙ 10am-5pm Wed-Mon) On the grounds of a 12th-century monastery, this gallery houses a noteworthy selection of paintings and sculptures by artists who spent time in Staraya Russa. The 1st floor is dedicated to works by well-known Soviet-era painter Vasily Svarog, while the ground floor has sculptures by Tomsky, including one of Lenin as a child.

Resurrection Cathedral CATHEDRAL

(Воскресенский собор; ul Vozrozhdeniya 1; ⊙ 7am-7pm) Sitting on the banks of the Polist River is this gorgeously restored 17th-century cathedral painted in red.

Church of the Holy Martyr Mina CHURCH

(Церковь святого великомученика Мины; ul Georgievskaya 44) If you like your churches photogenically abandoned, this one's for you. Legend has it that in the 17th century, Swedish invaders sought refuge in the church after a long day of looting and pillaging, only to be struck blind upon crossing the threshold. They were sent back to Sweden as proof of the miracles of Russian Orthodoxy.

Regional Museum MUSEUM

(Старорусский краеведческий музей; pl Timura Frunze; adult/student R100/60; ⊙ 10am-6pm Wed-Mon) Housed in an attractive white-washed 12th-century monastery, this museum offers the usual historical displays and religious relics, including some interesting religious etchings on bark, as well as artefacts from the area. You can also see fragments from the church's original frescoes dating to the 15th century.

Dostoevsky Cultural Centre ARTS CENTRE

(Научно-культурный центр Достоевского; ☑ 81652-37 285; ul Dostoevskogo 8; adult/student R180/110; ⊙ 10am-6pm Tue-Fri & Sun) This handsome little neoclassical building hosts temporary Dostoevsky-centric exhibitions, as well as exhibitions of Russian artists, and events dedicated to Russian writers.

🛏 Sleeping & Eating

Hotel Polist HOTEL $$

(Гостиница Полисть; ☑ 81652-37 547; www.hotel-polist.ru; ul Gostinodvorskaya 20; s/d incl breakfast from R1700/2400; ☎) This well-maintained hotel is a solid option with functional, basic rooms. It also houses a decent restaurant that passes for fancy around these parts.

★ Amaks Staraya Russa SPA HOTEL $$$

(Отель Старая Русса; ☑ 81652-57 888; www.russa.amaks-kurort.ru; ul Mineralnaya 62; s/d incl breakfast from R3000/4900; ☎ ⛱) A throwback to the town's heyday as a popular spa destination, this huge complex offers treatments, therapies and procedures for whatever ails you. There are loads of indulgent options, including massages and saunas. It's also great fun for kids. Comfortable rooms, an indoor pool and on-site restaurant round out the deal.

Cafe-Bar Bashnya RUSSIAN, EUROPEAN $$

(Кафе-бар БАШНЯ; ul Gostinodvorskaya 2; mains R250-650; ⊙ noon-midnight Mon-Thu & Sun, to 1am Fri & Sat; ☎) With a menu catering to all tastes and a central-square location, Bashnya is a good choice for lunch and coffee while sightseeing in Staraya Russa. Choose from Russian classics, European fare and, of course, the ever-present pizza and sushi options.

ⓘ Information

Tourist Information (☑ 81652-52 977; www.visitrussa.ru; ul Lenina 6; ⊙ 9am-7pm Mon-Fri, 10am-4pm Sat; ☎) No English is spoken but the staff here are friendly and helpful and there is an English brochure on the town. Also has a map of the town and free wi-fi.

ℹ Getting There & Away

BUS

There are regular buses to/from Veliky Novgorod (R230, 1½ hours). Travelling to Novgorod, tickets tend to sell out fast, so it's best to buy your ticket when you arrive in Staraya Russa. There are at least six daily buses to/from St Petersburg (from R370, 3½ hours).

TRAIN

The train station, next to the bus station, is on the route between Pskov (*platskart/kupe* R1279/1828, 3½ hours, one night bus) and Moscow (*platskart/kupe* R2006/2957, 7½ hours, one night bus); services are at inconvenient hours. There are no direct trains to or from St Petersburg.

ℹ Getting Around

From the bus station (next to the train station), you can either catch a taxi (R100) to Dostoevsky's old home or take a 40-minute walk. Head under the road bridge, cross the tracks, then continue along ul Karla Libknekhta until you hit the river. Cross it, turn right off the bridge and follow the riverside path south to the museum.

Pskov   Псков

☑ 8112 / POPULATION 206,730 / ⏱ MOSCOW

Only 30km from the Estonia border, church-studded Pskov is dominated by its mighty riverside kremlin, an enormous bulwark that has faced up to its fair share of invading armies down the centuries. Leafy lanes and parks wriggle their way round the attractive old quarter on the east bank, past weathered churches, city-wall ruins and handsome 19th-century brick residences.

Day trips include the old fortress and beautiful countryside at Stary Izborsk, the Technicolor church and spooky cave necropolis at Pechory, and Mikhailovskoe, the family estate and last resting place of Alexander Pushkin in Pushkinskie Gory.

History

Pskov's history is saturated with 700 years of war for control of the Baltic coast. It was first mentioned in early Russian chronicles in 903 when Prince Igor of Kyiv married the future saint Olga of Pskov. Teutonic Knights captured the town in 1240, but Alexander Nevsky routed them two years later in a famous battle on the ice of Lake Peipsi.

In the 14th century, like Veliky Novgorod, Pskov was its own sovereign republic and a member of the Hanseatic League. The Poles laid siege in the 16th century and the Swedes did likewise the following century. Peter the Great used Pskov as a base for his drive to the sea, Nicholas II abdicated at its train station and the Red Army fought its first serious battle against Nazi troops outside the city.

◉ Sights

★ **Cathedral of the Transfiguration of the Saviour**   CATHEDRAL
(Спасо-Преображенский Собор Мирожского монастыря; ☑ 8112-567 301; Spaso-Preobrazhensky Sobor, Mirozhsky Monastery; adult/student R200/150, tours R900; ⏱ 11am-5.30pm Tue-Sun) The Unesco-protected, nonworking Cathedral of the Transfiguration of the Saviour is the highlight of the **Mirozhsky Monastery** (Мирожский монастырь; ☑ 8112-576 403; www.mirozhsky-monastery.ru; nab Mirozhskaya 2; ⏱ 11am-5pm Tue-Sun, closed last Tue of the month). Its 12th-century frescos are considered to be one of the most complete representations of the biblical narrative to have survived the Mongols. The Byzantine-style frescos have been partially restored after centuries of damage from flooding, whitewashing and scrubbing; 80% of what you see today is original.

The cathedral was based on a 12th-century Greek model, formed around a symmetrical cross – you can still see traces of the original structure along exterior walls. The church closes often due to inclement weather – too hot, too cold or too wet – so it's best to call in advance.

★ **Pskov National Museum of History, Architecture & Art**   MUSEUM
(Псковский государственный объединённый историко-архитектурный и художественный музей-заповедник; ☑ 8112-663 311; www.muse-ums.pskov.ru; ul Nekrasova 7; Pogankin Chambers R250, art & history galleries R150; ⏱ 11am-6pm Tue-Sun, closed last Tue of the month) As you can guess from its name, this museum, spread over several buildings, includes history and art exhibitions. The architecture bit comes from the museum's key sight outside – the **Pogankin Chambers** (Поганкины палаты), the fortress-like house and treasury of a 17th-century merchant. Art from local

Pskov

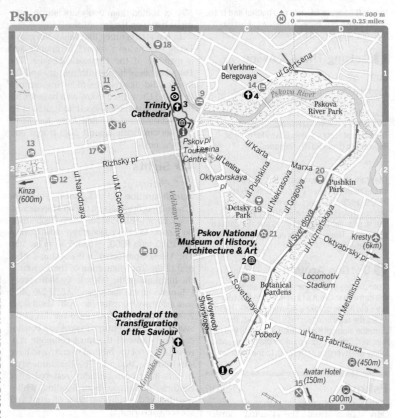

Pskov

◎ Top Sights

1 Cathedral of the Transfiguration	
of the Saviour	B4
2 Pskov National Museum of	
History, Architecture & Art	C3
3 Trinity Cathedral	B1

◎ Sights

Dovmont Town	(see 7)
4 Epiphany Church of Zapskovie	C1
5 Kremlin	B1
Mirozhsky Monastery	(see 1)
6 Pokrovskaya Bashnya	C4
7 Writ Chamber	B2

🛏 Sleeping

8 Dvor Podznoeva	C3
9 Golden Embankment Hotel	C1
10 Hostel Rus	B3
11 Hotel 903	B1
12 Hotel Arle	A2

| 13 Hotel Rizhskaya | A2 |
| 14 Old Estate Hotel & Spa | C1 |

⊗ Eating

Dvor Podznoeva	(see 8)
15 Grafin	D4
16 Hansa	B2
17 Pozharka Tavern	A2
Restaurant 903	(see 18)
Rusakov	(see 9)
Trapeznie Palat	(see 8)

🍸 Drinking & Nightlife

18 Beer Bar 903	B1
19 Old School Bar	C2
Pivnoi Dom	(see 9)
20 TIR	D2

✪ Entertainment

| 21 Pskov Region Philharmonia | C3 |

churches, many of which have closed, has been collected here. The museum offers a rare chance to thoroughly examine one particular style of iconography at close range. There are no English captions, but audio guides (R200) are available.

The maze of galleries in the chambers holds 14th-to-18th-century pottery, weaving and weaponry, including the original 15th-century sword of one of Pskov's princes. Equally impressive is the huge collection of silver artefacts, including beautifully crafted baroque-style bible covers. The largest, a 25kg beast, was originally housed at Pskov's Trinity Cathedral.

Equally worthwhile is the art gallery, with works spanning the 18th to 20th centuries, including paintings by Nikitin, Tropinin and Zhukovsky, plus representations from the Russian avant-garde, including a couple of Petrov-Vodkins.

The 2nd floor in the main building houses the war collection, with photos and artefacts from WWII and more recent conflicts.

★ **Trinity Cathedral** CHURCH
(Троицкий собор; Kremlin; ⊙11am-5pm) This blindingly white 72m-high structure, with its top dome shining gold, can be seen from miles away on a clear day. Consecrated in 1699, it's the fourth version of a church to have stood on this spot since the early 11th century, when a wooden one was commissioned by Princess Olga, an early convert to the Orthodox faith. The interior contains a large collection of bejewelled icons of the Madonna.

Kremlin HISTORIC SITE
(Псковский Кремль (Кром); ⊙9am-8pm) FREE Rising from a high narrow cape on the banks of the Velikaya River, Pskov's mighty kremlin (also known as the Krom) is the most complete portion of a fortress that once had five layers, 37 towers, 14 gates and an overall length of 9.5km. The walls and towers of the 15th-to-16th-century Outer Town (Окольный город) can still be seen along ul Sverdlova, the Velikaya River embankment and across the tributary Pskova River.

The largest tower – a whopping 90m in diameter and 50m tall – is the **Pokrovskaya Bashnya** (Intercession Tower). Dovmont Town can be found in the southern corner of the complex.

Writ Chamber MUSEUM
(Приказные Палаты; www.museums.pskov.ru; Kremlin; adult/student R100/50; ⊙11am-6pm Tue-Sun, closed last Tue of the month) This 17th-century stone building once held the administrative chambers of Pskov. Today it houses a small museum that gives some insight into the workings and officialdom of the old city; there's also a decent souvenir shop on the premises and an information centre. Outside, you'll find the preserved foundations of a dozen 12th-to-15th-century churches that once made up the independent city of **Dovmont Town** (Довмонтов город).

Epiphany Church of Zapskovie CHURCH
(Церковь Богоявления с Запсковья; ul Gertsena 7; ⊙8am-6pm) This attractive, working church overlooking the Pskova River was built in 1494 and includes a separately standing five-column belfry – its open gables and large pillars are distinctive of the Pskovian style. Around the church is a lovely stretch of park.

🛏 Sleeping

Avatar Hotel HOTEL $
(Аватар Отель; ☑8112-662 686; www.avatar-hotelpskov.ru; 3rd fl, ul Sovetskaya 111; s/d from R1100/1600; ☎) The building's rear entrance and the surrounding industrial area are less than appealing, but head up to the 3rd floor and you'll find the bright and colourful Avatar. It's a great choice for budget travellers looking for clean modern rooms and a handy location for the bus and train stations. Cheaper rooms have shared bathroom. There's also an on-site cafe.

Hostel Rus HOSTEL $
(Хостел Рус; ☑8-921-212 4505; www.hostelrusp-skov.ru; ul Lagernaya 5a; dm R500-700, d R1600; ☎) You'll be doubting your Google Maps directions when you wander around a back street to a random corner apartment building, but that's exactly where you'll find this spick-and-span hostel. Mixed four- to eight-bed dorms are bright with individual lamp, power point and curtain for privacy. The fully equipped kitchen, laundry and close-to-the-river location are added bonuses. No English is spoken.

★ **Hotel 903** HOTEL $$
(Гостиница 903; ☑8112-570 557, 8-911-880 0903; www.pskov903.ru; ul Maxima Gorkogo 2b; s/d incl breakfast from R2800/3000; ❄☎) This sparkling hotel has exceptional river and kremlin views, comfortable beds and lots of nice little extras, including free hot drinks all day and good hairdryers in the bathrooms. All

rooms have balconies and some have lovely exposed timber ceilings. Top-notch staff (Russian-speaking only) and a cute restaurant round out the deal.

Hotel Arle
HOTEL $$

(Отель Арль; ☑ 8112-298 080; pr Rizhsky 16; ☺ t-w/d incl breakfast from R1800/2300; ✳ 🛜) The 4th floor of an entertainment and shopping complex is not where you'd expect to find such a sparkling clean and great-value boutique-y hotel. Arle offers modern rooms with comfortable beds, helpful staff and a decent breakfast in the downstairs restaurant. Some rooms can receive a bit of noise from the entertainment complex, namely bowling pins crashing at the on-site alley!

Hotel Rizhskaya
HOTEL $$

(Гостиница Рижская; ☑ 8112-562 223; www.rijskaya.ru; Rizhsky pr 25; s/d R1700/3000; 🛜) Overlooking a grassy square, this old Intourist offers modern, renovated rooms with small bathtubs. Some of the friendly staff speak English. Buffet breakfast is R320 extra. Ask for a room with a view over the park.

Golden Embankment Hotel
HOTEL $$

(Отель Золотая Набережная; ☑ 8112-627 877; www.zn-hotel.ru; nab Sovetskaya 2; s/d incl breakfast R3200/3500; 🛜) With a prime position in the shadow of the kremlin, this intimate hotel, in an unmissable peach building, offers pleasant, spacious and reasonably priced rooms with a friendly welcome. Request a room with a kremlin view. Some English is spoken.

★ Dvor Podznoeva
HOTEL $$$

(Двор Подзноева; ☑ 8112-797 000; www.dvorpodznoeva.ru; ul Nekrasova 1; s/d R4410/4680; 🛜 🏊) This classy hotel in a 19th-century building is Pskov's best, with comfortable, nicely decorated rooms. An added perk is complimentary use of the pool, sauna and spa, where a range of massage treatments are available. Staff are friendly and professional, and some speak English. It's part of a complex of several eateries.

Old Estate Hotel & Spa
SPA HOTEL $$$

(☑ 8112-794 545; www.oldestatehotel.com; ul Verkhne-Beregovaya 4; s/d from R5100/5700; 🛜 🏊) Pskov's most upmarket option stands in a leafy street near the Pskova River. English-speaking staff is on hand and the service here matches the prices. Guests can use the spa with sauna, Jacuzzi and splash pool for free

between 7am and 10am (R500 afterwards). Nab a superior room for views.

✖ Eating

Restaurant 903
GRILL $

(ul Nabat 2a; mains R160-580; ☺ 11am-2am Mon-Fri, from noon Sat & Sun) This popular hang-out draws the crowds for all the right reasons: a lovely summer terrace with brilliant river views, a warm and woodsy interior and a menu for meat lovers with grilled meats prepared in its own smokehouse. Beer brewed at neighbouring Beer Bar 903 is available on tap.

Dvor Podznoeva
RUSSIAN $

(Двор Подзноева; www.dvorpodznoeva.ru; ul Nekrasova 1; dishes from R60; 🛜) There's something for everyone at this imaginatively designed complex: underground bakery cafe, beer house, well-stocked wine-and-cheese cellar, and the Trapeznie Palat.

★ Pozharka Tavern
GRILL $$

(Таверна Пожарка; ☑ 8-911-381 0065; www.pozharkapskov.ru; ul Paromenskaya 14; mains R350-650; ☺ 11am-2am Mon-Fri, from noon Sat & Sun) Although no longer in its riverside location, Pozharka still draws the crowds for its carnivore-pleasing menu that stars grilled meat and various treats prepared in the tavern's own smokehouse. The tender and juicy whole smoked trout is highly recommended and a steal at R120. There's a great range of beers too.

★ Rusakov
RUSSIAN $$

(Ресторан Русаков; ☑ 8112-201 480; www.caferp.ru; nab Sovetskaya 1/2; mains R260-690; ☺ noon-midnight; 🛜) Sitting on the riverside, plush upmarket Rusakov does classic Russian cuisine with a side of up-close kremlin and Trinity Cathedral views. Sink into comfy armchairs and peruse the menu of excellent dishes, such as pike dumplings, delicious homemade *pelmeni*, smoked trout, duck bliny and Russian wine from the Black Sea region.

Hansa
RUSSIAN $$

(☑ 8112-700 190; www.caferp.ru; ul Maksima Gorkogo 6a; mains R180-520; ☺ noon-1am; 🛜) This medieval-themed basement restaurant stays on the right side of kitsch with huge wooden chairs, exposed brick, lamp lighting and wrought-iron light fixtures. The menu features hearty comfort food, from Bavarian sausages and homemade *pelmeni* to warm-

MIKHAILOVSKOE

Russia's most beloved poet, Alexander Pushkin, lived several years at his family estate, **Mikhailovskoe** (Михайловское; ☑81146-22 321; www.pushkin.ellink.ru; with/without tour from R250/150; ☺10am-6pm, closed last Tue of month, Apr & mid-late Nov), near the small town of Pushkinskie Gory (Пушкинские Горы; Pushkin Hills), 120km south of Pskov.

The family first came to the area in the late 1700s, when Pushkin's great-grandfather Abram Hannibal was given the land by Empress Elizabeth. The family house was destroyed during WWII and has since been rebuilt. The surrounding 20-hectare park includes servants' quarters, orchards, cute bridges and a wooden windmill.

Pushkin's writing room has also been re-created, with his comfy leather chair, portraits of Byron and Zhukovsky (Pushkin's mentor, also a poet) and a small statue of Napoleon. The thick religious book on his writing table is the one he supposedly grabbed from the family bookcase and pretended to be reading whenever he saw the local priest coming for a visit.

At Pushkinskie Gory, about 1km north of the bus stop, is the **Svyatogorsky Monastery** (Святогорский монастырь), where Pushkin is buried. Monks remember him in their daily prayers.

Many travel agencies run excursions from Pskov on Saturdays with Russian-speaking guides only (R900, excluding admission fees); for an English-speaking guide, get in touch with the Pskov tourism office well in advance. See www.pushkin.ellink.ru for accommodation options.

You can catch a bus to Pushkinskie Gory from the Pskov bus station (R200 to R250, 2½ hours, at least six daily); the first bus leaves at 7.20am. The Pushkinskie Gory bus station is about 6km from Mikhailovskoe. If there's no local bus to cover the last leg, take a pleasant country walk. Turn left out of the bus station and walk for 1km along the road – you'll eventually see the Svyatogorsky Monastery on your left. From there a road leads off to the right towards Mikhailovskoe. However the best option is to hire a taxi from Pushkinskie Gory to take you around for the day; expect to pay between R1500 and R2000.

ing soups and chargrilled meats. German beers are also on offer.

Grafin INTERNATIONAL $$
(Графин; ☑8112-663 782; www.steakpskov.ru; ul Sovetskaya 83; mains R160-1200; ☺11am-2am Mon-Fri, from noon Sat & Sun) Grafin bills itself as a steakhouse, and while it does a mean mignon (R1300), there's plenty more than beef on the menu. Classics such as pork, lamb and chicken get a good workout, as do specialities such as rabbit and liver. They also do fish cooked on charcoal and homemade *pelmeni*, but there are slim pickings for vegos.

Kinza MIDDLE EASTERN $$
(☑8112-724 158; www.caferp.ru; pr Rizhskiy 54; mains R300-690; ☺noon-1am; ☺) In the basement of a residential building is this bright, sophisticated spot with exposed brick, Persian rugs and warm lighting. The menu features Middle Eastern fare from shashlyks (meat kebabs) and salads to pita wraps and homemade dips. There's no English menu but the friendly staff speak some English.

Trapeznie Palat RUSSIAN $$$
(Трапезные Палаты; ☑8112-797 111; ul Nekrasova 1; meals R640-1100; ☺noon-midnight) Part of the Dvor Podznoeva (p268) complex, this top-of-the-line restaurant occupies a re-created colourful interior of a 17th-century merchant's home. It serves traditional local dishes; soak them up with vodkas flavoured with ginger, horseradish, juniper and cedar.

 Drinking & Nightlife

Old School Bar CLUB
(3rd fl, Oktyabrskaya pr 20; ☺4pm-2am Sun-Thu, to 5am Fri & Sat) This mainstream rock bar has MTV on the screens and graffiti wall art. Join the young Pskovians here for late-night boogieing to thumping DJs, or just prop up the bar with some well-made cocktails from its extensive menu.

Beer Bar 903 MICROBREWERY
(☑8-900-990 3903; www.pivopskov.ru; ul Nabat 2a; ☺11am-midnight Sun-Thu, to 2am Fri & Sat) Enjoy mellow river views with delicious

beers brewed on-site at this rustic, chalet-like bar. Photo opps of the kremlin out front are some of the best you'll get. Also does meals.

TIR   BAR
(www.tirclub.ru; ul Sverdlova 52; ⊙noon-1am Mon-Thu & Sun, to 3am Fri & Sat; 🛜) This grungy, two-level hang-out is the hub of Pskov's underground music scene, staging local and national bands and DJs. Nibbles are available throughout the day and dirt-cheap beer is dispensed in big red brass samovars.

Pivnoi Dom   BAR
(Пивной Дом; 🖉 8112-627 800; www.zn-hotel.ru; Sovetskaya nab 1/2; ⊙noon-midnight Mon-Thu & Sun, to 2am Fri & Sat; 🛜) A cooling drink on the terrace of this joint facing the kremlin is perfect on a sunny day. It also does wonderfully fattening, German-style snacks.

☆ Entertainment

Pskov Region Philharmonia   CLASSICAL MUSIC
(Псковская областная филармония; 🖉 8112-668 920; www.philpskov.ru; ul Nekrasova 24; tickets from R150; ⊙box office 11am-8pm Mon-Fri, to 6pm Sat & Sun) Home of the city's classical orchestra; visit the website for concert details.

ℹ Information

Pskov Tourist Centre (Туристский информационный центр Красная Изба; www.tourism.pskov.ru; Administrative Chambers, Kremlin 4; ⊙10am-8pm) English-speaking staff can provide maps, advice and information on tours to Stary Izborsk or Mikhailovskoe. The tourist centre is usually located at pl Lenina 3, but at the time of research it was in a hard-to-find temporary location in the southwest corner of the kremlin; look for the old white building and call if you need directions.

ℹ Getting There & Away

AIR
Pskovavia (www.pskovavia.ru) operates irregular passenger flights (two hours, from R3865) between Moscow's Domodedovo Airport and Pskov's **Kresty Airport**, 6km southeast of the city centre; check the website for details. Note that flights in June and July tend to sell out months in advance.

BUS
Bus connections from Pskov **bus station** (ul Vokzalnaya) include St Petersburg (from R420, three to five hours, frequently), Veliky Novgorod (R530, 4½ hours, two daily) and Smolensk (from R750, seven to 10 hours, two daily and two night buses).

There are regular buses to/from Pechory (from R100, one hour), most of which stop en route in Stary Izborsk (from R78, 45 minutes).

Buses also cross the Estonian border to Tallinn (R1700, six hours, daily at 8.20am) and Tartu (from R570, three to four hours, two daily). Both pass through Stary Izborsk and Pechory – you could pick up the bus in either place rather than backtracking to Pskov. Details of other Russian and international services can be found at www.tourism.pskov.ru.

TRAIN
The **train station** (ul Vokzalnaya) is next to the bus station. Pskov is connected by one or two daily trains to Moscow (*platskart/kupe* from R1671/2359, 10 to 15 hours). For St Petersburg there's only one direct train, running on Sunday only (*obshchiy/kupe* R590/1223, four hours), so the bus is a better option. Otherwise you can catch a train to Luga (two to three hours), where there are connecting trains to St Petersburg (two hours).

For Latvia and Lithuania, you'll need to first catch a bus to Dedovichi (R250, 2¼ hours), from where there's an evening train to Rīga (*platskart/kupe* from R2389/4694, 11¾ hours) at 9.30pm, or Vilnius (*platskart/kupe* from R4412/8318, 13 hours) at 8.20pm.

ℹ Getting Around

Buses 11 and 17 run from the train station down Oktyabrsky pr and through the centre (R16). Bus 2 or 17 runs along Rizhsky pr from the station (taxis charge about R150). Bus 2 also runs past Mirozhsky Monastery.

Stary Izborsk
Старый Изборск
🖉 81148 / POPULATION 789 / ⊙ MOSCOW
Its name meaning 'old Izborsk', this sleepy village is indeed ancient – it celebrated its 1150th anniversary in 2012. The main attraction here is the ruined stone fortress, which overlooks lovely countryside, and there's the peaceful Gorodishchenskoye Lake further afield. There are a few small museums worth visiting and this is a great spot to take a break and get a taste of the Russian rural way of life for a day or so.

◉ Sights & Activities

Izborsk Museum organises a range of cultural tours and sightseeing in town; check their website for details. There are also a few more museums covering ethnology and archaeology along the main street.

Fortress FORTRESS
(Крепость; adult/student R100/50; ⏰9am-6pm) The ruins of this ancient stone fortress are among the oldest in Russia, and from its ridge location it overlooks a beautiful slice of countryside. Inside is the small 14th-century **Church of St Nicholas** and a **stone tower** with a viewing platform. A path behind the fortress leads to the tranquil **Gorodishchenskoye Lake** and **Slovenian Springs** (Словенские ключи), a 10-minute walk away. It's a pleasant spot with a few small cascading falls and moss-covered stones.

Locals carry their own water bottles to fill up at the springs – legend has it that the water will bring love, happiness, health and good luck.

Izborsk Museum MUSEUM
(Музей Изборск; www.museum-izborsk.ru; ul Pechorskaya 39; admission R100; ⏰10am-6pm May-Sep, to 5pm Oct-Apr) This museum houses displays of local archaeological finds and explanations, in Russian, of the town's rich history. The museum website has information on village festivals.

Horse Riding HORSE RIDING
(☑8-964-316 6393; per hr R800) Stary Izborsk's beautiful countryside is perfect for exploring on horseback.

⌁ Sleeping & Eating

★**Izborsk Park** GUESTHOUSE $$
(Изборск-Парк; ☑81148-23 327; www.izborsk-park.ru; ul Pechorskaya 43; d from R2500, mains R90-480; ⏰cafe 10am-8pm) This is country living, Russian style, at its finest. Rooms are inviting and cosy, the air smells of wood fires, and the grounds themselves are ridiculously Arcadian with roaming geese and chickens. The attached cafe serves up wholesome, hearty food such as soup and cabbage rolls, as well as beer on tap. There's a *banya* (R1800 for two hours) too.

Izborsk Hotel HOTEL $$
(Гостиничный комплекс Изборск; ☑8112-607 031, 8-921-703 7031; www.izborsk-hotel.ru; ul Pechorskaya 13; s/d incl breakfast from R2300/3000; ☎) This pretty complex ticks all the twee boxes: it's romantic and quaint with lace curtains and floral wallpaper. The attached craft shop sells charming hand-stitched teddies and cute gifts, and the restaurant cooks with locally sourced ingredients. You'll find it at the entrance to the village from the main road.

It also has a *banya* (R1200 for one hour) and bicycle hire (R150 per hour).

Gostevoy Dom GUESTHOUSE $$
(Гостевой Дом; ☑81148-96 612; ul Shkolnaya, 3; d/tr without bathroom R1500/2000, ste with bathroom R3500; ☎) Affiliated with Izborsk Museum, this bucolic guesthouse overlooks the valley from beneath the back of the fortress. The two-room *lyux* suite has a broad private balcony. Guests can use the communal kitchen.

Blinnaya RUSSIAN $
(Блинная; bliny from R110; ⏰8am-7pm) Just steps from the kremlin walls and fortress entrance is this sweet little cafe boasting 'Izborskian' bliny. There's also light meals such as *pelmeni* and potato fritters. Look for the big garden and dark-wood gate; the outside area is ideal for an afternoon drink.

ℹ Getting There & Away

Stary Izborsk is 32km from Pskov, on the road to Estonia. There are bus connections with Pskov (R100, 45 minutes, six daily) and Pechory (R69, 20 minutes, frequent). Several of the buses from Pskov to Pechory stop in Stary Izborsk, so it's easy to combine a trip to both places.

Pechory Печоры
☑81148 / POPULATION 11,195 / ⏰MOSCOW

This tiny town, just 2.5km from the Estonian border, is home to the photogenic Pechory Monastery and its eerie burial caves. You can wander the monastery grounds and visit most of the churches on your own. To visit the caves you'll have to join a tour; be sure to arrange this in advance.

Tours booked in nearby Pskov start from R700 and visit both Pechory and Stary Izborsk. With enough notice they should be able to arrange an English-speaking guide.

◎ Sights

Pechory Monastery MONASTERY
(Свято-Успенский Псково-Печерский монастырь; ⏰6am-8pm) Founded in 1473, this monastery sits in a ravine full of hermits' grottoes. With all the high ground outside, it's an improbable stronghold, but several tsars fortified it and depended on it. A path descends under the 1564 St Nicholas Church (Никольская церковь) into a Disneyesque palette of colours and architectural styles, where

several dozen monks still live and study. One of the highlights is the **burial caves** (admission by donation; ☺ near caves 10am-5pm, far caves 10am-5pm Tue-Thu, Sat & Sun), where some 10,000 bodies – monks, benefactors and others – are bricked up in vaults.

The central yellow church comprises two buildings. At ground level is the original Assumption Cathedral (Успенский собор), built into the caves. Upstairs is the 18th-century baroque Intercession Church (Покровская церковь). Below the belfry on the left is the entrance to the caves. Taking photos of the buildings is acceptable if you make a contribution at the front gate, but photographing the monks is taboo. Women must wear skirts and cover their heads and shoulders (shawls and skirts to be worn over trousers are available to borrow at the entrance). Men should wear long pants.

🛏 Sleeping & Eating

Hotel Pechory Park   HOTEL **$$**
(Гостиница Печоры-Парк; ☎ 81148-23 327; www.pechorypark.ru; ul Gagarin 2b; d/q R1895/3400; ☎) Just 500m from the monastery and offering city-style service, this hotel is your best option in Pechory. Rooms are small and basic. Some standard rooms have shared showers and no TV but do come with private toilet and washbasin. There's a cafe on site.

Old Tower Cafe   CAFE **$**
(Кафе Старая Башня; Oktyabrskaya pl 7; mains R110-350; ☺9am-9pm; ☎) Housed in an old brick water tower, this charming modern cafe offers simple, classic meals, such as *pelmeni* (Russian-style ravioli typically stuffed with meat) – veg options also available – and hearty soups.

❶ Information

Excursion Office (☎ 8-911-379 4815; www. pechori.ru; ☺10am-5pm) For Pechory Monastery and caves tours.

❶ Getting There & Away

You can cross the Estonian border to Tallinn (R1650, five hours, daily) and Tartu (R370, three hours, two daily) on buses originating in Pskov. Hourly buses shuttle between Pskov and Pechory (from R100, one hour) between 8am and 11pm. At least six buses a day make a stop in Stary Izborsk (R69, 25 minutes). See www. pechori.ru for updated timetable links.

Kaliningrad Region

Best Places to Eat

➡ Fish Club (p282)

➡ Madame Boucher (p281)

➡ Dom Rybaka (p288)

Best Places to Stay

➡ Skipper Hotel (p280)

➡ Dom Skazochnika (p287)

➡ Butik Hotel 12 (p288)

➡ Chaika (p280)

➡ Lumier Art Hotel (p287)

Why Go?

The Kaliningrad region's eponymous capital was the medieval seat of Prussia and an important port that was fought over for centuries. Today, fewer than 500,000 people visit each year. Until WWII, the province was almost entirely German; bratwurst made way for borsch after the war as Stalin repopulated the region with Russians. Though Kaliningrad is separated from Russia by Lithuania and Poland, the exclave is intimately attached to the motherland.

Yet for all of its chaotic history and cultural foibles – or perhaps because of them – 'Little Russia' is a fascinating place to visit. The city of Kaliningrad teems with interesting sights and surprisingly sophisticated accommodation and dining options; seaside towns Svetlogorsk and Zelenogradsk dish up old-world charm by the spadeful; sparkling Yantarny is the world's amber capital; and the dunes, pine forests and tranquil villages of Kurshskaya Kosa National Park make for a serene sojourn.

When to Go
Kaliningrad

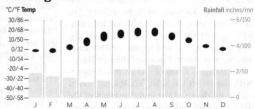

Jul Crowds descend on the beaches as the Baltic warms up.

Aug Summer is in full swing, and seaside Yantarny celebrates its Amberfest.

Sep & Oct Kaliningrad's lively cultural calendar helps soften the blow of a long dark season

Kaliningrad Region's Highlights

1 Kaliningrad Cathedral (p275) Paying your respects at philosopher Immanuel Kant's grave, then attending an organ concert.

2 Museum of the World Ocean (p275) Exploring Russia's maritime history on former expedition vessels and a submarine.

3 Kurshskaya Kosa National Park (p289) Soaking up the beauty of the Curonian Spit, where the forests dance and the dunes roll on as far as the eye can see.

4 Yantarny (p285) Visiting a working amber mine and then splashing in the Baltic.

5 Svetlogorsk (p286) Discovering old German villas and the sculptures of Herman Brachert while strolling this spa town's shady lanes.

6 Chernyakhovsk (p286) Seeing ruined castles and saddling up at the Georgenburg Stud Farm.

History

The Kaliningrad region is intimately connected with the Order of the Teutonic Knights, a band of Christian crusaders with historical ties to the Baltic Sea area. The town of Königsberg was founded by the knights in 1255, the name *könig* (German for 'king') referring to Bohemian King Ottakar II, who had led a crusade against the then-pagan Old Prussians. The city prospered and joined the Hanseatic League of northern European cities in 1340.

Following a series of battles and disputes with the Polish kingdom, Königsberg served as the residence of the grand masters of the Teutonic order and their successors, the dukes of Prussia. The area eventually emerged as the Duchy of Prussia in 1525, with Königsberg as its capital. Prussia's first king, Frederick I, was crowned in 1701 in the city's castle.

Königsberg's liberal atmosphere attracted scholars, artists and entrepreneurs from across Europe, and for the next couple of centuries the city flourished – in 1697 Peter the Great visited as part of his Grand Embassy and the 18th-century philosopher Immanuel Kant (1724–1804) lived there all his life. For four years of the Seven Years' War (1756–63), East Prussia – as the Duchy became known in the early 18th century – temporarily became part of the Russian Empire and, later, during the Napoleonic Wars, Russia and Prussia were allies.

Following Germany's defeat in WWI, East Prussia was separated from the rest of Germany when Poland regained statehood. Animosity caused by this division helped in part to explain the regional popularity of the emerging Nazi party in the 1930s. During WWII, the city of Königsberg suffered heavy bombing by the Royal Air Force (in 1944). Less than a year later, in April 1945, the Soviet Red Army captured the city in one of the fiercest battles of

WWII. There were massive casualties on both sides and Königsberg was left in ruins.

After the war, the region was renamed Kaliningrad in honour of Mikhail Kalinin, one of Stalin's more vicious henchmen, and the capital was rebuilt in grand Soviet concrete style, albeit tempered by parks, ponds, waterways and the Kaliningrad Lagoon. The surviving German population was relocated to far-flung corners of the Soviet Union, deported or killed. The Russian Baltic fleet was headquartered in Baltiysk, and the region was closed to foreigners for over 40 years.

Like much of Russia, Kaliningrad struggled through extreme economic difficulties in the early 1990s. The discovery of oil off the coast and the granting of special economic zone status have helped it turn the corner. With Kaliningrad one of the host cities for the 2018 FIFA World Cup, the region remains of key strategic importance to Russia.

Kaliningrad Калининград

☑ 4012 / POP 431,900 / ⊙ MOSCOW –1HR

While Königsberg revelled in regal architecture and a cosmopolitan European culture, Kaliningrad carries more than a whiff of its days as an outpost of the USSR. But despite vast swaths of brutal Stalin-stamped buildings and unmistakable Soviet monuments, the city is a pleasant one, softened by leafy parks, revitalised historical enclaves, exceptional museums, charming neighbourhoods and its trademark city gates. Kaliningrad is easy to navigate: public transport abounds, as do welcoming locals all too willing to lend visitors a hand.

After Kaliningrad Cathedral, the most visible remains of Königsberg are its red-brick fortification walls, bastions and gates, built between the 17th and 19th centuries. The remains of the city's castle were destroyed and replaced by the hideous Dom Sovietov (House of Soviets) in the 1960s. During the eyesore's construction it was discovered that the land below was hollow, housing a (now-flooded) four-level underground passage connecting to the cathedral. The decaying, half-finished building has never been used.

⊙ Sights

★ **Museum of the World Ocean** MUSEUM
(Музей Мирового Океана; ☑ 4012-538 915; www.world-ocean.ru; nab Petra Velikogo 1; adult/student R300/150, individual vessels R150/100; ⊙ 10am-6pm Wed-Mon) Strung along the banks of the Pregolya River are several ships, a submarine, maritime machinery and exhibition halls that together make up this excellent museum. The highlight is the handsome former scientific expedition vessel *Vityaz,* moored alongside the *Viktor Patsaev,* with its exhibits relating to space research; visits to this are by guided tour (included in the admission price; every 45 minutes). The pre-atomic B-413 submarine gives a taste of what life was like for its 300 former inhabitants.

A restored storehouse has interesting displays on the sea-connected history of Kaliningrad, as well as the remains of a 19th-century wooden fishing boat. There's also a pavilion with a sperm whale skeleton, and halls with small aquariums and general information about the ocean.

Kaliningrad Cathedral CHURCH
(Кафедральный собор Кёнигсберга; ☑ 4012-631 705; www.sobor-kaliningrad.ru; Kant Island; adult/student R200/100, concerts from R150; ⊙ 10am-6pm Mon-Thu, to 7pm Fri-Sun) Photos displayed inside this Unesco World Heritage Site attest to how dilapidated the cathedral was until the early 1990s – the original dates back to 1333. The lofty interior is dominated by an ornate organ used for regular **concerts.** Upstairs, the carved-wood **Wallenrodt Library** has interesting displays of old Königsberg.

The top floor is devoted to noted philosopher and Kaliningrad native Immanuel Kant (1724–1804); the exhibition includes his death mask. **Kant's Tomb** is on the building's outer north side.

Bunker Museum MUSEUM
(Музей Блиндаж; ul Universitetskaya 3; adult/student R150/70; ⊙ 10am-6pm Tue-Sun) The city's last German commander, Otto Lasch, capitulated to the Soviets from this buried command post on 9 April 1945, following the bloody Battle of Königsberg. Exhibits include wartime photographs and film, and a peek into the cell where Lasch surrendered. There's little English signage, but enough to get a general idea. The entrance is poorly marked. Find it in a small park just east of Leninsky pr.

Amber Museum MUSEUM
(Музей Янтаря; ☑ 4012-466 888; www.ambermuseum.ru; pl Marshala Vasilevskogo 1; adult/student R240/140; ⊙ 10am-7pm Tue-Sun; ♿) Housed in the 19th-century **Dohna Tower** (Башня Дона; pl Marshala Vasilevskogo) on the southern shore of the Upper Pond (Верхний пруд), this museum features over 6000 amber exhibits, including marvellous artworks, a whopping

KALININGRAD REGION KALININGRAD

Kaliningrad

Scale: 500 m / 0.25 miles

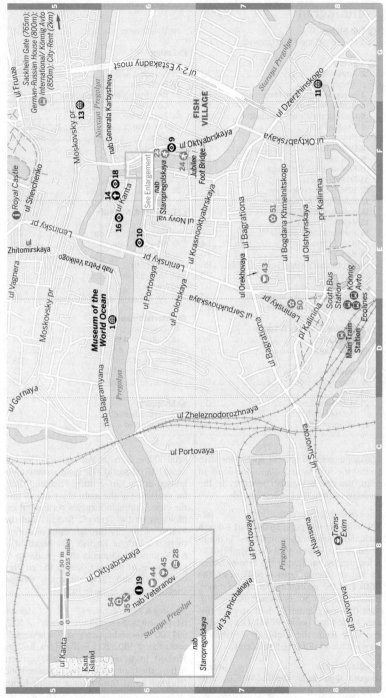

Kaliningrad

4.28kg nugget and ancient specimens with prehistoric insects and plants fossilised in resin. You can buy amber jewellery in the museum or from the vendors outside.

Kant Island & Riverside   AREA
This once densely populated island – now a parkland dotted with sculptures – is dominated by the Kaliningrad Cathedral (p275). A few nearby buildings – the **former Stock Exchange** (Биржа; Leninsky pr 83) from the 1870s and the neotraditional row of shops, restaurants and hotels known as **Fish Village** (Рыбная Деревня) – hint at what this area looked like before WWII. Get a bird's-eye view from the 31m-high **lighthouse viewing tower** (R100; ⊙10am-10pm).

Friedland Gate   MUSEUM
(Ворота Фридланд; ☎4012-644 020; www.fvmuseum.ru; ul Dzerzhinskogo 30; adult/child

R200/100; ⊙10am-7pm May-Aug, to 6pm Sep-Apr, closed 1st Fri of month) This history museum is housed in the 19th-century Friedland Gate, for years one of the main entry points into the city. Admission includes permanent exhibitions on the Teutonic Knights and the history of the city through eight centuries; there is a little in English. The highlight is a 30-minute multimedia show made up of projections of photos taken in the city between 1908 and 1913, and grainy footage shot around the castle in 1937.

History & Arts Museum   MUSEUM
(Историко-Художественный музей; ☎4012-994 900; www.westrussia.org; ul Klinicheskaya 21; adult/student R100/80; ⊙10am-6pm Tue-Sun) Housed in a reconstructed 1912 concert hall on the banks of the pretty Lower Pond (Нижний пруд), this museum mainly focus-

es on events since Russia's takeover of the region, though Kaliningrad's German past does get a look-in.

Central Park
PARK

(Центральный парк; main entrance pr Pobedy 1; ⊙24hr) **FREE** This forest-like park, on the grounds of an old German cemetery, has statues, funfair rides and an amphitheatre hosting summer concerts.

King's Gate
MUSEUM

(Королевские ворота; ul Frunze 112; adult/student R100/50; ⊙11am-7pm Wed-Sun) Focusing on Peter the Great's Grand Embassy to the city in 1697, this revamped gate also has good models of old Königsberg and exhibits on the personalities who shaped the region's history. A little south of here, where Moskovsky pr meets Litovsky val, is the twin-towered Sackheim Gate (Закхаймские ворота).

Kaliningrad Zoo
ZOO

(Калининградский Зоопарк; ☑4012-218 914; www.kldzoo.ru; pr Mira 26; Mon-Fri R100, Sat & Sun R270; ⊙9am-8pm May-Sep, to 5pm Oct-Apr; ⊕) This is one of the city's most popular attractions for families, so expect lines on the weekends. The zoo dates from 1896, when it was founded as the Königsberger Tiergarten. The destruction of WWII and funding shortfalls in the 1990s made things difficult for the animals, though the authorities are now working hard to improve the facilities. There are lots of big cats, though kids will love the bear and hippos the most.

Kaliningrad Art Gallery
GALLERY

(Калининградская художественная галерея; ☑4012-467 143; www.kaliningradartmuseum.ru; Moskovsky pr 60-62; adult/student R150/100; ⊙10am-7pm Tue & Wed, Fri-Sun, to 9pm Thu) This gallery contains modern and contemporary works by local artists, including some striking pieces from the Soviet decades. The gallery shop sells art books and local creations.

Ploshchad Pobedy
SQUARE

(Площадь победы) The city's central square has come a long way since 1934, when it was known as Adolf-Hitler Platz. Today it's surrounded by shopping malls and the gold-domed Cathedral of Christ the Saviour (Кафедральный Собор Христа Спасителя; pl Pobedy; ⊙8am-7pm), built in 2006 in the Russo-Byzantine style.

AMALIENAU

To the city's west along pr Mira is Amalienau (Амалиенау), Kaliningrad's most beautiful neighbourhood offering a glimpse of the city's prosperous pre-WWII past. Stroll along ul Kutuzova to find an eclectic range of villas. The streets connecting prs Pobedy and Mira are filled with beautiful prewar townhouses such as Altes Haus (☑tours 4012-335 060; www.alteshaus.ru; ul Krasnaya 11, Amalienau; R300; ⊙tours 11am, 1pm, 3pm Mon-Sat), a museum housed in a 1912 apartment house, which has been restored to its former state and stuffed with genteel period pieces and gorgeous antique furniture. Entry is by guided tour (in Russian). Visitors are given more or less free rein to sit on the furniture and generally carry on – politely – as if they owned the joint.

🏃 Activities

Amber Spa
SPA

(☑4012-592 200; www.amberspa.ru; ul Oktyabrskaya 6; from R1000, prices vary by the day; ⊙7am-10pm) Five different saunas, a medium-sized swimming pool, a spa and a swim-up bar make up this swish spa complex attached to the Hotel Kaiserhof (p280).

Boat Tours
BOATING

(adult/child R500/250; ⊙May-Sep) Small passenger boats leave from the promenade beside Fish Village and sail around Kant Island and down the Pregolya River (one hour).

✦ Festivals & Events

For a small city, Kaliningrad has a wealth of festivals in its calendar. See www.visit-kaliningrad.ru/en/events for the full rundown.

First Summer Music Festival
MUSIC

Local and international musicians rocking out reggae, punk and ska style. Held at the start of June.

Kaliningrad City Jazz Festival
MUSIC

(www.jazzfestival.ru) Open-air jazzfest held in Central Park at the end of July and the beginning of August.

🛏 Sleeping

Amalienau Hostel
HOSTEL $

(☑8-911-864 8686; www.amalienau-hostel.ru; ul Karla Marksa 19; dm/r from R540/1500) Clean,

KALININGRAD'S STATUES & MONUMENTS

Kaliningrad is littered with all manner of amusing, eclectic statues and monuments, celebrating everything from cosmonauts to Woody Allen. A **statue of Immanuel Kant** (ul A Nevskogo, Kant State University), Königsberg's most famous son, stands in front of the university named after him, tucked off Leninsky pr.

Along pr Mira, the **Cosmonaut Monument** (Памятник Землякам Космонавтам; next to pr Mira 41/43) is a gem of Soviet iconography, honouring the four Kaliningrad-born cosmonauts, including Alexey Leonov, the first man to conduct a space walk.

In the lobby of the nearby Scala cinema is a witty monument to **Woody Allen** (pr Mira 43), who was born Allen Konigsberg – a pair of the film director's trademark glasses jut from the wall. In Central Park, you'll find monuments to legendary tall-tale teller and supposed Kaliningrad visitor **Baron Munchausen** (pr Pobedy 1), and **Vladimir Vysotsky** (Памятник Владимиру Высоцкому; pr Pobedy 1), a massively popular singer from the 1960s and '70s.

friendly hostel in the historic Amalienau neighbourhood, about 3km west of the city centre. Accommodation is in 10-bed mixed, male-only or female-only rooms, with a few excellent-value private doubles available. Breakfast costs an extra R150.

Oh, my Kant   HOSTEL **$**
(☑ 4012-390 278; www.ohmykant.ru; ul Yablonevaya Alleya 34; dm/d from R500/1900; ☜) This well-maintained hostel is one of several budget accommodation options run by the 'Oh, my Kant' group. See the website for the other properties. The setting here is a charming house in a lovely part of town, about 2km west of the centre. The dorms are airy and bright, and the kitchen and common areas are super-clean.

★**Chaika**   HOTEL **$$**
(Чайка; ☑ 4012-210 729; www.hotelchaika.ru; ul Pugacheva 13; s/d from R3500/4000; ✻☜) On a leafy street near the picturesque Amalienau area, the 'Seagull' is a delightful 28-room property occupying an early-20th-century mansion and decorated with classy heritage touches. It also has a restaurant, comfy lounge and fitness room.

★**Skipper Hotel**   HOTEL **$$**
(Гостиница Шкиперская; ☑ 4012-307 237; www.skipperhotel.ru; ul Oktyabrskaya 4a; r from R3500; ✻☜) Location, ahoy! In a quaint period building with a superb riverside position in Fish Village, the Skipper is within stumbling distance of many of Kaliningrad's main attractions, cafes and bars. Rooms are clean with a nautical theme. Breakfast costs an additional R600. Ask for a room overlooking the river.

Hotel Paraiso   BOUTIQUE HOTEL **$$**
(Гостиница Параисо; ☑ 4012-216 969; http://ageevgroup.ru/hotels/paraiso; ul Turgeneva 32a; s/d from R2200/2500; @☜) This inviting mini-hotel comes over all country lodge, with ivy creeping over its old German-style walls and a delightful garden. Rooms are simple and comfortable, there's a small sauna, and the attached restaurant serves wholesome Russian and German meals.

Hotel Dona   HOTEL **$$**
(Отель Дона; ☑ 4012-351 612; http://ageevgroup. ru/hotels/dona; pl Marshala Vasilevskogo 2; s/d from R2700/3500; ✻☜) This modern, mirrored manse is hard to miss, and you'll be glad you didn't. The Dona has a fantastic location in a pretty part of town, English-speaking staff, good buffet breakfasts and the wonderful restaurant Dolce Vita (p282). See-through glass doors to the rooms' toilets are an interesting design touch.

Villa Severin   GUESTHOUSE **$$**
(Вилла Северин; ☑ 4012-365 385; www.villa-severin.ru; ul Leningradskaya 9a; r R2700-3500; ✻@☜) This villa looks like a doll's house, with an adorable garden and lovely setting by Upper Pond to match. There are a half-dozen comfortably furnished rooms, including one simple student room (R1300 without breakfast). It also has a small sauna and cafe.

Hotel Kaiserhof   HOTEL **$$$**
(Отель Кайзерхоф; ☑ 4012-592 222; www.kaiserhof-hotel.com/en; ul Oktyabrskaya 6a; s/d from R5000/6000; ✻@☜✹) Part of the Fish Village development, this nicely designed and furnished hotel has light-filled rooms and a

full-service spa and sauna. Rates are lower from Friday to Sunday.

Eating

Head to the lively **Central Market** (Центральный рынок; ul Chernyakhovskogo; ☺8am-6pm) for self-catering and engrossing people-watching.

First Coffee
INTERNATIONAL **$**

(Фёст; ☎4012-616 210; www.a-kovalsky.ru/project/first; Teatralnaya ul 30; mains R200-300; ☺9am-10pm; ☎) This combo restaurant and cafe on the northern edge of the Europe shopping centre, overlooking pl Pobedy, is a lunchtime lifesaver in a busy part of town. The long menu is filled with appetising salads, pizzas, sandwiches, grills and, of course, decent cakes and coffee. The pavement terrace is a fun perch for people-watching.

Borsch & Salo
RUSSIAN, UKRAINIAN **$$**

(Борщ и Сало; ☎4012-357 676; www.borshsalo.ru; pl Pobedy 10; meals R300-500; ☺noon-midnight Sun-Thu, to 2am Fri & Sat; ☎) Decked out like a Ukrainian hut, this cosy cafe has all the delicious, fattening treats you'd expect from its name, which translates loosely as 'borsch and bacon'. Alongside a wide range of Russian and Ukrainian dishes, the restaurant has a huge variety of flavoured brandies; if you're nice, they might even give you one on the house.

Madame Boucher
FRENCH **$$**

(Мадам Буше; ☎8-921-619 2595; ul Oktyabrskaya 2a; mains R300-500; ☺Mon-Sat 10am-11pm, Sun 11am-8pm) The specialities are sweet and savoury crêpes at this French-themed riverfront restaurant at the northern end of Fish Village, though the homemade cakes are enormous and also highly recommended, as are the lunch and dinner mains centred on fish and steaks. Dine out on the terrace or under the chandeliers in the lavish but tiny interior. Reservations highly recommended.

Zarya
RUSSIAN, EUROPEAN **$$**

(Заря; ☎4012-300 388; pr Mira 43; mains R300-500; ☺10am-11pm Sun-Thu, to 2am Fri & Sat; ☎) This fashionable brasserie in the Scala cinema lobby is beautifully decorated and has an attractive outdoor area. A popular hangout for pre- and post-movie nibbles, it whips up everything from steak and seafood to the unutterably sinful deep-fried camembert.

Moskva-Berlin
RUSSIAN **$$**

(Москва-Берлин; ☎4012-352 285; www.moskwa-berlin.ru; pr Mira 19-21; mains R200-500; ☺8am-2am; ☎) This upscale diner, complete with banquette seating along the windows, is a trendy pick for lunch or dinner. Pour over a menu of burgers, steaks, pasta and sushi at reasonable prices and settle in for good food and good times. There are decent cakes and homemade ice cream for dessert. The central location, across from the Kaliningrad Zoo, is convenient.

Parmesan
ITALIAN **$$**

(Пармезан; ☎4012-313 137; www.britannicaproject.ru; ul Karla Marksa 18; mains R300-500; ☺noon-1am; ☎♿) Excellent ingredients and attention to detail in the pizzas, pastas and grill dishes move this self-described trattoria a notch up over the usual pizza and pasta joints around town. There are minders on hand for the kids, and the outdoor terrace is the perfect spot for the adults to relax over a glass of wine and a grilled calamari appetiser.

Ashman Park
RUSSIAN, UZBEK **$$**

(Ашман Парк; ☎4012-770 203; www.otel39.ru/kafe/kafe-ashman-park; ul Gertsena 1a; mains R300-600; ☺noon-2am; ☎) The northern section of Kaliningrad is notoriously short of good restaurants, and this hybrid Russian-Uzbek-Italian option stands out as the best around. The chef appears equally adept at turning out very good Russian borsch, pizza or Central Asian–style minced-lamb kebabs. Our only quibble is the long prep time for meals. Reservations recommended.

Solar Stone
SEAFOOD **$$**

(Солнечный камень; ☎4012-539 106; www.sun-stone.ru; Rossgarten Gate; mains R400-800; ☺noon-2am) Housed in the **Rossgarten Gate**, this period-themed place specialises in upmarket seafood, though it does have other options on the menu. The skylighted, red-brick dining room is handsome and suited to special occasions. In nice weather, it's possible to eat outdoors towards the back.

Khmel
RUSSIAN **$$**

(Хмель; ☎4012-593 377; pl Pobedy 10; mains R300-500; ☺noon-1am; ☎) Situated in a shopping centre bordering central pl Pobedy, Khmel is a popular lunch spot. The interior resembles a brewery, with exposed pipes and brick walls. The ambitious menu draws from around Russia and features fish, caviar, duck, pork and just about everything else. There are four types of home-brewed beer, including an excellent dark, and *kvas* (fermented rye-bread water) that's slightly alcoholic.

Baklazhan
RUSSIAN $$

(Баклажан; ☑ 4012-357 575; ul Professora Baranova 40; meals R300-500; ◷ 11am-midnight Sun-Thu, to 3am Fri & Sat; ☎) One of the better options in the immediate pl Pobedy area, this cafe, restaurant and club (depending on the hour) offers dependable Russian and international dishes, including very good soups, salads and steaks. There's a covered terrace in nice weather. Come back for cocktails after dark.

Cheshskiy traktir 'U Gasheka'
CZECH $$

(Чешский трактир 'У Гашека'; ☑ 4012-919 182; www.ugasheka.ru; Leninsky pr 1; mains R300-500; ◷ 10am-midnight Mon-Fri, from noon Sat & Sun; ☎) The Czech Republic seems to hold a special place in the hearts of Kaliningrad residents, or at least Czech beer. Named after the author of classic Czech WWI novel *The Good Soldier Švejk*, this popular restaurant promises Czech beer on tap and Central European staples like roast pork and sausages, though the food is more filling than memorable.

Brittanica
INTERNATIONAL $$

(Британника; ☑ 4012-313 101; www.britannicaproject.ru; ul Karla Marksa 18; mains R300-600; ◷ noon-1am; ☎) Reservations are absolutely essential at this bustling English-pub-themed spot in a quiet residential neighbourhood west of the centre. The appeal is understandable: very good home-brewed beer, excellent grills, big salads and an airy terrace that's perfect on a warm summer night. There's a second branch, at ul Gorkogo 2, not far from the city's Central Market.

★ Fish Club
SEAFOOD $$$

(Рыбный клуб; ul Oktyabrskaya 4a; mains R500-1500; ◷ noon-midnight; ☎) For a seafood splurge with a view, this classy waterfront restaurant cannot be beaten. Everything on the menu is fresh and elegantly prepared, and the service is the best in the city. If you're not supping in the sunshine, ask for a table near the aquarium.

Dolce Vita
EUROPEAN, RUSSIAN $$$

(☑ 4012-351 612; http://ageevgroup.ru/restaurants/dolche-vita; pl Marshala Vasilevskogo 2; mains R500-1200; ◷ noon-midnight; ☎☑) One of a handful of destination restaurants in Kaliningrad, the Dolce Vita is located adjacent to the Hotel Dona (p280). Many of the inventive dishes appear overly fussy on the menu, but the competent chef makes them work. There's an excellent selection for vegetarians, superb seafood and divine pastas. Reservations recommended. Dine on the terrace in nice weather.

🍷 Drinking & Nightlife

★ Harry Johnson's Bar
COCKTAIL BAR

(☑ 8-911-450 6655; https://vk.com/harryjohnson; pr Mira 10-12; ◷ 24hr) Easily Kaliningrad's best cocktail bar, Harry Johnson's has the cred to back it up. It's named for the author (and possible Königsberg native) of the earliest *Bartenders' Manual*, first published in the US in 1882. As you'd expect, there are expertly prepared cocktails and bar snacks, served in a relaxed setting.

Kvartira
CAFE

(Квартира; ☑ 962-269 4200; ul Serzhanta Koloskova 13; ◷ 8am-11pm Mon-Fri, 11am-11pm Sat & Sun; ☎) Hiding on the ground floor of an apartment block, Kvartira is unquestionably one of Kaliningrad's coolest hang-outs. Lined with a fascinating range of pop-culture books, CDs, records and DVDs, all for sale or rent (as is everything else, including the stylish furniture), Kvartira – which means 'apartment' – also serves drinks and snacks.

WB17D
BAR

(☑ 4012-571 807; ul Yanalova 17d; ◷ 9pm-6am Thu-Sun) The 'WB' in the name stands for 'whiskey bar', and there certainly is a huge range of the liquor at this super-slick nightspot. Frock up and bring all the attitude you can muster; there are no wallflowers here. Cover charge from R60.

Labyrinth
CAFE

(Лабиринт; ul Orekhovaya 7-19; 1st hr R120, per min R2; ◷ 11am-1pm Sun-Thu, to 6am Fri & Sat; ☎) This popular 'anticafe' – where you pay for the time but not for snacks and drinks – offers free wi-fi, hot drinks, billiards, ping-pong and a slew of table and video games. The entrance is on the park-side of the building.

Magiya Kofe
CAFE

(Магия кофе; ☑ 4012-509 704; ul Oktyabrskaya 4; ◷ 10am-11pm) This handy riverfront cafe serves above-average coffees, plus the usual range of cakes and sweets, beer, wine and soft drinks. They also do good salads and light bites. Try to arrive at off-meal times to grab a coveted terrace table.

Amsterdam
CLUB

(☑ 4012-353 306; 38/11 Litovsky val; ◷ noon-6pm Mon-Thu, to 6am Fri, 10pm-6am Sat; ☎) This large, alternative, gay-friendly club is in an old brick building 200m west off Litovsky val (also accessible via per Griga). The cover charge is R500. During the week, the club morphs into a cafe-restaurant with a daily, good-value business lunch (R300).

Verf
WINE BAR

(Верфь; ul Oktyabrskaya 4a; ⏰11am-midnight; 📞) This relaxed wine bar has outdoor tables overlooking Kaliningrad Cathedral. It screens movies and provides coloured pencils and paper for doodling.

Kruassan Cafe
CAFE

(Круассан-кафе; ☎4012-389 462; www.kruassan.com; pr Mira 84; ⏰8am-11pm; 📞) This pr Mira branch is one of a number of 'Croissant Cafe' outlets scattered around the city. It's a reliable stop for a decent coffee as well as very good cakes, sweets, ice cream, sandwiches and, yes, croissants. The wine selection is surprisingly good for a coffee shop.

Cafe 'Laundry'
CAFE

(GS Coffee; ☎8-906-230 0595; https://vk.com/gscoffeeshop; pr Mira 74-76; ⏰8am-10pm Mon-Fri, 10am-10pm Sat & Sun) This tiny third-gen roaster is certainly in the running for the city's best coffee. Grab a to-go cup or take a seat in the small drinking room. The baristas specialise in AeroPress or more traditional filtered coffees, though they'll prepare it any way you please.

☆ Entertainment

★ Club Vagonka
LIVE MUSIC

(Клуб Вагонка; ☎4012-956 677; www.vagonka.net; Stanochnaya ul 12; ⏰11pm-5am Fri & Sat) Housed in a former German church about 3km from the city centre, Vagonka is one of the city's oldest and most popular venues for live rock, dance parties and general carousing. Performances take place in one of two concert halls, the biggest of which holds around 1000 people. Check the website for the current schedule.

Philharmonic Hall
CLASSICAL MUSIC

(Филармония; ☎tickets 4012-647 890; www.kenigfil.ru; ul Bogdana Khmelnitskogo 61a; tickets from R250; ⏰box office 10.30am-7pm) This beautifully restored neo-Gothic church has excellent acoustics, perfect for organ concerts, chamber-music recitals and the occasional symphony orchestra.

Drama Theatre
THEATRE

(Театр драмы и комедии; ☎box office 4012-212 422; www.dramteatr39.ru; pr Mira 4; tickets from R300; ⏰box office 11am-7pm Tue-Fri, to 6pm Sat & Sun) Several plays staged here are included

in the program of the annual **Baltic Season** (www.baltseasons.ru; ⏰Sep-Dec).

Club Planeta
LIVE MUSIC

(Планета; ☎4012-533 809; www.rk-planeta.ru; ul Chernyakhovskogo 26; ⏰noon-3am) Planeta is not just a club, it's an entertainment complex with a ground-floor restaurant, and the upper floors given over, depending on the night, to DJ dance music, karaoke and occasional live concerts. The central location, just a block away from pl Pobedy, is a big draw. Check the website for concerts and events.

Club Platinum
LIVE MUSIC

(Клуб 'Platinum'; ☎4012-384 848; www.club-platinum.ru; ul Dmitriya Donskogo 19; concerts from R400; ⏰11pm-5.30am Fri & Sat) There are regular appearances by popular rock and indie acts at this heaving, upscale dance club. Dress up to get through the front door. Check the website for concerts on during your visit.

House of Arts
ARTS CENTRE

(Дом Искусств; ☎4012-643 747; www.domiskusstv.com; Leninsky pr 155; ⏰box office 10am-7pm) The varied repertoire here features musical theatre, modern dance, ballet, classical music and children's performances. Check the website to see if something interesting is on during your visit. Buy tickets at the venue box office.

Puppet Theatre
PUPPET THEATRE

(Театр Кукол/Teatr Kukol; ☎tickets 4012-214 335; www.teatrkukol39.ru; pr Pobedy 1a; R200; ⏰box office 10am-5pm Fri-Sun; ♿) Performances are held on Saturdays and Sundays at noon in the 19th-century Lutheran Queen Luisa Church.

🔒 Shopping

You can hardly move in Kaliningrad without someone trying to sell you souvenirs made of amber – the hard resin of coniferous trees that grew in the region approximately 45 to 50 million years ago. Around 90% of the world's amber hails from the region. The region's sanatoriums even offer 'amber therapy', said to combat fatigue and other health disorders.

★ Kaliningrad Amber Factory
JEWELLERY

(Калининградский янтарный комбинат; www.ambercombine.ru; ul Oktyabrskaya 2; ⏰10am-9pm) Easily the biggest and best of several amber shops along the riverfront promenade in Fish Village. Counters full of amber stones, necklaces, bracelets and pendants at all price points. Enter from the river or the street-side of the building.

KALININGRAD REGION KALININGRAD

ⓘ Information

Emergency Hospital (Городская больница скорой медицинской помощи; ☑ emergency 4012-466 989; https://bsmp-39.ru; ul A Nevskogo 90; ⊙24hr)

Main Post Office (Почта; ☑ 4012-219 868; www.pochta.ru; ul Kosmonavta Leonova 22; ⊙8am-10pm Mon-Fri, 9am-6pm Sat & Sun) Located about 400m north of pr Mira. There's also a **post office** (Почта России; ☑ 4012-536 731; ul Chernyakhovskogo 32; ⊙8am-8pm Mon-Fri, 9am-6pm Sat, 9am-2pm Sun) near the Central Market.

Baltma Tours (☑ 4012-931 931; www.baltma.ru; 4th fl, pr Mira 94; ⊙9am-6pm Mon-Fri, to noon Sat) The multilingual staff here can arrange visas, accommodation, city tours and local excursions.

Konigsberg.ru (www.konigsberg.ru) Useful website with loads of info on visas, hotels and what's on in Kaliningrad.

Regional Tourism Information Centre (☑ 4012-957 980, 4012-555 200; www.visit-kaliningrad.ru; pr Mira 4; ⊙9am-8pm Mon-Fri, 11am-6pm Sat May-Sep, 9am-7pm Mon-Fri, 11am-4pm Sat Oct-Apr) Helpful, English-speaking staff and lots of information on the region.

Royal Castle (☑ 4012-350 782; www.kaliningradinfo.ru; Hotel Kaliningrad, Leninsky pr 81; ⊙8am-8pm Mon-Fri, 9am-4pm Sat; 🛜) Access the internet and book tours to the Curonian Spit (Kurshskaya Kosa) and elsewhere.

ⓘ Getting There & Away

AIR

Khrabrovo Airport (Аэропорт Храброво/KGD; ☑ 4012-610 620; www.kgd.aero) is 24km north of the city. Aeroflot and other Russian airlines offer several daily flights to Moscow's main airports as well as to St Petersburg and a handful of other Russian cities. Outside of Russia, service is available to Minsk, Warsaw, Riga and Barcelona.

BOAT

Trans-Exim (Транс-Эксим; ☑ ferries 4012-660 470; www.transexim.ru; ul Suvorova 45; ⊙10am-5pm Mon-Fri) has weekly car ferries between Baltiysk and Ust-Luga, 150km west of St Petersburg. See the website for the latest prices and schedules.

BUS

Kaliningrad has excellent local bus services to cities and towns around Kaliningrad province as well as to a handful of major cities in nearby countries, including Lithuania, Poland, Latvia and Germany. International services are operated by two main coach companies: **Ecolines** (☑ 4012-758 733; www.ecolines.net; ul Zheleznodorozhnaya 7; ⊙9.30am-10pm) and **König Avto** (☑ 4012-999 199; www.kenigauto.com). Nearly all buses, both local and international, depart from the **South Bus Station** (Автовокзал Южный, Yuzhny Bus Station; ul Zheleznodorozhnaya 7), though some coaches may use the city's **International Bus Station** (Международный Автовокзал Калининград; ☑ 4012-999 199; www.kenigauto.com; Moskovsky pr 184).

Buses are the easiest and often quickest way of reaching the main resorts on the Baltic Sea coast, including Yantarny (R100, 1½ hours, hourly), Svetlogorsk (R80, one hour, every 30 minutes) and Zelenogradsk (R60, 45 minutes, every 30 minutes), as well as to Chernyakhovsk (R150, two hours, six daily). Many, but not all buses, also stop at a small **bus stop** next to the North Train Station on Sovetsky pr. Buy tickets at station ticket windows or directly from the driver.

TRAIN

All long-distance and most local trains arrive at and depart from the **Main Train Station** (Южный вокзал, Yuzhny Vokzal; http://eng.rzd.ru; Zheleznodorozhnaya ul 15/23; ⊙5am-11pm). Some trains also pass through (but always stop at) the smaller but more centrally located **North Train Station** (Северный вокзал, Severny Vokzal; http://eng.rzd.ru; pl Pobedy 4a).

The train is a viable option for traveling to Svetlogorsk and Zelenogradsk, both of which have quick and frequent train services with the capital. Buy tickets at train station ticket counters.

INTERNATIONAL BUS SERVICES FROM KALININGRAD

DESTINATION	PRICE (R)	DURATION (HR)	FREQUENCY
Gdansk	400	4½	2 daily
Klaipėda	600	4	1-2 daily
Riga	1000	10	3 daily
Stuttgart	5200	24	1 weekly
Tallinn	2700	15	1 daily
Vilnius	900	8	2 daily
Warsaw	1000	9	1 daily

Local trains run on local time, but those that travel beyond the region to Moscow and St Petersburg have their arrival and departure times listed in Moscow time; if a Moscow-bound train is scheduled to depart at 10am, it will leave at 9am Kaliningrad time.

❶ Getting Around

Kaliningrad is a sprawling city and the public-transport network of buses, trams and trolleybuses is useful for getting around. Buy tickets (R18) from on-board conductors. Taxis are relatively cheap; getting between destinations within the city will cost R200 to R300. **Taxi Kaliningrad** (☑4012-585 858; www.taxi-kaliningrad.ru) is a reliable operator.

Bus 244E (R80, 45 minutes) shuttles between the airport and the South Bus Station, or you can order a taxi at kiosks stationed at the airport exit. A taxi to/from the airport is about R600.

Car rental is available from **City-Rent** (☑4012-509 191; www.city-rent39.com; pr Mira 26; ☺9am-9pm), which also has a branch at the airport. Rates start at R1900 per day.

Yantarny Янтарный

☑401532 / POP 5524 / ☺MOSCOW –1HR

Formerly known as Palmniken, the peaceful resort of Yantarny (Янтарный), 42km northwest of Kaliningrad and 24km southwest of Svetlogorsk, boasts arguably the nicest sandy beach in Kaliningrad. It's got a lovely seaside park and promenade and feels worlds away from the bustle of Kaliningrad city. It also happens to be the spot where 90% of the world's amber is sourced, and with some advanced booking it's possible to visit the amber mine and processing centre.

❍ Sights & Activities

While Yantarny's beach may be beautiful, the short swimming season runs most years only from July through August. There are public toilets at the beach, as well as scattered cafes to grab something to eat.

Another swimming option, with warmer water and easier waves, is at Yantarny Lake (Yantarnoe Ozero), a former quarry located 1km northeast of the town centre. There's a small beach adjacent to the Hotel Valtr. The lake, with crystal-clear water and a depth of up to 26m, also offers some of the best diving in Kaliningrad, and a couple of companies offer the chance to do so.

Diving is another possibility: contact the diving clubs **Poseidon 39** (☑8-906-238 6306; www.poseidon39.ru; Yantarny Lake) or **Demersus** (☑8-909-775 3222; www.demersus.ru; ul Ozernaya 1).

Becker Park   PARK
(ul Sovetskaya 70) **FREE** Enjoy a picnic in this park that stretches along the headland above the beach in the centre of Yantarny. Enter from behind the Schloss Hotel.

Kaliningrad Amber Plant   MINE
(Калининградский янтарный комбинат; ☑tours 40153-37 444; www.ambercombine.ru; ul Balebina 1; R180; ☺guided tours on the hour 9-11am & 1-4pm) The Kaliningrad Amber Plant offers tours of its amber-processing facility, including a view of an amber mill, an observation deck and the chance to see an enormous 'Amber Pyramid', a huge structure made of 800kg of amber. Visits are by guided tour (Russian only), which leave on the hour throughout the day. Tickets can be bought on-site, though it's best to call or email in advance.

✪ Festivals & Events

Amberfest   MUSIC
(www.amberfest.ru; ☺Aug) Celebrate the solar stone each August with amber-centric events and live music on the beach.

TRAIN SERVICES FROM KALININGRAD

DESTINATION	PRICE (R)	DURATION	FREQUENCY
Moscow	*platskart/kupe* from 2800/5000	20hr	1 daily
St Petersburg	*platskart/kupe* from 2700/4000	25hr	1 daily
Svetlogorsk	*obshchiy* 70	1hr	at least 6 daily
Vilnius	*platskart/kupe* from 2200/3800	6hr	2 daily
Zelenogradsk	*obshchiy* 60	40min	at least 4 daily

CHERNYAKHOVSK

Formerly the Prussian city of 'Insterburg', Chernyakhovsk (Черняховск) was founded by Teutonic Knights in 1336. Kaliningrad's second-largest city was thoroughly trashed during WWII. All that remains of its former grandeur are two ruined castles: **Georgenburg** (Замок Георгенбург; ul Tsentralnaya; tours R200; ☺10am-5pm) and **Insterburg** (Замок Инстербург; ☑40141-32 424; ul Zamkovaya 1; entry by donation; ☺8.30am-8pm). The estate of the former, about 3km north of Chernyakhovsk's town centre, now nudges the **Georgenburg Stud Farm** (☑40141-22 929, 40141-23 469; www.georgenburg.com; ul Tsentralnaya 18; tours per person R200; ☺9am-6pm) and its attached **hotel** (☑40141-23 501; www.georgenburg.com; ul Tsentralnaya 10; s/d from R2200/3000). Tranken horses have been bred at this impressive complex since 1812. The farm is also the location of the Georgenburg Cup, an international show-jumping tournament, typically held on the second weekend in September.

If horses aren't your thing stay at the cute **Pivnoy Dvor** (Пивной Двор; ☑40141-34 627; ul Suvorova 14; d R1500; ▣🅿🛜), opposite St Michael's Cathedral, one of Chernyakhovsk's last remaining examples of pre-WWII architecture. **Akvatoria** (Акватория; ☑40141-35 577; ul Lenina 11a; meals R250-500; ☺noon-midnight Sun-Thu, to 2am Fri & Sat) is a perfect in-town option for lunch or dinner, and the menu has something for everyone.

Chernyakhovsk's bus station is located at the southern end of ul Lenina, about 500m from the centre of the city. Buses and minibuses (R150, two hours, every 30 minutes) run to and from Kaliningrad's South Bus Station.

🛏 Sleeping

Galera
BUNGALOW $$

(Галера; ☑8-929-166 6061; www.a-kovalsky.ru; ul Sovetskaya 1; bungalows from R3000) These mega-modern beach bungalows, stacked one on top of the other like cubes, are located on the far northern end of Yantarny's beach and offer pretty sea views from huge glass doors. They have self-contained kitchens, or you can eat at the nearby Galera restaurant (open 11am to 11pm Sunday to Thursday, to 4am Friday and Saturday), shaped like a huge ship.

★ Schloss Hotel
HOTEL $$$

(☑4012-555 040; www.schloss-hotel.ru; ul Sovetskaya 70; s/d from R6800/8000; ▣🛜🛜) This decadent hotel offers elegance to the max. Its renovated, snow-white mansion was once the hunting lodge of Prussian King George Friedrich and today houses luxurious rooms (some with plunge baths and balconies), a sophisticated spa, upmarket bar and **res-taurant** (☑4012-555 040; www.schloss-hotel.ru; ul Sovetskaya 70; mains R600-1000; ☺11am-10pm; 🛜) and a summer terrace with sea views.

Becker Hotel
HOTEL $$$

(Отель Беккер; ☑4012-565 195; www.hotel-becker.ru; ul Sovetskaya 72; s/d incl breakfast from R4000/6000; 🛜) The Becker, a quick stroll to the beach and Becker Park, has a vaguely anti-septic feel (like a spa or hospital) but pleasantly furnished rooms; some have balconies. The attached **Becker Restaurant** (mains R400-600;

☺noon-11pm; 🛜) has a terrace overlooking the seaside. The hotel stands at the southern end of Yantarny, 400m beyond the town entrance if arriving by bus from Kaliningrad.

❶ Getting There & Away

Bus 120 runs to Yantarny from Kaliningrad (R100, 1½ hours, hourly). Buses 286 runs to Yantarny from Svetlogorsk (R50, one hour, four daily).

Note that there's no central bus station in Yantarny. Rather, buses stop at around 200m intervals along ul Sovetskaya. Tell the bus driver or conductor the name of your hotel to get off at the closest stop.

Svetlogorsk   Светлогорск

☑40153 / POP 10,772 / ☺MOSCOW –1HR

Known as Rauschen until 1947, Svetlogorsk (Светлогорск) is a peaceful, slow-paced spa town, 40km northwest of Kaliningrad. The narrow beach, backed by steep, sandy slopes, is nothing to speak of, but the pretty old German houses, revamped sanatoriums, top-class hotels and dappled forest setting make it worth a visit. Fairly untouched by WWII, Svetlogorsk has benefited from being declared a federal health resort, with good infrastructure and facilities.

⊙ Sights

Svetlogorsk's swimming season runs from early July through August. The best beach is west of the Grand Palace hotel. To find it, follow per

Beregovoy down from ul Lenina, turning left at the sea. The seafront promenade runs for about 2km; it's a pretty 30-minute stroll.

Svetlogorsk is spread out but easy to navigate on foot or by bicycle: rent bikes from the Svetlogorsk Tourist Information Centre (☑ 40153-22 098; www.svetlogorsk-tourism. ru; ul Karla Marksa 7a; ⊙ 10am-7pm Mon-Sat, to 4pm Sun; ☎).

Herman Brachert House-Museum MUSEUM
(Дом-музей Германа Брахерта; ☑ 40153-21 166; www.brachert.ru; ul Tokareva 7; R150; ⊙ 10am-5pm Mon-Thu, to 4pm Sat & Sun) This museum features the work of Herman Brachert (1890–1972), the sculptor whose work can be spotted all around Svetlogorsk; his bronze **Nymph statue** resides in a mosaic-decorated shell on the promenade. His small former home is decorated with more of his pieces and other works by contemporary sculptors. Head around 2km west along the main road from Svetlogorsk II train station to reach the suburb of Otradnoe.

Water Tower TOWER
(Kurortnaya ul 1) The elaborate 25m-high water tower just off ul Lenina is the symbol of Svetlogorsk. The tower was designed in a vaguely art nouveau style by architect Otto Walter Kukuck in 1908. The interior is closed to the general public.

Model of Medieval Königsberg SCULPTURE
FREE This sandbox-sized model of early-16th-century Königsberg is well worth the 200m walk west of the Svetlogorsk Tourist Information Centre along ul Gorkogo to see more than 500 buildings faithfully reconstructed, including the old Royal Castle and Cathedral. Find it beneath some trees across the street from the Dom Skazochnika hotel.

Sundial MONUMENT
(ul Morskaya, Seafront Promenade) **FREE** On the promenade, this impressive sundial is decorated with an eye-catching mosaic of the zodiac.

🛏 Sleeping

Most rates for Svetlogorsk accommodation include breakfast and are for the July/August season; prices can drop by a third or more at other times.

★ **Dom Skazochnika** GUESTHOUSE $$
(Дом Сказочника; ☑ 40153-22 396; www.hoffmann-house.ru; Skazochnika Gofmana per 2; s/d from R2800/3800, breakfast R200) The name

means 'House of the Storyteller', and what a fairy-tale place this is. Named in honour of fantasist Ernst Hoffman, this enchanting guesthouse has a *Babes in the Woods* setting, an art gallery and a delightful miniature sculpture garden. High-ceilinged rooms are comfortable, the service is superb and the attached restaurant is wonderful.

Stary Doktor HOTEL $$
(☑ 40153-21 362; www.alterdoktor.ru; ul Gagarina 12; d from R3500, attic with shared bathroom R2500) Set in an atmospheric 19th-century sanctuary in a graceful residential neighbourhood, this place oozes ye olde charm. Rooms are simple and cosy.

Hotel Georgensvaldye HOTEL $$
(Георгенсвальде; ☑ 40153-21 526; www.walde. ru; ul Tokareva 6; r from R3500) In the village of Otradnoe, about 2km west of Svetlogorsk, this historic four-storey hotel stands opposite the Herman Brachert House-Museum. It's an elegant place, with a gazebo and gardens, and ideal for those seeking peace and quiet.

Lumier Art Hotel BOUTIQUE HOTEL $$$
(Люмьер Арт-отель; ☑ 4012-507 750; www. hotellumier.ru; per Lermontovsky 2a; standard/ theme r from R5000/6000, breakfast R550; ❀☎) This playful boutique hotel has silver-screen-themed rooms ranging from *Little Red Riding Hood* to *Gone With the Wind*. Even the standard rooms come with cable TV and DVD players. Many rooms have balconies. The rooms at the back of the hotel are quieter.

Royal Falke Resort & Spa HOTEL $$$
(☑ 40153-21 600; www.falke-hotel.ru; ul Lenina 1b; s/d from R5200/6200; ❀@☎❀) This luxurious hotel is a good choice for pampering. Its indoor pool, surrounded by landscaping and murals, is big enough for a decent swim. Families with small children are exceptionally well taken care of here, with everything from babysitters to bottle warmers available.

🍴 Eating

Svetlogorsk lacks standout restaurants. The seafront promenade and the main drag, ul Lenina, are lined with pizza and kebab joints.

Kruassan INTERNATIONAL $
(Круассан-кафе, Croissant Cafe; ☑ 4012-389 469; www.kruassan.com; ul Lenina 33a; mains R150-300; ⊙ 9am-11pm) This popular bakery-cafe next to the Svetlogorsk II train station serves excellent coffee, with daily breakfasts until 2pm and comfy outdoor tables to watch the

world go by. Lunch and dinner offerings include a wide variety of soups, salads and sandwiches, as well as more ambitious fish and chicken dishes.

Dom Rybaka SEAFOOD **$$**
(Дом Рыбака; ☑ 8-909-790 9222; per Beregovoy 1; mains R400-600; ☺ noon-11pm) A pretty seaside setting and good fish dishes are a winning combination at one of the few above-average restaurants in town. Excellent fish soup, a scrumptious baked halibut and a long list of other fish-based mains (plus a few chicken and beef options) are the main drawcards. The dining room is simple but cosy; there are outside tables in summer.

Novy Ochag ARMENIAN **$$**
(Новый очаг; ☑ 8-906-211 0371; Oktyabrskaya ul 19; mains R300-400; ☺ 11am-midnight) The food is only so-so at this Armenian-inflected grill restaurant, just off ul Lenina, but the pretty setting, on a bluff overlooking the sea, is ample reason to stop by. Most diners opt for one of the big fish, pork or chicken kebabs, but there are lots of soups and salads on the menu, plus a long wine list.

☆ Entertainment

Organ Hall CONCERT VENUE
(Зал Органной музыки; www.organhall.ru; ul Kurortnaya 3) Svetlogorsk's organ-recital hall began life as a Prussian Catholic church. It fell into disrepair and was rebuilt for its current purpose in the mid-1990s. In season (May to September), daily organ concerts take place at noon and 8pm. Tickets range from R400 to R600 and can be purchased at the venue box office.

❶ Getting There & Away

From Kaliningrad take a train (R70, one hour, at least six daily) or bus (R80, one hour, every 30 minutes). Kaliningrad buses arrive at and depart from the **bus stop** in front of the Svetlogorsk II train station. The bus stops for **Yantarny** (R50, one hour, four daily) and **Zelenogradsk** (R60, one hour, four daily) are on pr Kaliningradsky, facing Lake Tikhoe.

Zelenogradsk Зеленоградск

☑ 40150 / POP 13,026 / ☺ MOSCOW −1HR
The long beach that gave Zelenogradsk (Зеленоградск; formerly known as 'Kranz') the status of a royal bathing resort for the Kingdom of Prussia is still the town's prime attraction. It's a low-key place with a nostalgic

atmosphere: crumbling Soviet eyesores, lovely German buildings and modern villas stand side by side. Renovation of the promenade has been going on for years, but it's still possible to enjoy a seaside perambulation. In addition to the beach, Zelenogradsk is the gateway to Kurshskaya Kosa (Curonian Spit) National Park.

◎ Sights

Murrarium MUSEUM
(☑ 40150-31 020; www.murarium.ru; ul Saratovskaya 2a; adult/child R280/230; ☺ noon-7pm Tue-Sun) Housed in an old brick water tower, the Murrarium features the largest private collection of cat-themed art in all of Russia, a feline-fixated country if there ever was one. There are more than 3500 pieces on display, some kitsch, some comely; even if you're not a cat person, the views from the tower make a visit worthwhile.

⛺ Sleeping

High season is in July and August and most rates include breakfast. Book well in advance as the town fills up during these months.

★ Butik Hotel 12 BOUTIQUE HOTEL **$$**
(☑ 40150-51 313; ul Lenina 32a; s/d R3400/4000; P ⛅) Who would have imagined such a smart boutique hotel in Zelenogradsk? The stylish, minimalist design features a lobby awash in colour and light. The rooms pick up the theme with light woods, splashes of bright colour and big windows. The location is 700m west of the bus and train stations, and 60m from the beach. There's an excellent on-site restaurant.

Koshkin Dom GUESTHOUSE **$$**
(Кошкин Дом; ☑ 40150-33 546; www.koshkin-dom.ru; ul Gagarina 1a; s/d from R2600/3800; P ⛅ ⛲) Zelenogradsk's famous 'Cat House' is a welcoming, homey spot 50m from the beach. Though it looks like a towering mansion from the street, there are only 10 rooms, including one well-priced single. In addition to the cornucopia of cat figurines and artworks, there's also a sauna, swimming pool, barbecue area and billiards room. Bike rental is R100 per hour.

Hotel Sambia HOTEL **$$$**
(Отель Самбия; ☑ 40150-36 221; www.sambiahotel.com; ul Volodarskogo 20; r from R4200; P ✳ ⛅ ⛲) The biggest hotel in Zelenogradsk and one of the best, this family-friendly complex has two restaurants, a spa, billiards

room and mini water park. It occupies a prominent spot at the eastern end of the seafront promenade and is popular with families. Some rooms have balconies with sea views. Find it 1km east of the bus and rail stations.

Crystal Hotel
HOTEL $$$

(☑ 40150-29 333; www.crystalhotel.ru; ul Gagarina 19a; s/d R3000/5000; ☎) The Crystal offers some of the cheapest in-season rooms and is also a nice place to bunk down. Some of the rooms, particularly on the upper floors, offer sea views. There's also a decent restaurant and spa on the premises. It's located about 50m inland from the beach and about 600m west of the bus and train stations.

Villa Lana
GUESTHOUSE $$$

(Вилла Лана; ☑ 40150-33 410; www.villa-lana.ru; ul Gagarina 3a; s/d/apt R5400/5600/6800; ☎) This professionally run guesthouse just 50m from the beach offers spacious, nicely decorated rooms, plus a separate self-catering apartment that sleeps four. Helpful staff speak six languages and can help arrange tours and airport transfers.

✖ Eating

Ambar
RUSSIAN, POLISH $$

(Амбар; ☑ 8-981-470 8002; www.ambar2010.ru; ul Volodarskogo 30; mains R300-500; ☺ 11am-midnight) Considered the best of many restaurants on the seafront promenade, Ambar sits on the far eastern end of the beach. It's meant to evoke a seafront log cabin. The menu is filled with grilled meats and fish dishes, with several Polish and Lithuanian mains on the menu, as well as very good Lithuanian beer. Book in advance.

Captain Flint
TAVERNA $$

(Капитан Флинт; ☑ 40150-32 459; www.taverna-flinta.ru; Kurortniy per 1; mains R300-400; ☺ noon-2am) An informal tavern-style restaurant that's dolled up in all matters mariner. It's situated away from the seafront promenade, so it's often easier to find a seat here than at places closer to the beach. Serves above-average kebabs and grilled meats, as well as lots of fish dishes and salads.

❶ Getting There & Away

Frequent buses run to and from Kaliningrad (R60, 45 minutes, every 30 minutes) from a small bus station in the centre of town, located next to the train station. Buses also leave from here to Svetlogorsk (R60, around one hour, four daily), with onward service to Yantarny (R100, around two hours).

At least five minibuses per day make the run from the bus station to the main towns on the Curonian Spit (Kurshskaya Kosa). All minibuses stop in Lesnoy (R30, 15 minutes), Rybachy (R75, 30 minutes) and Morskoe (R100, 45 minutes). These buses fill to the gills in summer, so check the timetable posted at the station and turn up well in advance of the departure time to get a seat.

Regular trains run to and from Kaliningrad (R60, 40 minutes, several daily).

Kurshskaya Kosa
Куршская Коса

☑ 40150 / ⊘ MOSCOW −1HR

Tall, windswept dunes, pristine beaches and dense pine forests teeming with wildlife lie along the 98km-long Curonian Spit (Kurshskaya Kosa; Куршская Коса), a Unesco World Heritage Site that divides the Baltic Sea (to the west) from the tranquil Curonian Lagoon (on the eastern side). The 50km of the spit within Russian territory (the rest is in Lithuania) constitutes **Kurshskaya Kosa National Park** (Национальный парк Куршская коса; ☑ 40150-45 119; www.park-kosa. ru; per person/car R50/300). The park is home to the highest drifting dunes in Europe, with some reaching a lofty 60m. Mellow fishing and holiday villages dot the eastern coast (along the lagoon). From south to north they are **Lesnoy** (Лесной; formerly Sarkau), **Rybachy** (Рыбачий; formerly Rossitten) and **Morskoe** (Морское; formerly Pilkoppen).

◉ Sights & Activities

Epha's Height
HIKING

(Высота Эфа; km42) About 3km south of Morskoe village, this photogenic 2.8km hiking trail has boardwalks stretching from one side of the spit to the other, climaxing at the 40m-high **Big Dune Ridge** (Коса Большая Дюна). Along the way you'll see Europe's highest drifting dune, the 62m-high **Orekhovoy Dune**. If travelling by bus, tell the driver this is where you'd like to stop.

Dancing Forest
FOREST

(Танцующий лес; km36) One of Kurshskaya Kosa National Park's most remarkable sights is this aptly named forest, where the pines have been sculpted into twisting shapes by the elements – they do indeed appear to be frozen mid-boogie.

National Park Museum
MUSEUM

(Национальный парк-музей; ☑ 40150-45 247; www.park-kosa.ru; km14; R100; ☺ 10am-5pm Tue-Sun May-Sep, 10am-4.30pm Tue-Sun Oct-Apr) This museum offers basic information about Kurshskaya Kosa National Park's habitat and history. The complex is also home to more than 100 carved-wood mythological characters at the **Museum of Russian Superstitions** (Музей Русских Суеверий; ☑ 4012-532 907; www.park-kosa.ru; km14; ☺ 10am-5pm) FREE. Prearrange an excursion to the **Fringilla Ornithological Station** (Орнитологическая станция Фрингилла; www.zin.ru/rybachy/index-_e.html; km23; tours R100; ☺ 9am-5pm Apr-Oct), a bird-ringing centre where enormous funnelled nets can trap an average of 1000 birds a day; the birds are then tagged, studied and released.

🛏 Sleeping

Chalet Dunes
CAMPGROUND $

(Турбаза Дюны; ☑ reception 40150-33 726, sales office 4012-384 320; turbazaduna39@gmail.com; km16; standard/luxury cabins R1000/1300) These simple cabins are strictly no-frills, budget options. Frankly, the property could be maintained better, but the 'luxury' cabins are not bad for the price and it's a short walk to the beach. There's no power, but there is an authentic *banya* (hot bath; R1000 per hour), a social barbecue area and bracing sea breezes. It's 3km north of Lesnoy.

Altrimo
HOTEL $$

(Гостиничный комплекс Альтримо; ☑ 8-658-863 4012; www.altrimo.ru; ul Pogranichnaya 11, Rybachy; r/ste from R3400/5000; ❋ 🅂) Rybachy's most upmarket option. Although the rooms and facilities feel dated, it has a quiet location next to the lagoon. Amenities include a pleasant open-air restaurant and a pretty garden for strolling and relaxing. It's popular with weddings and families, and there are jet-skis, kayaks and other watercraft available for rent.

Mayakovski Hotel
HOTEL $$$

(Маяковский; ☑ 40150-33 716; www.mayakovski-hotel.ru; seafront promenade, Lesnoy; r R5300-6500; ❋ 🅂) The Mayakovski feels fresh and well maintained and is easily one of the best places to stay on the Curonian Spit. It's located just off the beach in Lesnoy.

The setting is a seafront cabin and the 10 rooms mix rustic elements like hardwood floors and wood-beamed walls with modern touches. There's a **restaurant** (☑ 40150-33 716; www.mayakovski-hotel.ru; seafront promenade, Lesnoy; mains R400-600; ☺ 11am-11pm; 🅂), spa and pretty pool on-site.

Walde Park
HOTEL $$$

(☑ 4012-400 008; www.walde-park.ru; Tsentralnaya ul 17, Lesnoy; r from R5000; Ⓟ❋🅂) This cheery, modern hotel, about 500m from the beach and close to the highway, got a major refresh in 2016 with new carpets and baths. Rooms come in several varieties, including large family-sized suites. Rooms at the back are quieter and offer garden views. There's a restaurant and the hotel rents out bicycles (R120 per hour).

ℹ Getting There & Away

Buses depart from Zelenogradsk's bus station at roughly two-hour intervals throughout the day, calling on Lesnoy (R30, 15 minutes), Rybachy (R75, 30 minutes) and Morskoe (R100, 45 minutes). Buy tickets from the driver. There are also direct buses from Kaliningrad to Morskoe (R150, two hours, four daily), stopping at Zelenogradsk, Lesnoy and Rybachy along the way. Kaliningrad's Regional Tourism Information Centre (p284) has the current timetable.

ℹ Getting Around

The Curonian Spit is best explored with your own car, and it's possible to hire one in Kaliningrad (from around R1900 per day). Hotels in Zelenogradsk occasionally rent out cars as well. Ask at your reception desk.

Buses are the only public-transport option, with most of these departing from Zelenogradsk's central bus station or Kaliningrad's South Bus Station. From May to September around half a dozen buses per day move up and down the spit, at roughly two-hour intervals, making scheduled stops at Lesnoy, Rybachy and Morskoe, as well as request stops at various points along the highway. Unless you're travelling to one of the towns, tell the bus driver on entering the bus where you'd like to stop. Buy tickets from the driver.

Taxis are an expensive fallback; it's normally possible in summer to find a cab in Lesnoy or Rybachy. Expect to pay R300 for the ride back to Zelenogradsk; the ride from Rybachy will cost around R500.

Northern European Russia

Best Places to Eat

➡ Genatsvale (p296)

➡ Izba (p305)

➡ Karelskaya Gornitsa (p297)

➡ Sem Vecherov (p328)

➡ Terrasa (p323)

Best Places to Stay

➡ Hotel Angliter (p327)

➡ Hostel Troika (p310)

➡ Solovki Hotel (p305)

➡ Azimut Hotel Murmansk (p322)

➡ Mini-Hotel Ilma (p296)

Why Go?

Russia's far north, with its stunning and often harsh natural beauty, is a place of startling extremes, best typified by the perpetual darkness of polar night and the midnight sun of polar day.

The inspiration for the epic poetry of the *Kalevala,* this vast region contains some of Russia's most celebrated sights, including the iconic wooden architecture of Kizhi Island, the remote Solovetsky Islands whose monastery once housed a notorious Gulag camp, and the frigid shores of the Barents Sea. This is also one of the best places to witness the northern lights as well as to explore Soviet-era ruins.

Travelling in Northern European Russia takes a lot of patience at times, and the weather can be unpredictable, with blistering sunshine turning quickly into icy rainstorms. But the reward for perseverance is an insight into one of Russia's most mesmerising regions.

When to Go
Murmansk

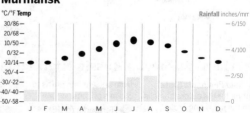

Early Mar–Apr Days are long and there's plenty of snow for dog sledding and skiing.

Early Jun–late Jul The fleeting summer is ideal for island access and fun in the midnight sun.

Late Nov–mid-Jan Scan the perpetually sunless skies for the gasp-inducing aurora borealis.

Northern European Russia Highlights

① **Kola Peninsula** (p312)
Hunting for the aurora borealis amid the sprawling Arctic wilderness.

② **Solovetsky Islands** (p301) Discovering these far-flung islands' long history,

from ancient labyrinths to Stalin's prisons.

③ **Teriberka** (p316)
Wandering the Arctic coastline in this ever-evocative fishing village.

④ **Kizhi** (p298) Spending

a day exploring this island's architectural wonders.

⑤ **Murmansk** (p317)
Swimming with the human walruses and boarding a nuclear icebreaker in the world's biggest Arctic city.

History

Petroglyphs and mysterious stone labyrinths attest to a now-mysterious religious life that existed as early as the 3rd millennium BC in this northern region.

From the 11th century AD, Russians from Novgorod made hunting, fishing and trapping expeditions to the White Sea area. Some of their seasonal camps eventually became permanent settlements. These Pomors (coast dwellers) developed a distinct material culture and their own lively dialect of Russian.

Moscow grabbed the Vologda area in the early 15th century and annexed the rest of the northwest from Novgorod in 1478. Shortly after, the unexpected arrival of English sailors seeking a northeast passage to China gave Ivan the Terrible the idea of founding a port and commencing trade with the west. That port, Arkhangelsk, bloomed, as did many towns on its river supply route. All this changed, however, once Peter the Great founded St Petersburg in 1703, offering much easier access to the sea. Formerly forgotten Karelia was suddenly the supply centre for building Peter's new capital, and Petrozavodsk was founded a year later to produce armaments for his wars with Sweden.

Founding Murmansk

The northwest's biggest city, Murmansk, was founded during WWI when embattled tsarist Russia was in desperate need of supplies from its Western allies. But no sooner had the Murmansk–Moscow railway been laid than the October Revolution changed circumstances entirely. The Western allies, which opposed the new Bolshevik regime, occupied Murmansk and Arkhangelsk for two years and at one point advanced south almost to Petrozavodsk.

From the 1920s the Murmansk railway helped Soviet governments unlock the Kola Peninsula's vast mineral resources, bringing new towns such as Monchegorsk and Kirovsk into existence. Gulag prisoners were part of the force that built the region's new factories and the White Sea–Baltic Canal.

WWII & After

Stalin invaded Finland in 1939–40. Having been independent from Russia only since 1917, Finland allied with Germany to counter-attack along the entire Soviet–Finnish border, eventually occupying Petrozavodsk. Once again, anti-German allies fought desperately to prevent a Russian defeat, sending highly risky supply convoys from Scot-land to embattled Murmansk and Arkhangelsk. Those ports held out but were both bombed to rubble by the Luftwaffe. In 1944 the Red Army fought back, pushing the Nazis out of Norway and claiming a chunk of southeastern Finland, which remains part of Russia's Republic of Karelia today. Many ethnic Finns and Karelians (a Finno-Ugric people related to Finns and Estonians) fled to Finland, and today only about 10% of the Republic of Karelia's 720,000 population is actually Karelian.

In the 1990s the Kola Peninsula's heavy industries and naval and military installations were especially hard hit by the collapse of the USSR's command economy, and cities suffered a big population decline. Despite ongoing problems, strong ties with Scandinavia mean the region's big cities have a progressive air that is unusual for provincial Russia.

REPUBLIC OF KARELIA

Stretching north and west of Petrozavodsk, Karelia is Russia's Land O' The Lakes, dotted with villages and with ample opportunities for fishing and hiking. Wild camping is permitted almost anywhere unless there are signs with the words 'Не разбивать палатку'. Signs saying 'Не разжигать костры' mean 'no campfires'. Lakes and rivers offer canoeing opportunities and some outfits offer rafting, albeit without many rapids. Culturally, the most rewarding day-trip destination from Petrozavodsk is Kizhi, a wonder of wooden architecture.

Petrozavodsk Петрозаводск

🖉 8142 / POP 277,111 / ⊘ MOSCOW

Set on a bay on vast Lake Onega, Petrozavodsk is the launching point for summer visits to two of the region's biggest attractions: Kizhi Island and Valaam Monastery. The name ('Peter's factory') refers to a munitions plant founded here by Peter the Great in 1703, and superseded 70 years later by the Alexandrovskiy Ironworks (still standing). But Petrozavodsk is by no means the gritty, industrial city its name would suggest. Its neoclassical facades, a large student population and connections with Finland all make for a distinctly European atmosphere, and the appealing lakefront promenade is made for strolling. There are no truly must-see sights here, but it's a pleasant enough place to spend a day or two before or after a trip to Kizhi.

Petrozavodsk

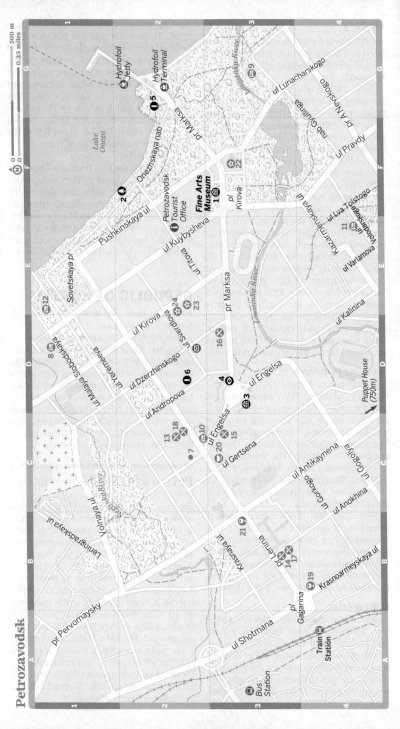

0 500 m
0 0.25 miles

Lake Onega

Hydrofoil Jetty
Hydrofoil Terminal

Onezhskaya nab
pr Marksa
ul Lunacharskogo
nab Gyullinga
pr A Nevskogo
ul Pravdy

Petrozavodsk Tourist Office
Fine Arts Museum 1

pl Kirova
22

Pushkinskaya ul
ul Kuybysheva
ul Titova
Kazarmenskaya ul
ul Lva Tolstogo
Volodarskogo
11
ul Varlamova

Sovetskaya pl
24
23
pr Marksa
Losossinka River
ul Kalinina

ul Kirova
ul Sverdlova
16

8
Matrosa Slobodskaya ul
ul Dzerzhinskogo
6
4
ul Engelsa
Puppet House (750m)

ul Yeremena
ul Andropova
3

13 18
10
15
ul Engelsa
ul Gertsena
ul Antikaynena
ul Gorkogo
ul Anokhina
ul Gogolya

7
20

21

pr Pervomaysky
Leningradskaya ul
Volnaya ul
Neglinka River
Krasnaya ul
pl Lenina
14 17
19
Krasnoarmeyskaya ul

pl Gagarina
ul Shotmana
Bus Station
Train Station

Petrozavodsk

NORTHERN EUROPEAN RUSSIA PETROZAVODSK

◎ Sights

★ Fine Arts Museum   MUSEUM
(Музей изобразительных искусств; www.art-museum.karelia.ru; pr Marksa 8; R400; ⊘ 10am-6pm Tue-Sun; 🚌 8, 12, 17, 19) Besides the permanent exhibitions that feature medieval icons, and folk art such as embroidery, weaving and birch-bark creations, there's a collection of 18th-century Russian Masters that includes a dark and creepy *Christ in Gethsemane* by Ilya Repin, and interesting temporary exhibitions.

Museum of Regional Studies   MUSEUM
(Карельский   государственный краеведческий музей; www.kgkm.karelia.ru; pl Lenina 1; R150; ⊘ 10am-5.30pm Tue-Sun; 🚌 5, 8, 12, 17, 19) Besides exhibitions on trade between Russia's north and the Byzantine world, the history of the city and regional trades, this excellent museum (with English captioning) introduces you to the mysteries of ancient stone labyrinths and the *Kalevala*, Finland's national epic, which was pieced together in the 19th century from northern Karelian song-poems.

Lakeside Promenade   PARK
(🚌 5, 19, 25, 29) On a fine summer's day, scores of strolling families, rollerbladers and cyclists take to the Lake Onega promenade – an appealing park area scattered liberally with summer cafes serving *shashlyk* (meat kebab) and beer, and a host of contemporary sculptures by home-grown and international talent. The most striking of them are the silver *Fishermen* throwing in a net and the elk-like *Sleeping Beauty*, symbolising unity between Karelian woman and nature.

Ploshchad Lenina   SQUARE
(Площадь Ленина) The circular pl Lenina is the original heart of neoclassical Petrozavodsk, skirted by matching semicircular buildings built in 1784. In its centre is a 1933 statue of Lenin. Steps pass an eternal flame into the pretty riverside park, from where a bridge crosses to the surprisingly grand facade of the former Alexandrovskiy Ironworks, now part of the vast Onezhskiy Tractor Factory.

Statue of Yury Andropov   MONUMENT
(Памятник Юрию Андропову; pl Andropova; 🚌 4, 5 , 12) Unveiled to protests and arrests in 2005, a youthful statue of Yury Andropov commemorates the USSR's 1982–84 supremo and chief of Petrozavodsk's Komsomol (Communist Party youth wing) some 50 years earlier. Andropov was a long-term KGB director and some believe that had he not died, he would have implemented necessary reforms without breaking up the Soviet Union, unlike Gorbachev.

Puppet House   MUSEUM
(Дом Кукол; http://kukla.karelia.ru; nab La Rochelle 13; R175; ⊘ noon-5pm Mon-Sat; 🚌 21) A remarkable and somewhat creepy collection of handmade creations by one of Russia's foremost puppet mistresses. Storybook heroes, mythological creatures and folk-tale evil-doers are re-created here and each doll is unique.

Statue of Peter the Great MONUMENT
(Памятник Петру I; pr Karla Marksa) Close to the hydrofoil terminal is a jaunty statue of Peter the Great pointing to the spot where Petrozavodsk would be founded.

🏃 Activities & Tours

Intourist-Petrozavodsk TOURS
(Интурист-Петрозаводск; ☑ 8142-592 900; http://ru.go-karelia.com; Hotel Severnaya, pr Lenina 21; ☐ 17, 1) Multilingual agency that can help arrange fishing, skiing and adventure tours around Karelia.

Nordic Travel TOURS
(☑ 8142-762 330; www.nordictravel.ru; ul Engelsa 10; ☐ 17) Tours of Karelia, the Russian Arctic and Solovetsky Islands.

RussiaDiscovery North-West ADVENTURE
(☑ 921-458 6465; www.russiadiscovery.ru) Specialist in active Karelia adventures such as quad-bike tours and snowmobile tours. Based in Moscow.

🎊 Festivals & Events

Hyperborea Festival FIESTA
(⊙ Jan-Feb) Chase the winter blues away at this festival celebrating all things snow and ice. Held lakeside.

🛌 Sleeping

★ Mini-Hotel Ilma HOTEL $$
(Гостиница Илма; ☑ 8-911-661 4516; www.ilmahotel.ru; ul Volodarskogo 10; s/d/dm from R2500/2500/650; ☎; ☐ 20) Well-located mini-hotel with a fresh colour scheme, friendly staff and a small guest kitchen. Also has a hostel out back with bunk beds in bright rooms. Breakfast costs an extra R150.

Hotel Severnaya HOTEL $$
(Гостиница Северная; ☑ 8-800-700 1670; www.otel-severnaya.ru; pr Lenina 21; s/d/ste R2250/2450/6000; ☎☎; ☐ 4, 5, 12) This centrally-located, refurbished Soviet-era hotel has a mixture of anonymous rooms and elegant en suite accommodation. Front-facing rooms suffer from street noise. The grand in-house restaurant (mains from R290) has its own brewery. Included breakfast buffet.

13 Chairs HOTEL $$
(Бутик-отель 13 Стульев; ☑ 8-921-220 4444; http://13hotel.ru; nab Neglinskaya 13; s/d/ste from R3300/3800/5500; ☎☎☎; ☐ 4, 8, 14) The rooms at this boutiquey hotel are designed

to imitate a romantic 19th-century fantasy without actually investing in period furniture. Extra (anachronistic) pampering comes in the form of a pool, sauna and spa.

Hotel Karelia HOTEL $$$
(Отель Карелия; ☑ 8142-733 333; www.kare-lia-hotel.ru; nab Gyullinga 2; s/d/apt/ste from R3000/3800/4400/10960; ☐☎☎; ☐ 19, 25) This bustling multistorey tower feels a little like an upmarket clinic, with a health-spa complex offering various massages, baths and beauty treatments. Many rooms have good lake views. The beds in the cheaper options aren't particularly comfortable.

Onego Palace HOTEL $$$
(Гостиничный комплекс Онего Палас; ☑ 8142-790 790; www.onegopalace.com; ul Kuybysheva 26; s/d/ste from R2500/3100/5700; ☎; ☐ 101) This monolith looks a bit like a UFO looming over the lake from which it takes its name. Thankfully its interior is a lot less gauche, with classically styled rooms and three upmarket restaurants. Athletic types will appreciate the gym and saunas; for everyone else, there's a 24-hour lobby bar.

🍴 Eating

Petrozavodsk is the best place to try traditional Karelian food, including the *kalitki* pastries that are sold everywhere. For self-catering, head to the well-stocked **Lotos** (Лотос; ul Anokhina 37; ⊙ 8am-midnight) or **Sigma** (Сигма; ul Lenina 18; ⊙ 8am-10pm; ☐ 17).

La Parisienne CAFE $
(Парижанка; www.parizhanka-cafe.ru; pr Marksa 22; mains from R230; ⊙ 8am-midnight; ☎; ☐ 17) Come to this spacious European-style cafe for the good coffee, tea, and tasty pastries. Order the dill-topped pizza at your peril, though.

Deja Vu FUSION $
(Дежавю; pr Lenina 20; mains from R195; ⊙ 9am-2am; ☎; ☐ 17) Small but inexpensive salads, soups and light mains served in an upbeat, youthful atmosphere where the déjà vu in question is the Eiffel Tower, a giant photo of which is echoed in ironwork motifs above the bar.

★ Genatsvale GEORGIAN $$
(Генацвале; pr Lenina 35; mains from R310; ☎) Despite a somewhat gaudy facade, Genyatsvale is a laid-back, tastefully decorated Georgian cafe with blown-up photos of the motherland on the walls. Serves perfectly

made *khachapuri po ajarski* (flatbread filled with melted cheese and a runny egg). Friendly staff and a good Georgian wine list.

★ **Karelskaya Gornitsa** KARELIAN $$
(Карельская Горница; www.gornica.ru; ul Engelsa 13a; mains R320-850; ⊙noon-midnight; 📖17) Claiming to be the first Karelian restaurant in the world, this ye-olde hot spot boasts excellent, hearty fare, including rabbit borsch and rich, gamey and fishy mains, washed down with its own *medovukha* (honey mead). The wild mushroom soup (*pokhlebka gribnaya*) is superb.

Dobra Khata UKRAINIAN $$
(Добра Хата; ul Engelsa 13; mains from R275; ⊙noon-midnight; 🖥️) The rustic Ukrainian theme is worked to the max here – expect a cheery stove, woven tablecloths, sunflowers, clay jugs and nostalgic sepia prints of Ukrainian peasantry. Maidens in traditional costume serve you all the favourites: *draniki* (potato fritters), *vareniki* (filled dumplings), borsch, grilled meats and tankards of *kvas* (fermented rye bread water).

🍷 Drinking & Nightlife

★ **Kivach** BAR
(Кивач; pr Lenina 28; ⊙8am-2am Sun-Thu, 8am-5am Fri & Sat; 🖥️; 📖4, 5, 12) Popular with a youngish crowd, this centrally-located bar-cafe serves pizza and grilled meat dishes (mains from R310), and has imported beers on tap. It also has table football.

Kaffee Haus CAFE
(Кофейный Дом; pr Lenina 23; ⊙9am-1am; 🖥️; 📖17) Widely acclaimed for Petrozavodsk's best coffee and cakes.

Fusion BAR
(Krasnoarmeyskaya ul 33; ⊙8.30am-2am; 🖥️; 📖17) This super-sleek Russo-Japanese-style hang-out by the train station dishes up lethal cocktails every bit as delicious as the authentic sushi snacks (from R85). Popular with the young trendies.

☆ Entertainment

Rock Bar FM LIVE MUSIC
(Рок-бар FM; www.vk.com/rockbarfm; ul Kirova 12; cover from R150; ⊙6pm until late; 📖12) This large student-oriented basement bar beneath the Philharmonia is where Peterozavodsk's fledgling and established rock bands come to strut their stuff.

Musical Theatre THEATRE
(Музыкальный театр; 🖃8142-783 738; www.mrteatr.onego.ru; pl Kirova 1; 📖5) This magnificent Parthenon pile stages light operas, plays, ballets and folk-group shows.

Philharmonia CLASSICAL MUSIC
(Филармония; 🖃8142-769 208; www.philharmonia.onego.ru; ul Kirova 12) The top place for classical music and 'sympho-jazz'.

Musical Theatre THEATRE
(Музыкальный Театр; 🖃8142-783 738; www.mrteatr.onego.ru; pl Kirova 1; ⊙ticket office 11am-8pm Mon-Fri, 10am-6pm Sat & Sun; 📖8, 12, 17, 20) International ballet and opera performances are hosted in the theatre's becolumned neoclassical building.

ℹ️ Information

Karelia Tourism Portal (www.ticrk.ru/en) Extremely useful website for all things Karelia.

Komart (www.komart.karelia.ru) Handy addresses and 'what's on' listings.

Petrozavodsk Tourist Office
(Информационный туристский центр РК; 🖃8142-764 835; www.ticrk.ru; ul Titova 3; ⊙9am-5pm Mon-Sat; 📖29) Very obliging English-speaking staff offer loads of information and advice.

Post Office (Почта; ul Dzerzhinskogo 5; ⊙8am-8pm Mon-Fri, 9am-6pm Sat) Main post office.

ℹ️ Getting There & Away

For updated transport timetables, both urban and intercity, consult www.ptz-trans.ru.

BOAT

In summer, hydrofoils leave up to five times daily from the **Hydrofoil Jetty** (off pr Marksa) to Kizhi (R2900 return). You can buy tickets in advance at the Hydrofoil Terminal (p299).

BUS

From the **bus station** (Автостанция; ul Chapaeva 3) there are departures every day except Saturday for Helsinki, Finland (R2700, 13 hours, 5am), St Petersburg (R900, 8½ hours, four to five daily), Sortavala (R680, four to seven hours, seven to eight daily), and Vologda (R1130, 12½ hours, 7.10am Tuesday, Thursday, Friday and Sunday). There's a handy bus schedule and price list in English pinned to the bus station wall.

TRAIN

From the train station, there are departures for Moscow (R1459, 12¾ to 16¼ hours, four to eight daily), with the ideal overnight choice being train 17, which departs at 8pm and arrives at 9am. The best timed of five services to St Petersburg is train 11 (R800), departing at 10.40pm and arriving at 6.24am. Between six and seven services run daily to/from Murmansk (R1417, 18¾ to 24 hours), the swiftest being train 16. Train 294 (departing at 7.40pm) is the best of a bunch of inconveniently timed trains for Kem (R860, 8½ hours), arriving at 4.03am, although you'll need to kill a few hours at the train station when you arrive before the 8am boat to the Solovetsky Islands.

ⓘ Getting Around

The 2GIS website (www.2gis.ru) provides up-to-date transport route info online and via its handy app. Trolleybuses and buses (R25) trundle up and down pr Lenina. From the train station, trolleybus 1 is the most useful, going straight through the heart of the city and down as far as the lake.

Kizhi   Кижи

This enchanting green sliver is by far the most visited of Lake Onega's 1600-plus islands. This is thanks to the magnificent Transfiguration Church, Russia's most iconic wooden landmark, which dominates the stunning Kizhi Museum Reserve.

Visitors typically get four hours on the island, which is more than enough time to visit the main reserve and stroll up to the lived-in Yamka village. Guided excursions are on offer but much of what you'll see is self-explanatory and placards are in English. Stay on the marked paths – a decline in the island's poisonous-snake population has led to proliferation of ticks that potentially carry encephalitis.

There is a small **cafe** (Кафе; near hydrofoil dock; kalitki R75; ⊗9am-7pm; 🛜), just as you get off the boat.

◉ Sights

★**Kizhi Museum Reserve**   MUSEUM
(Музей-заповедник 'Кижи'; www.kizhi.karelia. ru; R500, audio guide R150; ⊗8am-8pm Jun-Aug, 9am-4pm Sep–mid-Oct & 15-31 May, 10am-3pm mid-Oct–mid-May) One of Russia's unmissable attractions, the reserve is home to dozens of 18th- and 19th-century log buildings, some furnished in period style, which were moved here from Karelian villages during Soviet times. Topped with 30 miniature domes, the magnificent Transfiguration Church is its star. Be aware that renovation works expected to be completed by 2020–21 currently spoil the view somewhat.

Hydrofoils (R2900 return) from Petrozavodsk dock at a landing flanked by souvenir

kiosks. From the ticket office, head south into the main reserve.

An obvious coastal path loops around the main attractions, followed anticlockwise by most visitors, starting with the unmissable **Kizhi Enclosure** (Корпус музея 'Кижи'). It contains a striking pair of churches, their cupolas covered with wooden 'scales', a modest graveyard and an 1862 wooden bell tower. Kizhi's world-famous 1714 **Transfiguration Church** features a chorus of wooden domes, gables and ingenious decorations to keep water off the walls. Entry isn't allowed as it's undergoing extensive renovation. However, the lovely nine-domed **Church of the Intercession** (1764) next door hosts a rich collection of 16th-to-18th-century icons and a splendid iconostasis.

Directly south of the Kizhi Enclosure, the 1876 **Oshevnev House** is typical of larger historical Karelian rural homes where house and stable-barn were combined into one unit. Notice the 'bed cupboard' and the dried herbs hanging from the ceiling (Old Believers considered tea drinking a sin).

Further south is a **black banya**, a tiny wooden bathhouse hut so known because there was no chimney to allow the escape of smoke from the heater fires.

Outside the furnished 1880 **Elizarov House**, a craftsman carves little human and animal figures, while within the **Chapel of the Archangel Michael**, note the 'sky' – the wooden icons that make up the ceiling. A merry ringing of church bells usually accompanies your visit.

Just south of **Schepin House** is a working **smithy**, while in the southernmost **Sergiev House** an exhibition compares the coexisting worlds of male and female peasants in the late 19th century. Women were in charge of cooking, embroidery, sewing and child rearing, while men worked in the fields and fished. No surprises there.

Further north, the little 14th-century **Church of the Resurrection of Lazarus** from Murom monastery is the oldest structure on Kizhi – some claim it to be the oldest wooden building in Russia.

An interesting **carpentry exhibit** en route to **Yakovlev House** gives a great visual explanation of how wooden buildings were made without nails. The house itself is the most affluent of the lot, with lace tablecloths and a group of weavers who burst into Old Russian song as you walk in.

From here you could return to the dock past a carved wooden cross, a once common roadside waymarker in rural Karelia. Alternatively, stroll on to Yamka. You can also rent bicycles at the entrance to the reserve for R300 per hour. No deposit is required.

Yamka

VILLAGE

(Ямка) The village of Yamka is home to extravagantly bearded Old Believers, as well as genuinely lived-in (and well-labelled) historic houses. Its pretty lake-side setting is a 15-minute walk up the east coast of the island from the reserve. The reserve's seasonal staff sleep communally here in the 1905 **Pertyakov House**, with a traditional-style outdoor *banya* hut (like a sauna) at the waterside. Two doors south, outside **Moshikova House**, is a curious blue-eyed pagan totem that's somewhat reminiscent of an Easter Island *moai*.

Veronica's Veil Chapel

CHAPEL

(Часовня Спаса Нерукотворного из д. Вигово; Kizhi island) FREE Dating from the 17th century, the view from Veronica's Veil Chapel offers wonderful panoramas right across Kizhi. Walk west across the island from Yamaka village towards Vasilyevo village to get here. It's on top of a picturesque hill. An alternative path from here leads back to the hydrofoil landing for transport back to Petrozavodsk.

❶ Getting There & Away

From the end of May until late August, **hydrofoils** (return R2900) make the 90-minute-trip from Petrozavodsk to Kizhi between one and five times daily, according to demand and weather. In summer, there are scheduled departures at 10.30am, 11.30am and 12.15pm, returning at 3.45pm, 4.45pm and 5.30pm, with extra departures depending on demand. Check the Petrozavodsk Transport website (www.ptz-trans.ru/interurban/ships-interurban/timetable_ships.html) for up-to-date timetables. Double-check a day ahead at Petrozavodsk's **Hydrofoil Terminal** (pr Marksa). Sporadic boats run in early May and from September to mid-October.

In winter, some tour agencies can arrange visits to Kizhi by snowmobile or hovercraft.

Northern Lake Ladoga

The top attraction in Europe's largest lake is the monastery island of Valaam. Coming from Petrozavodsk, it's most conveniently reached via Sortavala, though there's an alternative hydrofoil connection from the historic castle town of Priozersk (formerly Käkisalmi) in Leningradsky Oblast, as well as pricey cruises from St Petersburg.

Sortavala   Сортавала

📞 81430 / POP 18,746 / ⏲ MOSCOW

Founded by the Swedes in 1632, sleepy Sortavala became better known as Serdobol during its first Russian phase (1721 to 1812), when its quarries provided much of the stone for St Petersburg's great palaces. It was part of Finland until WWII, when, after severe bombing, its population evacuated and the area was forced into the USSR.

Sortavala is primarily a launching point for reaching Valaam, but it's well worth peeking into the **Kronid Gogolev Museum** (Музей Кронида Гоголева; www.artgogolev.ru; ul Komsomolskaya 6; R125; ⏲10am-8pm) near the dock. The highlights here are the remarkable tableaux carved out of wood by local artist Kronid Gogolev.

A couple of blocks away is the statue of Karelian rune singer **Petri Shemeikka** (pl Vainamoinen) plucking a *kantele* (traditional Karelian stringed instrument)

🛌 Sleeping & Eating

Uyutnyy Dom Apartments

APARTMENT $

(📞8-921-224 8489; nikitkaonego@yandex.ru; Kirova 18; apt R1200-2000; ❄🏠) Uyutnyy Dom consists of several fully equipped apartments for two to four people, all within a few minutes' walk from the pier. Ideal for self-caterers. Call ahead so that the owner can meet you.

Hotel Kaunis

HOTEL $$

(Отел Каунис; 📞81430-24 910; www.hotelkaunis.ru; ul Lenina 3; s/d R2900/3650; 🏠) A good upmarket portside option. Rooms are spacious, with decent linen and powerful showers, but the lack of netting on windows means you either roast or become a mosquito buffet in summer (bring repellent). English is spoken and the restaurant (mains from R290) overlooks the water.

Hotel Piipun Piha

HOTEL $$

(Пийпун Пиха; 📞8-921-526 1111; www.piipunpiha.ru; ul Promishlennaya 44; s/d R3100/4000) A 15-minute walk from the centre, this lakeside hotel's bright and comfortable rooms all have terraces. There is also a good restaurant on the 1st floor serving Russian and European food (mains from R350). Staff will meet you at the bus or train station.

★**Kalitka**   KARELIAN $
(Калитка; ul Komsomolskaya 9; kalitki from R40)
This tiny, cosy cafe takes its name from the
ubiquitous *kalitki* (open-face pies) found all
over the region. Choose from tasty potato,
meat, cheese and spinach or cabbage fillings.

Boulevard   RUSSIAN $
(Бульвар; ul Karelskaya 35; mains R230-390;
⊙ 10am-2am Sun-Thu, 10am-2am Fri & Sat) Though
the diners boogieing down to Russian pop on
the dance floor take away from the Parisian
sophistication that Boulevard's wall prints intend to convey, the dishes are nicely presented and the service is congenial and prompt.
Choose from such delights as *ukha* (hearty
fish soup) with vodka, and chicken stuffed
with mushrooms. Best restaurant in town.

❶ Information

Sberbank (Сбербанк; ul Komsomolskaya 8)
has a 24-hour ATM.

❶ Getting There & Away

From Sortavala's **bus station** (Автовокзал;
ul Chapaeva 3), daily buses and scheduled
marshrutky (fixed-route minibuses) run to Petrozavodsk (R680, four to seven hours, up to six
daily). There are also daily bus departures to St
Petersburg at 1.31pm (R650, 6½ hours) and 5pm
(R600, four hours). Train 350 from St Petersburg
(R661, 5½ hours) arrives in Sortavala on Friday
at 8.21pm. However, there is no direct train link
from Sortavala to St Petersburg at present.

Valaam   Валаам

☑ 81430 / POP 200 / ⊙ MOSCOW

This beautiful, mostly forested archipelago in the north of Lake Ladoga consists of
around 50 isles tightly clustered around a
27.8-sq-km main island, where the **Transfiguration Monastery** (Валаамский Спасо-
Преображенский монастырь; www.valaam.
ru; Valaam; ⊙ 8am-7pm) 〖FREE〗 is the main
drawcard. If you're overwhelmed by the
stampede of pilgrims, explore a dozen other smaller churches, chapels and sketes
on pretty headlands, quiet inland bays or
bridged islets. It's by no means an essential
sight, however – if you are island-hopping in
the region and pressed for time, Kizhi and
the Solovetsky Islands have far more to offer.

Mystics like to claim that Valaam was
visited by St Andrew within a generation of
Christ's crucifixion. True or not, a monastery
was founded here around the late 14th century. Its dual role as fortress against Swedish invaders failed in 1611 when the Swedes

destroyed it completely. Rebuilt in the 18th
century with money from Peter the Great,
the monastery burned down again in 1754.
In the 19th century Valaam pioneered the
idea of sketes, sort of halfway houses between
hermitages and monasteries, where novice
monks could retreat and learn from more experienced peers.

When the Soviet Union took northern Lake
Ladoga from Finland in WWII, many of the
monks and much of the monastery's treasure
were moved to a site near Karvio, Finland,
where the Uusi Valamo (New Valaam) monastery remains active. Today there's a renewed
community of about 200 monks, the Transfiguration Monastery is beautifully restored and
several outlying sketes have been rebuilt.

One of the few parts of the island that's
easily accessible on foot from the monastery
is the forested Nikonovskaya area, dotted
with chapels and sketes.

Amid trees directly above the Nikonovskaya
jetty, the modest red-brick **Resurrection
Church** isn't a real attraction, but sporadic
minibuses (R70) shuttle visitors to the main
monastery from here. If none materialise, the
6km walk is blissfully peaceful.

Alternatively, walk 1km west along the
main track then, just beyond the pretty
wooden **Gethsemane Skete**, take the forest
footpath to the left, turning left again soon
after that. This path winds round past the
Ascension Chapel, with lovely views down
to a wood-lined bay, then curves down and
back around past the **Konevsky Skete** to
the Valaam monastery farm complex. From
here you can return to Gethsemane Skete, or
walk 2km back to the main track near Tikhvin Bridge and hope for a passing vehicle to
pick you up (not assured).

For a great picnic site, stroll about 20
minutes north of the Transfiguration Monastery to the quaint, heptagonal bell tower
of **Nikolski Skete**.

🛏 Sleeping

In summer, booking ahead is essential.

Hotel Zimnyaya   HISTORIC HOTEL $$
(Гостиница Зимняя; ☑ 8-921-629 3311, 8-921-728
7681; www.vp.valaam.ru; s/d from R2300/2550)
Don't be put off by the Gostiny Dvor building's
decrepit entrance and stairways: the Zimn-
yaya's vaulted cell-rooms are (aptly) austere
and overpriced for what they are, but they're
clean and cosily decorated. All but three have
shared bathrooms. In spite of its name, the
Winter Hotel receives guests year-round.

Hotel Letnaya
HOTEL **$$**

(Гостиница Летняя; ☑ 81430-44 593; ul Tsentralnaya; s R2600-3000, d R3200-3400) A tasteful alternative to traditional Valaam accommodation. From the outside, it looks more like a stately home than a monks' cloister. Rooms are modest, yet comfortable.

Hotel Igumenskaya
MONASTERY **$$**

(Гостиница Игуменская; ☑ 8-921-629 3311; www.valaam.com/hotels/73; s/d R3600/4000) Wood-panelled rooms inside the monastery with simple beds come complete with an icon in a corner niche. From the top of the main approach stairway, enter the first lilac-scented courtyard of the main monastery, turn right and press the buzzer at the third door. There's no sign. Not the best ratio of guest numbers to shared bathroom. Mainly caters to pilgrims.

🔓 Getting There & Away

From June till early September it's usually possible to reach the island daily from Sortavala, though not 100% guaranteed. Scheduled hydrofoils typically sail at 9.30am and 11am (R1600 return, 45 minutes), but they are reserved for tour groups, so solo travellers will only get a seat if there's space. In peak season, private speedboat captains round up solo travellers and charge the same as hydrofoils for the journey to/from Valaam. Double-check the return times from the island. Booking a tour with one of many Petrozavodsk agencies is a safer bet.

In February and March a hovercraft runs from Sortavala, ice conditions allowing. With a minimum of seven passengers, tickets cost around R2000 per person; book through Intourist (p296) in Petrozavodsk.

Overnight river cruises run regularly in summer from St Petersburg.

🔓 Getting Around

Most boats and hydrofoils from Sortavala arrive at the Monasterskaya landing, close to the main Transfiguration Monastery. Numerous souvenir stands at both ports sell useful, if flawed, maps of the archipelago. Electric bicycles are for rent (R300 per hour) at the landing point.

WHITE SEA БЕЛОЕ МОРЕ

Kem & Rabocheostrovsk
Кемь и Рабочеостровск

If you're heading for the Solovetsky Islands, the most reliable boat connection is from tiny Rabocheostrovsk, 12km northeast of the logging town of Kem and easily reachable by bus 1 (R60, 20 minutes, every 20 to 40 minutes from around 6.30am to 8.30pm) from Kem's railway station. A taxi to Rabocheostrovsk costs around R400. The ATMs at Kem's **Sberbank** (Кемовский Сбербанк; pr proletarskiy 19, Kem) and train station are your last chance to withdraw cash, as there are no ATMs on the Solovetsky Islands.

If you need somewhere to stay before or after heading to the islands, **Turkomplex Prichal** (Рабочеостровской Туркомплекс Причал; ☑ 81458-56 060; www.prichalk.ru/eng; Naberezhnaya 1, Rabocheostrovsk; s/d/tr from R1200/1600/2400; ☻☎) offers fairly bright, well-maintained, pine-furnished rooms in eight chalet-style blocks. 'Superior' rooms have fireplaces, while the windows in the cheapies don't open. An on-site cafe serves light meals (mains R275). Boats for Solovetsky Islands leave from behind the hotel; the helpful reception staff can book your ticket, ideally with advance notice.

There are eight daily trains from Murmansk (R1028, 11 to 13½ hours) to Kem, although only the 598, which goes via Petrozavodsk, will get you into town (4.03am) in time to catch the 8am boat from the islands. From Petrozavodsk, there are six trains daily to Kem (R845, eight to 11 hours).

If you catch the 4pm boat from the islands, you can make the night trains heading both north and south: the 21 to St Petersburg via Petrozavodsk leaves at 8.55pm (R1234), and there are two trains departing for Murmansk at 8.41pm and 8.51pm (R1028).

SOLOVETSKY ISLANDS
СОЛОВЕЦКИЕ ОСТРОВА

☑ 8183590 / POP 950 / ⊘ MOSCOW

Alternatively called Solovki, these distant, lake-dappled White Sea islands are home to one of Russia's best-known monasteries. Transformed by Stalin into one of the USSR's most notorious prison camps, Solovki was described in Solzhenitsyn's *Gulag Archipelago* as being so remote that a 'scream from here would never be heard'.

Visiting the islands is an adventure. The brief summer is pretty much your only window of opportunity as the autumn brings storms and soup-thick fog, and during the long winter Solovki are swept clean by howling blizzards. Solovki warrant several days'

ℹ VISITING THE MONASTERY

➡ Entry to the kremlin yard at Solovetsky Transfiguration Monastery, and to some churches within, is free. However, exhibition halls and linking corridors require a 'Riznitsa' (ризница) ticket, purchased inside the sacristy upstairs.

➡ Access to the towers and the prison is limited to those on guided tours.

➡ Dress code is typical for active monasteries: headscarves for women, trousers for men, and no shorts or short skirts allowed.

---

exploration to properly absorb the history and the silence of the forests, bays and outer islands. Bring mosquito repellent, warm clothes and plenty of patience.

The archipelago has six main islands and more than 500 lakes. By far the largest island, Bolshoy Solovetsky (24km by 16km) is home to the main monastery, which dominates the rural idyll of Solovetsky Village, the islands' main settlement.

History

Many millennia ago, the ancestors of the present-day Sami adorned these islands with stone 'labyrinths' and burial mounds, possibly considering Solovki a gateway to the spiritual world. Permanent occupation began in 1429 when monks from Kirillo-Belozersky Monastery founded a wooden hermitage at Savvatevo. Bequests and royal patronage meant the monastery rapidly grew into a rich landholder, and in the 1570s the complex became enclosed within vast fortress walls, useful as a defence against Swedish incursions. Ironically, greater damage was self-inflicted when, from 1668, the monastery endured an eight-year siege for opposing the ecclesiastical reforms of Patriarch Nikon – doubly ironic as Nikon had been a young monk here (on Anzer Island) – before being betrayed by one of its own.

In a bizarre sideshow to the Crimean War, two British frigates sailed by and bombarded the kremlin with nearly 2000 cannonballs. Given that Russia lost that war, punching a hole in one of the ships and not losing a single man put Solovki back into the minds of Russia's faithful. Donations rolled in and monks arrived to repopulate the monastery, which remained vibrant until the Soviet government closed it in 1920.

Three years later the islands were declared a work camp for 'enemies of the people'. At first, the prisoners were permitted to work fairly freely, keeping up the monastery's botanical garden and libraries. But it wasn't long until the camp was repurposed, turning into one of the USSR's most severe and dreaded Gulag camps. Over 350,000 prisoners from all over the Soviet Union and beyond passed through Solovki, and for 20,000 or so the islands became their grave. The prison was closed in 1939, and replaced by a naval training base.

Restoration work on the badly damaged monastery began in the 1960s. Monks started returning in the late 1980s and the islands acquired Unesco World Heritage listing in 1992. Today the monastic community is flourishing but reconstruction remains a long-term task. The islands are today a popular pilgrimage site for Russian Orthodox Christians.

In recent years, as President Putin has forged an alliance with the powerful Russian Orthodox Church, critics have alleged that the history of the Gulag camps on the islands is being downplayed. Some Orthodox officials have also called for strict limits to be placed on 'secular' tourism on the islands. For now, however, there is nothing to prevent you visiting.

⦿ Sights

◉ Bolshoi Solovetsky Island

★ Solovetsky Transfiguration Monastery MONASTERY (Спасо-Преображенский Соловецкий монастырь; www.solovky.ru; Bolshoy Solovetsky Island; R250; ⊘grounds 8am-10pm, museums 10am-6pm) This imposing, stone-walled monastery is the heart and soul of the Solovetsky Islands. Founded in 1429, it has played various roles throughout its existence: a hermit's retreat, a vibrant religious community, a rebel enclave that held out against the Patriarch of the Russian Orthodox Church, a fortress victorious against British warships, a gulag for the Soviet Union's damned and a museum. Revived post-*perestroika*, it flourishes once more as a spiritual institution.

The kremlin yard is contained within massive boulder-chunk walls with six sturdy fortress towers topped with conical wood-shingle roofs. These, along with a quivering flurry of church towers and domes, reflect magnificently in Svyatoe

Lake. The centrepiece is the 1566 Transfiguration Cathedral (Спасо-Преображенский собор), with its blend of Pomorsky architecture, powerful foundations and white-washed walls, clusters of domes covered in a dense carpet of wooden scales and a dazzling six-level iconostasis upstairs.

Upstairs is the vast dining room, connected to the rest of the complex by covered walkways. Next to it is the Assumption Church (Успенская церковь), a cavernous former refectory with sparse photo-history boards focusing especially on the 1992 return of the relics of monastery founders Saints Zosima, Savvaty and Herman.

The sacristy (ризница) upstairs was used to house the monastery's treasures, but many artefacts were carted off by the Bolsheviks and destroyed.

The tiny but magnificently mural-covered 1601 Annunciation Church (Благовещенская церковь) is entered through an unmarked door, one floor above the main gate.

The prison has been in use since the 16th century, first to house those who'd committed crimes against the faith and later to punish those who'd erred against the state. The harshest punishments (leg irons, dreadful food) was reserved for the 'secret' prisoners who arrived with nothing but accompanying papers stating the conditions in which they should be kept.

The monastery complex was heated using three powerful stoves and a series of heating vents that ran through the walls, with underfloor heating used to dry the grain before it was ground into flour. The 17th-century water mill, in turn, was powered by a network of canals that the industrious monks dug to connect the island's 500-something lakes.

★ Gora Sekirnaya   HISTORIC SITE
(Секирная гора; Bolshoy Solovetsky Island) Literally translated as Hatchet Mountain, this infamous 71m-high hill was the site of tortures and summary executions described in Aleksandr Solzhenitsyn's *Gulag Archipelago*. The unassuming hilltop Ascension Church (1857–62) that doubles as a lighthouse was used for solitary confinement. A faint path leads to the clearing where prisoners were dumped in unmarked graves. Crosses now mark some of these burial sites – the numbers on each indicate how many bodies were found at that spot.

Near the stairs leading up to the church, a larger 1992 cross commemorates all who died on Solovki. The site is about 10km from the village, 7km beyond the botanical garden towards Savvatyevsky minor monastery. Tours cost R480 and can be booked with the island's tourist office (p306). You could also hike or cycle there.

Solovetsky Forced Labour Camps
& Prison 1920–1939   MUSEUM
(Соловецкие лагеря и тюрьма особого назначения (1920–1939); ul Zaozyornaya 7, Bolshoy Solovetsky Island; adult/student R250/150; ☺10am-7.30pm) Inside former barracks, this excellent exposition (in Russian) takes you through the different stages of the Solovetsky gulag – from punishing 'counter-revolutionary elements' and providing a slave labour force to build the infamous Belomorsky Canal, to the summary mass executions during the Great Terror of 1937–38. Bold displays are

NORTHERN EUROPEAN RUSSIA SOLOVETSKY ISLANDS

PRISONERS OF THE MOTHERLAND

Billed 'the mother of the gulag' by Aleksandr Solzhenitsyn, Solovki was home to one of the USSR's first labour camps. Established in 1923, it was given the name SLON (Solovetsky Lager Osobogo Naznachenia; Solovetsky Special Purpose Camp). In Russian, 'slon' means 'elephant', and upon receiving their sentences, Solovki-bound prisoners grimly joked that they were 'off to see the elephant'.

Back-breaking logging duty, coupled with inadequate tools and clothing, very little sleep and starvation rations, was enough to reduce most prisoners to shells within weeks. Escape from the islands was very difficult, as prisoners had to break out in groups, navigate their way across the sea and then avoid all settlements en route to the Finnish border. In the gulag's history, only three escape attempts were successful.

This wasn't the first time the monastery was used for less-than-pious purposes – 'undesirables' had been shipped off to the White Sea outpost since the reign of Ivan the Terrible. Prisoners of note included Count Pyotr Tolstoy – forebear of novelist and anarcho-pacifist Leo Tolstoy – and Cossack leader Petro Kalnyshevsky, who was incarcerated here for 25 years and died on the island in 1803...aged 111!

interspersed with gulag prisoner testimonies. A tour by the knowledgeable local archivist (R550) makes the visit particularly worthwhile; book at the tourist office.

Botanical Garden
GARDENS

(Ботанический сад; Bolshoy Solovetsky Island; R250; ⊙9am-7.30pm) Around 3km northwest of the village, the botanical garden enjoys a special microclimate – monks have grown vegetables and hothouse fruits here for centuries. For views, climb nearby Alexander Hill, topped by the miniature **Alexander Nevsky Chapel** (1854).

Archaeological Exhibition
MUSEUM

(Экспозиция Подземные Археологические Соловки; Solovetsky Transfiguration Monastery, Bolshoy Solovetsky Island; R150; ⊙10am-6pm) Contains exhibits detailing the history of the monastery, including the ruins of monks' cells dating from the 16th century.

Annunciation Church
CHURCH

(Благовещенская церковь; Solovetsky Transfiguration Monastery, Bolshoy Solovetsky Island) `FREE` This tiny but magnificently mural-covered church dates from 1601.

⊙ Other Solovetsky Islands

★Bolshoy Zayatsky Island
ISLAND

(Большой Заяцкий остров; tour including entry to island R750) This small, wind-whipped island is famous for its 13 labyrinths, including the largest one in northern Russia. A boardwalk loops around the island from the dockside wooden church. Bolshoy Zayatsky Island was used for female solitary confinement during gulag years, but not a trace remains. Independent travel to the island is prohibited, but there is no obligation to stick with the tour guide once you arrive. Buy tickets for daily tours at the tourist office (p306). Boats make the trip in around 40 minutes.

Anzer Island
HISTORIC SITE

(Остров Анзер) The second-largest island in the archipelago, Anzer Island has its share of stone labyrinths and burial mounds, as well as a scattering of monastic sketes, the oldest dating back to the 17th century. One of these was used as a typhoid hospital in the 1920s, and hundreds of prisoners died here.

Full-day visits to Anzer costs R1600 per person and can be arranged at the tourist office (p306). Tours run from early May to October.

Bolshaya Muksalma Island
ISLAND

(Большая Муксалма) The third largest of the Solovetsky Islands, Bolshaya Muksalma is connected to the main island by a dam built by monks in the 19th century. It's an impressive sight and the trip here passes through some eye-catching natural landscapes. Tours can be arranged with the tourist office (p306) on Bolshoy Solovetsky Island.

🏃 Activities

Bicycle Rental
CYCLING

(Велопрокат; Bolshoy Solovetsky Island; bike rental per hour/day from R120/600) Rents everything from single-gear Soviet sturdies to mountain bikes – the latter are by far the best for tackling the unpaved, bumpy roads. A deposit in the form of a valuable (driver's license, watch, mobile phone) is required. There are a number of offices on the island, including one at the Solovetskaya Sloboda (p305) hotel. Look out for the signs that say Велопрокат.

Whale Watching
WILDLIFE

(Мыс Белужий) In early summer, white beluga whales breed off Cape Beluzhy (west coast) and raise their young here.

MYSTERIES IN STONES

Dating back around 4000 years, concentric swirls of shrub-covered stones known as **labyrinths** occur widely in northern Scandinavia, the Kola Peninsula and the outer Solovetsky Islands. Each has a single entrance and a cairn at its heart. Their purpose is still unknown, but since no human remains have been found in the few labyrinths excavated, it is assumed that they were used for religious ceremonies.

Human and animal remains have been found, however, underneath the **stone mounds** that dot the outer Solovetsky Islands. Given that the remains are relatively few in number, it is believed that only the most unquiet of souls were given a burial on remote islands.

Stones played an important spiritual role in the lives of the Sami ancestors. Anthropomorphic rocks and mounds of rocks scattered around the Kola Peninsula, known as **seids**, are believed to have been worshipped as deities.